ent Analysis Measures †

Liquidity	Capital structure and solvency	Financial market
Current ratio	Total debt ratio	Price-to-earnings
Working capital	Total debt to equity ratio	Price-to-book
Acid-test (quick) ratio	Long-term debt to equity	Earnings yield
Cash ratio	Times interest earned	Dividend yield
Collection period	Earnings to fixed charges	
Inventory turnover	Cash flow to fixed charges	
Days to sell inventory	Financial leverage ratio	
Accounts payable turnover	Financial leverage index	
Days' purchases in accounts payable	Altman Z-score	
Operating cash flow to current liabilities		
Operating cycle		

nore than one category.

asures ‡

Liquidity

Current ratio = current assets / current liabilities
Working capital = current assets − current liabilities
Acid-test (quick) ratio = (cash + cash equivalents + marketable securities + accounts receivable) / current liabilities
Cash ratio = (cash + cash equivalents + marketable securities) / current liabilities
Collection period = (average accounts receivable × 360) / sales
Inventory turnover = cost of sales / average inventory
Days to sell inventory = (average inventory × 360) / cost of sales
Accounts payable turnover = purchases / average accounts payable
Days' purchases in accounts payable = (accounts payable × 360) / purchases
Cash flow ratio to current liabilities = operating cash flow / current liabilities
Operating cycle= days' to sell inventory + collection period

Capital structure and solvency

Total debt ratio = total liabilities / total assets
Total debt to equity ratio = total liabilities / shareholders' equity
Long-term debt to equity = long-term liabilities / shareholders' equity
Times interest earned = income before interest and income taxes / interest expense
Earnings to fixed charges = earnings available for fixed charges / fixed charges {see chapter 10 for definitions}
Cash flow to fixed charges = pretax operating cash flow available for fixed charges / fixed charges (see Chapter 10 for definition)
Financial leverage ratio = total assets / common shareholders' equity
Financial leverage index = ROCE / ROA
Altman Z-score = 0.717(working capital/total assets) + 0.847(retained earnings/total assets) + 3.107(income before interest and taxes/total assets) + 0.420 (shareholders' equity/total liabilities) + 0.998(sales/total assets)

Financial market

Price-to-earnings = market price per common share / earnings per share
Price-to-book = market price per common share / book value per common share
Earnings yield = earnings per share / market price per common share
Dividend yield = annual cash dividends per common share / market price per common share

ions; 365 days is also commonly used.

FINANCIAL STATEMENT ANALYSIS

Theory, Application, and Interpretation

SIXTH EDITION

LEOPOLD A. BERNSTEIN

City University of New York at Baruch

JOHN J. WILD

University of Wisconsin at Madison

Boston, Massachusetts Burr Ridge, Illinois Dubuque, Iowa Madison, Wisconsin
New York, New York San Francisco, California St. Louis, Missouri

Irwin/McGraw-Hill

A Division of The ***McGraw-Hill*** *Companies*

FINANCIAL STATEMENT ANALYSIS: THEORY, APPLICATION, AND INTERPRETATION

This book is printed on acid-free paper.

1 2 3 4 5 6 7 8 9 0 DOW/DOW 9 0 9 8 7

ISBN 0-256-16704-4

Vice President and editorial director: *Michael W. Junior*
Executive editor: *Jeff Shelstad*
Sponsoring editor: *George Werthman*
Developmental editor: *Marc Chernoff*
Senior marketing manager: *Rhonda Seelinger*
Senior project manager: *Beth Cigler*
Production supervisor: *Scott Hamilton*
Designer: *Stuart D. Paterson/Image House, Inc.*
Compositor: *GAC/Shepard Poorman*
Typeface: *10/12 Garamond*
Printer: *R. R. Donnelley & Sons Company*

Library of Congress Cataloging-in-Publication Data

Bernstein, Leopold A.
Financial statement analysis: theory, application, and interpretation.—6th ed./ Leopold A. Bernstein, John J. Wild.
p. cm.
Includes index.
ISBN 0-256-16704-4 (acid-free paper)
1. Financial statements. I. Wild, John J. II. Title
HF5681.B2B46 1997
6571.3—dc21 97–5129

http://www.mhhe.com

To my wife Cynthia, children Debbie and Jeffrey, and Distinguished Professor Emanuel Saxe—Teacher, Colleague, and Friend

—*L. A. B.*

To my wife Gail and children Kimberly, Jonathan, and Stephanie

—*J. J. W.*

Preface

We are all aware of the exciting and dynamic practice of financial statement analysis, as well as its enormous implications for economic development, allocation of financial resources, and the economic well-being of a wide range of individuals. Because of these implications, financial statement analysis plays a very prominent role in how we educate the current and next generation of information users and providers. This book's goal is to give readers a distinct competitive advantage in an increasingly competitive marketplace as it continues to set the standard in showing students the keys to effective financial statement analysis. Our collective challenge is to equip today's student with the analysis skills necessary to compete in the business world and this book meets that challenge.

We know financial statements are relevant to many individuals, including investors, creditors, consultants, managers, auditors, directors, analysts, regulators, employees, and politicians. Yet our experience in teaching this material tells us we must engage students by showing the relevance of material and conveying its excitement. This book meets this need as it is aimed at students with broad business career interests as well as those specializing in accounting and finance fields. This broadens the book's appeal and the perspectives of those students not accustomed to thinking in the larger decision-making context. This book also fulfills another important need: it is written to meet the needs of today's instructors and students of financial statement analysis by allowing for flexibility and innovation in the classroom. It presents a new pedagogy that includes the impact of technology, all within a modern eye-catching design that satisfies the visual preferences of today's students.

Generally, three key considerations guided our efforts in writing the book: (1) to make the material *relevant* to students; (2) to encourage students to think in an *evaluative* or inferential manner; and (3) to make the material *accessible and interesting* to students. We describe next how we accomplish these important objectives.

Relevance

To engage students we must make the material relevant to them. We recognize that "users" include more than only creditors and equity investors. While these two user groups and their decisions are an important focus of this book, they are *not* the only focus. We have chosen to adopt a broader notion of the financial statement user by linking analysis to many other direct and indirect users of financial statements. This requires students to think about the relevance of financial statements from different and unique perspectives, including political and community activists, environmentalists, school board members, lawyers, and entrepreneurs. We design and frame the book to support this broader perspective, and several distinctive features help us in this regard.

- *Analysis Viewpoints.* Analysis Viewpoints are a unique feature that require students to assume the role of a financial statement user. We confront students with a situation requiring consideration of one or more aspects of financial statements. Traditional examples include a banker deciding loan eligibility and an investor analyzing a company's stock. Less traditional examples include a community activist evaluating corporate social responsibility and an environmentalist fighting for tougher pollution controls. An example follows:

ANALYSIS VIEWPOINT *. . . You are the director*

You are a new member of the board of directors of a toy merchandiser. You are preparing for your first meeting with the company's independent auditor. A stockholder has written you a letter raising concerns about earnings quality. What are some questions or issues that you can raise with the auditor to address these concerns and fulfill your fiduciary responsibilities to shareholders

- *Excerpts from practice.* Numerous excerpts from practice illustrate key points throughout this book. They continually reinforce the relevance of financial statement analysis and help us engage students. Excerpts include accounting and market data, annual report disclosures, newspaper clippings, and financial press cut-outs. An interesting revenue recognition policy is now reproduced:

The company sells certain whiskey in barrels in bond under agreements which provide for future bottling. In prior years, profits on such transactions were reflected as of the date of sale. The present company policy is to treat such profits as deferred income until the whiskey is bottled and shipped.

—Schenley Industries, Inc.

- *Annual Reports.* Financial statements from three companies are reproduced in this book and used for illustration purposes throughout. The innovative annual report of Adaptec is packaged with copies of this edition and is referenced often. Experience shows us that frequent use of annual reports heightens students' interest and learning. An annual report also exposes students to information beyond financial statements. A Comprehensive Case drawing on the financial statements of Campbell Soup Company serves as a capstone portrayal of our analysis techniques.
- *Assignment Material.* End-of-chapter assignments include numerous excerpts from practice or entire financial reports from many companies. These companies include: Quaker Oats, Toro, Columbia Pictures, Abbott, Kraft, Philip Morris, Merck, Mead, Armstrong World, and Coca-Cola. The five types of assignment materials, *Questions, Exercises, Problems, Cases, and Internet Activities*, are comprehensive, flexible, and reliable. Each assignment is individually titled to reflect its purpose and many assignments require critical thinking, communication skills, analysis, interpretation, decision making, and use of technology.

Evaluative

We believe students must learn to effectively evaluate evidence from financial statement analysis. While computations and analysis results are important, the evaluative task is crucial to reaping the benefits of analysis. After extensive feedback from financial statement analysis instructors, we designed this book to support an important objective: increased emphasis of the evaluative aspect of analysis. Part One, which covers Chapters 1 and 2, sets the tone for increased evaluative emphasis. Financial statements are introduced immediately in the book to begin our focus on evaluating a company's performance in planning, financing, investing, and operating activities. Our early analysis of Adaptec's financial statements allows us to focus directly and often on evaluation. Alternative views from different users are also introduced early and reinforced often. This book's unique introduction to financial statement analysis provides a natural springboard that leads to the accounting analysis in Part Two and the financial analysis in Part Three. We focus throughout on introducing analysis tools and techniques in an evaluative manner. Features helping us accomplish this include the following:

- *Assignment Material.* Many end-of-chapter assignments emphasize the evaluative and decision-making aspect of financial statement analysis. Mechanics and ratio computations are presented as a means to an end, with the end being strategic analysis and business decisions.
- *Chapter Linkages.* Linkages launch every chapter and establish bridges between topics and concepts in prior, current, and upcoming chapters. We have found these linkages to greatly assist students in developing a broader perspective on financial statement analysis, and the linkages show the applicability and relevance of analysis tools and techniques across topics.
- *Research Insights.* Research Insights describe research relevant to analysis of financial statements. These insights summarize and communicate important research that bears on our application and interpretation of financial statements. Examples include recent evidence on fundamental analysis, the relation between accounting numbers and stock prices, and the impact of company size for informativeness of prices. An example is reproduced on the next page.

Accessible and Interesting

Learning financial statement analysis is easier and more satisfying if the material is accessible and interesting. We have spent considerable time and effort attending to both instructors' and students' suggestions by designing a book that is user friendly and engaging. Several features are visibly apparent, others are more subtle. For example, we describe theoretical concepts and specialized analysis techniques in uncomplicated terms. We present data and illustrations in readable and understandable frameworks. We streamline chapters to move quickly to important points and emphasize concise writing. We introduce industry and economic data throughout the book, often in graphical form. Special features help us in making the material more accessible and interesting, including the following:

- *Visual Appeal.* Extensive use of graphs, charts, and tables show how topics relate to business practices of actual companies. These graphics draw on annual

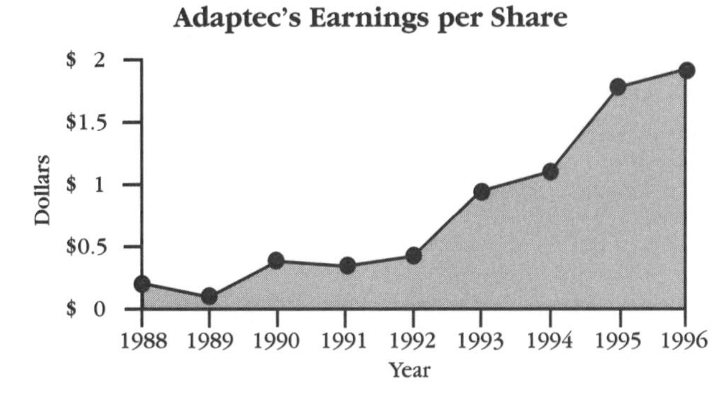

reports, surveys of business practices, and specialized reports of investor and creditor agencies.

- *Learning Objectives.* Chapters open with a list of key learning objectives that highlight important chapter goals. They help focus students' attention on the most important issues in a chapter.
- *Clarity.* We took great care in writing this book in a clear, readable, and lively style. Extensive reviews and feedback from financial statement analysis instructors helped us achieve this clarity.
- *Streamlining.* This book's streamlined presentation emphasizes succinct writing, a flexible design, and tightened organization. This book should especially appeal to analysis courses augmented with additional readings, cases, projects, research, and writing assignments.
- *Contemporary.* We carefully crafted this book to ensure that we included the most contemporary material and up-to-date techniques. Moreover, we convey current financial practices of companies through both graphical and textual presentations. For example, see the pie chart for lease accounting on the next page.

Analysis Research Insight 1.1

Accounting Numbers and Stock Prices

Do accounting numbers such as net income "explain" changes in a company's stock prices? The answer is yes. Evidence from research shows a definite link between the "news" conveyed in net income and the price changes in a company's stock (returns). "Good news" net income is accompanied by positive stock price changes, whereas "bad news" net income is associated with negative price changes. The more good or bad the net income, the greater the accompanying stock price reaction. Similar evidence is obtained for other summary financial statement numbers, such as book value.

Research also shows us that the relation between accounting numbers and stock prices is influenced by many factors. These include company factors such as risk, size, leverage, and variability, which decrease the influence of numbers like net income on prices, and factors such as growth and persistence, which increase its impact. Our analysis must recognize those influences that impact the relevance of accounting numbers for security analysis.

Fundamental analysis research offers guidance in our use of financial statement information for predicting *future* stock price changes. Evidence indicates that financial statements help to reveal the permanent and transitory portions of net income. Permanent portions are much more long-lasting in their impact on stock prices and are commensurately of greater magnitude in their influence on prices.

- *Previews.* Previews are included at the beginning of all three major parts of this book. These previews assist students in integrating the material and understanding linkages between sometimes difficult financial statement analysis topics.

Instructor feedback gives us confidence that we have achieved our goal of making financial statement analysis accessible and interesting to all students. We urge you to read Chapter 1, especially our analysis of Adaptec, to judge for yourself.

Lease Types for Companies

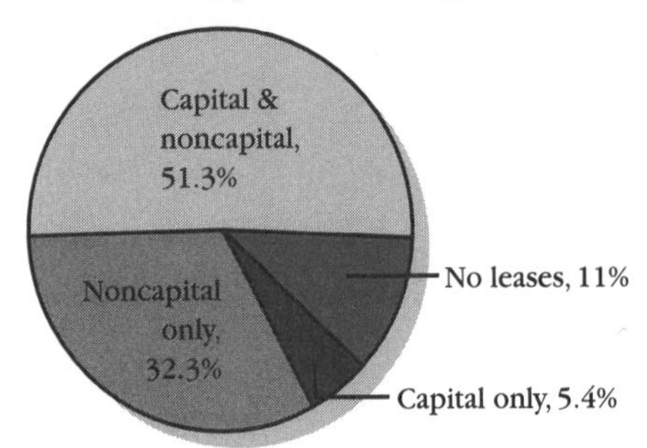

Source: *Accounting Trends & Techniques.*

Organization and Content

Flexibility and innovation are increasingly important in financial statement analysis education. This book's design encourages unique teaching strategies in presenting material to students. While the book is comprehensive in covering all topics of relevance for financial statement analysis, its organization encourages instructors to choose topics and depth of coverage as desired.

Many books lack a tight, integrated flow of topics from chapter to chapter. In this book students are told in Chapter 1 how the book's topics are related to each other. One way we achieve integration is by organizing material into three parts:

1. Overview
2. Accounting Analysis
3. Financial Analysis

Overview

Part One is an overview of financial statement analysis. We emphasize understanding business activities—planning, financing, investing, and operating. We describe strategies underlying business activities and their effects on financial statements, and we discuss the objectives of analysis. We demonstrate popular tools and techniques in analyzing and interpreting financial statements. Our attention is directed at users of financial statements whose well-being depends on reliable and relevant analysis. An important and unique feature is our use of Adaptec's annual report as a means to instill in students both the relevant and interesting nature of analysis. Two chapters comprise Part One.

- *Chapter 1.* We begin our analysis of financial statements by considering their relevance in business decisions. This leads us to focus on users, their needs, and how analysis addresses these needs. We describe business activities and how they are captured in financial statements.
- *Chapter 2.* This chapter begins by describing the analysis objectives of users. We discuss both stock and debt valuation. The importance and limitations of accounting data for our analysis are described and assessed.

Accounting Analysis

Part Two describes the accounting measurement and reporting practices underlying financial statements. We organize this presentation around financing (liabilities and equity), investing (assets), and operating (income and cash flow) activities. We show how operating activities are outcomes of changes in investing and financing activities. We provide insights into income determination and asset and liability measurement, and we discuss procedures and clues for analysis. For students to effectively reap all the benefits from financial statement analysis, they must understand accounting measurement and reporting practices. Five chapters comprise Part Two.

- *Chapter 3.* Chapter 3 begins our analysis of the financial numbers reflecting business activities and explains how these numbers are the raw material for all analyses. Our focus is on explaining, analyzing, and interpreting financing activities. We explore the relevance of book values and the implications of off-balance-sheet financing. We stress analyzing and adjusting accounting numbers in understanding financing activities.
- *Chapter 4.* Our analysis is extended to investing activities. We show how to analyze assets like cash, marketable securities, receivables, derivatives, inventories, property, equipment, and intangibles. An understanding of what these numbers reveal about company performance and financing is provided.
- *Chapter 5.* We extend our analysis to special investing activities—*intercompany and international activities.* We analyze both intercorporate investments and business combinations from the perspective of a "parent" company. We examine international investments and their reporting in financial statements. We show how interpreting disclosures on intercompany and international activities is an important part of analysis.
- *Chapter 6.* This chapter broadens our analysis to operating activities. We analyze *accrual* measures of both revenues and expenses in yielding net income. Understanding recognition methods of both revenues and expenses is emphasized. We interpret the income statement and its components for analysis purposes.
- *Chapter 7.* Chapter 7 expands our analysis of business activities to cash flows. We analyze cash flow measures for insights into all business activities, but with special emphasis on operations. Attention is directed at understanding company and business conditions when interpreting cash flows.

Financial Analysis

Part Three examines the processes and methods of financial statement analysis. We stress the objectives of many users and describe analytical tools and techniques for meeting those objectives. The means of analysis range from computation of ratio and cash flow measures to earnings prediction and valuation. We apply analysis tools that enable us to reconstruct the economic reality embedded in financial statements. We demonstrate how analysis tools and techniques enhance users' decisions—including company valuation and lending decisions. We show how financial statement analysis reduces our uncertainty and strengthens our confidence in making timely business decisions. Throughout the book we illustrate how an understanding of accounting supplemented by knowledge of the analysis tools and techniques improves business decisions, and this reinforces the integrated presentation of financial statement analysis in this book. Six chapters and a Comprehensive Case comprise Part Three.

- *Chapter 8.* Chapter 8 begins our study of the application and interpretation of analysis tools. We present analysis tools as means to reveal insights into company operations and future performance. Attention in this chapter is directed at accounting-based ratios, turnover, and operating activity measures, with special emphasis on assessing liquidity.
- *Chapter 9.* We study forecasting and pro forma analysis of financial statements in this chapter. We explain the flow of cash through a company's business activities and its implications for liquidity. Both short-and long-term forecasting of cash flows are described, and attention is directed at applying these analysis tools in practice.
- *Chapter 10.* This chapter focuses on capital structure and its implications for solvency. We analyze the importance of financial leverage and its effects on risk and return. Analytical adjustments to accounting book values are evaluated for solvency assessments. We also describe earnings-coverage measures and their interpretation.
- *Chapter 11.* Chapter 11 emphasizes return on invested capital and explains variations in its measurement. Special attention is directed at return on assets and return on common equity. We explore disaggregations of both these return measures and describe their relevance. Financial leverage is explained and analyzed.
- *Chapter 12.* This chapter expands our returns analysis to focus on profitability. We emphasize the components of income and their evaluation. Special attention is directed at sales, cost of sales, taxes, selling, and financing expenses. We explain break-even analysis and its relevance for assessing profitability. Profitability analysis tools are demonstrated, including their interpretation and adjustment.
- *Chapter 13.* Chapter 13 concludes returns analysis with earnings-based analysis and valuation. Our earnings-based analysis focuses on assessing earnings quality, earnings persistence, and earning power. Attention is directed at techniques to aid us in measuring and applying these analysis concepts. Our discussion of earnings-based valuation focuses on issues in estimating company value and forecasting earnings.
- *Comprehensive Case.* This case is a comprehensive analysis of financial statements and related notes. We describe steps in analyzing statements and the essential attributes of an analysis report. Our analysis is organized around the building blocks of financial statement analysis: liquidity, cash analysis, capital structure, solvency, return on invested capital, asset utilization, operating performance, and profitability.

Target Audience

This best-selling book is targeted to students and professionals of all business-related fields. Students and professionals alike find the book beneficial in their careers as they are rewarded with an understanding of both the techniques of analysis and the expertise to apply them. They also acquire the skills to successfully recognize business opportunities and the knowledge to capitalize on them. The book accommodates courses extending over one quarter, one semester, or two quarters, and is suitable for a survey course in financial statement analysis or for an upper-level capstone course. It is a valuable textbook for both undergraduate and graduate courses, as well as for professional programs. The book's contemporary design and practice orientation make it the book of choice in financial statement analysis education.

Supplement Package

This book is supported by a wide array of supplements aimed at the needs of both students and instructors of financial statement analysis. They include the following:

- *Financial Statement Analysis—**The Wall Street Journal Edition***. This version of the book includes a 10-week subscription to *The Wall Street Journal*, the leading business daily newspaper. The *Journal's* coverage of financial statement analysis issues illustrates many of this book's topics.
- *Book Web site*. The Internet is increasingly important for financial statement analysis, and this book is designed to take advantage of Internet resources to help students learn about this important medium. Chapter materials direct readers to World Wide Web sites relevant for financial analysis. This book has its own Web site (http://www.mhhe.com/business/accounting/wild) which is an excellent starting point for financial analysis resources on the Internet. This site includes current links to a large number of relevant sites as well as additional information for both instructors and students, including financial statement databases, up-to-date stock quote information, current accounting standards, regulatory requirements, and IEM assignment material.
- *Instructor's Solutions Manual*. An Instructor's Solutions Manual contains complete solutions for assignment material. It is carefully prepared, reviewed, and checked for accuracy and is available in both printed and electronic versions.
- *Test Bank*. A Test Bank contains a variety of test materials with varying levels of difficulty. All material is carefully reviewed for consistency with the book and thoroughly examined for accuracy. The Test Bank is available in both printed and electronic versions.
- *Instructor's Resource Manual*. An Instructor's Resource Manual contains chapter summaries, learning objectives, outlines and other helpful materials. We also include special transition notes for instructors for ease in moving from the fifth to the sixth edition. This includes complete cross-referencing of assignment material between both editions.
- *Instructor Resource File*. An electronic Resource File is available, comprising material contained in the Instructor's Resource Manual.
- *Casebook Support* (ISBN: 0-256-12584-8). An accompanying casebook is available. It includes analyses from practice that draw on financial statements and related disclosures, and it includes a model case from Coca-Cola along with cases of other high profile companies like GE, Apple, Abbott, Whirlpool, Pfizer, and Waste Management.
- *Custom Cases by Darden and Insead*. Instructors have the opportunity to select from a database of financial accounting cases developed at Darden and Insead.
- *IEM: Iowa Electronics Market*. IEM is a fully interactive, real-money electronics futures market designed as a teaching supplement. Students use real money accounts to trade contracts with payoffs based on actual events like companies' earnings announcements. Students have incentives to learn about markets and follow company, industry, and economic news. IEM is a user friendly, menu-driven technology and is easily accessed. Visit the IEM web site at http://www.biz.uiowa.edu/iem or telnet directly to iem.biz.uiowa.edu, and log into a free practice session.

- *Financial Accounting Video Library.* The *Financial Accounting Video Library* includes short, action-oriented videos for lively classroom discussion of accounting topics, including Ben & Jerry's disclosure practices, the purpose of the International Accounting Standards Committee, and the role of the Financial Accounting Standards Board.
- *Computerized Practice Sets.* Computerized Windows®-based practice sets by L. Mansuetti and K. Weildkamp help students understand basic accounting underlying financial statements. A corporate simulation practice set is provided with Wild Goose Marina, Inc.
- *Case Accompaniments.* Many instructors augment this book with additional case materials. While practical illustrations and case materials are abundant within the text, more are available:

  Financial Statement Analysis by R.J. Ball and S.P. Kothari (ISBN: 0-070-04645-X). This supplement contains research for using financial statement information in financial markets. It focuses on investing and lending decisions, risk assessment, bankruptcy prediction, takeovers and management buyouts, and forecasting.

  International Accounting: A Case Approach by J.A. Schweikart, S.J. Gray, and C.B. Roberts (ISBN: 0-070-55599-0). This case book consists of 40 class-tested international cases divided into five sections: financial reporting, financial statement analysis, management and control, auditing, and taxation.

  Financial Accounting and Corporate Reporting: A Casebook by K. Ferris (ISBN 0-256-11996-7). This casebook contains over 70 cases on financial accounting and analysis topics. Most cases use actual company data and five are international.
- *Customer Service.* Irwin/McGraw-Hill provides complimentary services, supplements, and supplement packages to adopters. They can be reached at 1-800-634-3963 or at Irwin/McGraw-Hill, 1333 Burr Ridge Parkway, Burr Ridge, IL 60521-6489.

Financial statement analysis is an exciting and dynamic field. The winds of change are upon us, and this book reflects these innovations and advances. We urge you to embrace this book and join us in our collective challenge to instill in readers the same feelings and passion for financial statement analysis that we hold.

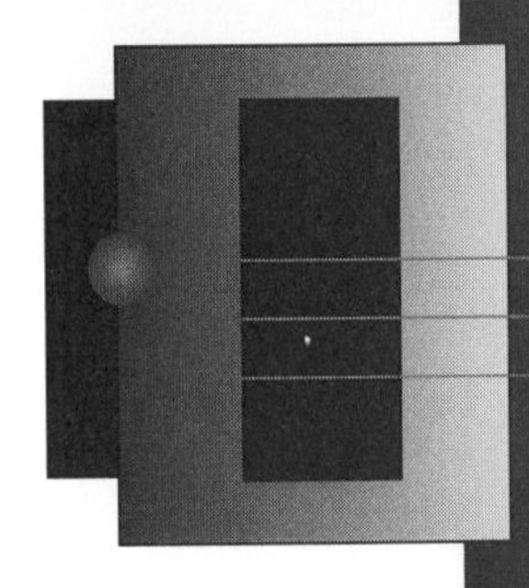

Acknowledgments

We are thankful for the encouragement, suggestions, and counsel provided by many instructors, professionals, and students in writing this book. It has been a team effort and we recognize the contributions of all of these individuals. They include the many professionals who read portions of this book in various forms:

Kenneth Alterman
(*Standard & Poor's*)

Clyde Bartter
(*Portfolio Advisory Co.*)

Hyman C. Grossman
(*Standard & Poor's*)

Richard Huff
(*Standard & Poor's*)

Michael A. Hyland
(*First Boston Corp.*)

Robert J. Mebus
(*Standard & Poor's*)

Robert Mednick
(*Arthur Andersen*)

William C. Norby
(Financial Analyst)

David Norr
(*First Manhattan Corp.*)

Thornton L. O'Glove
(*Quality of Earnings Report*)

Paul Rosenfield
(*AICPA*)

George B. Sharp
(*CITIBANK*)

Fred Spindel
(*Coopers & Lybrand*)

Frances Stone
(*Merrill Lynch & Co.*)

Jon A. Stroble
(*Jon A. Stroble & Associates, Ltd.*)

Jack L. Treynor
(*Treynor-Arbit Associates*)

Neil Weiss
(*Jon A. Stroble & Associates, Ltd.*)

Gerald White
(*Grace & White, Inc.*)

We also want to recognize the many instructors and colleagues who provided valuable comments and suggestions to further improve the book:

Rashad Abdel-Khalik
(*University of Florida*)

Robert N. Anthony
(*Harvard University*)

Hector R. Anton
(*New York University*)

Terry Arndt
(*Central Michigan University*)

Mark Bauman
(*University of Illinois—Chicago*)

William T. Baxter
(*CUNY—Baruch*)

Martin Benis
(*CUNY—Baruch*)

Shyam Bhandari
(*Bradley University*);

Fred Bien
(*Louisiana State University*)
John S. Bildersee
(*New York University*)
Vince Brenner
(*Louisiana State University*)
Abraham J. Briloff
(*CUNY—Baruch*)
Gary Bulmash
(*American University*)
Joseph Bylinski
(*University of North Carolina*)
Douglas Carmichael
(*CUNY—Baruch*)
Philip Chuey
(*Youngstown State University*)
Benny R. Copeland
(*North Texas State University*)
Maurice P. Corrigan
(*Teikyo Post University*)
Wallace N. Davidson III
(*North Texas State University*)
Harry Davis
(*CUNY—Baruch*)
Peter Lloyd Davis
(*CUNY—Baruch*)
Peter Easton
(*Ohio State University*)
Eric S. Emory
(*Sacred Heart University*)
William P. Enderlein
(*Golden Gate University*)
Calvin Engler
(*Iona College*)
Thomas J. Frecka
(*University of Notre Dame*)
John Gentis
(*Ball State University*)
Philip Gerdin
(*University of New Haven*)
Edwin Grossnickle
(*Western Michigan University*)
Peter M. Gutman
(*CUNY—Baruch*)
J. Larry Hagler
(*East Carolina University*)
Jerry Han
(*SUNY—Buffalo*)
Frank Heflin
(*Yale University*)
Yong-Ha Hyon
(*Temple University*)
Henry Jaenicke
(*Drexel University*)
Kenneth H. Johnson
(*Georgia Southern University*)
Homer Kripke
(*New York University*)
Russ Langer
(*San Francisco State University*)
Burton T. Lefkowitz
(*C.W. Post College*)
Steven Lillien
(*CUNY—Baruch*)
Thomas Lopez
(*Pace University*)
Mostafa Maksy
(*Northeastern Illinois University*)
Brenda Mallouk
(*University of Toronto*)
Martin Mellman
(*Hofstra University*)
Belinda Mucklow
(*University of Wisconsin*)
Hugo Nurnberg
(*CUNY—Baruch*)
Stephen Penman
(*University of California at Berkeley*)
Tom Porter
(*Boston College*)
Larry Prober
(*Rider University*)
William Ruland
(*CUNY—Baruch*)
Stanley C. W. Salvary
(*Canisius College*)
Emanuel Saxe
(*CUNY—Baruch*)
Lenny Soffer
(*Northwestern University*)

Reed Storey
(*Financial Accounting Standards Board*)
Rebecca Todd
(*Boston University*)
Jerrold Weiss
(*Lehman College*)
Kenneth L. Wild
(*University of London*)
Richard F. Williams
(*Wright State University*)
Philip Wolitzer
(*Marymount Manhattan College*)
Christine V. Zavgren
(*Clarkson University*)
Stephen Zeff
(*Rice University*)

We acknowledge permission to use problems adapted from examinations of the Institute of Chartered Financial Analysts and the American Institute of Certified Public Accountants. We also appreciate the support of Adaptec, Inc., and Cole Danehower for permission to use Adaptec's unique and innovative annual reports for educational purposes. This is an exciting partnership, and one that should benefit both instructor and student.

We are fortunate to work with a publisher committed to education. The Irwin/McGraw-Hill team working on this book did an outstanding job and we want to especially thank George Werthman, Sponsoring Editor; Jeff Shelstad, Publisher; Marc Chernoff, Development Editor; Beth Cigler, Senior Project Manager; Melissa Caughlin, Marketing Coordinator; and Rhonda Seelinger, Marketing Manager.

Mark Bauman, University of Illinois—Chicago, provided valuable advice and help in this edition. His contribution was exceptional and much appreciated.

Special thanks go to our families for their patience, understanding, and inspiration in completing this book, and we dedicate the book to them. We also thank Leonard and Mary Wild, Thomas and Darlene Kieliszewski, and Thomas, Rosemary, Karen, Robert, Shirley, and Kenneth. To you and to all who contributed to the book, we extend our sincere appreciation.

Leopold A. Bernstein
John J. Wild

About the Authors

Leopold A. Bernstein is Professor of Business at Bernard M. Baruch College, City University of New York. He received his MBA from Harvard University and his PhD from New York University. Professor Bernstein is a consultant to many financial institutions and accounting firms, and is a Certified Public Accountant.

Professor Bernstein has taught numerous courses and professional training programs in financial statement analysis and accounting. He is a recognized teacher, known for his expertise in financial statement analysis and his commitment to professional instruction and education. He is a recipient of several prestigious honors, including the Graham and Dodd Award from the Financial Analysts Federation for outstanding contribution, the Best Article Award from the *Journal of Accountancy*, and the Gold Medal Award from the Massachusetts Society of CPAs. He is sought after for expert witness testimony in financial statement analysis and company valuation, and he conducts professional training programs for major domestic and international financial institutions.

Professor Bernstein is active in several important organizations. He is also the author of several notable books including *Analysis of Financial Statements*, *Cases in Financial Statement Reporting and Analysis*, *Advanced Accounting*, and *Understanding Corporate Reports: A Guide to Financial Statement Analysis*. His more than 30 research publications appear in the *Financial Analysts Journal*, *Harvard Business Review*, *The Accounting Review*, *The Journal of Commercial Bank Lending*, *The Journal of Accountancy*, *The Financial Review*, *The CPA Journal*, and many other business and professional periodicals.

Professor Bernstein and his wife Cynthia enjoy biking, travel, and music. They make their home in Haworth, New Jersey.

John J. Wild is Professor of Business and Vilas Research Scholar at The University of Wisconsin at Madison. He has previously held appointments at Michigan State University and The University of Manchester in England. He received his BBA, MS, and PhD from The University of Wisconsin.

Professor Wild teaches courses in financial accounting and analysis at both the undergraduate and graduate levels. He has received the Mable W. Chipman Excellence-in-Teaching Award and the Departmental Excellence-in-Teaching Award at The University of Wisconsin. He also received the Beta Alpha Psi and Roland F. Salmonson Excellence-in-Teaching Award from

Michigan State University. Professor Wild is a past KPMG Peat Marwick National Fellow and is a prior recipient of Fellowships from The American Accounting Association, The Ernst and Young Foundation, The University of Wisconsin, and Michigan State University. He is a frequent speaker at universities and at national and international conferences.

Professor Wild is an active member of both The American Accounting Association and its sections, including Financial Reporting, International Accounting, and Auditing. He has served on several committees of these organizations, including the Outstanding Accounting Educator Award, National Program Advisory, Publications, and Research Committees. His research on financial accounting and analysis appears in *The Accounting Review*, *Journal of Accounting Research*, *Journal of Accounting and Economics*, *Contemporary Accounting Research*, *Journal of Accounting, Auditing & Finance*, *Journal of Accounting and Public Policy*, *Auditing: A Journal of Theory and Practice*, and other accounting and business periodicals. He is Associate Editor of *Contemporary Accounting Research*, and has served on editorial boards of several respected journals, including *The Accounting Review*, *Accounting and Business Research*, *The British Accounting Review*, and the *Journal of Accounting and Public Policy*.

Professor Wild, his wife, and three children enjoy travel, music, sports, and community activities. They make their home in Madison, Wisconsin.

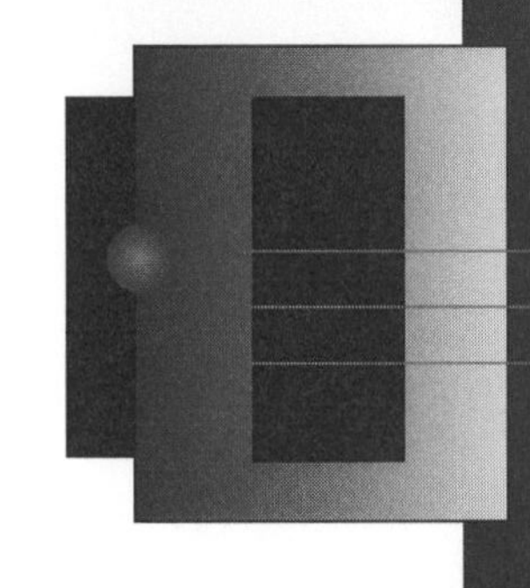

Contents in Brief

Contents

PART ONE

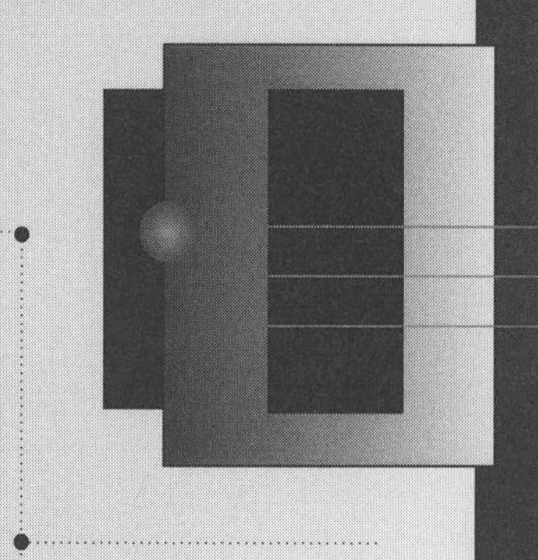

Financial Statement Analysis and Reporting

CHAPTER 1 *Overview of Financial Statement Analysis*

Chapter 1 introduces us to financial statement analysis and its importance in making business decisions. We see how financial statements capture and report on business activities. Financial reports of Adaptec are analyzed as an opening illustration of financial statement analysis. You'll learn about important financial features of several companies, including The Limited, McDonald's, Nike, PepsiCo, and Wal-Mart. During our reading you'll assume the role of a banker, an investor, and a community activist. We'll see how financial statement analysis fits with theories of market efficiency, and we'll also learn about financial statement analysis research and how financial numbers affect stock prices.

CHAPTER 2 *Analysis Objectives and Financial Reporting*

This chapter describes the primary users of financial statements, including creditors, investors, managers, auditors, directors, analysts, regulators, employees, and customers, and explains how this information affects their business decisions. We discuss the accounting dual-entry system and its measurement of business activities. Accounting requires estimates and assumptions, and we discuss how these limit the reliability and relevance of our analysis. We introduce specialized analysis techniques and discuss the usefulness of comparability analysis. In our reading, you'll assume the role of a director confronting a lawyer's warnings about litigation risk as well as an auditor seeking to use financial statement analysis techniques on a new client engagement. We'll learn about fundamental analysis research and the value of financial statements in predicting companies' values.

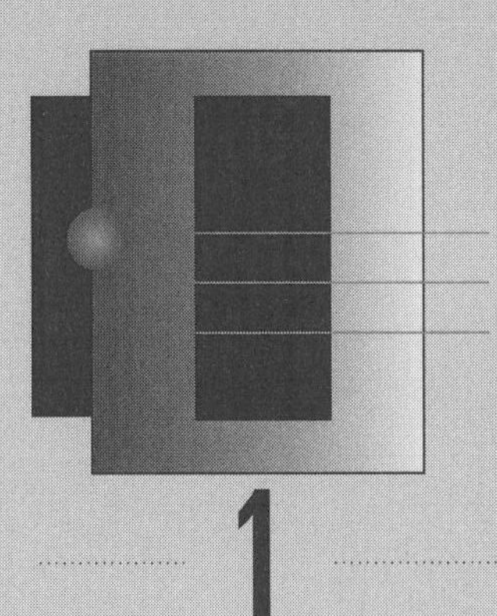

CHAPTER 1

Overview of Financial Statement Analysis

A Look at This Chapter

We begin our analysis of financial statements by considering their relevance in analyzing an actual company. This leads us to focus on financial statement users, their information needs, and how financial statement analysis helps address these needs. We describe the major types of business activities and how they are revealed in financial statements. We conduct a preliminary financial statement analysis of a company to illustrate these important concepts. We learn that financial statement analysis has several purposes and benefits.

A Look Ahead

Chapter 2 reviews objectives of financial statement analysis from the perspective of specific users. We consider the relevance and limitations of accounting information and describe specialized financial statement analysis techniques. Chapters 3 through 7 include detailed analysis of, and the adjustments necessary for, the accounting numbers underlying financial statement analysis. Chapters 8 through 13 focus on mastering the tools of financial statement analysis. A comprehensive financial statement analysis of a company completes the book.

Learning Objectives

- Explain why financial statement analysis is important.
- Identify financial statement users and information relevant for their decisions.
- Describe major types of business activities and their impact on financial statements.
- Explain the purpose of each financial statement and the linkages between them.
- Identify additional information in a financial reporting system and its relevance.
- Analyze and interpret the financial statements of an actual company as a preview to more fundamental analysis.
- Describe several financial statement analysis techniques and their relevance.
- Explain the purpose of financial statement analysis in an efficient market.
- Describe important investment theories and their implications for financial analysis (Appendix 1A).

PREVIEW OF CHAPTER 1

Financial statement analysis applies analytical tools and techniques to general-purpose financial statements and related data to derive estimates and inferences useful in business decisions. It is a screening tool in selecting investment or merger candidates, and is a forecasting tool of future financial conditions and consequences. It is a diagnostic tool in assessing financing, investing, and operating activities, and is an evaluation tool for managerial and other business decisions. Financial statement analysis reduces our reliance on hunches, guesses, and intuition, and in turn it diminishes our uncertainty in decision making. It does not lessen the need for expert judgment but rather establishes an effective and systematic basis for making business decisions. This chapter describes users of financial statements and explains business activities underlying financial statements. We introduce several fundamental tools and techniques of financial statement analysis. Special attention is devoted to a preliminary financial statement analysis of an actual company, Adaptec, Inc. The content and organization of this chapter are as follows:

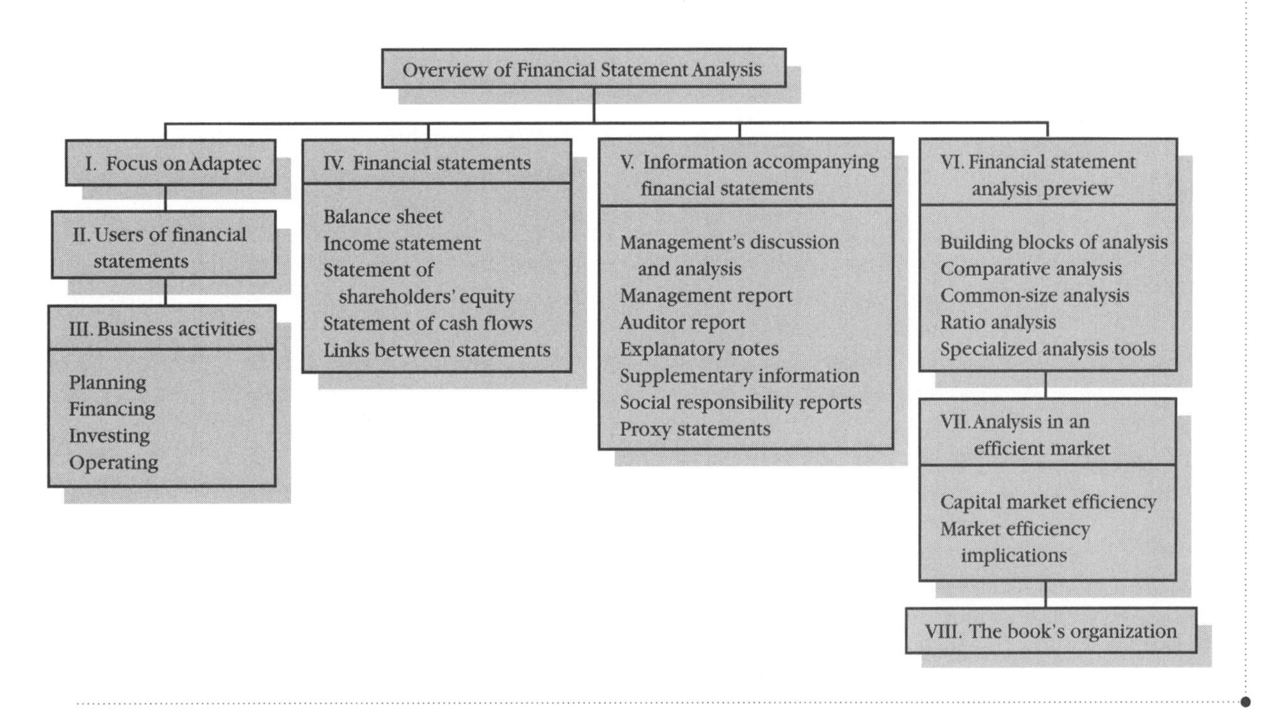

Focus on Analysis: Adaptec, Inc.

Financial statements report a company's past financial performance and current financial position. They are designed to provide information on four primary business activities: planning, financing, investing, and operating activities. This book emphasizes financial statement analysis by helping us read, understand, and use financial statements for making better decisions. Today's advanced

technology increases the importance of expert financial statement analysis. We are required to sort through a vast maze of information to gain insight into a company's current and future prospects. Analyzing financial statements helps us sort through and evaluate information, focusing attention on reliable information most relevant to our business decisions.

Adaptec, Inc., is a leading company in advanced communications and technology. Adaptec supplies computer hardware and software to facilitate interaction between computer systems and peripheral devices like printers, disk drives, CD-ROMs, and scanners. Its 1996 annual report is reproduced in Supplement A near the end of the book.

Adaptec requires considerable resources to finance its operations. The company's 1996 balance sheet reveals contributions from shareholders of more than $182 million and more than $134 million from creditors. Are we willing to contribute to the financing of Adaptec—either through an investment in stock or through a loan? Financial statement analysis helps us make this decision. A review of Adaptec's financial performance reveals considerable growth since 1992—net revenues (339%), net income (607%), and total assets (366%) show striking increases. Financial markets recognize this growth and, as noted in its annual report, Adaptec's common stock, valued between $14 and $19½ a share in the first quarter of 1995, traded between $35⅛ and $56⅜ by the fourth quarter of 1996 (see Selected Financial Data section in Supplement A). But what are its future prospects? Are you willing to buy Adaptec's shares at $35, or $45, or $55, or some other value? Financial statement analysis helps us answer these questions.

We use and rely on financial statements in making important decisions. Shareholders and creditors assess future company prospects for investing and lending decisions. Boards of directors, as shareholders' representatives, use financial statement information in monitoring management's decisions. Employees and unions use financial statements in labor negotiations. Suppliers use financial statements in establishing credit terms. Customers use financial statements in deciding whether to establish supplier relationships. Public utilities set customer rates by referring to financial statements. Information intermediaries, like Dunn & Bradstreet, Moody's, and Standard & Poor's, use financial statements in making buy-sell recommendations and setting credit ratings. Auditors use financial statements in assessing the "fair presentation" of their clients' financial statement numbers.

More specifically, when analyzing Adaptec, creditors perform financial statement analysis to answer the following type of questions:

- What are reasons for Adaptec's need for additional financing?
- What are Adaptec's likely sources for payment of interest and principal?

- How has Adaptec handled its prior short- and long-term financing?
- What are Adaptec's likely needs for future financing?

Shareholders and potential shareholders also require information in analyzing Adaptec. Financial statement analysis helps shareholders answer the following questions:

- What are Adaptec's current and long-term operating prospects?
- What is Adaptec's future earnings potential?
- Are Adaptec's earnings vulnerable to significant variability?
- What is Adaptec's current financial condition?
- What factors most likely determine Adaptec's financial position?
- What is Adaptec's capital (financing) structure?
- What risks and rewards do Adaptec's capital structure present?
- How does Adaptec compare with its competitors?

Sound decision making begins with identifying the most pertinent questions for the objectives at hand. While financial statement analysis does not provide all the answers, every decision is aided by such analysis. This book helps develop skills needed by financial statement users when making business decisions.

Users of Financial Statements

Financial statement users are broadly classified into two groups. **Internal users,** primarily the managers of a company, are involved in making operating and strategic decisions for the business. As employees, they typically have complete access to a company's information system. Internally generated financial reports are, therefore, specifically tailored to the unique information needs of an internal decision maker, such as a CEO, CFO, or internal auditor. **External users** are individuals not directly involved in the company's operations. These users must rely on information provided by management as part of the financial reporting process. This book stresses the analysis needs of external users of general-purpose financial statements. Nevertheless, many analysis techniques described here are usefully applied by internal users.

There are many classes of external users of financial statements. **Creditors** are bankers, bondholders, and other individuals who lend money to business enterprises. Creditors look to financial statements for evidence concerning the ability of the borrower to pay periodic interest payments and repay the principal amount when the loan matures. **Equity investors** include existing and potential shareholders of a company. Existing shareholders need financial information in deciding whether to continue holding the stock or sell it. Potential shareholders need financial information to help in choosing among competing alternative investments. Equity investors are generally interested in assessing the future profitability and/or riskiness of a company. **Merger and acquisition analysts** are interested in determining the economic value and assessing the financial and operating compatibility of potential merger candidates. **Auditors** use financial analysis techniques in determining areas warranting special attention during their examination of a client's financial statements. A company's **board of directors,** in their role as appointees of shareholders, monitors management's actions. **Regulatory agencies** utilize financial statements in the exercise of their supervisory functions, including the Securities and Exchange Commission which vigilantly oversees published financial statements for compliance with federal securities laws. Certain price-regulated industries, such as public utilities, submit financial reports to regulators for rate-determination purposes. Other users include **employees** (in evaluating the fairness of their wages and working conditions), **intermediaries** (in offering investment advice), **suppliers** (in determining the creditworthiness of customers), and **customers** (in evaluating the staying power of their suppliers). All of these users rely on the analysis of financial statements.

Business Activities in a Market Economy

A business pursues a number of activities in a desire to provide a saleable product and to yield a satisfactory return on investment. Adaptec supplies hardware and software products that enhance performance of computer-related tasks. Financial statements and related disclosures are designed to inform us about four major activities of a company: planning, financing, investing, and operating. It is important to understand each of these major business activities before we can effectively analyze a company's financial statements.

Planning Activities

A company exists to implement specific goals and objectives. Adaptec aspires to deliver high-quality technology-based computer products. A company's goals and objectives are captured in a **business plan** or strategy, that describes the company's purpose, strategy, and tactics for activities. A business plan assists managers in focusing their efforts and identifying expected opportunities and obstacles. Knowledge or insight into a business plan considerably aids our analysis of a company's current and future prospects. We look for information on company objectives and tactics, market demands, competitive analysis, sales strategies (pricing, promotion, distribution), management performance, and financial projections. Information of this type, in varying forms, is often revealed in financial reports to outsiders. It is also available through less formal means, such as press releases, industry publications, analysts' newsletters, and popular magazines.

Two important sources for information on a company's business plan are the Shareholders' Letter and Management's Discussion and Analysis. Adaptec, in its Shareholders' Letter from its 1996 annual report, discusses various business opportunities and plans: "a growing market for the expandability and speed offered by Adaptec's products . . . We have achieved strategic supplier status with several important customers . . . Our leadership position in this market was further underscored . . . We anticipate further growth with the market acceptance of new peripherals . . . acquiring complementary companies and technologies . . . prepare for new market opportunities in the longer term through ongoing development of products based on serial interfaces." Additional discussion appears in the Management's Discussion and Analysis section of Adaptec's financial report. These two sources are excellent starting points in constructing a company's business plan. Much more information on a company's business plan and strategy are found in its annual report and other direct and indirect sources.

It is important to stress business planning is not cast in stone and is fraught with expectations. Can Adaptec be certain of the future of high-performance connectivity or the delivery of digital data? Can Adaptec be certain silicon, semiconductors, or other raw material costs will not increase? Can Adaptec be sure how competitors will react? These and other questions add *risk* to our analysis. While all actions involve risk, some actions involve more than others. Financial statement analysis helps us estimate the degree of risk, or uncertainty, and yields more informed and better decisions. While information taken from financial reports does not provide irrefutable answers, it does help us gauge the soundness of a company's business opportunities and strategies, and better understand its financing, investing, and operating needs.

Financing Activities

A company requires financing to carry out its business plan. Adaptec needs financing in purchasing raw materials for production, in acquiring complementary companies and technologies, and in pursuing research and development. **Financing activities** are the means companies use to pay for these ventures. Because of their magnitude, and their potential in determining the success or failure of a venture, companies take care in acquiring and managing their financial resources.

There are two main sources of business financing: equity investors (also referred to as *owners* or *shareholders*) and creditors (also called *lenders*). Decisions concerning the composition of financing activities are not separate from conditions existing in financial markets. Financial markets are potential sources of business financing. In looking to financial markets, a company considers several issues including: the amount of financing necessary, source(s) of financing (owners or creditors), timing of repayment, and structure of the financing agreement(s). Decisions on these issues determine a company's organizational structure, affect its growth, influence its riskiness, and determine the power of outsiders in business decisions.

Equity investors are a major supplier of financing. Adaptec's balance sheet shows it raised more than $182 million by issuing stock to equity investors. Investors provide financing in a desire for a fair return on their investment, weighing both the return and risk of financing. **Return** is the equity investors' share of company earnings, and takes one of two forms: earnings distribution or earnings reinvestment. **Earnings distribution** involves a company paying cash or other assets to investors. **Dividend payout** refers to the amount of earnings distributed, and often is described as a percent: Dividend paid ÷ Earnings. Adaptec is a "growth company," which is evidenced by a zero dividend payout. **Earnings reinvestment** refers to increasing company value through earnings financing. **Equity growth** is the amount of earnings reinvested, and is often described as a percent: Equity growth ÷ Equity investors' value in the company. Adaptec's equity growth is 27.8 percent ($103,375/$371,644).

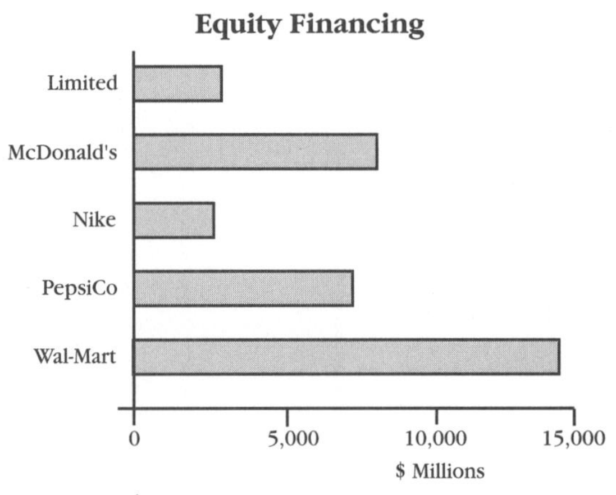

Source: Annual reports.

Equity financing can be in cash or any asset or service contributed to a company in exchange for shares.

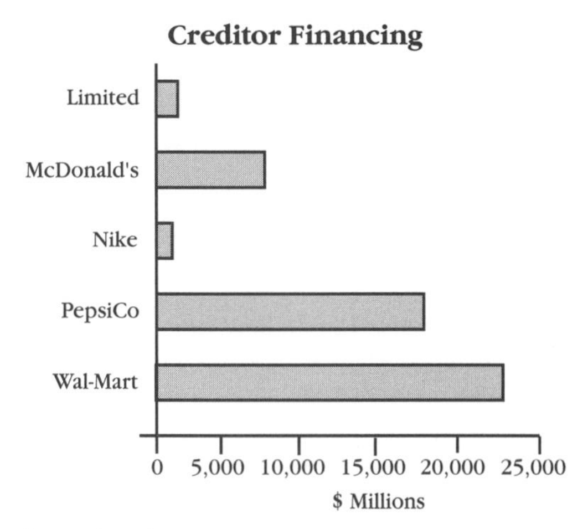

Source: Annual reports.

Private offerings of shares usually involve selling shares to one or more individuals or organizations. Public offerings involve selling shares to the public. There are significant costs with public offerings of shares, including government regulatory filings, stock exchange listing requirements, and brokerage fees to selling agents. Public offerings of shares provide substantial funds for business activities. Many corporations offer their shares for trading on organized exchanges like the New York, Tokyo, Singapore, and London stock markets. Adaptec's common stock trades in the over-the-counter market under the NASDAQ symbol ADPT.

Companies also obtain financing from creditors. Creditor financing of business activities often occurs through loans. Creditors include organizations like banks, savings and loans, and other financial or nonfinancial institutions. Creditors also include individuals, for example, a manager, an employee, or a financier. Adaptec's balance sheet shows that creditor financing is 20.8 percent ($134,541/$646,486) of total financing.

Creditor financing is different than equity financing in that an agreement, or **contract,** is usually established requiring repayment of the loan with interest at a specific date(s). While interest is not always expressly stated in these contracts, it is always implicit. Loan periods are variable and depend on the desires of both creditors and companies. Loans can be as long as 50 years or more or as short as a week or less. Even employees who are paid periodically, say weekly or monthly, are providing a form of credit financing. When employees provide services to the business but do not receive pay for a week, they are providing a source of short-term financing. Nearly 40 percent ($22,440/$56,717) of Adaptec's accrued liabilities relate to compensation and related taxes. There are numerous instances of this implicit creditor financing—utility, supplier, and tax payments.

Like equity investors, creditors are concerned with return and risk. Unlike equity investors, creditors' returns are usually specified in loan contracts. For example, a 20-year 10 percent fixed-rate loan is straightforward—that is, creditors receive a 10 percent annual return on their investment for 20 years. Adaptec's long-term loan is due in June 1998, requiring interest payments of 7.65 percent (see note 4 to statements). Equity investors' returns are not guaranteed and depend on the level of future earnings. Risk for creditors is the likelihood a business is unsuccessful and defaults in repaying its loans and interest. In this situation, creditors might not receive their money due, and bankruptcy or other legal remedies ensue. Such remedies always impose costs on creditors.

ANALYSIS VIEWPOINT *. . . You are the banker*

Adaptec requests a $50 million loan from your bank. How does the composition of Adaptec's financing sources (creditor and/or owner) affect your loan decision? Do you have any reluctance making the loan to Adaptec given its current financing composition? (Note: Solutions to analysis viewpoints appear at the end of each chapter.)

Investing Activities

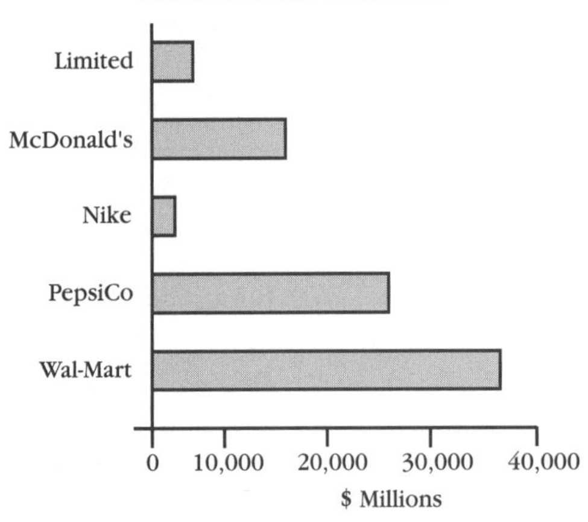

Source: Annual reports.

Investing activities are the acquisition and maintenance of investments by companies to sell products or provide services. Financing provides the funds necessary to acquire the investments needed to carry out business plans. Investments include land, buildings, equipment, legal rights (patents, licenses, copyrights), inventories, human capital (managers, employees), information systems, and all components necessary for operating a company. Adaptec's balance sheet shows its 1996 investment, or asset, base is $646 million.

Information on both financing and investing activities assists us in putting some of the puzzle together revealing business performance. Notice also that the value of investments always equals the value of financing obtained. Any excess financing not invested is simply reported as cash (or some other noncash asset). Companies differ in the amount and composition of their investments. Many companies demand huge investments in acquiring, developing, and selling their products, while others require little investment. Size of investment does not necessarily determine company success. It is the efficiency and effectiveness with which a company carries out its operations that determine earnings and returns to owners.

Investing decisions involve several factors including type of investment necessary (including technological and labor intensity), amount required, acquisition timing, asset location, and contractual agreement (purchase, rent, lease). Adaptec's assets are 72 percent current ($465,280/$646,486) and 28 percent noncurrent ($181,206/$646,486). Like financing activities, decisions on investing activities determine a company's organizational structure (centralized or decentralized operations), affect growth, and influence riskiness of operations. Nearly 40 percent of Adaptec's identifiable assets are in Asia ($259,179/$646,486) (see note 9 in its 1996 report).

Investment total and composition is of value to both insiders and outsiders of a company as a measure to assess earnings. Adaptec's income statement shows its 1996 net income is $103,375, and its return on beginning-of-year investment is 23.7 percent ($103,375 ÷ $435,708)—a seemingly adequate return. In comparison, if the same $103,375 income is obtained with investments of $10,000,000, we might question Adaptec's long-term viability in light of its low 1 percent return on investment. Such analysis, while revealing, is not a complete picture. We still need to consider costs of financing. For example, while a 16 percent return looks appealing, we might think otherwise if financing costs equal 17 percent.

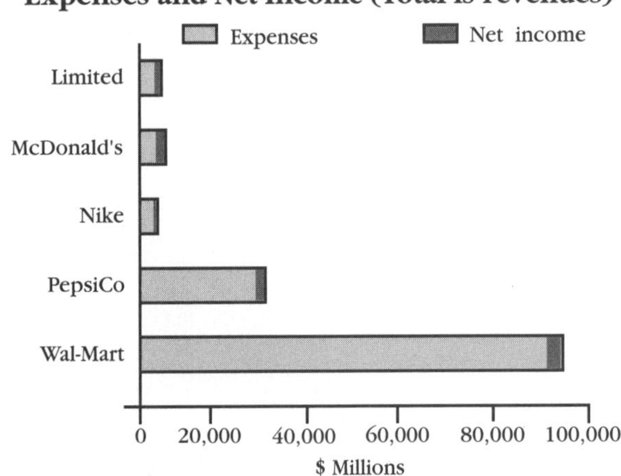

Source: Annual reports.

Operating Activities

One of the more important pieces in analyzing a company is operating activities. **Operating activities** represent the "carrying out" of the business plan given necessary financing and investing. These activities involve at least five basic components: research, purchasing, producing, marketing, and labor. A proper mix of key components of operating activities depends on the type of business, its plans, and "input" markets. Input markets for operating activities include raw materials for production. Examples are supplier markets, labor markets, technology markets, and consumer markets. Management decides on the most efficient and effective mix for their company's competitive advantage.

Operating activities are a company's primary source of income. Income measures a company's success in buying from input markets and selling in output markets. How well a company does in devising business plans and strategies, and deciding on materials comprising the mix of operating activities, determines business success or failure. Our analysis of income numbers, and their component parts, measures a company's success in efficiently and effectively managing these business activities.

Financial Statements Capture Business Activities

Business activities—planning, financing, investing, and operating—are synthesized into a cohesive picture of how businesses function in a market economy. Exhibit 1.1 portrays these business activities from the beginning to the end of one period; in practice, this process continues indefinitely. Step one for the company is formulating plans and strategies. Next, a company pursues financing from equity investors and creditors. Financing is used to acquire investments in land, buildings, equipment, merchandise, labor, and other resources to produce goods or services (the operating activities).

The top level of Exhibit 1.1 shows investing and financing activities at the business's inception (termed *beginning of period*). Actual amounts needed for investing and financing activities are specified in the business plan. Investing and financing are intentionally displayed opposite each other to emphasize their equality or balance. That is, financing is always in the form of investments, and investments cannot exceed their financing. Provided with financing and investments, a company commences its operating activities to carry out business plans. A merge symbol (∇) is used to stress that operating activities (lower apex) derive from a combination of planning (cohesive

EXHIBIT 1.1 Dynamics of Business Activities

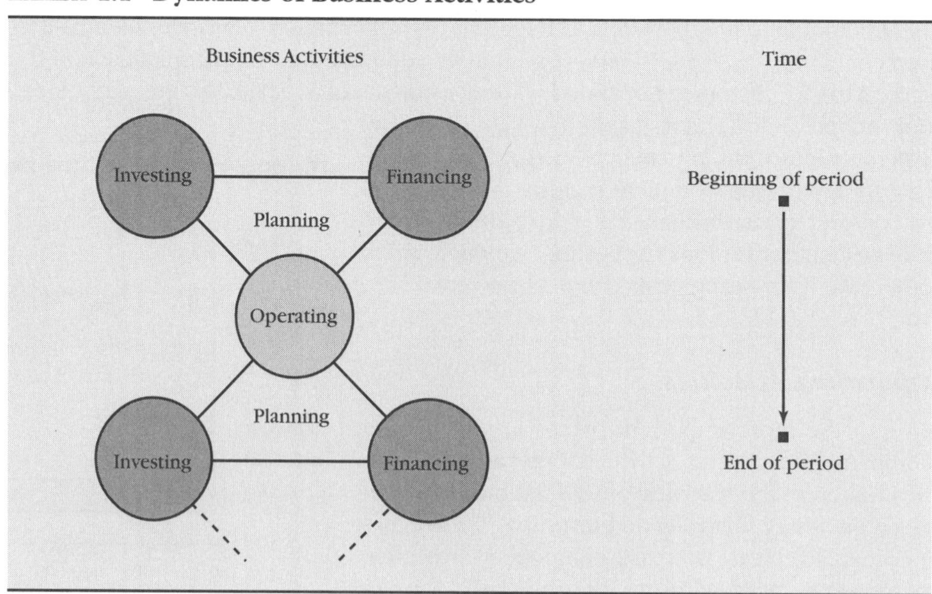

center), financing (right apex), and investing (left apex) activities. A company raises additional financing for further investments or repays suppliers of financing if investment requirements shrink. However, investing always equals financing (referred to as the accounting equation).

At the end of the period—typically quarterly or annually in practice—**financial statements** are prepared. An extract symbol (Δ) is used to indicate preparation of these statements. These statements update listings of financing and investing activities, and summarize operating activities for the most recent period(s). This is the role of financial statements and our object of analysis. Financial statement reporting of financing and investing activities occur at a point in time, whereas operating activities are reported for a period of time. In Exhibit 1.1, there are two disclosure points: beginning of period and end of period. Four primary financial statements are prepared: the balance sheet, the income statement, the statement of shareholders' (owners') equity, and the statement of cash flows.

Balance Sheet

The **accounting equation** is the basis of the financial reporting system:

$$\text{Assets} = \text{Liabilities} + \text{Shareholders' equity}$$

The left-hand side of this equation relates to the economic resources controlled by a company, or **assets.** These resources are valuable in representing potential sources of future revenues through operating activities. To engage in operating activities, a company obtains funding to invest in assets. The right-hand side of this equation identifies funding sources. **Liabilities** are funding from creditors and represent obligations of a company or, alternatively, claims of creditors on assets. **Shareholders' equity** is a total of (1) funding invested or contributed by shareholders (contributed capital) and (2) accumulated earnings since inception in excess of distributions to shareholders (retained earnings). From the shareholders' point of view, these amounts represent their claim on company assets.

A balance sheet summarizes the financial position of a company at a given point in time. Most companies are required under accepted accounting practices to present a classified balance sheet. In a classified balance sheet, assets and liabilities are separated into current and noncurrent accounts. **Current assets** are expected to be converted to cash or used in operations within one year or the operating cycle, whichever is longer. **Current liabilities** are obligations that the company must settle in the same time period. The difference between current assets and current liabilities is **working capital.**

It is revealing to rewrite the accounting equation in terms of underlying business activities:

$$\text{Investing activities} = \text{Financing activities}$$

Recognizing the two financing sources, this is rewritten as:

$$\text{Investments} = \text{Creditor financing} + \text{Shareholder financing}$$

Exhibit 1.2 shows balance sheets of Adaptec, dated March 31, 1996, and 1995. Adaptec's 1996 investments equal $646,486 million. Of this amount, creditors' claims total $134,541 million, while the remaining $511,945 million represent claims of shareholders. Adaptec's financial statements are also available at its web site [http://www.adaptec.com].

EXHIBIT 1.2 Adaptec Balance Sheet

Consolidated Balance Sheets

IN THOUSANDS

As of March 31	1996	1995
Assets		
Current assets		
Cash and cash equivalents	$ 91,211	$ 66,835
Marketable securities	204,283	179,911
Accounts receivable, net of allowance for doubtful accounts of $4,220 in 1996 and $4,431 in 1995	89,487	56,495
Inventories	55,028	31,712
Prepaid expenses and other	25,271	15,519
Total current assets	465,280	350,472
Property and equipment, net	92,778	67,863
Other assets	88,428	17,373
	$646,486	$435,708
Liabilities and Shareholders' Equity		
Current liabilities		
Current portion of long-term debt	$ 3,400	$ 3,400
Note payable	46,200	—
Accounts payable	23,974	22,008
Accrued liabilities	56,717	31,006
Total current liabilities	130,291	56,414
Long-term debt, net of current portion	4,250	7,650
Commitments (Note 7)		
Shareholders' equity		
Preferred stock		
Authorized shares, 1,000		
Outstanding shares, none	—	—
Common stock		
Authorized shares, 200,000		
Outstanding shares, 53,020 in 1996 and 51,677 in 1995	182,932	140,191
Retained earnings	329,013	231,453
Total shareholders' equity	511,945	371,644
	$646,486	$435,708

See accompanying notes.

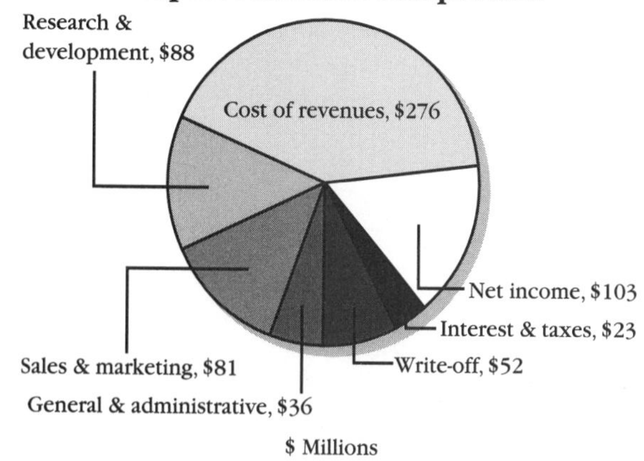

Source: Annual reports.

Income Statement

An income statement measures a company's financial performance between balance sheet dates and, hence, reflects a period of time. It lists revenues, expenses, gains, and losses of a company over a time period. The bottom line, or **net income,** shows the increase (or decrease) in net worth of a company (assets less liabilities), before considering distributions to and contributions from shareholders. In practice, net income is determined using the **accrual basis of accounting.** Under this method, revenues are recognized when a company sells goods and/or renders services, independent of receiving cash. Expenses, in turn, are recognized when related revenue is recorded, independent of

EXHIBIT 1.3 Adaptec Income Statement

Consolidated Statements of Operations

IN THOUSANDS, EXCEPT PER SHARE AMOUNTS

Year Ended March 31	1996	1995	1994
Net revenues	$659,347	$466,194	$372,245
Cost of revenues	275,939	205,596	189,526
Gross profit	383,408	260,598	182,719
Operating expenses			
Research and development	87,628	60,848	39,993
Sales and marketing	81,548	58,737	46,192
General and administrative	35,784	23,229	19,399
Write-off of acquired in-process technology	52,313	—	—
	257,273	142,814	105,584
Income from operations	126,135	117,784	77,135
Shareholder settlement	—	—	(2,409)
Interest income	12,694	7,932	5,183
Interest expense	(840)	(1,179)	(1,306)
	11,854	6,753	1,468
Income before income taxes	137,989	124,537	78,603
Provision for income taxes	34,614	31,135	19,653
Net income	$103,375	$ 93,402	$ 58,950
Net income per share	$ 1.89	$ 1.75	$ 1.10
Weighted average number of common and common equivalent shares outstanding	54,569	53,357	53,602

See accompanying notes.

paying cash. Income statements of Adaptec for fiscal years ended March 31, 1996, 1995, and 1994 appear in Exhibit 1.3. In 1996, Adaptec earned net revenues of $659,347 million. Of this amount, $555,972 million is offset with a variety of expenses, yielding net income of $103,375 million.

Statement of Shareholders' Equity

The statement of shareholders' equity reports changes in component accounts comprising equity. This statement is useful in identifying reasons for changes in shareholders' claims on the assets of a company. As we discuss in subsequent chapters, accepted practice excludes certain gains and losses from net income that, instead, are directly reported in the statement of shareholders' equity. Adaptec's statement of shareholders' equity for fiscal years ended March 31, 1996, 1995, and 1994, is shown in Exhibit 1.4. During the 1994–1996 period, individual equity account balances changed due to several reasons: selling stock under employee purchase and option

EXHIBIT 1.4 Adaptec Statement of Shareholders' Equity

Consolidated Statements of Shareholders' Equity

IN THOUSANDS

	Common Stock		Retained	
	Shares	Amount	Earnings	Total
Balance, March 31, 1993	50,714	$124,806	$100,349	$225,155
Sale of common stock under employee purchase and option plans	1,577	7,728	—	7,728
Income tax benefit of employees' stock transactions	—	5,783	—	5,783
Net income	—	—	58,950	58,950
Balance, March 31, 1994	52,291	138,317	159,299	297,616
Sale of common stock under employee purchase and option plans	1,426	11,245	—	11,245
Income tax benefit of employees' stock transactions	—	5,929	—	5,929
Repurchases of common stock	(2,040)	(15,300)	(21,248)	(36,548)
Net income	—	—	93,402	93,402
Balance, March 31, 1995	51,677	140,191	231,453	371,644
Sale of common stock under employee purchase and option plans	1,218	16,512	—	16,512
Issuance of common stock in connection with acquisition	385	17,232	—	17,232
Income tax benefit of employees' stock transactions	—	10,947	—	10,947
Repurchases of common stock	(260)	(1,950)	(5,815)	(7,765)
Net income	—	—	103,375	103,375
Balance, March 31, 1996	53,020	$182,932	$329,013	$511,945

See accompanying notes.

plans, repurchasing of stock, issuing stock for an acquisition, and reinvesting of net income. Particularly important is the change in Adaptec's Retained Earnings balance. Through this account, income statements link consecutive balance sheets. Specifically, Adaptec had retained earnings of $100,349 million in 1993 and reports net income of $58,950 million in 1994, resulting in $159,299 million ($100,349 + $58,950) of retained earnings in 1994. Since dividends represent distributions from retained earnings, the Retained Earnings balance generally represents an upper limit on the amount of potential dividend distributions. This is not yet an issue for Adaptec since, as indicated at the bottom of Selected Financial Data in its 1996 annual report, Adaptec "does not currently plan to pay cash dividends to its shareholders in the near future."

Statement of Cash Flows

Under accrual accounting, net income does not typically equal net cash flow except over the life of a company. Since accrual accounting yields numbers different from cash flow accounting, and cash flows are important, there is a need for periodic reporting

Analysis Research Insight 1.1

Accounting Numbers and Stock Prices

Do accounting numbers such as net income explain changes in a company's stock prices? The answer is yes. Evidence from research shows a definite link between the "news" conveyed in net income and the price changes in a company's stock (returns). "Good news" net income is accompanied by positive stock price changes, whereas "bad news" net income is associated with negative price changes. Also, the more good or bad is net income, the greater is the accompanying stock price reaction. Similar evidence exists for other summary financial statement numbers such as book value.

Research also shows us that many factors influence the relation between accounting numbers and stock prices. These include company factors, such as risk, size, leverage, and variability, which decrease the influence of numbers like net income on prices, and factors, such as earnings growth and persistence, which increase their impact. Our analysis must recognize those influences impacting the relevance of accounting numbers for security analysis.

Fundamental analysis research offers guidance in our use of financial statement information for predicting future stock price changes. Evidence indicates financial statements help reveal the permanent and transitory portions of net income. Permanent portions are much more long-lasting in their impact on stock prices and are commensurately of greater magnitude in their influence on prices.

of cash inflows and outflows. For example, analyses involving reconstruction and interpretation of business transactions often require the statement of cash flows. The statement of cash flows details cash inflows and outflows related to a company's operating, investing, and financing activities over a period of time. Adaptec's statement of cash flows for 1996, 1995, and 1994 appears in Exhibit 1.5. Adaptec's 1996 cash balance increased by $24,376 million, from $66,835 million to $91,211 million. Of this net cash change, Adaptec's operating activities provided $103,379 million, its investing activities used $95,297 million, and its financing activities provided $16,294 million.

Links between Financial Statements

Financial statements are linked at points in time and across time. These links are portrayed in Exhibit 1.6 using Adaptec's financial statements for 1995–1996. Notice Adaptec's statement of retained earnings is included in its statement of shareholders' equity. Adaptec began 1996 with the investing and financing amounts reported in the balance sheet on the far left side of Exhibit 1.6. Its investments, comprising both cash ($66,835) and noncash assets ($368,873), totaled $435,708. These investments are financed from both creditors ($64,064) and equity investors, the latter comprising receipts from both stock issuances ($140,191) and retained earnings ($231,453). Adaptec's 1996 operating activities are reported in the middle "column" of Exhibit 1.6. The statement of cash flows reports how operating, investing, and financing activities impact cash. Adaptec's $66,835 cash balance at the beginning of 1996 grew to $91,211 at year-end. This end-of-year cash figure is reported in the year-end balance sheet on

EXHIBIT 1.5 Adaptec Statement of Cash Flows

Consolidated Statements of Cash Flows

IN THOUSANDS

Year Ended March 31	1996	1995	1994
Cash Flows From Operating Activities:			
Net income	$103,375	$ 93,402	$ 58,950
Adjustments to reconcile net income to net cash provided by operating activities:			
Write-off of acquired in-process technology, net of taxes	39,686	—	—
Depreciation and amortization	17,593	15,662	11,489
Provision for doubtful accounts	250	150	2,069
Changes in assets and liabilities:			
Accounts receivable	(30,727)	(1,311)	(13,020)
Inventories	(20,516)	7,228	(5,563)
Prepaid expenses	(8,973)	460	(5,470)
Other assets	(19,111)	(4,107)	(11,478)
Accounts payable	(167)	2,354	(2,781)
Accrued liabilities	21,969	4,251	8,867
Net Cash Provided by Operating Activities	103,379	118,089	43,063
Cash Flows From Investing Activities:			
Purchase of Trillium, Future Domain and Power I/O, net of cash acquired	(31,177)	—	—
Investments in property and equipment	(39,748)	(31,576)	(17,314)
Investments in marketable securities, net	(24,372)	(32,291)	(20,250)
Net Cash Used for Investing Activities	(95,297)	(63,867)	(37,564)
Cash Flows From Financing Activities:			
Proceeds from issuance of common stock	27,459	17,174	13,511
Repurchase of common stock	(7,765)	(36,548)	—
Principal payments on debt	(3,400)	(3,400)	(2,968)
Net Cash Provided by (Used for) Financing Activities	16,294	(22,774)	10,543
Net Increase in Cash and Cash Equivalents	24,376	31,448	16,042
Cash and Cash Equivalents at Beginning of Year	66,835	35,387	19,345
Cash and Cash Equivalents at End of Year	$ 91,211	$ 66,835	$ 35,387

See accompanying notes.

the far right side of Exhibit 1.6. Adaptec's net income ($103,375) computed from revenues less expenses is reported in the income statement. The income figure helps explain the change in retained earnings reported in the statement of retained earnings. Adaptec chooses not to pay cash dividends and, thus, dividends do not affect its Retained Earnings balance. Adaptec's Retained Earnings balance is carried to the shareholders' equity section of its year-end balance sheet.

In sum, Adaptec's balance sheet is a listing of its investing and financing activities at a *point in time*. The three statements of (1) cash flows, (2) income, and (3) shareholders' equity explain changes (typically from operating activities) over a *period of time* in Adaptec's investing and financing activities. Every transaction captured in these three latter statements impacts the balance sheet. Examples are revenues and expenses affecting net income and subsequently carried to retained earnings, or cash transactions in the statement of cash flows and summarized by the cash balance on the balance sheet, or all revenue and expense accounts affecting one or more balance sheet accounts. Consequently, financial statements are inherently linked: point-in-time balance sheets are explained by the period-of-time income statement, statement of cash flows, and statement of shareholders' equity.

EXHIBIT 1.6 **Financial Statement Links for Adaptec**

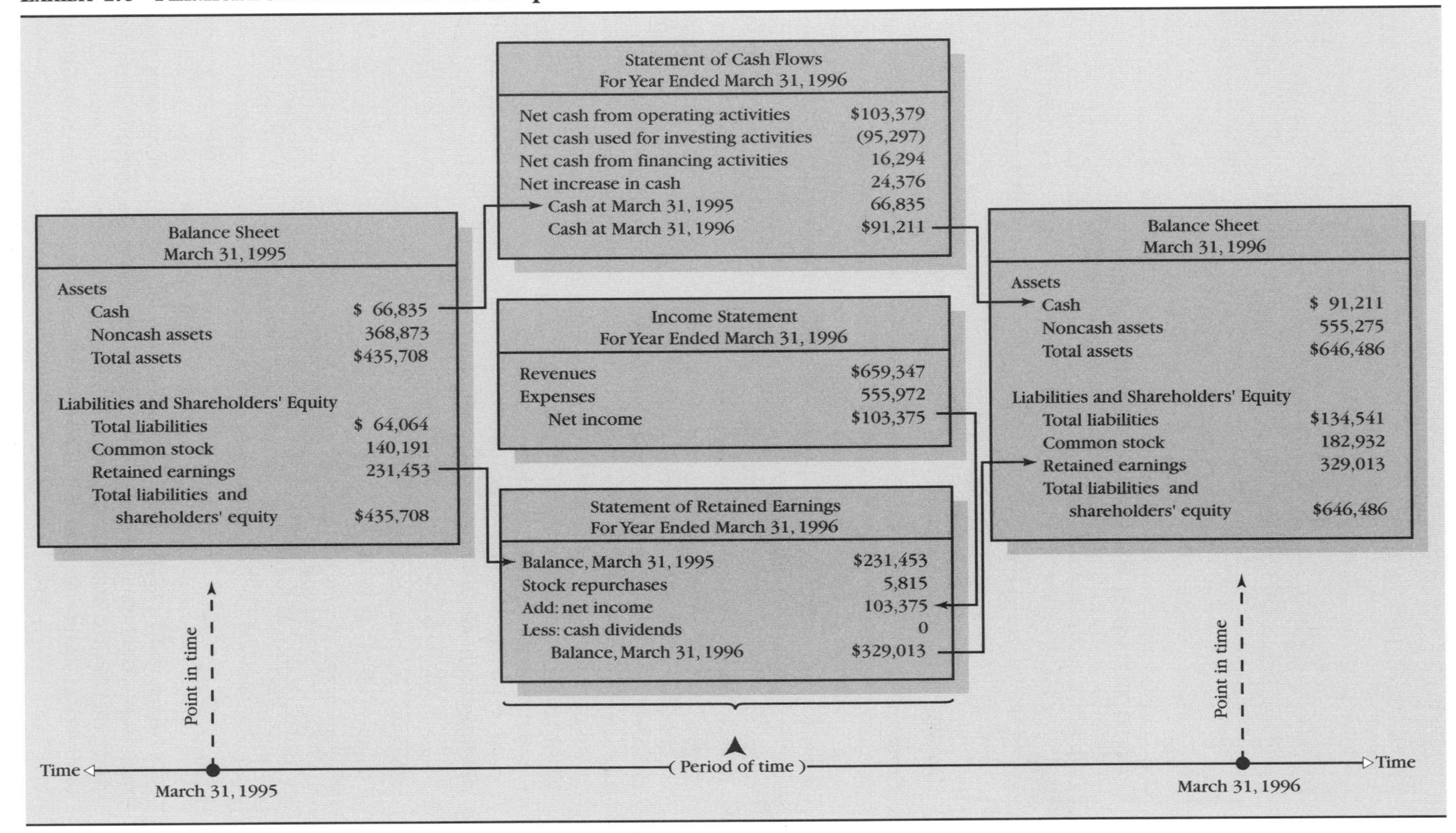

ANALYSIS VIEWPOINT . . . *You are the investor*

You are interested in buying Adaptec stock. Your review of Adaptec's financial statements reveals a near 25 percent decline in net cash flow for 1996, while net income increased by 10 percent. Based on your review of these statements, are you interested in buying Adaptec stock?

Information Accompanying Financial Statements

Formal financial statements are not the sole output of a financial reporting system. Additional information is communicated by companies through a number of sources. A thorough financial statement analysis involves examining these additional sources of information.

Management's Discussion and Analysis (MD&A)

Companies with publicly traded debt and equity securities are required by the Securities and Exchange Commission to provide a Management's Discussion and Analysis (MD&A) in their financial reports. The MD&A section reviews a company's financial condition and results of operations. Management must highlight any favorable or unfavorable trends and identify significant events and uncertainties affecting the company's liquidity, capital resources, and results of operations. They must also disclose prospective information involving material events and uncertainties known to cause reported financial information to not be indicative of future operating activities or of future financial condition. The MD&A also reports qualitative information regarding the effects of inflation and changing prices if material to financial statement trends. Companies are encouraged, but not required, to provide forward-looking information. The MD&A for Adaptec's 1996 financial statements includes a year-by-year analysis along with an analysis of its liquidity and capital resources by business activity (see Supplement A).

Management Report

A management report sets out the responsibilities of management in preparing a company's financial statements. The purposes of this report are (1) to reinforce senior management's responsibilities for the company's financial and internal control system, and (2) to reinforce the shared roles of management, directors, and auditor in preparing financial statements. Adaptec's Report of Management highlights the role of its Audit Committee of the Board of Directors in providing assurance on the integrity of its financial statements.

Auditor Report

An external auditor is an independent certified public accountant hired by management to assess whether the company's financial statements are prepared in conformity with generally accepted accounting principles. Auditors provide an important check on financial statements prior to their public release. There are four types of auditor opinions:

- **Unqualified (clean) opinion.** Financial statements "present fairly" (according to accepted accounting practices) a company's financial performance and position.

- **Qualified opinion.** This is an unqualified opinion except for the item(s) relating to the qualification.
- **Adverse opinion.** Financial statements do not "present fairly" a company's financial performance and position.
- **Disclaimer of opinion.** Audit is insufficient in scope to render an opinion.

Sound financial statement analysis requires a review of the auditor's report to ascertain whether the company received an unqualified opinion before conducting any analysis. Adaptec's Report of Independent Accountants, prepared by Price Waterhouse LLP, is shown in Exhibit 1.7. Adaptec received an unqualified opinion. The auditor's report (as is typical) stresses that with "reasonable," but not complete, assurance the financial statements are free of material misstatement, and in the auditor's opinion these statements "present fairly" the financial position of Adaptec.

Explanatory Notes

Explanatory notes accompanying financial reports play an integral role in financial statement analysis. Notes are a means of communicating additional information regarding items included and excluded from the body of the statements. It is the often technical nature of notes that creates a need for a certain level of accounting sophistication on the part of financial statement users. Explanatory notes include

EXHIBIT 1.7 Adaptec's Auditor Report

Report of Independent Accountants

To the Board of Directors and
Shareholders of Adaptec, Inc.:
In our opinion, the accompanying consolidated balance sheets and the related consolidated statements of operations, of cash flows and of shareholders' equity present fairly, in all material respects, the financial position of Adaptec, Inc. and its subsidiaries at March 31, 1996 and 1995, and the results of their operations and their cash flows for the years then ended in conformity with generally accepted accounting principles. These financial statements are the responsibility of the Company's management; our responsibility is to express an opinion on these financial statements based on our audits. We conducted our audits of these statements in accordance with generally accepted auditing standards which require that we plan and perform the audit to obtain reasonable assurance about whether the financial statements are free of material misstatement. An audit includes examining, on a test basis, evidence supporting the amounts and disclosures in the financial statements, assessing the accounting principles used and significant estimates made by management, and evaluating the overall financial statement presentation. We believe that our audits provide a reasonable basis for the opinion expressed above. The financial statements of Adaptec, Inc. as of and for the year ended March 31, 1994 were audited by other independent accountants whose report dated April 25, 1994 expressed an unqualified opinion on those statements.

Price Waterhouse LLP

San Jose, California
April 22, 1996

information on (1) accounting principles and methods employed, (2) detailed disclosures regarding individual financial statement elements, (3) commitments and contingencies, (4) business combinations, (5) transactions with related parties, (6) stock option plans, (7) legal proceedings, and (8) significant customers.

Supplementary Information

Certain supplemental schedules required by accounting regulatory agencies appear in either the notes to financial statements or, in the case of companies with publicly traded securities, in exhibits to Form 10-K filed with the Securities and Exchange Commission (SEC). Supplemental schedules include information on (1) business segment data, (2) export sales, (3) marketable securities, (4) valuation accounts, (5) short-term borrowings, and (6) quarterly financial data. Several supplemental schedules appear in the 1996 annual report of Adaptec. An example is the information on segment operations included as note 9 to Adaptec's financial statements. The SEC is responsible for overseeing financial reporting to external users for companies with publicly traded securities. It requires annual financial reports to be audited by independent auditors. Companies must file annual and quarterly reports with the SEC. Annual reports are referred to as **Form 10-K reports,** and much of this information overlaps with annual reports to shareholders. Quarterly reports are known as **10-Q reports.** Additional SEC filings are required if certain events occur. Examples include a **Form 8-K report** if a company changes auditors and a *registration statement* if a company issues new shares. Much of this information is available at the SEC's [http://www.sec.gov/edgarhp.htm] web site.

Social Responsibility Reports

Companies increasingly recognize their need for social responsibility. This recognition is not simply altruistic but, rather, translates often into meaningful financial benefits. In our analysis of financial statements, we scrutinize companies on their social responsibility. Our findings are based on management's commitment to employees, its integrity, its devotion to human resource development, and many nonquantifiable (yet relevant) analysis factors. Adaptec's social responsibility report is shown in Exhibit 1.8. This report declares Adaptec's commitment to "the importance of giving back to the communities where Wally and Molly are growing and learning . . . Adaptec in fiscal 1997 is making a special $150,000 donation to support literacy and reading programs to help children get a head start on their futures." While social responsibility reports like Adaptec's are increasing, there is as yet no standard format or accepted practice in this area.

Proxy Statements

Shareholder votes are solicited for electing directors and for votes on corporate actions such as mergers, acquisitions, and authorization of securities. A **proxy** is a means whereby a shareholder authorizes another person(s) to act for him/her at a meeting of shareholders. A **proxy statement** contains information necessary for shareholders in voting on matters for which the proxy is solicited. Proxy statements contain a wealth of information regarding a company including: identity of shareholders owning 5 or more percent of outstanding shares, biographical information on the board of directors, compensation arrangements with officers and directors, employee benefit plans, and certain transactions with officers and directors.

EXHIBIT 1.8 Adaptec's Social Responsibility Report

Adaptec in the Community

PROVIDING OPPORTUNITIES

Wally and Molly are the information users of tomorrow. But they are the children of today, and often children need our help. Adaptec believes in the importance of giving back to the communities where Wally and Molly are growing and learning. In fiscal 1996 we helped the groups and agencies below in their efforts to make our world more livable for children.

Through our commitment to children, Adaptec in fiscal 1997 is making a special $150,000 donation to support literacy and reading programs to help children get a head start on their futures.

The Children's Health Council
Make-A-Wish Foundation
United Way
The Tech Museum of Innovation
Leavey School of Business, Santa Clara University
Reading Research Center, Mission San Jose Elementary School
Junior Achievement
Second Harvest Food Bank
Ronald McDonald House
Leukemia Society of America
Adaptec Scholarship
Indian Peaks Elementary School
Milpitas High School
San Jose State University
Bellarmine College Preparatory
Girl Scouts of Santa Clara County
Los Altos Educational Foundation
Keys School

ANALYSIS VIEWPOINT . . . *You are the community activist*

You are an activist scrutinizing a company's commitment to its community. What can you learn about a company's community commitment from an analysis of financial statements?

Preview of Financial Statement Analysis

In analyzing financial statements, users have a variety of tools available from which to select those best suited to their specific needs. In this section, we introduce certain tools of analysis and apply them to Adaptec's 1996 annual report including: comparative financial statement analysis, common-size financial statement analysis, and ratio analysis. We briefly discuss other, more specialized, analyses (described more fully in latter parts of the book).

Building Blocks of Analysis

Whatever approach to financial statement analysis taken and whatever methods used, we always examine one or more important aspects of a company's financial condition and results of operations. Our financial analysis, motivated by various objectives, falls within any or all of the six areas of inquiry below—in any sequence and with the degree of relative emphasis required under the circumstances. These six areas of inquiry and investigation are the building blocks of financial statement analysis.

- **Short-term liquidity.** A company's ability to meet short-term obligations.
- **Funds flow.** Future availability and disposition of cash.
- **Capital structure and long-term solvency**. A company's ability to generate future revenues and meet long-term obligations.
- **Return on investment.** A company's ability to provide financial rewards sufficient to attract and retain suppliers of financing.
- **Asset utilization.** Asset intensity in generating revenues to reach a sufficient level of profitability.
- **Operating performance.** A company's success at maximizing revenues and minimizing expenses from long-run operating activities.

Each of these six areas of inquiry, and the tools used in analyzing them, receive emphasis throughout the book.

Comparative Financial Statement Analysis

Financial statement users conduct comparative financial statement analysis by setting consecutive balance sheets, income statements, or statements of cash flows side by side, and reviewing changes in individual categories on a year-to-year or multiyear basis. The most important item revealed by comparative financial statement analysis is *trend.* A comparison of statements over several years reveals direction, speed, and extent of a trend(s). Analysis also compares trends in related items. For example, a year-to-year 10 percent sales increase accompanied with a 20 percent increase in freight-out costs requires investigation and explanation. Similarly, a 15 percent increase in accounts receivable and a sales increase of only 10 percent warrants investigation into the reasons for this difference in the rate of increase. Comparative financial statement analysis is also referred to as *horizontal* analysis given the left-right (or right-left) movement of our eyes as they review comparative statements. Two techniques of comparative analysis are especially popular: year-to-year change analysis and index-number trend series analysis.

Year-to-Year Change Analysis

Comparing financial statements over relatively short time periods—two to three years—is performed with analysis of year-to-year changes in line items. A year-to-year change analysis for short time periods is manageable and understandable. It has the advantage of presenting changes in absolute dollar amounts as well as in percentages. Both change analyses are relevant since different dollar sizes of bases in computing percent changes can yield large percent changes inconsistent with their actual importance. For example, a 50 percent change from a base figure of $1,000 is generally less significant than the same percent change from a base of $100,000. Thus, reference to dollar amounts is necessary to retain a proper perspective and to make valid inferences on the relative importance of changes.

Computation of year-to-year changes is straightforward. However, a few clarifying rules should be borne in mind. When a negative amount appears in the base and a positive amount in the next period (or vice versa), we cannot compute a meaningful percent change. Also, when there is no figure for the base year, no percent change is computable. And, when an item has a value in the base year and none in the next period, the decrease is 100 percent. Each of these points is underscored in the following illustration:

Illustration 1.1

Complications and how we confront them in an analysis of changes are depicted under four scenarios:

			Change Analysis	
Scenario Item	***Year 1***	***Year 2***	***Amount***	***Percent***
Net income (loss)	$(4,500)	$1,500	$ 6,000	—
Tax expense	2,000	(1,000)	(3,000)	—
Notes payable	—	8,000	8,000	—
Notes receivable	10,000	—	(10,000)	(100%)

Comparative financial statement analysis typically reports both the cumulative total for the period under investigation and the average (or median) for the period. Comparing yearly amounts with an average computed over a number of years highlights unusual happenings for a particular period, as average values smooth out erratic or unusual fluctuations.

Exhibit 1.9 reports a year-to-year comparative analysis using Adaptec's 1995 and 1996 income statements. While net revenues increase by 41.4 percent, the cost of revenues increases by only 34.2 percent, resulting in a 47.1 percent boost in gross profit. Despite this boost in gross profit, income from operations increases by only 7.1 percent. A major reason for this relatively small income increase is Adaptec's write-off of in-process technology associated with its acquisition of several businesses.

Index-Number Trend Series Analysis

Comparing financial statements covering more than two or three periods using year-to-year change analysis is often cumbersome. An excellent procedure to effect longer-term trend comparisons is index-number trend series analysis. Analyzing data using index-number trend analysis requires choosing a base year, for all items, with a preselected index number usually set to 100. Since a base year represents a frame of reference for all comparisons, it is best to choose a "normal" year with regard to business conditions. One of the earliest years in the series often usefully serves this purpose, yet, if it is atypical, choose another year. As in computing year-to-year percent changes, certain changes, like those from negative to positive amounts, cannot be expressed by means of index numbers. Also, all index numbers are computed by reference to the base year.

EXHIBIT 1.9 Adaptec's Comparative Income Statements

	1996	*1995*	*Change ($)*	*Change (%)*
Net revenues	$659,347	$466,194	$193,153	41.4%
Cost of revenues	275,939	205,596	70,343	34.2
Gross profit	$383,408	$260,598	$122,810	47.1
Operating expenses:				
Research and development	87,628	60,848	26,780	44.0
Sales and marketing	81,548	58,737	22,811	38.8
General and administrative	35,784	23,229	12,555	54.0
Write-off of technology	52,313	0	52,313	—
Income from operations	$126,135	$117,784	$ 8,351	7.1
Interest income	12,694	7,932	4,762	60.0
Interest expense	(840)	(1,179)	(339)	(28.0)
Income before income taxes	$137,989	$124,537	$ 13,452	10.8
Provision for income taxes	34,614	31,135	3,479	11.2
Net income	$103,375	$ 93,402	$ 9,973	10.7%

Illustration 1.2

Century Technology's cash balance (in $ thousands) at December 31, Year 1 (the base year), is $12,000. The cash balance at December 31, Year 2, is $18,000. Using 100 as the index number for Year 1, the index number for Year 2 equals 150 and is computed as:

$$\frac{\text{Current} - \text{Year balance}}{\text{Base} - \text{Year balance}} \times 100 = \frac{\$18,000}{\$12,000} \times 100 = 150$$

The cash balance of Century Technology at December 31, Year 3, is $9,000. The index for Year 3 is 75 and is computed as:

$$\frac{\$9,000}{\$12,000} \times 100 = 75$$

When using index numbers, we compute percent changes by reference to the base year. The change in cash balance between Year 1 and Year 2 is 50 percent (index 150 – index 100), and is easily inferred from the index numbers. However, the change from Year 2 to Year 3 is not 75 percent (150 – 75), as a direct comparison might suggest, but rather is 50 percent (i.e., $9,000/$18,000). This latter computation involves computing the Year 2 to Year 3 change by reference to the Year 2 balance. The percent change is, however, computable using index numbers only, for example, 75/150 = 0.50, or a change of 50 percent.

In conducting index-number trend analysis, we need not analyze every item in financial statements. Rather, we should attempt to eliminate insignificant items. We should also exercise care in using index-number trend comparisons because of certain weaknesses attributed to changes in company and industry factors. In assessing changes in *current* financial condition, comparative statements of cash flows are often useful. An index-number trend comparison is also useful in comparing changes in the *composition* of working capital items over years.

Interpretation of percent changes, including those using index-number trend series, must be made with an awareness of potentially inconsistent applications of accounting principles over time. Where possible, we adjust for these inconsistencies. Also, the longer the time period for comparison, the more distortive are effects of price-level changes (Supplement C considers these effects). An important outcome of trend analysis is its power in conveying insight into management's philosophies, policies, and motivations (conscious or otherwise) underlying the changes revealed. The more diverse the economic environments comprising the periods of analysis, the better our picture of how a company deals with adversity and takes advantage of opportunities.

Index-number trend analysis for selected financial statement items of Adaptec are reported in Exhibit 1.10. Data used in preparing this analysis are taken from the Selected Financial Data in Adaptec's 1996 annual report. We see that net revenues increase by 439 percent over the period of analysis, while gross profit increases by an even greater 583 percent. The largest increase among operating expenses is a 500 percent increase in research and development (R&D). While this rate of increase exceeds that of net revenues, this is not necessarily cause for concern. The advanced computer technology business requires R&D for continual innovation and improvement. A slower rate of increase in R&D, while providing higher short-term earnings, is likely at the expense of long-term earnings. Total assets increase by 466 percent over this period, and the 439 percent increase in shareholders' equity indicates Adaptec has achieved asset growth without reliance on excessive borrowing.

Adaptec's Index-Number Trend Series for Gross Profit and Net Income

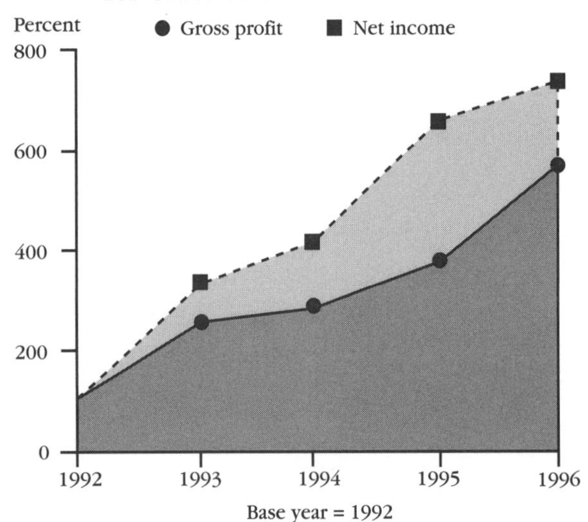

Source: Annual reports.

Data in Exhibit 1.10 use 1992 as the base year. To illustrate the sensitivity of inferences to the choice of base year, Exhibit 1.11 reports similar indices using 1993 as the base year. Notice growth rates for net revenues and gross profit are less than one-half those reported in Exhibit 1.10, implying 1992 might be a less than representative

EXHIBIT 1.10 Adaptec's Index-Number Trend Series (base year 1992)

	1996	*1995*	*1994*	*1993*	*1992*
Net revenues	439	310	248	207	100
Cost of revenues	326	243	224	206	100
Gross profit	583	396	278	209	100
Operating expenses:					
Research and development	500	347	228	150	100
Sales and marketing	382	275	216	152	100
General and administrative	340	221	184	148	100
Income from operations	769	718	470	383	100
Net income	707	639	403	338	100
Total assets	466	314	259	204	100
Shareholders' equity	439	319	255	193	100

starting point. In this regard, consider growth rates in selling and administrative expenses. In Exhibit 1.10, growth rates in sales and marketing expenses (382%) and general and administrative expenses (340%) are lower than the growth in net revenues. Yet in Exhibit 1.11, growth rates in sales and marketing expenses (251%) and general and administrative expenses (230%) exceed the 212 percent growth in net revenues. This simple exercise emphasizes the importance of proper base year selection.

Common-Size Financial Statement Analysis

Financial statement analysis benefits from knowing the proportion of a total group or subgroup an item represents. In analyzing a balance sheet, it is common to express total assets, liabilities, and capital each as 100 percent, and individual items within these categories as a percent of their respective total. In analyzing an income statement, net revenues is commonly set at 100 percent with other income statement items expressed as a percent of net revenues. Since the sum of these individual items totals 100 percent, this analysis technique is said to yield **common-size financial statements.** This technique is also referred to as **vertical analysis** given the up-down (or down-up) movement of our eyes as they review the statements. Common-size financial statement analysis is an inquiry into the internal structure of financial statements. In analyzing a balance sheet, a structural analysis focuses on two elements:

- Sources of financing, including the distribution of financing among current liabilities, noncurrent liabilities, and equity capital.
- Composition of investments, including current and noncurrent assets.

Common-size balance sheet analysis is often extended to examine the proportions comprising particular subgroups. For example, in assessing liquidity of current assets, it is often important to know what proportion of current assets is comprised of inventories, and not simply what proportion inventories are of total assets. Common-size income statement analysis is often of even greater importance. An income statement readily lends itself to a common-size analysis, where each item is related to a key quantity (e.g., sales). To varying degrees, sales level affects each expense, and it is instructive for our analysis to know what proportion of sales is absorbed by various expense items. An exception is income tax expense, which is related to pre-tax income, and not sales.

EXHIBIT 1.11 Adaptec's Index-Number Trend Series (base year 1993)

	1996	*1995*	*1994*	*1993*
Net revenues	212	150	120	100
Cost of revenues	158	118	109	100
Gross profit	280	190	133	100
Operating expenses:				
Research and development	333	231	152	100
Sales and marketing	251	181	142	100
General and administrative	230	149	125	100
Income from operations	201	188	123	100
Net income	209	189	119	100
Total assets	229	154	127	100
Shareholders' equity	227	165	132	100

Temporal (time) comparisons of common-size statements of a company are valuable in showing changing proportions of components within groups of assets, liabilities, expenses, and other financial statement categories. Nevertheless, we must exercise care in interpreting changes and trends.

Illustration 1.3

Account balances for patents and total assets of MicroDisc, Inc., for the most recent three years are:

	Year 3	*Year 2*	*Year 1*
Patents	$ 50,000	$ 50,000	$ 50,000
Total assets	$1,000,000	$750,000	$500,000
Patents/Total assets	5%	6.67%	10%

While the dollar amounts of patents remain unchanged during this period, increases in total assets progressively reduce patents as a percent of total assets. Since this percent varies with either the change in the absolute dollar amount of an item or the change in the total balance for its category, interpretation of common-size analysis requires examination of both actual figures and the basis for their computation.

Common-size statements are especially useful for intercompany comparisons because financial statements of different companies are recast in common-size format. Comparison of a company's common-size statements with competitors' or industry common-size statistics alerts our attention to differences in account structure or distribution; the reasons for these should be explored and understood. Yet common-size statements fail to reflect the relative sizes of companies under analysis. A comparison of selected common-size statement items of Campbell Soup Company to industry statistics is part of the Comprehensive Case at the end of the book.

Adaptec reports a common-size income statement in its 1996 annual report under the heading Results of Operations. At least two items are noteworthy. First, cost of revenues is decreasing as a percent of sales. Second, the write-off of acquired technology amounts to 8 percent of 1996 sales. Common-size balance sheets of Adaptec appear in Exhibit 1.12. A major change is the increase in other assets from 4.0 percent to 13.7 percent of total assets. Absent this increase, total current assets as a percent of total assets is similar to prior years. The financing side of the balance sheet reveals an increase in current liabilities, primarily due to notes payable. This, in turn, caused total liabilities to increase from 14.7 percent to 20.8 percent of total assets.

Ratio Analysis of Financial Statements

Ratios are among the most popular and widely used tools of financial analysis. Yet their function is often misunderstood and, consequently, their significance often overrated. A ratio expresses a mathematical relation between two quantities. A ratio of 200 to 100 is expressed as 2:1, or simply 2. While computation of a ratio is a simple arithmetic operation, its interpretation is far more complex. To be meaningful, a ratio must refer to an economically important relation. For example, there is a direct and crucial relation between an item's sales price and its cost. Accordingly, the ratio of cost

EXHIBIT 1.12 Adaptec's Common-Size Balance Sheets

	1996	*1995*
Current assets:		
Cash and cash equivalents	14.1%	15.3%
Marketable securities	31.6	41.3
Accounts receivable, net of allowance	13.8	13.0
Inventories	8.5	7.3
Prepaid expenses and other	3.9	3.6
Total current assets	71.9%	80.5%
Property and equipment, net	14.4	15.5
Other assets	13.7	4.0
Total assets	100%	100%
Current liabilities:		
Current portion of long-term debt	0.5%	0.8%
Note payable	7.1	0.0
Accounts payable	3.7	5.0
Accrued liabilities	8.8	7.1
Total current liabilities	20.1%	12.9%
Long-term debt	0.7	1.8
Common stock	28.3	32.2
Retained earnings	50.9	53.1
Total shareholders' equity	79.2%	85.3%
Total liabilities and equity	100%	100%

of goods sold to sales is a significant one. In contrast, there is no obvious relation between freight costs and the balance of marketable securities.

Ratios are tools providing us with clues and symptoms of underlying conditions. Ratios, properly interpreted, identify areas requiring further investigation. Analysis of a ratio reveals important relations and bases of comparison in uncovering conditions and trends difficult to detect by inspecting individual components comprising the ratio. Ratios, like other analysis tools, are future oriented, and we must adjust the factors affecting a ratio for their probable future trend and magnitude. We must also assess factors potentially influencing future ratios. Consequently, the usefulness of ratios depends on our skillful interpretation of them, and is the most challenging aspect of ratio analysis.

Illustration 1.4

Consider interpreting the ratio of gasoline consumption to mileage driven, referred to as miles per gallon (mpg). In comparing the ratio of gas consumption to mileage driven, person X claims to have the superior performing vehicle, that is, 28 mpg compared to person Y's 20 mpg. Is person X's vehicle superior?

Assuming they drive identical cars, there are several factors affecting gas consumption requiring analysis before we can properly interpret these ratios and judge whose performance is better: (1) weight of load driven, (2) type of terrain, (3) city or country driving, (4) grade of fuel used, and (5) travel speed of cars. Numerous as these factors influencing gas consumption are, evaluating a gas consumption ratio is, nevertheless, a more simple analysis than evaluating most financial statement ratios. This is because of the interrelations in business variables and the complexity of factors affecting them.

Factors Affecting Ratios

Beyond the internal operating conditions affecting a company's ratios, we must be aware of the effects of economic events, industry factors, management policies, and accounting methods. Our discussion of accounting methods later in the book highlights their influence on the measurements comprising ratios. Any weaknesses in accounting measurements impact the effectiveness of ratios. For instance, historical cost values are sometimes less relevant to a decision than current market values.

Prior to computing ratios, or similar measures like trend indices or percent relations, we must confirm that the numbers underlying their computation are valid and consistent. For example, when inventories are valued using LIFO (see Chapter 4) and prices are increasing, the current ratio is understated because LIFO inventories (the numerator) are understated. Similarly, certain pension liabilities are often unrecorded and disclosed in notes only (see Chapter 3). We normally want to recognize these liabilities when computing ratios like debt to equity. We must also recognize that when we make adjustments for one ratio, consistency often requires they be made for other ratios. For example, the omission of a pension liability implies understated pension expenses. Accordingly, net income numbers often require adjustment in ratio computation. We need also remember the usefulness of ratios depends on the quality of the numbers in their computation. When a company's internal accounting controls or other governance and monitoring mechanisms are unreliable in producing credible figures, the resulting ratios are equally unreliable.

Ratio Interpretation

Ratios must be interpreted with care since factors affecting the numerator can correlate with those affecting the denominator. For instance, companies can improve the ratio of operating expenses to sales by reducing costs that stimulate sales (e.g., research and development). If this cost reduction ultimately yields long-term declines in sales or market share, a seemingly short-term improvement in profitability can significantly damage a company's future prospects and must be interpreted accordingly. We should remember many ratios have important variables in common with other ratios. Consequently, it is not necessary for us to compute all possible ratios to analyze a situation. Ratios, like most techniques in financial analysis, are not significant in themselves and are interpretable only in comparison with (1) prior ratios, (2) predetermined standards, or (3) ratios of competitors. The variability of a ratio over time is often as important as its trend.

Illustration of Ratio Analysis

We often compute numerous ratios using a company's financial statements. Some ratios have general application in financial analysis, while others are unique to specific circumstances or industries. Exhibit 1.13 lists selected ratios having general applicability for most businesses; the ratios are grouped by major financial analysis objectives (see inside cover for definitions and additional ratios). Data used in this illustration are from Adaptec's 1996 annual report.

Several ratios are applicable in assessing **short-term liquidity.** Most common is the *current ratio*—reflecting current assets available to satisfy current liabilities. Adaptec's current ratio of 3.57 implies there are $3.57 of current assets available to meet each $1 of currently maturing obligations. A more stringent test of short-term liquidity, the *acid test ratio,* uses only the most liquid current assets (cash, short-term investments, accounts receivable). Adaptec has $2.95 of liquid assets to cover each $1

EXHIBIT 1.13 Financial Statement Ratio Computations for Adaptec

Short-Term Liquidity Ratios

$$\text{Current ratio} = \frac{\text{Current assets}}{\text{Current liabilities}} = \frac{\$465{,}280}{\$130{,}291} = 3.57$$

$$\text{Acid test ratio} = \frac{\text{Cash + Cash equivalents + Marketable securities + Accounts receivable}}{\text{Current liabilities}} = \frac{\$91{,}211 + \$204{,}283 + \$89{,}487}{\$130{,}291} = 2.95$$

$$\text{Collection period} = \frac{\text{Average accounts receivable}}{\text{Credit sales} \div 360} = \frac{(\$56{,}495 + \$89{,}487) \div 2}{\$659{,}347 \div 360} = 40 \text{ days}$$

$$\text{Days to sell inventory} = \frac{\text{Average inventory}}{\text{Cost of revenues} \div 360} = \frac{(\$31{,}712 + \$55{,}028) \div 2}{\$275{,}939 \div 360} = 57 \text{ days}$$

Capital Structure and Solvency Ratios

$$\text{Total debt to total capital} = \frac{\text{Current liabilities + Long-term liabilities}}{\text{Equity capital + Total liabilities}} = \frac{\$130{,}291 + \$4{,}250}{\$511{,}945 + \$130{,}291 + \$4{,}250} = 20.81\%$$

$$\text{Long-term debt to equity} = \frac{\text{Long-term liabilities}}{\text{Equity capital}} = \frac{\$4{,}250}{\$511{,}945} = 0.83\%$$

$$\text{Times interest earned} = \frac{\text{Income before income taxes + Interest expense}}{\text{Interest expense}} = \frac{\$137{,}989 + \$840}{\$840} = 165.27$$

Return on Investment Ratios

$$\text{Return on total assets} = \frac{\text{Net income + Interest expense (1 – Tax rate)}}{\text{Average total assets}} = \frac{\$103{,}375 + \$840(1 - 0.34)}{(\$435{,}708 + \$646{,}486) \div 2} = 19.21\%$$

$$\text{Return on common equity} = \frac{\text{Net income}}{\text{Average equity capital}} = \frac{\$103{,}375}{(\$371{,}644 + \$511{,}945) \div 2} = 23.4\%$$

of current liabilities. We also assess short-term liquidity by estimating the length of time needed for conversion of receivables and inventories to cash. Adaptec's *collection period* for receivables is approximately 40 days, and there are approximately 57 days between production and sale of inventories. These ratios together indicate an operating (or cash-to-cash) cycle of 97 (40 + 57) days.

To assess Adaptec's financing, we examine its **capital structure** and **long-term solvency.** The *debt-to-capital ratio* shows 20.8 percent of assets are financed by creditors, or 79.2 percent from equity investors. The *long-term debt to equity ratio* is 0.8 percent, highlighting Adaptec's greater reliance on short-term debt. The *times interest earned ratio* indicates over $165 of earnings is available to cover each $1 of interest. These ratios are especially reassuring for a credit analysis.

There are two popular ratios for assessing different aspects of **return on investment.** Adaptec's *return on total assets* of 19.21 percent implies a $1 asset investment generates 19.21¢ of earnings before after-tax interest. But shareholders are especially interested in management's performance using equity capital. Adaptec's *return on equity capital* of 23.4 percent is impressive. **Operating performance** ratios often link income statement line items to sales, and are not unlike results from common-size income statement analysis. Several operating ratios for Adaptec are reported in Exhibit 1.13. **Asset utilization** ratios, relating sales to different asset categories, are important determinants of return on investment. Adaptec's large working capital (i.e., the excess of current assets over current liabilities) is a potential hindrance to larger returns.

EXHIBIT 1.13 *(concluded)*

Operating Performance Ratios

$$\text{Gross profit ratio} = \frac{\text{Gross profit}}{\text{Net revenues}} = \frac{\$383{,}408}{\$659{,}347} = 58.15\%$$

$$\text{Operating profit to sales} = \frac{\text{Income from operations}}{\text{Net revenues}} = \frac{\$126{,}135}{\$659{,}347} = 19.13\%$$

$$\text{Pretax profit to sales} = \frac{\text{Income before income taxes}}{\text{Net revenues}} = \frac{\$137{,}989}{\$659{,}347} = 20.93\%$$

$$\text{Net income to sales} = \frac{\text{Net income}}{\text{Net revenues}} = \frac{\$103{,}375}{\$659{,}347} = 15.68\%$$

Asset Utilization Ratios

$$\text{Sales to cash} = \frac{\text{Net revenues}}{\text{Average cash}} = \frac{\$659{,}347}{(\$66{,}835 + \$91{,}211) \div 2} = 8.34$$

$$\text{Sales to accounts receivable} = \frac{\text{Net revenues}}{\text{Average accounts receivable}} = \frac{\$659{,}347}{(\$56{,}495 + \$89{,}487) \div 2} = 9.03$$

$$\text{Sales to inventories} = \frac{\text{Net revenues}}{\text{Average inventories}} = \frac{\$659{,}347}{(\$31{,}712 + \$55{,}028) \div 2} = 15.20$$

$$\text{Sales to working capital} = \frac{\text{Net revenues}}{\text{Average working capital}} = \frac{\$659{,}347}{[(\$350{,}472 - \$56{,}414) + (\$465{,}280 - \$130{,}291)] \div 2} = 2.10$$

$$\text{Sales to fixed assets} = \frac{\text{Net revenues}}{\text{Average fixed assets}} = \frac{\$659{,}347}{(\$67{,}863 + \$92{,}778) \div 2} = 8.21$$

$$\text{Sales to total assets} = \frac{\text{Net revenues}}{\text{Average assets}} = \frac{\$659{,}347}{(\$435{,}708 + \$646{,}486) \div 2} = 1.22$$

Market Measures

$$\text{Price to earnings ratio} = \frac{\text{Market price per share}}{\text{Earnings per share}} = \frac{\$48.25 \div 2}{\$1.89} = 25.53$$

$$\text{Earnings yield} = \frac{\text{Earnings per share}}{\text{Market price per share}} = \frac{\$1.89}{\$48.25 \div 2} = 3.92\%$$

$$\text{Dividend yield} = \frac{\text{Dividends per share}}{\text{Market price per share}} = \frac{0}{\$48.25 \div 2} = 0\%$$

$$\text{Dividend payout ratio} = \frac{\text{Dividends per share}}{\text{Earnings per share}} = \frac{0}{\$1.89} = 0\%$$

$$\text{Price to book ratio} = \frac{\text{Market price per share}}{\text{Book value per share}} = \frac{\$48.25}{\$511{,}945 \div 53{,}020} = 5.00$$

Ratio analysis yields valuable insights, as is apparent from our preliminary analysis of Adaptec. We must, however, keep in mind these calculations are based on the numbers reported in Adaptec's annual report. As we stress throughout this book, our ability to draw useful insights and make valid intercompany comparisons is greatly enhanced by our skill in *adjusting* reported numbers *prior to* inclusion in these analyses.

Specialized Analysis Tools

Beyond the multipurpose tools of financial statement analysis already discussed, we have available a variety of special-purpose tools. Special-purpose tools focus on specific financial statements or segments of statements, or they concentrate on a particular industry (e.g., occupancy-capacity analysis for hotels, hospitals, or airlines). They include cash forecasts, analysis of cash flows, statements of variation in gross profit, and break-even analysis. We describe each of these tools later in the book.

Financial Statement Analysis in an Efficient Capital Market

Capital Market Efficiency

The **efficient market hypothesis,** or EMH for short, deals with the reaction of market prices to financial and other data. The EMH has its origins in the **random walk hypothesis.** This hypothesis asserts that the size and direction of the next stock price change, at any point in time, is random. There are three common forms of this hypothesis. The *weak form* EMH asserts that prices reflect fully the information contained in historical price movements. The *semistrong form* EMH asserts that prices reflect fully all publicly available information. The *strong form* EMH asserts that prices reflect *all* information including "inside" information. There is considerable research on EMH. Early evidence so strongly supported both weak and semistrong form EMH that efficiency of capital markets became a maintained or generally accepted hypothesis. More recent research, however, questions the generality of EMH. A number of stock price anomalies have been uncovered suggesting investors can earn excess returns using "simple trading strategies." Nevertheless, as a first approximation, current stock price is a reasonable estimate of company value.

Market Efficiency Implications for Financial Statement Analysis

EMH assumes there exists competent and well-informed analysts using tools of analysis like those described in this book. It also assumes analysts are continually evaluating and acting on the regular stream of information entering the marketplace. Yet extreme proponents of EMH claim that if all information is instantly reflected in market prices, attempting to reap consistent advantages through financial statement analysis is futile. This position presents a paradox. On one hand, financial statement analysts are assumed capable in keeping our security markets efficient, yet these same analysts arguably fail to recognize their efforts to yield excess returns is futile. Moreover, should analysts suddenly realize their efforts are futile, the efficiency of our market ceases.

Several factors might explain this apparent paradox. Foremost among them is that EMH is built on aggregate, rather than individual, investor behavior. Focusing on macro- (or aggregate) behavior highlights average performance but ignores or masks individual performance based on ability, determination, and ingenuity, as well as superior individual timing in acting on information. Few doubt that important information travels fast, encouraged by the magnitude of financial stakes involved. Nor do we doubt securities markets are rapid processors of information. Indeed, we contend the speed and efficiency of our market is evidence of analysts at work, motivated by personal rewards.

EMH's alleged implication for the futility of financial statement analysis fails to recognize an essential difference between information and its proper interpretation. That is, even if all information available at a given point in time is impounded in security price, price does not necessarily reflect value. A security can be under- or overvalued, depending on the extent of an incorrect interpretation or evaluation of available information by the aggregate market. Market efficiency depends not only on availability of information but also on its correct interpretation. Financial statement analysis is complex and demanding. The spectrum of financial statement users varies from an institutional analyst who concentrates on but a few companies in one industry to an unsophisticated chaser of rumors. All act on information, but surely not

Analysis Research Insight 1.2

Informativeness of Stock Prices

Are stock prices equally informative across companies? The answer is no. Research shows small companies' stock prices are less informative than those of large companies. This is implied from evidence showing earnings reports of small companies yield larger and more prolonged stock price reactions. This implies earnings are more important in determining stock prices of small firms. This evidence also suggests *all* financial statement information relevant in setting prices is potentially more informative for small companies.

Analysis research indicates financial markets are less able to anticipate information conveyed in financial statements of small companies. This timing difference is likely tied to the lower quality and/or more sporadic disclosure of information about small companies. Research also reveals less accurate and more variable forecasts of financial numbers for small companies. Consequently, analysis and interpretation of small companies' financial statements are likely to demand more time and effort because of limited availability of alternative information.

with the same insights and competence. A competent analysis of information entering the marketplace requires a sound analytical knowledge base and an **information mosaic**—to fit new information links in the chain of analytical information for evaluation and interpretation. Not all of us possess the ability and preparation to expend efforts and resources needed in producing an information mosaic. The timing aspect also cannot be underestimated in the marketplace. Movement of new information, and its proper interpretation, flows from the well-informed and proficient segment of users to less-informed and inefficient users. This is consistent with a gradual pattern in processing new information.

Resources necessary for competent analysis of equity securities are considerable and imply that certain market segments are more efficient than others. Securities markets for our largest companies are more efficient (informed) because of a following by a greater number of analysts due to potential rewards from information search and analysis compared with smaller, less-prominent companies. Extreme proponents of EMH must take care in sweeping generalizations. In the annual report to shareholders of Berkshire Hathaway, chairman and famed investor Warren Buffet expresses amazement that EMH is embraced by many scholars and analysts. This, Buffet maintains, is because by observing correctly that the market is frequently efficient, they conclude incorrectly it is *always* efficient. Buffet declares, "the difference between these propositions is night and day."

We must also remember that the function and purpose of financial statement analysis of equity securities is often construed too narrowly by those who judge usefulness in an efficient market. While the search for over- and undervalued securities is an important function of financial analysis, the importance of assessing risk and avoiding losses in the total framework of business decision making cannot be overemphasized. Examples include credit and lending decisions, forming an audit opinion by the auditor, and valuing companies whose shares are not publicly traded. Prevention of serious losses or risk exposures is at least as important an objective of financial statement analysis as the discovery of misvalued securities. We must also recognize the value of fundamental financial analysis not only as a means of maintaining market efficiency and preserving the integrity of our capital markets, but also as a means by which we as users—having obtained, analyzed, and interpreted information—reap personal rewards. For us, rewards of financial statement analysis, long before its conversion to a "public good," are tangible and potentially large. Our rewards might not be discernible, however, in the performance of investor behavior aggregated to comprise major market segments, such as mutual funds. Instead, they remain as individual, but real, as the efforts expended to produce them. Financial statement analysis does not provide answers to all problems of security analysis or risk assessment. Yet it consistently directs us to the relevant underlying economics of the case at hand. It imposes the discipline of assessing future potentialities against past and present performance, and it is a safeguard against grievous errors of judgment recurringly made by individuals in times of speculative euphoria.

Preview of This Book's Organization

This book is organized into 13 chapters within three parts. It begins by looking at the environment of financial statement analysis, then at a company's business activities, and, finally, it looks at applying and interpreting financial statement analysis techniques (see Exhibit 1.14). Chapters 1 and 2, or Part One, describe the environmental context within which financial statement analysis occurs. These chapters preview financial statement analysis, describe its accounting and economic environment, and articulate the analysis objectives.

Part Two of this book (Chapters 3 through 7) focuses on the accounting measurement and reporting system, with special emphasis on their implications for financial statement analysis. We describe the important tools and techniques one can use to reconstruct from the highly summarized financial statements and related disclosures the transactions and economic events they represent. We stress the importance of understanding the accounting underlying financial statements for proper analysis and interpretation.

Part Three of this book (Chapters 8 through 13) investigates in great depth the primary areas of emphasis in financial statement analysis, the analytical adjustments to accounting reports, and the contemporary tools and techniques in practice.

In summary, the book begins by discussing the business and accounting environment of financial statement analysis before describing very specific ratios, tools, techniques, adjustments, computations, and strategies that users apply to survive and prosper in business.

The book concludes with a Comprehensive Case analysis of the financial statements of Campbell Soup Company. We apply and interpret many of the analysis techniques described in the book. Supplement A reproduces annual report excerpts from three companies that are often referred to in the book: Adaptec, Campbell Soup, and Quaker Oats. Supplements B and C discuss the analysis implications of auditing and changing price levels, respectively. Throughout this book, the relation of new material to topics covered in earlier chapters is described to reinforce how all the material comprises an integrated structure for financial statement analysis.

EXHIBIT 1.14 Organization of the Book

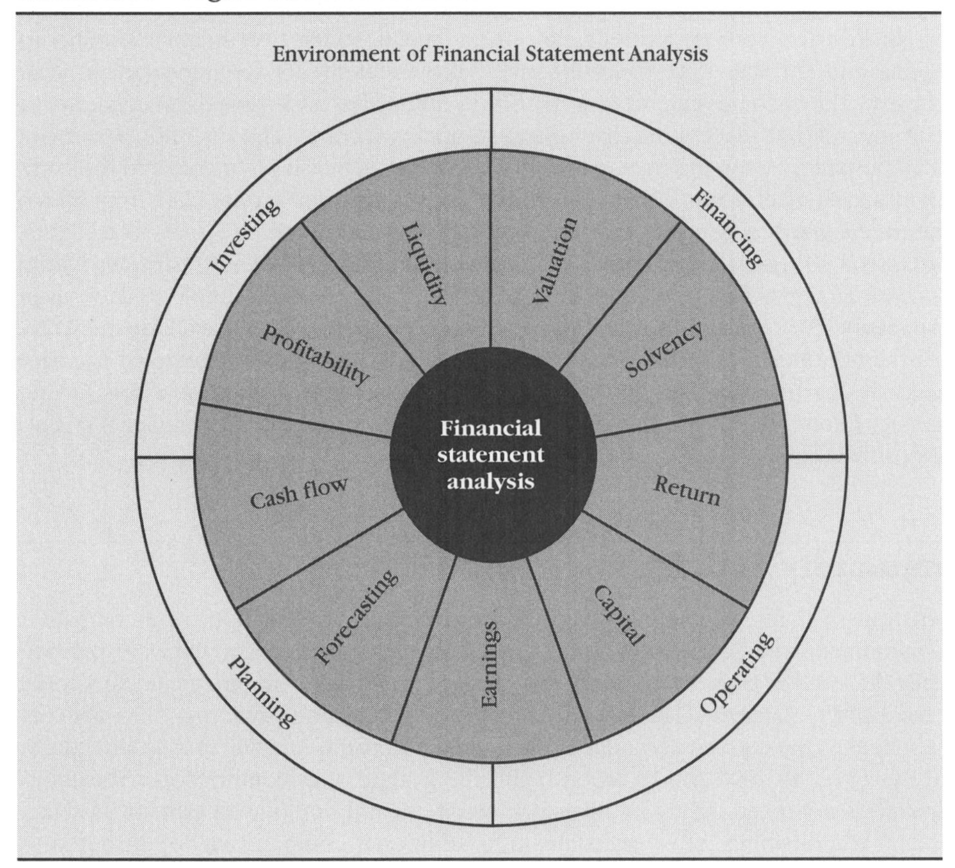

GUIDANCE ANSWERS TO ANALYSIS VIEWPOINTS

You Are the Banker

A banker is concerned about Adaptec's ability to satisfy its loan obligations. Concern about the composition of Adaptec's financing sources is twofold. First, the greater is owner financing, the lower is a banker's credit risk. This is because interest must be paid before dividends are distributed and, in event of liquidation, credit financing must be paid before shareholders are paid. Second, creditors are also concerned with Adaptec's other current and future creditor financing. Creditors often write **debt covenants** to restrict a company's future lending, or require collateral in case of default, or limit the amount of dividends payable to shareholders. For Adaptec, nearly 80% of financing is from shareholders. Moreover, current assets are more than three times current liabilities, suggesting short-term obligations are adequately covered. Accordingly, with adequate protection from debt covenants, your bank can confidently make the loan.

You Are the Investor

As an investor, your review of financial statements focuses on Adaptec's ability to create and maintain future net income. All the statements are important in your review. The income statement is especially important as it reveals management's current and past success in creating and sustaining income. The cash flow statement is important in assessing management's ability to meet cash payments and the company's cash availability. The balance sheet shows Adaptec's asset base from which future income is generated, and reports on liabilities and their due dates to creditors. Adaptec's 10% increase in earnings is strong, especially considering earnings would be 30% larger without the "one-time" write-off of in-process technology. Moreover, Adaptec's 25% decline in net cash flow is deceptive since (1) if we exclude the write-off then its operating cash flows increase significantly, and (2) its substantial decrease in cash due to investing activities involves the purchase of various assets having greater future returns possibilities. Thus, our analysis of Adaptec's statements reveals a positive future.

You Are the Community Activist

Analysis of financial statements can reveal important information on a company's commitment to its community. Major contributions to the community are periodically disclosed in notes to the statements. Increasingly, companies are including a social responsibility statement. This statement reports, albeit in summary form, important contributions to the community. Adaptec includes a statement, Adaptec in the Community, at the end of its 1996 annual report highlighting some of its contributions. This information is not taken lightly by investors, creditors, and others with a financial stake. Social responsibility often translates into additional company value attributed to employee morale and dedication, perceived integrity of management, and other subjective factors.

APPENDIX

1A

Investment Theory and Financial Statement Analysis

The practice of financial statement analysis is dynamic and challenging. Scholars actively scrutinize this practice and sometimes challenge conventional techniques and analyses. Various theories exist and are designed to provide insight into financial statement analysis processes. We briefly review some of the major theories.

Portfolio Theory

Considerable work is directed at the problem of portfolio construction. **Portfolio theory** maintains that both *risk and return* must be considered—provided a formal framework for quantifying both exists—and shows how the relation between security risks and returns is accounted for in portfolio construction. In its basic form, portfolio theory begins with the assumption that future security returns are estimable, and then equates risk with the variance of the returns distribution. Under certain assumptions, portfolio theory evidences a linear relation between risk and return. In this framework, it suggests how much of each security to hold in constructing a portfolio. The two-dimensional risk-return approach reinforces to an investor the trade-off between risk and return. Portfolio theory assumes **rational investors** resist increases in risk without commensurate increases in expected returns. Yet, by proper diversification, we lower risk while preserving expected returns. The relation between the risk accepted and the return expected is fundamental to all modern investing and lending decisions. While this may be obvious, it is worth emphasizing the greater the perceived degree of risk of an investment or of a loan, the greater is the required rate of return to compensate for this risk.

Categories of Risk

Risk is commonly linked with uncertainty surrounding outcomes of future events. While many investors and creditors make subjective evaluations of risk, scholars boast of statistical measures of risk arising from beta coefficient theory. **Beta coefficient theory** maintains that the total risk associated with an investment is comprised of two elements: **systematic risk,** the risk attributed to prevailing market movements, and **unsystematic risk,** the risk unique to a specific security. This theory offers a quantitative expression of systematic risk (referred to as **beta**). A beta of 1 implies security price moves with the volatility of the market. The higher (lower) a security's beta, the greater (lower) is its expected return. Treasury bills have a beta of zero because they are essentially riskless; that is, they do not fluctuate with the market. A stock with a beta of 1.20 is expected to rise or fall 20 percent faster than (but in the same direction as) the market. A stock with a beta of 0.90 is expected to yield market value changes 10 percent less in amplitude than those of the market. Thus, we expect higher returns from higher beta stocks in a *bull market* but larger than average declines in a *bear market.*

Unsystematic risk is the residual risk unexplained by market movements and, by definition, no unsystematic risk exists for the market. By that same reasoning, there is almost no unsystematic risk in a highly diversified portfolio of stocks. As portfolios become larger and more diversified, their unsystematic risk approaches zero. Proponents of portfolio theory maintain the market does not reward exposure to unsystematic risk when it is removable by proper diversification. They believe the implication of this theory for stock investors is to diversify, and if investors expect the market to rise, to increase the beta of their portfolios, and vice versa. Experimental studies indicate as much as 30 percent or more of a specific stock's price movements are due to market (systematic) risk and this influence is as high as 85 percent or more in a well-diversified portfolio of 30 or more stocks.

A portfolio manager who does not wish to rely only on market movements for returns, or who does not wish to forecast market movements, should seek **nondiversification**—that is, exposure to the amount of unsystematic risk required for achieving the desired rate of return. This strategy emphasizes analysis of individual securities, as emphasized in this book, as opposed to overall portfolio risk balancing. Thus, reaping the rewards of exposure to unsystematic risk depends on our ability to identify misvalued securities and to properly assess their risk.

Components of Unsystematic Risk

Those of us wishing to obtain our rewards from exposure to unsystematic or nonmarket risk through rigorous analysis of individual securities must focus on the various components of this risk. While these components are undoubtedly interrelated and subject to the influence of such elements of systematic risk as overall political, economic, and social factors, we can nevertheless usefully classify them as follows:

- **Economic risk.** Economic risks are inherent in a company's operating environment, including general economic risk (fluctuations in business activity), capital market risk (including changes in interest rates), and purchasing power risk (aspects we discuss in Supplement C).

- **Business risk.** Business risk is the uncertainty regarding a company's ability to earn a satisfactory return on its investments in light of the cost and revenue factors affecting this return, including factors of competition, product mix, and management ability.
- **Financial risk.** This refers to risks of capital structure and a company's ability to meet fixed and senior charges and claims.
- **Accounting risk.** Accounting risk is inherent in the selection and application of accounting methods, including management latitude in influencing the output of the accounting process.

Beta theorists assume investors are averse to risk and seek to diversify away a security's unsystematic risk, exposing investors only to market risk. Yet these theorists must recognize that historical betas for individual securities are quite unstable over time and, consequently, historical betas are seemingly imperfect predictors (at best) of a security's future betas. While theories are easier to apply to stock aggregates than to the evaluation of individual stocks, they are less reliable and inaccurate instruments for investment purposes.

Another, and perhaps more troublesome, issue is the assumption by beta theorists that past volatility is a sufficient measure of risk without reference to a security's current price. Is a security trading significantly above its true value, as determined by some method of fundamental analysis, no more risky than a security of equal volatility (beta) trading significantly below its true value? We know paying an excessive price for a stable, high-quality security is potentially as risky as investing in an unseasoned speculative security. While theorists have yet to effectively address this issue, they have braved the question of how the market values securities.

Relation between Accounting and Market Measures of Risk

Research shows accounting measures of risk, such as dividend payout ratios, capitalization ratios, coverage, and asset growth, are reflected in market risk measures like beta. Hence, selecting and ranking portfolios according to accounting risk measures is similar to portfolio formation using market-determined risk measures. Research also evidences a relation between systematic risk and a company's leverage (and other accounting risk measures). Research also considers the use of *fundamental betas,* where beta is a function of a company's changing fundamentals like earnings, asset structure, financial structure, and growth rates. An important implication is that the same economic (accounting-expressed) determinants that cause a stock to be more risky also cause it to have high systematic risk (beta).

Capital Asset Pricing Model

The capital asset pricing model (CAPM) extends portfolio theory in a manner intended to explain how prices of assets are determined—in short, in providing greater return for greater risk. This model assumes investors desire to hold securities in efficient portfolios providing maximum return for a given risk level. Several simplifying assumptions underlie the model, including:

- Existence of a riskless security.
- Investors able to borrow or lend unlimited amounts at the riskless rate.

- Investors possess identical investment horizons and act on the basis of identical expectations and predictions.

Using these assumptions, the expected return on an individual security, $E(R_i)$, relates to its systematic risk, β_i, in the following linear form:

$$E(R_i) = E(R_0) + [E(R_M) - E(R_0)]\beta_i$$

This return formulation suggests, under conditions of equilibrium, a security's (or any asset's) expected return equals the expected return of a riskless security, $E(R_0)$, plus a premium for risk taking. The risk premium consists of a constant, $[E(R_M) - E(R_0)]$, defined as the difference between the market expected return and the riskless security return (i.e., short-term government bond return) multiplied by a security's systematic risk (beta). CAPM implies each security's expected return is related to its risk. Risk is measured as the security's systematic movements with the market, and it cannot be eliminated by portfolio diversification. A major implication is only systematic (i.e., beta) risk is rewarded by the market, whereas holding unsystematic risk (potentially removable through diversification) earns no additional return.

QUESTIONS

1–1. Describe financial statement analysis.

1–2. Identify five classes of financial statement users.

1–3. Identify and discuss the four major activities of a business enterprise.

1–4. Explain how financial statements capture business activities.

1–5. Identify and discuss the four major financial statements of a business enterprise.

1–6. Explain why financial statements are important to the decisionmaking process in financial statement analysis.

1–7. Identify seven types of additional information items accompanying financial statements.

1–8. Identify and discuss the "building blocks" of financial statement analysis.

1–9. Identify and describe the four broad categories of financial statement analysis tools.

1–10. *a.* Explain the usefulness of comparative financial analysis.
b. Describe how financial statement comparisons are effectively made.
c. Discuss the necessary precautions required of an analyst in performing comparative analytical work.

1–11. Is past trend a good predictor of future trend? Justify your argument(s).

1–12. Compare the "absolute amount of change" with the "change in percent" as an indicator of significant change. Which is better?

1–13. Identify conditions preventing computation of a valid percent change. Provide an example.

1–14. Describe criteria in selecting a base year for index-number comparative analysis.

1–15. Explain what useful information is available from trend analysis.

1–16. *a.* Describe a common-size financial statement. Explain how one is prepared.
b. Explain what a common-size financial statement report communicates about a company.

1–17. Discuss the relative significance of ratios. Justify your response.

1–18. Describe limitations of ratio analysis.

1–19. *a.* Identify five ratios using balance sheet figures exclusively.
b. Identify five ratios using income statement data exclusively.
c. Identify seven ratios requiring data from both the balance sheet and income statement.

1–20. Identify four examples of special-purpose analytical tools commonly utilized by an analyst of financial statements.

1–21. Explain how the efficient market hypothesis (EMH) depicts the reaction of market prices to financial and other data.

1–22. Discuss implications of the efficient market hypothesis (EMH) for financial statement analysis.

1–23. Differentiate between systematic risk and unsystematic risk, and discuss the various components of unsystematic risk.

1–24. Discuss the capital asset pricing model (CAPM) and describe how it depicts the problem of securities valuation by the market.

1–25. Explain the concept of trade-off between risk and return, and its significance to portfolio construction.

1–26. Discuss implications of the capital asset pricing model (CAPM) for financial statement analysis.

EXERCISES

Exercise 1–1

Relations among Comparative Income Statements

Complete the following comparative operating analysis of Toro Corporation.

TORO CORPORATION
Operating Statement
For Years Ending on December 31
(in thousands)

	Year 6	*Year 5*	*Year 4*	*Cumulative Amount*	*Annual Average Amount*
Net sales	____	$3,490	$2,860	____	____
Cost of goods sold	$3,210	____	____	____	$2,610
Gross profit	3,670	680	1,050	____	1,800
Total operating expenses	____	____	____	____	____
Income before tazxes	2,740	215	105	____	____
Net income	1,485	145	58	____	____

Describe and comment on any significant findings in the comparative operating analysis of Toro.

Exercise 1–2

Analyzing Relations Using Index-Number Trend Data

Compute increases (decreases) from the preceding year in percents and fill in all missing data in the following table:

	Year 7		*Year 6*		*Year 5*
Statement Item	*Index No.*	*Change in Percent*	*Index No.*	*Change in Percent*	*Index No.*
Net sales	____	29%	100	____	90
Cost of goods sold	139	____	100	____	85
Gross profit	126	____	100	____	80
Total operating expenses	____	20%	100	____	65
Income before tax	____	14%	100	____	70
Net income	129	____	100	____	75

Discuss any significant results from this trend analysis.

Exercise 1–3

Discretion in Comparative Financial Statement Analysis

Comparative balance sheets and income (operating) statements are commonly applied tools of financial statement analysis and interpretation.

Required:

a. Discuss the inherent limitations of single-year statements for purposes of analysis and interpretation. Include in your discussion the extent these limitations are overcome by use of comparative statements.

b. Comparative balance sheets and income statements showing a company's financial history for each of the last 10 years can be misleading. Discuss factors or conditions contributing to misinterpretations. Include a discussion of additional information and supplementary data potentially includable in or provided with comparative statements to prevent misinterpretations.

Exercise 1–4

Analyzing Prospective and Strategic Information in the MD&A

Carefully read the Management's Discussion and Analysis in Adaptec's 1996 annual report in Supplement A. Identify and discuss those prospective disclosures and strategic analyses useful to a creditor or investor.

PROBLEMS

Problem 1–1

Financial Statement Relations: Balance Sheet Reconstruction

Assume you are a management consultant for Mesco Company. The following data are available in your financial analysis task:

Retained earnings, December 31, Year 4	$98,000
Gross profit on sales	25%
Acid-test ratio	2.5:1
Noncurrent assets	$280,000
Days' sales in inventory	45 days
Days' sales in receivables	18 days
Shareholders' equity to total debt	4:1
Sales for the year (all on credit)	$920,000
Common stock: $15 par value; 10,000 shares issued and outstanding; issued at $21 per share	

Required:

From these data, construct the December 31, Year 5, balance sheet for your analysis. All data are as of December 31, Year 5, unless otherwise indicated. Expenses (excluding taxes for Year 5) are $180,000 in addition to cost of goods sold. The tax rate is 40%. Assume a 360-day year in your computations. No dividends are paid in either Year 4 or Year 5. Current assets consist of cash, accounts receivable, and inventories.

Problem 1–2

Financial Statement Relations: Balance Sheet Reconstruction

You are a management consultant to Fox Company. The following data are available in your financial analysis task:

Current ratio	2
Accounts receivable turnover ratio	16
Beginning accounts receivable	$50,000

Return on equity	20%
Sales for the year (all on credit)	$1,000,000
Days' sales in inventory	36 days
Gross profit on sales	50%
Expenses (excluding cost of goods sold)	$450,000
Total debt to equity ratio	1
Noncurrent assets	$300,000

Required:

Construct the December 31, Year 2, balance sheet for your analysis. All data are as of December 31, Year 2, unless otherwise indicated. Current assets consist of cash, accounts receivable, and inventory. Balance sheet items include cash, accounts receivable, inventory, noncurrent assets, current assets, current and noncurrent liabilities, and equity.

Problem 1–3

Financial Statement Relations: Dividend and Balance Sheet Construction

It is Sunday and you just opened your briefcase to work with Vague Company's December 31, Year 6, balance sheet. To your dismay you discover the computer printouts your assistant stuffed into your briefcase contain only the following sketchy information:

1. Beginning and ending balances are identical for both accounts receivable and inventory.
2. Net income is $1,300.
3. Times interest earned is 5 (ignore income taxes). The company has 5 percent bonds issued at par outstanding.
4. Net income to sales ratio is 10 percent. Gross profit ratio is 30%. Inventory turnover is 5.
5. Days' sales in receivables is 72 days.
6. Sales to working capital is 4. Current ratio is 1.5.
7. Acid-test ratio is 1.0 (excludes prepaid expenses).
8. Plant and equipment is one-third depreciated.
9. Dividends paid on 8 percent nonparticipating preferred stock are $40. There is no change in common shares outstanding during Year 6. Preferred shares were issued two years ago at par.
10. Earnings per common share are $3.75.
11. Common stock has a $5 par value and was issued at par.
12. Retained earnings at January 1, Year 6, are $350.

Required:

Given the information available, complete the balance sheet below as of December 31, Year 6. Determine the amount of dividends paid on common stock in Year 6.

Cash	
Accounts receivable	
Inventory	
Prepaid expenses	
Plant and equipment (net)	$6,000
Total assets	
Current liabilities	
Bonds payable	
Stockholders' equity	
Total liabilities and equity	

Problem 1–4

Financial Statement Ratio Computations

The balance sheet and income statement for Chicago Electronics, Inc., are reproduced below. The tax rate is 40 percent.

CHICAGO ELECTRONICS, INC.
Balance Sheet
As of December 31
($ thousands)

	Year 4	*Year 5*
Assets		
Current assets:		
Cash	$ 683	$ 325
Accounts receivable	1,490	3,599
Inventories	1,415	2,423
Prepaid expenses	15	13
Total current assets	$3,603	$6,360
Property, plant, equipment, net	1,066	1,541
Other	123	157
Total assets	$4,792	$8,058
Liabilities		
Current liabilities:		
Notes payable to bank	$ —	$ 875
Current portion of long-term debt	38	116
Accounts payable	485	933
Estimated income tax	588	472
Accrued expenses	576	586
Customer advance payments	34	963
Total current liabilities	$1,721	$3,945
Long-term debt	122	179
Other liabilities	81	131
Total liabilities	$1,924	$4,255
Shareholders' Equity		
Common stock, $1.00 par value; 1,000,000 shares authorized; 550,000 and 829,000 outstanding, respectively	$ 550	$ 829
Preferred stock, Series A 10%; $25 par value; 25,000 authorized; 20,000 and 18,000 outstanding, respectively	500	450
Additional paid-in capital	450	575
Retained earnings	1,368	1,949
Total shareholders' equity	$2,868	$3,803
Total liabilities and shareholders equity	$4,792	$8,058

CHICAGO ELECTRONICS, INC.
Income Statement
Years Ending December 31
($ thousands)

	Year 4	*Year 5*
Net sales	$7,570	$12,065
Other income, net	261	345
Total revenues	$7,831	$12,410
Cost of goods sold	4,850	8,048
General, administrative, and marketing expense	1,531	2,025
Interest expense	22	78
Total costs and expenses	$6,403	$10,151
Net income before tax	1,428	2,259
Income tax	628	994
Net income	$ 800	$ 1,265

Required:

Compute the following for Year 5:

a. Acid-test ratio.
b. Return on assets.
c. Return on common equity.
d. Earnings per share.
e. Gross profit ratio.
f. Times interest earned.
g. Days inventory to sell.
h. Long-term debt to equity ratio.
i. Total debt to total capital.
j. Sales to working capital ratio.

(CFA Adapted)

Problem 1–5

Financial Statement Ratio Computations and Interpretations

As a consultant to MFG Manufacturing Company you are informed the company is planning to acquire the Lowland Corporation and requested to prepare certain financial statistics for Year 5 and Year 4 from the following statements of Lowland Corporation.

LOWLAND CORPORATION
Balance Sheet
December 31, Year 5, and Year 4

	Year 5	*Year 4*
Assets		
Current assets:		
Cash	$ 1,610,000	$ 1,387,000
Marketable securities	510,000	
Accounts receivable, less allowance for bad debts:		
Year 5, $125,000; Year 4, $110,000	4,075,000	3,669,000
Inventories, at lower of cost or market	7,250,000	7,050,000
Prepaid expenses	125,000	218,000
Total current assets	$13,570,000	$12,324,000
Plant and equipment, at cost:		
Land and buildings	$13,500,000	$13,500,000
Machinery and equipment	9,250,000	8,520,000
Total plant and equipment	$22,750,000	$22,020,000
Less: Accumulated depreciation	13,470,000	12,549,000
Total plant and equipment—net	$ 9,280,000	$ 9,471,000
Long term receivables	$ 250,000	$ 250,000
Deferred charges	$ 25,000	$ 75,000
Total assets	$23,125,000	$22,120,000
Liabilities and Shareholders' Equity		
Current liabilities:		
Accounts payable	$ 2,950,000	$ 3,426,000
Accrued expenses	1,575,000	1,644,000
Federal taxes payable	875,000	750,000
Current maturities on long-term debt	500,000	500,000
Total current liabilities	$ 5,900,000	$ 6,320,000
Other liabilities:		
5% sinking fund debentures, due January 1, Year 16 ($500,000 redeemable annually)	$ 5,000,000	$ 5,500,000
Deferred taxes on income, related to depreciation	350,000	210,000
Total other liabilities	$ 5,350,000	$ 5,710,000

Shareholders' equity:		
Capital stock:		
Preferred stock, $1 cumulative, $20 par, preference on liquidation $100 per share (authorized: 100,000 shares; issued and outstanding: 50,000 shares)	$ 1,000,000	$ 1,000,000
Common stock, $1 par (authorized: 900,000 shares; issued and outstanding: Year 5, 550,000 shares; Year 4, 500,000 shares)	550,000	500,000
Capital in excess of par value of common stock	3,075,000	625,000
Retained earnings	7,250,000	7,965,000
Total shareholders' equity	$11,875,000	$10,090,000
Total liabilities and shareholders' equity	$23,125,000	$22,120,000

LOWLAND CORPORATION
Statement of Income and Retained Earnings
For the Years Ended December 31, Year 5, and Year 4

	Year 5	*Year 4*
Revenues:		
Net sales	$48,400,000	$41,700,000
Royalties	70,000	25,000
Interest	30,000	
Total revenues	$48,500,000	$41,725,000
Costs and expenses:		
Cost of sales	$31,460,000	$29,190,000
Selling, general, and administrative	12,090,000	8,785,000
Interest on 5% sinking fund debentures	275,000	300,000
Provision for Federal income taxes	2,315,000	1,695,000
Total costs and expenses	$46,140,000	$39,970,000
Net income	$ 2,360,000	$ 1,755,000
Retained earnings, beginning of year	7,965,000	6,760,000
Total	$10,325,000	$ 8,515,000
Dividends paid:		
Preferred stock, $1.00 per share in cash	$ 50,000	$ 50,000
Common stock:		
Cash—$1.00 per share	525,000	500,000
Stock—(10%)—50,000 shares at market value of $50 per share	2,500,000	
Total dividends paid	$ 3,075,000	$ 550,000
Retained earnings, end of year	$ 7,250,000	$ 7,965,000

Additional Information:

1. Inventory at January 1, Year 4, is $6,850,000.
2. Market prices of common stock at December 31, Year 5, and Year 4, are $73.50 and $47.75, respectively.
3. Cash dividends for both preferred and common stock are declared and paid in June and December of each year. The stock dividend on common stock is declared and distributed in August of Year 5.
4. Plant and equipment sales and retirements during Year 5 and Year 4 are $375,000 and $425,000, respectively. Related depreciation allowances are $215,000 in Year 5 and $335,000 in Year 4. At December 31, Year 3, the plant and equipment asset balance is $21,470,000 and the related depreciation allowances are $11,650,000.

Required:

Prepare a schedule computing the following statistics for both Year 5 and Year 4. Identify and discuss any significant year-to-year changes.

At December 31:

a. Current ratio.
b. Acid-test ratio.
c. Book value per common share.

For Year Ended December 31:

d. Gross profit ratio.
e. Days to sell inventory.
f. Times interest earned.
g. Common stock price-earnings ratio (end-of-year value).
h. Gross capital expenditures.

(AICPA Adapted)

CASES

Case 1–1
Financial Statement Ratio Analysis and Interpretation of Adaptec

Assume you are hired by Eagle National Bank as a junior analyst. Your supervisor hands you the financial statements of Adaptec, Inc., and a list of ratios for 1996 (Exhibit 1.13). She asks you to "Please compute identical ratios for 1995," and adds, "Although it amounts to only a two-year comparison, please comment on whether each ratio change is favorable or unfavorable and why."

(*Hint:* Using your skills, you determine the 1994 year-end accounts receivable is $55,334, 1994 inventory is $38,940, and 1994 fixed assets (i.e., property and equipment) is $51,522. Total assets and total equity for 1995 are disclosed elsewhere in Adaptec's annual report in Supplement A. For market measures use the March 31, 1995, price of $33 per share.)

Required:

Write a report responding to the supervisor's request.

Case 1–2
Financial Statement Ratio Analysis and Comparison

Refer to Quaker Oats Company's financial statements reproduced in Supplement A.

Required:

a. Compute the following ratios for both Year 11 and Year 10.
 Short-term liquidity ratios:
  Current ratio.
  Acid-test ratio.
  Days sales in receivables.
  Days to sell inventory.
  Collection period.
 Capital structure and long-term solvency ratios:
  Total debt to total capital.
  Long-term debt to equity capital.
  Times interest earned.
 Return on investment ratios:
  Return on total assets.
  Return on common equity capital.
 Operating performance ratios:
  Gross margin ratio.
  Operating profits to sales.
  Pretax income to sales.
  Net income to sales.
 Asset utilization ratios:
  Sales to cash.

Sales to accounts receivables.
Sales to inventories.
Sales to working capital.
Sales to fixed assets.
Sales to total assets.

Market measures (Quaker's stock prices per share are $56\frac{1}{2}$ and $52\frac{1}{2}$ for Years 10 and 11, respectively.):

Price to earnings ratio.
Earnings yield.
Dividend yield.
Dividend payout ratio.

b. Price to book ratio. Comment on the significance of the year-to-year changes.

Case 1–3
Describing and Illustrating Business Activities

Explain a company's major business activities for a general audience (e.g., shareholders, employees). Include concrete examples for each of the business activities.

INTERNET ACTIVITIES

Internet 1–1
Ratio Analysis and Interpretation of Adaptec 1997–1998

Refer to the 1997 financial statements of Adaptec, Inc., on the Internet (http://www.adaptec.com) or other available source.

Required:

a. Compute financial ratios listed in Case 1–2 for Adaptec using fiscal 1997 reports.

b. (*Optional*) Refer to the 1998 financial statements of Adaptec, Inc., on the Internet or other available source and compute the same ratios as in *a*. Compare the ratios computed in *a* and *b* and comment on any significance in the year-to-year changes.

Internet 1–2
Ratio Analysis and Interpretation of Campbell Soup Company

Access one of the financial statement databases available on the Internet, (for example, SEC's on-line database EDGAR (http://www.sec.gov/edgarhp.htm). Web addresses sometimes change, so if the SEC or other site address does not work, access the Web site for this textbook (http://www.mhhe.com/business/accounting/wild) for updated links to financial databases. Retrieve current financial statements of Campbell Soup Company or a company selected by either you or your instructor and answer the following.

Required:

a. Compute the ratios listed in Case 1–2 for the most recent two years' data of Campbell Soup Company.

b. Write a report comparing the two years' ratios computed in *a* and comment on any significance in the year-to-year changes.

Internet 1–3
Financial Statement Ratio Analysis

Access one of the financial statement databases available on the Internet and retrieve current financial statements of a company (preferably a manufacturing or merchandising company) selected by either you or your instructor and answer the following.

Required:

a. Compute the ratios listed in Case 1–2 for the most recent two years.

b. Write a report comparing the two years' ratios computed in *a* and comment on any significance in the year-to-year changes.

Internet 1–4

Financial Information Availability

There is an enormous amount of financial statement information available on the Internet. These include the SEC's on-line database referred to as EDGAR (http://www.sec.gov/edgarhp.htm) and numerous other Web sites offering access to financial statement information or related data. (See, for example, the AICPA (http://www.aicpa.org/index.htm), the IRS (http://www.irs.ustreas.gov/), and the AAA (http://www.rutgers.edu/Accounting/raw/aaa/). You can access the Web site for this textbook (http://www.mhhe.com/business/accounting/wild) for updated links to several of these databases. After accessing one of these Web sites selected by either you or your instructor, answer the following.

a. Write a report describing the types of relevant information available at this Web site for financial analysis.

b. How would you rate the importance of the information available at this Web site for financial analysis?

Internet 1–5

Comparing Company and Industry Ratios

Visit a Web site (or library) to access financial statement statistics by industry (e.g., Dun and Bradstreet). Write down five key industry ratios from this source (choose from the set of key ratios described in this chapter). Next, access the financial statements of a company in this industry and compute the same five ratios. For example, use the SEC's on-line database EDGAR (http://www.sec.gov/edgarhp.htm). Write a report commenting on differences or similarities between the company's ratios and those of its industry.

CHAPTER

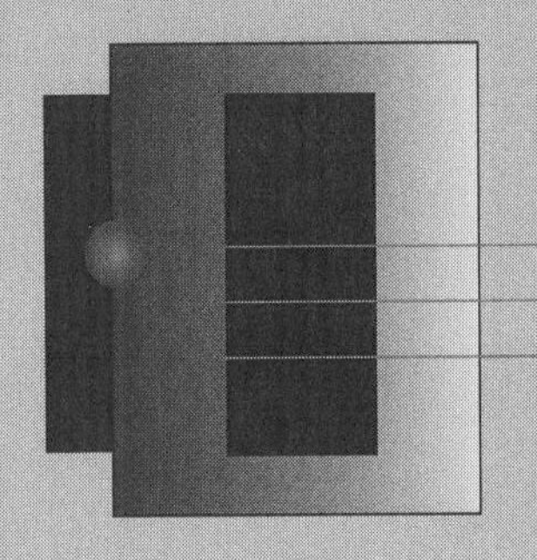

2

Analysis Objectives and Financial Reporting

Learning Objectives

- Identify the primary users of financial statements and discuss their objectives and information needs.
- Describe common stock valuation and compare it with the valuation of debt.
- Explain double-entry accounting and how it aids in measuring business activities.
- Describe the relevance of accounting information in financial statement analysis.
- Identify limitations of accounting data and their consequences for financial statement analysis.
- Discuss specialized financial statement analysis techniques.
- Explain how accounting rules are determined (Appendix 2A).
- Describe the role of technology in financial statement analysis (Appendix 2B).
- Identify sources of information for financial statement analysis (Appendix 2B).

A Look Back

We began our study of financial statement analysis with a preliminary analysis of Adaptec. We saw how financial statements report on important business activities, and the role of analysis in an efficient market.

A Look at This Chapter

We begin in this chapter by describing the financial statement analysis objectives of the primary users. We discuss stock valuation and contrast it with debt valuation. We describe and assess the importance and limitations of accounting data for financial statement analysis. We also identify specialized financial statement analysis techniques and their relevance to business decisions.

A Look Ahead

Chapter 3 launches our analysis of accounting numbers underlying financial statement analysis. We begin by focusing on financing activities. Chapters 4 and 5 extend this to investing activities. We explore various adjustments of these disclosures for analysis purposes.

PREVIEW OF CHAPTER 2

Financial statement analysis depends on the objectives of its users. While similarities exist, there are unique circumstances and objectives facing every user. To master financial statement analysis, we must understand users and their objectives. Financial statement analysis depends also on the accounting numbers comprising the statements. The recording function, the double-entry system, and classification are an integral part of accounting, one we must understand to fully exploit our analysis. Accounting information is subject also to certain limitations impairing our analysis. We must recognize and adapt our analysis for these limitations. This chapter describes the objectives and applications of primary users of financial statements. We introduce several important accounting functions and discuss their implications for analysis. We also discuss techniques of analysis that exploit our accounting knowledge. The content and organization of this chapter are as follows:

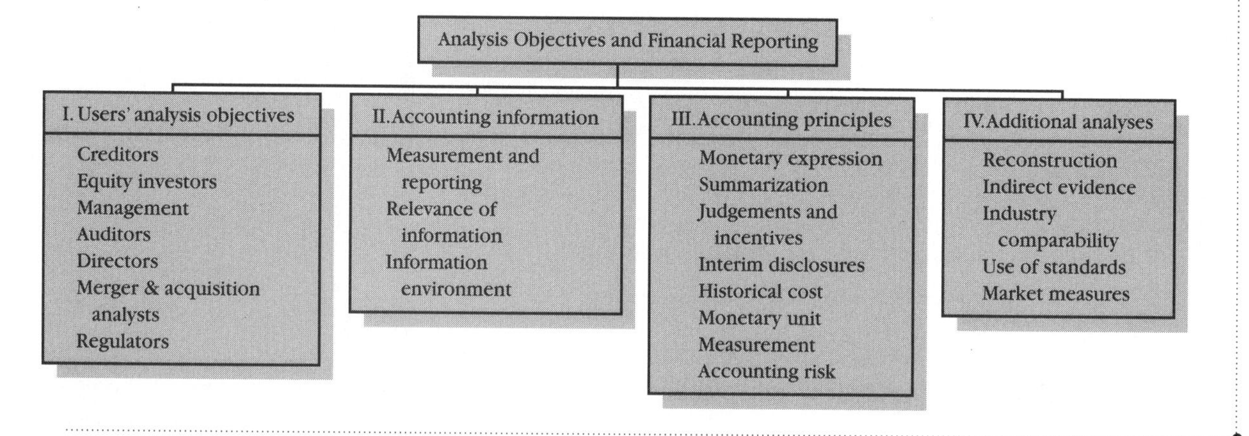

Objectives of Financial Statement Analysis

Learning financial statement analysis involves knowing and understanding the process of analysis with emphasis on its major objectives. The objectives of financial statement analysis depend on our perspective and the tasks confronting us. To understand this analysis and its objectives, we review information needs and analytical goals of some important users of financial statements: credit grantors, equity investors, management, auditors, directors, merger and acquisition analysts, and regulators.

Creditors

Credit grantors are lenders of funds to a company with a promise of repayment. This type of business financing is temporary since credit grantors expect repayment of their funds along with interest. Credit grantors lend funds in many forms and for a variety of purposes.

Trade creditors provide goods or services to a company and expect payment within a reasonable period, often determined by the industry norm. Most trade credit is short term, ranging from 30 to 60 days, with cash discounts occasionally given for early payment. Trade creditors do not usually receive (explicit) interest for an extension of credit. Instead, trade creditors' profits derive directly from profit margins on the business transacted.

Nontrade creditors provide financing to a company in return for a promise, usually in writing, of payment with interest (explicit or implicit) on specific future dates. This type of financing can be either short or long term, and can originate from a variety of sources.

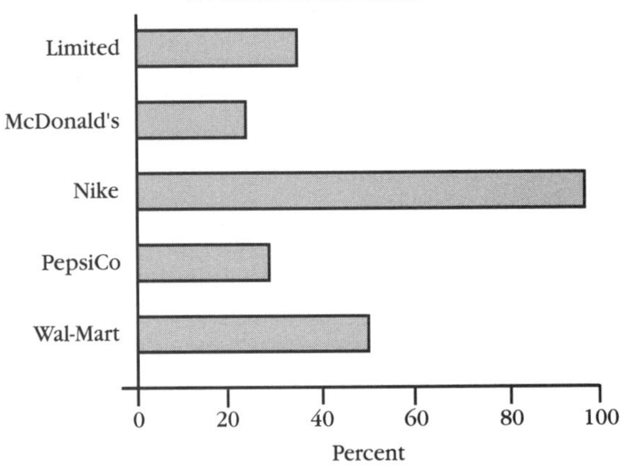

Source: Annual reports.

Companies often obtain short-term credit through banks or through the sale of commercial paper. They often obtain long-term credit through financial institutions like banks in the form of term loans or through insurance companies in the form of bonds or notes in private placements. Companies can also obtain long-term financing through public sale of notes or bonds in securities markets. Leasing and conditional sales are additional forms of financing.

Credit financing is also available through "hybrid" securities. Sales of **convertible bonds,** often subordinated, combine the borrowing of money with an added feature of an option to the lender. This option allows lenders to exchange their claims for equity interests should they consider it profitable. Issuance of **preferred stock,** stock senior to common equity but junior to debt, combines the "fixed" interest features of a loan with "unguaranteed" principal repayment of equity.

An important characteristic of all pure credit financing transactions is the fixed nature of rewards accruing to credit grantors. Should the company prosper, credit grantors' rewards are limited to a contractually fixed rate of interest or to the profit on goods or services provided. However, should the company incur losses or encounter adversities, a credit grantor's principal can be jeopardized. This "asymmetric" nature of a creditor's risk-return relation has a major effect on the creditor's perspective and the manner and objectives of credit analysis undertaken.

Credit grantors focus on the **security provisions** for their loans. These provisions are usually of two types: security in the form of the fair market value of assets pledged or other promises to limit business activities reducing company value (e.g., dividend payment restrictions) or security in repayment of principal and interest. For this purpose, credit grantors look to existing resources, and the reliability, timing, and stability of future cash flows. Creditors require definite links between management's projections and existing resources, along with demonstrated ability to achieve projections. Creditors are especially concerned with the sensitivity of earnings to recessionary periods. They generally are more conservative and heavily rely on financial statement analysis. Their analysis focuses on assessing a borrower's demonstrated ability to control cash flows and to maintain a sound financial base under varying economic and operating circumstances.

Techniques of financial statement analysis and the criteria of evaluation for credit grantors vary with the term, security, and purpose of a loan. With short-term credit, the grantor's primary concerns are current financial condition, the liquidity of current assets, and their rate of turnover. We fully describe these considerations in Chapter 8.

Evaluation of long-term credit, including valuation of bonds, requires more detailed and forward-looking inquiry and analysis. Long-term credit analysis includes projections of cash flows and evaluation of the extended earning power of the company. A company's extended earning power is a determining source of assurance of its ability to meet interest and principal payments arising from debt along with its other commitments under varying conditions. Thus, profit analysis is very important to long-term creditors. We examine these issues more completely in Chapters 11–13.

Credit analysis, whether long or short term, also looks at capital structure because it bears on risk and on the creditor's margin of safety. The relation of equity capital to creditor financing is an indicator of the risk exposure to credit grantors. This relation also reflects management's attitude toward risk and influences income coverage of fixed charges.

Creditors generally view asset values in the context of financial statement assumptions—namely, whether a company is a going concern. When a company's going-concern status is in doubt, liquidation values are more applicable. For this reason, creditors tend to conservatively adjust asset values, and make allowance for future contingencies, especially when a company is a doubtful going concern.

Equity Investors

Equity investors are providers of funds to a company in return for the risks, uncertainties, and rewards of ownership (there is no promise of repayment). Equity investors are the major providers of most business financing. Equity capital offers a cushion or safeguard for both preferred stock and credit financing that is senior to it. Equity investors are entitled to distributions only after the claims of senior securities are met—equity investors have a **residual interest**. With a going-concern entity, residual interest implies equity investors can receive distributions after satisfying obligations of senior claimants for debt interest and preferred dividends. In liquidation, equity investors have claims to the residual only after the claims of creditors and preferred stockholders. Thus, when a company prospers, equity investors reap gains above the amounts due senior claimants. But conversely, equity investors are the first to absorb losses when a company collapses, and their losses are generally limited to the amount invested.

Because of the risks confronting equity investors, their information needs are among the most demanding and comprehensive of all users of financial data. This is because equity investors' interests are affected by all aspects and phases of operations, financial condition, and capital structure. We briefly examine the kinds of difficulties equity investors confront.

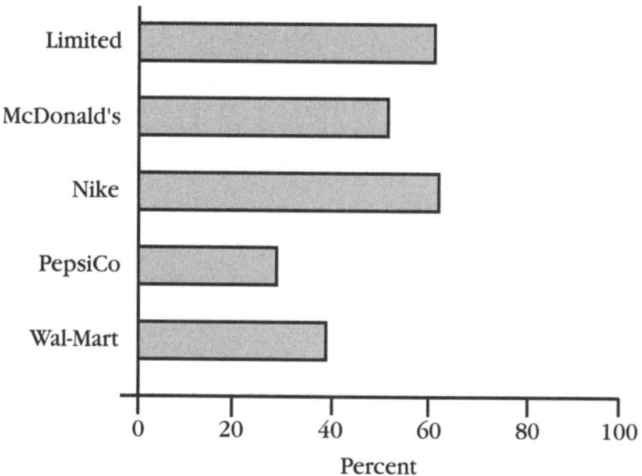

Source: Annual reports.

Common Stock Valuation

Valuation of common stock is a major objective of equity investors. It is a task involving financial statement analysis *plus* assessing factors like economic and industry conditions, competitive pressures, strategic advantages, and management and employee quality.

The equity investor, having no legal claim to a definite dividend or capital distribution, looks to three principal rewards: (1) current dividends, (2) special distributions such as rights, and (3) future capital gains from increasing market value. Ultimately, the most important determinant of both dividends and market value is earnings. Earnings, the source of dividends and retained earnings, along with earnings expectations, are major elements in determining the price of stock.

The theoretical basis of stock valuation is **present value theory.** This approach maintains the value of a stock at time t (V_t) equals the sum of all dividends expected, discounted to the present at an appropriate rate of interest:

$$V_t = BV_t + \frac{D_{t+1}}{(1+k)} + \frac{D_{t+2}}{(1+k)^2} + \ldots + \frac{D_{t+n}}{(1+k)^n} + \ldots$$

where D_{t+n} is the dividend in the $(t+n)$th year, and k is the discount rate or investors' required rate of return. Dividend distributions are the appropriate valuation attribute because only payouts to owners can increase their level of consumption.

Common Stock versus Debt Valuation

The present value model of stock valuation is similar to the conventional means of debt valuation. We calculate the value of debt (or purchase price) by discounting coupon payments and the principal repayment to the present using a discount rate equal to the desired yield. In stock valuation, the expected dividends correspond to the debt's coupons. The stock valuation model does not include a residual stock price because it assumes infinite dividend projections (consistent with the going-concern assumption). Because the discounting factor (the denominator) increases over time, the valuation impact of residual price is increasingly negligible. The logic and mathematical elegance of the stock valuation model is readily apparent, but we must recognize important differences between the inputs required of the stock and debt models. These differences are important since our purpose is to relate the scope and the techniques of financial statement analysis to valuation of equity securities.

In debt valuation, we typically know both the coupon payments and principal. Thus, as we described under the objectives of credit grantors, the major questions involve availability of funds for payment of interest and principal. While our assessment of the likelihood of funds availability involves the entire company's prospects, estimation is less difficult than obtaining inputs for the stock valuation model. The basic and important difference in an analysis of debt versus equity is with the *certainty of evidence.* No matter how "right" we are in making assumptions and forecasts, a major part of our reward from common stock analysis—future capital values—depends on other market participants (i.e., on ultimate market confirmation of our assessments). No such dependence on validation by the marketplace exists in our analysis of debt.

Stock Valuation Data Requirements

We require certain data to quantify the inputs for the stock valuation model. A fundamental problem with any dividend-based valuation model is the estimation of future distributions to owners. This task is all the more difficult due to the discretionary nature of dividend payments. However, we know dividend policies are slow to change. Companies are hesitant to increase dividend payouts unless they can indefinitely maintain higher levels with little likelihood of forced cuts in future payouts. Thus, observed dividend payouts are less indicative of company value except in the very long run. It is clear, however, that expected payouts are based largely on earnings and the earning power of assets. This reasoning underlies recent advances in developing an accounting-based equity valuation model. The model uses the accounting *clean surplus relation*:

$$BV_t = BV_{t-1} + NI_t - D_t$$

where

BV_t = Book value of common equity at end of period t
BV_{t-1} = Book value of common equity at end of period $t - 1$ (or beginning of period t)
NI_t = Net income for period t
D_t = Dividends declared during period t

Under clean surplus accounting, net income includes all changes to common equity other than those due to transactions with owners (capital contributions are treated as negative dividends). While income determination in practice does not always adhere to clean surplus accounting, it is a very reasonable approximation.

If we restate the clean surplus relation in terms of D, and substitute this relation for D in the stock valuation model, we obtain the following (equivalent) stock valuation formula expressed in terms of accounting data:

$$V_t = BV_t + \frac{NI_{t+1} - (k \times BV_t)}{(1+k)} + \frac{NI_{t+2} - (k \times BV_{t+1})}{(1+k)^2} + \ldots + \frac{NI_{t+n} - (k \times BV_{t+n-1})}{(1+k)^n} + \ldots +$$

The focus of discounting in this model is the stream of future **abnormal earnings**, or *residual income*, of the company [$(NI - (k \times BV)$]. Abnormal earnings are the excess of reported earnings over the level of earnings expected from multiplying the required rate of return by the company's beginning-of-period book value. The logic underlying calculation of abnormal earnings is intuitive. If a company achieves a rate of profitability in excess of its required rate of return, value is created (i.e., abnormal earnings are positive). If a company achieves a rate of profitability less than its required rate of return, abnormal earnings will be negative (i.e., value declines).

This accounting-based stock valuation model shows equity investors need not focus their analysis on estimation of future dividends—a focus on future earnings is sufficient. The projection of future earnings (see Chapter 13) is, of course, a demanding task subject to its own uncertainty. For example, financial statement users evaluate reported earnings and often adjust them to yield a valid basis for projection. The more distant the projections of earnings, the more uncertain the estimates. Another factor, for both models, is the appropriate level for the **discount factor**, k. This level depends to a large extent on the risk involved. *Risk* reflects factors such as industry stability, prior earnings variability, and a company's leverage.

No one stock valuation model has proved an accurate forecaster of stock prices under all conditions. Perhaps the factors bearing on determination of stock prices are too numerous or too complex for inclusion in a workable formula, or perhaps not all factors are adequately measured (maybe due to simplifying assumptions). But whatever method of stock valuation we use, be it a simple short-term projection of earnings capitalized at a predetermined rate or a more sophisticated model, the results are only as accurate or reliable as the inputs used in calculations. The reliability and validity of these inputs—be they earnings projections, expected payout ratios, risk factors, or capital structure assumptions—depend on the quality of our financial statement analysis.

Analysis Research Insight 2.1

Common Stock Valuation

Are accounting numbers useful in stock valuation? For many years, proponents of the efficient markets hypothesis followed an *informational perspective* of accounting—accounting numbers, and earnings in particular, were viewed as "signals" serving to alter investors' beliefs about future cash flows and dividends.

Recent analysis research encourages a *measurement perspective* on accounting. This approach asserts that the accounting system has properties useful in capturing the wealth-generating process of a company. Specifically, book value represents the worth of a company at a point in time, while earnings measure the change in company value over a period of time.

Research reveals the following findings:

- As the reporting period decreases, accounting earnings are more closely correlated with stock price change than is cash flow.
- The correlation between accounting earnings and stock price changes increases dramatically for longer reporting periods, especially for periods exceeding two or three years.
- Earnings less sensitive to accounting recognition criteria and assumptions are more highly correlated with stock price changes.
- Expected abnormal earnings are more highly correlated with stock prices than are expected dividends.

Management

Management are those individuals hired by the company's owners (or their representatives) to effectively and efficiently manage assets and liabilities. They are interested in the company's financial condition, profitability, and future possibilities. Management has a number of means available to monitor and stay abreast of the ever-changing circumstances of the company. Financial analysis is one important means of facilitating these objectives. Financial analysis by management is continual and comprehensive due to their constant and unlimited access to accounting information and other data. Their analysis of ratios, trends, economic relations, and other significant factors is often systematic and alert to changing business conditions. Timely detection and reaction to these changes is a major objective. Exhibit 2.1 lists benefits to management from analysis of financial statements.

Since management has superior access to inside information, what is their interest in analysis of financial statements? One important reason for management utilizing the tools of analysis is that such data compel them to view the company in the way important outsiders, like creditors and equity investors, must view it. This gives management an insight into valuation and other uses of financial data they might not otherwise gain. Analysis of financial statements can sometimes provide management with valuable clues to important changes in underlying operating, investing, and financing activities. Recognition of these changes and timely action to check adverse trends are the essence of managerial control. Management derives important advantages from systematic monitoring of financial data.

EXHIBIT 2.1 Benefits to Management from Monitoring Financial Statements

- Recognition that no business event occurs in isolation. Management aims to discern whether an event is the cause or consequence of additional, potentially underlying, conditions.
- Recognition that management must not blindly act on isolated events. There is a need for careful examination of related economic consequences. Management should ascertain the cause(s) of an event; positive or negative assessments should be withheld until a full analysis is undertaken.
- Organization of relevant data and analysis of patterns relative to prior experience or external conditions. This permits management to "see the forest through the trees"—minimizing the possibility of being lost among a maze of financial facts and figures.
- Encourages prompt and effective actions as conditions unfold—rather than "post mortem" analysis of causes and effects.

Auditors

Auditors are outsiders who examine and provide assurance that financial statements are prepared in accordance with accepted practices. The product of an audit is an expression of opinion on the fairness of financial statements. The basic objective of an audit is to provide some assurance about the absence of material errors and irregularities, intentional or otherwise, in financial statements. Financial statement analysis, and its tools and techniques, represent an important set of audit procedures. Because errors and irregularities can significantly affect various financial, operating, and investing relations, analysis of these relations can sometimes reveal their potentiality. Application of financial statement analysis as part of the audit program is often most effective in the early stages of an audit because it often reveals areas of greatest change and vulnerability—areas to which an auditor will want to direct attention. At the completion of an audit, these tools represent a final check on the reasonableness of financial statements as a whole.

Directors

Directors are elected representatives of shareholders who oversee their interests in the company. This representation typically involves oversight of dividend policy, establishing management compensation or incentive programs, hiring and firing of management and the external auditor, and setting company goals. Because of directors' responsibilities to shareholders, they should be vigilant overseers of the company's business activities. This demands an understanding and appreciation of financing, investing, and operating activities. Financial statement analysis aids directors in fulfilling their oversight responsibilities to shareholders.

Merger and Acquisition Analysts

Merger and acquisition analysts are individuals interested in valuing a company for purchase or for merger with one or more other entities. This task represents an attempt to determine economic value, the relative worth of merging entities, and/or the relative bargaining positions of interested parties. Financial statement analysis is a valuable technique in determining economic value and in assessing the financial and operational compatibility of merger candidates. Objectives of the merger and acquisition analyst are similar to an equity investor's except the analysis must often be extended and stress the valuation of assets, including intangible assets such as goodwill, and any off-balance-sheet liabilities in an acquisition or merger plan.

Regulators

Regulators are those with authority or significant influence over rules guiding the preparation of financial statements. Government agencies and politicians have both the authority over and demand for financial statement information. The Internal Revenue Service, a government agency, applies tools and techniques of financial statement analysis to both audit tax returns and check the reasonableness of reported amounts. Other regulatory agencies use analysis techniques in the exercise of their supervisory and rate-determination functions. Politicians often use financial statements to support the perceived need, or lack thereof, for legislation affecting companies. For example, excessive earnings in an industry can invite additional income tax levies.

Other Important Users

Financial statement analysis serves the needs of many other important users. *Financial intermediaries,* such as stockbrokers, use financial data in making investment recommendations. *Employees* of a company are interested in assessing the fairness of their wages and their future employment prospects. *Labor unions* use techniques of financial statement analysis in attempting to gain the upper hand in collective bargaining discussions. *Suppliers* must investigate a company's financial soundness prior to making sales on credit. *Customers* use analysis techniques to determine profitability (or staying power) of their suppliers, the suppliers' returns, and other relevant factors. *Lawyers* use analysis techniques to advance their investigative and legal work, and *economists* use them in research and policy debates.

ANALYSIS VIEWPOINT . . . *You are the director*

You are named a director of a major company. Your lawyer warns you about litigation risk and the need to constantly monitor management and the financial health of the company. How can financial statement analysis assist you in performing your director duties?

Accounting Information: Basis of Analysis

The analytical processes underlying the inferences of financial statement users make use of a vast array of information, including economic, industry, social, and political data. Yet, the most important quantitative data are financial accounting data. Since financial accounting data are the product of conventions, measurements, and judgments, their apparent precision is sometimes misleading. Skillful use of accounting data for financial analysis requires a thorough understanding of the accounting framework underlying their computation, including the practices governing measurement of assets, liabilities, equities, and operating results for a company.

Accounting Measurement and Reporting of Business Activity

Accounting is the quantitative expression of economic phenomena. Accounting emerged from a need for a framework for recording, classifying, and communicating economic phenomena. Contemporary accounting practice reflects modifications in response to changing social, cultural, and economic demands.

The accounting function is carried out at two levels. One is the **recording function.** This involves the mechanics of recording and summarizing transactions and economic events in a quantifiable manner. The second is the **measurement and reporting function.** This function is arguably more complex and subject to greater managerial discretion. It governs the methods, procedures, and principles determining how companies measure and report accounting data. This section considers the recording function, while subsequent chapters (see Part Two) take up the practices and principles governing accounting measurement and reporting.

The **principle of double-entry** governs the recording function in accounting. Understanding double-entry accounting aids our analysis of financial statements. Users find an understanding of double-entry accounting assists them with reconstructing business transactions from financial statements. The double-entry system uses the duality of every business transaction. For example, if a company borrows $1,000, it acquires both an asset (cash) and a claim against assets (a liability) in equal amounts. This duality and balance prevails in all transactions and provides order, consistency, and control. Exhibit 2.2 describes these counterbalancing effects for assets, liabilities, revenues, and expenses. At all times, a company's assets equal the sum of the claims from creditors and owners (this is the accounting equation discussed in Chapter 1). Under the double-entry system, all transactions are recorded, classified, and summarized using appropriate account designations. Financial statements are formal, condensed presentations of data derived from these accounts.

EXHIBIT 2.2 Counterbalancing Effects of Transactions in Financial Statements

Asset acquisition is counterbalanced with:
- Incurrence of a liability;
- Increase in ownership claim; and/or
- Disposal of another asset.

Liability extinguishment is counterbalanced with:
- disposal of an asset;
- increase in ownership claim; and/or
- incurrence of another liability.

Revenue earned is counterbalanced with:
- increase in assets;
- decrease in liabilities; and/or
- decrease in ownership claim.

Expenses incurred are counterbalanced with:
- decrease in assets;
- increase in liabilities; and/or
- increase in ownership claim.

Relevance of Accounting Information

Business decisions, like choosing equity investments or extending credit, require a variety of data with varying reliability and relevance. These data include information on economic conditions and industry trends, as well as information on intangible items like the integrity and motivations of management. Financial statements represent measurable indices of past performance and financial conditions. While the importance of nonquantifiable intangibles vis-à-vis quantified financial statements varies, financial statement users do not make any serious, well-grounded decisions without analysis of the quantifiable data in financial statements.

Financial statements are important because they are objective and report economic consequences of actual events. Moreover, they quantify and measure these consequences. The attribute of measurability endows financial statements with an important characteristic: **common monetary unit.** Since data are expressed in the common denominator of money, it enables us to add and combine data, to relate them to other data, and to manipulate them arithmetically.

Accounting for economic phenomena, however, is imperfect and has limitations. It is easy to become impatient with these imperfections and limitations and search for a substitute. There is no ready substitute. Financial accounting is and remains the only relevant and reliable system for systematic recording, classification, and summarization of business activities. Improvement rests with refinements in this time-tested system. It is thus incumbent on anyone who desires to analyze effectively the financial position and the results of operations of a company, to understand accounting, its terminology, and its practices, including its imperfections and limitations.

Analysis of financial statements is an indispensable part of lending, investing, and other financial decisions. We must understand that its relative importance varies considerably in any particular case. Since a lender's return derives primarily from the company, financial statement analysis is an important part of a lending decision. Financial statement analysis plays a different role in the equity investing decision. The equity investor looks to two different sources for a return: dividends and capital appreciation. Dividends depend on profitability, growth, and liquidity—elements lending themselves to evaluation by means of financial statement analysis. However, dividends are but one part, and often the smaller part, of the two sources of investor return. Indeed, many growing and successful companies, like Adaptec, pay no dividends. The often more important return derives from other investors' future willingness to pay more for the stock than we did. While the willingness of investors to pay more for the stock depends on earning power and growth, it can also depend on the psychology of the market, the valuation of earnings retained, and other factors such as rates of return available on alternative investments. Gauging the performance of equity security markets is challenging.

The importance of financial statement analysis for equity investing varies with circumstances and time. Its importance is relatively greater when market valuations are low than when these valuations are subject to general market euphoria. Its relative importance is also greater when directed to risk assessment and the detection of areas of vulnerability. Financial statement analysis is often of greater value for defensive investing and in the avoidance of loss than it is in uncovering investment opportunities.

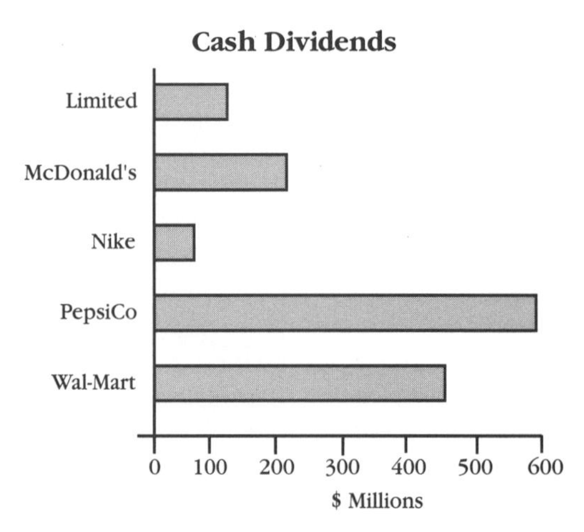

Source: Annual reports.

Information Environment for Financial Statement Analysis

We have discussed the relative importance of financial statement analysis to the total decision effort. The relevant information set a decision maker draws on includes financial statements and various other types of information. The relative importance of each varies from decision to decision. Exhibit 2.3 illustrates the composition of our entire information set. It is important to recognize that financial statements are but a portion of the entire information set available. Companies cannot effectively convey all relevant information in financial statements and better communicate some through other means (e.g., analysts' forecasts or recommendations). Certain information in financial reports is not overseen by accounting regulatory agencies. For example, accounting standards do not extend to Management's Discussion and Analysis. Nevertheless, this additional information is often relevant in our analysis.

Accounting Principles and Limitations

We must temper the importance of financial accounting data by the data's limitations for financial statement analysis. This section discusses the more important limitations.

Monetary Expression

An obvious accounting limitation is that information in financial statements must lend itself to quantification in a monetary unit. Not all important economic relations about a company lend themselves to quantification. For example, financial state-

EXHIBIT 2.3 Information Set for Financial Statement Analysis

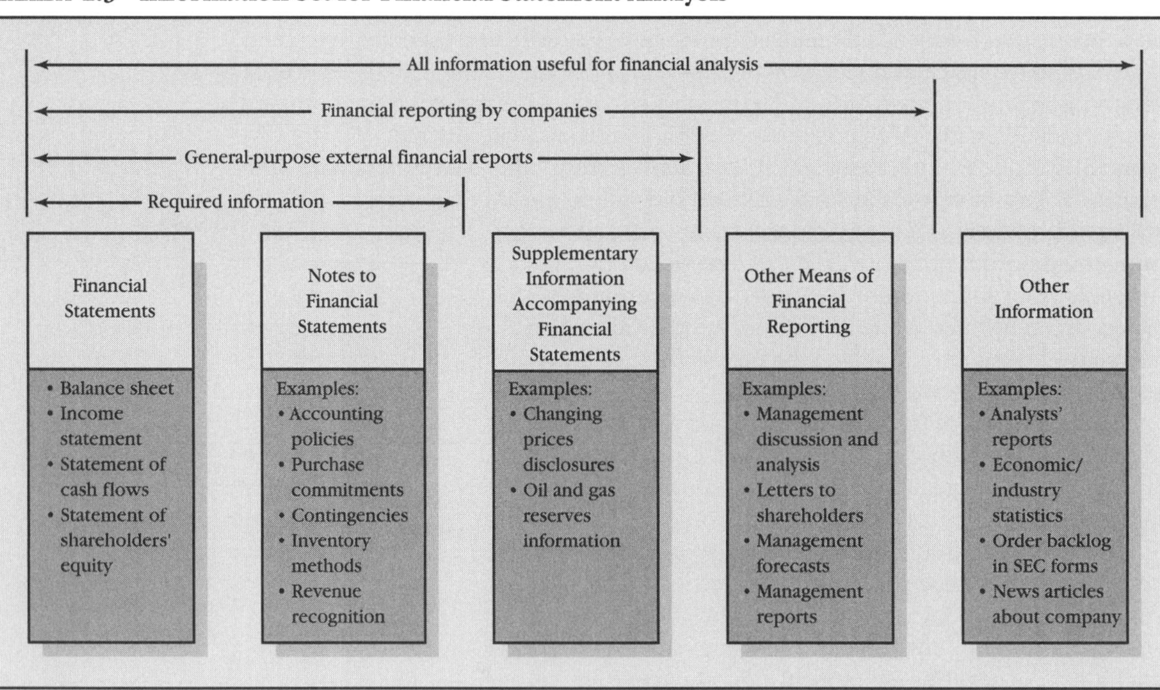

ments convey little if any direct information about the character, motivation, or experience of management or employees. They convey no disaggregate information on the quality of research and development efforts nor the extent of a company's marketing efforts. Nor do they typically convey any detailed information on product lines, machinery efficiency, or future plans. Also absent is information on organization structure, informal communication channels within and outside a company, and assessments on the importance of specific individuals' talents.

Simplification and Summarization

Financial statements simplify and summarize complex and diverse economic activities. Simplification is necessary in classifying the various economic events into a manageable number of categories. Summarization is also necessary to keep the quantity and detail of financial statements within reasonable bounds. Costs of statement preparation further encourage simplification and summarization. Yet simplification and summarization are at the expense of clarity and detail potentially useful in our analysis. Simplification and summarization inherent in accounting make it imperative that we analyze and reconstruct the events and transactions they represent. It is essential we be able to recover from financial statements the economic realities that underlie them or to recognize those realities whose recovery is futile—the latter yield meaningful questions for management and others able to provide additional information.

Judgment and Incentives

Preparation of financial statements requires judgment. Judgment is imperfect, yielding variability in the quality and reliability of accounting numbers. Since financial statements are general-purpose presentations, preparers' judgments are affected by their view of a typical user's requirements and expectations. These requirements and expectations do not necessarily coincide with those of a user with a specific task in mind. Accounting is also a *social science* and, therefore, is at least partially determined by human factors, including incentives. No assessment of financial statement quality or reliability is complete without considering these incentives. While the overriding purpose of accounting is supplying information useful in business decisions, we must recognize many parties are involved in the accounting function, each having their own interest in mind. Exhibit 2.4 lists several examples of how financial reports might reflect insiders' interests. Furthermore, parties external to a company have their own agenda and incentives. Governments want accounting to promote policies encouraging inflation control, good labor relations, continued economic growth, antitrust oversight, and equitable taxes. Accounting practitioners want accounting to increase the market for their services, maintain positive relations with clients, and assist clients in reaching their objectives. These biased interests do not, nor should they, affect objectives of accounting. Accounting regulatory agencies must represent society and ensure that accounting objectives mesh with society. Still, we must be aware of strong personal incentives at stake trying to bend practice to favor other interests. Society's countermeasures include regulatory institutions (e.g., Securities and Exchange Commission), the courts, and the accounting and auditing professions. Each of these institutions can impose punitive damages on the various parties.

EXHIBIT 2.4 Transactions or Events in Financial Reports Potentially Affected by Insiders' Interests

Obtaining credit to ensure a company's survival through difficult events.
Selling securities in the open market to facilitate company growth.
Enhancing compensation of executives or employees for personal gain.
Helping management fend off a hostile takeover attempt.
Permitting managers to enrich themselves at the expense of owners.
Increasing wealth of the company's current owners.

Interim Disclosures and Estimates

Useful accounting information is *timely*. Accordingly, disclosure of financial condition and results of operations occurs frequently. But the more frequent the disclosures—especially with an income statement—the greater the need for estimates. This greater need for estimates increases the uncertainty inherent in financial statements. Estimates are required for many items including: (1) amount and timing of cash collections on receivables, (2) expected selling prices and sales volume for inventory items, (3) benefit period and salvage value of depreciable assets, (4) future warranty claims, (5) portion complete and remaining costs of long-term sales contracts, (6) income and property taxes, and (7) loss reserves. The link between frequency of reporting, the length of period covered, and the degree of accounting uncertainty deserves explanation. Namely, many business transactions and events require a long period of time (several quarters or years) for completion and determination of results. For example, long-term depreciable assets benefit several periods extending years into the future. The longer the benefit period, the more tentative are estimates of their salvage value, benefit period, and payback pattern. As another example, the value, if any, of investments in mining or exploration ventures are often not apparent until many years subsequent to initial development efforts. Consequently, while we demand and receive interim accounting reports, we must recognize the lower reliability of such disclosures due to the increased need for estimates in interim reports.

Historical Cost Measurement

Accounting systems aim to report *fair and objective* information. Since the value of an asset determined through arm's-length bargaining is usually fair and objective, use of *historical cost* values in financial statements is common. These historical cost values enjoy an objectivity surpassing any other unrealized appraisals of value. Accounting practice adheres, with some exceptions, to this cost concept. The consequence of this objectivity when values subsequently change impairs the usefulness of financial statements. Historical cost balances do not, in most cases, represent current market values. Yet users of financial statements desire a balance between objectively determined values and the most current market values of assets and liabilities. Thus, while we must be aware of and adjust to valuation bases other than cost, historical cost measures represent a pragmatic compromise to a difficult circumstance.

Unstable Monetary Unit

Accounting reports generally deal with items expressed only in monetary terms. However, the purchasing power of money experiences periodic fluctuations with a typically declining trend. The monetary unit has not retained its attribute as a "standard of value" and, consequently, adding account balances across years can yield serious distortions. Practice recognizes this limitation. Yet, no reporting requirements currently exist for adjusting financial statements for changes in purchasing power.

Need to Understand Accounting Measurements and Disclosures

Substantial progress has been made by regulatory agencies in narrowing the range of acceptable accounting practices, in expanding meaningful disclosure, and in improving the quality and credibility of financial statements. This progress notwithstanding, the experienced user of financial statements recognizes continuing limitations and imperfections. We would be naive and unrealistic in hoping the time is near when we no longer need to "go behind the numbers" underlying financial statements and are able to "go forward from the numbers." Among the more important reasons for this conclusion are:

- Management has a vital interest in financial statements and, hence, exerts influence on accounting for and disclosure of financial results. While auditors increase the objectivity and credibility of financial statements, their influence is limited due to questions of independence and problems inherent in the accounting system. The latter include:

    Application of standards in practice. Accounting standards are rarely so explicit to eliminate judgment from accounting and auditing practice. Moreover, accounting standards typically apply only to *material* items—yet a standard definition of materiality eludes us.

    Accounting standards are not comprehensive. Several areas of accounting, including business combinations, goodwill, product cost accounting, and allocations, are provided limited guidance from accounting standards. This contributes to diversity and inconsistencies in practice.

    Accounting is slow to change. Emerging transactions, changing business practices, and the ingenuity of "financial engineers" yield an inevitable lag in standards behind practice. Accounting standards generally focus on existing problems vis-à-vis looming or anticipated problems.

- Powerful interest groups have and continue to limit progress on development of uniform and fair accounting standards. These groups exert pressure with regulatory agencies to enact standards in their best interests. An example is the extensive lobbying efforts of certain groups to prevent mandatory expense recognition of costs associated with stock-based compensation.
- Much of the data comprising financial statements is "soft." This is in spite of the precision conveyed by detailed and numeric presentations. Soft data refers to information dependent on subjective evaluations; forecasts of future conditions; and assumptions regarding the integrity, competence, intent, or motives of management.
- We cannot safely abdicate our analysis task of scrutinizing and evaluating the accounting numbers comprising financial statements. A prerequisite to our thorough and intelligent analysis is an understanding of the data relied on. Experience shows us that improvements in accounting standards are accompanied by increased complexity of data measures and disclosures.

Implications of Accounting Risk

Our analysis of financial statements recognizes a number of risks. There are the risks associated with all profit-seeking businesses, including the risk of losses, risk of adversities, risk of contingencies, and risk of information reliability. We must also recognize another type of risk, referred to as **accounting risk**. Accounting risk results from the need for judgments, estimates, and the imprecision inherent in the accounting system. Accounting risk increases our uncertainty in decision making. Accounting risk also involves accounting *conservatism*. Assumptions play an important role in accounting measurements, and these assumptions can be too conservative or optimistic. Thus, the degree of conservatism, or lack thereof, can confound our analysis (we return to this issue in Chapter 13). Partly in recognition of accounting risk, regulators currently require companies to disclose a summary of accounting policies underlying their financial statements. Companies are required to emphasize their accounting choices made from both accepted alternatives and unusual, innovative, or industry-unique practices. Adaptec summarizes its accounting policies in note one of its 1996 financial statements.

ANALYSIS VIEWPOINT . . . *You are the auditor*

You have just been informed your audit firm is the low bidder on a proposed audit engagement and you accept the assignment. How can you use financial statement analysis in your audit engagement of this new client?

Additional Analysis Techniques

Reconstruction of Business Activities and Transactions

An important part of our analysis is the ability to reconstruct business activities and transactions summarized in financial statements. **Accounting reconstruction** is the replication of the financial statement preparers' work in *reverse* order. This role reversal is portrayed as follows:

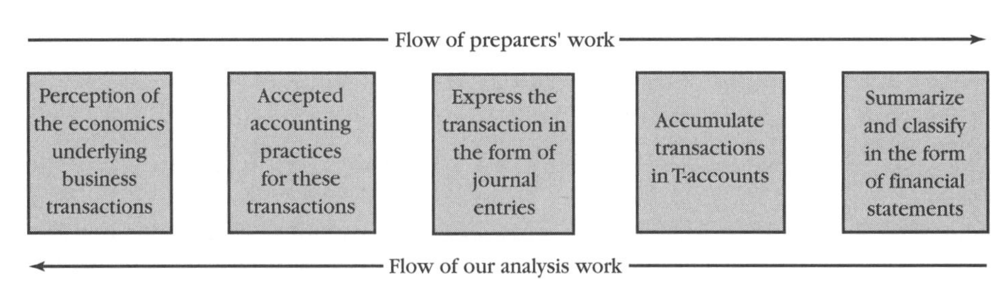

Preparers' efforts and skills are directed at understanding the economics underlying transactions or events. Preparers must then use their accounting knowledge to record the transaction, express it in the form of a journal entry, and carry it to the accounts. These basic concepts of journal entries and T-accounts are particularly useful in our analytical work. Preparers ultimately summarize and report all accounts of a period in the form of financial statements.

Our analysis work is in reverse order. It is important to recognize while preparers' efforts are primarily oriented to past events, our analysis focuses on future expectations. Our analysis works with financial statements made available by the company. Our task is to recapture, to the extent possible, the economics imbedded and summarized in financial statements. This analytical process requires us to visualize the journal entries made and reconstruct, in summary fashion, all or selected accounts in the financial statements. This task requires an understanding of the economics underlying business transactions and events as well as a knowledge of accounting practice.

Our reconstruction of business activities and transactions gives us insight into the changes in balance sheet accounts and the consequences of given transactions or events. It also permits us to answer questions like the following:

- What is the reason for an increase or decrease in investments?
- What are the consequences of debt refunding for working capital and cash?
- What amount of long-term debt is repaid this period?
- What is the effect of income taxes and how much tax is actually paid?

Reconstruction of business transactions and events requires accounting knowledge—the ability to know how a transaction is recorded and what kinds of activities or events increase or decrease specific accounts. It also requires the ability to read carefully, understand, and interpret financial statements and their notes. We need knowledge of what information is available in financial statements, where it is found, and how to reconstruct transactions (including the making of reasonable assumptions). Reconstruction depends on our knowledge of related disciplines—such as accounting, economics, finance, and psychology—and on our skills of derivation and inference. It also demands a degree of detective work based on marshaling all known facts while using the limited and incomplete data available. In reconstructing transactions and events, we work with known information in deducing unknown facts. The degree of accuracy expected in our reconstruction and analysis is not at nor need it approach the accuracy expected in the accounting and recording function.

The **T-account** is a very important analytical tool and we use it often. Our emphasis here is *not* on accounting mechanics but on the use of the T-account to reconstruct and understand transactions and events. Yet we must recognize that our understanding of the accounting function is a useful analytical technique. Use of T-account analysis depends on our ability to visualize transactions in journal form and summarize them in T-accounts. Illustration 2.1 shows us how a T-account is used to derive cash collections.

When there is inadequate information, we often must combine accounts and analyze them together. Having identified the missing information, we can pose informed questions to management or shareholder relations departments to obtain the desired information. We must also recognize what information is not available in financial statements, and attempt to secure it if sufficiently important. For example, specific information on commitments, lines of credit, and order backlogs is usually unavailable. A notes payable account or a loan-to-officers account can show little or no change in year-end balances but might have experienced significant interim balances liquidated during the year.

Illustration 2.1

Our financial statement analysis of Campbell Soup Company needs to determine the amount of cash collected from customers during Year 11. We decide to reconstruct Accounts Receivable to answer this question. We find accounts receivable on the balance sheet and know that reconstruction is key to determining the cash collected from customers (see the financial statements in Supplement A). We also need knowledge of the usual entries determining accounts receivable. Our first step is to establish the accounts receivable T-account with beginning and ending balances (details are in note 13 of Campbell's financial statements):

Accounts Receivable (net)

	Debit	Credit	
Beginning balance	534.1		
Net sales	6,204.1		Cash collections
		6,276.5	(plug & balance)
Ending balance	461.7		

Our second step is to determine the aggregate debits to this account. We must work with aggregates from financial statements rather than the detailed entries comprising them. Knowing debits to assets represent the counterpart of sales (a revenue item increasing equity), we debit the asset Accounts Receivable for the total sales of $6,204.1 (in millions). We know not all sales are for cash, but to arrive at cash collections from customers it does not matter whether the charges are cash sales or credit sales. The amount needed to balance the accounts receivable T-account is $6,276.5. This is our best estimate of cash collections from customers. We know this amount is overstated because it includes credits to customers for cash discounts and bad debts. Yet, to reconstruct the Allowance for Bad Debts account we would need at least the amount of bad debt expense charged to income during the year—an amount not always reported in financial statements. These residual accounts are, however, small relative to total collections and are not likely to materially affect our cash collection estimate.

Indirect Evidence and Evaluation

Financial statement analysis can provide indirect evidence bearing on important questions. For instance, analysis of past statements of cash flows can offer evidence as to the financing and investing tendencies of management. Moreover, analysis of operating statements offers evidence on management's skill in coping with fluctuations in a company's business activities. While indirect evidence and evaluation are often not precise or quantifiable, they provide insight into managerial decisions and preferences. Indirect evidence and evaluation is facilitated through **contrast analysis.** Contrast analysis rests on the proposition that no number by itself is meaningful but rather acquires meaning only in contrast to a comparable quantity. Contrast analysis focuses on *exceptions and variations,* and saves us the need to formulate individual norms and expectations. It also serves as an attention-directing and control device. Contrast analysis is accomplished by examining:

- External data from competitors or industry publications (i.e., external contrasts).
- Company performance over time (i.e., internal contrasts).
- Yardsticks compiled from standards, budgets, or forecasts.

Advantages of external data are their (1) objectivity and independence, (2) value as standards if derived from similar companies, and (3) comparability when derived from companies subject to similar economic and industry conditions. Reliable contrasts enjoy a consistent basis of compilation, comparable periods of analysis, and source credibility.

Industry Comparability Analysis of Financial Statements

One of the most popular and effective contrast tests is **industry comparability analysis.** Comparing financial statements of companies within an industry presents a number of challenges. We discuss the more significant challenges below.

Differing Reporting Periods

While the majority of companies use a calendar year-end, some use noncalendar year-ends for reporting purposes. Adjustment for differing year-ends depends on the extent of the year-end time difference. If the year-end time difference is under three months, adjustments are typically not necessary. If the year-end time difference exceeds three months, financial statement users can use quarterly reports to make data comparable for a reliable financial statement analysis. Through the addition of any four consecutive quarters, we can adjust year-ends for comparison purposes. The need to adjust for year-end time differences and the magnitude of adjustments depends on whether extraordinary events, like strikes or property damage, occur in a quarter. Moreover, the effects of seasonal and cyclical influences on comparability of time periods need careful evaluation.

Differing Accounting Principles

As we stress throughout, use of alternative accounting principles or methods renders data of companies noncomparable. This lack of comparability must be corrected by means of data adjustments before performing a reliable financial statement analysis. The following list is a sampling of alternative accounting principles requiring our attention (we list the chapters where we discuss their effects on financial statements).

Alternative Accounting Principles	*Chapter Coverage*
Leases (operating, capital)	3
Inventory valuation (acquisition cost, standard cost, lower of cost or market)	4
Inventory cost flow assumption (FIFO, LIFO, weighted average)	4
Investments in securities (trading, available for sale, held to maturity)	4, 5
Depreciation method (straight line, accelerated)	4, 6
Corporate acquisitions (purchase, pooling of interests)	5
Foreign currency translation (all current, temporal method)	5
Revenue recognition (percentage of completion, completed contract)	6

Restatement and Reclassification Requirements

Several cases require restatement of financial statements including:

- The merger of companies under the pooling method of accounting requires restating prior years' statements as if the companies had been merged from inception. As a practical matter only financial statements reported when the merger is announced are in restated form.
- Discontinuances or disposals of a segment of a business require that companies classify revenues and expenses of these segments, and any losses expected on disposal, in the income statement under discontinued operations. Similarly,

net assets of these segments appear separately on the balance sheet. Financial statements that include discontinuances are restated accordingly.

- Certain changes in accounting principles (e.g., changes in inventory cost flow assumptions or changes in income recognition on long-term contracts) require that companies restate any reported prior years' financial statements to reflect the newly adopted principle.

Difficulties often arise because the available restated period is less than the preferred time period for analysis. This is because companies typically report balance sheets for two years and income statements and statements of cash flow for three years. These are the periods for which restated financial statements are likely available, although restatements for longer periods are sometimes found in SEC filings (e.g., registration statements). We must also recognize any account classification differences across companies' financial statements. Some classification differences are easier to adjust for than others. For example, if one company includes depreciation expense in cost of goods sold while another shows this expense as a separate item, we can easily make adjustments to put analytical measures (like ratios) on a comparable basis.

Analytical Use of Accounting Standards and Assumptions

We review many accounting standards and assumptions underlying financial statements in this book. Our purpose is to examine their financial statement consequences when applied to similar transactions and circumstances, as well as the managerial latitude in interpretation and application of accounting standards. These consequences must be understood before making a meaningful analysis or reliable comparison. We highlight the importance of standards and assumptions in accounting determinations in Illustration 2.2.

In the illustration, our prospective buyer has at least two questions about this income statement: Can I rely on the income statement numbers? What adjustments are necessary for a reliable net income number in computing price?

Assurance about the fairness of financial statements is provided by an independent auditor. We assume an audit assures the financial statements accurately portray results of operations and financial position in accordance with generally accepted principles. An answer to our second question is more difficult. While an auditor's assurance extends to the fairness of the income statement, it does *not* imply income is the relevant figure to use in computing the price of the apartment building. Let us examine the information our buyer needs and what assumptions are necessary to arrive at a reliable income number for computing price. We pursue the following specific analyses:

Rental income. Does the $46,000 figure represent 100 percent occupancy during the year? If so, should we make an allowance for possible vacancies? What are rental trends in the area? What are rental expectations for the next five years? Next 10 years? Are demand factors for apartments in the area stable, improving, or deteriorating? Our aim is to adjust the yearly rental income number to approximate a level that, on average, we expect to prevail for the foreseeable future. Prior years' data are useful in judging this.

Real estate taxes. The trend of taxes over the years is important. This depends on the taxing authority and its tax demands and tendencies.

Mortgage interest. This item is relevant only if our buyer plans to assume the existing mortgage. Otherwise, substitute the interest expense related to our buyer's new financing.

Illustration 2.2

The owner of Lakeside Apartment Complex has an interested buyer. How is the price set? How is a buyer reassured in the soundness and profitability of this investment at a set price? There is more than one approach to set price, including analysis of comparable current values and reproduction costs. One of the most widely accepted methods for valuation of income-producing properties or investments is *capitalization of earnings.* If earnings is our major consideration, we focus on the income statement. Our prospective buyer is provided the income statement for the apartment (we have excluded income taxes because they depend on our owner's tax status):

LAKESIDE APARTMENT COMPLEX
Income Statement
For the Year Ending December 31

Revenue:		
Rental revenue	$46,000	
Garage rentals	2,440	
Other income from washer and dryer concession	300	
Total revenue		$48,740
Expenses:		
Real estate taxes	4,900	
Mortgage interest	2,100	
Electricity and gas	840	
Water	720	
Superintendent's salary	1,600	
Insurance	680	
Repairs and maintenance	2,400	13,240
Income before depreciation		$35,500
Depreciation		9,000
Net income*		$26,500

* Taxes are excluded.

Utilities. This item is scrutinized with a view to ascertaining whether they are at a representative level of future costs.

Superintendent's salary. Is this pay adequate to secure acceptable services? Can the services of the superintendent be retained?

Insurance. Are all foreseeable risks insured for? Is coverage adequate?

Repairs and maintenance. We must review these expenses over a number of years to determine a representative level. Is this level of expenses sufficient to afford proper maintenance of the property or is the expense account "starved" to show a higher net income?

Depreciation. This figure is not likely relevant to our buyer's decision unless the buyer's cost approximates the seller's. If cost to the buyer differs, then we compute depreciation using that cost and an acceptable method of depreciation over the building's useful life.

Our buyer must also ascertain whether any expenses expected are omitted from this income statement. An auditor's unqualified opinion does not diminish the importance of addressing these type of questions. For example, while accepted accounting principles require that insurance expense include accruals for the entire year, they do *not* attest to adequacy of insurance coverage. Nor are accounting principles concerned with a company's maintenance policy, or a superintendent's pay, or with any *expected* revenues and expenses.

Recognizing the many complex questions and problems in this simple income statement provides us with a sense of the complexities in a complete analysis of financial statements of a large business enterprise. It is essential that a reliable analysis includes an appreciation of what financial statements portray and what they do not or cannot portray. There are items that properly belong in statements and there are items that, because of an inability to quantify them or to determine them objectively, cannot be included. Our illustration of the apartment buyer shows, despite their limitations, financial statements are indispensable to business decisions. While our potential buyer can use the income statement without these assumptions and adjustments, our buyer is at a great disadvantage without them.

Traditional Market Measures

Analyses in practice use a variety of measures to evaluate the price and yield behavior of a company's securities. The **price-earnings ratio** measures the multiple at which the market is capitalizing the earnings per share of a company. The **earnings yield,** the inverse of the price-earnings ratio, represents the income-producing power of a share of common stock at the current price. The **dividend yield** is the cash return accruing to an investor on a share of stock based on the current dividend rate and current price. Recall that all or part of a company's earnings can be distributed as dividends and the balance retained. The **dividend payout ratio** measures the proportion of earnings currently paid out as common stock dividends.

Review Problem: Understanding Relations among Financial Statements

This exercise reviews our understanding of various intra- and interstatement relations and ratios. Our task is to reconstruct the balance sheet shown below using the information available.

Balance Sheet Information

Accounts:	
Cash	
Accounts receivable	
Inventory	$ 50
Building	
Land	
Current liabilities	
Common stock	
Retained earnings	$100

Additional information:

Assets – Liabilities = $600.
Stockholders' equity = 3 x Total liabilities.
Carrying amount of land is two-thirds of the building.
Acid-test ratio = 1.25.
Ending inventory turnover is 15.
Gross profit is 44 percent of the cost of goods sold.
Days' sales in accounts receivable is 20.

SOLUTION TO REVIEW PROBLEM

Assets		***Liabilities***	
Cash	$190	Current liabilities	$200
Accounts receivable	60	Shareholders' Equity	500
Inventory	50	Retained earnings	100
Buildings	300	Total liabilities and	
Land	200	shareholders' equity	$800
Total assets	$800		

Determination of this balance sheet is based on steps 1–6 described below:

Step 1:

Assets – Liabilities = $600
Stockholders' equity = 600
Retained earnings = 100 (as given)
Common stock = 500

Step 2:

Equity = 3 × Total liabilities
3 × Current liabilities (which equal total liabilities) = $600
Current liabilities = 200
Total assets = Current liabilities + Equity = $800

Step 3:

Acid test = 1.25

$$\frac{\text{Cash + Accounts receivable}}{\$200} = 1.25$$

Cash + Accounts receivable = $250

Step 4:

Inventory + Buildings + Land = $550 [i.e., Total assets – (Cash + Accounts receivable)]
Buildings + Land = $500 (since inventory is given at $50)

Land = $^2/_3$ of building; thus, if x = Carrying amount of building
$x + {}^2/_3\, x = \$500 \qquad x = \$300$ (building)
Land = $500 – $300 = $200

Step 5:

$$\frac{\text{Cost of goods sold (CGS)}}{\text{Ending inventory}} = \text{Inventory turnover; } \frac{\text{CGS}}{\$50} = 15$$

Cost of goods sold = $750

Gross profit=44% of $750 = $330

Step 6:

Cost of goods sold + Gross profit = $750 + $330 = Sales = $1,080

$$\text{Days' sales in receivables} = \frac{\text{Accounts receivable} \times 360}{\text{Sales}}$$

Accounts receivable = (20 × $1,080) ÷ 360 = $60

Cash = $250 – Accounts receivable ($60) = $190

GUIDANCE ANSWERS TO ANALYSIS VIEWPOINTS

You Are the Director

As a member of a company's board of directors, you are responsible for oversight of management and the safeguarding of shareholders' interests. Accordingly, a director's interest in the company is broad and risky. To reduce risk, a director uses financial statement analysis to monitor management and assess company profitability, growth, and financial condition. Because of a director's unique position, there is near unlimited access to internal financial and other records. Analysis of financial statements assists our director in (1) recognizing causal relations among business activities and events, (2) "seeing the forest through the trees," that is, helping directors focus on the company, and not on a maze of financial details, and (3) encouraging proactive and not reactive measures in confronting changing financial conditions.

You Are the Auditor

An auditor's primary objective is an expression of an opinion on the fairness of financial statements according to generally accepted accounting principles. As auditor, you desire assurance on the absence of errors and irregularities in financial statements. Financial statement analysis can help identify any errors and irregularities affecting the statements. Also, this analysis compels our auditor to understand the company's operations and its performance in light of prevailing economic and industry conditions. Application of financial statement analysis is especially useful as a preliminary audit tool, directing the auditor to areas of greatest change and unexplained performance.

A P P E N D I X

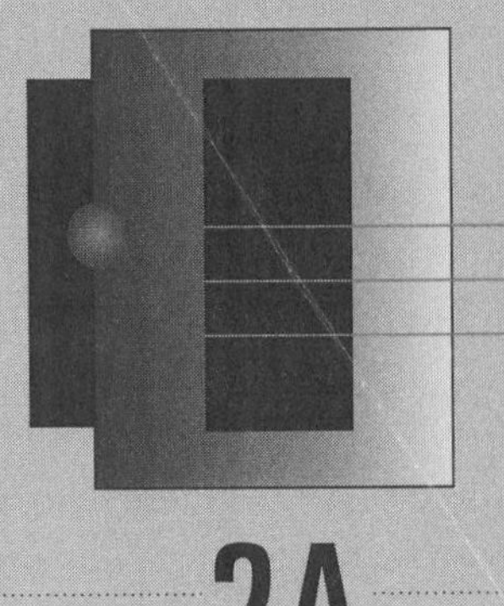

2A

Accounting Principles Underlying Financial Statements

Generally Accepted Accounting Principles

Generally accepted accounting principles (GAAP) are the rules and operative guidelines of accounting. These rules, or more accurately standards, determine such matters as how assets are measured, when liabilities are incurred, when income is recognized as earned, and when expenses and losses accrue. To the user of accounting data and statements, an understanding of these rules is essential. A user cannot undertake a reliable analysis of financial statements without ascertaining the accounting principles used in their preparation and how they are applied.

How Accounting Standards Are Established

Accounting principles have been long in developing and are subject to continual innovation, modification, and change. Accounting principles have changed in response to developments in, and the needs of, society and its requirements and expectations. It is generally accepted that primary responsibility for fair financial statements rests with management. However, responsibility for development of accounting standards that govern these statements is borne primarily by the accounting profession and the Securities and Exchange Commission (SEC) and, to a lesser extent, the American Accounting Association (AAA) and organized securities exchanges.

Influence of Accounting Profession

Reasons for the accounting profession's early leadership in development of accounting principles are readily apparent. One of the profession's major and unique functions is attesting to the fairness of financial statements. Yet, the term fairness requires a frame of reference. Accepted principles are intended to provide this frame of reference, and the accounting profession is presumed to have both the independence and the technical competence for their development. In pursuing the development of accounting principles, the profession is not only performing a vital public service but is also catering to its own self-interests.

The AICPA initially attempted to place the effort of developing accounting principles with a Committee on Accounting Procedure (CAP). Its purpose was to reduce the areas of difference in accounting and to narrow the choices available in the area of alternative accounting principles. This committee considered numerous accounting problems and issued pronouncements in the form of 51 *Accounting Research Bulletins (ARBs)*. The authority of *ARBs,* except where the CAP asks and secures formal adoption by the AICPA membership, rests on the general acceptability of its opinions. The Committee on Accounting Procedure was subsequently replaced with the Accounting Principles Board (APB). The APB, vested with greater authority and supported by an enlarged research staff, was charged with further narrowing the areas of differences in accounting principles and in promoting the written expression of generally accepted accounting principles. The APB issued 31 *Opinions;* some improved accounting practice (pension accounting), some inadequately changed practice (leasing), and some confused practice (earnings per share).

Currently, the Financial Accounting Standards Board (FASB), composed of seven full-time paid members, functions as the standard-setting body of the accounting profession. Board members are appointed by a group of trustees, including AICPA members and representatives from private industry, security analysts, and others. In spite of its limitations, the FASB is an improvement over its predecessors. Before issuing an accounting standard, the board issues, in most cases, a *discussion memorandum* for public comment. Written comments are filed with the board, and oral comments can be voiced at public hearings that generally precede the issuance of an Exposure Draft for a *Statement of Financial Accounting Standards (SFAS)*. After further exposure and comment, the FASB usually issues a final *SFAS*. It also issues interpretations of previously issued pronouncements from time to time. Another improvement in procedure is the inclusion in most *SFASs* of careful and elaborate explanations of the rationale of the board for the statements it issues, explanations of how comments to the board are dealt with, as well as examples of actual applications. The Financial Accounting Foundation (the FASB's parent body) also adopted a number of changes in the FASB structure to include greater participation by financial statement users in rule making.

Influence of the Securities and Exchange Commission

The SEC, an independent quasi-judicial government agency, administers the Securities Act of 1933 and the Securities Exchange Act of 1934. The primary purpose of the 1933 act is to ensure that a potential purchaser of a security offered for public sale is provided all material facts relating to it. A registration statement, which companies must file with the SEC, discloses these facts. The function of the SEC regarding a registration statement under the 1933 act is to ensure that a company makes full and accurate disclosure of all pertinent information relating to a company's business, its securities, its financial position and earnings, and the underwriting arrangements. Until the SEC approves this statement, amended as necessary, it can prevent the registration statement from becoming effective and the securities from being sold. The SEC is not, however, concerned with the merits of any security registered with it. The 1934 act prescribes disclosure requirements for issuers of securities listed and registered for public trading on our national securities exchanges. Following registration of their securities, registrants must file annual, quarterly, and other periodic reports.

Since its inception, the SEC has encouraged development and improvement of accounting and auditing practice. The commission has issued specific rules and regulations concerning the preparation of financial statements and the degree of detail they contain. The commission's prosecution of numerous accounting and auditing infractions of its rules results in a form of "case law" providing important clues and precedents in the area of accounting principles and auditing procedures. While many SEC positions on accounting and auditing matters confront specific instances and applications, the commission recognizes the impossibility of issuing rules to cover all possible scenarios. An important part of the SEC's influence on matters of accounting takes the form of conferences between companies, their accountants, and SEC staff, and the numerous unpublished rulings and guidelines that result.

The SEC has grown in competence and experience. It has considerable regulatory authority in accounting and the ability to enforce it. It recognizes the great difficulties and complexities involved in finding universally acceptable principles. It also recognizes that certification of financial statements with the commission places a heavy responsibility on the accounting profession. At the same time, the commission does not hesitate to criticize and prod, to take exception to accounting presentations, and to discipline members of the profession when circumstances warrant. The commission exemplifies not a rigid and arbitrary exercise of government authority but the sparing use of this authority.

The SEC approach toward accounting practice is, in large measure, determined by current public attitudes toward, and confidence in, financial reporting—and to some extent by the aggressiveness of its chief accountant. All of these influences change over the years and we see differing and sometimes unique approaches. In recent years, the SEC forced audit firms to consent to quality reviews of their practice by committees of peers, and confronted the FASB with numerous new SEC requirements in areas it considers as being under its jurisdiction. The SEC is increasingly aggressive in modifying FASB standards. The aggressive and constructive influence of these organizations in the development of accounting principles must not mislead us into believing that financial statements filed with the commission are more reliable than others. Less than effective methodologies and limited staffing weaken the SEC's ability to review thoroughly all documents submitted.

Influence of Other Organizations

Two other organizations are influential in formation of accounting principles: the American Accounting Association (AAA) and the organized securities exchanges, particularly the New York Stock Exchange. The AAA is comprised primarily of accounting educators. Being one step removed from practice, they have a more detached point of view and, by the very nature of their calling, a more scholarly and theoretical one. While AAA statements on accounting theory are influential in shaping accounting thought, they have no official standing and are not binding. The role of organized securities exchanges in formulating accounting theory is limited. Like the SEC, organized exchanges have the power to enforce adherence to standards. The basic instrument by which an exchange secures compliance to its standards is the listing agreement. This agreement defines, among other things, the minimum accounting disclosure required in the financial statements of the listed company. One important way the organized securities exchanges support efforts of the AICPA in the area of accounting improvements is by urging listed companies to comply with specific professional pronouncements.

Accounting Objectives and Concepts

Objectives of Financial Statements

While there is some degree of agreement with the proper accounting in specific areas, agreement on the basic bedrock objectives of accounting has, so far, eluded us. There is no broad consensus on objectives that help practitioners settle differences. Accounting is not an exact science. It is a social science—its concepts, rooted in the value system of our society, are socially determined and socially expressed. Consequently, broad agreement on useful generalizations regarding basic objectives is difficult to achieve. The setting of accounting standards is basically a political process involving many parties expressing their self-interests.

Concepts Underlying Financial Statements

The FASB has devised a **conceptual framework** whose purpose is establishing a coherent system of interrelated objectives and concepts for consistent measurement and reporting. These objectives and concepts are expected to guide selection of the events accounted for, the measurement of events, and the means of their summarization and communication to users. Without conceptual underpinnings, measures and reports provided by accountants are arguably matters of judgment and personal opinion. The more precise the conceptual framework, the less subjectivity involved.

The conceptual framework is represented by *Statements of Financial Accounting Concepts (SFACs).* Several *SFACs* are relevant to financial statement analysis. *SFAC No. 1,* "Objectives of Financial Reporting by Business Enterprises," establishes the objectives of general-purpose external financial reporting by business enterprises. This *Statement* asserts financial reporting best serves us by helping us predict the amount, timing, and uncertainty of future cash flows. Moreover, it asserts financial reporting should provide information about the economic resources of an enterprise, the claims to those resources, and the effects of transactions, events, and circumstances that change its resources and claims to those resources. A primary focus of financial reporting is information about earnings and its components. Financial reporting is also expected to provide information about an enterprise's financial performance during a period and about how management has discharged its stewardship responsibility to owners.

SFAC No. 2, "Qualitative Characteristics of Accounting Information," identifies the characteristics of accounting information that make it useful. Exhibit 2.5 illustrates these characteristics as a hierarchy of qualities where usefulness for decision making is first in importance. The hierarchy of accounting qualities separates user-specific qualities (e.g., understandability) from qualities inherent in the information. Information cannot be useful to decision makers unless they understand it regardless of how relevant it is.

Relevance and **reliability** are the primary qualities making accounting information useful for decision making. Information is relevant if it has the capacity to confirm or change a decision maker's expectations. If information is received by a user too late to have an effect on a decision, it is uninformative. Hence, *timeliness* is an important aspect of relevance. So is *predictive value,* usefulness as an input into a predictive process, and *feedback value,* information helping to confirm or adjust earlier predictions. Information is reliable if it is *verifiable*—that is, independent observers using the same measurement methods arrive at the same results. Reliability is enhanced when accounting numbers and disclosures represent what actually exists or happened (*representational faithfulness*). Reliability also implies *neutrality* of information—

EXHIBIT 2.5 Hierarchy of Accounting Qualities

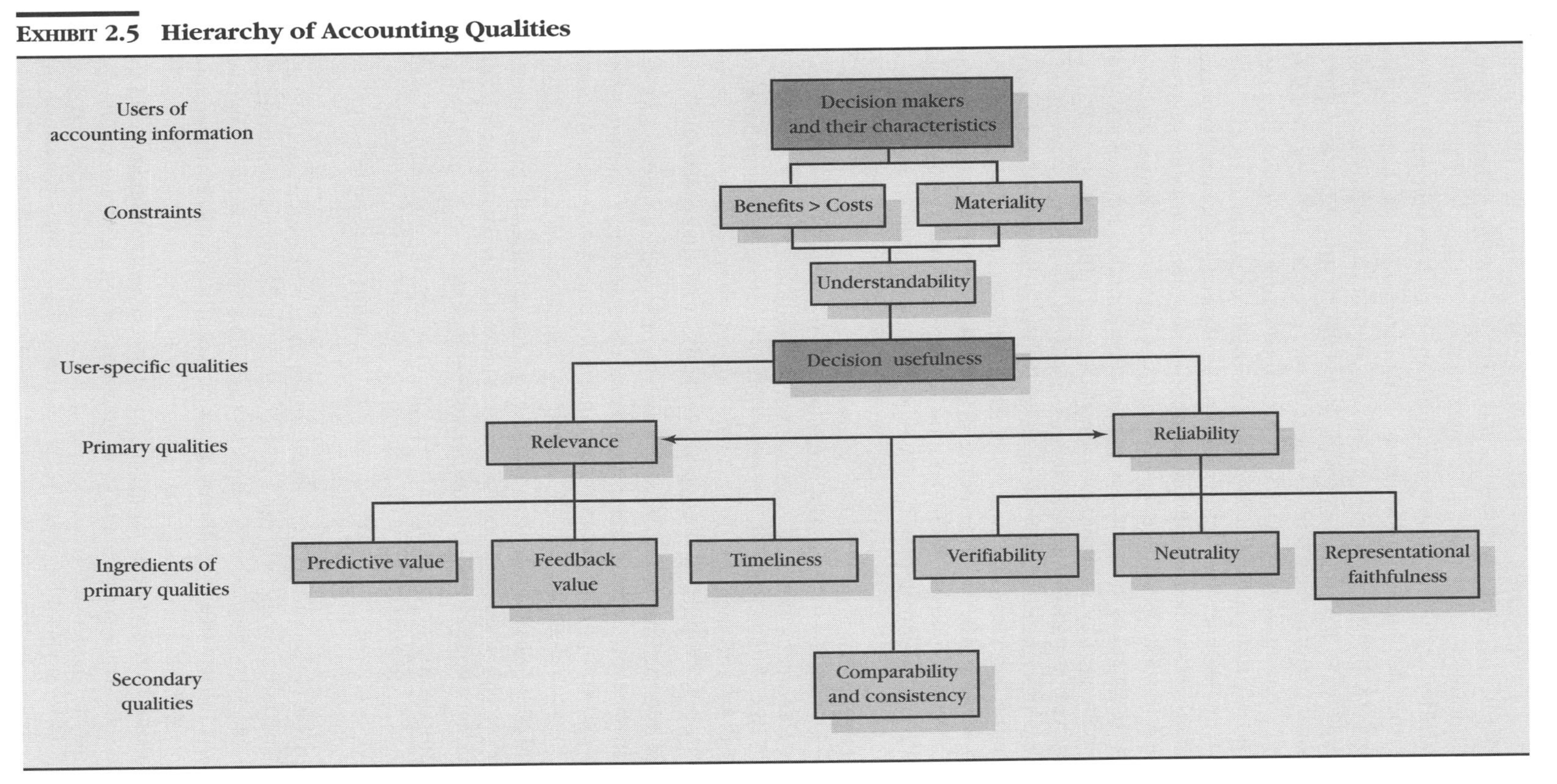

Source: FASB, *FAC No. 2*, "Qualitative Characteristics of Accounting Information" (Stamford, CT, 1980).

standard setters should not be swayed if proposed standards cause undesirable economic effects for a particular industry or company. Accounting information must be truthful and unbiased.

Comparability, including consistency, interacts with relevance and reliability to contribute to the usefulness of information. Comparison is one of the most basic and important tools of analysis for decision making. Almost all evaluations and alternative-choice judgments involve comparisons. The ability to compare sets of accounting data of the same company over time, or those of one company with another, is crucial.

Overriding these qualitative characteristics are *pervasive constraints* like **benefits versus costs** and **materiality.** Information is costly to gather, process, interpret, and use. As with other services, information is supplied only if its benefits exceed its costs. *Materiality* is defined as "the magnitude of an omission or misstatement of accounting information that, in the light of surrounding circumstances, makes it possible that the judgment of a reasonable person relying on the information would be changed or influenced by the omission or misstatement." In accounting, the concept of materiality assumes special significance because, by its nature, accounting information is not comprehended easily by readers. The main problem of materiality rests on the allegation that some preparers of financial statements and their auditors use it to avoid disclosing what they do not wish to. This aspect makes the concept significant to users of accounting data who must realize accountants do omit, reclassify, or ignore data and information on the basis of what they consider is material. There are no set criteria guiding either the accountant or user of information in distinguishing between what is material and what is not.

SFAC No. 3, "Elements of Financial Statements of Business Enterprises," describes 10 elements comprising financial statements (see Exhibit 2.6). Items qualifying as elements of financial statements and meeting criteria for recognition and measurement are accounted for and included in financial statements using accrual accounting. Accrual accounting and related concepts include the following processes:

- **Accrual accounting** recognizes noncash events and circumstances as they occur; specifically, accrual is the accounting process of recognizing assets, liabilities, and components of comprehensive income for amounts companies expect to receive or pay, usually in cash, in the future.
- **Deferral** is the accounting system process of recognizing a liability from a current cash receipt or an asset resulting from a current cash payment, with deferred recognition of components of comprehensive income.
- **Allocation** is the accounting process of (1) reducing a liability recorded as a result of a cash receipt by recognizing revenues or (2) reducing an asset recorded as a result of a cash payment by recognizing expenses or cost production payment.
- **Realization** is the process of converting noncash resources and rights into money and is most precisely used in accounting and financial reporting to refer to sales of assets for cash or claims to cash. The related terms, *realized* and *unrealized,* therefore, identify revenues or gains or losses on assets sold and unsold, respectively.
- **Recognition** is the process of formally recording or incorporating an item in the financial statements of an entity. Thus, an asset, liability, revenue, expense, gain, or loss may be recognized (recorded) or unrecognized (unrecorded). *Realization* and *recognition* should not be used as synonyms, as they sometimes are in accounting and financial literature.

EXHIBIT 2.6 Financial Statement Elements

- **Assets** are probable future economic benefits obtained or controlled by a particular entity as a result of past transactions or events. Once acquired, an asset continues as an asset of the enterprise until the enterprise collects it, transfers it to another entity, or uses it, or some other event or circumstance destroys the future benefit or removes the enterprise's ability to obtain it. Valuation accounts that reduce or increase the carrying amount of an asset are sometimes found in financial statements; these are part of the related assets and are neither assets in their own right nor liabilities.
- **Liabilities** are probable future sacrifices of economic benefits arising from present obligations of a particular entity to transfer assets or provide services to other entities in the future as a result of past transactions or events. Once incurred, a liability continues as a liability of the enterprise until the enterprise settles it, or another event or circumstance discharges it or removes the enterprise's responsibility to settle it.
- **Equity** is the residual interest in the assets of an entity that remains after deducting its liabilities. In a business enterprise, the equity is the ownership interest (owners' equity).
- **Investments by owners** are increases in net assets of a particular enterprise resulting from transfers to it from other entities of something valuable to obtain or increase equity (ownership interests). What the enterprise receives includes most commonly assets, but may also include services or satisfaction or conversion of liabilities of the enterprise. Investments by owners increase equity (ownership interests).
- **Distributions to owners** are decreases in net assets of a particular enterprise resulting from transferring assets, rendering services, or incurring liabilities by the enterprise to owners. Distributions to owners decrease equity (owners' interest). When an enterprise declares dividends, it incurs a liability to transfer assets to owners in the future, resulting in an equity reduction and a liability increase. Reacquisition by an entity of its own equity securities by transferring assets or incurring liabilities to owners is a distribution to owners.
- **Comprehensive income** is the change in equity (net assets) of an enterprise during a period from transactions and other events and circumstances from nonowner sources. It includes all changes in equity during a period except those resulting from investment by owners and distributions to owners (i.e., the clean surplus relation). Over the life of a business enterprise, its comprehensive income equals the net of its cash receipts and cash outlays (excluding cash investments by owners and cash distributions to owners).
- **Revenues** are inflows or other enhancements of assets of an entity or settlements of its liabilities (or a combination of both) during a period of delivering or producing goods, rendering services, or other activities that constitute the entity's ongoing major or central operations. Revenues represent actual or expected cash inflows (or the equivalent) that have occurred or will eventuate as a result of the enterprise's ongoing major or central operations during the period.
- **Expenses** are outflows or other using up of assets or incurrences of liabilities (or a combination of both) during a period of delivering or producing goods, rendering services, or carrying out other activities that constitute the enterprise's ongoing major or central operations. Expenses represent actual or expected cash outflows (or the equivalent) that have occurred or will eventuate as a result of the enterprise's ongoing major or central operations during the period.
- **Gains** are increases in equity (net assets) from peripheral or incidental transactions of an entity and from all other transactions and other events and circumstances affecting the entity during a period except those resulting from revenues or investments by owners.
- **Losses** are decreases in equity (net assets) from peripheral or incidental transactions of an entity and from all other transactions and other events and circumstances affecting the entity during a period except those that result from expenses or distributions to owners.

SFAC No. 5, "Recognition and Measurement in Financial Statements of Business Enterprises," endorses current recognition and measurement practices while allowing for gradual, evolutionary change. The basic approach to recognition is identification of information that financial statements report. Recognition of an item in financial statements is required when the item meets the following four criteria:

- Meets the definition of a financial statement element.
- Is measurable.
- Is relevant—it is capable of making a difference in users' decisions.
- Is reliable—it is representationally faithful, verifiable, and neutral.

This *Statement* fails to resolve the major measurement dilemma of current value versus historical cost. Several measurement attributes are used in practice, and the board expects the use of different attributes to continue. However, the board gives itself an option to pursue more extensive use of current values, stating that: "Information based on current prices should be recognized if it is sufficiently relevant and reliable to justify the costs involved and more relevant than alternative information."

Analysis Implications of Accounting Objectives and Concepts

The conceptual framework is an attempt to establish a logical and coherent structure of interrelated objectives and concepts to enhance the theoretical foundations of accounting standards and to promote confidence in and acceptance of these standards. We are understanding of the profession's efforts to establish a sound framework and are supportive of its goals, which are, ultimately, in our best interests. At the same time, we must be aware previous attempts at establishing conceptual frameworks have not yielded universally accepted concepts or "truths." The board admitted that *SFAC No. 5* "would not produce instant, indisputable answers to questions about whether a particular event should be recognized and when, and what amount best measures it." The board took the cautious position that establishing objectives and identifying concepts does not solve accounting and reporting problems. Rather, objectives give direction, and concepts are tools for solving problems. The board has seemingly concluded that change in accounting is an evolutionary process and is not the product of a conceptual framework.

The conceptual framework does contribute to a healthy debate on the objectives of accounting and the primary users of financial statements. It identifies qualitative characteristics of accounting information and the qualities that make it useful. It defines elements of financial statements, such as assets, liabilities, owners' equity, revenues, expenses, gains, losses, and comprehensive income. It presents superior definitions of accounting-related concepts. It can even contribute to a higher degree of internal consistency in promulgated standards. Nevertheless, it disappoints those who hoped it would provide a structure for resolving today's and tomorrow's vexing accounting problems. By relying on gradual change and evolution, the board admits it cannot meet the expectations of the conceptual framework. From the point of view of users of financial statements, this admission is a healthy development giving the board a more realistic view of what can and cannot be accomplished in accounting standard setting. Change in accounting comes mostly as a process where standard setters address problems demanding immediate action. Motivations for diligent effort and compromise were pressing and solutions found. This process is likely to continue. Resolution of these problems is always influenced by the cries and protests of those most affected by them. Many observers expect this. Social sciences do not have codified conceptual frameworks. There are none for law, economics, or finance. Board members who have experienced firsthand how difficult it is to settle even limited problems of practice—such as those of foreign operations, pensions, or taxes—realize developing a framework to settle important issues of accounting in advance is futile. Addressing accounting problems requires compromises and adjustments. In using financial statements, we must be alert to the practical considerations of self-interest governing accounting as much as logic and rational processes.

A P P E N D I X

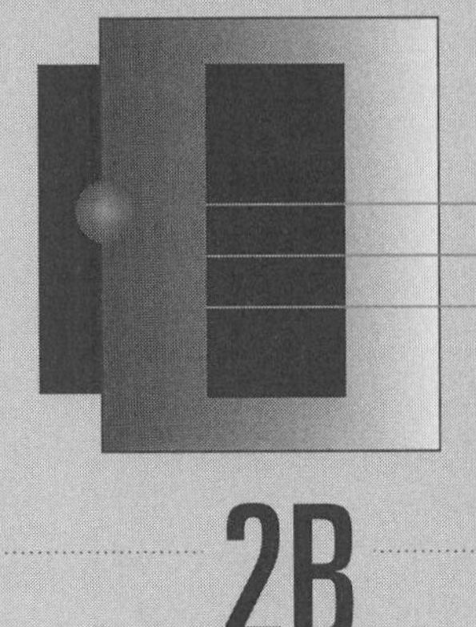

2B

Additional Tools and Sources for Financial Statement Analysis

Technology-Based Financial Analysis Tools

The major emphasis throughout this book is on the application of thoughtful and logical analysis using reliable and relevant data. Financial statement analysis does, however, involve significant work of a computational nature as well. We can utilize technology to our advantage here. Judicious use of technology in financial analysis depends on thorough understanding of its limitations. Technology lacks the ability to generate intuitive judgments or keen insights—capabilities that are essential to a competent and discerning financial analysis. We must always remember there is nothing technology adds that a competent user cannot. Yet technology significantly enhances the efficiency of our analysis, especially in statistical analysis.

With the exception of databases offering on-line access to complete financial statements, most databases for technological analysis do not include all information necessary to adjust accounting numbers to render them comparable or conforming to our specific needs. Reasons for this include the following:

- Databases often lack information on a company's accounting policies and principles. This information is essential to reliable comparisons and interpretations of data.
- Notes and other explanatory information are usually missing or incomplete.
- Lack of retroactive adjustments in the data—even if the data are subsequently revealed as erroneous or misleading.
- Lapses or omissions often occur when examining large masses of financial data on a uniform basis. Data can also be classified inconsistently across companies.

- Aggregation of dissimilar or noncomparable data yields a loss of vital distinctions and diminishes its meaning and value in our analysis.

While technology has its limitations, there are several significant uses to which it can be effectively and efficiently applied in financial analysis.

Data Storage, Retrieval, and Computation

An accessible and comprehensive database is essential to effective use of technology in most phases of our analysis. Technology allows us to store and easily access vast amounts of important data. It has the ability to probe these data, to manipulate them mathematically, to update and modify them, and to select from among them using various criteria (e.g., sales levels, returns, growth rates).

Specialized Financial Analyses

Technology is useful for financial analysis in credit extension and security analysis. In credit extension, technology assists financial analysis with:

- Storage of data for comparison and decision making.
- Projection of enterprise cash requirements under a variety of assumptions.
- Projection of financial statements under various assumptions, showing the impact of changes on key variables. Known as *sensitivity analysis,* this technique allows the user to explore the effect of systematically changing a variable by a predetermined amount.
- Inclusion of probabilistic inputs. We can insert data as probability distributions, either normally shaped or skewed, or random probability distributions, otherwise known as Monte Carlo trials.

In security analysis, technology assists with:

- Calculations using past data.
- Trend computations.
- Predictive models.
- Projections and forecasts.
- Sensitivity analysis.
- Probabilistic analysis.

An understanding of technology, both its capabilities and limitations, is increasingly important in the analysis of financial statements.

Sources of Relevant Analysis Information

For company data, and for comparative industry data, financial statements are often the best and most readily available source. This section presents a list of information sources on financial and operating data. These data, while valuable, must be used with care and with as complete a knowledge as possible of the basis of their compilation. A realistic and sometimes superior alternative for us to use as a basis of comparison are financial statements of one or more comparable industry competitors.

Annual reports to shareholders contain an increasing amount of information required by either GAAP or specific SEC rulings. Company filings with the SEC—

such as registration statements pursuant to the Securities Act of 1933, supplemental and periodic reports requiring filing (e.g., Forms 8-K, 10-K, 10-Q, 14-K, and 16-K), or proxy statements—contain a wealth of useful information for our analysis. Additional information is often available through alternative mechanisms. Some companies offer "investor services" or supplementary data on request. Federal or state regulatory agencies require publicly available filings for certain industries. Those able to exert a degree of influence have other avenues available. Bond rating agencies are often given financial and operating details beyond that in published financial statements. Major lenders and investors often have similar access to more detailed information.

To achieve familiarity with the wide variety of available financial and operating data, we classify some popular sources by type of agency compiling the data. This list is intended to exemplify the type of materials available and is *not* a comprehensive list:

Professional and Commercial Organizations

Dun & Bradstreet, Inc., Business Economics Division, New York, NY.

- Industry norms and key business ratios.
- Key business ratios. Important operating and financial ratios in numerous lines.
- Selected operating expense figures for many retailing, wholesaling, and manufacturing lines, as well as for contract construction; service/transportation/communication; finance/insurance/real estate; agriculture/forestry/fishing; mining.
- Cost-of-Doing Business Series. Typical operating ratios for numerous lines of business, showing national averages. They represent a percentage of business receipts reported by a representative sample of the total of all federal tax returns. Published irregularly.

Moody's Investor Service, New York, NY. Moody's manuals contain financial and operating ratios on the individual companies covered.

Nelson's Directory of Investment Research, Port Chester, NY. W. R. Nelson & Co./Nelson Publications, annual.

Robert Morris Associates, *Annual Statement Studies*. Financial and operating ratios for about 300 lines of business—manufacturers, wholesalers, retailers, services, and contractors—based on information obtained from member banks of RMA. Data are broken down by company size.

Standard & Poor's Corporation.

- *Analysts Handbook*. "Composite corporate per share data—by industries," for over 90 industries. Statistics and percentages cover several components, including sales, operating profits, depreciation, earnings, and dividends.
- *Industry Surveys*. Basic data on many important industries, with financial comparisons of the leading companies in each industry. Includes a "Basic Analysis" for each, revised annually, and a "Current Analysis" for each industry, published quarterly. A monthly "Trends and Projections" includes tables of economic and industry indicators.

Almanac of Business and Industrial Financial Ratios by Leo Troy. Englewood Cliffs, NJ: Prentice Hall. A compilation of corporate performance ratios (operating and financial). Explains the significance of these ratios. Covers all industries in the study, each industry subdivided by asset size.

Value Line Investment Survey, New York: Value Line Publishing, Inc., weekly updating.

Federal Government

Small Business Administration. Publications containing industry statistics (published sporadically—may not be up to date): *Small Marketers Aid, Small Business Management Series;* and *Business Service Bulletins.*

U.S. Department of Commerce. Census of business—wholesale trade—summary statistics, monthly wholesale trade report. Ratio of operating expenses to sales.

Department of the Treasury. Statistics of income, corporation income tax returns. Operating statistics based on income tax returns.

Federal Trade Commission—Securities and Exchange Commission. *Quarterly Financial Report for Manufacturing, Mining, and Trade Corporations.* Contains operating ratios and balance sheet ratios as well as the balance sheet in ratio format.

U.S. Internal Revenue Service, Washington, DC: U.S. Government Printing Office.

- *Source Book: Statistics of Income: Corporation Income Tax Returns.* Annual. Balance sheet, income statement, tax and investment credit items by major and minor industries, broken down by size of total assets.
- *Statistics of Income: Corporation Income Tax Returns.* Annual. Balance sheet and income statement statistics from a sample of corporate returns. Includes tables by major industry, by asset size, and so on. Includes historical summaries.

Industry Associations

Many retail and wholesale trade associations compile and publish periodic statistics. Few manufacturing associations compile statistics available to the public; and so we must rely on general sources or annual reports of specific companies.

American Meat Institute, *Annual Financial Review of the Meat Packing Industry,* Washington, DC. Includes operating ratios.

Federal Deposit Insurance Corporation, *Bank Operating Statistics,* annual.

Institute of Real Estate Management, Experience Exchange Committee, *A Statistical Compilation and Analysis of Actual (year) Income and Expenses Experienced in Apartment, Condominium and Cooperative Building Operation,* annual.

Discount Merchandiser, *The True Look of the Discount Industry,* June issue each year. Includes operating ratios.

National Electrical Contractors Association, *Operation Overhead,* annual.

National Farm & Power Equipment Dealers Association, *Cost of Doing Business Study,* annual.

National Retail Hardware Association, *Lumber/Building Material Financial Report,* Indianapolis, annual.

Journal of Commercial Bank Lending, "Analysis of Year End Composite Ratios of Installment Sales Finance and Small Loan Companies."

National Association of Music Merchants, *Merchandising and Operating Statistics,* New York, annual.

National Decorating Products Association, *NDPA's Annual Cost of Doing Business Survey,* St. Louis. Taken from *Decorating Retailer.*

National Office Products Association, *NOPA Dealers Operating Results,* Alexandria, VA, annual.

National Restaurant Association, *Restaurant Industry Operations Report for the United States,* Washington, DC, annual.

Computerized Databases

ABI/Inform, Ann Arbor, MI: University Microfilms International, weekly (on-line), monthly (CD-ROM).

Corporate Information Research Reports (CIRR), East Chester, NY: J. A. Micropublishing. Microfiche collection, on-line database, and CD-ROM database. Monthly.

Compact Disclosure, Bethesda, MD: Disclosure Incorporated. CD-ROM database. Monthly.

Compustat, New York: Standard & Poor's Compustat Services, Inc. Computer tape files and CD-ROM database. Weekly.

Lotus OneSource, Cambridge, MA: Lotus Development Corporation. CD-ROM database. Monthly.

QUESTIONS

2–1. The president of a local company contacts you, the financial officer of a banking institution, for a substantial loan. Describe steps you can take in making this decision.

2–2. Describe differences in points of view between creditors and equity investors. Explain how these differences reveal themselves in the manner these two groups use to analyze financial statements and in the objectives they seek.

2–3. Explain the difference between a bond valuation model based on the present value of future net cash inflows and a stock valuation model based on the same principles.

2–4. Discuss why the information needs of equity investors are among the most demanding of all users of financial statements.

2–5. Explain why measuring and evaluating earning power is a key element in the valuation of equity securities.

2–6. Explain why the reliability and validity of any stock valuation method, no matter how complete and sophisticated, depend on a quality analysis of financial statements.

2–7. Identify management uses for financial statement analysis.

2–8. Describe the use of financial statement analysis for the auditor of a company.

2–9. Define the accounting function.

2–10. Functions and purposes of accounting are performed at two levels; describe them.

2–11. Discuss the relative importance of financial statement analysis in business decisions.

2–12. Identify important limitations of accounting data.

2–13. Identify simplifications in the accounting system.

2–14. Explain how accounting concepts and standards, and the financial statements based on them, are subject to the pervasive influence of individual judgments and incentives.

2–15. Compare the flow of an analyst's work in reconstructing business transactions to that of an accountant's. Explain how reconstruction of accounts contributes to analysis of financial statements.

2–16. Identify cases requiring analytical restatement of financial statements.

2–17. Identify the traditional market measures used in evaluating the price and yield behavior of securities.

2–18. Describe what are accounting standards.

2–19. Explain how accounting standards are established.

2–20. Identify how the FASB is better than its predecessors in establishing accepted accounting principles.

2–21. Can users of financial statements depend on GAAP to produce reliable financial statements? What are the implications to financial statement analysis from the rate of progress in advancing accounting principles and practices?

2–22. Explain the objectives of the *conceptual framework* project in accounting.

2–23. Identify the prominent features of *SFAC No. 1*.

2–24. Describe the focus of *SFAC No. 2*. Identify and discuss the characteristics making accounting information useful.

2–25. Identify the financial statement elements listed in *SFAC No. 3*.

2–26. Identify the criteria specified in *SFAC No. 5* for an item to be included in financial statements.

2–27. Describe implications for analysis resulting from the *conceptual framework* project.

2–28. Discuss uses of technology for investment analysis.

2–29. Discuss the limitations and disadvantages of technology for security analysis.

EXERCISES

Exercise 2–1

Income Measurement and Interpretation

In a discussion of corporate profits, a user of financial statements alleges that "One of the real problems with profits is that you never really know what they are. The only way you can find out is to liquidate a corporation and reduce everything to cash. Then you can subtract what went into the company from what came out and the result is profits. Until then, profits are only a product of the accountants."

Required:

Discuss whether there is a practical solution to measurement problems with profits.

Exercise 2–2

Computation and Usefulness of Earnings and Balance Sheets

A financial statement analyst declares that "There are *reported earnings* and then there are *earnings*. There are balance sheets as produced by accountants and then there are "true" balance sheets. Accountants are concerned with accounting. After all, accountants do accounting."

Required:

Explain the kind of *earnings* the analyst is referring to when comparing it to *reported earnings*. Discuss who could produce these *earnings* and by what means. Indicate the likely source of the "true" balance sheets to which the financial analyst refers.

Exercise 2–3

Uniformity in Accounting Principles

Some financial statement users maintain that "Despite its intrinsic intellectual appeal, complete uniform accounting seems unworkable in a complex industrial society that relies, at least in part, on economic market forces."

Required:

a. Discuss at least three disadvantages of national or international accounting uniformity.

b. Explain whether uniformity in accounting necessarily implies comparability.

(CFA Adapted)

Exercise 2–4

Valuation of Corporate Debt (annual interest)

On January 1, Year 1, you are considering the purchase of $1,000 of Hannah Corporation's 9% bonds. The bonds are due in five years, with interest payable annually on December 31. Based on your analysis of Hannah Corporation, you determine that an 11 percent return is appropriate.

Required:

a. Calculate the price you are willing to pay for these bonds using the present value model. Round your answer to the nearest dollar.

b. Calculate the price you would pay if your required rate of return is 7 percent.

c. Describe risk and how it is reflected in your required rate of return.

Exercise 2–5

Company Valuation Using the Accounting-Based Equity Valuation Model

On January 1, Year 1, you are considering the purchase of Alayna, Inc., common stock. Based on your financial statement analysis of Alayna, Inc., you determine the following:

1. Book value at January 1, Year 1, is $100 per share.
2. Predicted net income for Year 1 is $30 per share, and net income is predicted to increase by $5 per share every year until Year 5.
3. Beginning in Year 6, abnormal earnings are predicted to remain at the Year 5 level.
4. Alayna, Inc., is not expected to pay dividends.
5. The required rate of return is 15 percent.

Required:

Calculate the per share price of Alayna, Inc.'s common stock using the accounting-based equity valuation formula. Round your answer to the nearest penny.

PROBLEMS

Problem 2–1

Financial Statement Analysis and Accounting Standard Setting

Financial statement users often liken accounting standard setting to a political process. One user asserted that

> My hypothesis is that the setting of accounting standards is as much a product of political action as of flawless logic or empirical findings. Why? Because the setting of standards is a social decision. Standards place restrictions on behavior; therefore, they must be accepted by the affected parties. Acceptance may be forced or voluntary or some of both. In a democratic society, getting acceptance is an exceedingly complicated process that requires skillful marketing in a political arena.

Many parties affected by proposed standards intervene to protect their own interests while disguising their motivations as altruistic or theoretical. People often say, "If you like the answer, you will love the theory." It is also alleged that those who are regulated by the standard-setting process have excessive influence over the regulatory process. Prior to his resignation, a former FASB member declared "The business community has much greater influence than it's ever had over standard setting. I think it's unhealthy. It is the preparer community that is really being regulated in this process, and if we have those being regulated having a dominant role in the regulatory process, that's asking for major trouble."

Required:

Discuss the relevance of the accounting standard-setting process to analysis of financial statements.

Problem 2–2

Neutrality of Measurements in Financial Statements

Financial reporting has been likened to cartography:

> Information cannot be neutral—it cannot therefore be reliable—if it is selected or presented for the purpose of producing some chosen effect on human behavior. It is this quality of neutrality which makes a map reliable; and the essential nature of accounting, I believe, is cartographic. Accounting is financial mapmaking. The better the map, the more completely it represents the complex phenomena that are being mapped. We do not judge

> a map by the behavioral effects it produces. The distribution of natural wealth or rainfall shown on a map may lead to population shifts or changes in industrial location, which the government may like or dislike. That should be no concern of the cartographer. We judge his map by how well it represents the facts. People can then react to it as they will.

Required:

a. Explain why neutrality is such an important quality of financial statements.
b. Identify examples of the lack of neutrality in accounting reports.

Problem 2–3

Analysts' Information Needs and Accounting Measurements

An editor of the *Financial Analysts Journal* reviewed the earlier edition of this book and asserted:

> Broadly speaking, accounting numbers are of two types: those that can be measured and those that have to be estimated. Investors who feel that accounting values are more real than market values should remember that, although the estimated numbers in accounting statements often have a greater impact, singly or together, than the measured numbers, accountants' estimates are rarely based on any serious attempt by accountants at business or economic judgment.
>
> Accountants are understandably nervous about this; . . . [the book] cites the following language from *Accounting Research Study No. 1:* "The function of accounting is (1) to measure the resources held by specific entities . . ." By "resources" presumably is meant inventory, bricks and mortar, machines. The accountant cannot "measure" such "resources"; he can only estimate their value. The main reason accountants shy away from precise statements of principle for the determination of asset values is that neither they nor anyone else has yet come up with principles that will consistently give values plausible enough that, if accounting statements were based on these principles, users would take them seriously.

Required:

a. Describe what is meant by measurement in accounting.
b. According to the editor, what are the kinds of measurements analysts want?
c. Discuss whether these aims of accounting measurement are reconcilable.

Problem 2–4

Accounting Standard Setting and Politics

An FASB member expressed the following view:

> Are we going to set accounting standards in the private sector or not? . . . Part of the answer depends on how the business community views accounting standards. Are they rules of conduct, designed to restrain unsocial behavior and arbitrate conflicts of economic interest? Or are they rules of measurement, designed to generalize and communicate as accurately as possible the complex results of economic events? . . . Rules of conduct call for a political process . . . Rules of measurement, on the other hand, call for a research process of observation and experimentation . . . Intellectually, the case is compelling for viewing accounting as a measurement process . . . But the history of accounting standard setting has been dominated by the other view—that accounting standards are rules of conduct. The FASB was created out of the ashes of predecessors burned up in the fires of the resulting political process.

Required:

a. Discuss your views on the difference between "rules of conduct" and "rules of measurement."
b. Explain how accounting standard setting is a political process. Identify arguments for and against viewing accounting standard setting as political.

Problem 2–5

Accounting Information and the Conceptual Framework

The purpose of *Statement of Financial Accounting Concepts No. 2,* "Qualitative Characteristics of Accounting Information" (*SFAC No. 2*), is to examine the characteristics making accounting information useful. The characteristics or qualities of information discussed in the statement are the ingredients that make information useful and are the qualities sought when accounting choices are made.

Required:

a. Identify and discuss the benefits expected from the FASB's conceptual framework.

b. Identify the most important quality for accounting information as asserted in *SFAC No. 2.* Explain why this quality is the most important.

c. *SFAC No. 2* describes a number of key characteristics or qualities for accounting information. Discuss the importance of any three of these qualities for financial reporting.

Problem 2–6

Accounting in Society

Consider the following excerpt from the *Financial Analysts Journal:*

> Strictly speaking, the objectives of financial reporting are the objectives of society and not of accountants and auditors, as such. Similarly, society has objective law and medicine—namely, justice and health for the people—which are not necessarily the objectives of lawyers and doctors, as such, in the conduct of their respective "business."
>
> In a variety of ways, society exerts pressure on a profession to act more nearly as if it actively shared the objectives of society. Society's pressure is to be measured by the degree of accommodation on the part of the profession under pressure, and by the degree of counter-pressure applied by the profession. For example, doctors accommodate society by getting better educations than otherwise and reducing incompetence in their ranks. They apply counter-pressure and gain protection by forming medical associations.

Required:

a. Describe ways in which society has brought pressure on accountants to better serve it.

b. Describe how the accounting profession has responded to these pressures. Could the profession have better responded?

Problem 2–7

Financial Reporting or Financial Subterfuge

Consider the following claim from a business observer:

> An accountant's job is to conceal, not to reveal. An accountant is not asked to give outsiders an accurate picture of what's going on in a company. He is asked to transform the figures on a company's operations in such a way that it will be impossible to recreate the original figures.
>
> An income statement for a toy company doesn't tell how many toys of various kinds the company sold, or who the company's best customers are. The balance sheet doesn't tell how many of each kind of toy the company has in inventory, or how much is owed by each customer who is late in paying his bills.
>
> In general, anything that a manager uses to do his job will be of interest to some stockholders, customers, creditors, or government agencies. Managerial accounting differs from financial accounting only because the accountant has to hide some of the facts and figures managers find useful. The accountant simply has to throw out most of the facts and some of the figures that the managers use when he creates the financial statements for outsiders.
>
> The rules of accounting reflect this tension. Even if the accountant thought of himself as working only for the good of society, he would conceal certain facts in the reports he helps write. Since the accountant is actually working for the company, or even for the management of the company, he conceals many facts that outsiders would like to have revealed.

Required:

a. Discuss this observer's misgivings on the role of the accountant in financial reporting.

b. Discuss what type of omitted information the business observer is referring to.

Problem 2–8

Valuation of Bonds (semiannual interest)

On January 1, Year 1, you are considering the purchase of $10,000 of Colin Company's 8 percent bonds. The bonds are due in 10 years, with interest payable semiannually on June 30 and December 31. Based on your analysis of Colin, you determine that a 6 percent return is appropriate.

Required:

a. Calculate the price you are willing to pay for the bonds using the present value model. Round your answer to the nearest dollar.

b. Calculate the price you would pay if your required rate of return is 10 percent.

c. Describe risk and explain how it is reflected in your required rate of return.

Problem 2–9

Company Valuation Using the Accounting-Based Equity Valuation Formula

On January 1, Year 1, you are considering the purchase of Nicholas Enterprises' common stock. Based on your analysis of Nicholas Enterprises, you determine the following:

1. Book value at January 1, Year 1, is $50 per share.
2. Predicted net income per share for Year 1 through Year 5 is $8, $11, $20, $40, and $30, respectively.
3. Beginning in Year 6 and all years after, predicted abnormal earnings are $0.
4. Nicholas is not expected to pay dividends.
5. The required rate of return is 20 percent.

Required:

Determine the purchase price per share of Nicholas Enterprises' common stock using the accounting-based equity valuation formula. Round your answer to the nearest penny. Comment on the strengths and limitations of this formula for investment decisions.

Problem 2–10

Reconstruction Analysis from Financial Statement Information

Flam Bay, Inc., is a victim of management fraud. Assume you are hired as a special consultant to reconstruct the December 31, Year 3, balance sheet from data not subject to these fraudulent activities. These available data are current as of December 31, Year 3. Additionally, all Flam Bay's liabilities are current, and total assets consist of cash, accounts receivable, inventory, land, and buildings.

Cash	$90
Gross profit on sales	50%
Expenses (excluding cost of goods sold)	$540
Current liabilities	$300
Total debt to equity	1:1
Return on equity (using end-of-year balance)	20%
Ending inventory turnover	10
Current ratio	0.8:1
Acid-test ratio	0.6:1
Total assets	$600
Retained earnings	$120
Carrying amount of land equals two-thirds of the buildings balance.	

Required:

Reconstruct Flam Bay, Inc.'s balance sheet for December 31, Year 3.

CASES

Case 2–1

Analysis of Adaptec's Financial Statements

Answer the following questions using the 1996 annual report of Adaptec, Inc.

a. Assume you are considering the purchase of Adaptec common stock and have acquired a copy of the latest annual report. What additional, nonfinancial information are you seeking before making your decision?

b. Compute the value of Adaptec's common stock using the present-value-of-dividends formula. Assume a required rate of return of 15 percent.

c. Calculate Adaptec's abnormal earnings for the most recent four years assuming a required rate of return of 15 percent.

d. Examine note 1 to Adaptec's financial statements. Identify each instance where management's judgment directly influences the reported financial statements.

e. Reconstruct the 1996 activities in each of the following using T-account analysis:

1. Marketable securities.
2. Accounts receivable.
3. Note payable.
4. Long-term debt.

f. Calculate Adaptec's *annual* net income using the information in note 11 and assuming the following fiscal year-ends:

1. December 31, 1995.
2. September 30, 1995.
3. June 30, 1995.

Case 2–2

Oil Industry Accounting and Analysis

There are two permissible methods for companies to account for the cost of drilling for oil. Under the *full-cost method,* a drilling company capitalizes costs both for successful wells and dry holes; in other words, it classifies all costs as assets on its balance sheet. A company charges these costs against revenues as it extracts and sells the oil. Under the *successful-efforts method,* a company expenses the costs of dry holes as they are incurred, resulting in immediate charges against earnings; the costs of successful wells are capitalized. Most small and mid-sized drilling companies use the full-cost method and, as a result, millions of dollars of drilling costs appear as assets on their balance sheets.

The SEC imposed a limit to full-cost accounting. Costs capitalized under this method cannot exceed a ceiling are defined as the present value of company reserves. Capitalized costs above the ceiling are expensed. Oil companies, primarily smaller ones, have been successful in the past in prevailing on the SEC to keep the full-cost accounting method as an alternative even though the accounting profession took a position in favor of the successful-efforts method as the only one to be permitted. Because the imposition of the ceiling rule occurred during a time of relatively high oil prices, the companies accepted it, confident that it would have no practical effect on them.

With the subsequent decline in petroleum prices many of the companies found that drilling costs carried as assets on their balance sheets exceeded the sharply lower ceilings. Thus they were faced with serious write-offs. Oil companies, concerned about the effect that big write-downs would have on their ability to conduct business, began a fierce lobbying effort to try to win a change in the commission's accounting rules so as to avoid sizable write-downs that threatened to lower their earnings as well as their equity capital. The SEC staff supported a suspension of the rules because, they maintained, oil prices could soon turn up and because companies would still be required to disclose the difference between the market value and book value of their oil reserves. The staff proposal would have temporarily relaxed the rules pending the results of a study by the Office of the Chief Accountant on whether to change or rescind the ceiling test. The proposal would have suspended the requirement to use current prices when computing the ceiling amount in determining whether a write-down of reserves is required. The commission rejected the staff proposal that would have enabled 250 of the nation's oil and gas producing companies to postpone write-downs on the declining values of their oil and gas reserves while acknowledging that the impact of the decision could trigger defaults on bank loans. The commission chairman said "the rules are not stretchable at a time of stress."

Tenneco Co. found a way to cope with the SEC's refusal to sanction postponement of the write-offs. It announced a switch to successful-efforts accounting along with nearly a billion dollars in charges against prior years' earnings. In effect, Tenneco would take the unamortized dry-hole drilling costs currently on its balance sheet and apply them against prior years' revenues. These costs would affect prior year results only and would not show up as write-offs against currently reported income.

Required:

a. Discuss what conclusions an analyst might derive from the evolution of accounting in the oil and gas industry.

b. Explain the potential effect Tenneco's proposed change in accounting method would have on the reporting of its operating results over the years.

INTERNET ACTIVITIES

Internet 2–1

Analyzing Non-Financial Statement Information

Access one of the financial statement databases available on the Internet, for example, SEC's on-line database EDGAR (http://www.sec.gov/edgarhp.htm) or the Web site for this book (http://www.mhhe.com/business/accounting/wild). Retrieve current financial statements of a company selected by either you or your instructor and answer the following questions:

a. Identify and read the company's Management's Discussion and Analysis section. Write a report describing the useful information conveyed in this document for financial statement analysis. What information about the company's strategic plans is communicated in this document?

b. Identify and read the company's letter to shareholders. What useful information is conveyed in this document for financial statement analysis?

c. Can you identify the company's most recent press release? Is there useful information in this press release for financial analysis?

d. Can you identify the company's most recent earnings announcement? How do the most recent earnings compare to the prior year's earnings?

Internet 2–2

Analyzing Earnings and Stock Price Changes

Access one of the financial statement databases available on the Internet (http://www.mhhe.com/business/accounting/wild). Retrieve current financial statements of a company selected by either you or your instructor and answer the following questions:

a. Identify the company's most recent two years' earnings. How do the most recent earnings compare to the prior year's earnings?

b. Identify the company's stock prices on the dates of the most recent three years' financial statements. Financial statements often report summary stock price information. Also, many financial services offer access to up-to-date stock quote information for thousands of companies; for example, see CNN's Financial Network (http://cnnfn.com/markets/quotes.html) or Time Warner's Pathfinder (http://quote.pathfinder.com/money/quote/qc). Compute the change in stock prices (adding back any dividends per share to the end-of-period price per share) for the most recent two years.

c. Write a report comparing the change in earnings with the change in stock prices for the most recent two years.

Internet 2–3

Estimating a Company's Value and Its Abnormal Earnings

Access one of the financial statement databases available on the Internet (http://www.mhhe.com/business/accounting/wild). Retrieve current financial statements of a company selected by either you or your instructor and calculate the following:

a. The value of the company's common stock using the present-value-of-dividends formula. Assume a required rate of return of 15 percent.

b. The company's abnormal earnings for the most recent two years assuming a required rate of return of 15 percent.

Internet 2–4

Analyzing Price-Earnings Ratios

Identify recent price-earnings (P/E) ratios for five companies using financial services on the Internet with access to up-to-date stock quote information for thousands of companies, such as CNN's Financial Network (http://cnnfn.com/markets/quotes.html) or Time Warner's Pathfinder (http://quote.pathfinder.com/money/quote/qc). Write a report comparing P/E ratios across these five companies.

Internet 2–5

Current Accounting Standards Information

Access the FASB's Web site (http://gsma62.rutgers.edu/raw/fasb/welcome.htm). Note: if FASB's site address changes you can access the Web site for this textbook (http://www.mhhe.com/business/accounting/wild) for an updated link. After accessing this database, write a report answering the following questions:

a. How would you describe the types of information available at this Web site for financial analysis?

b. How would you rate the importance of the information available at this Web site for financial analysis?

PART TWO

Accounting Analysis of Financial Statements

CHAPTER 3 *Analyzing Financing Activities*

Chapter 3 describes the financing of a company's activities. We learn about both creditor (liability) and owner (equity) financing, and analyze the accounting for financing activities. In our reading you will negotiate a labor contract involving postretirement benefits, make an investment decision concerning common versus preferred stock, and interpret a stock split announcement.

CHAPTER 4 *Analyzing Investing Activities*

Companies obtain financing to pursue investments. This chapter explains investments in assets and their relation to profitability. While studying investing activities, we will interpret cash flow information, audit a change in a receivables estimate affecting income, determine a buying price using inventory figures, evaluate investments of a competitor, and use intangible asset disclosures to persuade a congressional hearing on environmental controls.

CHAPTER 5 *Analyzing Investing Activities: Special Topics*

This chapter describes intercompany and international investing activities. We analyze and interpret these special investments and their implications for financial statement analysis. Along the way you will assess litigation risks from consolidation, consider accepting an investment banker engagement where pooling accounting is distortive, and rate an international bond issuance.

CHAPTER 6 *Analyzing Operating Activities: Income*

Operating activities are examined in this chapter using accrual measures of performance. We study income and its components in evaluating productivity, assessing risks, and predicting future income. During our reading you must decide on a loan when revenue recognition is aggressive, appraise an earnings announcement involving a change in discretionary research and development outlays, and establish credit terms for a customer with an extraordinary loss.

CHAPTER 7 *Analyzing Business Activities: Cash Flows*

Analyzing operations and other business activities using cash flows is the purpose of this chapter. We learn about cash analysis techniques allowing us to reconstruct crucial transactions. We see how cash flow and income measures complement one another. Along the way you will use cash flows to overturn a company's decision to not fund your school district's educational programs, interpret conflicting cash flow and income measures for investment purposes, and assess a client's credit rating when alternative cash flow measures differ.

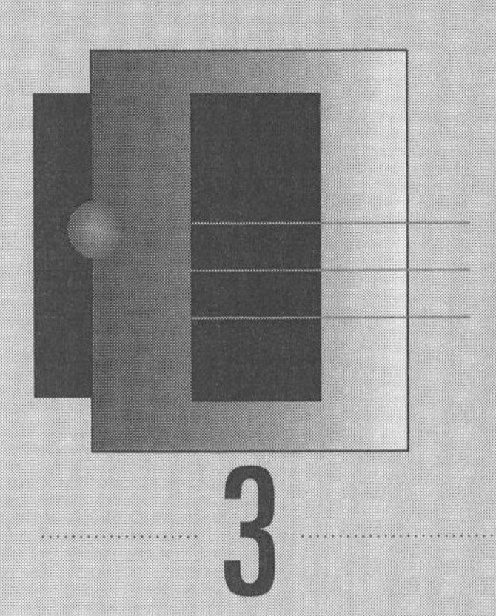

3

CHAPTER

Analyzing Financing Activities

A Look Back

We focused our attention in the first two chapters on overviewing financial statement analysis and learning the objectives, uses, and approaches to analysis. We discussed how financial statements report on financing, investing, and operating activities.

A Look at This Chapter

We begin in this chapter our analysis of the financial numbers underlying business activities. Financial numbers are the *raw material* for our analysis. We examine financing from both creditors and equity investors. Our focus is on explaining, analyzing, and interpreting financing activities. We explore the relevance of book values and implications of off-balance-sheet financing. We stress analyzing and adjusting accounting numbers in understanding financing activities.

A Look Ahead

Chapters 4 and 5 extend our analysis to investing activities. We examine various assets including intercompany and international investments.

Learning Objectives

- Identify principal characteristics distinguishing liabilities and equity.
- Interpret lease disclosures and their implications for future company performance.
- Analyze pension disclosures and their consequences for company valuation.
- Interpret postretirement obligations and funding implications for future performance.
- Analyze contingent liability disclosures and risks.
- Interpret deferred credits with reference to underlying transactions and events.
- Identify off-balance-sheet financing and consequences to risk analysis.
- Analyze and interpret liabilities at the edge of equity.
- Interpret capital stocks and identify their distinguishing features.
- Describe retained earnings and their distribution through dividends.
- Explain and interpret book values and their relevance in business valuation.

PREVIEW OF CHAPTER 3

Business activities are financed through either liabilities or equity. **Liabilities** are financing obligations requiring payment of money, rendering of future services, or dispensing of specific assets. They are claims against a company's present and future assets and resources. Such claims are usually senior to holders of equity securities. Liabilities include current obligations, long-term debt, capital leases, and deferred credits. This chapter also considers securities straddling the line separating liabilities and equity. **Equity** refers to claims of owners to the net assets of a company. While claims of owners are junior to creditors, they are residual claims to *all* assets once claims of creditors are satisfied. Equity investors expose themselves to the maximum risk associated with a business, but they are entitled to all residual rewards associated with it. Our analysis must recognize the claims of both creditors and equity investors, and their relationship, when analyzing financing activities. This chapter describes business financing and how companies report this to external users. We describe two major sources of financing—credit and equity—and the accounting underlying reports on these activities. We also consider off-balance-sheet financing, the relevance of book values, and liabilities "at the edge" of equity. We describe techniques of analysis exploiting our accounting knowledge. The content and organization of this chapter are as follows:

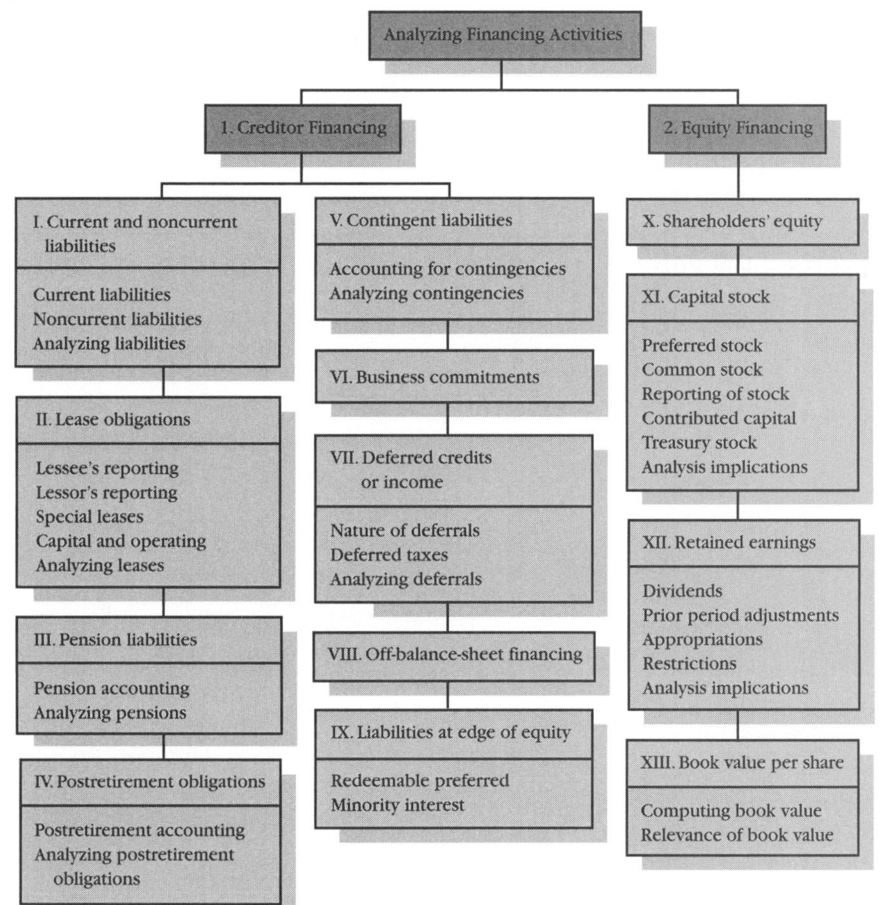

SECTION 1: CREDITOR FINANCING

Current and Noncurrent Liabilities

We describe both current and noncurrent liabilities in this section. We also discuss their implications to financial statement analysis.

Current Liabilities

Current (or short-term) liabilities are obligations whose liquidation requires the use of current assets or the incurrence of another current liability for settlement. The period over which companies expect to settle these liabilities is the longer of one year or the operating cycle. Theoretically, companies should record all liabilities at the present value of the cash outflow required to liquidate them. In practice, current liabilities are recorded at their maturity value due to the short time period until their liquidation. Ready availability of current assets for paying current liabilities does not justify offsetting one against another for reporting purposes.

Current liabilities are of two general types. The first type arises from operating activities. These include taxes payable, unearned income, advance payments, accounts payable, and other accruals of operating expenses. The second type of current liabilities arises from financing activities, and includes short-term loans and any current portion of long-term debt. Disclosure requirements (for SEC filings) for financing-related current liabilities are:

- Footnote disclosure of compensating balance arrangements, including those not in writing.
- Balance sheet segregation of (1) legally restricted compensating balances, and (2) unrestricted compensating balances relating to long-term borrowing arrangements if the compensating balance is computable at a fixed amount at the balance sheet date.
- Disclosure of short-term bank and commercial paper borrowings:

  Commercial paper borrowings separately stated in the balance sheet.

  Average interest rate and terms separately stated for short-term bank and commercial paper borrowings at the balance sheet date.

  Average interest rate, average outstanding borrowings, and maximum month-end outstanding borrowings for short-term bank debt and commercial paper combined for the period.
- Disclosure of amounts and terms of unused lines of credit for short-term borrowing arrangements (with amounts supporting commercial paper separately stated) and of unused commitments for long-term financing arrangements.

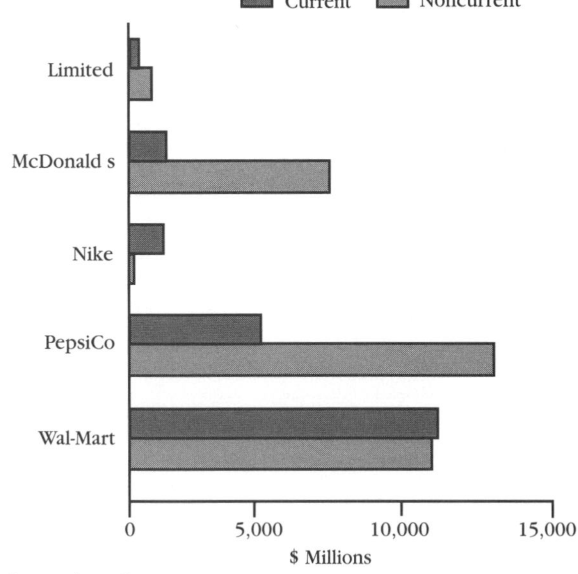

Source: Annual reports.

There are specific criteria for balance sheet classification of short-term obligations that companies expect to refinance. Companies classify short-term obligations as current unless the company intends to refinance them on a long-term basis and can demonstrate its ability to do so. Refinancing on a long-term basis means replacing short-term obligations with either long-term obligations or equity securities; or renewing, extending, or replacing them with other short-term obligations for a period extending beyond one year from the balance sheet date. A company demonstrates its ability to refinance on a long-term basis by either (1) having issued long-term obligations or equity securities to replace the short-term obligations after the balance sheet date but before its release, or (2) having entered into an agreement with a financing source permitting the refinancing of short-term obligations when coming due. Financing agreements that are cancelable for violation of a provision that can be evaluated differently by the parties to the agreement (such as "a material adverse change" or "failure to maintain satisfactory operations") do not meet this condition.

As discussed below, many borrowing agreements include provisions (or covenants) designed to protect the interests of creditors. A violation of a noncurrent debt covenant, such as a minimum level of working capital, does not require reclassification of the noncurrent liability to current provided one of the following conditions is met: (1) The lender either waives or loses the right to demand repayment for more than a year from the balance sheet date—for example, a lender might lose the right to demand repayment if a company subsequently cures a violation existing at the balance sheet date and the debt is no longer callable at the time of issuing financial statements; or (2) the obligation is not callable because it is probable that the company will cure a violation existing at the balance sheet date within a specified grace period (these circumstances are typically disclosed). This requirement does not apply to subjective covenants (for example, "if the lender deems itself insecure"); these would not by themselves trigger current liability classification. Following is an example of reclassification of noncurrent debt to current:

The third quarter loss, which included the $46,300 provision for loss on disposal of discontinued operations, placed the Company in default of net worth covenants under both its revolving credit and subordinated debt agreements. Because the defaults triggered a technical acceleration of the Company's senior (revolving credit) debt and allow the subordinated lenders to accelerate, the related debt has been classified as current at December 31. The Company intends to eliminate defaults under its debt agreements by restructuring the agreements through the use of proceeds from divestitures. Until the Company is able to reduce its debt through divestitures and achieve a related restructuring of its debt agreements, it will remain in default of, and subject to the lenders' rights of acceleration under, those agreements.

—BMC Industries

Noncurrent Liabilities

Noncurrent (or long-term) liabilities are obligations not payable within the longer of one year or the operating cycle. They include loans from financial institutions

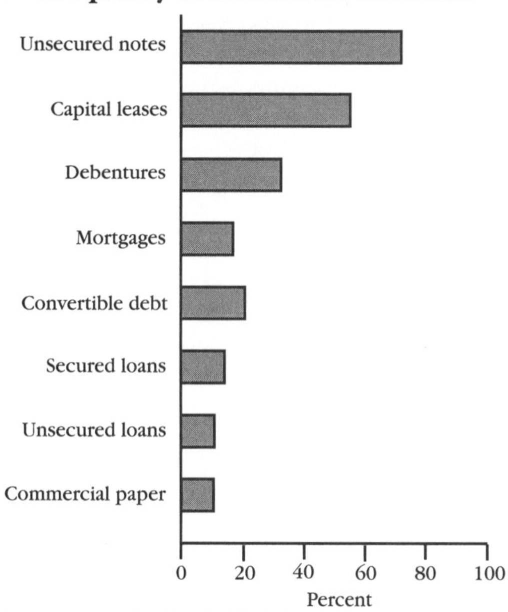

Source: *Accounting Trends & Techniques.*

such as banks, and more formal debt instruments such as bonds, debentures, and notes. These obligations can assume various forms, and their assessment and measurement requires disclosure of all conditions and covenants attached to them. This information includes the interest rate, maturity dates, conversion privileges, call features, subordination provisions, and restrictions. It also includes disclosure of collateral pledged (with indication of book and possible market values), sinking fund provisions, and revolving credit provisions. Companies must disclose any defaults of debt provisions, including defaults of interest and principal repayments.

A bond's par (or face) value helps determine the cash interest payments on the bond. Bond issuers sometimes sell bonds at a price either below par (at a discount) or in excess of par (at a premium). The discount or premium reflects an adjustment of the bond price to yield the market's required rate of return. A discount is amortized over the life of the bond and increases the effective interest rate paid by the borrower. Conversely, any premium received is similarly amortized but reduces the coupon rate of interest to the effective interest rate incurred. Noninterest-bearing obligations, or those bearing unreasonable rates of interest, are recorded at an amount reflecting the imputation of a reasonable interest rate. This not only shows the debt at an amount comparable to other interest-bearing debt obligations, but also provides for the computation of the interest charge reflecting the use of these funds. If debt results from acquisition of an asset, this treatment ensures that the company does not overstate the asset's cost.

Bond issuers offer a variety of incentives to promote the sale of bonds and reduce the interest rate required. These include convertibility features, attachments of warrants to purchase the issuer's common stock, or even warrants to purchase the stock of another company. To the extent these incentives are valuable, they impose costs on the issuing company. Whether these costs represent dilution of equity or a fixed price call on an investment, companies recognize these costs in financial statements as follows:

- Convertible feature. Recognized through its effect on computation of diluted earnings per share (see appendix to Chapter 6).
- Warrants. Recognized by assigning a discount factor at the time of debt issuance whose charge is amortized to income. Companies recognize the dilutive effects of warrants in diluted earnings per share.

A company can offer holders of its convertible debt an incentive to exercise their rights promptly to convert the debt to equity securities. We sometimes refer to this offer as a convertible debt sweetener. A company is required to recognize this conversion incentive as an expense, and cannot report it as an extraordinary item.

Another type of obligation relates to purchase commitments. For example, it is not uncommon for firms to agree to buy inventory months or even years in advance. Footnote disclosure is required of commitments under unconditional purchase obligations providing financing to suppliers and includes:

For purchase obligations *not* recognized on the purchaser's balance sheet:

- Description and term of obligation.
- Total fixed and determinable obligation.
- Description of any variable obligation.
- Amounts purchased under obligation.

For purchase obligations that are recognized on purchaser's balance sheet, a company must report payments for each of the next five years.

Disclosure is also required of future payments on long-term borrowings and redeemable stock including:

- Maturities and sinking funds requirements for each of the next five years.
- Redemption requirements for each of the next five years.

NEW YORK EXCHANGE BONDS

Quotations as of 4 p.m. Eastern Time
Wednesday, January 15, 1997

Volume $27,489,000

	Domestic Wed.	Domestic Tue.	All Issues Wed.	All Issues Tue.
Issues traded	319	326	327	334
Advances	138	181	144	186
Declines	115	100	117	103
Unchanged	66	45	66	45
New highs	11	14	12	16
New lows	8	5	8	6

SALES SINCE JANUARY 1
(000 omitted)

1997	1996	1995
$258,738	$277,973	$324,221

Dow Jones Bond Averages

–1996– High	–1996– Low	–1997– High	–1997– Low		–1997– Close	–1997– Chg.	–1997– %Yld	–1996– Close	–1996– Chg.
106.09	100.99	103.35	102.99	20 Bonds	103.35	+0.07	7.04	105.56	+0.22
102.43	97.46	100.37	99.99	10 Utilities	100.28	+0.01	7.21	102.01	+0.15
109.94	104.06	106.42	105.86	10 Industrials	106.41	+0.12	6.87	109.11	+0.28

CORPORATION BONDS
Volume, $26,659,000

Bonds	Cur Yld	Vol	Close	Net Chg
ADT Op zr10	...	8	64¼	+ ⅛
AMR 9s16	8.1	13	111⅛	+ ⅝
ATT 4¾98	4.8	59	98	– ⅛
ATT 4⅜99	4.6	100	96⅛	+ ⅜
ATT 6s00	6.1	20	98⅜	– 1
ATT 5⅛01	5.4	35	94¼	...
ATT 7⅛02	7.0	19	102½	+ ¼
ATT 6¾04	6.8	90	99⅞	– ⅛
ATT 7½06	7.2	4	103½	...
ATT 8⅛22	8.0	408	102⅛	– ½
ATT 8⅛24	7.9	127	102½	...
ATT 8.35s25	7.9	10	105¼	...
ATT 8⅝31	8.1	12	107	– ¼
Aames 10½02	10.2	3	103	...
AirbF 6¾01	cv	25	100½	– ¼
AlaPw 9¼21	8.8	30	105⅜	– ¼
AlskAr 6½05	cv	1	112	...
AlskAr 6⅞14	cv	41	100	+ 1½
AlldC zr98	...	10	89⅜	– ¼
AlldC zr99	...	15	83⅞	– ¼
AlldC zr09	...	60	39½	– ⅜
Allwst 7¼14	cv	10	95	+ 1¾
Alza 5s06	cv	43	94½	– ½
Alza zr14	...	50	41¼	+ ¾
AmBrnd 7½99	7.4	55	102	+ ⅛
AmBrnd 8½03	7.9	7	108	+ 1½
Amoco 8⅝16	8.2	30	104¾	...
Amresco 8¾99	8.7	10	100½	...
Anhr 8⅝16	8.3	35	104	...
AnnTaylr 8¾00	8.9	60	98	– ⅛
Argosy 12s01	cv	325	70¾	– 1
Argosy 13¼04	15.0	221	88½	– ½
Ashlnd 6¾14	cv	7	103	+ ½
AubrnHl 12⅝20f	...	1	150½	– ¾
Barnt 8½99	8.2	25	103¾	– ¾
BarBks 10⅞03	9.3	25	117	+ 1
Barnet 8½07	7.9	8	108	– 2
BellPa 7⅛12	7.2	103	99	+ 1
BellPa 7½13	7.4	17	101	– ¾
Bell[illegible] 6½00	[illegible]	[illegible]	100⅝	+ ⅛
[illegible]	[illegible]	[illegible]	[illegible]	⅛

Bonds	Cur Yld	Vol	Close	Net Chg
Masco 5¼12	cv	9	102½	+ ¾
Mascotch 03	cv	158	86¾	– ¼
Maxus 8½08	8.7	7	97⅜	...
McDnl 6¾03	6.7	5	101	+ ¼
McDnlDg 8⅝97	8.6	10	100 5/16	+ 1/32
Medtrst 7½01	cv	1	107½	+ 1½
Metrom 9½98	9.5	18	100⅜	+ ¼
MPac 5s45f	...	13	60½	– ⅛
Mobil 8⅜01	7.8	20	107⅝	+ ⅝
Moran 8¾08f	cv	10	85½	– 3½
Motrla zr13	...	10	80	– 1
Nabis 8s00	7.7	67	103⅜	...
NtEdu 6½[illegible]	cv	[illegible]	[illegible]	2½

Bonds	Cur Yld	Vol	Close	Net Chg
TmeWar 7¾05	7.7	15	100⅝	– ⅜
TmeWar 8.11s06	8.0	2	101½	...
TmeWar 8.18s07	8.0	12	102⅞	+ ½
TmeWE 7¼08	7.5	7	97	– ½
TmeWar 9⅛13	8.4	5	108⅝	– ⅜
TmeWar zr13	...	16	43	...
TmeWar 9.15s23	8.5	15	108⅛	– ⅜
TitanCp 03	cv	10	115	– 1¼
TolEd 7½02	7.6	8	99	– ⅞
TolEd 8s03	8.0	40	99¾	+ ½
TollCp 9½03	9.1	20	104⅜	+ 1½
Trimas 5s03	cv	5	106	– 1
TucEP 7.65s03	7.8	5	99¼	+ [illegible]

Illustrations of disclosures for current and noncurrent liabilities are found in notes 3 and 4 of the financial statements of Adaptec in Supplement A. Note 7 for Adaptec includes disclosure of several purchase agreements with suppliers of silicon wafers.

Analysis Implications of Liabilities

Since liabilities are claims against a company's assets and resources, we need assurance that companies account for all of them with proper details as to their amounts and due dates, including conditions, encumbrances, and limitations they impose on a company. We must realize most companies continually look for ways to reduce the amount of liabilities reported in their financial statements. We must also recognize that companies can misclassify or inadequately describe liabilities.

Auditors are one source of assurance in our identification of liabilities. Auditors use techniques like direct confirmation, review of board of director minutes, reading of contracts and agreements, and inquiry of those knowledgeable of company obligations to satisfy themselves that companies record all liabilities. Since double-entry accounting requires for every asset, resource, or cost acquired, a counterbalancing entry for the obligation or resources expended, the most difficult items are those relating to commitments and contingent liabilities requiring *no* entry. In this case, we must rely on information provided in notes to financial statements and in the management commentary in annual reports and related documents. We can also check the accuracy and reasonableness of debt disclosures by reconciling them to a company's required disclosures on the amounts of interest expensed and paid in cash. Any significant unexplained differences require further analysis or management explanation. When liabilities are understated, we must be aware of the upward bias to income attributed to lower or delayed expenses.

The SEC determined Ampex Corporation failed to fully disclose (1) its obligations to pay royalty guarantees to record companies totaling in excess of $80 million, (2) its sales of substantial amounts of prerecorded tapes improperly accounted for as "degaussed" or erased tapes to avoid payment of royalty fees, (3) a several million dollar understatement in the allowance for doubtful accounts receivable and provisions for losses arising from royalty contracts, and (4) income overstatements from inadequate credit allowances for returned tapes.

We need also review the terms and conditions of recorded liabilities. Our analysis must examine the description of liabilities and their terms, conditions, and encumbrances to satisfy us of their feasibility. Exhibit 3.1 is a list of important features for our analysis of liabilities. Minimum disclosure requirements as to debt provisions vary, but auditors are bound to disclose any breaches in loan provisions potentially

Analysis Research Insight 3.1

Accounting-Based Liability Restrictions

Do all bonds offer holders the same degree of security for safeguarding their investment? Are all bonds of equal risk? How might we choose among bonds with identical payment schedules and coupon rates? Analysis research on company liabilities provides us with some insight into these questions. Bonds are not of equal risk, and an important factor of this risk relates to restrictions, or lack thereof, in liability agreements. Creditors establish liability restrictions (or covenants) to safeguard their investment. These restrictions often limit management's behavior in ways that might harm the financial interests of creditors. Violating any restriction is usually grounds for "technical default," providing the creditor legal grounds to demand immediate repayment. Liability restrictions can reduce creditors' risk exposure.

Restrictions on management's behavior take many forms. The more common restrictions include:

- Dividend distribution restrictions.
- Working capital restrictions.
- Debt-to-equity ratio restrictions.
- Seniority of asset claim restrictions.
- Acquisition and divestment restrictions.
- Liability issuance restrictions.

These restrictions limit the dilution of net assets by constraining management's ability to distribute assets to new or continuing shareholders, or to new creditors. Details of these restrictions are often available in a liability's prospectus, a company's annual report, SEC report filings, and various creditor information services (e.g., *Moody's Manuals*). Many restrictions are in the form of accounting-based constraints. For example, dividend payment restrictions are often expressed in the form of a minimum level of retained earnings that companies must maintain. The selection and application of accounting procedures are, therefore, potentially affected by the existence of liability restrictions.

EXHIBIT 3.1 Important Features in Analyzing Liabilities

- Terms of indebtedness (e.g., maturity, interest rate).
- Restrictions on deployment of resources and freedom in business activities.
- Ability and flexibility in pursuing further financing.
- Requirements relating to working capital, debt to equity, and other financial figures.
- Dilutive conversion features that liabilities are subject to.
- Prohibitions on certain disbursements such as dividends.

limiting a company's freedom of action or increasing its risk of insolvency. Accordingly, we must be alert to any explanations or qualifications in the notes or in an auditor's report like the following example:

> The credit agreement was amended . . . converting the facility from a revolving credit arrangement to a demand note. Under the amended agreement, the Company is required to satisfy specified financial conditions and is also required to liquidate its indebtedness to specified maximum limits . . . the Company had satisfied all these requirements except for the working capital covenant. Subsequent to that date, the Company has not maintained its compliance as to maximum indebtedness. In addition, the tangible net worth requirement was not met . . . The Company has given notices to the agent bank of its failure to satisfy these requirements . . . In addition to the restrictions described above, this credit facility places restrictions on the Company's ability to acquire or dispose of assets, make certain investments, enter into leases and pay dividends . . . the credit agreement disallowed the payment of dividends.
>
> —American Shipbuilding Company

We aspire to foresee events like the American Shipbuilding case. One of our most effective tools in doing this is through financial analysis comparing the terms of indebtedness with the *margin of safety*—the extent existing compliance exceeds minimum requirements.

Lease Obligations

Lease obligations are contractual agreements between a lessor and a lessee giving the lessee a right to use assets owned by a lessor for the lease term in return for rental payments. Estimates show that companies lease more than $150 billion of assets, comprising nearly one-fourth of capital assets financed. Lease terms usually obligate a company to make a series of payments over a future period of time, and in many cases these payments contain elements of interest and principal amortization. A key factor in analyzing leases is examining the set of features that can either make

Lease Types for Companies

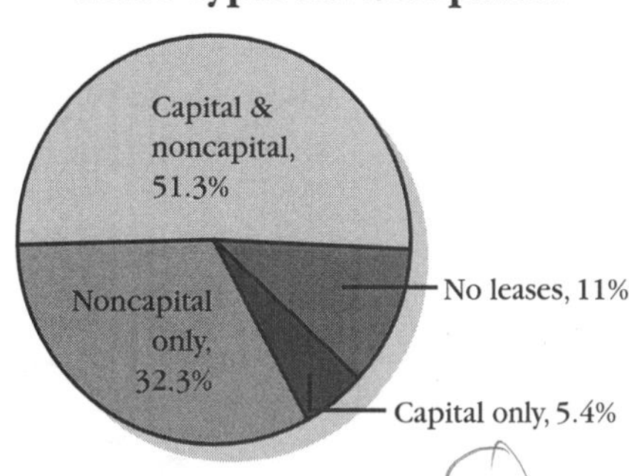

Source: *Accounting Trends & Techniques.*

it appear like a purchase (i.e., leasing as a means of financing) or appear like a long-term rental contract. Current accounting provisions hold that a lease transferring substantially all of the benefits and risks of ownership of property (**capital lease**) be treated like an asset acquisition and incurrence of liability by the *lessee*, and like a sale or financing transaction by the *lessor*. Companies account for all other leases as **operating leases**. These accounting provisions do not apply to leases relating to rights to explore natural resources or to licensing agreements.

Lessee's Reporting

A lessee classifies and accounts for a lease as a **capital lease** (recorded as an asset and associated liability) if, at the inception of the lease, it meets one of four criteria: (1) the lease transfers ownership of the property to the lessee by the end of the lease term, (2) the lease contains an option to purchase the property at a bargain price, (3) the lease term is equal to 75 percent or more of the estimated economic life of the property, or (4) the present value of the rentals and other minimum lease payments at the beginning of the lease term equals 90 percent of the fair value of the leased property less any related investment tax credit retained by the lessor. Regarding criteria (3) and (4), if the beginning of a lease term falls within the last 25 percent of the total estimated economic life of the leased property, the lessee applies neither the 75 percent of economic life criterion nor the 90 percent recovery criterion in classifying the lease—the lessee treats this lease as an operating lease. Lessees record a capital lease at an amount equal to the present value of minimum lease payments during the lease term, excluding executory costs (if determinable) like insurance, maintenance, and taxes paid by the lessor together with any profit thereon. This amount must not exceed the fair value of the leased property at inception of the lease, and if the lessee cannot determine executory costs from provisions of the lease, it estimates these costs. Amortization, in a manner consistent with the lessee's normal depreciation policy, is called for over the term of the lease except where the lease transfers title or contains a bargain purchase option; in the latter cases, amortization follows the estimated economic life. If the lease does not meet any of those criteria, the lessee classifies and accounts for it as an **operating lease**. In accounting for an operating lease, the lessee charges rentals to expense as they become payable except when rentals are not payable on a straight-line basis. In the latter case, lessees expense rentals when payable or on any systematic or rational basis reflecting the time pattern of benefits derived from the leased property. All lessees are required to disclose (1) future minimum lease payments separately for capital leases and operating leases, and in total, and for each of the five succeeding years, and (2) rental expense for each period they present an income statement. Lease disclosures for Adaptec appear in note 7 to its financial statements in Supplement A.

Lessor's Reporting

A lessor classifies and accounts for a lease (except leveraged leases) as a **sales-type lease** if it meets any one of the preceding four criteria for capital leases *plus* two additional criteria and if manufacturing or dealer profit is involved. If no manufacturing or dealer profit is involved, it is considered a **direct-financing lease**. The two additional criteria are (1) collectibility of minimum lease payments is reasonably predictable and (2) no important uncertainties surround the amount of unreimbursable costs yet to be incurred by the lessor under the lease. A lessor classifies and accounts for a lease not meeting these criteria as an operating lease. All lessors are required to disclose (1) future minimum lease payments they receive separately for sales-type, direct-financing, and operating leases; and (2) components of the investment in sales-type and direct-financing leases—estimated residual values and unearned income.

Sales-Type Leases

The major reporting and disclosure considerations with sales-type leases are:

- Lessor records the minimum lease payments plus the unguaranteed residual value accruing to the benefit of the lessor as the gross investment.
- The difference between gross investment and the sum of the present values of its two components is recorded as unearned income. The net investment equals gross investment less unearned income. Unearned income is amortized to income over the lease term to produce a constant periodic rate of return on the net investment in the lease. The lessor credits contingent rentals to income when they become receivable.
- At termination of the existing lease term of a lease being renewed, the lessor adjusts the net investment in the lease to the fair value of the leased property to the lessor at that date, and recognizes the difference, if any, as gain or loss. (The same procedure applies to direct-financing leases.)
- The lessor records the present value of the minimum lease payments discounted at the interest rate implicit in the lease as the sales price. The cost, or carrying amount, if different, of the leased property, plus any initial direct costs (of negotiating and consummating the lease) less the present value of the unguaranteed residual value is charged against income in the same period.
- The lessor periodically reviews the estimated residual value. If the value is excessive, the lessor revises the accounting for the transaction by using the changed estimate. The resulting reduction in net investment is recognized as a loss in the period in which the estimate changes. The lessor does not make an upward adjustment of the estimated residual value. (A similar provision applies to direct-financing leases.)

Direct-Financing Leases

The major reporting and disclosure considerations with direct-financing leases are:

- The lessor records the minimum lease payments (net of executory costs) plus the unguaranteed residual value plus the initial direct costs as the gross investment.
- The lessor records the difference between the gross investment and the cost, or carrying amount, if different, of the leased property, as unearned income. Net investment equals gross investment less unearned income. The unearned income is amortized to income over the lease term. The initial direct costs are amortized in the same portion as the unearned income. The lessor credits contingent rentals to income when they become receivable.

Operating Leases

Lessors include property accounted for as operating leases in their balance sheets and depreciate them in accordance with normal depreciation policies. They take rent into income over the lease term as it becomes a receivable, except if it departs from a straight-line basis, then they recognize income on this other basis or on another systematic or rational basis. Lessors defer initial costs and allocate them over the lease term.

Special Leases

Certain special leases yield unique disclosures. They include those involving real estate, sale-leasebacks, and leveraged leasing.

Real Estate Leases

These leases include cases of (1) land only, (2) land and buildings, (3) land and equipment, and (4) part of a building. Generally, the prior reporting requirements apply with the following exceptions:

- Where land only is involved, the lessee accounts for it as a capital lease if either criterion (1) or (2) applies. Land is not usually amortized.
- Concerning both land and building, if the capitalization criteria applicable to land are met, the lease retains the capital lease classification and the lessor accounts for it as a single unit. The lessee capitalizes the land and buildings separately, and the allocation of costs between these two is in proportion to their respective fair values at inception of the lease.
- If the capitalization criteria applicable to land are not met, and at the inception of the lease the fair value of the land is less than 25 percent of total fair value of the leased property, both lessor and lessee consider the property as a single unit. They attribute the estimated economic life of the building to the whole unit. In this case, if either criterion (3) or (4) is met, the lessee capitalizes the land and building as a single unit and amortizes it.
- If conditions in the immediately preceding point prevail, but the fair value of land is 25 percent or more of the total fair value of the leased property, both the lessee and the lessor consider the land and the building separately for purposes of applying capitalization criteria (3) and (4). If either criterion is met by the building element of the lease, the lessee accounts for it as a capital lease and amortizes it; the lessee accounts for the land element of the lease as an operating lease. If the building element meets neither capitalization criterion, both land and buildings are accounted for as a single operating lease.
- The lessor and the lessee consider separately equipment that is part of a real estate lease, and they estimate the minimum lease payments applicable to it by whatever means are appropriate in the circumstances.
- Leases of certain facilities like airports, bus terminals, or port facilities from governmental units or authorities are classified as operating leases.

Sale-Leaseback

When a lease meets criteria for treatment as a capital lease, the lessor defers any gain on its sale and amortizes it over the lease term in proportion to the amortization of the leased asset. When a capital lease is not implied, the lessor recognizes any gain at the time of sale if the fair rental for the lease term is equal to or greater than the rental prescribed by the lease. If the lease rental exceeds the fair rental, any gain on sale is reduced by the amount of this excess. When a leaseback is for only a portion of the property sold, the lessor makes an assessment as to whether the leaseback of the portion of property sold at a profit represents a continued involvement in the property sufficient to require deferral of all or part of the profit on the sale. The lessor accounts for a sale-leaseback involving real estate, including real estate with equipment, as a sale only if the transaction meets certain qualifications. Before any profit or loss is recognized on sales of real estate, the receivables from their sale must be collectible and the seller must have no significant remaining obligations.

Leveraged Leases

Leveraged leasing occurs when a lessor borrows heavily to finance a leasing transaction with small, or even negative (borrowing more than property cost), equity in the leased property. The accounting prescribed for use by lessors with leveraged leases is the *separate phases method*. This recognizes separate investment phases of a leveraged lease in which the lessor's net investment declines during the early years of the lease and rises during the later years. Lessees classify and account for leveraged leases in the same way as nonleveraged leases.

Capital and Operating Lease Implications

We consider numerical illustrations of capital and operating leases, and we contrast the two with respect to their implications for income and cash flow.

Reporting on Capital Leases: An Illustration

We consider the following lease terms and assumptions in our illustration:

- Lessor acquires equipment for lease at $10,000.
- Fair value of the leased equipment at inception of the lease, January 1, Year 1, is $10,000.
- Estimated economic life of the leased equipment is eight years.
- The lease has a fixed noncancelable term of five years with rental payments of $2,400 at the end of each year. The lessee guarantees a $2,000 residual value at the end of the five-year lease. The lessee receives any excess of the equipment's selling price over the guaranteed amount at the end of the lease. The lessee pays executory costs.
- Rental payments are fair, and the guarantees of residual value are expected to approximate realizable value. No investment tax credit is available.
- The lessee depreciates its equipment on a straight-line basis.
- The lessee's incremental borrowing rate is 10 percent per year.
- At the end of the lease term, the equipment is sold for $2,100.

Minimum lease payments for both the lessee and the lessor are computed as follows: (1) Minimum rental payments over the lease term equal ($2,400 × 5 years) or $12,000, plus (2) Lessee guarantee of the residual value at the end of the lease term or $2,000. Therefore, the total minimum lease payments equal $14,000.

Next, we determine the lessor's rate of interest implicit in this lease. This is the rate equating the recovery of the fair value of the equipment at the inception of the lease ($10,000) with the present value of both the minimum lease payments ($2,400 × 5) plus the lessee's guarantee of the residual value at the end of the lease ($2,000). This rate is arrived at here on a trial and error basis. At 10 percent, the two discounted amounts total $10,340; at 11 percent they total $10,057; and at 12 percent they equal $9,786. Through interpolation, we arrive at an implicit interest rate of 11.21 percent.

The lessee classifies this lease as a capital lease because the present value of the minimum lease payments at $10,340 (using its incremental borrowing rate of 10 percent) exceeds 90 percent of the fair value of the equipment at inception of the lease ($10,000). The lessee uses its incremental borrowing rate (10 percent) in discounting because it is less than the implicit interest rate in the lease. The lessor classifies this lease as a direct-financing lease because the present value of the minimum lease payments using the implicit rate of 11.21 percent ($10,000) exceeds 90 percent of the fair value of the equipment, and cost and fair value of the equipment are equal at inception of the lease, and all other conditions of capitalization are met.

Lessee's Accounting Implications

January 1, Year 1:

	Debit	Credit
Leased Property under Capital Leases	10,000	
Obligations under Capital Leases		10,000*
To record the capital lease at the fair value of the property.		

*Obligation due within one year will be classified as current.

December 31, Year 1:

	Debit	Credit
Obligations under Capital Leases	1,279	
Interest Expense	1,121†	
Cash		2,400
To record first-year rental payments.		

†Obligation balance outstanding × Implicit interest rate = $10,000 × 11.21% = $1,121.

	Debit	Credit
Depreciation Expense	1,600‡	
Accumulated Depreciation of Leased Property under Capital Leases		1,600
To record first-year depreciation.		

‡ $\frac{\text{Cost-residual value}}{\text{Term of lease}} = \frac{\$10,000 - \$2,000}{5} = \$1,600.$

December 31, Year 5 (selected journal entry):

	Debit	Credit
Cash	100	
Obligations under Capital Leases	2,000	
Accumulated Depreciation of Leased Property under Capital Leases	8,000	
Leased Property under Capital Leases		10,000
Gain on Disposition of Leased Property		100
To record liquidation of obligations under capital leases and receipt of cash in excess of guaranteed residual value.		

Lessor's Accounting Implications

January 1, Year 1:

	Debit	Credit
Equipment	10,000	
Cash		10,000
To record purchase of equipment for purpose of financing lease.		
Minimum Lease Payments Receivable	14,000	
Equipment		10,000
Unearned Income		4,000
To record investment in direct-financing lease.		

December 31, Year 1:

	Debit	Credit
Unearned Income	1,121§	
Earned Income		1,121
To recognize the portion of unearned income that is earned during first year of investment.		

§Net investment × Implicit interest rate = 10,000 × 11.21$ = $1,121

Cash	2,400	
Minimum Lease Payments Receivable		2,400
To record receipt of first year's rental.		

December 31, Year 5 (selected journal entry):

Cash	2,000	
Minimum Lease Payments Receivable		2,000
To record receipt of the lessee's guarantee.		

Capital Versus Operating Lease—Income Implications

Exhibit 3.2 shows the interest expense pattern of the capital lease mimics that of a fixed payment mortgage with interest expense decreasing over time as the principal balance decreases. The appeal of operating lease accounting to the lessee is readily apparent. Specifically, using capitalization, expenses incident to the lease (interest plus depreciation or $1,121 + $1,600) exceed rental expense by $321. As time passes, this excess reverses—over the lease period total expense under either method is equal. But the pattern of expense recognition is often an important consideration for many companies. The higher initial charge under capitalization is often a distinct disadvantage. Exhibit 3.2 also reveals the pattern of finance income recognition by the lessor that is proportional to the investment at risk.

Capital Versus Operating Lease—Cash Implications

With respect to cash flows, there is a yearly outflow of the $2,400 rental. Selection of the capital or operating lease method does not affect cash flows. However, classification of lease payments in the statement of cash flows differs according to the type of lease. Under capital lease accounting, cash from operations is reduced annually by declining interest charges (i.e., $1,121, $977, . . .), while payment of lease obligations represents a financing use of cash that increases yearly (i.e., $1,279, $1,423, . . .). The two amounts always equal the rental payment of $2,400. Amortization (depreciation) of the equipment's "property right" of $1,600 annually has no effect on cash since it is a noncash-using expense. Under operating lease accounting, the entire rental payment is included under cash from operations.

Analysis Implications of Lease Obligations

Leasing as a means of financing deserves scrutiny in our analysis. One of our major objectives is to make certain that "accounting form" does not mask "economic

EXHIBIT 3.2 Lease Payment Schedule for Numerical Illustration

	Rental	*Interest: Income (lessor)/ Expense (lessee)*	*Principal: Receipts (lessor)/ Payment (lessee)*	*Balance of Obligations*
Year 0	—	—	—	$10,000
Year 1	$ 2,400	$1,121	$1,279	8,721
Year 2	2,400	977*	1,423	7,298
Year 3	2,400	818	1,582	5,716
Year 4	2,400	641	1,759	3,957
Year 5	2,400	443	1,957	2,200
Total	$12,000	$4,000	$8,000	$ 2,000

*Year 2 interest is balance of obligation ($8,721) × 11.21%.

Analysis Research Insight 3.2

Capital versus Operating Leases

Are certain companies more prone to structure lease agreements as capital leases, or others as operating leases? What are possible incentives for management to choose capital leases over operating leases or vice-versa? Does the choice of capital versus operating lease matter? Analysis research offers us evidence on these issues. The most distinct factor is the tax implications of capital versus operating leases. Ownership of the asset provides the holder with tax benefits. This suggests that the entity with the *higher* marginal tax rate takes ownership of the property to take advantage of greater tax benefits. The entity with the *lower* marginal tax would lease the property. While accounting and tax reporting need not be identical, use of operating leases for financial reports creates unnecessary obstacles when claiming capital lease procedures for tax purposes.

Nontax factors are also evident in the capital versus operating lease decision. Capital lease treatment is more likely when (1) the lease term comprises much of the asset's benefit period, (2) companies do not express management compensation arrangements in terms of returns on investments, (3) companies do not express liability restrictions in accounting-based constraints (debt to equity), or (4) there is a comparative advantage in reselling the property. In sum, both tax implications and non-tax factors affect management's decision to structure lease agreements as capital or operating leases.

substance"—that financial statement users recognize debt and its effect on capital structure when appropriate, including exposure to fixed charges and the leverage effects. Many long-term leases possess most or all of the characteristics of debt. They create an obligation for payments under an agreement that is not cancelable. This represents a commitment to fixed payments and is the essence of debt. The adverse effects of debt are also present with a lease. An inability to cover lease payments signals, if not invites, insolvency. While there are statutory limitations on lease obligations in cases of bankruptcy, the relevant factor is information for assessing the probability of insolvency and the attendant adverse effects on asset values and credit standing. We need also assess the importance of leased property to company operations, since it is often vital and precludes abandonment of the lease.

It is often difficult for us to analyze the financial position of companies when they use different methods of financing, including purchases in the form of a lease. This extends to our comparison of companies' incomes, since with operating leases, rental payments are usually less than interest expense and amortization expenses in the early period of a lease agreement. Certain reporting requirements (described above) are of major help in our analysis. They provide us with information for properly assessing the impact of leases for financial statements and in evaluating their impact for financial position and results of operations. Yet we must be aware that assumptions of fair values, selling prices, residual values, implicit rates of interest, and incremental borrowing rates are not so tight as to preclude certain "management" of the accounting numbers by managers with strong incentives to do so. We discuss relevant analytical adjustment of items like the debt-to-asset ratio in Chapter 10.

Pension Liabilities

Pension liabilities are obligations of an employer to provide retirement benefits or payments to employees for services previously rendered. Pensions are a major employee-benefit cost designed to contribute to security after retirement. Current estimates are that pension plans, with assets exceeding $4 trillion (about 20% of U.S. assets), cover nearly 50 million individuals. Pension funds control about 25 percent of the value of NYSE common stock, and account for nearly one-third of daily trading volume. We consider the accounting and reporting requirements with pension liabilities in this section along with their implications for our analysis of financial statements. Chapter 6 considers issues involved in the determination of pension expenses.

Accounting and Reporting for Pensions

Pension commitments by companies are formalized through pension plans. As pensions grow in importance and magnitude for operating costs, so does the accounting for these costs. **Pension expense** is a measure of the current cost of providing for future promised benefits under pension plans. Pension expense derives from accrual accounting and is distinct from the funding of pensions. **Funding** refers to transfers of cash or other assets to a pension fund trustee to meet current and future pension payments.

Defined benefit pension plans specify the amount of pension benefits provided to retirees. Under defined benefit plans, the company bears the risk of pension fund performance. **Defined contribution** pension plans specify contributions required of the company, and the amount of pension benefits to retirees depends on the pension fund performance (a risk borne by employees). We primarily concern ourselves here with accounting for defined benefit pension plans. The reason is that defined benefit pension plans are by far the largest for asset value in our economy. The amount of retirees' benefits under these plans is determined by formulae involving actuarial variables like predicted retirement age, life expectancies, employee turnover rates, future salary levels, future returns on pension plan assets, and vesting provisions. *Vesting* is an employee's right to pension benefits regardless of whether the employee remains with the company or not. Once pension expense is determined based on plan provisions and actuarial assumptions, funding the expense becomes a managerial decision that is also influenced by legal and tax considerations. Tax law specifies minimum funding requirements to ensure the security of retirees' benefits. It also has tax deductibility limitations for overfunded pension plans. Minimum funding requirements also exist under the Employee Retirement Income Security Act (ERISA). A company can fund the expense exactly by providing assets to the plan trustee that equal the expense. It can *underfund* by recording a liability for accrued pension expenses, or it can *overfund* by prepaying future pension expenses.

Pension Illustration

To illustrate the process of funds accumulation for paying future pensions, we focus on the provision of a pension for one employee, named A. Worker. A. Worker joins the plan at age 45 and expects to retire at age 65. The plan specifies that A. Worker is entitled to a $20,000 annual pension and is expected to draw on it for 15 years (i.e., she has a life expectancy of 80 years). We assume the pension fund earns 7 percent on its assets. From the retirement date onward (i.e., during the pension disbursing period), the employer expects the fund to earn 8 percent on its assets. The process of accumulation and disbursement appears graphically in Exhibit 3.3. Under this scenario, assuming all expectations are accurate, the employer (company) makes the following annual accounting entry:

Pension Expense	4,176	
Cash (to Pension Trustee)		4,176

Accounting by the employer is more complex than implied here since assumptions are not always accurate. Provisions of pension accounting emphasize how to account for these ever-changing disparities between expectations and realizations.

The *pension trustee* (whose accounting we are not overly concerned with here) records payments received during the accumulation period as follows:

Cash	4,176	
Pension Liability		4,176

The trustee also records returns on investment from these pension funds. During the distribution period, the pension trustee continues to record income on these funds and discharges the pension obligation on a yearly basis as follows:

Pension Liability	20,000	
Cash		20,000

Pension Obligation Estimates

We need to understand the nature of pension liabilities when an employer promises a pension. There are three different estimates of pension obligations:

- *Projected benefit obligation (PBO)* is an estimate of an employer's pension obligations based on assumptions regarding workers' *future* compensation. Our illustration for A. Worker requires a fixed $20,000 annual pension. However, if A. Worker's pension depends on her average salary during the final five years of service, then her employer must make an assumption about future salary levels in computing PBO.
- *Accumulated benefit obligation (ABO)* is an estimate of an employer's pension obligations based on assumptions regarding workers' *current* compensation. No assumptions about future compensation are relevant. This amount is equivalent to an employer's current obligation if the plan is discontinued immediately, that is, as of the measurement date. In our illustration, A. Worker's pension depends on current compensation; thus, ABO and PBO are equal.

EXHIBIT 3.3 Pension Accumulation and Disbursement

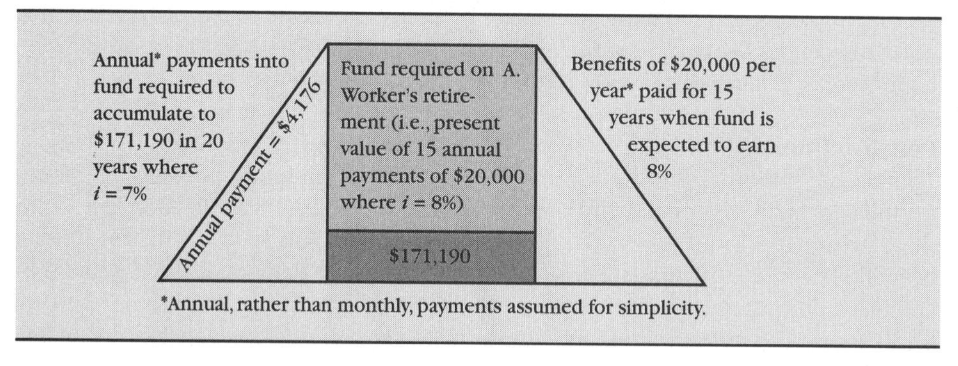

*Annual, rather than monthly, payments assumed for simplicity.

- *Vested benefit obligation (VBO)* is an estimate of an employer's pension obligations based on assumptions regarding workers' *current* compensation and for benefits *vested* to employees. For example, if A. Worker's pension plan stipulated her rights do not vest until she completes at least five years in employment, then the vested benefit obligation does not include her.

The tabulation below illustrates, in hypothetical amounts, the relations between the various amounts of the actuarial present value of benefit obligations:

	Vested benefits (VBO)	$10,000
+	Benefits not vested	3,000
=	Accumulated benefit obligation (ABO)	$13,000
+	Effect of future estimated compensation levels	2,000
=	Projected benefit obligation (PBO)	$15,000

Accounting and reporting requirements make it necessary that all three pension obligation estimates be known at each measurement date. There are also significant pension disclosure requirements. Exhibit 3.4 lists the more significant of these.

Overfunded Pension Plans

When the market value of pension fund assets exceeds the PBO, the pension fund is **overfunded**. There are various motivations for overfunding including tax-free accumulation of funds, outstanding company performance, or better than expected fund investment performance. Potential company raiders sometimes consider overfunded pension plans as sources of funds that can help finance their acquisitions. The implications of overfunded pension plans include:

- Companies can discontinue or reduce contributions to the pension fund until pension assets equal or fall below the PBO. Reduced or discontinued contributions have income and cash flow implications.
- Companies can withdraw excess assets. Recaptured amounts are subject to income taxes. Since companies often use pension funding as a tax shelter, reversion excise taxes are also often imposed. These actions impact cash flows.
- A change in expense accrual or funding policy might be unjustified if overfunding is due solely to favorable investment performance that is unpredictable and can reverse.

EXHIBIT 3.4 Significant Pension Disclosure Requirements

- Plan description including employee coverage, benefit formulas, funding policies, and assets held.
- Amount of net periodic pension cost for the period. Companies must show service cost, interest cost, and actual return on assets separately. Various amortization charges (e.g., unrecognized prior service costs, gains and losses) can be netted and disclosed as a single amount.
- Schedule reconciling the funded status of the pension plan with amounts reported in a company's financial statements.
- Assumptions, including the weighted-average assumed discount rate, the rate of compensation increase (if applicable) for measuring PBO, and the weighted-average expected long-term rate of return on plan assets.

Companies with overfunded pension plans have increased flexibility. They can reduce or eliminate pension contributions in the short run or can modify the plan to recapture excess assets. These are analytical considerations deserving our attention. Companies do not report excess pension fund assets as assets on the balance sheet. There are specific accounting practices when a company terminates a pension plan with assets in excess of accumulated benefits. Companies can recapture these excess assets for general use. There are also guidelines for treating gains from recapturing excess assets, for recording decreases in pension obligations, and for handling special termination events.

Additional Minimum Pension Liability

Reporting rules recognize an **additional minimum pension liability** in excess of amounts accrued as pension expenses. This additional liability is based on the ABO rather than the PBO, and represents a compromise between full recognition of pension liabilities and previous rulings requiring much less recognition. Rules require this additional pension liability when the ABO exceeds the fair value of pension plan assets. This yields an unfunded benefit obligation. Any debit balance in a Prepaid Pension Cost account increases the amount of this liability so that the balance sheet actually shows the minimum liability amount. Conversely, any credit balance in the Accrued Pension Cost account decreases the amount of this liability since that amount is taken into account in reporting the total minimum liability. For reporting purposes, companies combine the additional pension liability with the Accrued or Prepaid Pension Cost account. The table below illustrates the determination of this additional pension liability under different circumstances.

	Case 1	*Case 2*	*Case 3*	*Case 4*
		(in thousands)		
Accumulated benefit obligation	$1,000	$1,000	$1,000	$1,000
Less: Fair value of plan assets	700	700	700	1,400
Unfunded (overfunded) accumulated benefit obligation	$ 300	$ 300	$ 300	$(400)
Accrued pension cost (credit)	—	—	(200)	—
Prepaid pension cost (debit)	—	100	—	—
Additional minimum pension liability	$ 300	$ 400	$ 100	-0-*

*Balance not relevant because of overfunding.

While a company with an underfunded plan records an additional liability, if the company maintains a pension plan with assets in excess of accumulated benefits, it does not record an asset. Underfunding in one pension plan cannot be offset by overfunding in another plan. Recognition of this minimum pension liability in part remedies the unrecognized (i.e., unamortized) prior service costs, losses, and transition amounts reflecting the postponement (delay) in pension liability recognition. Recording this additional minimum pension liability as a credit to an appropriately designated liability account requires an offsetting debit to an intangible asset representing "a future economic benefit in the form of employee goodwill." However, if this intangible asset exceeds a company's unrecognized prior service costs, another approach is required. In this case, the company records its unrecognized net cost by charging the debit to a separate component of equity, net of any tax benefits from considering these losses as timing differences for tax purposes. Depending on circumstances, a company recording an additional minimum liability can create both an intangible pension asset and a contra shareholders' equity account.

To illustrate, assume for Case 1 in the preceding tabulation that the company has unrecognized prior service costs of $180,000. The company's entry to record the additional minimum liability is:

Intangible Pension Asset (*a*)	180,000	
Shareholders' Equity—Unrealized Pension Cost (*b*)	120,000	
Pension Liability		300,000

where (*a*) is an amount not to exceed unrecognized prior service cost, and (*b*) is a contra account to shareholders' equity. In absence of unrecognized prior service costs, the entire debit for the liability is to shareholders' equity. Each year the company makes a new determination of the additional minimum pension liability (if any) and adjusts the liability account accordingly.

Analysis Implications of Pension Liabilities

Accounting for pension liabilities does not fully recognize these obligations in all cases. While it does recognize a liability when the fair value of pension assets falls short of the ABO, it does not directly consider the PBO in this computation. The PBO recognizes future pay increases. Hence, when pension plans base benefits on future pay formulas (as many do), the liability computation fails to fully reflect the PBO and understates pension obligations. There is also a lack of accounting harmony. While companies ignore inflation effects when disregarding future pay increases, the interest rate used in discounting pension obligations to present value includes inflationary expectations. This reinforces the downward bias in the pension liability. The difference between the PBO and the fair value of pension plan assets is a preferred measure of pension liability. Yet, it does not measure the full pension obligations determined by the present value of amounts expected to be paid to employees based on total years service (past and present) and expected future salaries. The latter measure recognizes price-level changes on a company's pension obligation—a risky obligation indeed.

There are other limitations in pension accounting. The intangible asset created when recording certain pension liabilities is of doubtful economic significance. Recognition of this asset softens the effect of pension liabilities on a company's debt-to-equity ratio. There are also inherent inconsistencies in pension accounting. While the PBO is disregarded in computation of pension liabilities recorded, companies do use it in computing periodic pension service cost. Also, while underfunded pension plans lead to liability recognition, overfunded plans yield no asset recognition.

Our analysis must recognize that companies compute and evaluate pension liabilities annually and, unlike most liabilities, pension liabilities can and do fluctuate in value from period to period. Consequently, high-performing equity markets can reduce or eliminate pension liabilities. Poorly performing markets can increase pension liabilities, or make one appear where none existed.[1] The accounting rules encourage volatility with these liabilities. These rules measure pension obligations and the assets available to meet them at a point in time. Since factors affecting these accounts are ever-changing, it is inevitable that unfunded pension obligations are continually subject to change. This volatility is induced, as appropriate, by external factors and market conditions. Management, with the tacit assistance of auditors, pursues various means to reduce volatility and the increased risk it implies. Our analysis welcomes accounting that accurately portrays economic reality and the risks involved. One

[1] Pension assets rise when interest rates decline, but pension liabilities rise even faster. This is because long-term pension obligations cost more to fund in current dollars. The reverse prevails when interest rates rise. This leads some companies to try and manage assets and liabilities to reduce disparities between them.

useful way for us to view pension accounting is to consider a company's pension liability as an obligation not fully discharged by placing amounts charged to pension expense with an independent trustee. We can view pension plan assets like collateral or backup for an obligation that can change due to many factors, including inflation. This is reinforced in the following excerpt from practice:

> The Department of Labor filed suit against Maxxam, Inc., and Magnetex, Inc., who financed payments to retirees with annuities bought from an insurer whose financial problems later left it unable to meet all its obligations. These suits reinforce the ultimate obligation companies bear towards their retirees.

Postretirement Obligations Other Than Pensions

Postretirement obligations other than pensions refer to are health care and other welfare benefits to retirees and designated dependents. They include life insurance, medical care, housing assistance, legal and tax services, and eye and dental care. Nearly one-third of U.S. workers participate in postretirement health care plans, with a total unfunded liability in the $1 to $2 trillion range.

Accounting and Reporting for Postretirement Obligations

Recognition of postretirement obligations has, until recently, ranged from inadequate to nonexistent. Companies charged outlays for postretirement costs on a *pay-as-you-go* basis. IBM, for example, followed a policy of "terminal accrual" by providing for this liability only when an employee retired and not accruing any costs for active employees. When IBM ultimately recognized these liabilities, it yielded a $2.3 billion charge. We discuss accounting and reporting for postretirement obligations in this section, and their income implications in Chapter 6.

While reporting for postretirement obligations is similar to pensions, there are significant differences. One difference is in accounting for the unfunded postretirement obligation. This unfunded obligation at date of adoption, the *transition obligation,* is recognized as either (1) a cumulative effect of an accounting change (included as a charge to income) or (2) over future periods as a component of the annual postretirement expense over a period not to exceed 20 years. If a company elects to amortize its transition obligation over future years, then, unlike with pension accounting, it is not required to recognize immediately a minimum liability for the unfunded postretirement obligation attributable to present retirees and active employees eligible to receive benefits.

Another major difference from pension accounting is funding. Because no legal requirements exist for postretirement benefits (similar to ERISA requirements for pensions), and since funding postretirement benefits is not tax deductible like pension contributions, few companies fund their postretirement liabilities and are unlikely to do so in the near future. This yields large unrecorded, and growing, postretirement liabilities that are unfunded. Companies typically back these unrecorded liabilities by assets on their balance sheets and independent trustees have no control over these assets.

The components of accrued postretirement obligations (the balance sheet liability) are twofold: (1) **net annual postretirement cost**, which consists of (*a*) service cost, (*b*) interest cost, (*c*) any actual return on plan assets (a cost decrease), (*d*) amortization of unrecognized prior service cost, (*e*) amortization of actuarial gains or losses (cost increase or decrease), and (*f*) amortization of transition obligation if not recognized initially as a cumulative effect of an accounting change; and (2) **benefit payments**, which are the cash basis postretirement expenses. Components of the unrecognized postretirement obligation (unrecorded until recognized, generally on a straight-line basis over 20 years or less) are threefold: (1) unrecognized transition obligation measured on the date of adoption, and for which the company elects to amortize rather than charge to income immediately, less the sum of periodic amortization to net annual postretirement cost to date, (2) unamortized net gain or loss (unrecognized on balance sheet); and (3) unamortized prior service cost (unrecognized on balance sheet). Required disclosures for postretirement obligations include:[2]

- Description of postretirement benefit plans.
- Net periodic postretirement benefit expense and its components.
- Reconciliation of the funded status of the plan with amounts reported in employer's balance sheet.
- Assumed health care–cost trend rate in computing covered benefit costs for the next period, and description of the direction and pattern of change in these assumed rates.
- Weighted-average discount rate, rate of compensation, and expected long-term rate of return in measuring the accumulated postretirement benefit obligation.
- Effects on various balances due to a 1% increase in the health care–cost trend rate.
- Amounts and types of employer securities held.

Analysis Implications of Postretirement Obligations

Postretirement obligations are common and represent a long-standing practice for many companies. The magnitude of these obligations is estimated in the trillions of dollars and growing. Contributing to our need to vigilantly monitor postretirement obligations are two factors: (1) escalating expenses due to increasing medical costs, longer life expectancies, early retirement programs, and reduced Medicare reimbursements; and (2) limited management latitude in reducing or revoking postretirement benefits that are often upheld in our courts.

Our analysis recognizes that inclusion of postretirement obligations among companies' liabilities presents a more realistic, and leveraged, capital structure. Companies electing to amortize their unrecognized transition obligations over several years continue to hold substantial unrecorded liabilities. Companies that elected to immediately write-off this transition obligation show comparatively larger returns on equity because of decreased equity and reduced future income charges from the one-time writeoff. Most companies are likely to continue their practice of maintaining unfunded postretirement plans. Our analysis must recognize that whether postretirement liabilities are recorded or not, they are subject to extreme difficulties in measurement. Increased difficulties in measurement stem from the uncertainty in estimating health care and welfare costs several years into the future. Assumptions regarding intensity of services, medical service delivery methods, and the impact of technological advances in the health care industry make the estimation process more difficult. The health care–cost trend rate used by a company must be carefully evaluated. While the immediate cash

[2] See "Employers' Accounting for Postemployment Benefits" *Statement of Financial Accounting Standards No. 112* (Norwalk, Conn.: FASB, 1992).

flow effects from recording postretirement obligations are often minor, this is no cause for complacency. These obligations are real and likely require large future cash outflows to satisfy. Many factors affect our analysis of these future cash outflows for a company, including the ratio of active to retired employees and the age of its work force. We can use the current accounting disclosures, along with additional information, to compute our estimate of a company's immediate and future postretirement obligations.

ANALYSIS VIEWPOINT . . . *You are the labor negotiator*

As the head union negotiator on a new labor contract, you request that management sweeten postretirement benefits to employees. Management responds with no increase in postretirement benefits but with a commitment to fund a much larger portion of previously committed postretirement benefits, with these funds dispensed to an independent trustee. You are surprised and confused. Management already shows a large postretirement obligation on its financial statement. Should you accept management's counteroffer?

Contingent Liabilities

Contingencies refer to potential gains or losses whose resolution depends on one or more future events. Loss contingencies are potential claims on a company's resources (*contingent liabilities*). Contingent liabilities arise from litigation, threat of expropriation, collectibility of receivables, claims arising from product warranties or defects, guarantees of performance, tax assessments, self-insured risks, and catastrophic losses of property.

Accounting and Reporting for Contingencies

A loss contingency must meet two conditions before a company makes a provision for the loss and a charge to income. First, it must be *probable* that an asset is impaired or a liability incurred. Implicit in this condition is it must be probable that a future event(s) will occur confirming the loss. The second condition is the amount of loss must be *reasonably estimable*. Losses from uncollectible receivables and obligations related to product warranties and defects usually meet the two conditions for accrual at the time of sale. However, accrual for loss from self-insurance risks (injury to others, or damage to others' properties) or business interruption losses are not usually made until such loss occurs. Property and casualty insurance companies do not accrue catastrophic losses until such losses occur. Catastrophic losses do not meet the conditions for accrual because predictions of losses over relatively short time periods are unreliable. Accruals for losses from expropriation, litigation, claims, and assessments depend on the facts in each case. If a company does not make accrual for a loss contingency because one or both of the conditions for accrual are not met, the company discloses the contingency when there is at least a reasonable possibility that it has incurred a loss. This disclosure reports the nature of the contingency and offers an estimate of the possible loss or range of loss (or reports that such an estimate cannot be made). Appropriations of retained earnings are permitted for specific risks provided companies report them in shareholders' equity and do not use them to relieve the income statement of actual losses.

Consistent with conservatism in financial reporting, companies do not recognize gain contingencies in financial statements. They may, however, disclose contingencies in a footnote if the probability of realization is high.

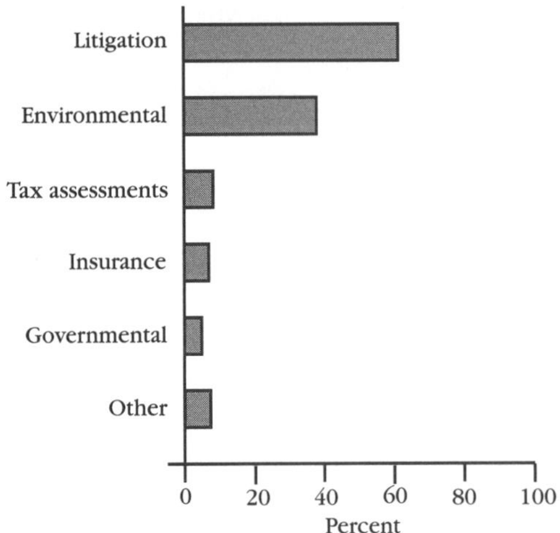

Source: *Accounting Trends & Techniques.*

Analysis Implications of Contingencies

Estimated liabilities for such items as service guarantees and warranties represent, in effect, revenue received for services not yet performed. Of importance to our analysis is the adequacy of these estimates. Companies often set these estimates on the basis of prior experience or future expectations. We must exercise care in accepting management's estimates on contingent liabilities. For example, Manville Corporation consistently argued it had substantial defenses to legal actions against it until the year it declared bankruptcy due to asbestos-related lawsuits. Concern with adequacy of amount is also a prime factor in our analysis of loss contingencies. For example, disclosure is required of indirect guarantees of indebtedness, such as advancing funds or covering fixed charges of another entity, and includes:

- Description of the obligation guaranteed and the degree of risk.
- Amount of exposure in the guarantee and how participation of others is treated in determining that exposure.
- Whether any reserves for losses are charged against income.

Still, our analysis must recognize that companies either do not recognize or underestimate some liabilities.[3] An example of disclosure for a contingent liability follows:

> There are various libel and other legal actions that have arisen in the ordinary course of business and are now pending against the Company. Such actions are usually for amounts greatly in excess of the payments, if any, that may be required to be made. It is the opinion of management after reviewing such actions with counsel that the ultimate liability which might result from such actions would not have a material adverse effect on the consolidated financial statements.
>
> —New York Times Company

Another example of measurement difficulties with contigent liabilities involves frequent flyer mileage.Unredeemed frequent flyer mileage credits entitle airline passengers to billions of miles of free travel. Frequent flyer programs assure customer loyalty and offer marketing benefits that are not cost-free. Yet airlines resist providing realistic estimates of these obligations.

---

[3] A recent study reported that of 126 lawsuits lost by publicly traded companies, nearly 40 percent were not disclosed in years preceding the loss. This implication that companies are reluctant to disclose pending litigation can affect our analysis, expecially in those cases where litigation risk is high.

Reserves for future losses is another category requiring our scrutiny. While conservatism in accounting calls for companies recognizing losses as they determine or foresee such losses, they tend, particularly in loss years, to overprovide for losses not yet incurred (referred to as a *big bath*)—typical costs are disposal of assets, relocation expenses, or plant closings. Overproviding for losses shifts expected future losses to the current period. A problem with these losses is once they are established there is no further accounting for the expenses and losses charged against them. Only in certain reports filed with the SEC (Form 10-K) are details of changes in these loss reserves required, and even here there is no requirement for detailed disclosure on the nature of any changes. Our analysis should always attempt to obtain details of reserves by category and amount. Two sources of useful information are (1) note disclosures in financial statements and (2) information in the Management's Discussion and Analysis section. Under the U.S. Internal Revenue Code, only a few categories of anticipated losses are tax deductible. Accordingly, our analysis of deferred taxes can detect undisclosed provisions for future expenses or losses—the accounting expense not tax deductible should yield an effect on deferred (prepaid) taxes. Yet little or no information is typically available, and our analysis must adopt a critical attitude toward establishing loss reserves and the means of their disposition. Reserves offer also a potential device for a company to manage or smooth income. They also do not protect against risk, have no cash flow consequences, and do not provide an alternative to insurance.

Cigna Corporation, a large property and casualty insurer, shows us how tenuous the reserve estimation process is. In a recent year, Cigna claimed it could look back on 10 years of a very stable pattern of claims (insurance reserves are designed to provide for such claims). During the following year, however, the incidence and severity of claims worsened. Cigna considered this an aberration and did *not* increase reserves for future losses. Only an intensive year-end review in the second year revealed enormous miscalculations. Early in the third year, Cigna announced a more than $1 billion charge to income to bring insurance reserves to required levels. In this and prior years the auditor's opinion was unqualified. Yet Cigna seriously misstated net income in these years.

The auditor's report gives us another perspective on contingencies, as shown below:

> The Company is subject to the Government exercising an additional option under a certain contract. If the Government exercises this option, additional losses could be incurred by the Company. Also, the Company has filed or is in the process of filing various claims against the Government relating to certain contracts. The ultimate outcome of these matters cannot presently be determined. Accordingly, no provision for such potential additional losses or recognition of possible recovery from such claims (other than relating to the Federal Excise Tax and related claims) has been reflected in the accompanying financial statements.
>
> —Harsco Corporation

In this case our analysis confronts auditors who express an inability to form an opinion on the outcome of certain events.

Banks have considerable exposure to losses that they often ignore or confine to notes. An example is losses on international loans when evidence points to impairments of assets but where banks and their auditors fail to fully react. Another example is with off-balance-sheet commitments of banks, including such diverse commitments as standby letters of credit, municipal bond and commercial paper guarantees, currency swaps, and foreign exchange contracts. Unlike loans, these commitments are promises banks expect they will not have to bear. Banks do not report these commitments on the balance sheet. This further increases the danger of not fully identifying risk exposures of banks.

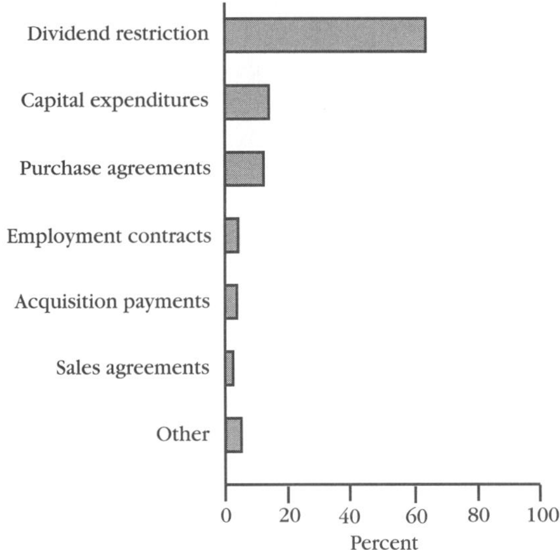

Source: *Accounting Trends & Techniques*.

Commitments

Commitments are potential claims against a company's resources due to future performance under a contract. They are not recognized in accounting reports since signing of an executory contract or issuance of a purchase order is not a completed transaction. Examples are long-term noncancelable contracts to purchase goods or services at specified prices and purchase contracts for fixed assets calling for payments during construction. A lease agreement is in some cases a form of commitment. Commitments call for disclosure of important factors surrounding the obligation including its amount, conditions, and timing. In Supplement A, Adaptec discloses commitments for the purchase of silicon wafers in note 7 of its financial statements. Two additional examples of commitments follow:

❖ ***Commitments and Contingent Liabilities*** In the normal course of business, there are various commitments outstanding and contingent liabilities that are properly not reflected in the accompanying financial statements. Losses, if any, resulting from these commitments are not anticipated to be material. The approximate amounts of such commitments are summarized below:

	In millions
Standby letters of credit	$ 2,400
Commercial and similar letters of credit	400
Commitments to extend credit*	17,300
Commitments to purchase futures and forward contracts	5,000
Commitments to purchase foreign and U.S. currencies	1,500

*Excludes credit card and other revolving credit loans.

Standby letters of credit include approximately $400 million of participations purchased and are net of approximately $300 million of participations sold. Standby letters of credit are issued to cover performance obligations, including those which back financial instruments (financial guarantees).

—Wells Fargo & Co.

> Company signed a patent license agreement with its former principal supplier of hand-held laser scanning devices. This agreement provides that the Company may manufacture and sell certain laser scanning products of its own design and that the Company pay minimum royalties and purchase minimum quantities of other products from that supplier.
>
> —Intermec Company

Deferred Credits or Income

Deferred credits (income) include a variety of items with varying characteristics. These items are often liabilities, but sometimes represent deferred income not yet earned. Companies sometimes use deferred credits to "manage" income. The difficulty in our analysis is compounded by a lack of agreement in accounting practice as to the exact nature of these items or their manner of presentation. Regardless of their nature or presentation, the key to our analysis rests in understanding the circumstances and transactions that spawned them.

Nature of Deferred Credits

Deferred credits span a range of categories. On one end are deferred credits like advances or billings on uncompleted contracts, unearned royalties and deposits, and customer service prepayments. The important characteristic of these items is their definite liability features. Although, as with advances of royalties, they can, after fulfilling certain conditions, find their way into income. Advances on uncompleted contracts are primarily means of financing this contractual work, and unearned deposits (like rent) are, as are customer service prepayments, security for performance of an agreement. These items are often more properly classified as distinct liabilities, yet are packaged with unlike items for reporting purposes. At the other end are deferred credits reflecting income or revenue received in advance. Companies earn these credits in future periods through the passage of time, the performance of services, or the delivery of goods. Examples are magazine subscription income representing receipts by magazine publishers of advance payment for long-term subscriptions, unearned rental income for receipt of advance rental payments, unearned finance charges, deferred profit on installment sales, deferred gain on sales-and-leaseback arrangements, and unrealized profit on lay-away sales. A typical case of deferred income from sales is reported as:

Deferred Credits of Companies

Other
Profit on sales
Unearned income
Deferred taxes
0 20 40 60 80 100
Percent

Source: *Accounting Trends & Techniques.*

> The company sells certain whiskey in barrels in bond under agreements which provide for future bottling. In prior years, profits on such transactions were reflected as of the date of sale. The present company policy is to treat such profits as deferred income until the whiskey is bottled and shipped.
>
> —Schenley Industries, Inc.

Deferred credits include a liability for future performance and often a potential profit component. Both are present in income received but not yet earned (e.g., subscription income). Deferred credits also include unearned finance charges that are already deducted but recognized in future periods with the passage of time. Also included are profits on installment sales that are deferred, not because they are unearned but because receivables from these sales are collected over a future time period. The preferred treatment is not to defer income on installment sales but to recognize them along with a provision for doubtful accounts.

Another category of deferred credits is so-called bargain purchase credits. *Bargain purchase credits* arise when the fair value of certain assets of an acquired company exceeds the consideration given (see Chapter 5). Companies often amortize these credits to income over an arbitrary period. These credits are benefits derived from presumably an advantageous acquisition. Companies often defer these benefits and recognize them in future income due to the desire to spread out, or smooth, their impact on income, and not because they are unearned.

Deferred Taxes

Deferred taxes are postponed tax effects attributed to temporary differences between taxable and accounting income. Deferred taxes are a complex and controversial topic, and often comprise the largest part of deferred credits. Deferred tax credits (or debits in reverse circumstances) arise from accounting tax allocation and the desire to match tax expense with pretax accounting income (see also Chapter 6).

To illustrate how deferred tax credits arise, consider a company electing accelerated depreciation for tax purposes and straight-line depreciation for accounting reports. Since depreciation is larger in earlier years for tax purposes, there are two consequences: (1) a tax deferral (savings) in early years, and (2) a tax "catch-up" in later years. These tax savings are temporary, and are accumulated as deferred taxes.

In practice, companies rarely pay deferred taxes in full. This is because as companies are expanding operations, and with inflation swelling nominal dollar amounts, there is accelerated depreciation on new facilities to balance—and often outweigh—the catch-up on older facilities. When companies' operations are decreasing, they are often unprofitable and, therefore, would not pay taxes.

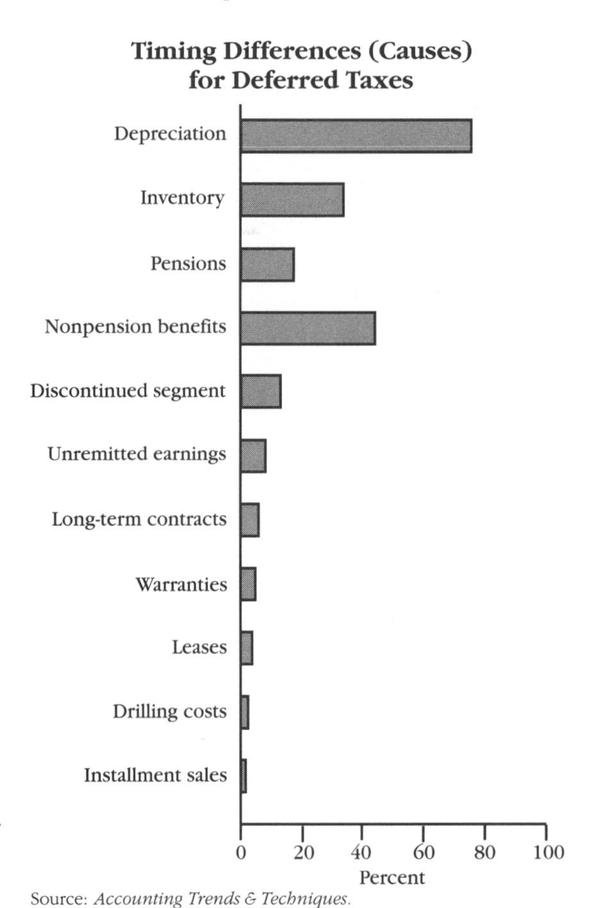

Source: *Accounting Trends & Techniques.*

Analysis Implications of Deferred Credits and Income

Our exposure to deferred credits highlights their unique and individual characteristics. Our analysis must reflect this and evaluate each item individually. The key to our analysis of deferred credits is a clear understanding of what spawned them. Items representing prepayments on services not yet performed or goods not yet delivered must be viewed as temporary sources of funds. For example, advances on contracts not yet executed serve as temporary financing for the supplier.

Our analysis of deferred income accounts includes items on their way to income. Examples are interest or deferred profit on installment sales that are earned with the passage of time and without incurring additional expense. We must not forget that certain deferred income accounts are not always comprised of pure income elements. An example is deferred subscription income representing advance payment for magazines not yet delivered. Earning subscription income typically requires paper, printing, editorial, and postage costs not usually provided for in the deferral. While items like advance subscriptions represent temporary financing, they are not sources of net income and can yield a net loss. Certain deferred income items lend themselves to income smoothing by management. The bargain purchase credit can smooth income over several years. And the ratable recognition of installment sales profit, motivated by concern for noncollection of sales, can smooth income.

One of the more difficult deferred credits for our analysis is deferred taxes. Its large magnitude heightens its importance. Deferred taxes often border between liabilities and equity. Deferred taxes often lack important characteristics of debt. Governments typically have no current claim on taxes nor is there a specific timetable for payment. While deferred taxes reflect forgone future deductibility of assets for tax purposes, its reduction to decrease tax expenses depends on future activities like asset acquisition and depreciation policies not entirely predictable. This uncertainty stresses why deferred taxes are not equity capital—they represent a postponement but not necessarily a savings of taxes. For our analysis, deferred taxes are often an important source of cash due to postponement of taxes, where the duration of postponement depends on factors like future growth or stability of the depreciable assets pool. Our assessment of these factors and their future likelihood is useful in analyzing deferred taxes. If we conclude that all or part of deferred taxes should be eliminated, we would make the following *analytical adjusting entry*:

Deferred Taxes (current and noncurrent credits)	X	
Deferred Taxes (current and noncurrent debits)		Y
Retained Earnings		Z

We can effect elimination of the annual provision for deferred taxes with the following adjusting entry:

Deferred Taxes	W	
Income Tax Expense		W

In certain cases, the debits and credits of this entry are reversed.

Off-Balance-Sheet Financing

Off-balance-sheet financing refers to the non-recording of certain financing obligations. We already have examined transactions that fit this mold—examples are operating leases that are indistinguishable from capital leases. In addition to these, there are other off-balance-sheet financing arrangements ranging from the simple to the highly complex. This is an ever-changing scenario, where as one requirement is brought in to better reflect the obligations from a certain off-balance-sheet financing transaction, new and innovative means are devised to take its place. One means to finance property, plant, and equipment is to have an outside party acquire them while a company agrees to use the assets and provide funds sufficient to service the debt. Examples of these arrangements are *through-put agreements,* where a company agrees to run a specified amount of goods through a processing facility, or *take-or-pay arrangements*, where a company guarantees to pay for a specified quantity of goods whether needed or not. A variation on these arrangements involves creating separate entities and then providing financing not to exceed 50 percent ownership (such as joint ventures or limited partnerships). Companies carry these variations as an investment at equity and do not consolidate them with the company's financial statements and, hence, exclude them from liabilities. Consider the following two practice conventions:

Avis Rent A Car set up a separate trust to borrow money to finance the purchase of automobiles that they then leased to Avis for its rental fleet. Because the trust is separate from Avis and its parent, the debt of about $400 million is kept off their balance sheets. The chief accounting officer of its parent company proclaimed: "One of the big advantages of off-balance-sheet financing is that it permits us to make other borrowings from banks for operating capital that we could not otherwise obtain." Two major competitors, Hertz and National Car Rental, bought rather than leased their rental cars.

Oil companies often resort to less than 50-percent-owned joint ventures as means to raise money for building and operating pipelines. While the debt service is the ultimate responsibility of the oil company, its notes simply report that the company might have to advance funds to help the pipeline joint venture meet its debt obligations if sufficient crude oil needed to generate the necessary funds is not shipped.

Another case involves companies financing inventory without reporting on their balance sheets the inventory or the related liability. These are referred to as *product financing arrangements* where a company sells and agrees to either repurchase inventory at a price equal to the original selling price plus carrying and related costs or sometimes guarantee a selling price to third parties. There are criteria for determining when these arrangements are "in substance" financing arrangements that are accounted for as a borrowing, and with repurchase costs treated as financing or holding expenses. A typical inventory financing agreement is disclosed as:

The Company entered into a five-year contract whereunder it agreed to purchase Scotch whiskey from a subsidiary of a British bank. The amount of the commitment is $28,279,000.

—Seagram Company

Guarantees with Off-Balance-Sheet Risk

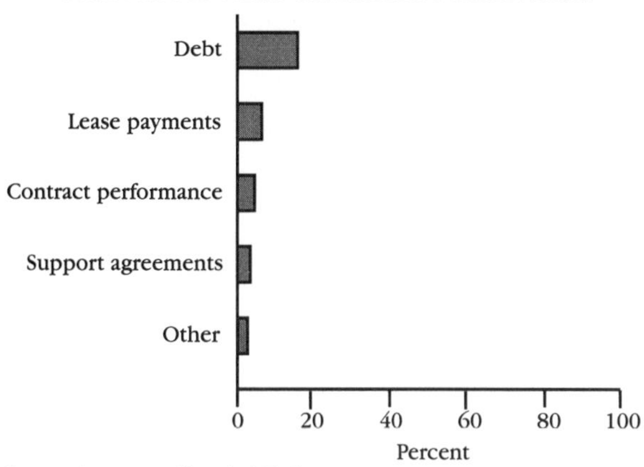

Source: *Accounting Trends & Techniques.*

Another means of off-balance-sheet financing is selling accounts receivable or other financial asset either with or without recourse. Reporting rules allow companies to sell their receivables with recourse (i.e., retaining risk of loss) and to record them as sales rather than as liabilities if they meet three criteria:[4]

- Seller is isolated from transferred assets.
- Seller surrenders effective control over transferred assets.
- Buyer has the right to pledge or exchange transferred assets.

If any one of these conditions is not met, the transfer of receivables is considered a loan with the receivables pledged as security. Companies are continuing to devise ways to not report obligations or to remove them from the balance sheet. Automakers and other major capital goods manufacturers have sold their receivables as backing for debt sold to the public. This "securitization" of loans removes these receivables (or mortgage loans in the case of savings and loan associations, or credit card receivables in the case of banks) and converts them into debt held by the public and backed by receivables. This enables companies to more quickly convert assets to cash, and to not fully record financing obligations. Companies need only report as liabilities the fraction of receivables they guarantee.

New and innovative financial instruments are emerging in response to deregulation, foreign exchange and interest rate volatility, tax law changes, and other factors. Many of these financial instruments hold considerable off-balance-sheet risks. Examples are outstanding loan commitments, standby and commercial letters of credit written, financial guarantees written, options written, and recourse obligations on receivables sold. Companies are required to disclose the following information about financial instruments with off-balance-sheet risk of accounting loss:

- Face, contract, or notional principal amount.
- Nature and terms of the instruments and a discussion of their credit and market risk, cash requirements, and related accounting policies.
- Accounting loss a company would incur if any party to the financial instruments failed completely to perform according to the terms of the contract, and the collateral or other security, if any, for the amount due proved of no value.
- Company's policy for requiring collateral or other security on financial instruments it accepts, and a description of collateral on instruments currently held.
- Information about significant concentrations of credit risk from an individual counterparty or groups of counterparties for all financial instruments.

These disclosure requirements extend only to credit and market risk. Adaptec's financial statements include a typical disclosure—see Concentration of Credit Risk in note 1 in Supplement A. Our analysis must continually be on the lookout for these and other off-balance-sheet obligations.

---

[4] See "Accounting for Transfers and Servicing of Financial Assets and Extinguishments of Liabilities," *Statement of Financial Accounting Standards No. 125* (Norwalk, Conn.: FASB, 1996).

Liabilities at the "Edge" of Equity

This section describes two items straddling liabilities and equity—redeemable preferred stock and minority interest.

Redeemable Preferred Stock

Our analysis must be alert to equity securities (typically preferred stock) that possess mandatory redemption provisions making them more akin to debt than equity. These securities require a company to pay funds at specific dates. A true equity security does not impose such requirements. Examples of these securities, under the guise of preferred stock, exist for many companies including Lockheed Corporation and Koppers Company. Tenneco's annual report (dates adapted) refers to its preferred stock's redemption provision as follows:

> The aggregate maturities applicable to preferred stock issues outstanding at December 31, Year 0, are none for the Year 1, $10 million for Year 2, and $23 million for each of the Years 3, 4, and 5.
>
> —Tenneco, Inc.

The Securities and Exchange Commission asserts that redeemable preferred stocks are significantly different from conventional equity capital and should *not* be included in shareholders' equity nor combined with nonredeemable equity securities. They also require disclosure of redemption terms and five-year maturity data. The accounting standards require disclosure of redemption requirements of redeemable stock for each of the five years subsequent to the balance sheet date. Companies whose shares are not publicly traded are not subject to SEC requirements, and can continue to report redeemable preferred stock as equity. Our analysis should treat them for what they are: an obligation to pay cash at a future date.

Minority Interest

Minority interest in consolidated companies is typically listed on the balance sheet between liabilities and equity, yet is not an immediate claim on company resources. Minority interest represents the proportionate stake of minority shareholders in a company's majority-owned subsidiary that is consolidated. Since the parent includes all net assets (i.e., assets less liabilities) of a consolidated subsidiary in its financial statements, it reports the minority's interest as a credit, or financing component, on the balance sheet. Discussion of the analytical treatment accorded minority interests is in Chapter 5.

Companies Reporting Minority Interest

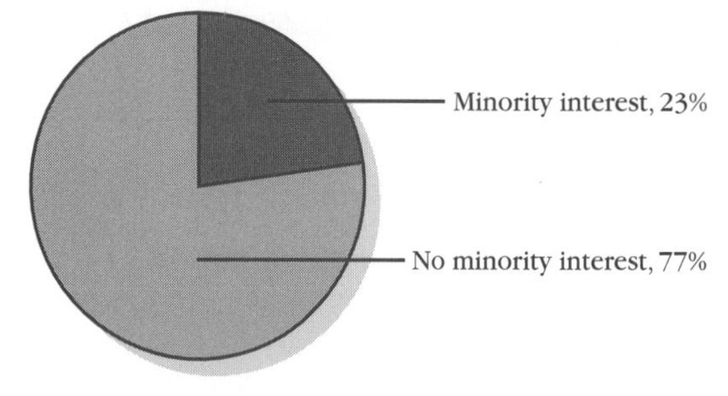

Source: *Accounting Trends & Techniques.*

SECTION 2: EQUITY FINANCING

Reporting for Shareholders' Equity

Our analysis must be aware of several measurement and reporting objectives underlying shareholders' equity including:

- Classifying and distinguishing among major sources of equity financing.
- Establishing rights for classes of shareholders and their priorities in partial or complete liquidation.
- Defining legal restrictions for distribution of equity funds.
- Reporting contractual, legal, managerial, and financial restrictions on distribution of retained earnings.
- Disclosing terms and provisions of convertible securities, stock options, and other arrangements involving future issuances of shares.

It is also important for us to distinguish between liability and equity instruments, especially when financial instruments have characteristics of both. Some of the more difficult questions that we must confront in our analysis include:

- Is a financial instrument like mandatory redeemable preferred stock or a put option written on a company's common stock—obligating a company to redeem them at specified amounts—a liability or equity instrument?
- Is a financial instrument like a stock purchase warrant or an employee stock option—obligating a company to issue its stock at specified amounts—a liability or equity instrument?
- Is a right to issue or repurchase a company's stock at specified amounts an asset or equity item?
- Is a financial instrument having features of *both* liabilities and equity sufficiently different from both to warrant separate presentation? If yes, what are the criteria for inclusion?

The following sections help us answer these and other issues confronting our analysis of financial statements. We first consider capital stock and then retained earnings.

Classification of Capital Stock

There are two basic types of capital stock: preferred and common. There are a number of different variations within each of these categories.

Companies with Preferred Stocks

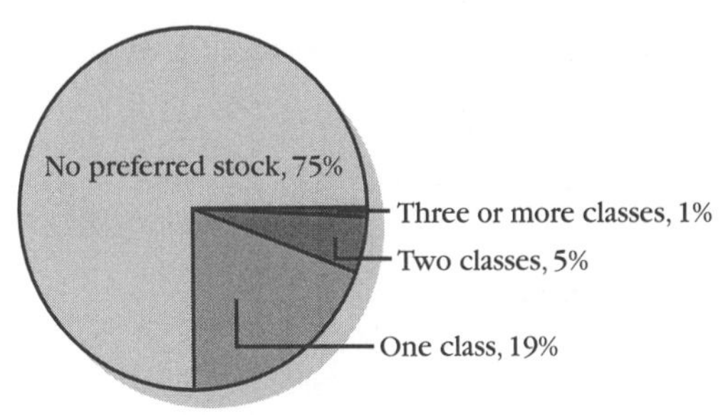

Source: *Accounting Trends & Techniques.*

Preferred Stock

Preferred stock is a special class of stock possessing preferences or features not enjoyed by common stock. The more typical features attached to preferred stock include:

- Dividend distribution preferences including participating and cumulative features.
- Liquidation priorities—especially important since the discrepancy between par and liquidation value of preferred stock can be substantial (General Aniline & Film Corporation had a preferred stock par value of $3.9 million versus a liquidation value of $85.7 million).

- Convertible (redemption) into common stock. The SEC requires separate presentation of these shares when preferred stock possesses characteristics of debt.
- Nonvoting rights. They can change with conditions like arrearages in dividends.
- Call provisions—usually protecting preferred shareholders against premature redemption (call premiums often decrease over time).
- Sinking fund provisions—infrequently established.

While often of higher priority, the preferred shareholders' rights to dividends are often fixed, but they can be cumulative, meaning they are entitled to arrearages (prior years) of dividends before common shareholders receive any dividends. Among preferred stock classes we find also a variety of preferences relating to dividend and liquidation rights. These features, and the fixed nature of their dividends, give preferred stock the appearance of liabilities. An important distinction between preferred shareholders and creditors is that preferred stock holders are typically not entitled to demand redemption of their shares. Nevertheless, there exist preferred stocks possessing set redemption dates that can include sinking funds—funds accumulated for expected repayment. Characteristics of preferred stock that would make them more akin to common stock are dividend participation rights, voting rights, and rights of conversion into common stock. Preferred stock often has a par value, but it need not be the amount at which it was originally issued.

NEW YORK STOCK EXCHANGE

Quotations as of 5 p.m. Eastern Time
Thursday, January 16, 1997

	52 Weeks Hi	52 Weeks Lo	Stock	Sym	Div	Yld %	PE	Vol 100s	Hi	Lo	Close	Net Chg
			-A-A-A-									
	31¼	17¾	AAR	AIR	.48	1.8	22	1819	27	26¼	26¼	– ⅝
s	20⅛	13½	ABM Indus	ABM	.40f	2.1	19	133	19¾	19½	19½	– ¼
	10⅜	9¼	ACM Gvt Fd	ACG	.90a	8.7	...	546	10⅜	10¼	10⅜	...
	7⅞	6⅝	ACM OppFd	AOF	.57	8.0	...	181	7¼	7⅛	7⅛	– ⅛
	9¼	8¼	ACM SecFd	GSF	.90	9.9	...	1517	9¼	9⅛	9⅛	– ⅛
	7¼	6	ACM SpctmFd	SI	.66	10.0	...	556	6⅝	6½	6⅝	+ ⅛
	12¾	10⅛	ACM MgmdInc	ADF	1.26	10.0	...	670	12⅝	12½	12⅝	...
	9⅞	8⅜	ACM MgdIncFd	AMF	.90	9.7	...	318	9⅜	9¼	9¼	– ⅛
	13¼	12	ACM MuniSec	AMU	.90	7.0	...	86	12⅞	12¾	12⅞	+ ⅛
	22½	14⅝	♣ACX Tch A	ACX		...	dd	325	19	18⅝	19	+ ⅛
	24¾	14	ADT	ADT		...	dd	3417	22⅞	22¾	22¾	...
	50⅛	21	♣AES Cp	AES		...	31	198	48⅝	47½	48½	+ ½
s	44	28¼	♣AFLAC	AFL	.40	.9	18	790	42⅞	42⅜	42½	– ½
s	31⅝	19¼	AGCO Cp	AG	.04	.1	12	2385	27⅛	26⅝	27⅛	+ ⅛
	22	17⅛	AGL Res	ATG	1.08f	5.1	15	799	21½	20⅞	21	– ⅜
	16⅞	8⅞	AgSvcAm	ASV		...	16	43	15⅞	15⅝	15⅞	+ ¼
	22¾	14¼	AJL PepsTr	AJP	1.44	9.4	...	1874	15½	14⅞	15⅜	+ ⅝
	23⅝	18⅞	♣AMLI Resdntl	AML	1.72	7.6	19	305	23⅛	22¾	22¾	– ¼
	46⅛	32⅞	♣AMP	AMP	1.00	2.4	21	4841	42¾	42	42⅜	– ¼
	97½	70½	AMR	AMR		...	17	13548	84½	83¼	83¾	+ ¼
	54	47⅛	♣ARCO Chm	RCM	2.80	5.6	12	87	50½	50¼	50¼	+ ⅛
	50½	33⅜	ASA	ASA	1.20	3.5	...	804	35	34⅜	34¾	+ ⅜
s	46¾	31⅝	AT&T	T	1.32	3.4	39	46829	38⅞	38	38⅜	– ½
n	33⅛	25¾	AXA ADR	AXA		...	...	194	32⅜	32⅛	32⅜	+ ⅛
s	61⅛	16¼	AamesFnl	AAM	.20	.5	23	3096	37¼	36⅜	37¼	+ 1⅛
n	25⅜	24¾	AbbeyNtl		.31p	...	...	14152	25¼	24 15/16	25⅛	– ⅛
	57⅜	38⅛	AbbotLab	ABT	.96	1.7	24	21372	55⅜	53⅞	55⅜	+ 2⅛
n	27	12⅝	Abercrombie A	ANF		...	...	709	15⅜	15	15⅛	+ ¼
	17⅜	12¼	Abitibi g	ABY	.40	...	...	1403	17⅜	17⅛	17⅛	– ¼
n	20⅛	14½	AC Nielsen	ART		...	...	2755	17	16⅝	16⅞	– ¼
	22½	13⅞	♣AcceptIns	AIF		...	9	103	19⅜	18⅝	18⅝	– ½
s	38	14 5/32	AccuStaff	ASI		...	49	8678	20⅝	20	20¼	– ⅛
	[illegible]	38	ACE Ltd	[illegible]	.72	1.2	[illegible]	[illegible]	59½	58½	58¾	– ½

Common Stock

Common stock is a class of stock representing ownership interest and bearing ultimate risks and rewards of company performance. Common stock represents **residual interests** having no preference, but reaping residual profits and assuming net losses. There is sometimes more than one class of common stock for major companies. The distinctions between common stock classes typically are differences in dividend, voting, or other rights. Common stock can carry a par value, if not, it is usually assigned a stated value. The par value of common stock is a matter of legal and historical significance; it usually has little substantive significance for our analysis.

Reporting of Capital Stock

Reporting of capital stock requires analysis and explanation of changes in the number of capital shares. This information is disclosed in the financial statements or related notes. Some reasons for changes in capital shares include:

Sources of increases in capital stock outstanding:

- Sales of stock.
- Conversion of debentures or preferred stock.
- Issuances pursuant to stock dividends or splits.
- Issuances of stock in acquisitions or mergers.
- Issuances pursuant to stock options or warrants exercised.

Companies with Par, No-Par, and Stated Value Common Stock

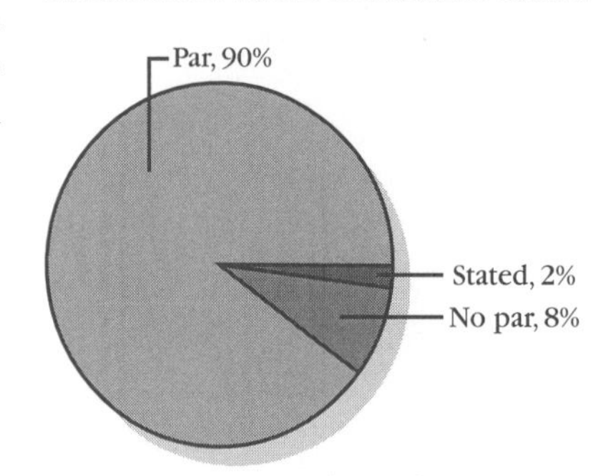

Source: *Accounting Trends & Techniques.*

Sources of decreases in capital stock outstanding:

- Purchases and retirements of stock.
- Purchases of treasury stock.
- Reverse stock splits.

Another important aspect of our analysis of the reporting of capital stock is the options held by others that, when exercised, cause the number of shares outstanding to increase and dilute ownership. These options include:

- Conversion rights of debentures or preferred stock into common.
- Warrants entitling holders to exchange them for stock under specified conditions.
- Stock options with compensation and bonus plans calling for issuances of capital stock over a period of time at prices fixed in advance. Examples are qualified stock option plans and employee stock ownership plans.
- Commitments to issue capital stock. An example is merger agreements calling for additional consideration contingent on the occurrence of an event like achieving a specific earnings level.

The importance of these disclosures is to alert us to the potential increase in the number of shares outstanding. In Supplement A, note 6 in the financial statements of Adaptec includes details on several stock plans. The extent of dilution in earnings and book value per share depends on factors like the amount received or other rights given up when converting securities. Alerted by the use of ever more complex securities, we must recognize that dilution represents a very real cost for a company—a cost that is given little formal recognition in financial statements. We examine the impact of dilution on earnings per share in the appendix to Chapter 6, while effects on the computation of book value are considered later in this chapter.

Contributed Capital

Contributed (or paid-in) capital is the total financing received from shareholders in return for capital shares. Contributed capital is usually divided into two parts. One part is assigned to the par or stated value of capital shares, the remainder is reported as **Additional Paid-in Capital** (or Paid-In Capital in Excess of Par or Stated Value, Additional Capital, or Paid-In Capital). In sum, these accounts signify the amounts paid in by shareholders for financing business activities. Other accounts in the contributed capital section of shareholders' equity arise from charges or credits from a variety of capital transactions, including (1) sale of treasury stock, (2) capital changes arising from business combinations, (3) capital donations, often shown separately as donated capital, (4) stock issuance costs and merger expenses, and (5) capitalization of retained earnings by means of stock dividends. Our analysis includes examining and assessing changes in capital accounts.

Companies Reporting Treasury Stock

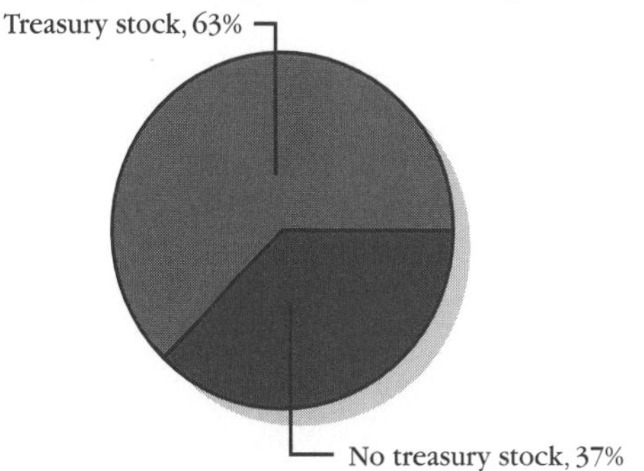

Source: *Accounting Trends & Techniques.*

Treasury Stock

Treasury stock represents shares of a company's stock reacquired after having been previously issued and fully paid. Purchasing treasury stock *reduces* both assets and shareholders' equity. Treasury stock is not an asset; it is a *contra equity account.* Treasury stock is typically recorded at *cost,* and the most common method of presentation is to deduct treasury stock cost from the total of shareholders' equity. When companies record treasury stock at par, they typically report it as a contra to its related class of stock. In rare cases, companies reserving treasury stock for purposes like profit sharing, contingent compensation, or deferred compensation plans, or for purposes of acquiring another company, sometimes report treasury stock among assets.

Analysis Implications for Capital Stock

Items comprising shareholders' equity do not have a marked effect on income determination and, as a consequence, do not seriously impact the analysis of income. For our analysis, the more relevant information relates to the composition of the capital accounts and to their applicable restrictions. Composition of equity is important because of provisions affecting the residual rights of common shares. Such provisions include dividend participation rights, conversion rights, and the variety of options and conditions that characterize complex securities frequently issued under merger agreements—most of which dilute common equity. It is important also that we know how to reconstruct and explain changes in these capital accounts.

ANALYSIS VIEWPOINT . . *You are the family "money manager"*

Your family has some extra money and you are responsible for investing it. You narrow your search to one company with two alternative securities: common stock and 10 percent preferred stock. The return for both securities (dividends and price appreciation) over the past few years is consistently around 10 percent. In which security do you invest your family's money?

Retained Earnings

Retained earnings is the earned capital of a company. It represents generally the accumulation of undistributed earnings or losses of a company since inception. This contrasts with the Capital Stock and Additional Paid-In Capital accounts that constitute contributed capital. Retained earnings is the primary source of dividend distributions to shareholders. Amounts distributed by charges to other accounts are not strictly dividends. Although several states permit distributions to shareholders from Additional Paid-In Capital, these distributions represent capital distributions.

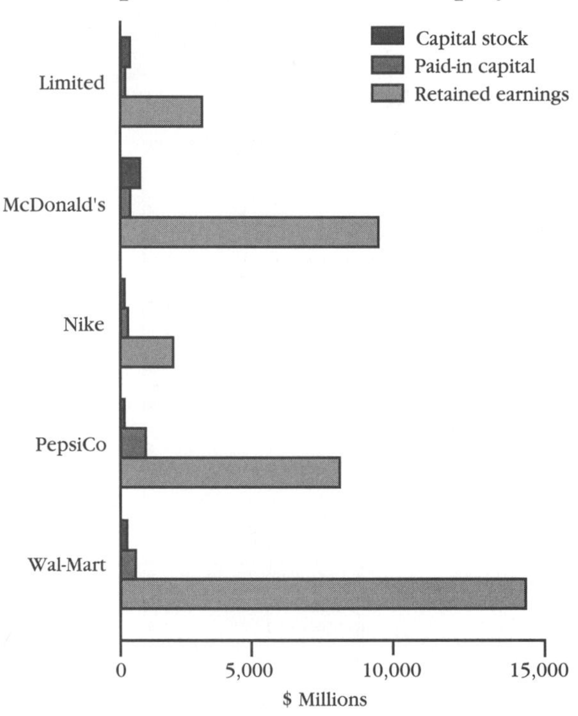

Cash and Stock Dividends

A **cash dividend** is a distribution of cash to shareholders. It is the most common form of dividend and, once declared, is a liability of a company. A similar form of dividend is the *dividend in kind* (or property dividend). These dividends are payable in the assets of a company, in goods (e.g., gold bars), or in the stock of another corporation. Such dividends should be valued at the fair market value of the assets distributed.

Ranchers Exploration and Development Corp. distributed a dividend in kind with gold bars. Dresser Industries, Inc., paid its dividend in kind with "a distribution on one INDRESCO share for every five shares of the Company's common stock."

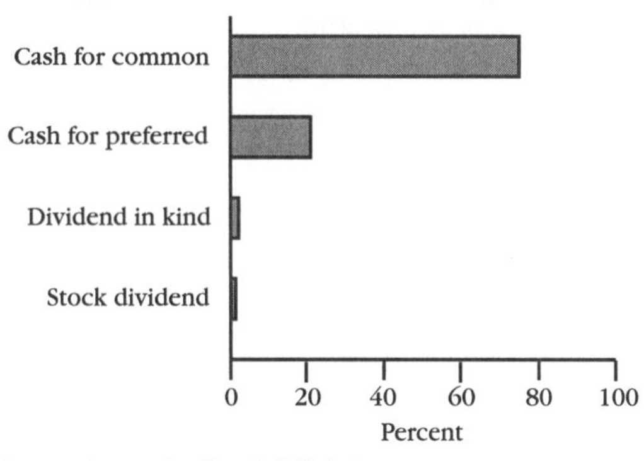

Source: *Accounting Trends & Techniques.*

A **stock dividend** is a distribution of a company's own shares to shareholders on a pro rata basis. It represents, in effect, a permanent capitalization of earnings. Shareholders receive additional shares in return for the reallocation of retained earnings to capital accounts. Accounting for *small* (or *ordinary*) *stock dividends*, typically less than 20 to 25 percent of shares outstanding, requires the stock dividend be valued at its fair market value on the date of declaration. This requirement is presumably designed to limit the number of shares issued as stock dividends. *Large stock dividends* (or "split-ups effected in the form of a dividend"), typically exceeding 25 percent of shares outstanding, require the stock dividend be valued at the par value of shares issued. We must not be misled into attaching substantive value to stock dividends. Companies sometimes encourage such inferences for their own self-interests.

Wickes Companies, Inc., announced a stock dividend "in lieu of the quarterly cash dividend." Management asserted this stock "dividend continues Wickes' 88-year record of uninterrupted dividend payments."

CORPORATE DIVIDEND NEWS

Dividends Reported January 15

Company	Period	Amt.	Payable date	Record date
REGULAR				
AAR Corp	Q	.12	3–5–97	2–3
Am Recreation Cnt	Q	.06½	4–8–97	3–18
Apogee Enterp	Q	n.09	2–12–97	1–28
n-Payable on pre-split shares.				
BHC Financial	Q	.03	2–14–97	2–1
Battle Mtn Gold	S	.02½	2–18–97	2–13
Battle Mtn Gold pf	Q	.81¼	2–18–97	2–3
Carnival Corp	Q	.11	3–14–97	2–28
Chaparral Steel	Q	.05	2–28–97	2–3
Clorox Co	Q	.58	2–14–97	1–31
Colonial Gas	Q	.32½	3–14–97	2–28
Community Inv Bcp	Q	.10	2–10–97	1–24
Dow Jones & Co	Q	.24	2–28–97	2–3
Dun & Bradstreet	Q	.22	3–10–97	2–20
Inco Ltd pfdE	Q	.68¾	3–3–97	2–3
Lindsay Mfg	Q	.05	2–28–97	2–14
MercuryFinance	Q	.07½	3–3–97	2–17
MerrLynch 6.5%strp	Q	.78	2–15–97	1–31
Modine Mfg	Q	.17	3–6–97	2–24
New Milford Bk&Tr	Q	.04½	2–7–97	1–27
Newhall Land&Farm	Q	.10	3–10–97	2–7

Prior Period Adjustments

Prior period adjustments are primarily corrections for errors in prior periods' financial statements. Companies exclude them from the income statement and report them as an adjustment (net of tax) to the beginning balance of Retained Earnings.

Appropriations of Retained Earnings

Appropriations of retained earnings are reclassifications of retained earnings for specific purposes. Through management action, and with board of directors' approval in compliance with legal requirements, companies can appropriate retained earnings. Appropriations of retained earnings (sometimes referred to as reserves) recognize that a company does not intend to distribute these amounts as dividends, but rather to reserve them for litigation, plant expansion, self-insurance, and other business contingencies. Appropriations do not set aside cash. Appropriations do not relieve the income statement of these potential charges.

Appropriations are reclassified as unappropriated retained earnings when their purpose is achieved. An appropriation of retained earnings at an amount equal to the cost of treasury stock purchased is an example of an appropriation established under legal requirements of certain states. This appropriation is reclassified as retained earnings once the treasury stock is sold, retired, or otherwise disposed of.

Restrictions on Retained Earnings

Restrictions (or covenants) on retained earnings are constraints or requirements on the retention of a certain retained earnings amount. A common and important restriction involves limitations on a company's distribution of dividends. Bond indentures and loan agreements are typical sources of restrictions. Companies often disclose restrictions in notes. Two examples stemming from debt indentures follow:

> Under the most restrictive of these agreements, approximately $33,000,000 was available for distribution of earnings to shareholders. Presently, the Company has no plans to declare any dividends.
>
> —Leslie Fay Companies

Allied Van Lines includes the following note:

> *Restrictive loan covenants.* The various loans include restrictive covenants which provide as follows: That the Company must maintain consolidated tangible net worth of $28,000,000 plus 50 percent of cumulative net income . . . ; current assets not less than 115 percent of current liabilities at all times and 120 percent at year-end; long-term debt not more than 35 percent of consolidated tangible net worth; income available for fixed charges not less than 125 percent of fixed charges; guarantees of loans made to or leases entered into by agents or owner-operators cannot exceed $3,500,000; the Company must maintain consolidated net working capital of not less than $6,000,000; and the sum of cash flow (principally working capital provided from operations) plus current notes receivable must be at least 130 percent of current maturities of long-term debt.
>
> —Allied Van Lines

Analysis Implications for Retained Earnings

Our analysis of restrictions imposed on distribution of retained earnings by loan or other agreements usually reveals a company's latitude in areas like dividend distributions or in maintaining required levels of working capital. These restrictions also reveal a company's bargaining strength and standing in credit markets. Knowledge of restrictive covenants enables us to assess a company's risk of default on these provisions.

ANALYSIS VIEWPOINT . . . *You are the shareholder*

You own common stock of US Enterprise Corporation. The price of US Enterprise stock has doubled in the past 12 months, and is currently selling at $66. US Enterprise today announces a 3:1 "stock split effected in the form of a dividend." How do you interpret this announcement?

Book Value per Share

Book value per share is the per share amount resulting from a company's liquidation at amounts reported on its balance sheet. *Book value* is conventional terminology referring to net asset value—total assets reduced by claims against them. The *book value of common stock* is equal to the total assets less liabilities and claims of securities senior to the common stock (such as preferred stock) at amounts reported on the balance sheet, but can also include unbooked claims of senior securities. A simple means of computing book value is to add up the common stock equity accounts and reduce this total by any senior claims not reflected in the balance sheet (including preferred stock dividend arrearages, liquidation premiums, or other asset preferences to which preferred shares are entitled).

Computation of Book Value per Share

Several cases portraying the measurement and relevance of book value per share follow.

Case 1

The shareholders' equity section of Kimberly Corporation for periods ending in Years 4 and 5 are reproduced below:

	Year 5	*Year 4*
Preferred stock,		
7% cumulative, par value $100 (authorized 4,000,000 shares; outstanding 3,602,811 shares)	$ 360,281,100	$ 360,281,100
Common stock		
Par Value $16⅔ per share (authorized 90,000,000 shares; outstanding 54,138,137 shares at December 31, Year 5, and 54,129,987 shares at December 31, Year 4)	902,302,283	902,166,450
Retained earnings	2,362,279,244	2,220,298,288
Total shareholder's equity	$3,624,862,627	$3,482,745,838

Note: Preferred stock is nonparticipating and callable at 105. Dividends for Year 5 are in arrears.

Our calculation of book value per share for both common and preferred stock at the end of Year 5 follows:

	Preferred +	Common =	Total
Preferred stock*(@$100)	$360,281,100		$ 360,281,100
Dividends in arrears (7%)	25,219,677		25,219,677
Common stock		$ 902,302,283	902,302,283
Retained earnings (net of amount attributed to dividend in arrears)		2,337,059,567	2,337,059,567
Total	$385,500,777	$3,239,361,850	$3,624,862,627
Divided by number of shares outstanding	3,602,811	54,138,137	
Book value per share	$107.00	$59.84	

* The call premium does not normally enter into computation of book value per share because the call provision is at the option of the company.

Case 2

The shareholders' equity section from the balance sheet of California Allied Corporation on June 30, Year 1, is reproduced below:

Preferred stock—authorized 200,000 shares, issued and outstanding 100,000 shares, par value $100; 6% cumulative, nonparticipating	$ 10,000,000
Common stock—authorized 375,000 shares, issued and outstanding 200,000 shares, par value $100	20,000,000
Capital contributed in excess of par value	5,000,000
Retained earnings (deficit)	(7,000,000)
Total stockholders' equity	$ 28,000,000

Note: Preferred stock has a liquidation value of $105 and is callable at $110. No dividends have been declared or paid by the company for the prior two years for either the preferred or common stock. Preferred stock has a preference on assets in liquidation.

Our computation of book value per share for California Allied's common and preferred stock as of June 30, Year 1, follows:

	Preferred	Common
Par value	$10,500,000	$ 20,000,000
Dividends in arrears	1,200,000	
Net deficit (all applicable to common stock)		(3,700,000)
Total	$11,700,000	$ 16,300,000
Divided by number of shares outstanding	100,000	200,000
Book value (equity) per share	$117.00	$81.50

Explanations:
1. Liquidation value for preferred shares ($105) is used; call value does not enter into the computation of book value per share.
2. Preferred shares are entitled to two years' dividends (12% of $10,000,000 = $1,200,000).
3. Preference of assets for preferred shares means that the deficit is wholly applicable to the common.
4. Computation of net deficit:

Retained earnings (deficit)	$(7,000,000)
Paid-in capital	5,000,000
Dividends in arrears	(1,200,000)
Preferred liquidation premium	(500,000)
Net deficit	$(3,700,000)

Cases 1 and 2 illustrate the major adjustments in book value per share computations arising from rights and priorities of securities senior to common stock. In most cases, these are attributed to premiums and liquidation priority rights of various classes of preferred stock. Care must be taken in determining the liquidation value of preferred stock. Some companies have preferred stock issues outstanding that provide a right to very substantial liquidation premiums far exceeding their par value. These liquidation premiums can substantially impact book value of common stock and other junior securities.

Case 3

The listing application of Glen Alden Corporation includes the following details regarding its book value computation:

Equity per share:

Equity per share of Glen Alden, Warner, and the Surviving Corporation, based on the initial redemption values of the preferred stocks and on the consolidated balance sheets of Glen Alden and Warner at December 31 and August 27, respectively, and the pro forma combined balance sheet follows:

Initial redemption per share values	*Capital stocks*	*Glen Alden, December 31*	*Warner, August 27*	*Pro forma surviving corporation*
$ 52.50	Senior stock	$52.50		$ 52.50
$107.00	Class B senior stock			$100.70
$110.00	Preferred stock	$88.89		None
$ 90.00	Class C stock	$72.73		None
None	Common stock	None	$19.51	None

Based on the pro forma combined balance sheet, there would be no book value attributable to the preferred stock, class C stock, and common stock of the Surviving Corporation when the equity applicable to the senior stock and the class B senior stock is considered at aggregate initial redemption value. The aggregate initial redemption value of the senior stock and class B senior stock exceeds total pro forma stockholders' equity by approximately $141,816,000.

The pro forma initial redemption and liquidation prices of the preferred stocks in the aggregate ($343,821,848) exceed their stated values by $296,179,211, and such excess exceeds the aggregate amount of common stock and surplus by approximately $141,816,000. Upon liquidation, the senior stock is first in order of preference followed by the class B senior stock. The preferred stock and class C stock are junior to the class B senior stock, but rank on a parity with each other. There are no restrictions upon surplus arising out of such excess.

Case 3 shows the liquidation premium of the senior stocks is sufficiently large to eliminate the entire residual book value of the junior preferred and common stock issues. We recognize the problem posed by preference rights substantially in excess of stated par values in the case of involuntary liquidation. Under this circumstance, the profession recommends the aggregate liquidation preference be prominently disclosed in the equity section of the balance sheet—including disclosure of call prices and dividend arrearages. In practice, the rules involving "dilutive securities" for computing earnings per share are not typically applied when computing book value per share. Nevertheless, our analysis should be aware of dilutive securties for book value computations.

Case 4

Global Technology Corporation's summarized balance sheet is reproduced below:

Assets less current liabilities	$1,000,000
Convertible debentures	100,000
Net assets	$ 900,000
Common shares	100,000

Note: Debentures are convertible into 20,000 shares of common stock. The company has warrants outstanding entitling holders to buy 10,000 shares at $6 per share. Stock options to buy 10,000 shares at an average price of $8 per share are also outstanding.

Our conventional method of computing book value per share yields a value of $9 per share (Net assets/Common shares = $900,000/$100,000). If we give effect to possible conversions in outstanding securities, our book value computation looks as follows:

Net assets (per above)	$ 900,000
Add convertible debentures	100,000
Proceeds from exercise of warrant (10,000 × $6)	60,000
Proceeds from exercise of stock options (10,000 × $8)	80,000
Adjusted net asset value	$1,140,000
Common shares outstanding	100,000
Add:	
Conversion of debentures	20,000
Exercise of warrants	10,000
Exercise of options	10,000
Adjusted number of common shares	140,000
Book value per share ($1,140,000/140,000)	$8.14

The effect from conversion of the debentures and options on book value depends on the conversion terms. If stock is converted at prices below conventional book value per share, the effect is *dilutive* as the above case illustrates. If conversion is at prices above conventional book value, the effect is *antidilutive.* Applying conservatism in our computation of book value per share, we ignore the antidilutive effects (i.e., those enhancing book value per share).

Relevance of Book Value per Share

Book value plays an important role in the analysis of financial statements. Recall the accounting-based stock valuation formula from Chapter 2:

$$V_t = BV_t + \frac{NI_{t+1} - (k \times BV_t)}{(1+k)} + \frac{NI_{t+2} - (k \times BV_{t+1})}{(1+k)^2} + \ldots + \frac{NI_{t+n} - (k \times BV_{t+n-1})}{(1+k)^n} + \ldots$$

From a valuation perspective, the analysis of financial statements begins with the book value figure, to which we add an estimate of future earnings. An estimate of the future profitability of a firm can be based directly on the earnings capacity of its asset base. There are several uses of book value per share in analysis of financial statements. These applications include:

- Book value, with potential adjustments, is frequently used in assessing merger terms.
- Book value approximates the rate base measure for public utilities.
- Analysis of companies comprised of mainly liquid assets (finance, investment, insurance, and banking institutions) relies extensively on book values.
- Analysis of high-grade bonds and preferred stock attaches considerable importance to asset coverage.

Our analysis must recognize the accounting considerations entering into the computation of book value per share. These include the following:

- Carrying values of assets, particularly long-lived assets like property, plant, and equipment, are usually reported at cost and can differ significantly from market values. Carrying values vary according to the accounting principles used. For instance, in times of rising prices, carrying values of inventories using the LIFO costing method are lower than under the FIFO method.
- Intangible assets of enormous value are often not reflected in book value, nor are contingent liabilities with a reasonable probability of occurrence.

Criticism of the use of book value can be at least partly attributed to deficiencies in accounting measurements. The exclusion from book value of most goodwill, patents, franchises, and other intangibles does not encourage its use and is unjustified. If book value is used in comparing the relative value of two companies engaged in merger negotiations, adjustments like the following are often required for useful comparisons:

- Carrying values of assets are adjusted to market values.
- Differences in applying accounting principles are adjusted for.
- Unrecorded intangibles are recognized.
- Contingent liabilities are assessed and recognized.

Other adjustments are also often necessary. For example, if preferred stock has characteristics of debt, it is appropriate to capitalize it as debt at the prevailing interest rate. We must also remember that unproductive assets are a real drain on scarce resources, often dragging down earnings due to necessary maintenance and management. Book value is a valuable analytical tool, but we must apply it with discrimination and understanding.

GUIDANCE ANSWERS TO ANALYSIS VIEWPOINTS

You Are the Labor Negotiator

To resolve this situation, we must realize that while postretirement benefits are accrued as liabilities on the company's balance sheet (and as expenses on the income statement), their funding is less than guaranteed. It is apparent from management's counteroffer that this company does not fully fund postretirement benefits—this is not a required part of accounting for these benefits. This situation can yield substantial losses in employee welfare if the company becomes insolvent and cannot be forced to fund these commitments. As labor negotiator, you must trade off desires for higher current wages with *both* postretirement benefits and assurance in receiving those benefits. It is also in a company's interest to limit recorded liabilities, although increasing funding commitments is not desirable as it depletes the company's available cash resources. Your task as labor's representative is to acquire both promises for postretirement benefits and assurance in actual funding of these benefits. Consequently, while the parameters of management's offer are likely negotiable, it must be viewed as a genuine offer.

You Are the Family "Money Manager"

Your decision involves aspects of both risk and return. From the perspective of risk, preferred stock is usually a senior claimant to the net assets of the company. This means that in the event of liquidation, preferred stock receives preference before any funds are paid to common shareholders. From the perspective of return, the decision is less clear. Your common stock return involves both cash dividends and price appreciation, while preferred stock return equates primarily to cash dividends. If recent returns are reflective of future returns, then your likely preference is for preferred stock given its equivalence in returns but reduced risk exposure.

You Are the Shareholder

Your interpretation of a stock split is likely positive. This derives from the "information signal" usually embedded in this type of announcement. A company wants to generally support its stock price. A lower price usually makes the stock more accessible to a broader group of buyers and can reduce transaction costs in purchasing stock. However, too low a price can create its own problems. Consequently, a split announcement is perceived as a signal of management's expectation (forecast) that the company will perform at the same or better level into the future. We should recognize that there is no tangible shareholder value in the split announcement itself—there is no income to shareholders. However, there is transfer of a balance from retained earnings to common stock.

QUESTIONS

3–1. Describe the nature of the two major types of current liabilities.

3–2. Describe the major disclosure requirements regarding terms of short-term debt.

3–3. Describe conditions required to demonstrate the ability of a company to refinance its short-term debt on a long-term basis.

3–4. Explain how bond discounts and premiums usually arise. Describe how they are accounted for.

3–5. Both the conversion feature of debt and that of warrants attached to debt aim at increasing the attractiveness of debt securities and lowering their interest cost. Describe how the costs of these two similar features are accounted for.

3–6. Describe the major disclosure requirements for long-term obligations.

3–7. Identify and explain any concerns when a company includes short-term bank debt in its current liabilities.

3–8. Explain how our analysis of financial statements evaluates a company's liabilities, both present and contingent.

3–9. *a.* Describe the criteria for classifying leases by a *lessee.*
b. Provide a summary of accounting for leases by a *lessee.*

3–10. *a.* Identify the different classifications of leases by a *lessor*. Describe the criteria for classifying each lease type.
b. Explain the accounting procedures for leases by a *lessor.*

3–11. Describe the provisions concerning leases involving real estate.

3–12. Explain the major disclosures required by both lessees and lessors.

3–13. Discuss the implications of lease accounting for the analysis of financial statements.

3–14. Companies use various financing methods to avoid reporting debt on the balance sheet. Identify and describe some of these financing methods.

3–15. Describe the criteria a company must meet before a transfer of receivables with recourse can be booked as a sale rather than as a loan.

3–16. Explain the following under contemporary financial reporting standards for pensions:

a. Accumulated benefit obligation.

b. Projected benefit obligation.

3–17. Accounting for postretirement employee benefits draws on the accounting for pensions, with some important differences. Explain these differences.

3–18. Discuss the required disclosures for postretirement benefit obligations.

3–19. *a.* Explain a loss contingency. Provide examples.

b. Explain the two conditions necessary before a company charges a provision for a loss contingency to income.

3–20. Describe what types of equity securities are similar to debt.

3–21. Discuss into what categories reserves and provisions can be usefully subdivided for purposes of financial statement analysis.

3–22. Explain why our analysis must be alert to the accounting for reserves for future costs and losses.

3–23. Distinguish between different kinds of deferred credits appearing on a balance sheet. Discuss how to analyze these accounts.

3–24. Describe the nature of deferred tax credits. Explain how we should interpret deferred taxes.

3–25. Describe the disclosure requirements for financial instruments with off-balance-sheet risk of accounting loss.

3–26. Identify objectives of the classifications and the footnote disclosures associated with the equity section of the balance sheet. Explain the relevance of these disclosures to our analysis of financial statements.

3–27. Identify the features of preferred stock that make it similar to debt. Identify the features that make it more like common stock.

3–28. Explain the importance of disclosing the liquidation value of preferred stock, if different from par or stated value, for our analysis.

3–29. Presidential Realty Corporation reports the following regarding its distributions paid on common stock: "The cash distributions on common stock were charged to Paid-In Surplus because the parent company has accumulated no earnings (other than its equity in undistributed earnings of certain subsidiaries) since its formation."

a. Explain whether these cash distributions are dividends.

b. Speculate as to why Presidential Realty made such a distribution.

3–30. Explain why the accounting for small stock dividends requires that the fair market value, rather than the par value, of the shares distributed be charged against retained earnings.

3–31. Identify what types of items can be treated as prior period adjustments.

3–32. Some companies present "minority interests in subsidiary companies" between the long-term debt and equity sections of a consolidated balance sheet; others present them as part of shareholders' equity.

a. Describe a minority interest.

b. Indicate where on the consolidated balance sheet it belongs. Discuss what different points of view these differing presentations represent.

3–33. Explain book value per share. Describe how to compute book value per share. Discuss its significance.

(CFA Adapted)

3–34. Describe relevant uses of book value in financial analysis.

3–35. Describe the accounting considerations entering into computation of book value per share and discuss their relevance for our analysis.

3–36. Indicate adjustments that are sometimes necessary to render book value per share comparable across two different companies.

EXERCISES

Exercise 3–1
Interpreting and Analyzing Debt Disclosures

Refer to the financial statements of Quaker Oats in Supplement A.

a. Determine the amount of long-term debt paid during Year 11.

b. Total debt increased by $217 million in Year 10. Describe the major cause for this increase.

c. Analyze and discuss the relative mix of debt financing for Quaker Oats.

Exercise 3–2
Understanding Accounting for Leases by the Lessee

On January 1, Year 8, Von Company entered into two noncancellable leases for new machines to be used in its manufacturing operations. The first lease does not contain a bargain purchase option and the lease term is equal to 80 percent of the estimated economic life of the machine. The second lease contains a bargain purchase option and the lease term is equal to 50 percent of the estimated economic life of the machine.

Required:

a. Explain the justification for requiring lessees to capitalize certain long-term leases. Do not limit your discussion to the specific criteria for classifying a lease as a capital lease.

b. Describe how a lessee accounts for a capital lease at inception.

c. Explain how a lessee records each minimum lease payment for a capital lease.

d. Explain how Von should classify each of the two leases. Provide justification.

(AICPA Adapted)

Exercise 3–3
Analyzing and Interpreting Deferred Tax Liabilities

On December 29, Year 7, Mother Prewitt's Handmade Cookies Corporation acquired a computer-controlled chocolate chip milling machine. Due to differences in tax and financial accounting, depreciation for tax purposes was $150,000 more than reported in published financial statements. This difference increases deferred taxes by $60,000. During the same year, Mother Prewitt sold $200,000 worth of cookies on an installment contract, and recognized the resulting $100,000 profit immediately. For tax purposes, $80,000 of the $100,000 profit will be recognized in the next accounting year. This transaction increases deferred taxes for Year 7 by an additional $32,000.

Required:

The deferred tax items confronted in this case do not reflect similar economic fundamentals—specifically, regarding a liability or a valuation adjustment. Explain how the two items are different.

(CFA Adapted)

Exercise 3–4
Distinguishing between Capital and Operating Leases

Capital leases and operating leases are two major classifications of leases from a lessee's perspective.

Required:

a. Describe how a lessee accounts for a capital lease both at inception of the lease and during the first year of the lease. Assume the lease transfers ownership of the property to the lessee by the end of the lease.

b. Describe how a lessee accounts for an operating lease both at inception of the lease and during the first year of the lease. Assume the lessee makes equal monthly payments at the beginning of each month of the lease. Describe any changes in the accounting when rental payments are not made on a straight-line basis.

Note: Do not discuss the criteria for distinguishing between capital and operating leases.

(AICPA Adapted)

Exercise 3–5

Analyzing and Interpreting Sales-Type and Financing Leases

Sales-type leases and direct financing leases are two common types of leases from a lessor's perspective.

Required:

Compare and contrast a sales-type lease with a direct financing lease on the following dimensions:

a. Gross investment in the lease.
b. Amortization of unearned interest income.
c. Manufacturer's or dealer's profit.

Note: Do not discuss the criteria for distinguishing between sales-type, direct financing, and operating leases.

(AICPA Adapted)

Exercise 3–6

Recognizing Unrecorded Liabilities for Analysis

Consider the following excerpt from an article published in *Forbes*:

> The Supersolvent—No longer is it a mark of a fuddy-duddy to be free of debt. There are lots of advantages to it. One is that you always have plenty of collateral to borrow against if you do get into a jam. Another is that if a business investment goes bad, you don't have to pay interest on your mistake.
>
> Debt-free, you don't have to worry about what happens if the prime rate goes to 12 percent again. You might even welcome it. You could lend out your own surplus cash at those rates.

The article went on to list 92 companies reporting no more than 5 percent of total capitalization in noncurrent debt on their balance sheets.

Required:

Explain how so-called "debt-free" companies (in the sense used by the article) can possess substantial long-term debt or other unrecorded noncurrent liabilities. Provide examples.

(CFA Adapted)

Exercise 3–7

Interpreting Disclosures for Loss Contingencies

Nearly all companies confront loss contingencies of various forms.

a. Describe what conditions must be met for a loss contingency to be accrued with a charge to income.
b. Explain when disclosure is required, and what disclosures are necessary, for a loss contingency that does not meet criteria for accrual of a charge to income.

Exercise 3–8

Understanding Shareholders' Equity and Book Value

Refer to the financial statements of Campbell Soup in Supplement A.

Required:

a. Describe what causes the $101.6 million increase in shareholders' equity for Year 11, and the $86.5 million decrease in Year 10.
b. Compute the book value of common stock at the end of Year 11.
c. What inferences can you draw from Campbell's book value?

Exercise 3–9

Analyzing Shareholders' Equity and Computing Book Value

Refer to the financial statements of Quaker Oats in Supplement A.

Required:

a. Explain the cause of the $116.5 million decrease in shareholders' equity for Year 11 and the $119.6 million decrease in Year 10.

b. Compute the book value of both common stock and preferred stock at the end of Year 11.

c. What inferences can you draw from Quaker Oats book values?

Exercise 3–10

Understanding and Interpreting Secret Reserves and Watered Stock

It is often asserted that using the LIFO inventory costing method during an extended period of rising prices, and the expensing of all human resource costs, are among accepted accounting practices helping create "secret reserves."

Required:

a. Describe a secret reserve. Explain how companies create or increase such reserves.

b. Explain the basis for saying the two specific practices cited create secret reserves.

c. Discuss the possibility of creating a secret reserve in connection with accounting for a liability. Explain and give an example.

d. Describe objections to the creation of secret reserves.

e. "Watered stock" is arguably the opposite of a secret reserve.

1. Explain the nature of watered stock.
2. Describe the general circumstances where watered stock can arise.
3. Discuss steps that can be taken to eliminate "water" from a firm's capital structure.

(AICPA Adapted)

Exercise 3–11

Interpreting Shareholders' Equity Transactions

Ownership interests in a corporation are customarily reported in the balance sheet under shareholders' equity and in the statement of shareholders' equity.

Required:

a. List the principal transactions or items reducing the amount of retained earnings. (Do not include appropriations of retained earnings.)

b. The shareholders' equity section of the balance sheet makes a distinction between contributed capital and earned capital. Discuss why this distinction is important.

c. There is frequently a difference between the purchase price and sale price of treasury stock. Yet, practitioners agree that a corporation's purchase or sale of its own stock cannot result in a profit or loss to the corporation. Explain why corporations do not recognize the difference between purchase and sale price as a profit or loss.

Exercise 3–12

Understanding Capital Stock

Capital stock is a major component of a corporation's equity. The term capital stock embraces both common and preferred stock issued by a corporation.

Required:

a. Identify the basic rights inherent in ownership of common stock, and explain how owners exercise them.

b. Describe preferred stock. Discuss various preferences often afforded preferred stock.

c. In our analysis and interpretation of various equity securities of a corporation, it is important to understand certain terminology. Describe the following equity items:

1. Treasury stock.
2. Legal capital.
3. Stock right.
4. Stock warrant.

Exercise 3–13 Pension Calculations

Use present value tables or computations to verify all amounts referred to in the A. Worker illustration in Exhibit 3.3.

PROBLEMS

Problem 3–1 Interpreting Notes Payable and Lease Disclosures

Refer to the financial statements of Campbell Soup Company in Supplement A.

a. Campbell Soup Company has zero coupon notes payable outstanding.
   1. Indicate the amount due noteholders on the maturity date of these notes.
   2. The liability for these notes is lower than its maturity value. Describe how this liability is reported in future years.
   3. Ignoring dollar amounts, prepare the annual journal entry that Campbell Soup Company makes to record the liability for accrued interest.

b. The note on leases reports future minimum lease payments under capital leases as $28.0 million and the present value of such payments as $21.5 million. Identify which amount is actually paid in future years.

c. Identify where in the financial statements Campbell Soup reports the payment obligation concerning operating leases of $71.9 million.

Problem 3–2 Capital Lease Implications for Financial Statements

On January 1, Year 1, Burton Company leases equipment from Nelson Company at an annual lease rental of $10,000. The lease term is five years, and the lessor's interest rate implicit in the lease is 8 percent. The lessee's incremental borrowing rate is 8.25 percent. The useful life of the equipment is five years, and it is estimated its residual value equals its removal cost. Annuity tables indicate that the present value of an annual lease rental of $1 (at 8 percent rate) is $3.993. The fair value of leased equipment equals the present value of rentals.

Required

Assume the lease is capitalized and:

a. Prepare entries required by Burton Company for Year 1.

b. Compute and illustrate the effect on the income statement for the year ended December 31, Year 1, and for the balance sheet as of December 31, Year 1.

c. Construct a table showing payments of interest and principal made every year for the five-year lease term.

d. Construct a table showing expenses charged to the income statement for the five-year lease term if the equipment is purchased. Show a column for (1) amortization, (2) interest, and (3) total expenses.

e. Discuss the income and cash flow implications from this capital lease.

Problem 3–3 Explaining and Interpreting Leases

On January 1, Borman Company, a lessee, entered into three noncancelable leases for new equipment identified as: Lease J, Lease K, and Lease L. None of the three leases transfers ownership of the equipment to Borman at the end of the lease term. For each of the three leases, the present value at the beginning of the lease term of the minimum lease payments, excluding that portion of the payments representing executory costs such as insurance, maintenance, and taxes to be paid by the lessor, including any profit thereon, is 75 percent of the excess of the fair value of the equipment to the lessor at the inception of the lease over any related investment tax credit retained by the lessor and expected to be realized by the lessor.

The following additional information is distinct to each lease:

- Lease J does not contain a bargain purchase option; the lease term is equal to 80 percent of the estimated economic life of the equipment.
- Lease K contains a bargain purchase option; the lease term is equal to 50 percent of the estimated economic life of the equipment.

- Lease L does not contain a bargain purchase option; the lease term is equal to 50 percent of the estimated economic life of the equipment.

Required:

a. Explain how Borman Company should classify each of these three leases. Discuss the rationale for your answer.

b. Identify the amount, if any, Borman should record as a liability at inception of the lease for each of these three leases.

c. Assuming that Borman makes the minimum lease payments on a straight-line basis, describe how Borman should record each minimum lease payment for each of these three leases.

d. Assess accounting practice in accurately portraying the economic reality for each lease.

(AICPA Adapted)

Problem 3–4

Interpreting Accounting for Bonds

One means for a corporation to generate long-term financing is through issuance of noncurrent debt instruments in the form of bonds.

Required:

a. Describe how to account for proceeds from bonds issued with detachable stock purchase warrants.

b. Contrast a serial bond with a term (straight) bond.

c. For a five-year term bond issued at a premium, explain why amortization in the first year of the life of the bond differs using the effective interest method of amortization versus the straight-line method. Include in your discussion whether the amount of amortization in the first year of the life of the bond is higher or lower using the effective interest method versus the straight-line method.

d. When a bond issue is sold between interest dates at a discount, prepare the journal entry made and explain how subsequent amortization of bond discount is affected. Include in your discussion an explanation of how the amounts of each debit and credit are determined.

e. Describe how to account for and classify the gain or loss from reacquisition of a long-term bond prior to its maturity.

f. Assess accounting for bonds in our analysis of financial statements.

Problem 3–5

Interpreting Accounting for Bonds

On November 1, Year 5, Abbott Company sells its five-year, $1,000 face value, 11 percent term bonds dated October 1, Year 5, at a discount yielding an effective annual interest rate (yield) of 12 percent. Interest is payable semiannually, and the first interest payment date is April 1, Year 6. Abbott uses an acceptable method of amortizing bond discount. It incurs bond issue costs in preparing and selling the bond issue.

On December 1, Year 5, Abbott sells its six-year, $1,000 face value, 9 percent nonconvertible bonds with detachable stock warrants at an amount exceeding the sum of the face value of the bonds and the fair value of the warrants.

Required:

a. Identify what factors determine that the 11 percent term bonds are sold at a discount. Explain.

b. Describe how all items related to the 11 percent term bonds (except cash) are reported/disclosed in a balance sheet prepared immediately after the term bond issue is sold, and for a balance sheet prepared at December 31, Year 5.

c. Identify the period of time for which Abbott amortizes the bond discount.

d. Compare the straight-line and effective interest methods of amortization. Explain which of the two methods is preferable.

e. Describe how Abbott should account for the proceeds from sale of the 9 percent nonconvertible bonds with detachable stock purchase warrants. Explain.

(AICPA Adapted)

Problem 3–6

Book Value, Financial Statement Analysis, and Business Valuation

Mother Prewitt's Handmade Cookie Corporation (MPH), relying on forecasts of increasing cookie consumption by aging baby boomers, constructed a highly sophisticated manufacturing facility. Unfortunately for MPH, recent medical findings encourage a shift in consumer preferences to high-fiber bran products and have resulted in lower cookie consumption. Following recent years' losses, the company is being offered for sale. You are asked to consult on the purchase of MPH. The current year's balance sheet follows:

Assets	
Current assets	$14,000,000
Plant & equipment (net)	14,000,000
Total assets	$28,000,000
Stockholders' Equity	
Preferred stock—authorized 200,000 shares, issued 100,000, par value $150, 5% cumulative, nonparticipating, liquidation value of $160, callable at $165	$15,000,000
Common stock—authorized 300,000 shares, issued 200,000 shares, par value $75	15,000,000
Capital contributed in excess of par value	100,000
Retained earning (deficit)	(2,100,000)
Total stockholders' equity	$28,000,000

Note: Preferred dividends are two years in arrears.

Required:

a. Calculate the book value per share of MPH common stock.

b. Describe the adjustments you might make to book value to arrive at an estimate of the fair market value of MPH common stock in your analysis.

(CFA Adapted)

Problem 3–7

Computing Book Value per Share

Fox Corporation is organized on January 1, Year 1, with the following capital structure:

10% cumulative preferred stock, par and liquidation value $100; authorized, issued, and outstanding 1,000 shares	$100,000
Common stock, par value $5; authorized 20,000 shares; issued and outstanding 10,000 shares	50,000

Fox's net income for the year ended December 31, Year 1, is $450,000, and no dividends are declared.

Required:

Compute Fox's book value per common share at December 31, Year 1. Describe the relevance of book value in your analysis.

Problem 3–8

Computing Book Value for Preferred and Common Stock

Grey, Inc., is organized on January 2, Year 4, with the following capital structure:

10% cumulative preferred stock, par value $100 and liquidation value $105; authorized, issued, and outstanding 1,000 shares	$100,000
Common stock, par value $25; authorized 100,000 shares; issued and outstanding 10,000 shares	250,000

Grey's net income for the year ended December 31, Year 4, is $450,000, and no dividends are declared.

Required:

a. Compute Grey's book value per preferred share at December 31, Year 4.

b. Compute Grey's book value per common share at December 31, Year 4.

c. Discuss the relevance of these book values for analysis purposes.

Problem 3–9

Interpreting Stock Prices and Their Link to Financial Statements

On a recent day, the stock of Superior Oil Corporation was being traded on the New York Stock Exchange for $1,492, while Getty Oil Company stock was trading at $64.

Required:

a. Explain how Superior Oil Corp. stock could be selling for a much larger price than Getty stock.

b. Indicate whether you can conclude anything about the relative profitability of these two companies from their stock prices.

c. On the previous day, Superior Oil stock was selling at $1,471, while Getty Oil sold for $62. Indicate which stock experienced the greater price increase.

d. If you purchased Getty Oil at $62 and sold it the next day for $64, describe what effect your purchase and sale of stock would have on the financial statements of Getty Oil Company.

CASES

Case 3–1

Analyzing and Interpreting Adaptec Liabilities

Use the 1996 annual report of Adaptec, Inc., in Supplement A to answer the following questions.

a. Identify Adaptec's three largest categories of liabilities. Identify which of these liabilities require recognition of interest expense.

b. Reconcile activity in the Noncurrent Debt account for 1996 using T-account analysis.

c. Determine the fair value of Adaptec's noncurrent debt according to its note 1. Identify factors that might change this value.

d. Describe the composition of Adaptec's Accrued Liabilities account using its note 2.

e. Identify any arrangement Adaptec has to borrow funds.

f. Describe the key features of Adaptec's noncurrent debt.

g. Examine Adaptec's note 7 regarding commitments.

1. Determine whether Adaptec is in compliance with the disclosure requirements for operating leases.
2. Identify any future outflows of cash not recorded on Adaptec's balance sheet.

Case 3–2

Analyzing and Interpreting Adaptec Shareholders' Equity

Use the 1996 annual report of Adaptec, Inc., in Supplement A to answer the following questions.

a. Calculate the book value per share of Adaptec common stock for fiscal year-ends 1993 through 1996.

b. Adaptec's common shares traded at $12¾, $18⅛, $33, and $48¼ at fiscal year-ends 1993 through 1996, respectively.

1. Calculate the price-to-book-value ratio at each of the above dates.
2. What do the observed price-to-book ratios indicate about investors' expectations regarding future profitability? *Hint:* Answer this question with reference to the accounting-based equity valuation model described in Chapter 2.

c. According to Adaptec's statement of shareholders' equity, identify reasons for issuing additional common shares over the last three years. Determine at what per share amounts Adaptec issued the shares.

d. Determine how many common shares Adaptec repurchased as treasury stock for the three years 1994, 1995, and 1996. Determine the price at which Adaptec repurchased the shares. Determine the price for which they were originally sold. Did Adaptec record a gain or loss on these treasury shares? Explain.

e. Identify the par value of Adaptec's common shares. Explain.
f. Determine the number of common shares authorized, issued, and outstanding at the end of fiscal years 1995 and 1996.

INTERNET ACTIVITIES

Internet 3–1

Analyzing Shareholders' Equity and Computing Book Value

Access one of the financial statement databases available on the Internet (http://www.mhhe.com/business/accounting/wild). Retrieve current financial statements of a company selected by either you or your instructor.

Required:

a. Explain changes in the company's shareholders' equity for both the current and prior years.
b. Compute the book value of common stock (and of any preferred stock) at the end of the current year.
c. What do these two analyses tell you about the company?

Internet 3–2

Analyzing and Interpreting Liabilities

Access one of the financial statement databases available on the Internet (http://www.mhhe.com/business/accounting/wild). Retrieve current financial statements of a company selected by either you or your instructor.

Required:

a. Identify the three largest categories of liabilities. Determine which of these liabilities requires recognition of interest expense.
b. Reconcile activity in the Long-Term Debt account using T-account analysis.
c. Describe the composition of any "accrued liabilities" accounts.
d. Identify any arrangement this company has to borrow funds.
e. Describe key features of this company's noncurrent liabilities.
f. Identify any future outflows of cash not recorded on this company's balance sheet.

Internet 3–3

Analyzing and Interpreting Shareholders' Equity

Access one of the financial statement databases available on the Internet (http://www.mhhe.com/business/accounting/wild). Retrieve current financial statements of a company selected by either you or your instructor.

Required:

a. Calculate book value per share of common stock for the most recent two fiscal year-ends.
b. Identify the common stock price at the date of the most recent two fiscal year-ends.
   1. Calculate price-to-book ratios using your answers to *a* and *b*.
   2. Write a report describing what these price-to-book ratios suggest about investors' expectations regarding future profitability. *Hint*: Answer this question with reference to the accounting-based equity valuation model described in Chapter 2.

c. Estimate the average issue price per share for common stock.
d. Identify any par or stated value for common stock.
e. Determine the number of common stock authorized, issued, and outstanding at the end of the most recent two fiscal years.

Internet 3–4

Analysis of Liabilities

Access one of the financial statement databases available on the Internet (http://www.mhhe.com/business/accounting/wild). Retrieve current financial statements of three companies in different industries selected by either you or your instructor.

Required:

a. Describe the major similarities and differences in these companies' liabilities.

b. Write a report comparing the components comprising these companies' liabilities.

Internet 3–5

Analysis of Shareholders' Equity

Access one of the financial statement databases available on the Internet (http://www.mhhe.com/business/accounting/wild). Retrieve current financial statements of three companies in different industries selected by either you or your instructor.

Required:

a. Describe the main similarities and differences in these companies' shareholders' equity.

b. Write a report comparing the components comprising these companies' shareholders' equity.

C H A P T E R

4

Analyzing Investing Activities

A Look Back

Our analysis of accounting components underlying financial statements began with financing activities. We saw how financing activities interact with operating and investing activities. We focused on analyzing and interpreting financing activities, and the importance of creditor versus equity financing.

A Look at This Chapter

Our analysis of accounting components extends to investing activities. We explore in detail how we analyze assets like cash, marketable securities, receivables, derivatives, inventories, property, equipment, and intangibles. We provide an understanding of how these numbers reflect on company performance and financing requirements. We see how adjustments to these numbers improve our analysis.

A Look Ahead

Chapter 5 extends our analysis of investing activities to intercompany and international activities. Analyzing and interpreting a company's investing activities requires consideration of these institutional and economic aspects. Chapters 6 and 7 focus on operating activities.

Learning Objectives

- Explain cash management and its interpretation for financial statement analysis.
- Analyze financial statement disclosures for marketable securities.
- Analyze receivables and provisions for uncollectible accounts.
- Describe analytical adjustments to receivables to reflect risk of ownership.
- Analyze disclosures for financial instruments.
- Interpret effects of inventory methods for analysis under varying business conditions.
- Analyze financial statement disclosure for noncurrent investments.
- Interpret valuations and disclosures for plant assets and natural resources.
- Describe and analyze intangible assets and their disclosures.
- Explain and interpret deferred charges for financial statement analysis.
- Analyze statements for unrecorded and contingent assets.

PREVIEW OF CHAPTER 4

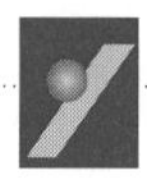

Assets are the driving force of profitability for companies. Assets produce revenues that compensate workers, repay lenders, reward owners, and fund growth. **Current assets** are resources or claims to resources readily convertible to cash. Major current assets include cash or cash equivalents, marketable securities, receivables, derivative financial instruments, inventories, and prepaid expenses. Our analysis of current assets provides insights into a company's liquidity. **Liquidity** is the length of time until assets are converted to cash. It is an indicator of a company's ability to meet financial obligations. The less liquid a company, the lower its financial flexibility to pursue promising investment opportunities, and the greater its risk of failure. **Noncurrent assets** are resources or claims to resources expected to benefit more than the current period. Major noncurrent assets include property, plant, equipment, intangibles, investments, and deferred charges. Our analysis of noncurrent assets provides insights into a company's solvency and operational capacity. **Solvency** refers to the ability of a company to meets its long-term (and current) obligations. **Operational capacity** is the ability of a company to generate future profits. This chapter shows how we use financial statements to better assess liquidity, solvency, and operational capacity using asset values, and to critically evaluate a company's financial performance and prospects. We describe the accounting practices underlying the measurement and reporting of current and noncurrent assets. We discuss the accounting for these assets and its implications for analysis of financial statements. This chapter gives special attention to various analytical adjustments helping us better understand current and future prospects. The content and organization of this chapter are as follows:

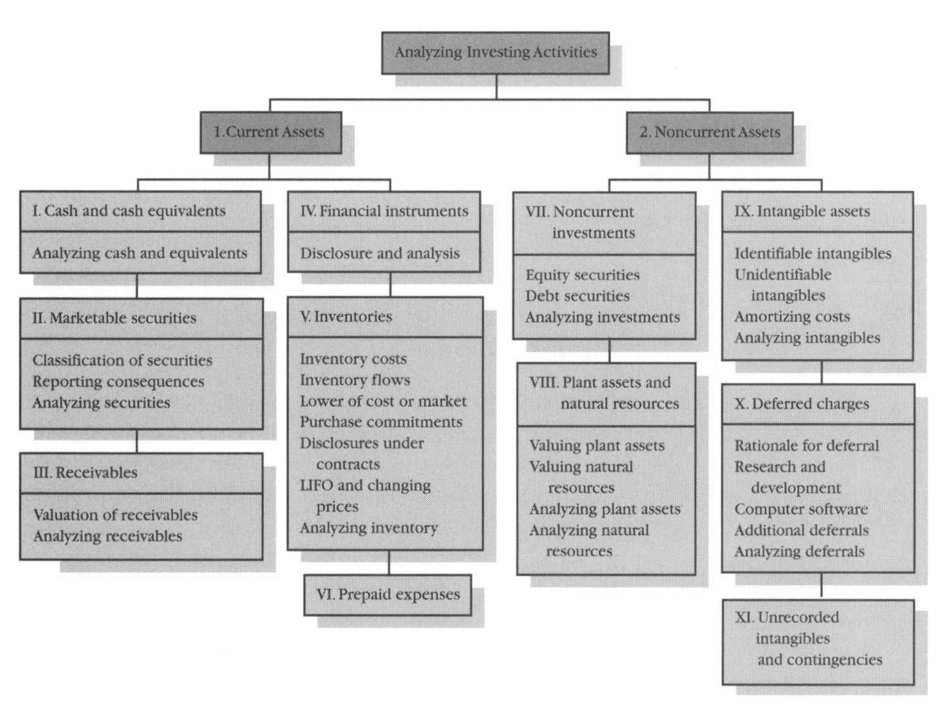

SECTION 1: CURRENT ASSETS

Cash and Cash Equivalents

Cash and Cash Equivalents as a Percentage of Assets

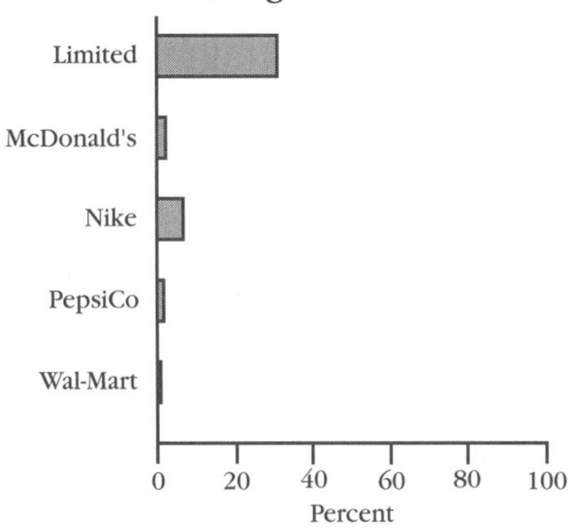

Source: Annual reports.

The vast majority of companies classify their most liquid assets in the cash and cash equivalents category. **Cash**, the most liquid asset, includes currency, available funds on deposit, money orders, and certified and cashier checks. **Cash equivalents** are highly liquid, short-term investments that are (1) readily convertible into cash, and (2) so near maturity they have minimal risk of price changes due to interest rate movements. These investments usually possess original maturities of three months or less. Examples of cash equivalents are treasury bills, commercial paper, and money market funds, often serving as temporary repositories of excess cash.

Cash does not present serious valuation problems because of its liquidity. However, cash requires special precautions against theft and defalcation, and care must be taken in analyzing and interpreting cash and cash equivalents when restrictions are placed on their disposition. Companies separately report temporary investments for special purposes like plant expansion or restricted balances for meeting sinking fund requirements, and typically show them among long-term investments. Restricted balances are not included in current assets since they are not available for paying current obligations. Similarly, companies usually segregate on the balance sheet cash set aside for debt service or maintenance under a bond indenture.

Cash and cash equivalents represent the starting point, and the finish line, of an operating cycle. An **operating cycle** is the circle of time from the commitment of cash for purchases until the collection of receivables resulting from sale of goods or services. The operating cycle is important in classifying assets and liabilities as current or noncurrent. Exhibit 4.1 portrays graphically a company's operating cycle. A company measures realization of a transaction by its sale and later by ultimate conversion of the consideration received into cash. Except for fixed commitments that are paid in cash, cash represents the point in the operating cycle where management has maximum discretion with deployment and use of resources.

Operating Cycle for Selected Industries

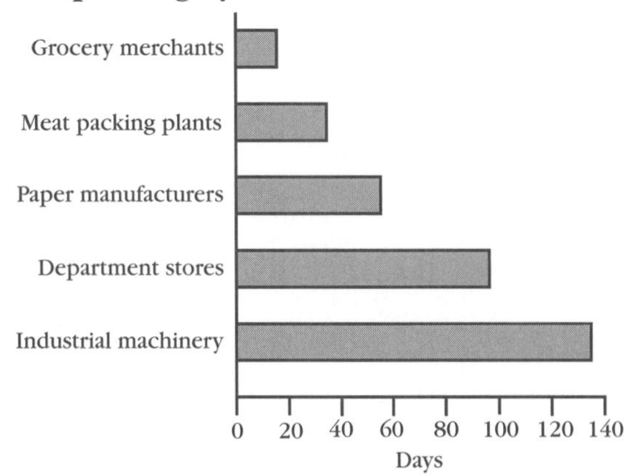

Source: Sonen, L. A. "Cash Conversion Cycle and Corporate Profitability" *Journal of Cash Management*, July/August 1993, p. 55.

Analysis Implications of Cash and Cash Equivalents

Compensating balances constitute part of a demand deposit maintained to support existing borrowing arrangements and to assure future credit availability. Accounting practice does not regard compensating balances maintained under a loan agreement as a restriction on cash because banks generally honor checks drawn against this balance. However, compensating balances must be segregated on the balance sheet if they are *legally restricted*. Compensating balances *not legally restricted* are disclosed in notes to financial statements. Although informal, such arrangements are of

EXHIBIT 4.1 Operating Cycle

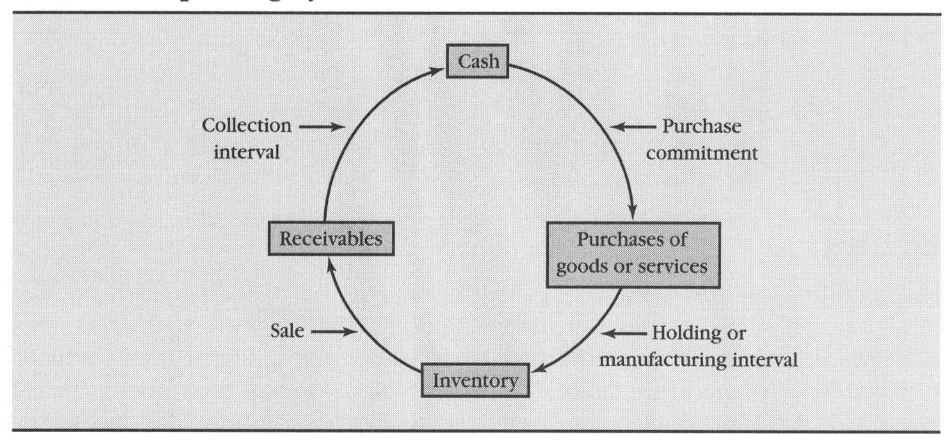

considerable practical significance. Accordingly, in assessing liquidity, we must consider the repercussions of potentially breaking a tacit agreement with a financial institution. This can involve loss of a credit source and can impact future financing. A company's exposure in this area is measured by the ratio of restricted cash to total cash.

In reporting cash, companies typically deduct float. **Float** refers to checks issued but not yet paid by a bank. Our analysis must be aware of the practice in some companies of including float in the cash balance and including outstanding checks in accounts payable.

Financial statements of Dominion Resources report a cash balance of $58.8 million. Among liabilities, Dominion reports "Cash due to banks" of $59.7 million, reflecting checks issued but not yet presented for payment.

This presentation of their float is not common but is in accordance with accepted practices forbidding companies from lumping together money they are owed by their bank (an asset) and money they owe their bank (a liability) unless the right of offset exists. In Dominion's statement of cash flows it reconciles net income to a negative cash balance of $900,000—this is inconsistent with its balance sheet presentation and with standards governing financial statements.

We must also be aware of "window-dressing" a cash balance. Consider the following case:

Blockbuster Entertainment reports a cash balance of $9 million. Management's Discussion and Analysis section reveals this entire cash amount is borrowed.

There is no rule prohibiting Blockbuster from window-dressing its cash balance in this manner.

ANALYSIS VIEWPOINT . . . *You are the investment analyst*

The management of Georgia-Pacific Corporation in its annual report claims "it is more important to focus on the cash flow generated by our business than on net income." Do you agree with management's claim?

Marketable Securities

Marketable securities, sometimes called *investment securities*, are often temporary repositories of excess cash held as marketable debt and/or equity securities. They can also include funds awaiting investment in plant, equipment, and other assets, or funds reserved for payment of liabilities. Companies typically report them among current assets. However, marketable securities that are temporary investments of cash specifically designated for special purposes such as plant expansion or the meeting of requirements under sinking fund provisions are reported among long-term investments.

Marketable debt securities are securities representing a creditor relationship with another entity; examples are corporate bonds, government bonds, and municipal securities. **Marketable equity securities** are securities representing ownership interest in another entity; examples are common stock and certain preferred stock. One important feature of accounting practice governing marketable securities is the requirement that companies carry many of these investments on the balance sheet at fair market value. We discuss implications of this requirement below.

Classification of Marketable Securities

Investments in debt and equity securities appear in financial statements under one of five categories:

- **Trading securities** are either debt or equity securities purchased with the intent to sell in the near future.
- **Held-to-maturity securities** are debt securities that management intends and is able to hold to maturity.
- **Available-for-sale securities** are either debt or equity securities that management does not intend to sell in the near future nor hold to maturity.
- **Influential securities** are equity investments representing between 20 percent and 50 percent ownership of the voting stock of another entity.
- **Controlling securities** are equity investments representing more than 50 percent ownership of the voting stock of another entity. These securities do not appear in consolidated statements.

Transfers of securities between categories are accounted for at fair market value. This fair value requirement ensures that a company transferring securities recognizes (in its income statement) changes in fair value and cannot conceal them by transferring securities to another category that does not recognize fair value changes in the income statement.

Financial Statement Consequences

Accounting guidelines for marketable securities differ depending on the type of security. We describe the effects for financial statements, categorized by security type, in this section.

Trading Securities

Trading securities are current assets. Companies report them at their aggregate fair value at the balance sheet date. Changes in fair value are directly reported in the income statement. In the case of equity trading securities, companies recognize dividends as income when received. For debt trading securities, interest income is accrued daily.

Held-to-Maturity Securities

Held-to-maturity securities are noncurrent assets except for the reporting period immediately prior to maturity when they are current assets. Companies report them in the balance sheet at amortized cost. Interest income, including amortization of any premium or discount, is accrued daily.

Available-for-Sale Securities

Available-for-sale securities are either current or noncurrent assets, depending on management's intentions regarding sale. Companies report them at fair value on the balance sheet date. Changes in fair value are directly reported as a separate component of stockholders' equity—bypassing the income statement. With equity securities, companies recognize dividends as income when received. For debt securities, interest income, including amortization of any premium or discount, is accrued daily.

Influential Securities

Influential securities are noncurrent assets unless their sale is imminent. Companies report them using the equity method, which we discuss later.

Controlling Securities

Controlling securities are not reported in consolidated financial statements.

Analysis Implications of Marketable Securities

There are a number of important items in accounting for investment securities that our analysis must consider. The importance of these items depends, to a certain extent, on the level (dollar magnitude) of a company's investment in debt and equity securities. Accordingly, analyzing these investments is crucial when examining financial institutions and insurance companies—these companies trade extensively in and hold large blocks of marketable securities as part of their normal operations.

Classification of investment securities (and its accounting treatment) depends on "management intent." **Management intent** refers to management's expressed objectives regarding disposition of securities. This intent rule can result in identical debt securities being classified as trading, held-to-maturity, or available-for-sale (in combination or in all three categories). This introduces arbitrariness in how changes in market values of securities are accounted for. Our analysis should assess the credibility of management intent by looking for "premature" sale of held-to-maturity securities. If premature sales occur, they undermine management's credibility. There is also disagreement on whether the manner for classifying securities is best for determining whether companies report changes in market values in income or not. While practice requires companies to report at fair value transfers of marketable securities from one category to another, category switching still permits some leeway in determining current and future income. Companies are *not* required to disclose the classification of specific investment securities in the balance sheet. Consequently, our analysis must examine notes to the statements to make this determination. For both available-for-sale and held-to-maturity securities, companies are encouraged to report aggregate fair value and unrealized holding gains or losses. In our analysis of the income statement effects of marketable securities, we look at companies' required disclosures on proceeds from sales, gains and losses from transfers, and unrealized holding gains or losses.

Accounting for investment securities is arguably one-sided. That is, if a company reports its investment securities at fair value, why not its liabilities? For many companies, especially financial institutions, asset positions are not managed independent of liability positions. As a result, accounting can yield earnings volatility exceeding what the true underlying economics suggest. This consideration led accounting regulators to exclude unrealized holding gains and losses on available-for-sale securities from net income. Excluding holding gains and losses from income affects our analysis of the income statement, but does not affect analysis of other statements. We should also treat with skepticism the amortization of any discount on available-for-sale debt securities (i.e., write-up of bond by crediting income) when evidence suggests they trade at a discount due to factors such as doubt of ultimate collectibility. We must be aware of these cases since interest income, including amortization, impacts net income while changes in fair values of available-for-sale debt securities bypass income and are reported directly in stockholders' equity.

Another concern is *gains trading* with available-for-sale and held-to-maturity securities. As noted, unrealized gains and losses on available-for-sale and held-to-maturity securities are excluded from net income. Companies can increase income by selling those securities with unrealized gains, and holding those with unrealized losses. In addition, in evaluating sales of securities, we must be aware of the various methods for determining securities' "cost" (e.g., specific identification, average cost) that affect income and assets.

Still another concern is the arbitrary and inconsistent definition of equity securities. For instance, convertible bonds are excluded from equity securities. Yet convertible bonds often derive all or most of their value from the conversion feature and are more akin to equity securities than debt. Accordingly, our analysis should question excluding convertible securities from equity. Redeemable preferred stocks are also not included in equity securities, and our analysis needs to investigate their characteristics to validate this treatment.

Accounting for available-for-sale securities using the portfolio method of aggregating unrealized gains and losses can also yield inconsistent effects on income recognition. We show this in three independent illustrations using a portfolio of trading or available-for-sale securities at the end of Year 1:

	Cost	*Market*
Security A	$10	$15
Security B	20	30
Security C	10	5
Security D	40	10
	$80	$60

Accounting practice for marketable securities prescribes a valuation allowance (loss) of $20 for this company's balance sheet at the end of Year 1. Illustration 4.1 considers the implications of recognizing holding gains and losses on a specific security.

Illustration 4.1

Assume security D is sold in Year 2 for $10, yielding a reported loss of $10—computed from the $30 holding loss on security D less elimination of the $20 allowance. In this case, the $30 holding loss from security D is recognized over two years rather than in Year 1 when it occurs.

Illustration 4.2 considers the dual effects from valuation allowance adjustments and recognition of holding gains and losses.

Illustration 4.2

Assume security C is sold in Year 2 for $5 and there is no change in the market prices of securities A, B, and C during Year 2 (their market prices are identical at the end of years 1 and 2). In this case, the $5 holding loss on security C is entirely offset by the $5 decrease in the allowance for unrealized losses (from $20 allowance down to $15). Consequently, the company's marketable securities yield a zero dollar impact on net income for Year 2.

Illustration 4.3 considers the aggregate versus individual recognition of holding gains and losses.

Illustration 4.3

Assume the following portfolio of marketable securities at the end of Year 2:

	Cost	*Market*
Security A	$10	$20
Security B	20	30
Security C	10	25
	$40	$75

Any individual security or combination of securities in this portfolio can decline up to $35 in value before any loss is recognized. Thus, security B can drop to $5 and security A to $10 (with C remaining unchanged) without any need for loss recognition. This is because as long as the aggregate market value of the portfolio remains above cost, no individual gains or losses are recorded.

Current market values of securities are always relevant in assessing management performance. An argument that unrealized gains are only *paper profits*—profits not yet realized—that can vanish before investments are actually sold or disposed of fails to recognize that management is responsible for the decision to hold or sell. A reduction in unrealized gains on investments is as much a loss as the decline in the value of inventories or equipment due to obsolescence.

Adaptec reports its short-term investments under the category "Marketable Securities" (See Adaptec's annual report in Supplement A). Notes 1 and 2 in Adaptec's 1996 annual report indicate its securities portfolio consists primarily of municipal securities classified as available-for-sale. At March 31, 1996, about 75 percent of Adaptec's securities ($153,996 ÷ $204,283) are due to mature in between one and three years, with the remainder maturing within one year. Management also discloses in the annual report that the market values of Adaptec's securities approximate cost.

Receivables

Receivables are amounts due that arise from the sale of goods or services, or the loaning of money. These include accrued amounts due such as rents and interest. **Accounts receivable** refer to oral promises of indebtedness due. **Notes receivable** refer to formal written promises of indebtedness due, although this characteristic does not necessarily make them more readily collectible than other receivables. Notes receivable are, however, more easily negotiable and pledged for loans than are accounts receivable. Certain receivables require separate disclosure by source. Examples are receivables from affiliated companies, corporate officers, company directors, or employees. Companies can establish receivables without formal billing of a debtor. For example, costs accumulated under a cost-plus-fixed-fee contract or some other types of government contracts are usually recorded as receivables as they accumulate. Claims for tax refunds are also often classified as receivables provided no substantial question of compliance exists.

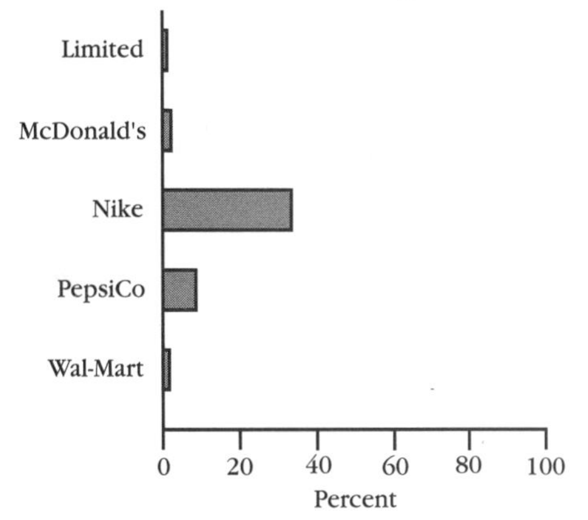

Source: Annual reports.

Companies expect receivables classified as current assets to be realized or collected within a year or the normal operating cycle of the business, whichever is longer. If the collection interval for receivables exceeds one year (e.g., long-term installment receivables), they are reported as current assets only if their collection interval is less than the normal operating cycle for the type of business the company is engaged in. The impact of an operating cycle is sometimes substantial as shown in the following annual report classification of assets and liabilities:

> Certain contracts entered into by the Company vary up to five years in length. For these contracts the Company classifies its contracting assets and liabilities as current.
>
> —Great Lakes Dredge & Dock Company

Valuation of Receivables

It is important to analyze receivables because of their impact on a company's asset position and income stream. These two effects of receivables are interrelated. Experience shows that companies do not collect all receivables nor necessarily collect them in their entirety. While judgment about collectibility can be made at any time, collectibility of receivables as a group is best estimated on the basis of past experience with suitable allowance for current economy, industry, and debtor conditions. The risk in this analysis is that past experience might not be an adequate measure of future loss, or that we fail to fully account for current conditions. Losses with receivables can be substantial and affect both current assets and current and future net income.

In practice, companies report receivables at their **net realizable value**—total amount of receivables less an allowance for uncollectible accounts. Management estimates the allowance for uncollectibles based on experience, customer fortunes, economy and industry expectations, and collection policies. Uncollectible accounts are written off against the allowance (often reported as a deduction from receivables in the balance sheet) and the expected loss is included in current operating expenses. Our assessment of earnings quality is often affected by an analysis of receivables and their collectibility. Our analysis must be alert to changes in the allowance—computed relative to sales, receivables, or industry and market conditions.

An interesting case involving valuation of receivables and its importance for analysis is that of Brunswick Corporation. In a past annual report, Brunswick made a "special provision for possible losses on receivables" or a write-off of $15 million after taxes. Management asserted circumstances revealed themselves that were not apparent to management or the auditor at the end of the previous year when a substantial amount of these receivables were reported as outstanding. Management explained these write-offs as follows (dates adapted):

> Delinquencies in bowling installment payments, primarily related to some of the large chain accounts, continued at an unsatisfactory level. Nonchain accounts, which comprise about 80 percent of installment receivables, are generally better paying accounts . . . In the last quarter of Year 3, average bowling lineage per establishment fell short of the relatively low lineage of the comparable period of Year 2, resulting in an aggravation of collection problems on certain accounts. The bowling business may have felt the competition of outdoor activities associated with the unseasonably warm weather during the latter part of Year 3. Some improvement in bowling lineage was noted in the early months of Year 4 which tends to confirm this view. However, the fact that collections were lower in late Year 3 contributed to management's decision to increase reserves. After the additional provision of $15 million, total reserves for possible future losses on all receivables amounted to $66 million, including $30 million transferred from deferred income taxes.
>
> —Brunswick Corporation

While it is impossible to precisely define the moment when collection of a receivable is sufficiently doubtful to require a provision, the relevant question is whether our analysis can warn us of an inadequate provision. In Year 2 of the Brunswick case, our analysis should have revealed the inadequacy of the bad debt provision in light of known industry conditions. Possibly not coincidentally, Brunswick's income peaked in early Year 2—the year benefiting from the insufficient provision.

Analysis Implications of Receivables

While an unqualified opinion of an independent auditor lends assurance to the validity and valuation of receivables, our analysis must recognize the possibility of error in audit procedure or judgment. We must also be alert to management's (and the auditor's) incentives in reporting income and assets. In this respect, two important questions confront our analysis of receivables.

Authenticity of Receivables

The first question is: Is the receivable genuine, due, and enforceable? The description of receivables in financial statements or notes is usually insufficient to provide reliable clues to whether receivables are genuine, due, and enforceable. Knowledge of industry practices and supplementary sources of information are used for added assurance. One factor affecting authenticity of receivables is a company's *credit policy*. Stringent credit policies imply higher quality, or lower risk, receivables. A company sometimes reports its credit policy in notes to the statements. Another factor affecting authenticity is the *right of merchandise return*. Customers in certain industries, like the compact disc, textbook, or toy industries, enjoy a substantial right of merchandise return. Our analysis must allow for return privileges in analyzing receivables quality. (Information on return policies is sometimes available in notes or other public [advertising] records.) Liberal return privileges can substantially impair quality of receivables. Illustration 4.4 emphasizes risks inherent in evaluating receivables.

Illustration 4.4

Topper Corporation is a manufacturer and marketer of toys. Topper's Year 1 financial statements report sales of $64 million. A terse footnote related to its accounts receivable of $31 million at December 31, Year 1, stated: "approximately $14 million of sales made in December Year 1 carried extended credit terms of five to eight months. The comparable amount for the prior year was $2 million." While the extended credit terms granted under Topper's December sales program are not unusual or excessively long, this casual footnote proved in retrospect an extraordinarily important piece of information for analysis purposes. Not only did Topper, in its desire to report higher sales and earnings as a means to obtain loans, grant its customers extended credit terms, free storage, and substantial discounts, it also granted them substantial rights of merchandise return and exchange to the point where risk of ownership did not in reality pass from Topper to its customers.

The auditors, who gave Topper a clean opinion for Year 1, claimed they first learned of the letters giving Topper's customers the right of merchandise return only in early Year 3. The auditors also withdrew their opinion on Year 1's financial statements a full year after rendering their clean opinion. In May of Year 3, Topper incurred huge write-downs of receivables and inventory, and one year later Topper was adjudged bankrupt. Losses to shareholders and to some large pension funds that extended credit on the basis of information contained in Year 2's prospectus were substantial.

Topper's case stresses that our analysis be alert to both risky agreements with customers offered by suppliers anxious to sell and changing demands that impair collectibility of receivables.

Our analysis of receivables must also be aware of international market conditions. Knowledge of international markets would have proved useful in assessing legitimacy of sales and receivables for Dayco Corporation (see the excerpt from practice at the top of page 163).

Receivables are also subject to various contingencies. Our analysis can reveal whether contingencies impair the value of receivables. A note to the financial statements of O.M. Scott & Sons Company revealed several contingencies (see the second excerpt from practice on page 163).

Dayco Corporation disclosed an after-tax write-off of $11.7 million in its annual report due to an international agent placing fictitious orders. Dayco ultimately wrote off $20 million in accounts receivable, inventories, and prepaid expenses related to this transgression.

Accounts receivable: Accounts receivable are stated net after allowances for returns, allowances, and doubtful accounts of $472,000. Accounts receivable include approximately $4,785,000 for shipments made under a deferred payment plan whereby title to the merchandise is transferred to the dealer when shipped; however, the Company retains a security interest in such merchandise until sold by the dealer. Payment to the Company is due from the dealer as the merchandise is sold at retail. The amount of receivables of this type shall at no time exceed $11 million under terms of the loan and security agreement.

—O.M. Scott & Sons Company

Under these conditions, a receivable might not represent an actual sale but, rather, a merchandise or service advance. Receivables like these cannot be valued like receivables without contingencies.

Companies can sell all or portions of their receivables to others. Receivables are sometimes sold with or without recourse to the seller (*recourse* refers to guarantee of collectibility). Sale of receivables *with recourse* does not effectively transfer risk of ownership of receivables from the seller, and sale of receivables *without recourse* does not *always* transfer risk of ownership from the seller. Our analysis must be alert to accounting procedures that view risk as having passed to the buyer when it has not. Transactions like these resemble sales with contingent liabilities for the seller—indeed, they might not be sales at all. Risks with receivables persist until the original debtor ultimately pays. Our analysis includes a useful analytical adjustment to correct for receivables sold when risk of ownership rests with the seller. This two-step analytical adjustment is: (1) Current assets + $Receivables sold, and (2) Current liabilities + $Receivables sold; or in double-entry form:

Receivables	$Receivables Sold	
Short-term Debt		$Receivables Sold

Collection Risk

The second question we confront is: Is the receivable's likelihood of collection properly assessed? Most provisions for uncollectible accounts are based on past experience, although they make allowance for current and emerging economic, industry, and debtor circumstances. In practice, management likely attaches more importance to past experience—for no other reason than economic and industry conditions are difficult to predict. Our analysis must bear in mind that while a formulaic approach to calculating the provision for bad debts is convenient and practical, it reflects a mechanical judgment that can miss changing or emerging conditions. Our analysis must rely on our judgment and knowledge of industry conditions to assess the provision for uncollectibles (recall the Brunswick case above).

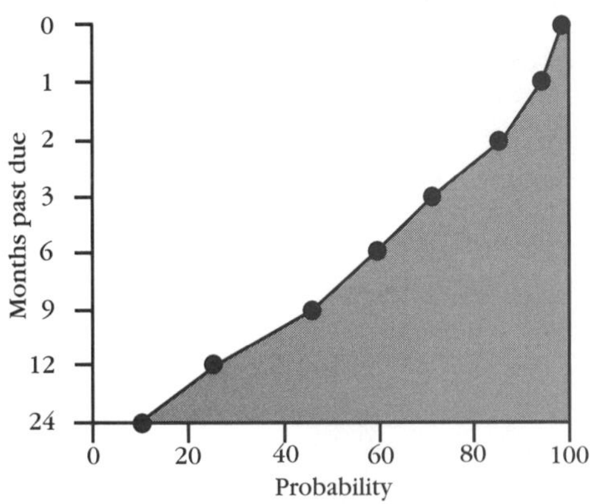

Source: "Annual Collectibility Survey," Commercial Collection Agency Section of the Commercial Law League of America, New Providence, NJ, April 1993.

Information to assess *collection risk* for receivables is not usually included in financial statements. Useful information must be obtained from other sources or from the company. Our analysis tools for investigating collectibility include:

- Determining patterns of receivables for competing companies as a percent of sales—vis-à-vis the company under analysis.
- Examining customer concentration. Risks increase when total receivables are concentrated among one or a few major customers.
- Investigating the age pattern of receivables (overdue and for how long).
- Determining the proportion of receivables that are renewals of previous accounts or notes receivable.
- Analyzing adequacy of allowances for trade discounts, returns, and other credits that customers are entitled to.

Our analysis of current financial position and a company's ability to meet current obligations—as reflected in measures like current ratio—must recognize the importance of operating cycle in classifying receivables as current. The operating cycle can permit installment receivables not collectible for several years or even decades (e.g., a winery business) in current assets. Our analysis of current assets, and their relation to current liabilities, must recognize and appropriately adjust for these *timing risks*.

ANALYSIS VIEWPOINT . . . *You are the auditor*

Your client, Research Technologies, reports preliminary financial results reflecting a 15 percent growth rate in earnings. This rate meets earlier predictions by management. In your audit, you discover management reduces its allowance for uncollectible accounts from 5 percent to 2 percent of gross accounts receivable. Absent this change, earnings shows a 9 percent growth rate. Should you be concerned about this change in estimate?

Financial Instruments

A **financial instrument** is defined as cash, evidence of an ownership interest in an entity, or a contract that both:

- Imposes on one entity a contractual obligation to deliver cash or another financial instrument to a second entity, or to exchange other financial instruments on potentially unfavorable terms with a second entity, and
- Conveys to a second entity a contractual right to receive cash or another financial instrument from the first entity, or to exchange other financial instruments on potentially favorable terms with the first entity.

This definition includes options, futures, swaps, and forwards—known as **derivative financial instruments** (or simply derivatives) because their value derives from another asset (e.g., stock, bond, commodity) or indicator (e.g., interest rates, domestic or international market indices).

Disclosure and Analysis of Financial Instruments

Current practice on disclosure of the fair value of financial instruments requires:

> An entity shall disclose, either in the body of the financial statements or in the accompanying notes, the fair value of financial instruments for which it is practicable to estimate that value. An entity also shall disclose the method(s) and significant assumptions used to estimate the fair value of financial instruments.

These disclosures are part of *supplemental information*—meaning that in reporting financial instruments, financial statements continue to rely primarily on cost and not fair value. What are credible sources of fair value? A *quoted market price*, if available, is reliable evidence of fair value. If a quoted market price is not available, management's (or our) best estimate of fair value can be based on the quoted market price of a financial instrument with similar characteristics, or derived using valuation techniques (e.g., present value of estimated future cash flows, option pricing models, market pricing models). Companies must disclose in financial statements why it is not practicable to estimate fair value if not reported. For trade receivables and payables, no disclosure is required when carrying amounts approximate fair values. An example of supplemental disclosure appears under "Fair Value of Financial Instruments" in note 1 of Adaptec's 1996 annual report found in Supplement A. Adaptec reports that "carrying amounts approximate fair value" for its financial instruments.

Some users view current reporting practices for financial instruments as a watershed position representing the beginning of a departure from historical cost accounting. However, there is a significant difference between *disclosure* and *recording* of fair value—the latter affecting actual reported financial position and measurement of income. Nevertheless, these disclosures allow us to better assess short-term liquidity and long-term solvency of companies. Disclosures of changes in the fair value of financial instruments are useful to us in adjusting income—thereby recognizing value changes not reflected in current accounting measures.

Inventories

Inventories refer to goods held for sale as part of a company's normal business operations or goods acquired (or in process of being readied) for sale. With the exception of certain service organizations, inventories are essential and significant assets of businesses. We scrutinize inventories because they are a major component of operating assets and directly affect determination of income. It is important we understand the difference between expensing and capitalizing inventory costs. **Expensing** inventory costs treats inventories like period costs, that is, costs expiring during the fiscal period incurred. Conversely, **capitalizing** treats inventory costs like product costs and does not charge them against current period income—remaining instead as a capitalized asset subsequently charged against future period(s) revenues benefiting from their sale. Capitalizing costs rather than expensing them shifts costs from current to future periods' income determinations—a timing difference.

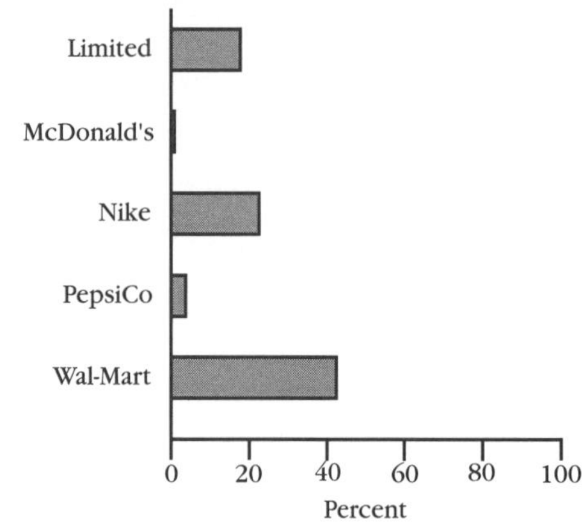

Inventory Costs

The importance of costing methods for inventory valuation, and the controversy surrounding them, are due to their impact on computing net income—through the cost of goods sold calculation. Assigning costs to inventory affects both income and asset measurements. Inventory costing methods are used to allocate cost of goods available for sale, consisting of beginning inventory and net purchases, between either cost of goods sold (an income deduction) or ending inventory (a current asset).

The **inventory equation** is useful in understanding inventory flows and is expressed as follows for a merchadising company:

Beginning inventory + Net purchases – Cost of goods sold = Ending inventory

Beginning inventory and net purchases are knowns—beginning inventory is taken from the prior period's statement and net purchases is computed from current period invoices. "Unknowns" are cost of goods sold and ending inventory—which must be computed by allocating cost of goods available for sale (sum of beginning inventory and net purchases). There are several accepted procedures for allocating cost of goods available for sale between cost of goods sold and ending inventory.

Another concern in inventory cost determination is the diversity of assumptions and practices involving the definition of **includable cost**—cost allocated to inventory. A simple example illustrates this difficulty. Take an office supply store that buys a desk for resale. The desk's invoice price is its primary cost. To that primary cost the store adds the costs of transportation-in and any costs of assembling. If the store imports the desk, then it can add duty and other direct costs of clearing customs. However, should costs associated with management's efforts in acquiring inventory be allocated to the desk? In practice, there is no direct answer. Companies sometimes allocate these costs to inventories, but they also sometimes expense these costs in the period incurred. Management's decision to allocate these costs or not can substantially affect reported income for current and future periods. Another issue is whether expenses incurred in selling the desk can be added to inventory costs. In this case, practice is more uniform in treating selling costs as period costs and not including them as costs of inventory.

In spite of its importance for analysis, disclosure or discussion of costs included in inventory is uncommon in financial statements. The following disclosure for Chrysler is unusual in both its detail and its revealing of inventory costing practices by a subsidiary:

> In accordance with industry practice (Program Accounting), Gulfstream Aerospace Corporation's inventoried costs relating to aircraft programs are stated at actual production costs, including factory overhead and tooling costs, reduced by costs attributed to units delivered based on the estimated average gross profit margins of all units expected to be produced. Revisions in the gross profits recognized are made on a prospective basis as the need for such changes becomes evident.
>
> —Chrysler Corporation

A more typical disclosure is that from Reebok, as its 1996 annual report succinctly describes its inventory accounting policy: "Inventory, substantially all finished goods, is recorded at the lower of cost (first-in, first-out method) or market." Similarly, the composition of Adaptec's inventory is concisely reported in one account labeled Inventories (see Adaptec's balance sheet in Supplement A).

Cost Accounting

The foregoing illustration involving inventoriable costs for a desk is relatively simple because it involved a retailer. Inventory valuation for a manufacturer creates additional complexities. Merchandising enterprises, like retailers, purchase merchandise requiring little or no additional work before resale. Manufacturing companies, however, require significant work with inventories before selling them. Inventories in manufacturing organizations are classified into three categories according to their stage of completion: **raw materials, work in process,** or **finished goods**. In our desk example, the manufacturer incurs three costs: (1) direct (raw) materials used in manufacturing, (2) direct labor to produce and assemble the desk, and (3) indirect manufacturing expenses including machinery depreciation, auxiliary supplies, utilities, factory occupancy (rent) costs, supervisory expenses, and management salaries. While the first two costs create some problems of classification, the third category finds the greatest variety of treatments and the most difficulty in practice. This third category of indirect expenses is often referred to as **overhead costs.** While it is feasible to identify direct material and direct labor costs, it is not practicable to trace specific overhead costs to desks. Such treatment requires allocation of an entire pool of costs to potentially numerous manufacturing products (e.g., desks, chairs, shelves, bookcases). Such allocation requires a number of assumptions and decisions regarding items included in overhead and the number of units over which companies allocate overhead costs. Difficulties in defining includable costs for overhead arise from the vast variety of expenses involved, the range of acceptable accounting methods, and the absence of meaningful restraints on practice. To underscore these difficulties, consider the following practicalities:

- Are costs of testing new designs and materials includable in inventory costs?
- On what basis and over how many units are overhead costs allocated?
- Are general and administrative expenses includable as inventory costs?

While reasonable answers exist, no single answer is necessarily more acceptable than another.

Allocation of overhead costs to inventory items must be *rational and designed to approximate actual cost.* Allocation difficulties stem from the sizeable portion of overhead that often reflects **fixed costs**—costs not varying with production but varying with time. Examples are rent payments and the factory manager's salary. In our illustration, assuming the store produces 10,000 desks, and fixed costs are $100,000, then the store assigns $10 of fixed costs to each desk. But if only 5,000 desks are produced, then $20 of fixed costs are assigned to each desk. Thus, level of activity is an important determinant of unit fixed cost, and wide fluctuations in output can yield wide fluctuations in unit fixed cost. These difficulties in both assignment of costs and overhead allocations produce significant variations in reported results.

Inventory Cost Flows

The assumption regarding flow of costs is another important decision in inventory cost determination affecting income and asset position. This assumption (LIFO, FIFO, average cost) need not conform to the flow of goods and, hence, is controversial. To illustrate the acceptable assumptions and their implications, we return to the retailer of office desks. For the year ending December 31, Year 2, inventory records for desks show:

Inventory on January 1, Year 2	100 @ $40	$ 4,000
First purchase in Year 2	200 @ $50	10,000
Second purchase in Year 2	100 @ $50	5,000
Third purchase in Year 2	200 @ $60	12,000
Total available for sale	600 desks	$31,000

A total of 50 desks remain in inventory at December 31, Year 2 (or 550 desks are sold in Year 2). How does the retailer value the 50 remaining desks? There are several measurement methods available in valuing these desks that carry the "generally accepted" label. We discuss the three methods most popular in practice.

First-In, First-Out (FIFO)

The **first-in, first-out** assumption probably best matches actual flow of goods in business—the first units produced or purchased are the first sold or used. This often conforms to the best inventory management practice. Under FIFO, the 50 desks are valued at $60 each—taken from the unit costs of the last 50 desks purchased, or $3,000. Cost of goods sold equals $28,000 ($31,000 cost of goods available for sale less the $3,000 value assigned to ending inventory).

Last-In, First-Out (LIFO)

The **last-in, first-out** method assumes the most recent (or last) units produced or purchased are the first sold or used, and is often likened to a "pile flow" of inventory. That is, if inventory consists of a pile of salt or coal, then the last quantity purchased is likely the first removed and sold. Concern with consistency between cost flow and physical flow of inventories ignores the primary intent of inventory valuation—selecting an assumption about the *flow of costs* rather than *flow of physical units*. An assumption about flow of costs is chosen not because it parallels the flow of physical units but, rather, because it achieves certain objectives of inventory valuation.

A major consequence of LIFO is charging cost of goods sold with the most recent costs incurred. When price levels are stable, reports using either FIFO or LIFO are the same. But when price levels are changing (like the increasing pattern in our desk example), reports using different inventory methods diverge, often dramatically. Use of LIFO in practice is encouraged by its acceptance for tax purposes. LIFO's charging of more recent and often higher prices to cost of goods sold can substantially reduce taxable income. Moreover, U.S. tax laws often stipulate that use of LIFO for tax purposes requires its adoption for financial reporting; the so-called **LIFO conformity rule** has led to many companies adopting LIFO. In our desk illustration, the ending inventory of 50 desks has a value using LIFO of $40 each, or $2,000. Using the inventory equation, cost of goods sold is $29,000 ($31,000 – $2,000). Notice the ending inventory of $2,000 reported on the balance sheet is 33 percent below current market (or at least one-third less than current cost—$40 versus $60). However, the income statement better matches current inventory costs (using $60 and $50 per unit costs) with current revenues. This reflects an important consequence of LIFO accounting: It better matches current expenses with current revenues when prices are changing (inflation or deflation). As we see later in this chapter, however, this result does not *always* occur in times of price-level changes.

Average Cost

The **average cost** method assumes units sold or used are priced at the weighted-average cost of all units available for sale or used during the period. The average cost method reduces the impact of cost fluctuations by using a weighted-average cost, where weights are the number of units produced or purchased, in valuing inventories and determining cost of goods sold. While computation of weighted-average cost of goods sold uses the *timing of sales* (referred to as the *moving average method*), for simplicity we compute the weighted-average cost per unit on the total cost of goods available (i.e., net purchases plus beginning inventory). This yields an average cost per desk of $51.67 ($31,000 ÷ 600 units), and the 50 desks in ending inventory are valued at $2,583.50 (50 units × $51.67). Cost of goods sold is $28,416.50 ($31,000 – $2,583.50).

To summarize, financial results using each of the three methods are:

	Beginning Inventory	+	*Net Purchases*	=	*Cost of Goods Sold*	+	*Ending Inventory*
FIFO	$4,000	+	$27,000	=	$28,000	+	$3,000
LIFO	$4,000	+	$27,000	=	$29,000	+	$2,000
Average	$4,000	+	$27,000	=	$28,416.5	+	$2,583.5

Beginning inventory in our example is identical under each method—in practice, this is rarely the case. Finally, if we assume sales of $35,000 for the period, the gross profit under each method equals:

	Sales	–	*Cost of Goods Sold*	=	*Gross Profit*
FIFO	$35,000	–	$28,000	=	$7,000
LIFO	$35,000	–	$29,000	=	$6,000
Average	$35,000	–	$28,416.5	=	$6,583.5

These differences in gross profit yield obvious tax implications if the same methods are used in computing taxable income. Overall, this illustration shows that the assumption about inventory cost flows can make a significant difference in *both* cost of goods sold and valuation of inventories—with direct repercussions to income and assets. Generally, FIFO provides a better inventory figure for the balance sheet by reflecting recent costs. In our illustration, FIFO ending inventory is $3,000 based on the $60 unit cost taken from the most recent purchase. LIFO yields an ending inventory of $2,000 using the least recent (oldest) unit cost of $40—a less faithful estimate of current costs. Yet LIFO yields a better matching of current expenses with revenues on the income statement. Average cost produces inventory and cost of goods sold figures between FIFO and LIFO—reflecting its averaging effect. In times of changing prices, as in our illustration, producing both inventory and cost of goods sold figures based on recent costs cannot be achieved simultaneously using any of these three historical-cost-based methods.

Frequency of Inventory Costing Methods in Practice*

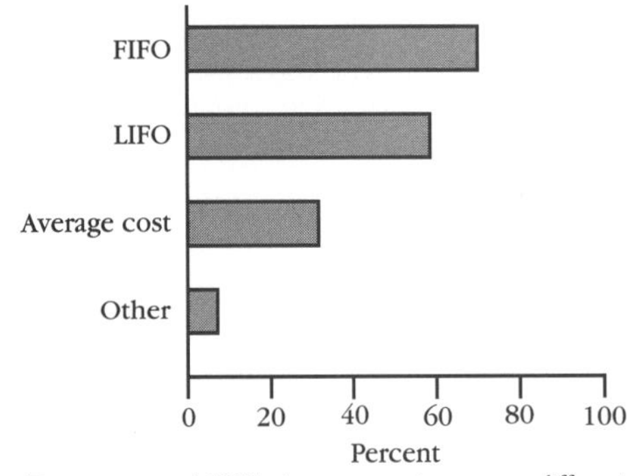

*Percents exceed 100% since companies can use different methods for different inventory groupings.

Source: *Accounting Trends & Techniques*.

Inventory Estimation

A commonly used method of inventory valuation for interim (less than one year) financial statements is the **gross profit method**. This method derives inventory by estimating cost of goods sold using a gross profit ratio based on past experience.

Analysis Research Insight 4.1

Inventory Method Choice

Why are all firms not using LIFO? Or FIFO? Or another method? Can the choice of inventory method inform our analysis of a company? Analysis research on inventory provides answers to some of these questions. Specifically, analysis research suggests that information on inventory method choice for a company can give us additional insights into the company and its environment.

For companies choosing LIFO, the following characteristics are common:

- Greater expected tax savings.
- Larger inventory balances.
- Less tax loss carryforwards.
- Lower variability in inventory balances.
- Less likelihood of inventory obsolescence.
- Larger in size.
- Less leveraged.
- Higher current ratios.

Accordingly, knowledge of inventory method choice can reveal information about a company's characteristics or circumstances otherwise obscured by the complexity of data or operations.

This method is accurate to the extent the gross profit ratio estimate is reliable and provided there are no unusual inventory shortages or spoilage. The **retail method** of inventory estimation is an extension of the gross profit method and is also common in practice. It computes physical inventory, priced first at retail, and then converts this retail inventory figure to "cost" using an estimated gross profit ratio(s). This method is typically more reliable than the gross profit method since gross profit ratios are estimated using current and past inventory cost-to-retail ratios.

Inventory Valued at Lower of Cost or Market

The generally accepted principle of inventory valuation is to value at the **lower of cost or market**. This simple phrase masks the complexities and variety of alternatives to which it is subject. It can significantly affect periodic income and inventory values. The lower-of-cost-or-market rule implies that if inventory declines in market value below its cost—for any reason, including obsolescence, damage, and price changes—then inventory is written down to reflect this loss. This write-down is effectively charged against revenues in the period the loss occurs. Since write-ups from cost to market are prohibited (except for recovery of losses up to the original cost), inventory is conservatively valued. **Market** is defined as current replacement cost through either purchase or reproduction. However, market value must not be higher than net realizable value nor less than net realizable value reduced by a normal profit margin. The upper limit of market value, or net realizable value, reflects completion and disposal costs associated with sale of the item. The lower limit ensures that if inventory is written down from cost to market, it is written down to a figure that includes realization of a normal gross profit on subsequent sale. **Cost** is defined as the acquisition cost of inventory. It is computed using one of the accepted inventory costing methods—for example, FIFO, LIFO, or average cost. Our analysis of inventory must consider the impact of the lower-of-cost-or-market rule. When prices are rising, this rule tends to *undervalue* inventories regardless of the cost method used. This depresses the current ratio. In practice, certain companies voluntarily disclose the current cost of inventory.

ANALYSIS VIEWPOINT . . . *You are the buying agent*

You are trying to reach agreement with a supplier on providing materials for manufacturing. To make its case for a higher price, the supplier furnishes an income statement revealing a historically low 20 percent gross margin. In your analysis of this statement, you discover a note stating that market value of inventory declined by $2 million this period and, therefore, ending inventory is revalued downward by that amount. Is this note relevant for your price negotiations?

Purchase Commitments for Inventory

Companies frequently contract with other entities to purchase inventory several months or years in advance. These contracts to purchase goods or services in advance are known as **purchase commitments**. Many commitments are cancelable at the option of the buyer and/or seller. As a general rule, no accounting entries are made to reflect these commitments since title to the goods has not passed to the buyer. However, companies can negotiate a noncancelable purchase contract. While no asset or liability is recorded at the date of the agreement (because neither party has fulfilled its part of the agreement), disclosure of contract details should exist. A formal entry is required only when both the agreed-upon price for the goods exceeds the market price and the company expects to incur this "loss" when the actual purchase occurs. Under these conditions, the loss and related liability are recorded. Consistent with conservatism, companies are not permitted to record gains if the market price exceeds the agreed-upon price.

Adaptec discusses several purchase commitments in note 7 of its 1996 annual report (see Supplement A). These agreements are designed to ensure availability of semiconductor wafers, a key raw material. With respect to certain agreements with TSMC, Adaptec has recorded in its accounts the payment of cash advances and the signing of a note payable.

Inventory Disclosures under Long-Term Contracts

Accumulation of costs under long-term contracts, reduced by progress billings, is a type of inventory. We encounter two common methods of accounting for these costs in our analysis, but circumstances dictate their use.

- **Completed-contract method.** When estimates of the final outcome or results of contracts are difficult or impossible to make and are too speculative to be reliable, the completed-contract method is used. Under this method, all costs of the contract, including related general and administrative costs, are accumulated and carried as assets (inventories) until completion of the contract when final net profit or loss is determined.

- **Percentage-of-completion method.** When estimates of cost and income at each stage of completion of the contract can be made, the percentage-of-completion method is used. Under this method, the estimated proportionate profit earned up to a particular point in time is credited to income and correspondingly included in accumulated costs (inventories).

Under either method, losses that are ascertainable at any point in time are recognized and accounted for when first determined. Accepted practice requires separate disclosure of inventoried costs related to long-term contracts—including methods of determining both cost and market, and description of the method used in removing amounts from inventory.

LIFO and Changing Inventory Prices

Increases in prices (or inflation) are typically accompanied by increasing adoptions of the LIFO method. One rationale for the switch to LIFO is it adjusts, at least partially, financial statements for inflation effects. In reality, LIFO merely postpones recognition of inflationary effects, although such postponement can be long term if prices continue to rise and the LIFO inventory base is not liquidated. Another reason for LIFO's popularity is its postponement of taxes when prices are increasing—a very real and tangible benefit to companies.

Analysis Implications of Inventory When Prices Are Changing

To understand the concept of inflation (or inventory) profits we compute a company's operating results using different inventory methods, as in Illustration 4.5.

Illustration 4.5

A company's quarterly inventory costs and selling prices per unit, beginning with the fourth quarter of Year 2, are reported below. Both costs and prices rise steadily in the first, second, and third quarters of Year 3, then level off in the fourth quarter, and decline in the first quarter of Year 4. For simplicity, we assume the company has a constant $200 markup on cost, has *three* units in inventory at all times, and both buys and sells *one* unit each quarter.

Per Unit	*4th Q Year 2*	*1st Q Year 3*	*2nd Q Year 3*	*3rd Q Year 3*	*4th Q Year 3*	*1st Q Year 4*
Selling price	$1,300	$1,400	$1,500	$1,600	$1,600	$1,500
Purchase cost	1,100	1,200	1,300	1,400	1,400	1,300

Exhibit 4.2 shows inventory and gross profit figures using the three inventory costing methods—FIFO, LIFO, and weighted average. The financial statement effects from these methods are analyzed in the remainder of this section.

FIFO Analysis

In the case of FIFO, the oldest unit (or first in) of inventory costing $1,100 is the first sold (or first out) in the second quarter of Year 3. Given a selling price of $1,500,

EXHIBIT 4.2 Financial Statement Effects of Changing Inventory Prices

TABLE 4.1 FIFO Inventory Figures

	Purchases						
Beginning of	*4th Q Year 2*	*1st Q Year 3*	*2nd Q Year 3*	*3rd Q Year 3*	*4th Q Year 3*	*1st Q Year 4*	*Balance Sheet Inventory Figure*
2nd Q Year 3	$1,100	$1,200	$1,300				= $3,600
3rd Q Year 3		1,200	1,300	$1,400			= 3,900
4th Q Year 3			1,300	1,400	$1,400		= 4,100
1st Q Year 4				1,400	1,400	$1,300	= 4,100

TABLE 4.2 FIFO Gross Profit Figures

	2nd Q Year 3	*3rd Q Year 3*	*4th Q Year 3*	*1st Q Year 4*
Sales	$1,500	$1,600	$1,600	$1,500
Cost	1,100	1,200	1,300	1,400
(when purchased)	(4thQ–Y2)	(1stQ–Y3)	(2ndQ–Y3)	(3rdQ–Y3)
Gross profit	$400	$400	$300	$100

TABLE 4.3 LIFO Inventory Figures

	Purchases						
Beginning of	*4th Q Year 2*	*1st Q Year 3*	*2nd Q Year 3*	*3rd Q Year 3*	*4th Q Year 3*	*1st Q Year 4*	*Balance Sheet Inventory Figures*
2nd Q Year 3	$1,100	$1,200	$1,300				= $3,600
3rd Q Year 3	1,100	1,200		$1,400			= 3,700
4th Q Year 3	1,100	1,200			$1,400		= 3,700
1st Q Year 4	1,100	1,200				$1,300	= 3,600

TABLE 4.4 LIFO Gross Profit Figures

	2nd Q Year 3	*3rd Q Year 3*	*4th Q Year 3*	*1st Q Year 4*
Sales	$1,500	$1,600	$1,600	$1,500
Cost	1,300	1,400	1,400	1,300
(when purchased)	(2ndQ–Y3)	(3rdQ–Y3)	(4thQ–Y3)	(1stQ–Y4)
Gross profit	$200	$200	$200	$200

gross profit equals $400 and is comprised of two elements. First, there is the normal $200 markup on cost. Second, there is an additional $200 profit resulting from matching an older, lower cost inventory item with a current selling price—this is

EXHIBIT 4.2 (*Concluded*)

TABLE 4.5 Average Cost Inventory Figures

		Purchases						
Beginning of	*Opening Average Cost*[a]	*4th Q Year 2*	*1st Q Year 3*	*2nd Q Year 3*	*3rd Q Year 3*	*4th Q Year 3*	*1st Q Year 4*	*Balance Sheet Inventory Figures*
2nd Q Year 3	—	$1,100	$1,200	$1,300				=$3,600.0
3rd Q Year 3	$2,400[(b)]				$1,400			= 3,800.0
4th Q Year 3	2,533.3[(c)]					$1,400		= 3,933.3
1st Q Year 4	2,622.2[(d)]						$1,300	= 3,922.2

[(a)]Balance sheet value of inventory – Average cost of goods sold (Prior balance sheet figure ÷ 3).
[(b)]$3,600 – ($3,600 ÷ 3) = $3,600 – $1,200 = $2,400.
[(c)]$3,800 – ($3,800 ÷ 3) = $3,800 – $1,266.7 = $2,533.3.
[(d)]$3,933.3 – ($3,933.3 ÷ 3) = $3,933.3 – $1,311.1 = $2,622.2.

TABLE 4.6 Average Cost Gross Profit Figures

	2nd Q Year 3	*3rd Q Year 3*	*4th Q Year 3*	*1st Q Year 4*
Sales	$1,500	$1,600	$1,600	$1,500
Cost (average)	1,200	1,266.7	1,311.1	1,307.4*
Gross profit	$ 300	$ 333.3	$ 288.9	$ 192.6

*Balance sheet value of inventory ÷ 3 = $3,922.2 ÷ 3 = $1,307.4.

referred to as **inflation profit**. If inflation continues at an identical rate, profits will continue to include both a normal $200 markup and a $200 inflation profit. This is again evident in the third quarter of Year 3 where gross profit remains at $400.

In the fourth quarter of Year 3, both selling price and cost stabilize (no inflation or deflation). This means a higher priced FIFO inventory cost unit (*layer*), compared with the prior quarter, flows into cost of goods sold. But, since there is no change in selling price, sales do not increase. There is a decline of 25 percent in gross profit from $400 to $300. The $300 gross profit is comprised of the $200 markup and a $100 inflation profit.

In the first quarter of Year 4, there is a $100 decline in both selling price and cost. FIFO assigns the oldest unit (the item purchased for $1,400 in the third quarter of Year 3) to cost of goods sold. This cost is matched against the reduced selling price of $1,500, yielding a gross profit of $100. This $100 profit is comprised of the $200 markup and a $100 *inflation loss*.

This illustration highlights a limitation of FIFO. FIFO inventory costs flow to cost of goods sold with a lag—the lag equaling the *inventory turnover period*. In periods of continuing inflation, this matching pattern (or lag) yields recurring inflation profits. When the rate of inflation declines, revenues typically and immediately reflect this change; but costs do not. For the duration of one inventory turnover period, costs continue to reflect the earlier rate of inflation or deflation and, hence, reflect an increasing or decreasing pattern. Therefore, a decline in the rate of inflation adversely affects profits of FIFO companies.

LIFO Analysis

In the case of LIFO, gross profit is identical for all quarters and equals the normal markup of $200. This occurs because under LIFO, the most recent purchase (last in) is the first deemed sold (first out). Thus, LIFO cost is similar to current cost, and the effects of inflation—both as price rises and falls—are generally negligible for the income statement. In practice, the correspondence between current cost and LIFO cost is not as exact as this illustration implies. Nevertheless, there are seldom significant income effects from changing prices when using LIFO, unless there is a reduction in inventory quantities. Consequently, the LIFO inventory method provides at least a temporary *correction* for the distorting effects of changing price levels—assuming purchases and sales are frequent and continual. In most cases, the price level at the time of the last-in purchase is similar to the price level at the time of sale. However, when purchases and sales occur at different times, such as with companies experiencing seasonal purchases and sales, the LIFO correction does not work as well. In this case, a time lag exists between purchase and sale, and reported income tends to behave more as if the company is on FIFO, even though it uses LIFO.

Average Cost Analysis

In the case of average cost, gross profits continue to vary with changing prices, but not to the extent as with FIFO. This occurs because the time lag, in matching older costs with current revenues, is shorter under average cost than under FIFO, but longer than under LIFO. Thus, the income effects of inflation for companies using average cost are similar to those using FIFO, but less extreme.

Analysis Implications of Inventory

Assessing Reliability of Inventory

The greater the accounting choices and methods available, the greater is management's latitude in reporting financial results. In accounting for inventory, where the impact of differing methods on income and asset position can be substantial, the possibility exists of management using this latitude to its personal advantage. One control on management's accounting choices is the auditor. An auditor's clean opinion provides assurance that companies uphold certain minimum standards in the exercise of managerial discretion in selecting and applying accounting principles. Yet in certain areas of inventory accounting, latitude is especially large such that our analysis must exercise care with inferences drawn from financial results. In particular, our analysis must understand what the managerial choices are, and evaluate these choices in light of existing conditions. Our analysis of inventory involves, at a minimum, acquiring information and assurance with respect to three questions.

Question 1. Does Inventory Physically Exist and Is It Fairly Valued? Audit procedures designed to give assurance about physical existence of inventories are better and, consequently, improve the reliability of inventory figures. Moreover, the board of directors, and its audit committee, are increasingly made more accountable for management abuses. Nevertheless, cases involving **manipulation of inventory** continue to arise. Cenco, Inc., nearly went insolvent due to a systematic inventory inflation scheme carried on over several years. This scheme, involving irregularities of nearly $25 million, forced Cenco's auditors to pay damages of $3.5 million. Another case involves Saxon Industries. To maintain its borrowings from banks along with other reasons, Saxon overstated inventories by about $50 million. Management had accurate inventory counts, but inflated them to meet predetermined goals. When management's scheme was exposed, Saxon filed for bankruptcy.

Other cases involve companies *aggressively* applying LIFO. Staufer Chemical Company is a case where the SEC alleges the company (1) improperly structured inventory layers to create artificial LIFO liquidations, (2) improperly recognized inventory profits from intracompany product transfers, and (3) prematurely recognized sales where extraordinary incentives were provided to distributors to stock up on chemicals in excess of actual sales needs. These actions resulted in a 25 percent overstatement in Staufer's earnings.

Given the substantial number of companies using LIFO, and the latitude available in its application, there is a conspicuous lack of authoritative guidelines. The AICPA has published and forwarded to the FASB an *Issues Paper* identifying more than 50 problematic financial accounting and reporting issues relating to LIFO. Accounting regulators have yet to act on these issues. The SEC issued a *Staff Accounting Bulletin* endorsing the AICPA's concerns and recommending companies and auditors use the AICPA's guidance in assessing acceptable LIFO practices. The SEC warns companies, if challenged, of their need to justify departures from the AICPA guidance. While there is no definitive guidance on establishing LIFO pools (layers), the AICPA does advocate valid business reasons for the number and composition of these pools. It is unacceptable to establish pools with the primary objective of facilitating inventory liquidations (that effectively decrease cost of goods sold).

Fairly valuing inventories is, of course, dependent not only on proper accounting for physical quantities but also on **proper inclusion** and **costing of items**. Our analysis must be alert to the types of costs included in inventory. For example, under Internal Revenue Service regulations, expenditures due to marketing, selling, advertising, distribution, interest, past service pension costs, and general and administrative expenses that pertain to overall (versus only manufacturing activities) are excluded from inventory overhead under a full-absorption cost system. A reading of notes can reveal unusual accounting policies regarding inventory carrying costs. In accounting for inventory costs in its aircraft division, Chrysler Corporation built some positive expectations about future profit margins into current costs:

The estimated number of aircraft to be produced from the date of acquisition under the combined Gulfstream III/IV program is 308. At year-end, 13 aircraft had been delivered under the program and the backlog included 3 Gulfstream III and 84 Gulfstream IV orders. The Gulfstream III/IV inventoried costs at year-end ($301.2 million) together with the additional estimated costs to complete the 87 orders exceeded the expected aggregate cost of sales of these aircraft by approximately $198.9 million. Chrysler anticipates that profit margins to be realized on delivery of aircraft against both existing unfilled orders and additional anticipated orders will be sufficient to absorb the inventoried costs.

—Chrysler Corporation

Analysis Research Insight 4.2

Predictions Using Inventory

Can our analysis use changes in a company's inventory levels to predict future sales and earnings? From one perspective, evidence of increased inventory can reveal management's expected increase in sales. From another, increased inventory can suggest excess inventory due to an unexpected sales decrease. Analysis research indicates we must cautiously interpret changes in inventory levels, even within types of industries and inventories.

For *manufacturing* companies, an increase in finished goods inventory is a useful predictor of increased sales but decreased earnings—evidence suggests companies reduce prices to dispose of undesirable inventory at lower profit margins. Periods subsequent to this increase in finished goods inventory do not fully recover—meaning future sales and earnings do not rebound to previous levels. In contrast, an increase in raw materials or work-in-process inventory tends to foreshadow both increased sales and earnings that persist.

Evidence with *retailing* companies suggests a slightly different pattern. Specifically, an increase in inventory implies future increased sales but decreased earnings. This pattern is consistent with less demand, subsequently followed by reduced inventory prices to dispose of undesirable inventory—yielding lower profit margins.

These research insights can be useful in our analysis of inventory. Yet we must not ignore the role of inventory methods and estimates. We must jointly consider these latter factors and adjust for them, in light of these research implications.

Under the going-concern assumption, companies are unconcerned with reporting inventory values on a basis other than in the normal course of business. Yet our own analysis, especially if for credit purposes, is often concerned with current values and, potentially, the composition of inventories. For example, raw material is generally more salable than work-in-process inventory since once raw material is converted into specific or unique components, it usually declines in value if liquidation of work-in-process inventory is necessary. The composition of inventory among raw materials, work in process, and finished goods can provide further analytical clues as to future production plans or to the existence of a divergence between actual and expected sales. A decline in raw materials against an increase in work in process and finished goods can imply a production slowdown, while an inventory divergence in the opposite direction can imply actual or expected increases in orders booked. Adaptec reports a breakdown of its inventory balance under Inventories in note 2 to its 1996 annual report (see Supplement A). Each of the three components increases significantly from 1995 to 1996, reflecting growth in operations.

Our analysis of the level of both inventories and accounts receivable, over time and in relation to sales, can hold important clues. Clues can provide insight into *inventory quality* (e.g., existence, worth) and the effects of factors like demand and returns. Consider the following two cases.

Toro Company's initial venture into snowblowers was less than successful. Toro reasoned that snowblowers were a perfect complement to its lawnmower business, particularly after two consecutive years of heavy snowfall. Toro tooled up and produced snowblowers as if snow was both a growth business and fell reliably as grass grows. When, in the third year, winter proved a snowless season, both Toro and its dealers were loaded with excess inventory. Dealers were so financially pressed that they were unable to finance needed lawnmower inventories for the summer season.

Regina Company experienced an unusually high rate of vacuum cleaner returns due to poor product quality. Early analytical clues to this problem included a near twofold increase in both finished goods inventories and receivables when sales increases were much less than expected. Yet many investors, creditors, and others were seemingly surprised when news of this problem became public. Regina also admitted their accounting disclosures were materially incorrect and withdrew its financial statements.

If our analysis includes access to management or investor relations departments, we should seek answers to additional questions about inventories including:

- How are LIFO inventories calculated—on an item-by-item basis or by use of dollar value pools where different items are grouped?
- Is income affected by changes in inventory pools and, if so, by how much?
- Is inventory affected by year-end purchasing decisions?
- Are additional expenses or losses recorded to offset income arising from involuntary liquidation of LIFO inventories?
- What assumptions concerning LIFO inventories underlie quarterly reports?

Question 2. Is Accounting for Inventories Consistent? Accepted reporting standards, including generally accepted auditing standards, require disclosure for changes in accounting principles and the impact of these changes. Our analysis must be alert to changes in principles of inventory accounting (e.g., from LIFO to FIFO). Our analysis must also be aware of accounting changes affecting comparability of financial statements that do not necessarily require disclosure in either the financial statements or auditor's report (e.g., number of LIFO pools).

Question 3. Can Effects of Different Inventory Methods Be Measured? Of the acceptable inventory methods, LIFO is the most complex. Use of LIFO has not only bookkeeping implications for management but ethical ones as well. The LIFO method increases management's latitude to manage earnings, and our analysis must be alert to this. Changing purchasing policies at the end of the year is one example that can affect reported results under LIFO as evidenced in Illustration 4.6. This scenario is not possible under FIFO.

Illustration 4.6

Pacific Rim Corp. illustrates the LIFO consequences of a change in purchasing policy. Pacific Rim purchased the following units in Year 1:

January to June	7,000 units at $1.00 per unit
July to November	5,000 units at $1.20 per unit
December	2,000 units at $1.30 per unit

Ending inventory equals 1,000 units. Under LIFO, Pacific Rim values ending inventory at a cost of $1 per unit. If, however, Pacific Rim purchased 3,000 units in December—an additional 1,000 at $1.30 each—its reported profits change. The additional purchase costs $1,300, but the addition to ending inventory is only $1,000 while there is a $300 increase in cost of sales. Thus, Pacific Rim's profits decline by $300. Under different conditions, buying more units can also increase profits.

We must also recognize that LIFO is not unitary but, rather, has many variations that can produce different results. It can be applied to all inventory components or a few; it can be applied to raw material costs and not to direct labor or overhead costs. Footnotes merely disclosing the variety of methods used without giving breakdowns of respective inventory amounts are of limited use. When a reduction in the LIFO inventory quantities (base) occurs, companies match less recent (older) LIFO costs with current revenues, resulting in increased profit margins when less recent costs are lower than current costs. The reduction in inventory quantities known as **LIFO layer liquidation** is the result of companies selling more units than purchased during a period, as seen in Illustration 4.7.

Illustration 4.7

Pacific Rim prices its product at 125 percent of the current cost. The operations of Pacific Rim for Year 2 are reflected in the following report:

Sales (2,000 @ $1.375)		$2,750
Cost of sales:		
Beginning LIFO inventory (1,000 @ $1)	$1,000	
Purchases (2,000 @ $1.10)	2,200	
Ending LIFO inventory (1,000 @ $1)	(1,000)	2,200
Gross profit		$ 550
Gross profit percentage		20%

In Year 3, Pacific Rim continues its policy of marking up units by 25 percent, while costs increase by 10 percent. A strike during Year 3 prevents replacement of inventory, and part of the LIFO base is liquidated. This increases profit margins as follows:

Sales (2,000 @ $1.5125)		$3,025
Cost of sales:		
Beginning LIFO inventory (1,000 @ $1)	$1,000	
Purchases (1,500 @ $1.21)	1,815	
Ending LIFO inventory (500 @ $1)	(500)	2,315
Gross profit		$ 710
Gross profit percentage		23.5%

Management can also adjust profit levels by dipping into LIFO inventory pools. Our analysis must search for disclosure of LIFO liquidations. The following is a disclosure by Federal Mogul Corporation:

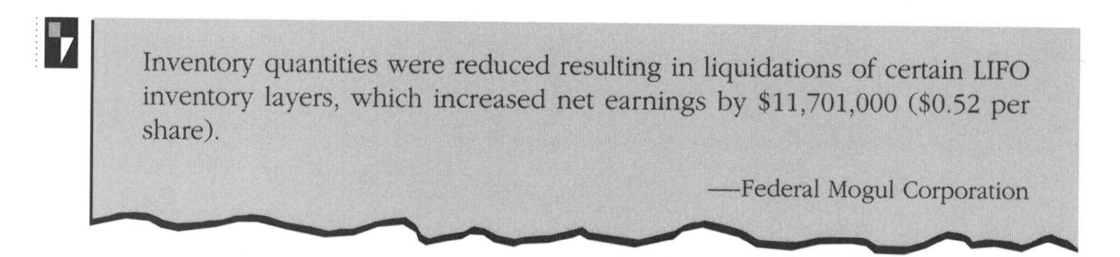

Inventory quantities were reduced resulting in liquidations of certain LIFO inventory layers, which increased net earnings by $11,701,000 ($0.52 per share).

—Federal Mogul Corporation

The amount of any LIFO liquidation gain, usually disclosed with its tax effect, can be considered separately as an unusual nonrecurring item by removing it from the cost of goods sold amount in a recast income statement. Identifying undisclosed LIFO inventory liquidations is sometimes difficult. A crude tool in our analysis is to see whether the dollar value of LIFO inventory has declined on a year-to-year basis. Information about inventory changes and liquidations is often reported in the Management's Discussion and Analysis section of annual reports.

Interim (quarterly) statements offer another challenge to our analysis of companies using LIFO. By application of tax law (conformity rule), LIFO is an *annual calculation*. For interim periods, preparation of financial statements requires forecasts of costs of inventory items purchased or produced as well as projections of future changes in inventory quantities and mix for the entire year. These estimates are subject to considerable managerial discretion—often impairing reliability of LIFO measurements for interim periods.

Analytical Restatement of LIFO Statements to FIFO

When financial statements are available using LIFO, and if LIFO is the method preferred in our analysis, the income statement requires no significant adjustment since cost of goods sold approximates current cost. The LIFO method, however, leaves inventories on the balance sheet at less recent, often understated costs. This can impair the usefulness of various measures like the current ratio or inventory turnover ratio.

Our preceding analysis shows LIFO understates inventory values *when prices are rising*. Consequently, LIFO understates the company's debt-paying ability (as measured, for example, by the current ratio), overstates inventory turnover, and provides a means of earnings management. To counter this we use an analytical technique for adjusting LIFO statements to approximate a pro forma situation assuming FIFO. This is possible when the amount by which current cost exceeds reported cost of LIFO inventories, the **LIFO reserve,** is disclosed. The following three-step pro forma adjustment of accounts is necessary:

Step 1. Inventory + LIFO reserve

Step 2. Deferred tax payable + [LIFO reserve × (1 − Tax rate)]

Step 3. Stockholders' equity + [LIFO reserve × Tax rate]

To calculate the effect on Year 11 net income from the restatement of inventories from LIFO to FIFO, we must compute the adjustment to beginning inventories.

Illustration 4.8

We illustrate restatement of LIFO inventories to FIFO using financial statements of Campbell Soup Co. for Years 10 and 11 in Supplement A. The inventory note 14 reports inventories are net of adjustments to reduce inventories to a LIFO basis (the LIFO reserve) of $89.6 million in Year 11 and $84.6 million in Year 10. To restate Year 11 inventories to a FIFO basis we use the following analytical entry:

Inventories[(a)]	89.6	
Deferred Tax Payable[(b)]		30.5
Retained Earnings[(c)]		59.1

(a) Inventories increase to approximate current replacement cost (a slow turnover can result in inventories at FIFO not being stated at the most current cost).
(b) Since inventories increase, a provision for taxes payable in the future must be made, using a tax rate of 34 percent (note 9). The reason for the tax deferral is the pro forma balance sheet entry reflects an accounting method different from that used for tax purposes.
(c) Higher ending inventories mean lower cost of goods sold and a higher cumulative net income flowing to the balance sheet into retained earnings (net of tax).

Recognize the analytical entry is strictly an adjustment for purposes of our financial analysis.

Illustration 4.9

	Year 11 (in thousands)		
	Under LIFO	*Difference*	*Under FIFO*
Beginning inventory	819.8[(a)]	84.6[(b)]	904.4
+ Purchases (P)[c]	P	—	P
− Ending inventory	(706.7)[(a)]	(89.6)[(b)]	(796.3)
= Cost of goods sold	P + 113.1	−5.0[(d)]	P + 108.1

(a) As reported per balance sheet or note 14.
(b) Per financial statement note 14.
(c) Since purchases are identical under either LIFO or FIFO, purchases need not be adjusted to arrive at the effect on cost of goods sold or net income. If desired, purchases for Year 11 are computed as: $4,095.5 (CGS per income statement) + $706.7 (ending inventory) − $819.8 (beginning inventory) = $3,982.4.
(d) Restatement to FIFO decreases CGS by $5.0 and increases net income by $5.0 × (1 − 0.34), or $3.3 using a 34 percent tax rate. When prices rise, LIFO net income is usually lower than FIFO net income. However, the net effect of restatement in any given year depends on the combined effect of the change in beginning and ending inventories and other factors including liquidation of LIFO layers.

To adjust Year 10 LIFO inventories to FIFO, we use the following analytical entry:

Inventories	84.6	
Deferred Tax Payable		28.8
Retained Earnings		55.8

The income restatement (net of tax) from LIFO to FIFO for Year 11 of $3.3 is reconciled with the credits to retained earnings in the preceding two entries:

Year 10 Credit to Retained Earnings	−	*Year 11 Credit to Retained Earnings*	=	*Increase in Year 11 Net Income*
$55.8		$59.1		$3.3

Prepaid Expenses

Prepaid expenses are advance payments for services or goods not yet received that extend beyond the current accounting period. Examples are advance payments for rent, insurance, utilities, and property taxes. Modest supplies of stationery or stamps are often included in prepaid expenses. Prepaid expenses are generally classified in current assets because they reflect services due that would otherwise require use of current resources during the ensuing operating cycle. Our analysis should be aware, for reasons of expediency and lack of materiality, that services due beyond one year are usually included among prepaid expenses classified as current. Generally, these items represent a small portion of current assets. For Adaptec, prepaid expenses comprise but 5 percent of total current assets for 1996 ($25,271/$465,280). However, when their magnitude is large, or when substantial changes occur, they warrant our scrutiny.

SECTION 2: NONCURRENT ASSETS

Noncurrent Investments

Noncurrent investments are typically of two types: equity securities and debt securities. Noncurrent investments in equity and debt securities are assets and represent resources owned or controlled by a company. These resources are expected to yield future benefits, either in the short or long term, depending on the revenue-generating potential of the investment. Reporting of investments depends on management's intent regarding the holding period, their marketability, and, in the case of equity securities, ownership percent.

Noncurrent Investments in Equity Securities

Equity securities represent ownership interests in another entity. Examples are common and preferred stock. They also include rights to acquire or dispose of ownership interests. Examples include warrants, rights, and call and put options. Redeemable preferred stock and convertible debt securities are not considered equity securities. There are two primary motivations for a company to purchase equity securities: (1) to exert influence over the directors and management of another entity (e.g., suppliers, customers), or (2) to yield dividend and stock price appreciation income. Investors report investments in equity securities according to their ability to influence or control the investee's activities. Evidence of this ability is based on the percent of voting securities controlled by the investor. These percentages are merely guidelines and can be overcome by other factors. For example, a minority interest (e.g., 15 percent) can provide effective control if other owners are widely dispersed and unorganized. Exhibit 4.3 identifies three levels of investor influence along with the valuation method prescribed. We discuss each of these three categories.

Holdings of Less Than 20 Percent

When equity securities are nonvoting preferred or less than 20 percent of an investee's voting stock, they are considered noninfluential. In these cases, investors are assumed to possess minimal influence over the investee's activities. These investments are classified as either trading or available-for-sale securities, based on the intent of management. Accounting for these securities is described in section one of this chapter.

EXHIBIT 4.3 Percent Ownership and Valuation of Equity Securities

	Ownership percent		
	Less than 20 percent	**Between 20 and 50 percent**	**More than 50 percent**
Influence	Minimal	Significant	Controlling
Valuation	Fair value	Equity	Consolidation

Holdings of between 20 Percent and 50 Percent

Security holdings of less than 50 percent of the voting stock can provide an investor the ability to exercise significant influence over an investee's business activities. Evidence of an investor's ability to exert significant influence over an investee's business activities is revealed in several ways such as in management representation and participation. But in the absence of evidence to the contrary, an investment (direct or indirect) of 20 percent or more in the voting stock of an investee is presumed to possess significant influence. When the ability to exercise significant influence is evident, the investor accounts for the investment using the equity method. The **equity method** prescribes investors record investments at cost and adjust them for the investor's proportionate share in the investee's income (or loss) since acquisition and decrease them by dividends received (including certain other adjustments). We discuss the mechanics of this method in Chapter 5. We should recognize while holdings in convertible preferred stock count toward percent ownership, they do not count in adjusting for the proportionate share of income, as shown in Illustration 4.10.

Illustration 4.10

Company A owns 15 percent of the common stock of Company B. Through additional holdings of convertible preferred stock, the total percent of voting power held is 20 percent. While total holdings entitle Company A to account for its investment in Company B using the equity method, it can record only 15 percent of Company B's net income since this is the percent of ownership in B's common stock.

Holdings of More Than 50 Percent

Holdings of more than 50 percent are referred to as **controlling interests**—where the investor is known as the **parent** and the investee as the **subsidiary. Consolidated financial statements,** discussed in Chapter 5, are prepared for holdings of more than 50 percent.

Noncurrent Investments in Debt Securities

Debt securities represent creditor relationships with other entities. Examples are government and municipal bonds, corporate bonds, and convertible debt. A recent survey revealed about 25 percent of companies held noncurrent debt securities (*Accounting Trends and Techniques*). As described earlier in this chapter, debt securities are categorized into one of three classes: held to maturity, available for sale, or trading. Categorization into these classes depends on management's intent. Only held-to-maturity and available-for-sale debt securities are potential noncurrent investments—depending on the securities' maturity dates and, in the case of available-for-sale securities, management's intent for disposition.

Analysis Implications of Noncurrent Investments

We must pay attention to several valuation consequences of accounting for noncurrent investments. One concern arises from using the equity method. Equity securities held by companies with a 20 percent or larger interest (and in certain instances even less than 20 percent) need not be adjusted to market. Rather, companies carry these equity securities at cost, which can be substantially different from market. For example, they can be undervalued due to the prohibition on write-up to market. Moreover, a company can report income from an investee's earnings or dividends while the investee's market value is declining. We must be alert to this potential impairment of value not reflected in financial statements. If separately disclosed, the income generated by equity securities can sometimes provide a clue to their fair value.

Another concern with the equity method is that income from investments can be substantially different from cash flow from investments. An investor company usually only receives cash from an investee's dividends, yet income from investments is often much larger due to recognition of the proportionate interest in the investee's income.

Kmart recently reported income from investments of $80 million. Cash flow (dividends) from these investments equaled $38 million. The difference of $42 million is due to "undistributed equity income."

The equity method can also conceal certain financing obligations—a form of off-balance-sheet financing since an investee's liabilities are not reported among the investor company's liabilities. We often find a summary of an investee's liabilities in the notes to an investor's financial statements. Knowledge of these off-balance-sheet liabilities can affect our liquidity and solvency assessment of an investor company.

We must also be aware of the presumption that an investment of 20 percent or more of the voting securities yields significant influence over an investee. This rule is arbitrary, but made in the interest of uniformity. If influence is absent, we must question an investor's ability to realize the equity valuation amount. Similarly, a company can sometimes exert significant influence over another entity when ownership is less than 20 percent. It is also possible to exert a controlling interest with less than 50 percent ownership, especially when there are no other large ownership blocks and remaining owners hold differing interests. For security holdings exceeding 20 percent, an investor must recognize a decline in value considered permanent like a loss in value on other long-term assets. An evaluation of "permanent" is left to management's judgment and interpretation. Experience shows companies are slow to recognize these losses on investments. We must be alert to situations where hope rather than reason supports the carrying value of an investment. Also, the equity method reflects only current operating losses and not capital losses due to the eroding earning power of investments as illustrated at the top of the next page.

Centran, a bank holding company, reports profits of $9.5 million for the year. Centran did not include losses of more than $120 million in its bond portfolio carried at cost—far exceeding market. Yet management and its directors *increased* dividends. When a hoped-for decline in interest rates failed to materialize, the subsequent periods' financial statements were compelled to reveal the bleak realities.

Joint ventures are another noncurrent investment. They represent investments by two or more entities in an enterprise with an objective of sharing supply sources, market development, or other types of risks and returns. A common form of joint venture is a 50-50 percent sharing of ownership, although other divisions of interest are found. Joint venture investments are accounted for using the equity method. A joint venture investment not evidenced by stock ownership can presumably be accounted for at cost.

ANALYSIS VIEWPOINT *. . . You are the competitor*

Toys "R" Us, a retailer in toys and games, is concerned about a recent transaction involving a competitor. Specifically, Marvel Entertainment Group, a comic book company, obtained 46 percent of equity securities in Toy Biz by granting Toy Biz exclusive worldwide license to use all of Marvel's characters (e.g., Spider-Man, Incredible Hulk, Storm) for toys and games. What is the primary concern of Toys "R" Us? What is Marvel's motivation for its investment in Toy Biz's equity securities?

Plant Assets and Natural Resources

Property, plant, and equipment (or plant assets) are noncurrent tangible assets used in the manufacturing, merchandising, or service processes. These assets contribute to these processes in a desire to generate revenues, and cash flows, for *more than one future period*. Accordingly, these assets have expected benefit periods (or useful lives) extending over more than one period. They are intended for use in operating activities, and are not acquired for sale in the ordinary course of business. Accordingly, their value or service potential diminishes with use. They are typically the largest of all operating assets. *Property* refers to the cost of real estate; *plant* refers to buildings and operating structures; and *equipment* refers to machinery used in operations. Property, plant, and equipment are also referred to as *productive assets, capital assets,* and *fixed assets*.

Valuing Property, Plant, and Equipment

The historical cost principle is used in valuing property, plant, and equipment. Historical cost valuation implies a company intially records an asset at its fair market

Property, Plant, and Equipment as a Percentage of Assets

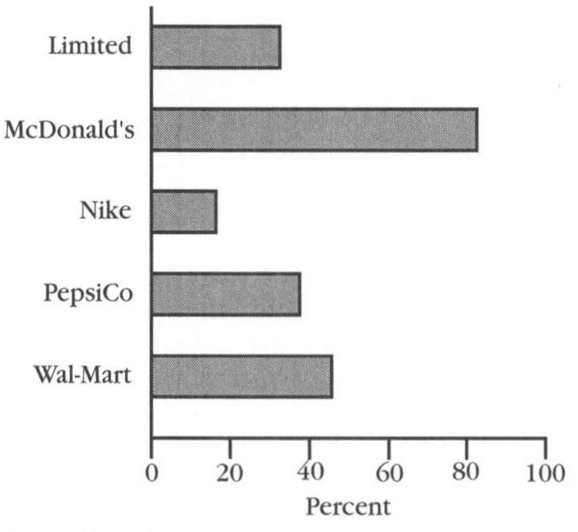

Source: Annual reports.

value or the fair market value of the asset(s) given up. This cost includes any additional expenses necessary to bring the asset to a useable or serviceable condition and location such as freight, installation, taxes, and set-up costs. All costs of acquisition and preparation are capitalized in the asset's account balance. Justification for historical cost includes:

- **Conservatism** in not anticipating subsequent replacement costs.
- **Accountability** in dollar amount for management.
- **Objectivity** in cost determination.

Capitalization and subsequent periods' allocation of plant asset costs, vis-à-vis expensing of these costs, are central to accounting practice and depend on the purpose of these costs, their benefit period, and materiality of amount. Historical cost valuation of plant assets, if consistently applied, does not lend itself to serious distortion. However, this is not the case when determining a benefit period and depreciation schedule. These issues are important to our analysis and we consider them in Chapter 6.

Interest costs during construction is one expenditure subject to debate. These costs result from funds being unavailable for use while an asset is being constructed and before it is productively utilized. Companies capitalize these costs and allocate them to future operations along with other capitalized costs. Despite this ruling, there is variety in practice relating to costs included when a company constructs a plant asset. While most direct costs are readily included, allocation of variable overhead and particularly fixed overhead costs is problematic. For example, when idle capacity is used to construct operating assets, inclusion of fixed overhead is arguable. If production is forgone to construct assets, there are grounds for capitalizing a proportionate share of overhead.

Another concern confronting our analysis of property, plant, and equipment is that historical cost fails to reflect changes in the measuring unit. Accumulation of costs acquired over different periods reflects aggregation of measuring units (dollars) with differing purchasing power. Since depreciation, the allocation of capitalized costs over the asset's benefit period, uses original cost, this distortion affects income. Thus, a case is made for adjusting historical cost for changes in purchasing power—not as an attempt to arrive at current market value. A case can also be made for computing depreciation using current replacement costs. Under either case, more "realistic" measures result in arguably more valid income statements with a better distinction between income and "real" capital, and present a fairer measure of management's success in managing invested funds.

All property, plant, and equipment assets are presumably part of continuing operating activities. If any of these assets are temporarily idle, companies are required to disclose this in notes to financial statements. Such disclosure might explain excess costs or lower profit margins. Should assets be idle for longer periods of time without definite prospects of use, companies exclude them from the Property, Plant, and Equipment account pending their reactivation, sale, or disposition. Their inclusion would distort relations like sales to operating assets, or return on operating assets. Idle assets represent investments with little or no return, and often require upkeep and maintenance. Kaiser Aluminum & Chemical Corporation includes a note in its annual report regarding idle assets:

> Idle facilities include the corporation's Chalmette, Louisiana, aluminum smelter which is temporarily closed because of high energy costs and generally poor market conditions for primary aluminum. The corporation wrote down its Baton Rouge, Louisiana, alumina refinery which had been included in idle facilities last year. Currently, production of alumina at Alumina Partners of Jamaica (ALPART) was temporarily suspended due to the continuing adverse economic conditions impacting the aluminum industry . . . Management believes that market conditions will improve and that operating costs of the idle facilities can be reduced sufficiently to permit economic operation of these facilities in the future. The corporation's policy is to continue normal depreciation for temporarily closed facilities.
>
> —Kaiser Aluminum & Chemical Corp.

Write-up of plant assets to market is not acceptable accounting. Yet conservatism permits a write-down if a permanent impairment of value and/or loss of utility occurs. A write-down relieves future periods of charges unrelated to operating activities. Amerada Hess Corporation reports the following asset write-down in its annual report:

> *Special Charge*
> The Corporation recorded a special charge to earnings of $536,692,000 ($432,742,000 after income taxes, or $5.12 per share). The special charge consists of a $146,768,000 write-down in the book value of certain ocean-going tankers and a $389,924,000 provision for marine transportation costs in excess of market rates.
>
> —Amerada Hess Corporation

While realities of business dictate numerous uncertainties, including accounting estimation errors, our analysis demands awareness of economic losses. Recent accounting rules for "impairments of long-lived assets" require companies to periodically review events or changes in circumstances for possible impairments.[1] Nevertheless, companies can still defer recognition of impairments beyond the time when management first learns of them. Subsequent write-downs can, hence, distort reported results. Under current rules, companies use a "recoverability test" to determine whether an impairment exists. A company must estimate future net cash flows expected from the asset and its eventual disposition. If these expected net cash flows (undiscounted) are less than the asset's carrying amount, it is impaired. The impairment loss is measured as the excess of the asset's carrying value over fair value, where fair value is the market value or present value of expected future net cash flows. In some cases, projects must be written down before becoming operative.

---

[1] See "Accounting for the Impairment of Long-Lived Assets and for Long-Lived Assets to Be Disposed Of," *Statement of Financial Accounting Standards No. 121* (Norwalk, Conn.: FASB, 1995).

Analysis Research Insight 4.3

Write-Down of Asset Values

Asset write-downs are increasingly conspicuous due to their escalating number and frequency in recent years. Are these write-downs good or bad signals about current and future prospects of a company? What are the implications of these asset write-downs for financial analysis? Are write-downs relevant for security valuation? Do write-downs alter users' risk exposures? Analysis research is beginning to provide us insights into these questions.

Evidence shows that companies previously recording write-downs are more likely to report current and future write-downs. This result adds an additional complexity to our analysis and interpretation of earnings. Research also examines whether companies take advantage of the discretionary nature of asset write-downs to manage earnings toward a "target" figure. Evidence on this question shows management tends to time asset write-downs for a period when their company's financial performance is already low relative to competitors. While this evidence is consistent with companies loading income with additional charges during years when earnings are unfavorable (referred to as a *big bath*), it is also consistent with management taking an appropriate reduction in asset value attributed to decreasing earnings potential. Regardless, our analysis of a company's financial statements that include write-downs must consider their implications in light of current business conditions and company performance.

Caterpillar Co. wrote off more than $200 million mostly due to the uneconomical nature of an unfinished parts center. In another case, Philip Morris, having overestimated U.S. beer consumption, incurred a nearly $300 million pretax loss in the write-down of a newly completed brewery that was promptly mothballed.

In other cases, operations can fail after a period of unsuccessful results, or political or economic conditions can undermine the viability of operations.

Pillsbury Co. recorded a more than $100 million loss in the sale or shutdown of several money-losing restaurant operations. In another case, Squibb Corporation declared its South American and Asian pharmaceutical operations permanently impaired due to adverse political and economic conditions—resulting in a $68 million write-down.

The method of acquiring assets should not bear on their valuation. Nevertheless, one method of acquisition deserves special mention—leasing. Acquiring assets through leasing is often a means of financing purchases. These leases are accounted for as purchases, and result in an asset equal in amount to the present value of future rental payments. When leasing is short term (covering a period less than the asset's useful life) and no property rights are acquired, no lease asset is recorded. A crucial characteristic with leasing is its means of financing, as discussed in Chapter 3.

Valuing Natural Resources

Natural resources, often referred to as **wasting assets**, are rights to extract or consume natural resources. Examples include purchase rights to minerals, timber, natural gas, and petroleum. Natural resources possess two important characteristics: (1) removal or consumption of the asset, and (2) replacement of the asset by natural progression. Timber is, of course, replenished by cutting and replanting, yet most natural resources once exhausted cannot be replenished (e.g., oil, coal, iron ore, sulfur). Companies report natural resources at historical cost plus costs of discovery, exploration, and development. The often substantial costs subsequent to discovery of natural resources are not given immediate recognition. Rather, they are recorded for income determination when the resource is removed, consumed, or sold. Companies typically allocate costs of natural resources over the total units of estimated reserves available. This allocation process is called depletion, and is discussed in Chapter 6 under reporting for oil exploration costs.

Analysis Implications of Plant Assets and Natural Resources

Valuation of property, plant, equipment, and natural resources emphasizes objectivity of historical cost, the conservatism principle, and accounting for the monies invested in these assets. There is no overt recognition of user needs in analyzing these assets. Rather, preparers often argue balance sheets do not purport to reflect market values. Historical costs are not especially relevant in assessing replacement values or in determining future need for operating assets. They are not directly comparable across different companies' reports, and are not particularly useful in measuring opportunity costs of disposal nor in assessing alternative uses of funds. In times of changing price levels, they represent a peculiar collection of expenditures reflecting different purchasing power.

Yet operating assets represent a company's capacity to produce goods or services. One of management's primary concerns rests in effectively and efficiently managing operating assets. It is sometimes argued the value of assets derives from their ability to earn a return and, consequently, their value rests with the income statement. While true in many ways, this is not the only avenue to evaluating an asset's worth. Asset worth is tied to its productive capacity and the skill of management.

We must also be aware of the increasing use of write-downs in practice. Examples include Diamond Shamrock Company's $600 million write-down of its oil and gas properties, and Standard Oil's $200 million write-down of its gas and oil reserves. Similarly, a change in the estimated benefit period can act like a form of write-down extending over more than one period.

> The Company reduced the estimated useful lives of its New Wales uranium plant assets because of the uncertainty whether sales contracts, covering most of the production, will be renewed when they expire . . . and whether the market price of uranium oxide will be favorable enough to warrant continued operation of the plant beyond that date . . . depreciation expense increased $4.3 million because of this change.
>
> —IMC Fertilizer Group

Asset valuation issues arise also with public utilities when operating assets are impaired due to reasons like cost overruns or inefficient operations. In assessing the value of operating assets after deregulation, American Telephone & Telegraph Co. recorded a $7.3 billion pretax write-down of network facilities and telephone equipment. There is an increasing reluctance of regulatory bodies to allow recovery of such costs through utility rate increases.

Intangible Assets

Intangible assets represent rights, privileges, and benefits of possession. Two common characteristics are high uncertainty regarding future benefits and lack of physical existence. Examples of some important categories of intangibles are shown in Exhibit 4.4. Intangible assets often (1) are nonseparable from a company, (2) have indefinite benefit periods, and (3) experience large valuation changes based on competitive circumstances. Historical cost, including costs necessary to ready the asset for its intended use, is the valuation rule for *purchased* intangibles. There is an important difference between accounting for tangible and intangible assets. If a company uses materials and labor in constructing a tangible asset, it capitalizes these costs and depreciates them over its benefit period. In contrast, a company spending monies advertising a product or training a sales force, or creating *internally developed* goodwill, cannot usually capitalize these costs even though they are often highly beneficial to future business activities. This treatment is attributed to conservatism—presumably due to increased uncertainty of realizing the benefits of intangibles (like advertising or training) vis-à-vis those of tangible assets.

Intangibles as a Percentage of Assets

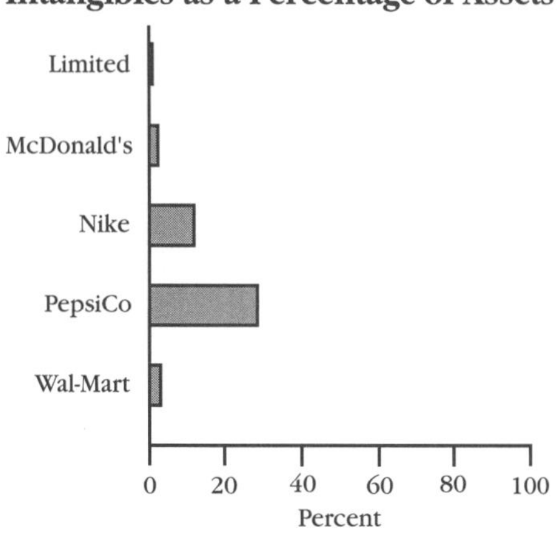

Source: Annual reports.

Identifiable Intangibles

Identifiable intangibles are separately identified and linked with specific rights or privileges having limited benefit periods. Likely candidates include patents, trademarks, copyrights, and franchises. Identifiable intangibles are developed internally, or acquired singly or in combination with a group of assets. Companies record them at cost and amortize them over their benefit periods. Writing off to expense the entire cost at acquisition is prohibited.

Unidentifiable Intangibles

Unidentifiable intangibles are rights or privileges either developed internally or purchased that are not specifically identifiable and often have indefinite benefit periods. They cannot be acquired singly, but rather are part of a larger collection of assets. A typical example is the excess of the price paid to acquire a company over the

EXHIBIT 4.4 Selected Categories of Intangible Assets

- Goodwill
- Patents, copyrights, and trademarks
- Leases, leaseholds, and leasehold improvements
- Exploration rights and natural resource development costs
- Special formulas, processes, and designs
- Licenses, franchises, memberships, and customer lists

EXHIBIT 4.5 Accounting for Intangible Assets

	Manner of Acquisition	
	Purchased	***Developed Internally***
Identifiable intangible	Capitalize and Amortize	Expense with some exceptions
Unidentifiable intangible	Capitalize and Amortize	Expense

sum of the fair values of all identifiable assets and liabilities. This excess cost is referred to as **goodwill**, and is the residual between acquisition cost and the sum of the fair values of tangible and identifiable intangible net assets. Companies expense as incurred the costs of developing, maintaining, or restoring unidentifiable intangibles. Exhibit 4.5 summarizes the accounting treatment for both types of intangible assets.

Goodwill is often a sizable asset and is recorded only upon purchase of another business entity or segment. Its description varies considerably—it can refer to an ability to attract and retain customers, or to qualities inherent in business activities such as organization, efficiency, and effectiveness. These qualities are apparent in the difference between a start-up company and a successful, on-going company. Goodwill is earning power. Since a given amount of invested capital expects a minimum return adjusted for risk, goodwill is tied to the level of earnings over and above this minimum return. These excess earnings are referred to as *superearnings*, and are similar to *abnormal earnings* described in Chapter 2.

Amortizing Costs of Intangibles

When costs are capitalized for both identifiable and unidentifiable intangible assets, they must be subsequently amortized over their presumed benefit periods. The duration of a benefit period depends on the type of intangible, demand conditions, competitive circumstances, and any other legal, contractual, regulatory, or economic limitations. Law, regulation, or agreement limit many benefit periods. Patents are rights conveyed by governments to an inventor, granting exclusive right to an invention for a specified term. Similarly, registered copyrights and trademarks convey exclusive rights for specific periods. Leaseholds and leasehold improvements are benefits of occupancy contractually limited by the lease. A benefit period for accounting amortization cannot exceed 40 years. Consistent with noncurrent tangible assets, if an intangible materially declines in value (applying the recoverability test), it is written down.

When a company acquires another business or segment, one needs to allocate the amount paid to all identifiable net assets in accordance with their fair market values. If any excess remains after this allocation, it is classified as goodwill. If the fair market values of net assets acquired exceed the purchase price, a "bargain purchase credit" (or *badwill*) results. After certain accounting adjustments, companies amortize any badwill to income over an arbitrary period not to exceed 40 years. Dun & Bradstreet Corporation describes its goodwill and intangible asset amortization policy as follows:

Frequency of Goodwill Amortization Benefit Periods

40 years
Not exceeding 40 years
25–30 years
20 years
10–15 years
Legal/estimated life
Other
0 20 40 60 80 100
Percent

Source: *Accounting Trends & Techniques*

Other Assets. Computer software ($86,332,000) and data files ($25,656,000), certain other intangibles ($99,118,000), and goodwill ($288,322,000) are being amortized, using principally the straight-line method, over 5 to 15 years, 12 to 40 years and 40 years, respectively.

—Dun and Bradstreet Corporation

Analysis Implications of Intangibles

Financial statement users often treat intangibles with suspicion when analyzing financial statements. Many users associate intangibles with riskiness. We encourage caution and understanding in evaluating their worth to a company. Intangibles are often one of the more valuable assets a company owns, and can be undervalued or carried at inflated amounts. An extremely conservative adjustment, absent any more substantive information, is to ignore intangibles in financial analysis. Analysis of goodwill reveals some interesting cases. We know goodwill is recorded only when acquired, thus, additional goodwill can exist off balance sheet. We also know that goodwill must eventually be reflected in superearnings. If superearnings are not evident, goodwill, whether purchased or not, is of little or no value. Goodwill is an advantage that must manifest itself in superearnings or fail to exist. While the write-off of goodwill reported by Inter City Gas Corporation is uncommon, it illustrates our point:

Pursuant to this reorganization and as a result of the losses incurred by KeepRite in the past two years, the Company has reassessed its investment in KeepRite Inc. As a result of this re-assessment, it has been determined that the value of the underlying assets in KeepRite have been impaired by an amount of $4,697,000. Accordingly, the Company has written off goodwill of $4,697,000 as an extraordinary charge against income.

—Inter City Gas Corporation

We must also be aware of management's latitude in amortizing intangibles. Since reducing amortization expense improves reported earnings, goodwill and other intangibles might be written off over longer than appropriate periods. While the 40-year

ANALYSIS VIEWPOINT . . . *You are the environmentalist*

You are testifying at congressional hearings demanding substantially tougher pollution standards for paper mills. The companies' spokesperson insists tougher standards cannot be afforded, and continually points to an asset to liability ratio of slightly above 1.0 as indicative of financial vulnerability. You counter by arguing the existence of undervalued and unrecorded intangible assets. The spokesperson insists any intangibles are worthless apart from the company, that financial statements are fairly presented and certified by an independent auditor, and that intangible assets are irrelevant to these hearings. How do you counter the spokesperson's arguments?

maximum benefit period for intangibles is arbitrary and can force excessive amortization, we can probably assume any bias is in the direction of too slow a rate of amortization. We can adjust these rates if armed with substantive information on intangibles' benefit periods.

In analyzing intangibles we must be prepared to form our own judgments regarding their valuation. We must also remember that goodwill recorded from business combinations before November 1970 does not require amortization—there remain billions of dollars of unamortized goodwill on today's balance sheets due to this ruling. Moreover, only in rare situations do auditors qualify their opinion with respect to the continuing value of unamortized goodwill.

Deferred Charges

Deferred charges are costs incurred but deferred because they are expected to benefit future periods or are prepaids benefitting future periods. Increasing complexities of business activities are expanding the number and types of deferred charges. Examples are prepaid pension costs, segregated cash or securities, and certain intangibles.

Rationale for Cost Deferral

Motivation for deferral of expenses and costs is the matching of costs to revenues they generate. If a cost incurred in the current period benefits a future period(s) by either a contribution to revenues or reduction in costs, then a company defers this cost until the future period(s). For example, if a company incurs start-up costs in operating new, better, or more efficient facilities, it can defer these costs and match (amortize) them to expected future benefit periods.

Research and Development Costs

Research and development costs are expenditures aimed at discovery of new knowledge or the translation of knowledge into a design for a new or revised product or process. Companies charge these costs to expense when incurred. This applies to either tangible or intangible assets purchased for use in a single project. However, if purchased assets are usable in more than one project, they are capitalized and their costs amortized to these projects. Research and development costs conducted for others under a contractual arrangement, including indirect costs specifically reimbursable, can also be recorded as work in progress or receivables under contracts and not immediately expensed. Some public utility regulatory commissions require deferral and amortization of research and development costs, and allow this accounting treatment in determining utility rates. Further discussion of implications from research and development is in Chapter 6.

Adaptec's 1996 research and development costs exceeded $87 million. This compares to Adaptec's 1996 net income of $103 million. Boeing Company's annual report disclosed research and development costs exceeding $2 billion in 1994, compared to a net income of $856 million.

Computer Software Costs

Computer software costs are expenditures to purchase or create software for either internal or external use in companies' business activities. Companies expense many computer software costs when incurred. If "technological feasibility" of the software is established, computer software costs are capitalized and amortized to current and future benefit periods. Technological feasibility is demonstrated in two ways. If a company's development process includes preparing a detailed program design (i.e., a blueprint usable by programmers for coding), then this must be completed to establish technological feasibility. If this detailed program design is not prepared, a working model must be established for capitalizing costs. Companies purchasing or developing software as an integral part of a product or process need to establish the software's technological feasibility, and complete research and development activities for other parts of the product or process prior to capitalizing costs. Companies amoritze capitalized software costs over the expected benefit period. The following note reveals capitalizing software costs increases earnings of Wang Laboratories, Inc., by nearly $20 million.

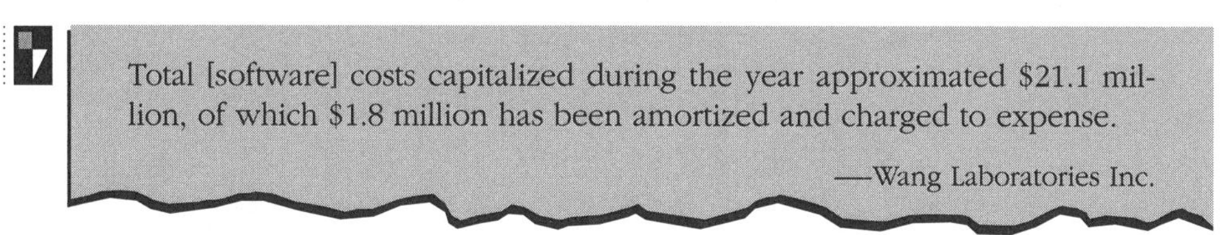
Total [software] costs capitalized during the year approximated $21.1 million, of which $1.8 million has been amortized and charged to expense.

—Wang Laboratories Inc.

Additional Deferred Charges

Companies often capitalize start-up costs as a deferred charge and amortize them over an expected future benefit period. Neptune International describes its deferral of start-up costs as follows:

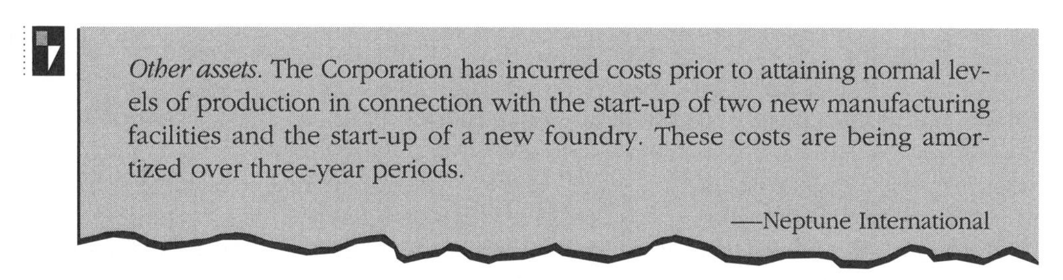
Other assets. The Corporation has incurred costs prior to attaining normal levels of production in connection with the start-up of two new manufacturing facilities and the start-up of a new foundry. These costs are being amortized over three-year periods.

—Neptune International

Relocation costs are another item often capitalized as a deferred charge. Willcox & Gibbs, Inc., includes the following note in its annual report:

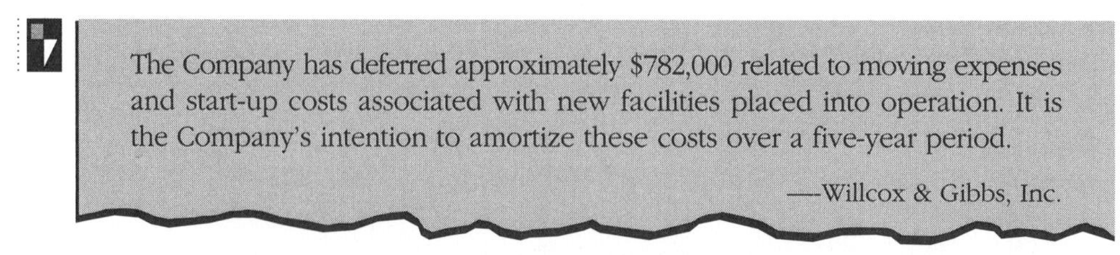
The Company has deferred approximately $782,000 related to moving expenses and start-up costs associated with new facilities placed into operation. It is the Company's intention to amortize these costs over a five-year period.

—Willcox & Gibbs, Inc.

There is disagreement on the merits of deferring start-up and relocation costs in practice. Increasing complexities in both technology and business practices have

EXHIBIT 4.6 Partial Listing of Possible Deferred Charges

Business Development, Expansion, Merger, and Relocation Costs
- Preoperating expenses, initial start-up costs, and tooling costs
- Initial operating losses or preoperating expenses of subsidiaries
- Moving, plant rearrangement, and reinstallation costs
- Merger or acquisition expenses
- Purchased customer accounts
- Noncompete agreements

Deferred Expenses
- Advertising and promotional expenses
- Imputed interest
- Selling, general, and administrative expenses
- Pension plan costs
- Property and other taxes
- Rental and leasing costs
- Vacation pay
- Seasonal growing and packing expenses

Intangible Costs
- Intangible drilling and development costs
- Contracts, films, copyright materials, and art rights
- Costs of computer software

Debt Issue Expenses

Future Income Tax Benefits

Organization Costs

Advance Royalties

expanded the Deferred Charges account. Since deferred charges often represent intangible future benefits, they are very similar in nature to intangible assets. Exhibit 4.6 offers a glimpse into the variety of deferred charges in financial statements. While we focus on the validity of these costs as deferred charges, we must remember it is not existence but timing of expense recognition that is relevant.

Analysis Implications of Deferred Charges

Deferred charges are often substantial and present challenges in our understanding and interpretation of financial statements. We can readily understand certain deferred charges like start-up costs or debt issue costs. Other deferred charges, like organization costs, are more difficult to justify and their amortization periods are arbitrary. Many users are not supportive of capitalization of software costs. They are concerned with rapid obsolescence of software and unjustified deferring of expenses. Users are also concerned the balance sheet excludes capitalizing more important assets like research and development. Validating many deferred charges, like relocation costs, promotional costs, or initial operating losses, depends on several estimates. Similarly, assessing the benefit period over which companies amortize deferred charges demands attention. Our analysis must be alert to deferred charges that do not represent future benefits. Experience shows us costs are sometimes carried forward under the guise of deferred charges so as not to burden current operating results with additional expenses. While an auditor's opinion and a company's description of deferred costs are helpful in our analysis, we must be prepared to evaluate evidence and information regarding deferrals on our own. We must also be aware that deferred charges are generally incapable of satisfying creditors' claims. Overall, our analysis of financial statements must examine the propensity of management to defer the costs of today into tomorrow. This is symptomatic of certain behavior in practice. Following is a classic case in point.

Lockheed Corporation experienced a time of unprofitable activity in its TriStar Jetliner program. Management repeated forecasts of future favorable developments, yet new orders consistently proved overoptimistic. Management deferred "initial planning and tooling and unrecovered production start-up costs," and adopted a policy of amortizing these deferred charges over a 10-year period. By the middle of this 10-year period, deferred TriStar costs grew to more than $280 million. Two-thirds into this period, Lockheed abandoned TriStar and was forced to recognize the inevitable—to write off the deferred charges that had overstated operating results for the past several years. Inventory write-downs added further to the losses with this program.

Unrecorded Intangibles and Contingent Assets

Our discussion of assets is not complete without mention of intangible and contingent assets not recorded in a balance sheet. One important asset is internally generated goodwill. In practice, expenditures toward creating goodwill are expensed when incurred. To the extent goodwill is created, and is saleable or generates superior earning power, a company's income is understated due to current expenses related to its development. Our analysis must recognize these cases and adjust assets accordingly. Another important category of unrecorded assets relates to service or idea elements. Examples are television programs carried at amortized cost (or nothing) but continuing to yield millions of dollars in licensing fees (e.g., *Gilligan's Island*, *M*A*S*H*, *Star Trek*), and current drugs taking years to develop but whose costs were written off many years earlier. Other examples are developed trade names like Coca-Cola, McDonald's, Nike, Kodak, and Pepsi; Exhibit 4.7 shows value estimates of some major trade names. In the end, the value of intangibles depends on producing super earnings

Contingent assets are another item not recognized in balance sheets. *Contingent assets* are rights or claims to resources whose existence is uncertain. Examples are pending court cases, donations, and bonuses. Contingent assets are disclosed in notes to financial statements only when there is a *very high likelihood* of existence. Allegheny Ludlum Industries, Inc., offers an example of a contingent asset disclosure:

A Federal District Court in Houston, Texas, following a jury trial completed earlier, entered judgment of approximately $18,900,000 in favor of Chemetron Corporation, a wholly-owned subsidiary of Allegheny, against Marathon Manufacturing Corporation and two individual defendants in a suit brought for securities law violations. That judgment has been appealed by the defendants and, since the outcome cannot be predicted at this time, no portion of the judgment has been reflected in the accompanying financial statements.

—Allegheny Ludlum Industries, Inc.

EXHIBIT 4.7 Valuation of Trade Names

Trade Name	*Company*	*Value ($billions)*
Marlboro	Philip Morris	$31.2
Coca-Cola	Coca-Cola	24.4
Budweiser	Anheuser-Busch	10.2
Pepsi-Cola	PepsiCo	9.6
Nescafé coffee	Nestlé	8.5
Kellogg cereals	Kellogg	8.4
Winston cigarettes	RJR Nabisco	6.1
Pampers diapers	Procter & Gamble	6.1
Camel cigarettes	RJR Nabisco	4.4
Campbell soups	Campbell	3.9
Nestlé sweets	Nestlé	3.7
Hennessy cognac	LVMH	3.0
Heineken beer	Heineken	2.7
Johnnie Walker scotch	Guinness	2.6
Louis Vuitton luggage	LVMH	2.6
Hershey sweets	Hershey	2.3
Guinness beer	Guinness	2.3
Barbie dolls	Mattel	2.2
Kraft cheese	Philip Morris	2.2
Smirnoff vodka	Grand Metropolitan	2.2

Source: *Financial World*, August 1992.

GUIDANCE ANSWERS TO ANALYSIS VIEWPOINTS

You Are the Investment Analyst

An investment analyst must consider *both* cash flow and net income. Cash flow is important for liquidity reasons—the company must pay employees, creditors, suppliers, and other providers to the business. Net income, on the other hand, only recognizes cash inflows as revenue when *earned* and cash outflows as expenses when actually *incurred*. Cash flow and net income differ only by the accounting accruals reflecting these differences.

You Are the Auditor

Yes, an auditor must be concerned about changes in estimates, especially when those changes exactly coincide with earlier predictions of management. An auditor must be certain the estimate of uncollectible accounts is reasonable in light of current industry, economic, and customer conditions.

You Are the Buying Agent

Yes, a buying agent should not necessarily compensate suppliers for potentially poor purchasing decisions. The supplier's 20 percent reported gross margin has the $2 million market adjustment "buried" in its cost of goods sold figure. The buyer should remove the market adjustment from cost of goods sold and place it among operating expenses in the income statement. Accordingly, the supplier's gross margin would be $2 million greater, and the buyer has a legitimately stronger negotiating position for a lower price.

You Are the Competitor

Toys "R" Us is concerned about the threat of the Marvel/Toy Biz agreement for its future sales in toys and games. Financial statement disclosure of this agreement is not only useful for those interested in Marvel and Toy Biz, but is also useful (and in some cases markedly more important) to the financial condition of competitors like Toys "R" Us. Because of this agreement, Marvel character-based toys are one of the leading boys' action figure lines, and Toy Biz recently introduced Marvel Interactive CD-ROM comics. Toy Biz is now arguably the fastest-growing toys and games company, and recently listed its securities on the New York Stock Exchange. The motivation for Marvel's acquisition of 46 percent of equity securities in Toy Biz is to retain some influence on the business activities of Toy Biz—especially as it relates to Marvel-related products. It is also an opportunity for Marvel to expand its operations using the existing expertise of Toy Biz and, thus, reduce its investment risk.

You Are the Environmentalist

This is a difficult issue to resolve. On one hand, the spokesperson's claim that intangibles are irrelevant is in error—intangible assets confer substantial economic benefits to companies and often comprise a major part of assets. Moreover, the spokesperson's reliance on the auditors certifying the fairness of financial statements according to accepted accounting principles is misguided. Since accounting principles do not permit capitalization of internally generated intangibles, do not require adjustment of intangibles to their market values, and do not value many intangibles (human resources, customer/buyer relationships), an auditor's certification is insufficient evidence on the worth of intangibles. On the other hand, the spokesperson is correct in questioning the value of intangibles apart from the company. Absent sale of a company or a segment of it, the cash inflow from intangibles is indirect—through above-normal earnings levels. In addition, most lending institutions do not accept intangibles as collateral in making credit decisions. In sum, resolution of these hearings must recognize the existence of intangibles, the sometimes high degree of uncertainty regarding value and duration of intangibles, the limited worth of intangibles absent liquidation of all or part of a company, and finally the need for a "political" decision reflecting the needs of society.

QUESTIONS

4–1. Following common practice, companies typically report compensating balances under a loan agreement as unrestricted cash classified within current assets.

a. For purposes of analysis of financial statements, is this a useful classification?

b. Describe how you would evaluate compensating balances.

4–2. *a.* Explain what is meant by a company's operating cycle.

b. Discuss the significance of the operating cycle to classification of current versus noncurrent items in a balance sheet.

c. Is the operating cycle concept useful in measuring the current debt-paying ability of a company and the liquidity of its working capital components?

d. Describe the effect of the operating cycle for classification of selected current assets in the following industries: (1) tobacco, (2) liquor, and (3) retailing.

4–3. Accounting for investments in debt and equity securities follows certain generally accepted procedures.

a. Describe the salient provisions in accounting requirements for investments.

b. Discuss the disclosures required for these investments.

4–4. Discuss some of the gaps and inconsistencies in accounting for debt and equity securities (*SFAS No.115*) of which we must be aware in our analysis.

4–5. *a.* Identify the primary concerns in our analysis of accounts receivable.

b. Describe information, other than that usually available in financial statements, we should gather to assess the risk of noncollectibility of receivables.

4–6. Explain why analysts typically attach great importance to inventories.

4–7. *a.* Discuss the consequences associated with the various methods available in accounting for the cost of inventories and determination of income.

b. Comment on the variation in practice as to inclusion of costs in inventories. Give examples of three types of such cost components.

4–8. Describe the significance of the level of activity on the unit cost of goods produced by a manufacturer. Allocation of overhead costs requires certain assumptions; explain and illustrate allocations and activity levels through an example.

4–9. Explain the major objective(s) of LIFO inventory accounting. Discuss the consequences of using LIFO on both the measurement of income and the valuation of inventories for analysis of financial statements.

4–10. Discuss current disclosures for inventory valuation methods in practice. Describe how these disclosures are useful in our analysis. Identify additional types of inventory disclosures that would be useful in our analysis.

4–11. Following common practice, companies generally apply the lower-of-cost-or-market (LCM) method for inventory valuation.

a. Define *cost* as it applies to inventory valuation.

b. Define *market* as it applies to inventory valuation.

c. Discuss the rationale behind the LCM rule.

d. Identify any arguments against use of LCM.

4–12. Compare and contrast effects of the LIFO and FIFO inventory costing methods on earnings during a period of inflation.

4–13. Discuss ways and conditions under which FIFO and LIFO inventory costing methods produce different inventory valuations. Do not discuss procedures for computing inventory cost.

4–14. Describe the accounting principles applying to noncurrent equity securities.

4–15. Describe accounting principles governing valuation and presentation of noncurrent investments. Distinguish between accounting for investments in equity securities of an investee when holding *(a)* less than 20 percent of voting shares outstanding, and *(b)* 20 percent or more of voting shares outstanding.

4–16. *a.* Evaluate accounting for investments when holding between 20 and 50 percent of equity securities of an investee from the view of an analyst of financial statements.

b. When are losses in noncurrent investments recognized? Evaluate the accounting governing recognition of these losses.

4–17. Describe weaknesses and inconsistencies in accounting for noncurrent investments of which we need be aware.

4–18. Explain how idle plant and equipment is reported in the balance sheet. Describe the reasons for this presentation.

4–19. Net income of companies exploring for natural resources sometimes bears little relation to the amount reported on the balance sheet for natural resources.

a. Explain how this can happen.

b. Describe circumstances where a more consistent relation is likely to exist.

4–20. From the view of a user of financial statements, describe objections to using historical cost as the basis of valuing tangible assets.

4–21. *a.* Identify the basic principles governing valuation of intangible assets.

b. Distinguish between accounting for internally developed and purchased intangibles.

c. Discuss the importance of distinguishing between identifiable intangibles and unidentifiable intangibles.

d. Explain the principles underlying amortization of intangible assets.

4–22. Describe analysis implications of the accounting for goodwill.

4–23. Identify five types of deferred charges and describe their rationale for deferral.

4–24. *a.* Describe two or more assets not recorded on the balance sheet.

b. Explain how an analyst evaluates unrecorded assets.

EXERCISES

Exercise 4–1
Components and Valuation of Cash

Accounting for cash is generally regarded as uncomplicated, yet certain complexities can arise for both domestic and multinational companies.

Required:

a. Describe the usual components of cash.

b. Identify circumstances giving rise to valuation problems with cash for our analysis.

Exercise 4–2
Analyzing Allowances for Uncollectible Receivables

On December 31, Year 1, Carme Company had significant amounts of accounts receivable as a result of credit sales to customers. Carme Company uses the allowance method based on credit sales to estimate bad debts. Based on past experience, Carme will normally not collect 1 percent of credit sales. Carme expects this pattern to continue.

Required:

a. Discuss the rationale for using the allowance method based on credit sales to estimate bad debts. Contrast this method with the allowance method based on the balance in the Trade Receivables accounts.

b. How should Carme Company report the Allowance for Bad Debts account on its balance sheet at December 31, Year 1? Describe the alternatives, if any, for presentation of bad debt expense in Carme Company's Year 1 income statement.

c. Explain your objectives in analyzing the reasonableness of Carme Company's Allowance for Bad Debts.

(AICPA Adapted)

Exercise 4–3
Analyzing Notes Receivable

On July 1, Year 1, Carmen Company, a calendar-year company, sold special-order merchandise on credit and received in return an interest-bearing note receivable from the customer. Carmen Company will receive interest at the prevailing rate for a note of this type. Both the principal and interest are due in one lump sum on June 30, Year 2.

Required:

a. When should Carmen Company report interest income from the note receivable? Discuss the rationale for your answer.

b. Assume that the bank discounts the note receivable without recourse on December 31, Year 1. How would Carmen Company determine the amount of the discount and what is the appropriate accounting for the discounting transaction?

c. What are your concerns when analyzing an interest-bearing note receivable?

(AICPA Adapted)

Exercise 4–4

Assessing Inventory Cost and Market

Steel Company, a wholesaler that has been in business for two years, purchases its inventories from various suppliers. During the two years, each purchase has been at a lower price than the previous purchase. Steel uses the lower-of-FIFO-cost-or-market method to value inventories. The original cost of the inventories is above replacement cost and below the net realizable value. The net realizable value less the normal profit margin is below the replacement cost.

Required:

a. What criteria should be used in determining costs to include in inventory?

b. Why is the lower-of-cost-or-market rule used in reporting inventory?

c. At what amount should Steel report its inventories on the balance sheet? Explain the application of the lower-of-cost-or-market rule in this situation.

d. What would be the effect on ending inventories and net income for the second year had Steel used the lower-of-average-cost-or-market inventory method instead of the lower-of-FIFO-cost-or-market inventory method? Explain.

(AICPA Adapted)

Exercise 4–5

Explaining Inventory Measurement Methods

Cost for inventory purposes should be determined by the inventory cost flow method most clearly reflecting periodic income.

Required:

a. Describe inventory cost flow assumptions for average cost, FIFO, and LIFO methods.

b. Discuss reasons for using LIFO in an inflationary economy.

c. When there is evidence the value of inventory, through its disposal in the ordinary course of business, is less than cost, what is the accounting treatment and what concept justifies this treatment?

(AICPA Adapted)

Exercise 4–6

Restating Inventory from LIFO to FIFO

Refer to the financial statements of Campbell Soup Company in Supplement A.

Required:

a. Compute Year 10 cost of goods sold under the FIFO method. (Note: At the end of Year 9, the excess of FIFO inventory over LIFO inventory was $88 million.)

b. Explain the potential usefulness of the LIFO to FIFO restatement.

Exercise 4–7

Identification of Unrecorded Assets

A balance sheet, which is intended to present fairly the financial position of a company, is frequently criticized for not reflecting certain liabilities. Similarly, the balance sheet is faulted for not reflecting certain assets.

Required:

List five examples of assets that are not presently included on balance sheets. Discuss their implications for financial statement analysis.

(CFA Adapted)

Exercise 4–8

Motivation and Classification of Marketable Securities

An important part of the accounting methods and procedures with respect to marketable securities, concerns the distinction between noncurrent and current classification of marketable securities.

Required:

a. Why does a company maintain an investment portfolio of current and noncurrent securities?

b. What factors should we consider in determining whether investments in marketable equity securities should be classified as current or noncurrent, and how do these factors affect the accounting treatment for unrealized losses?

Exercise 4–9

Determining Asset Valuation

Consider the following news item:

> The greatest nonevent in the annals of the sea occurred last Thursday in Japan, when the world's biggest oil tanker, the 484,377-ton *Nissei Maru*, was completed—and went straight into lay-up. Between the time the keel of the monster vessel was laid and its delivery, its hypothetical market value plunged 90 percent. Moreover, it will cost a small fortune to maintain it in lay-up. Then there is the delicate problem of accepting a ship without putting it through its sea trials. What will be the validity of the shipyard's guarantees if it is put through its paces for the first time two or three years hence?

Required:

a. What determines the value of assets?

b. Do contemporary accounting principles promptly recognize changes in economic values? Discuss.

c. What are the implications of asset valuation rules for our analysis of financial statements?

Exercise 4–10

Asset Identification

Which of the following items are classified as assets on a balance sheet?

a. Depreciation.
b. President's salary.
c. Cash.
d. Deferred income taxes.
e. Installment receivable (to be collected in three years).
f. Capital withdrawal.
g. Inventories.
h. Prepaid expenses.
i. Deferred charges.
j. Work in process.
k. Allowance for depreciation.
l. Allowance for bad debt.
m. Loan to officers.
n. Loan from officers.
o. A fully trained sales force.
p. Common stock of a subsidiary.
q. Trade name purchased.
r. Company developed goodwill.
s. Valuable franchise agreements obtained at no cost.

PROBLEMS

Problem 4–1

Restating and Analyzing Inventory from LIFO to Average Cost

Refer to the financial statements of Quaker Oats Company in Supplement A.

Required:

a. Quaker Oats uses primarily the LIFO cost assumption in determining its cost of goods sold and beginning and ending inventory amounts. Determine the gross profit of Quaker Oats for the following years if average cost is used for all items of inventory. (See note 1 and use a 34 percent tax rate.)

1. For Year 11.
2. For Year 10.

b. Compute the net income effect of using LIFO rather than average cost and comment on the differences for our analysis of finanacial statements.

c. Give the adjusting analytical entry to restate the financial statements from a LIFO to an average cost basis for Year 11. How does this help us in our analysis?

Problem 4–2

Interpreting and Restating Inventory from FIFO to LIFO

In analysis of the financial statements of ABEX Chemicals, Inc., you are concerned with certain accounting procedures potentially distorting operating results.

Required:

a. Data for ABEX is included in Case 10–3. Using the data in Table 4 of this case, describe how ABEX's use of the FIFO method of accounting for its petrochemical inventories affects its division's operating margin during each of the following periods:

1. Years 1 through 3.
2. Years 3 through 5.

b. ABEX is considering adopting the LIFO method of accounting for its petrochemical inventories in either Year 6 or Year 7. Recommend an adoption date for LIFO, and justify your choice.

(CFA Adapted)

Problem 4–3

Restating Inventory from LIFO to FIFO

Zeta Corporation uses LIFO inventory accounting. Footnotes to Zeta's Year 9 financial statements contain the following:

Inventories	*Year 8*	*Year 9*
Raw materials	$392,675	$369,725
Finished products	401,342	377,104
	$794,017	$746,829
Less LIFO reserve	(46,000)	(50,000)
	$748,017	$696,829

Zeta Corporation has a marginal tax rate of 35 percent.

a. Determine the amount by which Year 9 retained earnings of Zeta changes if FIFO is used.

b. Determine the amount by which Year 9 net income of Zeta changes if FIFO is used for both Years 8 and 9.

c. Discuss the usefulness of the LIFO to FIFO restatments in our analysis of Zeta.

(AICPA Adapted)

Problem 4–4

T-Account Analysis of Plant Assets

Refer to the financial statements of Campbell Soup in Supplement A.

Required:

By means of T-account analysis explain the changes in the Property, Plant, and Equipment account for Year 11. Provide as much detail as the disclosure enables you to supply. (*Hint:* Utilize information disclosed on the Form 10-K schedule.) Explain the usefulness of this analysis.

Problem 4–5

T-Account Analysis of Plant Assets

Refer to the financial statements of Quaker Oats in Supplement A.

Required:

By means of a T-account analysis explain changes in the Property, Plant, and Equipment account for Years 10 and 11. Provide as much detail as the disclosure enables you to supply. Explain the usefulness of this analysis.

Problem 4–6

Analyzing and Interpreting Marketable Securities

Presented below are four unrelated situations involving marketable equity securities:

Situation I. A noncurrent portfolio of available-for-sale equity securities with an aggregate market value in excess of cost includes one particular security whose market value has declined to less than one-half of the original cost.

Situation II. The balance sheet of a company does not classify assets and liabilities as current and noncurrent. The portfolio of available-for-sale equity securities includes securities normally considered current that have a net cost in excess of market value of $2,000. The remainder of the portfolio has a net market value in excess of cost of $5,000.

Situation III. An available-for-sale marketable equity security, whose market value is currently less than cost, is classified as noncurrent but is to be reclassified as current.

Situation IV. A company's noncurrent portfolio of marketable equity securities consists of the common stock of one company. At the end of the prior year, the market value of the security was 50 percent of original cost, and this effect was properly reflected in a Valuation Allowance account. However, at the end of the current year, the market value of the security had appreciated to twice the original cost. The security is still considered noncurrent at year-end.

Required:

Describe the effects for classification, carrying value, and earnings in each of these situations.

Problem 4–7

Property, Plant, and Equipment Accounting and Analysis

Among the principal topics related to accounting for the property, plant, and equipment of a company are acquisition and retirement.

Required:

a. What expenditures should be capitalized when a company acquires equipment for cash?

b. Assume that the market value of equipment acquired is not determinable by reference to a similar purchase for cash. Describe how the acquiring company should determine the capitalizable cost of equipment purchased by exchanging it for each of the following:

1. Bonds having an established market price.
2. Common stock not having an established market price.
3. Similar equipment having a determinable market value.

c. Describe the factors that determine whether expenditures relating to property, plant, and equipment already in use should be capitalized.

d. Describe how to account for the gain or loss on the sale of property, plant, and equipment for cash.

e. Discuss the important considerations in analyzing property, plant, and equipment.

Problem 4–8

Understanding Self-Constructed Assets

Jay Manufacturing, Inc., began operations five years ago producing probos, a new medical instrument it hoped to sell to doctors, dentists, and hospitals. The demand for probos far exceeded initial expectations, and the company was unable to produce enough probos to meet demand. The company was manufacturing its product on equipment that it built at the start of its operations. To meet demand, it needed more efficient equipment. The company decided to design and build the equipment since that currently available on the market was unsuitable for producing probos. A section of the plant was devoted to development of the new equipment and a special staff of personnel was hired. Within six months, a machine was developed at a cost of $170,000 that successfully increased production and reduced labor costs substantially. Sparked by the success of the new machine, the company built three more machines of the same type at a cost of $80,000 each.

Required:

a. In addition to satisfying a need that outsiders cannot meet within the desired time, why might a firm construct fixed assets for its own use?

b. In general, what costs should a company capitalize for a self-constructed fixed asset?

c. Discuss the propriety of including in the capitalized cost of self-constructed assets:

1. The increase in overhead caused by the self-construction of fixed assets.
2. A proportionate share of overhead on the same basis as that applied to goods manufactured for sale.

d. Discuss the proper accounting treatment of the $90,000 ($170,000 - $80,000) by which the cost of the first machine exceeded the cost of the subsequent machines.

(AICPA Adapted)

Problem 4–9

Intangible Assets (Patents)

On June 30, Year 1, your client, the Vandiver Corporation, was granted two patents covering plastic cartons that it has been producing and marketing profitably for the past three years. One patent covers the manufacturing process, and the other covers the related products. Vandiver executives tell you that these patents represent the most significant breakthrough in the industry in the past 30 years. The products have been marketed under the registered trademarks Safetainer, Duratainer, and Sealrite. Your client has already granted licenses under the patents to other manufacturers in the United States and abroad and is already receiving substantial royalties. On July 1, Vandiver commenced patent infringement actions against several companies whose names you recognize as those of substantial and prominent competitors. Vandiver's management is optimistic that these suits will result in a permanent injunction against the manufacture and sale of the infringing products and collection of damages for loss of profits caused by the alleged infringement. The financial vice president has suggested that the patents be recorded at the discounted value of expected net royalty receipts.

Required:

a. What is an *intangible asset*? Explain.

b.
1. What is the meaning of "discounted value of expected net receipts"? Explain.
2. How would such a value be calculated for net royalty receipts?

c. What basis of valuation for Vandiver's patents would be generally accepted in accounting? Give supporting reasons for this basis.

d.
1. Assuming no practical problems of implementation and ignoring generally accepted accounting principles, what is the preferable basis of evaluation for patents? Explain.
2. What would be the preferable theoretical basis of amortization? Explain.

e. What recognition, if any, should be made of the infringement litigation in the financial statements for the year ending September 30, Year 1? Discuss.

(AICPA Adapted)

CASES

Case 4–1

Analysis of Adaptec's Current Assets

Refer to the 1996 annual report of Adaptec, Inc., (in Supplement A) to answer the following questions:

a. What current asset accounts does Adaptec report on its balance sheet?

b. Which of the current asset accounts has the largest balance?

c. What portion of Adaptec's March 31, 1996, accounts receivable is expected to be uncollectible?

d. According to note 1, how does Adaptec define cash and cash equivalents?

Case 4–2

Inventory Valuation in the Film Industry

Financial statements of Columbia Pictures Industries, Inc., include the following footnote:

Inventories. The costs of feature films and television programs, including production advances to independent producers, interest on production loans and distribution advances to film licensors, are amortized on bases designed to write off costs in proportion to the expected flow of income.

The cost of general release feature productions is divided between theatrical exhibition and television exhibition, based on the proportion of net revenues expected to be derived from each source. The portion of the cost of feature productions allocated to theatrical exhibition is amortized generally by the application of tables which write off approximately 62 percent in 26 weeks, 85 percent in 52 weeks, and 100 percent in 104 weeks after release. Costs of two theatrical productions first released on a reserved-seat basis are amortized in the proportion that rentals earned bear to the estimated final theatrical and television rentals.

Because of the depressed market for the licensing of feature films to television and poor acceptance by the public of a number of theatrical films released late in the year, the company made a special provision for additional amortization of recent releases and those not yet licensed for television to reduce such films to their currently estimated net realizable values.

Required:

a. Identify the primary determinants for valuation of feature films, television programs, and general release feature productions by Columbia.

b. Are the bases of valuation reasonable?

c. Indicate additional information on inventory valuation an unsecured lender to Columbia would wish to obtain.

Case 4–3

Financial Statement Consequences of LIFO and FIFO

Falcon Store purchases its merchandise, a standard item, at the current market price and resells the same product at a price 20 cents higher. The purchase price remains constant throughout the year. Data on number of units in inventory at the beginning of year, unit purchases, and unit sales are shown below:

Number of units in inventory—beginning of year ($1 cost)	1,000 units
Number of units purchased during year @ $1.50	1,000 units
Number of units sold during year @ $1.70	1,000 units

The beginning-of-year balance sheet for Falcon Store lists the following:

Inventory	Equity
(1,000 units @ \$1) = \$1,000	\$1,000

Required:

a. Calculate the after-tax profit for Falcon Store using the (1) FIFO and (2) LIFO methods of inventory valuation if the company has no expenses other than cost of goods sold and it computes income taxes using a 50 percent rate. Taxes are accrued currently and paid the following year.

b. If all sales and purchases are for cash, construct the balance sheet at the end of the year using the (1) FIFO and (2) LIFO methods of inventory valuation.

c. Describe the significance of each of these methods of inventory valuation for profit determination and financial position in a period of increasing prices.

d. What problem does the LIFO method pose in constructing interim financial statements?

(CFA Adapted)

Case 4–4 Financial Statement Effects of Alternative Inventory Methods

Colin Company is a retailer dealing in a single product. Beginning inventory is zero at January 1, operating expenses for the year are \$5,000, and there are 2,000 common shares outstanding. The following purchases are made during the year:

	Units	Per Unit	Value
January	100	\$10	\$ 1,000
March	300	11	3,300
June	600	12	7,200
October	300	14	4,200
December	500	15	7,500
Total	1,800		\$23,200

Ending inventory at December 31 is 800 units. Assets, excluding inventories, amount to \$75,000, of which \$50,000 are current. Current liabilities amount to \$25,000, and long-term liabilities equal \$10,000.

Required:

a. Determine net income for the year using each of the following inventory accounting methods. Assume a sales price of \$25 per unit and ignore income taxes.

1. FIFO
2. LIFO
3. Average cost

b. Compute the following ratios under each of the inventory accounting methods (FIFO, LIFO, average cost).

1. Current ratio.
2. Debt-to-equity ratio.
3. Inventory turnover.
4. Return on total assets.
5. Gross margin as percent of sales.
6. Net profit as percent of sales

c. Discuss the effects of inventory accounting methods for financial statement analysis.

Case 4–5

Analysis of Adaptec's Noncurrent Assets

Refer to the 1996 annual report of Adaptec, Inc., (in Supplement A) to answer the following questions.

a. What categories of noncurrent assets appear on Adaptec's balance sheet?

b. According to note 2, what is the breakdown (in dollars) of Adaptec's property and equipment? What do these dollar amounts represent?

c. Which categories of plant and equipment increased the most from 1995 to 1996? What do these increases imply about future operating results?

d. According to note 1, what impact will the adoption of *SFAS No. 121* have on Adaptec's financial condition and results of operations? What does this imply about the balance sheet values of Adaptec's long-lived assets?

e. According to note 5, what assets were acquired by Adaptec in 1996? What happened to the "in-process technology" acquired by Adaptec?

f. According to note 8, where is Adaptec's manufacturing facility located? Why do you think Adaptec chose this location?

g. Use T-account analysis to explain the composition of "Other assets." Provide as much detail as the disclosure enables you to supply. (*Hint*: See notes 5 and 7.)

INTERNET ACTIVITIES

Internet 4–1

Analyzing Current Assets

Access the most recent financial statements of Adaptec (or another company selected by your instructor) on the Internet (http://www.adaptec.com) and answer the following:

a. What current asset accounts are reported on the balance sheet?

b. Which of the current asset accounts has the largest balance?

c. What portion of accounts receivable is expected to be uncollectible?

d. How are cash and cash equivalents defined?

Internet 4–2

Analyzing Noncurrent Assets

Access the most recent financial statements of Adaptec (or another company selected by your instructor) on the Internet (http://www.adaptec.com) and answer the following:

a. What categories of noncurrent assets are reported on the balance sheet?

b. Can you identify the breakdown (in dollars) of property and equipment? Why is this information useful?

c. Which categories of plant and equipment experience the largest increases in the most recent year? What do these increases imply about future operating results?

d. What assets are acquired in the most recent year?

e. Does the company have assets located outside its home country? What might explain this company's decision to locate assets outside or within its home country?

Internet 4–3

T-Account Analysis of Plant Assets

Access one of the financial statement databases available on the Internet (http://www.mhhe.com/business/accounting/wild). Retrieve current financial statements of a company selected by either you or your instructor.

Required:

By means of T-account analysis explain changes in Property, Plant, and Equipment accounts for the most recent two years. Provide as much detail as the disclosures enable you to supply.

Internet 4–4

Analysis of Assets

Access one of the financial statement databases available on the Internet (http://www.mhhe.com/business/accounting/wild). Retrieve current financial statements of three companies in different industries selected by either you or your instructor.

Required:

a. Describe the major similarities and differences in these companies' assets.

b. Compute the relative proportion of current, noncurrent investment, plant, intangible, and "other" assets as a percent of total assets.

c. Write a report explaining why these companies' assets are different.

Internet 4–5

Analysis of Asset Accounting Methods

Access one of the financial statement databases available on the Internet (http://www.mhhe.com/business/accounting/wild). Retrieve current financial statements of three companies in different industries selected by either you or your instructor.

Required:

a. Identify the accounting methods used by each company to account for inventories, investments, plant assets, and intangible assets.

b. Write a report discussing differences and similarities in the accounting methods identified in *a.*

c. What are the expected effects of these methods on each company's financial statements?

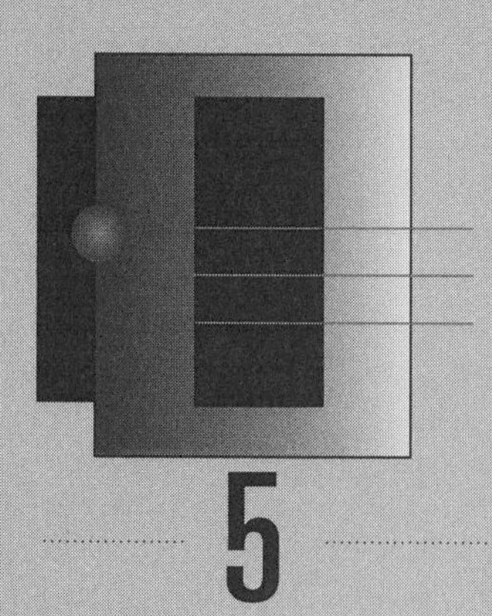

C H A P T E R

5

Analyzing Investing Activities: Special Topics

A Look Back

Our analysis of accounting components began with both financing and investing activities. We explained and analyzed these activities and interpreted them in terms of our expectations for company performance.

A Look at This Chapter

This chapter extends our analysis to special investing activities—intercompany and international. We analyze both intercorporate investments and business combinations from the perspective of the parent company. We also examine international investments and their reporting in financial statements. We show the importance of interpreting disclosures on intercompany and international activities for analysis of financial statements.

A Look Ahead

Chapter 6 extends our analysis to operating activities. We analyze the income statement as a means to understand and predict future company performance. We extend this analysis of operating and other activities to cash flows in Chapter 7.

Learning Objectives

- Analyze financial reporting for intercorporate investments.
- Interpret consolidated financial statements.
- Analyze implications of purchase and pooling accounting for business combinations.
- Interpret goodwill arising from business combinations.
- Describe international accounting and auditing practices.
- Analyze foreign currency translation disclosures.
- Distinguish between foreign currency translation and transaction gains and losses.

PREVIEW OF CHAPTER 5

Intercompany and international activities play an increasingly larger role in business activities. Companies pursue intercompany activities for several reasons including diversification, expansion, and competitive opportunities and returns. International activities provide similar opportunities but offer unique and often riskier challenges. This chapter considers our analysis and interpretation of these business activities as reflected in financial statements. We consider current reporting requirements from our analysis perspective—both for what they do and do not tell us. We describe how current disclosures are relevant for our analysis, and how we might usefully apply analytical adjustments to these disclosures to improve our analysis. We direct special attention to the unrecorded assets and liabilities in intercompany investments, the interpretation of international operations in financial statements, and the risks assumed in intercompany and international activities. The content and organization of this chapter are as follows:

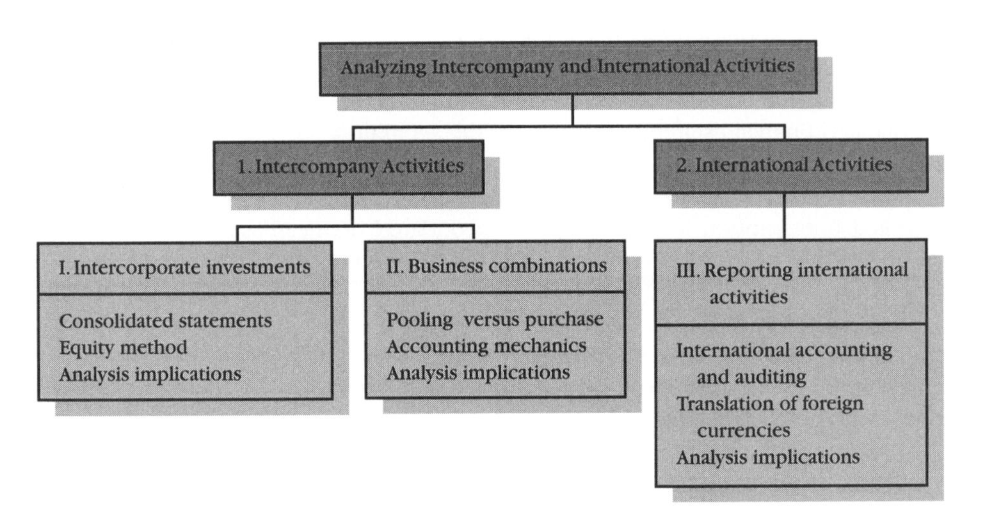

SECTION 1: INTERCOMPANY ACTIVITIES

Section 1 considers intercorporate investments and business combinations. We consider international activities in Section 2.

Intercorporate Investments

Intercorporate investments are investments by one corporation in the equity securities of another corporation. A **parent** corporation is one who controls, generally through ownership of equity securities, the activities of another separate legal entity known as a **subsidiary**. A **parent-subsidiary** relationship exists when one corporation owns all or a majority of the voting equity securities of another corporation. A parent corporation also often invests in **affiliates**. Although a parent might exercise influence over affiliates' activities, it does not control them. Reasons why one company pursues intercorporate investments, or buys control of another company, are many and varied. They include superior sources of supplies, growth in market share, entry into new lines of business, tax advantages, reduced risk exposure, government support, and technological and strategic alliances. There are two basic methods for a parent company to account for its ownership in a subsidiary: consolidated financial statements and equity method accounting. We consider these methods in this section. From our analysis perspective, these methods differ substantially in the amount of information they provide about financial condition and results of operations for the combined parent-subsidiary entity. We discuss implications of these methods for our analysis. Chapter 4 described investments where one company holds a minority of the voting securities of another company, including joint venture investments, and we do not discuss them here.

Consolidated Financial Statements

Consolidated financial statements report the results of operations and financial condition of a parent corporation and its subsidiaries in one set of statements. A parent company's financial statements evidence ownership of stock in a subsidiary through an investment account. From a legal point of view, a parent company owns the stock of its subsidiary. A parent does not own the subsidiary's assets nor is it usually responsible for the subsidiary's debts, although it frequently guarantees them. Consolidated financial statements disregard the separate legal identities of the parent and its subsidiary in favor of its "economic substance." That is, consolidated financial statements reflect a business entity controlled by a single company—the parent. There is a presumption in practice that consolidated financial statements are more meaningful than separate financial statements in reporting on this parent-subsidiary relationship.

Basic Technique of Consolidation

Consolidation involves two steps: *aggregation* and *elimination*. Consolidated financial statements aggregate the assets, liabilities, revenues, and expenses of subsidiaries with their corresponding items in the financial statements of the parent company. To the extent the parent does not own 100 percent of a subsidiary's equity securities, the **minority interest** of outsiders is recognized in the consolidation. Minority interest represents the portion of a subsidiary's equity securities owned by other than the parent company. If the parent owns all of a subsidiary's equity securities, the subsidiary is referred to as a *wholly owned subsidiary*.

The second step is to eliminate *intercompany transactions* (or reciprocal accounts) to avoid double counting or prematurely recognizing income. For example, a parent's account payable to its subsidiary's account receivable are both eliminated when preparing a consolidated balance sheet.

Illustration of Consolidation

Exhibit 5.1 reproduces the simplified balance sheet of Pharmaceutical Corporation (the parent) at the time of its acquisition of Silicon Supplies Company (the subsidiary). The assets and liabilities reported in the balance sheet of Silicon Supplies are at their fair market values at the time of acquisition. Pharmaceutical paid $78,000 (in millions) for 90% of Silicon Supplies' common stock (fair value of net assets acquired equal 90% of $80,000, or $72,000). Accounts receivable of Pharmaceutical include $4,000 owed to it by Silicon Supplies. Adjustments necessary to combine the two companies follow:

EXHIBIT 5.1

Pharmaceutical Corporation and Silicon Supplies Company
Consolidated Balance Sheet Worksheet
Date of Acquisition

	Pharma-ceutical Corporation	*Silicon Supplies Company*	*Adjustments and Elminiations Dr. (Cr.)*	*Minority Interest*	*Consoli-dated*
Assets					
Cash	16,000	11,000			27,000
Accounts receivable	32,000	19,000	(4,000)		47,000
Inventories	42,000	18,000			60,000
Fixed Assets	64,000	42,000			106,000
Investment in Silicon					
Fair value at acquisition	72,000	—	(72,000)		—
Excess of cost over fair value (goodwill)	6,000	—			6,000
Total assets	232,000	90,000			246,000
Liabilities and Equity					
Accounts payable	12,000	10,000	4,000		18,000
Capital stock:					
Pharmaceutical Corporation	120,000				120,000
Silicon Supplies Company		50,000	45,000	5,000	
Retained earnings:					
Pharmaceutical Corporation	100,000				100,000
Silicon Supplies Company		30,000	27,000	3,000	
Minority interest					8,000
Total liabilities and equity	232,000	90,000			246,000

1. The investment at acquisition is eliminated against 90% of the equity (capital stock plus retained earnings) of Silicon Supplies. The remaining 10% of Silicon Supplies' equity belongs to outside stockholders and is shown as minority interest in the consolidated balance sheet. The amount of $6,000 (i.e., $78,000 – $72,000) that Pharmaceutical paid in excess of the fair value of 90 percent of the tangible net assets of Silicon Supplies is carried as goodwill in the consolidated balance sheet. We describe the method of determining goodwill later in this chapter.
2. The accounts receivable of Pharmaceutical and the corresponding payable of Silicon Supplies are eliminated in consolidation. This entry is required because a single economic entity cannot have claims to and from itself.

Under consolidation, the income statement of Silicon Supplies is combined with that of Pharmaceutical, and the 10% share of the minority interest in the net income or loss of Silicon Supplies for the period is deducted from the consolidated income (or loss) and added to the minority's interest to show the consolidated net results of operations of the *total entity.* When consolidating the income statement of the subsidiary with the parent, intercompany profits on sales of inventories held by the consolidated entity at year-end, along with any intercompany profits on other asset transactions, must be eliminated. This is required so the equity interest in earnings of a consolidated entity relate to earnings from transactions with parties outside the entity. Transactions among parties within the entity yield unrealized profit.

ANALYSIS VIEWPOINT *. . . You are the lawyer*

One of your clients calls on you with a legal matter. Your client has nearly all of her savings invested in the common stock of NY Research Labs, Inc. Her concern stems from the financial statements of NY Research Labs released yesterday. These financial statements are, for the first time, consolidated statements involving a subsidiary, Boston Chemicals Corp. Your client is concerned her investment in NY Research Labs is now at greater risk due to several major lawsuits against Boston Chemicals. Some of these suits have the potential to bankrupt Boston Chemicals. How do you advise your client? Should she be more concerned about her investment in NY Research Labs because of the consolidation?

Principles Governing Consolidation

Accounting practice presumes consolidated statements are more meaningful than separate parent and subsidiary statements. Consequently, consolidation is considered the preferred method of reporting the financial statements of a parent and its subsidiaries. Accounting practice requires consolidation of a majority-owned subsidiary (the parent owns more than 50 percent of the voting stock) even if it has nonhomogeneous operations (e.g., credit, insurance, leasing), a large minority interest, or a foreign location. Practice requires that summarized information about the assets, liabilities, and results of operations (or separate statements) of previously unconsolidated majority-owned subsidiaries continues to be reported after these subsidiaries are consolidated. There are two conditions where a subsidiary should not be consolidated:

- *Control is incomplete or temporary.* To consolidate a subsidiary, a parent should have ownership or **effective management control** of a subsidiary. Ownership of over 50 percent of the voting stock is generally required for consolidation, and consolidation is inappropriate when control is temporary, does not rest with the majority owner, or when the subsidiary is to be disposed of.
- *Income is uncertain.* When there is substantial uncertainty about whether an increase in equity from a subsidiary has actually accrued to the parent, consolidation is inappropriate. Substantial uncertainty can arise, particularly with international subsidiaries, when there are restrictions on conversion of foreign currencies or on remittance of foreign earnings.

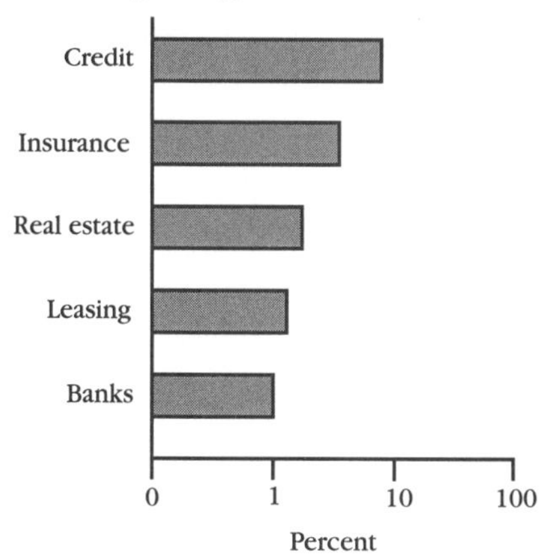

Source: *Accounting Trends & Techniques.*

Equity Method Accounting

Equity method accounting reports the parent's investment in the subsidiary, and the parent's share of the subsidiary's results, as line items in the parent's financial statements. Accordingly, the equity method is sometimes referred to as *one-line consolidation*. Equity method accounting is used in consolidated financial statements for investments in equity securities of all unconsolidated subsidiaries (international or domestic) where, for reasons described in the prior section, consolidation is inappropriate. Equity method accounting is not a valid substitute for consolidation and should not be used to justify exclusion of a subsidiary when consolidation is appropriate. Equity method accounting is generally used for investments representing 20 to 50 percent of the voting stock of a company's equity securities. It can, in certain cases, be appropriate for investments representing an interest of less than 20 percent (see Chapter 4). The primary difference between consolidation and equity method accounting rests in the level of detail reported in financial statements.

There is wide application of equity method accounting for investments in subsidiaries, joint ventures, and less than majority–owned investees. This method involves several important procedures (see Exhibit 5.2). Practice in this area emphasizes the need to consider *substance over form* in determining accounting for intercorporate investments. SEC regulations specifically address the possible need to consolidate a less than majority–owned subsidiary and to employ equity method accounting or a valuation allowance to achieve fair presentation.

EXHIBIT 5.2 Important Procedures in Equity Method Accounting

- Intercompany profits and losses are eliminated until realized by the investor or investee as if a subsidiary, corporate joint venture, or investee company is consolidated.
- Difference between the cost of an investment and the amount of equity in net assets of an investee is accounted for as if the investee is a consolidated subsidiary (amortization of any goodwill is required over a period not exceeding 40 years).
- Investment(s) in common stock is shown in the balance sheet of an investor as a single amount, and the investor's share of earnings or losses of an investee(s) is ordinarily shown in the income statement as a single amount except for any extraordinary items and prior period adjustments that are separately classified in the investor's income statement.
- Capital transactions of an investee affecting the investor's share in the equity of the investee are accounted for as if the investee is a consolidated subsidiary.
- Selling stock of an investee by an investor is accounted for as a gain or loss equal to the difference between the stock's selling price and carrying amount when sold.
- If an investee's financial statements are not sufficiently timely for an investor to apply the equity method, the investor should record its share of the earnings or losses of an investee from the most recent financial statements. Any lag in reporting should be consistent from period to period.
- Loss in value of an investment that is other than a temporary decline is recognized the same as a loss in value of other long-term assets. Evidence of a loss in value can include an inability to recover the carrying amount of investment, or a decline in market price.
- An investor should discontinue equity method accounting when the investment (and net advances) is reduced to zero, and should not provide for additional losses unless the investor has guaranteed obligations of the investee or is otherwise committed to providing further financial support to the investee. If the investee subsequently reports net income, the investor should resume equity method accounting only after its share of that net income equals the share of net losses not recognized during the period it suspended the equity method.
- When an investee has outstanding cumulative preferred stock, an investor computes its share of earnings (losses) after deducting the investee's preferred dividends, whether or not such dividends are declared.
- The carrying amount of an investment in common stock of an investee that qualifies for equity method accounting can differ from the equity in net assets of the investee. This difference affects determination of the investor's share of earnings or losses of an investee as if the investee is a consolidated subsidiary. If the investor is unable to link this difference to specific accounts of the investee, the difference is considered goodwill and amortized over a period not exceeding 40 years.

Analysis Implications of Intercorporate Investments

Our analysis confronts several important considerations due to intercorporate investments. We discuss below the more important implications.

Validity of Taking Up Earnings

Both consolidation and equity method accounting assume a dollar earned by a subsidiary is equivalent to a dollar's earnings for the parent. While disregarding the parent's potential tax liability from remittance of earnings by a subsidiary, the dollar-for-dollar equivalence of earnings cannot be taken for granted. Reasons include:

- A regulatory authority can sometimes have power to intervene in a subsidiary's dividend policy.
- A subsidiary can operate in a country where restrictions exist on remittance of earnings or where the value of currency can deteriorate rapidly. Political risks can further inhibit access to earnings.
- Dividend restrictions in loan agreements can limit earnings accessibility.
- Presence of a stable or powerful minority interest can reduce a parent's discretion in setting dividend or other policies.

Our analysis must recognize these factors in assessing whether a dollar earned by a subsidiary is the equivalent of a dollar earned by the parent.

Provision for Taxes on Undistributed Subsidiary Earnings

Including undistributed earnings of a subsidiary in the pretax accounting income of a parent company (either through consolidation or equity method accounting) can require a concurrent provision for taxes. The answer here depends on the action and intent of the parent company. Current practice assumes all undistributed earnings transfer to the parent and that a provision for taxes is made by the parent in the current period. Computation of the tax provision recognizes the tax-planning alternatives the company is entitled to. The basic assumption is overcome if persuasive evidence exists that the subsidiary either has or will invest undistributed earnings permanently or will remit earnings through a tax-free liquidation. Our analysis should be aware that the decision on whether taxes are provided on undistributed earnings is primarily that of management. Management must report the amount of earnings for which no income taxes are provided by the parent. Adaptec offers a disclosure on taxes for undistributed subsidiary earnings in note 8 of its 1996 annual report as follows:

> As of March 31, 1996, the Company had not accrued income taxes on $186,100,000 of accumulated undistributed earnings of its Singapore subsidiary, as these earnings will be reinvested indefinitely.
>
> —Adaptec, Inc.

An investor owning a 20 to 50 interest in an investee must make a provision for taxes on equity in earnings since a presumption of an ability to reinvest earnings is not made.

Debt in Consolidated Financial Statements

Liabilities in consolidated financial statements do not operate as a lien upon a common pool of assets. Creditors, whether secured or unsecured, have recourse in the event of default only to assets owned by the specific corporation that incurred the liability. If a parent company guarantees a liability of a subsidiary, then the creditor has the guarantee as additional security with potential recourse provisions. The consolidated balance sheet does not help us assess the margin of safety enjoyed by creditors. To assess the security of liabilities, our analysis must examine the individual financial statements of each subsidiary. We must remember that legal constraints are not always effective measures of liability, both pro and con. For example, American Express covered obligations of a warehousing subsidiary not because of any legal obligation, but because of concern for its own reputation.

Additional Limitations of Consolidated Financial Statements

Consolidated financial statements are generally meaningful representations of the financial condition and results of operations of the parent-subsidiary entity. Nevertheless, there are additional limitations to those already discussed.

- Financial statements of the individual companies comprising the larger entity are not always prepared on a comparable basis. Differences in accounting principles, valuation bases, amortization rates, and other factors can inhibit homogeneity and impair the validity of ratios, trends, and other analyses.
- Consolidated financial statements do not reveal restrictions on use of cash for individual companies. Nor do they reveal intercompany cash flows or restrictions placed on such flows. These factors obscure the relation between liquidity of assets and the liabilities they aim to meet.
- Companies in poor financial condition sometimes combine with financially strong companies, thus obscuring our analysis—since assets of one member of the consolidated entity cannot be seized to pay liabilities of another.
- Extent of intercompany transactions is unknown unless the procedures underlying the consolidation process are reported—consolidated statements generally reveal only end results.
- Consolidated retained earnings actually available for payment of dividends are difficult to establish unless reported.
- Composition of minority interest (e.g., between common and preferred) cannot be determined from a "combined" minority interest amount in the consolidated balance sheet.
- Accounting for the consolidation of finance and insurance subsidiaries can pose several problems for our analysis. Aggregation of dissimilar enterprises can distort ratios and other relations—for example, current assets of finance subsidiaries are not generally available to satisfy current liabilities of the parent. Assets and liabilities of separate entities are not interchangeable, and consolidated financial statements obscure the priorities of creditors' claims.

Business Combinations

Business combinations refer to the merger, acquisition, reorganization, or restructuring of two or more businesses to form another business entity. Business combinations alter the ownership and control of the acquired or divested businesses. They occur when one company acquires or divests itself of a substantial part of one or more other companies' equity securities. Business combinations require that subsequent financial statements report on the combined activities of this new entity. Accounting

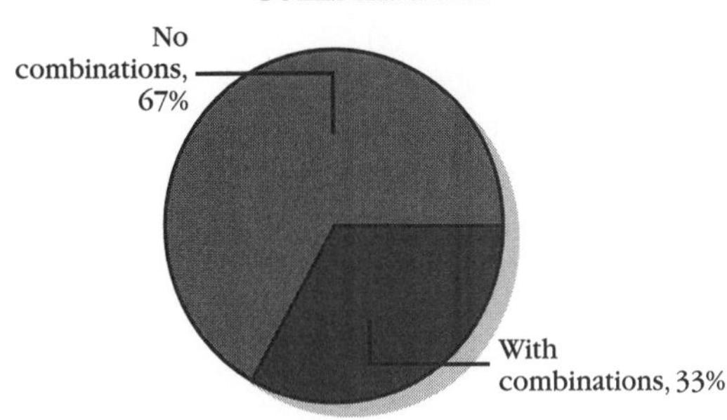

Source: *Accounting Trends & Techniques.*

for a business combination requires a decision on how to value the assets and liabilities of the new entity. This decision can involve a complete revaluation to market value of all assets and liabilities acquired, with substantial effects extending to current and future financial statements. This accounting decision is different from the intercorporate activities discussion in the prior section that focused not on the accounting for the "combination" but on the extent a subsidiary is viewed as an integral part of the parent. Our analysis of business combinations must recognize management's incentives, the accounting implications, and the need to evaluate and interpret financial statements of the new entity.

Business combinations with sound economic motivations have a long history. Business combinations arise also as a means to "glamorize" or enhance a company's image, its perceived growth potential, or its prosperity. It is also a means of increasing reported earnings. Among the economic reasons for business combinations are (1) acquiring valuable sources of materials, productive facilities, technology, marketing channels, or market share; (2) securing financial resources or access to them; (3) strengthening management; (4) enhancing operating efficiency; (5) encouraging diversification; (6) rapidity in market entry; (7) achieving economies of scale; and (8) acquiring tax advantages. We should also recognize certain intangible reasons for business combinations. In certain cases these intangibles are the best explanation for the high costs incurred. They include management prestige, compensation, and perquisites. Management's accounting choices in recording business combinations are often better understood when considering these motivations.

Financial "architects" can utilize methods in accounting for business combinations to deliver a picture of earnings growth that is, in large part, illusory. The means to achieve illusionary earnings growth include:

- Merging a growth company having a high price-earnings ratio with a company(ies) having lesser growth prospects, using payment in the high-growth company's stock. This transaction can contribute to further earnings per share growth, and can reinforce and even increase the acquiring company's high price-earnings ratio. Markets sometimes fail to fully account for the potential lower quality of acquired earnings. This is primarily a transitory problem inherent in the market evaluation mechanism, and it is not easily remedied by regulators.
- Utilizing latitude in accounting for business combinations. This is distinct from genuine economic advantages arising from combinations. We consider alternative accounting methods for business combinations in the next section.
- Issuing convertible securities with limited or no recognition given to their potential dilutive effects on common shareholders' equity. This technique is more difficult to accomplish today given accounting changes to recognize these dilutive effects.

Pooling versus Purchase Accounting for Business Combinations

Accounting for business combinations is controversial. Practice permits two methods of accounting for business combinations: pooling or purchase. They are not meant as alternatives, but to reflect the economic substance of the business combination. **Pooling accounting** is meant to reflect the merging of two shareholder groups through an exchange of equity securities to share in future risks and opportunities. The prior ownership interests continue and the recorded assets and liabilities of the constituent companies are carried forward to the combined entity at their recorded amounts. This method combines two or more streams of business activities into one entity. Since this is a pooling of interests, income of the combined entity includes income of the constituents for the entire fiscal period in which combination occurs. Prior periods' results are also restated to report the individual companies as merged since inception. **Purchase accounting** is meant to reflect the acquisition of one or more companies by another company. The acquiror continues operating, while the acquired company(ies) disappears. The acquisition is accounted for similar to the acquisition of any other asset. That is, the acquiror records the acquired assets (including goodwill) and liabilities at "cost"—fair values at date of acquisition. The acquiror records the income of the acquired companies only from date of acquisition. Reports on prior periods refer to activities of the acquiror only. If a business combination meets certain criteria (see below), it must be treated as a pooling of interests. Otherwise, it is treated as a purchase. We first evaluate the accounting under these two methods. We next interpret implications of accounting for business combinations in analysis of financial statements.

Accounting for Business Combinations

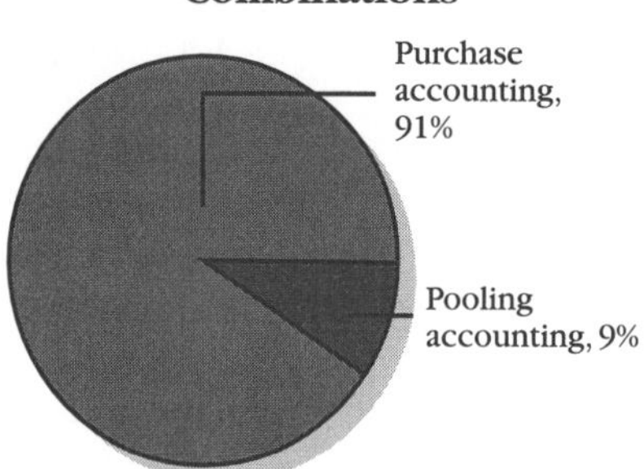

Source: *Accounting Trends & Techniques.*

Pooling Accounting Criteria

There are 12 conditions for a business combination to be treated as a pooling of interests. The 12 can be grouped under three categories: (1) attributes of the combining companies, (2) absence of planned transactions, and (3) manner of combining interests. These conditions attempt to identify a situation where ownership in net assets is not transferred from one group of owners to another—that is, there is clear continuity of ownership.[1] The most critical condition relates to the method of payment offered by the surviving (parent) corporation. This condition states that the surviving corporation must exchange at least 90 percent of the outstanding common stock of the combining company for voting common stock of the surviving corporation. This condition ensures that the common shareholders of the combining companies continue as voting common shareholders of the new combined entity. If a combining company remains a subsidiary of the issuing corporation after the combination, the combination can still be treated as a pooling provided all conditions for a pooling are met. A business combination meeting all 12 conditions must be treated as a pooling.

Purchase Accounting Concerns

Purchase accounting views a business combination as the acquisition of one entity by another. We consider several important accounting issues in this transaction.

Valuing the Consideration. A major problem in purchase accounting is determining the total cost of the acquired entity. The same accounting principles apply whether determining the cost of assets acquired individually, in a group, or in a business combination. It is the nature of the transaction determining the accounting principles to apply in arriving at total cost of assets acquired. No problems usually arise in determining the total cost of assets acquired for cash, since the amount of cash disbursed is the cost of acquired assets. Allocation of this cost to the individual assets acquired, however, is more difficult.

---

[1] Precise details of the conditions for a combination to be treated as a pooling are available in APB Opinion 16.

If a company acquires assets by incurring liabilities, the total cost of acquired assets is the present value of the amounts to be paid in the future. The present value of a debt security is the fair value of the liability. If the debt security is issued at an interest rate substantially above or below the current effective rate for a similar security, the appropriate amount of premium or discount is recorded. In some cases, the characteristics of a preferred stock are so similar to a debt security that it is valued in the same manner.

If a company acquires assets in exchange for stock, the total cost of acquired assets is the fair value of the stock given or the fair value of the net assets received, whichever is more clearly evident. The fair value of securities traded in an organized market is typically preferred over estimating the fair value of the acquired company. Quoted market price serves as a guide in determining total cost of an acquired company after considering factors like market fluctuations, quantities traded, and issue costs. If the quoted market price is not reliable, the fair value of net assets received, including goodwill, must be determined. In these cases, the best available means of estimation is used, including a detailed review of the negotiations leading up to the purchase and the use of independent appraisals.

Contingent Consideration. A company usually records the amount of any contingent consideration payable in accordance with a purchase agreement when the contingency is resolved and the consideration is issued or issuable. Two common types of contingencies are based on either earnings or security prices. Guidelines to accounting for contingent consideration include: (1) disclose a contingent issuance of additional consideration, but not as a liability or as outstanding securities unless the outcome of the contingency is determinable beyond a reasonable doubt; (2) record a contingent issuance of additional consideration based on future earnings as additional cost of the acquisition when the contingency is resolved—in this case, the total amount of consideration representing cost is not determinable at the date of acquisition; (3) adjust the amount originally recorded for securities at the date of acquisition for a contingent issuance of additional consideration based on future security prices.

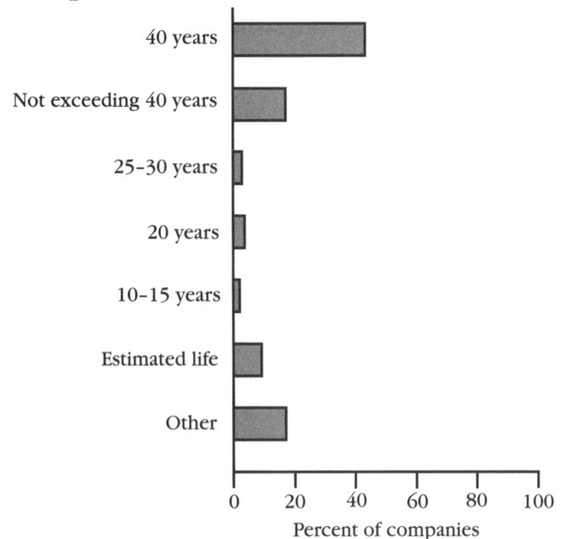

Source: *Accounting Trends & Techniques.*

Allocating Total Cost. Once a company determines the total cost of an acquired entity, it is necessary to allocate this cost to individual assets received. All identifiable assets acquired and liabilities assumed in a business combination are assigned a portion of the total cost, normally equal to their fair value at date of acquisition. The excess of total cost over the amounts assigned to identifiable assets acquired, less liabilities assumed, is recorded as goodwill. The company must amortize goodwill over a period not to exceed 40 years. It is possible that market or appraisal values of identifiable assets acquired, less liabilities assumed, exceed the cost of the acquired company. In those cases, values otherwise assignable to noncurrent assets acquired (except long-term investments in marketable securities) are reduced by a proportionate share of this excess. A company does not record negative goodwill unless the value assigned to such long-term assets is first reduced to zero. If this allocation yields an excess of net assets over cost, this excess is classified

Analysis Research Insight 5.1

Managers' Choice of Purchase or Pooling

Does management's choice of accounting for business combinations matter? Does the market perceive companies differently based on their decision to use purchase or pooling accounting? Is management's choice of purchase or pooling accounting useful for our analysis of companies? Analysis research offers us insight into these questions. Several studies reveal that companies choosing purchase accounting do experience substantial positive stock price changes for the period leading up to announcement of the business combination. However, companies choosing pooling accounting experience no significant changes in stock prices at or around the time of the business combination. This evidence does *not* imply that companies wishing for stock price increases choose purchase accounting for business combinations. But what does this evidence imply?

The evidence of increases in stock prices for companies using purchase accounting, but not for those choosing pooling accounting, likely reflects one of three sources of important economic differences:

- Business combination—tax status, percent acquired, and cash transaction.
- Acquiror—managerial ownership, debt restrictions, compensation plans, and dividend constraints.
- Acquired entity—debt level, relative size vis-à-vis acquiror, and performance.

Our analysis can potentially utilize the disclosure on the accounting choice to draw inferences regarding important underlying company characteristics. For example, management's choice of purchase accounting is likely to increase assets and equity. To the extent there exist accounting-based debt restrictions (e.g., debt-to-equity ratio), management has incentives to choose purchase accounting the nearer these restrictions are to a binding constraint. Another example is dividend restrictions in the form of retained earnings constraints. Since pooling likely increases retained earnings, management wishing to relax potentially binding dividend restrictions has incentives to choose pooling. We should view evidence on management's decision to choose purchase or pooling as an opportunity for us to obtain information about companies that we can use in our analysis.

as a deferred credit and amortized to income over the period estimated to be benefited, but not exceeding 40 years.

There are methods for assigning amounts to individual assets and liabilities acquired other than goodwill. Acquiring companies record marketable securities at current net realizable values. Receivables, accounts and notes payable, long-term debt, and other claims payable are stated at present value, determined at appropriate current interest rates. Finished goods inventories are recorded at selling prices less cost of disposal and reasonable profit allowance. Work-in-process inventories are stated at estimated selling prices of finished goods less the sum of the costs to complete, costs of disposal, and a reasonable profit allowance for the completing and selling effort of the acquired corporation. Raw materials and plant and equipment are recorded at current replacement costs. Other assets, such as land, natural resources, nonmarketable securities, and identifiable intangible assets are valued at appraised values. An acquiring corporation does not record as a separate asset goodwill previously recorded by an acquired company, and it does not record deferred income taxes previously recorded by an acquired company. Amounts assigned to identifiable assets and liabilities recognize that their value can be less, if part or all of their assigned value is not deductible for tax purposes. The acquiring corporation does not record deferred taxes for the tax effect of these differences at the date of acquisition.

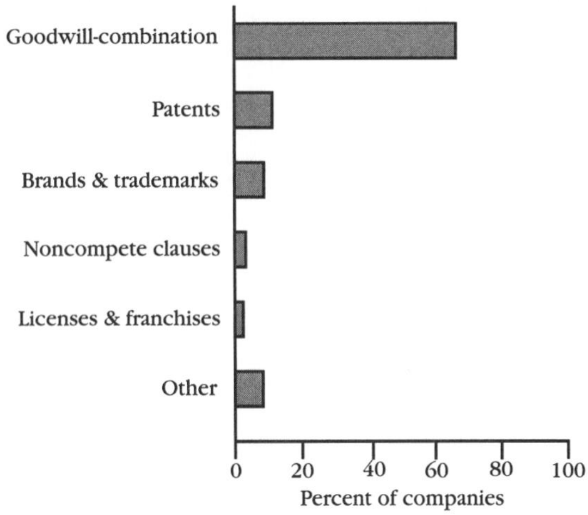

Source: *Accounting Trends & Techniques.*

Goodwill Treatment. For intangible assets acquired in a business combination, the method of allocating the total cost of the acquired company depends on whether or not the asset is identifiable (e.g., a patent) or unidentifiable (e.g., goodwill). The cost of an identifiable intangible asset is based on the fair value of the asset. The cost of an unidentifiable intangible asset is measured as the difference between total cost and the amount assigned to other assets acquired and liabilities assumed. The acquiring corporation does not write off the cost of an intangible asset in the period of acquisition but amortizes it based on its benefit period, not to exceed 40 years. The straight-line amortization method is used unless the company demonstrates another method is more appropriate. The company should disclose the method and amortization period.

Pro Forma Supplementary Disclosure. Notes to financial statements of the acquiring corporation for the period of the business combination include supplemental information for the following results of operations on a pro forma basis:(1) combined results of operations for the current period as though the companies had combined at the beginning of the period, unless acquisition is at or near the beginning of the period; and (2) if comparative financial statements are reported, combined results of operations for the immediately preceding period as though the companies combined at the beginning of that period. This supplemental pro forma information reports, at a minimum, revenue, income before extraordinary items, net income, and earnings per share.

ANALYSIS VIEWPOINT . . . *You are the investment banker*

Your client, LA Waste Management, requests your services in offering common stock to potential shareholders. You are excited about this engagement for, among other reasons, you are offered a 7% fee for services. Prior to accepting the engagement, you perform an analysis of the company and its financial statements. One matter concerns you. You discover LA Waste Management recently acquired Riverside Trucking. LA Waste Management accounts for this acquisition using pooling accounting. Your concern stems from pooling accounting and its understatement of assets for Riverside Trucking. There is a corresponding overstatement in income due to lower expenses attributed to less depreciation with the understated assets. Since Riverside Trucking's income is pooled with that of LA Waste Management's income, the income number and financial ratios based on income are *inflated*. The pooling accounting used by LA Waste Management is acceptable practice and is fully disclosed in the financial statements. Do you accept this engagement?

EXHIBIT 5.3 Merger of Company Sell into Company Buy

Summary of Pro Forma Combined Balance Sheet (in thousands)

	Company Buy	Company Sell	Combining Adjustments Debit	Combining Adjustments Credit	Combined
Total Assets	$157,934	$28,013	—	—	$185,947
Total Liabilities	$ 42,591	$11,218	—	—	$ 53,809
Stockholders' equity:					
Company Buy:					
Preferred stock	810	—	—	—	810
Common stock	7,572	—	—	$1,200	8,772
Company Sell:					
Common stock	—	1,285	$1,285	—	—
Additional paid-in capital	31,146	137	—	85	31,368
Retained earnings	75,815	15,373	—	—	91,188
Total stockholders' equity	$115,343	$16,795	$1,285	$1,285	$132,138
Total liabilities and equity	$157,934	$28,013	$1,285	$1,285	$185,947

Accounting Mechanics of Business Combinations

We illustrate the accounting mechanics of a business combination using both pooling and purchase accounting.

Mechanics of Pooling Accounting

We consider the following case: Company Buy agrees to acquire Company Sell in a transaction where it issues 1,200,000 of $1 par value common shares for all common shares of Company Sell. This transaction qualifies as a pooling and, consequently, the fair market value of Sell's assets and liabilities at the date of merger are not relevant for the accounting. Exhibit 5.3 lists in columnar manner the balance sheets of Company Buy and Company Sell with the adjustments to effect the combination under pooling accounting. Pooling accounting requires (1) accepting Sell's assets and liabilities at recorded amounts, and (2) carrying forward the equity account balances subject to adjustments required by differences in the par values of securities exchanged. Since the par value of Company Buy's common stock issued in the transaction ($1,200,000) is less than the par value of Company Sell's stock ($1,285,000), the difference is credited to Additional Paid-In Capital. If par value of Company Sell's stock exceeded Company Buy's, then additional par value is removed first from existing paid-in capital accounts of the constituents and, if insufficient, from Retained Earnings. Balances in Retained Earnings accounts are carried forward. The accounting entry made by Company Buy for the pooling with Company Sell is (in thousands):

	Debit	Credit
Assets	28,013	
Liabilities		11,218
Common stock		1,200
Additional Paid-In Capital ($137 + $85)		222
Retained Earnings		15,373

To record the issuance of 1,200,000 shares of $1 par value common stock for the merged net assets of Sell and to credit to Retained Earnings the balance of retained earnings of Sell at date of acquisition.

EXHIBIT 5.4 Merger of Company Buy and Company Sell (Company Sell remains as a wholly owned subsidiary of Company Buy)

Summary of Pro Forma Balance Sheet (in thousands)

	Company Buy	Company Buy Only		
		Adjustments		
	Before Pooling	*Debit*	*Credit*	*After Pooling*
Assets—before pooling	$157,934	—	—	$157,934
Investment in Company Sell	—	$16,795	—	16,795
Total Assets	$157,934	$16,795	—	$174,729
Total Liabilities	$ 42,591	—	—	$ 42,591
Stockholders' equity:				
Company Buy:				
Preferred stock	810	—	—	810
Common stock	7,572	—	$ 1,200	8,772
Company Sell: Common stock	—	—	—	—
Additional paid-in capital	31,146	—	222	31,368
Retained earnings	75,815	—	—	75,815
Retained earnings from pooled company	—	—	15,373	15,373
Total stockholders' equity	$115,343	—	$16,795	$132,138
Total liabilities and equity	$157,934	—	$16,795	$174,729

Exhibit 5.3 reflects the pooling as a "statutory merger." This implies the assets and liabilities of individual companies are combined and Company Sell ceases its separate existence. Rather, if we assume Company Sell continues as a wholly owned subsidiary of Company Buy, the pooling is recorded as shown in Exhibit 5.4. The accounting entry on Company Buy's books is as follows (in thousands):

Investment in Company Sell	16,795	
Common Stock		1,200
Additional Paid-In Capital		222
Retained Earnings from Pooled Company		15,373

To record the issuance of 1,200,000 shares of $1 par value common stock for the common stock of Sell and to credit to Retained Earnings the balance of retained earnings of Sell at date of acquisition.

The investment in Company Sell continues to be carried on an equity basis by Company Buy, the parent. In consolidation, the investment account in Company Sell is eliminated against Company Sell's common stock, additional paid-in capital, and the parent company's retained earnings from the pooled company, all in accordance with usual consolidation procedures.

Mechanics of Purchase Accounting

We now assume Company Buy acquires Company Sell for $25,000,000 in cash. This acquisition must be accounted for as a purchase, and we must determine the fair values of Company Sell's assets and liabilities. Note that a cash acquisition is not the only transaction requiring purchase accounting. Purchase accounting is required under several circumstances, including acquisition for stock.

The following tabulation compares Company Sell's recorded asset and liability amounts with fair values at the date of acquisition (in thousands):

	Amounts on Company Sell Books	*Fair Values Determined at Date of Acquisition*
Assets	$28,013	$34,000
Liabilities	11,218	13,000
Net assets	$16,795	$21,000
Cost to Company Buy	—	$25,000
Amount assigned to goodwill	—	4,000

Assets and liabilities are valued using accepted valuation principles. Company Buy assigns the excess of purchase price over the fair value of net assets acquired to goodwill and amortizes goodwill over its benefit period, not to exceed 40 years. Exhibit 5.5 reports the consolidated balance sheet of Company Buy immediately after purchasing Company Sell. Note at least three important differences in the mechanics of purchase accounting from that of pooling. (1) Assets and liabilities are recorded at fair value. Goodwill is recognized. Both of these differences result in higher charges to income, reflecting the higher net asset values acquired. (2) Total shareholders' equity is unchanged. There is an exchange of resources—Company

EXHIBIT 5.5 Purchase of Company Sell by Company Buy

Summary of Pro Forma Consolidated Balance Sheet (in thousands)

	Company Buy	*Company Sell (at fair values on date of acquisition)*	*Combining and Consolidating Adjustments*		*After Purchase*
			Debit	*Credit*	
Assets					
Assets (exclusive of goodwill)	$157,934	$34,000	—	$25,000	$166,934
Goodwill	—	—	$ 4,000	—	$ 4,000
Total assets	$157,934	$34,000	$ 4,000	$25,000	$170,934
Liabilities and Equity					
Liabilities	$ 42,591	$13,000	—	—	$ 55,591
Stockholders' equity:					
Company Buy:					
Preferred stock	810	—	—	—	810
Common stock	7,572	—	—	—	7,572
Additional paid-in capital	31,146	—	—	—	31,146
Retained earnings	75,815	—	—	—	75,815
Net assets at fair value of Company Sell	—	21,000	21,000	—	—
Total stockholders' equity	$115,343	$21,000	$21,000	—	$115,343
Total liabilities and equity	$157,934	$34,000	$25,000	$25,000	$170,934

Sell transfers $25,000,000 of net assets for Company Buy's cash. (3) Company Buy records the acquisition as follows:

Investment in Company Sell	25,000,000	
Cash		25,000,000

An example of a disclosure for business acquisitions is in note 5 of Adaptec's 1996 annual report in supplement A. Adaptec made four acquisitions in 1996 and accounted for them using purchase accounting. These acquisitions resulted in Adaptec recording $8.2 million in goodwill. Two additional acquisitions are made subsequent to 1996 year end: a $33 million cash acquisition accounted for as a purchase, and a $68 million stock acquisition accounted for as a pooling.

Analysis Implications of Business Combinations

For analysis we must examine the impact that accounting for business combinations has on results of operations and reports of financial position. We must also remember the objectives of management in many business combinations are to (1) reduce charges to current and future income that arise from assets acquired in a purchase; and (2) increase postacquisition income by understating assets acquired or by overproviding for future costs and contingencies. This section explains these analysis implications.

Analyzing Pooling and Purchase Accounting

At least three major transactions support pooling accounting:

- An offering of a company's unissued stock in an exchange involving no distribution of resources; instead, equity is increased. However, if cash is distributed in a business acquisition, an acquiror parts with resources.
- An exchange of common stock involving the seller receiving a part of itself *and* a part of the buyer. Since the company does not part with ownership of itself, there is no basis for establishing new asset and liability values.
- A transaction involving a combination of equals through exchanging stock when it is difficult to determine who acquired whom.

A few comments are in order regarding these transactions. The first transaction does not fully articulate why unissued stock is not a resource while cash is. That is, if stock is acceptable consideration to a seller, it must also command a value in the market. The ability to issue stock is often viewed like a license to print money. Valuation of noncash consideration like stock is a common problem in accounting. Moreover, if a combination fails to meet the conditions for a pooling, then it is necessary to value the stock issued in accounting for the combination as a purchase. The second transaction is credible, although for most business combinations the size of the pooled-in company relative to the surviving entity is small. The third transaction is inconsequential in most cases since there is no size constraint for pooling. Therefore, a large company can acquire a very small company and account for this combination as a pooling.

Regarding analysis implications of accounting for business combinations, it is the consequences from pooling accounting that especially concern us. The following example illustrates the large and extensive consequences to pooling. Assume Company B wants to acquire Company S. Company B's net income equals $1,000 this period and there are 500 common shares outstanding. The condensed balance sheet for Company S prior to the business combination is reproduced below:

Fixed assets*	$ 400	Liabilities	$ 200
Other assets	600	Equity	800
	$1,000		$1,000

*The Fixed Assets' market value is $600, and market value equals reported value for Other Assets and Liabilities.

Company S's net income for this period is $200 after deducting $20 for depreciation (10% of $400 fixed assets, less a 50% tax effect).

We consider the operating implications for Company B one period after acquiring Company S under two different scenarios: (1) cash payment, and (2) stock disbursement. Earnings of both companies for this period are identical to the prior year. The $1,400 purchase price for Company S is obtained as follows:

Fixed assets (market value)	$ 600
Other assets	600
Goodwill (estimated)	400
	$1,600
Less liabilities assumed	200
Purchase consideration	$1,400

If $1,400 cash is paid, the combined company's income statement is prepared using purchase accounting as follows:

Net Income of Company B			$1,000
Net Income of Company S (before depreciation)		$220	
Depreciation (10% of $600)	$30*		
Goodwill amortization (400 ÷ 40 years†)	5	35	185
Net income of the combined company			$1,185

*After-tax effect.
†Assuming amortization over 40 years, after tax.

If the $1,400 is dispersed in stock, the combined company's income statement using pooling accounting is:

Net Income of Company B	$1,000
Net Income of Company S	200
Net income of the combined company	$1,200

The difference in net income between purchase and pooling is due to pooling's inclusion of fixed assets at $400 (their original cost to Company S) and the omission of goodwill paid by Company B in acquiring Company S. This example emphasizes that reporting of income for the combined company at either $1,200 or $1,185 depends on how the purchase price is paid. We should note if the purchase price is paid in common stock and any of the other 11 conditions of a pooling are not met, then the acquisition is accounted for as a purchase, yielding income of $1,185 and not $1,200. Revaluation of assets and liabilities, or absence thereof, is the fundamental difference between pooling and purchase accounting. Pooling potentially understates assets and, consequently, overstates income in current and future periods. This heightens our concern with potentially inflated earnings from pooling accounting. Arguably, economic form prevails over economic substance in permitting pooling accounting in certain cases.

For our analysis, we summarize likely consequences from pooling accounting for the combined company that markedly distinguish it from purchase accounting:

- Assets are acquired and carried at book value and not market value as reflected in consideration given. To the extent goodwill is purchased, the acquiring company does not report it on its balance sheet.
- Understatement of assets yields understatement in combined company equity.
- Understatement of assets (including inventory, property, plant, equipment, goodwill, and other intangibles) yields understatement of expenses (such as cost of goods sold, depreciation, amortization) and overstatement of income.
- Understatement of assets yields not only understatement of expenses but potential overstatement of gains on asset disposition. The combined company reports in its operations any gains on sales of assets. Yet these gains potentially arise at time of acquisition and are carried forward at unrealistically low amounts only to be recognized at disposition.
- Understatement of invested equity or overstatement of income yields overstatement in return on investment.
- Retained earnings of the acquired entity are carried forward to the combined company.
- Income statements and balance sheets of the combined entity are restated for all periods reported. Under purchase accounting, they are combined and reported *postacquisition*—although pro forma statements showing preacquisition combined results are typically furnished.

Restating prior periods can lead to a type of double counting similar in effect to an acquiror of a pooled company reporting gains on the sale of undervalued acquired (pooled) assets.

Blockbuster Entertainment enhanced earnings by means of acquisitions accounted for as poolings. This arguably inflated its stock price—used to consummate additional poolings. Blockbuster acquired its largest franchisee, Video Superstore, for stock. Blockbuster's past sales of video tapes to Video Superstore contributed greatly to Blockbuster's profits. When Video Superstore was pooled, the revenues and profits related to the intercompany video tape sales were eliminated in comparative statements. With these prior sales and profits reported at now lower levels, Blockbuster's growth curve appeared all the more impressive.

One rough adjustment for omitted values in a pooling is to determine the difference between reported amounts and the market value of assets acquired. This difference can then be amortized against reported income on some reasonable basis to arrive at results comparable to those achieved under purchase accounting. Purchase accounting is designed to recognize the acquisition to which a buyer and seller in a business acquisition agree. It is more relevant for our analysis needs provided we are interested in market values at the date of a business combination rather than original costs of a seller.

Managerial Latitude in Accounting for Combinations

While practice provides specific provisions for valuation of assets and liabilities in business combinations, there remains latitude for abuses and baseless interpretations. Our analysis must also be alert to understatement of assets and overstatement of liabilities resulting from provisions for future costs and losses.

Gulf United's acquisition of Southwestern Drug Company highlights opportunities for earnings management in purchase accounting. Pro forma financial statements indicated approximately 1 million shares of Southwestern Drug were to be exchanged and purchased for cash. Their value was set at $16 million (or $16 per share), yielding a bargain purchase of Southwestern Drug not justified by its financial statements or recent earnings history. In a supplement to its prospectus, Gulf United subsequently increased its per share valuation to a more realistic $22.5 (Gulf United's stock was trading at $23.5). A review of the accounting by Gulf United for the Southwestern Drug acquisition reveals only 116,000 shares were purchased for cash at $22.5 per share. The remaining balance of 900,000 shares were exchanged on a one-for-one basis and valued at $16 per share. The accounting revalued Southwestern Drug's equipment to zero, and negative goodwill was recorded and used to increase Gulf United's income for the next 20 years through its amortization. Gulf United's eagerness to use purchase accounting in this acquisition is apparent by its inclusion as a contractual condition for completing the acquisition.

This illustration emphasizes our need to evaluate financial statement notes on the process of valuation in business combinations to effectively assess the implications of purchase accounting. This information can help us reach inferences on the fairness of presentation for the acquired company's assets and liabilities. We should direct particular attention to potential overprovision in future costs and losses.

When an acquisition accounted for as a purchase is effected for equity securities, our analysis must be alert to the valuation of net assets acquired. In periods of high market prices, purchase accounting tends to inflate values of net assets, particularly intangible assets, of acquired companies when valued using the market price of stock issued. Such values, while determined on potentially inflated stock prices, remain on a company's balance sheet and affect its operating results for years to come. Our analysis should be aware that acquiring companies using purchase accounting find it advantageous to provide (and overprovide) for costs like plant closings, excess employee costs, and termination benefits. Acquiring companies then include these costs in the costs of the purchase. For example, if a liability or provision for such a cost is established, then goodwill is correspondingly increased. While these cost provisions shield the income statement from charges it otherwise absorbs, goodwill amortization generally affects income over a more extended period of time. Practice has moved to restrict liabilities in purchase accounting, but our analysis must be aware of and adjust for earnings management techniques. In general, accounting for goodwill offers the potential for management to exercise considerable latitude in reporting financial performance.

Consequences of Accounting for Goodwill

The excess of the purchase price over the market value of identifiable net assets acquired represents payment for super (abnormal) earnings. Superearnings are attributed to brand names and other items offering superior competitive position. Superior

Source: *Annual reports.*

competitive position is subject to change from a myriad of economic and environmental forces. With effort and opportunity, a company can maintain a superior position. Nevertheless, goodwill is not permanent. Moreover, the present value of superearnings declines as they extend further into the future. The accounting compromise requires amortization of goodwill against the new entity's earnings over a period not exceeding 40 years. This implies that excess earnings are expected to continue in the acquiring entity's income statement for as long as 40 years. The SEC increasingly insists that companies relate the amortization period of goodwill to the nature of the business acquired. Accordingly, high-tech acquisitions require 5- to 7-year amortization and banks 15- to 20-year periods. International practice limits goodwill amortization to no more than 20 years.

Accounting for goodwill is subject to misuse for several reasons. One reason stems from its residual measurement as evidenced in the following case:

Alexander & Alexander purchased the British insurance broker Alexander Howden Group. It paid $300 million for this acquisition. Alexander Howden had $120 million in net assets and, hence, the $180 million balance was charged to goodwill. When Alexander & Alexander subsequently discovered $40 million of Alexander Howden's assets missing, they simply increased goodwill by the same amount. It took pressure from the SEC to force Alexander & Alexander to record this $40 million as a charge to earnings.

The residual measurement of goodwill gives rise to other uncertainties. Payments resulting from errors of estimation, of intense bidding contests, or of carelessness with owner or creditor resources get swept into goodwill. These payments can even include finder's fees, legal costs, investment banker fees, and interim financing costs. Warren Buffett, chairman of Berkshire Hathaway, Inc., recognized this residual measurement of goodwill in writing to his shareholders: "When an overexcited management purchases a business at a silly price . . . silliness ends up in the goodwill account. considering the lack of managerial discipline that created the account, under the circumstances it might better be labeled no-will." The crux of this issue is: Does goodwill represent superior earnings power and does its benefits extend over the amortization period? Our analysis must realize that in too many cases the answer is no, as suggested in the following case:

United Technologies purchased semiconductor maker Mostek Corporation for $345 million, of which $234 million represents goodwill. The expectation of substantial profits, if not superprofits, underlies payment of such a substantial premium. Mostek unfortunately continued its loss history (it lost $19 million in the year before its acquisition and $11 million in the preacquisition months of the acquisition year). Six years after the acquisition, United Technologies wrote off $75 million in inventories of its semiconductor division. But yet, amortization of goodwill continued at a slow 25-year pace unfazed by the apparent absence of goodwill.

If companies do write off goodwill in the face of substantial losses by purchased subsidiaries, the timing of the write-off seldom reflects prompt recognition of this loss in value.

Bangor Punta Corporation acquired Piper Aircraft for payment including a substantial amount for goodwill. Ultimately, payment was for superlosses rather than superprofits. In one period, Bangor Punta earned $3.1 million on a consolidated basis, while Piper Aircraft lost $22.4 million. Only when confronting an operating loss of $38.5 million by Piper Aircraft, and an overall consolidated loss, did Bangor Punta write off the Piper Aircraft goodwill of $54.7 million. It also appears that Bangor Punta did so on the basis of the "big bath." That is, recognition of the write-off was delayed until its impact was diminished by Bangor Punta's loss (i.e., take all the hits at one time). Write-offs do have the beneficial side effect of relieving Bangor Punta's future income of amortization charges.

To help our analysis, we might better understand accounting for goodwill and its implications to our analysis if we compare the accounting definition of goodwill to the usual analyst's definition:

Accounting definition of goodwill. Excess of cost over fair market value of net assets acquired in a purchase transaction—known as *goodwill.* No attempt is made to explicitly identify components of this asset or the economic values assigned to them. Whatever has been paid for and cannot be separately identified is assigned to goodwill. A requirement to amortize goodwill to income over a period of years, not to exceed 40, means that in many cases management will select the longest period allowable.

Analyst's definition of goodwill. Goodwill reflects real economic value such as that due to brand names requiring costly development and promotion. Goodwill can also reflect overpayments attributed to unrealistic expectations, undisciplined zeal, or lack of sound judgment and proper analysis. Evaluation of goodwill and its amortization requires careful analysis of a company's competitive market position and superior earning power with respect to the operations acquired. Goodwill represents a nonpermanent advantage that must manifest itself in superior earning power; if not, it does not exist.

Analysis of goodwill continues to be a difficult task. Billions of dollars in goodwill are on corporate balance sheets. In certain companies, it represents a substantial part of net worth or even exceeds total capital. Payment for superior earning power is warranted. But our analysis must be aware in many cases goodwill is nothing more than mechanical application of accounting rules giving no consideration to value received in return. The process by which billions of dollars in goodwill are placed on balance sheets is illustrated by the battle for control of RJR Nabisco:

Prior to the bidding battle for RJR Nabisco, the market (dominated by financial institutions holding 40% of its stock) valued the company at about $12 billion. A group, led by RJR Nabisco's CEO, started the bidding by offering $17 billion for the company—$5 billion more than the goodwill assigned to it by the market. RJR Nabisco was eventually sold for $25 billion, including $13 billion in goodwill. Undoubtedly swept into this account were significant costs of financing, professional and investment banking talent, and other expenses involved in this costly bidding war. A reasonable concern in our analysis is the extent to which goodwill reflects or does not reflect the present value of future excess earnings.

Our analysis must also realize that goodwill on corporate balance sheets reflects the part of a company's intangible earning power (due to market position, brand names, or other proprietary advantages) purchased. However, under generally accepted accounting principles, internally developed goodwill cannot be recorded as an asset, as seen in the case of Philip Morris:

Philip Morris, Inc., acquired General Foods Corporation for $5.8 billion, of which about $2.8 billion is payment for goodwill. General Foods' brand names possibly justify this premium. On Philip Morris's balance sheet, goodwill represents nearly 80% of net worth. Yet it does not include the considerable value of Philip Morris's own brand names.

Push-Down Accounting

Purchase accounting requires the assets and liabilities of an acquired company be included in the consolidated financial statements of the purchaser at their market values. A controversial question is how the acquired company reports these assets and liabilities in its separate financial statements (if that company survives as a separate entity). The SEC requires that purchase transactions resulting in an entity becoming substantially wholly owned (as defined in Regulation S-X) establish a new basis of accounting for the purchased assets and liabilities. For example, if Company A acquires substantially all the common stock of Company B in one or a series of purchase transactions, Company B's financial statements must reflect the new basis of accounting arising from its acquisition by Company A. When ownership is under control of the parent, the basis of accounting for purchased assets and liabilities should be the same regardless of whether the entity continues to exist or is merged into the parent's operations. That is, Company A's cost of acquiring Company B is "pushed down" and used to establish a new accounting basis in Company B's separate financial statements. The SEC recognizes that the existence of outstanding public debt, preferred stock, or significant minority interest in a subsidiary can impact a parent's ability to control ownership. In these cases, the SEC has not insisted on push-down accounting.

SECTION 2: INTERNATIONAL ACTIVITIES

Reporting of International Activities

When we analyze the financial statements of a company with international investments and operations, we must recognize obstacles unique to companies operating in more than one country. These obstacles subdivide into two categories:

- Obstacles due to differences in accounting practices peculiar to a country where operations exist.
- Obstacles arising from translation of assets, liabilities, and equities into the home-country measuring unit.

This section considers both of these obstacles for analysis of international activities.

International Accounting and Auditing Practices

Accounting practices vary considerably across countries. There are several reasons for cross-country variation in accounting, including lack of agreement on objectives of financial statements, differences in legal requirements, disparities in taxation laws, and variation in authority and maturity of local professional bodies (e.g., securities exchanges). Recent years have seen serious attempts at more conformity in international accounting practices. Establishment of international accounting standards through the International Accounting Standards Committee (IASC) is a major step toward uniformity. IASC's objective is to "formulate and publish in the public interest, basic standards to be observed in the presentation of audited accounts and financial statements and to promote their worldwide acceptance and observance." IASC has and continues to release standards for accounting and reporting on a number of important topics (e.g., changing prices, taxes, contingencies, pensions, earnings per share). These standards represent important steps toward narrowing differences in accounting practices across countries.

Perspectives on International Accounting

A key premise of this book is that analysis of financial statements requires understanding of the accounting underlying their preparation. When confronting analysis of international companies, we must possess a working familiarity with international accounting practices. Variation in international accounting is linked to differences in financial reporting objectives across countries. Accounting is a social science and its objectives are determined within societal settings. A country's history, culture, politics, geography, legal system, economic environment, and religion all affect financial reporting. For this reason, harmonization of international accounting practices is difficult. In the United States, financial statements are prepared with an emphasis on the interests of security holders. In Germany, the interests of creditors tend to dominate, while in France, the government and taxing authorities' interests take precedence. Moreover, in countries like Switzerland and Germany, the emphasis is on conservatism where reserves, including some unreported, are used to understate both assets and income or to overstate liabilities. We must recognize that not all countries share the view that accounting is a means to communicate economic data for investment and credit decisions.

There are at least four basic accounting systems, often referred to as the: (1) **British-American-Dutch system,** (2) **Continental system,** (3) **South American system,** and (4) **Socialist system.** The British-American-Dutch system is common in North America, India, Australia, and Britain. Countries adopting this system generally have proficient securities markets and market economies. The Continental system is familiar to Japan and many European countries. Governmental and creditor interests tend to dominate in this system. The South American system is common to most countries of South America. Accounting for changing prices (inflation) is central to this system, and uniformity in disclosure across business entities is routine. The Socialist system is prevalent in socialist economies where financial reporting is aimed to government and economic planners. Because of variations across these systems and societies, differences in accounting practices across countries can be substantial. Exhibit 5.6 lists a few differences indicative of international practices. Our analysis must use up-to-date sources in identifying significant international accounting differences. In consolidating international subsidiaries, U.S.–based multinationals usually require their subsidiaries' accounting to conform to the parent company.

EXHIBIT 5.6 Differences in International Accounting Practices

- Inventory reserves and other unrecorded ("secret") reserves sanctioned.
- Excessive depreciation recorded.
- Restatements of property accounts due to price-level changes.
- Legal reserves amounting to a fixed percent of income recorded.
- Tax allocation not practiced.
- Stock dividends recorded using the par value of stock issued.
- Pooling of interests accounting not sanctioned.
- Consolidation of parent and subsidiary financial statements not required.
- Pension liabilities not recognized.
- Provisions (reserves) and subsequent reversals used to manage income.
- Capitalization of lease obligations not acceptable.
- Certain assets (research and development) not recorded on financial statements.
- Little significance attached to consistency in accounting.
- Disclosure of accounting policies not required.

Perspectives on International Auditing and Governance

Auditing and governance activities are concerned with the reliability of financial reporting and ensuring managerial accountability. There is a variety of international auditing and governance practices. In countries like the United Kingdom and Canada, the auditing function is important and highly regarded, while in others its standing is weak and, consequently, the reliability of financial statements is dubious. An auditing firm of international repute can enhance the credibility of a company's financial statements regardless of its location. Our analysis must assess reliability of financial statements with knowledge of auditing and governance mechanisms in place.

ANALYSIS VIEWPOINT *. . . You are the bond rater*

Your supervisor assigns you the task of rating an international bond issue. Your analysis follows the usual procedures, including examination of numerous measures of both risk and return for the bonds involved. Upon completion, you submit your bond rating to the supervisor. Your supervisor responds with several questions as to how you dealt with international auditing and governance concerns. How do you satisfy your supervisor's concerns?

Translation of Foreign Currencies

The most common reason for nonconsolidation of international subsidiaries is substantial uncertainty about ultimate realization or transferability of foreign earnings. Accounting practice requires a parent company to recognize in its financial statements the equity in earnings or losses of unconsolidated foreign subsidiaries—this is similar to the accounting discussed earlier for income from corporate joint ventures and intercorporate investments for which the company exerts a significant influence. Consolidation of, and equity accounting for, foreign subsidiaries (and affiliates) requires their financial statements be translated into dollar equivalents. This is necessary before the accounts of foreign subsidiaries are combined with the parent company.

Methods of Foreign Currency Translation

The **current-noncurrent method** of foreign currency translation involves translating (1) *current* assets and liabilities at current rates, and (2) *noncurrent* assets and liabilities at historical rates. This method usually contains exceptions to the current-noncurrent distinction such as the translation of all payables and receivables at current rates. Another method, the **monetary-nonmonetary method** translates (1) *monetary* assets and liabilities at current rates, and (2) *nonmonetary* assets and liabilities at historical rates. Assets and liabilities are considered monetary if expressed in terms of fixed foreign currency units. Examples are cash, receivables, and payables expressed in foreign currency. All other assets and liabilities not expressed in foreign currency units are considered nonmonetary. Two other methods of foreign currency translation are also possible. The **current rate method** translates all assets and liabilities at current rates. The **temporal method** translates (1) cash, receivables, payables, and other assets and liabilities measured at present or future prices at current rates, and (2) assets and liabilities measured at past prices (historical costs) at historical rates.

Current practice emphasizes a "local perspective." That is, a foreign subsidiary is treated as a separate business entity, and financial statements of this business entity are prepared using the local currency. This is referred to as the **functional currency approach**. Two major objectives of accounting for foreign currency translation under this approach are to (1) provide information compatible with the expected economic effects of an exchange rate change on an entity's cash flows and equity, and (2) reflect in consolidated statements the financial results and relations of a subsidiary measured in the currency of the economic environment in which it operates—referred to as its *functional currency* (management determines the functional currency of a foreign subsidiary). Regarding the first objective, practice recognizes changes in exchange rates need not necessarily affect the operations of a foreign subsidiary. The second objective recognizes foreign subsidiaries operate in their own economic setting, which is likely different from the parent. Notice that translation should not affect financial relations such as a current ratio, inventory turnover ratio, or debt-equity ratio, which are products of the financial statements expressed in the functional currency. The functional currency approach does not translate foreign operations as if they were originally conducted in a parent company's currency (e.g., dollars). Instead, a functional currency approach reflects and retains the relations prevailing in the economic environment where the foreign subsidiary operates.

A major feature of the functional currency approach is the *current rate method* of translation. A foreign subsidiary's assets, liabilities, and operations are reported in the economic environment of its functional currency. It incurs costs in functional currency, and earns revenues in functional currency. Use of the current exchange rate retains historical costs and related measurements, but it restates them in the functional currency. It thereby preserves relations found in the subsidiary's economic environment. Use of the current exchange rate carries to the consolidated financial statements the inherent relations existing in a subsidiary's functional currency financial statements.

Another major feature of the functional currency approach is to *not* report in income of the period the gain or loss from *translation* of foreign financial statements. Rather, this translation adjustment is reported as a separate

Companies Reporting Foreign Currency Translation Adjustments

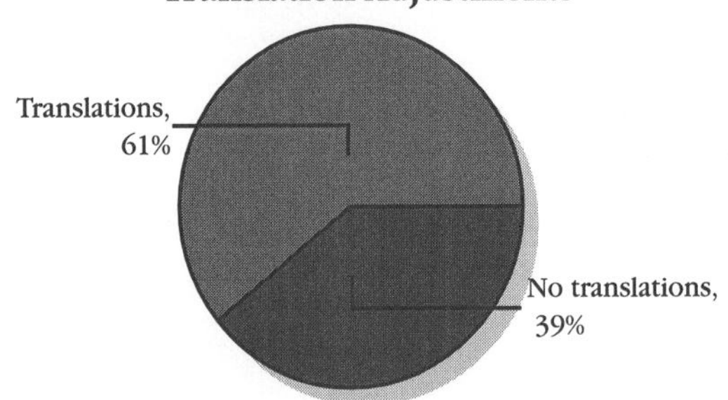

Source: *Accounting Trends & Techniques.*

Companies Reporting Foreign Currency Transaction Gains or Losses

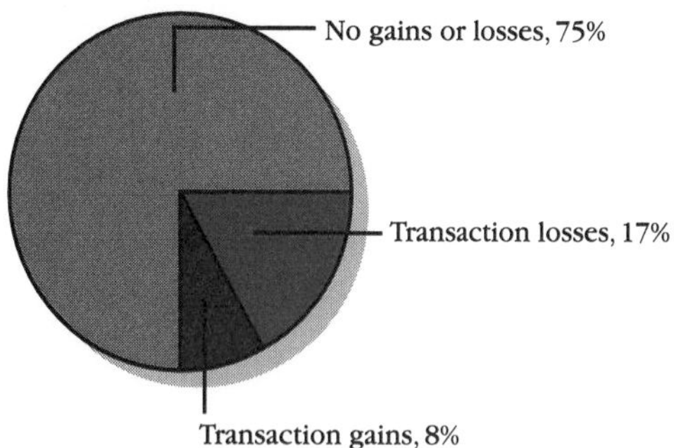

Source: *Accounting Trends & Techniques.*

component in shareholders' equity (a violation of the clean surplus relation). The translation adjustment must be distinguished from gains or losses on foreign currency *transactions*—the latter, with exceptions, are reported in income. Foreign currency transaction gains or losses include income from settled and unsettled transactions, arising when, for example, a U.S. parent assumes a 20-year debt denominated in Swiss francs.

A change in exchange rate between a dollar and a foreign currency yields a change in the dollar equivalent of the net investment, although there is no change in the net assets of the foreign entity measured in its functional currency. A strengthening of the foreign currency against the dollar enhances the dollar equivalent investment; a weakening reduces the dollar equivalent. Therefore, the translation adjustment reflects an economic effect of exchange rate changes. Yet a change in the dollar equivalent of the net investment is an *unrealized* increase or decrease, having no effect on the functional currency net cash flows generated by the foreign entity that can be reinvested

CURRENCY TRADING

EXCHANGE RATES

Wednesday, January 15, 1997

The New York foreign exchange selling rates below apply to trading among banks in amounts of $1 million and more, as quoted at 4 p.m. Eastern time by Dow Jones Telerate Inc. and other sources. Retail transactions provide fewer units of foreign currency per dollar.

	U.S. $ equiv.		Currency per U.S. $	
Country	Wed	Tue	Wed	Tue
Argentina (Peso)	1.0012	1.0012	.9988	.9988
Australia (Dollar)	.7762	.7805	1.2883	1.2812
Austria (Schilling)	.08958	.08921	11.163	11.210
Bahrain (Dinar)	2.6525	2.6525	.3770	.3770
Belgium (Franc)	.03050	.03044	32.787	32.854
Brazil (Real)	.9592	.9601	1.0425	1.0416
Britain (Pound)	1.6845	1.6713	.5936	.5983
30-Day Forward	1.6833	1.6702	.5941	.5987
90-Day Forward	1.6810	1.6732	.5949	.5977
180-Day Forward	1.6773	1.6643	.5962	.6009
Canada (Dollar)	.7453	.7399	1.3418	1.3516
30-Day Forward	.7469	.7415	1.3389	1.3486
90-Day Forward	.7497	.7443	1.3338	1.3436
180-Day Forward	.7540	.7483	1.3263	1.3363
Chile (Peso)	.002352	.002352	425.15	425.15
China (Renminbi)	.1201	.1201	8.3262	8.3264
Colombia (Peso)	.0009881	.0009926	1012.00	1007.50
Czech. Rep. (Koruna)	....	....	....	....
Commercial rate	.03633	.03633	27.528	27.524
Denmark (Krone)	.1651	.1647	6.0575	6.0705
Ecuador (Sucre)	....	....	....	....
Floating rate	.0002743	.0002740	3645.00	3650.00
Finland (Markka)	.2110	.2105	4.7395	4.7495
France (Franc)	.1866	.1859	5.3600	5.3805
30-Day Forward	.1869	.1857	5.3501	5.3858
90-Day Forward	.1876	.1852	5.3305	5.4003
180-Day Forward	.1888	.1847	5.2976	5.4135
Germany (Mark)	.6300	.6274	1.5872	1.5940
30-Day Forward	.6313	.6287	1.5841	1.5906
90-Day Forward	.6263	.6311	1.5968	1.5845
180-Day Forward	.6223	.6332	1.6069	1.5792
Greece (Drachma)	.004038	.004026	247.67	248.40
Hong Kong (Dollar)	.1292	.1292	7.7389	7.7385
Hungary (Forint)	.006048	.006073	165.35	164.67
India (Rupee)	.02789	.02789	35.850	35.855
Indonesia (Rupiah)	.0004205	.0004202	2378.25	2379.75
Ireland (Punt)	1.6488	1.6442	.6065	.6082
Israel (Shekel)	.3011	.3064	3.3209	3.2637
(Lira)	.00[illegible]460	.0006447	1548.00	1551.00
Japan (Yen)	.008558	.008552	116.85	116.93
30-Day Forward	.008595	.008590	116.35	116.41
90-Day Forward	.008668	.008662	115.37	115.45
180-Day Forward	.008785	.008777	113.83	113.93
Jordan (Dinar)	1.4075	1.4075	.7105	.7105
Kuwait (Dinar)	3.3278	3.3278	.3005	.3005
Lebanon (Pound)	.0006447	.0006447	1551.00	1551.00
Malaysia (Ringgit)	.4046	.4034	2.4715	2.4787
Malta (Lira)	2.7322	2.7397	.3660	.3650
Mexico (Peso)	....	....	....	....
Floating rate	.1282	.1282	7.8030	7.8000
Netherland (Guilder)	.5610	.5584	1.7824	1.7908
New Zealand (Dollar)	.7039	.7021	1.4207	1.4243
Norway (Krone)	.1576	.1565	6.3460	6.3885
Pakistan (Rupee)	.02520	.02520	39.680	39.680
Peru (new Sol)	.3833	.3833	2.6089	2.6089
Philippines (Peso)	.03802	.03800	26.305	26.318
Poland (Zloty)	.3437	.3436	2.9098	2.9100
Portugal (Escudo)	.006306	.006289	158.58	159.01
Russia (Ruble) (a)	.0001784	.0001786	5606.00	5599.00
Saudi Arabia (Riyal)	.2666	.2666	3.7503	3.7505
Singapore (Dollar)	.7117	.7119	1.4050	1.4047
Slovak Rep. (Koruna)	.03259	.03259	30.688	30.688
South Africa (Rand)	.2149	.2141	4.6525	4.6700
South Korea (Won)	.001178	.001178	848.95	848.55
Spain (Peseta)	.007511	.007504	133.13	133.26
Sweden (Krona)	.1441	.1436	6.9415	6.9655
Switzerland (Franc)	.7294	.7274	1.3710	1.3748
30-Day Forward	.7318	.7299	1.3665	1.3701
90-Day Forward	.7362	.7342	1.3583	1.3620
180-Day Forward	.7433	.7413	1.3454	1.3489
Taiwan (Dollar)	.03652	.03644	27.382	27.443
Thailand (Baht)	.03898	.03899	25.655	25.650
Turkey (Lira)	.00000892	.00000897	112160.00	111500.00
United Arab (Dirham)	.2723	.2723	3.6720	3.6720
Uruguay (New Peso)	....	....	....	....
Financial	.1136	.1136	8.8050	8.8050
Venezuela (Bolivar)	.002094	.002092	477.65	477.95
SDR	1.4193	1.4241	.7046	.7022
ECU	1.2214	1.2194	....	....

Special Drawing Rights (SDR) are based on exchange rates for the U.S., German, British, French, and Japanese currencies. Source: International Monetary Fund.

European Currency Unit (ECU) is based on a basket of community currencies.

...xing ...oscow Interbank Currency Exchange.

or distributed to the parent. It is for this reason that the translation adjustment is reported separately from net income.

Accounting for Foreign Currency Translation

The major provisions of accounting for foreign currency translation using a functional currency approach are:

- Translation requires identifying the functional currency of the entity. It is generally the currency of the country in which the subsidiary is located. All financial statement elements of the foreign entity are measured using the functional currency, but in conformity with the parent's accounting practices.
- Translation from the functional currency into the reporting currency is required, if they are different. This translation occurs at the *current* exchange rate, except for revenues and expenses that are translated at the *average* current exchange rate during the period. The functional currency approach typically considers the effect of exchange rate changes on the net investment in a foreign entity rather than on its individual assets and liabilities.
- Translation adjustments are not included in income. Rather, they are reported and accumulated as a separate component of shareholders' equity until such time the parent sells or completely or substantially liquidates the net investment in the foreign entity. Translation adjustments are removed from equity and included as gains or losses in determining income for the period when such sale or liquidation occurs.
- Exchange gains and losses attributable to intercompany foreign currency transactions, and balances that are of a trading nature, are included in income. But those attributable to long-term financing or capital transactions, where settlement is not expected for the foreseeable future, are reported as a separate component of equity.

Using current exchange rates to translate nonmonetary assets of foreign subsidiaries located in highly inflationary economies can produce distorted results. Under GAAP, if a foreign entity's functional currency is affected by cumulative inflation of 100 percent or more during a three-year period, it is considered not stable enough to serve as a functional currency. Consequently, the financial statements of this foreign entity are *remeasured* in the reporting (i.e., parent's) currency. This remeasurement is not unlike translation by the temporal method—an exception is the translation of deferred taxes at the current rate of exchange.

Illustration of Foreign Currency Translation

BritCo, a wholly owned British subsidiary of DollarCo, incorporates when the exchange rate is £1 = US$1.10. No capital stock changes occur since incorporation. The trial balance of BritCo at December 31, Year 6, expressed in £ units is reproduced in Step (5) below.

Additional Information for Translation:

1. BritCo's trial balance is adjusted to conform to DollarCo's accounting principles. The pound (£) is the functional currency of BritCo.
2. The Cumulative Foreign Exchange Translation Adjustment account at December 31, Year 5, is $30,000 (credit).

3. Dollar balance of Retained Earnings at December 31, Year 5, is $60,000.
4. Exchange rates are as follows:

January 1, Year 6	£1 = US$1.20
December 31, Year 6	£1 = US$1.40
Average for Year 6	£1 = US$1.30

5. All accounts receivable, payables, and noncurrent liability amounts are denominated in the local currency. Britco's December 31, Year 6, trial balance is:

Cash	£ 100,000
Accounts receivable	300,000
Inventories, at cost	500,000
Prepaid expenses	25,000
Property, plant, and equipment (net)	1,000,000
Long-term note receivable	75,000
	£2,000,000
Accounts payable	£ 500,000
Current portion of long-term debt	100,000
Long-term debt	900,000
Capital stock	300,000
Retained earnings, January 1, Year 6	50,000
Sales	5,000,000
Cost of sales	(4,000,000)
Depreciation	(300,000)
Other expenses	(550,000)
	£2,000,000

6. Sales, purchases, and all operating expenses occur evenly throughout the year. Accordingly, use of the average exchange rate produces results as if each individual month's revenues and expenses are translated using the rate in effect during each month. In this case, cost of goods sold is also convertible by use of the average rate.
7. Income tax consequences, if any, are ignored in this illustration.

Exhibit 5.7 reports the translation of the trial balance into both a balance sheet and income statement. The balance sheet highlights the reporting of translation adjustments as a separate component of shareholders' equity. A review of the translated financial statements of BritCo reveals the following:

- The company converts all income statement items using the average rate of exchange during the year.
- All assets and liabilities are translated at the current rate of exchange. Capital stock is translated at the historical rate. If all of a foreign entity's assets and liabilities are measured in its functional currency and are translated at the current exchange rate, then the net accounting effect of a change in the exchange rate is the effect on the entity's net assets. This accounting result is compatible with the concept of economic hedging, which is the basis of the net investment view. That is, no gains or losses arise from hedged assets and liabilities, and the dollar equivalent of the unhedged net investment increases or decreases as the functional currency strengthens or weakens.
- Notice that, after the translated net income for Year 6 of $195,000 is added to the retained earnings in the balance sheet, a translation adjustment of $85,000 must

EXHIBIT 5.7

BritCo
Translated Balance Sheet and Income Statement
Year Ended December 31, Year 6

	£	*Exchange Rate*	*Translation Code or Explanation*	*US $*
Balance Sheet				
Cash	100,000	1.4	C	140,000
Accounts receivable	300,000	1.4	C	420,000
Inventories, at cost	500,000	1.4	C	700,000
Prepaid expenses	25,000	1.4	C	35,000
Property, plant, and equipment (net)	1,000,000	1.4	C	1,400,000
Long-term note receivable	75,000	1.4	C	105,000
Total assets	2,000,000			2,800,000
Accounts payable	500,000	1.4	C	700,000
Current portion of long-term debt	100,000	1.4	C	140,000
Long-term debt	900,000	1.4	C	1,260,000
Total liabilities	1,500,000			2,100,000
Capital stock	300,000	1.1	H	330,000
Retained earnings:				
Balance, 1/1/Year 6	50,000		B	60,000
Current year net income	150,000		F	195,000
Balance, 12/31/Year 6	200,000			255,000
Cumulative foreign exchange translation adjustment:				
Balance, 1/1/Year 6			B	30,000
Current year translation adjustment			G	85,000
Balance, 12/31/ Year 6				115,000
Total stockholders' equity	500,000			700,000
Total liabilities and equity	2,000,000			2,800,000
Income Statement				
Sales	5,000,000	1.3	A	6,500,000
Cost of sales	(4,000,000)	1.3	A	(5,200,000)
Depreciation	(300,000)	1.3	A	(390,000)
Other expenses	(550,000)	1.3	A	(715,000)
Net income	150,000			195,000

Translation code or explanation:
C = Current rate.
H = Historical rate.
A = Average rate.
B = Balance in U.S. dollars at the beginning of the period.
F = Per income statement.
G = Amount needed to balance the financial statements.

be inserted to balance the statement. When this current year translation adjustment (credit) of $85,000 is added to the $30,000 beginning credit balance of the Cumulative Foreign Exchange Translation Adjustment account, the ending balance equals a credit of $115,000. This is the beginning balance of this equity account for January 1, Year 7.

- In this illustration only the translation adjustment required to balance the translated balance sheet affects the Cumulative Foreign Exchange Translation Adjustment account. In other circumstances this account is debited or credited for:

  Gains and losses attributable to a foreign currency transaction designated as, and effective as, an economic hedge of a net investment in a foreign entity.

  Gains or losses of a long-term financing or capital nature attributable to intercompany foreign currency transactions and balances.

Analysis of Translation Gain or Loss. Use of the current rate translation results in a balancing figure of $85,000 in the translated balance sheet. This yields a translation gain of $85,000 for BritCo that is added to the Cumulative Foreign Exchange Translation Adjustment account in equity. Exchange rate changes do not affect accounts translated at historical rates because such accounts are assigned the dollar amount prevailing at their origination. Accordingly, exchange gains or losses arise from translation of assets or liabilities at the current rate. Since companies translate only equity accounts at historical rates, the net assets that are translated at current rates are exposed to risk of changes in exchange rates. If the dollar strengthens against the foreign currency, the dollar value of foreign net assets declines and yields exchange losses. If the dollar weakens against the foreign currency, the dollar value of foreign net assets increases and yields exchange gains—this is the case with BritCo in Year 6.

The $85,000 translation gain for BritCo, that we computed indirectly, is also computable directly. We start with the beginning net asset position of £350,000 (i.e., capital stock of £300,000 + retained earnings of £50,000). We multiply the beginning balance of net assets by the change in exchange rate between the beginning and end of the year—in our illustration, this is a strengthening of $0.20 ($1.40 – $1.20) per pound. Since net assets increase in Year 6 the entire beginning balance is exposed to the change in exchange rate for the year, yielding a gain of $70,000 for this part of net assets. The second part is the *change* in net assets during the year. Here we multiply the change by the difference between the year-end rate ($1.40) and the rate prevailing at the date or dates when change(s) occur. We know in the BritCo example that the only change occurs due to income earned. Revenue and expense items are translated at the average exchange rate ($1.30). Therefore, we multiply the increase in net assets by the difference between the year-end rate and the average rate ($1.40 – $1.30) or $0.10. We can directly compute the translation gain as follows:

Translation gain on beginning net assets (£350,000 × [$1.40 – $1.20])	$70,000
Translation gain on increase in net assets for Year 6 (£150,000 × [$1.40 – $1.30])	15,000
Total	$85,000

When the cause of a change in net assets for the year is due to reasons other than those related to operations, the company needs to identify the reasons along with the rate of exchange for translation. These adjustments enter the computation of translation gain or loss consistent with the above.

Disclosing Foreign Currency Translation

Practice requires disclosure of the aggregate transaction gain or loss in income for the period. It also requires disclosure of analysis of changes during the period as a separate component of equity for cumulative translation adjustments. The SEC is concerned about the adequacy of disclosures for the effects of translating international operations. They encourage additional disclosure in Management's Discussion and Analysis section to supplement financial statements, including:

- Explaining how rate changes affect reported operating results (e.g., the depressing effect of weakening foreign currencies on reported sales).
- Identifying functional currencies used in measuring foreign operations.
- Describing the degree of exposure to exchange rate risks.
- Determining availability of cash flows from foreign operations in meeting company demands.
- Describing net investments by major functional currency.
- Identifying the company's intracompany financing practices.
- Interpreting the nature of translation components of equity.
- Analyzing the translation components of equity by functional currency or geographical region.

Foreign Currency Translation Adjustments

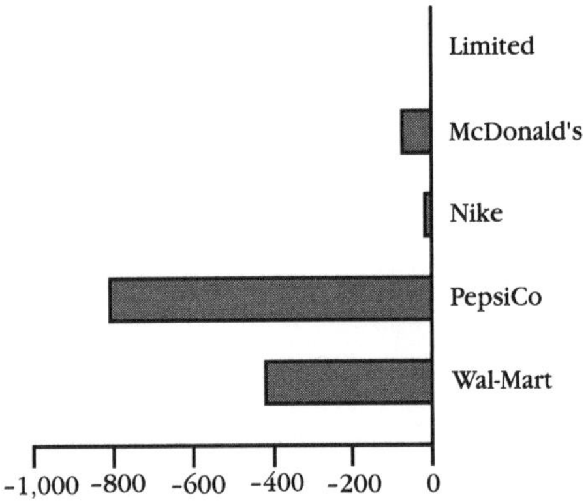

Limited
McDonald's
Nike
PepsiCo
Wal-Mart
-1,000 -800 -600 -400 -200 0
$ Millions

Source: *Annual reports.*

Accounting for Foreign Investment by Parent Company

When the parent company accounts for the investment in a foreign subsidiary by using the equity method, the parent records its proportionate share of the translation adjustment. In our illustration, DollarCo makes the following entries in Year 6 (in US$):

Investment in BritCo	195,000	
Equity in Earnings of Subsidiary		195,000
To record equity in BritCo's earnings.		
Investment in BritCo	85,000	
Translation Adjustment		85,000
To record current year translation adjustment.		

If DollarCo sells its investment in BritCo on January 1, Year 7, then DollarCo (1) records a gain or loss on the difference between the proceeds of the sale and the reported (book) value of the investment, and (2) transfers the Cumulative Foreign Exchange Translation Adjustment account, with a credit balance of $115,000, to income.

Analysis Implications of Foreign Currency Translation

Accounting for foreign currency translation is controversial, partly due to the difficulty and complexity of translation. Our analysis requires an understanding of both the economic underpinnings and the accounting mechanics to evaluate and predict effects of currency rate changes on a company's financial position.

The **temporal method** of translation is most faithful to and consistent with the historical cost accounting model. Under this method, nonmonetary items like property, plant, equipment, and inventories are stated at translated dollar amounts at date of acquisition. Similarly, companies translate depreciation and cost of goods sold on the basis of these historical-dollar costs. Since fluctuations in exchange rates do not affect the reported amounts of these nonmonetary assets, exposure to balance sheet translation gains and losses is measured by the excess (or deficit) of monetary assets over monetary liabilities (which are translated at current rates). For example, under the temporal method, if a foreign subsidiary has an excess of monetary liabilities over monetary assets (*high debt position*), then the following relations prevail:

Dollar Versus Local Currency	***Balance Sheet Translation Effect***
Dollar strengthens	Gain
Dollar weakens	Loss

If a foreign subsidiary has an excess of monetary assets over monetary liabilities (*high equity position*), then the following relations ensue:

Dollar Versus Local Currency	***Balance Sheet Translation Effect***
Dollar strengthens	Loss
Dollar weakens	Gain

Companies generally do not like translation gains and losses subjected to variation in economic environments as with the temporal method. They dislike even more the recording of these unpredictable gains and losses in income, yielding earnings volatility. Company criticism is not as strong when the translation process results in gains rather than losses. Current practice does *not* follow the temporal method *except* in two cases:

1. When a foreign entity is merely an extension of the parent and, thus, the functional currency is that of the parent.
2. When hyperinflation causes translation of nonmonetary assets to unrealistically low reported values because of using the current rate. The foreign currency, thus, loses its usefulness and a more stable currency is used.

Current practice applies the functional currency approach and uses current exchange rates. This approach selectively introduces current value accounting. It also allows gains and losses to bypass the income statement, violating clean surplus accounting. This removes from current operations certain risk effects of international operations and the risks of changes in exchange rates. Yet while insulating income from balance sheet translation gains and losses, as opposed to transaction gains and losses and income statement translation effects, the functional currency approach introduces a different translation exposure. While translation exposure for the temporal method is measured by the difference between monetary assets and monetary liabilities, the translation exposure for the functional currency approach is measured by the *size of the net investment*. This is because all balance sheet items, except net equity, are translated at the current rate. We illustrate this as follows.

SwissCo, a subsidiary of AmerCo, started operations on January 1, Year 1, with a balance sheet in Swiss francs (SF) as follows:

	SF		***SF***
Cash	100	Accounts payable	90
Receivables	120	Capital stock	360
Inventory	90		
Fixed assets	140		
	450		450

The income statement for the year ending December 31, Year 1, is:

	SF
Sales	3,000
Cost of sales (including depreciation of SF 20)	(1,600)
Other expenses	(800)
Net income	600

The December 31, Year 1, balance sheet is:

	SF		*SF*
Cash	420	Accounts payable	180
Receivables	330	Capital stock	360
Inventory	270	Retained earnings	600
Fixed assets (net)	120		
	1,140		1,140

The following exchange rates are applicable:

January 1, Year 1	$1 = SF 2.0
December 31, Year 1	$1 = SF 3.0
Year 1 average	$1 = SF 2.5

The beginning and ending balance sheets are translated into dollars as follows:

	January 1, Year 1			**December 1, Year 1**		
	SF	***Conversion***	***$***	***SF***	***Conversion***	***$***
Cash	100	÷2	50	420	÷3	140
Receivables	120	÷2	60	330	÷3	110
Inventory	90	÷2	45	270	÷3	90
Fixed assets	140	÷2	70	120	÷3	40
	450		225	1,140		380
Accounts payable	90	÷2	45	180	÷3	60
Capital stock	360	÷2	180	360	÷2	180
Retained earnings				600	*	240
Translation adjustment						(100)
	450		225	1,140		380

*Per income statement—since *each* individual income statement item is translated at the average rate, net income in dollars is SF 600 ÷ 2.5 = $240.

The translation adjustment account (a part of equity) is independently calculated as:

Total equity (equals net assets):		
In SF at December 31, Year 1	SF 960	
Converted into dollars at year-end rate (÷ 3)		$ 320
Less:		
Capital stock at December 31, Year 1, per converted balance sheet (in dollars)	$180	
Retained earnings balance at December 31, Year 1, per converted balance sheet (in dollars)	240	420
Translation adjustment—loss		$(100)

We can derive several analysis insights from this illustration. First, the translation adjustment (a loss of $100 in Year 1) is determined from the net investment in SwissCo at end of Year 1 (SF 960) multiplied by the change in exchange rates. The exchange rate declines from SF 2.0 per dollar for capital stock, and from SF 2.5 per dollar for retained earnings, to the year-end exchange rate of SF 3.0 per dollar. Consequently, the SF investment expressed in dollars suffers a loss of $100. This is intuitive—when an investment is expressed in a foreign currency and that currency weakens in relation to the dollar, then the investment value (in dollars) declines. The reverse occurs if that currency strengthens.

Second, under the functional currency approach, currency translation affects equity (but not income). This approach affects among other items the debt-to-equity ratio (potentially endangering certain debt covenants) and book value per share for the translated balance sheet (but not for the foreign currency balance sheet). Since the entire equity capital represents the measure of exposure to balance sheet translation gain or loss, that exposure is potentially more substantial than under the temporal method, especially with a subsidiary financed with low debt and high equity. Our analysis can estimate the translation adjustment impact by multiplying year-end equity by the estimated change in the period-to-period rate of exchange.

Third, we can examine the effect of a change in exchange rates on the translation of the income statement. If we assume in Year 2 SwissCo reports the same income but the SF *weakens* further to SF 3.5 (average for year) per dollar, then the translated income totals SF 600 ÷ 3.5 = $171, or a decline of $69 from the Year 1 level of $240. This loss is reflected in the translated income statement. In contrast, if the SF *strengthens* to SF 2.0 per dollar (average for year), the translated income totals SF 600 ÷ 2.0 = $300, or a gain of $60 from the Year 1 level of $240. This gain is reflected in income and recognizes income earned in SF is worth more dollars. Under the functional currency approach, translated income varies directly with changes in exchange rates. This makes our estimation of the income statement translation effect easier.

Our analysis must be aware that income also includes the results of completed foreign exchange transactions. Further, any gain or loss on translation of a current payable by the subsidiary to parent (which is not of a long-term capital nature) flows through consolidated income.

A substantial drop in the dollar relative to many important currencies has the effect of increasing the reported income of consolidated foreign subsidiaries. It often also increases shareholders' equity, in certain cases by substantial amounts. This effect lowers measures like return on equity. Should the dollar recover its value, the results are the opposite and reduce reported income.

Our analysis must be aware that if the dollar weakens, companies can, by designating the dollar as the functional currency, apply the temporal translation method to potentially yield better reported results. Conversely, a strengthening dollar often makes it advantageous to use the "all current" translation method of the functional currency approach. Our analysis must bear in mind that it is management's decision whether the functional currency is the local currency or the dollar.

The managements of Unocal, Occidental Petroleum, and Texaco designated the dollar as the functional currency of most of their foreign operations. In contrast, their competitors Mobil Oil, Exxon, and Amoco designated local currencies of their foreign businesses as the functional currencies.

While current practice yields smaller fluctuations in income relative to fluctuations in exchange rates, it yields substantial changes in shareholders' equity because of changes in the cumulative translation adjustment (CTA) account. For companies with a large equity base, these changes are arguably insignificant. But for companies with a small equity base these changes, which further reduce equity, yield potentially serious effects on debt-to-equity and other ratios, and can put a company at risk of violating its debt covenants. Exposure to changes in the CTA depends on the degree of exposure of foreign subsidiary net assets to changes in exchange rates. Companies can reduce this exposure by reducing net assets of their foreign subsidiaries. This can be achieved by withdrawing foreign investment through dividends or by substituting foreign debt for equity. We must recognize that an increasing debit balance in the CTA is often symptomatic of a failure to manage properly the foreign exchange exposure. This can result from investments denominated in persistently weak currencies, among other reasons.

GUIDANCE ANSWERS TO ANALYSIS VIEWPOINTS

You Are the Lawyer

Your client needs to be informed about a distinction between "economic substance" and "legal responsibility." Consolidated financial statements are meant to recognize the entire business entity under a centralized control. Economic substance suggests that all subsidiaries under a parent's control are its responsibility and should be reported as such—yielding consolidated statements. Legal responsibility is *not* the same. Shareholders like your client (and NY Research Labs) are *not* responsible for any losses incurred by lawsuits against Boston Chemicals Corporation. Shareholders' risks generally extend only to their investment in a corporation's stock. In sum, NY Research Labs is not responsible for lawsuits of Boston Chemicals because of consolidation. But the amount of NY Research Labs' investment in common stock of Boston Chemicals is subject to the risk presented from these lawsuits.

You Are the Investment Banker

There are two important aspects to this case. First, you require complete and accurate disclosure of your client's stock offering according to accepted practices. This includes your analysis of LA Waste Management's financial statements to ensure adherence with accepted accounting principles. On this dimension, you are entirely assured. Second, and not unrelated to the first point, you require that your client is not misrepresenting its financial position. This is important for your reputation and future business opportunities as an investment banker. Here is the dilemma. LA Waste Management properly reports their financial statements using pooling accounting for its acquisition of Riverside Trucking. Yet you know from your analysis that pooling does not entirely reflect the economic substance of this transaction. More specifically, you expect their common stock will fetch a price considerably higher than what their fundamentals suggest. To accept this engagement you would like to report pro forma statements for LA Waste Management assuming *purchase accounting* for Riverside Trucking. In this way you are comfortable in fairly representing the economic substance of your client's financial position. If LA Waste Management refuses to disclose any additional information than required under acceptable practices, you might be forced to decline this engagement.

You Are the Bond Rater

Analyzing auditing and governance factors for international bond issue rating decisions is demanding and crucial. You must decide on the role played by particular firms and institutions, and then assign a measure of reliance to their responsibility in safeguarding company assets. The less rigorous are auditing and governance mechanisms, the greater risk assigned to a bond issue. For example, bond covenants are of little value when auditors fail to encourage compliance or disclosure of violations. Audit firms and governance mechanisms do differ in quality and responsibility across countries, and bond ratings must reflect these. The supervisor is wise in questioning a rating's reliance on these factors. Our bond rating exercise must reflect and document reliance on these audit and governance factors in determining the rating.

QUESTIONS

5–1. Describe important information potentially disclosed in individual parent and subsidiary companies' financial statements not found in their consolidated statements.
(CFA Adapted)

5–2. Evaluate the following statement from our analysis viewpoint: "A parent company is not responsible for the liabilities of its subsidiaries nor does it own the assets of the subsidiaries. Therefore, consolidated financial statements distort legal realities."

5–3. Identify the cases requiring consolidated financial statements.

a. Parent company has a two-fifths ownership of a subsidiary.

b. Parent company has temporary but absolute control over a subsidiary.

c. Parent company has a controlling interest in a subsidiary but plans to dispose of it.

d. Parent company is to relinquish control of a subsidiary in the near future because of a minority shareholder's legal suit.

e. A conglomerate parent company has majority interest in diversified subsidiaries.

f. Parent company has a 100 percent interest in a foreign subsidiary located in a country where governmental authorities severly restricted conversion of currencies and transfer of funds.

g. Parent company has a 100 percent interest in a subsidiary whose principal business is leasing properties to the parent company and its affiliates.

5–4. What are some important limitations of consolidated financial statements?

5–5. The note below appears in the financial statements of the Best Company for the period ending December 31, Year 1:

> *Event subsequent to December 31, Year 1*: In January Year 2, Best Company acquired Good Products, Inc., and its affiliates by the issuance of 48,063 shares of common stock. Net assets of the combined companies amounted to $1,016,198, and net income for Year 1 approximated $150,000. To the extent the acquired companies earn in excess of $1,000,000 over the next five years, Best Company is required to issue additional shares not exceeding 151,500, and limited to a market value of $2,000,000.

a. Explain whether this disclosure is necessary and adequate.

b. If Good Products, Inc., is acquired in December Year 1, at what price does Best Company record this acquisition? Best Company's shares traded at $22 on the acquisition date.

c. Explain the contingency for additional consideration.

d. If the contingency materializes to the maximum limit, how does Best Company record this investment?

5–6. Describe how you determine the valuation of assets acquired in a purchase when:

a. Assets are acquired by incurring liabilities.

b. Assets are acquired in exchange of common stock.

5–7. Assume a company appropriately determines the total cost of a purchased entity. Explain how the company allocates the total cost to the following assets.

a. Goodwill.

b. Negative goodwill (bargain purchase).

c. Marketable securities.

d. Receivables.

e. Finished goods.

f. Work in process.

g. Raw materials.

h. Plant and equipment.

i. Land and mineral reserves.

j. Payables.

k. Goodwill recorded in the book of the acquired company.

5–8. One argument for pooling accounting is that no resource is given in exchange for the acquisition. Since the acquiring company furnishes its unissued stock, the acquisition is arguably not regarded as a purchase. Indicate and explain your agreement or disagreement with this argument.

5–9. Company A uses pooling accounting to account for the acquisition of Company B. Company B's market value of net assets is much higher than its book value. Describe the effect(s) of pooling accounting on Company A's (*a*) income statement, and (*b*) balance sheet.

5–10. Describe how goodwill is treated in an acquisition accounted for as a pooling of interests.

5–11. If assets are understated from the use of pooling accounting, describe the effect(s) this understatement has on the following items:

a. Capital account.

b. Expenses.

c. Disposition of assets acquired.

5–12. Describe whether our analysis can adjust an income statement using pooling accounting to be comparable with an income statement using purchase accounting.

5–13. From our analysis point of view, is pooling or purchase accounting for a business combination preferable and why?

5–14. When an acquisition accounted for as a purchase is effected for stock or other equity securities, discuss what our analysis should be alert to.

5–15. When a balance sheet reports a substantial amount for goodwill, discuss what we should be concerned with.

5–16. Resources, Inc., is engaged in an aggressive program of acquiring competing companies through the exchange of common stock.

a. Explain how an acquisition program might contribute to the rate of growth in earnings per share of Resources, Inc.

b. Explain how the income statements of prior years might be adjusted to reflect the potential future earnings trend of the combined companies.

(CFA Adapted)

5–17. Indicate factors that can change management's original estimates for the benefit periods of intangible assets.

5–18. Identify significant problem areas in accounting for foreign operations.

5–19. When a consolidated financial statement includes foreign operations, discuss what our analysis must be particularly alert to.

5–20. Discuss the major objectives of current accounting practice in foreign currency translation.

5–21. Identify and discuss the major provisions of accounting for foreign currency translation.

5–22. Describe circumstances where a company must employ the temporal method of translating foreign currency.

5–23. Discuss implications for our analysis resulting from the accounting for foreign currency translation.

EXERCISES

Exercise 5–1

Analyzing and Interpreting Intercorporate Investments

The diagram below portrays Company X (the parent or investor company), its two subsidiaries C1 and C2, and its "50 percent or less owned" affiliate C3. Each of the companies has only one type of stock outstanding, and there are no other significant shareholders in either C2 or C3. All four companies engage in commercial and industrial activities.

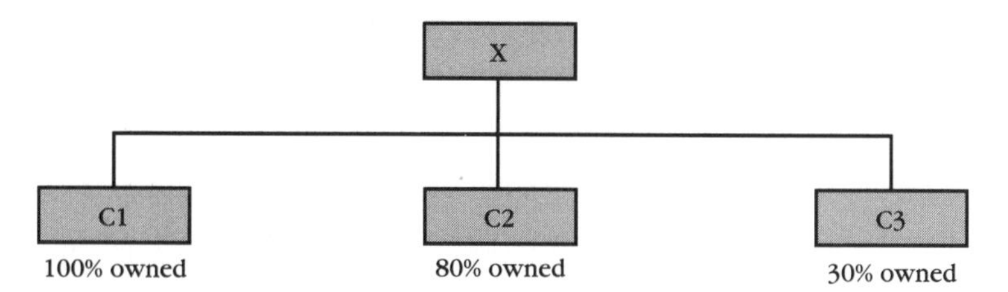

Required:

a. Explain whether each of the separate companies maintains distinct accounting records.

b. Identify the type of financial statements each company uses for financial reporting.

c. Assuming you have the ability to enforce your requests, describe the type of financial statements and other information about these companies (separate or consolidated) that you would request.

d. Explain what Company X reports in its assets regarding C1.

e. If C1 is legally dissolved into Company X, describe how Company X's balance sheet changes.

f. If C1 is legally dissolved into Company X, describe how the consolidated balance sheet changes.

g. In the consolidated balance sheet, explain how the 20 percent of C2 *not* owned by Company X is reported.

h. Identity what transaction is required before C3 is included line by line in the consolidated statements.

i. If "combined" statements are reported for C1 and C2, discuss the need for any elimination entries.

j. Suppose Company X sold its entire investment in C2 to C1 (C2 is then 80 percent owned by C1). Explain how the consolidated balance sheet changes.

k. If C1 sold additional common stock to Company X for cash, describe how the consolidated balance sheet changes.

Exercise 5–2

Interpreting Accounting for Business Combinations

Spellman Company acquires 90 percent of Moore Company in a business combination. The total consideration is agreed upon, yet the exact nature of Spellman's payment is not fully agreed upon. It is possible that this business combination can be accounted for as either a purchase or a pooling of interests. It is expected that at the date of the business combination, the fair value will exceed the book value of Moore's assets minus liabilities. Spellman desires to prepare consolidated financial statements that include the financial statements of Moore.

Required:

a. Explain how the method of accounting for a business combination affects whether goodwill is reported.

b. If goodwill is reported, explain how to determine the amount of goodwill.

c. Describe how the method of accounting for a business combination affects whether minority interest is reported. If minority interest reported differs across the two methods, explain why.

d. From a conceptual standpoint, explain why consolidated financial statements should be prepared.

e. From a conceptual standpoint, identify the usual first condition necessary before consolidated financial statements are prepared.

f. From a conceptual standpoint, discuss how the method of accounting for a business combination affects the decision to prepare consolidated financial statements.

Exercise 5–3

Analyzing Companies with International Operations

Assume your firm is considering investing in the equity securities of companies operating in several different countries. After a preliminary review of financial statements, you realize there is a range of international accounting practices that can materially affect net income and other financial data relevant for equity valuation purposes.

Required:

a. Discuss two plausible approaches to comparing companies operating in different countries and using different accounting principles.

b. Discuss how international variations in accounting for each of the following items affect reported net income:

1. Revaluation of fixed assets.
2. Treatment of acquired goodwill.
3. Discretionary reserves.

Exercise 5–4

Analyzing Foreign Currency Translation

Accounting rules for foreign currency translation are intended to apply to foreign currency transactions and financial statements of foreign branches, subsidiaries, partnerships, and joint ventures that are consolidated, combined, or reported under the equity method.

Required:

a. Describe the following key concepts of accounting for foreign currency translation:
   1. Functional currency.
   2. Translation.
   3. Remeasurement.

b. Describe the accounting for foreign currency translation with a multinational company located in a highly inflationary country.

Exercise 5–5

Analyzing Implications of Pooling Accounting for Mergers

Controversy exists concerning the widespread use of pooling accounting for mergers. Opponents of the use of pooling accounting assert that the surviving company often uses pooling (rather than purchase accounting) to hide the "true economic" effects of a merger.

Required:

a. Discuss what might be "hidden."

b. Describe how pooling accounting affects our analysis of a company's securities.

(CFA Adapted)

Exercise 5–6

Interpreting the Effects of Functional Currency

Bethel Company uses the U.S. dollar as its functional currency worldwide. Star Brite Company uses the local currency for each country in which it operates as its functional currency.

Required:

Explain how choice of functional currency affects each of the following:

a. Reported sales.

b. Computation of translation gains and losses.

c. Reporting of translation gains and losses.

(CFA Adapted)

PROBLEMS

Problem 5–1

Analyzing Intercorporate and International Investments

Refer to the financial statements of Campbell Soup Company in Supplement A.

Required:

a. As of July 28, Year 11, Campbell owned 33 percent of Arnotts Limited. Explain where Campbell reports the amounts representing this investment.

b. Note 18 contains disclosures regarding the market value of the company's investment in Arnotts Limited. Explain whether this market value is reflected in Campbell's financial statements beyond the disclosures referred to.

c. In July of Year 11, Campbell acquired the remaining shares of Campbell Canada. This is in addition to one other acquisition during Year 11. Describe what the relation between the purchase price paid for these acquisitions and the fair market value of acquired net assets tell us.

d. Prepare a composite journal entry recording the total Year 11 acquisitions.

e. Explain the likely causes of changes in the cumulative translation adjustment accounts for (1) Europe, and (2) Australia.

Problem 5–2

Interpreting Intercorporate Investments and Foreign Operations

Refer to the financial statements of Quaker Oats Company in Supplement A.

Required:

a. The financial statements of fiscal Year 10 and earlier years reflect the company's decision to discontinue (divest) the operations of Fisher-Price. Identify where in the financial statements the assets and liabilities of Fisher-Price are reflected in Year 10.

b. Quaker Oats reports no acquisitions in Years 10 and 11. Yet goodwill amortization, which Quaker Oats is amortizing on a straight-line basis, increases in both years. Explain how these events are reconcilable.

c. Quaker Oats has forward contracts to purchase and sell currencies to hedge balance sheet exposure. Describe where gains or losses on these contracts are reported.

d. The company reports on hyper-inflationary conditions in Brazil. Explain where in the financial statements the gains and losses on translation of Brazilian subsidiaries are reflected.

Problem 5–3

Analyzing Financial Statement Effects of Intercorporate Investments

The following data are from the annual report of Francisco Company, a manufacturer of cardboard boxes:

	Year 6	*Year 7*	*Year 8*
Sales	$25,000	$30,000	$35,000
Net income	2,000	2,200	2,500
Dividends paid	1,000	1,200	1,500
Book value per share (year-end)	$ 11.00	$ 12.00	$ 13.00

Note: Francisco had 1,000 common shares outstanding during the entire period. There is no public market for Francisco shares.

Potter Company, a manufacturer of glassware, made the following acquisitions of Francisco common shares:

January 1, Year 6	10 shares at $10 per share
January 1, Year 7	290 shares at $11 per share, increasing ownership to 300 shares
January 1, Year 8	700 shares at $15 per share, yielding 100% ownership of Francisco

Ignore income tax effects and the effect of lost income on funds used to make these investments.

Required:

a. Compute the effect of these investments on Potter Company's reported sales, net income, and cash flows for each of the Years 6 and 7.

b. Calculate the carrying value of Potter Company's investment in Francisco as of December 31, Year 6, and December 31, Year 7.

c. Discuss how Potter Company accounts for its investment in Francisco during Year 8. Describe any additional information necessary to calculate the impact of this acquisition on Potter Company's financial statements for Year 8.

(CFA Adapted)

Problem 5–4

Interpreting Pro Forma Balance Sheets under Purchase or Pooling

Your supervisor asks you to analyze the potential purchase of Drew Company by your firm, Pierson, Inc. You are provided the following information (in millions):

		Drew Company		
	Pierson, Inc., Historical Cost	*Historical Cost*	*Fair Value*	*Pro Forma Combined (pooling accounting)*
Current assets	$ 70	$ 60	$ 65	$130
Land	60	10	10	70
Buildings	80	40	50	120
Equipment	90	20	40	110
Total assets	$300	$130	$165	$430
Current liabilities	$120	$ 20	$ 20	$140
Shareholders' equity	180	110	—	290
Total liability & equity	$300	$130		$430

Required:

a. Prepare a pro forma combined balance sheet using purchase accounting. Pierson pays $180 million in cash for Drew where this cash is obtained by issuing long-term debt.

b. Discuss how differences between pooling and purchase accounting for acquisitions affect future reported earnings of the Pierson/Drew combination.

(CFA Adapted)

Problem 5–5

Intercorporate Investments under the Equity Method

Burry Corporation acquires 80 percent of The Bowman Company for $40 million on January 1, Year 6. At the time of acquisition, Bowman has total net assets with a fair value of $25 million. For the years ended December 31, Year 6, and December 31, Year 7, Bowman reported earnings and paid dividends as shown below:

	Net Income (loss)	*Dividends Paid*
Year 6	$2,000,000	$1,000,000
Year 7	(600,000)	800,000

The excess of the acquisition price over the fair value of net assets is amortized over 40 years.

Required:

a. Compute the value of Burry's investment in Bowman as of December 31, Year 7, under the equity method. Include the "earnings pickup" for Years 6 and 7.

b. Discuss the strengths and weaknesses of the income statement and balance sheet in reflecting the economic substance of this transaction using the equity method.

(CFA Adapted)

CASES

Case 5–1

Analysis of Adaptec Financial Statements

Answer the following using the 1996 annual report of Adaptec, Inc., in Supplement A.

a. During fiscal 1996, Adaptec acquired all of the outstanding capital stock of four companies (see its note 5). For each of these acquisitions, identify the following:

1. Name of company.

2. Consideration given.
3. Accounting treatment.

b. Subsequent to fiscal 1996, Adaptec acquired all of the outstanding capital stock of two companies (see its note 5). For each of these acquisitions, identify the following:
1. Name of company.
2. Consideration given.
3. Accounting treatment.

c. Describe how Adaptec's recent acquisitions fit into its business plan and strategy.

d. Under accepted accounting practice an acquiring company is permitted to determine the price for "in-process" research and development assets of an acquired company and immediately write them off.
1. Determine how much acquired "in-process technology" Adaptec wrote off in 1996.
2. If Adaptec is not permitted to record this write-off, explain how it would treat this amount.
3. Describe how Adaptec's write-off of this amount affects current and future financial position and operating results.

e. Determine the amount of goodwill included in Adaptec's March 31, 1996, balance sheet. In what account is goodwill recorded?

f. According to the Concentration of Credit Risk section of Adaptec's note 1, explain how Adaptec manages its foreign currency risk.

Case 5–2

Consolidating Intercorporate Investments

Axel Corporation acquired 100 percent of the stock of Wheal Company on December 31, Year 4. The following information pertains to Wheal Company on the date of acquisition:

	Book Value	*Fair Value*
Cash	$ 40,000	$ 40,000
Accounts receivable	60,000	55,000
Inventory	50,000	75,000
Property, plant, and equipment (net)	100,000	200,000
Secret formula	—	30,000
	$250,000	$400,000
Accounts payable	$ 30,000	$ 30,000
Accrued employee pensions	20,000	22,000
Long-term debt	40,000	38,000
Capital stock	100,000	—
Other contributed capital	25,000	—
Retained earnings	35,000	—
	$250,000	$ 90,000

Axel Corporation issues $110,000 par value ($350,000 market value on December 31, Year 4) of its own stock to the shareholders of Wheal Company to consummate the transaction, and Wheal Company becomes a wholly owned, consolidated subsidiary of Axel Corporation.

Required:

a. Prepare journal entries for Axel Corp. to record the acquisition of Wheal Company stock assuming (1) pooling accounting, and (2) purchase accounting.

b. Prepare working paper entries for Axel Corp. to eliminate the investment in Wheal Company stock in preparation for a consolidated balance sheet at December 31, Year 4 assuming (1) pooling accounting, and (2) purchase accounting.

c. Calculate consolidated retained earnings at December 31, Year 4 (Axel's retained earnings at this date are $150,000), assuming:
1. Axel Corporation uses the pooling of interests method for this business combination.
2. Axel Corporation uses the purchase method for acquisition of Wheal Company.

Case 5–3

Analyzing Translated Financial Statements

On December 31, Year 8, U.S. Dental Supplies (USDS) created a wholly owned foreign subsidiary, Funi, Inc. (FI), located in the country of Lumbaria. The condensed balance sheet of Funi as of December 31, Year 8, reported in local currency (the pont), is reproduced below:

FUNI, INC.
Balance Sheet
December 31, Year 8

	Ponts (millions)
Cash	180
Fixed assets	420
Total assets	600
Capital stock	600

Funi initially adopted the U.S. dollar as its functional currency and translated its Year 9 balance sheet and income statement in accordance with U.S. accounting practice. These statements are reproduced below:

FUNI, INC.
Balance Sheet
December 31, Year 9

	Ponts (millions)	*Exchange Rate (ponts/US$)*	*US$ (millions)*
Cash	$ 82	4.0	$ 20.5
Accounts receivable	700	4.0	175.0
Inventory	455	3.5	130.0
Fixed assets	360	3.0	120.0
Total assets	$1,597		$445.5
Accounts payable	$ 532	4.0	$133.0
Capital stock	600	3.0	200.0
Retained earnings	465		112.5
Total liabilities and shareholders' equity	$1,597		$445.5

FUNI, INC.
Income Statement
December 31, Year 9

	Ponts (millions)	*Exchange Rate (ponts/US$)*	*US$ (millions)*
Sales	$3,500	3.5	$1,000.0
Cost of sales	(2,345)	3.5	(670.0)
Depreciation expense	(60)	3.0	(20.0)
Selling expense	(630)	3.5	(180.0)
Translation gain (loss)	—		(17.5)
Net income	$ 465		$ 112.5

USDS subsequently instructed Funi to change its functional currency to the pont. The following exchange rates (pont per U.S. Dollar) are applicable:

January 1, Year 9	3.0
Average for Year 9	3.5
December 31, Year 9	4.0

Required:

a. Prepare a pro forma balance sheet as of December 31, Year 9, and an income statement for the year ending December 31, Year 9, for Funi. Prepare both statements in U.S. dollars, using the pont as the functional currency for Funi.

b. Describe the effects of the change in functional currency to the pont for Funi's:

1. U.S. dollar balance sheet as of December 31, Year 10.
2. U.S. dollar Year 10 income statement.
3. U.S. dollar financial ratios for Year 10.

(CFA Adapted)

Case 5–4

Analyzing Translated Financial Statements and Intercorporate Investments

The December 31, Year 8, trial balance of SwissCo Corporation, a Swiss company, is shown below (in Swiss francs, SFr).

	Debit	*Credit*
Cash	SFr 50,000	
Accounts receivable	100,000	
Property, plant, and equipment (net)	800,000	
Depreciation expense	100,000	
Other expenses (including taxes)	200,000	
Inventory, January 1, Year 8	150,000	
Sales		SFr2,000,000
Allowance for doubtful accounts		10,000
Accounts payable		80,000
Notes payable		20,000
Capital stock		100,000
Retained earnings, January 1, Year 8		190,000
Purchases	1,000,000	
	SFr2,400,000	SFr2,400,000

Additional Information:

1. SwissCo uses the periodic inventory system and the FIFO costing method for inventory and cost of goods sold. On December 31, Year 8, inventory on hand is SFr120,000. It is carried at cost.
2. SwissCo capital stock was issued six years ago when the company was established; the exchange rate at that time was SFr1 = $0.30. The company purchased plant and equipment five years ago when the exchange rate was SFr1 = $0.35; and the note payable was made out to a local bank at the same time.
3. Revenues and expenses are earned or incurred uniformly throughout Year 8. Inventory on hand on December 31, Year 8, is purchased throughout the second half of Year 8.
4. Retained Earnings in the December 31, Year 7, balance sheet (in U.S. dollars) of SwissCo Corporation is $61,000, and Inventory is $47,000.

5. The spot rates for SFr in Year 8 are:

January 1, Year 8	$0.32
Average for Year 8	$0.37
Average for second half of Year 8	$0.36
December 31, Year 8	$0.38

6. Management determined the functional currency of SwissCo is the Swiss franc.

Required:

a. Prepare a trial balance in U.S. dollars for SwissCo Corporation as of December 31, Year 8.

b. Prepare an income statement for the year ending December 31, Year 8, and the balance sheet at that date (both in U.S. dollars) for SwissCo Corporation.

c. Assume Unisco Corporation, a U.S. firm, purchases a 75 percent ownership interest in SwissCo Corporation at book value on January 1, Year 8. Prepare the entry Unisco makes at December 31, Year 8, to record its equity in SwissCo's Year 8 earnings. Unisco Corp. uses the equity method in accounting for its investment in SwissCo.

INTERNET ACTIVITIES

Internet 5–1

Analyzing Intercompany Activities

Access one of the financial statement databases available on the Internet (http://www.mhhe.com/business/accounting/wild). Retrieve current financial statements of a company selected by either you or your instructor.

Required:

a. Write a report summarizing the impact of any intercorporate investments on its financial statements.

b. Write a report summarizing the impact of any business combinations on its financial statements.

Internet 5–2

Analyzing International Activities from Financial Statements

Access one of the financial statement databases available on the Internet (http://www.mhhe.com/business/accounting/wild). Retrieve current financial statements of a company selected by either you or your instructor. Write a report summarizing the impact of this company's international activities on its financial statements.

Internet 5–3

Analysis of Intercompany and International Accounting Methods

Access one of the financial statement databases available on the Internet (http://www.mhhe.com/business/accounting/wild). Retrieve current financial statements of *three* companies in different industries selected by either you or your instructor.

Required:

a. Identify the accounting methods used by each company to account for (1) intercorporate investments, (2) business combinations, and (3) international activities (*note:* not all companies have these activities).

b. Write a report discussing differences or similarities in the accounting methods identified in *a.*

c. What are the expected effects of these methods on each company's financial statements?

Internet 5–4

Analyzing International Operations

Access one of the financial statement databases available on the Internet (http://www.mhhe.com/business/accounting/wild). Retrieve current financial statements of *three* companies in the same industry selected by either you or your instructor.

Required:

a. Identify information for each company regarding its international activities (*note:* not all companies have these activities).

b. Compute return on assets for domestic activity and for each international segment identified.

c. Write a report comparing the performance of domestic and international segments.

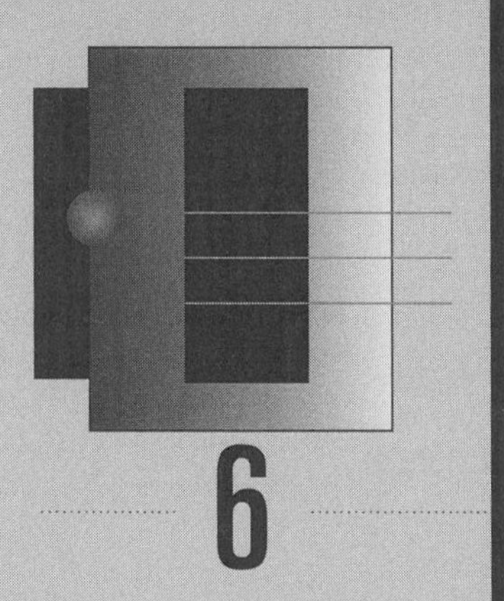

C H A P T E R

6

Analyzing Operating Activities: Income

A Look Back

The previous three chapters analyzed the accounting numbers describing financing and investing activities. We focused on their interpretation for financial liquidity, flexibility, and solvency. We also analyzed these activities for predicting operations.

A Look at This Chapter

This chapter extends our analysis to accounting numbers underlying operating activities. We analyze accrual measures of both revenues and expenses in yielding net income. Understanding recognition methods of both revenues and expenses is important and emphasized. We interpret the income statement and its components for financial analysis.

A Look Ahead

Chapter 7 extends our analysis to cash measures of operating and other activities. We analyze the cash flow statement for interpreting these activities. We show how both accrual and cash measures of business activities enhance our analysis of financial statements.

Learning Objectives

- Analyze revenue recognition and its risks for financial analysis.
- Describe depreciation and depletion of assets.
- Evaluate pension and other postretirement costs.
- Analyze expenditures for research, development, and exploration.
- Interpret goodwill and its implications for financial analysis.
- Describe interest expense and accounting for income taxes.
- Analyze extraordinary items and discontinued operations.
- Interpret accounting changes and error corrections.
- Analyze and interpret earnings per share data (Appendix 6A).

PREVIEW OF CHAPTER 6

Income is the residual of revenues and gains *less* expenses and losses. Income is one measure of operating activities and is determined using the accrual basis of accounting. Accrual accounting recognizes revenues and gains when earned, and recognizes expenses and losses when incurred. The income statement (also referred to as the *statement of operations or earnings*) reports net income for a period of time. This statement also reports income components: revenues, expenses, gains, and losses. We analyze income and its components to evaluate company performance, assess risk exposures, and predict amounts, timing, and uncertainty of future cash flows. While "bottom line" net income frames our analysis, income components provide pieces of a mosaic revealing the economic portrait of a company's operating activities. This chapter examines the analysis and interpretation of income components. We consider current reporting requirements and their implications for our analysis of income components. We describe how we might usefully apply analytical adjustments to income components and related disclosures to better our analysis. We direct special attention to revenue recognition and the recording of major expenses and costs. Part Three of this book further uses and analyzes income components. The content and organization of this chapter are as follows:

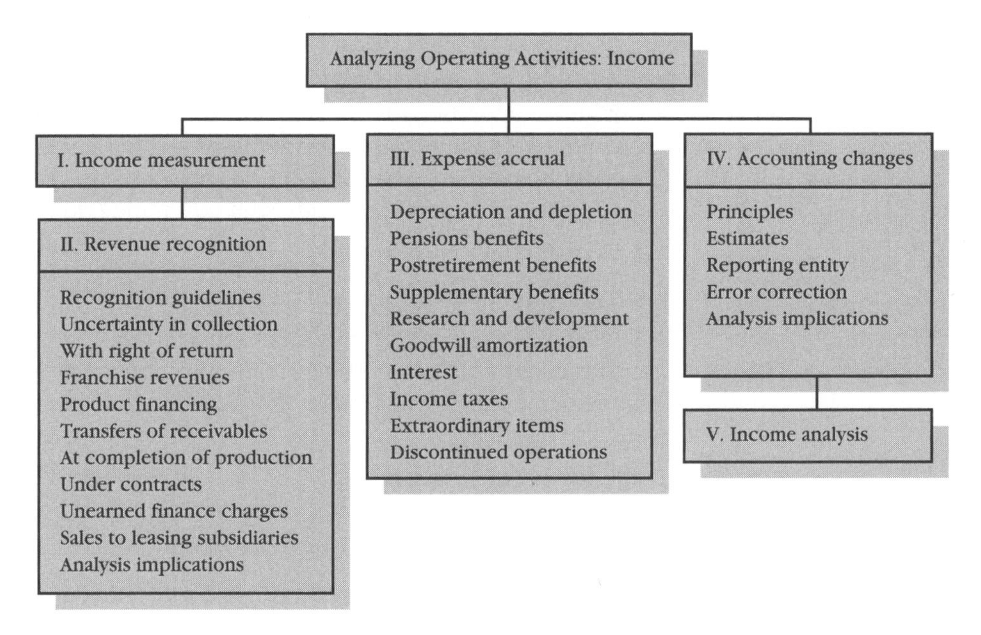

Income Measurement

An **income statement** portrays the net results of operating a company over a period of time. Since results are the ultimate objective of a business and since company valuation is, in large measure, determined by the magnitude and quality of these results, our analysis attaches great importance to income components. Scrutiny of income reveals differences of opinion regarding income definition and measurement. Consider a company with $100,000 in cash. This company uses the $100,000 to buy a plot of vacant land at the beginning of the period. At the end of the period the company is still holding the land. What is income? If the land's market price at year-end is $95,000, a $5,000 *economic* loss is evident. The accounting loss is less certain, depending on whether an impairment in the land's value has occurred. The economic loss, recognizing a decrease in capital of $5,000, implies the company is worse off at the end of the period than at the beginning. If, instead, the land's market price at year-end is $110,000, then the company recognizes an *economic* gain of $10,000. Because of historical cost accounting, there is no accounting gain. Another measure of income would be to value the land at the present value of future cash flows discounted at an appropriate rate(s) and use this amount in determining income. Measures of income usually avoid this approach because variables determining land value change frequently before final disposition of the land and are, therefore, not objective evidence warranting income recognition. Price-level changes are another matter, and we consider their effects in Supplement C.

Notice our simple case of a non-income-producing asset (vacant land), involving no complexities on the expense side, gives rise to genuine differences of opinion for income measurement. Extending this case, it is easy to see why determination of income for a company with multiple operations is no simple task. Principles of income determination must operate within this environment to best serve the needs of users. Notice also that economic income is the amount that a company can consume or distribute during a period and still maintain itself as "well off" at the end of the period as at the beginning. It is in measuring "well-offness" of a company that the gap between economic and accounting income is most apparent. *Accounting income* emphasizes objectivity, verifiability and conservatism. *Economic income* presumes capital value is measurable by the present value of future net receipts. But these receipts are subjective and involve uncertainty with estimates of future probabilities for net receipts and the discount factors applied. The degree of uncertainty associated with these estimates exceeds that involving many other estimates (e.g., benefit periods for plant and equipment, probability of debt collection). These marked differences in opinion are major causes for the variation in economic and accounting income.

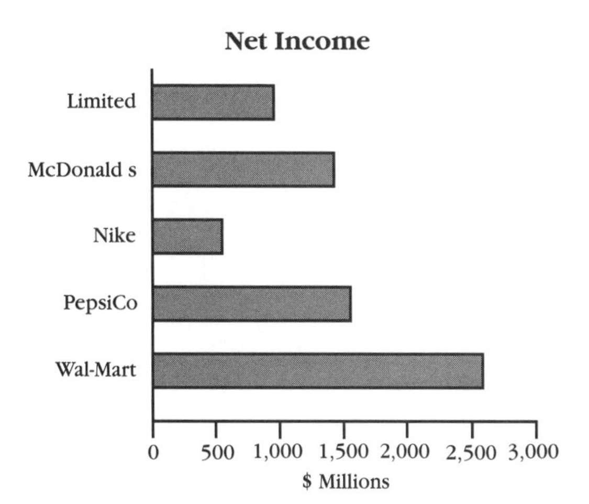

Source: *Annual reports.*

The *capital maintenance method* in measuring accounting income compares the capital balances at the beginning and end of a period. Since capital is the excess of assets over liabilities, the accounting challenge for income determination is inseparable from asset and liability measurement. While economic income focuses on comparing capital balances at successive points in time, the measurement of accounting income matches costs with revenues during a period of time. In our analysis of income, the accounting approach is more useful because of its focus on the components comprising net income.

EXHIBIT 6.1 Income Statement Components

Operating Section
- Revenue or sales
- Cost of goods sold
- Selling expenses
- General and administrative expenses

Nonoperating Section
- Other gains and revenues
- Other losses and expenses

Income Tax
Discontinued operations
Extraordinary items
Cumulative effect of change in accounting principle

Earnings per share data

Generally, the accounting process of income determination involves two steps: (1) identification and measurement of the revenues attributable to the period, and (2) recognizing costs associated with revenues of the period through either a direct link to products sold or a reasonable allocation. Our discussion in this chapter emulates an income statement, the common components of which appear in Exhibit 6.1. Exhibit 6.1 follows a *natural expense* classification common in merchandising and manufacturing companies. Retail companies often use a *functional expense* classification.

Revenue and Gain Recognition

Revenues are defined in practice as "inflows or other enhancements of assets of an entity or settlements of its liabilities" resulting from a company's "ongoing major or central operations." **Gains,** on the other hand, are increases in net assets (equity) resulting from "peripheral or incidental transactions" of a company. Distinguishing between revenues and gains depends on the usual business activities of a company. Since our analysis treats these items differently (e.g., revenues are expected to persist, while gains are not), their distinction is important. It is also important to understand when a company recognizes revenue. Our analytical adjustments sometimes modify income numbers using revenue recognition information. An important question is when, or at what point, in the sequence of revenue-earning activities in which a company is engaged, is it proper to recognize revenue as earned? This section addresses this question.

Types of Gains Reported by Companies

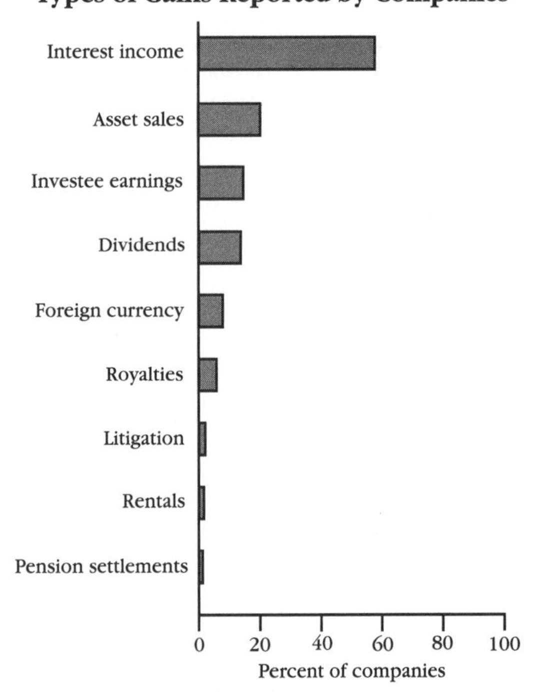

Source: *Accounting Trends & Techniques.*

Guidelines for Revenue Recognition

From our analysis perspective, inappropriate accrual recognition of revenues (or gains) can have one of two undesirable consequences:

EXHIBIT 6.2 Revenue Recognition Criteria

Earning activities creating revenue are substantially complete, and no significant effort is necessary to complete the transaction.

Risk of ownership in sales is effectively passed to the buyer.

Revenue, and the associated expense, are measured or estimated with substantial accuracy.

Revenue recognized normally yields an increase in cash, receivables, or securities. Under certain conditions it yields an increase in inventories or other assets, or a decrease in liabilities.

Business transactions yielding income are at arm's length with independent parties (i.e., not with controlled parties).

Transaction is not subject to revocation (e.g., carrying a right of return for merchandise sold).

- If a company records revenue prematurely or belatedly, then revenue is assigned to the wrong period.
- If a company records revenue prior to reasonable certainty of realization, then revenue might be recorded in one period and later cancelled or reversed in another—this overstates income in the first period and understates it in the latter period.

These two effects adversely affect our analysis. To counter this, accounting applies strict and conservative rules regarding revenue recognition. Generally, revenue is recognized when it is both realized (or realizable) and earned. Criteria are established to reduce premature recording of revenues. Exhibit 6.2 lists criteria that must be satisfied for revenue recognition. While these criteria are seemingly straightforward, they are subject to certain exceptions and have, in practice, been interpreted in different ways. To understand these variations, we consider next the application of these criteria under certain circumstances.

Uncertainty in Revenue Collection

Companies use a provision for doubtful (uncollectible) accounts to reflect uncertainty in the collectibility of receivables from sales. A company makes a judgment, based on the circumstances, when it can no longer reasonably assure the collectibility of receivables. This judgment can be conservative or it might use liberal or optimistic assumptions. When collectibility is no longer reasonably assured, practice follows various paths including three different methods of recognizing revenue.

Installment Sales Method

The installment sales method is sometimes used when a receivable is collected over a period of many months or years. Time is an important dimension in the assessment of collection risk. The more distant the time of collection, the more uncertain is collection. Accordingly, the length of time for collection is an important factor in assessing uncertainty in collection. The installment sales method is used when there is *no* reasonable basis for estimating doubtful accounts. In this case, a company recognizes revenue and expense from installment sales when sold, but defers the income to future periods when cash is collected and is recognized in proportion to the total amount of cash received.

Cost Recovery Method

The cost recovery method is used when there is no reasonable basis for estimating the degree of collectibility of receivables. It can be viewed as a more conservative version of the installment sales method. Under the cost recovery method, a company reports revenue and expense from the sale in the income statement, but defers the income and recognizes it only when the cost of the sale is fully recovered. This deferred income is offset against the related receivable. Once cost is fully recovered, subsequent collections are entirely recorded as income.

Real Estate Method

Sale of real estate is often characterized by payments extending over long periods. A long collection period increases uncertainty, and recognition of income from these sales depends on an ability to assess the probability of collection. In practice, accounting for real estate sales stipulates use of the usual accrual method when a seller's receivables from land sales are collectible and if the seller has no significant remaining construction or development obligations. When a sale does not meet these conditions, it is reported under the installment sales or percentage-of-completion methods. For sales of real estate *other than land sales*, use of the accrual method requires that the sale is consummated, the buyer's down payment and commitment for continuing investment in the property sold is adequate, and the seller does not have substantial continuing involvement with the property after the sale.

Revenue When Right of Return Exists

Revenue from sales where the buyer has a right to return the product is recognized at the time of sale *only* if the following conditions are met:

- Price is substantially fixed or determinable at the sale date.
- Buyer pays the seller or is obligated to pay the seller (not contingent on resale).
- Buyer's obligation to seller is unchanged in event of theft or physical damage to product.
- Buyer acquiring a product for resale has economic substance apart from that provided by the seller.
- Seller has no significant obligations for future performance to directly effect resale of product.
- Product returns are reasonably estimated.

If these conditions are met, sales revenue and cost of sales are recorded but reduced to reflect estimated returns and expenses; if not met, revenue recognition is postponed. These conditions do not apply to (1) service companies where all or part of their service revenue is returnable under cancellation privileges granted to the buyer, (2) transactions involving real estate or leases, or (3) sales transactions where a customer can return defective goods such as under warranty provisions. Right of return problems vary across industries. In newspaper and perishable foods industries, returns quickly follow sales. In contrast, returns can occur long after a sale in the book publishing industry.

> In accordance with industry practice, records, tapes, magazines and books are usually sold to customers with the right to return unsold items. Revenues from these and other sales represent gross sales less a provision for future returns. It is WCI's general policy to value returned goods included in inventory at estimated realizable value but not in excess of cost.
>
> —Warner Communications, Inc.

A company's ability to estimate future returns is an important consideration in accounting for returns. Items hindering one's ability to reasonably predict returns include:

- Susceptibility to factors such as technological obsolescence or market trends.
- Long return privilege periods.
- Lack of relevant experience with returns.

Franchise Revenues

Revenue from franchises is approximately $1 trillion per year. Franchises employ nearly 10 million individuals and make one-third of all retail sales. Accounting and reporting standards for franchisors require that franchise fee revenue from individual and area franchise sales be recognized only when all material services or conditions relating to the sale are substantially performed or satisfied by the franchisor. This applies also to continuing franchise fees, continuing product sales, agency sales, repossessed franchises, franchising costs, commingled revenue, and relationships between a franchisor and a franchisee. A typical franchise fee arrangement follows:

> *Application, License, and Royalty Fees.* All fees from licensed operations are included in revenue as earned. Management accelerated the revenue recognition for application fees from the time the site was approved or construction begun to the time cash is received. Management believes this method will more accurately relate the income recognition to performance of the related service . . . License fees are earned when the related store opens. Unearned license fees which have been collected are included in current liabilities. Royalty fees are based on licensee revenues and are recognized in the period the related revenues are earned.
>
> —Church Fried Chicken

Product Financing Arrangements

A *product financing arrangement* is an agreement involving the transfer or sponsored acquisition of inventory that (although it sometimes resembles a sale of inventory) is in substance a means of financing inventory. For example, if a company transfers ("sells") inventory to another company, and concurrently agrees to repurchase the inventory at a later date, this transaction is likely a product financing arrangement and not a sale and subsequent purchase of inventory. In essence, if a party bearing the risks and rewards of ownership transfers inventory to a purchaser, and in a related transaction agrees to repurchase the product at a specified price over a specified time, or guarantees some specified resale price for sales of the product to outside parties, the arrangement is a product financing arrangement and is accounted for as such. In this case the inventory remains on the seller's statements and the seller recognizes no revenue.

Transfers of Receivables with Recourse

An important revenue recognition question involves circumstances where transfers of receivables with recourse are accounted for as sales rather than borrowing transactions. Accounting practice requires a transferor to report as a sale a transfer of receivables with recourse, and to recognize any associated gain or loss, if the following conditions are met:

- Transferor is isolated from transferred assets.
- Transferor surrenders effective control over transferred assets.
- Transferee has the right to pledge or exchange transferred assets.

If these conditions are *not* met, proceeds from the transfer are reported as a liability. Transfers to wholly owned finance subsidiaries do not prohibit recognition as sales.

Recognition at Completion of Production

A basic principle of accounting is that gains accrue only at the time of sale and that gains are not anticipated by reflecting assets at their current selling prices. There are some exceptions to this principle, which primarily arise with smaller agricultural or precious metals producers who, facing difficult cost determination problems, often use the completion-of-production method. The *completion-of-production method* recognizes revenue from inventory as measured by the current selling price less estimated costs of disposition. This method essentially recognizes revenue when production is complete.

Seaboard Corporation recognizes revenue at completion of production: "Grain inventories are valued at market after adjustment of open purchases and sales contracts to market." Also, Handy and Harman Company reports: "Changes in the unit price of . . . precious metals result in corresponding changes in sales and cost of sales."

A variation of the completion-of-production method is to record a producer's "sale" to a cooperative as the basis for revenue recognition. This practice is controversial because the cooperative is not often sufficiently independent for this transaction to constitute an effective transfer of risk.

Revenue under Contracts

Recording income from short-term construction or production contracts poses no special problems. The seller typically recognizes revenue when the end product is complete and is accepted by a buyer. In contrast, accounting for *long-term* construction contracts for items like buildings, aircraft, ships, or heavy machinery is more challenging. One problem is the construction cycle can extend over several accounting periods while substantial costs accumulate, financed in part by progress billings to the buyer. Two accepted methods of accounting are in use:

- **Percentage-of-completion method.** This is the preferred method when there exists reasonably certain estimates of both costs to complete a contract and mearsures of progress toward completion of the contract. A common basis of profit estimation is to record part of the estimated total profit corresponding to the ratio of costs incurred to date divided by expected total costs. Other methods of estimation of

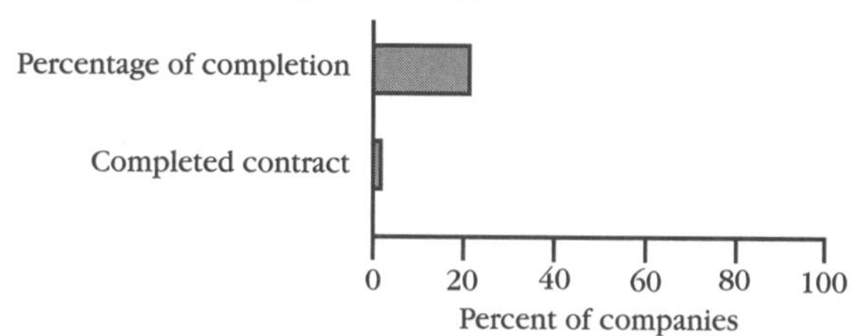

Source: *Accounting Trends & Techniques.*

completion are based on units completed, qualified engineering estimates, or units delivered.

▪ **Completed-contract method.** This method is preferable when conditions inherent in contracts present risks and uncertainties resulting in an inability to make reasonable estimates of costs and completion time. Problems with this method include assessing the point when completion is deemed to have occurred and identifying the kind of expenses for deferral. Some companies defer all costs to the completion date, including general and administrative overhead, while others consider these costs as period costs and expense them as incurred.

Under either method, current or anticipated losses are fully recognized in the period when they are initially identified.

> *Long-Term Contracts*—The Company enters into long-term contracts for the production of products. For financial statement purposes, sales are recorded as deliveries are made (units of delivery method of percentage-of-completion). Unbilled costs on these contracts are included in inventory. Progress payments are netted against the inventory balances. Provisions for estimated losses on uncompleted contracts are made in the period in which such losses are determined.
>
> —Parker Hannifin Corporation

Unearned Finance Charges

Accrual of interest revenue is typically a function of time. That is, income on a loan to another entity depends on principal outstanding, time elapsed, and rate. Finance companies, like those in the consumer or sales finance businesses, make loans and add a finance charge to the face amount—often referred to as *discount*. Several methods are available to recognize, or "take up," this discount. For example, if a 12-month note's face value is $2,400 and the cash advanced is $2,160, the $240 unearned finance charge can be taken up using one of the following methods:

- **Straight line.** Under this method, one-twelfth or $20 is taken up each month as the company collects installments.
- **Sum of the months' digits.** With this method, larger amounts of income are recognized in the early part of the loan contract. In the case of our 12-month loan, the sum of the digits is 78. Accordingly, in the first month, 12/78th of the finance charge ($36.92) is taken up into income; and in the last month, 1/78th ($3.14) is taken up. Interest earned bears a closer relation to funds at risk under this method as compared to the straight-line method. This is true of all methods that take up income in proportion to the decreasing balance of the loan outstanding.

A variation on either of these methods is available and involves taking into income, immediately on granting of the loan, an amount often referred to as the *acquisition factor* intended to offset the initial loan acquisition expenses. The remaining balance of the unearned finance charge is taken up into income using one of the alternative methods.

Recognizing "Sales" to Leasing Subsidiaries

For sales revenue to be considered realized, there must be an actual transfer of risk from seller to buyer. An interesting case involving this principle relates to the attempt by Memorex Corporation to record as a sale the transfer of equipment to its unconsolidated leasing subsidiary. Memorex's reporting failed on at least two accounts: (1) the subsidiary was not capitalized with third-party capital and consequently could not pay Memorex for the equipment, and (2) Memorex agreed to protect the subsidiary against losses. These two conditions imply there was no transfer of risk of ownership from Memorex to an independent party and, consequently, there was no bona fide sale. Memorex subsequently agreed to record the transfer of equipment as a lease rather than as a sale. There are also revenue recognition issues with companies leasing property to others. We discussed these issues and their methods of revenue recognition in Chapter 3. Similarly, when a company owns a part or the whole of another entity, the interest of the company in the investee's income is accounted for in several ways. Chapters 4 and 5 discussed these methods.

Analysis Implications of Revenue Recognition

The income statement is important to our analysis and the valuation of a company. This statement is also important to management for these same reasons and others, including its role in accounting-based contractual agreements, management pressure to achieve income-based results, management compensation linked to income, and the value of stock options. Given management's incentives, we rationally expect management to select and apply accounting principles that best meet their own interests but are still within acceptable accounting practice. It is possible that objectives of income reporting do not always align with management's incentives in this area. Our analysis must be alert to these management propensities and the accounting latitude available.

Datapoint Corporation recorded a significant amount of sales that hard-pressed sales representatives booked by asking customers to order millions of dollars of computer equipment months in advance with payment to be made later. In many of these cases, Datapoint recorded sales as revenue even though it had not even manufactured such equipment. It is reported these sales representatives were under intense pressure to achieve unreasonable or unattainable goals. Datapoint subsequently reversed these sales and consented to an order barring it from future violations of the Securities Exchange Act and SEC rules.

Recording of revenue is the first step in the process of income recognition. It is referred to as the critical event in income determination. Our analysis must take aim at accounting methods chosen to ascertain whether they properly reflect economic reality. For example, if a manufacturer records profits on sale to a dealer, our analysis must inquire about dealer inventories and market conditions—because real earnings activity consists of selling to the ultimate consumer. Another example of income recognition follows:

> The company sells certain whiskey in barrels in bond under agreements which provide for future bottling. In prior years, profits on such transactions were reflected as of the date of sale. The present company policy is to treat such profits as deferred income until the whiskey is bottled and shipped.
>
> —Schenley Industries, Inc.

Similarly, when a country club records a membership fee at the time a contract is signed, our analysis must determine whether the crucial earnings activity consists of selling memberships or in delivering services of the country club.

Managements' propensities and incentives to manage revenue recognition yields many pronouncements on the subject of income recognition by accounting regulatory agencies. In spite of these, our analysis must remain alert to certain accounting approaches skirting the spirit, if not the letter, of these pronouncements.

> Prime Motor Inns earns a major portion of its income, not from core operations, but rather from hotel sales, construction fees, and interest. In recording these nonrecurring earnings, Prime Motor Inns stretched recognition criteria by accepting notes and receivables of dubious value, and by guaranteeing to buyers of their hotels, and their bankers, certain levels of future income. While they recorded profits, they did not record many contingent liabilities associated with the profits.

Another technique of recording profits and not providing for related contingencies is extending loans in return for substantial fees. While such "consulting fees" are recorded as profit, the usual poor quality of these loans is not immediately provided for.

Aware of these revenue recognition problems, the SEC expressed its belief that significant uncertainties regarding a seller's ability to realize noncash proceeds received in transactions often arise when the purchaser is thinly capitalized, or highly leveraged, or when the purchaser's assets consist primarily of those purchased from the seller. These uncertainties raise doubt as to whether income recognition is appropriate. Circumstances fueling questions about income recognition include:

- Sale of assets or operations that have historically not produced cash flows from operations sufficient to fund future debt service and full dividend requirements.
- Lack of substantial equity capital in the purchasing entity other than that provided by the seller.
- Existence of contingent liabilities of a seller such as debt guarantees or agreements requiring the seller to infuse cash into the purchasing entity under certain conditions.

Even when a company receives cash proceeds, any guarantees or other agreements requiring the company to infuse cash into the purchasing entity impacts income recognition, especially when the first two circumstances listed above exist. Income should not be recognized until: (1) cash flows from operating activities are sufficient to fund debt service and dividend requirements (on an accrual basis), or (2) the company's investment in the purchasing entity is or can be readily converted to cash and the company has no further obligations under any debt guarantees or other agreements requiring it to make additional investments in the purchasing entity. Amounts of any deferred income, including deferral of interest or dividend income, are generally disclosed in a balance sheet as a deduction from the related asset account (e.g., investment in the purchasing entity). Notes to the financial statements usually offer a description of the transaction including any commitments and contingencies, and the accounting methods applied.

An emphasis on transactions rather than performance often results in anticipation of earnings prior to completion of the earnings process. Our analysis must be alert to problems related to timing of revenue recognition. We have examined the accounting concept of realization and reasons for the emphasis on objective and verifiable evidence. While justification for these procedures is debatable, our analysis is improved when we understand the implications of accounting practice in this area.

Current practice in realization generally does not allow for recognition of income in advance of sale. It is not typical to recognize increases in market value of property like land, equipment, or buildings; the accretion of values in growing timber or natural resources; or increases in the value of inventories. Yet the timing of sales is an important item that is partly within the discretion of management. This gives management certain latitude in timing revenue recognition.

Thousand Trails, a membership campground operator, recorded revenue from membership fees when a new member initially signed even though these fees were nearly 90 percent financed and many cancelled within days of signing. When their revenue recognition practices became public, Thousand Trails' stock price declined sharply.

Our analysis regarding companies with contracts must reflect that use of the completed-contract method occurs in cases where reasonable estimates of costs and degree of completion are unavailable. Accordingly, these companies' financial results are likely unpredictable and irregular. Companies using the percentage-of-completion method also present problems. Our analysis often cannot support the judgments of management, the internal cost allocations, or the degree of actual completion of contracts. The following two excerpts from practice highlight these concerns.

Stirling Homex, a company building modular homes, had strong incentives to report earnings growth given its "glamour" status and its need for financing. Applying percentage-of-completion contract principles, it recognized the earnings process as complete when housing modules were "manufactured and assigned to specific contracts." In reality, they applied this method as an earning-by-producing process. Their spurious revenues were subsequently reversed, triggering loan defaults and ultimately bankruptcy.

Four Seasons Nursing Centers reveals the dangers and pitfalls of percentage-of-completion contract accounting. During the audit of Four Seasons, the auditors deemed physical engineering estimates of job completion as unacceptable. Four Seasons subsequently based degree of contract completion on the percentage of costs incurred to date relative to total estimated costs. The company, at this time considered a glamour stock of Wall Street with strong incentives to generate increasing earnings, supplied auditors with fictitious or inappropriate cost invoices. This yielded higher percentage-of-completion estimates and income figures.

Cost incurrence is a convenient and not a precise method of estimating degree of contract completion. Auditors are required to make certain the cost-incurred method is a reliable substitute for more precise methods like engineering estimates. We also need to recognize that management has considerable latitude in classifying costs between contract costs and period costs.

ANALYSIS VIEWPOINT *. . . You are the banker*

Playground Equipment Company calls on you for a long-term loan to expand operations. Although you are their banker, they are a recent client with new management. In reviewing financial statements as part of their application, you notice they recognize revenue *during production*. Their statements report: "revenue is recognized during production because production activity is the critical event in the company's earnings process . . . and deferring revenue substantially impairs the usefulness of the financial statements." You ask a colleague for her opinion, and she feels their revenue recognition method is too liberal. She voices a preference for revenue recognition at point of sale or, possibly, when cash is received. Do you require Playground Equipment to restate their statements? What risks do you see in acting on their loan?

Expense and Loss Accruals

Expenses (or costs) are "outflows or other using-up of assets or incurrence of liabilities" resulting from a company's "ongoing major or central operations." **Losses** are decreases in a company's net assets from "peripheral or incidental transactions" of a company. Expenses and losses are resource and service potentials consumed, spent, or lost in the pursuit or production of revenues or gains. Accounting for expenses and losses involves their measurement and the timing of their allocation to reporting periods.

One objective of income measurement is linking expenses and losses to the revenues or gains recognized during a period. This is difficult since there are many kinds of expenses and losses behaving in various ways. Some expenses are specifically identified with a given item of revenue. Other expenses bear no identifiable relation to any specific revenue and are identified only with the time period where incurred.

Yet variation in expense behavior gives rise to a useful classification helpful in our analysis of matching and of allocation methods.

Variable expenses are costs varying in direct proportion to activity measured by means of sales, production, or similar gauges. For example, in manufacturing electric cable, consumption of copper wire is often said to vary in direct proportion to sales volume. The higher is cable sales, the higher is copper wire expense.

Fixed expenses are costs relatively constant over a considerable range of activity. Rent, property taxes, and insurance are examples of fixed expenses. No category of expense is fixed indefinitely. For example, after reaching a certain level of activity, a company must rent additional space, thereby increasing rent expense. Many expenses contain both fixed and variable elements and are referred to as **semivariable expenses.**

Expenses are classified in other ways depending on their purposes. One can identify **product expenses** attaching to specific goods or services where revenue is derived. Expenses that cannot be identified with goods or services are called **period expenses** because they are identified with the period incurred. We already touched on this distinction of expenses in our analysis of inventory and costs of goods sold in Chapter 4. Allocation of expenses to products sold, and especially manufactured products, gives rise to a distinction among three major classes of product expense:

Types of Losses Reported by Companies

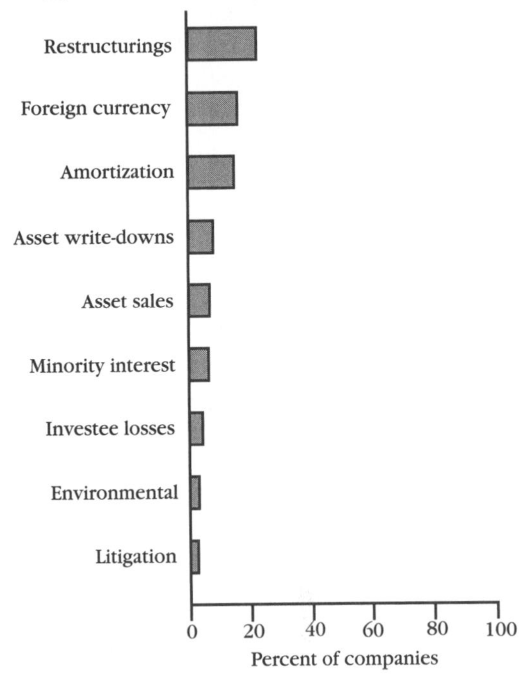

Source: *Accounting Trends & Techniques.*

- **Direct product expenses.** These expenses are charges identified with a product. Direct product expenses for a retailing business include the expense of the item sold, its direct freight, and additional acquisition expenses incurred in acquiring it. For manufacturing company, it includes the direct expense of material and labor in producing the item. Direct product expenses usually vary in proportion to revenues. This characteristic results in their being classified as variable expenses. Direct product expenses are often easily matched with specific revenue flows.
- **Indirect product expenses.** These expenses include costs associated with receiving, inspecting, purchasing, and storing products manufactured or acquired for resale. Most companies find it impractical to allocate expenses like indirect labor to specific products. They often allocate indirect product expenses to products on a reasonable basis. Many fixed expenses like depreciation and supervision are treated as indirect overhead expenses and allocated to products or services on a basis reflecting consumption or benefits derived.
- **Joint product expenses.** These expenses are not identified with specific products, but jointly benefit all or many products. These expenses are common, for example, in the meat-processing industry. Joint product expenses are often allocated on a reasonable basis reflecting selling prices of end products, relative sales volume, or net realizable values.

Methods of expense allocation are usually devised in response to characteristics of expense behavior.

Companies encounter accounting challenges in measuring and allocating expenses. Generally, an expense reflects service potential or utility awaiting use in current and/or future reporting periods. Expenses related to revenue of future periods are viewed as deferred expenses and reported as assets. Major items are (1) inventories; (2) property, plant, and equipment; (3) intangibles; and (4) deferred charges. Chapter 4 described accounting for these items. We further consider income implications of these expenses in this chapter.

Expenses are often chargeable to income in the current period. Most period expenses become current expenses; and certain categories of expenses like selling and administrative are not usually deferred. Measurement and allocation of expenses are complicated whenever a significant lapse of time occurs between their payment or incurrence of cost and the time of their use in operations. The longer the lapse of time, the more difficult and speculative the allocations and measurements. We next consider important categories of expenses, principles governing their allocation to revenue, and their implications to our analysis.

Depreciation and Depletion

Expenses of assets in productive use, or otherwise income producing, are allocated or assigned to periods comprising their useful life. A basic principle of income determination is that income benefiting from use of long-lived assets must bear a proportionate share of their cost.

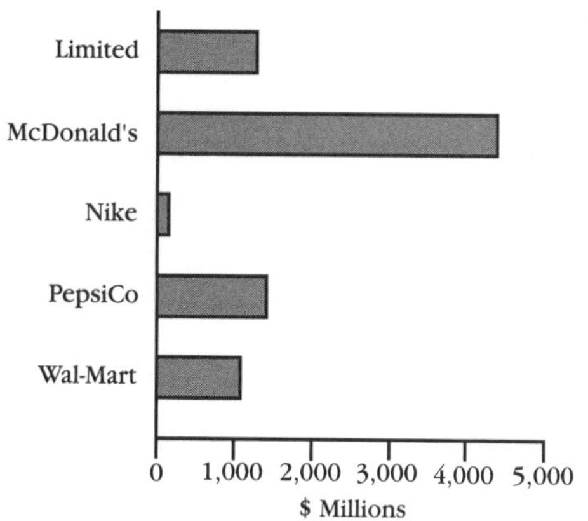

Source: *Annual reports and 10-Ks.*

Depreciation

Depreciation is the allocation of the cost of property, plant, and equipment over its useful life. The purpose of depreciation is to charge against operations, by means of allocation, the cost of an asset. If operations are unprofitable, depreciation becomes an unrecovered cost, that is, a loss. This is as true for depreciation as it is for all costs not recovered due to inadequate revenues. Depreciation does *not* provide funds for replacement of an asset. This objective is achieved through a financial policy to accumulate cash.

There is little dispute about the principles of depreciation accounting. Nevertheless, depreciation is an expense subject to some confusion among users of statements. Confusion stems from the methods and assumptions to allocate the cost of assets to operations.

Rate of Depreciation

Rate of depreciation depends on two factors: useful life and allocation method.

Useful Life. Nearly all assets are subject to physical deterioration. The general exception is land, which is not subject to depreciation. Yet while land has an indefinite life span, this does not ensure resistance to loss of economic value. Such a loss is not provided for by depreciation but recognized as and when it occurs (e.g., impairments). Useful lives of assets vary greatly. Assumptions regarding useful lives of assets are based on economic conditions, engineering studies, experience, and information about an asset's *physical* and *productive* properties. Physical deteriora-

EXHIBIT 6.3 Straight-Line Depreciation

End of Year	*Depreciation*	*Accumulated Depreciation*	*Undepreciated Asset Balance*
			$110,000
1	$10,000	$ 10,000	100,000
2	10,000	20,000	90,000
.			
.			
.			
9	10,000	90,000	20,000
10	10,000	100,000	10,000

tion is an important factor limiting useful life. Frequency and quality of maintenance bears on it. Maintenance can extend useful life but cannot prolong it indefinitely. Another limiting factor is obsolescence. *Productivity* or *obsolescence* views useful life as a function of progress in technology, consumption patterns, and economic forces. Ordinary obsolescence occurs when technological improvements make an asset inefficient or uneconomical before its physical life is complete. Extraordinary obsolescence occurs when revolutionary changes occur or radical shifts in demand ensue. Computer-based equipment is continually subject to rapid obsolescence. The integrity of depreciation, and that of income determination, depend on a reasonably accurate estimate of useful life. This estimate is ideally not influenced by management's incentives regarding timing of income recognition.

Allocation Method. Once the useful life of an asset is determined, periodic depreciation expense depends on the allocation method. Depreciation varies significantly depending on the method chosen. We consider two of the most common classes of methods: straight line and accelerated.

Depreciation Methods

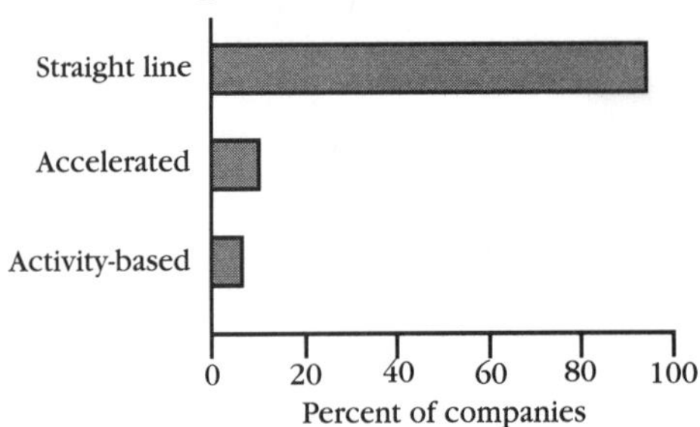

Percents exceed 100 percent because companies can use different methods for different assets.

Source: *Accounting Trends & Techniques.*

- **Straight line.** The straight line method of depreciation allocates the cost of an asset to its useful life on the basis of equal periodic charges. Exhibit 6.3 illustrates depreciation of an asset costing $110,000, with a useful life of 10 years and estimated salvage value of $10,000. Each of the 10 years is charged with one-tenth of the asset's cost less the salvage value.

The rationale for straight-line depreciation is that the process of physical deterioration occurs uniformly over time. This is a more valid assumption for fixed structures than with, say, machinery where utilization is a more important factor. The other determinant of depreciation, obsolescence, is not necessarily uniformly applicable over time. Yet in the absence of information on probable rates of depreciation, the straight-line method has the advantage of simplicity. This attribute, perhaps more than any other, accounts for its popularity.

There are conceptual flaws with straight-line depreciation. If the service value of an asset is charged evenly over its useful life, then loss of productivity and increased maintenance costs should not be ignored. Straight-line depreciation implicitly assumes, however, that depreciation in early years is identical to that in later years when the asset is likely less efficient and requires increased maintenance. Another flaw with straight-line depreciation, and one of special interest to our analysis, is the resulting distortion in rate of return on capital. Straight-line depreciation yields an increasing rate of return pattern over time. For example, assuming the asset depreciated in Exhibit 6.3 yields a constant income of $20,000 per year before depreciation, it produces an increasing rate of return on book value as shown below:

Year	Beginning Year Book Value	Income before Depreciation	Depreciation	Net Income	Return on Book Value
1	$110,000	$20,000	$10,000	$10,000	9.1%
2	100,000	20,000	10,000	10,000	10.0
3	90,000	20,000	10,000	10,000	11.1
10	10,000	20,000	10,000	10,000	100.0

Increasing maintenance costs adversely affect our assumption of constant income before depreciation, but it does not negate the overall effect of an increasing return on investment. An increasing return on investment for an aging asset is not entirely reflective of the economic realities of investments.

▪ **Accelerated.** Accelerated methods of depreciation allocate the cost of an asset to its useful life in a decreasing manner. Use of these methods is encouraged by their acceptance in the Internal Revenue Code. These methods' appeal in deferring income to later periods for tax purposes is apparent. The earlier an asset is written off for tax purposes, the greater the tax deferral to future periods and the more funds immediately available for operations. Conceptual support for accelerated methods is that charges for depreciation decrease over time and compensate for (1) increasing repair and maintenance costs, (2) decreasing revenues and operating efficiency, and (3) higher uncertainty of revenues in later years of aged assets (due to obsolescence).

There are two primary methods of accelerated depreciation: declining balance and sum of the years' digits. The *declining-balance method* applies a constant percent to the declining asset balance. In practice, an approximation of the exact rate of declining-charge depreciation is to apply it at some multiple of (often two times) the straight-line rate. For example, an asset with a 10-year useful life can be depreciated at a double-declining-balance rate of 20 percent (2 × [1/10]). The *sum-of-the-years'-digits method* applies a decreasing fraction to cost less salvage value. Specifically, the cost of an asset depreciated over a five-year period is written off by applying a fraction whose denominator is the sum of the years' digits ($1 + 2 + 3 + 4 + 5 = 15$), also computed as $n(n + 1)/2$ where n equals the useful life—and whose numerator is the remaining life from the beginning of the period. This yields a fraction of 5/15 for the first year progressing to 1/15 in the fifth and final year.

Exhibit 6.4 illustrates accelerated depreciation of an asset costing $110,000, with a salvage value of $10,000 and a useful life of 10 years. Since an asset is never depreciated below its salvage value, practice must take care to ensure that declining-balance methods do not violate this. When depreciation expense using the declining-balance method falls below the straight-line rate, it is common practice to use the straight-line rate for the final remaining periods.

EXHIBIT 6.4 Accelerated Depreciation

	Depreciation		Cumulative Amount	
Year	*Double-Declining*	*Sum-of-the Years'-Digits*	*Double-Declining*	*Sum-of-the Years'-Digits*
1	$22,000	$18,182	$22,000	$ 18,182
2	17,600	16,364	39,600	34,546
3	14,080	14,545	53,680	49,091
4	11,264	12,727	64,944	61,818
5	9,011	10,909	73,955	72,727
6	7,209	9,091	81,164	81,818
7	5,767	7,273	86,931	89,091
8	4,614	5,455	91,545	94,546
9	3,691	3,636	95,236	98,182
10	2,953	1,818	98,189	100,000

▪ **Special.** Special methods of depreciation are found in certain industries like steel and heavy machinery. These methods include relating depreciation charges to *activity* or intensity of asset use. For example, if a machine has a useful life of 10,000 running hours, the depreciation charge varies with hours of running time rather than the period of time. It is important when using activity methods that the estimate of useful life be periodically reviewed to remain valid under changing conditions. Bethlehem Steel Corporation reports the following depreciation policy:

Depreciation—Depreciation is based upon the estimated useful lives of each asset group, which for most steel producing assets is 18 years. Steel and most raw materials producing assets are depreciated on a straight-line basis adjusted by an activity factor. This factor is based on the ratio of production and shipments for the current year to the average production and shipments for the five preceding years at each operating location. Annual depreciation after adjustment for this activity factor is not less than 75 percent nor more than 125 percent of straight-line depreciation. The costs of blast furnace linings are depreciated on a unit-of-production basis. All other assets are depreciated on a straight-line basis.

—Bethlehem Steel Corporation

Depletion

Depletion is the allocation of the cost of natural resources on the basis of rate of extraction or production. The difference between depreciation and depletion is that depreciation is an allocation of the cost of a productive asset over time, while depletion is the exploitation of natural resources like coal, oil, minerals, or timber. Allocation of depletion is dependent on production: No production yields no depletion. For example, if an ore deposit costs $5,000,000 and contains an estimated 10,000,000 recoverable tons, the depletion rate per ton of ore mined is $0.50. Production of 100,000 tons yields a depletion charge of $50,000 and a net balance in the asset account at year-end of $4,950,000. Our analysis must be aware that, like depreciation, depletion can produce various complications. One is reliability of the estimate of recoverable resources. Companies must periodically adjust it to reflect new information. Another is the definition of cost. Cost is especially complex for property under development. Still another is the composition of the asset. In the case of oil fields, depletion varies with what constitutes an oil field. This is because depletion can be based on individual wells or an entire field. It is sometimes argued that the discovery value of a natural resource deposit is so large in relation to its cost that depletion is unnecessary. This is not a valid reason to ignore depletion, nor is the contention that estimating available natural reserves is tenuous.

Analysis Implications of Depreciation and Depletion

Most companies utilize long-lived productive assets in operating activities and, in these cases, depreciation is often a significant expense. Management makes decisions involving the depreciable base, useful life, and allocation method. These decisions can yield substantially different depreciation charges. Our analysis should include information on these factors to assess reported earnings or for comparative earnings analysis across companies.

A company's revision of the useful lives of fixed assets can produce more reliable allocations of costs. Our analysis must, however, approach these revisions with critical skepticism. Such revisions are sometimes used to shift or smooth income across periods, or to reduce depreciation charges in future periods. The following General Motors case had a major earnings impact:

> The corporation revised the estimated service lives of its plants and equipment and special tools . . . These revisions, which were based on . . . studies of actual useful lives and periods of use, recognized current estimates of service lives of the assets and had the effect of reducing . . . depreciation and amortization charges by $1,236.6 million or $2.55 per share on $1\frac{2}{3}$ par value common stock.
>
> —General Motors Corporation

In this case, GM's "studies of actual useful lives" were less than precise since three years later GM took a $2.1 billion charge to cover expenses of closing several plants and for plants not closing for several years. Our analysis leaves us wondering whether this is earnings management by a newly elected chairman who explained this as "a major element in GM's long-term strategic plan to improve the competitiveness and profitability of its North American operations." By charging current income for $2.1 billion of plant costs that otherwise would be depreciated in future periods it reduced future expenses and increased future income.

Information in annual reports regarding allocation methods varies and is often less complete than in SEC filings. Detailed information includes the method or methods of depreciation and the range of useful lives applied to various categories of assets. Two things are apparent regarding this information for our analysis. One is its limited usefulness. It is difficult to infer much from allocation methods used *without* quantitative information on the extent of its use and the assets affected. The second is its required disclosure. This information is not reported because of a company's conviction about its usefulness. Thus, information on ranges of useful lives and allocation methods contributes little to our analysis. A typical disclosure follows:

Depreciation—Estimated useful lives and depreciation methods are as follows:

	Estimated Useful Lives	***Predominant Methods in Use***
Buildings and additions	10–50 years	Straight line
Machinery and equipment	5–20 years	Sum of the-years' digits
Office equipment	10 years	Sum of the-years' digits
Automotive equipment	3–5 years	Declining balance

—Homasote Company

There is usually no disclosure on the relation between depreciation rates and the size of the asset pool, nor between the rate used and the allocation method. While use of the straight-line method enables us to approximate future depreciation charges, accelerated methods make this approximation less reliable unless we can obtain additional information not often disclosed.

Another challenge for our analysis arises from differences in allocation methods used for financial reporting and for tax purposes. Three common possibilities arise:

- Use of straight-line methods for both financial reporting and tax.
- Use of straight line for financial reporting and an accelerated method for tax. The favorable tax effect resulting from higher depreciation is offset through interperiod tax allocation discussed later in this chapter. The favorable tax effect is a company's ability to postpone tax payments, yielding cost-free use of funds.
- Use of accelerated methods for both financial reporting and tax. This yields higher depreciation in early years, and sometimes indefinitely in the case of an expanding company.

Disclosures about the impact of these differing methods is not always adequate. Adequate disclosure includes information on depreciation charges under the alternative allocations. If a company discloses deferred taxes arising from accelerated depreciation for tax, our analysis can approximate the added depreciation due to acceleration by dividing the deferred tax amount by the current tax rate. We discuss using these expanded disclosures for the composition of deferred taxes later in this chapter.

Our analysis should not ignore depreciation information, nor should it focus on income before depreciation under false pretenses. While we return to this issue in the next chapter, depreciation expense derives from cash spent *in the past* and does not require any current cash outlay. For this reason, a few analysts refer to income before depreciation as *cash flow*. This is an unfortunate oversimplification because it omits many factors comprising cash flow from operations. It is, at best, a limited simplification since it includes only selected inflows without considering a company's commitment to outflows like plant replacement, investments, or dividends.

Another misconception deriving from this cash flow simplification is that depreciation is but a "bookkeeping expense" and is different from expenses like labor or material and, thus, can be dismissed or accorded less importance than other expenses. Our analysis must not make this mistake. One potential reason for this misconception is the absence of any current cash outlay. Purchasing a machine with a useful life of five years is, in effect, a prepayment for five years of services. For example, take an assembly machine and assume its tasks are performed by a worker for eight hours a day. Although uncommon, if we contract with this worker for services over a five-year period and pay for it in advance, we would allocate this pay over the five years of work. At the end of the first year, one-fifth of the payment is expensed and the remaining four-fifths prepayment represent an asset in the form of a claim for future services. The similarity between the labor contract and the machine is apparent. In Year 2 of the labor contract, there is no cash outlay, but there is no doubt about the reality of the labor costs. Depreciation of machinery is no different.

Depreciation, a real and significant operating expense, is challenging for our analysis. Much of the information disclosed in published reports is not especially useful. Our analysis must tackle evaluation of depreciation with an understanding of these limitations, but with resolve. Assessing depreciation requires evaluation of its adequacy using measures like the ratio of depreciation to total assets or its relation to other size-related factors. These and other analytical measures are often useful in our analysis. There are several measures relating to plant age that are useful in comparing depreciation policies over time and for intercompany comparisons:

Average total life span of plant and equipment assets is estimated from:
Gross plant and equipment assets / Current year depreciation expense.
Average age of plant and equipment assets is computed as:
Accumulated depreciation / Current year depreciation expense.
Average remaining life of plant and equipment assets is estimated from:
Net plant and equipment assets / Current year depreciation expense.

These measures provide reasonably accurate estimates for firms using straight-line depreciation, but are less useful for companies using accelerated methods. Another mathematical relation often useful in our analysis is:

Average total life span = Average age + Average remaining life

When applicable, these measures help us in assessing a company's depreciation policies and decisions over time. Average age of plant and equipment is useful in evaluating several factors including profit margins and financing requirements. For example, capital-intensive companies with aged facilities often have profit margins not reflecting the higher costs of replacing aging assets. Similarly, the capital structure of these companies often do not reflect the financing necessary for asset replacement. When these analytical measures are used as bases of comparison with companies in the same industry, care must be exercised because depreciation expense varies according to the allocation method and assumptions of useful life and salvage value.

Pensions

Pensions are often a major employee expense. Since pension expenses are sometimes quite large and comprise a significant part of operating expenses, our analysis of them is important. Chapter 3 provides background information on pension accounting, but was aimed at the *liability* aspects of pensions (it is useful to review that discussion). This section addresses our analysis of pension *expenses*.

Components of Pension Expense

It is useful here to expand our analysis of the pension for A. Worker discussed in Chapter 3 (pp. 114–115). We examine six major components comprising periodic pension cost; we use the term *cost* here to emphasize that not all portions of the pension cost are expensed during a period, but rather some are capitalized into assets like inventory. The six components comprising net pension cost for a period are (1) service cost, (2) interest cost, (3) expected return on plan assets, (4) amortization of unrecognized prior service cost, (5) amortization of net unrecognized gains or losses, and (6) amortization of unrecognized transition cost or gain.

1. *Service cost* for a period is the actuarial present value of the pension benefit earned by A. Worker (or a group of employees) based on a pension benefit formula. Recall the pension formula for A. Worker in Chapter 3. This yielded a service cost for Year 1 of $4,176.

2. *Interest cost* must be recognized because the projected benefit obligation (PBO) carried from the preceding year must earn the assumed rate of interest if the future expected value (i.e., $171,190 in our A. Worker case) is realized. Interest cost is computed by multiplying PBO from the prior year-end by the discount rate. For example, in Year 2 the interest added to pension cost equals the PBO at end of Year 1 ($4,176) times 7 percent, or $292. In practice, the discount rate is based on the current price of settling the employer's obligation. For many companies this rate is determined by using the discount rates published by the Pension Benefit Guarantee Corporation.

Assumed Discount Rate in Pensions

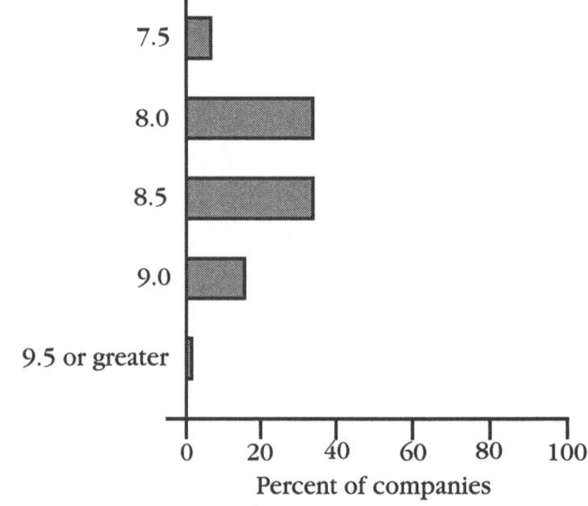

Source: *Accounting Trends & Techniques.*

3. *Expected return on plan assets* reduces the pension cost. Pension costs are reduced by the expected (rather than actual) return on plan assets because use of the actual return would subject pension costs to the fluctuations of financial markets and a concern that pension costs would be too volatile. Gains or losses representing the difference between expected and actual returns are deferred and amortized to reduce this volatility. As discussed below (under amortization of net unrecognized gains or losses), the deferred gain or loss on plan assets is amortized over an appropriate period of time and included in periodic pension cost. To understand the actual return on assets for the cost computation, the expected return on plan assets is included in Exhibit 6.5. For clarity of illustration, hypothetical amounts of pension cost components are included in this exhibit. The expected return on plan assets is reported as the difference between actual return on plan assets and the deferred gain or loss. Hence, the actual return on plan assets is disclosed and linked to the cost computation. Actual return on plan assets consists of investment income plus realized or unrealized appreciation or depreciation of plan assets during the period—its value is positive or negative. Expected return on plan assets is computed by multiplying the expected long-term rate of return on plan assets by the market-related value of plan assets at the beginning of the period. Market-related value of plan assets is either the fair value or a calculated value recognizing changes in fair value in a systematic manner over five years. Long-term rate of return on plan assets is estimated by the pension trustee.

4. *Amortization of unrecognized prior service cost* is one of three remaining components of pension cost linked to unrecognized pension liabilities (or assets). It is a recognition of delayed costs in pension expense. Prior service cost can arise from granting retroactive pension benefits at the initiation of a pension plan or by plan amendments. Referring to our case of A. Worker, her pension benefits can be increased

EXHIBIT 6.5 Illustration of Pension Expense Computation

Service cost		$1,000
Interest cost		200
Expected return on plan assets:		
Actual return on plan assets	($180)	
Add—unrecognized (deferred) loss on plan assets	(10)	(190)
Amortization of various cost elements:		
Unrecognized prior service cost		20
Unrecognized loss (gain)		(10)
Unrecognized transition cost		30
Total periodic pension cost		$1,050

after admission to the plan or retroactive benefits can be granted at inception of the plan. Practice does not require immediate recognition of costs of retroactive benefits granted. These costs do, however, increase PBO and are recognized as expense over the remaining employment of existing employees in the plan. Deferred recognition allows these costs of retroactive benefits to be matched against future economic benefits expected to be realized from their granting. Amortization is based on the future service period of employees or is applied on a straight-line basis.

5. *Amortization of net unrecognized gains or losses* arises from differences between actual results achieved and estimates of results used in computing pension costs. These differences stem from: (1) the difference between actual and expected return on plan assets, and (2) changes in PBO due to changes in assumptions. Changes in assumptions are typically due to actuarial assumptions that reflect changes in factors like compensation rates, turnover, mortality, retirement estimates, and discount rates. Practice specifies both a minimum value and a systematic method of amortizing net unrecognized gains and losses. A "corridor" approach shields actuarial gains and losses falling within a corridor from required amortization. This corridor is the greater of 10 percent of the market-related asset value or 10 percent of the PBO at the beginning of the year.

6. *Amortization of unrecognized transition cost or gain,* arises when a plan is initially adopted. In pension accounting, a company determines: (1) the PBO (from the actuary), (2) the fair value of plan assets (from the trustee), and (3) previously recognized unfunded or prepaid pension cost (from company records). The difference between the PBO and the sum of (2) and (3) is designated as the *unrecognized transition cost or gain.* Recognition of this transition cost or gain (usually cost) is amortized on a straight-line basis over the average remaining service period of qualified employees.

Analysis Implications of Pension Expense

Despite improvements in accounting for pensions, considerable management discretion and latitude remains in determining pension expense. Volatility in pension expenses is expected. If this volatility reflects changing economic conditions, then pension expenses offer us useful information for analysis. However, if volatility is induced by managing expense determination, our analysis can be impaired. We must evaluate pension expense with this in mind and, to the extent possible, distinguish between them.

The expected return on pension plan assets is an important item affecting pension costs. There is considerable accounting latitude here. For example, interest rate assumptions, typically in the range of 6 to 9 percent, can be increased by using higher market-related settlement rates. This settlement rate can be used regardless of a plan's actual investment holdings. Until now, high-yield investments were held to justify a high discount rate. This is no longer necessary. Management can, however, keep the expected rate of return on plan assets and the discount rate equal, as was often done previously. Also, when long-term interest rates (that determine settlement rates) increase, pension service costs decrease and vice versa.

There is also management latitude in selecting assumptions of inflation. This is not limited to the choice of discount rate, but extends to the choice of an expected rate of inflation for future compensation levels. Management can also achieve smoothing of results by valuing pension assets on a market-related basis rather than on a market basis, with up to five-year averaging of values permitted. Pension cost levels are also smoothed by deferring a variety of cost elements (e.g., prior service cost and unrecognized losses) representing in essence a sanction to remove a burden from current pension costs and defer them to future periods.

The intangible asset arising on a balance sheet through the recording of a pension liability (see Chapter 3) presents an interesting problem of interpretation for our analysis. This intangible is basically devoid of economic value and should not be included in computations like book value per share.

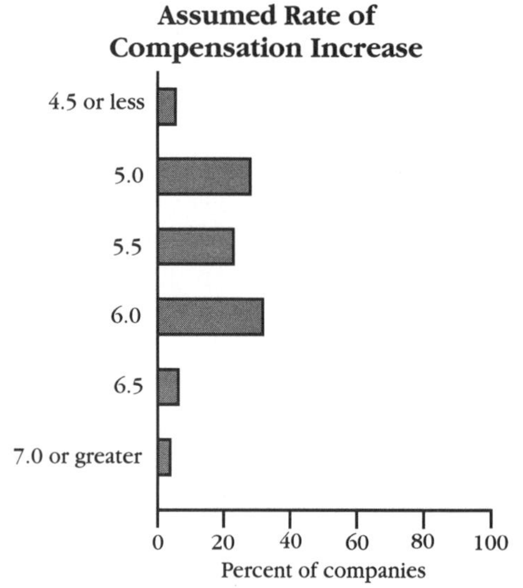

Source: *Accounting Trends & Techniques.*

Other Postretirement Employee Benefits

Accounting for postretirement employee benefits expense other than pensions (e.g., health benefits and life insurance) is similar to accounting for pensions. While there are significant differences, three important aspects are retained:

▪ *Net cost reporting.* Consequences of events and transactions affecting postretirement benefit plans are reported as a single amount. This amount includes at least three components: (1) present value of the accrued cost of deferred compensation promised in exchange for employee service, (2) interest cost accruing from the passage of time until these benefits are paid, and (3) returns from the investment in the plan's assets. These returns do not reduce the cost of many postretirement plans because, as discussed in Chapter 3, most are not funded.

▪ *Delayed recognition.* Certain changes in postretirement obligations, including those arising as a result of a plan initiation or amendment, and certain changes in the value of plan assets set aside to meet these obligations are recognized systematically over future periods and not as they occur. These measures are aimed to insulate current costs from fluctuations in values and other factors.

▪ *Offsetting.* Plan assets restricted for payment of postretirement benefits offset the accumulated postretirement benefit obligation in determining amounts recognized in the balance sheet.

Components of Postretirement Benefits Expense

The primary components of net annual postretirement employee benefits expense are listed below:

▪ *Service costs* are costs of postretirement benefit promises. The total actuarially determined costs of providing future benefits, the *expected postretirement benefit obligation (EPBO),* are recognized over the employee service period (i.e., the date an employee is fully eligible to receive benefits, even if that date precedes the expected retirement date). Practice mandates a single attribution method, the *benefits/years of service approach* to allocate (generally on a straight-line basis) the EPBO to each year in the service period. The portion of the EPBO "earned" by employee services as of a given date is the *accumulated postretirement benefit obligation (APBO).*

▪ *Interest costs* are the imputed growth in the APBO during the period using an assumed discount rate. Interest is compounded because the APBO is recognized on a present value basis.

▪ *Amortization of gains and losses* are costs arising when actual experience of the plan differs from initial estimates or if the expected return on assets differs from actual return. Because these gains and losses can fluctuate significantly, they are deferred. If the cumulative net amount of previously unrecognized gains or losses exceeds 10 percent of the APBO, this excess portion is amortized to income over the average remaining service period.

▪ *Amortization of unrecognized prior service costs* are costs arising from plan amendments that change benefits and are attributed to employee service rendered prior to the amendment date. These costs are recognized on a prospective basis by assigning equal amounts to remaining future service periods.

▪ *Amortization of unrecognized transition obligation* are costs arising from initial adoption. At adoption, an unfunded postretirement obligation, the *transition obligation,* is identified and measured as the difference between the APBO and plan assets (if any) minus any postretirement liabilities previously recorded. If a company does not recognize immediately the transition obligation with a charge to income (as a cumulative effect of an accounting change), periodic postretirement expense is increased by this amortization of unrecognized transition obligation. This obligation can be amortized over the remaining employee service period or over an optional period of 20 years.

▪ *Actual return on plan assets* reduces the net annual postretirement expense if all or part of the plan is funded. Exhibit 6.6 summarizes, with the use of hypothetical values, the interrelation between the postretirement benefits' expense, liability, and other balance sheet accounts. The APBO is reconciled to the accrued postretirement expense reported in Exhibit 6.6 as follows:

APBO at year-end		$25,400
Less: Unrecognized obligations – Deferrals representing deferred charges that are offset against APBO for balance sheet purposes:		
Unrecognized:		
Transition obligation	$19,000	
Prior service cost	2,800	
Net (gain) or loss	200	22,000
Net liability – Accrued postretirement (OPEB) cost		$ 3,400

EXHIBIT 6.6 Interrelation between Other Postretirement Employee Benefits (OPEB) Related Accounts ($ thousands)

	Accumulated Postretirement Benefit Obligation (APBO)	Unrecognized[a] *Transition Obligation*	Unrecognized[a] *Prior Service Cost*	Unrecognized[a] *Net (Gain) or Loss*[b]	*Accrued OPEB Cost*[c]	*Net Annual OPEB Cost*
Balance—on adoption of *SFAS No. 106*—or beginning	$(20,000)	$20,000				
Activity in period:						
Service cost	(1,600)					$1,600
Interest cost	(2,200)					2,200
Liability gain or loss	(200)			$200		
Plan amendments	(3,000)		$3,000			
Amortization of:						
Unrecognized prior service costs			(200)			200
Unrecognized transition obligation		(1,000)[d]				1,000
Net annual OPEB cost					(5,000)	$5,000
Benefit payments	1,600				1,600[e]	
Balance at year-end	$(25,400)	$19,000	$2,800	$200	$3,400	

Note: In this illustration the plan is not funded.

[a]Unrecognized liabilities represent unbooked deferred charges offsetting the APBO.

[b]Net gains and losses on assumptions or plan experience deemed below level requiring amortization.

[c]This is the balance sheet liability for OPEB costs.

[d]Here the transition is amortized over 20 years.

[e]Benefit payments represent a discharge of plan obligation—they represent also the cash basis OPEB outlay.

Analysis Implications of Postretirement Benefits Expense

While accounting provides us a framework for recognizing postretirement expenses and liabilities, our analysis must evaluate recorded *and* unrecorded postretirement obligations using our knowledge of accounting practice in this area. Accrual accounting requires an estimate of future postretirement costs. While the estimation process is similar to estimating pension costs, it is more difficult and subjective for two reasons. First, data about current costs are more difficult to obtain. Pension benefits involve either fixed dollar amounts or defined dollar amounts based on pay levels. Health benefits, by contrast, are estimates not easily computed by actuarial formulas. Many factors enter into these estimates including deductibles, age, marital status, and number of dependents. Second, more assumptions than those governing pension calculations are required. In addition to retirement dates, life expectancies, turnover, and discount rates, we require assumptions of the medical costs trend rate, Medicare reimbursements, and other related variables. One survey indicated more than 80 percent of companies assume a cost trend rate ranging from 10 to 15 percent. Our analysis must also realize in certain industries postretirement expenses bypass the income statement. For example, utilities can record these expenses as receivables to be recovered in the future from rate increases—see the following disclosure on postretirement expenses:

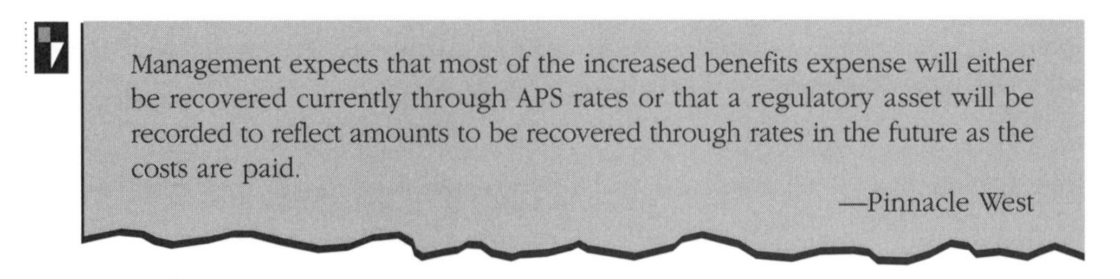

Management expects that most of the increased benefits expense will either be recovered currently through APS rates or that a regulatory asset will be recorded to reflect amounts to be recovered through rates in the future as the costs are paid.

—Pinnacle West

Defense contractors can also elect to pass on postretirement expenses to the government, resulting in these expenses being inventoried or deferred.

Supplementary Employee Benefits

Societal pressures, competition, and scarcity of employee talent have led to a proliferation of employee benefits supplementary to wages. Some fringe benefits like vacation pay, bonuses, profit sharing, and paid health or life insurance are identifiable with the period where they are earned or granted. These identifiable expenses do not pose problems of accounting recognition and accrual. Other supplementary benefit plans, due to their tentative or contingent nature, are not accorded full or timely accounting recognition. Certain supplementary benefits are handled better than others. We review the accounting for some of these benefits here.

▪ **Compensated absences** of employees are accounted for by accruing their expense on a current basis when the following conditions are met: (1) the company's obligation relating to an employee's rights to receive compensation for future absences is attributed to services already rendered, (2) the obligation relates to rights that vest or accumulate, (3) payment of the compensation is probable, and (4) the expense is reasonably estimated. Compensated absences include vacation, holiday, illness, or other personal allowances where it is expected an employee is paid.

▪ **Deferred compensation contracts** are promises to pay employees in the future, sometimes with contingencies. They are typically granted to executives the company wishes to retain or who desire deferring income to postretirement or potentially lower tax years. Provisions in these contracts often include noncompete clauses or specify an employee's availability for consulting services. These provisions are usually not significant enough to justify deferring recognition of expenses. Accounting practice requires at least the present value of deferred compensation be accrued in a systematic and rational manner over the period of active employment from the time the contract is entered into. An exception is when future services expected from the employee to the company are commensurate with the future payments or a portion of these future payments to be made. Similar accruals are required with contracts guaranteeing minimum payments to an employee or beneficiaries.

▪ **Stock appreciation rights (SARs)** are stock rights granted an employee on a specified number of shares. SAR awards are based on the increase in market value of

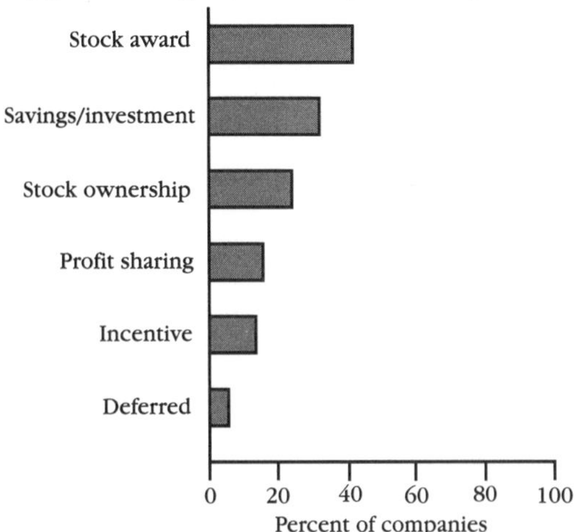

Percents can differ from 100% because companies can use any number of compensatory plans.

Source: *Accounting Trends & Techniques.*

a company's stock since date of grant, and can be awarded in either cash, stock, or a combination of both. Under these plans, a company records compensation expense at the end of each period. Expense is computed as the difference between the award market price of the shares and their grant date option price. Accounting also provides a method for apportioning expense over the service period. Changes in market price from period to period are reflected as adjustments to compensation expense.

▪ **Junior stock plans** allow employees to buy shares of a special class of stock at a fair market value (determined by independent appraisal) less than that of the company's common stock because of reduced voting, dividend, or liquidation rights. At a future date, junior stock is exchangeable for regular common stock if certain performance goals are achieved (e.g., sales or earnings increases). Accounting practice requires that junior stock awards are accounted for like stock appreciation rights. Expense is measured by the difference between the amount the company receives for the junior stock and the market price of common stock on the date conversion is certain. Companies start recognizing expense when it becomes probable that performance targets will be met and the junior stock will be converted to regular common. Periodic charges to income are based on end-of-period common stock prices and are subject to change until the final amount is set at the date conversion is certain.

▪ **Stock options** are incentive compensation devices where an employee receives a right to buy a number of shares at a certain price over a number of years subject to conditions designed to align an employee's interests with those of a company. Companies contend stock options enhance performance by giving employees a stake in the business. Stock options allow employees to build an endowment and offer tax advantages. Employee stock options fit into two broad categories: incentive and nonqualified. *Incentive* or *tax-favored (qualified) stock options* are not taxed until the stock is sold by the employee. These options must be granted at fair market value and the stock must be held for two years from the date of the grant and one year from the date they are exercised. The difference between the exercise price and the selling price is generally taxed as ordinary income. *Nonqualified stock options* do not have the tax benefits of qualified options. These options are sometimes granted at a discount from fair market value and employees are taxed at the time of exercise on the difference between the exercise price and the stock's fair market value. In this case, the company benefits from a tax deduction equal to the amount of income recognized by the employee.

Prior to 1995, accounting for stock options required no charge to income provided options are issued under a noncompensatory plan, a plan where all employees participate equally. If a plan is compensatory, the expense is measured as the excess of the fair value of the optioned shares over the option price. Since the spread, if any, between the market price and the option price at the date of grant is usually negligible, the expense for options has generally not been recorded because of immateriality. Does this accounting reflect economic reality? Consider a case where you are granted options to purchase 10,000 shares of your employer's common stock at the current price of $20 per share. The options allow you to exercise them at any time over the next 10 years. Prior to 1995, the accounting presumes you received nothing of value. Is this logical? What if the market price subsequently exceeds $20 during the next 10 years? You can then buy shares at $20, sell them at the higher market price, and reap the benefits. The possibility that market price can exceed the exercise price subsequent to the granting of the option gives it economic value.

In 1995, accounting for stock-based compensation changed (SFAS No. 123). Companies are now allowed to continue accounting for employee stock options as before, but must provide disclosure of pro forma net income and earnings per share numbers using an estimate of the fair value of the options granted. Companies must estimate this fair value of the options using an option pricing model such as the Black-Scholes model. For pro forma reports, the value of the options is charged to expense over the period where the employee provides the related service (usually the vesting period).

Analysis Implications of Supplementary Benefits Expense

Accounting for stock options prior to 1995 requires our analysis of the provisions of incentive stock plans to assess their potential impact on income. Since the impact on income of some of these plans depends on the price level of the company's stock, this evaluation is cumbersome. Our analysis must also recognize that even with current accounting for stock-based compensation there is considerable management latitude in determining compensation costs associated with employee stock options. As companies implement this new standard, the required disclosures regarding the option pricing model and its inputs will prove useful in our analysis. A positive feature in accounting for stock options is the earnings per share calculation. Stock options having a dilutive effect on earnings per share must enter into computation of this figure. Consequently, earnings per share reveals some of the compensation effect missing in reported income. We discuss computation and evaluation of earnings per share in the Appendix 6A. See Supplement A for how Adaptec discloses details of stock plans in note 6 of its annual report.

Research, Exploration, and Development

Companies undertake research, exploration, and development activities for several reasons, all aimed at either short-term benefits or long-term profit and enhanced market position. Some of these activities are directed at maintaining existing products, while others aim at developing new products and processes. **Research** is often separated into two types. The first type, *basic* (or *pure*) *research*, is directed at the discovery of new facts, natural laws, or phenomena without regard to immediate commercial application of results. Benefits from basic research are uncertain, but if successful, often most rewarding. *Applied research* is aimed at more specific goals. These include product improvement or the refinement of processes or techniques of production. **Exploration** is the search for natural resources. Exploration is an applied activity with definite and known objectives. **Development** begins where research or exploration end. Development is the activity devoted to bringing the fruits of research or the resources discovered by exploration to a commercially useful and marketable stage. Development can involve efforts to exploit an original product invention, oil well, mineral deposit, or tract of timber.

Research and Development Expenses

Research and development (R&D) activities are often one part of many strategic activities of a company. For some companies, especially in their formative stages, R&D activities are often the sole activities. Research activities aim at discovery, and development activities are a translation of research. R&D activities exclude routine or periodic alterations in ongoing operations, market research, and testing activities.

Analysis Research Insight 6.1

Valuing R&D Expenditures

Are R&D expenditures assets? Do R&D expenditures benefit periods other than the period of the outlay? Analysis research implies R&D expenditures are valued much like other long-lived assets. In valuing an expenditure, the market immediately reduces the value of the company for expenditures benefiting the current period only. Examples include rent, utilities, and property taxes. If an expenditure benefits future periods, and those benefits exceed its costs, the market does not reduce the value of the company—in fact, the expenditure *increases* company value. Research indicates the market assesses R&D expenditures in a manner similar to many long-lived assets like property, plant, and equipment. In several cases, the market is found to value R&D expenditures as possessing greater future value than many long-lived assets. This market assessment accorded R&D expenditures is inconsistent with the accounting treatment for them. R&D expenditures are generally expensed currently in financial reporting. Why the discrepancy? The accounting treatment is a convenient solution to a difficult valuation question. More research is needed to precisely estimate the net benefits of R&D expenditures before capitalization of their costs is likely. More important, we need research on a measurement system to better assess the future benefits of *specific* R&D expenditures. R&D expenditures are not all equal, and advances in accounting for R&D depend on better techniques to recognize these differences and appropriately account for them.

Accounting for R&D. Accounting for R&D expenses is problematic. Reasons for difficulties in R&D accounting include:

- High uncertainty of ultimate benefits deriving from R&D activities.
- An often significant lapse of time between initiation of R&D activities and determination of their success.
- Evaluation problems due to the intangible nature of most R&D activities.

It is this pervading uncertainty that causes difficulties in accounting for R&D activities. Because of this uncertainty, U.S. accounting practice requires companies to expense R&D expenditures when incurred. Accounting regulators maintain that only a small percent of R&D projects are successful (recognizing the difficulty in defining success), and, even if success could be predicted with reasonable accuracy, it is difficult to estimate the periods of future benefits. These regulators mandate, subject to certain exceptions, all R&D expenditures be charged to expense as incurred. Only costs of materials, equipment, and facilities having *alternative future uses* (in R&D projects or otherwise) are capitalized as tangible assets. Intangibles purchased from others for R&D activities having alternative future uses are also capitalized.

Costs identified with R&D activities are:

- Materials, equipment, and facilities acquired or constructed for a *specific* R&D project, or purchased intangibles having *no* alternative future uses (in R&D projects or otherwise).

- Materials consumed in R&D activities; and depreciation of equipment or facilities, and amortization of intangible assets used in R&D activities having alternative future uses.
- Salaries and other related costs of personnel engaged in R&D activities.
- Services performed by others in connection with R&D activities.
- Allocation of indirect costs, excluding general and administrative costs not directly related to R&D activities.

R&D expenses are reported in or disclosed with income statements. Government-regulated companies deferring R&D expenditures, in accordance with an exception in accounting standards, require additional disclosures. The uncertainty of future benefits from R&D activities is not unlike that encountered with expenditures for employee training programs, product promotions, and advertising. Like R&D expenditures, these costs are typically expensed when incurred.

Analysis Implications of R&D. Analysis of R&D expenditures is challenging. They are often of sufficient magnitude to warrant scrutiny in analysis of a company's current and future income. Accounting for R&D expenditures is a simple solution to a complex phenomenon. Future benefits are undoubtedly created by many R&D activities and, conceptually, these R&D expenditures should not be expensed as incurred. It is the uncertainty of these benefits that limit R&D capitalization. Yet expensing R&D costs impairs the usefulness of earnings. For example, when a company incurs a major R&D outlay in a desire for future benefits, there is a decline in earnings at the same time the market often revalues upward the company's stock price. Our analysis recognizes while current accounting virtually assures no overstatement in R&D assets, it is at the loss of reasonable measures of expenditures to match with revenues arising from R&D activities. Accounting ignores the productive experience of many ongoing R&D activities in favor of the uncertainty of one-shot research projects. It does, however, achieve a uniformity of accounting for R&D activities and avoids difficult judgments with a policy of capitalization and deferral. Nevertheless, current "nonaccounting" for R&D activities fails to effectively serve the needs and interests of our analysis of financial statements.

In spite of accounting problems, it is reasonable to assume companies pursue R&D projects with expectations of positive returns. Companies often have specific return expectations, and their realization or nonrealization can be monitored and estimated as R&D projects progress. A policy of deferral of R&D costs affords managements and their independent auditors, who regularly work with uncertainties and estimates, an opportunity to convey useful information for our analysis of the potential of R&D outlays. Currently, R&D outlays are treated as if they have no future benefits. Our analysis does not benefit from the insights of those in the best position to provide them.

To assess the quality and potential value of R&D outlays, our analysis needs to know more than the periodic R&D expense. We desire information on the types of research performed, R&D outlays by category, technical feasibility, commercial viability, and the potential of projects periodically assessed and reevaluated. We also desire information on a company's success/failure experience in R&D activities to date. Current accounting does not provide us this basic information. Except in cases of voluntary disclosure, or an investor or lender with sufficient influence, we are unable to obtain this information.

Our analysis can safely assume expensing of R&D outlays yields more conservative balance sheets. There are likely fewer "bad" news surprises from R&D activities. Our analysis must realize that with a lack of information about potential benefits, we are, unless our analysis probes widely and deeply, also unaware of potential disasters befalling a company tempted or forced to spend added funds in R&D projects whose promise was great but whose failure is imminent.

ANALYSIS VIEWPOINT *. . . You are the analyst*

The announcement of net income for California Technology Corporation shows an increase of 10 percent. Your analysis of its operating activities reveals the increase in income is due to a decrease in research and development expenditures. If R&D expenditures for California Technology equaled that for the previous year, income would be down by more than 15 percent. What is your assessment of the future profitability of California Technology Corporation based on their income announcement?

Computer Software Expenses

Development of computer software is a specialized activity that does not fit the usual expenditures of R&D activities. Development of software for marketing purposes is an ongoing activity leading directly to current or future revenues. At some point in the software's development cycle, its costs need to be deferred and matched against future revenues. Current practice in accounting for expenditures of computer software to be sold, leased, or otherwise marketed identifies a point referred to as *technological feasibility* where these costs are capitalized and matched against future revenues. Until the establishment of the point of technological feasibility, all expenditures are expensed as incurred (similar to R&D). Expenditures incurred after technological feasibility, and until the product is ready for general release to customers, are capitalized as an intangible asset. Additional costs to produce software from the masters and package it for distribution are inventoried and charged against revenue as a cost of the product sold.

Exploration and Development Expenses in Extractive Industries

The search for new deposits of natural resources is important to companies in extractive industries. These industries include oil, natural gas, metals, coal, and nonmetallic minerals. The importance of these industries and their special accounting problems deserve our separate attention. As with R&D activities, the search for and development of natural resources is characterized by high risk exposure. Risk involves uncertainty; and for income determination, uncertainty yields measurement and recognition problems. For extractive industries, problems rest with expenses. The problem is whether exploration and development costs that are reasonably expected to be recovered from sale of natural resources are expensed as incurred or capitalized and amortized over the expected future benefit period. While many companies expense exploration costs as incurred, some charge off a portion and capitalize the remainder. Few companies capitalize all development costs and amortize them over future periods.

Accounting for Extractive Industries. Accounting regulators have made various attempts to curtail these divergent practices. Early recommendations included:

- Expenditures for prospecting costs, indirect acquisition costs, and most carrying costs are expensed as incurred as part of current costs of exploration.
- Direct acquisition costs of unproved properties are capitalized and any estimated loss portion is amortized to expense on a systematic and rational basis as part of current costs of exploration.
- Unsuccessful exploration and development expenditures are expensed even though incurred on property where commercially recoverable reserves exist.

A special Committee on Extractive Industries (oil and gas) concluded:

> There exists in practice two basic concepts or philosophies regarding accounting in the oil and gas industry; namely, full-cost accounting and successful efforts accounting. The basic concept of the full-cost method is that all costs, productive and nonproductive, incurred in the search for oil and gas reserves should be capitalized and amortized to income as the total oil and gas reserves are produced and sold. The basic concept of the successful efforts method is that all costs which of themselves do not result directly in the discovery of oil and gas reserves have no future benefit in terms of future revenues and should be expensed as incurred. It was equally clear that the application of the two concepts in practice varies to such an extent that there are in fact numerous different methods of accounting.

Subsequent deliberations led to disagreements, indecision, and changes in direction—even between regulatory agencies. The FASB prescribed *successful efforts accounting* for oil and gas producing companies. This directs that exploration costs except costs of drilling exploratory wells are capitalized when incurred. These costs are later expensed if the resource is unsuccessful *or* reclassified as an amortizable asset if proved oil or gas reserves are discovered. The SEC disagreed and favored instead *reserve recognition accounting* (a current value method). This led the FASB to reconsider and, in effect, permitted the same alternatives to continue. The SEC consequently requested the FASB to develop supplementary disclosures, including value-based disclosures. The FASB responded with requiring the following supplementary *disclosures* for publicly owned oil and gas producers:

- Proved oil and gas reserve quantities.
- Capitalized costs relating to oil and gas producing activities.
- Costs incurred in acquisition, exploration, and development activities.
- Results of operations for oil and gas producing activities.
- Measures of discounted future net cash flows for proved reserves.

Both publicly traded and other companies are required to disclose the method of accounting for costs incurred in oil and gas producing activities and the manner of disposing of related capitalized costs. Companies are allowed to use historical cost/constant-dollar measures in presenting current cost information about oil and gas mineral interests. The SEC adopted these requirements with minor changes.

Disclosure is one thing and accounting measurement is another. The successful efforts accounting method has not received general support. Yet in sanctioning use of full-cost accounting, the SEC provided that costs under this method are capitalized up to a ceiling. This ceiling is determined by the present value of company reserves.

Capitalized costs exceeding this ceiling are expensed. When falling oil prices lower this ceiling, companies have and likely will continue to pressure the SEC to suspend or modify the rules.

Analysis Implications for Extractive Industries. The variety of acceptable methods of treating exploration and development costs in extractive industries hampers our comparison of results across companies. Accounting in this industry continues to exhibit diversity. The two methods in common use, and the variations on these methods, can yield significantly different results. Our analysis must be aware of this. Many analysts favor successful efforts accounting over full-cost accounting because it better matches costs with related revenues and is more consistent with current accounting practices. Successful efforts accounting requires a direct relation between costs incurred and specific reserves discovered before these exploration and development costs are capitalized. In contrast, full-cost accounting permits companies to label "dry holes" as assets.

Goodwill Amortization

Goodwill is the measure of value assigned to a rate of earnings above the norm. It is, in some respects, similar to a premium paid for a bond when the coupon rate exceeds the interest rate demanded, although the size and timing of excess earnings are much more uncertain.

Accounting for Goodwill

One major problem in accounting for goodwill is measuring its expiration. On one hand, it is not necessary to write off an asset against earnings when its value does not expire. Land is an obvious example. Unlike land, the superior earning power of a company is not indestructible or indefinite. It must be nurtured and renewed, and changes in management or market conditions can rapidly reduce its value. As the residual amount in computing the cost of a business purchase, goodwill is often a major component of consideration paid. As we discussed in Chapters 4 and 5, practice requires the excess paid over fair market value of tangible net assets acquired in a purchase—goodwill—be amortized to income over a period not exceeding 40 years.

Analysis Implications of Goodwill

If we ignore goodwill, our analysis overlooks assets of potentially great value. Ignorance is no solution, and it puts our analysis at risk. Even considering the limited amount of information available, we are far better off knowing the effects of accounting for goodwill on reported income and assets.

Our analysis should be also aware of a "historical quirk." Prior to 1970, companies often assigned as much of the purchase price as possible to goodwill or an account titled Excess of Cost over Book Value of Assets Acquired. The reason for this tendency was that costs assigned to assets like inventories, plant and equipment, patents, or future tax benefits must all ultimately be charged against income. Goodwill, prior to 1970, required amortization only when its value was impaired or expiring. Such assessments are difficult to prove, not to mention audit or second-guess. Accordingly, companies included as much of the purchase price as feasible in the Excess of Cost account and asserted the amount was not amortized because its value was undiminished. Our analysis should be aware of these still existing pools of goodwill for many companies, such as that for American Medical:

> Goodwill acquired prior to November 1, 1970, was $10,000,000 and is not being amortized since, in management's opinion, there has been no diminution in the value of these purchased businesses. Similar costs relating to subsequent acquisitions are being amortized on a straight-line basis over 40 years.
>
> —American Medical International, Inc.

Our analysis must be alert to the composition, valuation, and disposition of goodwill. Goodwill is written off when the superior earning power justifying its existence disappears. Disposition, or write-off, of goodwill is frequently timed by management for a period when it has the least impact on the market. This is often a period of loss or reduced earnings. An example of a write-off explanation follows:

> As a result of *Book Digest Magazine's* continuing losses, management concluded that there had been a substantial reduction in the value of the magazine's net assets. Accordingly . . . Excess of Cost over Net Assets of Businesses Acquired was reduced by $9,400,000.
>
> —Dow Jones & Company

Under normal circumstances, goodwill is not indestructible but is an asset with a limited useful life. Whatever the advantages of location, market dominance, competitive stance, sales skill, or product acceptance, they are not unaffected by ordinary changes in the business environment. Amortization of goodwill gives recognition to the expiration of a resource where capital is invested, a process similar to depreciation. Our analysis must recognize that a 40-year amortization period, while adhering to accounting practice, is a compromise position and might not reflect expiration of goodwill. We must assess the relevance of the amortization period by reference to evidence like the continuing value or profitability of units for which goodwill was originally paid.

Interest on Liabilities

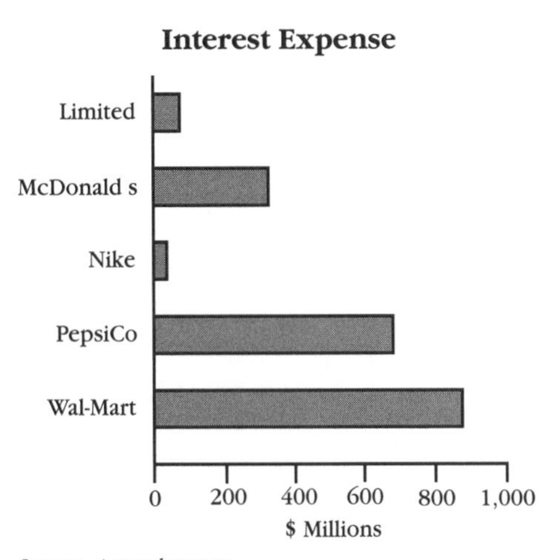

Interest is compensation for use of money. It is the *excess* cash paid or collected beyond the money (principal) borrowed or loaned. Interest is determined by several factors, and one of the most important is credit (nonpayment) risk of the borrower. *Interest expense* is determined by the interest rate, principal, and time.

Interest Computation

Interest expense for a company is the nominal rate paid on debt financing including, in the case of bonds, the amortization of any discount or premium. A complication arises when companies issue convertible debt or debt with warrants. These situations yield a nominal rate below the cost of similar debt not enjoying these added features. In the case of convertible debt, accounting practice considers the debt and equity features inseparable.

Therefore, no portion of the proceeds from issuance of convertible debt is accounted for as attributable to the conversion feature. In the case of debt issued with attached stock warrants, the proceeds attributable to the value of the warrants are accounted for as paid-in capital. The corresponding charge is to a debt discount account that is amortized over the life of the debt issue, increasing the effective interest cost.

Interest Capitalization

Interest expense typically accrues with the lapse of time. Exceptions arise in the case of public utilities, real estate companies, and other special instances. Under these exceptions, interest expense can be capitalized. Accounting practice requires capitalization of interest as part of the cost of assets constructed or otherwise produced for a company's *own use* (including assets constructed or produced for a company by others where deposits or progress payments are made). Inventory items routinely manufactured or produced in large quantities on a repetitive basis do not qualify for interest capitalization. The objectives of interest capitalization are to (1) measure more accurately the acquisition cost of an asset, and (2) amortize acquisition cost against revenues generated by an asset.

The amount of interest capitalized is based on a company's actual borrowings and interest payments. The interest rate used for capitalization is (in order): (1) a rate for specific borrowings associated with the assets; or (2) if borrowings are not specific for the asset, or if the cost of the asset exceeds specific borrowings, a weighted average of rates applicable to these other (or additional) borrowings. Alternatively, a company can use a weighted average of rates of all appropriate borrowings regardless of specific borrowings incurred to finance the asset. Interest capitalization cannot exceed the total interest paid during a period, nor is imputing interest cost to equity funds permitted. A company with no debt cannot capitalize interest. Capitalization can begin when three conditions are present: (1) expenditures are being incurred for the asset, (2) work on the asset is in progress, and (3) interest payments are being incurred. Interest capitalization ceases when the asset is ready for its intended use. Companies must disclose: (1) interest expense when interest is not capitalized, and (2) *both* interest expense and interest capitalized when interest is capitalized. Two examples follow:

In connection with various construction projects, interest of approximately $19,118,000, $30,806,000 and $17,393,000 was capitalized as property, plant and equipment.

—New York Times Company

Interest costs aggregating $2.7 [million] . . . for purchase and construction of long-term assets were capitalized and are being amortized over the related assets' estimated useful lives.

—Duracell International Inc.

Analysis Implications of Interest

Our analysis should realize current accounting for interest on convertible debt is controversial. Many contend that ignoring the value of a conversion privilege and using the coupon rate as the measure of interest ignores the real interest cost.

Somewhat contrary to this position, computation of diluted earnings per share uses the number of shares issuable *in the event of conversion of convertible debt.* This in effect creates an additional charge to the coupon rate through diluting earnings per share.

Accounting for interest capitalization is also disputable. The Financial Analysts Federation's position is interest represents a period cost and is not capitalizable. Our analysis must realize that several criteria and definitions in accounting for interest capitalization are vague, leading to variations in practice (e.g., qualifications for inventory). We should remember that capitalized interest is included in assets' costs and enters expense via depreciation or amortization. To assess the impact of interest capitalization on net income, our analysis must know the amount of capitalized interest currently charged to income via depreciation and amortization. We also need this amount to accurately compute the fixed-charge coverage ratio (see Chapter 10). Unfortunately, practice does not require disclosure of these amounts so our analysis is often handicapped. One potential source of this information is Schedule VI of SEC Form 10-K.

Our analysis must be aware of changes in the interest rate at which a company is borrowing money. An increase in the borrowing rate of interest, not explained by market trends, denotes deterioration in the credit rating of a company.

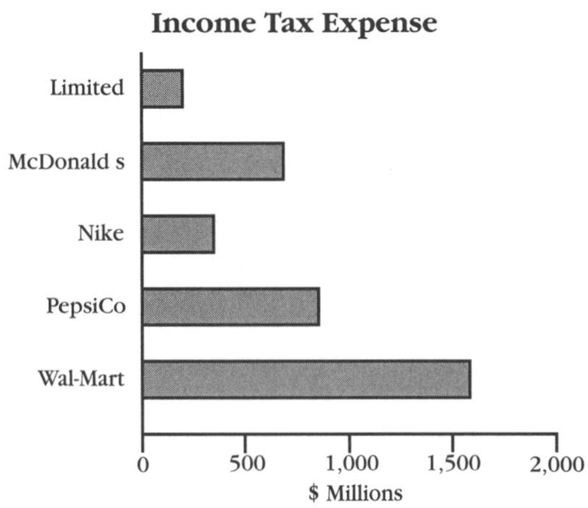

Income Tax Expense

Limited
McDonald s
Nike
PepsiCo
Wal-Mart
0 500 1,000 1,500 2,000
$ Millions

Source: *Annual reports.*

Income Taxes

Income tax expense is a substantial cost of business. Understanding accounting for income taxes is important to successful analysis of financial statements. Our discussion here focuses on the accounting and analysis of periodic income tax expense, and not on tax law.

Accounting for Income Tax

The accounting and reporting standards for income taxes resulting from a company's activities require an asset and liability approach. Specifically, deferred taxes are determined separately for each tax-paying component (an individual entity or group of entities consolidated for tax purposes) in each tax jurisdiction. Determination includes the following procedures:

- Identifying the types and amounts of temporary differences (discussed below) and the nature and amount of each type of operating loss and tax credit carryforward including the remaining length of the carryforward period.
- Measuring total deferred tax liability for taxable temporary differences using the applicable tax rate.
- Computing the total deferred tax asset for deductible temporary differences and operating loss carryforwards using the applicable tax rate.
- Measuring deferred tax assets for each type of tax credit carryforward.
- Reducing deferred tax assets by a valuation allowance if, based on the weight of available evidence, it is more likely than not (a more than 50 percent probability) some portion or all of deferred tax assets will not be realized.

The valuation allowance must be sufficient to reduce deferred tax assets to the amount likely to be realized. Deferred tax assets and liabilities are adjusted for effects of changes in tax rates or laws. These effects are included in income from continuing operations for that period. One notable provision of current practice is allowing a parent company to not recognize a liability for deferred taxes due to a subsidiary's unremitted earnings. Taxes paid on taxable income are governed by regulations. Certain regulations like those concerning depletion or legal credits can reduce the effective tax rate of a company below statutory levels. Practice requires information regarding reasons for deviations from normal tax levels.

Net income computed using accepted accounting principles is often different from taxable income computed using tax regulations. This is due to two general types of differences: (1) permanent differences, and (2) temporary differences. To analyze income tax expense, it is helpful to distinguish between permanent and temporary income tax differences.

Permanent Income Tax Differences

Permanent differences can result from tax regulations where:

- Items are nontaxable: for example, income on tax-exempt bonds and life insurance proceeds on an employee.
- Deductions are not allowed: for example, penalties for filing certain returns, government fines, and employee life insurance premiums.
- Special deductions are granted: for example, tax exclusion on dividends from unconsolidated subsidiaries or from other domestic corporations.

The effective tax rate paid by a company on net income can vary from the statutory rate for many reasons including:

- Basis of property differs for financial and tax accounting due to reorganizations or combinations.
- Nonqualified and qualified stock option plans.
- Special tax privileges, for example, in savings and loan associations, shipping lines, or insurance companies.
- Lower corporate income tax rate up to a certain level.
- Tax credits, for example, research and development credits, or foreign tax credits.
- Different tax rates on foreign income.
- Tax expense includes both state and local income taxes, net of federal tax benefit.
- Tax loss carryforward benefits.

We consider these differences permanent because they do not have future repercussions on a company's taxable income. We must take this into account when reconciling a company's actual (effective) tax rate to the statutory rate.

Temporary Income Tax Differences

Unlike permanent differences, temporary differences are expected to affect taxable income at some future time. That is, they are expected to *reverse*. For example, consider a company depreciating a $1,000 asset over 10 years on a straight-line basis. To conserve cash, the company elects for tax purposes to use double-declining-balance depreciation. In Year 1, accounting depreciation is $100 while tax depreciation is $200. Years later, accounting depreciation will eventually exceed tax depreciation because under either method total depreciation equals $1,000. Consequently, this

EXHIBIT 6.7 Categories of Temporary Income Tax Differences

Revenue or gain recognized in financial reporting but deferred for tax purposes.
Examples are:
Installment method for tax purposes and the accrual method for financial reporting.
Completed-contract method for tax purposes and percentage-of-completion method for financial reporting.

Expenses deducted for tax purposes *exceed* these expenses for financial reporting.
Examples are:
Accelerated depreciation for tax purposes and straight-line for financial reporting.
Land reclamation costs deducted for tax but capitalized and amortized for financial reporting.

Revenue or gain recognized for tax but *deferred* for financial reporting.
Examples are:
Rent income received in advance is recognized for tax purposes but not for accounting.
Unearned finance charges recognized currently for tax but over time in for accounting.

Expenses deducted for financial reporting *exceed* these expenses for tax.
Examples are:
Estimated expenses (repair, maintenance, warranty, vacation) are accrued for financial reporting but not deducted for tax.
Estimated refunds due the government for price redetermination and renegotiation are accrued for financial reporting but not for tax.

tax difference reverses and is temporary. Exhibit 6.7 goups temporary differences into four categories. We summarize these four categories as follows:

	Reported on		Initial Income Tax Journal Entries	
Category of Transaction	***Income Statement***	***Tax Return***	***Income Tax Expense***	***Balance Sheet Deferred Tax Accounts****
1. Revenue or gain	Earlier	Later	Debit	Credit
2. Expenses or loss	Later	Earlier	Debit	Credit
3. Revenue or gain	Later	Earlier	Credit	Debit
4. Expenses or loss	Earlier	Later	Credit	Debit

*These can reverse later. Some reversals occur in the normal course of business, while others occur due to a switch in policy, e.g., deferred installment profits reverse when receivables are sold to a bank and deferred tax must be paid; or tax deferrals due to accelerated depreciation reverse because the company switches from owning assets to leasing.

While all four categories exist in practice, the desirable temporary differences from a company's perspective are those yielding credits to the deferred tax account—thus postponing taxes paid. The third and fourth categories are least desirable in this regard (they yield "early" tax payments).

A balance sheet reports separately deferred tax liabilities and assets into current and noncurrent amounts. Deferred tax liabilities and assets are classified as current or noncurrent depending on the classification of the related asset or liability for financial reporting. A deferred tax liability or asset not related to an asset or liability for financial reporting, including deferred tax assets related to carryforwards, is classified according to the expected reversal period of the temporary difference. When a valuation allowance measuring the likelihood of realizing deferred tax assets is used, it is allocated between current and noncurrent deferred tax assets on a pro rata basis.

A basic problem with temporary differences is the differences between income before tax reported in the income statement and the taxable income on the tax return. If actual tax paid is considered as a period expense, it will not fit with pre-tax income on the income statement. This violates the basic accounting principle of matching income and related expenses. **Interperiod tax allocation** is designed to assure income reported on financial statements is charged with the tax applicable to it regardless of how this income is reported for tax purposes. This achieves the basic objective of recognizing tax consequences of an event in the same year it is recognized in financial statements.

Case 6.1: Consider a case illustrating principles of *interperiod tax allocation*. A retailer sells mountain bikes on installment. On January 1, Year 1, it sells a bike for $720 payable at the rate of $20 a month for 36 months. Ignoring finance charges, the gross profit to the retailer is 20 percent, and the tax rate is 50 percent. For financial reporting the retailer recognizes in Year 1 a gross profit of $144 (20 percent of $720). For tax purposes it recognizes profit based on actual cash collections as follows:

	Cash Collection	*Taxable Gross Profit (20%)*	*Actual Tax Payable*
Year 1	$240	$ 48	$24
Year 2	240	48	24
Year 3	240	48	24
Total	$720	$144	$72

With no interperiod tax allocation the retailer reports the following financial results:

	Pre-Tax Profit	*Tax Payable*	*Profit (Loss)*
Year 1	$144	$24	$120
Year 2	—	24	(24)
Year 3	—	24	(24)
Total	$144	$72	$ 72

The potential for misinterpretation in these reports is apparent. The financial reporting profit of Year 1 does not bear its proper share of tax. This yields a profit "overstatement" of $48. This misrepresentation carries over to Years 2 and 3, where profits are understated by $24 each since they bear a tax payment unrelated to any revenues from those years. These reports can mislead one to believe that in Year 1 our retailer is more profitable than, for example, a competitor who sells a mountain bike for cash ($720), realizes a gross profit of $144, pays tax of $72, and reports an after-tax profit of $72 (versus $120 for our retailer). Interperiod tax allocation is designed to remedy these distortions by means of a deferred tax account. This account is used to better match tax expense reported with revenue reported as follows:

		Taxes				
	Pre-Tax Profit	*Actual Payable*	*Deferred*	*Total*	*After-Tax Profit*	*Deferred Tax Account*
Year 1	$144	$24	$48	$72	$72	$48
Year 2	—	24	(24)	—	—	24
Year 3	—	24	(24)	—	—	—

This deferred tax account (e.g., $48 in Year 1) is a liability (in our case) and is adjusted for changes in tax laws and rates. The provision for deferred taxes does not require cash, and the tax credit arising from the reversal of deferred taxes is not a source of cash.

Our installment sale case is a simplification of a complex process. While the tax deferral on the mountain bike is, as shown in the case, entirely reversed at the end of Year 3, the aggregate tax deferral account usually does not entirely reverse. For example, if another mountain bike is sold in Year 2, the aggregate deferred tax account remains the same. If the retailer sells an increasing number of mountain bikes, the deferred tax account grows. In the case of differences in financial reporting and tax attributed to depreciation, and where assets are long lived, the deferred tax account often grows over time or at least is stable.

Intraperiod tax allocation concerns the distribution of tax across the various items of the income statement. The objective is to show each major item net of its tax effect. For example, an extraordinary item is shown net of its appropriate tax effect so the tax related to operating results is applicable to it. Other examples of intraperiod tax effects include discontinued operations, cumulative effects of accounting changes, and prior period adjustments.

Tax Loss Carrybacks and Carryforwards

A company incurring an operating loss can generally carry it back for a refund on taxes paid. If a loss cannot be entirely covered within the preceding 3 years, it can be carried forward for 15 years to apply against future taxes payable. The status of a tax loss carryback is usually simple to determine—it is either available or not. An asset is recognized for the amount of taxes paid in prior years that is refundable by carryback of an operating loss or unused tax credit. The value of a tax loss carryforward depends on a company's ability to earn taxable income in the future, which is not a certainty. An operating loss or tax credit carryforward is recognized as a reduction of a deferred tax liability for temporary differences expected to yield taxable amounts in the carryforward period. The tax benefit of an operating loss or tax credit carryforward that cannot be recognized as a reduction of a deferred tax liability is booked as a deferred tax asset. This asset is reduced by a valuation allowance if, based on available evidence, it is more likely than not that all or part of the deferred tax asset will not be realized. In the year of a loss when both a net operating loss (NOL) carryback *and* carryforward are available, a company makes the following entry:

Income Tax Refund Receivable	xxx	
Future Benefit from NOL Carryforward	xxx	
Income Tax Benefit from NOL Carryback		xxx
Income Tax Benefit from NOL Carryforward		xxx

Case 6.2: Consider the following case as illustrative of accounting for tax loss carrybacks and carryforwards. The Erratic Corporation's taxable income (loss) and related adjustments are reported below (this company is subject to a 50 percent tax rate):

Tax Return Data ($ thousands)

	Year 1	*Year 2*	*Year 3*	*Year 4*	*Year 5*	*Year 6*	*Year 7*
Taxable income (loss)	$120	$80	$160	$100	$(600)	$100	$220
Tax loss carryback[(a)]		$80	$160	$100			
Tax loss carryforward[(b)]						$100	$160
Refund of prior year taxes (carryback)[(c)]					($170)		
Carryforward benefits (reducing current taxes)[(d)]						$ 50	$ 80

[(a)]Taxable income of preceding three years—here $340, which is all usable being less than the Year 5 loss of $600.
[(b)]Having used up $340 of the $600 loss in carrybacks, the tax loss carryforward available at the end of Year 5 stood at $260 ($600 – $340) and can be carried forward to reduce taxes of the following 15 years.
[(c)]The tax refund amounts to 50 percent of $340. Regardless of tax rates prevailing at any given time, only taxes actually paid are recoverable.
[(d)]In Year 6, $100 in tax loss carryforwards are used up resulting in a $50 tax benefit. In Year 7, the remaining $160 tax loss carryforward is used up, which results in a $80 tax benefit.

The financial reporting data for Erratic Corp. over the same period are as follows:

Income Statement Data ($ thousands)

	Year 1	*Year 2*	*Year 3*	*Year 4*	*Year 5*	*Year 6*	*Year 7*
Income (loss) before taxes[e]	$120	$80	$160	$100	$(600)	$100	$220
Less: Tax expense	60	40	80	50	0	50[(a)]	110[(b)]
Tax refund[(c)] NOL carryback					(170)		
Tax benefit NOL carryforward					(130)[(d)]		
Net income (loss)	$ 60	$40	$ 80	$ 50	$(300)	$ 50	$110

[(a)]Credit is to an asset, Future Benefit from NOL Carryforward.
[(b)]$80 ($110 – $30) of this is credited to Future Benefit asset accounts; the balance of $30 results in taxes payable.
[(c)]For three years to Year 4—50 percent of income.
[(d)]The resulting asset subject to a valuation allowance (50% of 600, less 170), if needed.
[(e)]For convenience, financial reporting income (loss) is assumed equal to taxable income.

Tax reductions resulting from tax loss carryforwards show up in the reconciliation of tax expense to the amount based on applying domestic federal statutory rates to pre-tax income from continuing operations. Our analysis of this reconciliation often yields insights into a company's future effective tax rates.

Income Tax Disclosures

Companies disclose the following components of the net deferred tax liability or asset recognized on their balance sheets:

- Total deferred tax liabilities.
- Total deferred tax assets.
- Total valuation allowance recognized for deferred tax assets.

Additional disclosures are also available on components of income tax expense for each year reported, including:

- Current tax expense or benefit.
- Deferred tax expense or benefit (exclusive of effects of other components below).
- Investment tax credits.
- Government grants (when recognized as a reduction of income tax expense).

- Benefits of operating loss carryforwards.
- Tax expense resulting from allocating tax benefits to either contributed capital or goodwill deduction or another noncurrent intangible asset of an acquired entity.
- Adjustments in deferred tax liability or asset due to changes in tax laws or rates or status of a company.
- Adjustments in the beginning-of-the-year balance of the valuation allowance due to circumstances yielding a revised estimate of the realizability of the deferred tax asset in future periods.

Companies disclose a reconciliation between the effective income tax rate and the statutory federal income tax rate. Amounts and expiration dates of operating loss and tax credit carryforwards for tax purposes are also disclosed.

Analysis Implications of Income Taxes

Our analysis must understand the relation between pre-tax income and income tax expense. We should remember that procedures applied to loss carryforwards differ from those applied to carrybacks. Tax loss carrybacks result in a tax refund in the loss year and are recognized as an asset. A loss carryforward results in a *deferred* asset. This deferred tax asset is reduced by a valuation allowance to the extent "it is more likely than not" that all or part of it will not be realized by a reduction of taxes payable (on taxable income) during the carryforward period.

In spite of disagreements on tax allocation, the accounting yields a reasonable tax accrual and, hence, reasonable income numbers. Practice distinguishes tax strategy from financial reporting of income. It tempers motivation by management to adjust results through accounting techniques. Interperiod tax allocation is also sound from an analytical perspective. That is, assets whose future tax deductibility is reduced are not worth as much as those having greater tax deductibility. For example, consider two companies depreciating an identical asset costing $100,000 under different tax methods of depreciation resulting in first-year depreciation amounts of $10,000 and $20,000, respectively. At the end of Year 1, one company has an asset it can depreciate for tax purposes to the amount of $90,000. The other company can depreciate its asset only to the amount of $80,000. These two assets do not possess equal value. The tax deferral adjustment recognizes this economic reality.

A weakness with interperiod tax allocation is its lack of recognition of the present value of a future obligation or loss of benefits. These values should be discounted rather than reported at par as currently done in companies' deferred tax accounts. The FASB ignored the time value of money because of its alleged complexity, both in implementation and interpretation. Yet present value computations appear in many other areas including accounting for leases and pensions. Failure to discount these values hinders our analysis. This can contribute to the often steady increase of deferred tax liabilities that, while reducing income, do not represent a legal obligation. The FASB also bowed to pressure from various constituencies when it retained earlier provisions allowing parent companies to avoid providing deferred taxes on unremitted earnings of subsidiaries.

Our analysis of tax expense must also guard against a common error in this area. It is sometimes incorrectly assumed that deferred tax accounting acts as an entire offset to differences between tax and financial accounting methods. Rather, if we assume, for example, that accelerated depreciation for tax purposes is more realistic than straight line for financial reporting, then the effect of deferred taxes is to remove only about one-third of the overstatement in income resulting from straight-line depreciation for financial reporting.

Income tax disclosures provide an explanation of why the effective tax expense rate differs from the current statutory rate. This is an important tool in our analysis of whether present tax benefits or extra costs that a company enjoys or incurs are expected to continue. More reliable information can improve our predictions of cash flows and earnings. Benefits like the research and development credit, foreign tax shelters, depletion allowances, and capital gains treatment depend on legislative sanction and are subject to change, repeal, or expiration. Other differences, such as those arising from foreign tax differentials and tax loss carryforwards, depend on conditions demanding our attention. Some tax benefits may or may not remain in tax laws. The long-standing and substantial benefit of the investment tax credit was repealed in 1986—but is likely to return again. Other benefits depend on the company's ability to take advantage of them (e.g., capital expenditures) to earn investment tax credits when available.

Our analysis of underlying transactions includes assessing continuation of accounting-related differentials, such as those relating to use of the equity method income pick up. Also, a low effective tax rate leads us to investigate the likelihood of recurrence of tax benefits, as does a higher than normal tax rate demand our scrutiny. For example, a higher than normal effective tax rate can be due to subsidiary losses that a company might not be able to offset on its tax return. Useful information is also available in our analysis of the effective tax rate reconciliation. If, for example, our analysis indicates tax-free interest reduced taxes by $144,000, we can determine the amount of tax-free income by dividing $144,000 by 0.35 (assumed statutory tax rate), or $411,429.

Our analysis of *components* of deferred income tax expense can also yield insights. Through evaluation of components we can learn about capitalization of costs, early recognition of revenues, and other discretionary accrual adjustments. We can also acquire information about expected future reductions in deferred income taxes. These reductions can foretell higher tax expense cash outlays, and are valuable predictors for the liquidity implications they carry. For example, whenever a deferred tax credit "reverses," accounting tax expense is reduced by the amount of the reversal, but the actual tax payment is higher than the net expense reported in the income statement. The implication is a cash decrease.

Extraordinary Items and Discontinued Operations

Income components discussed so far are generally of the ordinary operating and recurring type. It is reasonable in these cases to assume that their inclusion in an income statement yields a figure reflecting a period's operating performance. These performance results are important in valuing securities, evaluating management, and many other analyses. Perhaps more important, income components are used as primary indicators of a company's earning power. Accordingly, treatment of gains or losses from unusual, extraordinary, or discontinuing operations is of major importance.

Extraordinary Items

Extraordinary items are distinguished by their unusual nature and by the infrequency of their occurrence. Examples include uninsured losses from a major casualty (earthquake, hurricane, tornado) or losses from expropriation. There are two schools of thought on how to handle extraordinary gains or losses. One is the *all-inclusive* view. This view recognizes in net income all items affecting changes in equity during a period except dividend payments and capital transactions (i.e., the clean surplus relation). The other is the *current operating performance* view. This view excludes from net income items that, if included, impair its significance as a measure of current earning power. Application of the current operating performance view led to dubious income reporting practices (e.g., management classified items as extraordinary those it did not want associated with predictions of recurring income). Accounting practice subsequently reacted with more refined definitions of what constitutes *extraordinary*. To qualify as extraordinary an item must be *both* unusual in nature and infrequent in occurrence. These are defined as follows:

- *Unusual nature.* An event or transaction has a high degree of abnormality and is unrelated to, or only incidentally related to, the ordinary and typical activities of the company (recognizing its environment).
- *Infrequent occurrence.* An event or transaction is not reasonably expected to recur in the foreseeable future (recognizing the company's environment).

Practice requires separate disclosure in income before extraordinary items of unusual or nonrecurring events or transactions not meeting both conditions for classification as extraordinary.

Practice also requires companies to *not* report certain gains and losses as extraordinary items because they are not unusual in nature and are expected to recur as a consequence of customary and continuing business activity. These examples include:

- Write-down or write-off of receivables, inventories, equipment leased to others, deferred R&D costs, or other intangible assets.
- Gains or losses on disposal of a business segment.
- Gains or losses from sale or abandonment of property, plant, or equipment.
- Effects of a strike, including those against competitors and major suppliers.
- Adjustment of accruals on long-term contracts.

In a desire to limit items qualifying as extraordinary, gains and losses on debt retirement were initially excluded from extraordinary and shown as ordinary items. Gains and losses on debt retirement arise when, due to changes in interest rates and/or credit standing, a debt is satisfied by repurchase in the open market or otherwise at an amount below (gain) or above (loss) its book value. When increasing interest rates reduce the price of low coupon bonds, companies are encouraged to exchange high coupon bonds of lower aggregate par values for outstanding low coupon bonds. The resulting "profits" can be substantial. Practice now requires that debt retirements of all kinds, except for sinking fund purchases, be separately disclosed as extraordinary items. Sinking fund gains and losses are aggregated and separately identified in the income statement.

Discontinued Operations

Accounting for and presentation of discontinued operations, including disposal of a segment of a business, are treated similar to extraordinary items. They are reported separately and net of their related tax effects. To qualify as discontinued, the assets and business activities of a segment must be clearly distinguishable (both physically and operationally) from the assets and business activities of the remaining entity. Our analysis must recognize when estimating future earning power that results from

EXHIBIT 6.8 Prototype of the Lower Part of an Income Statement

Income from continuing operations before income taxes		$xxx
Income taxes		xxx
Income from continuing operations		$xxx
Discontinued operations:		
Income (loss) from discontinued operations (less applicable taxes of $xxx)*	$xxx	
Loss on disposal of discontinued operations including provision of $xxx for operating losses during phaseout period (less applicable taxes of $xxx)†	xxx	xxx
Extraordinary item (less taxes of $xxx)		xxx
Cumulative effect of change in accounting principle (less taxes effect of $xxx)		xxx
Net income		$xxx

*Includes operating losses to date of commitment to formal disposition of a segment, that is, a separately identifiable entity—physically, operationally, and financially.

†Includes estimated operating losses from date of decision to discontinue to expected disposal date. (Expected net gains on disposal can be recorded only *when realized*.)

discontinued operations are treated differently than recurring (persistent) operations. They are treated analytically similar to extraordinary items. A prototype of the lower part of an income statement is shown in Exhibit 6.8.

Analysis Implications of Extraordinary Items and Discontinued Operations

It is important in our analysis that adequate disclosure accompany the income statement. Our analysis of the income statement is mostly predictive in nature. Analysis relies on factors whose stability and recurrence facilitate prediction. We also require adjustments for the sporadic and nonrecurring elements of reported income. We need details of all ordinary operating elements of revenue and expense, *and* information regarding the nature of and gains or losses from extraordinary items and discontinued operations. This is because of their magnitude and our need to form judgments on their treatment in assessing results of operations and probability of recurrence.

Our analysis should not assume that the accounting designation of an item as extraordinary renders it excludable from the measure of periodic operating performance. The best we can expect here is full disclosure of all credits and charges in the income statement regardless of their designation. Extraordinary items should never be disregarded because they often reveal a particular risk(s) that a company is subject to. While these items may not recur yearly, their occurrence attests to the possibility of their recurrence. In their monetary impact on a company, they are not different from operating items, although their persistence is different. For example, a loss from a flood affects a company's wealth as an equal loss on the sale of merchandise below cost. Moreover, the cumulative importance, and risk exposure, of extraordinary items can be considerable.

Our analysis should always be aware of management's reporting propensities in this area. Management has a certain latitude in determining both the magnitude and timing of these gains and losses. For instance, management can decide when to sell an asset, when to discontinue a product line, or when to provide for a future loss (under regulatory provisions). The *timing* of these decisions is seemingly too often affected by the probable impact on income. There is a "tendency" for extraordinary items to occur where gains are offset by losses. Management's motivations for this are frequently apparent: smoothing or management of earnings. Eaton Corporation reports a "bunching" of unusual and extraordinary items:

> The Company settled a portion of its obligation under several of its domestic pension plans through the purchase of annuity contracts by the pension funds. As a result, income from continuing operations included a settlement gain of $26 million, before income taxes of $9 million. Also included in income from continuing operations . . . was a provision of $24 million, before income tax credits of $9 million, for the estimated costs of closing several manufacturing plants.
>
> —Eaton Corporation

The propensity of management to offset gains with accruals for current and future losses can accomplish two "reporting objectives": (1) it removes from income an unusual profit boost that an earnings-trend conscious company can find difficult to match in subsequent years, and (2) it provides a discretionary "cushion" against which future losses and expenses can be charged to improve the earnings trend (or it can provide for losses that a company did not previously find expedient to accrue for). We should also recognize materiality as a factor in determining whether an item is extraordinary or not. For example, losses that are small and considered "operating" can be permitted to accumulate to a level where they are large enough to be labeled extraordinary. In evaluating extraordinary items, our analysis should be alert to management's use of these reporting opportunities. We must adopt an independent and critical attitude toward income components, be they classified as unusual, extraordinary, or whatever manner. Only when we obtain information on the nature of these items can we reach reliable conclusions on their impact on the earnings performance of a company.

ANALYSIS VIEWPOINT . . . *You are the supplier*

Your company supplies raw materials to Chicago Construction Corp. Your job is to annually assess customers for credit terms and policies. Chicago Construction's net income for this year is down by 12 percent. Your analysis of their financial statements shows this decrease is due to an extraordinary loss attributed to a construction site fire. Absent this extraordinary loss, income for Chicago Construction is up by 23 percent. What is your credit assessment of Chicago Construction?

Accounting Changes

To discourage management from unjustified switching from one accounting method to another, practice requires the following: "in the preparation of financial statements there is a presumption that an accounting principle once adopted should not be changed in accounting for events and transactions of a similar type. . . The presumption that an entity should not change an accounting principle may be overcome only if the enterprise justifies the use of an alternative acceptable accounting principle on the basis that it is preferable." Practice distinguishes among three types of accounting changes: a change in accounting principle, in accounting estimate, and in reporting entity.

Change in Accounting Principle

The *cumulative effect of a change in accounting principle (net of tax)* on the amount of retained earnings at the beginning of the period where the change is made is computed and included in income. It is reported in the income statement after extraordinary items and before net income. This computation is a "catch-up" adjustment. Previously published financial statements are *not* adjusted. Companies disclose the following information with an accounting principle change:

- Nature of and justification for the change in principle.
- Effect of the new principle on both net income and income before extraordinary items for the period of change, including related earnings per share data.
- Pro forma effects of retroactive application of the accounting change on net income and income before extraordinary items (and related earnings per share data); these are reported on all prior periods' income statements disclosed currently.

When pro forma effects are not determinable, the company discloses why these effects are not reported. A change in the method of allocating costs of long-lived assets, if adopted only for newly acquired assets, does not require this catch-up adjustment.

There are three exceptions to the requirement that previously issued financial statements need not be restated; they are:

- Change from LIFO to another inventory costing method.
- Change in accounting for long-term construction contracts.
- Change to or from full-cost accounting in extractive industries.

Case 6.3: The Switching Corporation's Year 5 annual report states: "Effective as of January 1, Year 4, the Company adopted the last-in, first-out (LIFO) method of determining inventory cost . . . LIFO inventories at December 31, Year 4, and Year 5 were $58,970,000 and $55,723,000, respectively. Under the average-cost method of accounting previously used, inventories would have been $14,580,000 and $19,311,000 higher than those reported at December 31, Year 4, and Year 5, respectively." The effect of the change from average cost to LIFO cost is computed below (in thousands):

	Debit (Credit)		
Changes on	***Year 5***	***Year 4***	***Year 3***
Income Statement:			
1. ΔCost of sales	$ 4,731	$14,580	
2. ΔTax expense	(1,609)	(4,957)	
3. ΔNet income (net decrease)	$ 3,122	$ 9,623	
Retained Earnings Statement:			
4. ΔBeginning balance	9,623	–0–	
5. ΔNet income	3,122	9,623	
6. ΔEnding balance	$12,745	$ 9,623	
Balance Sheet:			
7. ΔInventories	(19,311)	(14,580)	–0–
8. ΔTaxes payable—current	6,566	4,957	
9. ΔRetained earnings	$12,745	$ 9,623	

Note: The Δ denotes "change in."

Additional Explanation for Items 1–9:

1. The effect on cost of sales is calculated as the difference in the inventory change. In Year 5 the inventory reduction is higher at year-end than at the beginning, resulting in an increase in cost of goods sold of $4,731 ($19,311 – $14,580). In Year 4 the reduction in ending inventory of $14,580 (when comparing average cost to LIFO) results in an increase in cost of sales because opening inventory is not changed.
2. Since inventories are reduced (credited) under LIFO, tax expense is reduced (debited) by an assumed 34 percent rate on the amount of the inventory reduction. Lower ending inventories compared to the beginning of the period result in higher costs and lower income.
3. Sum of (1) and (2).
4. The change in beginning retained earnings is the result of the change in net income from the prior year. Since the company switched to LIFO on January 1, Year 4, there is no change in net income from the prior year (zero effect is reported for Year 4).
5. Change in net income of current year as reported in (3) above.
6. Sum of (4) and (5).
7. The change in inventories is reported in financial statements.
8. The reduction in inventories is accompanied by a reduction in taxes payable (i.e., a reduced cash outlay), computed using an assumed tax rate of 34 percent of ending inventories.
9. Concurs with (6).

Change in Accounting Estimate

Income measurement requires assessing future events like inventory obsolescence, asset lives, warranty costs, and uncollectibles. These are known as *accounting estimates*. Practice requires the following for changes in accounting estimates:

- Prospective application—changes are accounted for in the period of change and, if applicable, future periods (retroactive restatement is prohibited).
- Change in accounting estimate recognized by a change in accounting principle is reported as a change in estimate.
- Disclosure is required of the effect on both net income and income before extraordinary items (including related earnings per share data) for the current period even when a change in estimate also affects future periods.

Change in Reporting Entity

A change in reporting entity can occur in several ways, including:

- Initial publication of consolidated financial statements.
- Change in consolidation policy regarding subsidiaries.
- Pooling of interests.

Accounting practice requires restating all periods reported in financial statements and disclosing the nature of the change and its rationale.

Correction of an Error

Errors in financial statements can sometimes arise from arithmetic mistakes, mistakes in application of accounting principles, or mistakes of information disclosure. Practice does not consider correction of an error as an accounting change. Rather, the correction of an error is treated as a *prior period adjustment* to the beginning balance of Retained Earnings. Disclosure includes the nature of the error and the effect on net income and income before extraordinary items (and related earnings per share data).

Analysis Implications of Accounting Changes

It is important we recognize the requirement that changes in accounting principle only occur when the change is preferable. This judgment depends not only on management but on the independent auditors' assessment of preferable accounting. To reduce a propensity for liberal interpretation, the SEC expects consistency between audit clients when endorsing preferability judgments. Inclusion of a catch-up adjustment from a change in accounting principle in computing net income of the period when the change occurs reinforces our need to deemphasize the net income of any one year. Rather, we need to focus attention on the stream of earnings over time.

Our analysis often needs to assess the effect on financial statements from use of different accounting principles or estimates. This occurs because we sometimes want to adjust financial statements to reflect a different accounting principle for analytical purposes. It also occurs from our need to compare financial statements of companies using different accounting policies, or because we want to estimate the change's effect on components of current or past financial statements. Our analysis sometimes desires estimates of the effect of accounting changes on past financial statements where restatements are not provided. One excellent technique of analysis in these cases is to establish the journal entries required by each alternative method and then to compare them.

Comments on Income Analysis

Importance of the income statement to our analysis is due to several factors. One factor is that this statement reports the dynamic operating aspects of a company, the results of operations, and the success of its performance. This statement is also the basis for important projections of future performance. We see in this and preceding chapters the nonuniformity of accounting rules for measuring periodic income. We see also management's latitude in selecting and applying accounting methods. Consequently, we conclude our discussion by looking at some possibilities in distorting reported income.

If we accept the proposition of a "true" income, income determined when all facts are known and all uncertainties resolved, then reported income will deviate from this ideal. For example, we are never sure about the useful life of an asset until it is actually complete; nor can we be certain about the ultimate profitability of a contract until it is fulfilled; nor about the revenue received from a transaction until the sales price is actually collected. Uncertainties are a necessary part of business activities, and the best we expect is to estimate their ultimate disposition using the best information available. Periodic income reporting requires we not wait for final disposition of uncertainties but that companies estimate them as best they can. This system is subject to error—errors of estimation, errors of omission, and errors of commission. The better and more conscientious a company's management and the better its internal controls, the less likely these errors substantially distort reported income. Serious cases of income distortion arise when management sets out to "manage" reported results away from economic reality. Instead of portraying economic reality, management sometimes reports reality as they see it. We saw that distortions can be carried out through the timing of transactions, selecting certain accounting principles, introducing conservative or, alternatively, optimistic estimates, and choosing methods that require or do not require disclosing certain components of income.

A company engaging in practices to benefit current income at the expense of future income may use one or more of the following techniques:

- Selecting inventory methods to maximize inventory carrying values and minimize current charges to cost of goods or services sold.

- Choosing depreciation methods and useful lives of property to minimize current depreciation charges.
- Deferring costs to the future—examples are preoperating, moving, rearrangement, start-up, and marketing costs. These costs are carried as deferred charges or included with the costs of other assets like property, plant, and equipment.
- Amortizing assets and deferring costs over extended periods. Assets often affected include goodwill, leasehold improvements, patents, and copyrights.
- Selecting assumptions leading to the lowest possible pension and other employment compensation cost accruals.
- Capitalizing rather than expensing certain general and administrative costs and taxes.
- Choosing accelerated methods of income recognition in the areas of leasing, franchising, real estate sales, and contracting.

Exhibit 6.9 depicts the potential impact on reported income of but a few of the alternative accounting principles available to management.

GUIDANCE ANSWERS TO ANALYSIS VIEWPOINTS

You Are the Banker

Playground Equipment's recognition of revenue during production is probably too liberal. Recognizing revenue during production is acceptable only when total revenues and expenses are estimated with reasonable certainty *and* when realization (payment) is reasonably assured. For most companies, these conditions are not met. Unless we are highly confident that Playground Equipment's earnings process meets these stringent conditions, we should require restatement (or an alternative statement) using point of sale as the basis for revenue recognition. If Playground Equipment has considerable collection risks or costs, we might require restatement using revenue recognition when cash is received. The more conservative the statements used in our analysis, the less risky should be our loan agreement with Playground Equipment. The primary risk we are exposed to in acting on their loan is risk of nonpayment or default. Additional risks include interest rate changes, renegotiation potential, delayed payments, industry changes, and personal employment/promotion.

You Are the Analyst

All corporations wish to minimize expenses. When net income increases due to decreases in expenditures, this is generally good news. Nevertheless, our analysis must examine the source of the expenditure decreases *and* assess its potential ramifications. In the case of California Technology, our analysis reveals a less than comfortable situation. Since most R&D outlays are expensed as incurred, we know that each dollar decrease in R&D outlays increases current net income by a dollar. But since R&D is the essence of a high technology corporation, our analysis of California Technology is troubling. Unless R&D costs have generally fallen in the industry (which is unlikely), California Technology's decrease in R&D expenditures hints at a less than optimistic future. While short-term income rises from decreases in R&D outlays, long-run income is likely to suffer.

EXHIBIT 6.9 Effects of Various Accounting Principles on Income

RIVAL MANUFACTURING COMPANY
Consolidated Statement of Income
For Year Ended 20xx

	Method A	*Method B*
Net sales	$ 365,800,000	$ 365,800,000
Cost of goods sold (1) (2) (3) (4) (5)	(276,976,200)	(274,350,000)
Gross profit	$ 88,823,800	$ 91,450,000
Selling, general, and administrative expenses (5) (6)	(51,926,000)	(42,700,000)
	$ 36,897,800	$ 48,750,000
Other income (expenses):		
Interest expenses	(3,085,000)	(3,095,000)
Net income—subsidiaries	1,538,000	1,460,000
Amortization of goodwill (7)	(390,000)	(170,000)
Miscellaneous expenses	(269,000)	(229,000)
Income before taxes	$ 34,691,800	$ 46,716,000
Taxes:		
Income taxes—deferred	(556,000)	(850,000)
Income taxes—current	(13,906,500)	(18,639,500)
Net income	$ 20,229,300	$ 27,226,500
Basic earnings per share	$6.98	$9.39

Explanations:

(1) Inventories:
A uses last-in, first-out
B uses first-in, first out
} Difference = $1,780,000

(2) Administrative costs:
A includes some administrative costs as period costs
B includes some administrative costs as inventory costs
} Difference = $88,000

(3) Depreciation:
A uses sum of the years' digits
B uses straight line
} Difference = $384,200

(4) Useful lives of assets:
A uses conservative assumption—8 years (average)
B uses liberal assumption—14 years (average)
} Difference = $346,000

(5) Pension costs:
A uses realistic assumptions for rates of return on assets and future inflation
B uses less realistic assumptions for rates of return on assets and future inflation
} Difference = $78,000

(6) Executive compensations:
A compensates executives with cash bonuses
B compensates executives with stock options
} Difference = $840,000

(7) Goodwill from acquisition:
A amortizes over 10 years
B amortizes over 40 years
} Difference = $220,000

Note: This is not a complete list of differences.

You Are the Supplier

Your credit assessment of Chicago Construction is likely positive. While the company's extraordinary loss is real, it is not recurring. This implies the 23 percent increase in net income is more representative of the ongoing business activities of Chicago Construction, and not the 12 percent decrease after the extraordinary loss. You must also assess the extent to which the fire loss is extraordinary. That is, this loss might be more than what extraordinary implies, or it might signal a new risk exposure for Chicago Construction. Nevertheless, on the information provided, the credit terms should be at least as good and perhaps better in the coming year.

QUESTIONS

6–1. Explain why our analysis attaches great importance to evaluation of the income statement.

6–2. Describe what conditions are usually required before revenue is considered realized.

6–3. Identify what conditions are usually required before a sale with "right of return" is recognized as a sale and the resulting receivable is recognized as an asset.

6–4. An ability to estimate future returns (when right of return exists) is an important consideration. Identify factors impairing the ability to predict future returns.

6–5. Explain how accounting practice defines a product financing arrangement.

6–6. Distinguish between the two major methods used to account for revenue under long-term contracts.

6–7. Describe aspects of revenue recognition we must be especially alert to in our analysis.

6–8. Distinguish between variable, semivariable, and fixed expenses.

6–9. Depreciation accounting is imperfect for our analysis purposes. Comment on the following assertion:

> Our analysis cannot accept the depreciation figure unquestioningly. We must try to find the age and efficiency of plant assets. We can obtain help by comparing depreciation, current and accrued, with gross plant, and by comparisons among similar companies. We still cannot adjust earnings with the precision an accountant needs to balance the books, but our analysis doesn't need that much precision.

6–10. Identify some analytical tools used in evaluating depreciation expense. Explain why they are useful.

6–11. Why is the expected return on pension plan assets treated as a *reduction* of periodic pension cost?

6–12. In what ways do pension accounting methods serve to smooth pension expense?

6–13. In what ways can management exercise latitude over the amount of pension expense recorded?

6–14. Where do pension costs appear in the financial statements of a company?

6–15. Identify the aspects of pension accounting retained in the accounting for postretirement employee benefits.

6–16. Explain why estimation for postretirement costs is more difficult than for pension costs.

6–17. How is compensation granted by means of stock options measured? Does accounting practice require realistic recognition of the compensation cost inherent in stock options granted?

6–18 Discuss the standards that govern R&D costs as stipulated in accounting practice. What are the disclosure requirements?

6–19. What information does our analysis need regarding R&D outlays, especially in light of the limited disclosure requirements in practice?

6–20. To what aspects of the valuation and the amortization of goodwill must our analysis be alert?

6–21. Contrast the computation of total interest costs of a bond issue with warrants attached to an issue of convertible debt.

6–22 *a.* What is the main provision of accounting for capitalization of interest, and what are its objectives?

b. How is interest to be capitalized computed and how is the rate to be used ascertained?

c. What restrictions to capitalization are imposed in practice and when does the capitalization period begin?

6–23. Net income computed on the basis of financial reporting often differs from taxable income due to permanent differences. What are permanent differences and how do they arise?

6–24. What factors cause the effective tax rate to differ from the statutory rate?

6–25. What are the main requirements of accounting for income taxes?

6–26. List four circumstances giving rise to temporary differences between financial reporting and tax income.

6–27. What are the disclosure requirements of accounting for income taxes?

6–28. Name at least one flaw to which tax allocation procedures are subject.

6–29. How does accounting practice define an *extraordinary* item? Give three examples of such items.

6–30. What conditions are necessary before an item qualifies as a prior period adjustment?

6–31. In the debate on the treatment of extraordinary items, what should be our analysis' main interest?

6–32. Why is it impossible to arrive at an absolutely "precise" measure of periodic net income?

6–33. What are some types of methods by which income can be distorted?

6–34. For each of the three items below explain:
a. Two acceptable accounting methods for corporate reporting purposes.
b. How each of these two acceptable accounting methods affect current period earnings.
(1) Depreciation.
(2) Inventory.
(3) Installment sales.

(CFA Adapted)

6–35. Accounting practice distinguishes among different types of accounting changes. What are these accounting changes?

EXERCISES

Exercise 6–1
Analytical Measures of Plant Assets

Refer to the financial statements of Quaker Oats Company in Supplement A.

Required:

a. Compute the following analytical measures for Quaker Oats for Years 10 aand 11:
1. Average total life span of plant and equipment.
2. Average age of plant and equipment.
3. Average remaining life of plant and equipment.

b. Discuss the importance of these ratios for analysis of Quaker Oats.

Exercise 6–2
Analytical Measures of Plant Assets

Refer to the financial statements of Campbell Soup Company in Supplement A.

Required:

a. Compute the following analytical measures for Cambell Soup for Years 10 and 11:
1. Average total life span of plant and equipment.
2. Average age of plant and equipment.
3. Average remaining life of plant and equipment.

b. Discuss the importance of these ratios for analysis of Campbell Soup.

Exercise 6–3

Analysis of Revenue Recognition Timing

Revenue is usually recognized at the point of sale. Under special circumstances, moments other than the point of sale are used for timing of revenue recognition.

Required:

a. Why is point of sale usually used as the basis for the timing of revenue recognition?

b. Disregarding special circumstances when bases other than the point of sale are used, discuss the merits of both of the following objections to the sale basis of revenue recognition:

1. It is too conservative because revenue is earned throughout the entire process of production.
2. It is too liberal because accounts receivable do not represent disposable funds, sales returns and allowances can occur, and collection and bad debt expenses can be incurred in a later period.

c. Revenue can be recognized (1) during production and (2) when cash is received. For each of these two bases of timing revenue recognition, give an example of the circumstances where it is properly used and discuss the accounting merits of its use in lieu of the sales basis.

(AICPA Adapted)

Exercise 6–4

Analyzing Percentage-of-Completion Results

The Michael Company accounts for a long-term construction contract using the percentage-of-completion method. It is a four-year contract currently in its second year. Recent estimates of total contract costs indicate the contract will be completed at a profit to Michael Company.

Required:

a. What theoretical justification is there for Michael Company's use of the percentage-of-completion method?

b. How are progress billings accounted for? Include in your discussion the classification of progress billings in the Michael Company financial statements.

c. How is income recognized in the second year of the four-year contract using the cost-to-cost method of determining percentage of completion?

d. What is the effect on earnings in the second year of the four-year contract when using the percentage-of-completion method instead of the completed-contract method? Discuss.

(AICPA Adapted)

Exercise 6–5

Interpreting Revenue Recognition for Leases (book and tax effects)

Crime Control Company accounts for a substantial part of its alarm system sales under the sales-type (capitalized) lease method. Under this method the company computes the present value of the total receipts it expects to get (over periods as long as eight years) from a lease and records this present value amount as sales in the first year of the lease. Justification for this accounting is that the 8-year lease extends over more than 75 percent of the 10-year useful life of the equipment. While the sales-type lease method is used for financial reporting, for tax purposes the company reports revenues only when received. Since first-year expenses of a lease are particularly large, the company reports substantial tax losses on these leases.

Required:

a. Critics maintain the sales-type lease method "front-loads" income and that reported earnings may not be received in cash for years. Comment on this criticism.

b. Will financial reporting income benefit from the company's tax benefit?

c. The company insists it can achieve earnings results similar to those achieved by the sales-type lease method by selling the lease receivables to third-party lessors or financial institutions. Comment on this assertion.

(AICPA Adapted)

Exercise 6–6

Understanding Expensing and Capitalization of Costs

Our analysis must be familiar with the concepts involved in determining earnings of a business entity. The amount of earnings reported for a business entity depends on the proper recognition of revenues and expenses for a given time period. In certain cases, costs are recognized as expenses at the time of product sale; in other situations, guidelines are applied in capitalizing costs and recognizing them as expenses in future periods.

Required:

a. Explain the rationale for recognizing costs as expenses at the time of product sale.

b. What is the rationale underlying the appropriateness of treating costs as expenses of a period instead of assigning the costs to an asset? Explain.

c. Under what circumstances is it appropriate to treat a cost as an asset instead of as an expense? Explain.

d. Certain expenses are assigned to specific accounting periods on the basis of systematic and rational allocation of asset cost. Explain the underlying rationale for recognizing expenses on this basis.

e. Identify the conditions necessary to treat a cost as a loss.

(AICPA Adapted)

Exercise 6–7

Analyzing Discontinued Operations

Refer to the financial statements of Quaker Oats in Supplement A. In note 2, Discontinued Operations, various transactions are discussed concerning the operations and disposal of certain lines of business.

Required:

a. What is your best estimate of the summary journal entry recording the disposal of discontinued operations in Year 11?

b. What are the expenses of discontinued operations in Year 10?

c. Discuss the importance of discontinued operations in analyzing Quaker Oats.

Exercise 6–8

Interpreting Deferred Income Taxes

The Primrose Company appropriately uses the deferred method for interperiod tax allocation. Primrose reports depreciation expense for certain machinery purchases for the current year using the modified accelerated cost recovery system (MACRS) for income tax purposes and the straight-line basis for financial reporting. The tax deduction is the larger amount this year. Primrose also received rent revenues in advance this year. It included these revenues in this year's taxable income. For financial reporting, rent revenues are reported as unearned revenues, a current liability.

Required:

a. What is the conceptual underpinning for deferred income taxes?

b. How does Primrose determine and account for the income tax effect for both depreciation and rent? Why?

c. How does Primrose classify the income tax effect of both depreciation and rent on its balance sheet and income statement? Why?

Exercise 6–9

Understanding Defined Benefit Pension Plans

Carson Company sponsors a defined benefit pension plan. The plan provides pension benefits determined by age, years of service, and compensation. Among the components included in the recognized net pension cost for a period are service cost, interest cost, and actual return on plan assets.

Required:

a. Identify two accounting problems resulting from the nature of the defined benefit pension plan? Why do these problems arise?

b. How does Carson determine the service cost component of the net pension cost?

c. How does Carson determine the interest cost component of the net pension cost?

d. How does Carson determine the actual return on plan assets component of the net pension cost?

(AICPA Adapted)

Exercise 6–10

Analyzing Postretirement Benefits

The accounting treatment of postretirement benefits other than pensions requires that companies offering these benefits adopt accrual accounting (similar to the requirements for pension plans)—pay-as-you-go accounting is no longer acceptable.

You are now considering an investment in one of two companies offering postretirement benefits and are concerned about their relative impacts. The two firms are of roughly equal size and have identical retiree medical plans. However, one company is more labor intensive, and has a greater ratio of retirees to workers and an older, more strongly unionized work force than the other company.

Required:

a. Compare the relative impacts of accounting for postretirement benefits on the:
   1. Size of the postretirement benefit obligation recognized by each of the two firms.
   2. Size of the postretirement benefit cost reported by each of the two firms.

b. For each of the three forms of the efficient market hypothesis, explain the effect that adoption of this accounting has on the per share price of a firm. Comment on the applicability of these implications to actual markets.

(CFA Adapted)

Exercise 6–11

Analyzing Accounting Reserves

The following quote is taken from an article (by L. Bernstein) scrutinizing use of reserves to recognize future costs and losses. That is, are these reserves valid or merely means to manage earnings?

> The growing use of reserves for future costs and losses impairs the significance of periodically reported income and should be viewed with skepticism by the analyst of financial statements. That is especially true when the reserves are established in years of heavy losses, when they are established in an arbitrary amount designed to offset an extraordinary gain, or when they otherwise appear to have as their main purpose the relieving of future income of expenses properly chargeable to it. The basic justification in accounting for the recognition of future losses stems from the doctrine of conservatism which, according to one popular application, means that one should anticipate no gains, but take all the losses one can clearly see as already incurred.

Required:

a. Discuss the merits of Bernstein's arguments and apprehensions regarding reserves.

b. Explain how this perspective can be factored into your analysis of past earnings trends, estimates of future earnings, and valuation of common stock.

(CFA Adapted)

Exercise 6–12

Interpreting Disclosures of Accounting Changes

There are various types of accounting changes requiring different types of reporting treatments. Understanding the different changes is important to our analysis.

Required:

a. Under what category of accounting changes is the change from sum-of-the-years'-digits method of depreciation to the straight-line method for previously recorded assets defined? Under what circumstances does this type of accounting change occur?

b. Under what category of accounting changes is the change in expected service life of an asset (due to new information) defined? Under what circumstances does this type of accounting change occur?

c. Regarding changes in accounting principle:

1. How does a company calculate the effect?
2. How does a company report the effect?

Note: Do not discuss earnings per share requirements.

d. Why are accounting principles, once adopted, normally continued over time?

e. What is the rationale for disclosure of a change from one accounting principle to another?

(AICPA Adapted)

PROBLEMS

Problem 6–1

Revenue Recognition (multiple choice)

I. In preparing its Year 9 adjusting entries, the Singapore Company neglected to adjust rental fees received in advance for the amount of rental fees earned during Year 9. What is the effect of this error?

a. Net income is understated, retained earnings are understated, and liabilities are overstated.

b. Net income is overstated, retained earnings are overstated, and liabilities are unaffected.

c. Net income, retained earnings, and liabilities all are understated.

II. The Sutton Construction Company entered into a contract in early Year 8 to build a tunnel for the city at a price of $11 million. The company estimated total cost of the project at $10 million and three years to complete. Actual costs incurred (on budget) and billings to the city are as follows:

	Costs Incurred	*Billings to City*
Year 8	$2,500,000	$2,000,000
Year 9	4,000,000	3,500,000
Year 10	3,500,000	5,500,000

Using the percentage-of-completion method for revenue recognition, what does Sutton Construction report for revenues and profit for Year 9?

	Revenues	*Profit*
a.	$4,000,000	$300,000
b.	$4,400,000	$400,000
c.	$3,850,000	$350,000
d.	$3,500,000	$500,000

III. Using the percentage-of-completion method in accounting for long-term projects, a company can increase reported earnings by:

a. Accelerating recognition of project expenditures.

b. Delaying recognition of project expenditures.

c. Switching to completed-contract accounting.

d. Overestimating the total cost of the project.

IV. Revenue can be recognized at the time of:

a. Production.

b. Sale.

c. Collection.

d. All of the above.

V. In October, a company shipped a new product to retailers. Which one of the following conditions would prohibit immediate recognition of revenue?

a. Terms of the sale require the company to provide extensive promotional material to retailers before December 1.

b. Retailers are not obligated to pay the purchase price until February, after their Christmas sales are collected.

c. On the basis of past performance, reliable estimates are that 20 percent of the product is returned.

d. The company is unable to enforce agreements concerning discounting of the retail sales of the product.

VI. In accounting for long-term contracts, how does the percentage-of-completion method of revenue recognition differ from the completed contract method? (Choose one answer from the second list below.)

i. Present value of income tax payments is minimized.

ii. Revenue during each period of the contract reflects more closely the results of construction activity during the period.

iii. Current status of uncompleted contracts is reported more accurately.

iv. Percentage-of-completion method relies less on estimates for the degree of completion and the extent of future costs to be incurred.

a. *i* and *ii*.

b. *i* and *iii*.

c. *ii* and *iii*.

d. *ii* and *iv*.

VII. R. Lott Corporation, which began business on January 1, Year 7, uses the installment sales method of accounting. The following data are available for December 31, Year 7, and Year 8:

	Year 7	***Year 8***
Balance of deferred gross profit on sales account:		
Year 7	$300,000	$120,000
Year 8	—	$440,000
Gross profit on sales	30%	40%

The installment accounts receivable balance at December 31, Year 8, is:

a. $1,000,000

b. $1,100,000

c. $1,400,000

d. $1,500,000

(CFA Adapted)

Problem 6–2

Alternative Depreciation Methods

Sports Biz, a profitable company, built and equipped a $2,000,000 plant brought into operation early in Year 1. Earnings of the company (before depreciation on the new plant and before income taxes) is projected at: $1,500,000 in Year 1; $2,000,000 in Year 2; $2,500,000 in Year 3; $3,000,000 in Year 4; and $3,500,000 in Year 5. The company can use straight-line, double-declining-balance, or sum-of-the-years'-digits methods of depreciation for the new plant. Assume an income tax rate of 50 percent and that the plant's useful life is 10 years (with no salvage value).

Required:

Calculate the effect each of these methods of depreciation have on:

a. Income taxes.

b. Net income.

c. Cash flow.

(CFA Adapted)

Problem 6–3

Analyzing Pension Plan Disclosures

Refer to the financial statements of Campbell Soup in Supplement A. The note Pension Plans and Retirement Benefits describes computation of pension expense, projected benefit obligation (PBO), and other elements of the pension plan (all amounts in millions).

Required:

a. What is the service cost of $22.1 for Year 11?

b. What discount rate did the company assume for Year 11? What is the effect of the change from the discount rate used in Year 10?

c. How is the "interest on projected benefit obligation" computed?

d. Actual return on assets is shown as $73.4. Does this item enter in its entirety as a component of pension cost? Why or why not?

e. Campbell shows an accumulated benefit obligation (ABO) of $714.4. What is this obligation?

f. What is the PBO and what accounts for the difference between it and the ABO?

g. Has Campbell funded its pension expense at the end of Year 11?

Problem 6–4

Analyzing Income Tax Disclosures

Refer to the financial statements of Campbell Soup Company in Supplement A.

Required:

a. Estimate the amount of depreciation expense reported on Campbell's tax returns for Years 11, 10, and 9. Use a tax rate of 34 percent.

b. Identify the amounts and sources in Years 11, 10, and 9 for the following (combine federal, foreign, and state taxes).

1. Earnings before income taxes.
2. Expected income tax at 34 percent.
3. Total income tax expense.
4. Total income tax due to governments.
5. Total income tax due and not yet paid at end of Years 11, 10, and 9.

c. Why does the effective tax rate for Years 11, 10, and 9 differ from 34 percent of income before taxes? Compute dollar amounts of permanent differences.

d. There is a small tax benefit derived from the divestiture and restructuring charges in Year 10. What are possible reasons? Can you estimate the cash outlays for these charges in Year 10?

Problem 6–5

Analyzing Income Tax Disclosures

Refer to the financial statements of Quaker Oats Company in Supplement A.

Required:

a. Estimate the amount of depreciation expense reported on Quaker Oats' tax returns for Years 11, 10, and 9. Use a tax rate of 34 percent.

b. Identify the amounts and sources in Years 11, 10, and 9 for the following (combine federal, foreign, and state taxes).

1. Earnings before income taxes.
2. Expected income tax at 34 percent.
3. Total income tax expense.
4. Total income tax due to governments.
5. Total income tax due and not yet paid at the end of Years 11, 10, and 9.

c. Why does the effective tax rate for Years 11, 10, and 9 differ from 34 percent of income before taxes? Is it likely that the effective tax rate will continue to be high in the future?

d. Is the company's effective tax rate in Year 11 different from that in Year 10? If it is, what are the main reasons?

e. What is the increase or decrease in deferred tax (current) during Years 11, 10, and 9?

f. What is the increase or decrease in deferred tax (noncurrent) during Years 11, 10, and 9?

Problem 6–6

Understanding Revenue Recognition and Deferred Income Taxes

Big-Deal Construction Company specializes in building dams. During Years 3, 4, and 5, three dams were completed. The first dam was started in Year 1 and completed in Year 3 at a profit before income taxes of $120,000. The second and third dams were started in Year 2. The second dam was completed in Year 4 at a profit before income taxes of $126,000, and the third dam was completed in Year 5 at a profit before income taxes of $150,000. The company uses percentage-of-completion accounting for financial reporting and the completed-contract method of accounting for income tax purposes. The applicable income tax rate is 50 percent for each of the Years 1 through 5. Data relating to progress toward completion of work on each dam as reported by the company's engineers are below:

Dam	*Year 1*	*Year 2*	*Year 3*	*Year 4*	*Year 5*
1	20%	60%	20%		
2		30	60	10%	
3		10	30	50	10%

Required:

For each of the five years, Year 1 through Year 5, compute:

a. Financial reporting income.

b. Taxable income.

c. Change in deferred income taxes.

Problem 6–7

Analyzing Preoperating Costs and Deferred Income Taxes

Stead Corporation is formed in Year 4 to take over the operations of a small business. This business proved very stable for Stead, as is evidenced below (in thousands):

	Year 4	*Year 5*	*Year 6*
Sales	$10,000	$10,000	$10,000
Expenses (except taxes)	9,000	9,000	9,000
Income before taxes	$ 1,000	$ 1,000	$ 1,000

Stead expends $1,400,000 on preoperating costs for a new product during Year 4. These costs are deferred for financial reporting purposes but are deducted in calculating Year 4 taxable income. During Year 5, the new product line is delayed; and in Year 6, Stead abandons the new product and charges the deferred cost of $1,400,000 to the Year 6 income statement. The applicable tax rate is 50 percent.

Required:

a. Prepare comparative income statements for Years 4, 5, and 6. Identify all tax amounts as either current or deferred.

b. List each tax item on the balance sheet for Years 4, 5, and 6 (assume all tax payments and refunds occur in the year following the reporting year).

Problem 6–8

Accounting for Income Tax Expense

Playgrounds, Inc., is granted a distribution franchise by Shady Products in Year 1. Operations are profitable until Year 4 when certain of the company's inventories are confiscated and large legal expenses are incurred. Playgrounds' tax rate is 50 percent each year (Year 4 expenses are tax deductible). Relevant income statement data are (in thousands):

	Year 1	Year 2	Year 3	Year 4	Year 5	Year 6	Year 7	Year 8
Sales	$50	$80	$120	$ 100	$200	$400	$500	$600
Cost of sales	20	30	50	300	50	120	200	250
General and administrative	10	15	20	100	20	30	40	50
Net income before tax	$20	$35	$ 50	$(300)	$130	$250	$260	$300

Required:

Prepare financial reporting journal entries to record tax expense for each of Years 1 through 8, and present comparative income statements for these years.

General Energy Company uses accepted accounting methods for pensions. Net periodic pension expense is reported as:

	Year Ended December 31, Year 6 ($ thousands)
Service cost	$586
Interest cost	129
Actual return on plan assets	(196)
Deferred loss	(48)
Amortization of transition asset	(19)
Net periodic pension expense	$452

Problem 6–9

Predicting Pension Expense

The weighted-average discount rate used in determining the actuarial present value of the projected benefit obligation (PBO) is 8.5 percent, and the assumed rate of increase in future compensation is 7.5 percent. The expected long-term rate of return on plan assets is 11.5 percent. The PBO at the end of Year 6 is $2,212,000, and the accumulated benefit obligation is $479,000. Fair value of assets is $3,238,000, and a transition asset of $581,000 remains.

Required:

Predict General Energy Company's Year 7 net periodic pension expense given a 10 percent growth in service cost, amortization of deferred loss over 30 years, and no change in the other assumed rates. Show all calculations.

(CFA Adapted)

Problem 6–10

Disclosing Discontinued Operations

The *unaudited* income statements of Disposo Corporation are reproduced below.

	Year 8	Year 7
Sales	$1,100	$900
Costs and expenses	990	860
Loss on asset disposal	10	—
Income before taxes	$ 100	$ 40
Tax expense	50	20
Net income	$ 50	$ 20

Note: On August 15, Year 8, the company decided to discontinue its Metals Division. The business was sold on December 31, Year 8, at book value except for a factory building with a book value of $25 which was sold for $15. Operations of the Metals Division were:

	Sales	Income (Loss)
Year 7	$300	$ 8
Jan. 1 to Aug. 15, Year 8	250	(3)
Aug. 16 to Dec. 31, Year 8	75	(1)

Required:

Correct Year 7 and Year 8 income statements to reflect the proper reporting of discontinued operations.

Problem 6–11

Analyzing Depreciation Effects on Rates of Return

Assume that a machine costing $300,000 and having a useful life of five years (with no salvage value) generates a yearly income before depreciation and taxes of $100,000.

Required:

Calculate the annual rate of return on this machine (using the beginning-of-year book value) under the following depreciation methods:

a. Straight line.

b. Sum of the years' digits.

CASES

Case 6–1

Analyzing Adaptec's Revenue Recognition and Depreciation

Using the 1996 annual report of Adaptec, in Supplement A, answer the following questions:

a. According to note 1, when does Adaptec recognize revenue?

b. Does Adaptec's revenue recognition method allow management discretion over the amount of revenue recorded for a year? Explain.

c. Does Adaptec's revenue recognition method allow management discretion over the amount of revenue recorded over a number of years? Explain.

d. What method of depreciation does Adaptec use for its property and equipment? What useful lives are assumed?

e. Calculate the following amounts for Adaptec's depreciable property and equipment: average total life span, average age, and average remaining life. *Hint:* Depreciation and amortization expense is reported in the statement of cash flows.

Case 6–2

Analyzing Adaptec's Costs and Expenses

Using the 1996 annual report of Adaptec in Supplement A, answer the following questions:

a. Note 6 discusses four stock plans of Adaptec. For each of the plans, identify the:

1. Name of plan.
2. Shares authorized under plan.
3. Individuals eligible under plan.
4. Purchase price of shares.

b. According to the statement of shareholders' equity, Adaptec sold common shares under various employee stock plans over each of the last three years.

1. How many shares were sold in each of fiscal years 1994 through 1996?

2. Use the disclosure in note 6 to identify the plans under which shares were sold in 1996.

c. As of March 31, 1996, how many exercisable options did Adaptec have outstanding? Other than in note 6, is the potential effect of the exercise of these options reflected in the financial statements? If so, where?

d. Adaptec's research and development (R&D) expense ranges between 10 and 13 percent of net revenues over the most recent three years.

1. What is the dollar amount of R&D expense for each of the last three years?
2. What would be the short-run impact on Adaptec's financial statements if R&D expenditures are curtailed?
3. What would be the long-run impact on Adaptec's financial statements if R&D expenditures are curtailed?

e. Over what period of time is Adaptec amortizing its goodwill?

f. Use the information in note 8 to answer the following questions regarding Adaptec's income taxes.

1. What is Adaptec's percent split between domestic and foreign income before taxes from fiscal 1994 through 1996? What is the 1996 percent split *without* the write-off of in-process technology? Comment on the significance of any trend in the split.
2. The foreign component of Adaptec's provision for income taxes increases from $1,106,000 in 1995 to $15,074,000 in 1996. Speculate on the cause of this increase.
3. Where are Adaptec's deferred tax assets reported in its balance sheet? What is the amount of the valuation allowance recognized by Adaptec? What does this allowance amount imply about future profitability?
4. What is Adaptec's effective tax rate from fiscal 1994 through 1996? Why is the effective rate lower than the statutory rate? Will the effective rate continue to be lower in the future? Why?
5. Why has Adaptec not accrued income taxes on the undistributed earnings of its Singapore subsidiary?

g. Adaptec reported a $52,313,000 write-off of acquired in-process technology in 1996. How is this amount considered for our projections of future profitability for Adaptec? Why?

Case 6–3
Understanding Depreciation Accounting

Toro Manufacturing Company is organized on January 1, Year 5. During Year 5 it uses in its reports to management the straight-line method of depreciating its plant assets. On November 8, you (as consultant) have a conference with Toro's officers to discuss the depreciation method used for income tax and financial reporting. The president of Toro suggests the use of a new method he feels is more suitable than straight line for the needs of the company during this period of predicted rapid expansion of production and capacity. Following is an example of his proposed method applied to a fixed asset with an original cost of $32,000, an estimated useful life of five years, and a salvage value of $2,000.

Year	*Years of Life Used*	*Fraction Rate*	*Depreciation Expense*	*Accumulated Depreciation at End of Year*	*Book Value at End of Year*
1	1	1/15	$ 2,000	$ 2,000	$30,000
2	2	2/15	4,000	6,000	26,000
3	3	3/15	6,000	12,000	20,000
4	4	4/15	8,000	20,000	12,000
5	5	5/15	10,000	30,000	2,000

The president favors this new method because he asserts that it:

- Increases the funds recovered in years near the end of the assets' useful lives when maintenance and replacement disbursements are high.
- Increases write-offs in later years and thereby reduces taxes.

Required:

a. What is the purpose and principle of accounting for depreciation?

b. Is the president's proposal within the scope of generally accepted accounting principles? In making your decision discuss the circumstances, if any, where the method is reasonable and those, if any, where it is not.

c. The president requests your advice on the following.
   1. Do depreciation charges recover or create cash? Explain.
   2. Assuming the Internal Revenue Service accepts the proposed depreciation method, and if it is used for both financial reporting and tax purposes, how does it affect availability of cash generated by operations?

Case 6–4

Understanding Revenue Recognition

BIKE Company starts with $3,000 cash. Its business plan is to produce bike helmets using a simple assembly process. During the first month of business, the company signs sales contracts for 1,300 units (sales price of $9 per unit), produces 1,200 units (production cost of $7 per unit), ships 1,100 units, and collected in full for 900 units. Production costs are paid at the time of production. The company has only two other costs: (1) sales commissions of 10 percent of selling price paid when the company collects from the customer, and (2) shipping costs of $0.20 per unit paid at time of shipment. Selling price and all costs have been constant per unit and are likely to remain the same.

Required:

a. Prepare comparative (side-by-side) balance sheets and income statements for the first month of BIKE Company for each of the following three alternatives:
   1. Revenue is recognized at the time of shipment.
   2. Revenue is recognized at the time of collection.
   3. Revenue is recognized at the time of production.

   Note: Net income for each of these three alternatives is (1) $990, (2) $810, and (3) $1,080, respectively.

b. The method where revenue is recognized at time of collection, known as the *installment method,* is acceptable for financial reporting in unusual and special cases. Why is BIKE Company likely to prefer this method for tax purposes?

c. Comment on the usefulness of the installment method for a credit analyst.

INTERNET ACTIVITIES

Internet 6–1

Analyzing Operating Activities

Access one of the financial statement databases available on the Internet (http://www.mhhe.com/business/accounting/wild). Retrieve current financial statements of *three* companies in different industries selected by either you or your instructor.

Required:

a. Compute the relative proportion of individual revenues, expenses, gains, and losses in a common size income statement analysis (where sales is 100%).

b. For each company, write a report describing the major similarities and differences in the
   1. income statement components.
   2. accounting methods for income recognition and measurement.

Internet 6–2

Analyzing Revenues and Gains

Access one of the financial statement databases available on the Internet (http://www.mhhe.com/business/accounting/wild). Retrieve current financial statements of a company selected by either you or your instructor.

Required:

a. Identify the company's revenue recognition method(s). What is the effect of the revenue recognition method(s) for your analysis of this company's statements?

b. Does the company's revenue recognition method allow management discretion over the amount of revenue recorded for a year? Explain.

c. Does the company's revenue recognition method allow management discretion over the amount of revenue recorded over a number of years? Explain.

d. Identify any nonoperating gains in income. How do gains effect your analysis of income?

Internet 6–3

Analyzing Expenses and Costs

Access one of the financial statement databases available on the Internet (http://www.mhhe.com/business/accounting/wild). Retrieve current financial statements of a company selected by either you or your instructor.

Required:

a. What method of depreciation is used for property, plant, and equipment? What useful lives are assumed?

b. Calculate the following amounts for the company's depreciable property, plant, and equipment: average total life span, average age, and average remaining life. *Hint:* Depreciation and amortization expense is often reported in the statement of cash flows.

c. As of the current year, how many exercisable options, if any, does the company have outstanding? Is the potential effect of the exercise of options, if any, reflected in financial statements? If so, where?

d. Identify the company's research and development (R&D) expense for the most recent two years.

1. What is the dollar amount of R&D expense for each of the past two years?
2. What is the short-run impact on financial statements if R&D expenditures are curtailed?
3. What is the long-run impact on financial statements if R&D expenditures are curtailed?

e. Over what period of time is the company amortizing intangibles?

f. Use the company's income tax information (often disclosed in notes) to answer the following:

1. What is the company's percent split between domestic and foreign income before taxes for the most recent two years? Comment on the significance of any trend in the split.
2. Identify the foreign component of the company's provision for income taxes for the most recent two years. Speculate on the cause of any change in this component.
3. Where are the company's deferred tax assets, if any, reported in the balance sheet? What is the amount of the valuation allowance, if any, recognized by the company? What does this allowance amount imply about future profitability?
4. What is the company's effective tax rate for each of the most recent two years? Why is the effective rate different from the statutory rate?

g. Did the company have any nonoperating gains or losses? If yes, how are these amounts handled for projections of future profitability?

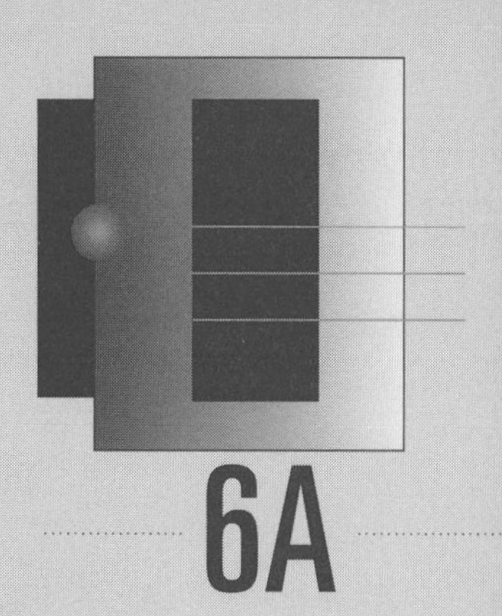

A P P E N D I X

6A

Earnings per Share: Computation and Analysis

Earnings per share (EPS) data are widely used in evaluating the operating performance and profitability of a company. This appendix describes the principles governing earnings per share computation and interpretation. A key feature in earnings per share computation is recognition of the potential impact of dilution. **Dilution** is the reduction in earnings per share (or increase in net loss per share) resulting from dilutive securities being converted into common stock, the exercise of options and warrants, or the issuance of additional shares in compliance with contracts. Since these adverse effects on earnings per share can be substantial, the earnings per share computation serves to call attention to the potentially dilutive effects of a firm's capital structure.

The computation and reporting requirements for earnings per share are in transition. For financial reports covering fiscal years ending *after* December 15, 1997 (see *SFAS 128,* "Earnings per Share"), the earnings per share computation is simpler and consistent with international accounting standards. This new requirement replaces *primary EPS* with *basic EPS.* It also requires dual presentation of basic and *diluted EPS* on income statements of companies with complex capital structures and requires a reconciliation of the numerator and denominator of basic EPS to the same figures of diluted EPS. To understand these computations and their interpretation, this appendix (1) explains simple and complex capital structures, (2) describes the various earnings per share measures, and (3) provides several case examples. Our discussion covers both the prior and new earnings per share reporting requirements.

Simple Capital Structure

A **simple capital structure** is one consisting only of common stock and nonconvertible senior securities and does not include potentially dilutive securities. For companies with simple capital structures, a single presentation of earnings per share is required and is computed as follows:

$$\text{Basic earnings per share} = \frac{\text{Net income} - \text{Preferred dividends}}{\text{Weighted average number of common shares outstanding}}$$

EXHIBIT 6A.1 Computation of Weighted-Average Number of Shares Outstanding

A. Transactions

Year 1	*Transactions in Common Stock*	*Number of Shares*
January 1	Outstanding	1,200
February 2	Stock options exercised	200
April 15	Issued a 5% stock dividend	70
August 16	Issued in pooling of interests	400
September 2	Sale for cash	300
October 18	Repurchase of treasury shares	(100)
		2,070

B. Computations

		Shares Outstanding		**Computation**
		Number	*Days*	*Number × Days*
Date of change:				
January 1		1,200		
Retroactive adjustment:				
For stock dividend (5%)		60		
Issued in pooling		400		
January 1—adjusted		1,660	32	53,120
February 2—stock option	200			
+ 5% stock dividend	10	210		
		1,870	212	396,440
September 2—sale for cash		300		
		2,170	46	99,820
October 18—repurchase		(100)		
		2,070	75	155,250
			365	704,630

Year 1 weighted-average number of shares $\frac{704,630}{365}$ = 1,930 shares

In the numerator of this computation, dividends of cumulative senior equity securities, whether earned or not, are deducted from net income or added to net loss.

The precise computation of weighted-average number of common shares is the sum of shares outstanding each day, divided by the number of days in the period. Less precise averaging methods, based on a monthly or quarterly computation where there is little change in the number of shares outstanding, are also accepted. Exhibit 6A.1 provides an example using the following rules for computing the weighted-average shares outstanding:

- Reacquired shares are excluded from date of acquisition.
- Shares sold or issued in a purchase of assets are included from date of issuance.
- Previously reported earnings per share data are adjusted retroactively for changes in outstanding shares resulting from stock splits or stock dividends.

Shares issued in a pooling of interests are included in the computation of earnings per share as of the beginning of all periods presented. This is because under pooling, the merged companies are assumed to be combined since their respective inceptions. For business purchases, earnings per share reflect new shares issued only from date of acquisition. Stock dividends are also adjusted retroactively. Issuances of stock (as a result of stock options or sale) and repurchases of stock all involve changes in entity resources and enter the computation only from the date of the transaction.

Basic earnings per common share is used only when the company has a simple capital structure and no agreements exist for contingent issuances of common stock (sometimes referred to as *potential common shares*). Earnings per share requirements prior to December 15, 1997 dictated a simple presentation of *primary* earnings per share if the total dilution from dilutive securities or other provisions did not exceed 3 percent. That is, if the adjusted net income divided by total shares (including dilutive securities) yields an earnings per share number not less than 97 percent of the per share number obtained without considering dilutive securities, a primary earnings per share computation was sufficient.

Complex Capital Structure

A company is viewed as having a **complex capital structure** if it has outstanding potentially dilutive securities like convertible securities, options, warrants, or other stock issue agreements. More than 25% of publicly traded companies have potentially dilutive securities. The relation between basic and diluted earnings per share for these companies is depicted as:

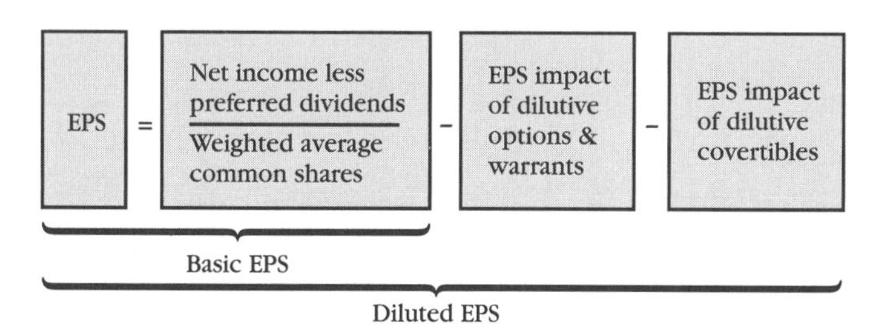

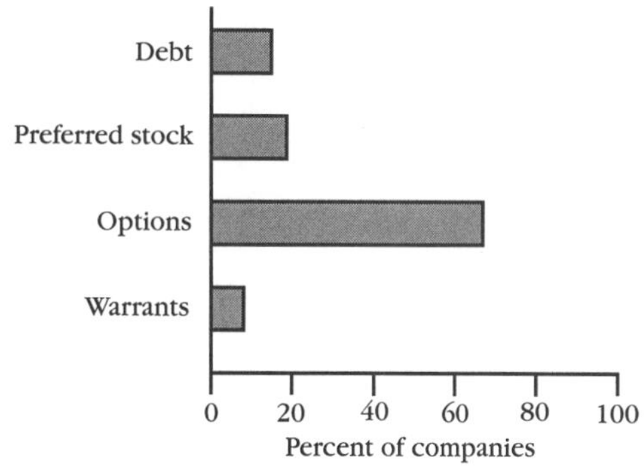

Source: *Accounting Trends & Techniques.*

This dual presentation warns users of the potential for dilution in earnings per share. Both earnings per share figures are reported with equal prominence on income statements of companies with complex capital structures. These companies need not report diluted earnings per share when potential common shares are antidilutive. **Antidilutive securities** are those that increase earnings per share when exercised or converted. Under the prior requirements for "primary and fully diluted" EPS, a company with a complex capital structure must have a dual presentation of earnings per share if the aggregate dilutive effect of convertible and other securities is more than 3 percent.

Basic and Primary Earnings per Share

This section describes the computation of both basic (the new requirement) and primary (the prior requirement) earnings per share figures.

Basic Earnings per Share

The basic earnings per share computation for companies with complex capital structures is identical to that for companies with simple capital structures. The basic earnings per share computation differs from the primary earnings per share computation (see below) in that *common stock equivalents* are not added to the denominator of basic EPS.

Primary Earnings per Share

Computation of primary earnings per share for companies with complex capital structures requires us to determine **common stock equivalents (CSEs).** A CSE denotes a security deriving its primary value from its common stock characteristics or conversion privileges. It is a security that because of the terms or circumstances attached to it is substantively equivalent to common stock. Examples of CSEs include:

EXHIBIT 6A.2 EPS Computations

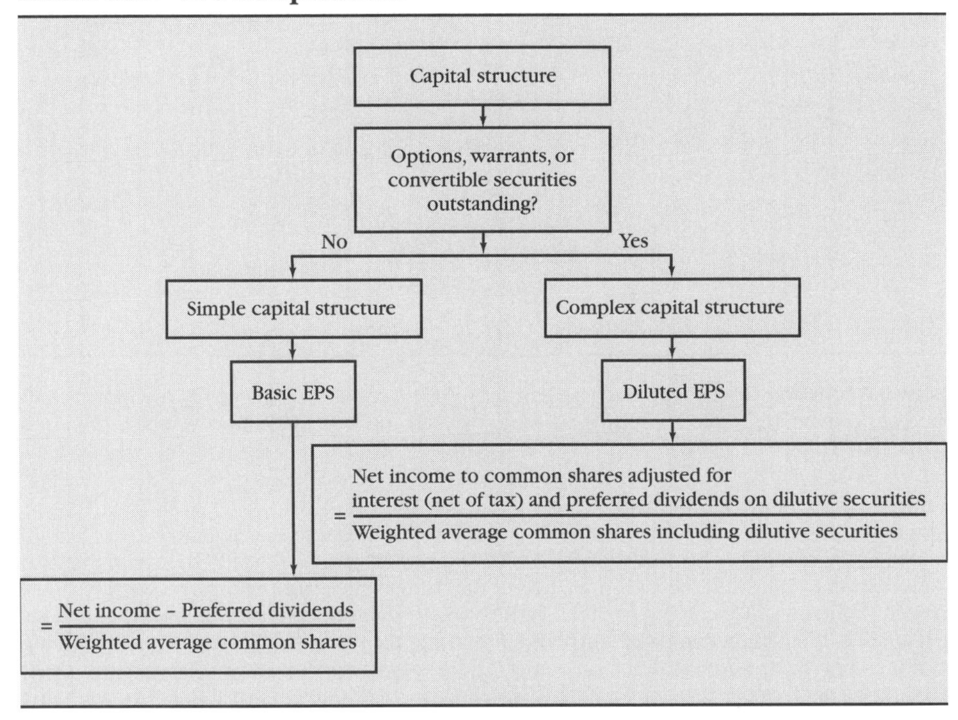

- *Stock options and warrants* (including stock purchase contracts) are always considered CSEs.
- *Convertible debt and convertible preferred stocks* are CSEs if they have an effective yield of less than $66\frac{2}{3}$ percent of the average Aa corporate bond yield at the time of issuance.
- *Participating securities and two-class common stocks* are CSEs if their participation features enable their holders to share in the earnings potential of the issuing corporation on substantially the same basis as common stock.
- *Contingent shares.* If shares are issuable in the future upon the mere passage of time, they are considered as outstanding for purposes of computing earnings per share.
- *Securities of subsidiaries* are often considered common stock equivalents and conversion or exercise assumed for computing consolidated or parent company earnings per share.

If CSEs with a dilutive effect exist, then primary earnings per share are based on the weighted-average number of shares of common stock and CSEs. This computation is also based on the assumption that convertible securities that are CSEs were converted at the beginning of the period (or at time of issuance, if later), and this requires adding back to net income any deductions for interest or dividends (net of tax) related to these securities. This procedure is referred to as the "if converted" method. It is computed as numerator divided by denominator, where

$$\frac{\text{Net income for the period} - \text{Preferred dividends applicable to preferred stock not considered CSEs} + \text{Tax-adjusted interest on convertible bonds considered CSEs}}{\text{Average shares outstanding} + \text{Number of common shares into which convertible preferred shares and convertible bonds (deemed to be CSEs) are convertible, adjusted for proportion of time outstanding}}$$

Diluted and Fully Diluted Earnings per Share

This section describes the computation of both diluted (the new requirement) and fully diluted (the prior requirement) earnings per share figures. Companies with complex capital structures report both basic and diluted EPS figures under the new requirements (or primary and fully diluted EPS under prior requirements). Exhibit 6A.2 portrays the computation of earnings per share for complex capital structures under the new requirements. Diluted EPS reflects *all*

EXHIBIT 6A.3 Treasury Stock Method Illustrated

Data for Illustrations:

1. 1,000,000 common shares outstanding (no change during year).
2. $80 average market price for the common stock for the year.
3. 100,000 warrants outstanding exercisable at $48.

Computation of Shares:

100,000	shares issuable on exercise of warrants (proceeds $4,800,000)
(60,000)	shares acquirable with $4,800,000 proceeds (at $80 per share)
40,000	CSEs
1,000,000	common shares
1,040,000	shares used for computing primary EPS

potential common shares that decrease earnings per share. We consider only the more familiar types of potentially dilutive securities—stock options and warrants, and convertible preferred stocks and bonds.

Stock Options and Warrants

Stock options and **warrants** are instruments entitling the holder to buy an amount (or fraction) of common shares at a specific price for a specified period of time (usually shorter in the case of options than with warrants). Computation of the dilutive effects of options and warrants must recognize the benefits accruing from the cash or "boot" that the converter of these instruments must pay to the issuing company. This gives rise to the **treasury stock method** of computing earnings per share when options, warrants, and their equivalents exist. The treasury stock method recognizes the use of proceeds from exercise of options and warrants in computing earnings per share. It assumes proceeds are used to purchase common stock at current market prices. Specifically, the treasury stock method of computing earnings per share is applied to options and warrants as follows: Earnings per share data are computed (1) as if options and warrants are exercised at the beginning of the period (or at time of issuance, if later), and (2) as if the funds obtained are used to purchase common stock at the *average* market price during the period. (Note: With primary EPS, the exercise is not reflected in earnings per share data unless the market price of the common stock obtainable is in excess of the exercise price for substantially all of three consecutive months, ending with the last month of the period where earnings per share are reported.) An example of the treasury stock method is shown in Exhibit 6A.3.

Exception to Treasury Stock Method. Warrants or debt indentures may permit or require special uses of funds when they are exercised. Examples are when (1) debt is permitted or required as tender toward the exercise price, (2) proceeds of exercise are required to retire debt, and (3) convertible securities require cash payments upon conversion. In these cases an **if converted method** assuming conversion on exercise at the beginning of the period is applied as if retirement or conversion of the securities had occurred and as if any excess proceeds are applied to the purchase of common stock under the treasury stock method.

Provisions Concerning Antidilution. **Antidilution** is an increase in earnings per share from assumed exercise of options and warrants. While stock options and warrants (and their equivalents) and stock purchase contracts are always considered potential common shares, they do not enter into earnings per share calculations unless the average market price of common stock exceeds the exercise price of the option or warrant for the reporting period.

Convertible Securities

Convertible bonds and convertible preferred stocks are instruments entitling the holder to exchange these securities for common shares. Diluted (and fully diluted) earnings per share are computed to reflect the maximum dilution from conversion of all convertible securities, provided they are dilutive. All conversions are assumed to take place at the beginning of the period (or at the time of issuance if the securities are issued during the period). Any interest charges applicable to convertible securities and nondiscretionary adjustments made to items based on net income or income before taxes—such as profit-sharing expense, certain royalties, investment credit—or preferred dividends applicable to the convertible securities are taken into account in determining the balance of income applicable to common stock. Accordingly, the numerator in the diluted earnings per share computation increases by any interest charges (net of tax) and the denominator increases by the number of additional shares assumed issued at conversion.

Computation of Diluted and Fully Diluted EPS

Both diluted and fully diluted earnings per share are designed to show the maximum potential dilution of current earnings per share on a prospective basis. To illustrate how these figures are computed, we consider Plex Corporation which has 1,000,000 shares of class A preferred stock and 1,500,000 shares of class B preferred stock outstanding. Both stock issues are convertible into common on a share-for-share basis. Plex also has two million shares of common outstanding. Class A preferred (which is a CSE) returns a $1.80 dividend; and class B preferred (not a CSE) carries a $1 dividend. Net income before either preferred stock dividend is $7,300,000. The basic (and primary) earnings per share figure of $2.00 ($1.93) for Plex Corporation is computed as follows:

	Shares	*Net Income*	*EPS*
Net income		$ 7,300,000	
Shares outstanding	2,000,000		
$1.80 preferred dividend		(1,800,000)	
$1.00 preferred dividend		(1,500,000)	
	2,000,000	4,000,000	
Basic EPS			$2.00
Assume conversion of CSE class A preferred	1,000,000	1,800,000	
	3,000,000	5,800,000	
Primary EPS			$1.93
Assume conversion of non-CSE class B preferred	1,500,000	1,500,000	
	4,500,000	$ 7,300,000	
Diluted EPS (beginning with primary EPS)			$1.62

Since the intent of diluted and fully diluted earnings per share is to reveal the maximum dilution conceivable, companies prepare a ranking of the impact of each convertible preferred stock (and convertible bond when applicable) on diluted earnings per share. Each dilutive convertible security is considered in a sequential order based on their ranking (most dilutive to least). When a dilutive convertible security does not decrease diluted earnings per share, it (and all lesser ranked dilutive securities) is not used in computing diluted earnings per share. Plex Corp. illustrates this situation as follows:

	Shares	*Net Income*	*EPS*
Shares outstanding and income after dividends	2,000,000	$4,000,000	
Assume conversion of non-CSE class B preferred	1,500,000	1,500,000	
	3,500,000	$5,500,000	
Diluted EPS—(beginning with basic EPS)			$1.57

If class A preferred stock is assumed converted, then diluted earnings per share increases to $1.62. This is because while class A preferred is dilutive for purposes of computing primary earnings per share, it is antidilutive for purposes of computing diluted and fully diluted earnings per share. Computations should exclude securities whose conversion, exercise, or other contingent issuance have the effect of increasing earnings per share. Accordingly Plex Corp. reports diluted (or fully diluted) earnings per share of $1.57, and not $1.62.

Fully Diluted EPS Exception to Treasury Stock Method. If the number of shares of common stock obtainable upon exercise of outstanding options and warrants in the aggregate exceeds 20 percent of the number of common shares outstanding at the end of the period, the treasury stock method is modified for fully diluted EPS. In these cases, all options and warrants are assumed to be exercised and the aggregate proceeds are applied in two steps: (1) as if the funds obtained are first applied to the repurchase of outstanding common shares at the average market price during the period (treasury stock method) but not exceeding 20 percent of the outstanding shares; and then (2) as if the balance of the funds are applied first to reduce any short-term or long-term borrowings and any remaining funds are invested in U.S. government securities or commercial paper, with appropriate recognition of any income tax effect. The results of steps (1) and (2) in this computation (whether dilutive or antidilutive) are aggregated, and if the net effect is dilutive, it enters into the earnings per share computation.

Comprehensive Earnings per Share Cases

This section illustrates several EPS computations and analyses.

EPS for Complex Capital Structures

Complex Corporation experienced the following changes in its capital structure during Year 6:

	Number of Shares
Common stock:	
Balance on January 1	500,000
April 1—issued in conversion of preferred stock	200,000
July 1—sold for cash	100,000
Balance on December 31	800,000
Preferred stock:	
$10 par 8 percent, each convertible into two common shares, issued in Year 3 at $12 per share when the average Aa corporate bond yield was 7½ percent (dividend requirement on outstanding shares is $80,000)	
Outstanding, January 1, Year 6	175,000
Converted on April 1, Year 6 (into 200,000 common)	100,000
Outstanding since April 1, Year 6 (and year-end)	75,000
Subordinated debentures:	
$800,000 of 4 percent debentures issued at par in year 4 when the average Aa corporate bond yield was 9 percent. The debentures are convertible into 12,000 shares of common and are all outstanding.	
Warrants:	
100,000 warrants issued in Year 4, each to purchase one common share at $80 per share until December 31, Year 9. So far none have been exercised.	
Additional information:	

	Average for Quarter	*End of Quarter*
Market prices of common stock for Year 6:		
First quarter	$78	$79
Second quarter	80	85
Third quarter	90	89
Fourth quarter	88	84

Preferred dividends paid in Year 6:	
First quarter	$ 35,000
Second quarter	15,000
Third quarter	15,000
Fourth quarter	15,000
Income before extraordinary item in Year 6	1,200,000
Extraordinary item—condemnation gain (net of tax effect)	300,000
Income tax rate	50%

Steps in computing EPS of the Complex Corporation for Year 6 are:

1. Compute weighted-average number of common shares outstanding in Year 6:

	Shares Outstanding	Number of Months	Shares × Months
January 1	500,000	3	1,500,000
April 1	700,000	3	2,100,000
July 1	800,000	6	4,800,000
		12	8,400,000

Weighted average: $\frac{8,400,000}{12} = 700,000$ shares

1a. Identify common stock equivalents (CSEs)—applicable to primary and fully diluted EPS:

Security	(A) Effective Yield at Issuance	(B) Two-Thirds of Average Aa Corporate Bond Rate at Date of Issuance	Classification and Elaboration
8% convertible preferred	$\frac{\$0.80}{\$12} = 6.67\%$	$\frac{2}{3}$ of $7\frac{1}{2}\% = 5\%$	Not a CSE because (A) exceeds (B)
4% subordinated debentures	4% (issued at par)	$\frac{2}{3}$ of $9\% = 6\%$	CSE because (B) exceeds (A)
Warrants	—	—	Warrants are considered a CSE

2. Compute basic EPS:

	Shares	Earnings
Income before extraordinary item		$1,200,000
Dividend requirements of outstanding preferred stock (paid in Year 6)		80,000
Income available for common before extraordinary item		1,120,000
Extraordinary item (net of tax)		300,000
Net income		820,000
Weighted average of common shares outstanding (see computation)	700,000	
Totals	700,000	1,120,000
Basic EPS		
Income before extraordinary item ($1,120,000/700,000)	$1.60	
Extraordinary item ($300,000/700,000)	0.43	
Net income ($820,000/700,000)	1.17	

2a. Compute primary EPS:

	Shares	Earnings
Income before extraordinary item		$1,200,000
Dividend requirements of outstanding preferred (paid in Year 6)		80,000
Income available for common shares before extrordinary item		1,120,000
Weighted average of common shares outstanding (see computation)	700,000	
Assumed conversion of 4% subordinated debentures	12,000	
Add back to income interest:		

4% of $800,000	$32,000			
Less tax effect at 50%	16,000			16,000
Effect of assumed exercise of warrants:				
1st and 2nd quarters	Assumed exercise of warrants should not be reflected until market price of common has been in excess of exercise price for substantially all of three consecutive months (a one-time test).			
3rd quarter	In this quarter the above condition was fulfilled.			
	Total shares issuable on exercise	100,000		
	$\frac{\text{Proceeds}}{\text{Average price for quarter}} = \frac{\$8{,}000{,}000}{\$90}$	88,889		
	Incremental shares for quarter	11,111		
4th quarter	Total shares available for exercise	100,000		
	$\frac{\text{Proceeds}}{\text{Average price for quarter}} = \frac{\$8{,}000{,}000}{\$88}$	90,909		
	Incremental shares for quarter	9,091		
	Total incremental shares for all quarters	20,202		
	20,202 ÷ 4		5,050	
Totals			717,050	$1,136,000

Primary EPS

Before extraordinary item ($1,136,000/717,050)	$1.58
Extraordinary item ($300,000/717,050)	0.42
Net income ($1,436,000/717,050	$2.00

3. Compute diluted EPS (identical to fully diluted EPS for Complex Corp.):

		Shares	*Earnings*
Income before extraordinary item			$1,200,000
Weighted average of common shares (as above)		700,000	
Add: Assumed conversion of 4% debentures[(a)]			
Assumed conversion of 8% convertible preferred (175,000 × 2)	350,000		
Less: Converted preferred already included in 700,000 weighted-average (200,000 × ¾ year)	150,000	200,000[(b)]	—
Warrants: Assumed exercise:			
Total shares available for exercise	100,000		
$\frac{\text{Proceeds}}{\text{Average market price}} = \frac{100{,}000 \times \$80^{(c)}}{\$84} =$	95,238		
Incremental shares		4,762	
		904,762	$1,200,000

Diluted EPS

Income before extraordinary item ($1,120,000/904,762)	$1.33
Extraordinary item ($300,000/904,762)	$0.33
Net income ($1,500,000/904,762)	$1.66

[(a)] These debentures are excluded from this computation because they are antidilutive (i.e., they result in an EPS increment of $1.33). Interest requirement is $32,000 (4 percent of 800,000) less 50% tax = $16,000. $16,000 ÷ 12,000 shares = $1.33. Thus, the inclusion of the debentures in the computation would increase EPS.

[(b)] Alternative proof:

	Shares	*Months*	*Shares × Months*
175,000 preferred × 2 outstanding 1st Q	350,000	3	1,050,000
75,000 preferred × 2 outstanding 3rd Q	150,000	9	1,350,000
			2,400,000 ÷ 12 = 200,000

[(c)] Note that a computation using individual quarters would have resulted in *fewer* incremental shares.

EPS for Business Combinations

This section illustrates EPS computations and analyses for business combinations.

Pooling of Interests

Assume on July 1, Year 2, Company A and Company B merged to form Company C. The transaction is accounted for as a pooling of interests. The following financial data illustrate the computation of earnings per share for Company C:

		Company A	*Company B*
Net income January 1 to June 30, Year 2		$100,000	$150,000
Outstanding shares of common stock at June 30, Year 2		20,000	8,000
Shares sold to public April 1, Year 2		10,000	
		Company C	
Net income July 1 to December 31, Year 2		$325,000	
Common shares issued for acquisition of:			
Company A		200,000	
Company B		400,000	
Computation:			
Net income ($100,000 + $150,000 + $325,000)		$575,000	
Average shares outstanding during year, using equivalent shares for pooled companies:			
Company A:			
100,000* × 3 months	300,000		
200,000† × 3 months	600,000		
Company B:			
400,000‡ × 6	2,400,000		
Company C:			
600,000 × 6	3,600,000		
	6,900,000		
Weighted-average (6,900,000 ÷ 12)	575,000		
Net income per weighted-average number of common stock outstanding during the year (equivalent shares used for pooled companies)		$1.00	

*10,000 × 10 (exchange ratio).
†20,000 × 10 (exchange ratio).
‡8,00 × 50 (exchange ratio)

Purchase

Assume at December 31, Year 2, Company X has outstanding 120,000 shares of common stock. On October 1, Year 2, Company X had issued 30,000 shares of its own common stock for another company. This transaction is accounted for as a purchase. Net income for Year 2 is $292,500. Earnings per share for Company X are computed as follows:

9 months × 90,000 shares outstanding		810,000
3 months × 120,000 shares outstanding		360,000
		1,170,000
Average shares (1,170,000/12)	97,500	
Net income per weighted-average number of common stock outstanding during the year ($292,500/97,500)		$3.00

EPS Restated for Prior Years

Whenever comparative earnings per share figures are reported for several prior years, they are restated to reflect changes in the number of common shares outstanding due to stock dividends, stock splits, issuance of shares in an acquisition accounted under the pooling of interests method, and prior period adjustments of net income. However, issuances of stock for cash, or in an acquisition or repurchase of stock, do not require adjustment because the earnings generated are deemed affected by the new resources acquired or relinquished in exchange for the shares. To illustrate computations for earnings per share when restatement is necessary we look at the case of Stock Splitters, Inc. Reported earnings per share figures for Stock Splitters, Inc., for the most recent six years are reproduced below:

	Year 9	*Year 8*	*Year 7*	*Year 6*	*Year 5*	*Year 4*
EPS	$5	$5	$9	$6	$3	$4

Stock Splitters, Inc., experienced the following changes in capitalization at the beginning of each of the years reported:

Year 5	100% stock dividend paid
Year 6	500,000 shares of common stock issued for cash
Year 7	200,000 shares of common stock issued on conversion of bonds
Year 8	3-for-1 stock split
Year 9	50% stock dividend paid

Notice that changes in capitalization are accounted for in their respective years' earnings per share computations (e.g., the 50% stock dividend occurring in Year 9 is already included in Year 9's earnings per share). However, all prior years' computations must be adjusted for changes (e.g., years prior to Year 9 reported earnings per share figures are multiplied by [100%/150%]). Computations for restatement of prior years' reported earnings per share figures are shown below:

Event		*Reported EPS*	*Adjustment*	*Adjusted EPS*
50% stock dividend	Year 9	$5.00	None	$5.00
3-for-1 stock split	Year 8	5.00	(100/150)	3.33
—	Year 7	9.00	(100/300)(100/150)	2.00
—	Year 6	6.00	(100/300)(100/150)	1.33
100% stock dividend	Year 5	3.00	(100/300)(100/150)	0.67
—	Year 4	4.00	(100/200)(100/300)(100/150)	0.44

EPS Disclosures in Financial Statements

Complex capital structures require disclosures either on the balance sheet or in its notes. Financial statements must include a description sufficient to explain the pertinent rights and privileges of the various securities outstanding. Specifically, earnings per share disclosure is required for:

- Basis on which the earnings per share figures are calculated—identifying the securities entering into computations.
- All assumptions and resulting adjustments in computations.
- Number of shares issued on conversion, exercise, and so forth, during the most recent year.

Exhibit 6A.4 is a comprehensive disclosure of an income statement. Notice the order of items—certain items (extraordinary) seldom occur.

EXHIBIT 6A.4 Income Statement Presentation

Net sales		$ x
Cost of sales		− x
Gross profit		$ x
Selling, general, and administrative		− x
Income from operations		$ x
Other revenues and gains		+ x
Other expenses and losses		− x
Income from continuing operations before income taxes		$ x
Income taxes		− x
Income from continuing operations		$ x
Discontinued operations:		
Income (loss) from operations of discontinued segment, net of tax	$x	
Income (loss) on disposal of discontinued segment, net of tax	x	+/−x
Extraordinary gain (loss), net of tax		+/−x
Cumulative effect of change in accounting principle, net of tax		+/−x
Net income		$ x
Per share of common stock:		
Income from continuing operations		$ #
Income (loss) from operations of discontinued segment, net of tax		#
Income (loss) on disposal of discontinued segment, net of tax		#
Income before extraordinary item and cumulative effect		$ #
Extraordinary item, net of tax		#
Cumulative effect of change in accounting principle, net of tax		#
Net income		$ #

Analysis Implications of Earnings per Share

Earnings per share requirements in accounting are often criticized because they extend to areas outside the usual realm of accountancy. Accounting for earnings per share relies on pro forma presentations influenced in large measure by market fluctuations. It also involves itself with areas of financial statement analysis. Whatever the merit of these criticisms, our analysis must welcome this initiative by the accounting profession. Factors comprising computation of earnings per share are varied and require considerable proprietary data, so it is appropriate this responsibility be placed on management and its auditors. Our analysis must, however, bring a thorough understanding of the bases on which earnings per share are computed so that we can draw reliable inferences.

The revised earnings per share requirements (for reporting periods ending after December 15, 1997) address several of the weaknesses and inconsistencies in previous requirements.

- Arbitrary benchmarks such as the 20 percent treasury stock repurchase cutoff and the $66\frac{2}{3}$ percent of the average Aa corporate bond rate test are eliminated.
- Under prior rules, determination of whether a security is a CSE or not is made only at the time of issuance. It is possible a security not originally a CSE is later recognized as one in the marketplace. Yet its status for computation of earnings per share did not change to recognize this reality. Elimination of CSEs from basic earnings per share avoids this problem.
- New rules require a reconciliation of the numerators and denominators of basic and diluted earnings per share computations. This entails disclosure of the individual income and share amount effects of all securities that affect earnings per share. Such disclosure provides us additional insights into companies' complex capital structures.

Despite these improvements in earnings per share computations and disclosures, serious barriers to effective analysis remain:

- While computation of basic earnings per share is simpler and less arbitrary than primary earnings per share, it ignores the potential effects of dilution from options and warrants. Consequently, the new rules "boost" the earnings per share of certain companies by 10 to 20 percent or more, while potentially obscuring the risk from issuances of new shares. Our analysis must study diluted earnings per share to avoid this pitfall.
- There are inconsistencies in treating certain securities as the equivalent of common stock for computing earnings per share while not considering them as part of shareholders' equity. Consequently, it is difficult in our analysis to effectively link reported earnings per share with the debt-leverage position pertaining to those earnings.
- The dilutive effects of options and warrants depend on the company's common stock price. This can yield a "circular effect," in that reporting of earnings per share can influence stock prices that, in turn, influence earnings per share. Hence, reported earnings per share can be affected by stock price and not solely reflect the economic fundamentals of the company. This also suggests that our projection of reported earnings per share consider not only future earnings but also future stock prices.

QUESTIONS

6A–1. Why is a thorough understanding of the principles governing computation of EPS important to our analysis?

6A–2. Discuss uses of EPS and reasons or objectives for the current method of reporting EPS.

6A–3. What is the purpose in reporting diluted EPS?

6A–4. How do cumulative dividends on preferred stock affect the EPS computation for a company with a loss?

6A–5. At the end of the year, a company has a simple capital structure consisting only of common stock, as all its preferred stock is converted into common shares during the year. Is a computation of diluted EPS required?

6A–6. If a warrant is not exercisable until seven years after the end of the current reporting period, is it excluded from the computation of diluted EPS?

6A–7. How does the payment of dividends on preferred stock affect the EPS computation?

6A–8. EPS can affect a company's stock prices. Can a company's stock prices affect EPS?

6A–9. What is meant by antidilution? Give an example of an antidilutive security.

6A–10. What is the treasury stock method? What is its purpose?

6A–11. Is the treasury stock method always used in computing EPS?

6A–12. Accounting for earnings per share has certain weaknesses that our analysis must consider for interpreting EPS data. Discuss these.

6A–13. In estimating the value of common stock, the amount of EPS is considered an important element.

a. Explain why EPS is important in the valuation of common stock.

b. Is EPS equally important in valuing a preferred stock? Why or why not?

(CFA Adapted)

EXERCISES

Exercise 6A–1 Analyzing Earnings per Share

Publicly traded companies are required to report earnings per share data on the face of the income statement.

Required:

Compare and contrast basic earnings per share with diluted earnings per share for each of the following:

a. The effect of dilutive stock options and warrants on the number of shares used in computing earnings per share data.
b. The effect of dilutive convertible securities on the number of shares used in computing earnings per share data.
c. The effect of antidilutive securities.

(CFA Adapted)

Exercise 6A–2

Interpreting Earnings per Share

Practice requires the presentation of earnings per share data on the face of the income statement.

Required:

a. Explain the meaning of basic earnings per share.
b. Explain how diluted earnings per share differ from basic earnings per share.
c. Explain how basic earnings per share differ from primary earnings per share.
d. Explain how diluted earnings per share differ from fully diluted earnings per share.

(CFA Adapted)

Exercise 6A–3

Earnings per Share Computations (multiple choice)

Champion had 2 million shares outstanding on December 31, Year 7. On March 31, Year 8, Champion paid a 10 percent stock dividend. On June 30, Year 8, Champion sells $10 million of 5 percent convertible debentures, convertible into common shares at $5 per share. The AA bond rate on the issue date is 10 percent.

I. Basic earnings per share for Year 8 is computed on the following number of shares:
   a. 2,050,000
   b. 2,200,000
   c. 3,200,000
   d. 4,200,000

II. Assume that Champion also has outstanding warrants to purchase 1 million shares at $5 per share. Assume that the price of Champion common shares is $8 per share at December 31, Year 8, and that the average share price for Year 8 is $4. For the computation of basic earnings per share, how many *additional* shares must be assumed to be outstanding because of the warrants?
   a. Zero
   b. 375,000
   c. 625,000
   d. 1,000,000

III. Given the same facts as in II, how many *additional* shares must be assumed to be outstanding because of the warrants when computing diluted earnings per share?
   a. Zero
   b. 375,000
   c. 625,000
   d. 1,000,000

(CFA Adapted)

PROBLEMS

Problem 6A–1

Earnings per Share Computations (multiple choice)

The financial data below should be used to answer the following two questions.

Wrestling Federation of America, Inc.
Capital Structure and Earnings for Year 7

Number of common shares outstanding on December 31, Year 7	2,700,000
Number of common shares outstanding during Year 7 (weighted average)	2,500,000
Market price per common share on December 31, Year 7	$25
Weighted-average market price per common share during Year 7	$20
Options outstanding during Year 7:	
Number of shares issuable on exercise of options	200,000
Exercise price	$15
Convertible bonds outstanding (December Year 3 issue):	
Number of convertible bonds	10,000
Shares of common issuable on conversion (per bond)	10
Coupon rate	5.0%
Proceeds per bond at issue (at par value)	$1,000
Average Aa corporate bond yield at time of issue	8.5%
Net income for Year 7	$6,500,000
Tax rate for Year 7	40.0%

I. Basic earnings per share for Year 7 is (choose one of the following):
   a. $2.41
   b. $2.57
   c. $2.60
   d. $2.50

II. Diluted earnings per share for Year 7 is (choose one of the following):
   a. $2.43
   b. $2.55
   c. $2.54
   d. $2.60

(CFA Adapted)

Problem 6A–2

Determining Earnings per Share

Fantasy, Inc., reports the following for Year 6:

Income before extraordinary item	$800,000
Extraordinary item—casualty loss (net of taxes)	200,000
Net income	$600,000

Current Year: At January 1, Year 6 there are 200,000 shares of common stock outstanding. On October 1, Year 6, an additional 60,000 shares are sold for cash.

Prior Years: In Year 4, 6 percent bonds are issued at par, $1,000,000. These are convertible into 20,000 shares of common stock. None have been converted. At date of issue, the AA bond rate is 8 percent.

In Year 3, 50,000 options are granted to purchase common stock (one option for each share) at $45 per share. None have been exercised. During Year 6, the average market price per share of common stock is $50 and on December 31, Year 6, the market price is $60.

In Year 2, 25,000 shares of $3 cumulative preferred stock are issued at $90 per share. Each preferred share is convertible into two shares of common stock. None have been converted. At date of issue, the AA bond rate is 9 percent. (*Note:* The income tax rate is 40 percent for all years.)

Required

a. Calculate basic earnings per share for Year 6.
b. Calculate diluted earnings per share for Year 6.
c Calculate primary earnings per share for Year 6.
d. Calculate diluted earnings per share for Year 6.

Problem 6A–3

Computing Earnings per Share

Company A's net income for the year is $4 million and the number of common shares outstanding is 3 million (there is no change in shares outstanding during the year). The company has options and warrants outstanding to purchase 1 million common shares at $15 per share.

Required:

a. If the average market value of the common share is $20, year-end price is $25, interest rate on borrowings is 6 percent, and the tax rate is 50 percent, then compute both basic and diluted EPS.
b. Do the same computations as in (*a*) assuming net income for the year is only $3 million, the average market value per common share is $18, and year-end price is $20 per share.
c. Calculate primary earnings per share under both sets of assumptions.
d. Calculate fully diluted earnings per share under both sets of assumptions.

Problem 6A–4

Analyzing Earnings per Share with Pooling of Interests

On October 1, Year 5, the management of Allen Corporation decides to merge with the Simon Corporation and the Duke Corporation. Following is additional information (the merger is accounted for as a pooling):

	Simon Corporation	*Duke Corporation*	*Allen Corporation*
Net income from 1/1/Year 5 to 9/30/Year 5	$100,000	$150,000	$250,000
Common shares outstanding on 10/1/Year 5	50,000	40,000	150,000
Shares issued on 7/1/Year 5	25,000		
Shares issued on 9/1/Year 5		10,000	
Net income from 10/1/Year 5 to 12/31/Year 5			$250,000
Number of shares issued for acquisition of:			
Simon Corporation (2 for 1)			100,000
Duke Corporation (5 for 1)			200,000

Required:

Compute earnings per share for the consolidated company on December 31, Year 5.

Problem 6A–5

Analyzing Earnings per Share with Pooling of Interests

On October 1, Year 5, the management of AM Corporation decides to merge with the PM Corporation and the NITE Corporation. Following is additional information (using pooling accounting):

	PM	*NITE*	*AM*
Net income from 1/1/Year 5 to 9/30/Year 5	$200,000	$300,000	$100,000
Common shares outstanding on 10/1/Year 5	100,000	80,000	300,000
Shares issued on 7/1/Year 5	50,000		
Shares issued on 9/1/Year 5		20,000	
Net income from 10/1/Year 5 to 12/31/Year 5			$400,000
Number of shares issued for acquisition of:			
PM Corp. (2 for 1)			200,000
NITE Corp. (5 for 1)			400,000

Required:

Compute earnings per share for the consolidated company on December 31, Year 5.

CASES

Case 6A–1

Analyzing Earnings per Share with Convertible Debentures

The officers of Environmental, Inc., considered themselves fortunate when the company sold a $9,000,000 subordinated convertible debenture issue on June 30, Year 1 with a 6 percent coupon. They had the alternative of refunding and enlarging the outstanding term loan, but the interest cost would have been one-half a point above the AA bond rate. The AA bond rate was as high as 8½ percent until March 29, Year 1, when it was lowered to 8 percent, the rate that prevailed until September 21, Year 1 when it was lowered again to 7½ percent. As of December 31, Year 1, Environmental, Inc., had the following capital structure:

7% term loan*	$3,000,000
6% convertible subordinated debentures †	9,000,000
Common stock, $1 par, authorized 2,000,000 shares, issued and outstanding 900,000	900,000
900,000 warrants, expiring July 1, Year 6‡	
Additional Paid-In Capital	1,800,000
Retained earnings	4,500,000

*Term loan (originally $5,000,000) is repayable in semiannual installments of $500,000.
†Convertible subordinated debentures, sold June 30, Year 1, are convertible any time at $18 until maturity. Sinking fund of $300,000 per year to start in Year 6.
‡Warrants entitle holder to purchase one share for $10 to expiration on July 1, Year 6.

Additional data for Year 1:

Interest expense	$ 500,000
Net income	1,500,000
Dividends paid	135,000
Earnings retained	900,000
Market prices December 31, Year 1 (equals averages for Year 1):	
Convertible debentures 6%	$107
Common Stock	$13.00
Stock Warrants	$4.50
Treasury bills interest rate at 12/31/Year 1	6%

Required:

a. Calculate and show computations for basic and diluted earnings per share figures for common stock for Year 1's annual report (assume a 50 percent tax rate).

b. What is the times-interest-earned ratio for Year 2 assuming net income before interest and taxes is the same as in Year 1 (a 50 percent income tax rate applies)?

(CFA Adapted)

Case 6A–2
Determining Earnings per Share

Part I. Information concerning the capital structure of Dole Corporation is reproduced below:

	December 31	
	Year 5	***Year 6***
Common stock	90,000 shares	90,000 shares
Convertible preferred stock	10,000 shares	10,000 shares
8% convertible bonds	$1,000,000	$1,000,000

During Year 6, Dole pays dividends of $1 per share on its common stock and $2.40 per share on its preferred stock. The preferred stock is convertible into 20,000 shares of common stock. The 8 percent convertible bonds are convertible into 30,000 shares of common stock. The net income for the year ended December 31, Year 6, is $285,000. The income tax rate is 50 percent.

Required:

a. Compute basic earnings per share for the year ended December 31, Year 6.

b. Compute diluted earnings per share for the year ended December 31, Year 6.

Part II. The R. Lott Company's net income for the year ended December 31, Year 6, is $10,000. During Year 6, R. Lott declares and pays $1,000 cash dividends on preferred stock and $1,750 cash dividends on common stock. At December 31, Year 6, 12,000 shares of common stock are issued and outstanding—10,000 of which were issued and outstanding throughout the year and 2,000 of which were issued on July 1, Year 6. There are no other common stock transactions during the year, and there is no potential dilution of earnings per share.

Required:

Compute the Year 6 basic earnings per common share of R. Lott Company.

INTERNET ACTIVITIES

Internet 6A–1
Analyzing Earnings per Share

Access one of the financial statement databases available on the Internet (http://www.mhhe.com/business/accounting/wild). Retrieve current financial statements of a company selected by either you or your instructor that reports both basic and diluted or (primary and fully diluted) earnings per share.

Required:

a. Describe the types of dilutive securities outstanding.

b. Explain how these securities affected the company's earnings per share.

C H A P T E R

7

Analyzing Business Activities: Cash Flows

A Look Back

In Chapter 6 we analyzed operating activities using accrual income. We examined revenue and expense recognition methods for interpretation of operations. Per share figures for income were also examined.

A Look at This Chapter

In this chapter we analyze cash flow measures for insights into *all* business activities, but with special emphasis on operations. Attention is directed at company and business conditions when interpreting cash flows. We also consider alternative measures of cash flows.

A Look Ahead

Chapter 8 begins Part Three where our focus is on more strategic application and analysis of financial statements. Analysis of short-term liquidity is the emphasis of Chapter 8. We explore various analytical tools in assessing current and anticipated liquidity.

Learning Objectives

- Explain the relevance of cash flows in analyzing business activities.
- Describe reporting of cash flows by business activities.
- Analyze cash flows through T-accounts and transaction reconstruction.
- Interpret cash flows from operating activities.
- Analyze cash flows under alternative company and business conditions.
- Describe alternative measures of cash flows and their usefulness.
- Illustrate analytical tools in evaluating cash flows (Appendixes 7A and 7B).

PREVIEW OF CHAPTER 7

Cash is the residual of cash inflows *less* cash outflows for all prior periods of a company. Net cash flows, or simply *cash flows,* refers to the current period's cash inflows less cash outflows. Cash flows are different from accrual measures of performance. Cash flow measures recognize inflows when cash is received but not necessarily earned, and outflows when cash is paid but not necessarily incurred. The statement of cash flows reports cash flow measures for three primary business activities: operating, investing, and financing. Operating cash flows, or cash flows from operations, are the cash basis counterpart to accrual net income. Information on cash flows helps us assess a company's ability to meet obligations, pay dividends, increase capacity, and raise financing. It also helps us assess the quality of earnings and the dependence of income on estimates and assumptions regarding future cash flows. This chapter describes cash flows and their relevance to our analysis of financial statements. We describe current reporting requirements and their implications for our analysis of cash flows. We explain useful analytical adjustments to cash flows using financial data. We direct special attention to transaction reconstruction, and T-account and conversion analyses. The content and organization of this chapter are as follows:

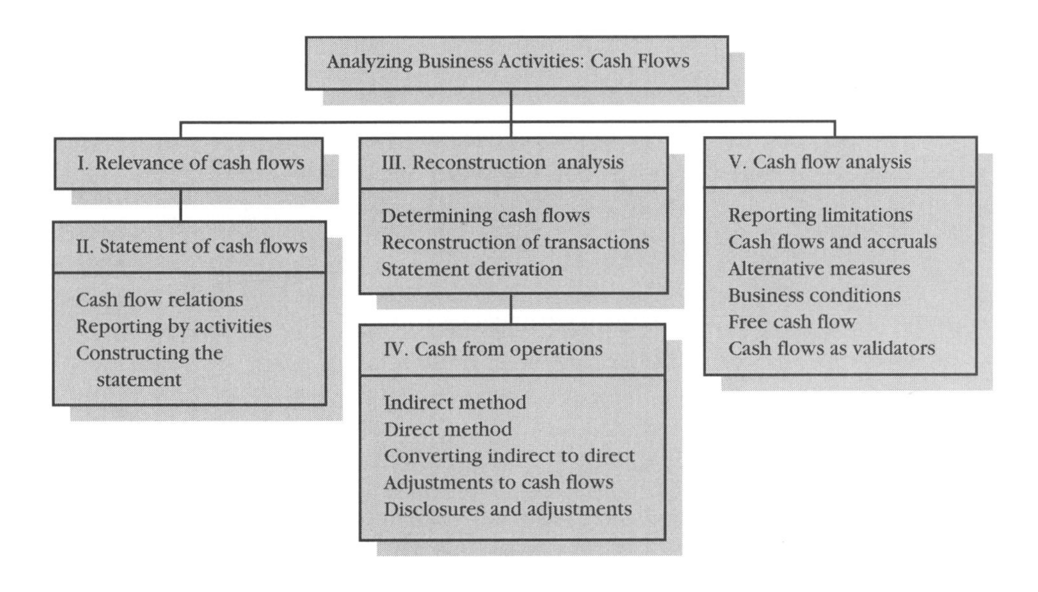

Relevance of Cash Flows

Cash is the most liquid of assets and offers a company liquidity and flexibility. It is both the beginning and the end of a company's operating cycle. A company's operating activities require cash conversion into various assets (e.g., inventories) that are used to yield receivables as part of sales. Operating results are realized when the collection process returns cash to the company enabling a new operating cycle to begin.

Our analysis of financial statements recognizes that accrual accounting, where companies recognize revenue when earned and expenses when incurred, differs from cash flows. Yet net cash flow is the end measure of profitability. It is cash, not income, that ultimately repays loans, replaces equipment, expands facilities, and pays dividends. Analyzing a company's cash inflows and outflows, and their operating, financing, or investing sources, is one of our most important investigative exercises. This analysis helps us assess liquidity, solvency, and financial flexibility. **Liquidity** is the nearness to cash of assets and liabilities. **Solvency** is the ability to pay liabilities when they mature. **Financial flexibility** is the ability to react and adjust to opportunities and adversities.

Total Cash Flows for Adaptec

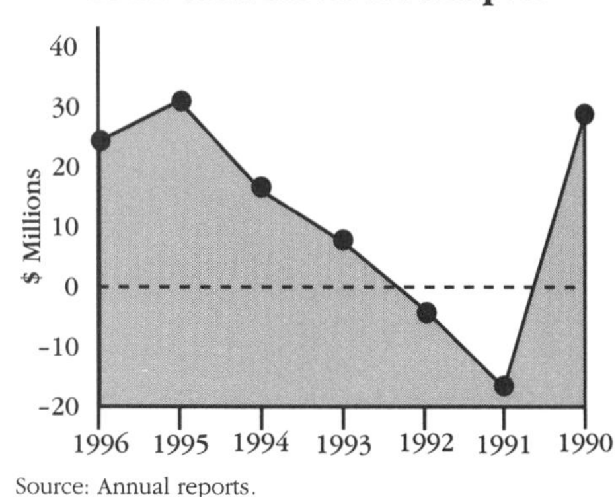

Source: Annual reports.

Useful but incomplete information on sources and uses of cash is available from comparative balance sheets and income statements. However, a comprehensive picture of cash flows is derived from the **statement of cash flows** (SCF). This statement is important to our analysis and provides information to help us address questions such as:

- How much cash is generated from or used in operations?
- What expenditures are made with cash from operations?
- How are dividends paid when confronting an operating loss?
- What is the source of cash for debt payments?
- What is the source of cash for redeeming preferred stock?
- How is the increase in investments financed?
- What is the source of cash for new plant assets?
- Why is cash lower when income increased?
- What is the use of cash from new financing?

Users of financial statements utilize cash flow analysis as an important analytical tool. The statement of cash flows is key to the reconstruction of many transactions, which is an important part of our analysis. Analysis of this statement requires our understanding of the accounting measures underlying its preparation and presentation. The first part of this chapter focuses on these important accounting fundamentals. We then focus on the analytical uses for the statement of cash flows and their implications for our analysis of financial statements.

Statement of Cash Flows

The purpose of the statement of cash flows is to provide us information on cash inflows and outflows for a period. It also distinguishes among the sources and uses of cash flows by separating them into operating, investing, and financing activities. This section discusses important cash flow relations and the layout of the cash flow statement.

Cash Flow Relations

Cash usually refers to cash and cash equivalents. **Cash equivalents** are short-term, highly liquid investments that are (1) readily convertible to known amounts of cash, and (2) near maturity with limited risk of price changes due to interest rate movements. Maturity within three months is typically used as a "nearness" cutoff. Examples of cash equivalents are treasury bills and money market funds.

To help us understand the relation between cash and other balance sheet accounts, consider two consecutive years' balance sheets divided into (1) cash, and (2) all other balance sheet accounts:

Accounts [Dr (Cr)]	*Year 1*	*Year 2*
Cash and cash equivalents	$ 3,000	$ 5,000
Noncash accounts:		
Noncash current assets	$ 9,000	$ 11,000
Noncurrent assets	6,000	8,000
Current liabilities	(8,000)	(10,000)
Long-term liabilities	(3,000)	(5,000)
Equity accounts	(7,000)	(9,000)
Net noncash balance	$(3,000)	$ (5,000)

Notice the net change in cash from Year 1 to Year 2 (an increase of $2,000) is matched exactly by the change in noncash balance sheet accounts between these two years (a $2,000 increase). This is because assets equal liabilities plus equity; and a change in one section of the balance sheet must be matched by an equal change in the remaining accounts. This relation between cash and noncash balance sheet accounts provides a useful means for understanding the preparation of the statement of cash flows. We can portray these two parts of the balance sheet as follows:

Balance Sheet

Group		
Group A	Cash and cash equivalents	
Group B	*Current*	
	Accounts receivable*	Accounts payable*
	Inventories*	Accrued liabilities*
	Prepayments*	Current portion—long-term debt
	Marketable securities	Dividends payable
	Noncurrent	
	Investments	Long-term debt
	Fixed assets	Deferred tax liabilities
	Intangibles	Capital stock accounts
	Other assets	Retained earning

*Related to operations (also referred to as *operating working capital* items).

These interrelations between cash and noncash balance sheet accounts can be generalized as:

- Net changes in cash (Group A) are explained by net changes in noncash balance sheet accounts (Group B). This implies the statement of cash flows contains items affecting *both* Groups A and B.
- Changes within or among noncash balance sheet accounts (Group B) do not affect cash. Practice does, require disclosure of all significant financing and investing activities; meaning noncash transactions (e.g., conversion of debt to equity, acquisition of assets through debt, exchanges of assets or liabilities) are reported in a separate schedule of noncash investing and financing activities.
- Changes within cash (Group A) are not reported. For example, if a company invests a larger share of its cash in cash equivalents, these investments or subsequent conversion of cash equivalents into cash need not be reported in the statement of cash flows.

Operating Cash Flows and Net Income of Adaptec

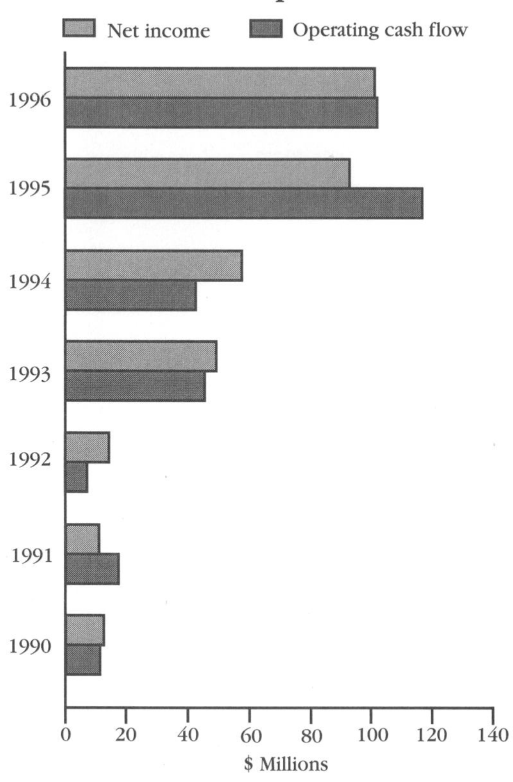

Source: Annual reports.

Investing and Financing Cash Flows of Adaptec

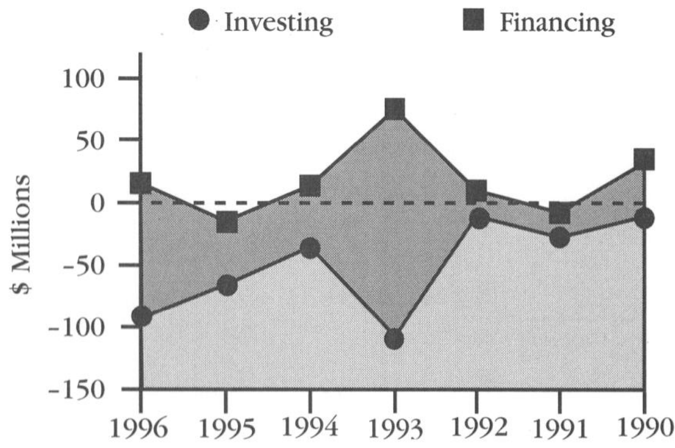

Source: Annual reports.

Reporting by Activities

The statement of cash flows reports cash receipts and payments by operating, financing, and investing activities—the primary business activities of a company.

Operating activities are the earning-related activities of a company. Beyond revenue and expense activities represented in an income statement, they include the net inflows and outflows of cash resulting from related operating activities like extending credit to customers, investing in inventories, and obtaining credit from suppliers. Operating activities relate to income statement items (with minor exceptions) and to balance sheet items relating to operations—usually working capital accounts like receivables, inventories, prepayments, payables, and accrued expenses. Practice also requires operating activities include transactions and events that do not fit into investing or financing activities (e.g., settlements in lawsuits).

Investing activities are means of acquiring and disposing of noncash (and noncash equivalent) assets. These activities involve assets expected to generate income for a company. They also include lending funds and collecting the principal on these loans.

Financing activities are means of contributing, withdrawing, and servicing funds to support business activities. They include resources from creditors and repaying of principal amounts borrowed. They also include contributions and withdrawals by owners and their return (dividends) on investment. Major investing and financing activities not involving cash are reported separately in either narrative or summary form.

The statement of cash flows reports effects of exchange rate changes on cash balances held in foreign currencies as a separate part of the reconciliation of cash. Except for special cases such as quick turnover items, investing and financing cash inflows and outflows are reported *separately* in the statement. For example, receipts from borrowing are reported separately from repayments, and asset purchases separately from asset sales. Practice permits banks, saving institutions, and credit unions to report certain net cash receipts and cash payments.

Because the statement of cash flows classifies transactions and events into business activities, we return to the balance sheet diagram and examine more specific examples for two categories: changes affecting both Groups A and B (i.e., changes affecting both cash and noncash accounts); and changes within Group B (changes within noncash accounts).

First, changes affecting both Groups A and B involve the interaction of cash with any item(s) in Group B. Examples are:

Transaction or Event	*Effect on Account*	*Activity*
Sales for cash	Credit (increase) retained earnings via income	Operating
Accounts receivable collection	Credit (decrease) receivable	Operating
Insurance paid in cash	Debit (decrease) retained earnings via income	Operating
Interest payment	Debit (decrease) retained earnings via income	Operating
Accounts payable paid	Debit (decrease) payable	Operating
Collection of noncurrent operating receivable	Credit (decrease) receivable	Operating
Payment for plant assets	Debit (increase) plant assets	Investing
Sale of investment	Credit (decrease) investments	Investing
Repayment of loans	Debit (decrease) loans	Financing
Payment of dividends	Debit (decrease) retained earnings	Financing

Second, changes within Group B do not affect cash. To understand their impact on the statement of cash flows it is useful to consider them in three subgroups:

- *Changes related to operating activities.* These are separated into (1) changes affecting operating working capital (e.g., purchase of inventory on account, sale of merchandise on account, accrued utilities expense), and (2) changes reflecting revenue or expense items (e.g., depreciation and amortization, accrual for deferred taxes, or equity in earnings of affiliated companies). The first class of transactions is part of the net change in operating working capital, and only those net changes affecting cash enter into cash from operations. The second class of items, while not affecting cash, affects noncash accounts like Accumulated Depreciation, Intangible Assets, or Investments in Affiliated Companies. These items reflect adjustments to income when converting from accrual to cash accounting.
- *Changes reflecting investing or financing activities.* Examples include converting debt to equity, purchasing assets for long-term debt (mortgage), or acquiring a subsidiary partially for debt or equity. These changes are reported in a separate schedule to the statement of cash flows detailing noncash investing or financing activities.

EXHIBIT 7.1

TORONTO TECHNOLOGY CORPORATION
Condensed Balance Sheets
(in thousands)

	December 31		Changes during Year 2*			
	Year 1	*Year 2*	*Operating Activity*	*Investing Activity*	*Financing Activity*	*Noncash Transactions*
[1] Cash	$ 120	$ 100				
[2] Accounts receivable	200	145	$ 55			
[3] Inventories	150	175	(25)			
[4] Fixed assets	660	874		$(214)		
[5] Accumulated depreciation	(200)	(244)	64	(20)		
[6] Intangible assets	150	100	50			
Total assets	$1,080	$1,150				
[7] Accounts payable	$ 150	$ 130	(20)			
[8] Long-term debt	420	400			$ (10)	$(10)
[9] Capital stock accounts	250	300			40	10
[10] Retained earnings	260	320	180		(120)	
Total liabilities and equity	$1,080	$1,150				
Totals			$304	$(234)	$ (90)	$ 0

▪ *Changes reflecting insignificant events not requiring separate reporting.* Potential examples are stock dividends and stock splits, write-off of fully depreciated assets, dividends declared and not paid, or reclassification of long-term debt to current.

Constructing the Cash Flow Statement

We focus on a case example to better understand how cash flows and its statement are determined. Exhibit 7.1 shows comparative balance sheets for Toronto Technology Corporation. Preparing a statement of cash flows requires details of account changes and supplementary data. These details are available in the descriptions below of the individual effects on cash or noncash transactions:

1. We first note the $20 cash decrease is the focus of explanation for the statement of cash flows. It is explained by changes in noncash balance sheet accounts.
2. The $55 decrease in accounts receivable is a positive (cash inflow) adjustment to income in arriving at cash flow from operations. It implies cash collections exceed accrual sales.
3. The $25 increase in inventories is a negative (cash outflow) adjustment to income because cash outlays for inventory exceed purchases in cost of sales.
4. A T-account is used to effectively summarize changes in fixed assets:

Fixed Assets

	Debit	Credit	
Beginning	660		
Acquisitions	314	100	Disposals
Ending	874		

Both acquisitions and disposals are part of investing activities. While each transaction is reported separately in the statement of cash flows, the balance sheet shows the net of $214 ($314 – $100).

5. A T-account summarizes changes in accumulated depreciation:

Accumulated Depreciation

	Debit	Credit	
		200	Beginning
Accumulated depreciation on assets disposed	20	64	Depreciation
		244	Ending

Depreciation ($64) is a noncash expense and reflects a change within Group B—a debit to income (retained earnings) and a credit to accumulated depreciation. It is added back to income in arriving at cash from operations. The $20 in accumulated depreciation relates to the $100 (original cost) of fixed assets sold at book value ($100 – $20 = $80). The $20 of accumulated depreciation adjusts the $100 amount included in investing activities.

6. The $50 decline in intangible assets reflects amortization. Amortization is a noncash expense similar to depreciation and is added back to income.
7. The $20 decrease in accounts payable is a negative (cash outflow) adjustment to income because amounts due suppliers declined.
8. The $20 decrease in long-term debt reflects a $10 repayment (a financing outflow) and a $10 reduction due to conversion of debt into equity (a noncash transaction).
9. The $50 increase in capital stock reflects a $40 issuance of stock (a financing inflow) and a $10 stock issuance by converting debt (a noncash transaction).
10. The $60 increase in retained earnings is summarized in T-account form:

Retained Earnings

	Debit	Credit	
		260	Beginning
Dividends paid	120	180	Net income
		320	Ending

The $180 net income, after adjustments, yields the source of cash from operations of $304. The $120 dividend is a financing cash outflow.

Drawing on the above analyses, the change in cash is explained as:

Cash flows from operating activities	$ 304
Cash flows from investing activities	(234)
Cash flows from financing activities	(90)
Net decrease in cash	$ (20)

Exhibit 7.2 reports these analyses in a statement of cash flows. While we constructed the statement of cash flows directly from the comparative balance sheets and information from Toronto Technology, a more structured and systematic method is available. In the next section, we illustrate the *T-account technique* for more systematic analysis of cash flows. We also analyze and interpret cash flow from operations.

EXHIBIT 7.2

TORONTO TECHNOLOGY CORPORATION
Statement of Cash Flows
For the Year Ended December 31, Year 2
(in thousands)

Cash flows from operating activities:		
Net income	$ 180	
Add (deduct) adjustments to cash basis:		
Depreciation	64	
Amortization of intangibles	50	
Decrease in accounts receivables	55	
Increase in inventory	(25)	
Decrease in accounts payable	(20)	
Net cash flows from operating activities		$ 304
Cash flows from investing activities:		
Purchase of fixed assets	$(314)	
Sale of fixed assets	80	
Net cash flows used in investing activities		(234)
Cash flows from financing activities:		
Sale of capital stock	$ 40	
Payment of dividends	(120)	
Repayment of long-term debt	(10)	
Net cash flows used in financing activities		(90)
Net increase (decrease) in cash		$ (20)
Schedule of noncash financing and investing activities:*		
Common stock issued in conversion of long-term debt		$ 10

*Can be presented in a footnote. Any amounts paid for interest and income taxes must also be disclosed.

ANALYSIS VIEWPOINT . . . *You are the school board member*

You are in your second two-year term on the school board. You have obtained substantial contributions from a publishing company to support educational programs in the school district. A new management team recently took control of the publishing company and earlier this week reported a $1.2 million annual loss. Net cash flows was an equally dismal $1.1 million decrease—with reported decreases in investing and financing equaling $1.9 million and $0.7 million, respectively. The new management warns you its contributions to educational programs are ending due to the company's financial distress, including this period's $1.3 million extraordinary loss. What is your course of action?

Reconstruction Analysis of Cash Flows

There are specific steps in determining cash flows as shown in our analysis of Toronto Technology in the prior section. Companies with more complicated transactions often require more extensive analysis including:

EXHIBIT 7.3

VATTER CORPORATION
Comparative Balance Sheet
As of December 31, Year 2
(in thousands)

	Year 1	*Year 2*	*Increase (decrease)*
Assets			
Current assets:			
Cash	$ 240	$ 120	$ (120)
Receivables	360	450	90
Inventories	750	1,053	303
Total current assets	$1,350	$1,623	$ 273
Fixed assets	4,500	6,438	1,938
Accumulated depreciation	(1,500)	(1,740)	(240)
Investment in affiliate	1,000	1,050	50
Goodwill	950	980	30
Total assets	$6,300	$8,351	$2,051
Liabilities and Equity			
Accounts payable	$ 360	$ 590	$ 230
Bonds payable	300	700	400
Deferred income taxes	240	260	20
Capital stock	2,400	3,200	800
Additional paid-in capital	900	1,300	400
Retained earnings	2,100	2,301	201
Total liabilities and equity	$6,300	$8,351	$2,051

- Analyzing net cash changes requiring more detailed information.
- Reversing or eliminating transactions within noncash accounts.
- Regrouping or reconstructing transactions within noncash accounts that explain changes in cash.

Methods used in these adjustments vary from elaborate electronic spreadsheets to summary adjustments performed intuitively. One of the most direct and flexible analytical tools is **reconstruction of transactions through T-accounts**. This tool is well suited to our analysis objectives. The aim of T-account analysis is to reconstruct in summary form the transactions affecting all balance sheet accounts during the reporting period. If the reconstructed transactions reveal a source or use of cash, it is recorded in our cash T-account. If a transaction does not affect cash, or is an insignificant investing or financing transaction, it is reversed in the relevant noncash T-accounts.

Determining Cash Flows by Activities

We illustrate reconstruction analysis using the comparative balance sheet and income statement of Vatter Corporation reproduced in Exhibits 7.3 and 7.4, respectively. The following additional information about Vatter for Year 2 is available:

EXHIBIT 7.4

VATTER CORPORATION
Income Statement
Year Ended December 31, Year 2
(in thousands)

Sales		$19,950
Cost of goods sold (includes $360 of depreciation)		11,101
Gross profit		$ 8,849
General, selling, and administrative expenses	$7,000	
Amortization of goodwill	30	7,030
		$ 1,819
Equity in earnings of unconsolidated affiliate*		50
Gain on sale of fixed assets		2
Income before taxes		$ 1,871
Income taxes:		
Current	$ 900	
Deferred	20	920
Net income		$ 951

*No dividends received.

1. On March 1, the company purchases for $510,000 cash a business with (a) fixed assets valued at $450,000, (b) current assets (no cash) equal to current liabilities, and (c) the excess of $60,000 over net assets treated as goodwill.
2. Machinery is sold for $18,000. It originally cost $36,000, and $20,000 depreciation is accumulated to date of sale.
3. In April, the company acquires $100,000 in fixed assets by issuing bonds for $100,000 par value.
4. In June, the company receives $1,000,000 cash for issuance of capital stock with a par value of $600,000; convertible bonds of $200,000 are converted to capital stock with a par value $200,000; and long-term bonds are sold for $500,000 (at par).
5. Fully depreciated assets of $100,000 are written off.
6. Dividends paid amount to $750,000.
7. General, selling, and administrative expenses include $50,000 of interest paid.
8. There are no liabilities for income taxes at the beginning or end of Year 2.

Using Vatter's financial statements and additional information we prepare a statement of cash flows for analysis by applying the following steps:

1. Set up a T-account for each noncash account in the balance sheet, and post the opening and closing balances in each T-account.
2. Set up a Cash T-account, separated into four sections: operating, investing, financing, and noncash transactions (illustrated in the case below).
3. Balances in T-accounts are reconstructed using information drawn from changes in noncash accounts by:
   a. Debiting or crediting items of income or loss, or converting items to a cash basis for the operating section.
   b. Debiting or crediting *non*operating items to one or more of the other three sections.
4. Prepare the statement of cash flows using details in the completed Cash T-account.

EXHIBIT 7.5 Relations between Income Statement and Balance Sheet Accounts

		Operating Working Capital				
Income Statement Item	***Cash***	***Accounts Receivable***	***Inventories***	***Prepayments***	***Accounts Payable and Accruals***	***Other Noncash Accounts***
Sales	X	X				
Cost of goods sold	X		X		X	
Depreciation						X
General, selling, and administrative expenses	X			X	X	
Amortization of goodwill						X
Equity in earnings of unconsolidated affiliate						X
Gain on sale of fixed assets						X
Income taxes—current	X				X	
Income taxes—deferred				X	X	X

The first step in reconstruction analysis is to determine net cash flows from operations (CFO). Items in Vatter Corporation's income statement relate to cash, operating working capital, or other balance sheet accounts. Exhibit 7.5 illustrates these relations. Certain items like sales, cost of goods sold, general selling and administrative expenses, and income taxes either produce or require cash. Others represent deferred cash receipts or payments in the form of receivables, payables, or other accruals (deferred income taxes) as part of operating working capital. They relate to operations and affect the conversion of accrual income to a cash basis. Still other items do not affect cash and must be added back to, or deducted from, net income in determining cash from operations. For instance, depreciation interacts with accumulated depreciation, amortization with intangibles, equity in investee earnings with investment in affiliates, and deferred tax expense with deferred tax liability. Further examples of items in the income statement with no cash flow implications are:

Income Statement item	***Related to the Following Noncash Balance Sheet Item***
Amortization of bond premium	Unamortized bond premium
Amortization of bond discount	Unamortized bond discount
Warranty expenses	Estimated noncurrent liability for warranty costs
Amortization of leasehold improvements	Leasehold improvements
Subscription income	Deferred noncurrent subscription income
Minority interest in income (loss)	Minority interest

More generally, this determination is summarized as:

Income Statement Item	***Related to Contra Account***	***Effect on Cash from Operations***
Debit expense or loss	Cr. to cash	Use of cash
	Cr. to noncash account	Add back—not using cash
Credit income or gain	Dr. to cash	Source of cash
	Dr. to noncash account	Deduct—not providing cash

Deserving separate consideration is the gain (or loss) on sale of fixed assets. The gain or loss from this transaction is removed from income because the cash received from its sale is reported in investing activities, and not because it did not bring in cash. If the gain on sale of fixed assets is not removed from Vatter's income, total proceeds from sale of fixed assets ($18,000) is reported in two locations: (1) in recovery of the $16,000 book value of fixed assets ($36,000 – $20,000), and (2) in gain on sale in net income.

Viewing operating activities as the earning-related activities of a company, we see how changes in operating working capital accounts affect operations. This is because the focus is not limited to revenues and expenses but includes cash inflows and outflows related to operating decisions—examples are extending credit to customers, investing in inventories, and securing credit from suppliers. As an illustration, consider the change in accounts receivable. For Vatter, accounts receivable increases by $90,000 during Year 2. This implies (on a net basis) sales for the year are $90,000 higher than cash collections from sales. This is also revealed by reconstructing the Accounts Receivable account for Year 2.

Accounts Receivable [B]

	Dr.	Cr.	
Beginning	360		
Sales	19,950	19,860	Cash collections*
Ending	450		

*In this simplified example we do not consider whether accounts receivable were net of an allowance for bad debts.

Practice requires changes in operations-related accounts, such as Accounts Receivable, be shown in the SCF adjusted for noncash entries such as the write-off of accounts receivable. Similarly, an increase in accounts receivable due to an acquisition must be adjusted to remove such increase from the computation of cash from operations and reclassified as an investing outlay of cash (part of the acquisition of a company).

Using similar analytical reasoning, we show changes in operating working capital accounts have the following cash flow effects:

Account	*Change: Dr. (debit) Cr. (credit)*	*Effect on Operations*
Accounts Receivable	Increase (Dr.)	Sales not collected in cash.
	Decrease (Cr.)	Collections exceed sales (i.e., some prior period receivables collected).
Inventories	Increase (Dr.)	Cash purchases exceed cost of sales.
	Decrease (Cr.)	Some cost of goods sold represents a reduction in inventories (i.e., cash purchases are less than cost of goods sold).
Prepaid Expenses	Increase (Dr.)	Cash paid for expenses that are charged to future periods (i.e., cash spent exceeds expenses in income statement).
	Decrease (Cr.)	Some expenses in the income statement were paid for in prior years and do not require a current cash outlay.
Trade Accounts or Notes Payable	Increase (Cr.)	Some purchases are not yet paid for.
	Decrease (Dr.)	Cash payments to suppliers exceed purchases for the period.

Our use of debit and credit designations for changes in these accounts is a useful check on the effects of changes in sources and uses of cash. For example, a credit change increases cash from operations while a debit change reduces it. The listed effects on operations assume only operating items flow through current assets and liabilities (e.g., accounts receivable do not include receivables for fixed asset sales, and accounts payable do not include payables for long-lived asset purchases). This is a necessary assumption for our analysis as outsiders and is usually proper.

Certain current assets or liabilities do not relate to operating activities but to either investing or financing activities. Examples are:

Account	*Activity*
Loans Receivable (e.g. from officers)	Investing
Current Portion of Long-Term Debt	Financing
Notes Payable to Bank	Financing
Dividends Payable	Financing

Vatter Corporation does not have any nonoperating current assets or liabilities in Years 1 or 2.

To summarize, we distinguish three categories of adjustments to convert accrual net income to cash flow from operations:

1. Expenses, losses, revenues, and gains not requiring or producing cash—these involve noncash accounts, except those in (2) below.
2. Net changes in noncash accounts (usually in operating working capital accounts) relating to operations—these adjustments affect accrual revenues and expenses (e.g., long-term receivables from ordinary sales).
3. Gains or losses (like sales of assets) transferred to another section of the statement of cash flows where their entire cash proceeds are recognized.

ANALYSIS VIEWPOINT . . . *You are the investor*

You are considering investing in D.C. Bionics. Earlier today D.C. Bionics announced a $6 million annual loss, however, net cash flows were a positive $10 million. How are these results possible?

Reconstruction of Transactions

In this section we describe actual reconstruction using T-accounts, and the analysis of transactions using accounting entries, for Vatter Corporation.

Reconstructed T-Accounts

Commensurate with reconstruction of transactions is the reconstruction of T-accounts. These two analytical tasks are best done concurrently. In this section we show reconstruction using T-accounts. Reconstruction of transactions is in the next section. The following T-accounts are the end result of our analysis of transactions ($ thousands). We use a **master T-account** for cash with subdivisions for operating, investing, financing, and noncash transactions.

Cash

Beginning		240			

Operations

Depreciation expense	(g)	360	2	—(b)	Gain on sale of fixed assets
Deferred income taxes	(k)	20	50	—(p)	Equity in earnings of —affiliate
Net income	(m)	951	90	—(q)	Increase in receivables
Goodwill amortization	(o)	30	303	—(r)	Increase in inventories
Increase in accounts —payable	(s)	230			

Investing

Sale of fixed assets	(b)	18	450	—(a)	Acquisition of fixed assets
			60	—(a)	Acquisition of goodwill
			1,524	—(f)	Acquisition of fixed assets

Financing

Bonds sold	(h)	500	750	—(n)	Dividends paid
Sale of stock	(l)	1,000			

Noncash Transactions

Bonds issued to —acquire fixed assets	(d)	100	100	—(c)	Fixed assets acquired with —bonds
Stock issued in —conversion	(j)	200	200	—(i)	Bond conversion to stock
End.		120			

Receivables

Beg.	360		
(q)	90		
End.	450		

Inventories

Beg.	750		
(r)	303		
End.	1,053		

Accounts Payable

		360	Beg.
		230	(s)
		590	End.

Fixed Assets

Beg.	4,500		
(a)	450	36	(b)
(c)	100	100	(e)
(f)	1,524		
End.	6,438		

Accumulated Depreciation

		1,500	Beg.
(b)	20	360	(g)
(e)	100		
		1,740	End.

Investment in Affiliate

Beg.	1,000		
(p)	50		
End.	1,050		

Goodwill

Beg.	950		
(a)	60	30	(o)
End.	980		

Bonds Payable

		300	Beg.
(i)	200	100	(d)
		500	(h)
		700	End.

Deferred Income Taxes

		240	Beg.
		20	(k)
		260	End.

Capital Stock

		2,400	Beg.
		200	(j)
		600	(l)
		3,200	End.

Paid-In Capital

		900	Beg.
		400	(l)
		1,300	End.

Retained Earnings

		2,100	Beg.
(n)	750	951	(m)
		2,301	End.

Reconstructed Entries

Our analysis of Vatter Corporation's individual accounts is described in this section. We use the accounting entry format, with debits and credits, to reconstruct these transactions. Alternatively, one can reconstruct these accounts in a more intuitive manner. We do not rely on intuitive methods since carrying dollar effects of transactions to the cash flow statement usually demands considerable experience and business insight. We consider all balance sheet accounts in our accounting entry analysis—reconstructed T-accounts are in the section above but periodic reference to them assists in understanding this analysis.

Fixed Assets. Vatter's acquisition of another business is reconstructed as:

		Debit	Credit
(a)	Fixed Assets	450,000	
	Goodwill	60,000	
	Cash—Investing		510,000

This acquisition is treated as an investing activity in the statement of cash flows. It is an acquisition of productive assets expected to generate revenues over a long period of time. We know current assets acquired (no cash) approximate current liabilities acquired. More often, increases (or decreases) in operating working capital items due to an acquisition require elimination so only changes in operating working capital due to operations are included in adjustments converting net income to cash from operations. Working capital items (e.g., receivables, payables) acquired are removed from adjustments in determining cash from operations and are considered part of cash outlays for acquisitions (investing activity).

Vatter's sale of equipment is reconstructed as:

		Debit	Credit
(b)	Cash—Investing	18,000	
	Accumulated Depreciation	20,000	
	Fixed Assets		36,000
	Cash—Operations (gain on sale)		2,000

The entire proceeds of $18,000 are debited to Cash from Investing Activities. In the statement of cash flows the sale of fixed assets is an investing activity. Cash from Operations is credited to remove the gain on sale of equipment from net income. This gain must be removed to match it with the recovery of book value of $16,000 and to show the entire proceeds as part of cash from investing activities.

Practice requires all significant investing and financing activities be disclosed whether or not cash is affected. Accordingly, the following entries are included to account for acquiring fixed assets through issuance of debt:

		Debit	Credit
(c)	Fixed Assets	100,000	
	Noncash Transactions		100,000
(d)	Noncash Transactions	100,000	
	Bonds Payable		100,000

The write-off of fully depreciated assets does not affect cash nor does it represent an important investing or financing activity. Therefore, it is not reflected in the statement of cash flows. We reconstruct this transaction as:

		Debit	Credit
(e)	Accumulated Depreciation	100,000	
	Fixed Assets		100,000

All known transactions are now posted to Fixed Assets. To arrive at the reported ending balance it is necessary to debit this account by $1,524,000. Our most probable conjecture is that Vatter acquired fixed assets at this amount for cash.

		Debit	Credit
(f)	Fixed Assets	1,524,000	
	Cash—Investing		1,524,000

Accumulated Depreciation. To balance Vatter's Accumulated Depreciation account, a credit of $360,000 is needed. This amount is the depreciation expense from the income statement.

		Debit	Credit
(g)	Cash—Operations	360,000	
	Accumulated Depreciation		360,000

Depreciation expense is added back to income because it is an expense not using cash.

Bonds Payable. Vatter's issuance of bonds is a financing activity. Our entry for issuance of bonds is:

		Debit	Credit
(h)	Cash—Financing	500,000	
	Bonds Payable		500,000

Converting bonds into common stock does not affect cash. However, as a significant financing activity it is disclosed in a separate schedule of the statement of cash flows.

		Debit	Credit
(i)	Bonds Payable	200,000	
	Noncash Transaction		200,000
(j)	Noncash Transaction	200,000	
	Capital Stock		200,000

Deferred Income Taxes. The charge for deferred income taxes does not require cash. It is an add-back to net income as an expense not requiring cash.

		Debit	Credit
(k)	Cash—Operations	20,000	
	Deferred Income Taxes		20,000

Capital Stock and Paid-In Capital. Vatter's sale of stock is a financing activity. Our entry for sale of stock is:

		Debit	Credit
(l)	Cash—Financing	1,000,000	
	Capital Stock		600,000
	Paid-In Capital		400,000

Retained Earnings. Net income of $951,000 is our starting point and it is adjusted for items needing conversion to a cash basis:

		Debit	Credit
(m)	Cash—Operations	951,000	
	Retained Earnings		951,000

Cash dividends paid to stockholders are a financing activity. Cash dividends paid amount to $750,000:

		Debit	Credit
(n)	Retained Earnings	750,000	
	Cash—Financing		750,000

Goodwill Amortization. Vatter's income statement reports $30,000 of goodwill amortization. Since this charge to income does not require cash, it is added back to net income:

		Debit	Credit
(o)	Cash—Operations	30,000	
	Goodwill		30,000

Investment in Affiliate. Equity in earnings of the unconsolidated affiliate (none are distributed as dividends) is a source of income not affecting cash. It is removed from net income:

		Debit	Credit
(p)	Investment in Affiliate	50,000	
	Cash—Operations		50,000

Accounts Receivable. The change in accounts receivable is necessary information in arriving at cash flow from operating activities. It is used to convert income from an accrual to a cash basis. An increase in accounts receivable implies some sales are not collected in cash. In Vatter's case, the $90,000 increase reduces cash flows from operations by an adjustment to income:

(q)	Accounts Receivable	90,000	
	Cash—Operations		90,000

Inventories. A change in inventories affects cash flows from operating activities. An increase in inventories implies purchases exceed cash outlays reported in cost of goods sold. An adjustment reducing cash flows from operations is proper:

(r)	Inventories	303,000	
	Cash—Operations		303,000

Accounts Payable. A change in accounts payable is important in arriving at cash flows from operating activities. Vatter's increase in accounts payable implies some purchases are not yet paid for. Expenses exceed cash outlays and require an adjustment to increase cash from operations.

(s)	Cash—Operations	230,000	
	Accounts Payable		230,000

Derivation of the Statement of Cash Flows

Once we reconstruct and analyze Vatter Corporation's transactions, we derive the statement of cash flows using the **master T-account** for cash. Vatter's statement of cash flows is reproduced in Exhibit 7.6. Exhibit 7.7 explains adjustments to convert Vatter's net income to a cash basis.

Operating Cash Flows and Net Income for Vatter Corporation

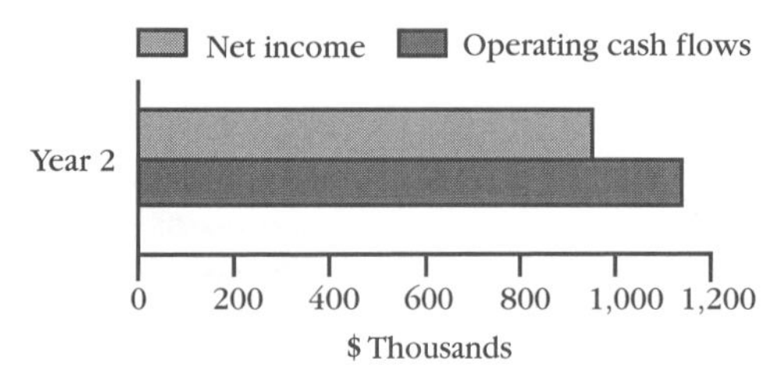

Reporting Cash Flows from Operations

There are two acceptable methods in reporting cash flows from operations (CFO): the indirect and direct methods. While both methods yield identical results, their format differs. However, these methods report identical formats for cash flows from investing and financing activities.

Indirect Method

The indirect method is used in Exhibits 7.6 and 7.7 and its accompanying analysis in determining cash flows from operations for Vatter Corporation. With the **indirect method,** net income is adjusted for noncash items requiring conversion to cash flows from operations. An advantage of this method is its reconciliation of differences between net income and operating cash flows. Some users predict cash flows by first predicting income and then adjusting income for leads and lags between

Companies Reporting Cash Flows using Indirect or Direct Formats

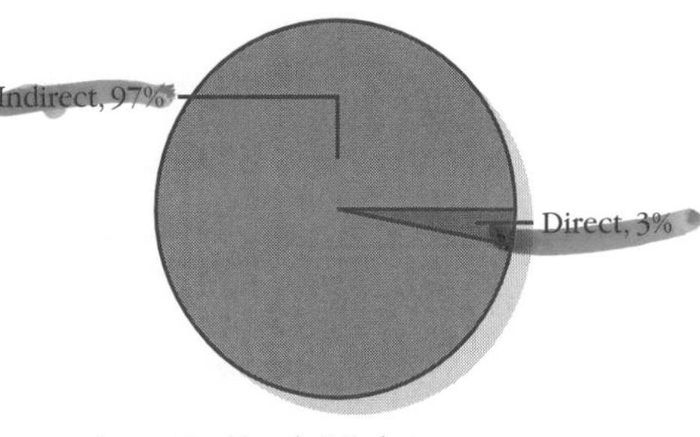

Source: *Accounting Trends & Techniques.*

EXHIBIT 7.6

VATTER CORPORATION
Statement of Cash Flows
For Year Ended December 31, Year 2
(in thousands)

Cash flows from operating activities:		
Net income	$ 951	
Add (deduct) adjustments to cash basis:		
Depreciation	360	
Amortization of goodwill	30	
Deferred income taxes	20	
Gain on sale of equipment	(2)	
Equity in earnings of affiliate	(50)	
Increase in receivables	(90)	
Increase in inventories	(303)	
Increase in accounts payable	230	
Net cash flows from operating activities		$ 1,146
Cash flows from investing activities:		
Purchase of fixed assets	$(1,974)	
Purchase of goodwill	(60)	
Sale of fixed assets	18	
Net cash flows used in investing activities		(2,016)
Cash flows from financing activities:		
Net proceeds from sale of bonds	$ 500	
Sale of capital stock	1,000	
Payment of dividends	(750)	
Net cash flows from financing activities		750
Net decrease in cash		$ (120)
Supplemental disclosure of cash flow information:		
Interest paid during year		$ 50
Income taxes paid during year		$ 900
Schedule of noncash investing and financing activities:		
Bonds issued to acquire fixed assets		$ 100
Stock issued in conversion of bonds		$ 200

income and cash flows—that is, using the noncash adjustments. Companies using the indirect method must disclose separately changes in inventory, receivables, and payables when reconciling income to operating cash flows. They must also report both interest and income taxes paid.

Direct Method

The **direct (or inflow-outflow) method** reports gross cash receipts and cash disbursements related to operations—essentially adjusting each income statement item from accrual to cash basis. A majority of respondents to the accounting *Exposure Draft* preceding current requirements for reporting cash flows, especially creditors, preferred the direct method. The direct method reports total amounts of cash flowing in and out of a company from operating activities. This offers us a better format to readily assess the amount of cash inflows and outflows for which management has

EXHIBIT 7.7 Deriving Operating Cash Flows from Income for Vatter Corp.

Item	*Amount (in thousands)*	*Explanation*
Net income, accrual basis	$ 951	Starting point of conversion
Add (deduct) adjustment to cash basis:		
Depreciation	360	Depreciation has no cash outflow.
Goodwill amortization	30	Amortization has no cash outflow.
Deferred income taxes	20	Deferred expense has no cash outflow.
Equity in earnings of affiliate	(50)	Item does not yield cash inflow.
Gain on sale of equipment	(2)	Remove gain (because it is nonoperating)—cash inflow is cash from investing activities.
Increase in receivables	(90)	Cash flow from sales is *less* than accrual sales.
Increase in inventories	(303)	Cash outflow for inventory *exceeds* accrual inventory cost included in cost of sales.
Increase in accounts payable	230	Cash outflows for purchases (included in cost of goods sold) is *less* than accrual purchases cost.
Cash flows from operations (Exhibit 7.6)	$1,146	

discretion. The risks to lenders are typically greater for fluctuations in cash flows from operations than in net income. Information on amounts of operating cash receipts and payments is important in assessing these fluctuations and risks. These important analytical considerations at first convinced regulators to require the direct method of reporting cash flows. But partly because preparers of information claimed this method imposes excessive implementation costs, regulators decided to encourage the direct method and to permit the indirect method. When companies report using the direct method, they must disclose a reconciliation of net income to cash flows from operations in a separate schedule. They also, at a minimum, must report the following cash receipts and payments:

Receipts:

- Cash from customers, including lessees, licensees, and similar.
- Interest and dividend payments received.
- Other operating cash receipts, if any.

Payments:

- Cash paid to employees and suppliers of goods or services, including suppliers of insurance, advertising, and similar.
- Interest paid.
- Income taxes paid.
- Other operating cash payments, if any.

Converting from Indirect to Direct Method

Because the vast majority of companies use the indirect method, we need to be prepared to convert cash flows from operations reported under the indirect method to the direct method. Accuracy of our conversion depends on adjustments using data

EXHIBIT 7.8 Converting Vatter's Operating Cash Flows from Indirect to Direct Format

Indirect Format		*Direct Format*	
Net income	$ 951	Total revenues ($19,950 + $50 + $2)	$20,002
Add: Depreciation	360	Remove gain on sale	(2)
Amortization	30	Less equity in earnings of affiliate	(50)
Deferred taxes	20	Less increase in receivables	(90)
Remove: Gain on sale of equipment	(2)	Cash receipts	$19,860
Deduct equity in earnings of affiliates	(50)		
Add (deduct) changes in:		Total expenses ($11,101 + $7,030 + $920)	$19,051
Receivables	(90)	Less: Depreciation	(360)
Inventories	(303)	Amortization	(30)
Payables	230	Deferred taxes	(20)
		Add increase in inventories	303
		Less increase in payables	(230)
		Cash payments	$18,714
Cash flows from operations	$1,146	Cash flows from operations	$ 1,146

available from external accounting records. The method of conversion we describe in this section (and in Appendix 7A) is sufficiently accurate for most analytical purposes.

Our conversion from the indirect to the direct format is portrayed in Exhibit 7.8 using values from Vatter Corporation. We begin by disaggregating (grossing up) net income ($951) into total revenues ($20,002) and total expenses ($19,051). Next, our conversion adjustments are applied to relevant categories of revenues or expenses. From these adjustments we report the direct format of Vatter Corporation's cash flows from operations in Exhibit 7.9. The equity in earnings of the affiliate (a noncash revenue item) and the gain from sale of equipment (transferred to investing activities) are omitted from the direct method presentation.

Adjustments to Cash Flow Components

Determining and analyzing cash flows from operations using the direct method is sometimes improved by relating adjustments to their applicable revenues and expenses. In certain cases these relations are clear. For example, the change in receivables (when used to adjust sales) approximates cash from customers. Similarly, the cash payment for taxes is determined as:

	Tax expense (accrual basis)
Add (deduct):	(Increase) decrease in deferred tax credits
	Increase (decrease) in deferred tax debits
	(Increase) decrease in taxes payable
	Increase (decrease) in tax refunds receivable
Equals	Cash paid for taxes

Since practice requires companies to disclose income taxes and interest paid, our analysis has these two amounts readily available.

EXHIBIT 7.9

VATTER CORPORATION
Cash Flows from Operations
For Year Ended December 31, Year 2
(in thousands)

Sales	$19,950	
Less increase in receivables	90	
Cash receipts		$19,860
Cash payments:		
Cost of goods sold	$11,101	
Less depreciation	360	
	$10,741	
Add: Increase in inventories	303	
	$11,044	
General, selling, and administrative expenses ($7,030 – $30)	7,000	
Less: Increase in accounts payable	(230)	$17,814
Income taxes—current ($920 – $20)		900
Total cash payments		$18,714
Cash flows from operations		$ 1,146

In certain cases, relating adjustments to revenues and expenses is inaccurate. For example, total depreciation expense can relate not only to cost of goods sold but also to general, selling, and administrative expenses. Similarly, payables, accruals, and prepayments can relate to more than one expense item. Our analytical adjustments depend on need, data availability, and degree of accuracy required. The more detailed the items of operating cash receipts and payments needed, the more detailed is the information required to determine their values.

Additional Disclosures and Adjustments

Practice requires companies who use the direct method in presenting cash flows from operations to also disclose cash flows from operations by the indirect method. To do this the preparer needs information generally available only from internal records. Our analysis assumes items in the reconciliation of income to cash flows from operations reflect adjustments using inside information. To ensure we understand these data, we analyze these required adjustments. Accurate adjustment of operating cash receipts and payments depends on segregating receivables and payables relating to operations from those relating to investing and financing activities. It also depends on eliminating the effects of noncash entries in Accounts Receivable, Accounts Payable, Inventories, and other relevant balance sheet accounts determining cash flows from operations.

In the case of Vatter Corporation, accounts receivable is shown net of an allowance for doubtful accounts. Because bad debts expense and the write-off of doubtful accounts are not disclosed, we approximate collections from customers as:

Receivables

	Debit	Credit	
Beginning	360		
Sales	19,950	19,860	Collections (plug)
Ending	450		

The collections of $19,860 are overstated because noncash entries to this account are not considered. However, if we knew the opening and closing balances of the Allowance for Doubtful Accounts are $20 and $25, respectively (often disclosed), and selling expenses include bad debts expense of $40 (occasionally disclosed), we can reconstruct these accounts and determine collections more accurately as:

Receivables

	Debit	Credit	
Beginning	380		
		35	(b)
Sales	19,950	19,820	Collections (plug)
Ending	475		

Allowance for Doubtful Accounts

	Debit	Credit	
		20	Beginning
(b)	35	40	(a)
		25	Ending

(*a*) Bad debt expense—reported.
(*b*) Bad debts written off—derived (plug).

Recognize that our prior estimate for collections of $19,860 is overstated by the bad debts expense amount.

Another example of a noncash entry occurs when a company includes certain depreciation costs in inventories. If a company does not disclose adjustments for these costs when reporting cash flows from operations using the indirect method, an increase in inventories is viewed incorrectly as a cash outflow. Another set of adjustments are required when a company purchases another company and consolidates its various assets and liabilities (details of all operations-related accounts are seldom disclosed). For example, assume Vatter Corporation purchases Bauman Enterprises in Year 2, including its inventories of $500. If we are unaware of this inventory amount, we would assume in our analysis the entire year-to-year increase in inventories of $303 relates to operations. This inventory increase is used to reduce cash flow from operations as reported in Exhibit 7.9. However, provided with this acquisition information we can now prepare an adjusting entry:

	Debit	Credit
Inventory	303	
Cash—Operations	197	
Cash—Investing		500

The $197 inventories decrease becomes an adjustment increasing cash flows from operations, and the $500 cash outlay is part of the amount paid for Bauman Enterprises included in investing activities. The ultimate effect of our lack of adjustments from the absence of inside information does *not* affect net cash flows, but does affect their classification across business activities.

Analysis Implications of Cash Flows

Cash flow information yields several analytical implications for our financial analysis. We discuss the more significant implications in this section.

Limitations in Cash Flow Reporting

The FASB argues a "more comprehensive and presumably more useful approach would be to use the direct method in the Statement of Cash Flows and to provide a reconciliation of net income and net cash flow from operating activities in a separate schedule—thereby reaping the benefit of both methods while maintaining the focus of the Statement of Cash Flows in cash receipts and payments." Yet the direct method is *not* required. Other limitations include:

- Practice does not require separate disclosure of cash flows pertaining to either extraordinary items or discontinued operations.
- Interest and dividends received, and interest paid, are classified as operating cash flows. Many users consider interest paid a financing outflow, and interest and dividends received as cash inflows from investing activities.
- Income taxes are classified as operating cash flows. This classification can distort our analysis of the three individual activities if significant tax benefits or costs are attributed to them in a disproportionate manner.
- Removal of pre-tax (rather than after-tax) gains or losses on sale of plant or investments from operating activities distorts our analysis of both operating and investing activities. This is because their related taxes are *not* removed, but left in total tax expense among operating activities.

Interpreting Cash Flows and Net Income

Our analysis of Vatter Corporation focused on the two primary financial statements directed to operating activities: the statement of cash flows and the income statement. In spite of practitioners' best efforts to explain the combined usefulness of both operating statements, not all users understand the dual information roles of cash flows and accrual net income. A recurrent misunderstanding among users is the meaning of *operations* and, also, the comparative relevance of cash flows and accrual net income in providing insights into operating activities. More simply, what different insights into operating activities do these two statements provide?

To help us understand their combined usefulness, we return to our analysis of Vatter Corporation. Exhibit 7.10 lists amounts side by side from both operating statements, and indicates their measurement objectives. We recognize the function of an income statement is to measure company profitability for a period. An income statement records revenues when earned and expenses when incurred. No other statement measures profitability in this manner. Yet an income statement does *not* show us the timing of cash inflows and outflows, nor the effect of operations on liquidity and solvency. This information is available to us in the statement of cash flows. The statement of cash flows provides us with this information separately for operating, investing, and financing activities.

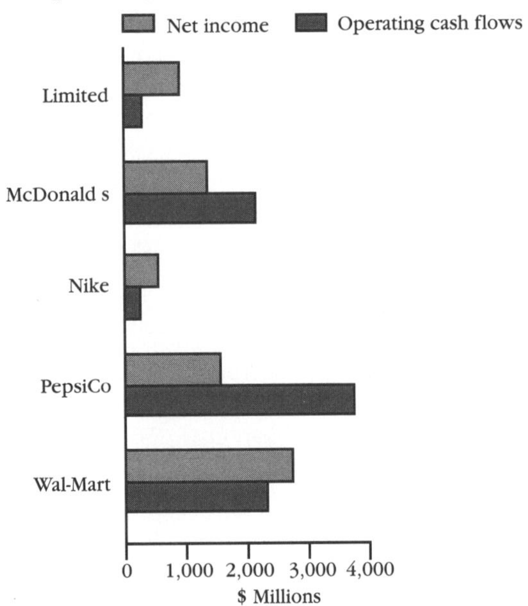

Source: Annual reports.

Cash flows from operations is a broader view on operating activities than is net income. Cash flows from operations encompass all earning-related activities of a company. This measure concerns not only revenues and expenses but also the cash demands of these activities. They include investing in customer receivables and inventories, and the financing provided by suppliers of goods and services. This difference is evident in Exhibit 7.10

Exhibit 7.10

VATTER CORPORATION
Comparison of Accrual and Cash Reporting

	Income Statement	***Operating Cash Flows***	
Sales	$19,950	$19,860*	Collections from customers
Equity in earnings of unconsolidated subsidiary	50	—	
Gain on sale of fixed assets	2	—†	
	$20,002	$19,860	Total collections
Cost of goods sold‡	$10,741	$10,814§	Payments to suppliers and labor
Depreciation	360	—	
General, selling, and administrative expenses	7,000	7,000	Payments for expenses
Amortization of goodwill	30	—	
Income taxes:			
Current	900	900	Payments for taxes
Deferred	20	—	
	$19,051	$18,714	Total disbursements
Net income	$ 951		
Cash from operations		$ 1,146	

*$19,950 (sales) – $90 (increase in receivables).

†Omitted because it is linked with proceeds from sales of assets under investing activities.

‡Exclusive of depreciation.

§$10,741 (cost of goods sold) + $303 (increase in inventories) – $230 (increase in payables). Note that the linkage of accounts payable to cost of goods sold is arbitrary because some may relate to other expense categories. However, no further breakdown is possible.

where we arrive at operating cash receipts and disbursements by adjusting items comprising the income statement using changes in operating assets and liabilities. Cash flow from operations focuses on the liquidity aspect of operations. It is *not* a measure of profitability because it does not include important costs like the use of long-lived assets in operations nor revenues like the noncash equity in earnings of subsidiaries or nonconsolidated affiliates.

We must bear in mind that a *net* measure, be it net income or cash flows from operations, is of limited usefulness. Whether our purpose of analysis is evaluation of prior performance or prediction of future performance, the key is information about **components** of these net measures. Our discussion in Chapter 13 emphasizes our evaluation of operating performance and future earning power depends not on net income but on the components comprising it.

Cash flows are often less subject to distortion than is net income. Accounting accruals determining net income rely on estimates, deferrals, allocations, and valuations. These considerations typically admit more subjectivity than factors determining cash flows. For this reason we often relate cash flows from operations to net income in assessing its quality. Certain users consider earnings of higher quality when the ratio of cash flows from operations divided by net income is greater. This derives from a concern with revenue recognition or expense accrual criteria yielding high net income but low cash flows. Cash flows from operations effectively serve as a check on net income, but not a substitute for net income. Cash flows from operations include a financing element and are useful for evaluating and projecting short-term liquidity and longer-term solvency.

Analysis Research Insight 7.1

Usefulness of Cash Flows

Are cash flow measures useful for users of financial statements? Do cash flow measures offer any additional information beyond accrual measures? Do securities markets react to cash flow information? Analysis research provides valuable insights into these important questions. Several studies of users identify a market shift away from traditional accrual measures like net income in favor of cash flow measures. These measures are increasingly used for credit analysis, bankruptcy prediction, assigning loan terms, earnings quality assessments, solvency forecasts, and setting dividend and expansion policies. Users of these measures include investors, analysts, creditors, auditors, and management.

Capital market studies provide evidence consistent with the use of cash flow measures. Namely, cash flows from operations explain changes in stock prices beyond those explained by net income. Research also suggests the usefulness of cash flow measures depends on the company and economic conditions prevailing. Evidence indicates the *components* of cash flows, and not the aggregate figure, are what drive the usefulness of cash flow data.

Cash flows from operations exclude, by definition, elements of revenues and expenses not currently affecting cash. Our analysis of operations and profitability should not proceed without considering these elements. Both the income statement and the statement of cash flows are designed to meet precise needs of users. The income statement uses accrual accounting in recognizing revenues earned and expenses incurred. Cash flows from operations report revenues received in cash and expenses paid. It is not an issue of which statement is superior to another—only a matter of our immediate analysis needs. Our use of these statements requires we bear in mind the statements' objectives and limitations.

Coca-Cola Enterprises, Inc., marketed a large initial share offering, not on the basis of traditional measures like price-earnings ratio (which was near 100), but on the basis of operating cash flows (specifically, earnings before taxes, depreciation, interest, and goodwill amortization). This latter measure substantially exceeded net income that was depressed due to heavy noncash charges.

Alternative Cash Flow Measures

Accrual accounting permits a variety of alternative accounting treatments and the potential for earnings management. Users sometimes use a crude measure of cash flows, defined as **net income plus major noncash expenses** (typically depreciation and amortization), to bypass these influences. This crude measure fails to provide for several important elements of cash flows and is an unreliable surrogate for cash flows. There is, however, at least one legitimate use of this measure. It is useful in comparing companies' income before depreciation and amortization—preferably these numbers are tax adjusted. Comparisons using this measure avoid differences arising from dissimilar depreciation methods and inconsistencies in estimates (useful life, salvage value).

The usefulness of this measure is demonstrated in the following case. Assume two companies (A and B) each invest $50,000 in machinery yielding $45,000 per year cash flows before depreciation. Assuming a five-year useful life and no salvage value for the machinery, results for the entire five-year period are:

	Five-Year Period
Cash provided by operations ($45,000 × 5 years)	$225,000
Cost of the machine	50,000
Income from operating machine	$175,000
Average yearly net income	$ 35,000

Under accrual accounting, the $175,000 five-year income is reported differently depending on the depreciation method adopted. Assuming company A adopts straight-line depreciation and company B adopts sum-of-the-years'-digits depreciation, annual income before and after depreciation (ignoring taxes) is:

		Company A: Straight-Line Depreciation		**Company B: Sum-of-the-Years'-Digits Depreciation**	
Year	*Income before Depreciation*	*Depreciation*	*Net Income*	*Depreciation*	*Net Income*
1	$ 45,000	$10,000	$ 35,000	$16,667	$ 28,333
2	45,000	10,000	35,000	13,334	31,666
3	45,000	10,000	35,000	10,000	35,000
4	45,000	10,000	35,000	6,667	38,333
5	45,000	10,000	35,000	3,332	41,668
Total	$225,000	$50,000	$175,000	$50,000	$175,000

Income before depreciation (or the "crude" cash flows measure) for these two companies is identical. This faithfully reveals identical earning power. However, income after depreciation, while identical for the entire five-year period, is considerably different for individual years. Accordingly, income before depreciation is a useful analytical tool provided we know its relevance and recognize its limitations.

Usefulness of cash flows is sometimes harmed by its misuse. Management dissatisfied with the reported income occasionally asserts cash flows are a better measure of performance. This is like asserting depreciation, or any costs not requiring immediate use of cash, are not genuine. When asked about cash flow measures, value-based investor Warren Buffett replied:

> We believe those numbers are frequently used by marketers of businesses and securities in attempts to justify the unjustifiable (and thereby to sell what should be the unsalable).

Net income is properly regarded as our measure of operating performance and is consistently linked with equity. If we add back depreciation to net income and compute return on investment, we are also in effect confusing the return *on* investment with return *of* investment in fixed assets. We should also realize that with inflation the depreciation allocated to sales is not likely sufficient for asset replacement because costs are probably higher. The primary source of cash from operations is sales to customers. It is from sales that companies pay expenses and make profits. If sales are insufficient to cover cash and accrual expenses, depreciation is not entirely covered.

Company and Economic Conditions

A balance sheet describes the assets of a company at a point in time and the manner in which those assets are financed. An income statement portrays the results of operations for a period of time. Income increases assets, including cash and noncash (both current and noncurrent) assets. Expenses are the consumption of assets (or incurrence of liabilities). Accordingly, net income is linked to cash flows through adjustments in balance sheet accounts.

It is conceivable that a profitable company can find it difficult to meet current obligations and need cash for expansion. Success through increasing sales can yield liquidity problems and restrict cash due to a growing asset base. Accordingly, there might be insufficient cash to cover maturing obligations. It is also important for us to distinguish performance across business activities. It is especially important to separate operating performance and profitability from investing and financing activities. All activities are essential and interconnected, but they are not identical and reflect on different aspects of companies. A statement of cash flows reveals the implications of earnings activities for cash. It reveals assets acquired and how they are financed. It describes how net income and cash flows from operations are different. The ability to generate cash flows from operations is vital to financial health. No business survives in the long term without generating cash from operations. Yet we must interpret cash flows and trends with care and an understanding of economic conditions.

While both successful and unsuccessful companies can experience problems with cash flows from operations, the reasons are markedly different. A successful company confronting increasing investments in receivables and inventories to meet expanding customer demand often finds its growing profitability useful in obtaining additional financing from both debt and equity suppliers. This profitability (positive accrual income) ultimately yields positive cash flows. An unsuccessful company experiences cash shortages from slowdowns in receivable and inventory turnovers, losses in operations, or combinations of these and other factors. The unsuccessful company can increase cash flows by reducing receivables and inventories, but usually this is done at the expense of services to customers, further depressing profits. These factors are signs of current and future crises and cash shortages, including declining trade credit. The unsuccessful company's decreasing cash flows have entirely different implications than for a successful one. Even if an unsuccessful manager borrows money, the costs and results of borrowing only magnify the ultimate loss. Profitability is our key variable; without it a company is doomed to failure.

We must also interpret changes in operating working capital items in light of economic circumstances. An increase in receivables can imply expanding consumer demand for products or it can signal an inability to collect amounts due in a timely fashion. Similarly, an increase in inventories (and particularly of raw materials) can imply anticipation of increases in production in response to consumer demand, or it can imply an inability to accurately anticipate demand or sell products (especially if finished goods inventory is increased).

Inflationary conditions add to the financial burdens and challenges of companies. The more significant challenges include replacing plant assets at costs exceeding depreciation expense, increasing investments in inventories and receivables, and dividend policies based on profits that do not provide for current costs of resources used in operations. While managerial decisions are not necessarily based on financial statements, we cannot dismiss their importance and implications. We look to the statement of cash flows for information on the effects, in current dollars, of how management copes under inflationary conditions. This yields a focus on cash flows from operations after capital expenditures and dividends.

Free Cash Flow

A useful analytical derivative of the statement of cash flows is the computation of **free cash flow**. As with other analytical measures, we must pay attention to components of the computation. Ulterior motives in reporting the components used in computing free cash flow can sometimes affect its usefulness. While there is not agreement on its exact definition, one of the more useful measures of free cash flow is:

	Cash flows from operations
Deduct:	Net capital expenditures required to maintain productive capacity
	Dividends on preferred stock and common stock (assuming a payout policy)
Equals	Free cash flow (FCF)

Positive free cash flow reflects the amount available for business activities after allowances for financing and investing requirements to maintain productive capacity at current levels. Growth and financial flexibility depend on adequate free cash flow. We must recognize that the amount of capital expenditures needed to maintain productive capacity is generally not disclosed. Rather it is part of total capital expenditures, which is disclosed, but can include outlays for expansion of productive capacity. Separating capital expenditures between these two components is problematic. The statement of cash flows rarely separates capital expenditures into maintenance and expansion components.

ANALYSIS VIEWPOINT *. . . You are the credit analyst*

You are a credit analyst at a credit-rating agency for industrial companies. A company you are rating has a strong history of positive (1) net cash flows, and (2) cash flows from operations. However, its free cash flow has recently turned negative and you expect it to remain negative into the foreseeable future. Do you change your credit rating of the company?

Cash Flows as Validators

The statement of cash flows is useful for our prediction of operating results on the basis of acquired and planned productive capacity. It is also of use in our assessment of a company's future expansion capacity, its capital requirements, and its sources of cash inflows. The statement of cash flows is an essential bridge between the income statement and the balance sheet. It reports a company's cash inflows and outflows, and a company's ability to meet current obligations. Moreover, the statement of cash flows provides us with important clues on:

- Feasibility of financing capital expenditures.
- Cash sources in financing expansion.
- Dependence on external financing (liabilities versus equity).
- Future dividend policies.
- Ability in meeting debt service requirements.
- Financial flexibility to unanticipated needs and opportunities.
- Financial practices of management.
- Quality of earnings.

The statement of cash flows is useful in identifying misleading or erroneous operating results or expectations. We recognize that cash flows are not easily managed, whereas net income can be managed through use of accruals using revenue recognition or expense deferral methods. Further discussion of earnings quality and the usefulness of cash flows as validators appears in Chapter 13. Nevertheless, like other statements, the statement of cash flows is more reliable and credible evidence of a company's actions and intentions than are predictions and press releases of management.

We must take care to examine relations among items in a statement of cash flows. Certain transactions are related—for example, purchasing assets by issuing debt. Yet our analysis must be careful not to infer relations among items where none exist. A change in cash, whether positive or negative, cannot be judged solely by the statement of cash flows. It must be analyzed in relation to other variables in a company's financial structure and operating results. For example, an increase in cash can arise from sacrificing a company's future earning power by selling valuable assets, or by taking on debt at high costs or unfavorable terms. Relations among financial statement items and their implications is important for the reliability of our analysis.

GUIDANCE ANSWERS TO ANALYSIS VIEWPOINTS

You Are the School Board Member

Your initial course of action is to verify management's claim of financial distress. A $1.2 million loss along with a $1.1 million decrease in net cash flows seemingly supports their claim. However, you should be suspicious of management's motives and its aversion to community activism. Consequently, you scrutinize the financial results, and your findings reveal a markedly different picture. You note cash flows from operations increased $1.5 million (– $1.1 = CFO – $1.9 – $0.7). You note that net income *before* the extraordinary loss is a positive $100,000. This is sufficient and powerful information with which to confront management. A serious and directed discussion is likely to yield reconsideration of this company's support of your educational programs.

You Are the Investor

Several factors can account for an increase in net cash flows when a loss is reported. Possibilities include: (1) early recognition of expenses relative to revenues generated (research and development), (2) valuable long-term sales contracts not yet recognized in income, (3) issuances of debt or equity to finance expansion, (4) selling of assets, (5) delayed cash payments, and (6) prepayment on sales. Our analysis of D.C. Bionics needs to focus on the components of both net income and net cash flows, and their implications for future performance.

You Are the Credit Analyst

The downward turn in free cash flow is an ominous sign. Free cash flow is the cash remaining after providing for commitments necessary to maintain operations at current levels. These commitments include a company's continuing operations, interest payments, income taxes, net capital expenditures, and dividends. A negative free cash flow implies a company must either sell assets or acquire financing (debt or equity) to maintain current operations. A significant change in free cash flow must be seriously analyzed in assigning a new credit rating.

A P P E N D I X

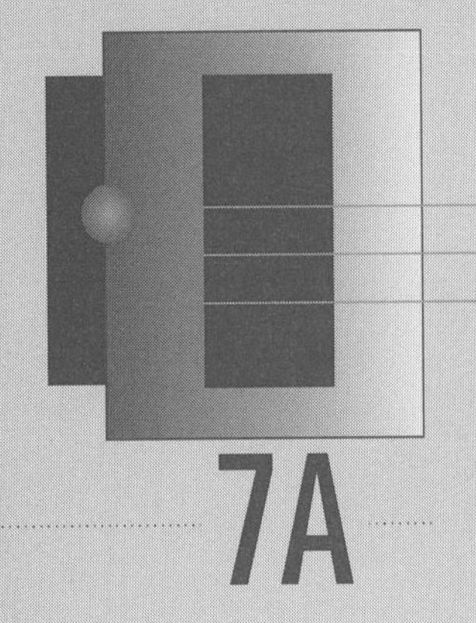

7A

Analytical Cash Flow Worksheets

This appendix provides us with usable worksheets to facilitate our converting of financial data to (1) direct (inflow-outflow) format for cash flows from operations, and (2) an *analytical* statement of cash flows.

Converting to a Direct Format

We often desire to convert a company's indirect format for cash flows from operations to an analytically more useful direct format. Exhibit 7A.1 displays a worksheet designed to simplify this conversion. The sources of data for this worksheet are the statement of cash flows, the income statement, and notes to these financial statements. Absent this disclosures, we might need to look at changes in balance sheet accounts or reconstruction of transactions (see Appendix 7B). Notes to the worksheet explain the items included, their sources, and their reconciliation to key financial statement items. Current disclosure requirements increase the accuracy and relevance of certain adjustments including those for noncash entries and acquisitions of operating assets and liabilities. In evaluating current cash flows and in forecasting of cash flows from operations, our analysis needs the cash effects of extraordinary items and discontinued operations. Since these disclosures are unavailable, their cash effects are available only if voluntarily disclosed by management or obtained in response to an inquiry.

Converting to an Analytical Statement

The analytical value of the statement of cash flows depends on its implementation potential. Specifically, some statements are reported in a format and with sufficient detail to meet our analysis needs. Our analysis must be prepared to adjust and recast published statements not meeting our needs. Exhibit 7A.2 is designed to facilitate our recasting of any statement of cash flows into an analytically useful statement. The conversion requires inserting amounts reported in the original statement and recasting them into our analytical statement of cash flows.

EXHIBIT 7A.1

FORM A
Worksheet to Compute Cash Flow from Operations (CFO)
Direct Presentation
For:____________
Year Ended __________
(in thousands)

	Line	Year		
		____	____	____
Cash receipts from operations:				
Net sales or revenues[(a)]	*1	$	$	$
Other revenue and income (see also lines 22 and 25)	*2			
(I) D in current receivables	3			
(I) D in noncurrent receivables[(b)]	4			
Other adjustments[(c)]	5			
Total Cash receipts	6			
Cash disbursements for operations:				
Total expenses (include interest and taxes)[(a)]	*7			
Less expenses and losses not using cash:				
– Depreciation and amortization	8			
– Noncurrent deferred income taxes	9			
– Other ______	10			
– Other ______	11			
– Other ______	12			
Changes in current operating assets and liabilities:				
I (D) in inventories	13			
I (D) in prepaid expenses	14			
(I) D in accounts payable	15			
(I) D in taxes payable	16			
(I) D in accruals	17			
I or D other ______	18			
I or D other ______	19			
I or D in noncurrent accounts[(b)]	20			
Total Cash disbursements[(d)]	21			
Dividends received:				
Equity in income of unconsolidated affiliates	*22			
Less undistributed equity in income of affiliates	23			
Dividends from unconsolidated affiliates	24			
Other cash receipts (disbursements)[(e)]	*25			
Describe ____________ (a)	25			
____________ (b)	25			
Total Cash flow from operations[(f)]	26			

Footnote all amounts that are composites or that are not self-evident. Indicate all sources for figures. I(D) refers to increases (decreases) in accounts.

*The sum of these five lines must equal reported net income per income statement.

[(a)]Including adjustment (grossing up) of revenue and expense of discontinued operations disclosed in footnote(s). Describe computation. Include other required adjustments and explain.

[(b)]Those relating to operations—describe in notes.

[(c)]Such as removal of gains included above—describe in notes.

[(d)]Which include (from supplemental disclosures):

Cash paid for interest (net of amount capitalized)	$____	____	____
Cash paid for income taxes	$____	____	____

[(e)]These include extraordinary items, discontinued operations and any other item not included above. The amount in line 25 is *after* adjustment to cash basis while the * refers to item(s) included in income *before* such adjustment. (Present details in notes.)

[(f)]Reconcile to amount reported by company. If not reported, reconcile to change in cash for period along with investing and financing activities.

EXHIBIT 7A.2

FORM B
Analytical Statement of Cash Flows*
For:_______________
Year Ended ___________
(in thousands)

		Year		
		______	______	______
Cash flows from operations:				
Income before extraordinary items	1	$	$	$
Add (deduct) adjustments to cash basis:				
Depreciation and amortization	2			
Deferred income taxes	3			
Equity in income of investees	4			
_______________(a)	5			
_______________(a)	6			
(I) D in receivables	7			
(I) D in inventories	8			
(I) D in prepaid expenses	9			
I (D) in accounts payable	10			
I (D) in accruals	11			
I (D) in taxes payable	12			
I or D in other current operating accounts[a]	13			
I or D in noncurrent operating accounts[a]	14			
Extraordinary items net of noncash items[b]	15			
Discontinued operations net of noncash items[b]	16			
Cash from operations[c]	17			
Cash flows from investing activities:				
Additions to properties	18			
Additions to investments (advances)	19			
Additions to other assets	20			
Cost of acquisition—net of cash	21			
Disposals of properties	22			
Decreases in other assets[a]	23			
Other[a]	24			
Cash from (used in) investing	25			
Cash flows from financing activities:				
Net I (D) in short-term debt	26			
I (D) in long-term debt	27			
I (D) of common and preferred stock[a]	28			
Dividends paid	29			
Other[a]	30			
Cash from (used in) financing	31			
Effect of exchange rate changes on cash:	32			
Net increase (decrease) in cash and equivalents	33			
Schedule of noncash activities[a]:				
_______________(a)	34			
_______________(a)	35			
_______________(a)	36			

*Use all figures from company's statement of cash flows. I (D) refers to increases (decreases) in accounts.

[a]Provide full details in statement or in separate notes.

[b]This information is not required to be disclosed. Provide details if this information is disclosed or can otherwise be obtained or reconstructed.

[c]To convert to the direct format use Form A in Exhibit 7A.1.

Adjusting the Statement of Cash Flows

Our analysis often needs to evaluate the statement of cash flows to determine whether explanations of changes in balance sheet accounts are adequate. When explanations are inadequate our analysis should reconstruct all or selected accounts in determining the necessary information or in limiting our conclusions. An entire reconstruction ensures that we consider all aspects of transactions in the statement, but such an extreme step is rarely necessary. Appendix 7B illustrates a reconstruction of transactions. Information from a reconstruction or analysis of disclosures should be included in our adjusted notes to the statement so we can use them in our analysis. The following are additional examples of adjustments.

Case 7A.1: When certain operations are discontinued, their effect on operations is usually reported in net or aggregate form (rarely disclosing more than revenues and expenses). Since changes in cash flows, and operating current assets and liabilities, are infrequently disclosed, it is difficult to separate the cash effects of discontinued operations from continuing operations. Our analysis must consider whether items on the income statement or statement of cash flows need adjustments. Adjustments are made by adding an adjustments column to our analytical statement of cash flows.

Case 7A.2: The *operating-nonoperating distinction* is not entirely clear. We view outlays for long-lived productive assets as *nonoperating* because their costs do not enter the income statement in the year of acquisition. The same is true of patent acquisitions that are amortized rather than immediately expensed, and motion picture films that are amortized over several periods. We choose to consider changes in noncurrent receivables as relating to operations provided they arose from the sale of operating assets like inventories. Our analysis must decide what a useful definition of operations is in a given situation. This information is difficult to obtain since it is not often revealed in financial statements. While practice requires management to use their informed judgment when classifying items in the statement, we need to be alert to misclassification.

Case 7A.3: When a company sells its receivables to a financial institution with recourse, the risk of ownership of these receivables often remains with the seller. Consequently, our analysis may not consider the reduction in receivables valid, but rather treat it as a short-term borrowing. Analytically, we accomplish this by reducing cash receipts from operations and increasing short-term borrowing (a financing source of cash).

Case 7A.4: When a business is purchased, information on operating working capital items acquired is often available only in the aggregate. Part of the change in receivables, inventories, or payables might be due to the acquisition and should not be used in adjusting sales and cost of sales which affect operating cash flows. Practice requires operating cash flows be adjusted for assets or liabilities acquired in a purchase of a business. If our analysis determines these adjustments are not adequately made, we must adjust the analytical statement. An example of adjustments necessary for the acquiring company in preparing a statement of cash flows follows. We start with the purchase entry ($ thousands):

Cash	20	
Accounts Receivable	200	
Inventories	300	
Other assets (including goodwill)	600	
Payables		120
Other liabilities		400
Cash		600

In preparing the statement, an investing cash outlay of $580 ($600 – $20) is shown and the gross changes in operating working capital items are adjusted as follows:

Accounts receivable reduced by $200.
Inventories reduced by $300.
Payables reduced by $120.

After adjusting all other assets and liabilities, the total equals the $580 investment. In this way the increase in accounts receivable of $200 is *not* attributed to uncollected sales (i.e., operations) but to part of the investing cash outflow.

Comprehensive Conversion and Adjustment Illustration

We illustrate the converting of Campbell Soup Company's published statement of cash flows into the analytically more useful formats presented in Exhibits 7A.1 and 7A.2. We also make the following assumption:

> We assume for this illustration only that Campbell disposed of a division in Year 11, having revenues of $1.2 million and an after-tax loss of $100,000. This after-tax loss is included in expenses. In the adjustment, we substitute for the after-tax loss of $100,000 the following—revenues of $1.2 million and expenses of $1.3 million minus the loss of $100,000 already included.

Exhibit 7A.3 reports our conversion of Campbell using Form A. Exhibit 7A.4 presents the conversion by means of Form B. Campbell acquires the balance of Campbell Canada in Year 11. In computing cash flows from operations and to conform with reporting requirements, Campbell probably adjusted operating assets and liabilities for amounts included in the acquisition (see item ⟨4⟩ in the table "Analysis of Unexplained Differences" in Appendix 7B).

EXHIBIT 7A.3

FORM A
Worksheet to Compute Cash Flow from Operations
Direct Presentation
For: Campbell Soup Company
Year Ended July 28, Year 11
(in millions)

	Line	*Year 11 Reported*	*Adjustments*	*Year 11 Revised*
Cash receipts from operations:				
Net sales	*1	$ 6204.1	$ 1.2[d]	$ 6202.9
Other revenue and income[e]	*2			
(I) D in current receivables	3	17.1		17.1
(I) D in noncurrent receivables	4			
Other adjustments	5			
Total cash receipts	6	$ 6221.2	$ 1.2	$ 6220.0
Cash disbursements for operations:				
Total expenses (include interest and taxes)[a][e]	*7	$ 5805.0	$ (1.2)[d]	$ 5803.8
Less expenses and losses not using cash:				
– Depreciation and amortization	8	(208.6)		(208.6)
– Noncurrent deferred income taxes	9	(35.5)		(35.5)
– Other, Net[c]	10	(57.4)		(57.4)
– Other ________	11			
– Other ________	12			
Changes in current operating assets and liabilities:				
I (D) in inventories	13	(48.7)		(48.7)
I (D) in prepaid expenses	14			
(I) D in accounts payable	15			
(I) D in taxes payable	16			
(I) D in accruals	17			
	18			
I or D other current assets & liabilities	19	(30.6)		(30.6)
I or D in noncurrent accounts	20			
Total cash disbursements	21	$ 5424.2	$ (1.2)	$ 5423.0
Dividends received:				
Equity in income of unconsolidated affiliates	*22	$ 2.4		$ 2.4
– Distribution in excess of income of affiliate 169A	23	5.8		5.8
Dividends from unconsolidated affiliates 169A	24	$ 8.2	$	$ 8.2
Other cash receipts (disbursements)	*25	$	$	$
Describe ________________ (a)	25	$	$	$
________________ (b)	25			
Cash flow from operations[b]	26	$ 805.2	$	$ 805.2

*The sum of these five lines must equal reported net income per income statement.

[a]Total expenses 22A + Taxes on earnings 27 + Minority interests 25 (or $5531.9 + $265.9 + $7.2).

[b]As reported.

[c]60 – (Line 24 – Line 22) ⇒ $63.2 – ($8.2 – $2.4) = $57.4. Dividends received from Armotts Ltd 169A $8.2 exceeds Equity in Earnings of affiliates 24 of $2.4. This difference is removed from other, net 60 of $63.2 and included on line 23.

[d]Revenues and expenses of discontinued operations of $1.3 million minus loss from discontinued operations of $1 million.

[e]It is acceptable to remove interest income of $26 from total expenses and include it on line 2.

EXHIBIT 7A.4

FORM B
Analytical Statement of Cash Flows*
For: Campbell Soup Company
Year Ended July 28, Year 11
(in millions)

Ref.		Line	*Year 11 Reported*	*Adjustments[(b)]*	*Year 11 Revised*
	Cash flows from operations:				
56	Income before extraordinary items	1	$ 401.5	$	$
	Add (deduct) adjustments to cash:				
57	Depreciation and amortization	2	208.6		
59	Deferred income taxes	3	35.5		
	Equity in income of investees	4			
60	Other—net	5	63.2		
	Decrease in dividend payable	6			
61	(I) D in receivables	7	17.1		
62	(I) D in inventories	8	48.7		
	(I) D in prepaid expenses	9			
	I (D) in accounts payable	10			
	I (D) in accruals	11			
	I (D) in taxes payable	12			
	I or D in other current operating accounts	13	30.6		
	I or D in noncurrent operating accounts[(a)]	14			
	Extraordinary items net of noncash items[(a)]	15			
	Discontinued operations net of noncash items[(a)]	16			
	Cash from operations	17	$ 805.2	$	$
	Cash flows from investing activities:				
65	Additions to properties	18	(361.1)		
	Additions to investments (advances)	19			
69	Additions to other assets	20	(57.8)		
67	Cost of acquisition—net of cash	21	(180.1)		
66	Disposals of properties	22	43.2		
68	Decreases in other assets[(a)]	23	67.4		
70	Other[(a)]—net change in temporary investments	24	9.7		
	Cash used in investing	25	$ (478.7)		
	Cash flows from financing activities:				
74 + 75 − 76	Net I (D) in short-term debt	26	$ (227.0)		
72 − 73	I (D) in long-term debt ($402.8 – $129.9)	27	272.9		
78 − 79	I (D) of common and preferred stock—treasury stock (net)[(a)] ($175.6 – $47.7)	28	(127.9)		
77	Dividends paid	29	(137.5)		
80	Other—net[(a)]	30	(0.1)		
	Cash used in financing	31	$ (219.6)		
82	Effect of exchange rate changes on cash:	32	$ (8.7)		
83	**Net increase (decrease) in cash and equivalents**	33	$ 98.2		
	Schedule of noncash activities[(a)]:				
	________	34			
	________	35			
	________	36			

*All figures from company's statements of cash flows.
[(a)]Provide full details in statement or in separate notes.
[(b)]No adjustments required in this case.

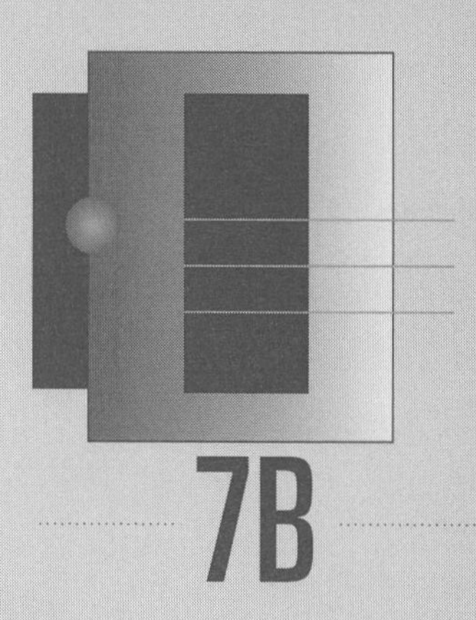

7B

A P P E N D I X

Analytical Reconstruction of Transactions

As we discussed in Appendix 7A, a *reconstruction* in the aggregate of all transactions for a period can (1) determine whether the statement of cash flows satisfactorily explains all changes in balance sheet accounts, (2) provide additional information helpful in understanding the statement, and (3) provide analytically useful insights into the aggregate transactions of a period and the relations among them.

In reconstruction, insight is obtained on summary transactions management has chosen to combine in categories often designated as "other." In addition to immaterial items and nonsignificant noncash transactions, adjustments like those relating to acquisitions and disposals yield unexplained differences in reconstruction. While these undisclosed adjustments relieve the statement of cash flows of unimportant details (like stock dividends or write-offs of fully depreciated assets), they can mask significant transactions (like new investments) for our analysis. Reconstruction also provides a check on management's classifications and descriptions of items.

Reconstruction is essentially the *reverse* of preparation. The steps of reconstruction are:

1. Establish T-accounts for all noncash accounts and one master T-account for cash with subdivisions for operations, investing, financing, and noncash transactions.
2. Insert opening and closing balances in all accounts. Verify that the individual debits and credits of all accounts are in balance.
3. Use all items in the statement of cash flows and additional information in other financial statements, notes, and elsewhere to reconstruct all T-accounts.
4. Items unable to post to T-accounts, and amounts needed to balance T-accounts, are posted to an Unexplained Differences account that must balance; if it does not, an error in posting or arithmetic exists. Based on all available information, we analyze and interpret the Unexplained Differences.

Exhibit 7B.1 presents reconstruction in T-accounts of Campbell Soup Company for Year 11. Notice all items in the statement of cash flows are listed in the Cash T-account. To not omit any items, it is best to list items in the order they appear on the statement of cash flows. Posting debits or credits to T-accounts requires knowledge of accounting and use of the information reported with the statement. As the posting entries indicate, most items are readily assigned to

EXHIBIT 7B.1

CAMPBELL SOUP COMPANY
Reconstruction of T-Accounts
For Year Ended July 28, Year 11

Cash and Cash Equivalents

	Debit	Credit	
Beg.	80.7		
Operations			
56 Net income	401.5		
57 Depreciation & amortization	208.6		
59 Deferred taxes	35.5		
60 Other, net	63.2		
61 Decrease in accounts receivable	17.1		
62 Decrease in inventories	48.7		
63 Net change in other current assets and liabilities	30.6		
Investing, Financing and Noncash Activities			
66 Sales of plant assets	43.2	361.1	65 Purchase of plant assets
68 Sales of business	67.4	180.1	67 Business acquired
70 Net change in other temporary investments	9.7	57.8	69 Increase in other assets
72 Long-term borrowings	402.8	129.9	73 Repayments of long-term borrowings
75 Other-short-term borrowings	117.3	137.9	74 Decrease in borrowings with less than 3 month maturities
79 Treasury stock issued	47.7	206.4	76 Repayments of other short-term borrowings
		137.5	77 Dividends paid
		175.6	78 Treasury stock purchases
		0.1	80 Other, net
		8.7	82 Exchange rate effect to cash
End.	178.9		

*These three categories can be shown separately.

Temporary Investments

	Debit	Credit	
Beg.	22.5	9.7	70
End.	12.8		

Accounts Receivable

	Debit	Credit	
Beg.	624.5	17.1	61
		80.0	A
End.	527.4		

Inventories

	Debit	Credit	
Beg.	819.8	48.7	62
		64.4	B
End.	706.7		

Prepaid Expenses

	Debit	Credit	
Beg.	118.0	25.3	C
End.	92.7		

Plant Assets

	Debit	Credit	
161A Beg.	2,734.9	174.1	D
65	361.1		
161A End.	2,921.9		

Accumulated Depreciation

	Debit	Credit	
E	80.2	1,017.2	Beg. 162
		194.5	57
		1,131.5	End. 162

Intangible Assets—Net

	Debit	Credit	
Beg.	383.4	14.1	57
F	66.2		
End.	435.5		

Other Assets

	Debit	Credit	
Beg.	349.0	2.2	G
69	57.8		
End.	404.6		

EXHIBIT 7B.1 *(concluded)*

Notes Payable

	Debit	Credit	
74	137.9	202.3	Beg.
76	206.4	117.3	75
		306.9	H
		282.2	End.

Payable to Suppliers & Others

	Debit	Credit	
I	42.8	525.2	Beg.
		482.4	End.

Accrued Liabilities

	Debit	Credit	
J	83.2	491.9	Beg.
		408.7	End.

Dividends Payable

	Debit	Credit	
		32.3	Beg.
		4.7	K
		37.0	End.

Accrued Income Taxes

	Debit	Credit	
		46.4	Beg.
		21.3	L
		67.7	End.

Long-Term Debt

	Debit	Credit	
73	129.9	805.8	Beg.
M	306.1	402.8	72
		772.6	End.

Deferred Income Taxes

	Debit	Credit	
N	12.1	235.1	Beg. 176
		35.5	59
		258.5	End. 176

Other Liabilities

	Debit	Credit	
O	5.5	28.5	Beg. 177
		23.0	End. 177

Minority Interest

	Debit	Credit	
P	32.8	56.3	Beg. 178
		23.5	End. 178

Common Stock

	Debit	Credit	
		20.3	Beg.
		20.3	End.

Capital Surplus

	Debit	Credit	
		61.9	Beg.
		45.4	Q
		107.3	End.

Retained Earnings

	Debit	Credit	
77	137.5	1,653.3	Beg.
R	4.7	401.5	56
		1,912.6	End.

Treasury Stock

	Debit	Credit	
Beg.	107.2	47.7	79
78	175.6		
S	35.3		
End.	270.4		

Cumulative Translation Adj.

	Debit	Credit	
T	39.9	63.5	Beg.
		23.6	End.

Unexplained Differences

		Debit	Credit		
67	Business acquired	180.1	63.2	60	Other, net
80	Other, net	0.1	30.6	63	Net change in other current assets and liabilities
82	Exchange rate effect on cash	8.7			
A	Account receivables	80.0	43.2	66	Sales of plant assets
B	Inventories	64.4	67.4	68	Sales of business
C	Prepaid expenses	25.3	80.2	E	Accumulated depreciation
D	Plant assets—net	174.1	66.2	F	Intangible assets
G	Other assets	2.2	42.8	I	Payable to suppliers and others
H	Notes payable	306.9	83.2	J	Accrued liabilities
K	Dividend payable	4.7	306.1	M	Long-term debt
L	Accrued income taxes	21.3	12.1	N	Deferred income taxes
Q	Capital surplus	45.4	5.5	O	Other liabilities
			32.8	P	Minority interest
			4.7	R	Retained earnings
			35.3	S	Treasury stock
			39.9	T	Cumulative translation adj.
		913.2	913.2		

their accounts. However, some items cannot be posted to a specific contra T-account and are posted to the Unexplained Differences T-account. These items are best analyzed after all items are posted.

Once posting is complete, we analyze each T-account to determine whether posted items explain the change in the opening to the closing balance. In some T-accounts, unexplained debit or credits are needed (plugged) to reconcile the account. These are posted on the opposite side (debit or credit) of the Unexplained Differences account and keyed with letters (A, B, C, . . .) for reference. In sum, items posted to Unexplained Differences include:

1. Items whose description in the statement of cash flows is inadequate to enable posting to a T-account. For example, "Other, net" items and "Effect of exchange rate changes on cash" are included here.
2. Items from complex transactions like "Businesses acquired," "Sales of businesses," and "Net change in other current assets and liabilities" represent aggregations of assets and liabilities relating to operations.
3. Items needed to balance T-accounts after all items from the statement of cash flows are posted. These are items identified as A, B, C, and so on.

Since plugged amounts in individual accounts must equal the unexplained items posted to the Unexplained Differences account, this account must balance. Posting all these items to the Unexplained Differences account helps in their analysis as we show below.

The entries below explain our posting of each item from Campbell's statement of cash flows to T-accounts.

		Debit	Credit
56	Cash—Operations	401.5	
	Retained Earnings		401.5
57	Cash—Operations	208.6	
	Accumulated Depreciation 187		194.5
	Intangible Assets—Net		14.1
59	Cash—Operations	35.5	
	Deferred Income Taxes		35.5
60	Cash—Operations	63.2	
	Unexplained Differences		63.2
	This amount is composed of several items. We transfer it to the unexplained T-account. After all items are posted we are in a better position to assign its amount to the proper accounts		
61	Cash—Operations	17.1	
	Accounts Receivable		17.1
62	Cash—Operations	48.7	
	Inventories		48.7
63	Cash—Operations	30.6	
	Unexplained Differences		30.6
	This amount is composed of several items related to current assets and liabilities. We post it to the unexplained T-account.		
65	Plant Assets—Net	361.1	
	Cash—Investing		361.1
66	Cash—Investing	43.2	
	Unexplained Differences		43.2
	Since we do not know the book value for assets sold, we transfer this amount to the unexplained T-account.		
67	Unexplained Differences	180.1	
	Cash—Investing		180.1
	This amount represents the business acquired that relates to a number of different accounts. We post it to the unexplained T-account.		

Ref.	Account	Debit	Credit
[68]	Cash—Investing	67.4	
	Unexplained Differences		67.4
	We do not have enough information on the sales of business. We transfer this amount to the unexplained T-account.		
[69]	Other Assets	57.8	
	Cash—Investing		57.8
[70]	Cash—Investing	9.7	
	Temporary Investments		9.7
[72]	Cash—Financing	402.8	
	Long-Term Debt		402.8
[73]	Long-Term Debt	129.9	
	Cash—Financing		129.9
[74]	Notes Payable	137.9	
	Cash—Financing		137.9
[75]	Cash—Financing	117.3	
	Notes Payable		117.3
[76]	Notes Payable	206.4	
	Cash—Financing		206.4
[77]	Retained Earnings	137.5	
	Cash—Financing		137.5
[78]	Treasury Stock	175.6	
	Cash—Financing		175.6
[79]	Cash—Financing	47.7	
	Treasury Stock		47.7
[80]	Unexplained Differences	0.1	
	Cash—Financing		0.1
	We post it to the unexplained T-account because we do not know to which accounts this amount is related.		
[82]	Unexplained Differences	8.7	
	Cash—Financing		8.7
	We do not know to what specific accounts these translation adjustments relate, so they are posted to the unexplained T-account.		

CAMPBELL SOUP COMPANY
Analysis of Unexplained Differences
For Year Ended July 28, Year 11

Ref. Items			
	<1>		
R	Retained Earnings	4.7	
K	Dividend Payable		4.7
	Noncash entry.		
	<2>		
M	Long-Term Debt	306.1	
H	Notes Payable		306.9
	Transfer from long-term debt to current, unexplained = 0.8.		
	<3>		
	Cash (or receivables)	22.5	
S	Treasury Stock	35.3	
Q	Capital Surplus		45.4
	Treasury stock issued—Management Incentive and Stock Option Plan—see data in 91—unexplained TS transactions		12.4

Ref. Items			
	<4>		
63	Net change in other current operating assets and liabilities	30.6	
I	Payable to suppliers and others	42.8	
J	Accrued Liabilities	83.2	
A	Accounts Receivable		80.0
B	Inventories		64.4
C	Prepaid Expenses		25.3
L	Accrued Income Taxes		21.3
	Unexplained*	34.4	
	*Difference is composed of adjustments to those accounts due to acquisitions and dispositions.		
	<5>		
66	Sales of Plant Assets—Cash	43.2	
68	Sales of Business—Cash	67.4	
E	Accumulated Depreciation	80.2	
N	Deferred Income Taxes	12.1	
P	Minority Interest	32.8	
T	Translation Adjustments		?
D	Plant Assets		174.1
	Incomplete entry relating to asset and business disposition.		
	<6>		
F	Intangible Assets	66.2	
T	Translation Adjustments	?	
67	Business Acquired—Cash		180.1
	Asset and Liabilities Acquired	?	
	(part of unexplained entry <4>)		?
	Incomplete entry relating to business and assets acquired.		

Our analysis of the transactions of Campbell provides us with insights into many undisclosed and unexplained items. It also provides a basis for informed questions to management. In extending the Campbell case to generalizations about reconstruction, we must emphasize that unexplained changes are *net*. That is, they can result from a number of significant debit and credit transactions but yield a relatively insignificant net amount. Moreover, these transactions can be informative about a company's activities (new or additional investments, losses) beyond the significance of amounts involved. Our analysis can identify the composition of these items up to a certain point. Beyond this point we need further information from management or to conduct additional analysis.

QUESTIONS

7–1. What information can a user of financial statements obtain from the statement of cash flows?

7–2. Describe the three major activities comprising the statement of cash flows.

7–3. Explain the three categories of adjustments in converting net income to cash flows from operations.

7–4. Describe the two methods of reporting cash flow from operations.

7–5. Contrast the purpose of the income statement with that of cash flow from operations.

7–6. What is the meaning of the term *cash flow*? Why is this term subject to confusion and misrepresentation?

7–7. Discuss the importance to analysis of the statement of cash flows. Identify factors entering into the interpretation of cash flows from operations.

7–8. Describe the computation of free cash flow. What is its relevance to financial analysis?

7–9. List insights that the statement of cash flows can provide to our analysis.

7–10. What is the objective of an analytical reconstruction of all transactions?

EXERCISES

Exercise 7–1

Relations in the Statement of Cash Flows

a. Practice requires the classification of cash inflows and outflows into three categories. Identify and describe them.

b. Which noncash activities are reported with the statement of cash flows and how are they reported?

c. First Corporation retains you to consult with them on preparation of the statement of cash flows using the indirect method for the year ended December 31, Year 8. Advise how the following items affect the statement of cash flows and how they are shown on the statement:

1. Net income for the fiscal year is $950,000, including an extraordinary gain of $60,000.
2. Depreciation expense of $80,000 is included in the income statement.
3. Uncollectible accounts receivable of $50,000 are written off against the allowance for uncollectible accounts. Bad debts expense of $24,000 is included in determining earnings for the year, and the same amount is added to the allowance for uncollectible accounts.
4. Accounts receivable increase by $140,000 during the year and inventories decline by $60,000.
5. Taxes paid to governments amount to $380,000.
6. A gain of $5,000 is realized on the sale of a machine; it originally cost $75,000 and $25,000 is undepreciated on the date of sale.
7. On June 5, Year 8, building and land are purchased for $600,000; First Corp. gave in payment $100,000 cash, $200,000 market value of its unissued common stock, and a $300,000 mortgage note.
8. On August 8, Year 8, First Corp. converts $700,000 face value of its 6 percent convertible debentures into $140,000 par value of its common stock. The bonds are originally issued at face value.
9. The board of directors declares a $320,000 cash dividend on October 30, Year 8, payable on January 15, Year 9, to stockholders of record on November 15, Year 8.
10. On December 15, Year 8, First Corp. declares a 2-for-1 stock split payable on December 25, Year 8.

Exercise 7-2

Analyzing Operating Cash Flows

The following data are taken from the records of Saro Corporation and subsidiaries for Year 1:

Net income	$10,000
Depreciation, depletion, and amortization	8,000
Disposals of property, plant, and equipment (book value) for cash	1,000
Deferred income taxes for Year 1 (noncurrent)	400
Undistributed earnings of unconsolidated affiliates	200
Amortization of discount on bonds payable	50
Amortization of premium on bonds payable	60
Decrease in noncurrent assets	1,500
Cash proceeds from exercise of stock options	300
Increase in accounts receivable	900
Increase in accounts payable	1,200
Decrease in inventories	850
Increase in dividends payable	300
Decrease in notes payable to banks	400

Required:

a. Determine the amount of cash flows from operations for Year 1.

b. For the following items explain their meaning, and their implications, if any, in adjusting net income to arrive at cash flows from operations.

1. Issuance of treasury stock as employee compensation.
2. Capitalization of interest incurred.
3. Amount charged to pension expense differing from the amount funded.

Exercise 7–3

Deriving Cash Flows from Financial Statements

Reproduced below are the balance sheets of Barrier Corporation as of December 31, Year 2, and Year 1, and the statement of income and retained earnings for the year ended December 31, Year 2.

BARRIER CORPORATION
Balance Sheets
As of December 31, Year 2, and Year 1

	Year 2	*Year 1*	*Increase (decrease)*
Assets			
Cash	$ 275,000	$ 180,000	$ 95,000
Accounts receivable	295,000	305,000	(10,000)
Inventories	549,000	431,000	118,000
Investment in Ort. Inc., at equity	73,000	60,000	13,000
Land	350,000	200,000	150,000
Plant and equipment	624,000	606,000	18,000
Less: accumulated depreciation	(139,000)	(107,000)	(32,000)
Goodwill	16,000	20,000	(4,000)
Total assets	$2,043,000	$1,695,000	$348,000
Liabilities and Stockholders' Equity			
Accounts payable	$ 604,000	$ 563,000	$ 41,000
Accrued expenses	150,000	—	150,000
Bonds payable	160,000	210,000	(50,000)
Deferred income taxes	41,000	30,000	11,000
Common stock, par $10	430,000	400,000	30,000
Additional paid-in capital	226,000	175,000	51,000
Retained earnings	432,000	334,000	98,000
Treasury stock, at cost	—	(17,000)	17,000
Total liabilities and equity	$2,043,000	$1,695,000	$348,000

BARRIER CORPORATION
Statement of Income and Retained Earnings
For Year Ended December 31, Year 2

Net sales		$1,937,000
Undistributed income from Ort. Inc.		13,000
Total net revenue		$1,950,000
Cost of sales		1,150,000
Gross income		$ 800,000
Depreciation expense	$ 32,000	
Amortization of goodwill	4,000	
Other expenses (including income taxes)	623,000	659,000
Net income		$ 141,000
Retained earnings, January 1, Year 2		334,000
		$ 475,000
Cash dividends paid		43,000
Retained earnings, December 31, Year 2		$ 432,000

Additional information:

- Capital stock is sold to provide additional cash.
- All accounts receivable and payable relate to operations.
- Accounts payable relate only to items included in cost of sales.
- There are no noncash transactions.

Required:

Determine the following amounts:

a. Cash collected from sales during Year 2.
b. Cash payments on accounts payable during Year 2.
c. Cash receipts during Year 2 *not* provided by operations.
d. Cash payments for noncurrent assets purchased during Year 2.

Exercise 7–4

Interpreting Cash Flows

Indicate if each transaction below is (1) a source of cash, (2) a use of cash, or (3) an adjustment leading to a source or use of cash. List also its placement in the statement of cash flows: operations (O), financing (F), investing (I), noncash significant (NCS), noncash nonsignificant (NCN), or no effect (NE).

Example **Transaction**	**Source**	**Use**	**Adjustment**	**Category in Statement of Cash Flows**
Cash dividend received	X			O

a. Increase in accounts receivable.
b. Pay bank note.
c. Issue common stock.
d. Sell marketable securities.
e. Retire bonds.
f. Declare stock dividend.
g. Purchase equipment.
h. Convert bonds to preferred stock.
i. Pay dividend.
j. Increase in accounts payable.

Exercise 7–5

Interpreting Cash Flows

Indicate if a transaction is (1) a source of cash, (2) a use of cash, or (3) an adjustment leading to a source or use of cash. List also its placement in the statement of cash flows: operations (O), financing (F), investing (I), noncash significant (NCS), noncash nonsignificant (NCN), no effect (NE).

Example **Transaction**	**Source**	**Use**	**Adjustment**	**Category in Statement of Cash Flows**
Sold bonds for cash	X			F

a. Decrease in inventory.
b. Paid current portion of long-term debt.
c. Retire treasury stock.
d. Buy marketable securities (noncurrent).
e. Issue bonds for property.
f. Declare stock dividend.
g. Sell equipment for cash.
h. Convert bonds to preferred stock.
i. Purchase inventory on credit.
j. Decrease in accounts payable from return of merchandise.

Exercise 7–6

Interpreting Economic Impacts of Transactions

During a meeting of the management committee of WEAK Corporation, a number of proposals are made to alleviate a weak cash position and improve income. Evaluate and comment on both the immediate *and* long-term effects of the following proposals on the measures indicated. Indicate increase (+), decrease (–), or no effect (NE).

	Effect on		
Proposal	***Net Income***	***Cash from Operations***	***Cash Position***
1. Substitute stock dividends for cash dividends.			
2. Delay needed capital expenditures.			
3. Reduce repair and maintenance outlays.			
4. Increase the provision for depreciation:			
a. For books only.			
b. For tax only.			
c. For both books and tax.			
5. Require earlier payment from clients.			
6. Delay payment to suppliers and pass up cash discounts.			
7. Borrow money short term.			
8. Switch from sum-of-the-years'-digits to straight-line depreciation for books only.			
9. Pressure dealers to buy more.			

Exercise 7–7

Depreciation as a Source of Cash

An economics book contains the following statement: "For the business firm there are, typically, three major sources of funds. Two of these, depreciation reserves and retained earnings, are internal. The third is external, consisting of funds obtained either by borrowing, or by the sale of new equities."

Required:

a. Is depreciation a source of cash? (Exclude all considerations pertaining to depreciation differences between taxable and financial accounting income.)

b. If depreciation is not a source of cash, what might explain the belief by some that depreciation is a source of cash?

c. If depreciation is a source of cash, explain the manner in which depreciation is a source of cash.

Exercise 7–8

Interpreting Differences between Net Income and Cash from Operations

Refer to the financial statements of Campbell Soup Company in Supplement A.

Required:

Explain how Campbell Soup Company can have net income of $401.5 million, but generate $805.2 million in cash from operations in Year 11. Explain this in language understood by a general businessperson. Illustrate your explanation by using the major reconciling items.

Exercise 7–9

Analyzing the Statement of Cash Flows

Refer to the financial statements of Campbell Soup Company in Supplement A.

Required:

a. How much cash does Campbell Soup collect from customers during Year 10? (*Hint:* Use the statement of cash flows to derive the beginning balance of receivables.)

b. How much is paid in cash dividends on common stock during Year 11?

c. How much is the total cost of goods and services produced and otherwise generated in Year 11? Consider all inventories.

d. How much is the deferred tax provision for Year 11? What effect did it have on current liabilities?

e. What effect does Year 11 depreciation expense have on cash from operations?

f. Why are the "Divestitures & restructuring" provisions in the statement of cash flows for Year 10 added back to net income in arriving at cash from operations?

g. What does the adjustment "Effect of exchange rate changes on cash" represent?

h. Note 1 to the financial statements discusses the accounting for disposal of property. Where is the adjustment of gain or loss found in the statement of cash flows?

Exercise 7–10

Analyzing the Statement of Cash Flows

Refer to the financial statements of Quaker Oats Company in Supplement A.

Required:

a. How much cash does Quaker Oats collect from customers during Year 10?

b. How much is paid in cash dividends on common stock during Year 11?

c. How much is the cost of goods and services produced and otherwise generated in Year 11? (*Hint:* Consider all inventories.)

d. If the company acquires property by issuing common stock, where in the statement of cash flows is this reported?

e. How much is the deferred tax provision for Year 11? What effect did it have on current liabilities?

f. What effect did the Year 11 depreciation expense have on cash from operations? Discuss as fully as you can.

g. What does the ($97.8) adjustment for receivables in the Year 11 statement of cash flows mean?

h. Does the cash flows from operations amount of $532.4 reported in Year 11 include discontinued operations?

i. How is it possible for Quaker Oats Company to have a Year 11 net income of $205.8 million but generate $532.4 million cash from operations? (Describe in general using selected figures; do not merely repeat the calculation shown in the statement.)

j. Where is the provision for uncollectible accounts probably included? How can this affect the presentation of the statement of cash flows?

k. Of the $532.4 million reported in Year 11 as cash flows from operations, what is your best estimate of cash provided by continuing operations?

PROBLEMS

Problem 7–1

Preparing and Analyzing the Statement of Cash Flows (Indirect)

A friend who is aware of your understanding of financial statements asks for your help in analyzing transactions and events of Zett Corporation. The following data are provided:

ZETT CORPORATION
Balance Sheet
At December 31, Year 2 and Year 1

	Year 1	*Year 2*
Cash	$ 34,000	$ 34,500
Accounts receivable (net)	12,000	17,000
Inventory	16,000	14,000
Investments (long term)	6,000	
Fixed assets	80,000	93,000
Accumulated depreciation	(48,000)	(39,000)
	$100,000	$119,500
Accounts payable	$ 19,000	$ 12,000
Bonds payable	10,000	30,000
Common stock	50,000	61,000
Retained earnings	21,000	28,000
Treasury stock		(11,500)
	$100,000	$119,500

Additional data for the period January 1, Year 2, through December 31, Year 2, are:

1. Sales on account, $70,000.
2. Purchases on account, $40,000.
3. Depreciation, $5,000.
4. Expenses paid in cash, $18,000 (including $4,000 of interest and $6,000 in taxes).
5. Decrease in inventory, $2,000.
6. Sale of fixed assets for $6,000 cash; cost $21,000 and two-thirds depreciated (loss or gain is included in income).
7. Purchase of fixed assets for cash, $4,000.
8. Fixed assets are exchanged for bonds payable of $30,000.
9. Sale of investments for $9,000 cash.
10. Purchase of treasury stock for cash, $11,500.
11. Retire bonds payable by issuing common stock, $10,000.
12. Collections on accounts receivable, $65,000.
13. Sold unissued common stock for cash, $1,000.

Required:

a. Prepare a statement of cash flows (indirect method) using the T-account approach for the year ending December 31, Year 2.

b. Prepare a side-by-side comparative statement contrasting two bases of reporting: (1) net income, and (2) cash flows from operations.

c. Which of the two statements in (b) better reflects profitability. Explain.

Problem 7–2

Analyzing the Statement of Cash Flows (Indirect)

Dax Corporation's genetically engineered flowers rapidly gain market acceptance and shipments to customers increase dramatically. The company prepares for significant increases in production. Management notes despite increasing profits the cash balance declines and it is forced to double debt in the current year. You are hired to advise management as to specific causes of the cash deficiency and how to remedy the situation. You are given the following balance sheets of Dax Corporation for Years 1 and 2 ($ thousands):

DAX CORPORATION
Balance Sheet
At December 31, Year 2 and Year 1

	Year 2		*Year 1*	
Cash		$ 500		$ 640
Accounts receivable (net)		860		550
Inventories		935		790
Prepaid expenses		25		—
Total current assets		$2,320		$1,980
Patents	$ 140			
Accumulated amortization	(10)	$ 130		—
Plant and equipment	$2,650		$1,950	
Accumulated depreciation	(600)	2,050	(510)	$1,440
Other assets	$ 200		$ 175	
Accumulated depreciation	(30)	170	(25)	150
Total noncurrent assets		$2,350		$1,590
Total assets		$4,670		$3,570
Accounts payable		$ 630		$ 600
Deferred income tax		57		45
Other current liabilities		85		78
Total current liabilities		$ 772		$ 723
Long-term debt		$1,650		$ 850
Common stock, $1 par		2,000		1,800
Retained earnings		248		197
Total long-term debt and equity		$3,898		$2,847
Total liabilities and equity		$4,670		$3,570

In addition, the following information is available:

1. Net income for Year 2 is $160,000 and for Year 1 is $130,000.
2. Cash dividends paid during Year 2 are $109,000 and during Year 1 are $100,000.
3. Depreciation expense charged to income during Year 2 is $95,000, and the provision for bad debts (expense) is $40,000. Expenses include cash payments of $28,000 in interest costs and $70,000 in income taxes.
4. During Year 2 the company purchases patents for $140,000 in cash. Amortization of patents during the year amount to $10,000.
5. Deferred income tax for Year 2 amounts to $12,000 and for Year 1 amounts to $15,000.

Required:

a. Prepare a statement of cash flows (indirect method) for Year 2 using the T-account approach.
b. Explain the discrepancy between net income and cash flows from operations.
c. Describe options available to management to remedy the cash deficiency.

Problem 7–3

Preparing the Statement of Cash Flows (Direct)

Using the income statement and balance sheets of Niagara Company below, prepare a statement of cash flows for the year ended December 31, Year 9, using the direct method.

NIAGARA COMPANY
Income Statement
Year Ended December 31, Year 9

Sales	$1,000
Cost of goods sold	(650)
Depreciation expense	(100)
Sales and general expense	(100)
Interest expense	(50)
Income tax expense	(40)
Net income	$ 60

NIAGARA COMPANY
Balance Sheets
As of December 31, Year 9 and Year 8

	Year 8	*Year 9*
Assets		
Cash	$ 50	$ 60
Accounts receivable	500	520
Inventory	750	770
Current assets	$1,300	$1,350
Fixed assets	500	550
Total assets	$1,800	$1,900
Liabilities and Capital		
Notes payable to banks	$ 100	$ 75
Accounts payable	590	615
Interest payable	10	20
Current liabilities	$ 700	$ 710
Long-term debt	300	350
Deferred income tax	300	310
Capital stock	400	400
Retained earnings	100	130
Total liabilities and capital	$1,800	$1,900

(CFA adapted)

Problem 7–4
Interpreting Cash Flow Effects of Transactions

Our ability to visualize quickly the effect of a transaction on the cash resources of a company is a useful analytical skill. This visualization requires an understanding of the economics underlying transactions and how they are accounted for. Expressing transactions in entry form can help us achieve a similar understanding of business activities.

Required:

A schematic statement of cash flows is reproduced below. The titles of lines in the schematic are given labels (letters). Several business activities of a company are listed below the schematic. For each of the activities listed, identify the lines affected and by what amount. Each activity is separate and unrelated to another, and the company closes its books once each year on December 31. Do not consider subsequent activities. Use the labels (letters) shown below. Do not indicate the effect on any line not given a label. If a transaction has no effect, write none. In indicating effects for lines *Y* and *C*, use a + to indicate an increase and a – to indicate a decrease. (*Hint:* Every activity with an effect, affects at least two lines—equal debits and credits. A journal entry is helpful in arriving at a solution.)

Schematic Statement of Cash Flows

Sources of Cash:

(Y)	Net income	________(Y)
(YA)	Additions and addbacks of expenses and losses not using cash	________(YA)
(YS)	Subtractions for revenues and gains not generating cash	________(YS)
	Changes in current operating assets and liabilities:	
(CC)	Add credit changes	________(CC)
(DC)	Deduct debit changes	________(DC)
(NC)	Add (deduct) changes in noncurrent operating accounts	________(NC)
	Cash flow from operations Y + YA – YS + CC – DC + or – NC	________
(DE)	Proceeds of debt and equity issues	________(DE)

Sources of Cash (continued):

(IL)	Increase in nonoperating current liabilities	________(IL)
(AD)	Proceeds of long-term assets dispositions	________(AD)
(OS)	Other sources of cash	________(OS)
	Total sources of cash	________

Uses of Cash:

(ID)	Income distributions	________(ID)
(R)	Retirements of debt and equity	________(R)
(DL)	Decreases in nonoperating current liabilities	________(DL)
(AA)	Long-term assets acquisitions	________(AA)
(OU)	Other uses of cash	________(OU)
	Total uses of cash	________
(C)	Increase (decrease) in cash	________(C)

Schedule of Noncash Investing and Financing Activities:

(NDE)	Issue of debt or equity	________(NDE)
(NCR)	Other noncash-generating credits	________(NCR)
(NAA)	Acquisitions of assets	________(NAA)
(NDR)	Other noncash-requiring debits	(NDR)

Examples:

i. Sales of $10,000 made on account.
ii. Dividends of $4,000 paid.
iii. Entered into long-term capital lease obligation (present value $60,000).

Answers in the form [Line, Amount]:

i. [DC, $10,000], [+ Y, $10,000]
ii. [ID, $4,000], [– C, $4,000]
iii. [NAA, $60,000], [NDE, $60,000]

Business Activities:

a. Provision for bad debt of $11,000 for the year is included in selling expenses.
b. Depreciation of $16,000 is charged to cost of goods sold.
c. Company acquires a building by issuance of a long-term mortgage note for $100,000.
d. Treasury stock with a cost of $7,000 is retired and canceled.
e. The company has outstanding 50,000 shares of common stock with par value of $1. The company declares a 20 percent stock dividend at the end of the year when the stock is selling for $16 a share.
f. Inventory costing $12,000 is destroyed by fire. The insurance company pays only $10,000 toward this loss, although the market value of the inventory is $15,000.
g. Inventories originally costing $25,000 are used by production departments in producing finished goods sold for $35,000 in cash and $5,000 in accounts receivable.
h. Accounts receivable of $8,000 are written off. There is an allowance for doubtful accounts balance of $5,000.
i. Long-lived assets are acquired for $100,000 cash on January 1. The company decides to depreciate $20,000 each year.
j. A machine costing $15,000 with accumulated depreciation of $6,000 is sold for $8,000 cash.

Problem 7–5

Interpreting Cash Flow Effects of Transactions

Complete the requirements of Problem 7–4 using the business activities listed below:

Part I

a. An annual installment of $100,000 due on long-term debt is paid on its due date.

b. Equipment originally costing $12,000 with $7,000 of accumulated depreciation is sold for $4,000 cash.

c. Obsolete inventory costing $75,000 is written down to zero.

d. Treasury stock costing $30,000 is sold for $28,000 cash.

e. A plant is acquired by issuing a $300,000 mortgage payable due in equal installments over six years.

f. The company's 30 percent-owned unconsolidated subsidiary earns $100,000 and pays dividends of $20,000. The company recorded its 30 percent share of these items using the equity method.

g. A product is sold for $40,000, to be paid $10,000 down plus $10,000 each year for three years. Interest at 10 percent of the outstanding balance is due. Consider only the effect at the time of sale (the company's operating cycle is less than one year).

h. The company uses a periodic inventory method. Certain inventory is mistakenly valued at $1,000—it should have been valued at $10,000. Show the effect of correcting the error.

i. Cash of $400,000 is used to acquire 100 percent of ZXY Manufacturing Company. At date of acquisition, ZXY has current assets of $300,000 (including $40,000 in cash); plant and equipment of $600,000; goodwill of $70,000; current liabilities of $160,000; and long-term debt of $410,000.

j. A provision for bad debt expense of $60,000 is made (calculated as a percent of sales for the period).

Part II

a. Investment of $120,000 cash in a 30 percent-owned company.

b. A 30 percent-owned subsidiary earns $25,000 (in total) and pays no dividends.

c. A 30 percent-owned subsidiary earns $30,000 (in total) and pays dividends of $10,000 (in total).

d. Equipment with an original cost of $15,000 and accumulated depreciation of $12,000 is sold for $4,000 cash.

e. The company borrowed $60,000 from its banks on November 30 payable on June 30 of next year.

f. Convertible bonds with a face value of $9,000 are converted into 1,000 shares of common stock with a par value of $2 per share.

g. Treasury stock with a cost of $4,000 is sold for $6,000 cash.

h. Common stock (par value $2) with a fair market value of $100,000 plus $100,000 cash are given to acquire 100 percent of ZYX Mfg. Co. At date of acquisition ZYX has current assets of $120,000 (including $40,000 cash); plant and equipment of $150,000; goodwill of $30,000; current liabilities of $60,000; and long-term debt of $40,000.

1. Identify the effect on the parent's statement.
2. Identify the effect on the consolidated statement.

i. The minority's share of income is $4,000.

j. Inventory with a cost of $80,000 is written down to its market value of $30,000.

k. Accounts receivable for $1,200 are written off. The company uses an allowance for doubtful accounts.

l. A noncancelable lease of equipment for 10 years with a present value of $120,000 is capitalized.

m. A 15 percent stock dividend is declared. The 60,000 shares of common stock issued as the dividend have a par value of $2 per share and a fair market value of $3 per share.

n. A provision of $27,000 for uncollectible accounts is made (calculated as a percent of sales for the period).

o. Dividends of $40,000 are declared on December 20 and are payable on January 20 of next year.

Problem 7–6

Reconstructing a Balance Sheet from Cash Flows

While on assignment you discover that you have misplaced the balance sheet of Bird Corporation as of January 1, Year 1. However, you do have the following data on Bird Corporation:

BIRD CORPORATION
Postclosing Trial Balance
December 31, Year 1

Debit balances:	
Cash	$ 100,000
Accounts receivable	120,000
Inventory	130,000
Property, plant, and equipment	550,000
Other noncurrent investments	200,000
	$1,100,000
Credit balances:	
Accounts payable	$ 100,000
Current portion of long-term debt	80,000
Accumulated depreciation	270,000
Long-term debt	200,000
Common stock	300,000
Retained earnings	150,000
	$1,100,000

BIRD CORPORATION
Statement of Cash Flows
For Year Ended December 31, Year 1

Cash from operations:			
Net income			$150,000
Add (deduct) adjustments to cash basis:			
Depreciation		$ 85,000	
Loss on sale of equipment		5,000	
Gain on sale of noncurrent investments		(50,000)	
Increase in accounts receivable		(30,000)	
Increase in inventories		(20,000)	
Increase in accounts payable		40,000	30,000
Cash from operations			$180,000
Investing activities:			
Additions to property and equipment		$(150,000)	
Sale of equipment		10,000	
Sale of investments		95,000	
Cash used for investing activities			(45,000)
Financing activities:			
Issuance of common stock		$ 10,000	
Additions to long-term debt	$ 15,000		
Decrease in current portion of long-term debt	(30,000)	(15,000)	
Cash dividends		(80,000)	
Cash used for financing activities			(85,000)
Increase in cash			$ 50,000

Required:

Reconstruct the T-accounts of Bird Corporation using the available data and information. Use T-accounts to prepare the balance sheet of Bird Corporation as of January 1, Year 1. (*Note:* Equipment sold had accumulated depreciation of $50,000.)

Problem 7–7
Analyzing Economic Impacts of Transactions

Indicate whether the following independent transactions increase (+), decrease (–), or do not affect (NE) the current ratio, the amount of working capital, and cash from operations. Also indicate the amounts of any effects. The company presently has a current ratio of 2 to 1 and current liabilities of $160,000.

	Current Ratio Effect	Working Capital *Effect $*	Cash from Operations *Effect $*
a. Paid accrued wages of $1,000.			
b. Purchased $20,000 worth of material on account.			
c. Received judgment notice from the court that the company must pay $70,000 damages for patent infringement within six months.			
d. Collected $8,000 of accounts receivable.			
e. Purchased land for factory for $100,000 cash.			
f. Repaid currently due bank note payable of $10,000.			
g. Received currently due note receivable of $15,000 from customer as consideration for sale of land.			
h. Received cash of $90,000 from stockholders as donated capital.			
i. Purchased machine costing $50,000; $15,000 down and the balance to be paid in seven equal annual installments.			
j. Retired bonds maturing five years hence at par of $50,000. Bonds have unamortized premium of $2,000.			
k. Declared dividends of $10,000 payable after year-end.			
l. Paid the above dividends in cash.			
m. Declared a 5% stock dividend.			
n. Paid the above stock dividend.			
o. Signed a long-term purchase contract of $100,000 to commence a year from now.			
p. Borrowed $40,000 cash for one year.			
q. Pays accounts payable of $20,000.			
r. Purchases a patent for $20,000.			
s. Writes off $15,000 of current marketable securities that became worthless.			
t. $8,500 of organization expenses are written off.			
u. Depreciation expense of $70,000 is recorded.			
v. Sold $28,000 of merchandise on account.			
w. A building is sold for $90,000. It has a book value of $45,000.			
x. A machine is sold at cost for $5,000; $2,500 down and the balance receivable in six months.			
y. Income tax expense is booked at $80,000, half of which is deferred (long term).			

Problem 7–8
Analyzing Operating Flow Measures

Your banker confides to you after looking at a number of financial statements that she is confused about the difference between two operating flow measures, net income and cash from operations.

Required:

a. Explain the purpose and significance of these two operating flow measures.

b. Several financial transactions or events are listed below. For each transaction or event, indicate whether it yields an increase (+), decrease (-), or no effect (NE) on each of the two measures.

	Effect of Transaction/Event on:	
	Net Income	***Cash from Operations***
1. Sale of marketable securities for cash at more than their carrying value.		
2. Sale of merchandise with deferred payments (one-half within one year and one-half after one year).		
3. Reclassify noncurrent receivable as current receivable.		
4. Payment of current portion of long-term debt.		
5. Collection of an account receivable.		
6. Recording the cost of goods sold.		
7. Purchase of inventories on account (credit terms).		
8. Accrual of sales commissions (to be paid at a later date).		
9. Payment of accounts payable (resulting from purchase of inventory).		
10. Provision for depreciation on a sales office.		
11. Borrowing cash from a bank on a 90-day note payable.		
12. Accrual of interest on a bank loan.		
13. Sale of partially depreciated equiment for cash at less than its book value.		
14. Flood damage to merchandise inventories (no insurance coverage).		
15. Declaration and payment of a cash dividend on preferred stock.		
16. Sale of merchandise on 90-day credit terms.		
17. Provision for uncollectible accounts receivable.		
18. Write-off of an uncollectible receivable.		
19. Provision for income tax expense (to be paid the following month).		
20. Provision for deferred income taxes (set up because depreciation for tax reporting exceeded depreciation for financial reporting).		
21. Purchase of a machine (fixed asset) for cash.		
22. Payment of accrued salary expense to employees.		

Problem 7–9

Preparing and Interpreting the Statement of Cash Flows

Following the acquisition of Kraft, the Philip Morris Companies released its Year 8 financial statements. The Year 8 financial statements and other data are reproduced below:

PHILIP MORRIS COMPANIES, INC.
Balance Sheets
As of December 31, Year 8 and Year 7
($ millions)

	Year 8	*Year 7*
Assets		
Cash and cash equivalents	$ 168	$ 90
Accounts receivable	2,222	2,065
Inventories	5,384	4,154
Current assets	$ 7,774	$ 6,309
Property, plant, and equipment (net)	8,648	6,582
Goodwill (net)	15,071	4,052
Investments	3,260	3,665
Total assets	$34,753	$20,608
Liabilities and Stockholders' Equity		
Short-term debt	$ 1,259	$ 1,440
Accounts payable	1,777	791
Accrued liabilities	3,848	2,277
Income taxes payable	1,089	727
Dividends payable	260	213
Current liabilities	$ 8,233	$ 5,448
Long-term debt	17,122	6,293
Deferred income taxes	1,719	2,044
Stockholders' equity	7,679	6,823
Total liabilities and stockholders' equity	$34,753	$20,608

PHILIP MORRIS COMPANIES, INC.
Income Statement
For Year Ending December 31, Year 8
($ millions)

Sales	$ 31,742
Cost of goods sold	(12,156)
Selling and administrative expenses	(14,410)
Depreciation expense	(654)
Goodwill amortization	(125)
Interest expense	(670)
Pre-tax income	$ 3,727
Income tax expense	(1,390)
Net income	$ 2,337
[Dividends declared $941 million]	

PHILIP MORRIS PURCHASE OF KRAFT
Allocation of Purchase Price
($ millions)

Accounts receivable	$ 758
Inventories	1,232
Property, plant, and equipment	1,740
Goodwill	10,361
Short-term debt	(700)
Accounts payable	(578)
Accrued liabilities	(530)
Long-term debt	(900)
Purchase price (net of cash acquired)	$11,383

Required:

a. Prepare a statement of cash flows (indirect method) for Philip Morris. (*Hint:* Acquisition of Kraft requires you to remove the assets acquired and liabilities incurred as a result of that acquisition from the balance sheet changes used in preparing the statement of cash flows. Philip Morris pays $11.383 billion for Kraft, net of cash acquired—see the Allocation of Purchase Price table.)

b. Calculate cash flows from operations using the direct method for Philip Morris.

c. Based on your answer to (*a*) compute Philip Morris's free cash flow for Year 8, and discuss how free cash flow impacts the company's future earnings and financial condition.

(CFA Adapted)

Problem 7–10

Analyzing Cash from Operations (Direct)

Refer to the financial statements of ZETA Corporation reproduced in Case CC–2 of the Comprehensive Case (following Chapter 13).

Required:

a. Prepare a worksheet computing cash flows from operations using the direct method. Include revenues and expenses of discontinued operations. Include a list of important assumptions and weaknesses as a note to your cash statement. Support all amounts shown. (*Hint:* Discontinued operations cannot be separated from continuing operations, but unadjusted income and expense of discontinued operations can be.)

b. ZETA's statement of cash flows reports income taxes paid in Year 6 of $2,600. Verify this amount independently.

c. Reconcile the change in "accounts payable and accruals" reported in the statement of cash flows with the number derived from the balance sheet. Explain the reason(s) for any difference. (*Hint:* Refer to notes 3 and 4.)

Problem 7–11

Converting Cash from Operations under Indirect Method to Direct

Refer to Campbell Soup Company's statement of cash flows in Supplement A. Convert Campbell's statement of cash flows for Year 11 to show cash flows from operations (CFO) using the direct method. For purposes of this problem only, *assume* the following:

i. Net change in other current assets and liabilities of $30.6 is comprised of:

Decrease in prepaid expenses	$(25.3)
Decrease in accounts payable	42.8
Increase in taxes payable	(21.3)
Increase in accruals and payrolls	(26.8)
	$(30.6)

ii. Campbell disposed of a division in Year 11 reporting revenues of $7.5 million and an after-tax loss of $5.3 million. The loss is included in expenses. The CFO presentation should include revenues and expenses of discontinued operations in Year 11.

Problem 7–12

Converting the Statement of Cash Flows to Alternative Formats

Refer to Campbell Soup Company's statement of cash flows in Supplement A. Convert Campbell's statement of cash flows for Year 10 to report:

a. Cash from operations under the direct method.

b. Analytical statement of cash flows divided into operating, investing, and financing activities.

(*Note:* For purposes of this assignment only, assume Campbell disposed of a division in Year 10 that had revenues of $7.5 million and an after-tax loss of $5.3 million. The loss is included in expenses. The CFO presentation should include revenues and expenses of discontinued operations in Year 10.)

Problem 7–13

Reconstruction of Transactions

Refer to the financial statements of Campbell Soup Company in Supplement A.

Required:

a. Verify that the changes in the company's balance sheets (beginning to end of Year 10) are explained in the statement of cash flows for Year 10.

b. Reconstruct T-accounts for balance sheet items showing the beginning and ending balances and a master T-account for cash (divided into [a] operations and [b] investing, financing, and other). Post all items shown in the Year 10 statement of cash flows to these T-accounts in the order they appear. "Key" each amount to an explanation using key references already provided. Use an Unexplained Differences T-account to accumulate all unexplained amounts requiring further analysis. Analyze carefully all differences. (*Hint:* Refer to notes and Form 10-K data and provide the best possible explanation for Unexplained Differences, using the format illustrated in this chapter.)

Problem 7–14

Computing Cash From Operations (direct)

Refer to the financial statements of Quaker Oats Company in Supplement A.

Required:

Determine cash flows from operations for Years 11, 10, and 9 using the direct approach. Use a worksheet to compute cash flows from operations and include revenues and expenses of discontinued operations.

Problem 7–15

Reconstruction of Transactions

Refer to the financial statements of Quaker Oats Company in Supplement A.

Required:

a. Verify that the changes in the company's balance sheets (beginning to end of Year 11) are explained in the Year 11 statement of cash flows.

b. Reconstruct T-accounts for the balance sheet items showing the beginning and ending balances and a master T-account for cash (divided into [a] operations, [b] investing, [c] financing, and [d] other). Post all items shown in the Year 11 statement of cash flows to these T-accounts in the order they appear. "Key" each amount to an explanation using key references already provided. Use an Unexplained Differences T-account to accumulate all unexplained amounts requiring further analysis. Analyze carefully all differences. (*Hint:* Refer to notes, MDA, and other disclosures for the best possible explanation.)

CASES

Case 7–1

Analysis of Adaptec's Financial Statements

Use the 1996 annual report of Adaptec in Supplement A to answer the following:

a. Compare Adaptec's net income to cash flows from operations over the most recent three years. Identify the major source(s) of any differences.

b. Adaptec uses the indirect method to prepare its statement of cash flows. Reconstruct the operating section for 1995 and 1996 using the direct method.

c. Why does Adaptec include changes in "Other Assets," a noncurrent account, in its operating section?

Case 7–2
Credit Analysis for a Leveraged Buyout

The management of Wyatt Corporation is frustrated because its parent company, SRW Corporation, repeatedly rejects Wyatt's capital spending requests. These refusals led Wyatt's management to conclude their operations play a limited role in the parent's long-range plans. Acting on this assumption, Wyatt's management approaches a merchant banking firm about the possibility of a leveraged buyout of their subsidiary. In their proposal, Wyatt management stresses the stable, predictable cash flows from Wyatt's operations as more than adequate to service the debt required to finance the proposed leveraged buyout. As a partner in the merchant banking firm, you investigate the feasibility of their proposal. You receive the balance sheet and supplementary information for Wyatt Corporation reproduced below. The management of Wyatt further discloses that, following their proposed purchase, they intend to acquire machinery costing $325,000 in each of the next three years to overcome the previous low level of capital expenditures while a subsidiary of SRW Corporation. Management argues these expenditures are needed for competitive reasons.

Required:

a. Using information in the balance sheet and the supplementary disclosures, prepare a statement of cash flows (indirect method) for the year ended December 31, Year 10.

b. Using the statement of cash flows from (*a*) and assuming that debt service is $300,000 per year after the leveraged buyout, evaluate the feasibility of management's proposal.

WYATT CORPORATION
Balance Sheet
As of December 31, Year 10, and Year 9

	Year 9	*Year 10*
Assets		
Current assets:		
Cash	$ 175,000	$ 192,000
Accounts receivable	248,000	359,000
Inventory	465,000	683,000
Total current assets	$ 888,000	$1,234,000
Noncurrent assets:		
Land	126,000	138,000
Buildings and machinery	3,746,000	3,885,000
Less accumulated depreciation	(916,000)	(1,131,000)
Total noncurrent assets	$2,956,000	$2,892,000
Total assets	$3,844,000	$4,126,000
Liabilities and Shareholders' Equity		
Current liabilities:		
Accounts payable	$ 156,000	$ 259,000
Taxes payable	149,000	124,000
Other short-term payables	325,000	417,000
Total current liabilities	$ 630,000	$ 800,000
Bonds payable	842,000	825,000
Total liabilities	$1,472,000	$1,625,000
Shareholders' equity		
Common stock	846,000	863,000
Retained earnings	1,526,000	1,638,000
Total shareholders' equity	$2,372,000	$2,501,000
Total liabilities and shareholders' equity	$3,844,000	$4,126,000

Supplementary Information:

1. Dividends declared and paid in Year 10 were $74,000.
2. Depreciation expense for Year 10 was $246,000.
3. Machinery originally costing $61,000 was sold for $34,000 in Year 10.

(CFA Adapted)

Case 7–3
Analyzing a Management Buyout Using the Statement of Cash Flows

The management of Dover Corporation claims that the securities market undervalues shares of its company. They propose to take it private by means of a leveraged buyout. Management's proposal contains the following features:

1. The leveraged buyout is expected to yield additional after-tax annual interest costs of $200,000.
2. To make Dover Corporation competitive, management plans to undertake:
   a. Annual investments in equipment of $180,000.
   b. Annual buildups in inventory of $60,000.
3. Management expects no additional financing demands beyond that listed in (1) and plans to use cash generated by operations as the primary financing source.

Management requests you to analyze the feasibility of their proposal. They provide you with the financial data listed below to assist in your analysis.

	December 31		
	Year 8	*Year 7*	*Net change*
Assets			
Cash	$ 471,000	$ 307,000	$ 164,000
Marketable equity securities, at cost	150,000	250,000	(100,000)
Allowance to reduce securities to market	(10,000)	(25,000)	15,000
Accounts receivable, net	550,000	515,000	35,000
Inventories	810,000	890,000	(80,000)
Investment in Top Corp., at equity	420,000	390,000	30,000
Property, plant, and equipment	1,145,000	1,070,000	75,000
Accumulated depreciation	(345,000)	(280,000)	(65,000)
Patent, net	109,000	118,000	(9,000)
Total assets	$3,300,000	$3,235,000	$ 65,000
Liabilities and Stockholders' Equity			
Accounts payable and accrued liabilities	$ 845,000	$ 960,000	$(115,000)
Note payable, long-term	600,000	900,000	(300,000)
Deferred income taxes	190,000	190,000	—
Common stock, $10 par value	850,000	650,000	200,000
Additional paid-in capital	230,000	170,000	60,000
Retained earnings	585,000	365,000	220,000
Total liabilities and stockholders' equity	$3,300,000	$3,235,000	$ 65,000

Additional Information:

1. On January 2, Year 8, Dover sells equipment costing $45,000, with a carrying amount of $28,000, for $18,000 cash.
2. On March 31, Year 8, Dover sells one of its marketable equity securities for $119,000 cash. There are no other transactions involving marketable equity securities.

3. On April 15, Year 8, Dover issues 20,000 shares of its common stock for cash at $13 per share.
4. On July 1, Year 8, Dover purchases equipment for $120,000 cash.
5. Dover's net income for Year 8 is $305,000. Dover pays a cash dividend of $85,000 on October 26, Year 8.
6. Dover acquires a 20 percent interest in Tops Corporation's common stock during Year 5. There is no goodwill attributable to the investment, which is accounted for using the equity method. Tops reports net income of $150,000 for the year ended December 31, Year 8. No dividend is paid on Tops' common stock during Year 8.

Required:

Prepare an analysis evaluating the financial feasibility of management's plans. (*Hint:* Prepare a statement of cash flows. Use the indirect method.)

INTERNET ACTIVITIES

Internet 7–1

Reconstructing Business Transactions from Financial Reports

Access one of the financial statement databases available on the Internet (http:// www.mhhe.com/ business/accounting/wild). Retrieve current financial statements of a company selected by either you or your instructor.

Required:

a. Verify that changes in the company's balance sheets (beginning to end of current year) are explained in the statement of cash flows.

b. Reconstruct T-accounts for balance sheet items showing the beginning and ending balances and a master T-account for cash dividend into operating, investing, financing, and noncash sections. Post all items shown in the current year's statement of cash flows to T-accounts in the order they appear. "Key" each amount with an explanation. Use an "Unexplained Differences" T-account to accumulate all unexplained amounts requiring further analysis.

c. Write a report describing your analysis of all differences (*Hint:* Refer to notes, MD&A, and other disclosures for possible explanations).

Internet 7–2

Analyzing Operating Cash Flows and Income

Access one of the financial statement databases available on the Internet (http:// www.mhhe.com/ business/accounting/wild). Retrieve current financial statements of a company selected by either you or your instructor.

Required:

a. Identify operating cash flows and net income for each of the past three years. Graph each of these numbers for the most recent three-year period.

b. Write a report explaining differences between operating cash flows and net income for the most recent three years. Describe any implications of these differences for the company's financial condition or future operating performance.

Internet 7–3

Analyzing Cash Flows Across Industries

Access one of the financial statement databases available on the Internet (http:// www.mhhe.com/ business/accounting/wild). Retrieve current financial statements of three companies in *different* industries selected by either you or your instructor.

Required:

a. Prepare a report analyzing cash flows from operating, investing, and financing activities for each company.

b. Write a report describing how activities and their cash flows differ in importance across companies.

PART THREE

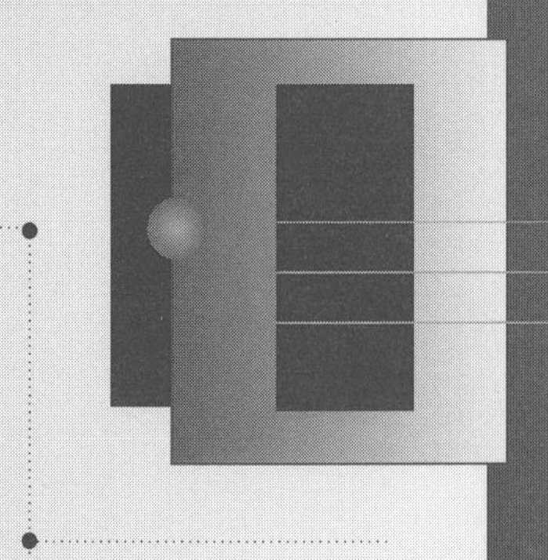

Financial Analysis Application and Interpretation

CHAPTER 8 *Short-Term Liquidity*

This chapter begins our application and interpretation of financial analysis. Our analysis tools explore accounting numbers for insights into company operations and future performance. We learn about and describe several measures of liquidity. In our reading you must assume the role of a banker to make a decision on a loan application and consult on estimated cost savings with improved inventory management.

CHAPTER 9 *Forecasting and Pro Forma Analysis*

In this chapter we study forecasting and pro forma analysis of cash flows and its implications for liquidity. We explain how cash circulates through a company's business activities. While studying forecasting and pro forma analysis, we must decide how to use forecasts in processing a loan application and analyze the disparity between cash and earnings forecasts for an initial public offering of stock.

CHAPTER 10 *Capital Structure and Solvency*

Capital structure and solvency are considered in this chapter. We learn how financial leverage affects both risk and return. We describe earnings-coverage measures, as well as analytical adjustments to book values and their interpretation. Along the way we assume the role of an entrepreneur to make a decision on whether to expand through debt financing, and we serve as an analyst who assesses preferred equity risk of two alternative investments.

CHAPTER 11 *Return on Invested Capital*

This chapter describes return on invested capital and its relevance for financial analysis. Attention is directed at *return on assets* and *return on common shareholders' equity*. We disaggregate these return measures, describe their importance, and evaluate the impact of financial leverage. During our reading we assume the role of an auditor to use returns analysis for substantive testing and we also serve as a management consultant in a review of company performance.

CHAPTER 12 *Profitability Analysis*

This chapter emphasizes returns analysis as applied to profitability and its components, including sales, cost of sales, taxes, selling, and financing expenses. We learn about break-even analysis and its relevance for profitability. Along the way, we decide on component information disclosure requirements as a securities listing director, we assess the relative strength of two loan applicants who differ on their level of diversification, and we scrutinize tax benefits granted to companies as a political activist.

CHAPTER 13 *Earnings-Based Analysis and Valuation*

This chapter concludes returns analysis by focusing on earnings-based analysis and valuation. Earnings-based analysis looks at earnings quality, persistence, and power. Earnings-based valuation focuses on forecasting earnings and estimating company value. In our reading we assess earnings quality as a member of the board of directors, and we analyze earnings persistence in preparing an earnings forecast for publication in an online forecasting service.

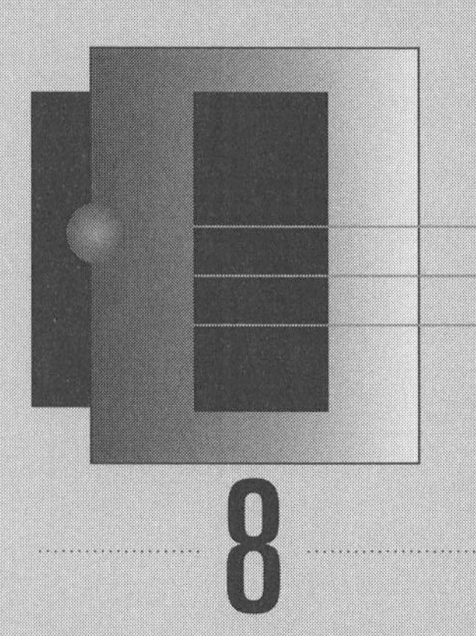

8

C H A P T E R

Short-Term Liquidity

A Look Back

Chapter 7 completed our study of the accounting analysis for financial statements. We examined cash flow measures of business activities and showed how this information complements our study of accrual measures in earlier chapters. We demonstrated the use of cash flow data in reconstructing business events and transactions.

A Look at This Chapter

We begin our study of the application and interpretation of analysis tools using financial statement numbers. Analysis tools exploit the accounting numbers to yield useful insights into company operations and future performance. This chapter highlights tools for assessing short-term liquidity. We explain liquidity and describe analysis tools capturing different aspects of it. Attention is directed at accounting-based ratios, turnover and operating activity measures of liquidity.

A Look Ahead

Chapter 9 extends our focus on analysis tools to cash flow prediction and analysis. We illustrate both short- and long-term forecasting procedures and discuss their reliability. Consideration is given to special cash-based measures in assessing companies' cash requirements.

Learning Objectives

- Explain the importance of liquidity in analyzing business activities.
- Describe working capital measures of liquidity and their components.
- Interpret the current ratio and cash-based measures of liquidity.
- Analyze operating cycle or turnover measures of liquidity and their interpretation.
- Describe other short-term liquidity measures and their usefulness for analysis.
- Illustrate what-if analysis for evaluating changes in company conditions and policies.

PREVIEW OF CHAPTER 8

Liquidity refers to the availability of company resources to meet short-term cash requirements. A company's short-term liquidity risk is affected by the timing of cash inflows and outflows along with its prospects for future performance. Our analysis of liquidity is aimed at companies' operating activities, their ability to generate profits from sale of products and services, and working capital requirements and measures. This chapter describes several financial statement analysis tools used to assess liquidity risk. We begin with a discussion of the importance of liquidity and its link to working capital. We explain and interpret useful ratios of both working capital and a company's operating cycle for assessing liquidity. We also discuss potential adjustments to these analysis tools and the underlying financial statement numbers. What-if analysis of changes in a company's conditions or strategies concludes our discussion. The content and organization of this chapter are as follows:

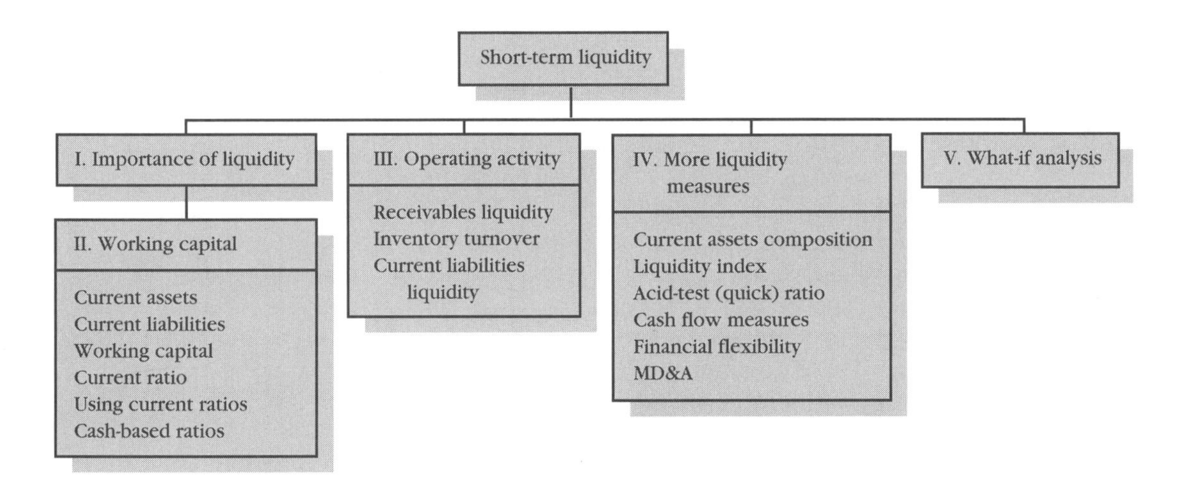

Importance of Short-Term Liquidity

A company's **short-term liquidity** refers to its ability to meet short-term obligations. *Liquidity* is the ability to convert assets into cash or to obtain cash. *Short term* is conventionally viewed as a period up to one year, though it is identified with the normal operating cycle of a company (the time period encompassing the buying-producing-selling-collecting cycle).

The importance of short-term liquidity is best seen by considering repercussions stemming from a company's inability to meet short-term obligations. Liquidity is a matter of degree. Lack of liquidity can signify a company unable to take advantage of favorable discounts or profitable opportunities. It also implies limited opportunities and constraints on management actions. More extreme liquidity problems reflect a company's inability to cover current obligations. This can lead to forced sale of investments and assets and, in its most severe form, to insolvency and bankruptcy.

For a company's shareholders, a lack of liquidity often precedes lower profitability and opportunity. It can foretell a loss of owner control or loss of capital investment. When a company's owners possess unlimited liability (proprietorships and certain partnerships), a lack of liquidity endangers their personal assets. To creditors of a company, a lack of liquidity can yield delays in collecting interest and principal payments or the loss of amounts due them. A company's customers and suppliers of products and services are affected by short-term liquidity problems. Implications include a company's inability to execute contracts and damage to important customer and supplier relationships.

These scenarios highlight why measures of liquidity are of great importance in our analysis of a company. If a company fails to meet its current obligations, its continued existence is doubtful. Viewed in this light, all other measures of analysis are of secondary importance. While accounting measurements assume indefinite existence of the company, our analysis must always assess the validity of this assumption using liquidity and solvency measures.

Analyzing Working Capital

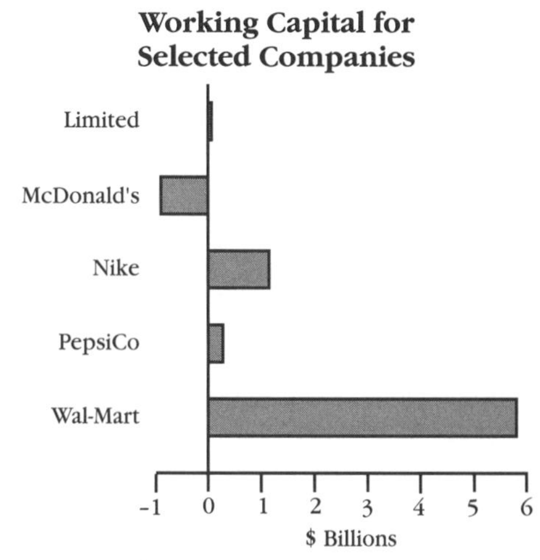

Source: Annual reports.

Working capital is a widely used measure of short-term liquidity. **Working capital** is defined as the excess of current assets over current liabilities. A working capital deficiency exists when current liabilities exceed current assets. When current assets exceed current liabilities, there is a working capital surplus.

Working capital is important as a measure of liquid assets providing a safety cushion to creditors. It is also important in measuring the liquid reserve available to meet contingencies and the uncertainties surrounding a company's balance of cash inflows and outflows. The importance attached by creditors, investors, and other users to working capital as a measure of liquidity and solvency causes some companies to stretch the definition of a current asset or a current liability. Our analysis must therefore evaluate the classification of items included in working capital.

Current Assets

Current assets are cash and other assets reasonably expected to be (1) realized in cash, or (2) sold or consumed, during the normal operating cycle of the company (or within one year if the operating cycle is less than a year). Note that the principle regarding ability to convert assets into cash within a year is subject to important qualifications. The most important qualification relates to the operating cycle. As we discussed in prior chapters, an operating cycle comprises the time period between acquisition of materials and services for operating activities until final cash realization of proceeds from sale of a company's products or services. This time period can be quite extended in industries requiring a long inventory holding period (e.g., tobacco, distillery, lumber) or for those selling on an installment plan. When a defined operating cycle is not evident, the one-year rule prevails. Common categories of current assets are briefly reviewed in this section. We discussed each of these assets in detail in Chapter 4.

Cash is the ultimate current asset since most current liabilities are paid off in cash. Cash marked for specific purposes like plant expansion should not be considered a current asset, and compensating balances under bank loan agreements should not, in most cases, be regarded as available cash. *Cash equivalents* are temporary investments of excess cash often made for purposes of earning a return. These investments must be short term and of high quality to ensure their sale without loss. *Marketable securities* are debt or equity securities held as investments. These securities are classified as current assets when (1) management intends to sell them in the near future (e.g., trading and available-for-sale securities), and/or (2) they are comprised of debt securities scheduled to mature in the next period. *Accounts receivable*, net of provisions for uncollectible accounts, are current assets. An exception is when they represent receivables from sales not in the ordinary course of business and are due beyond one year. Installment receivables from routine sales usually fall within the operating cycle of a company. Our analysis must be alert to the valuation and validity of receivables. This is especially important when those "sales" are on consignment or subject to return privileges. Receivables from affiliated companies or employees are current only if collectible in the ordinary course of business and within one year—or for installment receivables, within the operating cycle.

Inventories are current assets except when they are in excess of current production/sale requirements. These excess inventories should be shown as noncurrent and must be distinguished from typical inventories. The variations in practice are considerable and our analysis must carefully scrutinize them. Our analysis must pay special attention to inventory valuation. For example, measurement of inventories using LIFO can understate working capital. *Prepaid expenses* are also current assets. This is not because they can be converted to cash, but rather because they reflect advance payments for services and supplies that otherwise require current cash outlays.

Certain trucking companies include tires on their trucks as current assets. These companies presumably justify this practice on the basis the tires are used up during the company's normal operating cycle.

The mere ability of a company to convert an asset to cash is not the sole determinant of its classification as current. It is both management's intent and normal industry practice that governs classification. Intent is not always sufficient. For example, the cost of fixed assets intended for sale is included in current assets only if a company has a contractual commitment from a buyer to purchase these assets at a specific price within the year or operating cycle. Champion International Corporation classified "operations held for disposition" as current assets and reported it as:

> The company has entered into an agreement to sell three paperboard mills, its corrugated box manufacturing operations and all but one of its bag manufacturing operations to Stone Container Corporation ("Stone") for cash and Stone common stock. Upon consummation of the sale to Stone, the company expects to receive $372,900,000 in cash, subject to adjustment in certain circumstances.
>
> —Champion International Corporation

Attempts by management to stretch the definition of a *current asset* reinforces the importance that our analysis does not rely exclusively on financial statements. Rather, we need to exercise vigilance in our use of ratios and other analytical measures to render our own judgments. Attempts by management to stretch the rules to present a situation as better than it is serves as a warning of added risk.

Current Liabilities

Current liabilities are obligations expected to be satisfied with either (1) use of current assets, or (2) creation of other current liabilities, within a relatively short period of time, usually one year. Current liabilities include accounts payable, notes payable, short-term bank (and other) loans, taxes payable, accrued expenses, and the current portion of long-term debt. Additional description of current liabilities appears in Chapter 3 and is not repeated here. As with current assets, our analysis must not assume current liabilities are always properly classified.

> Penn Central Company excluded current maturities of long-term debt from current liabilities and included them in long-term debt. This treatment resulted in an excess of current assets over current liabilities of $21 million. Alternatively, including current debt maturities in current liabilities would have yielded a working capital deficit of $207 million. This disclosure decision by management foreshadowed Penn Central's financial collapse.

Our analysis must assess whether all current obligations with a reasonably high probability of eventual payment are reported in current liabilities. Their exclusion from current liabilities handicaps analysis of working capital. Three examples are:

- Contingent liabilities associated with loan guarantees. We need to assess the likelihood of this contingency materializing when we compute working capital.
- Future minimum rental payments under noncancelable operating lease agreements.
- Contracts for construction or acquisition of long-term assets often call for substantial progress payments. These obligations for payments are reported as

"commitments" and *not* as liabilities. When computing working capital, our analysis should often include these commitments.

We should recognize that current deferred tax assets (debits) are no more current assets than current deferred tax liabilities (credits) are current liabilities. Current deferred tax assets do not always represent expected cash inflows in the form of tax refunds. These assets usually serve to reduce future cash payments to taxing authorities. An exception is the case of net operating loss carrybacks. Similarly, current deferred tax liabilities do not always represent future cash outflows. Examples are temporary differences of a recurring nature (such as depreciation) that do not necessarily result in payment of taxes because their reversing differences are offset by equal or larger originating differences.

Many companies with fixed assets as their main "working assets," like certain trucking and leasing companies, carry as current assets their prospective receipts from billings—from which their current equipment purchase obligations are met. Also, certain companies do not distinguish between current and noncurrent on their balance sheets (e.g., real estate companies, banks, insurance companies). These reporting policies are attempts by these companies to convey "special" financing and operating circumstances. They claim the current versus noncurrent distinction is not applicable and that there is no parallel with manufacturing or merchandising companies. While some of these special circumstances are likely valid, they do not necessarily change the relation between current obligations and the liquid funds available or expected to be available to meet them. It is this relation that our analysis, confronted with evaluating liquidity, must focus attention on.

Working Capital Measure of Liquidity

The working capital measure of liquidity and of short-term financial strength is a common analytical tool. Credit grantors regularly rely on the difference between current assets and current liabilities. Loan agreements and bond indentures often contain stipulations for maintenance of minimum working capital levels. Financial analysts assess the magnitude of working capital for investment decisions and recommendations. Government agencies compute aggregates of companies' working capital for regulatory and policy actions. And nearly all published financial statements distinguish between current and noncurrent assets and liabilities in response to these and other user needs.

Yet the amount of working capital is more relevant to users' decisions when related to other key financial variables like sales or total assets. It is of limited value for direct comparative purposes and for assessing the adequacy of working capital. This is seen in Illustration 8.1.

Illustration 8.1

	Company A	*Company B*
Current assets	$300,000	$1,200,000
Current liabilities	100,000	1,000,000
Working capital	$200,000	$ 200,000

These companies have an equal amount of working capital. Yet even a quick comparison of the relation of current assets to current liabilities indicates Company A's working capital position is superior to Company B's.

Current Ratio Measure of Liquidity

The illustration above highlights the need to consider *relative* working capital. That is, a $200,000 working capital excess yields a different conclusion for a company with $300,000 in current assets than one with $1,200,000 in current assets. A common relative measure in practice is the current ratio. The **current ratio** is defined as:

$$\text{Current ratio} = \frac{\text{Current assets}}{\text{Current liabilities}}$$

In our illustration, the current ratio is 3:1 ($300,000/$100,000) for Company A and 1.2:1 ($1,200,000/$1,000,000) for Company B. This ratio reveals different pictures for companies A and B, and this ability to differentiate between Companies results in the widespread use of the current ratio for assessing a company's short-term liquidity.

Relevance of the Current Ratio

Reasons for the current ratio's widespread use as a measure of liquidity include its ability to measure:

- *Current liability coverage*. The higher the amount (multiple) of current assets to current liabilities, the greater assurance we have in current liabilities being paid.
- *Buffer against losses*. The larger the buffer, the lower the risk. The current ratio shows the margin of safety available to cover shrinkage in noncash current asset values when ultimately disposing or liquidating them.
- *Reserve of liquid funds*. The current ratio is relevant as a measure of the margin of safety against uncertainties and random shocks to a company's cash flows. Uncertainties and shocks, such as strikes and extraordinary losses, can temporarily and unexpectedly impair cash flows.

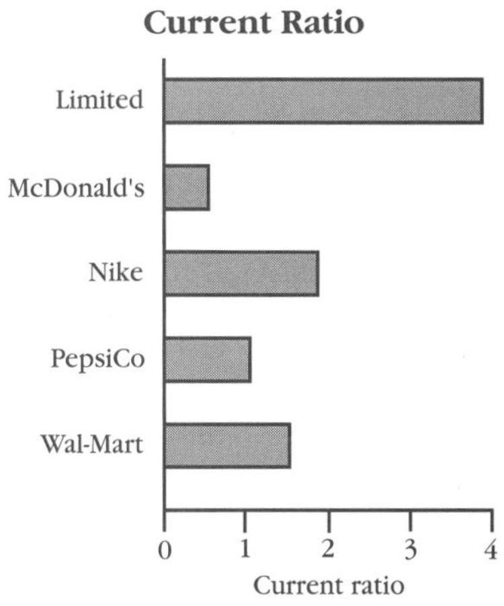

Current Ratio

Limited
McDonald's
Nike
PepsiCo
Wal-Mart
0 1 2 3 4
Current ratio

Source: Annual reports.

While the current ratio is a relevant and useful measure of liquidity and short-term solvency, it is subject to certain limitations we must be aware of. Consequently, before we describe the usefulness of the current ratio for our analysis, we discuss its limitations.

Limitations of the Current Ratio

A first step in critically evaluating the current ratio as a tool for liquidity and short-term solvency analysis is for us to examine both its numerator and denominator. If we define *liquidity* as the ability to meet cash outflows with adequate cash inflows, including an allowance for unexpected decreases in inflows or increases in outflows, then it is appropriate for us to ask: Does the current ratio capture these important factors of liquidity? Specifically, does the current ratio:

- Measure and predict the pattern of future cash inflows and outflows?
- Measure the adequacy of future cash inflows to outflows?

The answer to both these questions is generally no. The current ratio is a static (or "stock") measure of resources available at a point in time to meet current obligations. The current reservoir of cash resources does not have a logical or causal relation to its future cash inflows. Yet future cash inflows are the greatest indicator of liquidity. These cash inflows depend on factors excluded from the ratio, including sales, cash expenditures, profits, and changes in business conditions. To clarify these limitations, we need to examine more closely the individual components of the current ratio.

Numerator of the Current Ratio

We discuss each individual component comprising current assets and its implications for our analysis using the current ratio.

Cash and Cash Equivalents. Cash held by a well-managed company is primarily of a precautionary reserve intended to guard against short-term cash imbalances. For example, sales can decline more rapidly than cash outlays for purchases and expenses in a business downturn requiring availability of excess cash. Since cash is a nonearning asset and cash equivalents are usually low-yielding securities, a company's investment in these assets is minimized. The cash balance has little relation to the existing level of business activity and is unlikely to convey predictive implications. Further, many companies rely on cash substitutes in the form of open lines of credit not entering into the computation of the current ratio.

Marketable Securities. Cash in excess of the precautionary reserve is often spent on investment securities with returns exceeding those for cash equivalents. These investments are reasonably viewed as available to discharge current liabilities. Since investment securities are reported at their fair values (see Chapter 4), much of the guesswork from estimating their net realizable value is removed. Our analysis must recognize that the further removed the balance sheet date, the greater likelihood for unrecorded changes in these investment's fair values.

Accounts Receivable. A major determinant of accounts receivable is sales. The relation of accounts receivable to sales is governed by credit policies and collection methods. Changes in receivables correspond to changes in sales, though not necessarily on a directly proportional basis. Our analysis of accounts receivable as a source of cash must recognize, except in liquidation, the revolving nature of this asset. The collection of one account is succeeded by a new extension of credit. Accordingly, the level of receivables is not a measure of future net cash inflows.

Inventories. Like receivables, the major determinant of inventories is sales or expected sales—not the level of current liabilities. Since sales are a function of demand and supply, methods of inventory management (e.g., economic order quantities, safety stock levels, and reorder points) maintain inventory increments varying not in proportion to demand but by lesser amounts. The relation of inventories to sales is underscored by the observation that sales initiate the conversion of inventories to cash. Determination of future cash inflows from the sale of inventories depends on the profit margin that can be realized since inventories are reported at the lower of cost or market. The current ratio does not recognize sales level or profit margin, yet both are important determinants of future cash inflows.

Prepaid Expenses. Prepaid expenses are expenditures for future benefits. Since these benefits are typically received within a year or the company's operating cycle, they preserve the outlay of current funds. Prepaid expenses are usually small relative to other current assets. However, our analysis must be aware of the tendency of companies with weak current positions to include in prepaid expenses deferred charges and other items of dubious liquidity. We should exclude such items from our computation of working capital and the current ratio.

Denominator of the Current Ratio

Current liabilities are the focus of the current ratio. They are a source of cash in the same way receivables and inventories use cash. Current liabilities are primarily determined by sales, and a company's ability to meet them when due is the object of working capital measures. For example, since purchases giving rise to accounts payable are a function of sales, payables vary with sales. As long as sales remain constant or are rising, the payment of current liabilities is a refunding activity. In this case the components of the current ratio provide little, if any, recognition to this activity or to its effects on future cash flows. Also, current liabilities entering into the computation of the current ratio do not include prospective cash outlays—examples are commitments under construction contracts, loans, leases, or pensions.

Using the Current Ratio for Analysis

From our discussion of the current ratio we can draw at least three conclusions.

1. Liquidity depends to a large extent on *prospective* cash flows and to a lesser extent on the level of cash and cash equivalents.
2. No direct relation exists between balances of working capital accounts and likely patterns of future cash flows.
3. Managerial policies regarding receivables and inventories are directed primarily at efficient and profitable asset utilization and secondarily at liquidity.

These conclusions do not bode well for the current ratio as an analysis tool and we might question why it enjoys widespread use in analysis. Reasons for using the current ratio include its understandability, its simplicity in computation, and its data availability. Its use also derives from the creditor's (especially banker's) propensity in viewing credit situations as conditions of last resort. They ask themselves: What if there were a complete stoppage of cash inflows? Would current assets meet current liabilities? This extreme analysis is not always a useful way of assessing liquidity. Two other points are also pertinent. First, our analysis of short-term liquidity and solvency must recognize the relative superiority of cash flow projections and pro forma financial statements versus the current ratio. These analyses require information not readily available in financial statements, including product demand estimation (see Chapter 9). Second, should our analysis use the current ratio as a static measure of the ability of current assets to satisfy current liabilities, we must recognize this is a different concept of liquidity from the one described above. In our context, liquidity is the readiness and speed that current assets are convertible to cash and the extent conversion results in shrinkage in current asset values.

It is not our intent to reject the current ratio as an analysis tool. But it is important for us to know its relevant use. Our consideration of the current ratio's limitations indicates any analysis process of "adjusting" for them is not feasible. Consequently, to what valuable use can our analysis apply the current ratio? The relevant use of the current ratio is recognizing its limitations and restricting its use to appropriate situations. This means limiting its use to measuring the ability of current assets to discharge existing current liabilities. Second, we can consider the excess of current assets, if any, as a liquid surplus available to meet imbalances in the flow of funds and other contingencies. These two applications are applied with our awareness that the ratio assumes company liquidation. This is in contrast to the usual going-concern situation where current assets are of a revolving nature (e.g., collecting receivables is replaced with new receivables) and current liabilities are of a refunding nature (e.g., covering payables is met with new payables).

Provided we apply the current ratio in the manner described, there are two components that we must evaluate and measure before the current ratio can usefully form a basis of analysis:

1. Quality of both current assets and current liabilities entering into the ratio's computation.
2. Turnover rate of both current assets and current liabilities—that is, time period necessary for converting receivables and inventories into cash and for paying current liabilities.

Several adjustments, ratios, and other analysis tools are available to accomplish these tasks and enhance our use of the current ratio (see below). The remainder of this section describes relevant applications of the current ratio in practice.

Comparative Analysis

Analyzing the trend in the current ratio is often enlightening. Two tools of analysis described in Chapter 1 are useful here. One is *trend analysis*, where components of working capital and the current ratio are converted to indexes and examined over time. The other is *common-size analysis*, where the composition of current assets is examined over time. These comparative time analyses, along with intra-industry comparisons of these trends, are useful for our analysis.

Changes in the current ratio over time must be interpreted with caution. Changes in this ratio do not necessarily imply changes in liquidity or operating performance. For example, during a recession a company might continue to pay current liabilities while inventory and receivables accumulate, yielding an increase in the current ratio. Conversely, in a successful period, increases in taxes payable can lower the current ratio. Company expansion often accompanying operating success can create larger working capital requirements. This "prosperity squeeze" in liquidity decreases the current ratio and is illustrated in the case of company expansion unaccompanied by an increase in working capital.

Illustration 8.2

Technology Resources, Inc., experiences a doubling of current assets and a quadrupling of current liabilities with *no change* in its working capital. This yielded a prosperity squeeze evidenced by a 50 percent decline in the current ratio.

	Year 1	***Year 2***
Current assets	$300,000	$600,000
Current liabilities	100,000	400,000
Working capital	$200,000	$200,000
Current ratio	3:1	1.5:1

Inflation can produce a similar effect by increasing the balances of current assets and current liabilities.

Ratio Management

Our analysis must look for "management" of the current ratio, also known as *window dressing*. Toward the close of a period, management will occasionally press the collection of receivables, call in advances to officers for temporary repayment, reduce inventory below normal levels, and delay normal purchases. Proceeds from these activities are then used to pay off current liabilities. The effect of these activities is to increase the current ratio.

Illustration 8.3

Technology Resources, Inc., increases its current ratio by making an earlier-than-normal payoff of $50,000 of current liabilities:

	Before Payoff	***After Payoff***
Current assets	$200,000	$150,000
Current liabilities	100,000	50,000
Working capital	$100,000	$100,000
Current ratio	2:1	3:1

In a related situation, given management's desire to offset liabilities against assets, practice restricts offsets to situations where the legal right to offset exists. Our analysis should also go beyond annual measures and use interim measures of the current ratio. Interim analysis makes it more difficult for management to window dress and allows us to gauge seasonal effects on the ratio. For example, a strong current ratio in December can be misleading if a company experiences a credit squeeze at its seasonal peak in July.

Current Ratio for Selected Industries

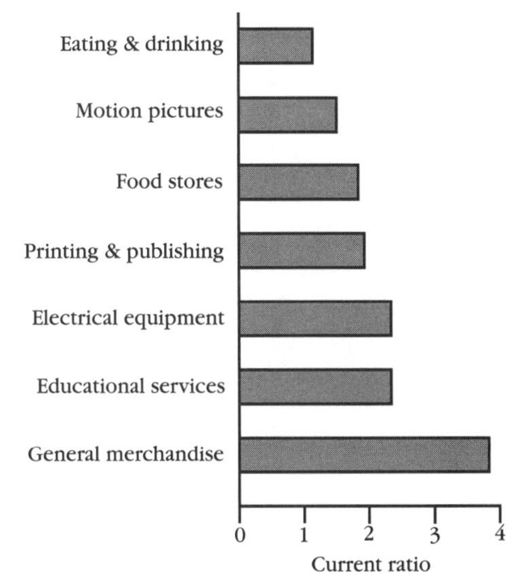

Source: Dun & Bradstreet.

Rule of Thumb Analysis

A frequently heard rule of thumb is if the current ratio is 2:1 or better, then a company is financially sound, while a ratio below 2:1 suggests increasing liquidity risks. At one time this "norm" was 2.5:1. This change in the rule of thumb may reflect lenders', and particularly bankers', reduced conservatism. It might also reflect better accounting, allowing bankers and lenders to reduce the "cushion" acceptable as their minimum protection. The 2:1 norm implies there are $2 of current assets available for every $1 of current liabilities or, alternatively viewed, the value of current assets can in liquidation shrink by as much as 50 percent and still cover current liabilities. A current ratio much higher than 2:1, while implying superior coverage of current liabilities, can signal inefficient use of resources and a reduced rate of return. Our evaluation of the current ratio with any rule of thumb is of dubious value for two reasons:

1. Quality of current assets, and the composition of current liabilities, are more important in evaluating the current ratio (e.g., two companies with identical current ratios can present substantially different risks due to variations in the quality of working capital components).
2. Working capital requirements vary with industry conditions and the length of a company's net trade cycle.

Net Trade Cycle Analysis

A company's working capital requirements are affected by its desired inventory investment and the relation between credit terms from suppliers and those extended to customers. These considerations determine a company's **net trade cycle**. Computation of a company's net trade cycle is illustrated below:

Illustration 8.4

Selected financial information from Technology Resources, Inc., for the end of Year 1 is reproduced below:

Sales for Year 1	$360,000
Receivables	40,000
Inventories*	50,000
Accounts payable†	20,000
Cost of goods sold (including depreciation of $30,000)	320,000

*Beginning inventory is $100,000.
†We assume these relate to purchases included in cost of goods sold.

We estimate Technology Resources' purchases per day as:

Ending inventory	$50,000
Cost of goods sold	320,000
	$ 370,000
Less: Beginning inventory	(100,000)
Cost of goods purchased and manufactured	$ 270,000
Less: Depreciation in cost of goods sold	(30,000)
Purchases	$ 240,000

Purchases per day = $240,000 ÷ 360 = $666.67

The net trade cycle for Technology Resources is computed as in days:

$$\text{Accounts receivable} = \frac{\$40{,}000}{\$360{,}000 \div 360} = 40.00 \text{ days}$$

$$\text{Inventories} = \frac{\$50{,}000}{\$320{,}000 \div 360} = \underline{56.24} \text{ days}$$

$$96.24 \text{ days}$$

$$\text{Less: Accounts payable} = \frac{\$20{,}000}{\$666.67} = \underline{30.00} \text{ days}$$

$$\text{Net trade cycle (days)} = \underline{\underline{66.24}} \text{ days}$$

Notice the numerator and denominator are adjusted on a consistent basis. Specifically, accounts receivable reported in sales dollars are divided by sales per day, inventories reported at cost are divided by cost of goods sold per day, and accounts payable reported in dollars of purchases are divided by purchases per day. Consequently, while the day measures are expressed on different bases, our estimation of the net trade cycle is on a consistent basis. Our analysis shows Technology Resources has 40 days of sales tied up in receivables, maintains 56.24 days of goods available in inventory, and receives only 30 days of purchases as credit from its suppliers. The longer the net trade cycle, the larger is the working capital requirement. Reduction in the number of days' sales in receivables or cost of sales in inventories lowers working capital requirements. An increase in the number of days' purchases as credit received from suppliers lowers working capital needed. Working capital requirements are determined by industry conditions and practices. Comparisons using industry current ratios, and analysis of working capital requirements using net trade cycle measures, are useful in our analysis of the adequacy of a company's working capital.

Sales Trend Analysis

Our analysis of the liquidity of current assets should include a review of the trend in sales. Since sales are necessary to convert inventory into receivables or cash, an upturn in sales implies the conversion of inventories into liquid assets is more likely than when sales are stable. Declining sales delay the conversion of inventories into liquid assets.

> **ANALYSIS VIEWPOINT** . . . *You are the banker*
>
> International Machines Corporation (IMC) calls on you for a short-term one-year $2 million loan to finance expansion in the United Kingdom. As part of your loan analysis of IMC you compute a 4:1 current ratio on current assets of nearly $1.6 million. Analysis of industry competitors yields a 1.9:1 average current ratio. What is your decision on IMC's loan application using this limited information? Would your decision change if IMC's application is for a 10-year loan?

Cash-Based Ratio Measures of Liquidity

Cash and cash equivalents are the most liquid of current assets. In this section, we examine cash-based ratio measures of liquidity.

Cash Ratio

The ratio of "near-cash" assets to the total of current assets is a measure of the degree of current asset liquidity. This measure, known as the **cash ratio**, is computed as:

$$\frac{\text{Cash} + \text{Cash equivalents} + \text{Marketable securities}}{\text{Current assets}}$$

The larger this ratio, the more liquid are current assets. This ratio has minimal danger of loss in value in case of liquidation and there is nearly no waiting period for conversion of these assets into usable cash. Our analysis should recognize possible restrictions on these near-cash assets. For example, lenders sometimes expect borrowers to maintain compensating balances. While these balances are relevant, the analyst must assess the effect on a company's credit standing and credit availability, and its banking relationship, of a breach of this tacit agreement not to draw on a compensating cash balance. Two additional factors bearing on our evaluation of the cash ratio should be recognized. One relates to cash management practices leading to efficient use of cash by companies and a lower threshold for cash required. The other is open lines of credit and standby credit arrangements that are effective substitutes for cash and should be considered in our analysis.

Cash to Current Liabilities Ratio

Another ratio measuring cash adequacy is the **cash to current liabilities ratio.** It is computed as:

$$\frac{\text{Cash} + \text{Cash equivalents} + \text{Marketable securities}}{\text{Current liabilities}}$$

This ratio measures the cash available to pay current obligations. This is a severe test ignoring the refunding nature of current assets and current liabilities. It supplements the cash ratio in measuring cash availability from a different perspective. To view this ratio as an extension of the quick ratio (see below) is, except in extreme cases, a too severe test of short-term liquidity. Nevertheless, the importance of cash as the ultimate form of liquidity should not be underestimated. The record of business failures provides many examples of insolvent companies with sizable noncash assets (both current and noncurrent) and an inability to pay liabilities or to operate.

Operating Activity Analysis of Liquidity

Operating activity measures of liquidity are important in our analysis. This section considers three operating activity measures based on accounts receivable, inventory, and current liabilities.

Accounts Receivable Liquidity Measures

For most companies selling on credit, accounts and notes receivable are an important part of working capital. In assessing liquidity, including the quality of working capital and the current ratio, it is necessary to measure the quality and liquidity of receivables. Both quality and liquidity of accounts receivable are affected by their turnover rate. *Quality* refers to the likelihood of collection without loss. A measure of this likelihood is the proportion of receivables within terms of payment set by the company. Experience shows that the longer receivables are outstanding beyond their due date, the lower is the likelihood of their collection. Their turnover rate is an indicator of the age of receivables. This indicator is especially useful when compared with an expected turnover rate computed using the permitted credit terms. *Liquidity* refers to the speed in converting accounts receivable to cash. The receivables turnover rate is a measure of this speed.

Accounts Receivable Turnover

The **accounts receivable turnover** ratio is computed as:

$$\frac{\text{Net sales on credit}}{\text{Average accounts receivable}}$$

Receivables Turnover for Selected Industries

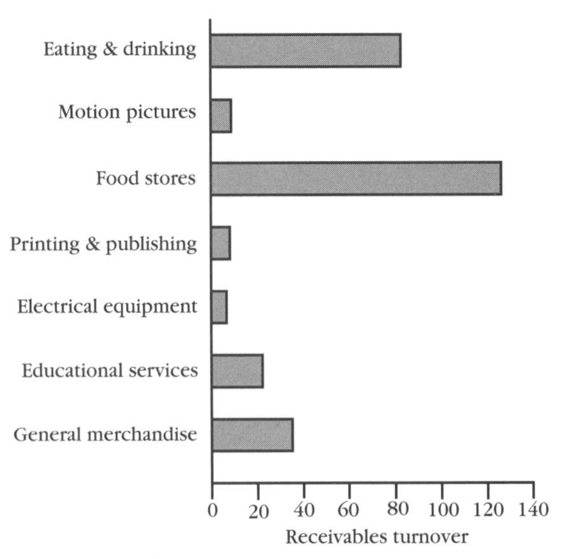

Source: Dun & Bradstreet.

The most direct way for us to determine *average* accounts receivable is to add beginning and ending accounts receivable for the period, and divide by two. Using monthly or quarterly figures yields more accurate estimates. The more sales fluctuate, the more likely distorted is this ratio. We should include notes receivable from normal sales when computing accounts receivable turnover. We should also include only credit sales when computing this ratio because cash sales do not create receivables. Since financial statements rarely disclose both cash and credit sales, our analysis often must compute this ratio using total net sales (i.e., assuming cash sales are insignificant). If they are not insignificant, then this ratio is less useful. However, if the proportion of cash sales to total sales is relatively stable, year-to-year comparisons of changes in the receivables turnover ratio are more relevant. The receivables turnover ratio indicates how often, on average, receivables revolve—that is, are received and collected during the year.

Illustration 8.5

Consumer Electronics, Inc., reports sales of $1,200,000, beginning receivables of $150,000, and year-end receivables of $250,000. Its receivables turnover ratio is computed as:

$$\frac{\$1{,}200{,}000}{(\$150{,}000 + \$250{,}000) \div 2} = \frac{\$1{,}200{,}000}{\$200{,}000} = 6$$

Collection Period for Selected Industries

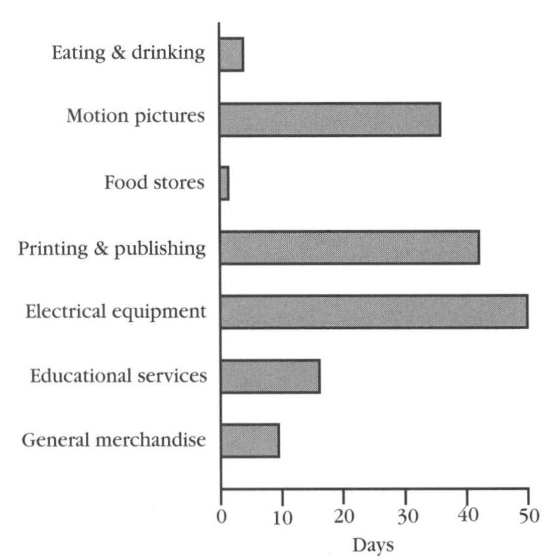

Source: Dun & Bradstreet.

Accounts Receivable Collection Period

While the receivables turnover ratio measures the speed of collections and is useful for comparison purposes, it is not directly comparable to the terms of trade a company extends to its customers. This latter comparison is made by converting the turnover ratio into days of sales tied up in receivables. The **receivables collection period** measures the number of days it takes, on average, to collect accounts (and notes) receivable. It is computed by dividing the average accounts receivable turnover ratio into 360 days (the approximate number of days in a year):

$$\text{Collection period} = \frac{360}{\text{Accounts receivable turnover}}$$

Using the figures from Consumer Electronics, Inc., in the above illustration, the receivables collection period is:

$$\frac{360}{6} = 60 \text{ days}$$

An alternative computation, known as **days' sales in reeivables**, is to divide *ending* accounts receivable by average daily sales as follows:

$$\text{Accounts receivable} \div \frac{\text{Sales}}{360}$$

This measure differs from the foregoing collection period computation. The accounts receivable collection period uses *average* accounts receivable, while the latter alternative computation uses *ending* accounts receivable. Using data from Consumer Electronics, Inc., the alternative computation yields:

$$\text{Average daily sales} = \frac{\text{Sales}}{360} = \frac{\$1{,}200{,}000}{360} = \$3{,}333$$

$$\frac{\text{Accounts receivable}}{\text{Average daily sales}} = \frac{\$250{,}000}{\$3{,}333} = 75 \text{ days}$$

Interpretation of Receivables Liquidity Measures

Accounts receivable turnover rates and collection periods are usefully compared with industry averages or to the credit terms given by the company. When the collection period is compared with the terms of sale allowed by the company, we can assess the extent of customers paying on time. For example, if usual credit terms of sale are 40 days, then an average collection period of 75 days reflects one or more of the following conditions:

- Poor collection efforts.
- Delays in customer payments.
- Customers in financial distress.

The first condition demands corrective managerial action, while the other two reflect on both the quality and liquidity of accounts receivable and demand judicious managerial action. An initial step is to determine whether accounts receivable are representative of company sales activity. For example, receivables may be sheltered in a captive finance subsidiary of the company. In this case, bad debts may also relate to receivables not on the company's books. It is also possible an *average* figure is not representative of the receivables population it represents. For example, the 75-day average collection period might not represent an across-the-board delay in payment by customers, but rather is due to the extreme delinquency of one or two customers. An excellent tool to investigate an extreme collection period is to *age* accounts receivable, listing the distribution of each account by the number of days past due. An aging schedule like the one shown below reveals whether the delay is widespread or concentrated:

		Days Past Due			
	Current	***0–30***	***31–60***	***61–90***	***Over 90***
Accounts receivable	$____	$____	$____	$____	$____

An aging analysis of receivables leads to more informed conclusions regarding the quality and liquidity of receivables. It also improves managerial decisions to take action necessary to remedy the situation. However, information to perform an aging analysis is often unavailable to us. Another measure of receivables quality is the credit rating from agencies like Dun & Bradstreet who often have access to other data.

Certain other areas deserve our attention. We must scrutinize notes receivable because, while they are normally more negotiable than open accounts, they are sometimes of lower quality. This is especially the case if they originate as a means to extend the payment period of an unpaid open account. Our analysis should also recognize that converting receivables into cash, except for their use as collateral for borrowing, cannot be achieved without a cutback in sales volume. The sales policy aspect of a collection period evaluation must be kept in mind. A company might be willing to accept slow-paying customers who provide overall profitable business. In this case, profit on sales compensates for the extended use by the customer of the company's funds. This circumstance can alter our analysis regarding the quality of receivables but not their liquidity. A company might also extend more liberal credit in cases where (1) a new product is launched, (2) sales are made to utilize excess capacity, or (3) special competitive conditions prevail. Accordingly, we must consider the relations between receivables, sales, and profits when evaluating the collection period.

Certain trend analyses also merit our study. The trend in collection period over time is important in assessing the quality and liquidity of receivables. Another trend to watch is the relation between the provision for doubtful accounts and gross accounts receivable, computed as:

$$\frac{\text{Provision for doubtful accounts}}{\text{Gross accounts receivable}}$$

Increases in this ratio over time suggest a decline in the collectibility of receivables. Conversely, decreases in this ratio suggest improved collectibility or the need to reevaluate the adequacy of the doubtful accounts provision. Overall, accounts receivable liquidity measures are important in our analysis. They are also important as measures of asset utilization, a subject we address in Chapter 11.

Inventory Turnover Measures

Inventories often comprise a substantial proportion of current assets. The reasons for this often have little to do with a company's need to maintain adequate liquid funds. Reserves of liquid funds are seldom kept in the form of inventories. Inventories are investments made for purposes of obtaining a return. This return is derived from the expected profits resulting from sales to customers. In most companies, a certain level of inventory must be kept. If inventory is inadequate, sales volume declines below an attainable level. Conversely, excessive inventories expose a company to storage costs, insurance, taxes, obsolescence, and physical deterioration. Excessive inventories also tie up funds used more profitably elsewhere. Due to risks in holding inventories, and given inventories are further removed from cash compared to receivables, they are normally considered the least liquid current asset. This is not always the case since items like commodities and raw materials enjoy ready markets and can usually be sold with little effort, expense, or loss. Yet fashion merchandise, special components, or perishable items can rapidly lose value unless sold on a timely basis. Our evaluation of short-term liquidity and working capital, which includes inventories, must include an evaluation of the quality and liquidity of inventories. Measures of inventory turnover are excellent tools for this analysis.

Inventory Turnover

The **inventory turnover ratio** measures the average rate of speed inventories move through and out of a company. Inventory turnover is computed as:

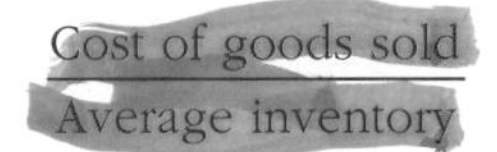

$$\frac{\text{Cost of goods sold}}{\text{Average inventory}}$$

Consistency in valuation requires we use cost of goods sold in the numerator because, like inventories, it is reported typically at cost. Sales, in contrast, includes a profit margin. Cost of goods sold is regularly reported in income statements. Yet our analysis is occasionally confronted with the unavailability of cost of sales figures. In this case, sales is often used as the numerator in a "modified" ratio. Dun & Bradstreet reports modified inventory turnover ratios. While use of sales impairs the usefulness of the turnover ratio, this modified ratio can be used for comparative (trend) analysis, especially if used consistently and where changes in profit margins are small. Average inventory is computed by adding the opening and closing inventory balances, and dividing by two. This averaging computation can be refined by averaging quarterly or monthly inventory figures. When we are interested in evaluating the *level* of inventory at a specific date, such as year-end, we compute the inventory turnover ratio using the inventory balance at this date as the denominator. Our analysis must also examine composition of inventory and make any necessary adjustments (e.g., from LIFO to FIFO).

Sales-Based Inventory Turnover Ratio for Selected Industries

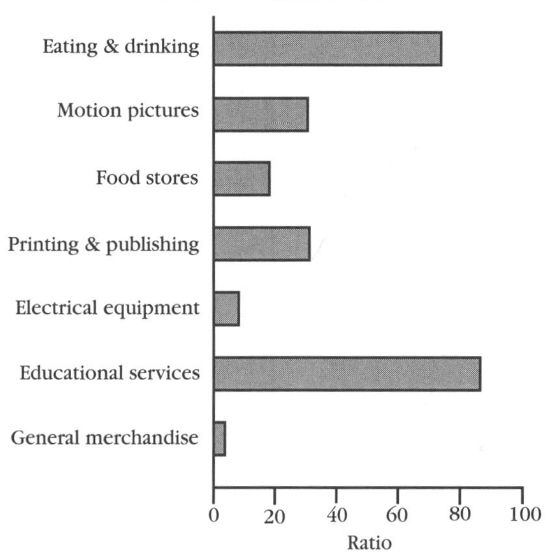

Source: Dun & Bradstreet.

Days to Sell Inventory

Another measure of inventory turnover useful in assessing purchasing/production policy is the number of days to sell inventory. The **days to sell inventory ratio** is computed as:

$$\frac{360}{\text{Inventory turnover}}$$

This ratio tell us the number of days a company takes in selling *average* inventory for that year. An alternative computation, referred to as the **days' sales in inventory**, is computed as:

$$\frac{\text{Ending inventory}}{\text{Cost of average day's sales}}$$

This alternative ratio tells us the number of days required to sell *ending* inventory, assuming a given rate of sales. The cost of average day's sales is computed as:

$$\frac{\text{Cost of goods sold}}{360}$$

Sales-Based Days to Sell Inventory for Selected Industries

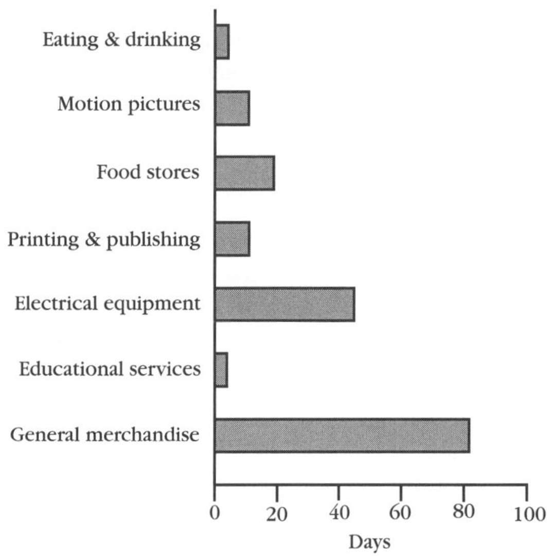

Source: Dun & Bradstreet.

Illustration 8.6

Selected financial information from Macon Resources, Inc., for the end of Year 8 is reproduced below:

Sales	$1,800,000
Cost of goods sold	1,200,000
Beginning inventory	200,000
Ending inventory	400,000

Inventory turnover ratios using *average* inventory are computed as:

$$\text{Inventory turnover ratio} = \frac{\$1,200,000}{(\$200,000 + \$400,000) \div 2} = 4$$

$$\text{Days to sell inventory ratio} = \frac{360}{4} = 90 \text{ days}$$

Inventory turnover ratios based on *ending* inventory equal:

$$\text{Cost of average days' sales} = \frac{\$1,200,000}{360} = \$3,333$$

$$\text{Days' sales in inventory} = \frac{\$400,000}{\$3,333} = 120 \text{ days}$$

Interpreting Inventory Turnover

The current ratio views current asset components as sources of funds to potentially pay off current liabilities. Viewed similarly, inventory turnover ratios offer measures of both the quality and liquidity of the inventory component of current assets. *Quality of inventory* refers to a company's ability to use and dispose of inventory. When our analysis assumes inventory liquidation, then cost recovery is the objective. Yet in the normal course of business, inventory is usually sold at profit. Assuming this usual state, the normal profit margin is important since funds obtained and deemed available for paying current liabilities include *both* profit and cost components. Our analysis of inventory under either liquidation or normal sales must reduce proceeds by any costs of selling inventory. We should also recognize a continuing company does not use inventory for paying current liabilities since any serious reduction in normal inventory levels likely cuts into sales volume.

When inventory turnover decreases over time, or is less than the industry norm, it suggests slow-moving inventory items attributed to obsolescence, weak demand, or nonsalability. These conditions question the feasibility of a company recovering inventory costs. We need further analysis to see if decreasing inventory turnover is due to inventory buildup in anticipation of sales increases, contractual commitments, increasing prices, work stoppages, inventory shortages, or other legitimate reason. We also must be aware of inventory management (e.g., just-in-time systems) aimed at keeping inventory levels low by integrating ordering, producing, selling, and distributing. Effective inventory management increases inventory turnover.

We can improve our evaluation of inventory turnover by computing separate turnover rates for major inventory components like raw materials, work in process, and finished goods. Similarly, computing department or division turnover rates yields more useful inferences concerning inventory quality. We should not forget that inventory turnover is an aggregate of varying turnover rates for diverse inventory groupings. One problem confronting our analysis when computing inventory turnover ratios by various groupings is availability of data. Companies do not frequently report inventory component data in financial statements. Certain companies are willing to provide these data when requested.

Inventory turnover is also a gauge of liquidity in measuring the speed with which inventory is converted to cash. A useful inventory liquidity measure is its **conversion period** or **operating cycle**. This measure combines the collection period of receivables with the days to sell inventories to obtain the time interval to convert inventories to cash. Using results computed from our two independent illustrations above, we compute the conversion period as:

Days to sell inventory	90
Collection period	60
Operating cycle	150

This implies it takes 150 days to sell inventory on credit and to collect receivables.

In evaluating inventory turnover, our analysis must be alert to the influence of alternative accounting principles for valuing the ratio's components. Our discussion of accounting for inventory in Chapter 4 is relevant here. Use of the LIFO method of inventory valuation can seriously impair the usefulness of both turnover and current ratios. For example, inventory valuation affects both the numerator and denominator of the current ratio—the latter through its effect on taxes payable. Information is often available in the financial statements enabling us to adjust unrealistically low LIFO inventory values in times of rising prices, making these values useful for inclusion in turnover and current ratios. Notice if two companies use the LIFO method for inventory valuation, their inventory-based ratios are likely *not* comparable because their LIFO inventory pools (bases) are almost certainly acquired in different years with different price levels. We must also remember companies using a "natural year" may have at year-end an atypically low inventory level. This can increase a turnover ratio to an abnormally high level.

Conversion Period for Selected Industries

Source: Dun & Bradstreet.

Liquidity of Current Liabilities

Current liabilities are important in computing both working capital and the current ratio for two related reasons:

- Current liabilities are used in determining whether the excess of current assets over current liabilities affords a sufficient margin of safety.
- Current liabilities are deducted from current assets in arriving at working capital.

ANALYSIS VIEWPOINT *. . . You are the consultant*

King Entertainment, Inc., engages your services as a management consultant. One of your tasks is to streamline costs of inventory. After studying prior performance and inventory reports, you propose to strategically reduce inventories through improved inventory management. Your proposal expects the current inventory turnover of 20 will increase to 25. Money not invested in inventory can be used to decrease current liabilities—the costs of holding current liabilities average 10 percent per year. What is your estimate of cost savings if predicted sales are $150 million and predicted cost of sales is $100 million?

In using working capital and the current ratio, our point of view is one of liquidation and *not* of continuing operations. This is because in normal operations current liabilities are not paid off but are of a refunding nature. Provided sales remain stable, both purchases and current liabilities will remain steady. Increasing sales usually yield increasing current liabilities. The trend and direction of sales is a good indicator of future current liabilities.

Quality of Current Liabilities

The quality of current liabilities is important in our analysis of working capital and the current ratio. Not all current liabilities represent equally urgent or forceful payment demands. At one extreme, we find liabilities for various taxes that must be paid promptly regardless of current financial pressures. Collection powers of federal, state, and local government authorities are formidable. At the other extreme are current liabilities to suppliers with whom a company has a long-standing relationship and who depend on and value its business. Postponement and renegotiation of these liabilities in times of financial pressures are both possible and common.

The quality of current liabilities must be judged on their degree of urgency in payment. We should recognize if fund inflows from current revenues are viewed as available for paying current liabilities, then labor and similar expenses requiring prompt payment have a first call on revenues. Trade payables and other liabilities are paid only after these outlays are met. We examine this aspect of funds flow in the next chapter.

Our analysis must also be aware of unrecorded liabilities having a claim on current funds. Examples are purchase commitments and certain postretirement and lease obligations. When long-term loan acceleration clauses exist, a failure to meet current installments can render the entire debt due and payable.

Days' Purchases in Accounts Payable

A measure of the extent accounts payable represent current and not overdue obligations is obtained by calculating the **days' purchases in accounts payable ratio**. This ratio is computed as:

$$\text{Days' purchases in accounts payable} = \frac{\text{Accounts payable}}{\text{Purchases} \div 360}$$

One difficulty we often encounter when computing this ratio is purchases are usually not separately reported in financial statements. For merchandising companies, an approximation of purchases is obtained by adjusting cost of goods sold for depreciation, other noncash charges, and changes in inventories as follows:

Purchases = Adjusted cost of goods sold + Ending inventory − Beginning inventory

If cost of goods sold contains significant cash charges, this can reduce the reliability of computations based on our approximation of purchases on credit.[1]

Additional Short-Term Liquidity Measures

Current Assets Composition

Composition of current assets is an indicator of working capital liquidity. Use of common-size percentage comparisons facilitates our evaluation of comparative liquidity, regardless of the dollar amounts. Consider the following case example.

Illustration 8.7

Texas Electric Corp.'s current assets along with their common-size percentages are reproduced below for Years 1 and 2:

	Year 1		Year 2	
Current assets:				
Cash	$ 30,000	30%	$ 20,000	20%
Accounts receivable	40,000	40%	30,000	30%
Inventories	30,000	30%	50,000	50%
Total current assets	$100,000	100%	$100,000	100%

Our analysis of Texas Electric's common-size percentages reveals a marked deterioration in current asset liquidity in Year 2 relative to Year 1. This is evidenced by the 10 percent decline in both cash and accounts receivable.

Liquidity Index

Our assessment of the liquidity of current assets is aided by use of a **liquidity index.** Computation of the liquidity index is illustrated in the following case.

The liquidity index is expressed in days and its computation is a weighting mechanism. Its usefulness depends on the validity of assumptions implicit in the weighting process. Increases in the index signify a deterioration in liquidity, while decreases signify improved liquidity. The liquidity index must be interpreted with caution. The

[1] Another useful measure is **accounts payable turnover**. It is computed as: Purchases ÷ Average accounts payable. This ratio indicates the speed at which a company pays for purchases on account.

Illustration 8.8

Using the financial data of Texas Electric Corp. reported in the illustration above, along with additional data, we find their conversion of inventories into accounts receivable takes 50 days (on average) and their conversion of receivables into cash takes 40 days (on average). The liquidity index for Texas Electric is computed as:

Year 1:

	Amount	×	*Days Removed from Cash*	=	*Product Dollar × Days*
Cash	$ 30,000		—		—
Accounts receivable	40,000		40 days		1,600,000
Inventories	30,000		90 days		2,700,000
Total	$100,000 (*a*)				4,300,000 (*b*)

$$\text{Liquidity index} = \frac{b}{a} = \frac{4{,}300{,}000}{\$100{,}000} = 43 \text{ days}$$

Year 2:

	Amount	×	*Days Removed from Cash*	=	*Product Dollar × Days*
Cash	$ 20,000		—		—
Accounts receivable	30,000		40 days		1,200,000
Inventories	50,000		90 days		4,500,000
Total	$100,000				5,700,000

$$\text{Liquidity index} = \frac{5{,}700{,}000}{\$100{,}000} = 57 \text{ days}$$

Computation of the liquidity indexes of Texas Electric for Years 1 and 2 is consistent with results from the common-size analysis of current assets composition—liquidity has deteriorated in Year 2 relative to Year 1.

index is a number without direct meaning. It becomes meaningful when comparing one index number with another. It is best used as a measure of period-to-period change in liquidity or as a company-to-company comparison of relative liquidity.

Acid-Test (Quick) Ratio

A more stringent test of liquidity uses the **acid-test (quick) ratio**. This ratio includes those assets most quickly convertible to cash and is computed as:

$$\frac{\text{Cash + Cash equivalents + Marketable securities + Accounts receivable}}{\text{Current liabilities}}$$

Inventories are often the least liquid of current assets and are removed from the acid-test ratio. Another reason for excluding inventories is their valuation typically involves more managerial discretion than required for other current assets. Yet we must remember certain inventories are more liquid than slow-paying receivables. Interpretation of the acid-test ratio is similar to that of the current ratio. The acid-test ratio is a more stringent test of liquidity, and our analysis must assess the merits of excluding inventories in evaluating liquidity.

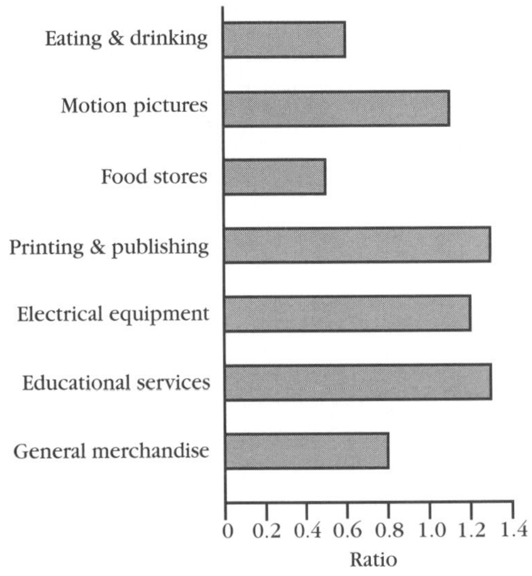

Source: Dun & Bradstreet.

Cash Flow Measures

The static nature of the current ratio and its inability (as a measure of liquidity) to recognize the importance of cash flows in meeting maturing obligations has led to a search for a dynamic measure of liquidity. Since liabilities are paid with cash, a comparison of operating cash flow to current liabilities is important. A ratio comparing operating cash flow to current liabilities overcomes the static nature of the current ratio since its numerator reflects a flow variable. For analysis purposes, operating cash flow for a period should be compared with current liabilities for that period. This **cash flow ratio** is computed as:

$$\frac{\text{Operating cash flow}}{\text{Current liabilities}}$$

The cash flow ratio computation for Campbell Soup in Year 11 is (data taken from financial statements reproduced in Supplement A):

$$\frac{\$805.2}{\$1{,}278} = 0.63$$

A ratio of operating cash flow to current liabilities of 0.40 or higher is common for healthy companies.

Financial Flexibility

In addition to the usual analysis tools for short-term liquidity, there are important *qualitative* considerations bearing on short-term liquidity. These are usefully characterized as depending on the financial flexibility of a company. **Financial flexibility** is the ability of a company to take steps to counter unexpected interruptions in the flow of funds. It can mean the ability to borrow from various sources, to raise equity capital, to sell and redeploy assets, or to adjust the level and direction of operations to meet changing circumstances. A company's capacity to borrow depends on several factors and is subject to change. It depends on profitability, stability, size, industry position, asset composition, and capital structure. It also depends on credit market conditions and trends. A company's capacity to borrow is important as a source of cash and in turning over short-term debt. Prearranged financing or open lines of credit are reliable sources of cash. Additional factors bearing on our assessment of a company's financial flexibility are (1) ratings of its commercial paper, bonds, and preferred stock, (2) any restrictions on its sale of assets, (3) the extent expenses are discretionary, and (4) ability to respond quickly to changing conditions (e.g., strikes, demand shifts, breaks in supply sources).

Management's Discussion and Analysis

As we discussed in Chapter 1, the Securities and Exchange Commission requires companies to include in their annual reports an expanded management discussion and analysis of financial condition and results of operations (MD&A). The financial condition section requires a discussion of liquidity—including known trends, demands, commitments, or uncertainties likely to impact on the company's ability to generate adequate cash. If a material deficiency in liquidity is identified, management must discuss the course of action it has taken or proposes to take to remedy the deficiency. Internal and external sources of liquidity and any material unused sources of liquid assets must be identified and described. Our analysis benefits from management's discussion and analysis. Adaptec includes a discussion titled Liquidity and Capital Resources in its MD&A section (see Supplement A).

What-If Analysis

What-if analysis is a useful technique to trace through the effects of changes in conditions or policies on the cash resources of a company. What-if analysis is illustrated in this section using the following selected financial data from Consolidated Technologies, Inc., at December 31, Year 1:

	Debit	*Credit*
Cash	$ 70,000	
Accounts receivable	150,000	
Inventory	65,000	
Accounts payable		$130,000
Notes payable		35,000
Accrued taxes		18,000
Fixed assets	200,000	
Accumulated depreciation		43,000
Capital stock		200,000

The following additional information is reported for Year 1:

Sales	$750,000
Cost of sales	520,000
Purchases	350,000
Depreciation	25,000
Net income	20,000

Consolidated Technologies anticipates 10 percent growth in sales for Year 2. All revenue and expense items are expected to increase by 10 percent, except for depreciation, which remains the same. All expenses are paid in cash as they are incurred, and Year 2 ending inventory is projected at $150,000. By the end of Year 2, Consolidated Technologies expects to have notes payable of $50,000 and a zero balance in accrued taxes. The company maintains a minimum cash balance of $50,000 as a managerial policy.

Case 8.1: Consolidated Technologies is considering a change in credit policy where ending accounts receivable reflect 90 days of sales. What impact does this change have on the company's cash balance? Will this change affect the company's need to borrow? Our analysis of this what-if situation is as follows:

Cash, January 1, Year 2			$ 70,000
Cash collections:			
Accounts receivable, January 1, Year 2		$150,000	
Sales		825,000	
Total potential cash collections		$975,000	
Less: Accounts receivable, December 31, Year 2		(206,250)[(a)]	768,750
Total cash available			$838,750
Cash disbursements:			
Accounts payable, January 1, Year 2	$130,000		
Purchases	657,000[(b)]		
Total potential cash disbursements	$787,000		
Accounts payable, December 31, Year 2	(244,000)[(c)]	$543,000	
Notes payable, January 1, Year 2	$ 35,000		
Notes payable, December 31, Year 2	(50,000)	(15,000)	
Accrued taxes		18,000	
Cash expenses[(d)]		203,500	749,500
Cash, December 31, Year 2			$ 89,250
Cash balance desired			50,000
Cash excess			$ 39,250

Explanations:

(a) $\$825{,}000 \times \frac{90}{360} = \$206{,}250.$

(b)

Year 2 cost of sales*: $520,000 × 1.1 =	$572,000
Ending inventory (given)	150,000
Goods available for sale	$722,000
Beginning inventory	(65,000)
Purchases	$657,000

* Excluding depreciation.

(c) $\text{Purchases} \times \frac{\text{Beg. accounts payable}}{\text{Year 1 purchases}} = \$657{,}000 \times \frac{\$130{,}000}{\$350{,}000} = \$244{,}000$

(d)

Gross profit ($825,000 − $572,000)		$253,000
Less: Net income	$ 24,500*	
Depreciation	25,000	(49,500)
Other cash expenses		$203,500

*110 percent of $20,000 (Year 1 N.I.) + 10 percent of $25,000 (Year 1 depreciation).

This change in credit policy would yield an excess in cash and no required borrowing.

Case 8.2: What if Consolidated Technologies worked to achieve an *average* accounts receivable turnover of 4.0 (instead of using *ending* receivables as in the previous case)? What impact does this change have on the company's cash balance? Our analysis of this what-if situation follows:

Excess cash balance as computed above		$39,250
Change from *ending* to *average* accounts receivable turnover increases year-end accounts receivable to:		
Average A. R. = $\frac{\$825,000}{4}$ = $206,250		
Ending A. R. = [$206,250 × 2] − $150,000 =	$262,500[a]	
Less: Accounts receivable balance from Case 8.1	206,250	56,250 (cash decrease)
Cash required to borrow		$17,000

[a] $\frac{\text{Sales}}{\text{Average A. R.. turnover}}$ = Average A.R.; Ending A.R. = [(Average A.R.) × 2] − Beginning A. R.

Consolidated Technologies would be required to borrow funds to achieve expected performance under the conditions specified.

Case 8.3: What if, in addition to the conditions prevailing in Case 8.2, the company's suppliers require payment within 60 days? What is the effect of this payment requirement on the cash balance? Our analysis of this case is as follows:

Cash required to borrow (from Case 8.2)		$ 17,000
Ending accounts payable (from Case 8.1)	$244,000	
Ending accounts payable under 60-day payment:		
Purchases × $\frac{60}{360}$ = $657,000 × $\frac{60}{360}$ =	109,500	
Additional disbursements required		134,500
Cash to be borrowed		$151,500

This more demanding payment schedule from suppliers would place additional borrowing requirements on Consolidated Technologies.

GUIDANCE ANSWERS TO ANALYSIS VIEWPOINTS

You Are the Banker

Your decision on IMC's one-year loan application is positive for at least two reasons. First, your analysis of IMC's short-term liquidity is assuring. IMC's current ratio of 4:1 suggests a considerable margin of safety in its ability to meet short-term obligations. Second, IMC's current assets of $1.6 million and current ratio of 4:1 implies current liabilities of $400,000 and a working capital excess of $1.2 million. This working capital excess totals 60 percent of the loan amount. The evidence supports approval of IMC's loan application. However, ixf IMC's application is for a 10-year loan, our decision is less optimistic. While the current ratio and working capital suggest a good safety margin, there are indications of inefficiency in operations. First, a 4:1 current ratio is in most cases too excessive and characteristic of inefficient asset use. Second, IMC's current ratio is more than double that of its competitors. Our decision regarding a long-term loan is likely positive, *but* substantially less optimistic than a short-term loan.

You Are the Consultant

Cost savings are assumed to derive from paying off current liabilities with money not invested in inventory. Accordingly, cost savings equal Inventory reduction × 10%. Under the old system, inventory equaled $5 million. This is obtained using the inventory turnover ratio: 20 = $100 million/Average inventory. With the new system inventory equals $4 million, computed using the new inventory turnover: 25 = $100 million/Average inventory. The cost savings are $100,000—computed from $5 million – $4 million × 10%.

QUESTIONS

8–1. Why is short-term liquidity important in our analysis of financial statements? Explain its importance from the viewpoint of more than one user.

8–2. Working capital equals current assets less current liabilities. Identify and describe factors impairing the usefulness of working capital.

8–3. What are *cash equivalents?* How should our analysis treat them?

8–4. Are fixed assets potentially includable in current assets? If your answer is yes, describe situations where inclusion is possible.

8–5. Certain installment receivables are not collectible within one year. Why are these receivables sometimes included in current assets?

8–6. Are all inventories included in current assets? Why or why not?

8–7. What is the justification for including prepaid expenses in current assets?

8–8. Assume a company under analysis has few current liabilities but substantial long-term liabilities. Notes to the financial statements report the company has a "revolving loan agreement" with a bank. Is this disclosure relevant to your analysis?

8–9. Certain industries are subject to peculiar financing and operating conditions calling for special consideration in drawing distinctions between *current* and *noncurrent.* How should our analysis recognize this in evaluating short-term liquidity?

8–10. Your analysis of two companies reveals identical levels of working capital. Are you confident in concluding their liquidity positions are equivalent?

8–11. What is the current ratio? What does the current ratio measure? What are reasons for using the current ratio for analysis?

8–12. Since cash generally does not yield a return, why does a company hold cash?

8–13. Is there a relation between level of inventories and sales? Are inventories a function of sales? If there is a relation between inventories and sales, is it proportional?

8–14. What are management's objectives in determining a company's investment in inventories and receivables?

8–15. What are the limitations of the current ratio as a measure of liquidity?

8–16. What is the appropriate use of the current ratio as a measure of liquidity?

8–17. What are cash-based ratios of liquidity? What do they measure?

8–18. How can we measure "quality" of current assets?

8–19. What does accounts receivable turnover measure?

8–20. What is the collection period for accounts receivable? What does it measure?

8–21. Assume a company's collection period is 60 days in comparison to 40 days for the prior period. Identify at least three possible reasons for this change.

8–22. What is an accounts receivable aging schedule? What is its usefulness in analyzing financial statements?

8–23. What are the repercussions to a company of (*a*) overinvestment, and (*b*) underinvestment, in inventories?

8–24. What problems are expected in an analysis of a company using the LIFO inventory method in an inflationary economy? What effects do price changes have on the (*a*) inventory turnover ratio, and (*b*) current ratio?

8–25. Why is the composition of current liabilities relevant to our analysis of the quality of the current ratio?

8–26. A seemingly successful company can have a poor current ratio. Identify possible reasons for this result.

8–27. What is window dressing? How can we recognize whether financial statements are window dressed?

8–28. What is the rule of thumb governing the expected size of the current ratio? What risks are there in using this rule of thumb for analysis?

8–29. Describe the importance of sales in assessing a company's current financial condition and liquidity of current assets.

8–30. What is the liquidity index? What is the usefulness of liquidity index numbers for our analysis?

8–31. Identify important qualitative considerations in our analysis of a company's short-term liquidity. What SEC disclosures help our analysis in this area?

8–32. What is the importance of what-if analysis on the effects of changes in conditions or policies for a company's cash resources?

EXERCISES

Exercise 8–1

Interpreting Effects of Transactions on Liquidity Measures

The Lux Company experienced the following unrelated events and transactions during Year 1. The company's existing current ratio is 2:1 and its quick ratio is 1.2:1.

1. Lux estimates $5,000 of accounts receivable are uncollectible.
2. A bank notifies Lux that a customer's check for $411 is returned marked insufficient funds. The customer is bankrupt.
3. The owners of Lux Company make an additional cash investment of $7,500.
4. Inventory costing $600 is judged obsolete when a physical inventory is taken.
5. Lux declares a $5,000 cash dividend to be paid during the first week of the next reporting period.
6. Lux purchases long-term investments for $10,000.
7. Accounts payable of $9,000 are paid.
8. Lux borrows $1,200 from a bank and gives a 90-day, 6 percent promissory note in exchange.
9. Lux sells a vacant lot for $20,000 that had been used in its business.
10. A three-year insurance policy is purchased for $1,500.

Required:

Separately evaluate the immediate effect of each of the transactions for the company's:

a. Current ratio.
b. Quick (acid-test) ratio.
c. Working capital.

Exercise 8–2

Interpreting Effects of Transactions on Liquidity Measures

Interpret the effect of the following six *independent* events and transactions for the:

a. Accounts receivable turnover (equals 3.0 prior to the event).
b. Collection period.
c. Inventory turnover (equals 3.0 prior to the event).

The three columns to the right of each event and transaction are identified as (*a*), (*b*), and (*c*) corresponding to the three liquidity measures. For each event and transaction indicate the effect as an increase (I); decrease (D); or no effect (NE).

Events and Transactions	*(a)*	*(b)*	*(c)*
1. Beginning inventory understatement of $500 is corrected this period.	______	______	______
2. Sales on account are underreported by $10,000.	______	______	______
3. $10,000 of accounts receivable are written off by a charge to the allowance for doubtful accounts.	______	______	______
4. $10,000 of accounts receivable are written off using the direct method.	______	______	______
5. Under the lower-of-cost-or-market method, inventory is reduced to market by $1,000.	______	______	______
6. Beginning inventory overstatement of $500 is corrected this period.	______	______	______

Exercise 8–3

Interpreting Effects of Transactions on Liquidity Measures

Interpret the effect of the following six *independent* events and transactions for the:

a. Accounts receivable turnover (equals 4.0 prior to the event).

b. Collection period.

c. Inventory turnover (equals 4.0 prior to the event).

The three columns to the right of each event and transaction are identified as (*a*), (*b*), and (*c*) corresponding to the three liquidity measures. For each event and transaction indicate the effect as an increase (I); decrease (D); or no effect (NE).

Events and Transactions	*(a)*	*(b)*	*(c)*
1. $5,000 of accounts receivable are written off by a charge to allowance for doubtful accounts.	______	______	______
2. Beginning inventory understatement of $1,000 is corrected this period.	______	______	______
3. Under the lower-of-cost-or-market method, inventory is reduced to market by $2,000.	______	______	______
4. Obsolete inventory of $3,000 is identified and written off.	______	______	______
5. Beginning inventory overstatement of $2,000 is corrected this period.	______	______	______
6. Sales on account are overstated by $10,000 and corrected this period.	______	______	______

Exercise 8–4

Identifying Window Dressing

The management of a corporation wishes to improve the appearance of its current financial position as shown in the current and quick ratios.

Required:

a. Describe four ways in which management can window dress the financial statements to accomplish this objective.

b. For each technique you identify in (*a*), describe the procedures, if any, you can use in your analysis to detect the window dressing.

(CFA Adapted)

PROBLEMS

Problem 8–1

Analyzing Measures of Short-Term Liquidity

Refer to the financial statements of Campbell Soup Company in Supplement A.

Required:

a. Compute the following liquidity measures for Year 10:
  1. Current ratio.
  2. Acid-test ratio.
  3. Accounts receivable turnover (accounts receivable balance at end of Year 9 is $564.1).
  4. Inventory turnover (inventory balance at end of Year 9 is $816.0).
  5. Days' sales in receivables.
  6. Days' sales in inventory.
  7. Conversion period (operating cycle).
  8. Cash ratio.
  9. Cash and cash equivalents to current liabilities.
  10. Liquidity index (assume prepaid expenses last for 100 days).
  11. Days' purchases in accounts payable.
  12. Net trade cycle.
  13. Cash flow ratio.

b. For Year 10, compute ratios 1, 4, 5, 6, and 7 using inventories valued on a FIFO basis (FIFO inventory at the end of Year 9 is $904).

c. What are the limitations of the current ratio as a measure of short-term liquidity?

d. How can our analysis of other related measures enhance the usefulness of the current ratio?

Problem 8–2

What-If Analysis of Cash Requirements

Selected financial data of Future Technologies, Inc., for December 31, Year 1, are reproduced below:

Account	***Debit***	***Credit***
Cash	$ 42,000	
Accounts receivable	90,000	
Inventory	39,000	
Fixed assets	120,000	
Notes payable		$ 21,000
Accrued taxes		10,800
Accumulated depreciation		25,800
Capital stock		120,000
Accounts payable		78,000
Retained earnings		35,400

The following additional information is available for Year 1:

Sales	$450,000
Cost of goods sold (excluding depreciation)	312,000
Purchases	210,000
Depreciation	15,000
Net income	12,000

For Year 2, Future Technologies anticipates a 5 percent sales growth. To counterbalance this lower than expected growth rate, the company implements cost-cutting strategies to reduce cost of goods sold by 2 percent from the Year 1 level. All other expenses are expected to increase by 5 percent. Expected net income for Year 2 is $20,000. Ending Year 2 inventory is estimated at $90,000 and there is no expected balance in accrued taxes. The company requires $175,000 to buy new equipment. The minimum desired cash balance is $30,000. The company offers a discount of 2 percent of sales if payment is received in 10 days. It is expected that 10 percent of sales takes advantage of this discount, while the remaining 90 percent are collected (on average) in 60 days.

Required:

Prepare a what-if analysis of cash needs for Year 2. Will Future Technologies need to borrow money?

Problem 8–3

What-If Analysis of Changes in Credit Policy

Reproduced below are selected financial accounts of RAM Corporation as of December 31, Year 1:

Account	*Debit*	*Credit*
Cash	$ 80,000	
Accounts receivable	150,000	
Inventory	65,000	
Accounts payable		$130,000
Notes payable		35,000
Accrued taxes		20,000
Fixed assets	200,000	
Accumulated depreciation		45,000
Capital stock		200,000

The following additional information is available for Year 1:

Sales	$800,000
Cost of sales (excludes depreciation)	520,000
Purchases	350,000
Depreciation	25,000
Net income	20,000

RAM Corporation anticipates growth of 10 percent in sales for the coming year. All corresponding revenue and expense items are expected to increase by 10 percent, except for depreciation, which remains the same. All expenses are paid in cash as incurred during the year. Year 2 ending inventory is predicted at $150,000. By the end of Year 2 the company expects a notes payable balance of $50,000 and no accrued taxes. The company maintains a minimum cash balance of $50,000 as a managerial policy.

Required:

Consider each of the following circumstances separately and independently of each other and focus only on changes described. (*Hint:* Prepare an analysis of cash needs for Year 2, and then calculate the effect of each of these three alternative scenarios.)

a. RAM Corporation is considering changing its credit policy. This change implies ending accounts receivable would represent 90 days of sales. What is the impact of this policy change on RAM Corp.'s current cash position? Will the company be required to borrow?

b. RAM Corporation is considering a change to a 120-day collection period based on ending accounts receivable. What is the effect(s) of this change on its cash position?

c. Suppliers are considering changing their policy of extending credit to RAM Corp. to require payment on purchases within 60 days; there would be no change in RAM Corp.'s collection period. What is the effect(s) of this change on its cash position?

Problem 8–4
What-If Analysis of Cash Demands

Reproduced below are selected financial data at the end of Year 5, and *forecasts* for the end of Year 6, of Top Corporation:

Account	*Year 5*	*Year 6*
Cash	$ 35,000	?
Accounts receivable	75,000	?
Inventory	32,000	$ 75,000
Accounts payable	65,000	122,000
Notes payable	17,500	15,000
Accrued taxes	9,000	0
Fixed assets	100,000	100,000
Accumulated depreciation	21,500	25,000
Capital stock	100,000	100,000

Additional Estimates for Year 6:

Sales	$412,500
Cost of sales	70% of sales
Net income	$10,000
Days' sales in receivables	90 days

Required:

Assuming all expenses are paid in cash when incurred and that cost of sales is exclusive of depreciation, estimate the ending cash balance for Year 6. If Top Corp. wishes to maintain a minimum cash balance of $50,000, must it borrow?

Problem 8–5
Qualitative Assessment of Liquidity

You are an investment analyst at Valley Insurance. Robert Jollie, a CFA and your superior, recently asked you to prepare a report on Gant Corporation's liquidity. Gant Corporation is a manufacturer of heavy equipment for the agricultural, forestry, and mining industries. Most of its plant capacity is located in the United States and a majority of its sales are international. Gant Corporation's investment bankers are offering Valley Insurance a participation in a private placement debenture issue. Beyond the traditional ratio analysis, your memo to Jollie stresses the following:

1. Gant Corporation's current ratio is 2:1.
2. During the prior fiscal year, Gant Corp.'s working capital increased substantially.
3. While Gant Corp.'s earnings are below record levels, rigorous cost controls yield an acceptable level of profitability and provide a basis for continued corporate liquidity.

After reviewing your memo, Jollie dismisses it as "totally inadequate"—not because it did not include a quantitative analysis of financial ratios, but because it did not effectively address corporate liquidity. Jollie wrote:

Liquidity is a cash phenomenon, and liquidity analysis is a process of evaluating the risk of whether a company can pay its debts as they come due. The vagaries and inconsistencies of working capital definitions do not adequately address this issue. Working capital analysis simply accounts for the change in a company's working capital position and adds little to an assessment of liquidity.

Required:

a. Identify five key information items directly impacting Gant's liquidity that should attempt to derive from this company's financial statements and management interviews.

b. Identify five *qualitative* financial and economic assessments specific to Gant and its industry that you should consider in further analyzing Gant's liquidity.

(CFA Adapted)

Problem 8–6

Interpreting Measures of Short-Term Liquidity

As lending officer for Prudent Bank you are analyzing the financial statements of ZETA Corporation (see Case CC-2 in the Comprehensive Case following Chaper 13) as part of ZETA's loan application. Your superior requests you evaluate ZETA's short-term liquidity using the two-year financial information available. The following additional information is acquired (in $thousands):

Inventory at January 1, Year 5	$32,000
Accruals:	
Year 5	3,000
Year 6	4,000

Required:

a. Compute the following measures for both Years 5 and 6:

1. Current ratio.
2. Days' sales in receivables.
3. Inventory turnover.
4. Days' sales in inventory.
5. Days' purchases in accounts payable (assume all cost of sales items are purchased).
6. Cash flow ratio.
7. Liquidity index (base number of days to sell inventory on cost of goods sold; assume prepaid expenses are 90 days removed from cash).

b. Comment on the significance of the year-to-year changes.

CASES

Case 8–1

Analyzing Adaptec's Liquidity and Financial Flexibility

Use the 1996 annual report of Adaptec, Inc., in Supplement A to answer the following questions.

a. Calculate the following short-term liquidity measures for 1996 and 1995.

1. Common-size composition of current assets.
2. Common-size composition of inventory (see note 2).
3. Allowance for doubtful accounts as percent of gross accounts receivable.
4. Working capital.
5. Current ratio.
6. Acid-test (quick) ratio.
7. Cash ratio.
8. Cash to current liabilities ratio.
9. Collection period (accounts receivable at fiscal year-end 1994 is $55,334).
10. Days to sell inventory (inventory at year-end 1994 is $38,940).
11. Operating cycle.
12. Cash flow ratio.

b. Using note 7 and the MD&A, assess Adaptec's financial flexibility.

c. Using your analysis in (*a*) and (*b*), assess Adaptec's liquidity.

Case 8–2

Assessing Short-Term Liquidity and Cash Requirements

Answer the following questions using the financial statements of Quaker Oats Company in Supplement A.

Part I

a. Construct a table containing the following short-term liquidity ratios for Years 9 through 11.

1. Current ratio.
2. Acid-test ratio.
3. Cash ratio.
4. Accounts receivable turnover.
5. Collection period.
6. Inventory turnover.
7. Days to sell inventory.
8. Days' purchases in accounts payable.
9. Operating cycle (conversion period).
10. Net trade cycle.
11. Liquidity index.
12. Cash flow ratio.

b. Based on your computations in (*a*), prepare a memorandum analyzing and evaluating Quaker Oats' short-term liquidity.

Part II

Management projects for Year 12 a 15 percent growth in sales, purchases and expenses. The inventory turnover for Year 12 is expected to be 6.5. To achieve these operating goals, management set the receivable collection period at 40 days, based on *year-end* accounts receivable. Ending accounts payable for Year 12 is expected to be $380 million and accounts payable turnover is 8.0. Also, $40 million in notes are to be paid off. Management desires to maintain a minimum cash balance of $70 million. The effective income tax rate for Year 12 is expected to be 45 percent and 10 percent of tax expense is expected to be deferred. Dividends will be $4.3 million on preferred stock and $128 million for common stock.

Required:

Will Quaker Oats need to borrow money in Year 12? (*Hint*: Prepare a projected income statement and cash flow statement for Year 12.)

Case 8–3

Preparing and Interpreting Cash Flow Forecasts

Fax Corporation's income statement and balance sheet for the year ended December 31, Year 1, is reproduced below:

FAX CORPORATION
Income Statement
For Year Ended December 31, Year 1

Net sales		$960,000
Cost of goods sold (excluding depreciation)		550,000
Gross margin		$410,000
Depreciation	$30,000	
Selling and administrative expenses	160,000	190,000
Income before taxes		$220,000
Income taxes (state and federal)		105,600
Net income		$114,400

FAX CORPORATION
Balance Sheet
As of December 31, Year 1

Assets		
Current assets:		
Cash	$ 30,000	
Marketable securities	5,500	
Accounts receivable	52,000	
Inventory	112,500	
Total current assets		$200,000
Plant and equipment	630,000	
Less: Accumulated depreciation	130,000	500,000
Total assets		$700,000
Liabilities and Equity		
Current liabilities:		
Accounts payable	$ 60,000	
Notes payable	50,000	
Total current liabilities		$110,000
Long-term debt		150,000
Equity:		
Capital stock	250,000	
Retained earnings	190,000	440,000
Total liabilities and equity		$700,000

Additional Information:

1. Purchases in Year 1 are $480,000.
2. In Year 2 management expects 15 percent sales growth and a 10 percent increase in all expenses except for depreciation, which increases by 5 percent.
3. Management expects an inventory turnover ratio of 5.5 for Year 2.
4. A receivable collection period of 90 days, based on *year-end* accounts receivable, is planned for Year 2.
5. Year 2 income taxes at the same rate of pre-tax income in Year 1 will be paid in cash.
6. Notes payable at the end of Year 2 will be $30,000.
7. Long-term debt of $25,000 will be paid in Year 2.
8. FAX desires a minimum cash balance of $20,000 in Year 2.
9. The ratio of accounts payable to purchases for Year 2 is the same as in Year 1.
10. All selling and administrative expenses will be paid in cash in Year 2.
11. Marketable securities and equity accounts at the end of Year 2 are the same as in Year 1.

Required:

a. Prepare a statement of expected cash inflows and outflows (what-if analysis) for the year ending December 31, Year 2.

b. Will FAX Corporation have to borrow money in Year 2?

Case 8–4

Preparing and Interpreting Cash Flow Forecasts

Kopp Corporation's income statement and balance sheet for the year ending December 31, Year 1, are reproduced below:

KOPP CORPORATION
Income Statement
For Year Ended December 31, Year 1

Net sales		$960,000
Cost of goods sold		550,000
Gross margin		$410,000
Depreciation	$ 30,000	
Selling and administrative expenses	160,000	190,000
Income before taxes		$220,000
Income taxes (48%)		57,600
Net income		$162,400

KOPP CORPORATION
Balance Sheet
As of December 31, Year 1

Assets		
Current assets:		
Cash	$ 30,000	
Marketable securities	5,500	
Accounts receivable	52,500	
Inventory	112,000	
Total current assets		$200,000
Plant and equipment	630,000	
Less: Accumulated depreciation	130,000	500,000
Total assets		$700,000
Liabilities and Equity		
Current liabilities:		
Accounts payable	$ 60,000	
Notes payable	50,000	
Total current liabilities		$110,000
Long-term debt		150,000
Equity:		
Capital stock	250,000	
Retained earnings	190,000	440,000
Total liabilities and equity		$700,000

Additional Information:

1. Purchases in Year 1 are $450,000.
2. In Year 2 management expects 15 percent sales growth and a 10 percent increase in all expenses except for depreciation, which increases by 5 percent.
3. Inventory turnover for Year 1 is 5.0, and management expects an inventory turnover ratio of 6.0 for Year 2.
4. A receivable collection period of 90 days, based on *year-end* accounts receivable, is planned for Year 2.
5. Year 2 income taxes at the same rate on pre-tax income in Year 1 will be paid in cash.
6. Notes payable of $20,000 will be paid in Year 2.
7. Long-term debt of $25,000 will be repaid in Year 2.
8. Kopp desires a minimum cash balance of $20,000 in Year 2.
9. The ratio of accounts payable to purchases will remain the same in Year 2 as in Year 1.

Required:

a. Prepare a statement of expected cash inflows and outflows (what-if analysis) for the year ending December 31, Year 2.

b. Will Kopp Corporation have to borrow money in Year 2?

Case 8–5
Making a Lending Decision

Ian Manufacturing Company was organized five years ago and manufactures toys. Its most recent three years' balance sheets and income statements are reproduced below:

IAN MANUFACTURING COMPANY
Balance Sheets
As of June 30, Year 5, Year 4, and Year 3

	Year 5	*Year 4*	*Year 3*
Assets			
Cash	**$ 12,000**	$ 15,000	$ 16,000
Accounts receivable, net	**183,000**	80,000	60,000
Inventory	**142,000**	97,000	52,000
Other current assets	**5,000**	6,000	4,000
Plant and equipment (net)	**160,000**	110,000	70,000
Total assets	**$502,000**	$308,000	$202,000
Liabilities and Equity			
Accounts payable	**$147,800**	$ 50,400	$ 22,000
Federal income tax payable	**30,000**	14,400	28,000
Long-term liabilities	**120,000**	73,000	22,400
Common stock, $5 par value	**110,000**	110,000	80,000
Retained earnings	**94,200**	60,200	49,600
Total liabilities and equity	**$502,000**	$308,000	$202,000

IAN MANUFACTURING COMPANY
Condensed Income Statements
For Years Ended June 30, Year 5, Year 4, Year 3

	Year 5	*Year 4*	*Year 3*
Net sales	**$1,684,000**	$1,250,000	$1,050,000
Cost of goods sold	**927,000**	810,000	512,000
Gross margin	**$ 757,000**	$ 440,000	$ 538,000
Marketing and administrative costs	**670,000**	396,700	467,760
Operating income	**$ 87,000**	$ 43,300	$ 70,240
Interest cost	**12,000**	7,300	2,240
Income before federal income tax	**75,000**	36,000	68,000
Income tax	**$ 30,000**	$ 14,400	$ 28,000
Net income	**$ 45,000**	$ 21,600	$ 40,000

A reconcilation of retained earnings for years ended June 30, Year 4, and Year 5, follows:

IAN MANUFACTURING COMPANY
Statement of Retained Earnings
For Years Ended June 30, Year 5 and Year 4

	Year 5	*Year 4*
Balance, beginning	**$ 60,200**	$49,600
Add: net income	**45,000**	21,600
Subtotal	**$105,200**	$71,200
Deduct: Dividends paid	**11,000**	11,000
Balance, ending	**$ 94,200**	$60,200

Additional Information:

1. All sales are on account.
2. Long-term liabilities are owed to the company's bank.
3. Terms of sale are net 30 days.

Required:

a. Compute the following measures for both Years 4 and 5:
   1. Working capital.
   2. Current ratio.
   3. Acid-test ratio.
   4. Accounts receivable turnover.
   5. Collection period of receivables.
   6. Inventory turnover.
   7. Days to sell inventory.
   8. Debt-to-equity ratio.
   9. Times interest earned.

b. Using Year 3 as the base year, compute an index-number trend series for:
   1. Sales.
   2. Cost of goods sold.
   3. Gross margin.
   4. Marketing and administrative costs.
   5. Net income.

c. Based on your analysis in (*a*) and (*b*), prepare a report regarding a recommendation on whether to grant a loan to Ian Manufacturing? Support your recommendation with relevant analysis.

INTERNET ACTIVITIES

Internet 8–1
Loan Analysis

Access one of the financial statement databases available on the Internet (http://www.mhhe.com/business/accounting/wild). Retrieve current financial statements of a company selected by either you or your instructor.

Required:

a. Compute the liquidity measures listed in Case 8–2 (*a*) for the most recent two years.

b. Using three years prior as the base year, compute an index-number trend series for: (1) Sales, (2) Cost of sales, (3) Gross margin, (4) Operating expenses, and (5) Net income.

c. Using your analysis in (*a*) and (*b*), write a report recommending whether to grant a short-term loan to this company. Support your recommendation with relevant analysis.

Internet 8–2
Liquidity Analysis and Credit Rating

Access one of the financial statement databases available on the Internet (http://www.mhhe.com/business/accounting/wild). Retrieve current financial statements of *three* companies in different industries selected by either you or your instructor. Make certain the companies are covered in Standard & Poor's (or Moody's) bond ratings service.

Required:

a. Using the analysis techniques described in this chapter, evaluate each company's short-term liquidity.

b. Use Standard & Poor's (or Moody's) bond ratings to identify the credit ratings for these three companies.

c. Write a report explaining why these companies have different or similar credit ratings given the analysis in (*a*).

Internet 8–3

Liability Analysis and Liquidity

Access one of the financial statement databases available on the Internet (http://www.mhhe.com/business/accounting/wild). Retrieve current financial statements of *three* companies in different industries selected by either you or your instructor.

Required:

a. Identify the major similarities and differences in these companies' current assets and liabilities.

b. Describe the relative amounts of different items comprising these companies' current assets and liabilities.

c. Write a report assessing the relative liquidity of these companies using your analysis in (*a*) and (*b*).

Internet 8–4

Credit Rating, Credit Risk, and Liquidity

Identify a recent article in the financial press (e.g., *The Wall Street Journal*, *Fortune*, *Barron's*) discussing a company that had its commercial paper or bond rating changed. Make a copy of the article. Next, access one of the financial statement databases available on the Internet (http://www.mhhe.com/business/accounting/wild) to retrieve the financial statements of this company.

Required:

a. Compute the financial ratios identified in Case 8–2 (*a*) for this company for the prior three years.

b. Write a report analyzing whether the financial ratios in (*a*) are useful in explaining the credit rating change for this company. Attach a copy of the article to your report.

C H A P T E R 9

Forecasting and Pro Forma Analysis

A Look Back

Chapter 8 began our study of the application and interpretation of financial statement analysis tools. We described analysis tools using financial data for assessing short-term liquidity. We demonstrated accounting-based, turnover, and activity measures of liquidity and explained their relevance for analyzing different aspects of liquidity.

A Look at This Chapter

We study forecasting and pro forma analysis of financial statements in this chapter. We explain the flow of cash through a company's business activities and its implications for liquidity. Both short- and long-term forecasting of cash flows are described. We direct attention at applying these analysis tools.

A Look Ahead

Chapter 10 expands our analysis of a company to capital structure and long-term solvency. We analyze capital structure and interpret its implications for future company performance and solvency. Several useful analysis tools are described and illustrated for interpretation of financial statements.

Learning Objectives

- Describe cash flow patterns in a company's business activities.
- Explain short-term forecasting and pro forma analysis of financial statements.
- Analyze cash flow patterns for long-term forecasting.
- Describe forecasting of operating, investing, and financing cash flows.
- Explain what-if forecasting scenarios and their relevance.
- Interpret specialized cash flow adequacy and reinvestment ratios.

PREVIEW OF CHAPTER 9

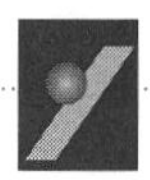

Future liquidity is as important to our analysis of financial statements as our assessment of past and current liquidity. This chapter shows how our analysis of future liquidity benefits from forecasts of cash inflows and outflows. For long-term cash forecasting horizons, we show the usefulness of forecasts framed by the statement of cash flows. The forecast tools described in this chapter are extremely useful in analyzing a company's future liquidity, solvency, and financial flexibility. We demonstrate these tools with actual financial statements. Our analysis relies on a more *dynamic* representation of liquidity than traditional static ratio analysis based on past financial statement data. The static nature of traditional analysis, relying on financial reports listing claims against an enterprise and the resources available to meet these claims, fails to capture the dynamic nature of liquidity. We show how the analysis techniques in this chapter build on reliable patterns of past performance, incorporate estimates of future plans and conditions, and forecast the future availability and disposition of cash. These techniques are subject to feasibility tests using pro forma analysis and the discipline inherent in the accounting system. The content and organization of this chapter are as follows:

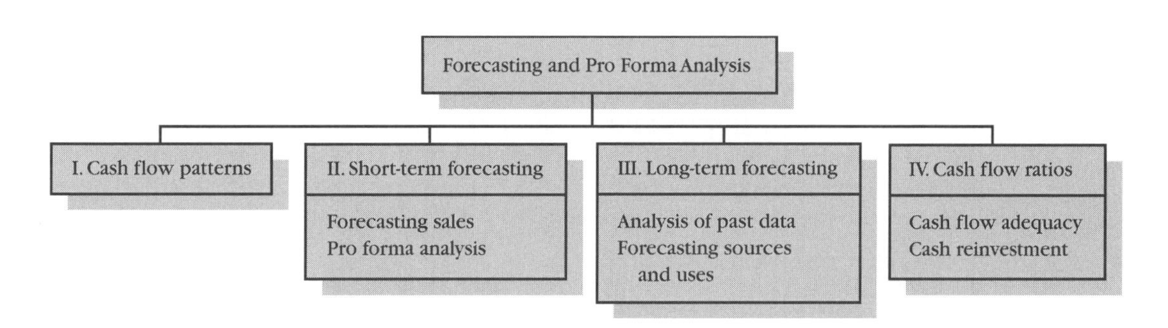

Cash Flow Patterns

It is important for us to review the nature of cash flow patterns before examining models for cash flow analysis and projection. Cash and cash equivalents (hereafter simply *cash*) are the most liquid of assets. Nearly all management decisions to invest in assets or pay expenses require the immediate or eventual use of cash. This results in management's focus on cash rather than on other concepts of liquid funds. Although some users (like creditors) sometimes consider assets like receivables and inventories part of liquid assets given their near-term conversion into cash.

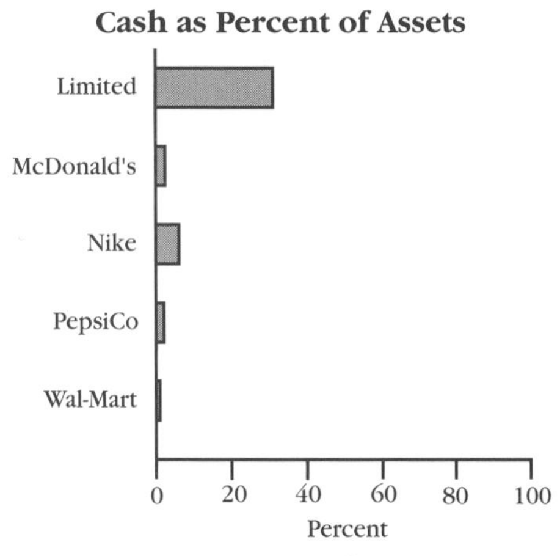

Source: Annual reports.

Holding cash provides little or no return and, in times of rising prices, cash (like all monetary assets) is exposed to purchasing power loss. Nevertheless, holding cash represents the least exposure to risk. Management is reponsible for the decisions to invest cash in assets or to pay immediate costs. These *cash conversions* increase risk because the ultimate recovery of cash from these activities is less than certain. Risks associated with these cash conversions are of various types and degrees. For instance, risk in converting cash into temporary investments is less than the risk in committing cash to long-term payout assets like plant and equipment. Investing cash in assets or costs aimed at developing and marketing new products carries often more serious risks of cash recovery. Both short-term liquidity and long-term solvency depend on the recovery and realizability of cash outlays.

Cash inflows and outflows are interrelated. A failure of any aspect of the company's business activities to successfully carry out its assigned task affects the entire cash flow system. A lapse in sales affects the conversion of finished goods into receivables and cash, leading to a decline in cash availability. A company's inability to replace this cash from sources like equity, loans, or accounts payable can impede production activities and produce losses in future sales. Conversely, restricting expenditures on items like advertising and marketing can slow the conversion of finished goods into receivables and cash. Long-term restrictions in either cash outflows or inflows can lead to company insolvency.

Our analysis must recognize the interrelations between cash flows, accruals, and profits. Sales is the driving source of operating flows. When finished goods representing the accumulation of many costs and expenses are sold, the company's profit margin produces an inflow of liquid funds through receivables and cash. The higher the profit margin, the greater the growth of liquid funds. Profits often primarily derive from the difference between sales and cost of sales (gross profit) and have enormous consequences to cash flows. Many costs, like those flowing from utilization of plant and equipment or deferred charges, do not require cash outlays. Similarly, items like long-term installment sales of land create noncurrent receivables limiting the relevance of accruals for cash flows. Our analysis must appropriately use these measures in assessing cash flow patterns.

Cash flows are limited in another respect. As cash flows into a company, management has certain discretion in its disbursement. This discretion depends on commitments to outlays like dividends, inventory accumulation, capital expenditures, or debt repayment. Cash flows also depend on management's ability to draw on sources like equity and debt. With noncommitted cash inflows, referred to as free cash flows, management has considerable discretion in their use. It is this noncommitted cash component that is of special interest and importance for our analysis.

Short-Term Cash Forecasting

In our analysis of short-term liquidity, one of our most useful tools is **short-term cash forecasting**. Short-term cash forecasting is of interest to internal users like management and auditors in evaluating a company's current and future operating activities. It is also of interest to external users like short-term creditors who need to assess a company's ability to repay short-term loans. Our analysis stresses short-term cash forecasting when a company's ability to meet current obligations is in doubt. The accuracy of cash flow forecasting is inversely related to the *forecast horizon*—the longer the forecast period, the less reliable the forecasts. This is due to the number and complexity of factors influencing cash inflows and outflows that cannot be reliably estimated in the long term. Even in the case of short-term cash forecasting, the information required is substantial. Since cash flow forecasting often depends on publicly available information, our objective is "reasonably accurate" forecasts. By studying and preparing cash flow forecasts, our analysis should achieve greater insights into a company's cash flow patterns.

Importance of Forecasting Sales

The reliability of our cash forecast depends importantly on the *quality of the sales forecast*. With few exceptions, such as funds from financing or funds used in investing activities, most cash flows relate to and depend on sales. Our forecasting of sales includes an analysis of:

- Directions and trends in sales.
- Market share.
- Industry and economic conditions.
- Productive and financial capacity.
- Competitive factors.

These components are typically assessed along product lines potentially affected by forces peculiar to their markets. Later examples illustrate the importance of sales forecasts.

ANALYSIS VIEWPOINT . . . *You are the loan officer*

As a recently hired loan officer at Intercontinental Bank you are processing a loan application for a new customer, DEC Manufacturing. In their application materials DEC submits short-term sales forecasts for the next three periods of $1.1, $1.25, and $1.45 million, respectively. You notice the most recent two periods' sales are $0.8 and $0.65 million, and you ask DEC management for an explanation. DEC's response is twofold: (1) recent sales are misleading due to a work stoppage and an unusual period of abnormally high raw material costs due to bankruptcy of a major supplier; and (2) recent industry volatility tied to consumer demand. Do you use their forecasts in your loan analysis?

Cash Flow Forecasting with Pro Forma Analysis

The reasonableness and feasibility of short-term cash forecasts are usefully checked by means of **pro forma financial statements**. We accomplish this by using assumptions underlying cash forecasts to construct a pro forma income statement for the forecast period and a pro forma balance sheet for the end of the forecast period. Financial ratios and other relations are derived from these pro forma financial statements and checked for feasibility against historical relations. These comparisons must recognize adjustments for factors expected to affect them during the cash forecast period.

We illustrate cash flow forecasting using financial data from IT Technologies, Inc. IT Technologies recently introduced a new electronic processor that has enjoyed excellent market acceptance. IT's management estimates sales ($thousands) for the next six months ending June 30, Year 1, as: $100, $125, $150, $175, $200, and $250 (see the bar graph). The current cash balance at January 1, Year 1, is $15,000. In light of the predicted increase in sales, IT's treasurer hopes to maintain *minimum* monthly cash balances of $20,000 for January; $25,000 for February; $27,000 for March; and $30,000 for April, May, and June. The treasurer foresees a need for additional funds to finance sales expansion. The treasurer expects new equipment valued at $20,000 will be purchased in February by giving a note payable to the seller. The note is paid, beginning in February, at the rate of $1,000 per month. The new equipment is not planned to be operational until August of Year 1.

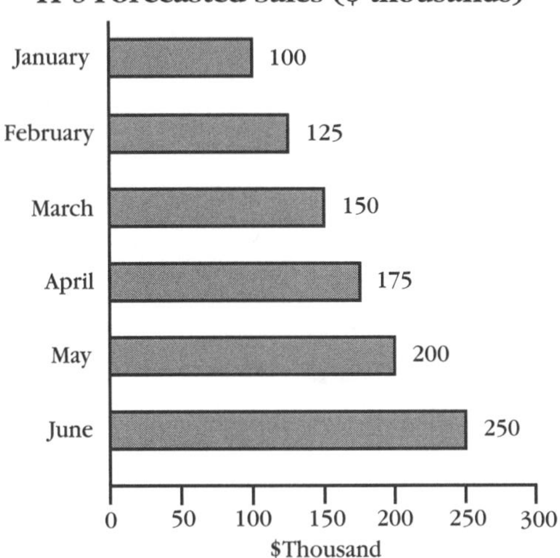

The treasurer plans several steps to fund these financing requirements. First, she obtains a financing commitment from an insurance company to acquire $110,000 of IT's long-term bonds (less $2,500 issue costs). These bond sales are planned for April ($50,000) and May ($60,000). She plans to sell real estate for additional financing, including $8,000 in May and $50,000 in June, and will sell equipment (originally costing $25,000 with a book value of zero) for $25,000 in June. The treasurer approaches IT's banker for approval of short-term financing to cover additional funding needs. The bank's loan officer requires the treasurer to prepare a *cash forecast* for the six months ending June 30, Year 1, along with *pro forma financial statements* for that period, to process her request. The loan officer also requests IT Technologies specify its uses of cash and its sources of funds for loan repayment. The treasurer recognizes the importance of a cash forecast and proceeds to compile data necessary to comply with the loan officer's request.

As one of her first steps, the treasurer estimates the pattern of receivables collections. Prior experience suggests the following collection pattern:

Collections	*Percent of Total Receivables*
In month of sale	40%
In second month	30
In third month	20
In fourth month	5
Written off as bad debts	5
	100%

EXHIBIT 9.1

Estimates of Cash Collections
For Months January–June, Year 1

	January	*February*	*March*	*April*	*May*	*June*
Sales	$100,000	$125,000	$150,000	$175,000	$200,000	$250,000
Collections of sales:						
1st month—40%	$ 40,000	$ 50,000	$ 60,000	$ 70,000	$ 80,000	$100,000
2nd month—30%		30,000	37,500	45,000	52,500	60,000
3rd month—20%			20,000	25,000	30,000	35,000
4th month—5%				5,000	6,250	7,500
Total cash collections	$ 40,000	$ 80,000	$117,500	$145,000	$168,750	$202,500
Write-offs—5%				5,000	6,250	7,500

This collection pattern along with expected product sales allows the treasurer to construct estimates of cash collections shown in Exhibit 9.1.

Analyzing expense patterns in prior periods' financial statements yields expense estimates based on either sales or time. Exhibit 9.2 shows these expense relations. IT Technologies pays off these expenses (excluding the $1,000 monthly depreciation) when incurred. The only exception is for purchases of materials, where 50 percent is paid in the month of purchase and 50 percent in the following month. Materials inventory on January 1, Year 1, is $57,000. The treasurer estimates materials inventory for the end of each month from January to June of Year 1 as: $67,000, $67,500, $65,500, $69,000, $67,000, and $71,000, respectively. She also estimates the pattern of payments on accounts payable for these materials. Exhibit 9.3 shows these expected payments. Since the electronic processor is manufactured to specific order, no finished goods inventories are expected to accumulate.

The treasurer's resulting cash forecast for each of the six months ending June 30, Year 1, is shown in Exhibit 9.4. Exhibit 9.5 shows IT Technologies' pro forma income statement for the six months ending June 30, Year 1. Both actual and pro forma balance sheets of IT Technologies as of January 1 and June 30, respectively, of Year 1 are shown in Exhibit 9.6.

Our cash flow analysis should critically examine the pro forma statements and submit them to *feasibility tests* on both their forecasts and their assumptions. We should evaluate both ratios and relations revealed in pro forma financial statements and compare them to historical ratios to determine their reasonableness and feasibility. As an example, IT Technologies' current ratio increases from 2.6 on January 1, Year 1, to 3.5 in the pro forma balance sheet of June 30, Year 1. In addition, for the six months ended June 30, Year 1, the projected return on average equity exceeds 8 percent. These and other measures such as turnover, trends, and common-size comparisons should be evaluated. Unexpected variations in important relations should be either explained or adjustments made to assumptions and expectations if errors are identified. These steps increase the reliability of pro forma statements for our analysis.

IT's Forecasted Cash ($ thousands)
(from Exhibit 9.4)

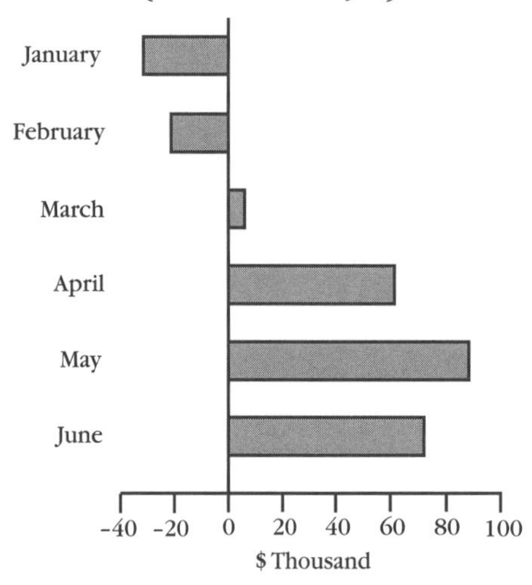

EXHIBIT 9.2

Expense Estimates
For Months January–June, Year 1

Materials	30% of sales
Labor	25% of sales
Manufacturing overhead:	
Variable	10% of sales
Fixed	$8,000 per month (includes $1,000 depreciation per month)
Selling expenses	10% of sales
General and administrative expenses:	
Variable	8% of sales
Fixed	$7,000 per month

EXHIBIT 9.3

Estimates of Cash Payments for Materials
For Months January–June, Year 1

	January	*February*	*March*	*April*	*May*	*June*
Materials purchases*	$40,000	$38,000	$43,000	$56,000	$58,000	$79,000
Payments:						
1st month—50%	$20,000	$19,000	$21,500	$28,000	$29,000	$39,500
2nd month—50%		20,000	19,000	21,500	28,000	29,000
Total payments	$20,000	$39,000	$40,500	$49,500	$57,000	$68,500

*These reconcile with material costs and changes in inventories.

We should recognize that electronic spreadsheet programs are available to assist us in pro forma analysis. The ease of changing variables for sensitivity tests improves the usefulness of pro forma statements. Nevertheless, we should not confuse the ease and flexibility of these programs with the crucial need to develop and verify estimates and assumptions underlying their output. The reasonableness of important estimates and assumptions, and the usefulness of this analysis, depend on our critical evaluation and judgment and *not* on our technology.

Long-Term Cash Forecasting

Short-term cash forecasting using pro forma statements is a very useful and reliable aid in assessing liquidity. However, the reliability and feasibility of cash forecasting using pro forma statements decline in longer time horizons. When the time horizon exceeds two or three years, the uncertainties in using pro forma analysis likely preclude detailed and accurate cash forecasts. **Long-term cash forecasting,** instead of focusing on items like receivables collections and payments for labor and materials, focuses on projections of income, operating cash flows, and other sources and uses

Exhibit 9.4

IT TECHNOLOGIES, INC.
Cash Forecast
For Months January–June, Year 1

	January	February	March	April	May	June	Six-Month Totals
Cash balance—beginning	$15,000	$20,000	$ 25,750	$ 27,250	$ 30,580	$ 30,895	$ 15,000
Add cash receipts for:							
Cash collections (Exh. 9.1)	40,000	80,000	117,500	145,000	168,750	202,500	753,750
Sale of real estate‡					8,000	50,000	58,000
Sale of bonds‡				47,500	60,000		107,500
Sale of equipment‡						25,000	25,000
Total cash available	$ 55,000	$100,000	$143,250	$219,750	$267,330	$308,395	$959,250
Less disbursements for:							
Material (Exh. 9.3)	$20,000	$39,000	$40,500	$ 49,500	$57,000	$ 68,500	$274,500
Labor†	25,000	31,250	37,500	43,750	50,000	62,500	250,000
Fixed overhead†	7,000	7,000	7,000	7,000	7,000	7,000	42,000
Variable overhead†	10,000	12,500	15,000	17,500	20,000	25,000	100,000
Selling expenses†	10,000	12,500	15,000	17,500	20,000	25,000	100,000
General and administrative†	15,000	17,000	19,000	21,000	23,000	27,000	122,000
Taxes§						19,000	19,000
Purchase of fixed assets‡		1,000	1,000	1,000	1,000	1,000	5,000
Total cash disbursements	87,000	120,250	135,000	157,250	178,000	235,000	912,500
Tentative cash balance (deficit)	$(32,000)	$(20,250)	8,250	$ 62,500	$ 89,330	$ 73,395	$ 46,750
Minimum cash required‡	20,000	25,000	27,000	30,000	30,000	30,000	
Borrowing required	$ 52,000	$ 46,000	$ 19,000	—	—	—	$117,000
Repayment of loan				$ 30,000	$ 58,000	$ 29,000	(117,000)
Interest paid on balance*				1,920	435	145	2,500
Ending cash balance	$ 20,000	$ 25,750	$ 27,250	$ 30,580	$ 30,895	$ 44,250	$ 44,250
Loan balance	$ 52,000	$ 98,000	$117,000	$ 87,000	$ 29,000	—	—

* Interest is computed at the rate of ½ percent per month and paid at month-end. Any loan is taken out at the beginning of a month.

† Estimates computed using information from Exhibit 9.2.

‡ Treasurer's expectations taken from information on page 450.

§ Taxes total a 40 percent combined state and federal rate. Taxes of $19,000 are paid in June, with the balance accrued.

EXHIBIT 9.5

IT TECHNOLOGIES, INC.
Pro Forma Income Statement
For Six Months Ending June 30, Year 1

		Source of Estimate
Sales	$1,000,000	Forecasted sales
Cost of sales:		
Materials	$ 300,000	Exhibit 9.2
Labor	250,000	Exhibit 9.2
Overhead	148,000	Exhibit 9.2
	$ 698,000	
Gross profit	$ 302,000	
Selling expense	$ 100,000	Exhibit 9.2
Bad debts expense	18,750	Exhibit 9.1
General and administrative expense	122,000	Exhibit 9.2
	$ 240,750	
Operating income	$ 61,250	
Gain on sale of equipment	25,000	Treasurer
Interest expense	(2,500)	Exhibit 9.4 note
Income before taxes	83,750	
Income taxes (40% rate)	33,500	
Net income	$ 50,250	

of cash. Long-term forecasting of cash flows often involves two steps. First, we analyze prior periods' cash flow statements. Second, we introduce adjustments to cash flow data based on relevant information and estimates about future uses and sources of cash to generate our forecasts. This section describes both of these tasks.

Analysis of Prior Cash Flows for Forecasting

We previously analyzed the principles underlying preparation of the statement of cash flows (SCF) and identified useful inferences from this statement. We now focus further on analysis of the statement of cash flows—paying special attention to its use in projecting future cash flows. In our analysis of financial statements, recent years' data are likely the most relevant since they represent a company's prevailing business activities. Since there is inherent continuity in business activities, recent performance is likely most relevant for forecasting purposes.

While we emphasize recent performance, it is important we obtain financial statements for several prior years if possible. This is especially important when analyzing the statement of cash flows. This is because planning and execution of plant expansions, modernization strategies, working capital changes, and financing policies likely involve multiyear horizons. For our analysis of management's plans and their execution, it is useful to analyze several prior years' statements of cash flows. This enables us to perform a more comprehensive analysis of management's strategies and their performance.

EXHIBIT 9.6

IT TECHNOLOGIES, INC.
Balance Sheets

	Actual January 1, Year 1		*Pro Forma June 30, Year 1*	
Assets				
Current assets:				
Cash	$ 15,000		$ 44,250	
Accounts receivable (net)	6,500		234,000	
Inventories—materials	57,000		71,000	
Total current assets		$ 78,500		$ 349,250
Real estate	$ 58,000		—	
Fixed assets	206,400		$ 201,400	
Accumulated depreciation	(36,400)		(17,400)	
Net fixed assets		228,000		184,000
Other assets		3,000		3,000
Deferred bond issue costs		—		2,500
Total assets		$ 309,500		$ 538,750
Liabilities and Equity				
Current liabilities:				
Accounts payable	$ 2,000		$ 41,500	
Notes payable	28,500		43,500	
Accrued taxes	—		14,500	
Total current liabilities		$ 30,500		$ 99,500
Long-term debt	$ 15,000		$ 125,000	
Common stock	168,000		168,000	
Retained earnings	96,000		146,250	
		279,000		439,250
Total liabilities and equity		$ 309,500		$ 538,750

Since conditions vary from company to company, it is difficult to formulate a "standard" analysis of cash flows. Nevertheless, certain commonalities exist. First, our analysis must establish the prior *major* sources of cash and their uses. A common-size analysis of the statement of cash flows aids in this year-to-year comparison. In assessing trends, it is useful to total the major sources and uses of cash over a period of years since annual or quarterly reporting periods are often too short for meaningful inferences. For example, financing of major projects often spans several years. In evaluating sources and uses of cash, the analyst should focus on questions like:

- Are asset replacements financed from internal or external funds?
- What are the financing sources of expansion and business acquisitions?
- Is the company dependent on external financing?
- What are the company's investing demands and opportunities?
- What are the requirements and forms of financing?
- Are managerial policies (e.g., dividends) highly sensitive to cash flows?

Case Analysis of Cash Flows for Forecasting

We illustrate the analysis of prior years' statements of cash flows for Campbell Soup Company in the Comprehensive Case following Chapter 13. Our analysis covers the six-year period ending July 28, Year 11. Exhibit CC.15 presents these statements in common-size format.

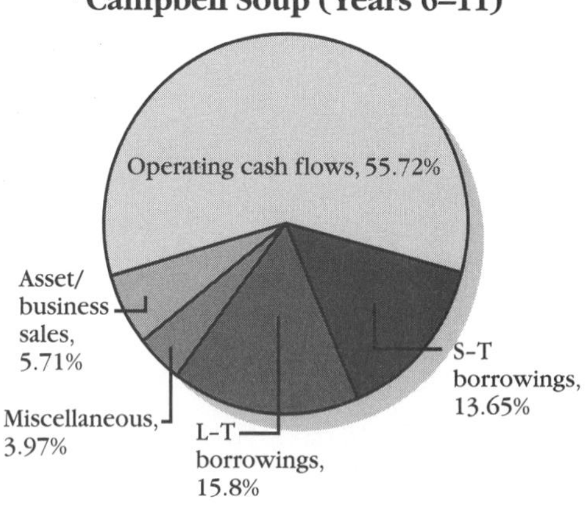

Our analysis of these statements reveals several insights. During this six-year period the major sources of cash are operations ($3,010 million), long-term debt ($854 million), and short-term debt ($737 million)—see Exhibit CC.14 and Campbell's statements in Supplement A. Major uses are plant purchases (net of sales) of $1,647 million, business acquisitions (net of sales) of $718 million, and cash dividends of $649 million. During this six-year period, cash and cash equivalents increased by $24 million. Sources of cash from operations as a percent of total sources average 55.7 percent, with a low of 31.3 percent in Year 9. Year 11 is the most profitable of the six, reflecting a recovery after two years of poor performance and restructuring activities. For this six-year period, cash from operations covered net cash used in investing activities and nearly all dividends paid. Cash flows are partially insulated from the sharp declines in earnings for Years 9 and 10 because restructuring charges of $682 million involved no cash outlays.

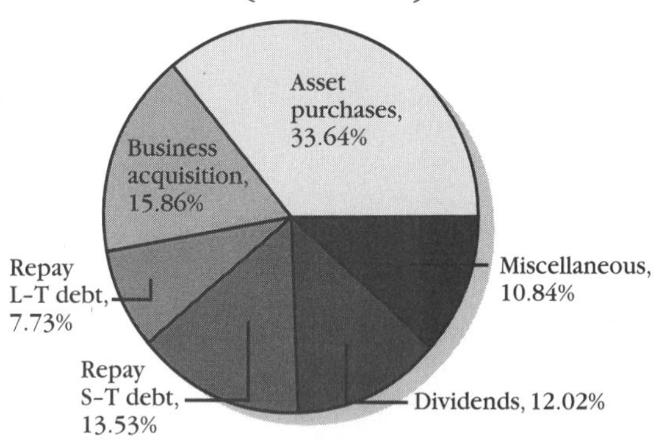

Our analysis of prior years' statements of cash flows is a useful basis for cash flow forecasting. A forecast of future cash flows must consider the above-mentioned relations—including the relation between cash and income, the components of the income to operating cash flow conversion, asset acquisitions, and the relation of sales to growth in operating cash flows. Noncash adjustments like depreciation depend on future depreciation and acquisition policies. Acquisition policies and write-offs for tax purposes partially determine deferred tax adjustments. The more we know about these and other factors, the more reliable our cash flow forecasts.

Forecasting Inferences from Analysis of Cash Flows

Our analysis of the statement of cash flows is, as the previous case suggests, an important step in forecasting cash flows. The Campbell Soup case illustrates the range of useful insights drawn from our analysis of cash flows. We must remember our analysis of the statement of cash flows is performed within the framework of our overall analysis of financial statements. Accordingly, inferences from our analysis of cash flows are corroborated or refuted through analysis of other financial statements.

Nevertheless, there are useful generalizations we can make about potential inferences from analysis of the statement of cash flows. First, our analysis of the statement of cash flows enables us to appraise the quality of management's decisions over time and their impact on the company's results of operations and financial position. When our analysis covers a long time period, it can yield insights into management's success in responding to changing business conditions and their ability to seize opportunities and overcome adversities.

Inferences from our analysis of cash flows include where management committed its resources, where it reduced investments, where additional cash derived from, and where claims against the company are reduced. Inferences also pertain to the disposition of earnings and the investment of discretionary cash flows. Analysis also enables us to infer the size, composition, pattern, and stability of operating cash flows.

We previously described patterns of cash flows through a company. Cash flows are used for labor, material, and overhead. They are also used for long-term assets like plant and equipment where conversion through the product-cost stream is at a slower rate. But eventually all uses of cash enter the sales process and are converted into receivables or cash. Profitable operations yield cash recoveries exceeding amounts invested and, consequently, increase cash inflows. Losses yield a reverse effect.

Our inferences must explain the variation in cash flow segmentation. Most view operating cash flows as an index of management's ability to redirect funds away from unprofitable opportunities to those of greater profit potential. Yet not all operating cash flows can be so judged because of commitments for items like debt retirements, stock redemptions, equipment replacements, and dividend payments. Nor is operating cash flows the only potential inflow since management can draw on external financing sources. We must also examine the components of operating cash flows. Components often hold important clues about the stability of cash sources. For example, depreciation is a stable component representing a "recovery" of investments in fixed assets from sales. Cash recovered from depreciation is normally reinvested in maintaining productive assets. Similarly, while goodwill amortization is also a stable component, any recovered amount of this noncash charge is not typically reinvested in those assets. Our inferences from analysis of cash flows include earnings quality assessment. One factor in the quality of earnings is the impact of changes in business conditions for cash flows. The statement of cash flows also reveals noncash income components bearing on our inferences of earnings quality. Inferences can involve assessments of future earnings potential implying demands for additional financing. Our analysis of the statement of cash flows can provide us insights into likely sources of this needed cash and its potential impacts, including any dilution of earnings per share.

Forecasting Sources and Uses of Cash Flows

Our analysis of prior periods' cash flows enables us to prepare estimates of future sources and uses of long-term cash flows. Credible cash forecasts of all business activities, especially investing and financing activities, improve the reliability of our long-term cash forecasting. We desire dependable forecasts of the cash needed for carrying out the operating activities planned and of the cash sources required to support planned activities. For example, if we forecast a company's expansion of sales and profits, we must assess whether the company has the "financial horsepower" to support this expansion. We do this by analyzing the likelihood and costs for both internal and external sources of future cash.

The statement of cash flows is a good analytical structure to assist us in long-term forecasting. Forecasting the statement of cash flows begins with a careful estimate of expected changes in individual asset categories and the cash acquired or used by these changes. Important factors for us to consider when performing this task include:

- Net income forecasts need adjusting for noncash items like depreciation, depletion, deferred income taxes, and nonremitted earnings of subsidiaries and investees for reliable estimates of operating cash flows.

- Forecasts of operating working capital are obtained by estimating required levels of working capital components like receivables, inventories, and payables. If necessary, working capital needed to support forecasted sales is also estimated on an aggregate (net) basis—often using the relation between incremental sales and working capital requirements.
- Estimates of cash sources from items like asset disposals, investment sales, and issuance of stock and bonds are required.
- Capital expenditure forecasts are based on current operations adjusted for productive capacity, forecasts of activity implied by profit projections, and estimates of asset replacement costs.
- Estimates of debt retirements and dividend payments are required.

Case Forecast of the Statement of Cash Flows

This section illustrates our forecasting of the statement of cash flows for Campbell Soup Company for Years 12 and 13. We use our analysis of both prior years' cash flows and the other financial statements in the Comprehensive Case following Chapter 13. Results of other analyses and important assumptions underlying our forecasts include the following ($ millions):

1. Sales forecasts are $6,350 in Year 12 and $6,800 in Year 13.
2. Forecast of net income for Year 12 is taken from our Year 12 forecasted income statement (see Exhibit CC.16). Forecast of net income for Year 13 is 7.9 percent of forecast sales.
3. Net income for Years 9 and 10 is used in our forecasting procedures *before* the net effects of divestitures, restructurings, and unusual charges totaling $260.8 in Year 9 and $301.6 in Year 10.
4. Forecasts of depreciation and amortization for Years 12 and 13 are based on their relation to net income. We use the relation of average depreciation and amortization for Years 9 through 11 to the average net income over the same period.
5. Deferred income taxes in Year 12 are estimated using the relation of total deferred taxes to total net income for Years 10 and 11. It changes in Year 13 by the percent change in Year 13 forecasted net income relative to Year 12 forecasted net income.
6. Forecast of "Other, net" in Year 12 reflects the relation of "Other, net" to net income from Years 9 through 11. Its forecast changes in Year 13 by the percent change in Year 13 forecasted net income relative to Year 12 forecasted net income.
7. Operating working capital items like accounts receivable, inventory, and payables (excluding cash and temporary investments) for Years 12 and 13 are forecasted as follows:
   a. Compute the percent relation between operating working capital items and sales for Year 11.
   b. Multiply the percent relation in (*a*) by forecasted sales in Years 12 and 13.
8. Forecasts of cash and temporary investments reflect their relation to forecasted sales in Years 12 and 13 using the relation of cash and temporary investments to sales from Year 11.

9. Other amounts in our forecast of the statement of cash flows are estimated (marked by est.) using available information. This includes items where we use the moving average of the prior six years' data.

Using these analyses and assumptions we compute forecasts for Years 12 and 13 in the structure of the statement of cash flows for Campbell Soup. Exhibit 9.7 shows our forecasted statements. Calculations underlying these forecasts are reported in the notes to this exhibit. More refined relations and computations underlying forecasts are possible with more detailed analysis and understanding of company and industry performance.

ANALYSIS VIEWPOINT . . . *You are the stockbroker*

You are analyzing the long-term cash forecasts of Boston Biotech, Inc., that are reported along with a scheduled initial public offering (IPO) of its common stock for next month. You notice Boston Biotech's forecasts of net cash flows are zero or negative for the next five years. During this same time period, Boston Biotech is forecasting net income at more than 10 percent of shareholders' equity. Your co-workers at the securities firm question the reliability of these forecasts. Can you identify potential explanations for the disparity between the five-year forecasts of cash flows and income?

What-If Forecasting of Cash Flows

Our use of forecasts from the statement of cash flows extends to our ability to assess the impact of unexpected changes or adversities confronting a company—a variation on traditional *what-if analysis.* Unexpected events usually manifest themselves through a significant change in cash inflows or outflows. These events include recessions, strikes, loss of a major customer, and market shifts. Forecasting the statement of cash flows is often a first step in assessing the defensive posture and capabilities of a company. The basic question addressed by this analysis is: What are the company's options and what resources (internal and external) are available to respond to unexpected changes in cash flows? This analysis is relevant for assessing a company's financial flexibility. We can use forecasts of the statement of cash flows to assess resources available to meet adversities and pursue opportunities. We can trace through the effects of these events for operating cash flows and on the sources and uses of cash. Forecasts of this statement are also useful in planning changes in managerial strategies to confront changing business environments. Forecasting is also a valuable tool for creditors in assessing risk exposures.

Specialized Cash Flow Ratios

The following two ratios are often useful in analyzing a firm's flow of funds.

Cash Flow Adequacy Ratio

The **cash flow adequacy ratio** is a measure of a company's ability to generate sufficient cash from operations to cover capital expenditures, investments in inventories, and

EXHIBIT 9.7

CAMPBELL SOUP COMPANY
Forecasted Statements of Cash Flows
($ millions)

	Year 13	*Year 12*
Cash flows from operating activities:		
Net earnings[(a)]	$ 540.0	$ 480.0
To reconcile net earnings to net cash from operations:		
Depreciation and amortization[(b)]	331.1	294.3
Deferred taxes[(c)]	30.0	26.7
Other, net[(d)]	65.5	58.3
(Increase) decrease in accounts receivable[(e)]	(38.2)	(12.4)
(Increase) decrease in inventories[(f)]	(51.2)	(16.6)
Net change in other current assets and liabilities[(g)]	85.9	27.9
Net cash provided by operating activities	$ 963.1	$ 858.2
Cash flows from investing activities:		
Purchases of plant assets[(b)]	$ (443.1)	$ (400.0)
Sale of plant assets (est.)[(i)]	31.5	28.4
Businesses acquired (est.)[(i)]	(85.3)	(77.0)
Sale of businesses (est.)[(i)]	25.5	23.0
Increase in other assets (est.)[(i)]	(53.9)	(48.6)
Net change in other short-term investments (est.)[(i)]	12.3	11.1
Net cash used in investing activities	$ (513.0)	$ (463.1)
Cash flows from financing activities:		
Long-term borrowings (est.)	$ 132.0	$ 142.3
Repayments of long-term borrowings[(j)]	(218.9)	(227.7)
Increase (decrease) in short-term borrowings[(k)]	(200.3)	(95.7)
Other short-term borrowings (est.)	131.2	122.9
Repayments of other short-term borrowings (est.)[(l)]	(140.4)	(200.0)
Dividends paid (est.)	(108.8)	(108.2)
Treasury stock purchases (est.)	(49.4)	(42.4)
Treasury stock issued (est.)	15.6	14.2
Other, net (est.)	9.1	10.4
Net cash provided (used in) financing activities	$ (429.9)	$ (384.2)
Effect of exchange rate changes on cash (est.)	$ (7.5)	$ (6.7)
Net increase (decrease) in cash and cash equivalents[(m)]	12.7	4.2
Cash and cash equivalents at the beginning of year[(m)]	183.1	178.9
Cash and cash equivalents at the end of year[(m)]	$ 195.8	$ 183.1

Notes:

[(a)] Projected net income for Year 12 is 7.6% of projected sales, and for Year 13 is 7.9% of projected sales. These projections are corroborated in the *Value Line Investment Survey*.

[(b)] Average percent of depreciation and amortization to net income in Years 9–11:

$$\frac{\text{Total depreciation and amortization}}{\text{Total net income *}} = \frac{\$601.8}{\$981.4} = 61.32\%$$

Depreciation and amortization for Year 12 = $480.0 × 0.6132 = $294.3
Depreciation and amortization for Year 13 = $540.0 × 0.6132 = $331.1

[(c)] Average percent of deferred taxes to net income in Years 10–11:

$$\frac{\text{Total deferred taxes}}{\text{Total net income *}} = \frac{\$39.4\ \boxed{59}}{\$707.5} = 5.57\%$$

Deferred taxes for Year 12 = $480.0 × 0.0557 = $26.7
Percent change of Year 13 net income to Year 12 net income = $540.0 / $480.0 = 112.5%
Deferred taxes for Year 13 = $26.7 × 1.125 = $30.0

EXHIBIT 9.7 (Concluded)

(d) Average percent of "Other, net" to net income in Years 9–11:

$$\frac{\text{Total "Other, net"}}{\text{Total net income}^*} = \frac{\$119.1\ \boxed{60}}{\$981.4} = 12.14$$

"Other, net" for Year 12 = $480.0 × 0.1214 = $58.3

Percent change of Year 13 net income to Year 12 net income = 112.5%

"Other, net" for Year 13 = $58.3 × 1.125 = $65.5

(e) Percent of year-end accounts receivable to sales in Year 11:

$$\frac{\text{A.R.}\ \boxed{33}}{\text{Sales}\ \boxed{13}} = \frac{\$527.4}{\$6,204.1} = 8.5\%$$

Fiscal year-end A.R. in Year 12 = $6,350.0 × 0.085 = $539.8

Fiscal year-end A.R. in Year 13 = $6,800.0 × 0.085 = $578.0

Change in A.R. in Year 12 = $539.8 – $527.4 = $12.4 increase

Change in A.R. in Year 13 = $578.0 – $539.8 = $38.2 increase

Data in the Comprehensive Case indicate that over a 10-year period A.R. had year-to-year increases over 9 years.

(f) Percent of year-end inventories to sales in Year 11:

$$\frac{\text{Inventories}\ \boxed{34}}{\text{Sales}\ \boxed{13}} = \frac{\$706.7}{\$6,204.1} = 11.39\%$$

Fiscal year-end inventories in Year 12 = $6,350.0 × 0.1139 = $723.3

Fiscal year-end inventories in Year 13 = $6,800.0 × 0.1139 = $774.5

Change in inventories in Year 12 = $723.3 – $706.7 = $16.6 increase

Change in inventories in Year 13 = $774.5 – $723.3 = $51.2 increase

(g) Percent of year-end net other current assets and liabilities (NOCACL) to sales in Year 11:

$$\frac{\text{Total current liabilities}\ \boxed{45} - \text{Prepaid expenses}\ \boxed{35}}{\text{Sales}\ \boxed{13}} = \frac{\$1,278.0 - \$92.7}{\$6,204.1} = 19.11\%$$

Fiscal year-end NOCACL in Year 12 = $6,350.0 × 0.1911 = $1,213.2

Fiscal year-end NOCACL in Year 13 = $6,800.0 × 0.1911 = $1,299.1

Change in NOCACL in Year 12 = $1,213.2 – $1,185.3 = $27.9 increase in liabilities

Change in NOCACL in Year 13 = $1,299.1 – $1,213.2 = $85.9 increase in liabilities

(h) For Year 12 see item [11] of MD&A under "statements of cash flows" within investing activities. For Year 13: Percent change in capital expenditures from Year 11 to Year 12:

$$\frac{\$400.0}{\$361.1\ \boxed{65}} = 110.8\%$$

Projected capital expenditures = $400.0 × 110.8% = $443.1

(i) From *(h)*, a percent of 110.8% of last year's balance is used also in relatively similar areas.

(j) See item [172] and [173], for maturity dates of LTD. For Year 13, $100.0 million is due in Year 16 at interest rate of 10.5%, but is redeemable in Year 13. If interest rates continue to fall, it may call for refinancing.

(k) Net amount needed to balance the statement.

(l) For Year 12, see item [170], 13.99% notes due Year 12. For Year 13, estimated using average of Years 7–12.

(m) Cash and cash equivalents balance is assumed related to net sales of that year.

$$\text{For Year 11} = \frac{\$178.9\ \boxed{31}}{\$6,204.1\ \boxed{13}} = 2.88\%$$

For Year 12 = $6,350.0 × 0.0288 = $183.1

For Year 13 = $680.0 × 0.0288 = $195.8

* *Income Numbers*	*For Year 11*		*For Year 10*		*For Year 9*		
Total net income =	$401.5	+	(4.4 + 301.6)	+	(13.1 + 260.8)	=	$981.4
For Year 10 and Year 11 =	401.5	+	(4.4 + 301.6)			=	$707.5

cash dividends. To remove cyclical and other random influences, a five-year total is typically used in computing this ratio. The cash flow adequacy ratio is calculated as:

$$\frac{\text{Five-year sum of cash from operations}}{\text{Five-year sum of capital expenditures, inventory additions, and cash dividends}}$$

Investment in other important working capital items like receivables is omitted because they are financed primarily by short-term credit (e.g., growth in accounts payable). Accordingly, only additions to inventories are included. Note in years where inventories decline, the downward change is treated as a zero change in computing the ratio. Using the financial statement data from Campbell Soup Company in Supplement A we compute its (five-year) cash flow adequacy ratio:

$$\frac{\$2{,}545.8^{(a)}}{\$2{,}418.5^{(b)} + \$117.1^{(c)} + \$544.8^{(d)}} = 0.83$$

(a) Cash from operations—item 64.
(b) Property additions—items 65 and 67.
(c) Inventory additions—item 62.
(d) Cash dividends—item 77.

Proper interpretation of the cash flow adequacy ratio is important. A ratio of 1 indicates the company exactly covered these cash needs without a need for external financing. A ratio below 1 suggests internal cash sources are insufficient in maintaining dividends and current operating growth levels. For Campbell Soup Company the ratio indicates that for the five years ending in Year 11, Campbell's operating cash flows fell short of covering dividends and operating growth. While not illustrated here, if we computed a six-year ratio, a more favorable ratio results. The cash flow adequacy ratio also reflects inflationary effects for funding requirements of a company. As with other analyses, inferences drawn from this ratio should be supported with further analysis and investigation.

Cash Reinvestment Ratio

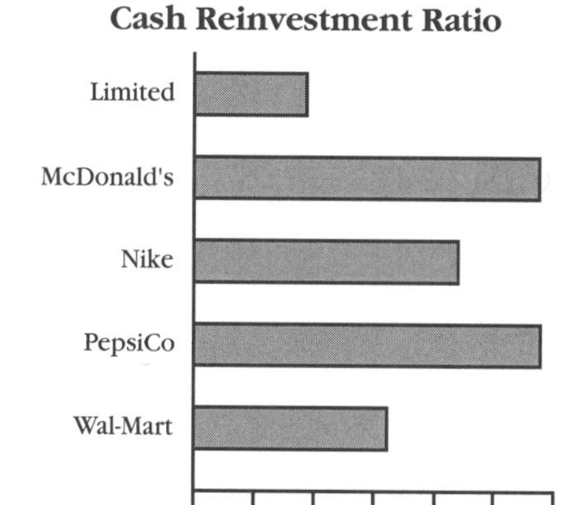

Source: Annual reports.

The **cash reinvestment ratio** is a measure of the percent of investment in assets representing operating cash retained and reinvested in the company for both replacing assets and growth in operations. This ratio is computed as:

$$\frac{\text{Operating cash flow} - \text{Dividends}}{\text{Gross plant} + \text{Investment} + \text{Other assets} + \text{Working capital}}$$

A reinvestment ratio in the area of 7 to 11 percent is generally considered satisfactory. Using the financial statements of Campbell Soup Company, we compute the cash reinvestment ratio for Year 11:

$$\frac{\$805.2^{(e)} - \$137.5^{(f)}}{(\$2{,}921.9 + \$477.6)^{(g)} + \$404.6^{(h)} + (\$1{,}518.5 - \$1{,}278.0)^{(i)}} = 16.5\%$$

(e) Cash from operations–item 64.
(f) Cash dividends–item 77.
(g) Gross plant assets–items 158 thru 161; plus: intangibles–items 163 and 164.
(h) Other assets–item 39.
(i) Total current assets–item 36; less: total current liabilities–item 45.

GUIDANCE ANSWERS TO ANALYSIS VIEWPOINTS

You Are the Loan Officer

Your first step is to corroborate or refute management's explanation for decreased sales in recent years. If their explanations are *not* validated with objective evidence, then you should reject DEC's application—hint of unscrupulous behavior is reason enough for immediate nonapproval. If you are able to verify management's explanations, your next step is to assess the *level and uncertainty* of DEC's sales forecasts. Your analysis of sales forecasts should consider important economic factors, including consumer demand, industry competition, supplier costs, and DEC's productive capacity/quality. Perhaps more important under DEC's circumstances is your assessment of uncertainty with sales. For example, sales might be objectively forecasted at $1 million, but the range of likely sales might extend anywhere from $0.5 to $1.5 million. Recent turmoil in consumer demand, material costs, and supplier relations suggests substantially greater risk than normal. Your assessment of increased risk can yield a response extending from a slight increase in interest rates or increased collateral demands to ultimate loan rejection. Consequently, while DEC's sales forecasts might be unbiased, we must recognize differences in uncertainty associated with sales forecasts in practice.

You Are the Stockbroker

The disparity in Boston Biotech's forecasts of cash flows and income is not necessarily of concern. Many growing companies experience little to no positive cash flows in the near term. Of course, these low near-term cash flows are expected to yield above-average cash flows in the future. Boston Biotech could potentially be recording substantial operating cash flows that are offset by large cash outflows in new investments, debt retirements, or dividends. Our analysis must look to the components of both cash flows and income to address our potential interest in Boston Biotech's IPO of common stock. Instead of spurning the stock of Boston Biotech, we might find it a lucrative and underpriced security due to our superior knowledge of accounting in financial statements.

QUESTIONS

9–1. Describe the primary difference between "funds flow" analysis and ratio analysis. Which analysis technique is preferred and why?

9–2. It is often asserted: From an operational point of view, management focuses on cash rather than working capital. Do you agree with this statement? Why or why not?

9–3. Describe the relation between inflows and outflows of cash.

9–4. Why are short-term cash forecasts important for our analysis of financial statements?

9–5. What is the usual first step in preparing cash forecasts, and what considerations are required in this step?

9–6. What are pro forma financial statements? How are they used with cash flow forecasts?

9–7. What limitations are associated with short-term cash forecasting?

9–8. If the usefulness of short-term cash forecasts is limited, what analytical tool is available to us for analyzing future cash flows?

9–9. What questions do we focus on in evaluating sources and uses of cash?

9–10. What useful information is available to us in our analysis of past statements of cash flows?

9–11. What considerations must we recognize when forecasting future statements of cash flows?

9–12. What are the differences between short-term and long-term financial forecasts?

9–13. What useful analytical role does the common-size statement of cash flows serve?

9–14. Why is a forecasted statement of cash flows necessary when we have historical data and statements based on actual performance?

9–15. If unexpected events affect company operations, what use is there for a forecasted statement of cash flows?

9–16. Cash flow per share is occasionally used in common stock analysis in the same way as earnings per share. In financial analysis, should the former be used more often than the latter? Explain.

(CFA Adapted)

EXERCISES

Exercise 9–1

Forecasting Income and Income Components

Refer to the financial statements of Quaker Oats Company in Supplement A. Prepare a forecasted income statement for Year 12 using the following assumptions ($ millions):

1. Revenues are forecast to equal $6,000.
2. Cost of sales forecast uses the average percent relation between cost of sales and sales for the four-year period ending June 30, Year 11.
3. Selling, general, and administrative expenses are expected to increase by the same percent increase as from Year 10 to Year 11.
4. Other expenses are predicted to be 8 percent higher than in Year 11.
5. A $2 million loss (net of taxes) is expected from disposal of net assets from discontinued operations.
6. Interest expense, net of interest capitalized and interest income, is expected to increase by 6 percent due to increased financial needs.
7. The effective tax rate is equal to that of Year 11.

Exercise 9–2

Financial Analysis Using Cash Flow Ratios

Refer to the financial statements of Quaker Oats Company in Supplement A.

Required:

a. Compute Quaker's cash flow adequacy ratio for Year 11. To remove cyclical and random influences, use a *three-year* total in computing this ratio for Quaker.

b. Discuss the importance and significance of the cash flow adequacy ratio.

c. Compute the cash reinvestment ratio for both Years 10 and 11.

d. Discuss the importance and significance of the cash reinvestment ratio.

Exercise 9–3

Preparing a Short-Term Cash Forecast

The Lyon Corporation is a merchandising company. Prepare a short-term cash forecast for July of Year 6 following the format of Exhibit 9.4. Selected financial data from Lyon Corporation for July of Year 6 are reproduced below ($ thousands):

Cash on hand, July 1, Year 6	$ 20
Accounts receivable, July 1, Year 6	20
Forecasted sales for July	150
Forecasted accounts receivable, July 31, Year 6	21
Inventory, July 1, Year 6	25
Desired inventory, July 31, Year 6	15
Depreciation expense	4
Miscellaneous outlays	11
Minimum cash balance desired	30
Accounts payable, July 1, Year 6	18

Additional Information:

1. Gross profit equals 20 percent of cost of goods sold.
2. Lyon purchases all inventory on the first day of the month and receives it the following week.
3. Lyon pays 75 percent of payables within the month of purchase and the balance in the following month.
4. All remaining expenses are paid in cash.

PROBLEMS

Problem 9–1
Forecasting the Statement of Cash Flows

Refer to the financial statements of Quaker Oats Company in Supplement A. Using Quaker's financial statements and the analysis guidance from the chapter, prepare a forecasted statement of cash flows for Year 12 using the following forecast information:

Selected Forecast Data ($ millions)

Item	*Year 12*
Sources of cash:	
Assets retirements	$ 20
Uses of cash:	
Repayment of long-term debt	45
Capital expenditures—Property, plant, & equipment	300
Cash dividends on capital stock	135
Other cash expenditures	30
Revenue forecast	6,000

Additional assumptions for your forecasting task include:

1. Income from continuing operations in Year 12 is expected to equal the average percent of income from continuing operations to sales prevailing in the three-year period ending June 30, Year 11.
2. The depreciation and amortization forecast for Year 12 uses the average percent relation of depreciation and amortization to income from continuing operations for the period Year 9 through Year 11. The average percent relation is computed at 82.33 percent.
3. Forecasts of deferred income taxes (noncurrent portion) and other items in Year 12 reflect the past three years' relation of deferred taxes (noncurrent) and other items to total income from continuing operations.
4. Provisions for restructuring charges are predicted to be zero for Year 12.
5. Days' sales in receivables is expected to be 42 for Year 12.
6. Days' sales in inventory of 55 and a ratio of cost of sales to sales of 0.51 is forecasted for Year 12.
7. Changes in other current assets are predicted to be equal to the average increase/decrease over the period Year 9 through Year 11.
8. Days' purchases in accounts payable of 45 is forecasted for Year 12, and purchases are expected to increase in Year 12 by 12 percent over Year 11 purchases of $2,807.2.
9. Change in other current liabilities are predicted to be equal to the average increase/decrease over the period Year 9 through Year 11.
10. There are no more changes expected with Fisher-Price and no expected changes in net current assets of discontinued operations.
11. Decreases in short-term debt are predicted at $40 million each year.
12. No cash inflows are expected from issuance of debt for spin-off and no cash effects from purchases or issuances of common and preferred stock.
13. Predicted year-end cash needs are equal to a level measured by the ratio of cash to revenues prevailing in Year 11.
14. Additions to long-term debt in Year 12 are equal to the amount needed to meet the desired year-end cash balance.

Problem 9–2

Analyzing and Interpreting Common-Size Statements of Cash Flows

Refer to the financial statements of Quaker Oats Company in Supplement A. Using common-size statements (where total sources = 100%), prepare and analyze the statements of cash flows for Quaker Oats covering the three-year period ending June 30, Year 11. Include in your analysis the interpretation and discussion of major sources and uses of cash.

Problem 9–3

Preparing Pro Forma Financial Statements

Telnet Corporation is a newly formed computer manufacturing corporation. Telnet plans to begin operations on January 1, Year 2. Selected financial information is available for the preparation of Telnet's six-month forecasted performance covering the period January 1 to June 30 of Year 2.

Forecasted *monthly* sales	$250,000
Monthly operating expenses:	
Labor	30,500
Rent for factory	10,000
Variable overhead	22,500
Depreciation on equipment	35,000
Amortization of patents	500
Selling and administrative expenses	47,500
Materials	125,000

Additional Information:

1.	Collection period	45 days
2.	Purchase terms	n/30
3.	Ending finished goods inventory	$100,000
4.	Ending raw material inventory	$35,000
5.	Effective tax rate	50%
6.	Beginning cash balance	$60,000
7.	Minimum cash balance required	$40,000
8.	Prepaid expenses on June 30, Year 2	$7,000

Required:

Prepare a pro forma income statement and balance sheet to portray the forecasted financial position of Telnet Corporation at the end of the six-month period ending June 30, Year 2. Your analysis should assume the following:

1. No inventory is in process on June 30, Year 2.
2. Sales are made evenly throughout the year.
3. Expenses are paid in cash (unless otherwise indicated).
4. Telnet Corporation's balance sheet data on January 1, Year 2, appear as:

Cash	$ 60,000
Equipment	1,200,000
Patents	40,000
Shareholders' equity	1,300,000

CASES

Case 9–1
Analyzing, Interpreting, and Forecasting Adaptec's Financial Statements

Using the 1996 financial statements of Adaptec in Supplement A, answer the following:

a. Prepare and analyze common-size statements of cash flows (express total sources of cash as 100 percent) for the:
   1. Fiscal years 1994, 1995, and 1996.
   2. Three-year period ending March 31, 1996.

b. Compute and interpret the following cash-based measures for (*i*) each of the most recent three fiscal years, and (*ii*) the three-year period ending March 31, 1996:
   1. Cash flow adequacy ratio.
   2. Cash reinvestment ratio.

c. Adaptec's sales revenue (in thousands) for the year ending March 31, 1997, is forecasted at $934,000. Using this sales forecast, prepare a complete set of forecasted financial statements—income statement, balance sheet, and statement of cash flows—for fiscal 1997. Discuss your forecasts and note any assumptions you make.

Case 9–2
Preparing and Analyzing Cash Forecasts

Miller Company is planning to construct a two-unit facility for the loading of beverage barrels into ships. On or before January 1, Year 2, stockholders will invest $100,000 in the company's capital stock to provide the initial working capital. To finance the construction program (total planned cost is $1,800,000) the company will obtain a commitment from a lending organization for a loan of $1,800,000. This loan is to be secured by a 10-year mortgage note bearing interest at 5 percent per year on the unpaid balance. The principal amount of the loan is to be repaid in equal semiannual installments of $100,000 beginning June 30, Year 3. Since loan proceeds will only be required as construction work progresses, the company agrees to pay a commitment fee beginning January 1, Year 2, equal to 1 percent per year on the unused portion of the loan commitment. This fee is payable when amounts are "drawn down" except for the first draw-down.

Work on the construction of the facility will commence in the fall of Year 1. The first payment to the contractors is due on January 1, Year 2, at which time the commitment and loan agreement become effective and the company will make its first draw-down for payment to the contractors in the amount of $800,000. As construction progresses, additional payments will be made to the contractors by drawing down the remaining loan proceeds as follows (payments to contractors are made on the same dates as the loan proceeds are drawn down):

April 1, Year 2	$500,000
July 1, Year 2	300,000
December 31, Year 2	100,000
April 1, Year 3	100,000

Because of weather conditions, the facility operates from April 1 through November 30 of each year. The construction program will permit the completion of the first of two plant units (capable of handling 5,000,000 barrels) in time for its use during the Year 2 shipping season. The second unit (capable of handling an additional 3,000,000 barrels) will be completed in time for the Year 3 season. It is expected 5,000,000 barrels will be handled by the facility during the Year 2 season. Thereafter, barrels handled are expected to increase in each subsequent year by 300,000 barrels until a level of 6,500,000 barrels is reached.

The company's revenues are derived by charging the consignees of the beverage for its services at a fixed rate per barrel loaded. All revenues are collected in the month of shipment. Based upon past experience with similar facilities elsewhere, Miller Company expects operating profit to average $0.04 per barrel before charges for interest, financing fees, and depreciation. Depreciation is $0.03 per barrel.

Required:

Prepare a cash forecast for each of the three calendar years: Year 2, Year 3, and Year 4. Evaluate the sufficiency of cash obtained from the sale of capital stock, draw-downs on the loan, and the operating facility to cover cash payments to the contractor and the creditor (principal and interest).

Case 9–3

Preparing a Cash Forecast for a Company in Distress

Royal Company has incurred substantial losses for several years and is insolvent. On March 31, Year 5, Royal petitions the court for protection from creditors, and submits the following balance sheet:

ROYAL COMPANY
Balance Sheet
March 31, Year 5

	Book Value	*Liquidation Value*
Assets:		
Accounts receivable	$100,000	$ 50,000
Inventories	90,000	40,000
Plant and equipment	150,000	160,000
Total assets	$340,000	$250,000
Liabilities and Stockholders' Equity:		
Accounts payable–general creditors	$600,000	
Common stock	60,000	
Retained earnings	(320,000)	
Total liabilities and equity	$340,000	

Royal's management informed the court that the company developed a new product and a prospective customer is willing to sign a contract for the purchase of (at a price of $90 per unit) 10,000 units during the year ending March 31, Year 6; 12,000 units during the year ending March 31, Year 7; and 15,000 units during the year ending March 31, Year 8. The product can be manufactured using Royal's current facilities. Monthly production with immediate delivery is expected to be uniform within each year. Receivables are expected to be collected during the calendar month following sales. Production costs per unit for the new product are:

Direct materials	$20
Direct labor	30
Variable overhead	10

Fixed costs (excluding depreciation) amount to $130,000 per year. Purchases of direct materials are paid during the calendar month following purchase. Fixed costs, direct labor, and variable overhead are paid as incurred. Inventory of direct materials are equal to 60 days' usage. After the first month of operations, 30 days' usage of direct materials is ordered each month.

Creditors have agreed to reduce their total claims to 60 percent of their March 31, Year 5, balances under two conditions:

- Existing accounts receivable and inventories are liquidated immediately with the proceeds going to creditors.
- Remaining balance in accounts payable is paid as cash is produced from future operations—but in no event later than March 31, Year 7. No interest is paid on these obligations.

Under this proposal, creditors would receive $110,000 more than the current liquidation value of Royal's assets. The court engages you to determine the feasibility of this proposal.

Required:

Prepare a cash forecast for years ending March 31, Year 6, and Year 7. Ignore any need to borrow and repay short-term funds for working capital purposes, and show the cash expected to be available to pay creditors, the actual payments to creditors, and the cash remaining after payments to creditors.

(AICPA Adapted)

Case 9–4

Comprehensive Analysis of Loan Request

You are a loan officer for Pacific Bank. The senior loan officer submits to you the following selected financial information as of September 30, Year 6 for Union Corporation, which has filed a loan application:

Current assets:	
Cash	$ 12,000
Accounts receivable	10,000
Inventory	63,600
Plant and equipment—net	100,000
Total liabilities	–0–
Actual sales:	
September, Year 6	$ 40,000
Forecasted sales:	
October, Year 6	48,000
November, Year 6	60,000
December, Year 6	80,000
January, Year 7	36,000

Sales are 75 percent for cash and 25 percent on account. Receivables are collected in full in the month following the sale. For example, the accounts receivable balance of $10,000 on September 30, Year 6 equals 25 percent of sales during September, of which all $10,000 is paid in October. Gross profit averages 30 percent of sales *before* purchase discounts. Therefore, the gross invoice cost of goods sold is 70 percent of sales.

Union Corp. carries $30,000 of inventory plus additional inventory sufficient to provide for the anticipated sales of the following month. Purchase terms are 2/10, n/30. Since purchases are made early in each month and all discounts are taken, payments are consistently made in the month of purchase.

Salaries and wages average 15 percent of sales, rent averages 5 percent of sales, and all other expenses (except depreciation) average 4 percent of sales. These expenses are paid in cash when incurred. Depreciation expense is $750 per month, computed on a straight-line basis. Equipment expenditures are forecasted at $600 in October and $400 in November. Depreciation on these new expenditures is not recorded until Year 7.

Union Corp. is to maintain a minimum cash balance of $8,000. Any borrowings are made at the beginning of the month and any repayments are made at the end of the month, both in multiples of $1,000 (excluding interest). Interest is paid when the principal is repaid, equal to a rate of 6 percent per year.

Required:

a. The senior loan officer requests you prepare the following schedules for the months of October, November, December, and the total three months (quarter) ending in December of Year 6:

1. Estimated total cash receipts.
2. Estimated cash disbursements for purchases (purchases are 70 percent of sales for the following month).

3. Estimated cash disbursements for operating expenses.
4. Estimated total cash disbursements.
5. Estimated net cash receipts and disbursements.
6. Estimated financing required.

b. For the three months (quarter) ending in December of Year 6, prepare a:
1. Forecasted income statement.
2. Forecasted balance sheet.

INTERNET ACTIVITIES

Internet 9–1
Cash Flow Ratios in Financial Analysis

Access one of the financial statement databases available on the Internet (http://www.mhhe.com/business/accounting/wild). Retrieve current financial statements of a company selected by either you or your instructor.

Required:

a. Compute the company's cash flow adequacy ratio for the most recent year using (1) current year figures, and (2) three-year cumulative figures.
b. Discuss the importance and usefulness of the cash flow adequacy ratio.
c. Compute the cash reinvestment ratio for the most recent two years.
d. Discuss the importance and usefulness of the cash reinvestment ratio.

Internet 9–2
Forecasting Income and Income Components

Access one of the financial statement databases available on the Internet (http://www.mhhe.com/business/accounting/wild). Retrieve current financial statements of a company selected by either you or your instructor. Prepare a forecasted income statement for the next year with the following assumptions:

1. Next year's revenues are forecasted to equal the current year's revenues *plus* the percent change in current year's revenues.
2. The cost of sales forecast is based on the average percent relation between cost of sales and sales for the most recent two-year period.
3. Operating expenses (except interest and taxes) are expected to change by their same percent change in the most recent year.
4. Interest expense, net of interest capitalized and interest income, is expected to equal the effective interest rate multiplied by total interest-bearing debt.
5. The effective tax rate is expected to equal the current year's rate.
6. State any additional assumptions necessary for your forecasted income statement.

Internet 9–3
Analyzing, Interpreting, and Forecasting Funds Flow

Access one of the financial statement databases available on the Internet (http://www.mhhe.com/business/accounting/wild). Retrieve current financial statements of a company selected by either you or your instructor.

a. Prepare and analyze common-size statements of cash flow sources less uses (where *total sources* of cash equal 100 percent) for:
1. Each of the most recent three years.
2. The cumulative three-year period ending with the current year.

b. Compute and interpret the following measures for (1) each of the recent three years, and (2) the cumulative three-year period ending with the current year:
1. Cash flow adequacy ratio.
2. Cash reinvestment ratio.

c. Assume the company's revenues for next year are predicted to equal current year revenues *plus* the current year's percent change in revenues. Using this revenue forecast, prepare a set of forecasted financial statements—income statement, balance sheet, and statement of cash flows—for next year. State any assumptions you make.

Internet 9–4

Analyzing and Interpreting Common-Size Statements of Cash Flows

Access one of the financial statement databases available on the Internet (http://www.mhhe.com/business/accounting/wild). Retrieve current financial statements of a company selected by either you or your instructor. Using common-size statements (where total sources equal 100 percent), analyze and interpret the statements of cash flow sources less uses for the company over the recent two-year period. Include in your response a discussion of the major sources and uses of cash.

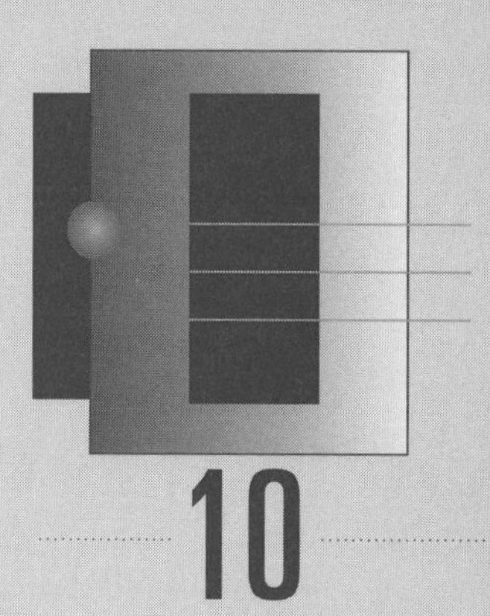

C H A P T E R

10

Capital Structure and Solvency

A Look Back

The prior two chapters focused on analysis tools for evaluating a company's liquidity. We described both turnover and activity-based measures and their relevance for analysis. We also explained how forecasting and pro forma analysis are useful in statement analysis.

A Look at This Chapter

This chapter focuses on capital structure, or a company's financing, and its implications for solvency. We analyze the importance of financial leverage and its effects on risk and return. Analytical adjustments to accounting book values are evaluated for solvency assessments. We also describe earnings-coverage measures and their interpretation for financial statement analysis.

A Look Ahead

In Chapter 11 our analysis shifts to the concept of return. We analyze return on investment, asset utilization, and other measures of performance that are relevant to a wide class of financial statement users. We describe several tools of analysis to assist in evaluation of company performance.

Learning Objectives

- Describe capital structure and its relation to solvency.
- Explain financial leverage and its implications for company performance and analysis.
- Analyze adjustments to accounting book values to assess capital structure.
- Describe analysis tools for evaluating and interpreting capital structure composition and assessing solvency.
- Analyze asset composition and coverage for solvency analysis.
- Explain earnings-coverage analysis and its relevance in evaluating solvency.
- Describe capital structure risk and return and its relevance to financial statement analysis.
- Interpret ratings of organizations' debt obligations (Appendix 10A).
- Describe prediction models of financial distress (Appendix 10B).

PREVIEW OF CHAPTER 10

Solvency is an important factor in our analysis of a company's financial statements. **Solvency** refers to a company's long-run financial viability and its ability to cover long-term obligations. All business activities of a company—financing, investing, and operating—affect a company's solvency. One of the most important components of solvency analysis is the composition of a company's capital structure. **Capital structure** refers to a company's sources of financing and its economic attributes. This chapter describes capital structure and explains its importance to solvency analysis. Since solvency depends on success in operating activities, the chapter examines earnings and the ability of earnings to *cover* important and necessary company expenditures. This chapter also describes various tools of solvency analysis, including leverage measures, analytical accounting adjustments, capital structure analysis, and earnings-coverage measures. We demonstrate these analysis tools with data from financial statements. We also discuss the relation between risk and return inherent in a company's capital structure and its implications for financial statement analysis. The content and organization of this chapter are as follows:

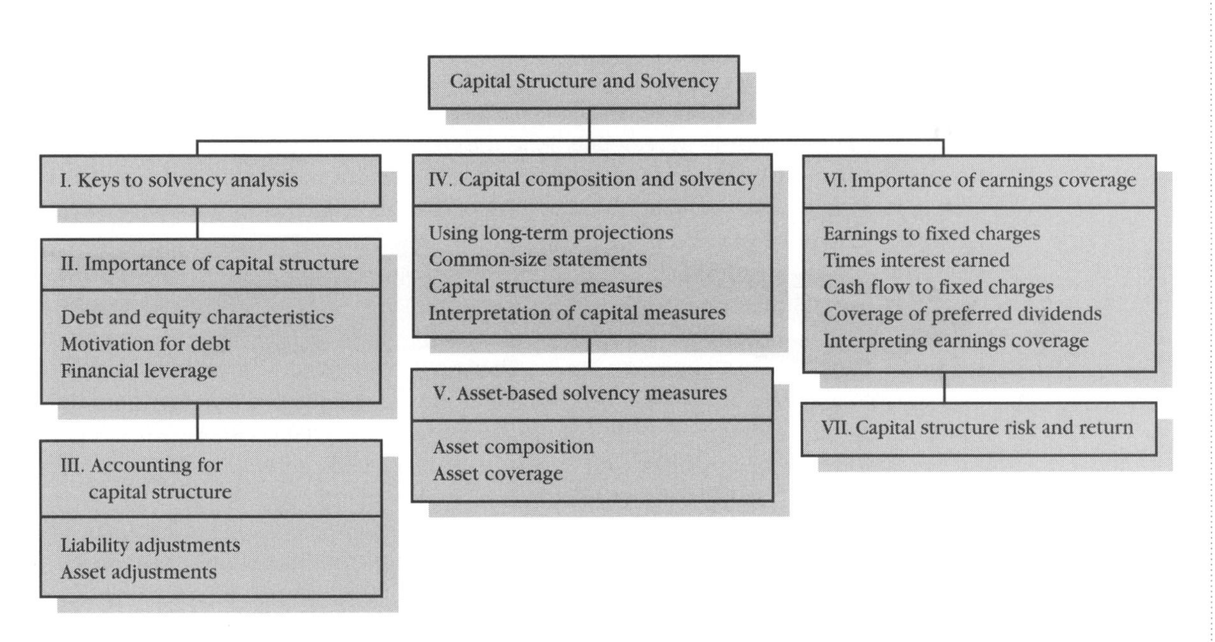

Keys to Solvency Analysis

Analyzing long-term solvency of a company is markedly different from analyzing short-term liquidity. In liquidity analysis, the time horizon is sufficiently short for reasonably accurate forecasts of cash flows. Long-term forecasts are less reliable and, consequently, our analysis of long-term solvency uses less precise but more encompassing analytical measures.

Our analysis of solvency involves several key elements. Analysis of capital structure is one of these. *Capital structure* refers to the sources of financing for a company. Financing forms range from relatively permanent equity capital to more risky or temporary short-term financing sources. Once a company obtains financing, it subsequently invests it in various assets. Assets represent secondary sources of security for lenders and range from loans secured by specific assets to assets available as general security to unsecured creditors. These and other factors yield different risks associated with different assets and financing sources.

Another key element of long-term solvency is *earnings* or *earning power*—implying the recurring ability to generate cash from operations. Earnings-based measures are important and reliable indicators of financial strength. Earnings is the most desirable and reliable source of cash for long-term payment of interest and debt principal. As a measure of cash inflows from operations, earnings is the gauge in covering interest and other fixed charges. A stable earnings stream is an important measure of a company's ability to borrow in times of cash shortage. It is also a measure of the likelihood of a company rebounding from conditions of financial distress.

Lenders guard themselves against company insolvency and financial distress by including in the lending agreements loan *covenants* or *pledges* of specific assets as security. Loan covenants define *default* (and the legal remedies available when it occurs), often defined using accounting data, to allow a lender the opportunity to collect on the loan before severe financial distress. Covenants are often designed to (1) emphasize key measures of financial strength like the current ratio and debt to equity ratio, (2) prohibit the issuance of additional debt, or (3) ensure against disbursement of company resources through excessive dividends or acquisitions. Covenants cannot assure lenders against operating losses—invariably the source of financial distress. Covenants and protective provisions also cannot substitute for our alertness and monitoring of a company's results of operations and financial condition.[1] The enormous amount of both public and private debt financing has led to standardized approaches to its analysis and evaluation. While this chapter explains many of these approaches, Appendix 10A discusses the analysis of debt securities by rating agencies, and Appendix 10B describes the use of ratios as predictors of financial distress.

Importance of Capital Structure

Capital structure is the equity and debt financing of a company. It is often measured in terms of the relative magnitude of the various financing sources. A company's

[1] Lenders must recognize that senior positions in the debt hierarchy do not always ensure the safety they seem to afford. Subordinated (junior) debt is not like capital stock because subordinated creditors have a voice in determining whether a debtor should be rescued or thrown into bankruptcy. This interdependence between junior and senior lenders leads some to buy the highest *yielding* obligation of a company under the presumption any situation affecting the value of junior securities is likely to affect senior securities.

financial stability and risk of insolvency depend on its financing sources and the types and sizes of various assets it owns. Exhibit 10.1 portrays a typical company's asset distribution and its financing sources. This exhibit highlights the potential variety in investing and financing items comprising a company—depicted within the accounting framework of assets equal liabilities plus equity.

Capital Structure

Current liabilities
Noncurrent liabilities
Shareholders equity

Limited
McDonald s
Nike
PepsiCo
Wal-Mart

0 25 50 75 100
Percent

Source: Annual reports.

Characteristics of Debt and Equity

The importance of analyzing capital structure derives from several perspectives, not the least is the difference between debt and equity. **Equity** refers to the *risk capital* of a company. Characteristics of equity capital include its uncertain or unspecified return and its lack of any repayment pattern. Capital that can be withdrawn at the contributor's option is *not* equity capital and has, instead, characteristics of debt capital. Equity capital contributes to a company's stability and solvency. It is usually characterized by a degree of permanence, persistence in times of adversity, and a lack of any mandatory dividend requirement. A company can confidently invest equity financing in long-term assets and expose them to business risks without threat of recall. Loss of equity capital for whatever reason does not necessarily jeopardize a company's ability to pay its fixed claims.

EXHIBIT 10.1 A Typical Company's Asset Distribution and Capital Structure

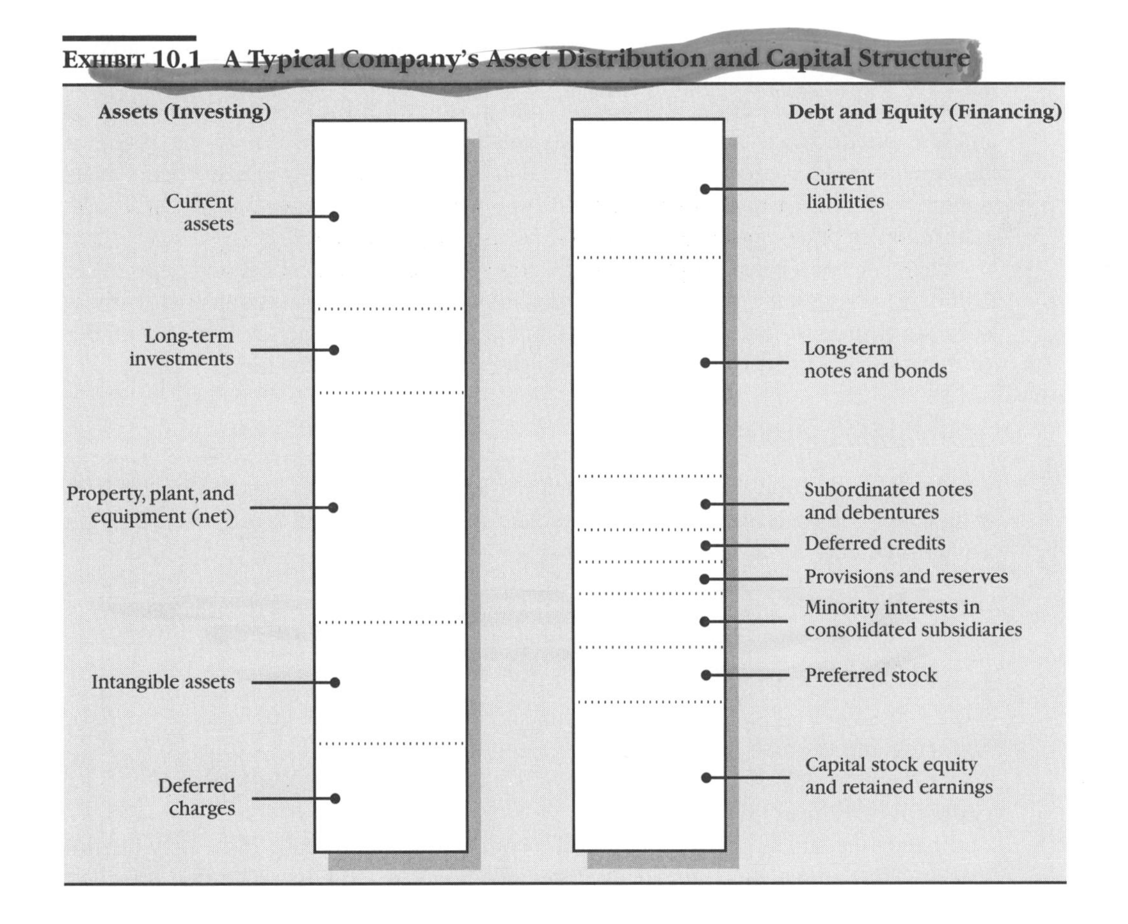

Unlike equity capital, both short-term and long-term **debt** capital must be repaid. The longer the debt repayment period and the less demanding its repayment provisions, the easier it is for a company to service debt capital. Still, debt must be repaid at specified times regardless of a company's financial condition, and so too must periodic interest on most debt. Failure to pay principal or interest typically results in proceedings where common shareholders can lose control of the company and all or part of their investment. If a company's equity capital is entirely taken by losses, creditors can also lose part or all of the principal and interest due them. When the proportion of debt in the total capital structure of a company is larger, the higher are the resulting fixed charges and repayment commitments. This also increases the likelihood of a company's inability to pay interest and principal when due.

For investors in common stock, debt reflects a risk of loss of the investment, balanced by the potential of profits from financial leverage. **Financial leverage** is the use of debt to increase earnings. Leverage magnifies both managerial success (profits) and failure (losses). It increases risks due to factors like commodity price fluctuations or technological obsolescence. Excessive debt limits management's initiative and flexibility for pursuing profitable opportunities. For creditors, increased equity capital is preferred as protection against losses from adversities. Lowering equity capital as a proportionate share of a company's financing decreases creditors' protection against loss and consequently increases risk.

While there is debate over whether the *cost of capital* for a company varies with different capital structures (mixes of debt and equity), the issue is relatively clear from an analysis perspective (creditors or investors). When analyzing companies, creditors expose themselves to increased risk if lending to a company with a greater proportion of debt financing, all else equal. Using the *Modigliani-Miller hypothesis*, a company's cost of capital in a perfect market is, except for the tax deductibility of interest, unaffected by the debt-to-equity relation. This result is due to the assertion that a shareholder can introduce personal risk preferences through portfolio management of stock. Under this hypothesis, the advantage of debt is offset by a company's lower price-earnings ratio.

Whatever one's perspective on the relation between cost of capital and debt, every company possesses a risk of loss for our investment. Our analysis task is to measure the degree of risk resulting from a company's capital structure. The remainder of this section looks at the motivation for debt capital and measuring its effects.

Motivation for Debt Capital

A primary motivation for a company financing its business activities through debt is its potential for lower cost. From a shareholder's perspective, debt is *less expensive* than equity financing for at least two reasons:

- Interest on most debt is fixed, and provided interest is less than the return earned from debt financing, the excess return goes to the benefit of equity investors.
- Interest is a tax-deductible expense whereas dividends are not.

We discuss each of these factors in this section due to their importance for debt financing and our risk analysis.

Concept of Financial Leverage

Companies' capital structures are typically comprised of both debt and equity financing. Creditors are generally unwilling to provide financing without protection provided by equity financing. Financial leverage refers to the amount of debt financing that pays a fixed return in a company's capital structure. Companies with financial leverage are said to be **trading on the equity**. This indicates a company is using equity capital as a borrowing base in a desire to reap excess returns.

Exhibit 10.2 illustrates trading on the equity. This exhibit computes the returns achieved for two companies referred to as Risky, Inc., and Safety, Inc. These two companies have identical assets and earnings before interest expense. Risky, Inc., derives 40 percent of its financing from debt while Safety, Inc., is debt-free, or *unlevered*. For Year 1, when the average return on total assets is 12 percent, the return on stockholders' equity of Risky, Inc., is 16 percent. This higher return to stockholders is due to the excess return on assets over the *after-tax* cost of debt (12 percent versus 6 percent, the latter computed as $10[1 - 0.40]$). Safety, Inc.'s return on equity always equals the return on assets since there is no debt. For Year 2, the return on assets of Risky, Inc., equals the after-tax cost of debt and, consequently, the effects of leverage are neutralized. For Year 3, leverage is shown to be a double-edged sword. Specifically, when the return on assets is *less* than the after-tax cost of debt, Risky, Inc.'s return on equity is lower than the return of equity for debt-free Safety, Inc. To generalize from this example: (1) an unlevered company's return on assets is identical to its return on equity, (2) a levered company is *successfully* trading on the equity when return on assets exceeds the after-tax cost of debt (alternatively stated, return on assets is less than return on equity), (3) a levered company is *unsuccessfully* trading on the equity when return on assets is less than the after-tax cost of debt (alternatively stated, return on assets exceeds return on equity), and (4) effects of leveraging are magnified in both good *and* bad years (for example, when return on assets drops below the after-tax cost of debt, a levered company's return on equity drops even farther).

Liability and Equity Financing

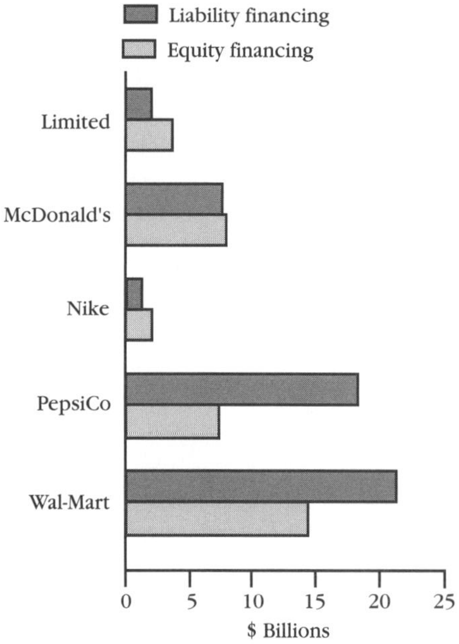

Liability financing
Equity financing
Limited
McDonald's
Nike
PepsiCo
Wal-Mart
0 5 10 15 20 25
$ Billions

Source: Annual reports.

Tax Deductibility of Interest

One reason for the advantageous position of debt is the *tax deductibility of interest*. We illustrate this tax advantage by extending the case in Exhibit 10.2. Let us reexamine the two companies' results for Year 2:

Year 2 Financials	*Risky, Inc.*	*Safety, Inc.*
Income before interest and taxes	$100,000	$100,000
Interest (10% of $400,000)	40,000	—
Income before taxes	$ 60,000	$100,000
Taxes (40%)	24,000	40,000
Net income	$ 36,000	$ 60,000
Add back interest paid to bondholder	40,000	—
Total return to security holders (debt and equity)	$ 76,000	$ 60,000

Recall the leverage effects are neutral in this year. But notice even when the return on assets equals the after tax cost of debt, the total amount available for distribution to debt and equity holders of Risky, Inc., is $16,000 higher than the amount available for the equity holders of Safety, Inc. This is due to the lower tax liability for Risky, Inc. We must remember the value of tax deductibility of interest depends on

EXHIBIT 10.2 Trading on the Equity—Returns for Different Earnings Levels ($ thousands)

		Financing Sources		*Income before Interest and Taxes*	*10 Percent Debt Interest*		*Net*	*Net Income + [Interest*	*Return on*	
	Assets	*Debt*	*Equity*			*Taxes**	*Income*	*× (1 – Tax Rate)]*	*Assets*†	*Equity*‡
Year 1:										
Risky, Inc.	$1,000,000	$400,000	$ 600,000	$200,000	$40,000	$64,000	$ 96,000	$120,000	12.0%	16.0%
Safety, Inc.	1,000,000	—	1,000,000	200,000	—	80,000	120,000	120,000	12.0	12.0
Year 2:										
Risky, Inc.	1,000,000	400,000	600,000	100,000	40,000	24,000	36,000	60,000	6.0	6.0
Safety, Inc.	1,000,000	—	1,000,000	100,000	—	40,000	60,000	60,000	6.0	6.0
Year 3:										
Risky, Inc.	1,000,000	400,000	600,000	50,000	40,000	4,000	6,000	30,000	3.0	1.0
Safety, Inc.	1,000,000	—	1,000,000	50,000	—	20,000	30,000	30,000	3.0	3.0

* Tax rate is 40 percent.

† Return on assets = Net income + Interest (1 – 0.40)/Assets.

‡ Return on equity = Net income/Shareholders' equity.

having sufficient earnings (unrecovered interest charges can be carried back and carried forward as part of tax loss carryovers permitted by tax law). To generalize from this example: (1) interest is tax deductible while cash dividends to equity holders are not, (2) because interest is tax deductible the income available to security holders can be much larger, and (3) nonpayment of interest can yield bankruptcy whereas nonpayment of dividends does not.

Other Effects of Leverage

Beyond advantages from excess return to financial leverage and the tax deductibility of interest, a long-term debt position can yield other benefits to equity holders. For example, a growth company can avoid earnings dilution through issuance of debt. In addition, if interest rates are increasing, a leveraged company paying a fixed lower interest rate is more profitable than its nonleveraged competitor. However, the reverse is also true. Strategically increasing debt capital prior to adverse operating performance is often advantageous to the borrower because availability or cost of debt financing likely changes. Finally, in times of inflation, monetary liabilities (like most debt capital) yield price-level gains.

Measuring Effects of Financial Leverage

As we saw in our examples above, the effect of financial leverage on operating results is positive when the return on equity capital *exceeds* the return on assets. This difference in returns isolates the return on borrowed money from the return on equity capital. We can use the measures in this section to effectively assess the effects of financial leverage.

Source: Dun & Bradstreet.

Financial Leverage Index

One measure of the effect of financial leverage is the **financial leverage index** and is computed as:

$$\frac{\text{Return on common equity}}{\text{Return on assets}}$$

A financial leverage index greater than 1.0 indicates favorable effects from leverage, a value less than 1.0 suggests unfavorable effects from leverage, and a value of exactly 1.0 suggests neither favorable nor unfavorable effects. Using the financial data in Exhibit 10.2, we compute the financial leverage indexes of Risky, Inc., for Years 1, 2, and 3:

$$\text{Year 1: } \frac{16.0\%}{12.0\%} = 1.33 \qquad \text{Year 2: } \frac{6.0\%}{6.0\%} = 1.00 \qquad \text{Year 3: } \frac{1.0\%}{3.0\%} = 0.33$$

For Year 1, when return on equity exceeds the return on assets, the financial leverage index equals 1.33, implying favorable effects of leverage. In Year 2, when return on equity equals the return on assets, the index is 1.00. This index of 1.00 reflects a neutralization of financial leverage. For Year 3, the index equals 0.33, well below 1.0. This suggests unfavorable effects of financial leverage in Year 3. We further discuss return on investment in Chapter 11.

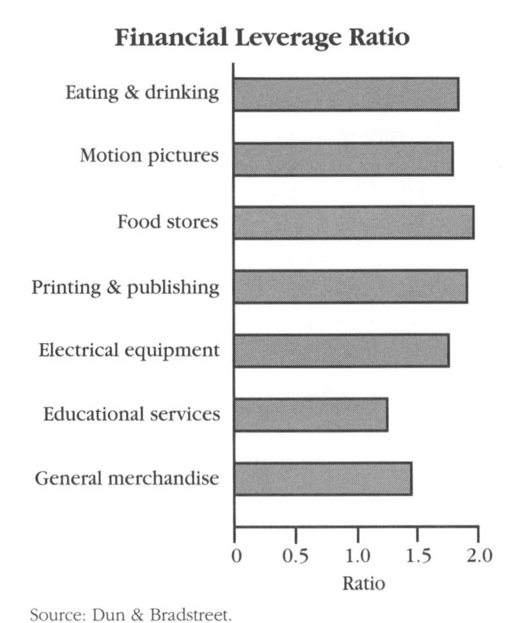

Source: Dun & Bradstreet.

Financial Leverage Ratio

The **financial leverage ratio** measures the relation between total assets and the common equity capital that finances assets. It is expressed as:

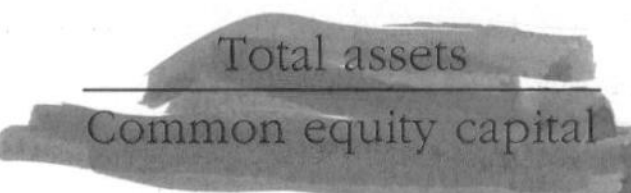

$$\frac{\text{Total assets}}{\text{Common equity capital}}$$

The greater the proportion of assets financed by common equity capital, the lower the financial leverage ratio. For a company successfully utilizing leverage, a higher financial leverage ratio enhances return on equity. Concurrently, the risk inherent in a change in profitability is greater when the financial leverage ratio is higher. The financial leverage ratio of Risky, Inc., (see Exhibit 10.2) at the end of Year 3 is:

$$\frac{\$1,000,000}{\$600,000} = 1.67$$

This financial leverage ratio indicates that every dollar of common equity commands $1.67 in assets for the company. We show in Chapter 11 how the financial leverage ratio can be viewed as a component of the analytical disaggregation of return on equity.

> **ANALYSIS VIEWPOINT** . . . *You are the entrepreneur*
>
> You are the entrepreneur and sole shareholder of a small, start-up restaurant. Your business is unlevered and doing well. The most recent year's return on assets is 9 percent, on assets of $200,000 (the tax rate is 40%). You are considering expanding your business but need to take on debt to finance expansion. What is your criterion in deciding whether to expand by adding debt?

Accounting Implications for Capital Structure Analysis

Measurement and disclosure of liability (debt) and equity accounts in financial statements are governed by the application of accepted accounting principles. We discussed principles governing measurement and disclosure of liability and equity accounts in Chapter 3. Our analysis must remember these principles when analyzing capital structure and its implications for solvency.

Adjustments to Book Values of Liabilities

The relation between liabilities and equity capital, the two major sources of a company's financing, is an important factor in assessing long-term solvency. An understanding of this relation is therefore essential in our analysis. There exist liabilities not fully reflected in balance sheets and there are financing-related items whose accounting classification as debt or equity must not be blindly accepted in our analysis. Our identification and classification of these items depend on a thorough understanding of their economic substance and the conditions to which they are subject.

The discussion in this section supplements the important analytical considerations in Chapter 3.

Deferred Income Taxes

Deferred income taxes is a deferred liability that is both significant in size and important to our analysis. We explained in Chapter 3 that deferred taxes is not a liability in the usual sense because the government does not have a definite short-term or even long-term claim against a company for these taxes. Yet we showed how deferred taxes represent the aggregate exhaustion in tax deductibility of assets and other items over and above that recorded in financial statements. This means at some point in the future the Deferred Tax liability account (credit) is used to reduce the higher income tax expense corresponding to the *increased* tax liabilities. Even if the likelihood of the Deferred Tax account "reversing" in the foreseeable future is high, there remains the question of whether the present value of future expected reversals should be used instead of the nominal face value amount of the deferred credit. Most other liabilities on the balance sheet (including pensions and leases) are carried at present value. The higher the borrowing rate (cost of debt) applicable to a company, the more significant the impact of discounting for present value. Accounting standard setters considered requiring the discounting of deferred taxes but decided against it.

For our analysis, an important question is whether we treat deferred taxes as a liability, as equity, or as part debt and part equity. Our answer depends on the nature of the deferral, past experience of the account (e.g., its growth pattern), and the likelihood of future reversals. In reaching our decision, we must recognize, under normal circumstances, deferred taxes reverse and become payable when a company's size declines. A company declining in size is usually accompanied by losses rather than by positive taxable income. In this case the drawing down of deferred taxes likely involves credits to tax loss carryforwards or carrybacks rather than payments in cash. To the extent future reversals are a remote possibility, as conceivable with timing differences from accelerated depreciation, deferred taxes should be viewed like long-term financing and treated like equity. However, if the likelihood of a drawing down of deferred taxes in the foreseeable future is high, then deferred taxes (or part of them) should be treated like long-term liabilities. As an example, if we decide the proper treatment of deferred tax credits is as equity (either in whole or in part), we can make the following type of *analytical* entry:

Deferred Income Taxes—Current	xx	
Deferred Income Taxes—Noncurrent	xx	
Shareholders' Equity		xx

There are other deferred credits (e.g., bond premiums) that represent allocation accounts designed to aid in measuring income. These types of deferred credits are typically insignificant in size and unimportant for our analysis. However, *deferred income* items like 'subscription income received in advance' represent obligations for future services and are properly treated as liabilities.

Operating Leases

Current accounting practice requires most financing long-term noncancelable leases be shown as debt. Yet companies have certain opportunities to structure leases in ways to avoid reporting them as debt (see Chapter 3). For example, if our analysis encounters noncancelable operating leases that should be capitalized, we can make the following *analytical* entry using data from Quaker Oats:

	Debit	Credit
Leasehold Assets[2]	93.8	
Liabilities under Long-Term Leases		93.8

Off-Balance-Sheet Financing

In determining the debt for a company, our analysis must be aware that some managers attempt to understate debt, often with new and sometimes complex means. We discuss several means for doing this in Chapter 3 including take or pay contracts, sales of receivables, and inventory repurchase agreements. Our critical reading of notes and management comments, along with inquiries to management, can often shed light on existence of unrecorded liabilities.

Pensions and Postretirement Benefits

Current accounting practice recognizes that if the fair value of pension assets falls short of the accumulated pension benefit obligation, a liability for pensions exists. This liability does not consider the projected benefit obligation, which recognizes estimates of future pay increases for pension plans using future pay formulas. Our analysis must be aware of this potential understatement, and estimate its impact on the pension liability when appropriate.

We discussed in Chapter 3 how companies can recognize the unfunded obligation on other postretirement employee benefits immediately or over as many as 20 years. Under the latter amortization option a company is, unlike with pensions, not required to record a minimum liability. Our analysis needs to assess the present value of this unrecorded liability related to postretirement benefits.

There is an important distinction between pension (and probably postretirement) liabilities and many other types of liabilities in that pensions are not often an immediate threat to a company's solvency. While the *Pension Benefit Guaranty Corporation* has authority to take control of an underfunded plan and place a lien on company assets for the protection of employee benefits, it moves very cautiously in this area. Also, the Internal Revenue Service has established procedures where companies in financial difficulty can obtain waivers to defer their pension fund contributions.

Unconsolidated Subsidiaries

The method of reporting financial statements for a parent and its subsidiaries in consolidated form is discussed in Chapter 5. From our analysis perspective we prefer consolidated statements. Separate financial statements of the consolidated entities are useful in certain cases like when utilization of assets of a subsidiary is not subject to the full discretion of the parent. Information on unconsolidated subsidiaries is also useful in our analysis when bondholders of subsidiaries must rely on subsidiaries' assets as security. Also, bondholders of a parent company (particularly holding companies) sometimes derive a significant portion of their fixed-charge coverage from the dividends of unconsolidated subsidiaries. The parent's bondholders can also be in a junior position to the subsidiary's bondholders, which is important in the event of a subsidiary's bankruptcy. When financial statements of a subsidiary are *not* consolidated with a parent, consolidation can be effected as an analytical adjustment:

---

[2] This capitalized amount is the present value of Quaker's rentals on noncancelable operating leases (see item **154**) and is computed as: $\$93.8 = \$16.5/1.1 + \$16.5/1.1^2 + \$15.7/1.1^3 + \$15.2/1.1^4 + \$15.0/1.1^5 + 66.8/1.1^{7.2}$ (or $93.8 = $15 + $13.6 + $11.8 + $10.4 + $33.6). We assume a 10 percent discount rate. We also assume rentals after Year 16 continue at the Year 16 level of $15. This means the $66.8 is paid over the next 4.45 years ($66.8/$15.0) or, on average, it is paid in 2.2 years (4.45/2) after Year 16. Therefore, the discount factor for the *average* rental in the $66.8 is $1.1^{7.2}$, which is 7.2 years from Year 11. This adjustment affects subsequent analyses (e.g., see Appendix 10C).

Subsidiary's Assets	xx	
Subsidiary's Liabilities		xx
Parent's Investment in Subsidiary		xx

If a subsidiary has unrecorded lease or pension liabilities, they too are consolidated for purposes of our analysis.

Contingent Liabilities

Contingencies such as product guarantees and warranties represent obligations to offer future services or goods that are classified as liabilities. Typically, reserves created by charges to income are also considered liabilities. Our analysis must make a judgment regarding the likelihood of commitments or contingencies becoming actual liabilities and then treat these items accordingly. For example, guarantees of indebtedness of subsidiaries or others that are likely to become liabilities should be treated as liabilities.

Minority Interests

Minority interests in consolidated financial statements represent the book value of ownership interests of minority shareholders of subsidiaries in the consolidated group. These are *not* liabilities similar to debt because they have neither mandatory dividend payment nor principal repayment requirements. Capital structure measurements concentrate on the mandatory payment aspects of liabilities. From this point of view, minority interests are more like outsiders' claims to a portion of equity or an offset representing their proportionate ownership of assets. Minority interests are currently reported at book value. If our analysis wants to assess what a parent company must pay to acquire the minority interest, market rather than book value is the relevant measure.

Convertible Debt

Convertible debt is usually reported among liabilities. If conversion terms imply this debt will be converted into common stock, then it can be classified as equity for purposes of our capital structure analysis.

Preferred Stock

Most preferred stock requires no obligation for payment of dividends or repayment of principal. These characteristics are similar to those of equity. However, as we discussed in Chapter 3, preferred stock with a fixed maturity or subject to sinking fund requirements should from our analytical perspective be considered debt. Preferred stock with mandatory redemption requirements is also similar to debt and we should consider it as debt in our analysis. This is in spite of certain cases where default by a company on redemption provisions does not carry repercussions as severe as those from nonpayment of debt. An example of financing with redeemable preferred stock is BFGoodrich:

> BFGoodrich has issued 250,000 shares of $7.85 Cumulative Preferred Stock, Series A. In order to comply with sinking-fund requirements, each year on August 15, BFGoodrich must redeem 12,500 shares . . . The redemption price is $100 per share, plus dividends accrued at the redemption date.
>
> —BFGoodrich

Adjustments to Book Values of Assets

Because shareholders' equity of a company is measured by the excess of assets over liabilities, analytical revisions of asset book values necessarily change the amount of equity. For this reason, in assessing capital structure our analysis must evaluate whether book values of assets are sufficiently reliable. We describe several examples of potential adjustments. Different or additional adjustments are sometimes necessary depending on circumstances.

Recognition of Market Values

In certain industries like mining, petroleum, timber, and real estate, the market value of assets can significantly differ from the book values reported on companies' balance sheets. Adjustments of book values to market values for these assets have a corresponding effect on equity. The adjusted values of these assets are reflected in a company's earning power *and* in a company's fixed-charge coverage measure—an effect that does not depend on our analytical adjustments discussed here. These adjustments assume market value is better reflective of a company's financial condition than its current accounting procedures. We discuss market adjustments to three important asset categories. These adjustments should be viewed as representative of other asset adjustments often required in our analysis of financial statements.

Inventories

Inventories reported using the LIFO costing method are typically understated in times of rising prices. Companies usually disclose (often in notes) the amount by which inventories computed using FIFO (which are more similar to replacement cost) exceed inventories computed using LIFO. This difference is referred to as the **LIFO reserve**. This reserve enables us to adjust inventory amounts and corresponding equity amounts (after tax) to reflect current values.

Analysis Research Insight 10.1

LIFO Reserve and Company Value

What is the relation between the LIFO reserve and company value? A common assumption is that the LIFO reserve represents an unrecorded asset. Under this view, the magnitude of the LIFO reserve reflects the current value adjustment to inventory. Analysis research has investigated this issue, with interesting results.

Contrary to the "unrecorded asset theory," evidence from practice is consistent with a *negative* relation between the LIFO reserve and company market value. This implies the higher is the LIFO reserve, the lower is company value. Why this negative relation? An "economic effects theory" suggests that companies adopt LIFO if the present value of expected tax savings exceeds the costs of adoption (e.g., administrative costs). If we assume the present value of tax savings is related to the anticipated effect of inflation on inventory costs (a reasonable assumption), a negative relation might reflect the decline in the real value of a company due to anticipated inflation. Our analysis must therefore consider the possibility that companies using LIFO and companies using FIFO are inherently different and that any adjustments using the LIFO reserve reflect this difference.

Marketable Securities

We described in Chapter 4 how current practice requires marketable securities be reported at market value (except for held-to-maturity securities). However, for fiscal years beginning *before* December 16, 1993, marketable securities were often stated at cost when their book value was below market value. When examining financial statements from these earlier periods, our analysis should use parenthetical, footnote, or other information to make an analytical adjustment—increasing both the securities to market and equity (after tax) by a corresponding amount.

Intangible Assets

Intangible assets and deferred asset items reported on the balance sheet affect computation of a company's equity. To the extent our analysis cannot assess or form a reliable opinion on the value or future utility of these assets, they should probably be excluded from our consideration. This conservative adjustment reduces equity (after tax) by the book values of these assets. The arbitrary exclusion of all intangible assets from equity is an unjustified exercise in overconservatism. Similarly, if our analysis yields information suggesting revisions in asset book values, our analysis should make these analytical revisions to both assets and equity.

ANALYSIS VIEWPOINT *. . . You are the analyst*

You are an analyst for a securities firm. Your supervisor asks you to assess the relative risk of two potential *preferred equity* investments. Your analysis indicates these two companies are identical on all aspects of both returns and risks with the exception of their financing composition. The first company is financed 20 percent by debt, 20 percent from preferred equity and 60 percent from common equity. The second is financed 30 percent by debt, 10 percent from preferred equity, and 60 percent from common equity. Which company presents the greater preferred equity risk?

Capital Structure Composition and Solvency

The fundamental risk with a leveraged capital structure is the risk of inadequate cash under conditions of adversity. Debt involves a commitment to pay fixed charges in the form of interest and principal repayments. While certain fixed charges can be postponed in times of cash shortages, the fixed charges related to debt cannot be postponed without adverse repercussions to a company's shareholders and creditors. A leveraged capital structure also runs a risk from loss of financing flexibility. A company's ability to raise needed funds is impaired when it has a highly leveraged capital structure, especially in periods of adverse market conditions.

Long-Term Projections in Analyzing Solvency

Having sufficient cash to service debt is important for a levered company's continued viability. A direct and relevant risk measure of a levered company's capital structure is the *projection of future cash resources and inflows* available to meet debt requirements. These projections typically assume the worst possible economic conditions. This "bad news" analysis is a valuable safety test from the creditor's perspective. If we examine only prosperous or normal conditions, creditors would not need their senior position to equity, *and* would be better off with an equity position where potential rewards are higher.

We typically consider short-term horizons as involving periods of up to one year. Long-term horizons cover a wide range of periods exceeding one year. Examples include solvency analysis covering a three-year term loan and the evaluation of risk with a 30-year bond issue. Meaningful long-term projections covering interest and principal of a three-year loan are reasonable. Yet projections of funds flow for the 30-year bond issue are unrealistic. This is one reason why long-term debt often contains **sinking fund provisions** to reduce risk from long-term horizons, and often stipulates additional security in the form of assets pledged as collateral. Long-term debt also often contains provisions requiring maintenance of minimum working capital levels or restrictions on dividend payments. Both of these help protect creditors against severe deterioration in a company's financial position. However, these provisions cannot prevent adverse operating performance—the most serious cause of cash flow deficiencies.

We described in the previous chapter detailed long-term cash flow projections. We showed how the statement of cash flows can be effectively used and that it requires less detail than projections of *all* cash flows. Nevertheless, projections for long time horizons are less reliable than short-term horizons even when using the statement of cash flows. Since long-term cash flow projections are less reliable, several measures of long-term solvency are available to assist our analysis. These long-term solvency measures are typically static and include analysis of capital structure and both asset and earnings coverage.

Common-Size Statements in Solvency Analysis

A common measure of financial risk for a company is its capital structure composition. **Composition analysis** is performed by constructing a **common-size statement** of the liabilities and equity section of the balance sheet. Exhibit 10.3 illustrates a common-size analysis for Tennessee Teletech, Inc. An advantage of common-size analysis of capital structure is in revealing the relative magnitude of financing sources for a company. We see Tennessee Teletech is primarily financed from common (35.6%) and preferred (17.8%) stock and liabilities (41.2%)—and a small amount of earnings is retained in the company (4.5%). Common-size analysis also lends itself to direct comparisons across different companies. A variation of common-size analysis is to perform the analysis using ratios. Another variation focuses only on long-term financing sources, excluding current liabilities.

Common-Size Analysis of Tennessee Teletech's Capital Structure

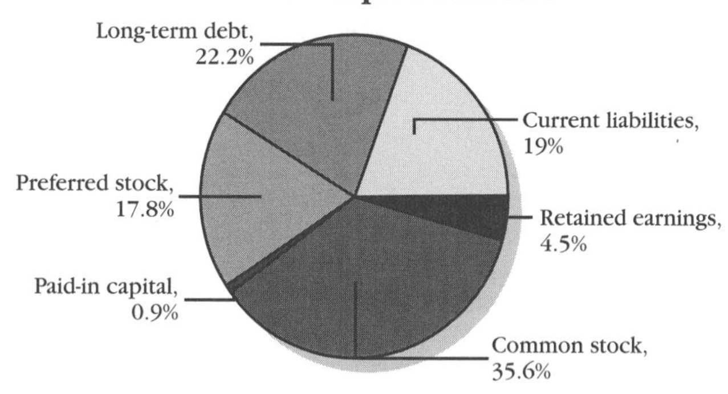

Capital Structure Measures for Solvency Analysis

Capital structure ratios are another means of solvency analysis. Ratio measures of capital structure relate components of capital structure to each other or their total. In this section we describe the most common of these ratios. We must take care before applying any measure or ratio that we understand its meaning and computation.

EXHIBIT 10.3 Tennessee Teletech's Capital Structure: Common-Size Analysis

Current liabilities	$ 428,000	19.0%
Long-term debt	$ 500,000	22.2
Equity capital:		
Preferred stock	$ 400,000	17.8
Common stock	800,000	35.6
Paid-in capital	20,000	0.9
Retained earnings	102,000	4.5
Total equity capital	$1,322,000	58.8
Total liabilities and equity capital	$2,250,000	100.0%

Total Debt to Total Capital

A comprehensive ratio is available to measure the relation between total debt (Current debt + Long-term debt + Other liabilities determined by our analysis, e.g., deferred taxes and redeemable preferred) and total capital (Total debt + Stockholders' equity [including preferred]). The **total debt to total capital ratio** (also called **total debt ratio**) is expressed as

$$\frac{\text{Total debt}}{\text{Total capital}}$$

The total debt to total capital ratio for Year 11 of Quaker Oats Company (financial statements are in Supplement A) is computed as:

$$\frac{\$926.9^{(a)} + \$701.2^{(b)} + \$115.5^{(c)} + \$366.7^{(d)}}{\$99.3^{(e)} + \$806.5^{(f)} + \$2{,}100.3^{(g)}} = \frac{\$2{,}110.3}{\$3{,}016.1} = 0.70$$

(a) Current liabilities.
(b) Long-term debt.
(c) Other liabilities.
(d) Deferred income taxes.
(e) Preferred stock outstanding.
(f) Shareholders' equity.
(g) Total debt (numerator).

This measure is often expressed in ratio form, 0.70, or described as debt comprising 70 percent of Quaker Oats' capital structure.

Total Debt to Equity Capital

Another measure of the relation of debt to capital sources is the ratio of total debt (as defined above) to *equity* capital. The **total debt to equity capital ratio** is computed as:

$$\frac{\text{Total debt}}{\text{Shareholders' equity}}$$

The total debt to equity capital ratio for Year 11 of Quaker Oats is computed as:

$$\frac{\$2{,}110.3}{\$99.3 + \$806.5} = 2.33$$

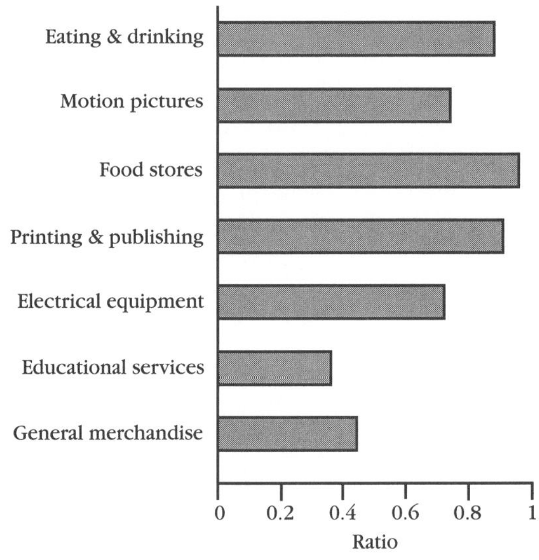

Source: Dun & Bradstreet.

This ratio implies that Quaker Oats' total debt is 2.33 times its equity capital. Alternatively stated, Quaker Oats' credit financing equals $2.33 for every $1 of equity financing.

Creditors often prefer the reciprocal measure of this ratio. This ratio, the **equity capital to total debt ratio,** is computed as:

$$\frac{\text{Shareholders' equity}}{\text{Total debt}}$$

Computation of this ratio for Year 11 of Quaker Oats equals:

$$\frac{\$905.8}{\$2{,}110.3} = 0.43$$

Creditors interpret this ratio as implying every dollar of debt is backed by 43 cents of equity capital. This ratio emphasizes that owners contribute a smaller share of the financing of Quaker Oats than do creditors.

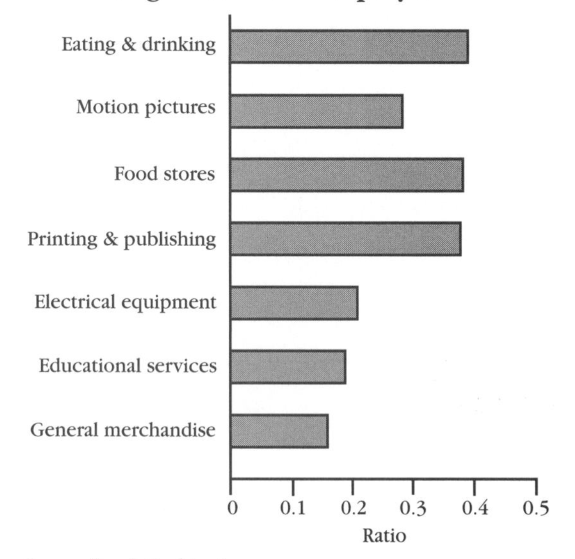

Source: Dun & Bradstreet.

Long-Term Debt to Equity Capital

The **long-term debt to equity capital ratio** measures the relation of long-term debt (usually defined as all noncurrent liabilities) to equity capital. A ratio in excess of 1:1 indicates greater long-term debt financing compared to equity capital. This ratio is commonly referred to as the **debt to equity ratio** and it is computed as:

$$\frac{\text{Long-term debt}}{\text{Shareholders' equity}}$$

For Year 11 of Quaker Oats the long-term debt to equity ratio equals:

$$\frac{\$2{,}110.3^{(a)} - \$926.9^{(b)}}{\$905.8^{(c)}} = 1.31$$

(a) Total debt.
(b) Total current liabilities.
(c) Shareholders' equity.

Short-Term Debt to Total Debt

The ratio of debt maturing in the short term relative to total debt is an important indicator of the short-run cash and financing needs of a company. Short-term debt, as opposed to long-term debt or sinking fund requirements, is an indicator of enterprise reliance on short-term (primarily bank) financing. Short-term debt is usually subject to frequent changes in interest rates.

Equity Capital at Market Value

Accounting practice emphasizes historical costs rather than market values. Since shareholders' equity is the residual of assets minus liabilities, equity book values can substantially differ from market values. This difference is especially meaningful when equity book values enter into the computation of important ratios. A common means of adjusting equity book values is to restate asset values from historical cost to market value. While company disclosures sometimes include replacement cost data, information on market value data is difficult to construct. One solution to this problem is computing equity capital at current (or average) market value of the stock comprising it. This technique assumes the securities market recognizes current values of assets and their earning power. The resulting *market value of equity* is then used in ratio computations that use equity values.

This method is less useful when stock prices fluctuate widely and when, in times of overspeculation or market uncertainty, prices may not be representative of a company's "fundamentals." Motivation for using stock prices derives from evidence that the marketplace provides a good approximation (or at least as good as any other judgmental process) of equity values. Also, use of *average* market prices diminishes the impact of transitory price changes. Use of reliable equity values can improve certain ratio analyses and provide more realistic measures of asset protection for creditors.

Evidence of equity book values consistently in excess of equity market values is usually interpreted as financial weakness and restricted financial capabilities. This affects a company's ability to issue additional equity or debt capital. Conversely, evidence of equity market values exceeding equity book values is interpreted as protection for creditors. This implies a company's ability to obtain capital at favorable prices and is an indicator of financial strength. Use of market values introduces a notion inherent in earnings-coverage measures. We discuss earnings-coverage measures later in this chapter; such measures benefit from a focus on the earning power of assets and not on asset book values. Equity market values also recognize the earning power of a company's assets. In this way, ratio measures using equity market values are consistent with earnings-coverage ratios.

We can compute the total debt to equity ratio of Quaker Oats for Year 11 using the average common stock market price for Year 11 (financial data reported in Supplement A):

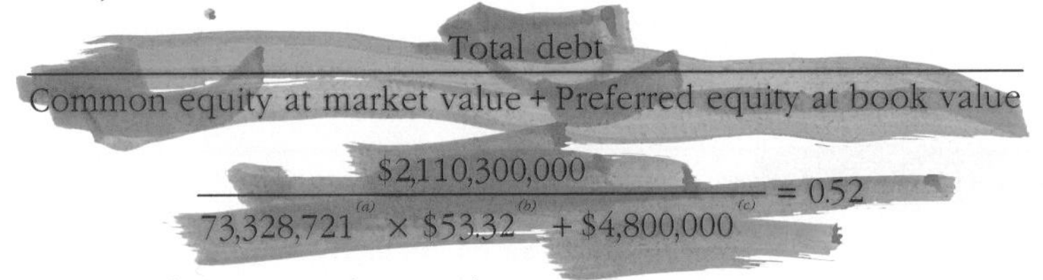

$$\frac{\text{Total debt}}{\text{Common equity at market value + Preferred equity at book value}}$$

$$\frac{\$2{,}110{,}300{,}000}{73{,}328{,}721^{(a)} \times \$53.32^{(b)} + \$4{,}800{,}000^{(c)}} = 0.52$$

(a) Number of shares of common stock outstanding.
(b) Average stock price for Year 11 (range is 41.75–64.88).
(c) Preferred stock at book value (market value unavailable).

Equity market values reflect the earning power of assets and possess a long-term perspective. If we compare the 0.52 we get when using equity market value to the 2.33 computed using book value, our interpretation is that the market value ratio is more favorable.

Interpretation of Capital Structure Measures

Common-size and ratio analyses of capital structure are primarily measures of the *risk* of a company's capital structure. The higher the proportion of debt, the larger the fixed charges of interest and debt repayment, and the greater the likelihood of insolvency during periods of earnings decline or hardship. Capital structure measures serve as *screening devices*. For example, when the ratio of debt to equity capital is relatively small (10 percent or less), there is no apparent concern with this aspect of a company's financial condition—our analysis is probably better directed elsewhere. Should our analysis reveal debt is a significant part of capitalization, then further analysis is necessary. Extended analysis should focus on several different aspects of a company's financial condition, results of operations, and future prospects.

Analysis of short-term liquidity is always important because before we assess long-term solvency we want to be satisfied about the near-term financial survival of the company. We described various analyses of short-term liquidity in the two previous chapters, and we would also assess the size of working capital to that of long-term debt. Loan and bond indenture covenants requiring maintenance of minimum working capital levels attest to the importance of current liquidity in ensuring a company's long-term solvency. Additional analytical tests of importance include our examination of debt maturities (as to size and timing), interest costs, and risk-bearing factors. The latter factors include a company's earnings stability or persistence, industry performance, and composition of assets.

Adjustments of Long-Term Debt to Equity Ratio

There are certain analytical adjustments we can make in our analysis of financial statements when using the debt to equity ratio. We illustrate these adjustments in Appendix 10C.

Event and Other Risk Factors

There are additional risk-bearing factors for creditors that are not easily measured and must be recognized in protective bond-indenture provisions or similar means. One risk factor is the possibility the company issues additional debt of equal or higher priority. This risk is referred to as **event risk** and occurs most often with leveraged buyouts, tender offers, and going-private transactions. These transactions typically yield serious declines in the value of outstanding debt. Additional risk of loss arises when a company increases shareholders' dividends to unreasonable levels, invests in riskier assets, or pursues business activities increasing risk of debt.

Asset-Based Measures of Solvency

This section describes two categories of asset-based analyses of a company's solvency.

Asset Composition in Solvency Analysis

The assets a company employs in its operating activities determine to some extent the sources of financing. For example, fixed and other long-term assets are typically not financed with short-term loans. These long-term assets are usually financed with equity capital. Debt capital is also a common source of long-term asset financing, especially in industries like utilities where revenue sources are stable.

Asset composition analysis is an important tool in assessing the risk exposure of a company's capital structure. Asset composition is typically evaluated using common-size statements of asset balances. Exhibit 10.4 shows our common-size analysis of Tennessee Teletech's

Common-Size Analysis of Tennessee Teletech's Asset Composition

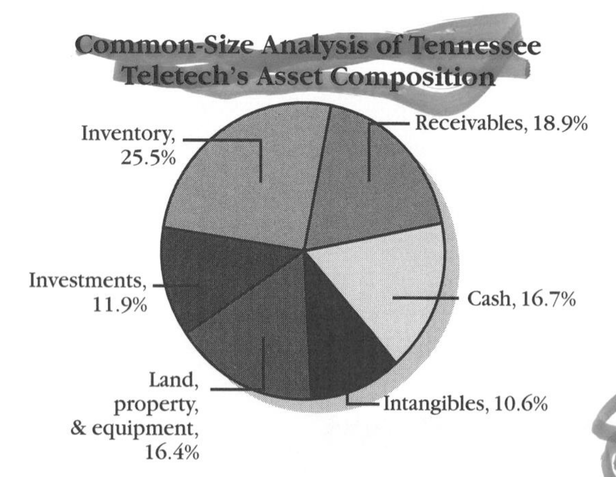

Source: Annual reports.

EXHIBIT 10.4 Tennessee Teletech's Asset Composition: Common-Size Analysis

Current assets		
Cash	$ 376,000	16.7%
Accounts receivable (net)	425,000	18.9
Merchandise inventory	574,000	25.5
Total current assets	$1,375,000	61.1
Investments	$ 268,000	11.9
Land, property, and equipment (net)	368,000	16.4
Intangibles	239,000	10.6
Total assets	$2,250,000	100.0%

assets (its liabilities and equity were analyzed in Exhibit 10.3). Judging by the distribution of assets and the related capital structure, it appears that since a relatively high proportion of assets is current (61 percent), a 41 percent total liabilities position is not excessive. Further analysis and measurements might alter or reinforce this preliminary interpretation.

Asset Coverage in Solvency Analysis

Asset coverage is an important factor in evaluating long-term solvency. Assets provide protection to creditors both because of their earning power and liquidation value. Assets represent the base a company relies upon for additional financing requirements. The relation between asset groups and selected items of capital structure is often usefully expressed in ratio form for our analysis. The **fixed assets to equity capital** ratio measures the relation between long-term assets and equity. A ratio in excess of 1:1 implies a portion of fixed assets are financed with debt. The ratio of **net tangible assets to long-term debt** is a measure of asset coverage for long-term obligations. It is a conservative measure—it excludes assets of sometimes doubtful realizability or value (intangibles). This ratio is interpreted as a measure of safety for creditors assuming asset liquidation at book values. The **total liabilities to net tangible assets** ratio (including net working capital) is a measure of the relation between debt and a company's investment in operating assets. This analysis tool measures the property collateral enjoyed by creditors. This ratio is especially useful when analyzing companies whose book values are understated.

Importance of Earnings Coverage

Our discussion of capital structure measures recognizes their usefulness as screening devices. They are a valuable means of deciding whether risk inherent in a company's capital structure requires further analysis. One limitation of capital structure measures is their inability to focus on availability of cash flows to service a company's debt. As debt is repaid, capital structure measures typically *improve* whereas annual cash requirements for paying interest or sinking funds remain *fixed* or *increase* (examples of the latter include level payment debt with balloon repayment provisions or zero coupon bonds). This limitation highlights our important emphasis on a company's

earnings coverage, or *earning power*, as the source of interest and principal repayments. While highly profitable companies can in the short term face liquidity problems because of asset composition, we must remember that long-term earnings are the major source of liquidity, solvency, and borrowing capacity.

Relation of Earnings to Fixed Charges

The relation of earnings to fixed charges is part of **earnings-coverage analysis**. Earnings-coverage measures focus on the relation between debt-related fixed charges and a company's earnings available to meet these charges. These measures are important factors in debt ratings (see Appendix 10A). Bond indentures often specify minimum levels of earnings coverage for additional issuance of debt. Securities and Exchange Commission regulations require the ratio of *earnings to fixed charges* be disclosed in the prospectus of all debt securities registered. The typical measure of the **earnings to fixed charges** ratio is:

$$\frac{\text{Earnings available for fixed charges}}{\text{Fixed charges}}$$

The concept underlying this measure is straightforward. Yet application of this measure is complicated by what is included in both "earnings available for fixed charges" and "fixed charges."

Computing Earnings Available for Fixed Charges

We previously discussed differences between income determined using accrual accounting and cash from operations (see Chapters 6 and 7). For example, certain revenue items like undistributed subsidiary earnings and sales on extended credit terms do not generate immediate cash inflows (although a parent can determine dividends for controlled subsidiaries). Similarly, certain expenses like depreciation, amortization, depletion, and deferred tax charges do not require cash outflows. These distinctions are important since fixed debt charges are paid out of cash, not earnings. Our analysis must recognize that unadjusted net income is not necessarily a good measure of cash available for fixed charges. Using earnings as an approximation of cash from operations is sometimes appropriate while in others it can misstate the amount available for servicing fixed charges. Our approach to this problem lies not with generalizations but in careful analysis of noncash revenue and expense items comprising income. For example, in analyzing depreciation as a noncash expense, we must remember the long-run necessity of a company replacing plant and equipment. Our analysis of the earnings available for fixed charges requires consideration of several of these important factors that are discussed below.

Extraordinary Gains and Losses. As discussed in Chapters 6 and 13, extraordinary gains and losses enter into the determination of long-term average earning power. They must be recognized as a factor that can over the long term contribute to or reduce cash available to pay fixed charges. Our computation of earnings-coverage measures using average earnings must recognize extraordinary gains and losses. This is especially true of earnings-coverage ratios where we measure the risk of loss of cash sources for paying fixed charges.

Preferred Dividends. Preferred dividends are not deducted from income because paying these dividends is not mandatory. In consolidated financial statements, preferred dividends of a subsidiary whose income is consolidated are deducted because they represent a charge having priority over the distribution of earnings to the parent.

Earnings Attributed to Minority Interests. These earnings are usually deducted from earnings available for fixed charges even though minority shareholders can rarely enforce a cash claim. An exception arises when a consolidated subsidiary has fixed charges. In this case, the coverage ratio should be computed using earnings before deducting minority interests. Another case arises when a subsidiary (having a minority interest) reports a loss. In this case, the credit to income from the minority's share in the loss should be excluded from consolidated earnings in computing our coverage ratio. The parent in most cases meets fixed-charges obligations of its subsidiary to protect its own credit standing, whether or not legally obligated.

Income Taxes. Income taxes in the computation of earnings-coverage ratios demand careful scrutiny. For example, since interest is tax deductible, it is paid from pre-tax earnings. In contrast, preferred dividends or sinking fund payments are not tax deductible and are paid from after-tax earnings.

Adding Back Fixed Charges. To determine pre-tax earnings available for fixed charges, the fixed charges deducted in arriving at pre-tax earnings must be added back to pre-tax earnings in the numerator of earnings-coverage ratios.

Income Level. The income level used in computing earnings-coverage ratios deserves attention. We must consider the question: What level of income is most representative of the amount actually available in future periods for paying debt-related fixed charges? Average earnings from continuing operations that span the business cycle and are adjusted for likely future changes are probably a good approximation of the average cash available from future operations to pay fixed charges. If one objective of an earnings-coverage ratio is to measure a creditor's maximum exposure to risk, an appropriate earnings figure is one that occurs at the low point of the company's business cycle.

Computing Fixed Charges

The second major component in the earnings to fixed charges ratio is fixed charges. In this section we examine the fixed charges typically included in the computation. Analysis of fixed charges requires us to consider several important components.

Interest Incurred. Interest incurred is the most direct and obvious fixed charge arising from debt. Yet reported interest expense includes amortization of any discount or premium. *Discount* and issuance expenses represent an amount by which par value exceeded proceeds from the debt issuance. Discount amortization increases reported interest expense. *Premium* is the reverse of a discount and represents proceeds exceeding par value. Premium amortization reduces reported interest expense. Both discount and premium amortization do not typically affect cash flows. They reflect expense or revenue allocations over the debt period. Another probable adjustment is when low coupon bonds are near maturity and it is likely they will be refinanced with higher coupon bonds. In this case the fixed charges should probably be adjusted to include the expected higher interest costs. Another issue arises from lack of information. When information is so limited to preclude our computation of interest incurred from interest capitalized, we can approximate the amount of interest incurred by referring to the mandatory disclosure of *interest paid* in the statement of cash flows. Interest incurred differs from the reported interest paid due to reasons that include (1) changes in interest payable, (2) interest capitalized being netted, and (3) discount and premium amortization. In the absence of information, interest paid is a good approximation of interest incurred.

Capitalized Interest. Current practice requires capitalization of certain interest costs (see Chapter 6). We must use care in dealing with capitalized interest in computing both the numerator and denominator of the earnings to fixed charges ratio. To begin, let's clarify the role of interest in reported income. Interest paid or obligated to be paid by a company for a period is *interest incurred*. This is the amount we focus on as needing coverage with earnings. Interest incurred that is charged to an asset is *interest capitalized*. Interest incurred less interest capitalized equals *interest expense*. Since interest expense is subtracted in computing pre-tax earnings, it should be added back to pre-tax earnings of the ratio's numerator to arrive at pre-tax pre-interest earnings. The ratio's denominator includes as a fixed charge the interest incurred whether capitalized or not. Interest capitalized in one period finds its way into the income statements of subsequent periods in the form of expenses like depreciation or amortization of assets capitalized. This amortized interest previously capitalized should be added back to pre-tax income. Failure to add back this interest yields earnings in the numerator computed *after* interest expenses rather than *before* interest expenses, understating the earnings to fixed charges ratio. Since the amount of previously capitalized interest that is amortized in a period does not require disclosure, our analysis must obtain this amount voluntarily from companies or derive it from other disclosures like those relating to deferred taxes. Quaker Oats in note 14 of its financial statements (in Supplement A) reports details of interest expense allocable to continuing operations, discontinued operations, and interest expense capitalized.

Interest Implicit in Lease Obligations. We discussed accounting recognition of leases as financing devices in Chapter 3. When a lease is capitalized, the interest portion of the lease payment is included in interest expense on the income statement, while most of the balance is usually considered repayment of the principal obligation. A question arises when our analysis discovers certain leases that should be capitalized but are not. This question goes beyond the accounting question of whether capitalization is appropriate or not. We must remember a long-term lease represents a fixed obligation that must be given recognition in computing the earnings to fixed charges ratio. Long-term leases that conceptually need not be capitalized can consist of fixed charges requiring inclusion in the earnings to fixed charges ratio. One problem is extracting the interest portion from the long-term lease payment. Our analysis can sometimes obtain the rate of interest implicit in a lease from note disclosures. Absent this, a rule of thumb (e.g., interest is approximately one-third of rental payments) might be our only solution. The Securities and Exchange Commission accepts this rule of thumb by registrants if management believes it represents a reasonable approximation of the interest factor.

Preferred Stock Dividend Requirements of Majority-Owned Subsidiaries. These are viewed as fixed charges because they have priority over the distribution of earnings to the parent. Items that would be or are eliminated in consolidation should not be viewed as fixed charges. We must remember that all fixed charges not tax deductible must be tax adjusted. This is done by increasing them by an amount equal to the income tax required to yield an after-tax income sufficient to cover these fixed charges. The preferred stock dividend requirements of majority-owned subsidiaries are an example of a non-tax-deductible fixed charge. We make an adjustment to compute the "grossed-up" amount:

$$\frac{\text{Preferred stock dividend requirements}}{1 - \text{Income tax rate}}$$

The tax rate used should be based on the relation between income tax expense on income from continuing operations and the amount of pre-tax income from continuing operations (this is a company's *effective tax rate*). We use the effective tax rate rather than the statutory rate since this is the SEC's requirement.

Principal Repayment Requirements. Principal repayment obligations are from a cash outflow perspective as onerous as interest obligations. In the case of rental payments a company's obligations to pay principal and interest must be met simultaneously. Several reasons are advanced as to why requirements for principal repayments are not given recognition in earnings to fixed charges ratio calculations, including:

- The earnings to fixed charges ratio is based on income. It assumes if the ratio is at a satisfactory level, a company can refinance obligations when they become due or mature. Accordingly, they need not be met by funds from earnings.
- If a company has an acceptable debt to equity ratio it should be able to reborrow amounts equal to principal repayments.
- Inclusion can result in double counting. For example, funds recovered by depreciation provide for debt repayment. If earnings reflect a deduction for depreciation, then fixed charges should not include principal repayments. There is some merit to this argument if debt is used to acquire depreciable fixed assets and if there is some correspondence between the pattern of depreciation and principal repayments. We must recognize depreciation is recovered typically only from profitable or at least break-even operations. Therefore, this argument's validity is subject to these conditions. We must also recognize the definition of *earnings* in the earnings to fixed charges ratio emphasizes cash from operations as that available to cover fixed charges. Using this concept eliminates the double-counting problem since noncash charges like depreciation would be added back to net income in computing earnings coverage.
- A problem with including debt repayment requirements in fixed charges is not all debt agreements provide for sinking funds or similar repayment obligations. Any arbitrary allocation of indebtedness across periods would be unrealistic and ignore differences in pressures on cash resources from actual debt repayments across periods. In the long run, maturities and balloon payments must all be met. One solution rests with our careful analysis of debt repayment requirements. This analysis serves as the basis in judging the effect of these requirements for long-term solvency. Assuming debt can be refinanced, rolled over, or otherwise paid from current operations is risky. Rather, we must recognize debt repayment requirements and their timing in analysis of long-term solvency. Including sinking fund or other early repayment requirements in fixed charges is a way of recognizing these obligations. Another way is applying debt repayment requirements over a period of 5 to 10 years into the future and relating these to after-tax funds expected to be available from operations.

Guarantees to Pay Fixed Charges. Guarantees to pay fixed charges of unconsolidated subsidiaries or of unaffiliated persons (suppliers) should be added to fixed charges if the requirement to honor the guarantee appears imminent.

Other Fixed Charges. While interest payments and principal repayment requirements are the fixed charges most directly related to the incurrence of debt, there is no reason to restrict our analysis of long-term solvency to these charges or commitments. A thorough analysis of fixed charges should include all long-term rental payment obligations[3] (not only the interest portion), and especially those rentals that must be met under noncancelable leases. The reason short-term leases can be excluded from consideration in fixed charges is they represent obligations of limited duration, usually less than three years. Consequently, these leases can be discontinued in a period of financial distress. Our analysis must evaluate how essential these leased items are to the continued operation of the company. Additional charges not directly related to debt, but considered long-term commitments of a fixed nature, are long-term noncancelable purchase contracts in excess of normal requirements.

Computing Earnings to Fixed Charges

The conventional formula, and one adopted by the SEC, for computing the earnings to fixed charges ratio is:

$$\frac{\left[\begin{array}{c}(a)\text{ Pre-tax income from continuing operations } \textit{plus } (b)\text{ Interest expense } \textit{plus}\\ (c)\text{ Amortization of debt expense and discount or premium } \textit{plus } (d)\text{ Interest portion}\\ \text{of operating rental expenses } \textit{plus } (e)\text{ Tax-adjusted preferred stock dividend requirements}\\ \text{of majority-owned subsidiaries } \textit{plus } (f)\text{ Amount of previously capitalized interest}\\ \text{amortized the period } \textit{minus } (g)\text{ Undistributed income of less than 50-percent-owned}\\ \text{subsidiaries or affiliates}\end{array}\right]}{\left[\begin{array}{c}(h)\text{ Total interest incurred } \textit{plus } (c)\text{ Amortization of debt expense and discount or}\\ \text{premium } \textit{plus } (d)\text{ Interest portion of operating rental expenses } \textit{plus } (e)\text{ Tax-adjusted}\\ \text{preferred stock dividend requirements of majority-owned subsidiaries}\end{array}\right]}$$

Individual components in this ratio are labeled *a–h* and are explained in detail below:

a. Pre-tax income before discontinued operations, extraordinary items, and cumulative effects of accounting changes.

b. Interest incurred less interest capitalized.

c. Usually included in interest expense.

d. *Financing leases* are capitalized so the interest implicit in these is already included in interest expense. However, the interest portion of *long-term operating leases* is included on the assumption many long-term operating leases narrowly miss the capital lease criteria, but have many characteristics of a financing transaction.

e. Excludes all items eliminated in consolidation. The dividend amount is increased to pre-tax earnings required to pay for it.[4]

f. Applies to *non*utility companies. This amount is not often disclosed.

---

[3] Capitalized long-term leases affect income by the interest charge implicit in them and by the amortization of the property right. To consider the "principal" component of these leases as fixed charges (after income is reduced by amortization of the property right) can yield double counting.

[4] Computed as [Preferred stock dividend requirements]/[1 – Income tax rate]. The income tax rate is computed as [Actual income tax provision]/[Income before income taxes, extraordinary items, and cumulative effect of accounting changes].

g. Minority interest in income of majority-owned subsidiaries having fixed charges can be included in income.

h. Included whether expensed or capitalized.

For ease of presentation, two items (provisions) are left out of the ratio above:

1. Losses of majority-owned subsidiaries should be considered in *full* when computing earnings.
2. Losses on investments in less than 50-percent-owned subsidiaries accounted for by the equity method should not be included in earnings *unless* the company guarantees subsidiaries' debts.

The SEC requires that if the earnings to fixed charges ratio is less than 1.0, the amount of earnings insufficient to cover fixed charges should be reported (rather than the ratio).

Case Illustration of Earnings to Fixed Charges Ratio

This section illustrates actual computation of the earnings to fixed charges ratio. Our first case focuses on CompuTech Corp., whose income statement is reproduced in Exhibit 10.5 along with additional financial information. Using the financial data of CompuTech ($ thousands) we compute the earnings to fixed charges ratio as (letter references are to the ratio definition):

$$\frac{\$2,200(a) + \$700(b \text{ and } c) + \$300(d) + \$80(f) - \$600(g) + \$200^{*}}{\$840(h) + \$60(c) + \$300(d)} = 2.40$$

*Note: The SEC permits including in income the minority interest in the income of majority-owned subsidiaries having fixed charges. This amount is added to reverse a similar deduction from income.

Our second case uses the Year 11 financial statements of Quaker Oats reproduced in Supplement A ($ millions). The Year 11 earnings to fixed charges ratio for Quaker Oats is computed as (letter references are to the ratio definition):

$$\frac{(a)\$411.5^{(1)} + (b)\$101.9^{(2)} + (d)\$14.8^{(3)}}{(h)\$103.8^{(4)} + (d)\$14.8^{(3)}} = 4.45$$

(1) Income from continuing operations before taxes—item 7.
(2) Interest expense—item 156.
(3) One-third of operating lease rentals or one-third of $44.5 = $14.8 —item 154.
(4) Interest incurred $101.9 + $1.9 = $103.8—item 156.

Pro Forma Computation of Earnings to Fixed Charges

In situations where fixed charges not yet incurred are recognized in computing the earnings to fixed charges ratio (e.g., interest costs under a prospective debt issuance), it is acceptable to estimate offsetting benefits expected from these future cash inflows and include them in pro forma earnings. Benefits derived from prospective debt can be measured in several ways, including interest savings from a planned refunding operation, income from short-term investments where proceeds can be invested, or other reasonable estimates of future benefits. When the effect of a prospective refinancing plan changes the ratio by 10 percent or more, the SEC usually requires a pro forma computation of the ratio reflecting changes to be effected under the plan.

Times Interest Earned Analysis

Another earnings-coverage measure is the **times interest earned ratio**. This ratio considers interest as the only fixed charge needing earnings coverage:

EXHIBIT 10.5

COMPUTECH CORPORATION
Income Statement

Net sales		$13,400,000
Income of less than 50%-owned affiliates (all undistributed)		600,000
Total revenue		$14,000,000
Cost of goods sold	$7,400,000	
Selling, general, and administrative expenses	1,900,000	
Depreciation (excluded from above costs)[3]	800,000	
Interest expense[1]—net	700,000	
Rental expense[2]	800,000	
Share of minority interests in consolidated income[4]	200,000	11,800,000
Income before taxes		$ 2,200,000
Income taxes:		
Current	$ 800,000	
Deferred	300,000	1,100,000
Income before extraordinary item		$ 1,100,000
Extraordinary gain (net of $67,000 tax)		200,000
Net income		$ 1,300,000
Dividends:		
On common stock	$ 200,000	
On preferred stock	400,000	600,000
Earnings retained for the year		$ 700,000

Selected notes to the financial statements:

[1]Interest expense is composed of the following:

Interest incurred (except items below)	$740,000
Amortization of bond discount	60,000
Interest portion of capitalized leases	100,000
Interest capitalized	(200,000)
Interest expense	$700,000

[2]Interest implicit in noncapitalized leases amounts to $300,000.

[3]Depreciation includes amortization of previously capitalized interest of $80,000.

[4]These subsidiaries have fixed charges.

Additional information (during the income statement period):

Increase in accounts receivable	$310,000
Increase in inventories	180,000
Increase in accounts payable	140,000
Decrease in accrued taxes	20,000

$$\frac{\text{Income + Tax expense + Interest expense}}{\text{Interest expense}}$$

The times interest earned ratio is a simplified measure. It ignores most adjustments to both the numerator and denominator that we discussed with the earnings to fixed charges ratio. While its computation is simple, it is potentially misleading and not as effective an analysis tool as the earnings to fixed charges ratio.

Relation of Cash Flow to Fixed Charges

Accrual accounting for net income does not always give us a good measure of the cash provided by operations that is available to cover fixed charges. Companies must pay fixed charges in cash while net income includes earned revenues and incurred expenses that do not necessarily generate or require immediate cash. This section describes a cash-based measure of fixed-charges coverage to address this limitation.

Cash Flow to Fixed Charges Ratio

The **cash flow to fixed charges ratio** is computed using *cash from operations* rather than earnings in the numerator of the earnings to fixed charges ratio. Cash from operations is reported in the statement of cash flows. The cash flow to fixed charges ratio is computed as:

$$\frac{\text{Pre-tax operating cash flow} + \text{Adjustments } (b)N - (g) \text{ on page 496}}{\text{Fixed charges}}$$

Using financial data from CompuTech in Exhibit 10.5 we can compute pre-tax cash from operations for this ratio as:

Pre-tax income	$2,200,000
Add (deduct) adjustments to cash basis:	
Depreciation	800,000
Deferred income taxes (already added back)	—
Amortization of bond discount	60,000
Share of minority interest in income	200,000
Undistributed income of affiliates	(600,000)
Increase in receivables	(310,000)
Increase in inventories	(180,000)
Increase in accounts payable	140,000
Decrease in accrued tax	(20,000)
Pre-tax cash from operations	$2,290,000

Fixed charges needing to be added back to pre-tax cash from operations are:

Pre-tax cash from operations	$2,290,000
Interest expensed (less bond discount added back above)	640,000
Interest portion of operating rental expense	300,000
Amount of previously capitalized interest amortized during period*	—
Total numerator	$3,230,000

*Assume included in depreciation (already added back).

Notice the numerator does not reflect a deduction of $600,000 (undistributed income of affiliates) because it, being a noncash source, is already deducted in arriving at pre-tax cash from operations. Also the "share of minority interests in consolidated income" is already added back in arriving at pre-tax cash from operations. Fixed charges for the ratio's denominator are:

Interest incurred	$ 900,000
Interest portion of operating rentals	300,000
Fixed charges	$1,200,000

CompuTech's cash flow to fixed charges ratio is computed as:

$$\frac{\$3,230,000}{\$1,200,000} = 2.69$$

As another example, we compute Quaker Oats' pre-tax cash from operations plus fixed charges for the numerator in the cash flow to fixed charges ratio as:

Numerator of cash flow to fixed charges ratio	***$ millions***
Cash from operations—item [31]	532.4
Add back:	
Income tax expense (except deferred)[(a)]—item [158]	161.4
Interest expense—item [156]	101.9
One-third of operating lease rentals of 44.5[(c)]	14.8
Amortization of previously capitalized interest (already added back)—presumably included in item [20]	—
Total numerator of ratio	810.5

Quaker Oats' cash flow to fixed charges ratio is computed as:

$$\frac{\$810.5}{\$103.8^{(b)} + \$14.8^{(c)}} = 6.83$$

[(a)] Deferred tax already added back in computing cash from operations.
[(b)] Interest incurred—item [156] ($101.9 + $1.9).
[(c)] One-third of operating lease rentals of $44.5—item [154].

Permanence of Cash from Operations

The relation of a company's cash flows from operations to fixed charges is important to our analysis of long-term solvency. Because of this relation's importance, we assess the "permanence" of operating cash flows. We typically do this in evaluating the components comprising operating cash flows. For example, the depreciation add-back to net income is more permanent than net income because recovery of depreciation from sales precedes receipt of any income. For all businesses, selling prices must (in the long run) reflect the cost of plant and equipment used in production. The depreciation add-back assumes cash flow benefits from recovery of depreciation are available to service debt. This assumption is true only in the short run. In the long run, this cash recovery must be dedicated to replacing plant and equipment. An exception can occur with add-backs of items like amortization of goodwill that are not necessarily replaced or depleted. Permanence of changes in the operating working capital (operating current assets less operating current liabilities) component of operating cash flows is often difficult to assess. Operating working capital is linked more with sales than with pre-tax income and therefore is often more stable than operating cash flows.

Earnings Coverage of Preferred Dividends

Our analysis of preferred stock often benefits from measuring the earnings coverage of preferred dividends. This analysis is similar to our analysis of how earnings cover debt-related fixed charges. The SEC requires disclosure of the ratio of combined fixed charges and preferred dividends in the prospectus of all preferred stock offerings. Computing the earnings coverage of preferred dividends must include in fixed charges all expenditures taking precedence over preferred dividends.[5] Since preferred dividends are not tax deductible, after-tax income must be used to cover them. Accordingly, the **earnings coverage of preferred dividends** ratio is computed as:

$$\frac{\text{Pre-tax income} + \text{Adjusted } (b) - (g) \text{ on page 496}}{\text{Fixed charges} + \left(\dfrac{\text{Preferred dividends}}{1 - \text{Tax rate}}\right)}$$

Using the financial data from CompuTech Corp. in Exhibit 10.5 we compute the earnings coverage of preferred dividends ratio. This is identical to using CompuTech's ratio of earnings to fixed charges (computed earlier) and adding the tax-adjusted preferred dividend requirement. Computation of the earnings coverage to preferred dividends ratio is ($ thousands):

$$\frac{\$2{,}200\,(a) + \$700\,(b \text{ and } c) + \$300\,(d) + \$80\,(f) - \$600\,(g) + \$200^{*}}{\$840\,(b) + \$60\,(c) + \$300\,(d) + \dfrac{\$400^{\dagger}}{1 - 0.50}} = 1.44$$

Note: Letters refer to individual components in the earnings to fixed charges ratio (see page 496).
* Minority interest in income of majority-owned subsidiaries (see prior discussion).
† Tax-adjusted preferred dividend requirement.

If there are two or more preferred issues outstanding, this coverage ratio is usually computed for each issue by omitting dividend requirements of junior issues and including all prior fixed charges and semior issues of preferred dividends.

Interpreting Earnings-Coverage Measures

Earnings-coverage measures provide us insight into the ability of a company to meet its fixed charges out of current earnings. There exists a high correlation between earnings-coverage measures and the default rate on debt—the higher the coverage, the lower the default rate. A study of creditor experience[6] with debt revealed the following default and yield rates for debt classified according to times interest earned ratios:

Times Interest Earned	*Default Rate*	*Promised Yield*	*Realized Yield*	*Loss Rate*
3.0 and over	2.1%	4.0%	4.9%	–0.9%
2.0–2.9	4.0	4.3	5.1	–0.8
1.5–1.9	17.9	4.7	5.0	–0.3
1.0–1.4	34.1	6.8	6.4	0.4
Under 1.0	35.0	6.2	6.0	0.2

Our attention on earnings in coverage measures is sensible since creditors place considerable reliance on the ability of a company to meet its obligations and continue

[5] Care must be exercised in comparing coverage ratios because some analysts and financial services include only the preferred dividend requirements in fixed charges.

[6] See H. B. Hickman, *Corporate Bond Quality and Investor Experience* (Princeton, NJ: Princeton University Press, 1958).

operating. An increased yield rate on debt seldom compensates creditors for the risk of losing principal. If the likelihood of a company meeting its obligations through continuing operations is not high, creditors' risk is substantial.

Importance of Earnings Variability and Persistence for Earnings Coverage

An important factor in evaluating earnings-coverage measures is the behavior of earnings and cash flows across time. The more stable the earnings pattern of a company or industry, the lower is the acceptable earnings-coverage measure. For example, a utility experiences little in the way of economic downturns or upswings and therefore we accept a lower earnings-coverage ratio. In contrast, cyclical companies like machinery manufacturers can experience both sharp declines and increases in performance. This uncertainty leads us to impose a higher earnings-coverage ratio on these companies. Both *earnings variability* and *earnings persistence* are common measures of this uncertainty across time. Our analysis can use one or both of earnings measures in determining the accepted standard for earnings coverage. Earnings persistence is usually measured as the (auto) correlation of earnings across time.

Importance of Measurements and Assumptions for Earnings Coverage

Determining an accepted standard for earnings-coverage depends on the method of computing an earnings-coverage measure. We described several earnings-coverage measures in the chapter. Many of these measures assume different definitions of *earnings* and *fixed charges*. We expect lower standards for earnings-coverage measures employing the most demanding and stringent definitions. Both the SEC and our computation of the earnings to fixed charges coverage ratio use earnings *before* discontinued operations, extraordinary items, and cumulative effects of accounting changes. While excluding these three items yields a less variable earnings stream, it also excludes important components that are part of a company's business activities. Accordingly, we suggest these components be included in computing the *average* coverage ratio over several years. The accepted standard also varies with the measure of earnings—for example, earnings measured as the average, worst, best, or median performance. The quality of earnings is another important factor that we examine in Chapter 13. We should not compute earnings-coverage ratios using shortcuts or purposefully conservative means. For example, using after-tax income in computing coverage ratios where fixed charges are tax deductible is incorrect and uses conservatism improperly. Our accepted standard of coverage must ultimately reflect our willingness and ability to incur risk (relative to our expected return). Appendix 10A refers to accepted standards of coverage ratios used by rating agencies in analyzing debt securities.

Capital Structure Risk and Return

It is useful for us to consider recent developments in "financial innovations" for risk inherent in a company's capital structure. A company can increase risks (and potential returns) of equity holders by increasing leverage. A leveraged buyout of a company uses increased leverage and often other factors (undervalued assets saleable for cash) favorable to buyers. Specifically, a *leveraged buyout* uses debt to take a company private by "buying out" equity holders. The acquirors rely on future cash flows to service the increased debt and on anticipated asset sales to reduce debt.

Another benefit of leverage is the tax deducibility of interest while dividends paid to equity holders are not tax dedcutible.

Substitution of debt for equity yields a riskier capital structure. This is why bonds used to finance certain leveraged buyouts are called *junk bonds*. A junk bond, unlike its high-quality counterpart, is part of a high-risk capital structure where its interest payments are minimally covered by earnings. Economic adversities rapidly jeopardize interest payments and principal of junk bonds. Junk bonds possess the risk of equity more so than the safety of debt.

Financial experience continually reminds us of those who forget the relation between risk and return. It is no surprise that highly speculative financial periods spawn risky securities. Our surprise is the refusal by some to appreciate the adjective *junk* when applied to bonds. Similarly, zero coupon bonds defer all payment of interest to maturity and offer several advantages over standard debt issues. However, when issued by companies with less than outstanding credit credentials, the risk with zero coupon bonds is substantially higher than with standard debt—due to the uncertainty of receiving interest and principal many years into the future. Another financial innovation called *payment in kind (PIK) securities* pay interest by issuing additional debt. The assumption is a debtor, possibly too weak to pay interest currently, will subsequently be successful enough to pay it later. While innovations in financing companies' business activities continue, and novel terms are coined, our analysis must focus on substance over form. The basic truth about the relation between risk and return in a capital structure remains.

Factors contributing to risk and our available tools of analysis discussed in this and preceding chapters point to our need for thorough and sound financial analysis. Relying on credit ratings or others' rankings is a delegation of our analysis and evaluation responsibilities. It is risky for us to place partial or exclusive reliance on these sources of analysis. No matter how reputable, these sources *cannot* capture our unique risk and return expectations. We need to exercise and improve our abilities to analyze risk and return in a company's capital structure to avoid situations like the following:

World of Wonder, Inc., raised $80 million from selling convertible debentures through the reputable investment banking firm of Smith Barney, Inc. Before paying its first coupon on these debentures, World of Wonder filed for protection from its creditors under Chapter 11 of the Bankruptcy Act. These debenture bonds, initially selling for $1,000 each, were trading at $75 each after this filing.

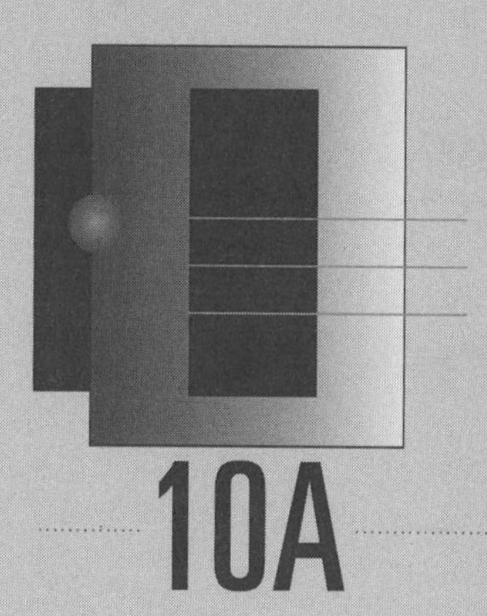

APPENDIX

Rating Debt Obligations

A comprehensive and complex system for rating debt securities is established in the world economy. Ratings are available from several highly regarded investment research firms: Moody's, Standard & Poor's (S&P), Duff and Phelps, and Fitch Investors Service. Many financial institutions also develop their own in-house ratings.

Treasury and Company Bond Yield Rates (One-Year Maturity)

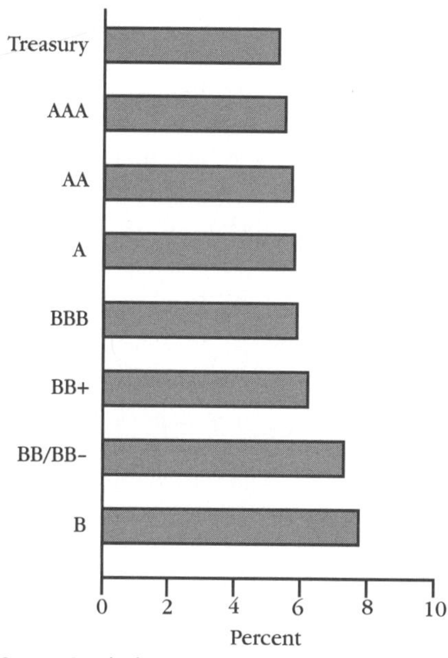

Source: Standard & Poor's, December 1996.

Bond Credit Ratings

The bond credit rating is a composite expression of judgment about the *creditworthiness* of the bond issuer and the quality of the specific security being rated. A rating measures credit risk, where *credit risk* is the probability of developments unfavorable to the interests of creditors. This judgment of creditworthiness is expressed in a series of symbols reflecting degrees of credit risk. Specifically, the top four rating grades from Standard & Poor's are:

AAA Bonds rated AAA are highest-grade obligations. They possess the highest degree of protection as to principal and interest. Marketwise, they move with interest rates and provide maximum safety.

AA Bonds rated AA also qualify as high-grade obligations, and in the majority of instances differ little from AAA issues. Here, too, prices move with the long-term money market.

A Bonds rated A are regarded as upper-medium grade. They have considerable investment strength but are not free from adverse effects of changes in economic and trade conditions. Interest and principal are regarded as safe. They predominantly reflect money rates in their price behavior, and to some extent economic conditions.

BBB Bonds rated BBB, or medium-grade category, are borderline between sound obligations and those where the speculative element begins to predominate. These bonds have adequate asset coverage and normally are protected by satisfactory earnings. Their susceptibility to changing conditions, particularly economic downturns, necessitates constant monitoring. Marketwise, these bonds are more responsive to business and trade conditions than to interest rates. This grade is the lowest qualifying for commercial bank investment.

There is a lower selection of ratings, including **BB,** lower-medium grade to marginally speculative; **B,** very speculative; and **D,** bonds in default.

A major reason why debt securities are widely rated while equity securities are not is because there is far greater uniformity of approach and homogeneity of analytical measures in analyzing creditworthiness than in analyzing future market performance of equity securities. This wider agreement on what is being measured in credit risk analysis has resulted in acceptance of and reliance on published credit ratings for several purposes.

	Bond Quality Ratings	
Rating Grades	*Standard & Poor's*	*Moody's*
Highest grade	AAA	Aaa
High grade	AA	Aa
Upper medium	A	A
Lower medium	BBB	Baa
Marginally speculative	BB	Ba
Highly speculative	B	B, Caa
Default	D	Ca, C

Criteria determining a specific rating are never precisely defined. They involve both *quantitative* (ratio and comparative analyses) and *qualitative* (market position and management quality) factors. Major rating agencies refuse to disclose their precise mix of factors determining ratings (which is usually a committee decision). They wish to avoid arguments about the validity of qualitative factors in ratings. These rating agencies use the analysis techniques discussed throughout this book. The following description of factors determining ratings is based on published sources and from discussions with officials of rating agencies.

Rating Company Bonds

In rating an industrial bond issue the rating agency focuses on the issuing company's asset protection, financial resources, earning power, management, and specific provisions of the debt. Also important are company size, market share, industry position, cyclical influences, and general economic conditions.

Asset protection refers to the extent a company's debt is covered by its assets. One measure is net tangible assets to long-term debt. One rating agency uses a rule of thumb where a bond needs a net tangible asset to long-term debt value of 5:1 for a AAA rating; 4:1 for a AA rating; 3 to 3.5:1 for a A rating; and 2.5:1 for a BBB rating. Concern with undervalued assets, especially with companies in the natural resources or real estate industries, leads to adjustments to these rating levels. Another rule of thumb suggests the long-term debt to total capital ratio be under 25 percent for a AAA, near 30 percent for a AA, near 35 percent for a A, and near 40 percent for a BBB rating. Additional factors entering rating agencies' consideration of asset protection include book value; composition of working capital; the quality and age of property, plant, and equipment; off-balance-sheet financing; and unrecorded liabilities.

Financial resources refer to liquid resources like cash and working capital accounts. Analysis measures include the collection period of receivables and inventory turnover. Their values are assessed relative to industry and absolute standards. Raters also analyze the issuer's use of both short-term and long-term debt, and their mix.

Future earning power and the issuer's cash-generating ability is an important factor in rating debt securities because the level and quality of future earnings determine a company's ability to meet its obligations. Earning power is usually a more reliable source of protection than are assets. One common measure of protection due to earning power is the earnings to fixed charges coverage ratio. A rule of thumb suggests an acceptable earnings to fixed charges ratio is 5:1 to 7:1 for a AAA rating, over 4:1 for a AA rating, over 3:1 for a A rating, and over 2:1 for a BBB rating. Another measure of debt servicing potential is cash flow from operations to long-term debt. A rule of thumb suggests this ratio be over 65 percent for a AAA, 45 to 60 percent for a AA, 35 to 45 percent for a A, and 25 to 30 percent for a BBB rating.

Management's abilities, foresight, philosophy, knowledge, experience, and integrity are important considerations in rating debt. Through interviews, site visits, and other analyses, the raters probe management's goals, strategies, plans, and tactics in areas like research and development, product promotion, product planning, and acquisitions.

Specific debt provisions are usually written in the bond indenture. Raters analyze the specific provisions in the indenture designed to protect interests of bondholders under a variety of conditions. These include analysis of stipulations (if any) for future debt issuances, security provisions like mortgaging, sinking funds, redemption provisions, and restrictive covenants.

Rating Municipal Bonds

Buyers and raters of municipal bonds analyze different factors from those of company debt. Municipal bonds are issued by state and local governments and are of several types. Many are *general obligation bonds* backed by the government unit issuing them. *Special tax bonds* are limited in protection to a particular tax used to service and retire them. *Revenue bonds* are protected by revenues of municipal enterprises. Others include *housing authority bonds* and *tax anticipation notes*. The amount of information disclosed to buyers of municipal bonds is of diverse quality, but legislative actions are attempting to remedy this.

Raters require a variety of information from issuers of municipal debt. With general obligation bonds, the debt relies on the issuer's ability and willingness to repay it from general revenues. The major revenue source is the taxing power of the municipality. Accordingly, raters' information needs include current population, trend and composition of population, largest taxpayer listing, market values of taxable properties, gross indebtedness, net indebtedness (e.g., deducting self-sustaining obligations and sinking funds), annual reports, budgets, estimates of capital improvements, future borrowing programs, and description of the area's economy. Rating techniques have similar objectives to those with company bonds. Yet the ratios are adapted to the unique factors associated with municipal debt. Consequently, the debt to market value of real estate ratio is important, where 10 percent is viewed as high and 3 to 5 percent as low. Moreover, annual debt expense of 10 percent of revenue is acceptable whereas percentages exceeding the upper teens are not. Another measure is per capita debt, where $400 or less is viewed as low and $900 to $1,000 is considered high (unfavorable). Raters also desire tax delinquencies not exceeding 3 to 4 percent. Additional factors include unfunded pension liabilities and the trend of indebtedness. An increase in indebtedness is undesirable. Management of the municipality is equally important for rating debt.

Limitations in the Ratings Game

Debt ratings are useful to a large proportion of debt issuances. Yet we must understand the inherent limitations of the standardized ratings procedures of rating agencies. As with equity security analysis, our analysis can improve on these ratings. Debt issuances reflect a wide range of characteristics. Consequently, they present us with opportunities to identify differences within rating classes and assess their favorable or unfavorable impact within their ratings class. Also, there is evidence that rating changes lag the market. This lag effect presents us with additional opportunities to identify important changes prior to their being reported by rating agencies.

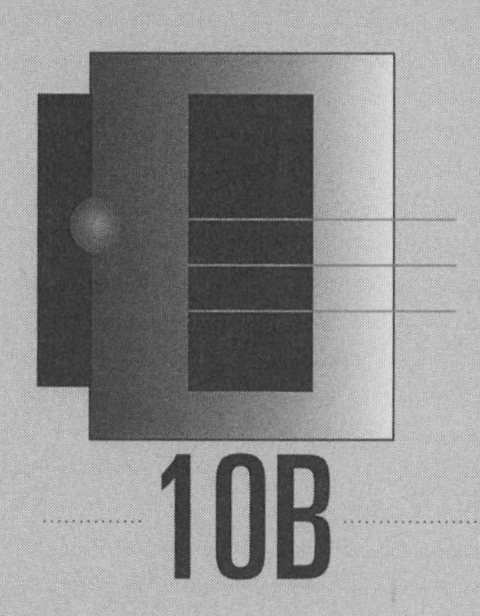

10B

APPENDIX

Predicting Financial Distress

A common use of financial statement analysis is in identifying areas needing further investigation and analysis. One of these applications is **predicting financial distress**. Research has made substantial advances in suggesting various ratios as predictors of distress. This research is valuable in providing us additional tools in analyzing long-term solvency. Models of financial distress, commonly referred to as **bankruptcy prediction models**, examine the trend and behavior of selected ratios. Characteristics of these ratios are used in identifying the likelihood of future financial distress. Models presume evidence of distress appears in financial ratios and we can detect it sufficiently early for us to take actions to avoid risk of loss or to capitalize on this information.

Altman *Z*-Score

Probably the most well-known model of financial distress is **Altman's *Z*-score**. Altman's *Z*-score uses multiple ratios to generate a predictor of distress.[7] Altman's *Z*-score uses a statistical technique (multiple discriminant analysis) to produce a predictor that is a linear function of several explanatory variables. This predictor classifies or predicts the likelihood of bankruptcy or nonbankruptcy. Five financial ratios are included in the *Z*-score: X_1 = Working capital/Total assets, X_2 = Retained earnings/Total assets, X_3 = Earnings before interest and taxes/Total assets, X_4 = Shareholders' equity/Total liabilities, and X_5 = Sales/Total assets. We can view X_1, X_2, X_3,

[7] See E. Altman, "Financial Ratios, Discriminant Analysis, and the Prediction of Corporate Bankruptcy," *Journal of Finance* 22 (September 1968), pp. 589–609. Also see J. Begley, J. Ming, and S. Watts, "Bankruptcy Classification Errors in the 1980s: An Empirical Analysis of Altman's and Ohlson's Models," *Review of Accounting Studies* (1997).

X_4, and X_5 as reflecting (1) liquidity, (2) age of firm and cumulative profitability, (3) profitability, (4) financial structure, and (5) capital turnover rate, respectively. The Altman *Z*-score is computed as:

$$Z = 0.717\,X_1 + 0.847\,X_2 + 3.107\,X_3 + 0.420\,X_4 + 0.998\,X_5$$

A *Z*-score of less than 1.20 suggests a high probability of bankruptcy, while *Z*-scores above 2.90 imply a low probability of bankruptcy. Scores between 1.20 and 2.90 are in the gray or ambiguous area.

Distress Models and Financial Statement Analysis

Research efforts identify a useful role for ratios in predicting financial distress. However, we must *not* blindly apply this or any other model without informed and critical analysis of a company's fundamentals. There is no evidence to suggest computation of a *Z*-score is a better means of analyzing long-term solvency than is the integrated use of the analysis tools described in this book. Rather, we assert the use of ratios as predictors of distress is best in complementing our rigorous analysis of financial statements. Evidence does suggest the *Z*-score is a useful screening, monitoring, and attention-directing device.

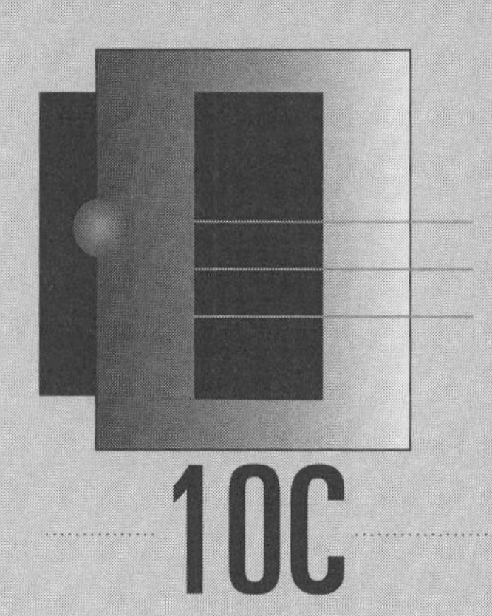

10C

APPENDIX

Analytical Adjustments to the Long-Term Debt to Equity Ratio

The conventional long-term debt to equity ratio is expressed as:

$$\frac{\text{Long-term debt}}{\text{Shareholders' equity}}$$

We can make useful analytical adjustments to increase its reliability:

$$\frac{LTD + NFL}{SE + NDT + LR + MSA}$$

LTD = Long-term debt consisting of all long-term liabilities inclusive of (1) noncurrent deferred taxes *likely* to reverse, and (2) other noncurrent liabilities.

NFL = Estimated present value of noncapitalized financial leases.

SE = Shareholders' equity, including minority interests.

NDT = Noncurrent deferred taxes assessed as *unlikely* to reverse in the foreseeable future.

LR = LIFO reserve (excess of disclosed FIFO value of ending inventory over reported LIFO amount).

MSA = Excess of market value of marketable securities over cost (for analysis of financial statements prior to 1994).

Using the Year 11 financial data of Quaker Oats reproduced in Supplement A, we compute this ratio as:

$$\frac{\$701.2^{(a)} + \$115.5^{(b)} + \$147^{(c)} + \$93.8^{(h)}}{\$806.5^{(d)} + \$99.3^{(g)} + \$220^{(e)} + \$18.9^{(f)}} = 0.92$$

(a) Long-term debt—item [79].
(b) Other liabilities—item [80].
(c) 40% of deferred income taxes—item [81], assumed liability portion.
(d) Shareholders' equity—item [91] less item [83].
(e) 60% of deferred income taxes—item [81], assumed equity portion.
(f) Excess of mostly average cost over LIFO—item [143].
(g) Preferred stock outstanding—item [82] less item [84].
(h) See discussion and footnote on pages 481–482.

GUIDANCE ANSWERS TO ANALYSIS VIEWPOINT

You Are the Entrepreneur

The primary criterion in your analysis is to compare the restaurant's return on assets to the after-tax cost of debt. If your restaurant can continue to earn 9 percent on assets, then the *after-tax* cost of debt must be less than 9 percent for you to successfully trade on the equity. Since the tax rate is 40 percent, you could successfully trade on the equity by adding new debt with an interest rate of 15 percent or less (9 %/[1 – 0.40]). The lower the interest rate is from 15 percent, the more successful is your trading on the equity. You must recognize that taking on debt increases the riskiness of your business (due to the risk of unsuccessfully trading on the equity). This is because if your restaurant's earnings decline to where return on assets falls below the after-tax cost of debt, then return on equity declines even further. Accordingly, your assessment of earnings stability, or *persistence*, is a crucial part of the decision to add debt.

You Are the Analyst

The preferred equity risk is greater for the second company. For the first company, senior securities (to preferred equity) comprise 20 percent of financing. However, for the second company, senior securities comprise 30 percent of financing. In a situation of bankruptcy, 30 percent of residual value must be paid to debtors prior to payments to preferred equity holders. In addition, financial leverage for the second company is potentially greater, although precise assessment of leverage risk depends on the features of preferred stock (e.g., features like fixed return, cumulative, nonparticipating, redeemable, and nonvoting make preferred stock more like debt).

QUESTIONS

10–1. Identify key elements in the evaluation of long-term solvency.

10–2. Why is analysis of a company's capital structure important?

10–3. What is meant by *financial leverage*? Identify one or more cases where leverage is advantageous.

10–4. Dynamic Electronics, Inc., a successful and high-growth company, consistently experiences a favorable difference between the rate of return on its assets and the interest rate paid on borrowed funds. Explain why this company should not increase its debt to the 90 percent level of total capitalization and thereby minimize any need for equity financing.

(CFA Adapted)

10–5. How should we treat deferred income taxes in our analysis of capital structure?

10–6. In analysis of capital structure, how should lease obligations not capitalized be treated? Under what conditions should they be considered equivalent to debt?

10–7. What is off-balance-sheet financing? Provide one or more examples.

10–8. What are liabilities for pensions? What factors should our analysis of a company's pension obligations take into consideration?

10–9. When is information on unconsolidated subsidiaries important to our analysis of long-term solvency?

10–10. Would you classify items below as equity or liabilities? State your reason(s) and any assumptions.
a. Minority interest in consolidated financial statements.
b. Appropriated retained earnings.
c. Guarantee for product performance on sale.
d. Convertible debt.
e. Preferred stock.

10–11. *a.* Why might our analysis need to adjust the book value of assets?
b. Give three examples of the need for possible adjustments to book value.

10–12. In evaluating solvency, why are long-term projections necessary in addition to a short-term analysis? What are some limitations of long-term projections?

10–13. What is the difference between common-size analysis and capital structure ratio analysis? Explain how capital structure ratio analysis is useful to financial statement analysis.

10–14. Equity capital on the balance sheet is reported using historical cost accounting and at times differs considerably from market value. How should our analysis allow for this, if at all, in analyzing capital structure?

10–15. Why is our evaluation of asset composition useful for capital structure analysis?

10–16. What does the earnings to fixed charges ratio measure? What does this ratio add to our other tools of analysis?

10–17. In computing the earnings to fixed charges ratio, what are your criteria for including an item in fixed charges?

10–18. A company you are analyzing has a purchase commitment of raw materials under a noncancelable contract that is substantial in amount. Under what conditions do you include this purchase commitment in computing fixed charges?

10–19. Is net income generally a reliable measure of funds available to meet fixed charges?

10–20. Company B is a wholly owned subsidiary of Company A. Company A is also Company B's principal customer. As a potential lender to Company B, what particular facets of this relationship concern you most? What safeguards, if any, do you require in any loan contract?

10–21. Comment on the assertion: "Debt is a supplement to, not a substitute for, equity capital."

10–22. A company in need of additional equity capital sells convertible debt. This action postpones equity dilution and the company ultimately sells its shares at an effectively higher price. What are the advantages and disadvantages of this action?

10–23. *a.* What is the reason for restrictive covenants in long-term debt indentures?
b. What is the reason for provisions regarding:
1. Maintenance of minimum working capital (or current ratio)?
2. Maintenance of minimum shareholders' equity?
3. Restrictions on dividend payments?
4. Ability of creditors to elect a majority of the board of directors of the debtor company in the event of default under terms of the loan agreement?

10–24. Why are debt securities regularly rated while equity securities are not?

10–25. What factors do rating agencies emphasize in rating an industrial bond? Describe these factors.

10–26. *a.* Municipal securities comprise several types. Describe these types.
b. What factors are considered in rating municipal securities?

10–27. Can our analysis improve on published bond ratings? Explain.

EXERCISES

Exercise 10–1

Ratio Analysis Using Market Values

Refer to the financial statements of Quaker Oats Company in Supplement A.

Required:

a. Using Quaker Oats' average common stock market price for Year 11 (see Quaker's Eleven-Year Selected Financial Data), compute the ratio of total liabilities to common equity at market value.

b. Discuss the importance and significance of ratios using equity capital at market value.

Exercise 10–2

Computing and Interpreting the Financial Leverage Index

Financial information for companies Alpha, Beta, and Gamma is reproduced below:

	Alpha, Inc.	*Beta, Inc.*	*Gamma, Inc.*
Total assets	$1,000,000	$2,000,000	$3,000,000
Total liabilities	$ 300,000	—	$1,200,000
Interest rate on liabilities	10%	—	5%
Operating income	$ 80,000	$ 210,000	$ 300,000
Percent of operating income to assets	8%	10.5%	10%

Required:

Compute financial leverage indexes for Alpha, Beta, and Gamma. The tax rate is 40 percent. Interpret the value of the financial leverage index for each of these companies.

Exercise 10–3

Determining Effect of Transactions on Solvency Ratios

Financial data ($ thousands) for Wisconsin Wilderness, Inc., are reproduced below:

Short-term liabilities	$ 500
Long-term liabilities	800
Equity capital	1,200
Cash from operations	300
Pre-tax income	200
Interest expense	40

Indicate the effect that each of the Wisconsin Wilderness transactions or events (*a* through *j*) has on each of the four ratios below. (Each transaction or event is independent of others—consider only the immediate effect.) Use I for increase, D for decrease, and NE for no effect.

A. Total debt to equity.

B. Long-term debt to equity.

C. Earnings to fixed charges (exceeds 1.0 before transactions or events).

D. Cash flow to fixed charges (exceeds 1.0 before transactions or events).

	A	*B*	*C*	*D*
a. Increase in tax rate.				
b. Retire bonds—paid in cash.				
c. Issue bonds to finance expansion.				
d. Issue preferred stock to finance expansion.				
e. Depreciation expense increases.				
f. Collect accounts receivable.				
g. Refinance debt resulting in higher interest cost.				
h. Capitalize higher proportion of interest expense.				
i. Convert convertible debt into common stock.				
j. Acquire inventory on credit.				

Exercise 10–4

What-If Analysis of Capital Structure Ratios (multiple choice)

The following information is relevant for Questions I and II:
Austin Corporation's Year 8 financial statement notes include the following information:

1. Austin recently entered into operating leases with total future payments of $40 million that equal a discounted present value of $20 million.
2. Long-term assets include held-to-maturity debt securities carried at their amortized cost of $10 million. Fair market value of these securities is $12 million.
3. Austin guarantees a $5 million bond issue, due in Year 13. The bonds are issued by Healey, a nonconsolidated 30 percent-owned affiliate.

You decide to adjust Austin's balance sheet for each of these three items.

I. Among the effects of these adjustments for the times interest earned coverage ratio is (choose one of the following):
   a. Lease capitalization increases this ratio.
   b. Lease capitalization decreases this ratio.
   c. Recognizing the debt guarantee decreases this ratio.
   d. Held-to-maturity debt securities adjustment increases this ratio.

II. Among the effects of these adjustments for the long-term debt to equity ratio is (choose one of the following):
   a. Only the held-to-maturity debt securities adjustment decreases this ratio.
   b. Only lease capitalization decreases this ratio.
   c. All three adjustments decrease this ratio.
   d. All three adjustments increase this ratio.

III. What is the effect of a cash dividend payment on the following ratios (all else equal)?

	Times Interest Earned	*Long-Term Debt to Equity*
a.	Increase	Increase
b.	No effect	Increase
c.	No effect	No effect
d.	Decrease	Decrease

IV. What is the effect of selling inventory for profit on the following ratios (all else equal)?

	Times Interest Earned	*Long-Term Debt to Equity*
a.	Increase	Increase
b.	Increase	Decrease
c.	Decrease	Increase
d.	Decrease	Decrease

V. The existence of uncapitalized operating leases is to (choose one of the following):
   a. Overstate the earnings to fixed charges coverage ratio.
   b. Overstate fixed charges.
   c. Overstate working capital.
   d. Understate the long-term debt to equity ratio.

(CFA Adapted)

Exercise 10–5

Effect of Capitalizing Interest for Ratio Analysis

Rogan Development Co., a real estate developer, is pursuing one major development project in Year 7—an office complex in Charlottesville, Virginia. Rogan's account titled Building under Construction has an average balance of $10,000,000. Rogan's long-term debt outstanding during Year 7 is comprised of:

	Average Balance	*Interest Rate*
Development loan	$ 6,000,000	11%
Mortgage debt	10,000,000	9
Senior debentures (secured)	40,000,000	10

Required:

a. Calculate the interest incurred, capitalized interest, and interest expense for Year 7. Show calculations.

b. As a bond analyst, list and justify your adjustments to the times interest earned ratio for Rogan and other companies who report significant amounts of capitalized interest.

(CFA Adapted)

PROBLEMS

Problem 10–1

Computing and Interpreting Solvency Ratios

Refer to the financial statements of Quaker Oats Company in Supplement A.

Required:

a. Compute the following ratios for Years 9, 10, and 11. Assume a statutory income tax rate of 34 percent in all ratios except the fixed-charge coverage ratios (where you are to use the effective tax rate). Consider all deferred taxes as liabilities. Assume fixed charges include the interest portion of operating rental expense, equal to one-third of the operating lease expense.

1. Financial leverage index.
2. Long-term debt to equity.
3. Total debt ratio.
4. Total debt to equity.
5. Preferred stock to equity (use stated value of preferred stock for all years).
6. Analytically adjusted long-term debt to equity for Year 10 (consider 50 percent of deferred income taxes as debt for this ratio only).
7. Earnings to fixed charges.
8. Cash flow to fixed charges.
9. Cash from operations to total debt.
10. Earnings coverage of preferred dividends.
11. Equity capital to net fixed assets.

b. Discuss the importance of both level and trend for each of the above measures.

Problem 10–2

Calculating Solvency Ratios

Refer to the financial statements of Campbell Soup Company in Supplement A. Assume 50 percent of deferred income taxes will reverse in the foreseeable future (the remainder should be considered equity).

Required:

a. Compute the following measures for Year 10.

1. Total debt to equity.
2. Total debt ratio.
3. Long-term liabilities to equity.
4. Analytically adjusted long-term debt to equity.
5. Total equity to total liabilities.
6. Fixed assets to equity.
7. Short-term liabilities to total debt.
8. Earnings to fixed charges.
9. Cash flow to fixed charges.
10. Working capital to total debt.

b. Under the heading "Balance Sheets" in its Management's Discussion and Analysis section, Campbell refers to the ratio of total debt to capitalization. Verify Campbell's computation for Year 10.

Problem 10–3 Computing and Analyzing Earnings-Coverage Ratios

The income statement of Kimberly Corporation for the year ended December 31, Year 1, is reproduced below:

KIMBERLY CORPORATION
Consolidated Income Statement
For Year Ended December 31, Year 1
($ thousands)

Sales	$14,000	
Undistributed income of less than 50%-owned affiliates	300	
Total revenue		$14,300
Cost of goods sold	$ 6,000	
Selling and administrative expenses	2,000	
Depreciation	600	
Rental expense	500	
Share of minority interest in consolidated income	200	
Interest expense	400	9,700
Pre-tax income		$ 4,600
Income taxes:		
Current	$ 900	
Deferred	400	1,300
Net income		$ 3,300
Dividends:		
Common stock	$ 300	
Preferred stock	400	$ 700
Earnings retained for the year		$ 2,600

Additional Information:

1. The following changes occurred in current assets and liabilities for Year 1:

Current accounts	*Increase (decrease)*
Accounts receivable	$900
Inventories	(800)
Dividend payable	(100)
Notes payable to bank	(200)
Accounts payable	700

2. The effective tax rate is 40 percent.
3. Shares of minority interests in consolidated income do not have fixed charges.
4. Interest expense includes:

Interest incurred (except items below)	$600
Amortization of bond premium	(300)
Interest on capitalized leases	140
Interest incurred	$440
Less—interest capitalized	40
Interest expense	$400

5. Amortization of previously capitalized interest (included in depreciation) is $60.
6. Interest implicit in operating lease rental payment (included in rental expense) is $120.

Required:

a. Compute the following earnings-coverage ratios:
   1. Earnings to fixed charges.
   2. Cash flow to fixed charges.
   3. Earnings coverage of preferred dividends.

b. Analyze and interpret the earnings-coverage ratios in (*a*).

Problem 10–4

Computing and Analyzing Earnings-Coverage Ratios

The income statement of Lot Corporation for the year ended December 31, Year 1, is reproduced below:

LOT CORPORATION
Income Statement
For Year Ended December 31, Year 1
($ thousands)

Sales	$27,400	
Undistributed income of less than 50%-owned affiliates	400	
Total revenue		$27,800
Less: Cost of goods sold		14,000
Gross profit		$13,800
Selling and administrative expenses	$ 3,600	
Depreciation[a]	1,200	
Rental expense[b]	1,400	
Share of minority interest in consolidated income[c]	600	
Interest expense[d]	1,200	8,000
Pre-tax income		$ 5,800
Income taxes:		
Current	$ 2,000	
Deferred	1,000	3,000
Net income		$ 2,800
Dividends:		
Preferred stock	$ 400	
Common stock	1,000	$ 1,400
Earnings retained for the year		$ 1,400

[a]Represents depreciation excluded from all other expense categories and includes $100 amortization of previously capitalized interest.

[b]Includes $400 of interest implicit in operating lease rental payments that should be considered as having financing characteristics.

[c]These subsidiaries have fixed charges.

[d]Interest expense includes:

Interest incurred (except items below)	$ 880
Amortization of bond discount	100
Interest portion of capitalized leases	340
Interest capitalized	(120)
	$1,200

Additional Information

1. The following changes occurred in current assets and liabilities for Year 1:

Current accounts	*Increase (decrease)*
Accounts receivable	$(1,600)
Inventories	2,000
Dividend payable	240
Notes payable	(400)
Accounts payable	2,000

2. The tax rate is 40 percent.

Required:

a. Compute the following earnings-coverage ratios:
   1. Earnings to fixed charges.
   2. Cash flow to fixed charges.
   3. Earnings coverage of preferred dividends.

b. Analyze and interpret the earnings-coverage ratios in *(a)*.

Problem 10–5 Analyzing Coverage Ratios

Your supervisor is considering purchasing the bonds and preferred shares of ARC Corporation. She furnishes you the income statement of ARC Corporation (reproduced below) and expresses concern about the coverage of fixed charges.

ARC CORPORATION
Consolidated Income Statement
For Year Ended December 31, Year 5

Sales	$27,400	
Income of less than 50%-owned affiliates (note 1)	800	
Total revenue		$28,200
Cost of goods sold		14,000
Gross profit		$14,200
Selling and administrative expenses	$ 3,600	
Depreciation (note 2)	1,200	
Rental expenses (note 3)	1,400	
Share of minority interests in consolidated income (note 4)	600	
Interest expense (note 5)	1,200	8,000
Income before income taxes		$ 6,200
Income taxes:		
Current	$ 2,000	
Deferred	1,000	3,000
Net income		$ 3,200
Dividends:		
Preferred stock	$ 400	
Common stock	1,000	$ 1,400
Increase in retained earnings		$ 1,800

Notes:
1. For the income from affiliates, $600 is undistributed.
2. Includes $80 amortization of previously capitalized interest.
3. Includes $400 of interest implicit in operating lease rental payments.
4. These subsidiaries do *not* have fixed charges.

5. Interest expense includes:

Interest incurred (except items below)	$ 880
Amortization of bond discount	100
Interest portion of capitalized leases	340
Interest capitalized	(120)
	$1,200

6. The following changes occurred in balance sheet accounts:

Accounts receivable	$(600)
Inventories	160
Payables and accruals	120
Dividends payable	(80)
Current portion of long-term debt	(100)

7. The tax rate is 40 percent.

Required:

a. Compute the following earnings-coverage ratios:
   1. Earnings to fixed charges.
   2. Cash flow to fixed charges.
   3. Earnings coverage of preferred dividends.

b. Analyze and interpret the earnings-coverage ratios in *(a)*.

Problem 10–6

Calculating Financial Ratios on Debt and Equity Securities

Answer the following questions using the financial data of Fox Industries Ltd. reproduced below:

FOX INDUSTRIES LIMITED
Condensed Income Statement
($ thousands)

	Fiscal Year Ended				
	Year 7	***Year 6***	***Year 5***	***Year 4***	***Year 3***
Earnings before depreciation, interest on long-term debt, and taxes	$8,750	$8,250	$8,000	$7,750	$7,250
Less: Depreciation	4,000	3,750	3,500	3,500	3,250
Earnings before interest on long-term debt and taxes	$4,750	$4,500	$4,500	$4,250	$4,000

FOX INDUSTRIES LIMITED
Capitalization as of December 31, Year 7
($ thousands)

Long-term debt:	
First mortgage bonds:	
5.00% serial bonds due Year 8 to Year 10	$ 7,500
6.00% sinking fund bonds due Year 15 (note 1)	17,500
Debentures:	
6.50% sinking fund debentures due Year 16 (note 1)	10,000
Total long-term debt	$35,000
Capital stock:	
$1.10 cumulative redeemable preferred, stated value $5.00 per share (redeemable at $20.00 share)	$ 1,500
400,000 Class A shares, no-par value (note 2)	14,000
1,000,000 common shares, no par value	6,000
Total capital stock	$21,500
Paid-in capital	7,000
Retained earnings	18,500
Total long-term debt and equity	$82,000

Notes:
1. Combined annual sinking fund payments are $500,000.
2. Subject to the rights of the preferred shares, the Class A shares are entitled to fixed cumulative dividends at the rate of $2.50 per share per annum, and are convertible at the holder's option, at any time, into common shares on the basis of two common shares for one Class A share.

Required:

a. Compute the (1) earnings-coverage ratio for Year 7, and (2) average annual earnings-coverage ratio for the five-year period Year 3 through Year 7 (inclusive), on the first mortgage bonds and on the sinking fund debentures at the end of Year 7.

b. Compute the long-term debt to equity ratio as of December 31, Year 7, and identify the proportion of equity represented by shares senior to common shares.

c. Assuming a 50 percent income tax rate, calculate earnings coverage on the $1.10 cumulative redeemable preferred shares for the end of Year 7.

d. Assuming a 50 percent income tax rate and full conversion of the Class A shares, calculate earnings per common share for the end of Year 7.

(CFA Adapted)

Problem 10–7

Analyzing Alternative Financing Strategies

TOP Company is planning to invest $20,000,000 in an expansion program expected to increase earnings before interest and taxes by $4,000,000. TOP Company currently is earning $5 per share on 1,000,000 shares of common stock outstanding. TOP Company's capital structure prior to the investment is:

Total debt	$20,000,000
Shareholders' equity	50,000,000
Total capitalization	$70,000,000

Expansion can be financed by the sale of 400,000 shares at $50 each or by issuing long-term debt at 6 percent. TOP Company's most recent income statement is reproduced below:

Sales		$100,000,000
Variable costs	$60,000,000	
Fixed costs	20,000,000	
Total costs		$ 80,000,000
Earnings before interest and taxes		$ 20,000,000
Interest		1,000,000
Earnings before taxes		$ 19,000,000
Taxes (40%)		7,600,000
Net earnings		$ 11,400,000

Required:

a. Assuming TOP Company maintains its current earnings level and achieves the expected earnings from expansion, what will be TOP Company's earnings per share:
1. If expansion is financed by debt?
2. If expansion is financed by equity?

b. At what level of earnings before interest and taxes will earnings per share be equal under both alternatives?

Problem 10–8

Analytical Adjustment of Debt to Capitalization Ratio

You are a senior portfolio manager with Reilly Investment Management reviewing the biweekly printout of equity value screens prepared by a brokerage firm. One of the screens used to identify companies is a "low long-term debt/total long-term capital ratio." The printout indicates this ratio for Lubbock Corporation is 23.9 percent. Your reaction is that Lubbock might be a potential takeover target and you proceed to analyze Lubbock's balance sheet reproduced below:

LUBBOCK CORPORATION
Condensed Balance Sheet
December 31, Year 7 ($ millions)

Assets	
Cash and equivalents	$ 100
Receivables	350
Marketable securities	150
Inventory	800
Other current assets	400
Total current assets	$1,800
Net plant and equipment	1,800
Total assets	$3,600
Liabilities and Equity	
Note payable	$ 125
Accounts payable	175
Taxes payable	150
Other current liabilities	75
Total current liabilities	$ 525
Long-term debt	675
Deferred taxes (noncurrent)	175
Other noncurrent liabilities	75
Minority interest	100
Common stock	400
Retained earnings	1,650
Total liabilities and equity	$3,600

Further analysis of Lubbock's financial statements reveals the following notes:

- "A subsidiary, Lubbock Property Corp., holds, as joint venture partner, a 50 percent interest in its head office building in Chicago, and 10 regional shopping centers in the United States. The parent company has guaranteed the indebtedness of these properties, which totaled $250,000,000 at December 31, Year 7."
- "The LIFO cost basis was used in the valuation of inventories at December 31, Year 7. If the FIFO method of inventory was used in place of LIFO, inventories would have exceeded reported amounts by $200,000,000."
- "The company leases most of its facilities under long-term contracts. These leases are categorized as operating leases for accounting purposes. Future minimum rental payments as of December 31, Year 7 are: $90,000,000 per year for Year 8 through Year 27. These leases carry an implicit interest rate factor of 10 percent, which translates to a present value of approximately $750,000,000."

Required:

a. Explain how the information in each note is used to adjust items on Lubbock's balance sheet. Calculate an adjusted *long-term debt to total long-term capitalization* ratio. Ignore potential income tax effects.

b. As a potential investor, you consider other accounting factors in evaluating Lubbock's balance sheet including:
1. Valuation of marketable securities.
2. Treatment of deferred taxes.

Discuss how each of these accounting factors can impact Lubbock's *long-term debt to total long-term capitalization* ratio.

(CFA Adapted)

Problem 10–9 Analyzing and Interpreting Financial Ratios

You are analyzing the bonds of ZETA Company (see Case CC.2 in the Comprehensive Case following Chapter 13) as a potential long-term investment. As part of your decision-making process, you compute various ratios for Years 5 and 6. Additional data and information to be considered only for purposes of this problem ($ thousands) follow:

	Year 6	Year 5
A. Interest is comprised of:		
Interest incurred (except items below)	$ 9,200	$ 5,000
Amortization of bond discount	2,500	2,000
Interest portion of capitalized leases	80	—
Interest capitalized	(1,780)	(1,000)
	$10,000	$ 6,000

B. Depreciation includes amortization of previously capitalized interest of $1,200 for Year 6 and $1,000 for Year 5.

C. Interest portion of operating rental expense considered a fixed charge: $20 in Year 6 and $16 in Year 5.

D. The associated company is less than 50 percent owned.

E. Deferred taxes constitute a long-term liability.

F. Present value of noncapitalized financing leases is $200 for both years.

G. Excess of the projected pension benefit obligation over the accumulated pension benefit obligation is $2,800 for both years.

H. End of Year 4 total assets and equity capital are $94,500 and $42,000, respectively.

I. Average market price per share of ZETA's common stock is $40 and $45 for Year 6 and Year 5, respectively.

Required:

a. Compute the following analytical measures for both Year 6 and Year 5:
1. Financial leverage index.
2. Total debt ratio.
3. Total debt ratio (based on market value of common equity).
4. Total debt to equity.
5. Long-term debt to equity.
6. Earnings to fixed charges.
7. Cash flow to fixed charges.

b. Analyze and interpret both the level and year-to-year trend in these measures.

c. Compute the analytically adjusted long-term debt to equity ratio for both Year 6 and Year 5. Analyze and interpret this ratio (for this ratio assume 60% of deferred taxes constitute a long-term liability).

CASES

Case 10–1 Analyzing Adaptec's Capital Structure and Solvency

Use the 1996 annual report of Adaptec, Inc., in Supplement A to answer the following:

a. Perform an analysis of Adaptec's 1996 and 1995 capital structure and solvency. Your analysis should (at a minimum) include analysis and interpretation of the following:
1. Financial leverage index.
2. Financial leverage ratio.
3. Common-size analysis.
4. Capital structure ratios.
5. Asset composition.

6. Asset coverage.
7. Both earnings and cash flow to fixed charges ratios.
8. Relevant qualitative considerations.

b. In analyzing the capital structure and solvency of Adaptec, what adjustments to the book values of liabilities and assets would you make? Be specific.

c. Estimate the present value of Adaptec's minimum future payments on operating leases (see note 7).

Case 10–2
Determining Bond Rating

Philip Morris Companies is a major manufacturer and distributor of consumer products. It has a history of steady growth in sales, earnings, and cash flows. In recent years Philip Morris has diversified with acquisitions of Miller Brewing and General Foods. In Year 8, Philip Morris acted to further diversify by announcing an unsolicited cash tender offer for all the 124 million outstanding shares of Kraft at $90 per share. After negotiation, Kraft accepts a $106 per share all-cash offer from Philip Morris. Assume you are an analyst with Investment Service, and that soon after the cash tender offer you are requested by your supervisor to review the potential acquisition of Kraft and assess its impact on Philip Morris' credit standing. You assemble various information using the projected Year 8 and Year 9 financial data reproduced below:

PHILIP MORRIS COMPANIES, INC.
Projected Financial Data
($ millions)

		Year 9 Estimate			
	Year 8 Estimate Excluding Kraft	*Before Kraft*	*Kraft Only*	*Adjustments*	*Consolidated*
Selected Income Statement Data					
Sales:					
Domestic tobacco	$ 8,300	$ 8,930			$ 8,930
International tobacco	8,000	8,800			8,800
General Foods	10,750	11,600			11,600
Kraft			$11,610		11,610
Beer	3,400	3,750			3,750
Total sales	$30,450	$33,080	$11,610		$44,690
Operating income:					
Domestic tobacco	$ 3,080	$ 3,520		$ 35	$ 3,555
International tobacco	800	940			940
General Foods	810	870			870
Kraft			$ 1,050	50	1,100
Beer	190	205			205
Other	105	125			125
Goodwill amortization	(110)	(110)		(295)	(405)
Total operating income	$ 4,875	$ 5,550	$ 1,050	$ (210)	$ 6,390
Percent of sales	16.0%	16.8%	9.0%		14.3%
Interest expense	(575)	(500)	(75)	(1,025)	(1,600)
Corporate expense	(200)	(225)	(100)	(40)	(365)
Other expense	(5)	(5)			(5)
Pre-tax income	$ 4,095	$ 4,820	$ 875	$(1,275)	$ 4,420
Percent of sales	13.4%	14.6%	7.5%		9.9%
Income taxes	$(1,740)	$(2,000)	$ (349)	$ 493	$(1,856)
Tax rate	42.5%	41.5%	40.0%		42.0%
Net income	$ 2,355	$ 2,820	$ 526	$ (782)	$ 2,564
Selected Balance Sheet Data at End of Year 8					
Short-term debt	$ 1,125	$ 1,100	$ 683		$ 1,783
Long-term debt	4,757	3,883	895	$11,000	15,778
Stockholders' equity	8,141	9,931	2,150	(2,406)	9,675

Other Selected Financial Data					
Depreciation and amortization	720	750	190	295	1,235
Deferred taxes	100	100	10	280	390
Equity in undistributed earnings of unconsolidated subsidiaries	110	125			125

Required:

a. You arrange a visit with Philip Morris management. Given the information you have assembled above, identify and discuss five major industry considerations you should pursue when questioning management.

b. Additional information is collected showing median ratio values along with their bond rating category for three financial ratios. Using this information reported in the excerpt below, along with the projections above:

1. Calculate these same three ratios for Philip Morris for Year 9 using:
   i. Amounts *before* accounting for the Kraft acquisition.
   ii. Consolidated amounts *after* the Kraft acquisition.
2. Discuss and interpret the two sets of ratios from part 1 compared to the median values for each bond rating category. Determine and support your recommendation on a rating category for Philip Morris *after* the Kraft acquisition.

(CFA Adapted)

Additional Information:
Median Ratio Values According to Bond Rating Categories

Ratio	*AAA*	*AA*	*A*	*BBB*	*BB*	*B*	*CCC*
Pre-tax interest coverage	14.10	9.67	5.40	3.63	2.25	1.58	(0.42)
Long-term debt as a percent of capitalization	11.5%	18.7%	28.3%	34.3%	48.4%	57.2%	73.2%
Cash flow* as a percent of total debt	111.8%	86.0%	50.9%	34.2%	22.8%	14.1%	6.2%

*For the purpose of calculating this ratio, Standard & Poor's defines *cash flow* as net income plus depreciation, amortization, and deferred taxes, less equity in undistributed earnings of unconsolidated subsidiaries.
Source: Standard & Poor's.

Case 10–3
Comprehensive Analysis of Creditworthiness

Assume you are an analyst at a brokerage firm. One of the companies you follow is ABEX Chemicals, Inc., which is rapidly growing into a major producer of petrochemicals (principally polyethylene). You are uneasy about competitors in the petrochemical business, their aggressive expansion, and the possibility of a recession in the next year or two. In response, you compile a summary of relevant industry statistics. Your analysis suggests prices of petrochemicals produced by ABEX will likely decline over the next 12 to 18 months. Primarily for this reason, you consider ABEX's credit standing as risky. You also note that ABEX common stock recently declined from $15 to $9 per share. Because of this price decline and subsequent stability, you extend your credit analysis of ABEX. You focus on the external environment, company fundamentals, and stock price behavior. A description of your findings follows:

External environment. While uncertainty about the economy persists, you conclude the key issue for the petrochemical industry is not demand but overcapacity. As revealed in Exhibit I, polyethylene production is expected to remain flat in Year 10 and capacity to increase, causing operating rates to fall. The result is increased competition and lower product prices. In the long run you expect use of polyethylene to grow 4 percent per annum and prices to rise 5 percent per annum, beginning in Year 12.

Company fundamentals. ABEX's operating earnings depend primarily on two businesses: pipeline distribution of natural gas (gas transmission) and petrochemical production. The gas transmission business is declining due to lower gas production and price constraints, but your outlook is for modest increases in volume and transmission rates. Your summary of key statistics for pipeline operations is included in Exhibit I. The more unpredictable component of ABEX's operating income is the petrochemical operation. Operating earnings from petrochemicals are sensitive to selling price, production costs, and volume of polyethylene sales. A key to estimating operating earnings is estimation of future prices and costs, and ABEX's market share. ABEX's management is confident their lower cost structure makes them price competitive and permits a higher capacity operating rate than their competitors. Exhibit I includes a summary of key statistics for polyethylene operations.

Stock price evaluation. Some investors value companies using discounted cash flows, but you are increasingly emphasizing the quality of cash flow, earning power, yield, book value, and earnings components. You also assemble financial statements and key financial ratios for ABEX (see Exhibits II–IV).

EXHIBIT I

Total U.S. Polyethylene Capacity, Production, and Prices

	Year 5	*Year 6*	*Year 7*	*Year 8*	*Year 9*	*Projected Year 10*	*Projected Year 11*	*Compound Annual Growth*
Total production (lbs. millions)	15,600	16,100	17,600	18,900	19,700	19,700	19,800	
Growth rate	7.6%	3.2%	9.3%	7.4%	4.2%	0.0%	0.5%	4.5%
Total capacity (lbs. millions)	17,600	17,700	18,600	20,100	21,200	23,400	24,300	
Growth rate	2.9%	0.6%	5.1%	8.1%	5.5%	10.4%	3.8%	5.2%
Capacity operating rate	88.6%	91.0%	94.6%	94.0%	92.9%	84.2%	81.5%	
Average price per pound	$0.41	$0.37	$0.36	$0.51	$0.52	$0.47	$0.57	
Percent change	–9.8%	–10.8%	–2.7%	24.4%	2.0%	–9.6%	21.3%	1.2%

ABEX CHEMICALS, INC.
Selected Key Statistics

	Year 5	*Year 6*	*Year 7*	*Year 8*	*Year 9*	*Projected Year 10*
Polyethylene operations:						
Production (lbs. millions)	1,840	1,975	2,870	4,835	5,000	4,950
Approximate capacity (lbs. millions)	1,900	2,100	2,950	5,000	5,500	5,500
Capacity operating rate	97%	94%	97%	97%	91%	90%
Average price received	$0.411	$0.367	$0.356	$0.511	$0.515	$0.470
Average cost/pound produced	$0.338	$0.307	$0.285	$0.350	$0.394	$0.370
Pipeline transportation operations:						
$/1,000 cubic feet (price)	$0.286	$0.253	$0.248	$0.221	$0.192	$0.187
Gas transported (trillion cubic feet)	4.64	4.88	4.67	5.00	5.85	6.29
Operating profit margin	25.6%	27.2%	27.3%	25.9%	26.8%	27.0%

Required:

Your firm's fixed income portfolio manager asks you to further extend your investigation of ABEX. The manager wants your assessment of whether the credit quality (risk) of ABEX's debt has changed during the most recent three years—Year 7 through Year 9. You decide to analyze key financial ratios for ABEX, focusing on areas of asset protection, short-term liquidity, and earning power.

a. Identify *five ratios* from Exhibit IV relevant to at least one of these three areas of analysis. Discuss and interpret both levels and trends in these five key ratios from Year 7 through Year 9.

b. Compare and analyze the pipeline and petrochemical divisions using three *qualitative* measures relevant to ABEX's credit quality for the period Year 7 through Year 9.

c. Using your analysis from *(a)* and *(b)*, discuss whether ABEX's credit quality has changed from Year 7 through Year 9.

(CFA Adapted)

EXHIBIT II

ABEX CHEMICALS, INC.
Consolidated Income Statements
($ millions)

	Year 5	*Year 6*	*Year 7*	*Year 8*	*Year 9*
Revenues:					
Petrochemicals	$ 757	$ 725	$ 1,021	$ 2,472	$ 2,575
Pipelines	1,328	1,235	1,156	1,106	1,123
Total revenues	$ 2,085	$ 1,960	$ 2,177	$ 3,578	$ 3,698
Operating costs:*					
Petrochemicals	(622)	(607)	(818)	(1,691)	(1,970)
Pipelines	(988)	(899)	(840)	(820)	(822)
Total operating costs	$(1,610)	$(1,506)	$(1,658)	$(2,511)	$(2,792)
Operating income:					
Petrochemicals	135	118	203	781	605
Pipelines	340	336	316	286	301
Total operating income	$ 475	$ 454	$ 519	$ 1,067	$ 906
Interest on long-term debt:					
Petrochemicals	(60)	(84)	(78)	(211)	(266)
Pipelines	(169)	(166)	(166)	(172)	(178)
Total interest expense	$ (299)	$ (250)	$ (244)	$ (383)	$ (444)
Administrative expenses	(22)	(24)	(23)	(28)	(40)
Rental expenses	(15)	(17)	(17)	(20)	(22)
Income from investments	25	8	4	7	4
Earnings before taxes	$ 234	$ 171	$ 239	$ 643	$ 405
Income taxes:					
Current	(78)	(30)	(45)	(40)	(44)
Deferred	(23)	(35)	(67)	(201)	(136)
Total taxes	$ (101)	$ (65)	$ (112)	$ (241)	$ (180)
Net income	133	106	127	402	225
Preferred dividends	(77)	(74)	(26)	(17)	(17)
Net available for common	$ 56	$ 32	$ 101	$ 385	$ 208
Average shares outstanding† (millions)	128	135	185	231	253
Basic earnings per common share	$0.44	$0.24	$0.54	$1.67	$0.82
Common dividends per share	0.40	0.40	0.40	0.40	0.50
Cash flow per common share	2.52	2.44	2.26	3.85	2.85

*Operating costs are costs of goods sold including depreciation as follows ($ millions):

Depreciation:					
Petrochemicals	$ 48	$ 60	$ 62	$135	$233
Pipelines	96	95	97	98	102
Total depreciation	$144	$155	$159	$233	$335

†Year 10 estimate is 305 million shares outstanding.

EXHIBIT III

ABEX CHEMICALS, INC.
Consolidated Balance Sheets
($ millions)

	Year 5	*Year 6*	*Year 7*	*Year 8*	*Year 9*
Assets					
Current assets:					
Cash & short-term investments	$ 45	$ 48	$ 74	$ 102	$ 133
Accounts receivable	279	300	414	868	923
Inventories	125	121	128	501	535
Total current assets	$ 449	$ 469	$ 616	$1,471	$1,591
Investments & other assets	631	380	167	252	400
Goodwill	35	90	105	330	560
Property, plant, & equipment:					
Petrochemicals	1,184	1,245	1,323	2,670	3,275
Pipelines	2,282	2,484	2,547	2,540	2,530
Total assets	$4,581	$4,668	$4,758	$7,263	$8,356
Liabilities					
Current liabilities:					
Bank indebtedness	$ 226	$ 77	$ 72	$ 215	$ 245
Accounts payable & accrued liabilities	333	312	377	768	787
Current portion of long-term debt	99	70	76	86	136
Other current payables	35	33	32	34	54
Total current liabilities	$ 693	$ 492	$ 557	$1,103	$1,222
Long-term debt:					
Petrochemicals	553	743	721	2,017	2,176
Pipelines	1,686	1,648	1,638	1,702	1,725
Advances—gas contracts	115	135	186	290	210
Deferred income taxes	125	160	227	428	564
Total liabilities	$3,172	$3,178	$3,329	$5,540	$5,897
Shareholders' Equity					
Preferred shares	$ 861	$ 826	$ 329	$ 216	$ 216
Common shares & retained earnings	548	664	1,100	1,507	2,243
Total shareholders' equity	$1,409	$1,490	$1,429	$1,723	$2,459
Total liabilities & shareholders' equity	$4,581	$4,668	$4,758	$7,263	$8,356
Average shares outstanding (millions)*	128	135	185	231	253

*Year 10 estimate is 305 million shares outstanding.

EXHIBIT IV

ABEX CHEMICALS, INC.
Selected Financial Ratios

	Year 5	*Year 6*	*Year 7*	*Year 8*	*Year 9*
Petrochemicals operating margin	17.8%	16.3%	19.9%	31.6%	23.5%
Pipeline operating margin	25.6%	27.2%	27.3%	25.9%	26.8%
Return on assets (EBIT/total assets)	10.1%	9.0%	10.2%	14.1%	10.2%
Pre-tax profit margin	11.2%	8.7%	11.0%	18.0%	10.9%
Tax rate	43.0%	38.0%	46.9%	37.5%	44.4%
Petrochemicals asset turnover (sales/fixed assets)	0.64	0.58	0.77	0.93	0.79
Pipelines asset turnover (sales/fixed assets)	0.58	0.50	0.45	0.44	0.44
Turnover (sales/total assets)	0.46	0.42	0.46	0.49	0.44
Debt to common equity	4.30	3.80	2.31	2.66	1.83
Net tangible assets to long-term debt	58.4%	55.4%	52.0%	34.7%	46.2%
Long-term debt to total capitalization	62.6%	62.9%	64.0%	70.0%	62.6%
Total assets to total shareholders' equity	3.25	3.13	3.33	4.22	3.40
Pre-tax interest coverage	1.63	1.46	1.80	2.54	1.84
Operating cash flow to long-term debt	20.2%	18.0%	20.4%	26.6%	22.1%
Collection period	48 days	55 days	68 days	87 days	90 days
Inventory turnover	11.0	11.0	12.0	7.2	4.7
Short-term debt to total debt	12.1%	5.5%	5.8%	7.5%	9.3%
Petrochemicals average cost of long-term debt	10.9%	11.3%	10.8%	10.5%	12.2%
Pipeline average cost of long-term debt	10.0%	10.1%	10.1%	10.1%	10.3%
Average cost of preferreds	8.9%	9.0%	7.9%	7.9%	7.9%

INTERNET ACTIVITIES

Internet 10–1 Market Values in Ratio Analysis

Access one of the financial statement databases available on the Internet (http://www.mhhe.com/business/accounting/wild). Retrieve current financial statements of a company selected by either you or your instructor.

Required:

a. Using the company's average (or average of high and low) common stock market price for the most recent year in computing common equity, calculate the (1) total debt to equity ratio, (2) long-term debt to equity ratio, and (3) financial leverage ratio.

b. Discuss the importance and significance of ratios that use equity capital at market value.

Internet 10–2 Financial Leverage Index Analysis

Access one of the financial statement databases available on the Internet (http://www.mhhe.com/business/accounting/wild). Retrieve current financial statements of three companies in different industries selected by either you or your instructor.

Required:

Compute the financial leverage indexes for these companies (use their effective tax rates). Interpret the financial leverage index for each of these companies and discuss any differences.

Internet 10–3

Solvency Ratios in Financial Analysis

Access one of the financial statement databases available on the Internet (http://www.mhhe.com/business/accounting/wild). Retrieve current financial statements of a company selected by either you or your instructor.

Required:

a. Compute the ratios listed in Problem 10–1 (a) for the most recent two years of this company. Assume a statutory income tax rate of 35 percent for all ratios except the fixed charge coverage ratios where you should use the effective tax rate. Consider any deferred taxes as liabilities. Assume fixed charges include any interest portion of operating rental expense which equals one-third of the operating lease expense.

b. Discuss the importance of analyzing both the level and trend of the ratios in (*a*).

Internet 10–4

Capital Structure and Solvency

Access one of the financial statement databases available on the Internet (http://www.mhhe.com/business/accounting/wild). Retrieve current financial statements of a company selected by either you or your instructor.

Required:

a. Perform a comprehensive analysis of the company's capital structure and solvency. Your analysis should (at a minimum) include analysis and interpretation of the measures listed in Case 10–1(*a*).

b. In analyzing capital structure and solvency for this company, what adjustments to the book values of liabilities and assets would you make? Be specific.

C H A P T E R

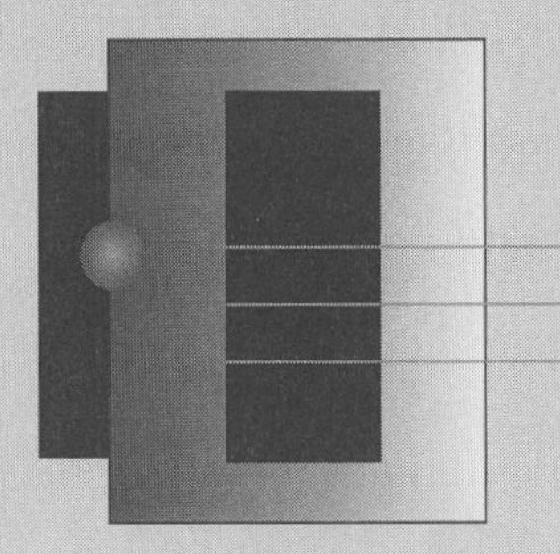

11

Return on Invested Capital

Learning Objectives

- Describe the usefulness of return measures in financial statement analysis.
- Explain return on invested capital and variations in its computation.
- Analyze return on total assets and its relevance in our analysis.
- Describe disaggregation of return on assets and the importance of its components.
- Analyze return on common shareholders' equity and its role in our analysis.
- Describe disaggregation of return on common shareholders' equity and the relevance of its components.
- Explain financial leverage and how to assess a company's success in trading on the equity by individual financing sources.

A Look Back

The previous three chapters focused primarily on risk. We analyzed a company's ability to cover both short- and long-term obligations. We described several useful analytical tools and applied them to illustrate their relevance for risk analysis. We explained also how capital structure affects the returns to shareholders.

A Look at This Chapter

This chapter focuses on return. We emphasize return on invested capital and explain variations in its measurement. Special attention is directed at return on assets and return on common shareholders' equity. We explore disaggregations of both these return measures and describe their relevance to our analysis. Financial leverage is explained and analyzed using the return measures in this chapter.

A Look Ahead

Chapter 12 extends our analysis of return to focus on profitability. We analyze operating activities using several techniques, including component analysis, break-even analysis, gross profit analysis, and income tax analysis. We describe operating leverage and its implications for profitability.

PREVIEW OF CHAPTER 11

Return on invested capital is important in our analysis of financial statements. Financial statement analysis involves our assessing both risk and return. The prior three chapters focused primarily on risk, whereas this chapter extends our analysis to return. *Return on invested capital* refers to a company's earnings relative to both the level and source of financing. It is a measure of a company's success in using financing to generate profits, and is an excellent measure of a company's solvency risk. This chapter describes return on invested capital and its relevance to financial statement analysis. We also explain variations in measurement of return on invested capital and their interpretation. We also disaggregate return on invested capital into important components for additional insights into company performance and future operations. The role of financial leverage and its importance for returns analysis is examined. This chapter demonstrates each of these analysis techniques using financial statement data. The content and organization of this chapter are as follows:

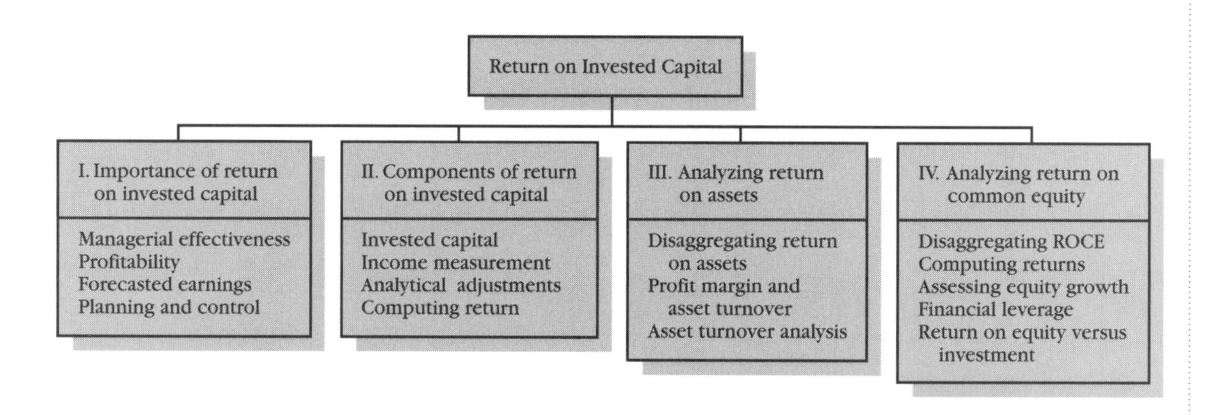

Importance of Return on Invested Capital

We can analyze company performance in several possible ways. Revenue, gross profit, and net income are performance measures in common use. Yet none of these measures *individually* are useful as a comprehensive measure of company performance. The reason stems from their interdependency and the interdependency of business activities. For example, increases in revenue are desirable only if they increase profits. The same applies to sales volume. To assess gross profit or net income we must relate them to invested capital. For example, a profit of $1 million is assessed differently if a company's invested capital is $2 million or $200 million.

Analysis of company performance demands *joint* analysis, where we assess one measure relative to another. The relation between income and invested capital, referred to as **return on invested capital** or *return on investment (ROI)*, is probably the most widely recognized measure of company performance. It allows us to compare companies on their success with invested capital. It also allows us to assess a company's return relative to its capital investment risk, and we can compare the return on invested capital to returns of alternative investments. Government treasury bonds reflect a minimum return due to their low risk. Riskier investments are expected to yield higher returns. Analysis of return on invested capital compares a company's income, or other performance measure, to the company's level and source of financing. It determines a company's ability to succeed, attract financing, repay creditors, and reward owners. We use return on invested capital in several areas of our analysis including: (1) managerial effectiveness, (2) level of profitability, (3) earnings forecasting, and (4) planning and control.

Measuring Managerial Effectiveness

The level of return on invested capital depends primarily on the skill, resourcefulness, ingenuity, and motivation of management. Management is responsible for a company's business activities. It makes financing, investing, and operating decisions. It selects actions, plans strategies, and executes plans. Return on invested capital, especially when computed over intervals of a year or longer, is a relevant measure of a company's managerial effectiveness.

Measuring Profitability

Return on invested capital is an important indicator of a company's long-term financial strength. It uses key summary measures from both the income statement (profits) and the balance sheet (financing) to assess profitability. This profitability measure has several advantages over other long-term measures of financial strength or solvency that rely on only balance sheet items (e.g., debt to equity ratio). It can effectively convey the return on invested capital from varying perspectives of different financing contributors (creditors and shareholders). It is also helpful in short-term liquidity analysis.

Measure of Forecasted Earnings

Return on invested capital is useful in earnings forecasting. This measure effectively links past, current, and forecasted earnings with total invested capital. Its use in our analysis and forecasting of earnings adds discipline and realism. It identifies overly optimistic or pessimistic forecasts relative to competitors' returns on invested capital, and it yields managerial assessments of financing sources when forecasts are different from expectations. Expectations are determined from historical and incremental rates of return, projected changes in company and business conditions, and expected returns for new projects. Return on invested capital is used as either a primary or supplementary means of earnings forecasting and to evaluate the reasonableness of forecasts from other sources.

Measure for Planning and Control

Return on invested capital serves an important role in planning, budgeting, coordinating, evaluating, and controlling business activities. This return is comprised of the returns (and losses) achieved by the company's segments or divisions. These segment returns are also comprised of the returns achieved by individual product lines, projects, and other components. A well-managed company exercises control over returns achieved by each of its profit centers and rewards its managers on these results. In evaluating investing alternatives, management assesses performance relative to expected returns. Out of this assessment come strategic decisions and action plans for the company.

ANALYSIS VIEWPOINT . . . *You are the auditor*

You are the audit manager responsible for substantive audit tests of a manufacturing client. Your analytical procedures reveal a 3 percent increase in sales from $2 to $2.06 (millions) and a 4 percent decrease in total expenses from $1.9 to $1.824 (millions). Both changes are within your "reasonableness" criterion of ±5 percent. Accordingly, you do not expand audit tests of these accounts. The audit partner in charge questions your lack of follow-up on these deviations and expressly mentions *joint* analysis. What is the audit partner referring to?

Components of Return on Invested Capital

Analyzing company performance using return on invested capital is conceptually sound and appealing. **Return on invested capital** is computed as:

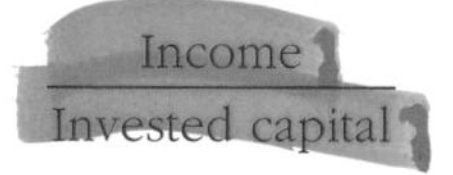

$$\frac{\text{Income}}{\text{Invested capital}}$$

There is, however, not complete agreement on the computation of either the numerator or denominator in this relation. These differences are valid and stem from the diverse perspectives of financial statement users. This section describes these differences and explains how different computations are relevant to different users or analyses. We begin with a discussion of invested capital, followed by consideration of income.

Invested Capital for a Typical Company

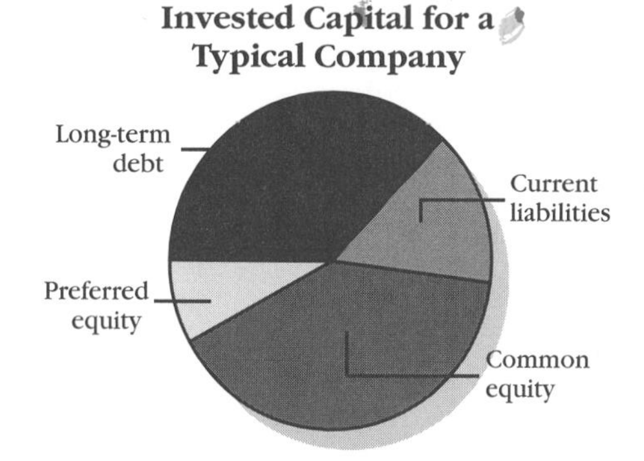

Defining Invested Capital

There is no universal measure of invested capital from which to compute rate of return. Return on invested capital reflects fundamental and accepted concepts of income and financing levels. The different measures of invested capital used reflect users' different perspectives. In this section we describe different measures of invested capital and explain their relevance to different users and interpretations.

Total Debt and Equity Capital

A company's return can be assessed from the perspective of its total financing base—*liabilities plus equity,* or simply *total assets.* This **return on total assets** is a relevant measure of operating efficiency. It reflects a company's return from all assets (or financing) entrusted to it. This measure does not distinguish return by financing sources. By removing the effect of financing of assets, our analysis can concentrate on evaluating or forecasting operating performance. The total asset base for computing return on invested capital is sometimes subject to adjustments. We describe three types of adjustments below.

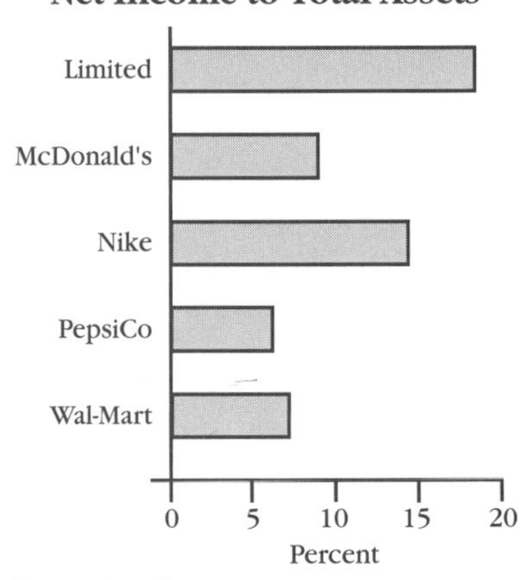

Source: Annual reports.

Unproductive Asset Adjustment. One type of adjustment relates to unproductive assets. The *unproductive asset adjustment* removes idle plant, facilities under construction, surplus plant, surplus inventories, surplus cash, and deferred charges from the invested capital base. These exclusions assume management is not responsible for earning a return on invested capital not in operations. While this argument is sometimes valid for internal analysis as a management and control tool, it is not justified when used to evaluate overall management effectiveness. Management is entrusted with funds by shareholders and creditors, and it has discretion over their investment. Management can dispose of assets with no return and repay creditors or pay dividends. If there are reasons for maintaining these investments, then there is no reason to exclude them from invested capital. Moreover, if long-run profitability benefits by maintaining these assets, then longer-term return reflects these benefits. Accordingly, our external analysis should not typically remove assets from invested capital because they are unproductive or fail to earn a return.

Intangible Asset Adjustment. Another type of adjustment excludes intangible assets from invested capital. This adjustment derives from skepticism regarding their value or earnings contribution to a company. In practice, intangibles are reported at amortized cost. If this cost exceeds their future utility, they are written down or sometimes reported with an "uncertainty reference" regarding their value in the auditor's report. Similar to our discussion for unproductive assets, this adjustment lacks merit. Excluding intangible assets from invested capital must be justified on substantive evidence and not lack of information or unsupported suspicion on their value.

Accumulated Depreciation Adjustment. A third adjustment relates to whether the invested capital base includes an addback for accumulated depreciation on depreciable assets (note that earnings are still reported *net* of depreciation). This adjustment is sometimes referred to as the *Du Pont method* due to its endorsement from that same company as an internal management tool. Advocates argue that since plant assets are maintained in prime working condition during their useful life, it is inappropriate to assess return relative to *net* assets. They also argue if accumulated depreciation is not added back, earnings in succeeding periods relate to an ever-decreasing investment base. Accordingly, even with stable earnings, return on investment continually rises and would fail to reveal true company performance. Relating earnings to invested capital that is stable would arguably offer a sound basis for comparing profitability of assets employed across years. This addback also compensates for the effects of inflation on assets expressed at historical cost. In our discussion of price-level accounting in Supplement C, we show that price-level adjustments are valid only with a complete restatement of financial statements. Crude adjustments like these are likely misleading and often worse than no adjustment.

In evaluating the Du Pont method we must remember its focus on the internal control of separate productive units and of operating management. Our analysis is different, focusing on the operating performance of an entire company. For analysis of an entire company, it is better to not add back accumulated depreciation to invested capital. This is consistent with computation of income net of depreciation expense. The increase in return due to decreasing depreciable assets is offset by the acquisition of new depreciable assets through capital recovered from depreciation. These new assets must also earn a return. We must also recognize that maintenance and repair costs commonly increase as assets age, tending to offset the reduction (if any) in the invested capital base.

Long-Term Debt Plus Equity Capital

Another computation of invested capital includes long-term debt capital and equity capital, often referred to as long-term capitalization. This computation differs from total debt and equity capital by excluding current liability financing. The aim of this calculation is to focus on the two main suppliers of long-term financing—long-term creditors and equity shareholders.

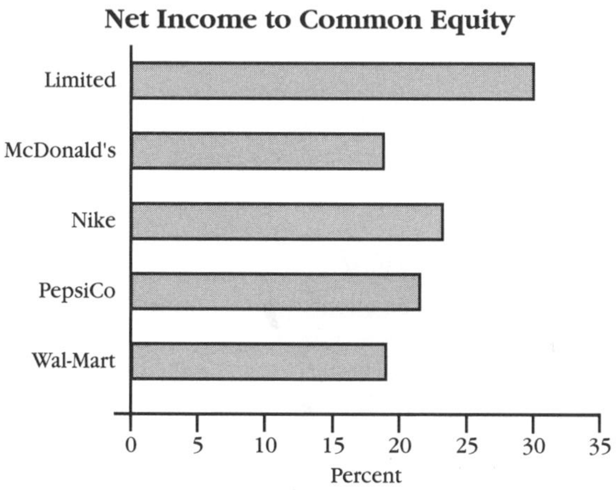

Net Income to Common Equity

Source: Annual reports.

Equity Capital

Our use of equity capital as the definition of invested capital gives us a measure of the return on shareholders' equity. This implies a focus on the return to equity holders. As we discussed in the context of financial leverage in the previous chapter, return on equity captures the effect of leverage (debt) capital on shareholders' return. Since preferred stock typically receives a fixed return, we exclude it from our calculation of equity capital.

Book versus Market Value of Invested Capital

Return on invested capital is typically computed using reported values from financial statements rather than market values. Yet market values are sometimes more relevant for our analysis because certain assets are not recognized in financial statements (patents, trademarks, reputation, human resources). Additionally, earnings by companies are sometimes delayed due to overly conservative accounting recognition criteria. One adjustment is to use the market value of invested capital. This adjustment substitutes the market value of invested capital (debt and equity) for its reported value in computing return.

Investor versus Company Invested Capital

In computing return on invested capital, we must distinguish between a company's invested capital and an investor's invested capital. An investor's invested capital is the price paid for a company's securities. Except when an investor acquires securities at book value, an investor's invested capital differs from the company's invested capital. Our analysis of return on invested capital focuses on the company and not on individual shareholders. Later in this chapter we come back to this issue and focus on shareholder return.

Computing Invested Capital for the Period

Regardless of our *invested capital* definition, we compare the return for the period with its investment base. The invested capital for the period is typically computed using the *average* capital available to a company during the period. An average is used to reflect changes in invested capital during the period. The most common method is adding beginning and ending year invested capital and dividing by 2. We must use care in applying averaging. Companies in certain industries choose a "natural" rather than calendar business year. For example, in retailing the natural business year ends when inventories and sales are low (e.g., January 31 after the holiday season). In this case, averaging year-ends yields the lowest rather than the average invested capital during the period. A more accurate method is to average interim amounts—for example, adding month-end invested capital amounts and dividing by 12.

Defining Income

Our analysis of return on invested capital requires a measure of **income.** The definition of *income,* or *return,* depends on our definition of *invested capital.* If *invested capital* is defined as total debt and equity capital, then income *before* interest expense is used. Excluding interest from income is necessary because interest is viewed as payment to suppliers of debt capital. Similar reasoning is used to exclude dividends—viewed as payments to suppliers of equity capital. Hence, income *before* interest expense and dividends is used when computing both return on assets and return on long-term debt plus equity capital (assuming interest expense is from long-term debt).

The income of a consolidated company that includes a subsidiary that is partially owned by a minority interest typically reflects a deduction for the minority's share of income. The company's consolidated balance sheet, however, includes the subsidiary's assets. Since invested capital (denominator) includes assets of the consolidated company, income (numerator) should include total company income (or loss), not just the parent's share. For this reason we add back the minority's share of earnings (or loss) to income when computing return on assets. When we define *invested capital* (denominator) as equity capital excluding minority interest, we need *not* add back the minority's share of earnings (or loss) to income.

Return on common equity capital uses income defined as net income *after* deductions for interest and preferred dividends. If preferred dividends are cumulative, they are deducted in computing income whether these dividends are declared or not. This is because common shareholders' claims are junior to preferred shareholders.

Measures of income in computing return on invested capital must reflect all applicable expenses including income taxes. Some users exclude income taxes in their computations. These users claim it is to isolate the effects of tax management from operating performance. Others claim changes in tax rates affect comparability across years. Still others claim companies with tax loss carryforwards add confusion and complications to return on invested capital computations. We must recognize that income taxes reduce a company's income and we should include them in measuring income, especially for the return on shareholders' equity. Later in the chapter we disaggregate return on invested capital where one component reflects the company's tax situation.

Adjustments to Invested Capital and Income

Our analysis of return on invested capital uses reported financial statement numbers as a starting point. As we discussed in several prior chapters, certain accounting numbers call for analytical adjustment. Also certain numbers not reported in financial statements need to be included. Much of our discussion in Chapter 10 regarding accounting adjustments is applicable here. Some adjustments, like those relating to inventory, affect both the numerator and denominator of return on invested capital, moderating their effect.

Computing Return on Invested Capital

This section applies our discussion to an analysis of return on invested capital. We illustrate the different measures of both income and invested capital for the computations. For this purpose, we draw on the financial statements of Excell Corporation reproduced in Exhibits 11.1 and 11.2. Our return on invested capital computations below are for Year 9 and use amounts rounded to the nearest million.

Return on Total Assets

Return on assets (both debt and equity capital) of Excell Corporation for Year 9 is computed as:

$$\frac{\text{Net income} + \text{Interest expense}\,(1 - \text{Tax rate}) + \text{Minority interest in income}}{(\text{Beginning total assets} + \text{Ending total assets}) \div 2}$$

$$\frac{\$64{,}569 + \$20{,}382\,(1 - 0.40) + \$0}{(\$1{,}333{,}982 + \$1{,}371{,}621) \div 2} = 5.677\%$$

Our tax adjustment of interest expense recognizes interest is tax deductible. This implies that if interest expense is excluded, the related tax benefit must be excluded from income. We assume a *marginal* corporate tax rate of 40 percent—the tax incidence with respect to any one item (like interest expense) can be measured by the marginal tax rate. There is no minority interest in the income of Excell, and the assets are averaged using year-end figures.

Return on Long-Term Debt Plus Equity

Return on long-term debt plus equity, also called *return on long-term capitalization,* of Excell Corporation for Year 9 is computed as:

EXHIBIT 11.1

EXCELL CORPORATION
Income Statement
For Years Ended December 31, Year 8, and Year 9
($ thousands)

	Year 8	*Year 9*
Net sales	$1,636,298	$1,723,729
Costs and expenses	1,473,293	1,579,401
Operating income	$ 163,005	$ 144,328
Other income, net	2,971	1,784
Income before interest and taxes	$ 165,976	$ 146,112
Interest expense*	16,310	20,382
Income before taxes	$ 149,666	$ 125,730
Less federal and other income taxes	71,770	61,161
Net income	$ 77,896	$ 64,569
Less cash dividends:		
Preferred stock	2,908	2,908
Common stock	39,209	38,898
Net income reinvested in the business	$ 35,779	$ 22,763

*In Year 9, interest on long-term debt is $19,695.

EXHIBIT 11.2

EXCELL CORPORATION
Balance Sheet
At December 31, Year 8, and Year 9
($ thousands)

	Year 8	*Year 9*
Assets		
Current assets:		
Cash	$ 25,425	$ 25,580
Marketable securities	38,008	28,910
Accounts and notes receivable—net	163,870	176,911
Inventories	264,882	277,795
Total current assets	$ 492,185	$ 509,196
Investments in and receivables from nonconsolidated subsidiaries	33,728	41,652
Miscellaneous investments and receivables	5,931	6,997
Funds held by trustee for construction	6,110	—
Land, buildings, equipment, and timberlands—net	773,361	790,774
Deferred charges to future operations	16,117	16,452
Goodwill and other intangible assets	6,550	6,550
Total assets	$1,333,982	$1,371,621
Liabilities		
Current liabilities:		
Notes payable to banks	$ 7,850	$ 13,734
Accounts payable and accrued expenses	128,258	144,999
Dividends payable	10,404	10,483
Federal and other taxes on income	24,370	13,256
Long-term indebtedness payable within one year	9,853	11,606
Total current liabilities	$ 180,735	$ 194,078
Long-term indebtedness	350,565	335,945
Deferred taxes on income	86,781	101,143
Total liabilities	$ 618,081	$ 631,166
Equity		
Preferred, 7% cumulative and noncallable, par value $25 per share; authorized 1,760,000 shares	$ 41,538	$ 41,538
Common, par value $12.50 per share; authorized 30,000,000 shares	222,245	222,796
Capital in excess of par value	19,208	20,448
Retained earnings	436,752	459,515
Less: Common treasury stock	(3,842)	(3,842)
Total equity	$ 715,901	$ 740,455
Total liabilities and equity	$1,333,982	$1,371,621

$$\frac{\text{Net income} + \text{Interest expense}\,(1 - \text{Tax rate}) + \text{Minority interest in income}}{(\text{Average long-term debt} + \text{Average equity})}$$

$$\frac{\$64{,}569 + \$20{,}382\,(1 - 0.40) + \$0}{(\$437{,}088 + \$715{,}901 + \$437{,}346 + \$740{,}455) \div 2} = 6.59\%$$

Decisions of how to classify items like deferred taxes between debt and equity must be made following our discussion in Chapter 10. For Excell, deferred taxes are included in long-term liabilities. In computing return on long-term debt plus equity, there is no need to classify deferred taxes because this computation includes both debt and equity. A classification problem does arise when computing return on shareholders' equity. In the cases that follow, deferred taxes possess characteristics more like a long-term liability than equity. Yet we must always assess this in practice since its classification can significantly affect return.

Return on Common Shareholders' Equity

Return on common equity typically excludes from invested capital all but common shareholders' equity. The **return on common equity** of Excell Corporation for Year 9 is computed as:

$$\frac{\text{Net income} - \text{Preferred dividends}}{\text{Average common shareholders' equity}}$$

$$\frac{\$64,569 - \$2,908}{(\$674,363 + \$698,917) \div 2} = 8.98\%$$

Excell's higher return on common shareholders' equity as compared to its return on total assets reflects the favorable effects of financial leverage. Excell is successfully trading on the equity. There is another method to compute the return on common shareholders' equity using a ratio of two often reported figures as follows:

$$\frac{\text{Basic earnings per share}}{\text{Book value per share}}$$

The return from this latter computation is often slightly different due to rounding. When *convertible* debt sells at a substantial premium above par and is held by investors primarily for its conversion feature, there is justification for treating it as an equivalent of equity capital. This is especially true when a company has the right to force conversion by calling it in.

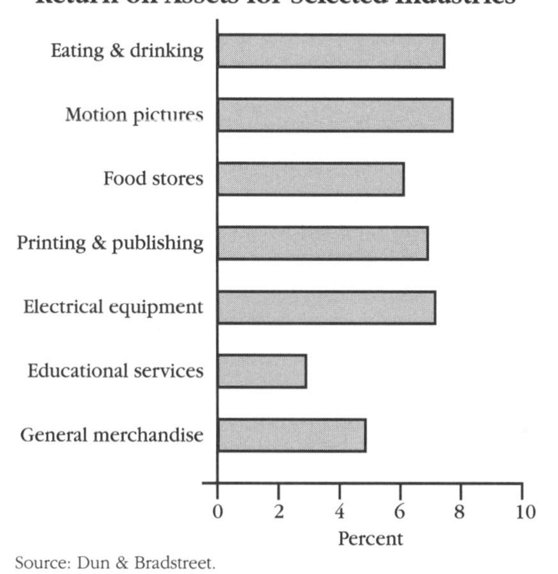

Source: Dun & Bradstreet.

Analyzing Return on Assets

Return on invested capital is useful in management evaluation, profitability analysis, earnings forecasting, and planning and control. Our use of return on invested capital for these tasks requires a thorough understanding of this return measure. This is because the return measure includes components with the potential to contribute to our understanding of company performance. This section examines this return when invested capital is viewed independently of its financing sources, using debt and equity capital (total assets), commonly referred to as **return on assets (ROA)**.

Disaggregating Return on Assets

Recall that the return on assets (or return on total capital) in its most *simplified form* is computed as:

$$\frac{\text{Income}}{\text{Assets}}$$

We can disaggregate this return into meaningful components relative to sales. We do this because these component ratios are useful in our analysis of company performance. Sales is an important criterion to judge company profitability and is a major indicator of company activity. This disaggregation of return on assets is:

Return on assets = Profit margin × Asset turnover

$$\frac{\text{Income}}{\text{Assets}} = \frac{\text{Income}}{\text{Sales}} \times \frac{\text{Sales}}{\text{Assets}}$$

The income to sales relation is called **profit margin** and measures a company's profitability relative to sales. The sales to assets relation is called **asset turnover** or **utilization** and measures a company's effectiveness in generating sales from assets. This decomposition highlights the role of these components, profit margin and asset turnover, in determining return on assets. Profit margin and asset turnover are useful measures that require our analysis to gain further insights into a company's profitability. We describe the major components determining return on assets in Exhibit 11.3. The "first level" of analysis focuses on the interaction of profit margin and asset turnover. The "second level" of analysis highlights other important factors determining profit margin and asset turnover. This section emphasizes the first level of analysis. The next two chapters explore the second level—Chapter 12 with analysis of operating results, and Chapter 13 with analysis and forecasting of earnings.

EXHIBIT 11.3 Disaggregating Return on Assets

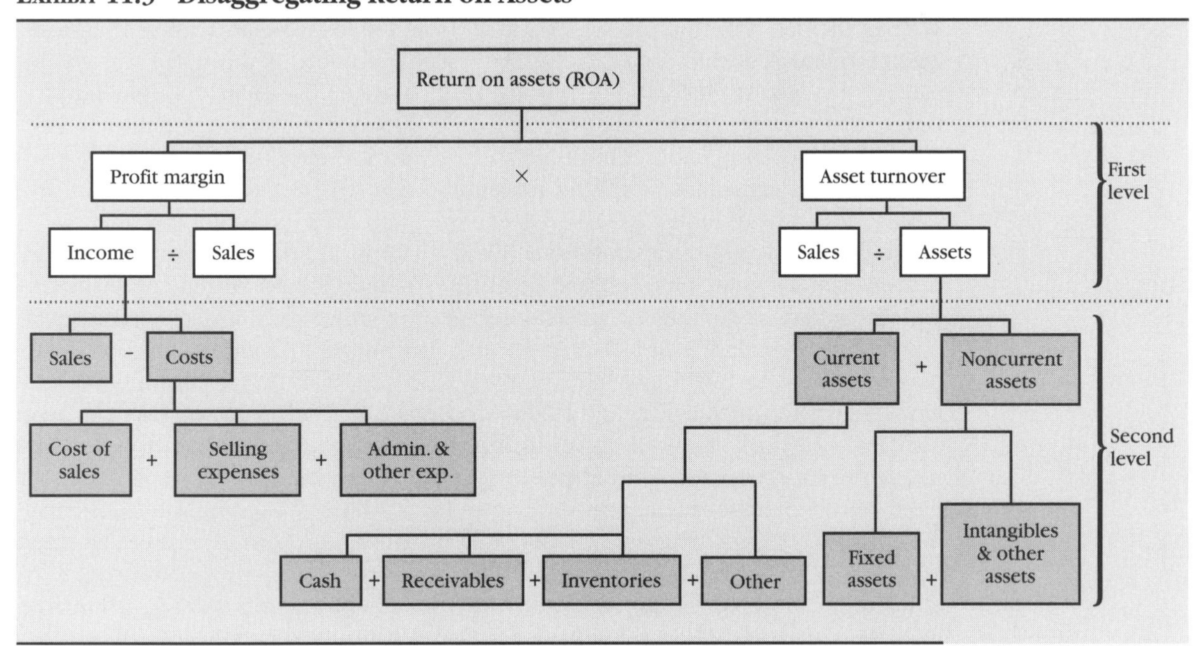

EXHIBIT 11.4 Analysis of Return on Assets

	Company X	*Company Y*	*Company Z*
Sales	$5,000,000	$10,000,000	$10,000,000
Income	500,000	500,000	100,000
Assets	5,000,000	5,000,000	1,000,000
Profit margin	10%	5%	1%
Asset turnover	1	2	10
Return on assets	10%	10%	10%

Relation between Profit Margin and Asset Turnover

The relation between profit margin and asset turnover is illustrated in Exhibit 11.4. As defined, return on assets (in percent) equals profit margin (in percent) multiplied by asset turnover. As Exhibit 11.4 shows, Company X achieves a 10 percent return on assets with a relatively high profit margin and a low asset turnover. In contrast, Company Z achieves the same return on assets but with a low profit margin and high asset turnover. Company Y's return is between these two companies, a 10 percent return with a profit margin one-half that of Company X and an asset turnover double that of Company X. This exhibit indicates there are many combinations of profit margins and asset turnovers yielding a 10 percent return on assets.

We can generalize the returns analysis of Exhibit 11.4 to show a continuous range of possible combinations of profit margins and asset turnovers yielding a 10 percent return on assets. Exhibit 11.5 portrays graphically this relation between profit margin (horizontal axis) and asset turnover (vertical axis). The curve drawn in this exhibit traces all combinations of profit margin and asset turnover yielding a 10 percent return on assets. This curve slopes from the upper left corner of low profit margin and high asset turnover to the lower right corner of high profit margin and low asset turnover. We plot the data from Companies X and Y (from Exhibit 11.4) in Exhibit 11.5—designated points X and Y, respectively. The remaining points A through P are combinations of profit margins and asset turnovers of other companies in a sample industry. Graphing returns of companies within an industry around the 10 percent return on asset curve (or other applicable return curve) is a valuable method of comparing profitability. More important, graphing reveals the relation between profit margin and asset turnover determining ROA and is extremely useful in our company analysis.

Disaggregating return on assets as in Exhibit 11.5 is useful in assessing companies' strategic actions to increase returns. Companies B and C must concentrate on restoring profitability. Assuming the industry represented in Exhibit 11.5 has a representative profit margin and asset turnover, the evidence suggests Company P should focus on improving asset turnover while Company D should focus on increasing profit margin. Other companies like H and I best concentrate on both profit margin and asset turnover. Our analysis to this point treats profit margin and asset turnover as independent. Yet profit margin and asset turnover are *interdependent*. As we stress in our discussion of break-even analysis in Chapter 12, when fixed expenses are substantial, a higher level of asset turnover increases profit margin. This is because in a certain range of activity, costs increase proportionally less than sales. In comparing companies in an industry, we must consider companies with low asset turnovers having potential to increase return through increased asset turnover (sales expansion).

EXHIBIT 11.5 Relation between Profit Margin, Asset Turnover, and Return on Assets

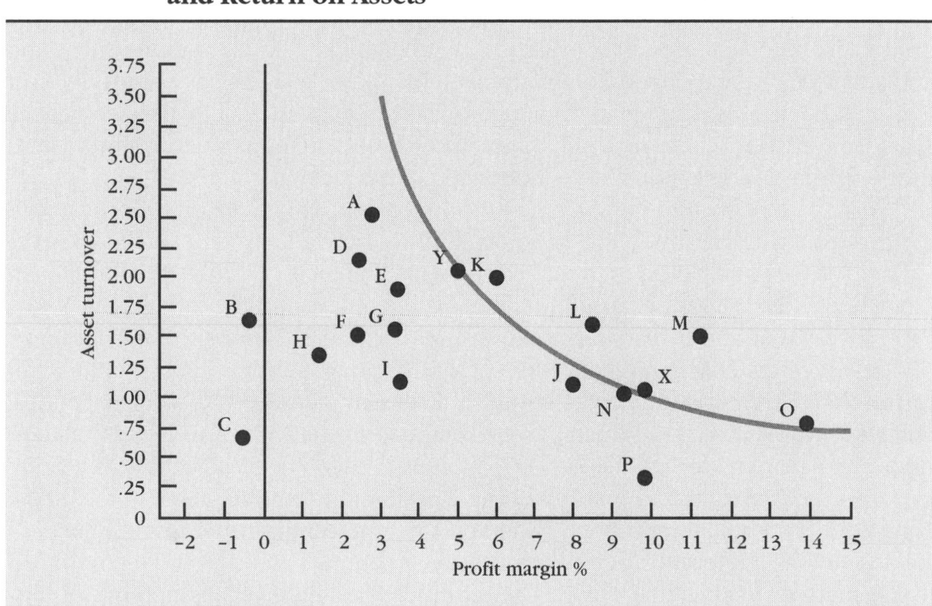

Analysis of return on assets can reveal additional insights into strategic activity. As another example, consider two companies in the same industry with identical returns on assets.

	Company AA	*Company BB*
Sales	$ 1,000,000	$20,000,000
Income	100,000	100,000
Assets	10,000,000	10,000,000
Profit margin	10%	0.5%
Asset turnover	0.1	2
Return on assets	1%	1%

Both companies' returns on assets are poor. Strategically, corrective action for each is different. Our analysis must evaluate the likelihood of managerial success and other factors in improving performance. Company AA has a 10 percent profit margin (near the industry average) while Company BB's is considerably lower. A dollar invested in assets supports only $0.10 in sales for Company AA, whereas Company BB achieves $2 in sales for each dollar invested. Our analysis focuses on Company AA's assets, asking questions such as: Why is turnover so low? Are there assets yielding little or no return? Are there idle assets requiring disposal? Are assets inefficiently or ineffectively utilized? Company AA can achieve immediate improvements by concentrating on increasing turnover (by increasing sales, reducing investment, or both). It is likely more difficult for Company AA to increase profit margin much beyond the industry norm.

Company BB confronts a much different scenario. Our analysis suggests Company BB should focus on correcting the low profit margin. Reasons for low profit margins are varied but often include inefficient equipment or production methods, unprofitable product lines, excess capacity with high fixed costs, or excessive selling and administrative expenses. Companies with low profit margins sometimes discover that changes in tastes and technology require increased investment in assets to finance sales. This implies that to maintain its return on assets, a company must increase its profit margin or else production is no longer moneymaking.

There is a tendency to view a high profit margin as a sign of high earnings quality. Yet we must emphasize the importance of return on invested capital (however defined) as the ultimate test of profitability. A supermarket is content with a profit margin of 1 percent or less because of its high asset turnover owing to a relatively low asset investment and a high proportion of leased assets (like stores and fixtures). Similarly, a discount store accepts a low profit margin to generate high asset turnover (primarily in inventories). In contrast, capital-intensive industries like steel, chemicals, and automobiles having large asset investments and low asset turnovers must achieve high profit margins to be successful. Exhibit 11.6 portrays graphically the relation between profit margin and asset turnover. This figure extends Exhibit 11.5 to show components for actual industries. We graph the 5 percent return on assets curve in Exhibit 11.6 as a reference point for analysis.

We must remember that analysis of returns for a single year is potentially misleading. The cyclical nature of many industries yields swings in profit margins where some years' profits can be excessive while others are not. Companies must be analyzed using returns computed over several years and spanning a business cycle.

EXHIBIT 11.6 Profit Margin, Asset Turnover, and Return on Assets for Selected Industries

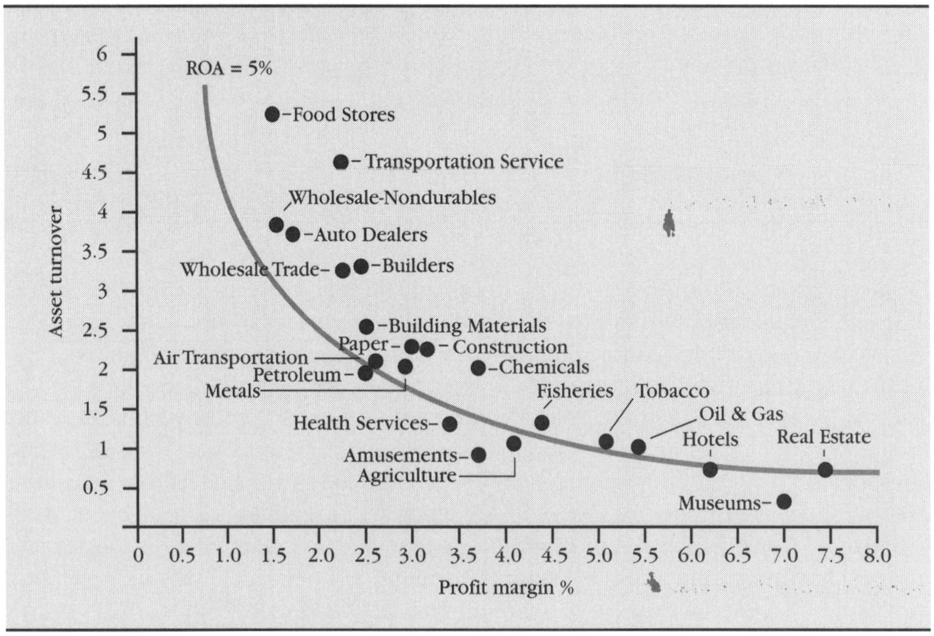

ROA = 5%
Food Stores
Transportation Service
Wholesale-Nondurables
Auto Dealers
Wholesale Trade
Builders
Building Materials
Paper
Construction
Air Transportation
Petroleum
Chemicals
Metals
Fisheries
Tobacco
Oil & Gas
Health Services
Hotels
Real Estate
Amusements
Agriculture
Museums
Asset turnover
0.5 1 1.5 2 2.5 3 3.5 4 4.5 5 5.5 6
0 0.5 1.0 1.5 2.0 2.5 3.0 3.5 4.0 4.5 5.0 5.5 6.0 6.5 7.0 7.5 8.0
Profit margin %

Source: Dun & Bradstreet.

Asset Turnover Analysis

Asset turnover measures the intensity with which companies utilize assets. The most relevant measure of asset utilization is the amount of sales generated because sales are essential to profits. In special cases like start-up or development companies, our analysis of turnover must recognize that most assets are committed to future business activities. Also, unusual supply problems or work stoppages are conditions affecting asset utilization and require special evaluation and interpretation. This section describes various analyses using disaggregation of asset turnover.

Disaggregation of Asset Turnover

The standard measure of asset turnover in determining return on assets is:

$$\frac{\text{Sales}}{\text{Assets}}$$

Further evaluation of changes in turnover rates for individual assets can be useful in our company analysis. This section examines asset turnover for *component asset accounts.*

Sales to Cash. Cash and cash equivalents are held primarily for purposes of meeting day-to-day transactions and as a liquidity reserve to prevent shortages arising from imbalances in cash inflows and outflows. All businesses have and must maintain a relation between sales and cash. A too high cash turnover can be due to a cash shortage that might signal a liquidity crisis if a company has no ready source of cash. A low cash turnover might signal idle or excess cash. Cash accumulated for specific purposes or known contingencies often yields temporary decreases in turnover. The basic trade-off is between liquidity and accumulation of funds yielding little or no return.

Sales to Receivables. A company selling on credit knows that the level of its receivables is a function of sales. A low receivables turnover is likely due to overextending credit, an inability of customers to pay, or poor collection activity. A high receivables turnover can imply a strict credit policy, or a reluctance or inability to extend credit. Receivables turnover often involves a trade-off between increased sales and accumulation of funds in receivables.

Sales to Inventories. Maintaining sales typically requires inventories. The sales to inventories relation varies across industries depending on the variety of types, models, colors, sizes, and other inventory classes necessary to lure and retain consumers. Both the length of production cycle and type of item (luxury versus necessity, or perishable versus durable) has a bearing on inventories turnover. A low inventory turnover often suggests overstocked, slow-moving, or obsolete inventories. It can also signal overestimation of sales. Temporary conditions like work stoppages or slowdowns with important customers can yield low turnover. A high turnover can imply underinvestment in inventory, threatening customer relations and future sales. Inventory turnover involves a trade-off between funds accumulated in inventory and the potential loss of customers and future sales.

Sales to Fixed Assets. The relation between sales and property, plant, and equipment is long term and fundamental to most companies. There are temporary conditions affecting this relation. Temporary conditions include excess capacity, inefficient plants, obsolete equipment, demand changes, and interruptions in raw materials supply. Our analysis must remember increases in fixed assets are typically *not* gradual, but occur in large increments. This process can create changes in fixed asset turnover. Leased facilities and equipment, often not appearing on the balance sheet, can distort this turnover. The fixed asset turnover involves a trade-off between fixed asset investments having high break-even points vis-à-vis more efficient, productive capacity with high sales potential.

Sales to Other Assets. Other assets often include patents, deferred charges, or other miscellaneous deferred expenditures. While a relation between other assets and sales is not always evident, no assets should be held unless they contribute to sales or income. For example, deferred R&D costs should reflect potential for future sales. Our analysis of other assets turnover must consider these potentialities.

Sales to Current Liabilities. The relation between sales and current trade liabilities is a predictable one. A company's short-term trade liabilities depend on its sales (demand for its goods and services). Short-term credit is relatively cost free and reduces a company's funds accumulated in working capital. Also, a company's available credit line depends on its sales and income.

Factors in Asset Turnover

Our analysis of return on assets involves several additional factors. In Chapter 13 we consider extraordinary gains and losses and how our analysis adjusts for them. The effect of discontinued operations must be similarly evaluated. Our analysis of the trend in return on assets must consider the effects of acquisitions accounted for as poolings of interest (Chapter 5) and their likelihood of recurrence. Supplement C discusses effects of price-level changes on our return computations and necessary adjustments to our analysis. An internal analysis (by managers, auditors, consultants) can often obtain return data by segments, product lines, and divisions. These disaggregated data increase the reliability of and insights from our analysis. Where bargaining power or position permits, an external analysis can sometimes obtain and analyze disaggregated data. A problem arises when the level of individual assets (or total assets) changes during a period and adversely affects turnover computation. Accordingly, we use averages of individual and total asset levels. Specifically, the **denominator in computing asset turnover is an average of beginning and ending balances.** Provided data are available, an average can be computed using monthly or quarterly balances.

A consistently high return on assets is the earmark of effective management. Such management can distinguish a growth company from one experiencing merely a cyclical or seasonal pickup in business. Examining all factors comprising return on assets usually reveals the source and limitations of a company's return. Neither profit margin nor asset turnover can increase indefinitely. Increasing assets through external financing and/or internal earnings retention is necessary for further earnings growth.

Analyzing Return on Common Equity

Return on common shareholders' equity (ROCE), or simply return on common equity, is of great interest to the shareholders of a company. Return on common shareholders' equity differs from return on assets due primarily to what is excluded from invested capital. Return on common shareholders' equity excludes assets financed by creditors and preferred shareholders. Creditors usually receive a fixed return on their financing or in some cases no return. Preferred shareholders usually receive a fixed dividend. Yet common shareholders are provided no fixed or promised returns. These shareholders have claims on the *residual* earnings of a company only after all other financing sources are paid. Accordingly, the return on shareholders' equity is most important to common shareholders. The relation between return on shareholders' equity and return on assets is also important as it bears on the analysis of a company's success with financial leverage.

Return on common shareholders' equity serves a key role in equity valuation. Recall the accounting-based stock valuation formula from Chapter 2 (pages 55–56):

$$V_t = BV_t + \frac{NI_{t+1} - (k \times BV_t)}{(1+k)} + \frac{NI_{t+2} - (k \times BV_{t+1})}{(1+k)^2} + \ldots + \frac{NI_n - (k \times BV_{t+n-1})}{(1+k)^n} + \ldots$$

Through algebraic simplification, the formula can be restated in terms of *future* returns on common shareholders' equity:

$$V_t = BV_t + \frac{(ROCE_{t+1} - k)BV_t}{(1+k)} + \frac{(ROCE_{t+2} - k)BV_{t+1}}{(1+k)^2} + \ldots + \frac{(ROCE_{t+n} - k)BV_{t+n-1}}{(1+k)^n} + \ldots$$

where ROCE is equal to net income available to common shareholders (i.e., *after* preferred dividends) divided by the beginning-of-period balance of common equity. This formula is intuitively appealing. Namely, it implies that companies with ROCE greater than the investors' required rate of return (k) increase value in excess of that implied by book value alone.

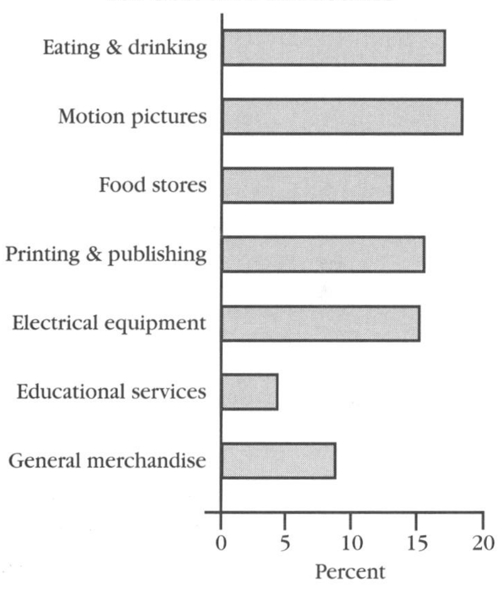

Source: Dun & Bradstreet.

Disaggregating Return on Common Equity

While ROCE in the above formula is computed using the beginning-of-period balance of common equity, in practice we use the *average* balance during the period under analysis. Like with return on assets, disaggregating return on common equity into components is extremely useful for our analysis. Recall that the return on common shareholders' equity is computed as:

$$\frac{\text{Net income} - \text{Preferred dividends}}{\text{Average common shareholders' equity}}$$

We can disaggregate return on common shareholders' equity to obtain:

***ROCE* = Adjusted profit margin × Asset turnover × Leverage**

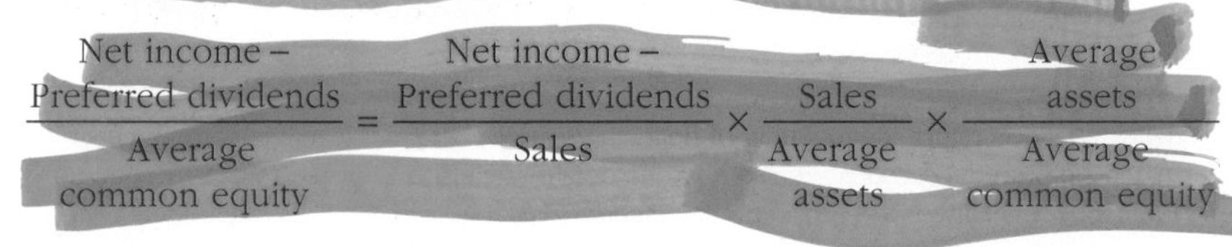

$$\frac{\text{Net income} - \text{Preferred dividends}}{\text{Average common equity}} = \frac{\text{Net income} - \text{Preferred dividends}}{\text{Sales}} \times \frac{\text{Sales}}{\text{Average assets}} \times \frac{\text{Average assets}}{\text{Average common equity}}$$

Adjusted profit margin reflects the portion of every sales dollar remaining for common shareholders after providing for all costs and claims (including preferred dividends). Asset turnover is exactly as defined above for return on assets, and **leverage** (or *common leverage*) is the common shareholders' leverage ratio measuring the proportion of assets financed by common shareholders. The larger the leverage ratio, the smaller the proportion of assets financed by common shareholders and the greater the financial leverage. These components are useful in both our analysis of company performance and in assessing returns to shareholders.[1]

Drawing on the financial statements of Excell Corporation in Exhibits 11.1 and 11.2, we can compute the disaggregated ROCE for Year 9 as (in $ millions):

$$\frac{\$65 - \$3}{(\$674 + \$699) \div 2} = \frac{\$65 - \$3}{\$1{,}724} \times \frac{\$1{,}724}{(\$1{,}334 + \$1{,}372) \div 2} \times \frac{\$1{,}334 + \$1{,}372) \div 2}{(\$674 + \$699) \div 2}$$

or

***ROCE* = Adjusted profit margin × Asset turnover × leverage**

$$8.98\% = 3.577\% \times 1.274 \times 1.970$$

We can compute additional variations on the disaggregated ROCE of Excell Corporation to provide us further insights into different aspects of its business. One way is to merge asset turnover and leverage. In Excell's operations, every dollar of common equity is used to obtain an *incremental* $0.97 of non-common equity financing (e.g., creditor and preferred equity). The *total* financing of $1.97 generates $2.51 in sales. We obtain this insight from recognizing that assets (equaling total debt and equity financing) are turning over (generating sales) at a rate of 1.274—in formula form, $1.97 × 1.274 = $2.50. This highlights that $2.51 in sales earn an adjusted profit margin (*after* all costs and preferred dividends) of 3.577 percent, yielding a return on common shareholders' equity of 8.98 percent ($2.51 × 3.577%).

Another variation of this analysis disaggregates adjusted profit margin into its pre-tax and tax retention components. When *pre-tax* adjusted profit margin is multiplied by (1 – Effective tax rate), or **retention rate,** of the company, we get adjusted profit margin:

Adjusted profit margin = Pre-tax adjusted profit margin × Retention rate

$$\frac{\text{Net income} - \text{Preferred dividends}}{\text{Sales}} = \frac{\text{Pre-tax earnings} - \text{Preferred dividends}}{\text{Sales}} \times \frac{\text{Net income} - \text{Preferred dividends}}{\text{Pre-tax earnings} - \text{Preferred dividends}}$$

[1] An alternative disaggregation of return on common equity is a variant of the return on assets (ROA). This disaggregation is:

***ROCE* = ROA × Earnings leverage × Common leverage**

$$\frac{\text{Net income} - \text{Preferred dividends}}{\textit{Average}\text{ common shareholders' equity}} = \frac{\text{Net income} + \textit{Interest}\,(1 - \textit{Tax}\text{ rate}) + \textit{Minority}\text{ interest in earnings}}{\text{Average assets}} \times \frac{\text{Net income} - \text{Preferred dividends}}{\text{Net income} + \textit{Interest}\,(1 - \textit{Tax}\text{ rate}) + \textit{Minority}\text{ interest in earnings}} \times \frac{\text{Average assets}}{\textit{Average}\text{ common shareholders' equity}}$$

Return on assets reflects return independent of financing sources. The two leverage components reflect the effect of using both creditor and preferred shareholder financing to increase return to common shareholders. **Earnings leverage** is the proportion of income available to common shareholders (*after* removing costs of both creditor [interest] and preferred [dividend] financing) relative to income available to creditor and equity financing sources (*before* removing these costs). **Common leverage** reflects the proportion of assets financed by common shareholders.

The purpose of this profit margin disaggregation is to separate pre-tax margin, a measure of *operating effectiveness*, from retention rate, a measure of *tax-management effectiveness*. In the case of Excell Corporation, the adjusted profit margin of 3.6 percent is disaggregated as:

$$3.577\% = \frac{\$126 - \$3}{\$1,724} \times \frac{\$65 - \$3}{\$126 - \$3} = 7.125\% \times 50.204\%$$

ANALYSIS VIEWPOINT . . . *You are the consultant*

You are the management consultant to a client seeking a critical review of its performance. As part of your analysis you compute ROCE and its components (industry norms in parenthesis): asset turnover = 1.5 (1.0); leverage = 2.1 (2.2); pre-tax adjusted profit margin = 0.05 (0.14); and retention rate = 0.40 (0.24). What does your preliminary analysis of these figures suggest?

Computing Return on Invested Capital

This section applies our analysis of return on invested capital to the financial statements of Campbell Soup Company reproduced in Supplement A.

Return on Assets

Return on assets is measured as (including reference to Campbell's relevant financial statement items):

$$\frac{\text{Net income } \boxed{28} + [\text{Interest expense } \boxed{18} \times (1 - \text{Tax rate})] + \text{Minority interest in earnings } \boxed{25}}{\text{Average assets } \boxed{39A}}$$

Computation of this return for Year 11 of Campbell yields ($ millions):

$$\frac{\$401.5 + \$116.2(1 - 0.34) + \$7.2}{(\$4,149.0 + \$4,115.6)/2} = \frac{\$485.4}{\$4,132.3} = 11.75\%$$

Disaggregated Return on Assets

We can disaggregate Campbell's Year 11 return on assets into its profit margin and asset turnover components:

$$\text{Return on assets} = \text{Profit margin} \times \text{Asset turnover}$$

$$\text{ROA} = \frac{\text{Net income} + \text{Interest } (1 - \text{Tax rate}) + \text{Minority interest in earnings}}{\text{Sales}} \times \frac{\text{Sales}}{\text{Average assets}}$$

$$11.75\% = \frac{\$485.4}{\$6,204.1} \times \frac{\$6,204.1}{\$4,132.3} = 7.8\% \times 1.5$$

Return on Common Equity

Return on common shareholders' equity is defined as (including reference to Campbell's relevant financial statement items):

$$\frac{\text{Net income } \boxed{28} - \text{Preferred dividends}}{\text{Average common equity * } \boxed{54}\boxed{176}}$$

* Includes 50 percent of deferred taxes we assume as equity.

Computation of return on common equity for Year 11 of Campbell yields ($ millions):

$$\frac{\$401.5}{[(\$1{,}793.4 + \$129.3) + (\$1{,}691.8 + \$117.5)]/2} = \frac{\$401.5}{\$1{,}866} = 21.52\%$$

Disaggregated Return on Common Equity

We disaggregate Campbell's Year 11 return on common equity into its components:

$$ROCE = \text{Adjusted profit margin} \times \text{Asset turnover} \times \text{Leverage}$$

$$ROCE = \frac{\text{Net income} - \text{Preferred dividends}}{\text{Sales } \boxed{\mathbf{13}}} \times \frac{\text{Sales}}{\text{Average assets}} \times \frac{\text{Average assets}}{\text{Average common equity}}$$

$$= \frac{\$401.5}{\$6{,}204.1} \times \frac{\$6{,}204.1}{\$4{,}132.3} \times \frac{\$4{,}132.3}{\$1{,}866.0}$$

$$21.52\% = 6.47\% \times 1.50 \times 2.22$$

Further disaggregation of Campbell's adjusted profit margin into its *pre-tax* and *tax retention* components yields:

$$\text{Adjusted profit margin} = \text{Pre-tax adjusted profit margin} \times \text{Retention rate}$$

$$= \frac{\text{Pre-tax earnings}}{\text{Sales}} \times \frac{\text{Net earnings}}{\text{Pre-tax earnings}}$$

$$= \frac{\$667.4 \boxed{\mathbf{26}}}{\$6{,}204.1} \times \frac{\$401.5 \boxed{\mathbf{28}}}{\$667.4}$$

$$6.5\% = 10.8\% \times 60.2\%$$

We conduct a comparative analysis of these ratios across time in our analysis of return on invested capital section of the Comprehensive Case chapter. Analysis of return on invested capital measures across time is often revealing of company performance. If ROCE declines, it is important for us to identify the component(s) responsible for this decline to assess past and future company performance. We can also assess areas of greatest potential improvement in ROCE and the likelihood of a company successfully pursuing this strategy. For example, if leverage is high and not likely to increase, our analysis focuses on adjusted profit margin and asset turnover. Our analysis of company strategies and potential for improvements depends on industry and economic conditions. We ask questions like: Is profit margin high or low in comparison with the industry? What is the potential improvement in asset turnover in this industry? Evaluating returns using the structured approach described in this chapter and interpreting them in their proper context can greatly aid our analysis.

Further Disaggregation of Return on Common Equity

Further disaggregation of return on common equity is sometimes useful for our analysis. Specifically, we can separate both *interest* and *tax* components from net income as follows:

EBIT [$783.6] = Net income [$401.5] + Interest [$116.2] + Taxes [$265.9 **27**] where EBIT is earnings (income) *before* interest and taxes (and *before* preferred dividends, if applicable). We use these net income components and merge them into the ROCE disaggregation formula as follows:

$ROCE$ = [(EBIT profit margin × Asset turnover) – Interest turnover] × Leverage × Retention rate

where EBIT profit margin equals EBIT divided by sales, interest turnover equals interest expense divided by average assets, and the other components are as defined above. Interest turnover is referred to as *interest burden*. This derives from the notion that the higher the interest burden, the lower the ROCE. Also, the higher the tax retention, the higher the ROCE. Computation of the disaggregation of ROCE for Year 11 of Campbell yields ($ millions):

$$ROCE = \left[\left(\frac{\$783.6}{\$6{,}204.1} \times \frac{\$6{,}204.1}{\$4{,}132.3}\right) - \frac{\$116.2}{\$4{,}132.3}\right] \times \frac{\$4{,}132.3}{\$1{,}866.0} \times (1.000 - 0.398)$$

$$21.52\% = \left[(0.126 \times 1.50) - 0.028\right] \times 2.22 \times 0.602$$

This disaggregation highlights *both* effects of interest and taxes on Campbell's ROCE.

Assessing Growth in Common Equity

Equity Growth Rate

We can assess the common equity growth rate of a company through earnings retention. This analysis emphasizes equity growth *without* resort to external financing. To assess equity growth we assume earnings retention *and* a constant dividend payout over time. The **equity growth rate** is computed as:

Analysis Research Insight 11.1

Return on Common Shareholders' Equity

How does a company's return on common shareholders' equity (ROCE) behave across time? Do certain companies consistently have high or low ROCE? Do companies' ROCEs tend to move toward an average ROCE? Analysis research has addressed these important questions. *On average*, a company's ROCE for the current period is a good predictor of its ROCE for the next period. However, as the time horizon increases, a company's ROCE tends to converge toward the average economywide ROCE. This is usually attributed to the effects of competition. Companies that are able to sustain high ROCEs typically command large premiums over book value.

A large portion of the variability in companies' ROCEs is due to changes in ROA. This is because, on average, leverage factors do not vary significantly over time. Two factors are important in predicting ROCE. First, disaggregating net income into operating and nonoperating components improves forecasts. Second, the conservatism inherent in accounting practice must eventually "reverse." This accounting reversal predictably yields an increase in ROCE.

$$\text{Equity growth rate} = \frac{\text{Net income} - \text{Preferred dividends} - \text{Dividend payout}}{\text{Average common stockholders' equity}}$$

The equity growth rate for Year 9 of Excell Corporation, using its financial statements reproduced in Exhibits 11.1 and 11.2, is computed as:

$$3.35\% = \frac{\$65 - \$3 - \$39^{*}}{(\$674 + \$699) \div 2}$$

*Common stock dividend payout.

This measure implies Excell Corporation can grow 3.35 percent per year without increasing its current level of financing.

Sustainable Equity Growth Rate

The **sustainable equity growth rate,** or simply sustainable equity growth, recognizes that internal growth for a company depends on *both*: (1) earnings retention and (2) return earned on the earnings retained. Specifically, the **sustainable equity growth rate** is computed as:

$$\text{Sustainable equity growth rate} = \text{ROCE} \times (1 - \text{Payout rate})$$

For Excell Corporation (see Exhibits 11.1 and 11.2), we find the dividend payout rate for Year 9 equals 65 percent ($41,806/$64,569). We then compute Excell's sustainable equity growth rate for Year 9 as:

$$3.17\% = 8.98\% \times (1 - 0.647)$$

Excell experienced an earnings decline from Year 8 ($77,896) to Year 9 ($64,569). This along with a constant dividend payout produced a declining sustainable growth rate. When estimating future equity growth rates it is often advisable to average (or otherwise recognize) sustainable growth rates for several recent years. We should also recognize potential changes in earnings retention and forecasted ROCE.

Financial Leverage and Return on Common Equity

This section analyzes effects of financial leverage for the return on common equity. *Financial leverage* refers to the extent of invested capital from other than common shareholders. For purposes of our analysis, we use financial statements of Excell Corporation. Our first step is to list the *average* amounts of all financing sources for Excell Corporation taken from its December 31, Year 9 and Year 8, balance sheets ($ thousands):

Current liabilities (excluding current portion of long-term debt)		$ 176,677
Long-term debt	$343,255	
Current portion of long-term debt	10,730	353,985
Deferred taxes		93,962
Preferred stock		41,538
Common shareholders' equity		686,640
Total financing		$1,352,802

We also reproduce relevant financial data from Excell's income statement for Year 9 ($ thousands):

Income before taxes	$125,730
Income taxes	61,161
Net income	$ 64,569
Preferred dividends	2,908
Income accruing to common shareholders	$ 61,661
Total interest expense	$ 20,382
Assumed interest on short-term notes (5%)	687
Balance of interest on long-term debt	$ 19,695

We can compute Excell Corporation's return on assets as:

$$ROA = \frac{\text{Net income} + \text{Interest} \times (1 - \text{Tax rate})}{\text{Average assets}}$$

$$5.677\% = \frac{\$64{,}569 + \$20{,}382(1 - 0.40)}{\$1{,}352{,}802}$$

Excell's 5.677 percent return on assets is relevant for assessing the effects of financial leverage. This implies that if suppliers of capital (other than the common shareholders) receive a less than 5.677 percent return, then common shareholders benefit. The reverse occurs when suppliers of capital receive more than a 5.677 percent return. The greater the difference in returns between common equity and other capital suppliers, the more successful (or unsuccessful) is the trading on the equity.

A thorough analysis of Excell's financial leverage appears in Exhibit 11.7. This exhibit shows an analysis of the relative contribution and return for each of the major financing suppliers. It also shows the influence of each financing suppliers' returns on ROCE. A few findings deserve mention. The $9,618 accruing to common shareholders from use of current liabilities is largely due to them being free of interest costs. The $8,279 accruing to shareholders from long-term debt is primarily due to tax deductibility of interest. The value of tax deferrals is evident where Excell's use of cost-free funds yields an annual advantage of $5,334. Since preferred dividends are *not* tax deductible, the low return on assets (5.677 percent) yields a leverage disadvantage to common shareholders of $550.

We can further extend our analysis of leverage to its component parts. Excell's return on common shareholders' equity is ($ thousands):

$$\frac{\text{Net income} - \text{Preferred dividends}}{\text{Average common equity}} = \frac{\$61{,}661^{*}}{\$686{,}640} = 8.98 \text{ percent}$$

*Identical to income accruing to common shareholders in Exhibit 11.7.

We know the net benefit to common shareholders from financial leverage is $22,681 (see Exhibit 11.7). As a percent of common equity, this benefit is computed as:

$$\frac{\text{Earnings in excess of return to suppliers of funds}}{\text{Average common equity}} = \frac{\$22{,}681}{\$686{,}640} = 3.303 \text{ percent}$$

Our analysis of return on common equity can view return as comprosed of two components:

EXHIBIT 11.7 Analyzing Leverage on Common Equity ($ thousands)

Financing Supplier	*Average Funds Supplied*	*Earnings on Funds Supplied at Rate of 5.677 Percent*	*Payment to Suppliers of Funds*	*Accruing to (Detracting from) Return on Common Equity*
Current liabilities	$ 176,677	$10,030	$ 412[a]	$ 9,618
Long-term debt	353,985	20,096	11,817[b]	8,279
Deferred taxes	93,962	5,334	none	5,334
Preferred stock	41,538	2,358	2,908[c]	(550)
Earnings in excess of return to suppliers of funds				$22,681
Add: Common equity	686,640	38,980	—	38,980
Totals	$1,352,802	$76,798	$15,137	
Total return to shareholders				$61,661

[a]Short-term interest expense of $687 less 40 percent tax (from Exhibit 11.1).

[b]Long-term interest expense of $19,695 less 40 percent tax (from Exhibit 11.1).

[c]Preferred dividends (from Exhibit 11.1)—not tax deductible.

Return on assets	5.677%
Leverage advantage accruing to common equity	3.303
Return on common equity	8.980%

Return on Common Shareholders' Equity versus Investment

Return on common shareholder's equity measures the relation of net income (attributable to common shareholders) to common shareholders' equity. Common shareholders' equity is measured using book values reported in the balance sheet. These values do not necessarily reflect how individual shareholders like us might fare in terms of return on our personal investment (price we pay for common stock). This is important since shareholders do not typically buy common stock at book value—they often pay a multiple of book value. The price we pay for stock plays an important role in determining **return on shareholders' investment (ROSI),** computed as (using all per share figures):

$$ROSI = \frac{\text{Dividends} + \text{Market value of earnings reinvested}}{\text{Share price (cost)}}$$

To illustrate, consider the following financial data from Austin Technics, Inc. (per share rounded to nearest dollar):

Net income	$ 6
Cash dividends to common	(2)
Earnings reinvested	$ 4
Book value of common equity	$60
Ratio of market value to book value	2:1
Market valuation of earnings reinvested	$ 4

The return on common shareholders' equity for Austin Technics is 10 percent ($6/$60). However, since a shareholder must pay the market share price (2 × $60), the shareholders' ROSI is only 5 percent—computed as:

$$5\% = \frac{\$2 + \$4}{2 \times \$60}$$

One component in computing shareholders' return on investment is the assumption that the market uses earnings reinvested at their reported amount. It is important for the shareholder to consider how the market values earnings reinvested and make an informed assumption. In the case of Austin Technics' earnings of $6 per share, shareholders benefit from: (1) earnings paid out as dividends [$2], and (2) the value the market places on the earnings reinvested [$4]. If we assume the market value of earnings reinvested is valued at more than their reported value, say $5.2 per share, then we can compute a **shareholder multiple** as (per share):

$$\frac{\$2 \text{ (dividend)} + \$5.2 \text{ (market valuation of } \$4 \text{ earnings reinvested)}}{\$6 \text{ (earnings)}} = \frac{\$7.2}{\$6} = 1.20$$

This shareholder multiple implies a dollar earned and reinvested by the company enriches shareholders by $1.20 (ignoring tax effects). Evidence in practice suggests a wide variation in the shareholder multiple across companies, where earnings do not always yield increased dividends or higher stock values. There is some evidence that the correlation between ROCE and ROSI is low (recall ROCE does not include the market's valuation of earnings reinvested or other measures).[2] The ROSI critically depends on market valuation. As we discussed in Chapter 2, our valuation of equity securities must include analysis of both financial statements *and* market prices. This distinction between the value of a company and its stock is extremely important. For example, our financial statement analysis might reveal a company is well managed and fundamentally sound. Yet this company might be a poor investment because its stock is overvalued (unless we can sell it short). Conversely, a poor performing company can be a good investment because its stock is undervalued.

GUIDANCE ANSWERS TO ANALYSIS VIEWPOINTS

You Are the Auditor

Joint analysis is where one measure of company performance is assessed relative to another. In the case of our manufacturing client, both *individual* analyses yield percent changes within the ±5 percent acceptable range. However, a joint analysis would suggest a more alarming situation. Consider a joint analysis using profit margin (net income/sales). The client's profit margin is 11.46 percent ($2,060,000 – $1,824,000/ $2,060,000) for the current year compared with 5.0 percent ($2,000,000 – $1,900,000/ $2,000,000) for the prior year—a 129 percent increase in profit margin! This is what the audit partner is concerned with, and encourages expanded audit tests including joing analysis to verify or refute the client's figures.

[2] See B. Ball, "The Mysterious Disappearance of Retained Earnings," *Harvard Business Review* (July–August 1987).

You Are the Consultant

Your preliminary analysis highlights deviations from the norm in (1) asset turnover, (2) pre-tax adjusted profit margin, and (3) retention rate. Asset turnover for your client is better than the norm. Your client appears to efficiently use its assets. One note of warning: we need to be assured all assets are accounted for and properly valued, and we want to know if the company is sufficiently replacing its aging assets. Your client's pre-tax adjusted profit margin is 60 percent lower than the norm. This is alarming, especially in light of the positive asset turnover ratio. Our client has considerably greater costs than the norm, and we need to direct efforts to identify and analyze these costs. Retention rate is also considerably worse than competitors. Our client is paying a greater proportion of its income in taxes than the norm. We need to utilize tax experts to identify and appropriately plan business activities with tax considerations in mind.

QUESTIONS

11–1. Why is return on invested capital one of the most relevant measures of company performance? How do we use this measure in our analysis of financial statements?

11–2. How is return on invested capital used as an internal management tool?

11–3. Discuss the motivation for excluding "nonproductive" assets from invested capital when computing return. What circumstances justify excluding intangible assets from invested capital?

11–4. Why is interest added back to net income when computing return on total assets?

11–5. What circumstances justify including convertible debt as equity capital when computing return on shareholders' equity?

11–6. Why must minority interest's share in net income be added back when computing return on total assets?

11–7. Why must net income used in computing return on invested capital be adjusted to reflect the capital base (denominator) used in the computation?

11–8. What is the relation between return on invested capital and sales?

11–9. Company A acquires Company B because the latter has a profit margin (net income to sales) exceeding the industry norm. After acquisition, a shareholder complains that the acquisition lowered return on invested capital. Discuss possible reasons for this happening.

11–10. Company X's profit margin is 2 percent of sales. Company Y has an asset turnover of 12. Both companies' returns on assets are 6 percent and are considered unsatisfactory by industry norms. What is the asset turnover of Company X? What is the profit margin for Company Y? What strategic actions do you recommend to the managements of the respective companies?

11–11. What is the purpose of measuring asset turnover for different asset categories?

11–12. What factors enter into our evaluation of return on invested capital measures?

11–13. How is the equity growth rate computed? What does it measure?

11–14. *a.* How do return on assets and return on common equity differ?
b. What are the components of return on common shareholders' equity? What do the components measure?

11–15. *a.* Equity turnover is sales divided by average shareholders' equity. What does equity turnover measure? How is it related to return on common equity?
b. "Growth in per share earnings from an increase in equity turnover is unlikely to continue indefinitely." Do you agree or disagree? Explain your answer and discuss alternative causes of an increase in equity turnover.

(CFA Adapted)

EXERCISES

Exercise 11–1
Analyzing Returns and Strategies of Alternative Financing

Roll Corporation's return on assets is 10 percent and its tax rate is 40 percent. Its assets ($10 million) are financed entirely by common shareholders' equity. Management is considering using bonds to finance an expansion costing $6 million. It expects return on assets to remain unchanged. There are two alternatives to finance the expansion:

1. Issue $2 million bonds with 5 percent coupon, and $4 million common stock.
2. Issue $6 million bonds with 6 percent coupon.

Required:

a. Compute Roll's current operating income (income before interest and taxes).
b. Determine operating income for each alternative financing plan.
c. Compute return on common shareholders' equity for each alternative.
d. Explain any difference in the two returns computed for (*c*).

Exercise 11–2
Analyzing Financial Leverage for Alternative Financing Strategies

Fit Corporation's return on assets is 10 percent and its tax rate is 40 percent. Its total assets ($4 million) are financed entirely by common shareholders' equity. Management is considering using bonds to finance an expansion costing $2 million. It expects return on assets to remain unchanged. There are two alternatives to finance the expansion:

1. Issue $1 million bonds with 12 percent coupon, and $1 million common stock.
2. Issue $2 million bonds with 12 percent coupon.

Required:

a. Determine operating income (income before interest and taxes) for each alternative.
b. Compute return on common shareholders' equity for each alternative.
c. Calculate the financial leverage index for each alternative.
d. Explain the level of the financial leverage index for each alternative.

Exercise 11–3
Disaggregating and Analyzing Return on Common Equity

Refer to the financial data in Case 10–3. In analyzing the entire company, You feel it is important to differentiate between operating success and financing decisions.

Required:

a. Explain the difference between ABEX's ROCE in Year 5 and in Year 9. Your analysis should include computation and discussion of the components determining return on common shareholders' equity.
b. Explain why ABEX's earnings per share nearly doubled between Year 5 and Year 9 despite the decline in its return on common shareholders' equity.

(CFA Adapted)

Exercise 11–4
Disaggregating Return Measures for Analyzing Leverage

Selected financial information from Rolf Corporation is reproduced below:

1.	Asset turnover (average assets equal ending assets)	2
2.	Net profit margin	5%
3.	Financial leverage ratio	1.786
4.	Sales	$5,000,000
5.	Capital structure is composed of $100,000 minority interests; 10 percent current liabilities (average interest expense is 5 percent for one-half of current liabilities); 30 percent long-term debt (average interest expense is 6 percent); and common equity.	
6.	Tax rate is 40 percent.	
7.	Minority interest in earnings	$1,000

Required:

a. Compute return on common equity using its three major components.

b. Compute return on assets.

c. Analyze the disaggregation of return on common equity as in Exhibit 11.7. What is the leverage advantage (in percent return) accruing to common shareholders?

Exercise 11–5

Analyzing Financial Leverage for Shareholders' Returns

Rose Corporation's condensed balance sheet for Year 2 is reproduced below:

Assets	
Current assets	$ 250,000
Noncurrent assets	1,750,000
Total assets	$2,000,000
Liabilities and Equity	
Current liabilities	$ 200,000
Noncurrent liabilities (8% bonds)	675,000
Stockholders' equity	1,125,000
Total liabilities and equity	$2,000,000

Additional Information:

1. Net income for Year 2 is $157,500.
2. Income tax rate is 50 percent.
3. Amounts for total assets and shareholders' equity are the same for Years 1 and 2.

Required:

a. Determine whether financial leverage (long-term debt) benefits Rose's shareholders.

b. If Rose Corporation achieves a 20 percent return on assets, compute both its return on common equity and its financial leverage index.

c. What can you conclude from the financial leverage index computed in (*b*)?

Exercise 11–6

Analyzing Returns and Effects of Financial Leverage

Selected financial information for ADAM Corporation is reproduced below:

1.	Asset turnover (average assets equal ending assets)	3
2.	Net income to sales	7%
3.	Financial leverage ratio (total assets to total equity)	1.667
4.	Sales	$12,000,000
5.	Capital structure is composed of $200,000 minority interests; 15 percent current liabilities (average interest expense is 4 percent for one-third of current liabilities); 20 percent long-term debt (average interest expense is 5 percent); and 60 percent common equity.	
6.	Tax rate is 50 percent.	
7.	Minority interest in earnings	$2,000

Required:

a. Compute return on common equity using its three major components.

b. Compute return on assets.

c. Prepare an analysis of the composition of return on common equity describing the advantage or disadvantage accruing to common shareholders' equity from use of leverage (see Exhibit 11.7).

Exercise 11–7

Understanding Return Measures (multiple choice)

I. Which of the following situations best correspond with a ratio of "sales to average net tangible assets" exceeding the industry norm? (Choose one answer.)
  a. A company expanding plant and equipment during the past three years.
  b. A company inefficiently using its assets.
  c. A company with a large proportion of aged plant and equipment.
  d. A company using straight-line depreciation.

II. Return on assets is equivalent to (choose one answer):
  i. Profit margin × Total asset turnover.
  ii. Profit margin × Total asset turnover × Leverage/Interest expense.
  iii. $\frac{\text{Net income} + \text{Interest expense } (1 - \text{Tax rate}) + \text{Minority interest in earnings}}{\text{Average assets}}$.
  iv. $\frac{\text{Net income} + \text{Minority interest in earnings}}{\text{Average assets}}$.

  a. *i* only.
  b. *i* and *iii.*
  c. *ii* only.
  d. *ii* and *iv.*

III. A measure of asset utilization (turnover) is (choose one answer):
  a. Sales divided by working capital.
  b. Return on assets.
  c. Return on common equity.
  d. Operating income divided by sales.

IV. Return on assets depends on the (choose one answer):
  a. Interest rates and pre-tax profits.
  b. Debt to equity ratio.
  c. After-tax profit margin and asset turnover.
  d. Sales and fixed assets.

PROBLEMS

Problem 11–1

Analyzing Return Measures for Investment Decisions

Refer to the financial statements of Campbell Soup Company in Supplement A. Assume our analysis reveals that one-half of deferred income taxes should be treated as equity.

Required:

a. Compute the following measures for Year 10 of Campbell Soup:
  1. Return on assets.
  2. Return on common equity.
  3. Return on long-term liabilities and equity.
  4. Financial leverage index.
  5. Equity growth rate.

b. Disaggregate Campbell's return on common equity and interpret the results.

c. Compute Campbell's Year 10 asset turnover for individual asset categories (for this part only, use year-end balances for individual assets).

d. Assume you are considering investing in Campbell's common stock. There is another investment of equal quality and risk having a 12.7 percent return on common equity.

Do you prefer one investment over the other? Is there other information you require to make a decision?

Problem 11–2 Analyzing Company Returns and Proposed Wage Increases

Zear Company produces an electronic processor and sells it wholesale to manufacturing and retail outlets at $10 each. In Zear's Year 8 fiscal period it sold 500,000 processors. Fixed costs for Year 8 total $1,500,000, including interest costs on its 7.5 percent debentures. Variable costs are $4 per processor for materials. Zear employs about 20 hourly paid plant employees each earning $35,000 in Year 8.

Zear is currently confronting labor negotiations. The plant employees are requesting substantial increases in hourly wages. Zear forecasts a 6 percent increase in fixed costs and no change in either the processor's price or in material costs for the processors. Zear also forecasts a 10 percent growth in sales volume for Year 9. To meet the necessary increase in production due to sales demand, Zear recently hired two additional hourly plant employees.

The condensed balance sheet for Zear at the end of fiscal Year 8 is reproduced below (the tax rate is 50 percent):

Assets		***Liabilities and equity***	
Current assets:		Current liabilities	$2,000,000
Cash	$ 700,000	Long-term 7½% debenture	2,000,000
Receivables	1,000,000	6% preferred stock, 10,000 shares, $100 par value	1,000,000
Other	800,000		
Total current assets	$2,500,000	Common stock and retained earnings	3,000,000
Fixed assets (net)	5,500,000		
	$8,000,000		$8,000,000

Required:

a. Compute Zear's return on invested capital for Year 8 where invested capital is:
1. Debt and equity capital at end of Year 8.
2. Long-term debt and equity capital at end of Year 8.
3. Common equity capital at end of Year 8.

b. Calculate the maximum annual wage increase Zear can pay each plant employee and show a 10 percent return on long-term debt and equity capital (invested capital computed at the end of Year 8 data).

(CFA Adapted)

Problem 11–3 Determining Return on Invested Capital (conceptual)

Quaker Oats Company in its Year 11 annual report disclosed the following:

Financial Objectives: Provide total shareholder returns (dividends plus share price appreciation) that exceed both the cost of equity and the S&P 500 stock index over time.
Quaker's total return to shareholders for Year 11 was 34 percent. That compares quite favorably to our cost of equity for the year, which was about 12 percent, and to the total return of the S&P 500 stock index, which was 7 percent. Driving this strong performance, real earnings from continuing operations grew 7.4 percent over the last five years, return on equity rose to 24.1 percent. [Note: Quaker Oats approximate stock prices at the beginning and end of Year 11 were $48 and $62, respectively.]

The Benchmark for Investment
We use our cost of capital as a benchmark, or hurdle rate, to ensure that all projects undertaken promise a suitable rate of return. The cost of capital is used as the discount rate in determining whether a project will provide an economic return on its investment. We estimate a project's potential cash flows and discount these cash flows back to present value. This amount is compared with the initial investment costs to determine whether incremental value is created. Our cost of capital is calculated using the approximate market value weightings of debt and equity used to finance the Company.

Cost of equity + Cost of debt = Cost of capital

When Quaker is consistently able to generate and reinvest cash flows in projects whose returns exceed our cost of capital, economic value is created. As the stock market evaluates the Company's ability to generate value, this value is reflected in stock price appreciation.

The cost of equity. The cost of equity is a measure of the minimum return Quaker must earn to properly compensate investors for the risk of ownership of our stock. This cost is a combination of a "risk-free" rate and an "equity risk premium." The risk-free rate (the U.S. Treasury Bond rate) is the sum of the expected rate of inflation and a "real" return of 2 to 3 percent. For Year 11, the risk-free rate was approximately 8.4 percent. Investors in Quaker stock expect the return of a risk-free security plus a "risk premium" of about 3.6 percent to compensate them for assuming the risks in Quaker stock. The risk in holding Quaker stock is inherent in the fact that returns depend on the future profitability of the Company. In Year 11, Quaker's cost of equity was approximately 12 percent.

The cost of debt. The cost of debt is simply our after-tax, long-term debt rate, which was around 6.4 percent.

Required:

a. Quaker reports the "return to shareholders" for Year 11 to be 34 percent.
  1. How is this return computed (report calculations)?
  2. How is this return different from return on common equity?
  3. Compare Quaker Oats' concept of "return to shareholders" to the concept of return on shareholder's investment (ROSI) discussed in the chapter.
  4. Can you verify Quaker Oats' computation of 24.1 percent for return on equity?

b. Explain how Quaker Oats arrives at a 3.6 percent "risk premium" needed by common shareholders as compensation for assuming the risks of Quaker Oats' stock.

c. Explain how Quaker Oats determined the 6.4 percent cost of debt.

Problem 11–4
Disaggregating and Analyzing Return on Invested Capital

You are a financial analyst at a debt-rating agency. You are asked to analyze return on invested capital and asset utilization (turnover) measures for ZETA Corporation. Selected financial information for Years 5 and 6 of ZETA Corporation are reproduced in the Comprehensive Case chapter (see Case CC–2). You are provided the following additional account balances (for this problem only) at December 31, Year 4 ($ thousands):

Total assets	$94,500
Long-term debt	11,200
Deferred income taxes (assume long-term liability)	1,000
Minority interest	800
Shareholders' equity	42,000

Interest expense on long-term debt is $4,000 in Year 6 and $3,000 for Year 5 (tax rate is 50 percent).

Required:

a. Compute the following return measures for Year 5 and Year 6:
  1. Return on assets.
  2. Return on long-term debt plus equity capital.
  3. Return on common equity.
  4. Equity growth rate.

b. Comment on the year-to-year changes in the measures in (*a*).

c. Disaggregate ROCE and explain the usefulness of this disaggregation.

d. Analyze and interpret the disaggregation of ROCE for Year 6 as in Exhibit 11.7.

e. What is the relevance of the analysis in (*d*)?

Problem 11–5

Disaggregating and Analyzing Return on Common Equity

Selected financial statement data from Texas Telecom, Inc., for Years 5 and 9 are reproduced below ($ millions):

	Year 5	Year 9
Income Statement Data:		
Revenues	$542	$979
Operating income	38	76
Depreciation and amortization	3	9
Interest expense	3	0
Pre-tax income	32	67
Income taxes	13	37
Net income	19	30
Balance Sheet Data:		
Fixed assets	$ 41	$ 70
Total assets	245	291
Working capital	123	157
Total liabilities	16	0
Total shareholders' equity	159	220

Return on common equity can be disaggregated into five components:

Profit margin (Net income/Sales).
Asset turnover (Sales/Average assets).
Interest turnover (Interest expense/Average assets).
Leverage (Average assets/Average Common equity).
Effective tax rate (Tax expense/income before income tax).

Required:

a. Calculate each of the five components of return on common equity (ROCE) for Years 5 and 9. Use end-of-year values for computations requiring an average.

b. Calculate return on common equity for Years 5 and 9 using each of the five components. Use end-of-year values for computations requiring an average.

c. Analyze and interpret changes in asset turnover and leverage for the change in ROCE from Year 5 to Year 9.

Problem 11–6

Disaggregating and Interpreting Return on Common Equity

Selected income statement and balance sheet data from Merck & Co. for Year 9 are reproduced below:

MERCK & COMPANY, INC.
Year 9 Selected Financial Data
($ millions)

Income Statement Data:	
Sales revenue	$7,120
Depreciation	230
Interest expense	10
Pre-tax income	2,550
Income taxes	900
Net income	1,650

Balance Sheet Data:	
Current assets	$4,850
Net fixed assets	2,400
Total assets	7,250
Current liabilities	3,290
Long-term debt	100
Shareholders' equity	3,860
Total liabilities & shareholders' equity	7,250

Values for each of the components determining return on common equity of Merck & Co. for Year 4 are reported below. (*Note*: Some of Merck's measures are defined slightly different from those in the chapter.)

Profit margin (Net income/Sales)	0.245
Asset turnover (Sales/Total assets)	0.724
Interest burden (Pre-tax income/EBIT)	0.989
Leverage (Total assets/Common shareholders' equity)	1.877
Income tax rate (Net income/Pre-tax income)	0.628

Required:

a. Calculate each of the five components of ROCE for Merck in Year 9.

b. Calculate return on common equity for Year 9 using the five components.

c. Analyze and interpret your calculations in (*a*) and (*b*). Describe how each component contributes to the change in Merck's ROCE between Year 4 and Year 9, and suggest reasons for the change in Merck's ROCE.

CASES

Case 11–1

Analyzing Adaptec's Return on Invested Capital

Using the 1996 annual report of Adaptec in Supplement A, answer the following:

a. Compute return on assets for 1994 through 1996. (*Hint*: Use Selected Financial Data from Adaptec's report.)

b. Compute return on common equity (ROCE) for 1994 through 1996.

c. Prepare a disaggregation of ROCE for 1994 through 1996 into adjusted profit margin, asset turnover, and leverage.

d. Analyze and interpret the results from *a*, *b*, and *c*.

e. Adaptec enjoys a 70 percent share of the market where it competes. Discuss the ability of Adaptec to maintain its current returns in light of increasing competition.

Case 11–2

Comprehensive Analysis of Return on Invested Capital

Refer to the financial statements of Quaker Oats Company reproduced in Supplement A.

Required:

a. Compute the following return on invested capital ratios of Quaker Oats for Years 11 and 10:
1. Return on assets.
2. Disaggregated return on assets.
3. Return on long-term liabilities plus equity.
4. Return on common equity.
5. Equity growth rate.
6. Disaggregated return on common equity into adjusted profit margin, asset turnover, and leverage.

b. Compute the following assets turnover ratios for Quaker Oats for Years 11 and 10.

1. Sales to cash.
2. Sales to receivables.
3. Sales to inventories.
4. Sales to property, plant, and equipment.
5. Sales to "other current assets."
6. Sales to total assets.

c. Using your computations in *(a)* and *(b)*, analyze and evaluate Quaker Oats' return on invested capital and asset turnover for Years 11 and 10.

d. For Year 11, construct a table showing net amounts accruing to (or detracting from) return on common equity from financing sources (including current liabilities). Discuss the results in your table (identify any assumptions you make and use averages for financing suppliers).

e. Compute return on invested capital for Year 11 when invested capital is measured as:
1. Gross productive assets (assume 20 percent of "other current assets" are unproductive).
2. Market value of common stock (assume market value equals the average market price for Year 11).

Case 11–3 Comprehensive Analysis of Return on Common Equity

You are the analyst at Investment Counselors, Inc. The senior portfolio manager at your firm makes a decision to increase communication stocks in the firm's managed funds. You are assigned to recommend one stock as an initial investment to meet this long-run objective. You diligently analyze and evaluate all communication stocks and narrow the decision to two newspaper publishers: Thomson Newspapers, Ltd., and Southam, Inc.

Thomson Newspapers, Ltd., is one of the largest nondiversified newspaper companies in North America. It owns and publishes predominantly small town daily newspapers. Thomson is usually the dominant newspaper advertising vehicle in individual markets. Its successful record of acquisitions assures future growth opportunities without jeopardizing earnings.

Southam, Inc., is a diversified communications company. It derives 70 percent of income from newspaper publishing, with the remainder from commercial printing, book retailing, and information services in Canada and the United States. Southam is Canada's largest daily newspaper company with publishing operations primarily in large competitive markets. While Southam is diversified into higher growth segments of communications to augment growth, its more cyclical large city newspapers continue to dominate earnings performance.

The senior portfolio manager requests that you discuss the internal sources of earnings growth for each company. You decide to disaggregate and analyze the internal growth components for each company to explain any trends in your variable of interest, *return on common shareholders' equity.* You identify five key components: profit margin, interest turnover. income taxes, asset turnover, and leverage. Summary measures using these components are reproduced below:

THOMSON NEWSPAPERS, LTD.

Year	*Assets/ Common Equity*	*Net Profit Margin*	*Income Tax Rate*	*Revenues/ Assets*	*EBIT*/ Revenues*	*Interest/ Assets*	*Return on Common Equity*
Year 11E	1.53	21.2%	28.0%	0.61	32.2%	1.9%	❑
Year 10	1.31	21.0	38.1	0.77	33.5	0.5	20.5%
Year 9	1.32	19.5	43.8	0.86	35.4	0.6	22.1
Year 8	1.41	19.0	41.6	0.80	34.2	1.5	21.2
Year 7	1.41	18.9	43.0	0.84	34.4	1.0	22.3
Year 6	1.45	17.9	44.3	0.86	33.2	1.0	22.2
Year 5	1.60	14.9	42.9	0.98	28.4	2.2	23.5
Year 4	1.67	15.0	45.7	0.91	30.8	3.2	22.6
Year 3	1.48	14.5	48.5	0.95	30.9	3.0	20.0
Year 2	1.37	19.4	46.9	0.81	38.1	1.3	21.4
Year 1	1.34	18.5	48.0	0.81	37.0	1.4	19.9

SOUTHAM, INC.

Year	Assets/ Common Equity	Net Profit Margin	Income Tax Rate	Revenues/ Assets	EBIT*/ Revenues	Interest/ Assets	Return on Common Equity
Year 11E	2.39	4.6%	43.0%	1.29	7.3%	2.7%	❑
Year 10	2.22	5.4	44.7	1.38	8.9	3.1	11.3%
Year 9	2.20	5.6	42.7	1.37	9.4	3.1	12.4
Year 8	2.47	4.2	42.7	1.46	8.9	3.6	13.3
Year 7	2.82	4.1	46.4	1.61	9.9	4.3	17.6
Year 6	2.70	4.5	46.7	1.57	10.2	3.3	18.2
Year 5	2.65	2.3	46.0	1.54	7.9	5.8	9.1
Year 4	2.73	5.4	46.1	1.62	13.5	6.2	23.2
Year 3	2.39	6.1	45.9	1.54	12.9	4.1	20.4
Year 2	2.03	7.0	44.3	1.62	13.0	2.5	21.1
Year 1	1.85	8.2	41.1	1.64	12.2	1.1	20.6

E = Estimated values

*Earnings before interest and taxes.

Required:

a. Compute return on common equity for Year 11 for both Thomson and Southam using their disaggregated data.

b. Discuss how the recent 10-year trend in each of the five components affects return on common equity for each company.

INTERNET ACTIVITIES

Internet 11–1
Analyzing Return Measures

Access one of the financial statement databases available on the Internet (http://www.mhhe.com/business/accounting/wild). Retrieve current financial statements of a company selected by either you or your instructor. Assume one-half of any deferred income taxes is equivalent to equity.

Required:

a. Compute the measures in Problem 11–1(*a*) for the company's most recent year.

b. Disaggregate return on common equity (*a*) and interpret the results.

c. Compute asset turnover for individual asset categories and interpret the findings.

d. Assume you are considering investing in the company's common stock. Write a report recommending an investment strategy for this stock.

Internet 11–2
Return on Invested Capital

Access one of the financial statement databases available on the Internet (http://www.mhhe.com/business/accounting/wild). Retrieve current financial statements of a company selected by either you or your instructor.

Required:

a. Compute the return on assets for the most recent two years.

b. Compute the return on common equity (ROCE) for the most recent two years.

c. Prepare a disaggregation of ROCE for the most recent two years.

d. Analyze and interpret results from (*a*), (*b*), and (*c*).

Internet 11–3

Comprehensive Analysis of Return

Access one of the financial statement databases available on the Internet (http://www.mhhe.com/business/accounting/wild). Retrieve current financial statements of a company selected by either you or your instructor.

Required:

a. Compute the company's return on invested capital ratios listed in Case 11–2(*a*) for of the prior two years.

b. Compute the company's asset turnover ratios listed in Case 11–2(*a*) for each of the prior two years.

c. Using your computations in (*a*) and (*b*), analyze and evaluate the company's return on invested capital and asset turnover for these years.

d. For the current year, construct a table showing net amounts accruing to (or detracting from) return on common shareholders' equity from financing sources. Discuss the results in your table (identify any assumptions you make).

e. Compute return on invested capital for the current year when invested capital is measured as:

1. Gross productive assets.
2. Market value of common stock (use year-end or average market value).

Internet 11–4

Profit Margin, Asset Turnover, and Return on Assets

Access one of the financial statement databases available on the Internet (http://www.mhhe.com/business/accounting/wild). Retrieve current financial statements of three companies in different industries selected by either you or your instructor.

Required:

a. Compute profit margin, asset turnover, and return on assets for each company.

b. Write a report analyzing and comparing these companies using the results in (*a*).

Internet 11–5

Return on Common Shareholders' Equity

Access one of the financial statement databases available on the Internet (http://www.mhhe.com/business/accounting/wild). Retrieve current financial statements of three companies in different industries selected by either you or your instructor.

Required:

a. Compute return on common equity (ROCE).

b. Disaggregate ROCE and interpret the results.

c. Write a report comparing these three companies using results from (*a*) and (*b*).

d. What are the effects from financial leverage for ROCE for each company? Does financial leverage affect company risk?

C H A P T E R

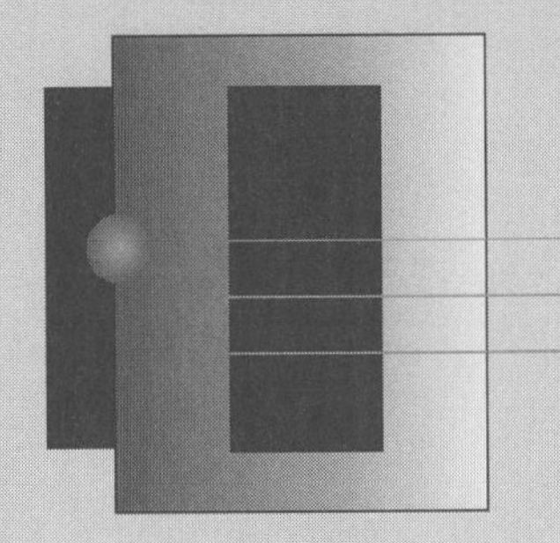

12

Profitability Analysis

Learning Objectives

- Describe the importance of profitability analysis and the necessity of analyzing and adjusting income.
- Analyze the sources, persistence, measurement, and recognition of revenues for assessing profitability.
- Explain gross profit and its evaluation using volume, price, and costs of sales.
- Analyze operating and nonoperating expenses using common-size, index number, and ratio analyses.
- Describe the effective tax rate and the analysis of income tax disclosures.
- Explain break-even analysis and its relevance in assessing profitability.
- Interpret operating leverage and its implications for profitability.

A Look Back

The preceding chapter described return on invested capital and explained its relevance for analysis. Return on assets and return on common equity were shown to be useful tools of analysis. We disaggregated both return measures and explained their value in assessing financial leverage.

A Look at This Chapter

This chapter expands our return analysis to emphasize profitability. Our analysis focuses on the components of income and their evaluation. We direct special attention at sales, cost of sales, taxes, and selling and financing expenses. We explain break-even analysis and its relevance. We demonstrate the use of profitability analysis tools, emphasizing interpretation and adjustments.

A Look Ahead

Chapter 13 extends our analysis to focus on earnings quality, persistence, and prediction. We describe how to assess earnings quality and explain analytical adjustments to income. We analyze management's incentives in reporting income and their implications for analysis. Earnings forecasting and its use of accounting disclosures are discussed.

PREVIEW OF CHAPTER 12

Profitability analysis is important in analyzing financial statements and complements the return analysis discussed in the previous chapter. Profitability analysis goes beyond the accounting measures—such as sales, cost of sales, and operating and nonoperating expenses—to assess their sources, persistence, measurement, and key economic relations. Results from this assessment enable us to better estimate both the return and risk characteristics of a company. Profitability analysis also allows us to distinguish between performance primarily attributed to management (operating decisions) and those results less tied to management decisions (taxes and selling prices). This chapter describes tools of analysis enabling us to make these distinctions. We also describe break-even analysis and its relevance for assessing profitability. Both analytic and graphic analysis of break-even points are explained. We also describe operating leverage and its importance for profitability. Throughout this chapter we emphasize the application of these analysis tools with several illustrative cases. The content and organization of this chapter are as follows:

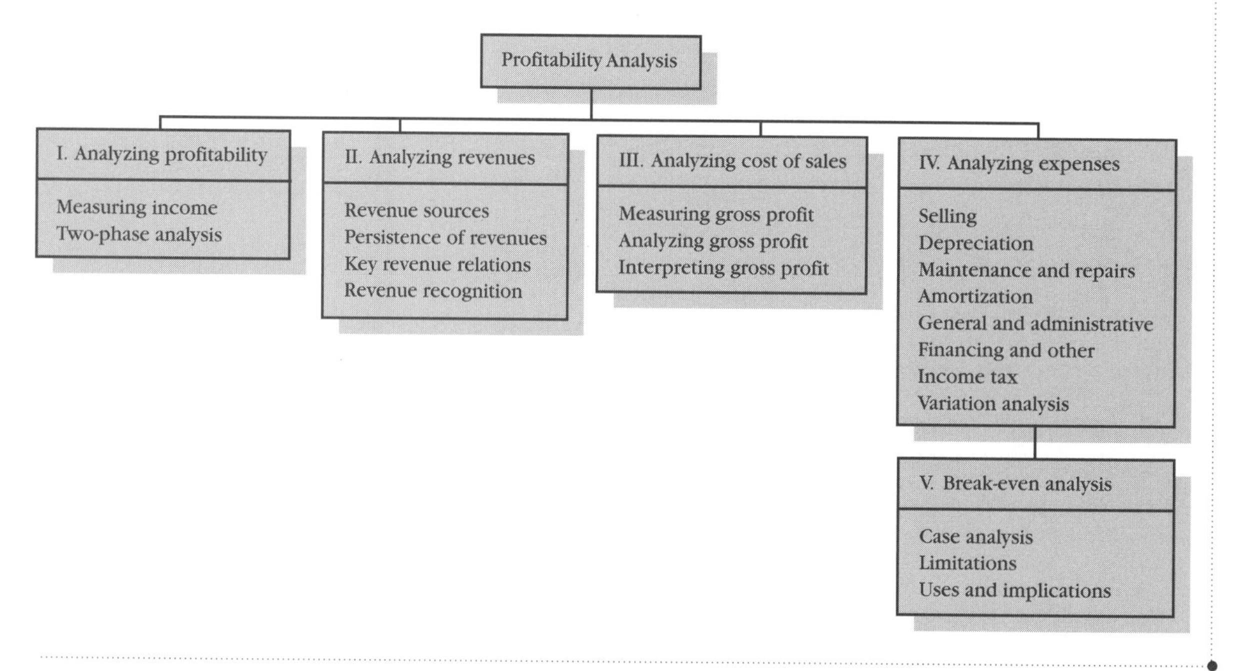

Analyzing Company Profitability

Analyzing company profitability is a major part of financial statement analysis. All financial statements are pertinent to profitability analysis, but none is more important than the income statement. The income statement reports a company's operating results over a period of time. Operating results are the primary purpose of a company, and play an important role in determining company value, solvency, and liquidity.

Profitability analysis is critically important for all users but especially equity investors and creditors. For equity investors, income is often the single most important determinant of changes in security values. Measuring and forecasting income are among the most critical tasks of investors. For creditors, income and operating cash flows are common and desirable sources of interest and principal repayments. When we evaluate company profitability, our analysis focuses on several questions including:

- What is the company's relevant income measure?
- What is the quality of income?
- What income components are most important for income forecasting?
- How persistent (including stability and trend) are income and its components?
- What is a company's earning power?

Factors in Measuring Company Income

Income is defined as revenues less expenses over a reporting period. This presumably simple concept creates many challenges in practice. Users' frustrations are reflected in questions like: Why is it so difficult to determine income under specific circumstances? What is "true income"? Does accounting identify and measure true income? Part Two of this book describes why we cannot expect accounting to provide us with a true income measure. Income is not a unique amount awaiting the perfection of a measurement system to precisely value it. We discuss several reasons for this in this section.

Estimation Issues

Income measurement depends on estimates of the outcome of future events. These estimates are a matter of judgment and probabilities. They require allocation of revenues and expenses across current and future periods. They involve determining future usefulness of many asset types and estimation of future liabilities and obligations. While we expect the judgments of skilled and experienced professionals to reveal some consensus (less variability), income measurement requires certain discretion.

Accounting Methods

Accounting standards governing income measurement are the result of professional experience, regulatory agendas, business happenings, and other social influences. They reflect a balance in these factors, including compromises on differing interests and views toward income measurement. We discussed some of these factors in Chapter 6. There is also latitude in the application of accounting to accommodate different business circumstances as explained in the following illustration.

Illustration 12.1

Our financial analysis uses knowledge of the company and industry to adjust reported income. We adjust income for estimated changes needed for revenue and expense items. These can include adjustments for bad debts, depreciation, research expenses, advertising, and extraordinary or unusual gains and losses. Comparative analysis with other companies demand similar adjustments.

Incentives for Disclosure

Practitioners are ideally concerned with fairly presenting financial statements. This implies accounting would be neutral and give expression and effect to business events without affecting how those events are perceived. Practitioners would choose from alternative principles those most applicable to the circumstances, and disclose relevant information, favorable and unfavorable, affecting users' decisions. However, all of us have opinions, we see the world a little differently, and we experience life from different perspectives. These yield *incentives* that affect much of what we do—and so it is for practitioners. Pressures of management, competition, finances, and family all bear on financial statements and income measurement. Managers bring strong views to the table. Directors expect certain results. Shareholders concentrate on the bottom line. Creditors want safeguards. And the incentives of accounting preparers and auditors are determined by these pressures—especially in gray areas of accounting. These incentives create pressure to choose "acceptable" measures rather than "appropriate" measures given the business circumstances. Our analysis must recognize these incentives and evaluate income accordingly.

Diversity across Users

Financial statements are general-purpose reports serving diverse needs of many users. It is unlikely that one simple income figure is relevant to all users. Certain users value only the bottom line, others value employment opportunities, and still others value social responsibility. This diversity of views implies that our analysis must use income as an initial measure of profitability. We then use information from financial statements and elsewhere to appropriately adjust income consistent with our interests and objectives as illustrated below.

Illustration 12.2

Consider the case where we wish to purchase an income-producing property. Depreciation expense for the property based on the seller's cost is not relevant to us but is to the seller. Our projection of income from this property must use depreciation based on expected purchase price, not on the seller's cost.

This illustration makes clear that the importance of measuring income is *secondary* to our analysis objective of gathering relevant information to adjust income consistent with our needs. This chapter describes analysis tools useful in this task and in evaluating income components. The next chapter considers questions regarding the quality of earnings, usefulness of income components for forecasting, persistence of income, and earning power.

Two-Phase Analysis of Income

Our analysis of income and its components involves two phases. The first phase is our *analysis of accounting and its measurements*. This requires an understanding of the accounting for revenue and expenses. It also requires an understanding of accounting for assets and liabilities since many assets reflect costs deferred and some liabilities represent deferred income. We must understand and assess the implications of using one type of accounting versus another, and its effect on income measurement and comparative analysis. Part Two of this book emphasized this important phase of financial statement analysis.

Our second phase is *applying analysis tools to income (and its components) and interpreting the analytical results.* Applying analysis tools is aimed at achieving our respective objectives in analyzing income. These objectives include income forecasting, assessing income persistence and quality, and estimating earning power. We devote the remainder of this chapter to describing these tools and interpreting their results.

ANALYSIS VIEWPOINT . . . *You are the securities listing director*

You are responsible for setting companies' listing requirements for a regional securities exchange. Several analyst groups request that you increase information disclosure requirements for income, regarding both income components and note disclosures. You also receive requests from certain labor unions, activist groups, and small investors to streamline and condense financial reports and improve the usefulness of aggregate income. What are some reasons for the apparent differences in these groups' requests? How do you balance their information needs?

Analyzing Company Revenues

This section focuses on analyzing a company's revenues (commonly called *sales*). Our analysis of revenues focuses on several questions including:

- What are the major sources of revenue?
- How persistent are revenue sources?
- How are revenues, receivables, and inventories related?
- When is revenue recorded and how is it measured?

PepsiCo's Revenue Sources

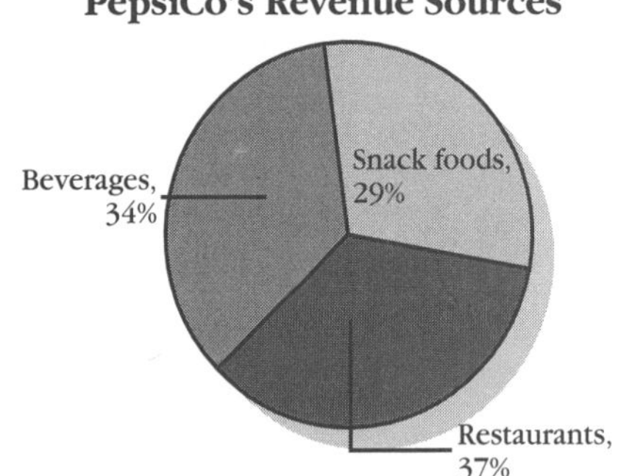

Percent of revenue total

Major Sources of Revenues

Knowledge of major sources of revenues is important in our analysis of income. This information is especially important if our analysis is of a *diversified* company. With diversified companies, each market or product line often has its own growth pattern, profitability, and future potential. An excellent means to analyze sources of revenues is common-size analysis. *A common-size analysis* shows the percent of each major class of revenue to its total. A useful tool for this purpose is to portray graphically the sources of revenue on an absolute dollar basis as shown in Exhibit 12.1 for GT Electronics. This graphical analysis is especially useful across periods. Another common approach is to portray revenue sources in a *pie chart* for specific periods or segments. Adjacent to this paragraph we show a pie chart presentation of PepsiCo for (1) total revenues, and (2) restaurant revenues.

PepsiCo's *Restaurant* Revenue Sources

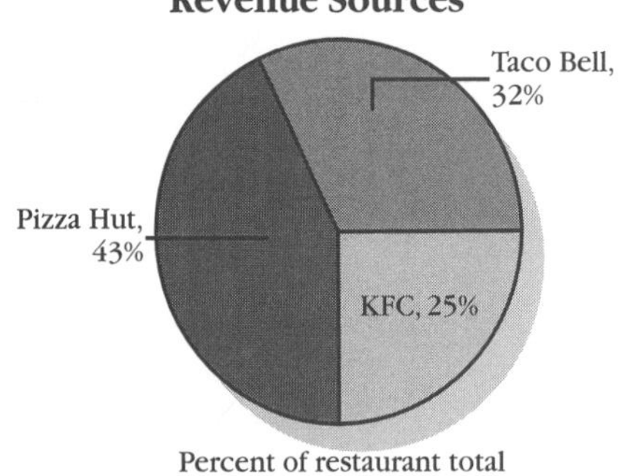

Percent of restaurant total

EXHIBIT 12.1 Analysis of GT Electronics' Revenues by Product Line across Periods

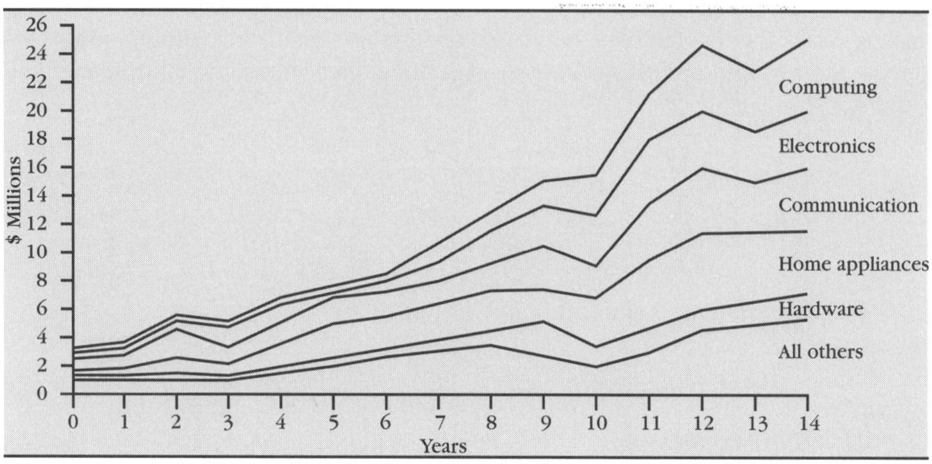

Challenges of Diversified Companies

Our analysis of financial statements of diversified companies must separate and interpret the impact of individual business segments on the company as a whole. This is challenging because different segments or divisions can experience varying rates of profitability, risk, and growth opportunities. Their existence is an important reason why our analysis requires considerable detailed information by business segment. Our evaluation, projection, and valuation of earnings requires this information be separated into segments sharing characteristics of variability, growth, and risk. Asset composition and financing requirements of segments often vary and demand separate analysis. A creditor is interested in knowing which segments provide cash and which are cash users. Knowing the make-up of investing and financing activities, the size and profitability of segments, and the performance of segment management is important information. We show in Chapter 13 that income forecasting benefits from forecasting by segments. Our evaluation of income growth opportunities also benefits from segment information. One analysis tool available to us is the **segmented earnings contribution matrix**. This matrix is useful in assessing earnings quality and growth opportunities, and for valuing aggregate earnings. Examples of variations on this matrix are reported in Exhibits 12.2 and 12.3 for Land's, Ltd. Land's has three major segments that are further subdivided. Both matrixes reveal that leisure goods dominate Land's business, and that its growth opportunities are greatest in this segment.

Reporting by Segments

Information reported on operating results and financial position by segments varies. Full disclosure would provide detailed income statements, balance sheets, and statements of cash flow for each important segment. However, full disclosure by segments is rare in practice because of difficulties in separating segments and management's reluctance to release information that can harm its competitive position.

Regulatory agencies have established reporting requirements for industry segments, international activities, export sales, and major customers. Evaluating risk and return is a major objective of financial statement analysis, and practice recognizes the value of segment disclosures in this evaluation. Analysis of companies operating across

EXHIBIT 12.2 Land's, Ltd., Earnings Contribution and Growth Rates by Segments

Segments	*Earnings Contributions ($ thousands)*	*Growth Rate of Earnings Contribution for Past Three Years*
Leisure goods:		
Camping equipment	$100	11%
Fishing equipment	50	2
Boats and accessories	72	15
Sporting goods	12	3
	$234	
Clothing apparel:		
Dress	$ 85	2%
Casual	72	8
Sports	12	15
	$169	
Education:		
Text publishing	$ 40	3%
Papers and supplies	17	6
	$ 57	
Total	$460	

EXHIBIT 12.3 Land's, Ltd., Segmented Earnings Contribution Matrix

	Growth Rate (in percent)			
Segment	*0–5*	*5–10*	*10–15*	*Total*
Leisure goods	$ 62	$ 0	$172	$234
Agribusiness	85	72	12	169
Education	40	17	0	57
Total	$187	$89	$184	$460

industry segments or geographic areas, which often have different rates of profitability, risk, and growth, is aided by segment data. These data assist us in analyzing uncertainties affecting the timing and amount of expected cash inflows and outflows.

Practice considers a segment significant if its sales, operating income, *or* identifiable assets comprise 10 percent or more of their relevant total amounts. Companies must disclose information for these segments. To ensure that these segments comprise a substantial portion of a company's operations, the combined sales of all segments reported must be at least 75 percent of the company's total sales. Practice suggests *10 segments* as a practical limit on the

Types of Segment Disclosures†

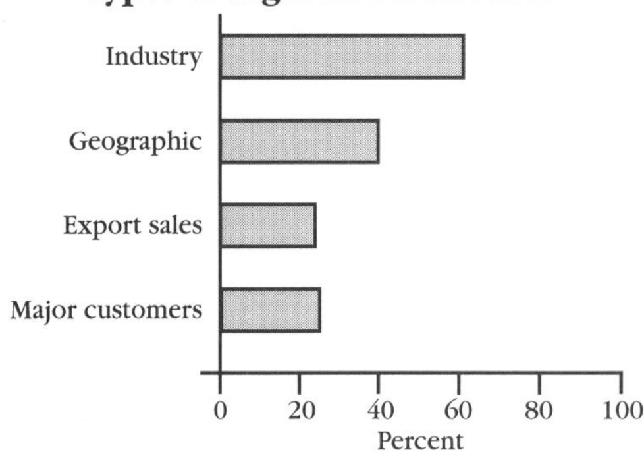

† Total can exceed 100% because companies can report one or more types of segments.
Source: *Accounting Trends & Techniques*.

number of industry segments reported. For each segment, companies must report annually the following items: (1) sales—both intersegment and to unaffiliated customers, (2) operating income—revenue less operating expenses, (3) identifiable assets, (4) capital expenditures, and (5) depreciation, depletion, and amortization expense. Practice does not prescribe methods of accounting for transfer pricing or cost allocation, but does require their disclosure. Practice also requires that if a company derives 10 percent or more of revenues from sales to a single customer, revenues from this customer must be reported. Guidelines are provided in determining a company's international operations and export sales, and for segmenting operations by geographic areas. Information similar to that required for industry segments (except capital expenditures and depreciation) is reported for these additional segments. The SEC also requires a narrative description of the company's business by segments including information on competition, customer dependence, principal products and services, backlogs, sources and availability of raw materials, patents, research and development costs, number of employees, and the seasonality of its business. Segment information for Adaptec is reported in note 9 of its 1996 annual report in Supplement A.

Analysis Implications of Segment Reports

Diversified companies, and the loss of identity for subsidiary companies in consolidated financial statements, creates challenges for our analysis. While segment information is available, our analysis must be careful in using this information for profitability tests. The more specific and detailed is segment information, the more dependent it is on accounting allocations of revenues and expenses. Allocation of common costs as practiced in internal accounting is often based on notions of fairness, reasonableness, and acceptability to managers. These notions are of little relevance to our profitability analysis. Allocations of joint expenses are often arbitrary and limited in their validity and precision. Examples are research and development costs, promotion expenses, advertising costs, interest, pension costs, federal and state income taxes, and general and administrative costs. There are no accepted principles in allocating or transferring costs of one segment to another. We must recognize these limitations when relying on segment reports.

Companies do not typically disclose internal accounting practices unless it is in their interest. Management of Murray Ohio Manufacturing Company felt it advantageous to disclose, in federal court, that its annual report did not reveal the true story in profitability or loss by product line. They admitted to understating losses in its bicycle division by millions of dollars to fend off hostile takeover advances by a Swedish company. Murray Ohio feared that the potential closing of a nonprofitable bicycle division would appeal to a potential acquirer. They therefore chose not to allocate $17 million in overhead to its bicycle division. This case offers us a rare glimpse into the murky area of overhead allocation and the many possibilities companies have to report misleading segment data.

Accounting practice recognizes limitations with segment data. This accounts for companies not being required to disclose segment profit contribution (revenue less those operating expenses *directly* traceable to a segment). The FASB also requires revenues from intersegment sales or transfers be accounted for on *whatever* basis the company uses to price intersegment sales or transfers—no single basis is prescribed. They also recognized certain items of revenues and expenses do not relate to segments or cannot be allocated objectively to segments. Consequently, there is no requirement that income be disclosed by segments. The FASB notes that identifying "segments must depend to a considerable extent on the judgment of the management of the enterprise."

The analysis implications of these limitations in financial statements (lack of firm guidelines and definitions) are serious. Segment reports are and must be analyzed as "soft" information—information subject to manipulation and preinterpretation by management. It must be treated with uncertainty, and inferences drawn from these data must be subjected to alternative sources of verification. Nevertheless, when alternative evidence supports the reliability of segment data, they are extremely useful for our analysis. Specifically, segment data can aid our analysis in:

- *Analyzing sales growth.* Analysis of trends in sales by segments is useful in assessing profitability. Sales growth is often the result of one or more factors including: (1) price changes, (2) volume changes, (3) acquisitions/divestitures, and (4) changes in exchange rates. A company's Management's Discussion and Analysis section usually offers insights into the causes of sales growth.
- *Analyzing asset growth.* Analysis of trends in identifiable assets by segments is relevant for our profitability analysis. Comparing capital expenditures to depreciation can reveal the segments undergoing "real" growth. When analyzing geographic segment reports, our analysis must be alert to changes in foreign currency exchange rates that can significantly affect reported values.
- *Analyzing profitability.* Measures of operating income to sales and operating income to identifiable assets by segment are useful in analyzing profitability. Due to limitations with segment income data, our analysis should focus on trends versus absolute levels.

Exhibit CC.1 in the Comprehensive Case chapter reports a summary of segment information for Campbell Soup Company. Note 2 of Campbell Soup's financial statements also reports Geographic Area Information.

Analysis Research Insight 12.1

Usefulness of Segment Data

Analysis research provides evidence that segment disclosures are useful in forecasting future profitability. We know that total sales and earnings of a company equals the sum of the sales and earnings of all segments (less any intercompany transactions). As long as different segments are subject to different economic factors, the accuracy of segment-based forecasts should exceed that of forecasts based on consolidated data.

Combining company-specific segment data with industry-specific forecasts improves the accuracy of sales and earnings forecasts. Evidence shows that the introduction of segment reporting requirements increased the accuracy and reduced the dispersion of earnings forecasts made by professional securities analysts. This implies that our profitability analysis can also benefit from segment data.

Persistence of Revenues

The stability and trend, or *persistence*, of revenues are important to our analysis of profitability. To the extent we can assess the persistence of revenues by segments, profitability analysis is enhanced. This section considers two useful analysis tools for assessing persistence in revenues: (1) trend percent analysis, and (2) evaluation of Management's Discussion and Analysis.

Trend Percent Analysis

A useful method in assessing persistence of revenues either in total or by segments is **trend percent analysis**. A five-year trend percent analysis of revenues by product lines for Madison, Inc., is shown in Exhibit 12.4. In this case Year 1 revenues are set equal to 100 percent and all years' revenues compared to it (e.g., Year 2 percent equals Year 2 revenues divided by Year 1 revenues). Revenue indexes by segments are often correlated and compared to industry norms or to similar measures for specific competitors. We can also compute *(auto)correlations* for revenues across periods to measure persistence in revenues. Additional considerations bearing on our analysis of revenues' persistence include:

- Demand sensitivity of revenues to business conditions.
- Ability to anticipate demand with new or revised products and services.
- Customer analysis—concentration, dependence, and stability.
- Revenues' concentration or dependence on one segment.
- Revenues' reliance on sales staff.
- Geographical diversification of markets.

As an illustration, our analysis of Micron Products, Inc., yields concern with overreliance on a few major customers.

> Sales to three major customers amounted to approximately 32 percent, 25 percent and 11 percent of the Company's net sales.
>
> —Micron Products, Inc.

Management's Discussion and Analysis

The Management's Discussion and Analysis (MD&A) of a company's financial condition and operating results is often useful in our analysis of persistence in revenues. The SEC requires several disclosures of an interpretative or explanatory nature in MD&A. This information aids us in understanding and evaluating period-to-period changes in financial accounts including revenues. Management is required to report on changes in revenue and expense components relevant for understanding operating activities. These include unusual events affecting operating income, trends or uncertainties affecting or likely to affect operations, and impending changes in revenue and expense relations like increases in material or labor costs. Management must also report on whether they attribute growth in revenues to increases in prices, volume,

EXHIBIT 12.4 Trend Percent Analysis of Revenues by Product Line for Madison, Inc. (Year 1 = 100)

Segment	*Year 1*	*Year 2*	*Year 3*	*Year 4*	*Year 5*
Bridges	100	110	114	107	121
Roadways	100	120	135	160	174
Landscaping	100	98	94	86	74
Engineering	100	101	92	98	105

inflation, or new product introduction. Management is encouraged to describe financial results, report forward-looking information, and discuss trends and forces not evident in the financial statements. The SEC asserts that MD&A provides information relevant to analyzing financial condition and operating results by evaluating the amounts and uncertainty of cash flows.

Reporting guidelines for management in preparing MD&A are few. Management has considerable discretion in communicating relevant information. The aim is meaningful disclosure in narrative form by management, and to supply useful information not typically available in financial statements. Its success in achieving this aim depends on management's attitudes and incentives. While our analysis using information in MD&A is likely "soft," we must remember that management cannot risk being careless or deceptive with this information because of potential SEC-related consequences. Accordingly, our analysis often benefits from this information. It usually provides useful insights, offers us management's perspective, and cannot readily be obtained in other ways. We can use these disclosures as analytical supplements for both the information offered (especially when independently verified) and as insight into management's strategic plans and actions.

Relations between Revenues, Receivables, and Inventories

The relations between revenues and accounts receivable, and revenues and inventories often provide important clues for our evaluation of operating results. They are also often useful in predicting future performance.

Revenues and Accounts Receivable

We discussed the relation between accounts receivable and revenues in Chapter 8 in the context of short-term liquidity. We assessed the quality (collectibility) of receivables and their liquidity (nearness to cash collection). Another important dimension of our analysis is the relation between revenues and receivables in evaluating earnings quality. If accounts receivable grow at a rate exceeding revenues, we need to analyze this to identify the causes. Causes can include revenues being driven by increased incentives, generous extension of credit, or an "in-the-door" strategy in anticipation of future revenue. These conditions bear on future revenues, both favorably and unfavorably. Additionally, such conditions often affect collectibility of receivables.

Illustration 12.3

The relation between revenues and accounts receivable of Toyland, Inc., for a recent five-year period is reflected in the following chart ($ thousands):

	Year ended				
	Year 6	*Year 5*	*Year 4*	*Year 3*	*Year 2*
Net revenues	$199	$227	$175	$198	$290
Percent change	−12.4%	29.7%	−11.3%	−31.9%	—
Accounts receivable	$271	$225	$190	$276	$328
Percent change	20.6%	18.2%	−31.1%	−15.9%	—

In Year 6, revenues declined by 12.4 percent whereas accounts receivable increased by 20.6 percent. This relation contrasts with relations prevailing in preceding years where increases and decreases in revenue or accounts receivables were met with increases and decreases in the other. This negative correlation warrants our special attention and analysis.

Revenues and Inventories

We discussed the relation of inventories to cost of goods sold in Chapter 8 in analyzing short-term liquidity. Also, our discussion in Chapter 11 showed how inventory turnover is related to inventory quality and asset turnover. Our analysis of inventory components often reveals valuable clues to future revenues and operating activity. For example, when increases in finished goods are accompanied by decreases in raw materials and/or work in process, we expect a decline in production.

Illustration 12.4

The relation between revenues and inventories (and inventory components) for Burroughs Corporation for a recent five-year period is reported in the chart below ($ millions):

	Year ended				
	Year 6	*Year 5*	*Year 4*	*Year 3*	*Year 2*
Net revenues	$ 762.7	$ 793.9	$ 689.8	$ 559.0	$ 560.0
Inventories:					
Finished goods	907.1	830.6	631.6	677.9	699.9
Work in process and raw materials	609.0	664.7	561.2	467.7	379.2
Total inventories	$1,516.1	$1,495.3	$1,192.8	$1,145.6	$1,079.1

This table reveals that during the most recent two years, finished goods inventories increase while work in process and raw materials decline. This relation usually foreshadows a production decline. An increase of inventories (especially in finished goods) with a decline in revenues is indicative of a failure of revenues to keep up with production. This is another cause for an expected decline in production.

Revenue Recognition and Measurement

There are various criteria in the recognition and measurement of revenue. We described revenue recognition and measurement in Chapter 6. We know that certain methods are more conservative than others. Our analysis must recognize the revenue recognition methods used by a company and their implications. We must also be aware of potential differences in revenue recognition methods used by different companies in any comparative analysis. When forecasting revenue, one consideration is whether the revenue recognition method used reflects the relevant measure of business performance and operating activities.

ANALYSIS VIEWPOINT *. . . You are the banker*

You are considering loan requests from two companies. Analysis of both companies' financial statements indicates similar risk and return characteristics, and both are marginal applicants. In discussing these cases with your senior loan officer, she points out that one company's income is dispersed across 10 different segments while the other is concentrated in one industry. How does this additional information influence your loan decision? Does it impact your comparison of these companies?

Analyzing Company Cost of Sales

Cost of sales or services provided is, as a percent of revenues, the single largest cost item for most companies. We discussed several methods of determining cost of sales in Chapter 6. There is also, especially in unregulated industries, no generally accepted cost classification method yielding a clear distinction between expenses such as cost of sales, administrative, general, selling, and financing. This is particularly true in classifying general and administrative expenses. Our analysis must be ever alert to methods of cost classification and the effect they have on individual cost assessments and comparative analysis within or across companies.

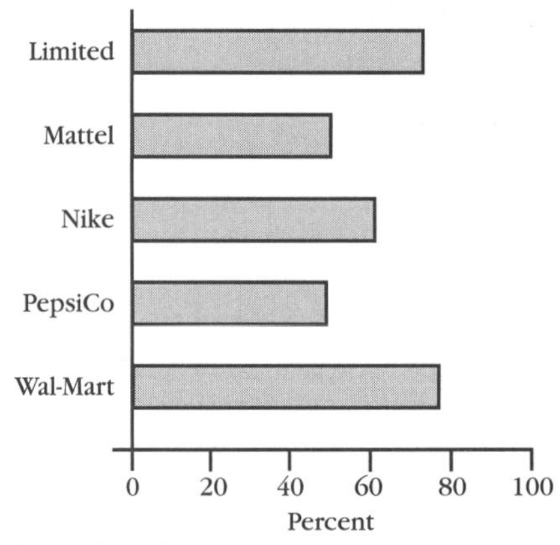

Source: Annual reports.

Measuring Gross Profit (Margin)

Gross profit, or *gross margin,* is measured as revenues less cost of sales. It is frequently reported and described as a percent. A recent year's gross profit for New York Jewelry, Inc., is ($ thousands):

Sales	$11,950	100%
Cost of sales	8,604	72
Gross profit	$ 3,346	28%

The gross profit or gross profit percent is a key performance measure. New York Jewelry's gross profit is $3,346,000 or 28 percent of sales. All other costs must be recovered from gross profit, and any income earned is the balance remaining after these costs. A company must produce a sufficient gross profit to be profitable. Also, gross profit must be sufficiently large to finance essential future-directed discretionary expenditures like research and development, marketing, and advertising. Gross profits vary across industries depending on factors like competition, capital investment, and the level of costs that must be recovered from gross profit.

Analyzing Changes in Gross Profit

Our analysis of gross profit directs special attention to the factors explaining variations in sales and cost of sales. Analyzing changes in gross profit is usually performed internally because it often requires access to nonpublic data, including number of units sold, unit selling prices, and unit costs. Unless a company sells a single product, this analysis benefits from data by product line. For internal analysis (and for external analysis when data permits), evaluating changes in gross profit is part of a useful analysis.

Case 12.1: This case show us an analysis of changes in gross profit for Pennsylvania Printers, Inc. (PPI). Selected financial data of PPI for the most recent two years are reproduced below:

	Year Ended December 31		Year-to-Year Change	
Item	*Year 1*	*Year 2*	*Increase*	*Decrease*
1. Sales ($ millions)	$657.6	$687.5	$29.9	
2. Cost of sales ($ millions)	237.3	245.3	8.0	
3. Gross profit ($ millions)	$420.3	$442.2	$21.9	
4. Units sold (in millions)	215.6	231.5	15.9	
5. Sales price per unit (1 ÷ 4)	$ 3.05	$ 2.97		$0.08
6. Cost per unit (2 ÷ 4)	1.10	1.06		0.04

Drawing on these financial data, we prepare an analysis of changes in PPI's gross profit of $21,900,000 from Year 1 to Year 2. Our analysis focuses sequentially on changes in sales and then cost of sales. The following steps underlie our analysis, and the results are reported in Exhibit 12.5.

Step 1. We focus first on year-to-year change in volume assuming unit selling price remains unchanged from Year 1. The volume change (15.9) is then multiplied by the constant unit selling price ($3.05) yielding a positive change in sales ($48.5).

Step 2. We focus next on year-to-year change in selling price assuming volume is constant. This decrease in selling price (–$0.08) is then multiplied by the constant volume (215.6) yielding a decline in sales (–$17.2).

Step 3. We recognize that assumptions in steps 1 and 2—that volume is constant while unit price changes and vice versa—are simplifications to highlight causes for change. Our analysis must recognize these assumptions ignore *joint* changes in

EXHIBIT 12.5 Analysis Statement of Changes in Gross Profit

PENNSYLVANIA PRINTERS, INC.
For Year 1 and Year 2 ($ millions)

Analysis of Variation in Sales	
1. Change in volume of products sold:	
Change in volume (15.9) × Year 1 unit selling price ($3.05)	$48.5
2. Change in selling price:	
Change in selling price (–$0.08) × Year 1 sales volume (215.6)	–17.2
	$31.3
3. Combined change in sales volume (15.9) and unit price (–$0.08)	– 1.3
Increase in net sales	$30.0*
Analysis of Variation in Cost of Sales	
1. Change in volume of products sold:	
Change in volume (15.9) × Year 1 cost per unit ($1.10)	$17.5
2. Change in cost per unit sold:	
Change in cost per unit (–$0.04) × Year 1 sales volume (215.6)	– 8.6
	$ 8.9
3. Combined change in volume (15.9) and cost per unit (–$0.04)	– 0.6
Increse in cost of sales	$ 8.3*
Net variation in gross profit	$21.7*

* Differences are due to rounding.

volume and unit price. Specifically, the positive volume change (15.9) along with the decrease in unit selling price (–$0.08) yields a net decline in sales (–$1.3).

Step 4. Steps 1 to 3 explain the $30 net increase in sales. Adding the effects on sales due to a (1) volume change (48.5), (2) price change (–17.2), and (3) combined volume and price change (–1.3), we obtain the components explaining the sales increase.

Our analysis of the increase in cost of sales ($8.3) follows the same four steps. Exhibit 12.5 reports results from analysis of both sales and cost of sales components of gross profit.

Interpreting Changes in Gross Profit

Analyzing changes in sales and cost of sales is useful in identifying major causes of changes in gross profit. The types of changes often consist of one or a combination of the following factors:

- Increase in sales volume.
- Decrease in sales volume.
- Increase in unit selling price.
- Decrease in unit selling price.
- Increase in cost per unit.
- Decrease in cost per unit.

The potential for a combined change in volume and unit selling price or a combined change in volume and unit cost poses no particular problem for our analysis.

Interpreting the results of our analysis of changes in gross profit requires identifying the major factors responsible for these changes. It also requires assessing the reasons underlying changes in the factors responsible for gross profit changes. We often extend our analysis to focus on strategic business activities to remedy or improve (through volume, price, or cost) gross profit. If we determine the reason for a decrease in gross profit is a decline in unit selling prices and this reflects overcapacity in the industry with necessary price cutting, then our analysis of the company is pessimistic given management's lack of strategic actions when confronting this condition. However, if the reason for a decrease in gross profit is an increase in unit costs, then our analysis is more optimistic yielding a wider range of potential strategic activities for management.

When interpreting cost of sales and gross profit, especially for comparative analysis, we must direct attention to potential distortions arising from accounting methods. While this is applicable to all cost analysis, it is especially important with inventories and depreciation accounting. These two items, considered in detail in Chapters 4 and 6, merit special attention because they represent costs that are usually substantial in amount and are subject to alternative accounting methods that can substantially affect their measurement.

Analyzing Company Expenses

Most expenses have an identifiable and measurable relation to revenues. This is because revenues are the primary measure of a company's operating activity. Three useful tools for our analysis are based, in part, on the relation between revenues and expenses:

- *Common-size analysis.* Common-size income statements express expenses in terms of their percent relation with revenues. This relation between expenses and sales is then traced over several periods or compared with the experience of competitors. Our analysis of Campbell Soup Company (see the Comprehensive Case chapter) includes common-size income statements spanning several years.
- *Index number analysis.* Index number analysis of income statements expresses income and its components in an index number related to a base period. This analysis highlights relative changes in these items across time allowing us to trace and assess their significance. Changes in expenses are readily compared with changes in both revenues and related expenses. Using index number analysis *with* common-size balance sheets, we can relate percent changes in expenses to changes in assets and liabilities. For example, a change in revenues or revenue-related expenses might explain a change in inventories or accounts receivable. Index number analysis is illustrated in our analysis of Campbell Soup in the Comprehensive Case.
- *Operating ratio analysis.* The operating ratio measures the relation between operating expenses (or its components) and revenues. It equals cost of goods sold plus other operating expenses divided by net revenues. Interest and taxes are normally excluded from this measure due to its focus on operating efficiency (expense control) and not financing and tax management. It is useful for analysis of expenses within or across companies, and can be viewed as an intermediate step in our common-size analysis of income. Properly interpreting this measure requires analysis of the reasons for variations in its components, including gross margin, selling, marketing, general, and administrative expenses.

This section applies these analytical tools in an analysis of a company's expenses.

Selling Expenses

Our analysis of selling expenses focuses on three primary areas:

- Evaluating the relation between revenues and key expenses.
- Assessing bad debts expense.
- Evaluating the trend and productivity of future-directed marketing expenses.

Relation of Selling Expenses to Revenues

The importance of the relation between selling expenses and revenues varies across industries and companies. In certain companies, selling expenses are primarily commissions and are highly variable, while in others they are largely fixed. Our analysis must attempt to distinguish between these variable and fixed components. These components are then usefully analyzed relative to revenues. The more detailed the components, the more meaningful the analysis. A component analysis of selling expenses for Sporting Goods, Inc., is reported in Exhibit 12.6. Our analysis of this exhibit reveals that selling expenses are rising faster than revenues from Year 1 to Year 4. Specifically, selling expenses in Year 4 comprised 5.6 percent more of revenues than in Year 1 ($360/$1,269 versus $180/$791). This is driven by increases, as a percent of revenue, of 1.0 percent in sales staff salaries, 3.6 percent in advertising, and 2.2 percent in branch expenses. Special attention should be directed at the 3.6 percent increase in advertising to determine its cause—for example, is it due to promotion of new products or development of new branches benefiting future sales? The 1.2 percent decline in delivery expense is partially offset with a 0.7 percent increase in freight costs.

When selling expenses as a percent of revenues show an increase, we should focus attention on the increase in selling expense generating the associated increase in revenues. Beyond a certain level of selling expenses there are lower marginal increases in revenues. This can be due to market saturation, brand loyalty, or increased expense in new territories. It is important for us to distinguish between the percent of selling expenses to revenues for new versus continuing customers. This has implications on our forecasts of profitability. If a company must substantially increase selling expenses to increase sales, its profitability is limited or can decline.

EXHIBIT 12.6 Component Analysis of Selling Expenses

SPORTING GOODS, INC.
Comparative Statement of Selling Expenses
($ thousands)

	Year 4		Year 3		Year 2		Year 1	
Sales	$1,269		$935		$833		$791	
Sales trend percent (Year 1 = 100%)		160.0%		118.0%		105.0%		100.0%
Selling expenses†								
Advertising	$ 84	6.6%	$ 34	3.6%	$ 28	3.4%	$ 24	3.0%
Branch expenses*	80	6.3	41	4.4	38	4.6	32	4.1
Delivery expense (own trucks)	20	1.6	15	1.6	19	2.3	22	2.8
Freight-out	21	1.7	9	1.0	11	1.3	8	1.0
Sales staff salaries	111	8.7	76	8.1	68	8.1	61	7.7
Sales staff travel expense	35	2.8	20	2.1	18	2.2	26	3.3
Miscellaneous selling expenses	9	0.7	9	1.0	8	0.9	7	0.9
Total selling expense	$ 360	28.4%	$204	21.8%	$190	22.8%	$180	22.8%

* Includes rent, regional advertising, and promotion.
†Selling expenses are reported in both dollars and as percent of that year's sales amount.

Bad Debts Expense

Bad debts expense is usually regarded as marketing expenses. Since the level of bad debts expense is related to the level of "allowance for doubtful accounts," it is usefully analyzed by examining the relation between the allowance and (gross) accounts receivable. We illustrate this analysis with interim data from Toyland, Inc. ($ thousand):

	Year 3—Quarter			
Item	*1st Quarter*	*2nd Quarter*	*3rd Quarter*	*4th Quarter*
Allowance for doubtful accounts	$ 13,500	$ 12,900	$ 10,600	$ 15,800
Gross receivables	343,319	223,585	179,791	305,700
Allowance as percent of gross receivables	3.93%	5.77%	5.90%	5.17%

	Year 2—Quarter			
Item	*1st Quarter*	*2nd Quarter*	*3rd Quarter*	*4th Quarter*
Allowance for doubtful accounts	$ 16,600	$ 15,000	$ 12,200	$ 18,500
Gross receivables	331,295	215,660	172,427	285,600
Allowance as percent of gross receivables	5.01%	6.96%	7.07%	6.48%

Notice the significant decline in Toyland's Year 3 allowance for doubtful accounts in relation to gross receivables as compared with Year 2. Potential reasons include improved collectibility of receivables or inadequate allowances resulting in understated bad debts expense. Further analysis is necessary to identify the reasons.

Future-Directed Marketing Expenses

Certain sales promotion expenses, particularly advertising, yield current *and* future benefits. Measuring future benefits from these expenses is extremely difficult. Yet it is reasonable for us to assume a relation between current expenditures for advertising and promotion and current *and* future revenues. Expenditures for these future-directed marketing activities are largely discretionary, and our analysis must consider year-to-year trends in these expenditures. Beyond the ability of these expenditures to influence future sales, they provide insights into management's tendency to "manage" reported earnings. We consider the effect of these and other discretionary expenses on earnings quality in the next chapter.

Depreciation Expense

Depreciation expense is often substantial in amount, especially for manufacturing and many service companies. Depreciation is usually considered a fixed cost in that it is often computed based on elapsed time. If its computation uses operating activity, it is a variable cost. In contrast to most expenses, the relation of depreciation to income is not usually meaningful due to its fixed nature. The relation of depreciation to gross plant and equipment is often more meaningful. A measure of this relation is the ratio of depreciation to depreciable assets:

$$\frac{\text{Depreciation expense}}{\text{Depreciable assets}}$$

The purpose of this ratio is to help us detect changes in the composite rate of depreciation. This is useful in evaluating depreciation levels and in detecting any adjustments (smoothing) to income. It is often useful to compute this ratio by asset categories. Analyzing the age of assets is also important and is discussed in Chapter 6.

Maintenance and Repairs Expenses

Maintenance and repairs expenses vary with investment in plant and equipment and with the level of productive activity. They affect cost of goods sold and other expenses. Maintenance and repairs comprise both variable *and* fixed expenses and therefore do not vary directly with sales. Accordingly, the relation of sales to maintenance and repairs expenses, both across companies and time, must be interpreted with care. To the extent our analysis can distinguish between variable and fixed portions of these expenses, we can better interpret their relation to sales. We also must remember that maintenance and repairs are largely discretionary expenses. Many of these expenses can be timed to not detract from one period's income or to preserve liquid resources. For example, companies can postpone or limit much preventive maintenance and many repairs; there are, of course, certain expenses that cannot be postponed without losses in productivity. Management's decisions in this regard bear on earnings quality. We should also consider a company's maintenance and repairs expenses when evaluating depreciation expense. We estimate assets' useful lives using many assumptions including their upkeep and maintenance. If maintenance and repairs are cut back, assets' useful lives likely decline. We may need to adjust upward the depreciation expense to counter the overstatement in income.

Amortization of Special Costs

Certain companies and industries have special costs related to items like tools, dies, jigs, patterns, and molds. The auto industry has considerable special costs related to frequent style and design changes. How a company amortizes these costs affects reported income and is important to our profitability analysis, including comparative analysis. Measures used to analyze changes in the deferral and amortization policies of these costs focus on the relation of the costs to revenues or asset categories. For example, the annual *expenditure* for special costs can be related to and expressed as a percent of (1) revenues and (2) net property and equipment. Similarly, the annual *amortization* of special costs can be related to (1) revenues, (2) unamortized special costs, and (3) net property and equipment. Comparison of annual trends in these relations can aid our analysis of consistency in reporting of income. Comparisons can be extended to evaluation of the income of two or more companies in an industry.

General and Administrative Expenses

Most general and administrative expenses are fixed. This is largely because these expenses include items like salaries and rent. There is a tendency for increases in these expenses, especially in prosperous times. When analyzing these expenses, our analysis should direct attention at both the trend in these expenses and the percent of revenues they consume.

Financing and Other Expenses

This section describes our analysis of financing expenses and "other" expenses.

Financing Expenses

Financing expenses are largely fixed (an exception is interest on short-term debt). Experience shows most creditor financing is eventually refinanced and not removed unless replaced with equity financing. Interest expense often includes amortization of any premium or discount on the debt along with any issue expenses. A useful tool in our analysis of a company's cost of borrowed money and credit standing is its **average effective interest rate** and is computed as:

$$\frac{\text{Total interest incurred}}{\text{Average interest-bearing indebtedness}}$$

As an example, compute Quaker Oats' average effective interest rate for Year 11 using data in Supplement A as $ millions:

$$\frac{(\$43.3 + \$60.5)^{(a)}}{(\$814.7 + \$1{,}115.8)^{(b)} \div 2} = 10.75\%$$

[a] Total interest costs (before deduction for interest capitalized)—item 156.

[b]		
Short-term debt 147	Year 10: $ 343.2	Year 11: $ 81
Current portion of long-term debt 148	32.3	33
Long-term debt 148	740.3	701
Total liabilities subject to interest	$1,115.8	$815

The average effective interest rate is usefully compared across years or companies. Quaker Oats includes a good discussion of debt in the Liquidity and Capital Resources section of its MD&A and in its disclosure on weighted-average interest rates of debt (see note 5 to its financial statements). We can also measure a company's sensitivity of interest rate changes by determining the portion of debt tied to market rates like the prime rate. In periods of rising interest rates, a company with debt tied to market rates is exposed to increased risk through higher interest expenses. Conversely, declining interest rates yield increased returns for these companies.

"Other" Expenses and Revenues

"Other" expenses and revenues are often of limited value in assessing company profitability. They usually small in relation to a company's total expenses and are nondescript in nature. Yet they sometimes obscure component expenses that are useful in assessing profitability but cannot be extracted from the total. For example, nonrecurring components are sometimes included and are often useful in our analysis. It is useful for us to analyze "other revenues" since they can include income from investments in new ventures and information not available elsewhere. These investments can have future implications, favorable or unfavorable, far exceeding their current revenue or expense. We must be alert to management's tendency to offset other expenses against other revenues. The problem is one of obscuring important information as we attempt to gather data on items comprising these expenses and revenues.

Volume of Sales Activity by Type of Organization

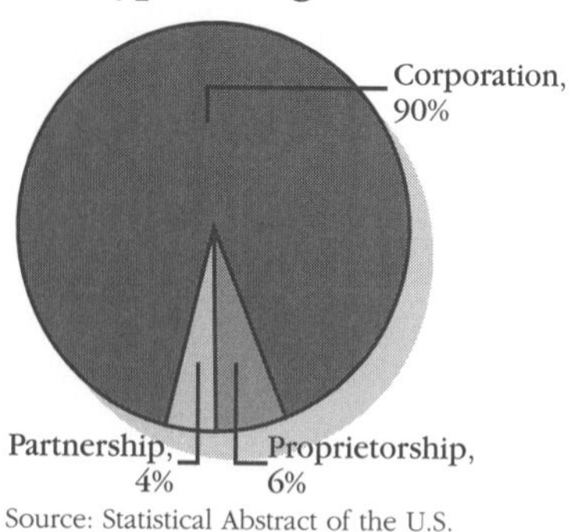

Source: Statistical Abstract of the U.S.

Income Tax Expenses

Income taxes essentially reflect a distribution of profits between a company and governmental agencies. They usually comprise a substantial portion of a company's income before taxes. For this reason our analysis must pay special attention to income taxes. Since corporations conduct nearly 10 times more sales activity than other forms of businesses combined (see pie chart), we focus primarily on *corporate* income taxes in this section.

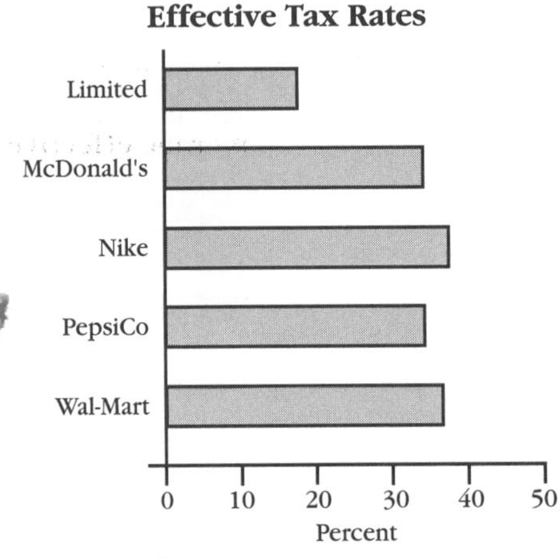

Measuring Effective Tax Rate

Except for a graduated rate on lower levels of income, corporate income is taxed at a uniform rate determined by tax law (35 percent). Differences in timing of recognition for revenues or expenses between taxable income and accrual income should not influence the effective tax rate. This is because interperiod income tax allocation aims to match tax expense with accrual income regardless of when taxes are paid. The relation between the income tax accrual and the pre-tax income, referred to as the **effective tax rate** or *tax ratio*, is also influenced by *permanent* tax differences. Examples include differences due to state and local taxes, foreign tax rate differentials, various tax credits, untaxed income and nondeductible expenses. We discuss both income tax allocation and permanent differences in Chapter 6. The effective tax rate is computed as:

$$\frac{\text{Income tax expense}}{\text{Income before income taxes}}$$

For Quaker Oats the effective tax rate for Year 11 is computed as:

$$\frac{\$175.7^{(a)}}{\$411.5^{(b)}} = 42.7\%$$

[(a)] Provision for income taxes—item [8] in Supplement A.

[(b)] Income from continuing operations before income taxes—item [7] in Supplement A.

The 42.7 percent effective tax rate corresponds to the rate computed by the company (see note 16 of its annual report in Supplement A). Notice the effective tax rate uses income from continuing operations rather than net income. If we want to compute the effective tax rate incurred by the company on *all* items of income during a period, including discontinued operations and extraordinary items, then a different computation is required. We use Quaker Oats to illustrate this:

Income (loss)	*Before Tax*	*Related Tax*	*After Tax*
Income from continuing operations before income taxes and other items	$411.5 [7]	$175.7 [8]	$235.8 [9]
Loss from discontinued operations	(50)	(20) [144]*	(30) [10]
Net income	$361.5*	$155.7*	$205.8 [11]

*Derived amount.

The effective tax rate using *all* items in net income is:

$$\frac{\$155.7}{\$361.5} = 43.1\%$$

We might also notice in our analysis of Quaker Oats' income that preferred dividends are reported net of tax. This is an unusual case of preferred dividends yielding a tax benefit of undisclosed amount. We must consider this type of tax effect bypassing net income (similar to tax effects relating to stock options and reported in equity) when reconciling all tax-related accounts to understand a company's tax position and amounts paid. We discuss this later in the chapter.

In evaluating income level, trend, and forecasts, we must identify the reasons why an effective tax rate deviates from the normal or expected rate. Income taxes are of such magnitude that small changes in the effective tax rate can yield major changes in income. Knowledge of the reasons for deviations and changes in the effective tax rate of a company is important to our profitability analysis and income forecasting. Practice requires several disclosures of current and deferred income taxes. Our analysis of these and other aspects of tax disclosures are important and is described next.

Analyzing Income Tax Disclosures

Our analysis of income tax disclosures can be undertaken with specific or general objectives. The more general objectives of our analysis include:

- Assess tax implications on income, assets, liabilities, and cash sources and uses.
- Evaluate tax effects for future income and cash flows.
- Appraise the effectiveness of tax management.
- Identify unusual gains or losses revealed in tax disclosures.
- Signal areas of concern requiring further analysis or management inquiry.
- Analyze the adequacy of tax disclosures.

The following *analytical strategy* is useful in analyzing income tax disclosures.

Step 1. Our first step is to establish a T-account for each tax-related account in the balance sheet and income statement. A current tax liability and/or a current tax receivable (for a refund) should be identifiable. There are also one or two deferred tax accounts (one current and one noncurrent) in the balance sheet. We must take care to identify income taxes (current and possibly deferred) relating to the separate income statement sections: (1) continuing operations, (2) discontinued operations, (3) extraordinary items, and (4) cumulative effect of changes in accounting principles. Their separate income tax effects are sometimes identified outside the income statement (e.g., Quaker Oats' preferred dividend tax benefit)—in parenthetical and financial statement notes, in schedules like those reconciling owner's equity, and in sections containing management discussion.

Step 2. Reconstruct the period's summary entry for recording tax expense. It is often helpful to split this into two or more entries: at least one for current tax expense and one for deferred tax expense.

Step 3. Once the opening and closing balances of all tax-related balance sheet T-accounts are entered, post the tax expense entries and income statement accounts to their relevant T-accounts. We should use all available information to reconstruct these accounts. Changes in deferred tax on the balance sheet should agree with the deferred tax expense reported in the income statement or in related footnotes. Information like noncash adjustments to income reported in the statement of cash flows is often useful. If our attempts at reconciliation are unsuccessful, we might look for either a deferred tax account combined with or reported under another caption in the balance sheet or an undisclosed entry for correcting errors or similar adjustment. We can always obtain the necessary balancing amount and enter it. We must realize our conclusions regarding balancing (plugged) amounts in a reconciliation are subject to the assumptions implicit in this balancing. For deferred tax accounts not fully reconciled, we transfer the amounts needed to reconcile them to Current Taxes Payable or to Tax Refunds Receivable. The tax T-accounts are now fully reconstructed.

Step 4. Use taxes paid during the period as a "plug" to the current Taxes Payable account. A credit plug reflects a tax refund.

We must recognize the usefulness of our analysis depends on the quality of disclosures in financial statements. Poor disclosures require more analytical adjustments like combining accounts (e.g., current tax receivable and payable accounts). Our analysis must also be aware that acquisition or disposition of businesses can result in related additions or deductions to balance sheet tax accounts. For example, acquisition of a company can require accepting its tax liabilities.

Illustration of Income Tax Analysis. To illustrate income tax analysis we use Quaker Oats' Year 11 annual report in Supplement A. Our *first step* is to establish T-accounts for each tax-related balance sheet account and for each income tax expense and tax effect account in Quaker's Year 11 income statement. We identify income tax payable and deferred income taxes (noncurrent account) in the balance sheet. We also identify the provision for income taxes and accounts below this (reported net of tax) in the income statement (the tax effect of the loss from discontinued operations ($20) is in note 2). Quaker Oats' financial statements do not disclose the preferred dividends' tax effect. We therefore compute its tax effect as (where PD is preferred dividends before tax and the assumed marginal tax rate is 34 percent):

$$PD\,(1 - 34\%) = \$4.3 \;\boxed{12}\; \text{ or } PD = \$6.5$$

Then, the preferred dividends' tax effect is simply:

$$\$6.5 - \text{Tax effect} = \$4.3 \text{ or Tax effect} = \$2.2$$

Our *second step* is to enter opening and ending balances in T-accounts. Tax-related accounts in income statements do not have opening balances and their ending balances are closed via the income statement to retained earnings. Opening balances must sometimes be derived using changes reported in the statement of cash flows.

Income Tax Payable [75]

	Debit	Credit	
		36.3	Beg.
(b)	20.0	161.4	*(a)*
(d)	24.7	2.2	*(c)*
Assumed paid	110.1		
		45.1	End.

Deferred Income Tax [81]

	Debit	Credit	
		327.7	Beg.
		14.3	*(a)*
		24.7	*(d)*
		366.7	End.

Income Tax Expense [8]

	Debit	Credit	
(a)	175.7		

Tax Effect—Discontinued Operations [144]

	Debit	Credit	
		20.0	*(b)*

Tax Effect—Preferred Dividends

	Debit	Credit
(c)	2.2	

Our *third step* is to enter the tax-related activity during year into the T-accounts using all available information, especially the tax note. We achieve this by using analytical entries and posting to relevant T-accounts. The tax expense (including tax effects of items shown net of tax) can be combined, but it is often easier to enter them separately as shown here:

Income Tax Expense	175.7	
Income Tax Payable (item **158**)		161.4
Deferred Income Tax (item **158**)		14.3
161.4Income Tax Payable	20.0	
Tax Effect—Discontinued Operation		20.0
Tax Effect—Preferred Dividends	2.2	
Income Tax Payable		2.2

Having entered all tax-related transactions in T-accounts, we then determine whether these entries explain the changes in all tax-related accounts except Tax Payable. For Quaker we find the change in Deferred Income Tax is not explained and requires a plugging entry as follows:

Income Tax Payable	24.7	
Deferred Income Tax (plug)		24.7

Our *fourth step* is to estimate taxes paid during the period and is only made after changes in the balances of all tax-related accounts, except Tax Payable (or Tax Receivable), are accounted for. Once done, as in our example here, we determine the taxes paid (or received) as a balancing figure (plug) in Tax Payable. For Quaker, the plug of $110.1 is on the debit side, indicating a tax payment. The tax paid (or received) should be reconciled (as feasible) to taxes paid as reported in the statement of cash flows. Quaker reports taxes paid in Year 11 of $88.7 million (item **159**). This is considerably less than the $110.1 million from our analysis. A complete explanation of Quaker's tax policies requires management (or inside) information.

We also explain how a company's tax rate is different from the "legal" rate. In Quaker's case it reports Year 11 pre-tax income from continuing operations of $411.5. This income yields $175.7 in tax expense, of which $161.4 are current federal income taxes. We explain this as follows:

Reconciliation to Legal Rate	***Computation***	***Item***	***$ Millions***
Expected federal income tax at 34%	$411.5 × 0.34	7	$139.9
Add: State tax net of federal benefit	$411.5 × 0.041	158c	16.9
			$156.8
Add permanent differences **158c**:			
Repatriation of foreign earnings	$4.3		
Non-U.S. tax rate differential	8.2		
Miscellaneous (rounded)	6.4		18.9
			$175.7
Less total deferred taxes			14.3
Total current federal, non-U.S. and state taxes		158	$161.4

Consideration of Pre-Tax Income

Our focus on net income and earnings per share requires an analysis of changes in the effective tax rate. Pre-tax income is also relevant for certain analyses. This is due to the importance attached to pre-tax operating results. Pre-tax operating results derive from management skills in operating the business as compared with performance due to variations in the effective tax rate. Management is likely to have less control over the company's tax performance relative to its operating activities.

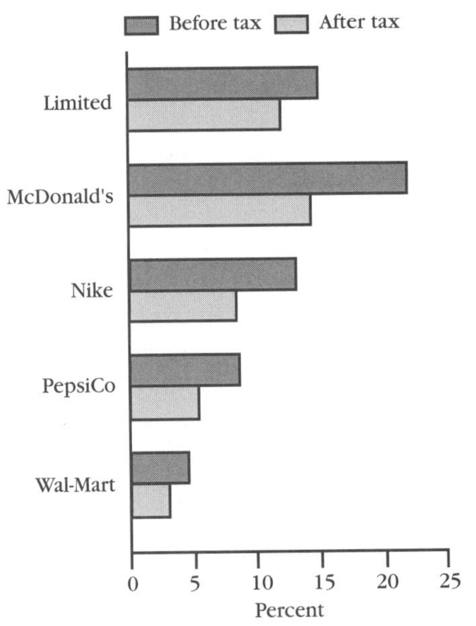

Source: Annual reports.

Variation Analysis of Income and Its Components

In our analysis of year-to-year changes in income, it is useful to measure components contributing to increases and decreases in income. This analysis is referred to as **variation analysis**. A common method of variation analysis indicating the percent increase or decrease in income components uses the *statement of variations in income and income components*. Exhibit 12.7 presents this statement for Campbell Soup Company using its annual report in Supplement A.

> **ANALYSIS VIEWPOINT** . . . *You are the political activist*
>
> You are the campaign manager for a first-time candidate running for state representative. The incumbent's campaign is financed almost exclusively by a major forest products company in your district. The incumbent fought for and received state and local logging cost benefits for this company in the past two years. One of your goals is to repeal these benefits if elected. The incumbent counters that this company is the largest employer in the district and points to this company's income *after* these benefits, which is similar to its competition. You look at the financial statements and find gross margin is 40% of sales while the industry norm is 20%. Yet profit margin is at the industry norm of 10%—the difference between gross and profit margin is primarily due to executive compensation. Is this useful information?

Break-Even Analysis

Break-even analysis focuses on the relation between a company's revenues and expenses. An important part of break-even analysis is distinguishing among two classes of expenses: variable and fixed. Variable expenses vary directly with revenues while fixed expenses remain essentially constant over a wide range of revenue levels.

Break-Even Analysis Case

Distinguishing between expenses according to their variable or fixed behavior is best understood with a case example. To focus on the information required and the analysis techniques involved, we consider the following scenario:

EXHIBIT 12.7

CAMPBELL SOUP COMPANY
Statement of Variations in Income and Income Components
Three-Year Period Year 6–Year 8 (Average) compared
to Three-Year Period Year 9–Year 11 (Average)
(in millions)

			Percent Change
Components Tending to Increase Net Income			
Increase in net sales:			
Net sales (Year 9–Year 11)	$6,027.3		
Net sales (Year 6–Year 8)	4,548.7	$1,478.6	32.5%
Deduct the increase in costs of goods sold:			
Cost of products sold (Year 9–Year 11)	$4,118.4		
Cost of products sold (Year 6–Year 8)	3,218.7	$ 899.7	28.0
Net increase in gross margin		$ 578.9	
Increase (decrease) in interest income:			
Interest income (Year 9–Year 11)	$ 27.3		
Interest income (Year 6–Year 8)	30.0	(2.7)	(9.0)
Total items tending to increase net income		$ 576.2	
Components Tending to Decrease Net Income			
Increase in marketing and sales expenses:			
Marketing and sales expenses (Year 9–Year 11)	$ 918.5		
Marketing and sales expenses (Year 6–Year 8)	634.6	$ 283.9	44.7
Increase in administrative expenses:			
Administrative expenses (Year 9–Year 11)	$ 283.2		
Administrative expenses (Year 6–Year 8)	214.1	$ 69.1	32.3
Increase in R&D expenses:			
R&D expenses (Year 9–Year 11)	$ 52.6		
R&D expenses (Year 6–Year 8)	44.6	$ 8.0	17.9
Increase in interest expenses:			
Interest expenses (Year 9–Year 11)	$ 107.3		
Interest expenses (Year 6–Year 8)	53.9	$ 53.4	99.1
Increase in other expenses:*			
Other expenses (Year 9–Year 11)	$ 32.2		
Other expenses (Year 6–Year 8)	5.0	$ 27.2	544.0
Increase in income tax expenses:			
Income tax (Year 9–Year 11)	$ 178.1		
Income tax (Year 6–Year 8)	160.5	$ 17.6	11.0
Total items tending to decrease net income		$ 459.2	
Change in net effect of equity in earnings of affiliates and minority interests (MI):			
Equity in earnings of affiliates and MI (Year 9–Year 11)	$ 2.7		
Equity in earnings of affiliates and MI (Year 6–Year 8)	3.6	(0.9)	(25.0)
Increase in net income:†			
Net income (Year 9–Year 11)	$ 367.0		
Net income (Year 6–Year 8)	250.9	$ 116.1	46.3

* Includes foreign exchange losses.

† Income before divestitures, restructuring and unusual charges; and before cumulative effect of change in accounting for income taxes.

Case 12.2: A local electronics company placed an ad in the college newspaper announcing an opportunity for an individual to sell compact cassette players with special discount coupons at an upcoming analysts' convention on campus. This position requires that one purchase a $10 vendor's license from the convention organizing committee and to rent a $140 sales booth. The electronics company charges the salesperson $3 for each cassette player with the right to return any that are unsold. The company also specifies an $8 selling price per player. Each cassette player purchase is packaged with discount coupons from the company. You must decide whether to accept this job. You wonder how many cassette players you must sell to break even. We analyze this case scenario using break-even analysis.

Equation-Based Break-Even Analysis

An equation-based analysis of break-even begins with the income equation:

Sales = Variable expenses + Fixed expenses + Profit (or *minus* Loss)

Break-even analysis assumes a zero profit or loss—this reflects common usage of the term break-even. If profit or loss is zero, the income equation is simplified as:

Sales = Variable expenses + Fixed expenses

For the above case, sales can be expressed as $8 multiplied by the number of cassette players sold. Similarly, variable expenses equal $3 multiplied by cassette players sold, and fixed expenses equal the $10 license plus the $140 booth. Substituting these relations into the income equation yields:

$$\$8X = \$3X + \$150$$

where:

Sales = $8 (unit selling price) × X
Variable expenses = $3 (unit variable cost) × X
Fixed expenses = $10 (license fee) + $140 (booth fee)

Fixed expenses are incurred regardless of the number of cassette players sold. We can solve the equation for X as follows:

$$(\$8 - \$3)X = \$150$$

$$X = 30 \text{ units to break even}$$

Knowing the number of cassette players necessary to be sold just to break even is important for your decision to accept or reject this job opportunity. Once you have this information you can assess the likelihood of at least selling the break-even number of units. This focus on break-even *units* is primarily limited to *single product* companies.

Companies typically sell multiple products. This would be the case in the scenario above if you sold calculators and headphones along with cassette players. In this case the break-even *units* computation is not appropriate. Rather, we focus on break-even *dollar* sales. Applying the break-even dollar sales analysis to the scenario above using the income equation yields (where Y is the break-even dollar sales):

$$Y = (\text{Variable expense as percent of price}) \times Y + \text{Fixed expenses}$$
$$Y = 0.375Y + \$150$$
$$0.625Y = \$150$$
$$Y = \$240$$

EXHIBIT 12.8 Graphic-Based Break-Even Analysis

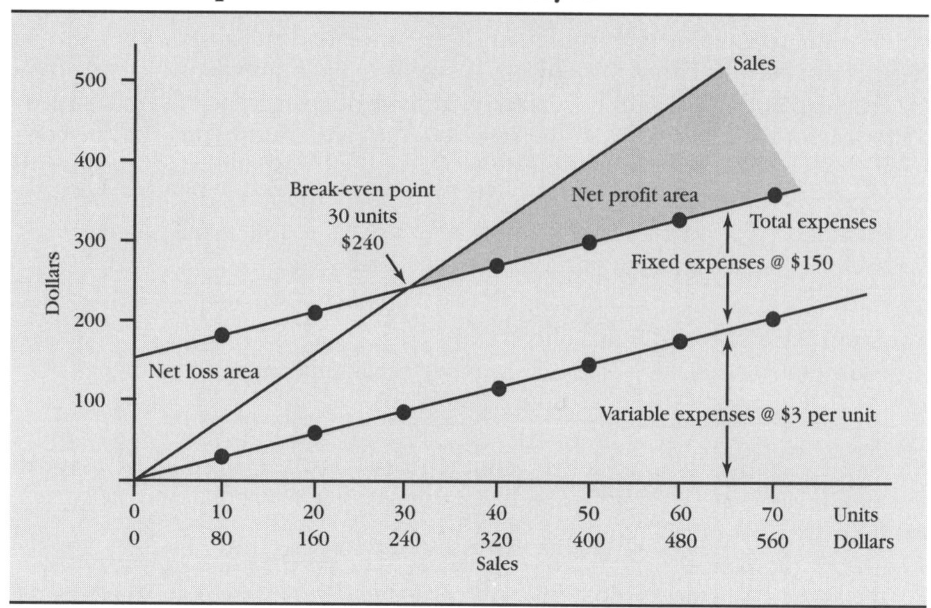

This indicates one must sell $240 of cassette players to break even. The $240 is equivalent to the 30 break-even units calculated above (at $8 per player). The variable expense percent is the ratio of variable expenses ($3) to selling price ($8). This percent is interpreted as a dollar of sales generates $0.375 of variable expenses, or variable expenses comprise 37.5 percent of sales.

Graphic-Based Break-Even Analysis

We can also estimate break-even points using graphic-based analysis. Using information from our cassette player scenario we portray graphically break-even analysis in Exhibit 12.8. A graph drawn to scale yields a solution identical to equation-based analysis, although graphic-based analysis is usually less precise. An especially nice feature of graphic-based analysis is the portrayal of the break-even point *and* a wide range of profitable scenarios above this point and losses below it.

Contribution Margin Break-Even Analysis

Contribution margin analysis is another method to assess break-even points. This method can provide additional insights into the relation between sales, expenses, and profits. **Contribution margin** is what remains after deducting variable expenses from sales. This contribution must cover fixed expenses before any profit is earned. Using the cassette player case, *contribution margin per unit* is computed as:

Selling price per cassette player	$8
Variable expenses per cassette player	3
Contribution margin per unit	$5

Since each unit (cassette player) sold contributes $5 to cover fixed expenses, the break-even point in units is:

$$\frac{\text{Fixed expenses}}{\text{Contribution margin per unit}} = \frac{\$150}{\$5} = 30 \text{ units}$$

This implies that after 30 units are sold fixed expenses are covered and each additional unit sold yields a profit equal to the unit contribution margin, or $5.

Contribution margin analysis can also be performed using sales dollars to compute the break-even point. This analysis uses the contribution margin ratio rather than the contribution margin per unit. The **contribution margin ratio** is computed as:

$$\frac{\text{Contribution margin per unit}}{\text{Selling price per unit}} = \frac{\$5}{\$8} = 0.625$$

For our cassette player case, the dollar break-even point is calculated as:

$$\frac{\text{Fixed expenses}}{\text{Contribution margin ratio}} = \frac{\$150}{0.625} = \$240$$

Contribution margin analysis is an important tool in assessing break-even points. We discuss further uses of contribution margin analysis later in this section.

Further Considerations in Break-Even Analysis

The break-even methods described in this section lend themselves to a variety of assumptions, requirements, and what-if analysis. We reveal some of these advantages in Illustrations 12.5 and 12.6. These illustrations use information from our cassette player scenario (unless explicit changes are mentioned).

Illustration 12.5

Assume one requires a profit of $400 to pursue selling of cassette players. How many cassette players must you sell before you achieve this profitability level? We use the equation-based analysis to answer this question (S equals sales):

$$\begin{aligned} \text{Sales} &= (\text{Variable expense percent})\,(\text{Sales}) + \text{Fixed expenses} + \text{Profit} \\ S &= 0.375\, S + \$150 + \$400 \\ 0.625\, S &= \$550 \\ S &= \$880 \\ \$880 \div \$8 &= 110 \text{ units} \end{aligned}$$

Limitations in Break-Even Analysis

The usefulness of break-even analysis depends on overcoming certain limitations. This section discusses those limitations and the assumptions underlying break-even analysis.

Identifying Fixed, Variable, and Semivariable Expenses

Our illustrations of break-even analysis clearly identified fixed and variable expenses. Yet many expenses are not easily separable into fixed and variable components. They either do not remain constant over major changes in sales volume or do not respond in exact proportion to changes in sales. Expenses for food supermarkets are a typical case. Many of their fixed expenses do not vary within a wide range of sales including rent, depreciation, certain maintenance, utilities, and supervisory labor. Yet they can sometimes change independent of sales, for example, management can increase the grocery manager's salary. In addition, variable expenses like

Illustration 12.6

The analysts' convention committee offers to provide you with a free booth if you agree to imprint the analysts' organization seal on the cassette player. You discuss this with the electronics company and they agree subject to the stipulation of an increase in cost from $3 to $4 per unit. What is the break-even point if you accept the convention committee's offer? To answer this, remember that their offer would reduce fixed expenses by $140 but increase variable expenses by $1 per unit. We can compute the break-even point in units sold (X) as follows:

$$\text{Sales} = \text{Variable expenses} + \text{Fixed expenses}$$
$$\$8X = \$4X + \$10$$
$$\$4X = \$10$$
$$X = 2.5 \text{ (or rounded up to 3)}$$

This offer involves a much lower break-even point and hence reduces your risk. However, it also lowers the contribution margin, which reduces profits at higher sales levels. Before you make a decision it is useful for you to compute the level of unit sales where the initial offer of $3 per unit variable expenses and $150 fixed expenses equals the committee's offer involving $4 per unit variable expenses and $10 fixed expenses. This is calculated as follows, where X is the number of units sold:

$$\$4X + \$10 = \$3X + \$150$$
$$\$1X = \$140$$
$$X = 140 \text{ units}$$

This result implies that if you sell *more* than 140 cassette players, the committee's offer involving the $3 variable expense is more profitable.

merchandise, trading stamps, supplies, and manual labor vary directly with sales. Nevertheless, there are expenses comprised of both fixed and variable components. Examples of these **semivariable expenses** are repairs, materials, indirect labor, fuel, and payroll taxes. Even utilities and rent can include variable components tied to sales activity. Break-even analysis requires the variable component of these expenses be separated from the fixed component. This is often difficult for our analysis without availability of internal data.

Assumptions in Break-Even Analysis

Break-even analysis typically includes several simplifying assumptions. While assumptions do not negate its results, our break-even analysis must be aware of assumptions and their potential effects. Important assumptions in break-even analysis include:

Assumptions about Expenses and Revenues:

- Expenses are separable into fixed and variable components.
- Variable expenses vary directly with sales volume.
- Fixed expenses are constant over the relevant range of analysis.
- Unit selling prices are constant over the relevant range of analysis.

Assumptions about Operating and Environmental Factors:

- Sales mix is unchanged over the analysis range.
- Operating efficiency remains constant.

- Prices of cost factors are constant.
- Volume is the only factor affecting expenses.
- Beginning and ending inventory levels remain essentially unchanged.
- General price levels are essentially constant.

This list of assumptions highlights the importance of *sensitivity tests* for break-even analysis. These tests examine how sensitive our conclusions are to changes in assumptions. For example, assuming the selling price does not change with volume is contrary to economic theory and experience—indeed, our sales line should be curved rather than straight. The degree of error in our analysis depends on the actual deviation of the sales line from our assumed straight line. We must also remember that not all assumptions are equally important or influential. We assume volume is the major factor affecting expenses, yet we know many factors like strikes, politics, legislation, and competition are influential. Our analysis must keep these assumptions in mind and be aware of factors or conclusions requiring adjustments.

Uses and Implications of Break-Even Analysis

Break-even analysis is a valuable analytical tool if we recognize its limitations and properly interpret its results. Its use extends beyond computing a break-even (zero profit) point. Break-even analysis is useful in examining revenue, expense, and profit projections under a wide range of future conditions (assumptions). Moreover, both internal (managerial) and external applications of break-even analysis are many. *For management,* it is useful in price determination, expense control, and profitability forecasts. It provides a basis for pricing decisions under differing levels of activity along with standard cost systems. It is a useful tool for expense control in conjunction with flexible budgets. It is also useful in providing break-even charts to measure the impact of specific managerial decisions like plant expansion and new product introduction, or even the impact of external influences on company profitability for various activity levels. *For external analysis,* the use of break-even analysis for profitability projections is useful in estimating the impact on profitability of various economic conditions and managerial strategies.

Application of Break-Even Analysis

This section shows how a reliably constructed break-even analysis is useful in forecasting profits, assessing operating risk, and evaluating profitability levels. We illustrate this through a break-even analysis of Cola-Company, a multiproduct business. We begin with a break-even chart for Cola-Company, shown in Exhibit 12.9 (numbers in thousands). This break-even chart is subject to the assumptions we described above including our ability to identify fixed and variable expense components. *At the break-even point,* Cola-Company's income statement appears as follows:

Sales		$1,387,000
Expenses:		
Variable	$887,000	
Fixed	500,000	1,387,000
Net income		$ –0–

The relevant break-even points are sales of $1,387,000; sales units of 1,156,000; and average selling price per unit of $1.20. The variable expense percent is $887/$1,387, or 64 percent. This implies that, on average, 64 cents of every sales dollar goes to cover variable expenses. The contribution margin ratio is 36 percent (100 minus the variable expense percent of 64). This indicates that each dollar of sales generates 36 cents toward covering fixed expenses and the earning of profit beyond break-even. Cola-Company's contribution margin earned on sales of $1,387,000 is exactly sufficient to cover $500,000 in fixed expenses. The lower are fixed costs, the less sales are necessary to cover them and the lower is the break-even point. If a business has only variable expenses (all costs vary directly with sales), there is no break-even point—this type of company makes a profit beginning with its first sale.

Cola-Company's break-even chart reflects revenues and expenses under its current product mix. Since each product has different revenue and expense patterns and profit margins, changes in product mix affect the break-even point and the relation between revenues, expenses, and profits. While Exhibit 12.9 shows the number of sales units on the horizontal axis, this number and the average selling price per unit are limited to the current product mix. The relevance of break-even analysis is confined to cases where the product mix is fairly stable, at least in the short term. It is also confined to cases where there are not dramatic and frequent fluctuations in selling prices or in costs of production like raw materials.

Exhibit 12.9 assumes fixed expenses of $500,000 will prevail up to a sales level of $2,400,000 (or 2,000 units). This is Cola-Company's point of nearly 100 percent capacity. The break-even point is near 60 percent of capacity, while current sales are near 75 percent of capacity. This implies that at 100 percent capacity, fixed expenses might require an upward revision. If Cola-Company is reluctant to expand capacity, and increase fixed expenses and its break-even point (assuming the variable expense rate does not change), it can consider alternatives including: (1) sacrificing sales growth, (2) increasing variable expenses (adding shift work), or (3) subcontracting

EXHIBIT 12.9 Cola-Company's Break-Even Chart

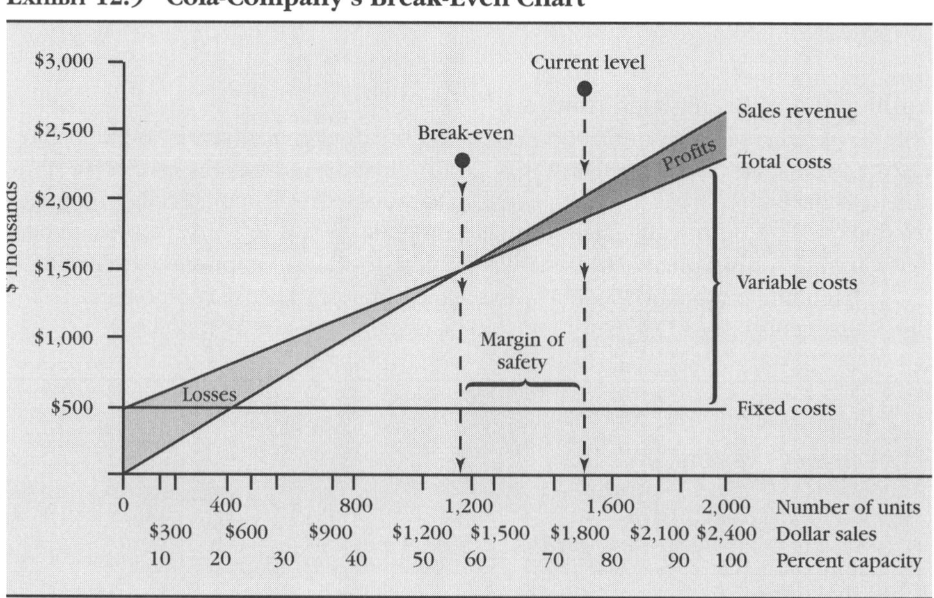

work to outsiders and giving up some profit margin. The break-even chart also portrays Cola-Company's current position relative to its break-even. Its current sales of $1,800,000 are about $413,000 above break-even. This is referred to as the **safety margin**. Safety margin is the company's gap or buffer from the break-even point. We can use safety margin to indicate the point on the chart where a company earns a desired return on investment. It can also be used to indicate the point where common dividends are in jeopardy or where current earnings no longer cover preferred dividends.

Operating Leverage and Break-Even Analysis

Operating leverage refers to changes in sales with a certain level of fixed expenses resulting in larger than proportionate changes in profitability. Like financial leverage (see Chapter 10), which utilizes fixed interest financing to generate greater returns for equity investors, operating leverage utilizes fixed expenses for greater profitability. Specifically, increases in profits that exceed fixed expenses magnify the return on equity financing and vice versa. Until a company generates sales sufficient to cover fixed expenses, it incurs losses. Having covered fixed expenses, further increments in sales result in more than proportionate increases in profitability.

The following case illustrates the effects of operating leverage. Book World, Inc., has the following expense structure: fixed expenses of $100,000; and variable expense percent of 60. The chart below describes Book World's profit or loss at successively higher levels of sales activity. It also compares relative percent changes in sales volume with those in profitability.

					Percent Increase over Prior Period	
Year	*Sales*	*Variable Expenses*	*Fixed Expenses*	*Profit (Loss)*	*Sales*	*Profit*
1	$100,000	$ 60,000	$100,000	$(60,000)	—	—
2	200,000	120,000	100,000	(20,000)	100%	—
3	250,000	150,000	100,000	—	25	—
4	300,000	180,000	100,000	20,000	20	Infinite
5	360,000	216,000	100,000	44,000	20	120%
6	432,000	259,200	100,000	72,800	20	65

The effects of operating leverage are evident with Book World. Relative to the break-even period (Year 3), the 20 percent sales increase for Year 4 results in an infinite increase in profits because of zero profits for the prior year. Year 5's 20 percent increase in sales results in a 120 percent profit increase relative to Year 4, and Year 6's 20 percent sales increase results in a 65 percent profit increase relative to Year 5. Notice the effects of operating leverage diminish as sales progressively increase above the break-even level because the base on which increases in profits are compared gets progressively larger. Operating leverage also has downside risk. Notice that a drop in sales from $200,000 to $100,000 (Year 2 to Year 1), representing a 50 percent decrease, results in a tripling of the loss.

Our analysis must be aware that companies performing near their break-even point have relatively larger percent changes in both profits and losses due to changes in sales. Consequently, *volatility in sales* increases a company's risk from operating leverage. On the upside, volatility is desirable. But on the downside, it can yield results much worse than those suggested by changes in sales alone. Our analysis must also be aware of operating potential, sometimes erroneously referred to as *leverage.* **Operating potential** refers to a case of high sales and very low profit margins. The potential rests with improvement in profit margins. Relatively minor changes in profit margins applied to a high sales level can produce dramatic changes in profits, both good and bad. We can make a similar analogy to sales volume per share and its link to earnings per share. That is, changes in profitability due to operating leverage or potential yield proportionately larger earnings per share changes.

Analysis Research Insight 12.2

Operating Leverage and Equity Risk

Analysis research has examined the relation between accounting data and the risk associated with investing in a company's equity securities. In economic terms, *total risk* is related to the riskiness of the company's capital structure (*financial risk*) and its asset structure (operating risk). *Operating risk* is comprised of variability in sales and operating leverage.

Evidence indicates the existence of a positive association between operating leverage and total risk. There is also evidence of a negative relation between companies' financial leverage and operating leverage, especially for companies with a high degree of total risk. This implies that companies are strategically attempting to trade off financial risk and operating risk in their business activites.

Relevance of the Variable Expense Percent

Volatility of profits also depends on the variable expense percent. A company with a low variable expense percent achieves higher profits for a given increase in sales once break-even operations are reached relative to a company with a high variable expense percent. We show this in the illustration below:

Illustration 12.7

Company A has fixed expenses of $700,000 and variable expenses of 30 percent of sales. Company B has fixed expenses of $300,000 and variable expenses of 70 percent of sales. Both companies are operating at sales of $1,000,000 and are at break-even. Notice that a $100,000 increase in sales of both companies yields a profit of $70,000 for Company A but only $30,000 for Company B. Company A has greater operating leverage and can, as a result, incur greater risks in pursuing an extra $100,000 in sales than can Company B.

This illustration shows that the break-even point is *not* the only criterion of risk assessment. Rather, our analysis must also pay attention to the variable expense percent.

Relevance of the Fixed Expense Level

The higher are fixed costs, the higher is a company's break-even point when assuming no change in the variable expense percent. Provided other factors are constant, percent changes in fixed expenses yield equal percent changes in the break-even point. For example, Storytime, Inc.'s break-even income statement is:

Sales		$100,000
Variable expenses	$60,000	
Fixed expenses	40,000	100,000
Net income		$ -0-

If fixed expenses for Storytime increase by 20 percent for a total of $48,000, the break-even sales level must also increase by 20 percent to cover increases in both fixed and variable expenses as shown below:

Sales (increase of 20%)		$120,000
Variable expenses (60% of sales)	$72,000	
Fixed expenses ($40,000 × 120%)	48,000	120,000
Net income		$ -0-

An increase in the break-even point usually increases *operating risk*. This means that a company depends on higher sales to break even. Alternatively viewed, it means that a company is more vulnerable to economic downturns relative to having a lower break-even point. Airline companies often have high operating risk. Their large aircraft investment yields high break-even points. While large aircraft lower the variable expense per passenger, they depend on projected increases in passengers. When this fails to happen, airlines' profit margins deteriorate rapidly and losses are likely. There are other repercussions to high levels of fixed expenses. A higher break-even point often yields less freedom to accommodate other needs like labor demands. Higher fixed expenses make strikes more expensive and increase pressures to submit to higher wage demands. Increases in fixed expenses are common in areas of technological innovation to save variable costs like labor and to improve efficiency. These strategic actions can be very profitable in periods of at least reasonably good demand. Yet when demand declines, the higher fixed expenses are burdensome due to operating leverage that yields declining profits or increasing losses. High fixed expenses reduce a company's ability to maintain profits when sales decline.

We must recognize that investments in fixed assets, especially those requiring skilled operators, can yield increases in fixed expenses far exceeding the costs of maintaining and replacing these assets. The skills required to operate these assets can require high-cost personnel that a company is often reluctant to dismiss when operations decline for fear of not being able to replace them when operations improve. This situation transforms variable expenses into de facto fixed expenses.

While fixed expenses are often incurred to increase capacity or to decrease variable expenses, it is often more advisable to cut fixed expenses to reduce risks associated with a high break-even point. A company can reduce, for example, fixed expenses by switching from a salaried sales force to one paid by sales commissions. It can also avoid fixed expenses by extending work shifts, buying ready-made parts, subcontracting work, or discontinuing less profitable product lines. When we analyze past and potential profitability of a company, our analysis must remember the effects of fixed expenses on operating results. In forecasting profitability, our analysis must also remember that assuming constant fixed expenses is valid to the limits of practical capacity within a range of product mixes. Beyond this practical capacity, profitability forecasts must take into consideration increases in both fixed expenses and financing requirements to fund the expansion.

Importance of Contribution Margin

Our analysis must be alert to the absolute size of a company's contribution margin since operating leverage depends on it. We must also be aware of factors influencing contribution margin: changes in variable expenses and selling prices. While our discussion has focused on the individual factors affecting expenses, revenues, and profitability, changes often result from a combination of factors. Projected increases in sales will increase profits if fixed and variable expenses are controlled and kept within projected limits. Break-even analysis assumes efficiency remains constant. Experience indicates cost controls are more lax in prosperous times than in times of distress. Our analysis cannot blindly assume constant efficiency any more than we can assume constant product mix. Both are important variables demanding our attention. Questions of why a company achieved lower profits on higher sales are often explained, at least in part, by changes in product mix.

Break-even analysis, in spite of limitations, is an important analysis tool. Its value depends on our ability to separate expenses into fixed and variable components and use information available to estimate the necessary factors for analysis. Disclosure of cost components like materials, labor, and various overhead categories are especially helpful. The more detailed the expense breakdowns and other information, the more reliable is our break-even analysis.

GUIDANCE ANSWERS TO ANALYSIS VIEWPOINTS

You Are the Securities Listing Director

Differences in users' information requests stem from their expertise and planned applications with financial data. Analysts' compensation depends on their ability to accurately assess and predict future risk and return characteristics of securities. Information that aids them in this task is welcome. Analysts typically possess the necessary expertise and training to effectively use this information. Unions, activists, and less sophisticated investors often do not possess the expertise, time, or motivation to seriously analyze financial statements. These users would prefer one number that captures a company's current financial position and future performance potential. Balancing these information needs (or analysis limitations) is delicate and demands consideration of both economic, political, *and social* factors. Social factors include public "access" to markets, fairness across users, costs to society, and other resource allocation implications. Establishing information listing requirements demands a broad perspective on fairness and is not unlike environmental or tax law.

You Are the Banker

Additional segment information can cause you to reassess risk and return characteristics. The fact that a company's income is derived from 10 different segments generally lowers its riskiness. This is because a downturn in one segment has less of an impact on overall company profitability. In contrast, an economic downturn in the segment of the single industry company can have severe negative consequences. A comparative analysis of these two companies including segment information would favor the multisegment company. The segment information is especially important in this situation given the *marginal* status of both companies and the unlikelihood of accepting additional risk.

You Are the Political Activist

This information is extremely valuable to your candidate. While income for this company is similar to the industry norm, its executive compensation is substantially *higher* than the norm. Logging benefits appear to have substantially lowered this company's cost of sales, as indicated by its high gross margin, but excess profits are being paid to top executives of the company at a rate far exceeding the norm. This information is not only useful in your candidate's campaign, but hints at less than ethical practices.

QUESTIONS

12–1. What are the major objectives of profitability analysis?

12–2. Why is *income* not a unique, specific quantity?

12–3. Two phases are identifiable in our analysis of income. Describe them.

12–4. Why is knowledge of major sources of revenue (sales) of a company important in our analysis of income?

12–5. Why are information and detailed segment data for diversified companies important for profitability analysis?

12–6. Disclosure of various types of information by line of business is required. Comment on the value of this segment information and the feasibility of reporting it in financial statements.

12–7. What are the major disclosure requirements for segment reporting?

12–8. Identify limitations of segment data that we must be aware of in our analysis of financial statements.

12–9. Describe important considerations bearing on the quality and persistence of revenue.

12–10. How are disclosures of an interpretive or explanatory nature in MD&A useful for profitability analysis?

12–11. Identify examples of subjects covered in MD&A.

12–12. What are the objectives of MD&A?

12–13. What are the most important components in analyzing gross profit?

12–14. What is a useful measure of the adequacy of current depreciation?

12–15. Maintenance and repairs expenses can be meaningfully related to what items?

12–16. What are the main objectives of our analysis of selling expenses?

12–17. How is bad debts expense most meaningfully evaluated? What are potential reasons for a decline in the allowance for doubtful accounts?

12–18. *a.* What is the effective tax rate and how is it computed?
b. What are the objectives of an analysis of income taxes?

12–19. What is the basic principle underlying break-even analysis? What are fixed expenses? Variable expenses? Semivariable expenses?

12–20. Certain assumptions underlie break-even analysis. Identify these.

12–21. In break-even analysis, what is the variable expense percent? What is its relation to the contribution margin ratio?

12–22. What alternatives to increases in fixed expenses can a company consider when approaching 100 percent of operational capacity?

12–23. What is operating leverage? What is the relation between operating leverage and fixed expenses? What are the analytical implications of operating leverage?

12–24. What is the relevance to our analysis of (*a*) the break-even point, and (*b*) the variable expense percent?

EXERCISES

Exercise 12–1

Analyzing Income for Diversified Companies

The statement of consolidated income for Standard Industries, Inc., is reproduced below:

STANDARD INDUSTRIES, INC.
Statement of Consolidated Income
For the Year Ended March 31, Year 8

Revenue:	
Net sales	$38,040,000
Other revenue	408,600
Total revenue	$38,448,600
Costs and expenses:	
Cost of products sold	$27,173,300
Selling and administrative expenses	8,687,500
Interest expense	296,900
Total costs and expenses	$36,157,700
Income before income taxes	$ 2,290,900
Provision for income taxes	1,005,000
Net income	$ 1,285,900

In its annual report, Standard's president reports the company is engaged in the pharmaceutical, food processing, toy manufacturing, and metal-working industries. Standard does not disclose separately the profit earned in each of its component industries. Further, several items appearing on the statement of consolidated retained earnings are not included on the income statement—specifically, a gain of $633,400 on the sale of the furniture division in early March of the current year and an assessment of additional income taxes of $164,900 resulting from an audit of tax returns covering the years ended March 31, Year 5, and Year 6.

Required:

a. Explain what is meant by the term *diversified* company.

b. Discuss the accounting problems involved in measuring net profit by industry segments within a diversified company.

c. With reference to Standard Industries' statement of consolidated income, identify the specific items where we might encounter difficulty in measuring profit by each of its industry segments and explain the nature of the difficulty.

d. What criteria should be applied in determining whether a gain or loss is excluded from net income?

e. What criteria should be applied in determining whether a gain or loss that is properly included in net income should be reported in the results of continuing operations or shown separately as an extraordinary item after all other revenues and expenses?

f. How should both the gain on sale of the furniture division and the assessment of additional taxes be reported in Standard's financial statements?

(AICPA adapted)

Exercise 12–2

Applying Segment Reporting Requirements

Selected financial information for Superior Corporation's three business segments is reproduced below ($ millions):

	Segment		
	Aerospace	***Building***	***Computing***
Segment information:			
Sales to unaffiliated customers	$ 12,200	$ 800	$300
Sales to affiliated customers	200	500	200
Operating profit	700	(50)	30
Identifiable assets	11,500	1,360	420
Depreciation and depletion	1,200	140	110
Capital expenditures	1,600	80	230

Consolidated information:		
Total operating profit		$680
Less:		
General expenses	$ 20	
Interest expense	35	
Minority interest income	15	
Income taxes	300	370
Net income		$310

The management of Superior hires you to advise them on the need to report segment data in their annual report. Your review of current reporting standards indicates that an industry segment is reportable if, in the most recent period reported on, one or more of the following apply:

- Its revenue is 10 percent or more of the combined revenue of all industry segments.
- Its operating profit (loss) is 10 percent or more of the greater of (1) the combined operating profit of all segments that did not incur a loss, or (2) the combined operating loss of all segments that did incur a loss.
- Its identifiable assets are 10 percent or more of the combined identifiable assets of all industry segments.

Required:

According to the above criteria, which of Superior Corporation's segments are reportable segments? (Support your answer with computations.)

Exercise 12–3

Analyzing Income Tax Disclosures

Refer to the financial statements of Quaker Oats Company in Supplement A.

Required:

a. Reconstruct all entries related to income taxes for Year 10. Post these entries to all T-accounts affected by taxes and reconstruct them as best possible. Identify any assumptions you make.

b. Compute the expected amount of income taxes paid from your analysis of taxes, and compare it with that disclosed by Quaker Oats.

Exercise 12–4

Preparing a Statement of Variations in Income and Income Components

Refer to the financial statements of Quaker Oats Company in Supplement A.

Required:

Prepare a statement of variations in income and income components for Quaker Oats focusing on Years 11 and 10. Analyze and interpret your results. (*Hint:* Management's Discussion and Analysis is useful for this analysis.)

Exercise 12–5

Analyzing Income Tax Disclosures

Refer to the financial statements of Campbell Soup Company in Supplement A.

Required:

a. Reconstruct all entries related to income taxes for Year 11. Post these entries to all T-accounts affected by taxes and reconstruct them as best possible. Identify any assumptions you make.

b. Calculate the expected amount of income taxes paid in Year 11 from your analysis of taxes, and compare it to that disclosed by Campbell Soup.

c. Explain how Campbell Soup, with income before tax of $667.4 in Year 11, reports $185.8 of current federal income tax when the statutory tax rate was 34 percent.

Exercise 12–6

Analyzing Depreciation Expense

Refer to the financial statements of Campbell Soup Company in Supplement A.

Required:

Compute and interpret the following analytical measures for Year 10:

a. Accumulated depreciation as a percent of gross plant assets subject to depreciation.

b. Depreciation expense as a percent of gross plant assets subject to depreciation.

c. Depreciation expense as a percent of sales.

Exercise 12–7

Preparing a Statement of Variations in Income and Income Components

Refer to the financial statements of Campbell Soup Company in Supplement A.

Required:

Prepare a statement of variations in income and income components for Campbell Soup focusing on Years 11 and 10. Analyze and interpret your results. (*Hint:* Management's Discussion and Analysis is useful for this analysis.)

Exercise 12–8

Break-Even Analysis with Sensitivity Tests

The NIKEY Corporation manufactures tennis balls. This corporation has been operating for several years. Because NIKEY experiences significant business swings, both up and down, the corporation retains you to analyze its cost structure and develop certain cost/price relations. Selected financial data for NIKEY are:

Fixed expenses are $100,000 per year.

Variable expenses per unit are $1.50.

Selling price per unit is $3.50.

Required:

a. Determine the break-even point in sales units.

b. Assuming current sales are 120,000 units, determine the increase (decrease) in profits resulting from each of the following independent business strategies:
1. Fifteen percent increase in sales units.
2. Fifteen percent decrease in sales units.

c. Assuming current sales are 150,000 units, determine the increase (decrease) in profits resulting from each of the following independent business strategies:
1. Ten percent decline in selling price.
2. Twenty percent decrease in variable expenses.
3. Twenty percent increase in sales units.
4. Combined effect of 1–3 above.

Exercise 12–9

Break-Even Analysis and Its Interpretation

Warner Publishing Company disclosed the following data related to one of its newly released publications:

Variable expenses per copy:	
Printing, binding, and paper	$1.30
Bookstore discounts	2.00
Authors' royalties	1.30
Commissions	0.40
General and administrative expenses	1.00
Total variable expenses per copy	$6.00
Fixed expenses:	
Editorial costs	$ 6,000.00
Illustrations	12,000.00
Typesetting	22,000.00
Total fixed expenses	$40,000.00
List price per copy	$10.00

Required:

a. Compute the number of copies produced at the break-even point. Interpret this value.

b. Prepare and label a break-even chart illustrating the various components of the analysis. Interpret the chart.

Exercise 12–10

Break-Even Analysis for a Multiproduct Company

All Seasons, Inc., produces three products: lanterns, coolers, and tents. The revenue and variable expenses for these products are described below:

	Lanterns	*Coolers*	*Tents*
Selling price per unit	$20.0	$30.0	$50.0
Variable expenses	15.0	20.0	25.0
Contribution margin	$ 5.0	$10.0	$25.0

Fixed expenses for All Seasons total $130,000. The product mix is approximately 1:2:3 for lanterns, coolers, and tents, respectively.

Required:

Compute the number of units of each product that must be sold to reach the break-even point. Interpret your results.

Exercise 12–11

Analyzing the Relation between Revenues and Expenses

A press report carried the following news item: *General Motors, Ford, and Chrysler are expected to post losses on fourth-quarter operations despite sales gains. Automakers' revenues are based on factory output rather than retail sales by dealers, and last quarter's sales increases were from the bulging inventories at the end of the third quarter, rather than from models produced in the fourth quarter.*

Required:

Discuss likely reasons for the expected fourth-quarter losses of automakers.

PROBLEMS

Problem 12–1

Analyzing Line-of-Business Data

Selected data from Kemp Corporation are reproduced below:

KEMP CORPORATION
Product-Line Information
(in thousands)

	Year 1	*Year 2*	*Year 3*	*Year 4*
Data communications equipment:				
Net sales	$4,616	$ 5,630	$ 4,847	$ 6,890
Income contribution	570	876	996	1,510
Inventory	2,615	2,469	2,103	1,897
Time recording devices:				
Net sales	3,394	4,200	4,376	4,100
Income contribution	441	311	34	412
Inventory	1,193	2,234	2,574	2,728
Hardware for electronics industry:				
Net sales	—	—	1,564	1,850
Income contribution	—	—	771	919
Inventory	—	—	331	287
Home sewing products:				
Net sales	1,505	1,436	1,408	1,265
Income contribution	291	289	276	342
Inventory	398	534	449	526
Corporate totals:				
Net sales	9,515	11,266	12,195	14,105
Income contribution	1,302	1,476	2,077	3,183
Inventory	4,206	5,237	5,437	5,438

Required:

a. List the products by variability of their income contribution trend. (Identify and explain your chosen measure of variability.)

b. For Year 4, list the products by dollars invested in ending inventory to generate a dollar of:
   1. Sales.
   2. Income contribution.

c. List products by consistency in contribution to growth of total income contribution.

d. Compute the percent of each product line's income contribution to the total for each year. Interpret this evidence.

e. Assume you can invest in one product line. Comment on the desirability of an investment in each product line.

Problem 12–2

Common-Size Analysis of Comparative Income Statements

Comparative income statements of Spyres Manufacturing Company for Years 8 and 9 are reproduced below:

	Year 9	*Year 8*
Net sales	$600,000	$500,000
Cost of goods sold	490,000	430,000
Gross margin	$110,000	$ 70,000
Operating expenses	101,000	51,000
Income before taxes	$ 9,000	$ 19,000
Income taxes	2,400	5,000
Net income	$ 6,600	$ 14,000

Required:

a. Prepare common-size statements showing the percent of each item to sales for both Year 8 and Year 9. Include a column reporting the percent of increase or decrease of Year 9 relative to Year 8 (round numbers to the tenth of 1 percent).

b. Interpret the trend shown in your percent calculations. What areas should be a matter of managerial concern?

Problem 12–3

Analyzing Measures of Company Profitability

Refer to the financial statements of Quaker Oats Company in Supplement A.

Required:

a. Compute the following analytical measures for Years 11 and 10:
1. Ratio of depreciation expense to depreciable assets.
2. Effective interest rate on liabilities subject to interest.
3. Ratio of tax expense to income before tax (effective tax rate).
4. Ratio of cost of goods sold plus other operating expenses to net sales.
5. Ratio of net income to total revenues.

b. Comment on both the level and trend of these analytical measures.

Problem 12–4

Analyzing Changes in Gross Margin

Johnson Corporation sells primarily two products: (A) consumer cleaners, and (B) industrial purifiers. Its gross margin components for the past two years are:

	Year 7	*Year 6*
Sales revenue:		
Product A	$60,000	$35,000
Product B	30,000	45,000
Total	$90,000	$80,000
Deduct cost of goods sold:		
Product A	$50,000	$28,000
Product B	19,500	27,000
Total	$69,500	$55,000
Gross margin	$20,500	$25,000

In Year 6, the selling price of A is $5 per unit, while in Year 7 it is $6 per unit. Product B sells for $50 per unit in both years. Security analysts and the business press expressed surprise at Johnson's 12.5 percent increase in sales and $4,500 decrease in gross margin for Year 7.

Required:

Prepare an analysis statement of the decline in gross margin. Discuss and show the effects of changes in quantities, prices, costs, and product mix on gross margin.

Problem 12–5

Break-Even Analysis, Interpretation, and Application

The following cost structures are available for Atlas Company and Globe Inc.:

	Atlas Co.	*Globe Inc.*
Fixed expenses	$12,000	$10,000
Variable expenses (% of sales)	40%	60%

Required:

a. Compute the break-even points in sales dollars for both companies.

b. Compute net income when sales are $18,000 for both companies.

c. Compute net income when sales are $27,000 for both companies.

d. Assume sales can be increased to $30,000. What percent of accounts receivable must each company collect to break even? (All sales are credit sales.)

e. What additional costs beyond the break-even point do each company require to increase sales to $30,000? (Assume all sales on credit are collectible.)

f. What is the rate of incremental profits on additional costs at a sales level of $30,000 from *d*?

g. Past experience indicates bad debts expenses amount to 10 percent of accounts receivable. What sales level is necessary if each company desires a profit of $10,000?

h. Assume current sales are $30,000 and that a maximum sales level of $40,000 is achievable with additional fixed expenses of $4,000 while variable expenses per unit remain the same. The bad debts ratio is 10 percent of sales. What is the net income for each company when sales are (1) $30,000, and (2) $40,000?

i. Are lower fixed expenses always advantageous?

j. Which company is in a better position to take the marginal risk in *h*?

Problem 12–6

Break-Even Analysis and Sensitivity Tests

Seco Corporation is a wholesale supply company using *independent* sales agents to market their product lines. Sales agents currently receive 20 percent commission on sales, but they are demanding an increase to 25 percent of sales for the Year 9 calendar year. Seco prepared its Year 9 budget before learning of the agents' demand. Seco's pro forma income statement using this earlier budget is reproduced below:

SECO CORPORATION
Pro Forma Income Statement
For the Year Ending December 31, Year 9

Sales		$10,000,000
Cost of sales		6,000,000
Gross margin		$ 4,000,000
Selling and administrative costs:		
Commissions	$2,000,000	
All other costs (fixed)	100,000	$ 2,100,000
Income before income tax		$ 1,900,000
Income tax (30%)		570,000
Net income		$ 1,330,000

Seco is studying the possibility of employing its own salespersons. It would be necessary to hire three individuals at an estimated annual salary of $30,000 each, plus commissions of 5 percent on sales. A sales manager would also be necessary at a fixed annual salary of about $160,000. All other fixed expenses, and variable expense percents, would remain the same as the estimates in the Year 9 pro forma income statement.

Required:

a. Compute Seco's break-even point in sales dollars for the year ending December 31, Year 9, based on the pro forma income statement prepared by the company.

b. Compute Seco's break-even point in sales dollars for the year ending December 31, Year 9, if Seco employs its own salespersons.

c. Compute the sales dollars necessary for the year ending December 31, Year 9, to yield the same net income as projected in the pro forma income statement if Seco continues to use independent sales agents with a 25 percent sales commission.

d. Compute the sales dollars necessary to yield an identical net income for the year ending December 31, Year 9, if (1) Seco employs its own salespersons, or (2) Seco uses independent agents and pays a 25 percent commission.

(AICPA Adapted)

Problem 12–7

Analyzing Income Tax Disclosures

Selected financial data from the annual report of Armstrong World Industries, Inc., are reproduced below:

Consolidated Statement of Income
($ millions)

	Year 2	*Year 1*
Earnings from continuing operations before income taxes	$218.5	$239.4
Income taxes	75.3	84.5
Earnings from continuing operations	$143.2	$154.9
Discontinued operation:		
Earnings (losses), net of income tax benefit of $0.7 in Year 2 and tax expense of $7.6 in Year 1	(1.1)	11.0
Provision for (loss) gain on disposition of discontinued operation, net of income tax benefit of $3.8 in Year 2 and tax expense of $8.0 in Year 1	(9.1)	21.7
Cumulative effect of change in accounting for income taxes	8.0	—
Net earnings	$141.0	$187.6

Consolidated Balance Sheets
($ millions)

	Year 2	*Year 1*
Current liabilities:		
Income taxes payable	$ 18.6	$ 20.3
Noncurrent liabilities:		
Deferred income taxes	167.5	167.7

Consolidated Statement of Cash Flows ($ millions)

	Year 2	Year 1
Supplemental cash flow information:		
Interest paid	$ 37.7	$ 42.9
Income taxes paid	$ 67.7	$ 87.6

Shareholders' Equity Changes ($ millions):

	Year 2	Year 1
Foreign currency translation: Cr (Dr)		
Balance at beginning of year	$ 21.9	$ 24.1
Translation adjustments and hedging activities	21.2	(2.9)
Allocated income taxes	5.2	0.7
Balance at end of year	$ 48.3	$ 21.9

Details of Income Taxes ($ millions)

	Year 2	Year 1
Income taxes:		
Payable:		
Federal	$ 24.6	$ 54.4
Foreign	32.5	30.0
State	1.5	9.2
	$ 58.6	$ 93.6
Deferred:		
Federal	$ 10.5	($ 9.3)
Foreign	1.3	0.8
State	4.9	(0.6)
	$ 16.7	($ 9.1)
Total income taxes	$ 75.3	$ 84.5

Reconciliation to Statutory U.S. Federal Income Tax Rate

	Year 2	Year 1
Effective tax rate	34.4%	35.3%
State income taxes	(2.0)	(2.4)
Benefit of ESOP dividend	3.0	1.4
Taxes on foreign income	(1.9)	(0.9)
Other items	0.5	0.6
Statutory tax rate	34.0%	34.0%

Required:

a. Use T-account and other analyses to reconcile as best as possible the Year 2 tax-related accounts of Armstrong World.

b. Compute the expected amount of income taxes paid in Year 2.

c. Compare your estimate of taxes paid to the amount of taxes paid as reported by Armstrong World. Interpret any difference.

Problem 12–8

Preparing a Statement of Variations in Income and Income Components

At a meeting of your company's Investment Policy Committee the possibility of investing in ZETA Corporation (see Case CC.2 in the Comprehensive Case chapter) is considered. During discussions a committee member asked about the major factors explaining the change in ZETA Corporation's income from Year 5 to Year 6.

Required:

Prepare a statement of variations in income and income components for ZETA Corporation focusing on Years 6 and 5. Analyze and interpret your results. (*Hint:* ZETA's notes are useful in your analysis.)

Problem 12–9

Analyzing Income Tax Disclosures

Refer to the financial statements of ZETA Corporation in Case CC.2 in the Comprehensive Case chapter.

Required:

a. Reconstruct all entries and T-accounts related to income taxes for Year 6 and estimate the amount of income tax paid.

b. Estimate the amount of depreciation expense reported for tax purposes.

CASES

Case 12–1

Analyzing Adaptec's Profitability and Profitability Components

Use the 1996 annual report of Adaptec, Inc., in Supplement A to answer the following.

a. Prepare a statement of variations in income and income components on Adaptec for 1996 and 1995. Interpret and comment on your results.

b. Using T-account analysis reconcile as best as possible the 1996 tax-related accounts and estimate the amount of income taxes paid in 1996. Compare your estimate to the amount of tax paid as reported by Adaptec. Comment on your evidence.

c. Note 9 to Adaptec's financial statements reports segment information.

1. Does Adaptec report industry segments, geographic segments, or both?
2. How does Adaptec define *income from operations?*
3. How does Adaptec report write-offs of acquired in-process technology?
4. Which segment has the largest amount of intercompany sales? Why?
5. How are the prices for intercompany sales determined? What implication does the use of this method have for our analysis of segment profitability?
6. Analyze sales growth, asset growth, and profitability for Adaptec's two largest segments. Interpret your results.

Case 12–2

Analyzing Line-of-Business Data

Selected financial data for Petersen Corporation's revenue and income (contribution) are reproduced below:

Line of Business	*Year 1*	*Year 2*	*Year 3*	*Year 4*
Revenue:				
Manufactured and engineered products:				
Engineered equipment	$ 30,341	$ 29,807	$ 32,702	$ 43,870
Other equipment	5,906	5,996	6,824	7,424
Parts, supplies and services	29,801	29,878	33,623	44,223
Total manuf. & engineered products	$ 66,048	$ 65,681	$ 73,149	$ 95,517
Engineering and erecting services	—	—	$ 12,261	$ 36,758
Total environmental systems group	$ 66,048	$ 65,681	$ 85,410	$132,275
Frye Copysystems	$ 25,597	$ 28,099	$ 31,214	$ 39,270
Sinclair & Valentine	—	53,763	57,288	60,973
A. L. Garber	16,615	15,223	20,445	24,808
Total graphics group	$ 42,212	$ 97,085	$108,947	$125,051
Total consolidated revenue	$108,260	$162,766	$194,357	$257,326
Income:				
Manufactured and engineered products	$ 3,785	$ 3,943	$ 9,209	$ 10,762
Engineering and erecting services	—	—	1,224	3,189
International operations	2,265	2,269	2,030	2,323
Total environmental systems group	$ 6,050	$ 6,212	$ 12,463	$ 16,274
Frye Copysystems	$ 1,459	$ 2,011	$ 2,799	$ 3,597
Sinclair & Valentine	—	3,723	4,628	5,142
A. L. Garber	(295)	926	1,304	1,457
Total graphics group	$ 1,164	$ 6,660	$ 8,731	$ 10,196
Total divisional income	$ 7,214	$ 12,872	$ 21,194	$ 26,470
Unallocated expenses and taxes	$ (5,047)	$ (8,146)	$(13,179)	$(16,449)
Total income from continuing operations	$ 2,167	$ 4,726	$ 8,015	$ 10,021

Required:

a. Use common-size statements to analyze every division's (1) contribution to total consolidated revenue, (2) contribution to total divisional income, and (3) ratio of income to revenue.

b. Interpret and comment on the trends revealed by your computations in (*a*).

Case 12–3

Analyzing Income Tax Disclosures

Selected data drawn from the financial statements of Biotech, Inc., are reproduced below:

Statements of Cash Flows
($ millions)

	Year 6	*Year 5*
Cash from Operations:		
Add (deduct) items not using (providing) cash:		
Deferred income taxes	$(22)	($94)

Balance Sheet
($ millions)

	Year 6	*Year 5*
Current assets:		
Recoverable income taxes	$ 56	$ 33
Current liabilities:		
Taxes payable	122	114
Long-term liabilities:		
Deferred income taxes	49	—

Income Taxes
($ millions)

	Years Ended October 31	
	Year 6	*Year 5*
Income (Loss) from Continuing Operations before Income Taxes Segregated as to U.S. or Foreign Source:		
U.S. source	$(22)	$(124)
Foreign source	59	51
Total income (loss) from continuing operations before income taxes	$ 37	$ (73)
Summary of Income Tax Expense:		
Currently payable:		
Federal	$ 13	$ 8
Foreign	43	51
State and local	7	13
Adjustment of estimated income tax liabilities	—	(16)
Deferred:		
Federal	37	(89)
Foreign	1	(1)
State and local	4	(5)
Charge equivalent to tax effects for:		
Use of foreign loss carryforwards	—	2
Use of foreign tax credit carryforwards	—	7
Taxes related to:		
Discontinued operations	(12)	(16)
Extraordinary gains on debt repurchases and early retirements	—	—
Cumulative effect of change in pension reversion	(59)	—
Total income taxes attributable to continuing operations	$ 34	$ (46)
Extraordinary Credits:		
Foreign loss and tax credit carryforwards	$—	$ 9
Gains on debt repurchases and early retirements (21 cents a share)	—	—
Total extraordinary credits	$—	$ 9

Income Statements
($ millions)

	Year 6	Year 5
Income (loss) from continuing operations before taxes	$37	$(73)
Income taxes	34	(46)
Income (loss) from continuing operations	$ 3	$(27)
Discontinued operations	16	21
Income (loss) before extraordinary item and cumulative effect of accounting change	$19	$ (6)
Extraordinary gain	—	9
Cumulative effect of change in pension reversion accounting	66	—
Net income	$85	$ 3

Required:

a. Use T-account analysis to reconcile as best as possible the Year 6 tax-related accounts of Biotech, Inc.

b. Estimate the amount of income taxes paid in Year 6.

Case 12–4

Analyzing Income Tax Disclosures

Selected financial data from the annual report of Mead Corporation are reproduced below:

Consolidated Statements of Earnings
($ millions)

	Year 2	Year 1
Earnings from continuing operations before income taxes	$148.0	$147.0
Income taxes (note M)	54.3	52.3
Earnings from continuing operations before equity in net earnings (loss) of jointly owned companies	$ 93.7	$ 94.7
Equity in net earnings (loss) of jointly owned companies (note C)	(18.1)	11.7
Earnings from continuing operations	$ 75.6	$106.4
Loss from discontinued operation (note N)	(10.0)	(74.8)
Earnings before extraordinary item and cumulative effect of change in accounting principle	$ 65.6	$ 31.6
Extraordinary gain on retirement of debt		6.9
Cumulative effect of change in accounting principle (note P)	(58.7)	
Net earnings	$ 6.9	$ 38.5

Consolidated Balance Sheets
($ millions)

	Year 2	Year 1
Current liabilities:		
Taxes, other than income	$ 57.4	$ 52.8
Other current liabilities	196.4	152.3
Noncurrent liabilities:		
Deferred income taxes	248.8	294.5

Note M—Income taxes (millions)

	December 31	
	Year 2	*Year 1*
Currently payable:		
Federal	$ 29.3	$ 43.0
Federal alternative minimum tax	29.6	12.3
State and local	5.3	(0.8)
Foreign	3.2	5.2
	$ 67.4	$ 59.7
Deferred:		
Excess tax depreciation	26.1	33.9
Alternative minimum tax carryforward	(29.6)	(12.3)
Pension income	7.7	7.5
Employee benefits		(8.6)
Other expenses	(10.3)	(25.6)
Miscellaneous	(7.0)	(2.3)
	$(13.1)	$ (7.4)
	$ 54.3	$ 52.3

Reconciliation between statutory federal rate and effective rate:	December 31	
	Year 2	*Year 1*
Federal income tax rate	34.0%	34.0%
State and local income taxes, net of federal benefit	(1.1)	(1.2)
Other	3.8	2.8
Effective tax rate	36.7%	35.6%

Note N—Discontinued operations ($ millions)	*Year 2*
Insurance operations:	
Provision for loss in runoff of insurance operations, net of $6.0 tax benefit	$(10.0)
Loss from discontinued operations	$(10.0)

Note P—Postretirement benefits other than pensions

In Year 2, the company adopted *Statement of Financial Accounting Standards No. 106*, "Employers' Accounting for Postretirement Benefits Other than Pensions." The company elected to immediately recognize the cumulative effect of the change in accounting for postretirement benefits of $93.5 million ($58.7 million net of income tax benefit), which represents the accumulated postretirement benefit obligation (APBO) existing at January 1, Year 2, of $107.9 million, less $14.4 million recorded in prior years.

Note S—Additional information on cash flows (millions)

	December 31	
	Year 2	*Year 1*
Cash paid during the year for:		
Interest (net of amount capitalized)	$112.5	$93.2
Income taxes	$ 41.9	$43.3

Mead Corporation does not report Income Taxes Payable as a separate line item in its balance sheets. Assume income taxes payable are included in "Other current liabilities" and that the beginning balance of Income Taxes Payable as of January 1, Year 2, is $50 million.

Required:

Using T-account analysis, post all the income tax–related transactions, and estimate the ending balance of Income Taxes Payable as of December 31, Year 2.

Case 12–5 Analyzing Income Tax Disclosures

Selected financial statement items and notes relating to income taxes from the annual report of Abbott Laboratories are reproduced below:

Consolidated Statement of Earnings (thousands)

	Year 2	*Year 1*
Earnings before taxes	$1,544,222	$1,350,733
Taxes on earnings	455,545	384,959
Earnings before extraordinary gain and accounting change	$1,088,677	$ 965,774
Extraordinary gain, net of tax $74,068	128,182	—
Cumulative effect of accounting change, net of tax $78,151	(128,114)	—
Net earnings	$1,088,745	$ 965,774

Consolidated Balance Sheets (thousands)

	Year 2	*Year 1*
Assets:		
Prepaid income taxes	$425,442	$296,861
Current liabilities:		
Income taxes payable	194,255	234,338
Other liabilities and deferrals:		
Deferred income taxes	347,245	409,090

Consolidated Statement of Shareholders' Investment (thousands)

	Year 2	*Year 1*
Common shares:		
Issued at beginning of year	$297,522	$241,576
Issued under incentive stock programs	49,423	49,266
Tax benefit from sale of option shares	19,000	16,683
Retired	(4,937)	(10,003)
Issued at end of year	$361,008	$297,522
Cumulative translation adjustments Cr (Dr):		
Balance at beginning of year	$ 74,328	$ 18,289
Translation adjustments	(36,750)	59,787
Allocated income taxes	43	(3,748)
Balance at end of year	$ 37,621	$ 74,328

Note 2—Taxes on Earnings

The related provisions for taxes on earnings are as follows:	*Year 2*	*Year 1*
Taxes on earnings (thousands):		
Current:		
U.S. federal and possessions	$316,377	$266,454
State	50,758	41,903
Foreign	140,559	109,129
Total current	$507,694	$417,486
Deferred:		
Domestic	($ 49,998)	($ 34,582)
Foreign	(2,151)	2,055
Total deferred	($ 52,149)	($ 32,527)
Total	$455,545	$384,959

Consolidated Statement of Cash Flows (thousands)

	Year 2	*Year 1*
Supplemental cash flow information:		
Interest paid	$ 59,915	$ 94,204
Income taxes paid	651,442	353,623

Required:

a. Reconstruct all entries related to income taxes for Year 2. Post these entries to the T-accounts affected by taxes and reconstruct them as best possible.

b. Estimate income taxes paid in Year 2 and compare it to that disclosed by Abbott Labs.

INTERNET ACTIVITIES

Internet 12–1

Income Tax Disclosures

Access one of the financial statement databases available on the Internet (http://www.mhhe.com/business/accounting/wild). Retrieve current financial statements of a company selected by either you or your instructor.

Required:

a. Reconstruct all entries related to income taxes for the current year. Post these entries to T-accounts affected by income taxes and reconstruct accounts as best as possible. Identify any assumptions you make.

b. Compute your expected amount of income taxes paid and compare it with the amount disclosed by the company.

Internet 12–2

Statement of Variations in Income and Income Components

Access one of the financial statement databases available on the Internet (http://www.mhhe.com/business/accounting/wild). Retrieve current financial statements of a company selected by either you or your instructor.

Required:

Prepare a "Statement of Variations in Income and Income Components" for each of the prior two years. Analyze and interpret your findings.

Internet 12–3

Analysis of Depreciation

Access one of the financial statement databases available on the Internet (http://www.mhhe.com/business/accounting/wild). Retrieve current financial statements of a company selected by either you or your instructor. Compute and interpret the following analytical measures for the most recent two years:

a. Accumulated depreciation as a percent of gross depreciable plant assets.

b. Depreciation expense as a percent of gross depreciable plant assets.

c. Depreciation expense as a percent of sales.

d. Write a brief report interpreting the analysis in *a*, *b*, and *c*.

Internet 12–4

Analyzing Company Profitability

Access one of the financial statement databases available on the Internet (http://www.mhhe.com/business/accounting/wild). Retrieve current financial statements of two companies in different industries selected by either you or your instructor.

Required:

a. Compute the following measures for the two most recent years for both companies:
   1. Ratio of depreciation expense to depreciable assets.
   2. Effective interest rate on interest-bearing liabilities.
   3. Ratio of tax expense to income before tax (effective tax rate).
   4. Ratio of cost of goods sold plus other operating expenses to net sales.
   5. Ratio of net income to total revenues.

b. Write a report discussing both the level and trend of these analytical measures for each company. Include in your report a comparison of these companies.

Internet 12–5

Profitability and Its Components

Access one of the financial statement databases available on the Internet (http://www.mhhe.com/business/accounting/wild). Retrieve current financial statements of a company selected by either you or your instructor.

a. Prepare a "Statement of Variations in Income and Income Components" for each of the prior two years. Write a short report summarizing and interpreting your results.

b. Using T-account analysis reconcile as best as possible the current year's tax-related accounts and estimate the amount of income taxes paid. Compare your estimate to the amount of tax paid.

C H A P T E R

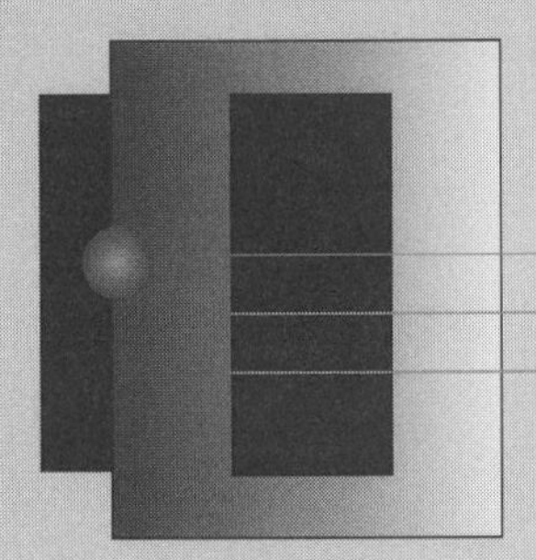

13

Earnings-Based Analysis and Valuation

LEARNING OBJECTIVES

- Describe earnings quality, its measurement, and its importance to the analysis of company performance.
- Analyze earnings persistence, its determinants, and its relevance for earnings forecasting.
- Explain recasting and adjusting of earnings and earnings components for analysis.
- Describe earnings-based valuation and its relevance for financial analysis.
- Analyze earning power and its usefulness for forecasting and valuation.
- Explain earnings forecasting, its mechanics, and its effectiveness in assessing company performance.
- Analyze interim reports and consider their value in monitoring and revising earnings estimates.

A LOOK BACK

The preceding two chapters dealt with analysis of company returns, both profitability and return on invested capital. Emphasis was on rate of return measures, disaggregation of returns, accounting analysis of earnings components, and break-even analysis. These return-based chapters complement earlier chapters that focused on risk, including liquidity and solvency.

A LOOK AT THIS CHAPTER

This chapter concludes returns analysis by emphasizing earnings-based analysis and valuation. Our earnings-based analysis focuses on assessing earnings quality, earnings persistence, and earning power. Attention is directed at techniques to aid us in measuring and applying these analysis concepts. Our discussion of earnings-based valuation focuses on issues in estimating company values and forecasting earnings.

A LOOK AHEAD

The Comprehensive Case applies many of the financial statement analysis tools and insights described in the book. These are illustrated using financial information from Campbell Soup Company. Explanation and interpretation accompany all analyses.

PREVIEW OF CHAPTER 13

Earnings-based financial statement analysis is the focus of this chapter. The two previous chapters examined return and profitability analyses of financial statements. This chapter extends these analyses to consider earnings quality, persistence, valuation, and forecasting. *Earnings quality* refers to the relevance of earnings in measuring company performance. Its determinants include a company's business environment and its selection and application of accounting principles. *Earnings persistence* is broadly defined and includes the stability, predictability, variability, and trend in earnings. We also consider earnings management as a determinant of persistence. Our *valuation* analysis emphasizes earnings and other accounting measures for computing company value. *Earnings forecasting* considers earning power, estimation techniques, and monitoring mechanisms. This chapter describes several useful tools for earnings-based financial analysis. We describe recasting and adjustment of financial statements. We also distinguish between recurring and nonrecurring, operating and nonoperating, and extraordinary and nonextraordinary earnings components. Throughout the chapter we emphasize the application of earnings-based analysis with several illustrations. The content and organization of this chapter are as follows:

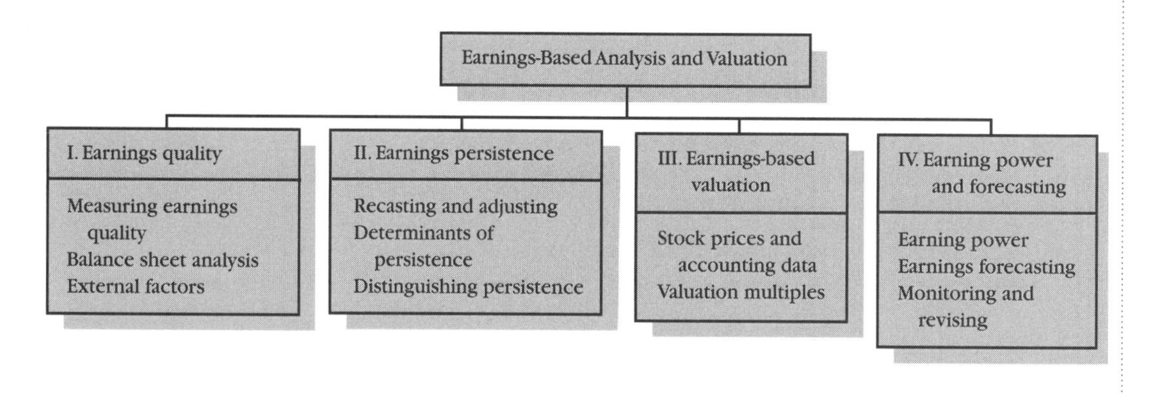

Earnings Quality

We know earnings (or income) measurement and recognition involve estimation and interpretation of business transactions and events. Our prior analysis of earnings emphasized that accounting earnings is not a unique amount but depends on the assumptions used and principles applied. Complicating earnings measurement are differences between accrual and cash accounting. Accrual accounting recognizes revenue when earned and expenses when incurred, while cash accounting recognizes inflows and outflows of cash irrespective of whether cash flows are earned or incurred. Despite limitations in cash flows, they are important to successful business operation and liquidity. For these reasons, we are interested in *both* cash and accrual measures of earnings.

The need for estimation and interpretation in accrual accounting has led some individuals to question the reliability of *all* accrual measures. This is an extreme and unwise reaction because of the considerable wealth of relevant information communicated in accrual measures. We know accrual accounting consists of adjusting cash flows to reflect universally accepted concepts: earned revenue and incurred expenses. What our analysis must focus on are the assumptions and principles applied, and the adjustments appropriate for our analysis objectives. We should use the information in accruals to our competitive advantage and to help us better understand current and future company performance. We must also be aware of both *accounting and audit risks* to rely on earnings. Improvements in both accounting and auditing have decreased the incidence of fraud and misrepresentation in financial statements. Nevertheless, management fraud and misrepresentation is far from eliminated, and audit failures do occur (e.g., Miniscribe, Phar-Mor, Leslie Fay, W.T. Grant, Equity Funding, Frigitemp, ESM Government Securities, Drysdale Securities, Crazy Eddie, Regina, and ZZZ Best). Our analysis must always evaluate accounting and audit risk, including the character and propensities of management, in assessing earnings.

Our evaluation of earnings persistence (trend and level) is linked with our evaluation of management. Similarly, evaluation of management cannot be separated from the earnings achieved. While other factors are relevant, earnings performance is the acid test of management's ability. Their ability is an extremely important (unquantifiable) factor in earnings forecasting. Our analysis must be alert to management changes and assess the company's dependence on management's ability, character, and risk taking.

Measuring Earnings Quality

Measuring earnings quality arose out of a need to compare earnings of different companies and a desire to recognize differences in quality for earnings-based valuation. There is not complete agreement on what earnings quality comprises. This section considers factors typically identified as comprising earnings quality and some examples of their assessment.

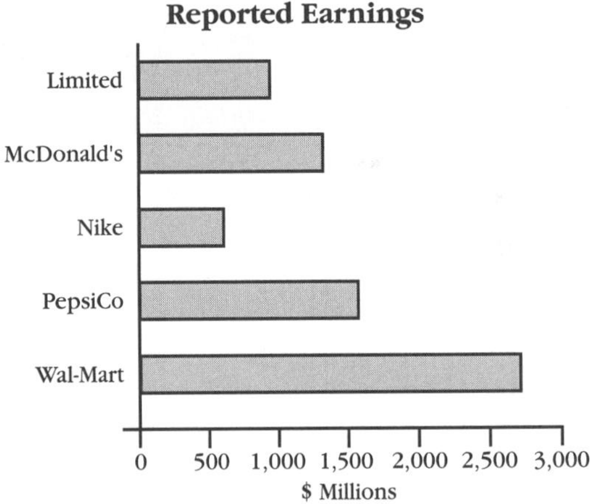

Source: Annual reports.

Determinants of Earnings Quality

Three factors are often identified as comprising earnings quality. We discuss them below.

Accounting Principles. One determinant of earnings quality is the discretion of management in *selecting accepted accounting principles.* This discretion can be liberal (optimistic) or conservative. The quality of conservatively determined earnings is perceived higher because they are less likely to overstate current and future performance expectations compared with those determined in a liberal manner. Conservatism reduces the likelihood of earnings overstatement and retrospective changes. Examples of conservative choices are LIFO inventory accounting in conjunction with rising prices and accelerated depreciation methods. However, excessive conservatism, while contributing temporarily to earnings quality, reduces the reliability and relevance of earnings in the long run. Examining the accounting principles selected can provide clues to management's propensities and attitudes.

Accounting Application. Another determinant of earnings quality is management's discretion in *applying* accepted accounting principles. Application of accounting relates to decisions such as whether adequate provision is made for asset reinvestment or for maintaining and increasing earning power. Management has discretion over the amount of earnings through their application of accounting principles determining revenues and expenses. Discretionary expenses like advertising, marketing, repairs, maintenance, research, and development can be *timed* to manage the level of reported earnings (or loss). Earnings reflecting timing elements unrelated to operating or business conditions can detract from earnings quality. Our analysis task is to identify the implications of management's accounting application and assess its motivations.

Business Risk. A third determinant of earnings quality is the relation between earnings and business risk. It includes the effect of cyclical and other business forces on earnings level, stability, sources, and variability. For example, earnings variability is generally undesirable and its increase harms earnings quality. Higher earnings quality is linked with companies more insulated from business risk. While business risk is not primarily a result of management's discretionary actions, this risk can be lowered by skillful management strategies.

Analyzing Discretionary Accounting Choices

Important determinants of earnings quality are management's selection and application of accounting principles. This section focuses on several important discretionary accounting expenditures to help us to assess earnings quality. *Discretionary expenditures* are outlays that management can vary across periods to conserve resources and/or influence reported earnings. For this reason, they deserve special attention in our analysis. We assess their adequacy relative to current business conditions, prior periods' levels, and current and future expectations.

Maintenance and Repairs. As discussed in the prior chapter, management has considerable discretion in performing maintenance and some discretion with repairs. Our analysis can compare these costs to the level of activity that drives these expenditures. Two ratios are especially useful in comparing repairs and maintenance levels from year to year. The first ratio relates *repairs and maintenance costs to the level of operating activity:*

$$\frac{\text{Repairs and maintenance expenses}}{\text{Sales}}$$

In the absence of major inventory changes, sales are a good indicator of business activity. If year-to-year inventory levels change appreciably, an adjustment can be made. This adjustment is twofold: (1) estimate ending inventories at selling prices and add them to sales, and (2) estimate beginning inventories at selling prices and deduct them from sales.

The second ratio relates *repairs and maintenance costs to the level of investment* from which these costs are incurred:

$$\frac{\text{Repairs and maintenance expenses}}{\text{Property, plant, and equipment (excluding land) net of accumulated depreciation}}$$

Depending on the extent of information available to us, we can compute the ratio of repairs and maintenance costs to specific categories of assets. Evidence of substandard repairs and maintenance of assets can cause us to revise assumptions of useful lives for depreciation.

Trends in repairs and maintenance costs from year to year can be expressed in terms of index numbers and compared to related accounts. The purpose of this analysis and the two ratio measures are to determine whether repairs and maintenance are at normal and necessary levels or whether they are being "managed" in a way that affects earnings quality and its projection for valuation.

Illustration 13.1

Our analysis of maintenance and repairs expense for Campbell Soup Company using its annual report data in Supplement A reveals the following:

	Year 11	*Year 10*	*Year 9*
Maintenance and repairs ÷ net sales	2.8%	2.9%	3.1%
Maintenance and repairs ÷ property, plant, and equipment—net*	12.2%	13.0%	13.1%

*Omitting land and construction in progress.

Evidence reveals a slight decline in these expenditures, requiring our further analysis.

Advertising. A major portion of advertising outlays has effects beyond the current period. This yields a weak relation between advertising outlays and short-term performance. This also implies management can in certain cases cut advertising costs with no immediate effects on sales. However, long-run sales are likely to suffer. Our analysis must look at year-to-year variations in advertising expenses to assess their impact on future sales and earnings quality. Management's Discussion and Analysis for Adaptec in Supplement A reported that its 39 percent increase in sales and marketing expenses is primarily due to "advertising and promotional programs aimed at generating demand in the consumer and enterprise computer markets." There are several ways of assessing the trend in advertising outlays. One is to convert them into *trend percents* using a "normal" year as a base. We then compare these trend percents to the trend in sales, gross profits, and earnings. Another measure is the ratio of advertising outlays to sales:

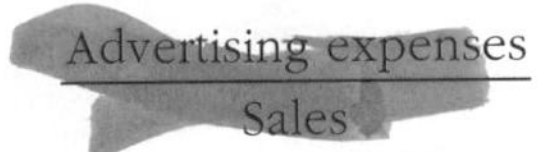

$$\frac{\text{Advertising expenses}}{\text{Sales}}$$

We examine this ratio across periods to look for shifts in advertising expenditures. Analysis of advertising to sales over several years can reveal the degree of dependence for a company on a particular promotional strategy.

Illustration 13.2

Analyzing the ratio of advertising expense to sales for Campbell Soup reveals a decline from 3.5 percent in Year 10 to 3.1 percent in Year 11. Our analysis should pursue reasons for this decline because this ratio was as high as 4.1 percent in Year 6.

Another useful ratio compares advertising to total selling outlays:

$$\frac{\text{Advertising expenses}}{\text{Total selling costs}}$$

This ratio is often useful in identifying shifts to and from advertising to other methods of sales promotion. Comparison of both these ratios with those of competitors reveals the degree of market acceptance of a company's products *and* the relative promotional efforts needed for sales.

Research and Development Costs. Research and development costs are among the most difficult expenditures in financial statements to analyze and interpret. Yet they are important, not necessarily because of their amount but because of their effect on future performance. Interestingly, research and development costs have acquired an aura of productive potential in analysis exceeding that often warranted by experience. There exist numerous cases of successful research and development activities in areas like genetics, chemistry, electronics, photography, and biology. But for each successful project there are countless failures. These research failures represent vast sums expensed or written off without measurable benefits. There is also the question of what constitutes research and the potential for distortion. The research label has been used in reference to first-rate scientific inquiry and also for superficial or routine "testing" activities.

Our analysis must pay careful attention to research and development costs, and to their absence. They often represent substantial costs, many of them fixed, reflecting the key to future company performance. Our analysis must also distinguish between nonquantifiable (or qualitative) and quantifiable factors. *Qualitative factors* include research quality. *Research quality* involves the caliber of the staff and organization, reputation of its leaders, and its commercial applicability. This qualitative analysis must accompany other analyses. A distinction should also be drawn between external (including government) sponsored research and company-sponsored research. The latter is more likely to be identified with the company's objectives. It is clear that we cannot evaluate research on the basis of amounts spent alone. Research outlays represent an expense or an investment depending on how they are applied. Far from guaranteeing results, they represent highly speculative ventures depending on the application of extraordinary scientific as well as managerial skills for success.

Quantifiable factors are also useful in our analysis of research and development outlays. Our intent is to determine the amount of current research and development costs having future benefits. These benefits are often measured by relating research and development outlays to:

- Sales growth.
- New products.
- Plant asset acquisitions (to exploit success).
- Profitability.

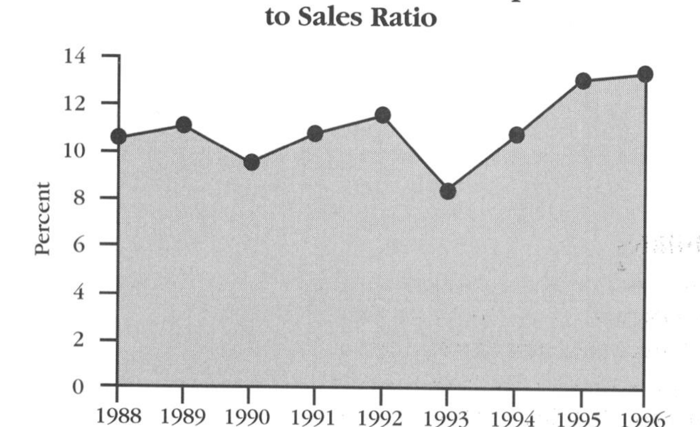

Another important measure of research and development outlays is their magnitude relative to a company's operating activities. While these outlays include fixed costs of research and development departments, most of these outlays are subject to the discretion of management, often with no immediate effects on sales. With regard to earnings quality, our analysis must evaluate year-to-year changes in research and development outlays. This is achieved through both trend percent analysis and ratio analysis. A useful ratio is:

$$\frac{\text{Research and development outlays}}{\text{Sales}}$$

Our careful comparison of this and similar ratios across periods reveals whether these research and development efforts are sustained or vary with operating activity. Transient research efforts usually lack the predictability or quality of a sustained long-term program.

Other Discretionary Future-Directed Costs. There are other future-directed outlays. Examples are costs of training, selling, and managerial development. While these human resource costs are usually expensed in the period incurred, they often have future utility. Our analysis should recognize this in assessing current earnings and future prospects.

Balance Sheet Analysis of Earnings Quality

Reported asset and liability values hold clues to our analysis of earnings quality. A **balance sheet analysis** is an important complement to our earnings-based analysis techniques. This section describes three variations of balance sheet analysis.

Conservatism in Reported Assets

The relevance of reported asset values is linked (with few exceptions like cash, held-to-maturity investments, and land) with their ultimate recognition as reported expenses. We can state this as a general proposition: When assets are *overstated,* cumulative earnings are *overstated.* This is because earnings are relieved of charges necessary to bring these assets down to realizable values. The converse is also true: When assets are *understated,* cumulative earnings are *understated.* At least two accounting practices qualify this proposition: conservatism and pooling accounting. Conservatism yields recognition of gains only when realized. While there is some movement away from strict interpretation of conservatism (e.g., trading securities), most assets are reported at cost even when their current or realizable values far exceed cost. Pooling of interests with business combinations allows an acquiring company to carry forward old book values of the assets of the acquired company even though such values can be far less than current market values or the consideration given for them (see Chapter 5). Pooling accounting allows the recording of profits when the values of understated assets are realized. This recording often represents recognition of previously understated assets. Since these profits are previously "purchased and paid for," they do not represent either earning power or the operating performance of management.

Conservatism in Reported Provisions and Liabilities

Our analysis must be alert to the proposition relating provisions and liability values to earnings: When provisions and liabilities are *understated,* cumulative earnings are *overstated.* This is because earnings are relieved of charges necessary to bring the provisions or liabilities up to their market values. Examples are understatements in provisions for taxes, product warranties, or pensions that yield overstatement in cumulative earnings. Conversely, an *overprovision* for current and future liabilities or losses yields an *understatement* of earnings (or overstatement of losses). We described in Chapter 6 how provisions for future costs and losses that are excessive shift the burden of costs and expenses from future income statements to the current period. Bearing in mind our propositions regarding the earnings effects from reported values of assets and liabilities, the critical analysis of these values represents an important factor in assessing earnings quality.

Risks in Reported Assets

There is another dimension to balance sheet analysis bearing on earnings quality. This dimension is based on exploiting the varying risks associated with future realizations of different assets. These risks span a spectrum of possibilities. Future realization of accounts receivable is typically higher than the realization of inventory costs. Similarly, future realization of inventory costs is typically higher than realization of goodwill or deferred start-up costs. Our analysis of assets by risk holds clues to earnings quality. If the reporting process yields deferrals of outlays with considerable risk of future realization, then earnings quality is lowered. To illustrate, we describe risk analysis on three specific assets to assess earnings quality.

Accounts Receivable. Sales quality depends on properly valuing accounts receivable. This valuation must recognize the risk of default and the time value of money. If receivables do not arise from transactions with customers or suppliers in the normal course of business with terms not exceeding a year, then, with minor exceptions, they are valued using the interest rate applicable to similar debt instruments. For example, if a receivable bears interest of 8 percent while similar receivables at the time bear interest of 12 percent, both the receivable and its corresponding sale are restated at the lower discounted amount. The level of accounts receivable and its relation to sales hold clues to earnings quality. If an increase in accounts receivable represents merely a shifting of inventory from the company to its distributor because of aggressive sales promotion or costly incentives, then these sales are nothing more than "borrowings" of future sales—reducing earnings quality.

Inventories. Overstated inventories yield overstated earnings. Overstatements can occur due to errors in quantities, costing, pricing, or valuation (of work in process). The more complex the inventory item or the more dependent is valuation on internally developed cost records, the more vulnerable are cost estimates to errors and misstatements. Overstatements are most likely when costs that companies should write off to expense are retained in inventory. Understatements of inventories derive from write-offs possessing future benefits that should be inventoried. An understatement of inventory results in understatement of current earnings and an overstatement of future earnings.

Deferred Charges. Deferred charges like deferred tooling, start-up, or preoperating costs must be scrutinized because their value depends vitally on estimates of future conditions. Experience shows these estimates are often overoptimistic or contain insufficient provisions for future contingencies. Risk of failure in achieving expectations with deferred charges is typically higher than with other assets.

External Factors and Earnings Quality

Earnings quality is affected by factors external to a company. These external factors make earnings more or less reliable. One factor is the quality of *foreign earnings.* Foreign earnings quality is affected by the difficulties and uncertainties in repatriation of funds, currency fluctuations, political and social conditions, and local customs and regulation. In certain countries companies lack flexibility in dismissing personnel which essentially converts labor into a fixed cost. Another factor affecting earnings quality is *regulation.* For example, the regulatory environment confronting a public utility affects its earnings quality. An unsympathetic or hostile regulatory environment can affect costs and selling prices and thereby diminish earnings quality due to increased uncertainty of future profits. Also, the stability and reliability of *earnings sources* affect earnings quality. Government defense–related revenues are dependable in times of high international tensions, but affected by political events in peacetime. *Changing price levels* affect earnings quality. When price levels are rising, "inventory profits" or understatements in expenses like depreciation lower earnings quality. Finally, because of uncertainties due to *complexities of operations,* earnings of certain conglomerates are considered of lower quality.

ANALYSIS VIEWPOINT . . . *You are the director*

You are a new member of the board of directors of a toy merchandiser. You are preparing for your first meeting with the company's independent auditor. A stockholder writes you a letter raising concerns about earnings quality. What are some questions or issues that you can raise with the auditor to address these concerns and fulfill your fiduciary responsibilities to shareholders?

Earnings Persistence

A good analysis identifies components in earnings streams exhibiting stability and predictability, or *persistent* components. We separate these from random or nonrecurring components. This distinction aids us in producing reliable forecasts of earning power for valuation. Our analysis must be alert to earnings management or income smoothing. Earnings management or income smoothing can impart more stability and predictability than implied by the underlying characteristics. Company management often asserts that such activities remove distortions or peculiarities from operating results. Yet these activities can mask natural and cyclical irregularities that are part of a company's environment and experience. Identifying these influences is important for us in assessing a company's risk. This section considers elements bearing on our analysis of earnings persistence: earnings level, trend, and components.

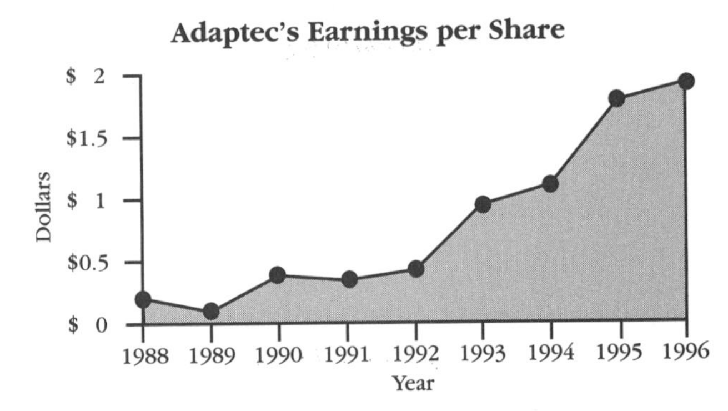

Recasting and Adjusting Earnings for Analysis

Our objective in this part of our analysis is to recast earnings and earnings components so that stable, normal and continuing elements comprising earnings are separated and distinguished from random, erratic, unusual and nonrecurring elements. The latter elements require separate analytical treatment or investigation. Recasting also aims to identify elements included in current earnings that should more properly be included in the operating results of one or more prior periods.

Information on Earnings Persistence

The income statement and other financial disclosures represent the natural starting point for our earnings analysis. We prefer an income statement containing detailed component information and disclosure. The exact composition and treatment of earnings and earnings components depends on one's perspective. One position claims that gains or losses should be included or excluded from earnings on the basis of management's interpretation of "normal operations." This position is controversial and subject to various criticisms. Another position adopts an approach approximating the clean surplus relation. A clean surplus approach results in most gains and losses being reported in earnings in the period they occur. There is also the question of how to handle, if at all, restatement of prior periods' results. With few exceptions like corrections of errors, current practice discourages restatements.

Our analysis of operating results for the recasting and adjustment of earnings requires reliable and relevant information. The major sources of this information include:

- Income statement, including its subdivisions.
  - Income from continuing operations.
  - Income from discontinued operations.
  - Extraordinary gains and losses.
  - Cumulative effect of changes in accounting principles.
- Other financial statements and notes.
- Management commentary in financial statements.
- Management's Discussion and Analysis.

We often find "unusual" items separated within the income statement (typically on a pre-tax basis), but their disclosure is optional. Their disclosure does not always include sufficient information to assess significance or persistence. We access all available sources and management, if possible, to obtain this information. Relevant information includes that affecting earnings comparability and interpretation. Examples are product-mix changes, technological innovations, work stoppages, and raw material constraints.

Recasting Earnings and Earnings Components

Once we secure all available information, the income statements of several years (typically at least five) are recast and adjusted to assess earnings persistence. Recasting and adjusting earnings aids us in also determining the earning power of a company. We consider recasting in this section and adjusting in the next, although both can be performed in one statement.

Recasting aims at rearranging earnings components to provide a meaningful classification and relevant format for analysis. Components can be rearranged, subdivided, or tax effected, but the total must reconcile to net income of each period as reported. Analytical reclassification of components within a period helps in evaluating earnings level. Discretionary expenses should be segregated. The same applies to components like equity in income (loss) of unconsolidated subsidiaries or affiliates often reported net of tax. Components reported pre-tax must be removed along with their tax effects if reclassified apart from income from continuing operations.

Income tax disclosures enable us to separate factors that either reduce or increase taxes. This permits us to analyze the recurring nature of these factors. All permanent tax differences and credits are included. This analytical procedure involves computing taxes at the statutory rate (35 percent) and deducting tax benefits arising from various items including tax credits, capital gains rates, tax-free income, or lower foreign tax rates. We need also add factors like additional foreign taxes, nontax-deductible expenses, and state and local taxes (net of federal tax benefit). Immaterial items can be considered in a lump sum labeled *other*.

Analytically recast income statements contain as much detail as necessary for our analysis and are supplemented by notes. Exhibit 13.1 shows the analytically recast income statements for Campbell Soup. These statements are annotated with key numbers referencing Campbell's financial statements in Supplement A. Financial data preceding Year 10 are taken from company reports summarized in the Comprehensive Case chapter, which also contains a discussion and an integration of Exhibit 13.1.

Adjusting Earnings and Earnings Components

The adjusting stage uses data from recast income statements and other available information to assign earnings components to periods where they most properly belong. We must be especially careful with assigning extraordinary or unusual items (net of tax) to periods. Also, the income tax benefit of a carryforward of operating losses should normally be moved to the year of the loss occurrence. Costs or benefits from settlements of lawsuits can relate to one or more preceding periods. Similarly, gains or losses from disposal of discontinued operations usually relate to operating results of several years. For changes in accounting principles or estimates, all years under analysis should be adjusted to a comparable basis. If the new principle is the desirable one, prior years should be restated to this new method. This restatement redistributes the "cumulative effect of change in accounting principle" to the relevant prior years. Changes in estimates are accounted for prospectively in practice with few exceptions (see Chapter 6). Our ability to adjust all periods to a comparable basis depends on information availability.

Before we assess earnings persistence it is necessary to obtain the best earnings estimate possible with our adjustments. Exhibit 13.2 shows the adjusted income statements of Campbell Soup Company. All earnings components must be considered. If we decide a component should be excluded from the period it is reported, we can either (1) shift it (net of tax) to the operating results of one or more prior periods, or (2) spread (average) it over earnings for the period under analysis. We should only spread it over prior earnings if it cannot be identified with a specific period. While spreading (averaging) helps us in determining earning power, it is not helpful to us in determining earnings trend. We must also realize moving gains or losses to other periods does not remedy the misstatements of prior years' results. For example, a damage award for patent infringement in one period implies prior periods suffered from lost sales or other impairments. We return to discuss the datails of Exhibit 13.2 in our Comprehensive Case.

Our analysis must also recognize certain characterizations of revenue or expense items as unusual, nonrecurring, infrequent, and extraordinary are attempts to reduce earnings volatility or minimize certain earnings components. These characterizations also extend to the inclusion in equity of certain transactions like gains or losses on available-for-sale securities or foreign currency translation adjustments. We often exclude equity effects from our adjustment process. Yet these items are part of a company's lifetime earnings. These items increase or decrease owners' equity and

EXHIBIT 13.1 Recast Income Statements

CAMPBELL SOUP COMPANY
Recast Income Statements For Years 6 to 11
($ millions)

Reference Item		Year 11	Year 10	Year 9	Year 8	Year 7	Year 6
13	Net sales	$6,204.1	$6,205.8	$5,672.1	$4,868.9	$4,490.4	$4,286.8
19	Interest income	26.0	17.6	38.3	33.2	29.5	27.4
	Total revenue	$6,230.1	$6,223.4	$5,710.4	$4,902.1	$4,519.9	$4,314.2
	Costs and expenses:						
	Cost of products sold (see Note 1 below)	$3,727.1	$3,893.5	$3,651.8	$3,077.8	$2,897.8	$2,820.5
	Marketing and selling expenses (see Note 2 below)	760.8	760.1	605.9	514.2	422.7	363.0
145	Advertising (see Note 2 below)	195.4	220.4	212.9	219.1	203.5	181.4
144	Repairs and maintenance (see Note 1 below)	173.9	180.6	173.9	155.6	148.8	144.0
16	Administrative expenses	306.7	290.7	252.1	232.6	213.9	195.9
17	Research and development expenses	56.3	53.7	47.7	46.9	44.8	42.2
102	Stock price–related incentive programs (see Note 3 below)	15.4	(0.1)	17.4	(2.7)	—	8.5
20	Foreign exchange adjustment	0.8	3.3	19.3	16.6	4.8	0.7
104	Other, net (see Note 3 below)	(3.3)	(2.0)	(1.4)	(4.7)	(0.4)	(9.0)
162A	Depreciation (see Note 1 below)	194.5	184.1	175.9	162.0	139.0	120.8
103	Amortization of intangible and other assets (see Note 3 below)	14.1	16.8	16.4	8.9	5.6	6.0
18	Interest expense	116.2	111.6	94.1	53.9	51.7	56.0
	Total costs and expenses	$5,557.9	$5,712.7	$5,266.0	$4,480.2	$4,132.2	$3,930.0
23	Earnings before equity in earnings of affiliates and minority interests	$ 672.2	$ 510.7	$ 444.4	$ 421.9	$ 387.7	$ 384.2
24	Equity in earnings of affiliates	2.4	13.5	10.4	6.3	15.1	4.3
25	Minority interests	(7.2)	(5.7)	(5.3)	(6.3)	(4.7)	(3.9)
26	Income before taxes	$ 667.4	$ 518.5	$ 449.5	$ 421.9	$ 398.1	$ 384.6
	Income taxes at statutory rate*	(226.9)	(176.3)	(152.8)	(143.5)	(179.1)	(176.9)
	Income from continuing operations	$ 440.5	$ 342.2	$ 296.7	$ 278.4	$ 219.0	$ 207.7
135	State taxes (net of federal tax benefit)	(20.0)	(6.6)	(3.8)	(11.8)	(8.6)	(8.0)
	Investment tax credit	—	—	—	—	4.4	11.6
137	Nondeductible amortization of intangibles	(4.0)	(1.6)	(1.2)	(2.6)	(1.4)	—
138	Foreign earnings not taxed or taxed at other than statutory federal rate	2.0	(2.2)	(0.2)	3.2	11.1	15.2
139	Other: Tax effects	(17.0)	(2.2)	(0.1)	(3.7)	7.5	(4.7)
	Alaska Native Corporation transaction	—	—	—	—	4.5	—
22	Divestitures, restructuring, and unusual charges	—	(339.1)	(343.0)	(40.6)	—	—
	Tax effect of divestitures, restructuring, and unusual charges (Note 4)	—	13.9	64.7	13.9	—	—
	Gain on sale of businesses in Year 8 and subsidiary in Year 7	—	—	—	3.1	9.7	—
	Loss on sale of exercise equipment subsidiary, net of tax	—	—	—	—	(1.7)	—
	LIFO liquidation gain (see Note 1 below)	—	—	—	1.7	2.8	1.4
	Income before cumulative effect of accounting change	$ 401.5	$ 4.4	$ 13.1	$ 241.6	$ 247.3	$ 223.2

Ref.	Item						
153A	Cumulative effect of accounting change for income taxes	—	—	—	32.5	—	—
28	Net income as reported	$ 401.5	$ 4.4	$ 13.1	$ 274.1	$ 247.3	$ 223.2
14	(Note 1) Cost of products sold	$4,095.5	$4,258.2	$4,001.6	$3,392.8	$3,180.5	$3,082.8
144	Less: Repair and maintenance expenses	(173.9)	(180.6)	(173.9)	(155.6)	(148.8)	(144.0)
162A	Less: Depreciation[(a)]	(194.5)	(184.1)	(175.9)	(162.0)	(139.0)	(120.0)
153A	Plus: LIFO liquidation gain[(b)]	—	—	—	2.6	5.1	2.6
		$3,727.1	$3,893.5	$3,651.8	$3,077.8	$2,897.8	$2,821.4
15	(Note 2) Marketing and selling expenses	$ 956.2	$ 980.5	$ 818.8	$ 733.3	$ 626.2	$ 544.4
145	Less: Advertising	(195.4)	(20.4)	(212.9)	(219.1)	(203.5)	(181.4)
		$ 760.8	$ 960.1	$ 605.9	$ 514.2	$ 422.7	$ 363.0
21	(Note 3) Other expenses (income)	$ 26.2	$ 14.7	$ 32.4	$ (3.2)	$ (9.5)	$ 5.5
102	Less: Stock price–related incentive programs	(15.4)	0.1	(17.4)	2.7	—	(8.5)
103	Less: Amortization of intangible and other assets	(14.1)	(16.8)	(16.4)	(8.9)	(5.6)	(6.0)
	Less: Gain on sale of businesses (Year 8) and subsidiary (Year 7)	—	—	—	4.7	14.7	—
104	Other, net	$ (3.3)	$ (2.0)	$ (1.4)	$ (4.7)	$ (0.4)	$ (9.0)
	(Note 4) Tax effect of divestitures, restructuring, and unusual charges at statutory rate	—	$ 115.3[(c)]	$ 116.6[(d)]	$ 13.9	—	—
136	Nondeductible divestitures, restructuring, and unusual charges	—	(101.4)[(e)]	(51.9)[(f)]	—	—	—
		—	$ 13.9	$ 64.7	$ 13.9	—	—

*The statutory federal tax rate was 34% in Year 8 through Year 11, 45% in Year 7, and 46% in Year 6.

†This amount was not disclosed for Year 6.

(a)We assume most depreciation is included in cost of products sold.

(b)LIFO liquidation gain before tax. For example, for Year 8 this is $2.58 million, computed as $1.7/(1 – 0.34).

(c)$339.1 **22** × 0.34 = $115.3.

(d)$343.0 **22** × 0.34 = $116.6

(e)$179.4 **26** × 0.565 **136** = $101.4.

(f)$106.5 **26** × 0.487 **136** = $51.9.

EXHIBIT 13.2 Adjusted Income Statements

CAMPBELL SOUP COMPANY
Adjusted Income Statements For Year 6 through Year 11
($ millions)

	Year 11	*Year 10*	*Year 9*	*Year 8*	*Year 7*	*Year 6*	*Total*
Net income as reported	$401.5	$ 4.4	$ 13.1	$274.1	$247.3	$223.2	$1,163.6
Divestitures, restructuring & unusual charges		339.1	343.0	40.6			
Tax effect of divestitures, restructuring, etc.		(13.9)	(64.7)	(13.9)			
Gain on sale of businesses (Year 8) and sale of subsidiary (Year 7), net of tax				(3.1)	(9.7)		
Loss on sale of exercise equipment subsidiary					1.7		
Alaska Native Corporation transaction					(4.5)		
LIFO liquidation gain				(1.7)	(2.8)	(1.4)	
Cumulative effect of change in accounting for income taxes				(32.5)			
Adjusted net income	$401.5	$329.6	$291.4	$263.5	$232.0	$221.8	
Total net income for the period							$1,163.6
Average earnings for the period							$ 193.9

affect earning power. Accordingly, even if we omit these items from our adjustment process, they belong in our analysis of average earning power.

Determinants of Earnings Persistence

After recasting and adjusting earnings for forecasting and valuation purposes, our analysis next focuses on determining earnings persistence. Earnings variability, trend, management, and incentives are all potential determinants of earnings persistence. We should assess earnings persistence over both the business cycle and the long term.

Earnings Variability and Persistence

Earnings fluctuating up and down with the business cycle are less desirable than earnings with a large degree of stability. This is because earnings variability is associated with stock price fluctuations. We can use standard variability measures for this purpose. In evaluating earnings variability, our analysis must recognize the limitations of examining a limited period of earnings. Depending on our objectives, our analysis considers at least two alternatives to the limited information provided by earnings variability measures:

1. *Average earnings*. Computed typically using 5 to 10 years of data. Averaging smooths erratic, extraordinary, and cyclical factors, and can provide a more reliable measure of earning power.
2. *Minimum earnings*. Typically selected from the most recent business cycle. Use of minimum earnings can be helpful in analyses sensitive to high-risk factors. Minimum earnings reflect a worst-case scenario.

Earnings Trends and Persistence

Earnings reflecting steady growth trends are desirable. We can assess earnings trends by purely statistical means or with **trend statements**. Examples of trend statements for selected financial data of Campbell Soup are reported in Exhibits CC.8 and CC.9 in the Comprehensive Case chapter. Trend analysis uses earnings numbers from our recasting and adjusting procedures as exemplified in Exhibit 13.2. Earnings trends often contain important clues to a company's current and future performance (cyclical, growth, defensive) and bear on the quality of management. We must be alert to accounting distortions affecting trends. Especially important are changes in accounting principles and the effect of business combinations, particularly purchases. We must make adjustments for these changes. Probably one major motivation of earnings management is to effect earnings trends. Earnings management practices assume earnings trends are important for valuation. They also reflect a belief that retroactive revisions of earnings previously reported have little effect on security prices. That is, once a company incurs and reports a loss, its existence is often as important as its magnitude for valuation purposes. These assumptions and the propensities of some managements to use accounting as a means of improving earnings trend has led to sophisticated earnings management techniques, including income smoothing.

Earnings Management and Persistence

There are several requirements for our specification of *earnings management.* These requirements are important as they distinguish earnings management from misrepresentations and distortions. Earnings management uses "acceptable" accounting principles for purposes of reporting specific results. It uses the available discretion in selecting and applying accounting principles to achieve these ends, and is arguably performed within the framework of accepted practice. It is a matter of form rather than of substance. It does not affect actual transactions (e.g., postponing expenses to later periods to shift earnings) but does affect a redistribution of credits or charges across periods. A major objective is to moderate earnings variability across periods by shifting earnings between good and bad years, between future and current years, or various combinations. Actual earnings management takes many forms. Some forms of earnings management that we should be especially alert to include:

- *Changes in accounting methods or assumptions.* Examples of companies who changed methods or assumptions include Chrysler, who revised upward the assumed rate of return on its pension portfolio and substantially increased earnings when sales were slumping, and Union Carbide, who switched to more liberal accounting methods and increased earnings.
- *Offsetting extraordinary/unusual gains and losses.* This practice removes unusual or sudden earnings effects that can adversely impact earnings trend (see Chapter 6 for further discussion).
- *Big baths.* This technique recognizes future periods' costs and losses in the current period, when the current period is unavoidably badly performing. This practice relieves future periods' earnings of these costs and losses.
- *Write-downs.* Write-downs of operating assets like plant and equipment or intangibles like goodwill when operating results are poor is another technique. Companies often justify write-downs by arguing that current economics do not support reported asset values. An example is CSX who wrote down $533 million of assets in a restructuring. Especially objectionable is writing down operating assets to a level meeting management's targeted return on invested capital.
- *Timing revenue and expense recognition.* This technique times revenue and expense recognition to manage earnings, including trend. Examples are the timing of revenues, asset sales, research expenditures, advertising, maintenance,

and repairs. Unlike most earnings management techniques, these decisions can involve the timing of actual transactions. An example is Franklin Mint, who inflated earnings by premature recognition of sales.

- *Aggressive accounting applications.* Aggressive accounting applications, sometimes borderline misstatements, are used to redistribute earnings across periods. Examples include creating an excessive number or unusual categories of inventory pools to influence reported earnings. These practices occasionally are outside of accepted norms.

McCormick Co. managed earnings by having its advertising agency delay mailing invoices until later periods.

Management Incentives and Persistence

We previously described the impact of management incentives for the accounting measurements in our analysis of financial statements (see Parts One and Two). This is especially relevant in assessing earnings persistence and other analyses (investing and lending). Experience shows that certain managements, owners, or employees sometimes manipulate or distort reported earnings to serve personal objectives and interests. Companies in financial distress are particularly vulnerable to these pressures. These practices are too often justified by these individuals as a battle for survival. Prosperous companies also sometimes try to preserve hard-earned reputations as earnings growth companies through earnings management. Compensation plans and other accounting-based incentives or constraints provide motivation for management to manage earnings. The impact of management incentives reveal themselves in the following cases:

Second-level divisional executives at H. J. Heinz used *earnings manipulation* to meet earnings targets. This occurred without knowledge of top management. Divisional executives created *hidden reserves* by prepaying for services not yet received like advertising, and they improperly recognized sales.

To meet its profit goals, the syndication division of J.W.T. Grant falsified records. This division bought programming from independent producers and sold them to television stations in return for future commercial time. This created "commercial time banks" for sale to agency clients. It involved creating fictitious time banks, clients, and revenues over several years. The deception was so successful that top management invested additional capital in the division.

Our analysis must recognize the incentives confronting management when reporting earnings. Earnings management is often initially achieved by understating reported earnings. This creates a "reserve" to call on in future low earnings periods. For example, Firestone Tire and Rubber Company concealed earnings in undisclosed accounts for purposes of drawing on these during lean years. Interestingly, some companies suggest earnings management can help users better assess their true earning power. While this point is arguable, this is not the purpose of financial reporting. We are better served by full disclosure of earnings components along with management's explanation. We can then average, smooth, or adjust reported earnings in accordance with our analysis objectives. A probable instance of earnings management is that of General Motors.

Illustration 13.3

GM reported a revision in useful lives of its plant and equipment. This reduced depreciation and amortization charges by $1.2 billion. GM's chairperson reported "*GM earned $3.6 billion for the year, up 21 percent . . . despite a 9 percent reduction in worldwide unit sales.*" Yet without the $1.2 billion decline in depreciation and amortization, earnings would have decreased. This accounting change followed a year-before provision of $1.3 billion for plant closings and restructurings. Yet only $0.5 billion had been charged against this provision four years later, leaving the rest to absorb future years' costs. Four years after this provision there was a change in leadership at GM. This change is accompanied by another $2.1 billion charge to earnings to cover costs of closing several plants, including closings planned several years into the future. This sequence of events impairs confidence in both financial statements and management. Accordingly, we need to reliably estimate earning power using techniques like averaging, recasting, and adjusting of earnings.

Today's accounting practices discourage earnings management. Yet given the incentives of management and the use of accounting numbers to control and monitor performance, our analysis must recognize the potential for earnings management and even misstatements. Our analysis must distinguish between companies' incentives to manage earnings, and especially scrutinize these companies' accounting practices to ensure the integrity of financial statements.

Persistence of Extraordinary Items in Earnings

Recasting and adjusting earnings, including assessing earnings levels and trends, for valuation purposes relies on separating stable, persistent earnings components from random, transitory components. Persistence is important in determining earning power. Earnings forecasting also relies on persistence. A crucuial step in our analysis is to assess the persistence of gains and losses. This section describes how we can determine the persistence of nonrecurring, unusual, or extraordinary items. We also discuss how they should be handled in evaluating earnings level, management performance, and earnings forecasting.

Companies Reporting Extraordinary Items

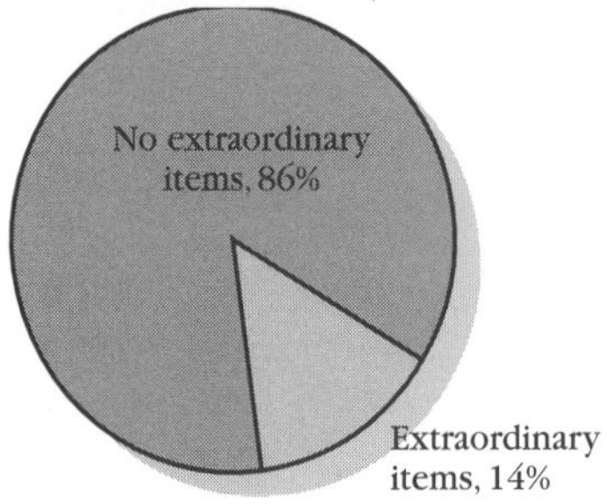

No extraordinary items, 86%

Extraordinary items, 14%

Source: *Accounting Trends & Techniques.*

Reporting of Extraordinary Items

The value of financial reporting depends on its usefulness to those making decisions based on financial statements. The reporting of extraordinary items is affected by its importance to both management and users of financial statements. Management is concerned with both measuring and reporting operating results. This concern reflects a widespread belief that many users accept reported numbers and their accompanying explanations as true measures of performance. Accordingly, extraordinary items are often means to modify reported numbers and to explain performance. These explanations are usually subjective and designed to communicate management's view of events. Practice recognizes the role of management's incentives in procedures governing the reporting of extraordinary items through explicit disclosure requirements and their inclusion in earnings.

Analyzing and Interpreting Extraordinary Items

Our purpose in analyzing and interpreting extraordinary items is twofold:

1. Determine whether an item is extraordinary (less persistent) for our analysis. This involves assessing whether an item is unusual, nonoperating, or nonrecurring.
2. Determine adjustments necessary given our assessment of persistence. Special adjustments are sometimes necessary for both evaluating and forecasting earnings.

We describe both of these analyses in this section.

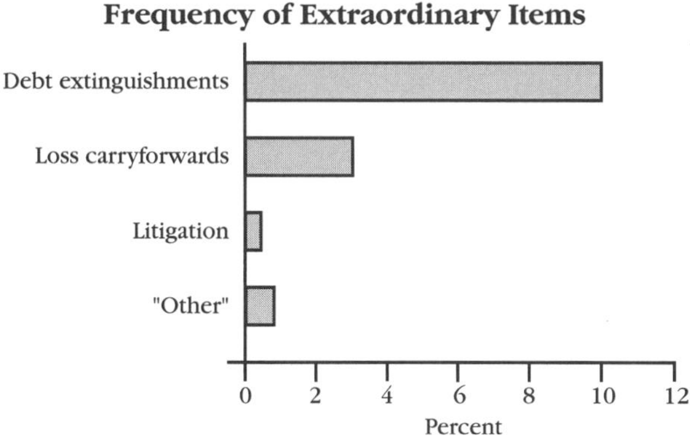

Source: *Accounting Trends & Techniques.*

Determining Persistence (Extraordinary Nature) of Items. Given the incentives confronting management in reporting extraordinary items, we must render our independent evaluation of whether a gain or loss is extraordinary—including where it fits on the spectrum of highly persistent to transitory earnings. We need also determine how to adjust for it. For this purpose we can arrange items into three broad categories: nonrecurring operating; recurring nonoperating; and nonrecurring nonoperating.

- *Nonrecurring operating gains or losses.* These gains or losses relate to operating activities but recur infrequently or unpredictably. Operating items relate to a company's *normal* business activities. The concept of normal operations is far less clear than many realize. A machine shop's operating revenues and expenses are those associated with the workings of the shop. In contrast, proceeds from selling available-for-sale marketable securities are nonoperating gains or losses. But a gain (or loss) on the sale of a lathe, even if disposed of to make room for a more productive one, is a nonoperating item. The other important concept, that of *recurrence,* is one of frequency. There are no predetermined generally accepted boundaries separating a recurring event from a nonrecurring one. For example, a regular event generating a gain or loss is classified as recurring. An unpredictable event, which occurs infrequently, is classified as nonrecurring. Yet an event occurring infrequently but whose occurrence is predictable raises questions as to its classification. An example is the relining of blast furnaces. They endure for many years and their replacement is infrequent, but the need for it predictable. Some companies provide for these types of replacements with a reserve.

Our analysis of nonrecurring operating gains and losses must recognize their inherent infrequency and lack of recurring patterns. We treat them as belonging to results of the reporting period. We must also address the question of normal operations. It is a bakery's purpose to bake bread, rolls, and cakes, but it is presumably outside normal activities to buy and sell marketable securities for gain or loss, or even to sell baking machinery that is replaced with more efficient machinery. This limited interpretation of operating activities can be challenged. Some argue the objective is not baking but for management to increase owners' equity, or common stock valuation. This is accomplished through strategic application of financing, investing, and operating activities. It is not limited to a narrow view of normal operations. We can usefully evaluate a much wider range of gains and losses as being derived from operating activities. This view results in many nonrecurring operating gains and losses considered as part of operating activities in the year they occur.

Our analysis of nonrecurring operating items does not readily fit a mechanical rule. We must review the information and will doubtless find some items more likely to be recurring than others and some more operating than others. This affects our recasting, adjusting, and forecasting of earnings. We should also recognize the magnitude of an item as an important factor. Once we complete our analysis of recurring earnings, we often need to focus on *average earnings* experience over a few years rather than the result of a single year. A focus on average earnings is especially important for companies with fluctuating amounts of nonrecurring and other extraordinary items. A single year is too short and too arbitrary a period to evaluate the earning power of a company or for forecasting earnings.

Illustration 13.4

In the past few years we have seen several large charges to earnings for reorganization, redeployment, or regrouping. Companies taking substantial write-offs include ($ billions) AT&T $2.6, Occidental Petroleum $2, Continental Airlines $1.8, Digital Equipment $1, Columbia Gas System $.8, General Dynamics $.6, and Bethlehem Steel $.6. Information supplied with these events is often limited, but there is no denying these companies' enormous "revisions" of previously reported results. In one stroke, these write-offs *correct* prior years' overreporting of earnings. Our analysis must also be alert to aggressive write-offs to relieve future periods of charges properly attributable to them.

- *Recurring nonoperating gains or losses.* These include items of a nonoperating nature that recur with some frequency. An example is the recurring amortization of a bargain purchase credit. Other possible examples are interest income and rent received from employees renting company-owned houses. While these items can be classified as unusual in financial statements, the limited definition of *nonoperating* and their recurrent nature are reasons why we should consider their potential inclusion in current operating earnings. They typically result from management's planned activities, and their recurrence requires the inclusion of these gains or losses in forecasts of future results.
- *Nonrecurring nonoperating gains or losses.* These items are nonrepeating and unpredictable, and fall outside normal operations. Events driving these items are typically extraneous, unintended, and unplanned. Yet they are rarely entirely unexpected. Business is subject to risks of adverse events and random shocks, be they natural or man-made. Business transactions are subject to the same. An example is damage to plant facilities due to the crash of an aircraft when your plant is not located near an airport. Other examples might include: (1) substantial uninsured casualty losses not within the usual risks of the company, (2) expropriation by a foreign government of assets owned

by the company, or (3) seizure or destruction of property from war, insurrection, or civil disorders when not expected. These occurrences are typically nonrecurring but their relation to operating activities varies. All are occurrences in the regular course of business. Even assets destroyed by acts of nature are acquired for operating activities and are subject to all risks. The third example is close to meeting the criterion of extraordinary. But unique events are rare. What often appears unique is frequently symptomatic of new risks affecting earning power and future operations. Our analysis must consider this possibility. But barring evidence to the contrary, these items are regarded as extraordinary and omitted from operating results of a single year. They are, nevertheless, part of the long-term performance of a company.

Adjustments to Extraordinary Items Reflecting Persistence. Our second step in analyzing extraordinary, or transitory, items is to consider their effects on both the resources of the company and our evaluation of management.

- *Effects of extraordinary items on company resources.* Every extraordinary gain or loss has a dual effect. For example, when recording a gain, a company also records an increase in resources. Similarly, a loss results in a decrease in resources. Since return on invested capital measures the relation of net income to resources, extraordinary gains and losses affect this measure. The larger the extraordinary item, the larger its effect on return. If we use earnings and current events in forecasting, then extraordinary items convey more than past performance. If an extraordinary loss decreases capital for expected returns, then future returns are lost. Conversely, an extraordinary gain increases capital and future expected returns. In forecasting profitability and return on investment, our analysis must take account of the effects of recorded extraordinary items and the likelihood of future events causing extraordinary items.
- *Effect of extraordinary items on evaluation of management.* One implication frequently associated with extraordinary gains and losses is their lack of association with normal or planned business activities. Because of this they are often not used when evaluating management performance. Our analysis should question their exclusion from management performance evaluation. What are the normal or planned activities that relate to management's decisions? Whether we consider securities transactions, plant asset transactions, or activities of divisions and subsidiaries, these all reflect actions taken by management with specific purposes. These actions typically require more consideration or deliberation than ordinary operating decisions because they are often unusual in nature and involve substantial amounts. All of these actions reflect on management's ability.

Standard Oil Co. reported an extraordinary charge of $1.15 billion in writing down its ill-fated investment in Kennecott. This loss implies prior years' earnings are overstated *and* questions about the ability of management..

Management should be aware of the risks of natural or manmade disasters or impediments. Business decisions are their responsibility. For example, a decision to pursue international activities is made with the knowledge of the special risks involved. A decision to insure or not is a normal operating decision. Essentially nothing is entirely unexpected or unforeseeable. Management does not engage, or is at least not expected to engage, in business activities unknowingly. Decision making is within the expected activities of a business. Every company is subject to inherent risks, and management should not blindly pursue activities.

In our assessment of operating results, distinguishing between normal and extraordinary items is sometimes meaningless. Management's beliefs about the quality of its decisions are nearly always related to the normalcy, or lack thereof, of business conditions. This is evident in the Management Discussion and Analysis. Yet the best management anticipates the unexpected. When failures or shortcomings occur, poor management typically takes time to "explain" these in a way to avoid responsibility. While success rarely requires explanation, failure evokes long explanations and blame to unusual or unforeseeable events. In a competitive economy, normal conditions rarely prevail for any length of time. Management is paid to anticipate and expect the unusual. Explanations are not a substitute for performance.

ANALYSIS VIEWPOINT . . . *You are the analyst/forecaster*

You are analyzing a company's earnings persistence in preparing its earnings forecasts for publication in your company's online forecasting service. Its earnings and earnings components ("net income" and "income from continuing operations") are stable and exhibit a steady growth trend. However, you find "unusual gains" relating to litigation comprising 40 percent of current earnings. You also find "extraordinary losses" from environmental costs. How do these disclosures affect your earnings persistence estimate?

Earnings-Based Valuation

Company valuation is an important responsibility for many users of financial statements. Reliable estimates of value enable us to make buy/sell/hold decisions regarding securities, assess the value of a company for credit decisions, estimate prices for business combinations, determine prices for public offerings of a company's securities, and many other useful applications. This section introduces us to accounting-based equity valuation and incorporates it within our analysis of financial statements. Many of the elements comprising accounting-based valuation are described in this and prior chapters but are not explicitly assimilated in a valuation framework.

Traditional descriptions of company equity valuation rely on the *discounted cash flow (DCF) method*. Under the DCF method, the value of a company's equity is computed based on forecasts of cash flows available to equity investors. These forecasts are then discounted using the company's cost of equity capital.[1] It is important to emphasize that the accounting-based equity valuation model introduced earlier in this book and discussed in this section is theoretically consistent with the DCF method. If correctly applied, the accounting-based and DCF methods yield identical value estimates.

[1] A common alternative is to discount expected cash flows available to both debt and equity holders using the company's weighted-average cost of debt and equity capital. This yields an estimate of the total value of the company. The value of a company's equity is obtained by subtracting the value of its debt.

Relation between Stock Prices and Accounting Data

Recall the accounting-based equity valuation model introduced in Chapter 2 and expanded upon in Chapter 11:

$$V_t = BV_t + \frac{(ROCE_{t+1} - k) \times BV_t}{(1+k)} + \frac{(ROCE_{t+2} - k) \times BV_{t+1}}{(1+k)^2} + \ldots + \frac{(ROCE_{t+n} - k) \times BV_{t+n-1}}{(1+k)^n} + \ldots$$

This model indicates a company's equity value (V_t) at time t equals its book value (BV_t) at time t plus the present value of future abnormal earnings. Abnormal earnings equal the difference between a company's return on common shareholders' equity ($ROCE_t$) and its cost of equity capital (k), multiplied by beginning period book value (BV_{t-1}).[2] The model directly shows the importance of future profitability in estimating company value—by using estimates of future ROCE and book values. Accurate estimates of these measures can be made only after consideration of the quality and persistence of a company's earnings and earning power.

A common criticism of accounting-based valuation methods is that earnings are subject to manipulation and distortion at the hands of management whose personal objectives and interests depend on reported accounting numbers. Indeed, a good portion of the book focuses on the need for our analysis to go "beyond the numbers." A reasonable question, therefore, is: Does the potential manipulation of accounting data influence the accuracy of accounting-based estimates, or forecasts, of company value? The answer is both yes *and* no.

The numerical example in Problem 13–5 confirms the "no" part of the answer. We demonstrate in that problem that accounting choices necessarily affect both earnings and book value. Aggressive (income increasing) accounting choices lead to higher earnings and book values. Yet this is only in the short run, as all costs must eventually flow through the income statement (assuming clean surplus accounting). Later periods' earnings for companies making aggressive accounting choices are lower than those employing conservative accounting choices. The "yes" part of the answer is based on the reality that analysis uses reported accounting data (and other information) as a basis for projecting future profitability. To the extent accounting choices mask the current true economic performance of the company, a less experienced analyst can be misled regarding the company's current and future performance. Consequently, the analysis techniques described in this book are important to our analysis even though the accounting-based valuation model is mathematically free from accounting manipulations.

Fundamental Valuation Multiples

Two widely cited valuation measures are the price-to-book (PB) and price-to-earnings (PE) ratios. Users often base investment decisions on the observed values of these ratios. We describe how our analysis can arrive at "fundamental" PB and PE ratios without referring to the trading price of a company's shares. By comparing our fundamental ratios to those implicit in current stock prices, we can evaluate the investment

[2] Abnormal earnings (NI_t^a) can also be computed as net income (NI_t) less the quantity of beginning period book value (BV_{t-1}) multiplied by the cost of equity capital (k).

Analysis Research Insight 13.1

Earnings Persistence

Earnings persistence plays an important role in company valuation. Analysis research indicates nonrecurring earnings increase company value on a dollar-for-dollar basis, while the stock price reaction to persistent sources of earnings is higher and positively associated with the degree of persistence.

An analyst cannot rely solely on income statement classifications in assessing the persistence of a company's earnings. Research indicates many types of nonrecurring items can be included in income from continuing operations. Examples include gains/losses on asset disposals, changes in accounting estimates, asset writedowns, and provisions for future losses. Our analysis must carefully examine the financial statement notes, MD&A, and other disclosures for the existence of these items.

Evidence also shows that extraordinary items and discontinued operations ("special items") may be partly predictable and can provide information regarding future profitability.

Recent analysis research indicates that companies currently reporting negative income along with special items are more likely to report special items in the following year. These subsequent years' special items are likely to be of the same sign. Although profitable companies with discontinued operations are more likely to report higher earnings in subsequent years.

merits of a publicly traded company. For those companies whose shares are not traded in active markets, the fundamental ratios serve as a means for estimating equity value.

Price-to-Book (PB) Ratio

The **price-to-book (PB) ratio** is expressed as:

$$\frac{\text{Market value of equity}}{\text{Book value of equity}}$$

By substituting the accounting-based expression for equity value in the numerator, the PB ratio can be expressed in terms of accounting data as follows:

$$\frac{V_t}{BV_t} = 1 + \left[\frac{(ROCE_{t+1} - k)}{(1+k)}\right] + \left[\frac{(ROCE_{t+2} - k)}{(1+k)^2} \times \frac{BV_{t+1}}{BV_t}\right] + \left[\frac{(ROCE_{t+3} - k)}{(1+k)^3} \times \frac{BV_{t+2}}{BV_t}\right] + \ldots$$

This expression yields several important insights. As future ROCE and growth in book value increase, the PB ratio increases. As the cost (risk) of equity capital, k, increases, the PB ratio decreases. Recognize that PB ratios deviate from 1.0 when the market expects abnormal earnings (both positive and negative) in the future. If the present value of future abnormal earnings is positive (negative), the PB ratio is greater (less) than 1.0.

Price-to-Earnings (PE) Ratio

The **price-to-earning (PE) ratio** is expressed as:

$$\frac{\text{Market value of equity}}{\text{Net income}}$$

By substituting the accounting-based expression for equity value in the numerator and simplifying, the PE ratio can be expressed in terms of accounting data as follows:

$$\frac{V_t}{NI_t} = \overline{PE} + \frac{\overline{PE}}{NI_t}\left[\frac{\Delta NI^a_{t+1}}{(1+k)} + \frac{\Delta NI^a_{t+2}}{(1+k)^2} + \ldots\right] - \frac{d_t}{NI_t}$$

where $\overline{PE}$ [equaling $(1+k)/k$] is a "normal" PE ratio, ΔNI^a_{t+1} is the expected change in abnormal earnings for year t+1 compared to the prior year (i.e., $NI^a_{t+1} - NI^a_t$) and d_t is dividends for year t.

This expression yields a number of key insights. As the cost of equity capital increases, the PE ratio decreases. PE ratios deviate from a normal $\overline{PE}$ whenever investors expect abnormal earnings in the future. If future abnormal earnings are increasing (decreasing), the PE ratio is greater (less) than normal $\overline{PE}$. In the presence of future abnormal earnings, the extent to which PE deviates from normal $\overline{PE}$ depends on the current level of earnings. As the level of current earnings increases (decreases), the PE ratio decreases (increases).

Articulation of PB and PE Ratios

By studying actual PB and PE ratios jointly, our analysis gains insight into the market's expectations of future profitability.[3] As we showed, the PB ratio is a function of future profitability relative to book value and growth in book value, while the PE ratio is a function of future profitability relative to the current level of earnings. The following table summarizes the implications of various combinations of PB and PE ratios:

	Low PB	*High PB*
Low PE	Earnings expected to grow slowly or decline relative to current level, with low expected ROCE.	Earnings expected to grow slowly or decline relative to current level, but with high expected ROCE.
High PE	Earnings expected to grow quickly relative to current level, but with low expected ROCE.	Earnings expected to grow quickly relative to current level, with high expected ROCE.

Illustration of Earnings-Based Valuation

We illustrate earnings-based valuation using financial information from Christine Company. The book value of equity for Christine Company at January 1, Year 1, is $50,000. The company has a 15% cost of equity capital (k). After careful study of the company and its prospects using analysis techniques described in this book, we obtain the following predictions of accounting data:

[3] For more detail on this issue, see S. H. Penman, "The Articulation of Price-Earnings Ratios and Market-to-Book Ratios and the Evaluation of Growth," *Journal of Accounting Research*, Autumn 1996. For an excellent summary of the accounting-based equity valuation model, see M. P. Bauman, "A Summary of Fundamental Analysis Research in Accounting," *Journal of Accounting Literature*, 1996.

	Year 1	Year 2	Year 3	Year 4	Year 5
Sales	$100,000	$113,000	$127,690	$144,290	$144,290
Operating expenses	77,500	90,000	103,500	118,000	119,040
Depreciation	10,000	11,300	12,770	14,430	14,430
Net income	$ 12,500	$ 11,700	$ 11,420	$ 11,860	$ 10,820
Dividends	6,000	4,355	3,120	11,860	10,820

For Year 6 and beyond we predict both accounting data and dividends will approximate Year 5 levels. To apply the accounting-based valuation model we compute expected future book values and ROCEs using our accounting predictions above. Provided with these data, estimation of book value is straightforward. For example, book value at January 1, Year 2, is computed as $56,500 ($50,000 beginning book value + $12,500 net income – $6,000 dividends). Expected book values at January 1, Years 3 through 5, are $63,845, $72,145, and $72,145, respectively.

Recall that the accounting-based valuation model uses ROCEs computed using *beginning-of-period* book value. Therefore, expected ROCE for Year 1 is 25% ($12,500 ÷ $50,000). Expected ROCEs for Years 2 through 5 are 20.71%, 17.89%, 16.44%, and 15%, respectively.

The value of Christine Company's equity at January 1, Year 1, is computed using the valuation model on page 642 and equals:

$$\$58,594 = 50,000 + \frac{(0.25 - 0.15) \times 50,000}{1.15} + \frac{(0.2071 - 0.15) \times 56,500}{1.15^2} + \frac{(0.1789 - 0.15) \times 63,845}{1.15^3} + \frac{(0.1644 - 0.15) \times 72,145}{1.15^4} + 0 + \ldots + \frac{(0.15 - 0.15) \times 72,145}{1.15^5} + 0 + \ldots$$

This accounting-based valuation implies that Christine's stock should sell at a PB ratio of 1.17 ($58,594 ÷ $50,000) at January 1, Year 1. To the extent expectations of stock market participants differ from those implied by the valuation model, the PB ratio using actual stock price will differ from 1.17. In this case, we must consider two possibilities: (1) estimates of future profitability are too optimistic or pessimistic, and/or (2) the company's stock is mispriced. This determination is a major part of fundamental analysis. Three additional observations regarding this illustration are important.

1. Expected ROCE equals 15% fro Year 5 and beyond. This 15% return is equal to Christine Company's cost of capital for those years. Since ROCE equals the cost of capital for Year 5 and beyond, these years' results do not change the value of Christine Company (i.e., abnormal earnings equal zero for those years). Our assumption that ROCE gradually nears the cost of capital arises from basic economics. That is, if companies in an industry are able to earn ROCEs in excess of the cost of capital, other companies will enter the industry and drive abnormal earnings to zero.[4] The anticipated effects of competition are implicit in our estimates

[4] Even if abnormal earnings are zero, conservatism in accounting principles can create the *appearance* of abnormal profitability. While this issue is not pursued here, our analysis must consider the effects of conservative accounting principles on future ROCEs. For example, due to mandated expensing of most research and development costs, firms in the pharmaceutical industry are characterized by relatively high ROCEs.

of future profitability. For example, net income as a percent of sales steadily decreases from 12.5% ($12,500 ÷ $100,000) in Year 1 to 7.5% ($10,820 ÷ $144,290) in Year 5 and beyond.

2. Since PE ratios are based on both *current* and *future* earnings, a PE ratio for Christine Company as of January 1, Year 1 cannot be calculated since prior years' data are unavailable. We can compute the PE ratio at January 1, Year 2. It is calculated as follows (We calculate Christine's abnormal earnings in Problem 13–6):

$$4.91 = \frac{1.15}{0.15} + \frac{\left(\frac{1.15}{0.15}\right)}{12{,}500}\left[\frac{3{,}225 - 5{,}000}{1.15} + \frac{1{,}844 - 3{,}226}{1.15^2} + \frac{1{,}039 - 1{,}845}{1.15^3} + \frac{0 - 1{,}039}{1.15^4}\right] - \frac{6{,}000}{12{,}500}$$

3. Our valuation estimates assume dividend payments occur at the end of each year. A more realistic assumption is that, on average, these cash outflows occur midway through the year. To adjust valuation estimates for mid-year discounting, we multiply the present value of future abnormal earnings by $(1 + k/2)$. For Christine Company the adjusted valuation estimate equals $59,239. This is computed as $50,000 plus $(1 + [.15/2]) \times$ $8,594.

Earning Power and Forecasting for Valuation

This section expands on the role of earning power and earnings forecasts for valuation. We also discuss our use of interim reports to monitor and revise these valuation inputs.

Earning Power

Earning power refers to the earnings level for a company that is expected to persist into the foreseeable future. With few exceptions, earning power is recognized as a primary factor in company valuation. Accounting-based valuation models include the capitalization of earning power, where capitalization involves using a factor or multiplier reflecting the cost of capital and future expected risks and returns. Most analyses of earnings and financial statements are also aimed at determining earning power.

Measuring Earning Power

Earning power is a concept derived from financial analysis, not accounting. It focuses on the stability and persistence of earnings and earnings components. Financial statements are used in computing earning power. This computation requires knowledge, judgment, experience, and perspective. Many valuation models use future cash flows (although Chapter 2 showed we can restate these models using earnings). Accrual earnings involve adjustments to cash flows in recording revenue when earned and expenses when incurred. Earnings are our most reliable and relevant measure for valuation purposes. While valuation is future oriented, we must recognize the relevance of current and prior company performance for estimating future performance. Recent periods' earnings extending over a business cycle represent actual operating performance and provide us a perspective on operating activities from which we can estimate future performance. We know valuation is extremely important to many users (e.g., in investing, lending, tax planning, adjudication of valuation disputes).

Accordingly, valuation estimates must be credible and defensible, and we must scrutinize departures from the norm. This is the reason courts and others are reluctant to replace past performance (earning power) with future estimates.

Time Horizon for Earning Power

A one-year period is often too short a period to reliably measure earnings. This is because of the long-term nature of many investing and financing activities, the effects of business cycles, and the existence of various nonrecurring factors. We can usually best measure a company's earning power by using average (or cumulative) earnings over several years. The preferred time horizon in measuring earning power varies across industries and other characteristics. A typical horizon is from 5 to 10 years in computing average earnings. This extended period is less subject to distortions, irregularities, and other transitory effects impairing the relevance of a single year's results. A five-year earnings computation often retains an emphasis on recent experience and avoids including less relevant performance results.

Our discussion of both earnings quality and persistence emphasizes the importance of several earnings attributes including trend. Earnings trend is an important factor in measuring earning power. If earnings exhibit a sustainable trend, we can adjust the averaging process to weigh recent earnings more heavily. As an example, in a five-year earnings computation, the most recent earnings is given a weight of 5/15, the next most recent earnings a weight of 4/15, and so on until earnings from five years ago receives a weight of 1/15. The more a company's recent experience is representative of future activities, the more relevant it is in the earnings computation. If recent performance is unlike a company's future plans, then less emphasis is placed on prior earnings and more on earnings forecasts.

Adjusting Earnings per Share

Earning power is measured using *all* earnings components. Every item of revenue and expense is part of a company's operating experience. The issue is to what year we assign these items when computing earning power. In certain cases our earnings analysis might be limited to a short time horizon. As described earlier in this chapter, we adjust short time series of earnings for items that better relate to other periods. If this is done on a per share basis, every item must be adjusted for its tax effect using the company's effective tax rate unless the applicable tax rate is specified. All items must also be divided by the number of shares used in computing earnings per share (see Appendix 6A). An example of analytical adjustments for A. H. Robins Company appears on the next page.

Earnings Forecasting

A major part of financial statement analysis and valuation is earnings forecasting. From our analytical perspective, evaluating earnings level is closely related to forecasting earnings. This is because a relevant forecast of earnings involves an analysis of earnings components and assessing their future levels. Accordingly, much of this chapter's previous discussion is applicable to earnings forecasting. Earnings forecasting follows our analysis of earnings components and estimates of their future levels. We should consider interactions among components and future business conditions. We should also consider persistence and stability of earnings components. This includes analysis of permanent (recurring) and transitory (nonrecurring) elements.

Example of Per Share Earnings Adjustment

Item	Year 2	Year 1
Effective tax rate change	+$0.02	
Settlement of litigation	+0.07	+$0.57
Change to straight-line depreciation	+0.02	
Reserves for losses on foreign assets	+0.02	−0.15
Loss on sale of divisions	−0.19	
Change to LIFO	−0.07	
Litigation settlements and expense	−0.09	−0.12
Foreign exchange translation	−0.03	−0.04
R&D expenditures exceeding prior levels	−0.11	
Higher percent allowance for doubtful accounts	−0.02	
±Per share earnings impact	−$0.38	+$0.26
Per share earnings as reported	$1.01	$1.71
Add back negative (−) impact to Year 2	*0.38*	
Subtract positive (+) impact from Year 1		*(0.26)*
Adjusted earnings per share	$1.39	$1.45

Mechanics of Earnings Forecasting

Chapter 9 considered certain mechanics of forecasting for short-term forecasting of cash flows. Forecasting requires us to effectively use all available information, including prior periods' earnings. Forecasting also benefits from disaggregation. Disaggregation involves using data by product lines or segments, and is especially useful when these segments differ by risk, profitability or growth. Divisional earnings for TechCom, Inc., reveal how strikingly different divisional performance is masked by aggregate results:

	TechCom Earnings ($ millions)			
	1995	*1996*	*1997*	*1998*
Electronic products	$1,800	$1,700	$1,500	$1,200
Customer services	600	800	1,100	1,400
Total net income	$2,400	$2,500	$2,600	$2,600

We must also differentiate forecasting from extrapolation. *Extrapolation* typically assumes the continuation of a trend and mechanically projects that trend into the future. A *projection* also differs from a forecast in that it depends on certain assumptions that are not necessarily the most probable.

Analysis research reveals various statistical properties in earnings. Annual earnings growth often behaves in a random fashion. Some users interpret this as implying earnings growth cannot be forecasted. We must remember these studies reflect aggregate behavior and not individual company behavior. Furthermore, reliable earnings forecasting is *not* done by naive extrapolation of past earnings growth or trends. It is done by analyzing earnings components and considering all available information, both quantitative and qualitative. It involves forecasting these components and speculating about future business conditions.

An often useful source of relevant information for earnings forecasting is Management's Discussion and Analysis. It contains information on management's views and attitudes about the future, along with a discussion of factors influencing company performance. While companies have been slow to respond to the market demand for forecasts, they are encouraged to report forward-looking information in this report.

Elements in Earnings Forecasting

While earnings forecasting depends on future prospects, the forecasting process must rely on current and past evidence. We forecast expected future conditions in light of this evidence. Our analysis must assess continuity and momentum of company performance, including its industry, but it should be put in perspective. We should not confuse a company's past with its future and the uncertainty of forecasting. We must also remember that earnings is total revenues less total costs, and that earnings forecasts reflect forecasts of these same components. Recognizing that earnings represents a relatively small portion of either component, we see how a relatively minor change in a component can cause a large change in earnings.

Another element in earnings forecasting is checking on a forecast's reasonableness. We often use return on invested capital for this purpose. If the earnings forecast yields returns substantially different from returns realized in the past or from industry returns, we should reassess our forecasts and the process. Differences in forecast returns must be explained, not necessarily to revise our forecast but to increase its reliability. We showed that return on invested capital depends on earnings—where earnings are a product of management quality and asset management.

- *Management quality.* It takes resourceful management to "breathe life" into assets by profitably and efficiently using them. Assuming stability of relations and trends implies there is no major change in the skill, depth, and continuity of management. It also implies no major changes in the type of business where management's skills are proven.
- *Asset management.* A second element of profitable operations is asset management and success in financing those assets. Companies require assets to expand operations. Continuity of success and forecasts of growth depend on financing sources and their effects on earnings.

A company's financial condition is another element to earnings forecasting. Lack of liquidity can constrain a successful management, and risky capital structure can limit management's actions. These and other economic, industry, and competitive factors are relevant to earnings forecasting. In forecasting earnings we must add expectations about the future to our knowledge of the past. We should also evaluate earnings trends with special emphasis on indicators of future performance like capital expenditures, order backlogs, and demand trends for products or services. It is important for us to realize that earnings forecasting is accompanied by considerable uncertainty. Forecasts may prove quite different from realizations because of unpredictable events or circumstances. We counter uncertainty by continual monitoring of performance relative to forecasts and revising forecasts as appropriate.

Reporting Earnings Forecasts

Recent years have witnessed increasing interest in disclosures of earnings forecasts by companies. Britain requires forecast disclosures under certain situations and there is a growing belief in practice that management forecasts would be useful additions to annual reports. We should recognize that management (insider) forecasting is different from forecasts made by financial analysts (outsiders). The reliability of forecasts depends on information access and assumptions made. Use of management or analyst forecasts in our analysis depends on our assessment of the assumptions underlying them. The SEC encourages forecasts made in *good faith* and that have a reasonable basis. It recommends they be reported in financial statement format and accompanied by information adequate for investors to assess reliability. To encourage forecast disclosures, the SEC has "safe harbor" rules protecting companies from lawsuits in case their predictions do not come true. These rules protect companies provided their forecasts are reasonably based and made in good faith. Because of practical legal considerations, few companies avail themselves of these safe harbor rules and publish forecasts.

> The Company cautions that any forward-looking statements . . . involve risks and uncertainties, and are subject to change based on various important factors . . . changes in consumer spending patterns, consumer preferences and overall economic conditions, the impact of competition and pricing, changes in weather patterns, political stability, currency and exchange risks and changes in existing or potential duties, tariffs or quotas, postal rate increases and charges, paper and printing costs, availability of suitable store locations at appropriate terms, ability to develop new merchandise and ability to hire and train associates.
>
> —The Limited, Inc.

Interim Reports for Monitoring and Revising Earnings Estimates

Assessing the earning power or earnings forecasts of a company relies on estimates of future conditions not amenable to verification. Our analysis must continually monitor company performance and compare it with our most recent forecasts and assumptions. We should regularly revise our forecasts incorporating current business conditions. Interim (less than one year) financial statements are a valuable source of information for monitoring performance. Interim statements are usually issued quarterly and are designed to meet users' needs. They are useful in revising our estimates of earning power and earnings forecasts. Yet we must recognize certain limitations in interim reporting related to difficulties in assigning earnings components to periods of under one year in length. The remainder of this chapter describes these limitations and their effects on interim reports.

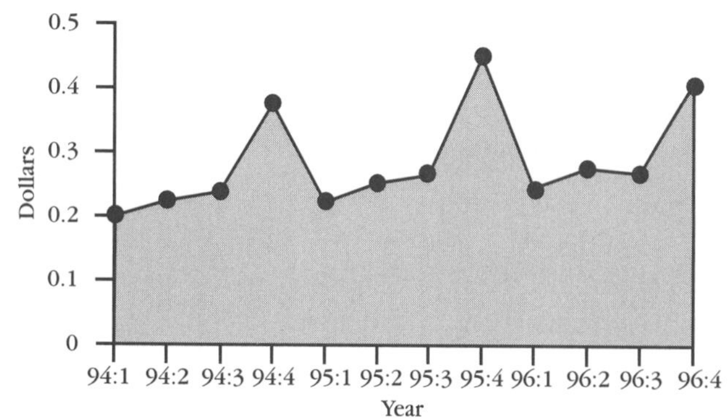

Source: Annual report.

Period-End Accounting Adjustments

Determining operating results for a one-year period requires many adjustments including use of accrual accounting. These year-end adjustments are often complex, time-consuming, and costly. Examples include revenue recognition, determining inventory costs, allocating overhead, obtaining market values of securities, and estimating bad debts. These adjustments for interim periods are often less complete and use less reliable information than their year-end counterparts. This likely yields a less accurate earnings measure for interim periods.

Seasonality in Business Activities

Many companies experience seasonality in their business activities. Sales, production, and other operating activities are often unevenly distributed across interim periods. This can distort comparisons of interim earnings. It also creates problems in allocating certain discretionary costs like advertising, research, development, repairs, and maintenance. If these expenses vary with sales, they are usually accrued on the basis of expected sales for the entire year. Reporting problems also extend to allocating fixed costs across interim periods.

Illustration 13.5

Seasonality led to the following adjustments in the interim reports of Toronto Electech: "Because of seasonality in the production cycle, and in accordance with practices followed by the Company in reporting interim financial statements, $435,000 of unabsorbed factory overhead is deferred at June 30, 1998. Due to uncertainties in production and sales for the entire 1998 year, $487,000 of unabsorbed overhead is expensed during the first 6 months of the year."

Integral Reporting Method

Interim reports are generally reported in a manner consistent with annual reporting requirements. Adopting the view that quarterly reports are integral to the entire year rather than a discrete period, practice requires accrual of revenues and expenses across interim periods. This includes accruals for inventory shrinkages, quantity discounts, and uncollectible accounts. Also, losses are not usually deferred beyond the interim period in which they occur, and extraordinary items are reported in the interim period when they occur. But accrual of advertising costs is not acceptable on the basis that their benefits cannot be anticipated. Similarly, LIFO inventory liquidations are not considered for interim periods, and only permanent declines in inventory values are recorded for interim reports. Yet income taxes are accrued using the effective tax rate expected for the annual period.

SEC Interim Reporting Requirements

The SEC is keenly interested in interim reporting. It requires quarterly reports (Form 10-Q), reports on current developments (Form 8-K), disclosure of separate fourth-quarter results, and details of year-end adjustments. There exist several reporting requirements for interim reports filed with the SEC. Principal requirements include:

- Comparative interim and year-to-date income statement data—can be labeled *unaudited* but must be included in annual reports (small companies are exempt).
- Comparative balance sheets.
- Year-to-date statement of cash flows.
- Pro forma information on business combinations accounted for as purchases.
- Conformity with accepted accounting principles, and disclosure of accounting changes including a letter from the auditor reporting whether the changes are preferable.

- Management's narrative analysis of operating results, with explanations of changes in revenues and expenses across interim periods.
- Disclosure as to whether a Form 8-K is filed during the period—reporting either unusual earnings adjustments or change of auditor.

These disclosures are believed to assist users in better understanding a company's business activities. They are also believed to assist users in estimating the trend in business activities across periods in a timely manner. We can see Adaptec's interim disclosure in note 11 of its 1996 annual report in Supplement A.

Analysis Implications of Interim Reports

Our analysis must be aware of estimation errors and the discretion inherent in interim reports. The limited involvement of auditors with interim data reduces their reliability relative to yearly audited financial statements. Exchange regulations offer some, albeit limited, assurance. Yet not all reporting requirements for interim reports are necessarily best for our analysis. For example, including extraordinary items in the interim period in which they occur requires adjustment for use in our analysis. Similarly, while accruing expenses across interim periods is reasonable, our analysis must remember there are no precise rules governing these accruals. Shifting expenses across periods is often easier than shifting revenues. Therefore, our analysis often emphasizes interim revenues as a measure of interim performance. We should also remember that common stock prices influence a company's earnings per share (see Appendix 6A). Our analysis of per share results should separate price effects from operating performance. Certain seasonality problems with interim reports are overcome by computing *year-to-date cumulative numbers*, including the results of the most recent quarter. This is a very effective means to monitor a company's recent performance.

GUIDANCE ANSWERS TO ANALYSIS VIEWPOINTS

You Are the Director

Your concern with earnings quality is to ensure earnings accurately reflect the company's return and risk characteristics. Low earnings quality implies *inflated earnings* (returns) and/or *deflated risk* not reflecting actual return or risk characteristics. Regarding inflated earnings (returns), you can ask the auditor for evidence of management's use of liberal accounting principles or applications, aggressive behavior in discretionary accruals, asset overstatements, and liability understatements. Regarding deflated risk, you can ask about earnings sources, stability, variability, and trend. Additional risk-related questions can focus on the character or propensities of management, the regulatory environment, and overall business risk.

You Are the Analyst/Forecaster

More persistent earnings reflect recurring, stable, predictable, and operating elements. Your estimate of earnings persistence should consider these elements. More persistent earnings comprise recurring operating elements. Finding 40% of earnings from unusual gains implies less persistence because its source is nonoperating. You can also question classification of litigation gains as "unusual"—they are sometimes better viewed as extraordinary. The extraordinary loss component also implies less persistence. In this case you need to assess whether environmental costs are truly extraordinary for this company's business. Together, these components suggest less persistence than suggested by the stable and steady growth trend in aggregate earnings. This lower persistence should be reflected in both the level and uncertainty of your earnings forecast.

Questions

13–1. Distinguish between earnings and cash flows. Why is there a distinction between these two measures?

13–2. What is meant by *earnings quality*? Why do users assess earnings quality? What major elements determine earnings quality?

13–3. What are discretionary expenses? What is the importance of discretionary expenses to our analysis of earnings quality?

13–4. Why is our analysis of research and development expenses important in assessing and forecasting earnings? What are some concerns in analyzing research and development expenses?

13–5. What is the relation between the reported values of assets and reported earnings? What is the relation between the reported values of liabilities, including provisions, and reported earnings?

13–6. How does balance sheet analysis provide a check on the validity and quality of earnings?

13–7. Discuss the riskiness of an asset and its implications for earnings quality.

13–8. Explain the relation between earnings quality and the following balance sheet items:
a. Accounts receivable.
b. Inventories.
c. Deferred charges.

13–9. What is the effect of external factors on earnings quality?

13–10. What is our purpose in recasting the income statement for analysis?

13–11. Where do we find the data necessary for analysis of operating results and for their recasting and adjustment?

13–12. What is the aim of the recasting process in analysis? Describe the recasting process.

13–13. Describe our adjustment of the income statement for financial statement analysis.

13–14. Explain earnings management. How is earnings management distinguished from fraudulent reporting?

13–15. Identify and explain three types of earnings management.

13–16. What factors and incentives motivate companies (management) to engage in earnings management? What are the implications of these incentives for our financial statement analysis?

13–17. Why is management interested in the reporting of extraordinary gains and losses?

13–18. What are our analysis objectives in evaluating extraordinary items?

13–19. What categories can unusual or extraordinary items be usefully subdivided into for purposes of our analysis? Provide examples for each category. How should our analysis treat items in each of these categories? Is a certain treatment implied under all circumstances? Explain.

13–20. Describe the effects of extraordinary items on:
a. Company resources.
b. Management evaluation.

13–21. Comment on the following statement: "Extraordinary gains or losses do not result from 'normal' or 'planned' business activities and, consequently, they should not be used in evaluating managerial performance." Do you agree?

13–22. Can accounting manipulations influence earnings-based estimates of company valuation? Explain.

13–23. *a.* Identify major determinants of PB and PE ratios.
b. How can the analyst use jointly the values of PB and PE ratios in assessing the merits of a particular stock investment?

13–24. What is the difference between forecasting and extrapolation of earnings?

13–25. How do disclosure requirements aid in earnings forecasting?

13–26. What is earning power? Why is earning power important for financial statement analysis?

13–27. How are interim financial statements used in analysis? What accounting problems with interim statements must we be alert to in our analysis?

13–28. Interim financial reports are subject to limitations and distortions. Discuss the reasons for this.

13–29. What are major disclosure requirements for interim reports? What are the objectives of these requirements?

13–30. What are the implications of interim reports for financial analysis?

EXERCISES

Exercise 13–1

Analyzing and Interpreting Maintenance and Repairs Expense

Refer to the financial statements of Quaker Oats Company in Supplement A.

Required:

a. Prepare a chart where maintenance and repairs expense is shown (i) as a percent of revenues and (ii) as a percent of property, plant, and equipment (net) for:
1. Years 9 and 10.
2. Average of Years 9 and 10.
3. Year 11.

b. Interpret the comparison of the spending level for maintenance and repairs in Year 11 with the average level of spending for Years 9 and 10.

Exercise 13–2

Interpreting Extraordinary Items

The president of Vancouver Viacom made the following comments to shareholders:

> Regarding management attitudes, Vancouver Viacom has resisted joining an increasing number of companies who along with earnings announcements make extraordinary or non-recurring loss announcements. Many of these cases read like regular operating problems. When we close plants, we charge earnings for the costs involved or reserved as we approach the event. These costs in my judgment are usually a normal operating expense and something that good management should expect or anticipate. That, of course, raises the question of what earnings figure should be used in assessing a price-earnings ratio and the quality of earnings.

Required:

a. Discuss your reactions to these comments.

b. What factors determine whether a gain or loss is extraordinary?

c. Explain whether you would classify the following items as extraordinary and why.
1. Loss suffered by foreign subsidiaries due to a change in the foreign exchange rate.
2. Write-down of inventory from cost to market.
3. Loss attributable to an improved product developed by a competitor.
4. Decrease in net income from higher tax rates.
5. Increase in income from liquidation of low-cost LIFO inventories due to a strike.
6. Expenses incurred in relocating plant facilities.
7. Expenses incurred in liquidating unprofitable product lines.

8. Research and development costs written off from a product failure (non-marketed).
9. Software costs written off because demand for a product was weaker than expected.
10. Financial distress of a major customer yielding a bad debts provision.
11. Loss on sale of rental cars by a car rental company.
12. Gains on sales of fixed assets.
13. Rents received from employees who occupy company-owned houses.
14. Uninsured casualty losses.
15. Expropriation by a foreign government of an entire division of the company.
16. Seizure or destruction of property from an act of war.

Exercise 13–3

Extraordinary Items in Financial Statement Analysis

A financial analyst's comments on classification in reporting follows:

> We should drop the word extraordinary and leave it to users to decide whether items like a strike will recur next year or not, and to decide whether a lease abandonment will recur or not. We need an all-inclusive statement with no extraordinary items. Let users apply the income statement for predictive purposes by eliminating items that will not recur. But let the record show all events that have an impact—there are really no values that "don't count." The current operating performance approach to reporting has no merit. I argue that everything is relevant and needs to be included. It is all part of operations. By omitting items from current operating performance we are relegating them to a lesser role. I do not believe this is conceptually correct. We include everything to better evaluate management and forecast earnings. Users can individually decide on the merits of an inventory write-off or the planned sale or abandonment of a plant. Both items deserve to adversely affect income because they reflect management performance. Both items can be excluded by the user in forecasting earnings. The current system yields abuses. Even an earthquake is part of the picture. A defalcation in Basel is part of banking. A lease abandonment recurs in the oil industry. No man is wise enough to cut the Gordian knot on this issue by picking and choosing what is extraordinary, recurring, typical, or customary.

Required:

a. Describe your views on this statement.

b. What is your opinion on how extraordinary items should be reported?

c. Discuss how extraordinary items should be treated in financial analysis.

Exercise 13–4

Interpreting Disclosures in Interim Financial Statements

Interim accounting statements comprise a major part of financial reporting. There is ongoing discussion considering the relevance of reporting on business activities for interim periods.

Required:

a. Discuss how revenues are recognized for interim periods. Comment on differences in revenue recognition for companies (1) subject to large seasonal fluctuations in revenue, and (2) having long-term contracts accounted for using percentage of completion for annual periods.

b. Explain how product and period costs are recognized for interim periods. Discuss how inventory and cost of goods sold can be given special accounting treatment for interim periods.

c. Describe how the provision for income taxes is computed and reported in interim reports.

(AICPA Adapted)

Exercise 13–5

Identifying Sources of Variability in Financial Data

Identify factors affecting variability in earnings per share, dividends per share, and market price per share that derive from (*a*) the company, and (*b*) the economy.

(CFA Adapted)

PROBLEMS

Problem 13–1 Recasting of the Income Statement

Refer to the financial statements of Quaker Oats Company in Supplement A.

Required:

a. Recast Quaker Oats' income statements for Years 11, 10, and 9 (*Hint:* Use notes 13, 14, and 15 for discretionary expenses, and estimate federal tax at the statutory rate of 34 percent).

b. Interpret trends revealed by the recast income statements.

Problem 13–2 Recasting of the Income Statement

Refer to the financial statements of Campbell Soup Company in Supplement A.

Required:

a. Recast Campbell Soup's income statements for Years 11, 10, and 9. Show computations.

b. Interpret trends revealed by the recast income statements.

Problem 13–3 Analyzing Pre- and Post-acquisition Financial Statements

You are considering the purchase of all outstanding stock of Finex, Inc., for $700,000 on January 2, Year 2. Finex's financial statements for Year 1 are reproduced below:

FINEX, INC.
Balance Sheet
As of December 31, Year 1

Cash	$ 55,000
U.S. government bonds	25,000
Accounts receivable (net)	150,000
Merchandise inventory	230,000
Land	40,000
Buildings (net)[(a)]	360,000
Equipment (net)[(b)]	130,000
Total assets	$990,000
Accounts payable	$170,000
Notes payable (current)	50,000
Bonds payable (due Year 12)[(c)]	200,000
Preferred stock (6%, $100 par)	100,000
Common stock ($100 par)	400,000
Paid-in capital	43,000
Retained earnings[(d)]	27,000
Liabilities and equity	$990,000

Income Statement
For Year Ended December 31, Year 1

Net sales	$860,000
Cost of good sold	546,000
Gross profit	$314,000
Selling and administrative expenses	240,000
Net operating income	$ 74,000
Income tax expense	34,000
Net income	$ 40,000

[a] Accumulated depreciation on buildings, $35,000. Depreciation expense in Year 1, $7,900.
[b] Accumulated depreciation on equipment, $20,000. Depreciation expense in Year 1, $9,000.
[c] Bonds are sold at par.
[d] Dividends paid in Year 1: preferred, $6,000; common, $20,000.

You need to adjust net income to estimate the earnings potential under your ownership after the purchase. The company uses the FIFO method of inventory valuation and all inventories can be sold without loss. With the change in ownership you expect an additional 5 percent of accounts receivable to be uncollectible. You assume sales and all financial relations are constant except as changed by the required adjustments.

Required:

a. What reported value is individually assigned to Land, Buildings, and Equipment after the proposed purchase? (*Hint:* Allocate the amount paid for these three assets in proportion to their respective book values on the Year 1 balance sheet.)

b. Prepare a balance sheet for Finex, Inc., immediately after your proposed purchase.

c. Estimate Finex, Inc.'s net operating income for Year 2 under your ownership. (*Hint:* Use the same ratio of depreciation expense to assets; and one-third of depreciation is charged to cost of goods sold.)

d. Assuming your minimum required ratio of net operating income to net sales is 8 percent, should you purchase Finex, Inc.?

Problem 13–4

Analyzing Creditworthiness for a Bank Loan

Aspero, Inc., has sales of approximately $500,000 per year. Aspero requires a short-term loan of $100,000 to finance its working capital requirements. Two banks are considering Aspero's loan request but each bank requires certain minimum conditions be satisfied. Bank America requires at least a 25 percent gross margin on sales, and Bank Boston requires a 2:1 current ratio. The following information is available for Aspero for the current year:

Sales returns and allowances are 10 percent of sales.
Purchases returns and allowances are 2 percent of purchases.
Sales discounts are 2 percent of sales.
Purchase discounts are 1 percent of purchases.
Ending inventory is $138,000.
Cash is 10 percent of accounts receivable.
Credit terms to Aspero's customers are 45 days.
Credit terms Aspero receives from its suppliers are 90 days.
Purchases for the year are $400,000.
Ending inventory is 38 percent greater than beginning inventory.
Accounts payable are the only current liability.

Required:

Assess whether Aspero, Inc., qualifies for a loan from either or both banks. Show computations.

Problem 13–5

Effects of Accounting Choice on Equity Value

Consider two identical companies. These companies use the same accounting methods and are expected to report net income ($ millions) of $20 in all future years. At December 31, Year 1, each company has a book value of $50 and incurs an expenditure of $10. Company "A" decides to capitalize the expenditure and depreciate it over the next two years under the straight-line method. Company "B" chooses to expense the expenditure immediately. Each company has a cost of equity capital of 12 percent and does not intend to pay dividends in the foreseeable future. Ignore income taxes.

Required:

a. Determine the following amounts for each company:

1. Net income for Years 1, 2, and 3. (*Hint:* You must consider additional depreciation expense for Company A.)

2. Book value at December 31, Years 1, 2, and 3.
3. ROCE for Years 2 and 3, computed using the beginning-of-period book value.

b. Which company is using more conservative accounting? Explain your reasoning.

c. Use the accounting-based equity valuation model to determine the value of each company at December 31, Year 1. ROCE equals 15% for Years 3 and beyond. Comment on your results.

d. Does the choice of accounting methods influence company value? Explain.

Problem 13–6

Accounting-Based Equity Valuation

Use the data from Christine Company in the chapter to answer the following.

a. Calculate the company's abnormal earnings for Years 1 through 5.

b. Use the accounting-based equity valuation model to estimate the value of Christine's equity at January 1, Years 2 through 5.

c. Adjust the estimates in (*a*). for mid-year discounting.

d. The chapter's discussion of Christine Company assumes that accounting for book value is not conservative. How does the use of conservative accounting principles affect the accounting-based valuation task?

e. Use the PB formula to determine the PB ratio at January 1, Years 2 through 5.

f. Use the PE formula to determine the PE ratio at January 1, Years 3 through 5.

CASES

Case 13–1

Analyzing Adaptec's Earnings and Earnings Components

Use the 1996 annual report of Adaptec, Inc., in Supplement A to answer the following.

Required:

a. Recast Adaptec's income statements from 1994 through 1996. Show computations.

b. Interpret trends revealed in Adaptec's recast income statements.

c. Analyze Adaptec's research and development expenses from 1994 through 1996.

d. Interpret trends revealed in Adaptec's research and development expenses.

e. Discuss how Adaptec's write-offs of acquired in-process technology should be treated in assessing current and future earning power.

Case 13–2

Analyzing and Interpreting Trends in Earnings and Earnings Components

Income statements of Ferro Corporation, along with its note 7 on income taxes and selected information from its Form 10-K, are reproduced below:

Consolidated Statement of Income
Years Ended December 31, Year 6, and Year 5 ($ thousands)

	Year 6	*Year 5*
Net sales	$376,485	$328,005
Cost of sales	266,846	237,333
Selling and administrative expenses	58,216	54,140
Research and development	9,972	8,205
Operating expenses	$335,034	$299,678
Operating income	$ 41,451	$ 28,327
Other income:		
Equity in net earnings of affiliated companies	$ 1,394	$ 504
Royalties	710	854
Interest earned	1,346	1,086
Miscellaneous	1,490	1,761
	$ 4,940	$ 4,205

Other charges:		
Interest expense	4,055	4,474
Unrealized foreign currency translation loss	4,037	1,851
Miscellaneous	1,480	1,448
	$ 9,572	$ 7,773
Income before taxes	$ 36,819	$ 24,759
U.S. and foreign income taxes (note 7)	16,765	11,133
Net income	$ 20,054	$ 13,626

Notes to Financial Statements:

7. Income tax expense is comprised of the following components ($ thousands):

	U.S. Federal	*Foreign*	*Total*
Year 6:			
Current	$5,147	11,125	16,272
Deferred	353	140	493
Total	$5,500	11,265	16,765
Year 5:			
Current	$2,974	8,095	11,069
Deferred	180	(116)	64
Total	$3,154	7,979	11,133

Deferred income taxes were mainly the result of using accelerated depreciation for income tax purposes and straight-line depreciation in the consolidated financial statements. State and local income taxes totaling approximately $750,000 and $698,000 in Year 6 and Year 5, respectively, are included in other expense categories. A reconciliation between the U.S. federal income tax rate and the effective tax rate for Year 6 and Year 5 follows:

	Year 6	*Year 5*
U.S. federal income tax rate	48.0%	48.0%
Earnings of consolidated subsidiaries taxed at rates less than the U.S. federal income tax rate	(5.3)	(5.3)
Equity in after-tax earnings of affiliated companies	(1.4)	(0.8)
Unrealized foreign exchange translation loss	5.3	3.6
Additional U.S. taxes on dividends from subsidiaries and affiliates	0.8	1.0
Investment tax credit	(1.5)	(0.9)
Miscellaneous	(0.4)	(0.6)
Effective tax rate	45.5%	45.0%

The following information from Form 10-K is available:

	Year 6	*Year 5*
Cost of sales includes ($ thousands):		
Repairs and maintenance	$15,000	$20,000
Loss on disposal of chemicals division	—	7,000
Selling and administrative expenses include ($ thousands):		
Advertising	$ 6,000	$ 7,000
Employee training program	4,000	5,000

Required:

a. Recast Ferro's income statements for Years 5 and 6. Show computations.

b. Identify factors causing income tax expense to differ from 48 percent of pre-tax income. Identify any random or unstable factors.

c. What significant changes can you identify in Ferro's operating policies for Year 6? (*Hint:* Limit your analysis to outlays for repairs and maintenance, advertising, and employee training programs.)

Case 13–3

Assessing Earnings Quality and Proposed Accounting Changes

Canada Steel, Ltd., produces steel castings and metal fabrications for sale to manufacturers of heavy construction machinery and agricultural equipment. Early in Year 3 the company's president sent the following memorandum to the financial vice president:

TO: Robert Kinkaid, Financial Vice President

FROM: Richard Johnson, President

SUBJECT: Accounting and Financial Policies

Fiscal Year 2 was a difficult year for us, and the recession is likely to continue into Year 3. While the entire industry is suffering, we might be hurting our performance unnecessarily with accounting and business policies that are not appropriate. Specifically:

(1) We depreciate most fixed assets (foundry equipment) over their estimated useful lives on the "tonnage-of-production" method. Accelerated methods and shorter lives are used for income tax purposes. A switch to straight-line for financial reporting purposes could. (a) eliminate the deferred tax liability on our balance sheet, and (b) leverage our profits if business picks up in Year 4.

(2) Several years ago you convinced me to change from the FIFO to LIFO inventory method. Since inflation is now down to a 4 percent annual rate, and balance sheet strength is important in our current environment, I estimate we can increase shareholders' equity by about $2.0 million, working capital by $4.0 million, and Year 3 earnings by $0.5 million if we return to FIFO in Year 3. This adjustment is real—these profits were earned by us over the past several years and should be recognized.

(3) If we make the inventory change, our stock repurchase program can be continued. The same shareholder who sold us 50,000 shares last year at $100 per share would like to sell another 20,000 shares at the same price. However, to obtain additional bank financing, we must maintain the current ratio at 3:1 or better. It seems prudent to decrease our capitalization if return on assets is unsatisfactory and our industry is declining. Also, interest rates are lower (11 percent prime) and we can save $60,000 after taxes annually once our $3.00 per share dividend is resumed.

These actions would favorably affect our profitability and liquidity ratios as shown in the *pro forma* income statement and balance sheet data for Year 3 ($ millions):

	Year 1	Year 2	Year 3 Estimate
Net sales	$ 50.6	$ 42.3	$ 29.0
Net income (loss)	2.0	(5.7)	0.1
Net profit margin	4.0%	—	0.3%
Dividends	$ 0.7	$ 0.6	$ 0.0
Return on assets	7.2%	—	0.4%
Return on equity	11.3%	—	0.9%
Current assets	$ 17.6	$ 14.8	$ 14.5
Current liabilities	6.6	4.9	4.5
Long-term debt	2.0	6.1	8.1
Shareholders' equity	17.7	11.4	11.5
Shares outstanding (000s)	226.8	170.5	150.5
Per common share:			
Book value	$ 78.05	$ 66.70	$ 76.41
Market price range	$42–34	$65–45	$62–55*

*Year to date.

Please give me your reaction to my proposals as soon as possible.

Required:

Assume you are Robert Kinkaid, the financial vice president. Appraise the president's rationale for each of the proposals. You should place special emphasis on how each accounting or business decision affects earnings quality. Support your response with ratio analysis.

(CFA Adapted)

Case 13–4
Accounting-Based Equity Valuation

After careful financial statement analysis, we obtain the following predictions for Colin Technology:

Year	*Net Income*	*Beginning Book Value*
1	$1,034	$5,308
2	1,130	5,292
3	1,218	5,834
4	1,256	6,338
5	1,278	6,728
6	1,404	7,266
7	1,546	7,856

Colin Technology's cost of equity capital is estimated at 13 percent.

Required:

a. Abnormal earnings are expected to be $0 per year after Year 7. Use the accounting-based equity valuation model to estimate Colin's value at the beginning of Year 1.

b. Determine Colin's PB ratio using the results in *(a)*. Colin's actual market-based PB ratio is 1.95. What do you conclude?

c. Determine Colin's PE ratio using the results in *(a)*. Colin's actual market-based PE ratio is 10. What do you conclude?

d. If we expect Colin's sales and profit margin to remain unchanged after Year 7 with a stable book value of $8,506, use the accounting-based equity valuation model to estimate Colin's value at the beginning of Year 1.

INTERNET ACTIVITIES

Internet 13–1
Recasting of Income Statements

Access one of the financial statement databases available on the Internet (http://www.mhhe.com/business/accounting/wild). Retrieve current financial statements of a company selected by either you or your instructor.

Required:

a. Recast the company's income statements for the prior two years.

b. Write a report interpreting trends revealed by the recasted income statements.

Internet 13–2
Analyzing Earnings and Earnings Components

Access one of the financial statement databases available on the Internet (http://www.mhhe.com/business/accounting/wild). Retrieve current financial statements of a company selected by either you or your instructor.

a. Recast the company's income statements from the prior two years.

b. Interpret trends revealed in the recast income statements.

c. Analyze and interpret the company's operating expenses for the prior two years.

d. Analyze and interpret the company's research and development expenses for the prior two years.

Internet 13–3

Accounting Choices and Equity Value

Access one of the financial statement databases available on the Internet (http://www.mhhe.com/business/accounting/wild). Retrieve current financial statements of two companies in different industries selected by either you or your instructor. If necessary, you can assume each company has a cost of equity capital of 10%.

Required:

a. Determine the following amounts for each company:
   1. Book value for the prior two years.
   2. Net income for the prior two years.
   3. ROCE for the prior two years.

b. Which company is using more conservative accounting? Explain your reasoning.

c. Use the accounting-based equity valuation model to determine the value of each company. Discuss your findings.

d. Does choice of accounting methods influence these companies' equity values? Explain.

Internet 13–4

Stock Prices and Earnings

Access one of the financial statement databases available on the Internet (http://www.mhhe.com/business/accounting/wild). Retrieve current financial statements of three companies selected by either you or your instructor.

Required:

a. Collect fiscal year-end stock price and earnings per share information for each company for the prior five years.

b. Prepare a chart depicting the relation between each company's stock price and earnings per share for the prior five years.

c. Write a report summarizing the relation between stock price and earnings for each company.

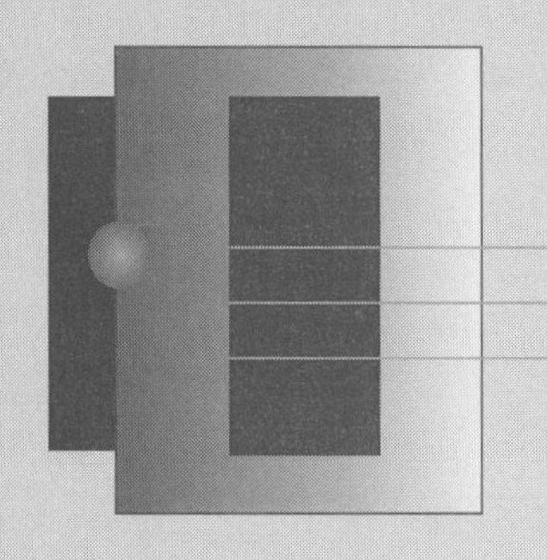

Applying Financial Statement Analysis

Learning Objectives

- Describe the steps in analyzing financial statements.
- Review the building blocks of financial statement analysis.
- Explain important attributes of reporting on financial statement analysis.
- Describe implications to financial statement analysis from evaluating companies in specialized industries or with unique characteristics.
- Analyze in a comprehensive manner the financial statements and notes of Campbell Soup Company.

A Look Back

Part One of the book provided us a broad overview of financial statement analysis using Adaptec as a primary example. Part Two described the accounting for financing, investing, and operating activities, and offered us insights into company performance. Part Three emphasized key financial statement analysis tools and techniques.

A Look at This Case

This case is a comprehensive analysis of financial statements and related notes. We use Campbell Soup Company as our focus. We describe the steps in analyzing financial statements, the building blocks of analysis, and essential attributes of an analysis report. We support our analysis using many of the tools and techniques described throughout the book. Explanation and interpretation accompany all of our analyses.

A Look Ahead

We describe the auditor's report and its implications for analysis in Supplement B. The effects of price changes on our analysis are explained in Supplement C.

Preview of Comprehensive Case

Comprehensive case analysis of the financial statements and notes of Campbell Soup Company is our focus. The three major parts of the book have prepared us to tackle all facets of financial statement analysis. This comprehensive case analysis provides us the opportunity to illustrate and apply these analysis tools and techniques. This case also gives us the opportunity to show how we draw conclusions and inferences from detailed analysis. We review the basic steps of analysis, the building blocks, and key attributes of an expert analysis report. Throughout the case we emphasize applications and inferences associated with financial statement analysis. The content and organization of this chapter are as follows:

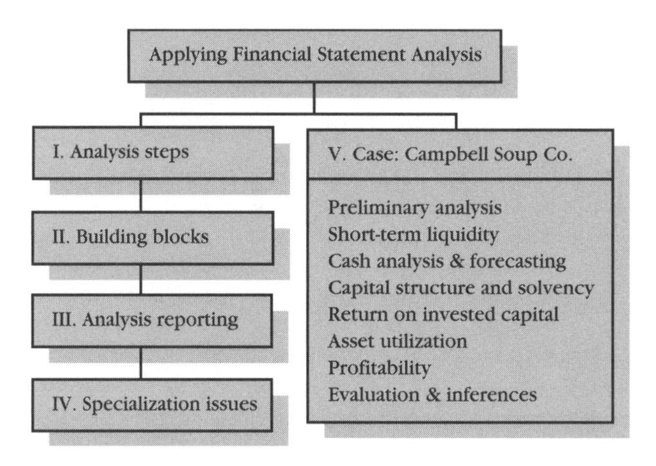

Steps in Analyzing Financial Statements

Our task in analyzing financial statements can be usefully summarized for consistency and organizational efficiency. There are generalizations and guidelines that help us conduct financial statement analysis. Although we must remember that analysis depends on our judgments and should be flexible. This flexibility is necessary because of the diversity of situations and circumstances in practice, and the need for us to aggressively apply ideas, experience, and knowledge.

Financial statement analysis is oriented toward achieving definite objectives. *Our first step is to explicitly define the analysis objectives.* Our evaluation of the issues and concerns leading up to specification of objectives is an important part of analysis. This evaluation helps us develop an understanding of pertinent and relevant objectives. It also helps eliminate extraneous objectives and to avoid unnecessary analysis. Identifying objectives is important to our effective and efficient analysis. Effectiveness in analysis implies a focus on the important and relevant elements of financial statements. Efficiency in analysis implies economy of time and effort.

Illustration CC.1a

Assume you are a bank loan officer handling a request for a short-term loan to finance inventory. A reasonable objective is for you to *assess the intent and ability of the borrower to repay the loan in a timely manner.* Your analysis concentrates on what information is necessary to assess the borrower's intent and ability. You need not focus on extraneous issues like long-term industry conditions affecting the borrower's long-run performance.

Our second step in analysis is to formulate specific questions and criteria consistent with the analysis objectives. Answers to these questions should be relevant in achieving the analysis objectives and reliable in making business decisions. Criteria for answers must be consistent with our risk and return requirements.

Illustration CC.1b

In your role as bank loan officer you need to specify relevant questions and criteria for making the above loan decision. Questions for the borrower include:

- Willingness to repay the short-term loan?
- Ability to repay the short-term loan (liquidity)?
- What are your future sources and uses of cash during the loan period?

Addressing these questions and defining criteria depend on a variety of information sources, including those bearing on the borrower's character. Financial statement analysis can answer many of these questions, but not all. Tools other than financial statement analysis must be used to answer some important questions.

Our third step in analysis is identifying the most effective and efficient tools of analysis. These tools must be relevant in answering the questions posed and the criteria established, and appropriate for the business decision at hand. These tools include many of the procedures and techniques discussed throughout the book.

Illustration CC.1c

Your role as loan officer requires decisions regarding what financial statement analysis tools to use for the above short-term loan request. You will probably choose one or more of the following tools:

- Short-term liquidity measures.
- Inventory turnover measures.
- Cash flow forecasts.
- Pro forma analysis.

Many of these analysis tools include estimates and projections of future conditions. This future orientation is a common thread of all analysis tools.

Our fourth step in analysis is interpreting the evidence. Interpretation of financial data and measures is the basis of our decision and subsequent action. This is a critical and difficult step in analysis, and requires us to apply our skills and knowledge of business and nonbusiness factors. It is a step demanding study and evaluation. It requires us to picture the business reality behind the numbers. There is no mechanical substitute for this step. Yet the quality of our interpretation depends on properly identifying the objectives of analysis, defining the questions and their criteria, and selecting efficient and effective analysis tools.

Illustration CC.1d

Your loan decision requires you to integrate and evaluate the evidence, and then interpret it for purposes of reaching a decision on whether to make the loan or not. It can also include various loan parameters: amount, interest rate, term, payment pattern, and loan restrictions.

This step is similar to requirements of many professions. For example, weather forecasting offers an abundance of analytical data demanding interpretation. Most of us exposed to weather information could not reliably interpret barometric pressure, relative humidity, or wind velocity. We only need to know the weather forecast resulting from the professional interpretation of weather data. Medicine, law, engineering, biology, and genetics provide similar examples.

Our analysis and interpretation of financial statements must remember that these data depict a richer reality. Analysis of financial data result in further levels of abstraction. As an example, no map or picture of the Rocky Mountains conveys their magnificence. One must visit these mountains to fully appreciate them because maps or pictures, like financial statements, are abstractions. This is why it is often advantageous for us to go beyond financial statements and "visit" companies—that is, use their products, buy services, visit stores, talk with customers, and immerse oneself in companies' business activities. The static reality portrayed by abstractions in financial statements is unnatural. Reality is dynamic and evolving. Recognizing the limitations of financial statements is necessary in analysis. This does not detract from their importance. Financial statements are the means by which a company's financial realities are reduced to a common denominator. This common denominator is quantifiable, can be statistically evaluated, and is amenable to prediction.

Building Blocks of Financial Statement Analysis

Financial statement analysis focuses on one or more elements of a company's financial condition or operating results. Our analysis emphasizes six areas of inquiry—with varying degrees of importance. We described these six areas of inquiry and illustrated them throughout the book. They are considered "building blocks" of financial statement analysis.

- **Short-term liquidity.** Ability to meet short-term obligations.
- **Cash flow and forecasting.** Future availability and disposition of cash.

- **Capital structure and solvency.** Ability to generate future revenues and meet long-term obligations.
- **Return on invested capital.** Ability to provide financial rewards sufficient to attract and retain financing.
- **Asset turnover.** Asset intensity in generating revenues to reach a sufficient profitability level.
- **Operating performance and profitability.** Success at maximizing revenues and minimizing expenses from operating activities over the long run.

Applying the building blocks to financial statement analysis involves determining:

1. Objectives of our analysis.
2. Relative emphasis among the building blocks.

For example, an equity investor when evaluating the investment merit of a common stock often emphasizes earnings- and returns-based analyses. This involves assessing operating performance and return on invested capital. A thorough analysis requires an equity investor to assess other building blocks although with perhaps lesser emphasis. Attention to these other areas is necessary to assess risk exposure. This usually involves some analysis of liquidity, solvency, and financing. Further analysis can reveal important risks that outweigh earning power, and lead to major changes in the financial statement analysis of a company.

We distinguish among these six building blocks to emphasize six distinct aspects of a company's financial condition or performance. Yet we must remember these areas of analysis are interrelated. For example, a company's operating performance is affected by availability of financing and short-term liquidity conditions. Similarly, a company's credit standing is not limited to satisfactory short-term liquidity, but depends also on its operating performance and asset turnover. Early in our analysis, we tentatively determine the relative emphasis of each building block and their order of analysis. Order of emphasis and analysis can subsequently change due to evidence collected.

Reporting on Financial Statement Analysis

The foundation of a reliable analysis is an understanding of the objectives. This understanding leads to efficiency of effort, effectiveness in application, and relevance in focus. Most analyses face constraints on availability of information. Decisions must be made using incomplete or inadequate information. One goal of financial statement analysis is reducing uncertainty through a rigorous and sound evaluation. A **financial statement analysis report** helps us on each of these points by addressing all the building blocks of analysis. It helps us identify weaknesses in inference by requiring explanation, and it forces us to organize our reasoning and to verify the flow and logic of analysis. The report serves as our communication device with readers. The writing process reinforces our judgments and vice versa, and it helps us refine inferences from evidence on key building blocks.

A good report separates interpretations and conclusions of analysis from the information underlying them. This separation enables readers to see our process and rationale of analysis. It also enables the reader to draw personal conclusions and make modifications as appropriate. A good analysis report typically contains at least six distinct sections devoted to:

1. **Analysis overview.** Background material on the company, its industry, and its economic environment.
2. **Evidential matter.** Financial statements and information used in the analysis. This includes ratios, trends, statistics, and all analytical measures assembled.
3. **Assumptions.** Identification of important assumptions regarding a company's industry and economic environment, and other important assumptions for estimates or forecasts.
4. **Crucial factors.** Listing of important favorable and unfavorable factors, both quantitative and qualitative, for company performance—usually listed by areas of analysis.
5. **Inferences.** Includes forecasts, estimates, interpretations, and conclusions drawing on all four prior sections of the report.

An analysis report should begin with an **Executive Summary** section. The executive summary is brief and focuses on important analysis results. We must remember that *importance* is defined by the user. The analysis report should also include a brief table of contents to help readers focus on those areas most relevant to their decisions. All irrelevant matter must be eliminated. For example, century-old details of the beginnings of a company and a detailing of the miscues of our analysis are irrelevant. Ambiguities and qualifications to avoid responsibility or hedge inferences should also be eliminated. Finally, writing is important. Mistakes in grammar and errors of fact compromise the credibility of our analysis.

Specialization in Financial Statement Analysis

Our analysis of financial statements is usually viewed from the perspective of a "typical" company. Yet we must recognize the existence of several distinct factors (e.g., unique accounting methods). These factors arise from several influences including special industry conditions, government regulations, social concerns, and political visibility. Our analysis of financial statements for these companies requires we understand their accounting peculiarities. We must prepare for this by learning the specialized areas of accounting relevant to the company under analysis. For example, analysis of an oil and gas company would require knowledge of accounting concepts peculiar to that industry, including determining cost centers, prediscovery costs, discovery costs, and disposing of capitalized costs. In addition, analysis of an oil and gas company would confront special problems in analyzing exploratory, development, and related expenditures, and in amortization and depletion practices. Another example is life insurance accounting. This analysis would require knowledge of the industry and its regulation. Challenges arise in understanding recognition of premium revenues, accounting for acquisition costs of new business, and determination of policy reserves. Another example is public utilities. Regulation results in specialized accounting concepts and problems for analysis. There are questions related to the adequacy of provisions for depreciation, and problems concerning the utility's "rate base" and the method used in determining it. Like any profession, specialized areas of inquiry require specialized knowledge. Financial statement analysis is no exception.

Comprehensive Case: Campbell Soup Company

We illustrate the major components of financial statement analysis using information and data from Campbell Soup Company.

Preliminary Financial Analysis

Campbell Soup Company is one of the world's largest food companies focusing on convenience foods for human consumption. The company's operations are organized within three divisions: Campbell North America, Campbell Biscuit and Bakery, and Campbell International. Within each division there are groups and business units. Major groups within the Campbell North America division are Soups, Convenience Meals, Grocery, Condiments, and Canadian operations.

The company's products are primarily for home use, but various items are also manufactured for restaurants, vending machines, and institutions. The company distributes its products through direct customer sales. These include chain stores, wholesalers, distributors (with central warehouses), institutional and industrial customers, convenience stores, club stores, and government agencies. In the United States, sales solicitation activities are conducted by subsidiaries, independent brokers, and contract distributors. No major part of Campbell's business depends on a single customer. Shipments are made promptly after receipt and acceptance of orders as reflected in no significant backlog of unfilled orders.

Sales Analysis by Source

Campbell's sales by division from Year 6 through Year 11 are shown in Exhibit CC.1. Its North American and International divisions are the largest contributors of sales, accounting for 68.7 percent and 19.7 percent, respectively, in Year 11.

Campbell's Sales by Divisions

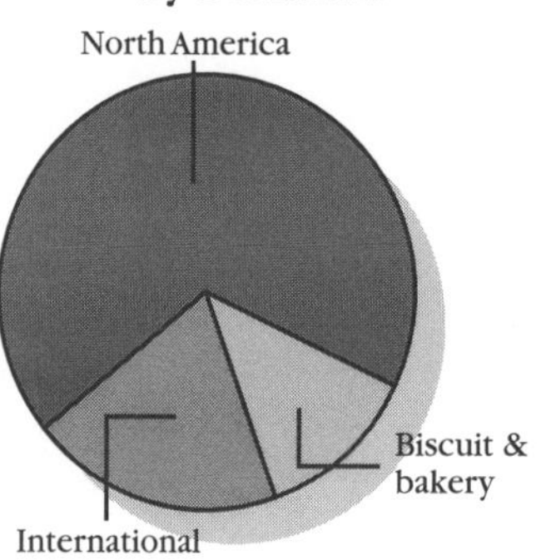

Source: Annual report.

Soup is the primary business of Campbell U.S., capturing about 60 percent of the entire soup market. This includes recent introductions of dry, ramen noodle, and microwavable soups. Other Campbell Soup brands include ready-to-serve soups: Home Cooking, Chunky, and Healthy Request. An integral part of the soup business is Swanson's canned chicken broth. Americans purchase more than 2.5 billion cans of Campbell's soups each year, and on average have nine cans in their pantry at any time during the year.

Fiscal Year 11 is a successful transition year for Campbell. It has completed major divestitures and accomplished significant restructuring and reorganization projects. Corporate goals concerning earnings, returns, and cash flows are being exceeded. The North American and International divisions produced exceptionally strong earnings results. The company enters Year 12 with a reconfigured product portfolio, positioned to support a continued strong financial performance. The solid margin growth gives Campbell an opportunity to increase consumer advertising and to further the introduction of new product line and continue support for flagship products.

Comparative Financial Statements

Complete financial statements and related information for Campbell Soup are in Supplement A. These reports include information from SEC Form 10-K. Comparative financial statements for Campbell for Years 6 through 11 are presented in Exhibits CC.2, CC.3, and CC.4. The auditor's opinions on their financial statements for the past six years are unqualified.

EXHIBIT CC.1

CAMPBELL SOUP COMPANY
Sales Contribution and Percent of Sales by Division
($ millions)

	Year 11	*Year 10*	*Year 9*	*Year 8*	*Year 7*	*Year 6*
Sales Contribution:						
Campbell North America:						
Campbell U.S.A	$3,911.8	$3,932.7	$3,666.9	$3,094.1	$2,881.4	$2,910.1
Campbell Canada	352.0	384.0	313.4	313.1	312.8	255.1
	$4,263.8	$4,316.7	$3,980.3	$3,407.2	$3,194.2	$3,165.2
Campbell Biscuit and Bakery:						
Pepperidge Farm	$ 569.0	$ 582.0	$ 548.4	$ 495.0	$ 458.5	$ 420.1
International Biscuit	219.4	195.3	178.0	—	—	—
	$ 788.4	$ 777.3	$ 726.4	$ 495.0	$ 458.5	$ 420.1
Campbell International	$1,222.9	$1,189.8	$1,030.3	$1,036.5	$ 897.8	$ 766.2
Interdivision	(71.0)	(78.0)	(64.9)	(69.8)	(60.1)	(64.7)
Total sales	$6,204.1	$6,205.8	$5,672.1	$4,868.9	$4,490.4	$4,286.8
Percent of Sales:						
Campbell North America:						
Campbell U.S.A.	63.0%	63.4%	64.7%	63.6%	64.2%	67.9%
Campbell Canada	5.7	6.2	5.5	6.4	6.9	5.9
	68.7	69.6	70.2	70.0	71.1	73.8
Campbell Biscuit and Bakery:						
Pepperidge Farm	9.2	9.4	9.7	10.2	10.2	9.8
International Biscuit	3.5	3.1	3.1	—	—	—
	12.7	12.5	12.8	10.2	10.2	9.8
Campbell International	19.7	19.2	18.2	21.3	20.0	17.9
Interdivision	(1.1)	(1.3)	(1.2)	(1.4)	(1.3)	(1.5)
Total sales	100.0%	100.0%	100.0%	100.0%	100.0%	100.0%

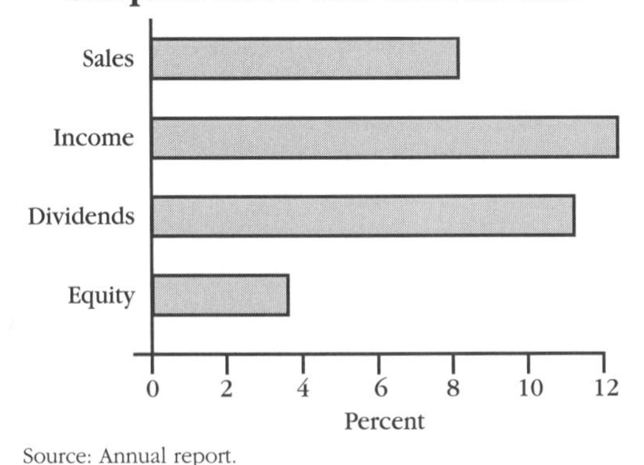

Source: Annual report.

Further Analysis of Financial Statements

Growth rates for important financial measures, annually compounded, are reported in Exhibit CC.5. These rates are computed using four different periods and are based on per share data (see Exhibit CC.9). Most impressive is the growth in net income per share over the past five years (12.93%). Growth in sales per share over the same recent five-year period is at a rate less than that of net income. Equity per share growth in the recent 5-year period declined compared to the 10-year period. This finding, including the two negative growth rates in the exhibit, is due to divestitures and restructurings in Years 9 and 10. We also compute common-size income statements and balance sheets in Exhibits CC.6 and CC.7. Exhibit CC.8 presents the trend indexes of selected accounts for Campbell Soup. Exhibit CC.9 presents Campbell Soup's per share results.

Exhibit CC.2

CAMPBELL SOUP COMPANY
Income Statements (millions)
For Years 6 through 11

	Year 11	*Year 10*	*Year 9*	*Year 8*	*Year 7*	*Year 6*
Net sales	$6,204.1	$6,205.8	$5,672.1	$4,868.9	$4,490.4	$4,286.8
Costs and expenses:						
Cost of products sold	$4,095.5	$4,258.2	$4,001.6	$3,392.8	$3,180.5	$3,082.7
Marketing and selling expenses	956.2	980.5	818.8	733.3	626.2	544.4
Administrative expenses	306.7	290.7	252.1	232.6	213.9	195.9
Research and development expenses	56.3	53.7	47.7	46.9	44.8	42.2
Interest expense	116.2	111.6	94.1	53.9	51.7	56.0
Interest income	(26.0)	(17.6)	(38.3)	(33.2)	(29.5)	(27.4)
Foreign exchange losses, net	0.8	3.3	19.3	16.6	4.8	0.7
Other expense (income)	26.2	14.7	32.4	(3.2)	(9.5)	5.5
Divestitures, restructuring, and unusual charges	0.0	339.1	343.0	40.6	0.0	0.0
Total costs and expenses	$5,531.9	$6,034.2	$5,570.7	$4,480.3	$4,082.9	$3,900.0
Earnings before equity in earnings of affiliates and minority interests	$ 672.2	$ 171.6	$ 101.4	$ 388.6	$ 407.5	$ 386.8
Equity in earnings of affiliates	2.4	13.5	10.4	6.3	15.1	4.3
Minority interests	(7.2)	(5.7)	(5.3)	(6.3)	(4.7)	(3.9)
Earnings before taxes	$ 667.4	$ 179.4	$ 106.5	$ 388.6	$ 417.9	$ 387.2
Taxes on earnings	265.9	175.0	93.4	147.0	170.6	164.0
Earnings before cumulative effect of accounting change	$ 401.5	$ 4.4	$ 13.1	$ 241.6	$ 247.3	$ 223.2
Cumulative effect of change in accounting for income taxes	0	0	0	32.5	0	0
Net earnings	$ 401.5	$ 4.4	$ 13.1	$ 274.1	$ 247.3	$ 223.2
Earnings per share	$ 3.16	$ 0.03	$ 0.10	$ 2.12*	$ 1.90	$ 1.72
Weighted-average shares outstanding	127.00	126.60	129.30	$ 129.30	$ 129.90	129.50

* Including $0.25 per share bumulative effect of change in accounting for income taxes.

Alternative Perspectives on Analysis

We analyze the financial statements of Campbell Soup Company from the perspective of three alternative points of view. These alternative perspectives yield different objectives and emphases in our final analysis. The three perspectives are:

- **Extending bank credit line**. The company requests our bank to make available a line of credit (for short-term operating purposes) of up to $60 million.
- **Private purchase of debt**. The company wishes to privately place $50 million of 25-year bonds with our insurance company.
- **Equity investment**. As an equity investor we consider a substantial investment in the company's common stock.

These diverse perspectives have commonalities in requiring us to analyze all major aspects of the company's financial condition and operating results. We also draw on industry composite figures for comparative purposes. These figures are drawn primarily from *Dun & Bradstreet Industry Norms and Key Business Ratios*, and are based on Year 11 financial statements of companies in SIC classification 2033. We will return to these perspectives at the end of our analysis.

EXHIBIT CC.3

CAMPBELL SOUP COMPANY
Balance Sheets
For Years 6 to 11 ($ millions)

	Year 11	*Year 10*	*Year 9*	*Year 8*	*Year 7*	*Year 6*
Assets						
Current assets:						
Cash and cash equivalents	$ 178.90	$ 80.70	$ 120.90	$ 85.80	$ 145.00	$ 155.10
Other temporary investments	12.80	22.50	26.20	35.00	280.30	238.70
Accounts receivable	527.40	624.50	538.00	486.90	338.90	299.00
Inventories	706.70	819.80	816.00	664.70	623.60	610.50
Prepaid expenses	92.70	118.00	100.40	90.50	50.10	31.50
Total current assets	$1,518.50	$1,665.50	$1,601.50	$1,362.90	$1,437.90	$1,334.80
Plant assets, net of depreciation	$1,790.40	$1,717.70	$1,540.60	$1,508.90	$1,349.00	$1,168.10
Intangible assets, net of amortization	435.50	383.40	466.90	496.60	—	—
Other assets	404.60	349.00	323.10	241.20	310.50	259.90
Total assets	$4,149.00	$4,115.60	$3,932.10	$3,609.60	$3,097.40	$2,762.80
Liabilities and Shareowners' Equity						
Current liabilities:						
Notes payable	$ 282.20	$ 202.30	$ 271.50	$ 138.00	$ 93.50	$ 88.90
Payable to suppliers and others	482.40	525.20	508.20	446.70	374.80	321.70
Accrued liabilities	408.70	491.90	392.60	236.90	182.10	165.90
Dividend payable	37.00	32.30	29.70	—	—	—
Accrued income taxes	67.70	46.40	30.10	41.70	43.40	49.60
Total current liabilities	$1,278.00	$1,298.10	$1,232.10	$ 863.30	$ 693.80	$ 626.10
Long-term debt	$ 772.60	$ 805.80	$ 629.20	$ 525.80	$ 380.20	$ 362.30
Other liabilities, mainly deferred income tax	305.00	319.90	292.50	325.50	287.30	235.50
Shareowner's equity:						
Preferred stock; authorized 40,000,000 sh.; none issued	—	—	—	—	—	—
Capital stock, $0.15 par value; authorized 140,000,000 sh.; issued 135,622,676 sh.	20.30	20.30	20.30	20.30	20.30	20.30
Capital surplus	107.30	61.90	50.80	42.30	41.10	38.10
Earnings retained in the business	1,912.60	1,653.30	1,775.80	1,879.10	1,709.60	1,554.00
Capital stock in treasury, at cost	(270.40)	(107.20)	(70.70)	(75.20)	(46.80)	(48.40)
Cumulative translation adjustments	23.60	63.50	2.10	28.50	11.90	(25.10)
Total shareowner's equity	$1,793.40	$1,691.80	$1,778.30	$1,895.00	$1,736.10	$1,538.90
Total liabilities and shareowners' equity	$4,149.00	$4,115.60	$3,932.10	$3,609.60	$3,097.40	$2,762.80

Short-Term Liquidity

Important measures of short-term liquidity for the most recent six years are reported in Exhibit CC.10. This exhibit also reports industry composite data for Year 11. The current ratio in Year 11 is at its lowest level for the past six years. Its value of 1.19 is measurably lower than the industry composite of 1.86. This is due in part to growth in current liabilities over recent years. Current liabilities are double what they were in Year 6, while current assets in Year 11 are but 114 percent of its Year

EXHIBIT CC.4

CAMPBELL SOUP COMPANY
Statements of Cash Flows
For Years 6 to 11 ($ millions)

	Year 11	*Year 10*	*Year 9*	*Year 8*	*Year 7*	*Year 6*	*Total*
Cash flows from operating activities:							
Net earnings	$ 401.5	$ 4.4	$ 13.1	$ 274.1	$ 247.3	$ 223.2	$ 1,163.6
To reconcile net earnings to net cash provided by operating activities:							
Depreciation and amortization	208.6	200.9	192.3	170.9	144.6	126.8	1,044.1
Divestitures and restructuring provisions	—	339.1	343.0	17.6	—	—	699.7
Deferred taxes	35.5	3.9	(67.8)	13.4	45.7	29.0	59.7
Other, net	63.2	18.6	37.3	43.0	28.0	16.6	206.7
Cumulative effect of accounting change	—	—	—	(32.5)	—	—	(32.5)
(Increase) decrease in accounts receivable	17.1	(60.4)	(46.8)	(104.3)	(36.3)	(3.6)	(234.3)
(Increase) decrease in inventories	48.7	10.7	(113.2)	54.2	(3.9)	23.1	19.6
Net change in other current assets and liabilities	30.6	(68.8)	(0.6)	30.2	42.9	48.7	83.0
Net cash provided by operating activities	$ 805.2	$ 448.4	$ 357.3	$ 466.6	$ 468.3	$ 463.8	$ 3,009.6
Cash flows from investing activities:							
Purchases of plant assets	$(361.1)	$(387.6)	$(284.1)	$(245.3)	$(303.7)	$(235.3)	$(1,817.1)
Sale of plant assets	43.2	34.9	39.8	22.6	—	29.8	170.3
Businesses acquired	(180.1)	(41.6)	(135.8)	(471.9)	(7.3)	(20.0)	(856.7)
Sale of businesses	67.4	21.7	4.9	23.5	20.8	—	138.3
Increase in other assets	(57.8)	(18.6)	(107.0)	(40.3)	(50.1)	(18.0)	(291.8)
Net change in other temporary investments	9.7	3.7	9.0	249.2	(60.7)	(144.1)	66.8
Net cash used in investing activities	$(478.7)	$(387.5)	$(473.2)	$(462.2)	$(401.0)	$(387.6)	$(2,590.2)
Cash flows from financing activities:							
Long-term borrowings	$ 402.8	$ 12.6	$ 126.5	$ 103.0	$ 4.8	$ 203.9	$ 853.6
Repayments of long-term borrowings	(129.9)	(22.5)	(53.6)	(22.9)	(23.9)	(164.7)	(417.5)
Increase (decrease) in short-term borrowings*	(137.9)	(2.7)	108.2	8.4	(20.7)	4.6	(40.1)
Other short-term borrowings	117.3	153.7	227.1	77.0	89.3	72.9	737.3
Repayments of other short-term borrowings	(206.4)	(89.8)	(192.3)	(87.6)	(66.3)	(88.5)	(730.9)
Dividends paid	(137.5)	(124.3)	(86.7)	(104.6)	(91.7)	(104.6)	(649.4)
Treasury stock purchases	(175.6)	(41.1)	(8.1)	(29.3)	—	—	(254.1)
Treasury stock issued	47.7	12.4	18.5	0.9	1.6	4.0†	85.1
Other, net	(0.1)	(0.1)	23.5	2.3	18.6	17.9	62.1
Net cash provided (used in) financing activities	$(219.6)	$(101.8)	$ 163.1	$ (52.8)	$ (88.3)	$ (54.5)	$ (353.9)
Effect of exchange rate change on cash	$ (8.7)	$ 0.7	$ (12.1)	$ (10.8)	$ (7.1)	$ (3.7)	$ (41.7)
Net increase (decrease) in cash and cash equivalents	98.2	(40.2)	35.1	(59.2)	(28.1)	18.0	23.8
Cash and cash equivalents at the beginning of year	80.7	120.9	85.8	145.0	173.1	155.1	760.6
Cash and cash equivalents at end of year	$ 178.9	$ 80.7	$ 120.9	$ 85.8	$ 145.0	$ 173.1	$ 784.4

* With less than three month maturities.

† 2.8 issued for a pooling of interest.

EXHIBIT CC.5

CAMPBELL SOUP COMPANY
Five-Year Growth Rates*
(annually compounded)

Per share	*Years 6 to 11*	[*Average for Years 6 to 8*] to [*Average for Years 9 to 11*]
Sales	8.09%	5.95%
Net income	12.93	−10.53
Dividends	11.50	6.69
Equity	3.55	0.53

Ten-Year Growth Rates*
(annually compounded)

Per share	*Years 1 to 11*	[*Average for Years 1 to 3*] to [*Average for Years 9 to 11*]
Sales	8.51%	7.22%
Net income	12.19	−0.44
Dividends	8.18	6.62
Equity	6.22	5.13

* Growth rates (annually compounded) are computed using the compound interest method (where n = Compounding period, and r = Rate of growth):

$$\text{Future value }(FV) = \text{Present value }(PV) \times \left(1 + \frac{r}{100}\right)^n$$

For example, net sales per share during Years 6 to 11 grew at a rate of:

$$FV = PV\left(1 + \frac{r}{100}\right)^n \Leftrightarrow \$48.85 = \$33.10\left(1 + \frac{r}{100}\right)^5$$

$$r = 8.09\%$$

6 level. A substantial amount of notes payable are reclassified as long-term debt in Year 10. This helps improve the current ratio. Exhibit CC.11 reveals that cash and cash equivalents in Year 11 represent a larger proportion of current assets (11.78%) compared with the industry (5.60%).

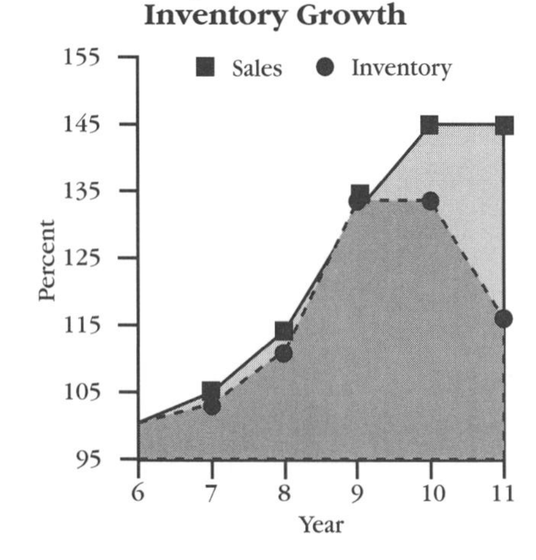

Campbell's acid-test ratio for the past three years (0.56) is slightly below the Year 11 industry composite (0.61). The assets and liabilities comprising the acid-test ratio can be compared against the industry composite using Exhibit CC.7. This exhibit along with Exhibit CC.11 reveals that inventories comprise a lower proportion of total assets (17%) and total current assets (47%) than they do for the industry (39% and 64%, respectively). Also, inventory turnover for Campbell in Year 11 is 5.37 versus 2.53 for the industry. These measures indicate Campbell has less funds invested in inventory relative to the industry. This conclusion is supported with evidence from Exhibit CC.8 where inventory growth is less than sales growth (116% versus 145%). These improvements in inventory management are concurrent with Campbell's launching of the just-in- time inventory system. This improvement is especially evident with raw

Exhibit CC.6

CAMPBELL SOUP COMPANY
Common-Size Income Statements
For Years 6 to 11

	Year 11	*Year 10*	*Year 9*	*Year 8*	*Year 7*	*Year 6*
Net sales	100.00%	100.00%	100.00%	100.00%	100.00%	100.00%
Costs and expenses:						
Cost of products sold	66.01%	68.62%	70.55%	69.68%	70.83%	71.91%
Marketing and selling expenses	15.41	15.80	14.44	15.06	13.95	12.70
Administrative expenses	4.94	4.68	4.44	4.78	4.76	4.57
Research and development expenses	0.91	0.87	0.84	0.96	1.00	0.98
Interest expense	1.87	1.80	1.66	1.11	1.15	1.31
Interest income	(0.42)	(0.28)	(0.68)	(0.68)	(0.66)	(0.64)
Foreign exchange losses, net	0.01	0.05	0.34	0.34	0.11	0.02
Other expense (income)	0.42	0.24	0.57	(0.07)	(0.21)	0.13
Divestitures, restructuring, and unusual charges	—	5.46	6.05	0.83	—	—
Total costs and expenses	89.17%	97.23%	98.21%	92.02%	90.93%	90.98%
Earnings before equity in earnings of affiliates and minority interests	10.83%	2.77%	1.79%	7.98%	9.07%	9.02%
Equity in earnings of affiliates	0.04	0.22	0.18	0.13	0.34	0.10
Minority interests	(0.12)	(0.09)	(0.09)	(0.13)	(0.10)	(0.09)
Earnings before taxes	10.76%	2.89%	1.88%	7.98%	9.31%	9.03%
Taxes on earnings	4.29	2.82	1.65	3.02	3.80	3.83
Earnings before cumulative effect of accounting change	6.47%	0.07%	0.23%	4.96%	5.51%	5.21%
Cumulative effect of change in accounting for income taxes	—	—	—	0.67	—	—
Net earnings	6.47%	0.07%	0.23%	5.63%	5.51%	5.21%

materials. Exhibit CC.12 reports inventory data showing a decline in the proportion of raw materials to total inventories consistent with our inference.

The LIFO inventory method is used in accounting for approximately 70 percent of inventories in Year 11 and 64 percent in Year 10 (see annual report note 14 in Supplement A). Exhibit CC.13 compares income and cost of goods sold using the LIFO and FIFO inventory methods. When prices are rising, LIFO income is typically lower than FIFO. In Campbell's case LIFO yielded income less than FIFO in Years 7, 9, and 11. During other years the reverse occurs. This might be due to declining costs or inventory liquidation.

Campbell's accounts receivable turnover has been declining over the past six years, but it is still above the industry level in Year 11 (see Exhibit CC.10). We also see from Exhibit CC.8 that accounts receivable are growing faster than sales, reaching a peak in Year 10 (209) with a decline in Year 11 (176). This is suggestive of a more aggressive credit policy. The collection period for accounts receivable (see Exhibit CC.10) worsened between Years 6 and 10, but improved slightly in Year 11. Similar behavior is evidenced with the inventory conversion period, with a general worsening from Years 6 through 10. Yet the conversion period in Year 11 returns to 92.7 days versus the 96.4 days for Year 6. This is primarily due to an improved inventory turnover, and helps Campbell in comparison to industry norms.

EXHIBIT CC.7

CAMPBELL SOUP COMPANY
Common-Size Balance Sheets
For Years 6 to 11

	Year 11	*Year 10*	*Year 9*	*Year 8*	*Year 7*	*Year 6*	*Year 11 Industry Composite*
Current assets:							
Cash and cash equivalents	4.31%	1.96%	3.07%	2.38%	4.69%	5.61%	3.4%
Other temporary investments	0.31	0.55	0.67	0.97	9.05	8.64	
Accounts receivable	12.71	15.17	13.68	13.49	10.94	10.82	16.5
Inventories	17.03	19.92	20.75	18.41	20.13	22.10	38.6
Prepaid expenses	2.23	2.87	2.55	2.51	1.62	1.14	2.2
Total current assets	36.60%	40.47%	40.73%	37.76%	46.43%	48.31%	60.70%
Plant assets, net of depreciation	43.15%	41.74%	39.18%	41.80%	43.55%	42.28%	21.0%
Intangible assets, net of amortization	10.50	9.32	11.87	13.76	—	—	
Other assets	9.75	8.48	8.22	6.68	10.02	9.41	18.3
Total assets	100.00%	100.00%	100.00%	100.00%	100.00%	100.00%	100.00%
Current liabilities:							
Notes payable	6.80%	4.92%	6.90%	3.82%	3.02%	3.22%	6.7%
Payable to suppliers and others	11.63	12.76	12.92	12.38	12.10	11.64	10.2
Accrued liabilities	9.85	11.95	9.98	6.56	5.88	6.00	15.8
Dividend payable	0.89	0.78	0.76	—	—	—	
Accrued income taxes	1.63	1.13	0.77	1.16	1.40	1.80	
Total current liabilities	30.80%	31.54%	31.33%	23.92%	22.40%	22.66%	32.70%
Long-term debt	18.62%	19.58%	16.00%	14.57%	12.27%	13.11%	19.7%
Other liabilities, mainly deferred taxes	7.35	7.77	7.44	9.02	9.28	8.52	1.5
Shareowner's equity:							
Preferred stock; authorized 40,000,000 sh.; none issued	—	—	—	—	—	—	
Capital stock, $0.15 par value; authorized 140,000,000 sh.; issued 135,622,676 sh.	0.49	0.49	0.52	0.56	0.66	0.73	
Capital surplus	2.59	1.50	1.29	1.17	1.33	1.38	
Earnings retained in the business	46.10	40.17	45.16	52.06	55.19	56.25	
Capital stock in treasury, at cost	−6.52	−2.60	−1.80	−2.08	−1.51	−1.75	
Cumulative translation adjustments	0.57	1.54	0.05	0.79	0.38	−0.91	
Total shareowner's equity	43.22%	41.11%	45.23%	52.50%	56.05%	55.70%	46.10%
Total liabilities and equity	100.00%	100.00%	100.00%	100.00%	100.00%	100.00%	100.00%

Campbell's success in managing current liabilities is varied. While the period in paying accounts payable increased from Year 6 through Year 8, the recent three years' payment period has leveled off (see Exhibit CC.10). Similarly, its average net trade cycle fluctuates over the past six years. But by Year 11 (47 days) it is below the Year 6 level of 57 days. This finding is consistent with the company's improving liquidity.

Cash Flow Analysis and Forecasting

Our cash flow analysis of Campbell Soup has two primary objectives:

EXHIBIT CC.8

CAMPBELL SOUP COMPANY
Trend Index of Selected Accounts
(Year 6 = 100)

	Year 11	*Year 10*	*Year 9*	*Year 8*	*Year 7*	*Year 6*
Cash and cash equivalents	115%	52%	78%	55%	93%	$ 155.1
Accounts receivable	176	209	180	163	113	299.0
Temporary investments	5	9	11	15	117	238.7
Inventory	116	134	134	109	102	610.5
Total current assets	114	125	120	102	108	1,334.8
Total current liabilities	204	207	197	138	111	626.1
Working capital	34	52	52	70	105	708.7
Plant assets, net	153	147	132	129	115	1,168.1
Other assets	156	134	124	93	119	259.9
Long-term debt	213	222	174	145	105	362.3
Total liabilities	192	198	176	140	111	1,223.9
Shareowners' equity	117	110	116	123	113	1,538.9
Net sales	145	145	132	114	105	4,268.8
Cost of products sold	133	138	130	110	103	3,082.7
Admin. and research expenses	157	148	129	119	109	195.9
Marketing and sales expenses	176	180	150	135	115	544.4
Interest expense	199	191	161	104	101	58.5
Total costs and expenses	142	155	143	115	105	3,900.0
Earnings before taxes	172	46	28	100	108	387.2
Net income	180	2*	6*	123	111	223.2

* Excluding the net effect of divestitures, restructuring, and unusual charges will change these amounts to: Year 10—$137 and Year 9—$123.

EXHIBIT CC.9

CAMPBELL SOUP COMPANY
Per Share Results

	Year 11	*Year 10*	*Year 9*	*Year 8*	*Year 7*	*Year 6*
Sales	$48.85	$47.88	$43.87	$37.63	$34.57	$33.10
Net income	3.16	0.03	0.10	2.12	1.90	1.72
Dividends	1.12	0.98	0.90	0.81	0.71	0.65
Book value	14.12	13.09	13.76	14.69	13.35	11.86
Average shares outstanding (mil.)	127.0	129.6	129.3	129.4	129.9	129.5

- Analyze the statement of cash flows to assess long-term cash flows (solvency) and investigate cash flow patterns.
- Extend our analysis of static measures of short-term liquidity to include cash forecasting.

We begin by analyzing cash flows from operations. Campbell reports cash flows from operations using the indirect method and we recast these to the more relevant inflow-outflow format (direct method). Results of our recasting are shown in Exhibit CC.14. This analysis reveals operating cash flows are a steady and growing source of

Exhibit CC.10

CAMPBELL SOUP COMPANY
Short-Term Liquidity Analysis

Units	Measure	*Year 11*	*Year 10*	*Year 9*	*Year 8*	*Year 7*	*Year 6*	*Year 11 Industry Composite*
1. Ratio	Current ratio	1.19	1.28	1.30	1.58	2.07	2.13	1.86
2. Ratio	Acid-test ratio	0.56	0.56	0.56	0.70	1.10	1.11	0.61
3. Times	Accounts receivable turnover	10.77	10.68	11.07	11.79	14.08	15.13	8.37
4. Times	Inventory turnover	5.37	5.21	5.41	5.27	5.15	5.14	2.53
5. Days	Days' sales in receivables	30.60	36.23	34.15	36.00	27.17	25.11	43.01
6. Days	Days' sales in inventory	62.12	69.31	73.41	70.53	70.59	71.29	142.03
7. Days	Approximate conversion period	92.72	105.54	107.56	106.53	97.76	96.40	185.32
8. Percent	Cash to current assets	11.78%	4.84%	7.55%	6.30%	10.14%	11.62%	5.60%
9. Percent	Cash to current liabilities	14.00%	6.22%	9.81%	9.94%	20.90%	24.77%	10.40%
10. Days	Liquidity index	59.87	72.62	72.55	71.46	52.29	52.07	130.62
11. M$'s	Working capital	240.50	367.40	369.40	499.60	744.10	708.70	54.33
12. Days	Days' purchases in accounts payable	46.03	46.56	46.20	49.30	44.25	39.33	
13. Days	Average net trade cycle	46.69	58.98	61.36	57.23	53.51	57.07	
14. Percent	Cash provided by operations to average current liabilities	62.51%	35.44%	34.10%	60.22%	71.36%	77.34%	

Notes:
For Year 11 (in millions):

(3) $\frac{\text{Net sales } \boxed{13}}{\text{Average accounts receivable } \boxed{33}} = \frac{6{,}204.1}{(527.4 + 624.5)/2} = 10.77$

(4) $\frac{\text{Cost of products sold } \boxed{14}}{\text{Average inventory } \boxed{34}} = \frac{4{,}095.5}{(706.7 + 819.8)/2} = 5.37$

(5) $\frac{\text{Ending accounts receivable } \boxed{33}}{\text{Sales } \boxed{13}/360} = \frac{527.4}{6{,}204.1/360} = 30.6$

(6) $\frac{\text{Ending inventory } \boxed{34}}{\text{Cost of products sold } \boxed{14}/360} = \frac{706.7}{4{,}095.5/360} = 62.12$

(7) Approximate conversion period = (5) Days' sales in receivables + (6) Days' sales in inventory

(10)

Financial item		*Days Removed from Cash*		*Product*
Cash and temporary investments 31 + 32	191.7 ×	0	=	0
Accounts receivable 33	527.4 ×	30.6	=	16138
Inventories 34	706.7 ×	92.7	=	65511
Prepaid expenses 35	92.7 ×	100*	=	9270
	1,518.5			90919

*Assumed number.

Liquidity index $= \frac{90919}{1518.5} = 59.87$ days

(12) $\frac{\text{Accounts payable } \boxed{41}}{\text{Purchases per day}^{\dagger}} = \frac{482.4}{10.48} = 46.03$

†From Exhibit CC.12.

(13) Number of days' sales in:

Accounts receivable	30.60
Inventories	62.12
	92.72
Less: accounts payable	46.03
	46.69

(14) $\frac{\text{Cash from operations } \boxed{64}}{\text{Beginning + Ending current liabilities } \boxed{45} \div 2} = \frac{805.2}{1{,}288} = 62.51$

EXHIBIT CC.11

CAMPBELL SOUP COMPANY
Common-Size Analysis of
Current Assets and Current Liabilities

	Year 11	*Year 10*	*Year 9*	*Year 8*	*Year 7*	*Year 6*	*Year 11 Industry Composite*
Current assets:							
Cash and cash equivalents	11.78%	4.85%	7.55%	6.30%	10.09%	11.62%	5.60%
Other temporary investments	0.84	1.35	1.64	2.57	19.49	17.88	—
Accounts receivable	34.73	37.50	33.59	35.72	23.57	22.40	27.18
Inventories	46.54	49.22	50.95	48.77	43.37	45.74	63.60
Prepaid expenses	6.11	7.08	6.27	6.64	3.48	2.36	3.62
Total current assets	100.00%	100.00%	100.00%	100.00%	100.00%	100.00%	100.00%
Current liabilities:							
Notes payable	22.08%	15.58%	22.04%	15.99%	13.48%	14.20%	20.49%
Payable to suppliers and others	37.75	40.46	41.25	51.74	54.02	51.38	31.19
Accrued liabilities	31.98	37.89	31.86	27.44	26.25	26.50	} = 48.32
Dividend payable	2.89	2.49	2.41	—	—	—	
Accrued income taxes	5.30	3.58	2.44	4.83	6.25	7.92	
Total current liabilities	100.00%	100.00%	100.00%	100.00%	100.00%	100.00%	100.00%

EXHIBIT CC.12

CAMPBELL SOUP COMPANY
Inventory Data
($ millions)

	Year 11	*Year 10*	*Year 9*	*Year 8*	*Year 7*	*Year 6*
1. Beginning inventory	$ 819.8	$ 816.0	$ 664.7	$ 623.6	$ 610.5	$ 623.1
2. Plus: production inputs	3,982.4	4,262.0	4,152.9	3,433.9	3,193.6	3,070.1
3. Goods available for sale	$4,802.2	$5,078.0	$4,187.6	$4,057.5	$3,804.1	$3,693.2
4. Less: Ending inventory	706.7	819.8	816.0	664.7	623.6	610.5
5. Cost of products sold	$4,095.5	$4,258.2	$4,001.6	$3,392.8	$3,180.5	$3,082.7
6. Depreciation	$ 208.6	$ 200.9	$ 192.3	$ 170.9	$ 144.6	$ 126.8
7. (2) − (6) = Purchases	3,773.8	4,061.1	3,960.6	3,263.0	3,049.0	2,943.3
8. (7)/360 = Purchases per day	$ 10.48	$ 11.28	$ 11.00	$ 9.06	$ 8.47	$ 8.18
Ending inventories:						
Raw materials, containers, and supplies	$ 342.3	$ 384.4	$ 385.0	$ 333.4	$ 333.6	$ 340.4
Finished products	454.0	520.0	519.0	412.5	372.4	348.1
	$ 796.3	$ 904.4	$ 904.0	$ 745.9	$ 706.0	$ 688.5
Less: Adjustment of inventories to LIFO	89.6	84.6	88.0	81.2	82.4	78.5
Total ending inventories	$ 706.7	$ 819.8	$ 816.0	$ 664.7	$ 623.6	$ 610.5
Raw materials, containers, and supplies	43.0%	42.5%	42.6%	44.7%	47.3%	49.4%
Finished products	57.0	57.5	57.4	55.3	52.7	50.6
	100.0%	100.0%	100.0%	100.0%	100.0%	100.0%

EXHIBIT CC.13

CAMPBELL SOUP COMPANY
Inventory Data Using FIFO versus LIFO
($ millions)

	Year 11	*Year 10*	*Year 9*	*Year 8*	*Year 7*	*Year 6*
Beginning inventory	$ 904.4	$ 904.0	$ 745.9	$ 706.0	$ 688.5	$ 707.0
Production inputs (same as LIFO)	3,982.4	4,262.0	4,152.9	3,433.9	3,193.6	3,070.1
Goods available for sale	$4,886.8	$5,166.0	$4,898.8	$4,139.9	$3,882.1	$3,777.1
Less: Ending inventory	796.3	904.4	904.0	745.9	706.0	688.5
Cost of products sold (FIFO)	$4,090.5	$4,261.6	$3,994.8	$3,394.0	$3,176.1	$3,088.6
Cost of products sold (LIFO)	$4,095.5	$4,258.2	$4,001.6	$3,392.8	$3,180.5	$3,082.7
Effect of restatement to FIFO increases (decreases) cost of products sold by:	$ (5.0)	$ 3.4	$ (6.8)	$ 1.2	$ (4.4)	$ 5.9
Net of tax* effect of restatement to FIFO decreases (increases) net income by:	$ (3.3)	$ 2.2	$ (4.5)	$ 0.8	$ (2.4)	$ 3.2

*Tax rate is 34% for Years 8 through 11, 45% for Year 7, and 46% for Year 6.

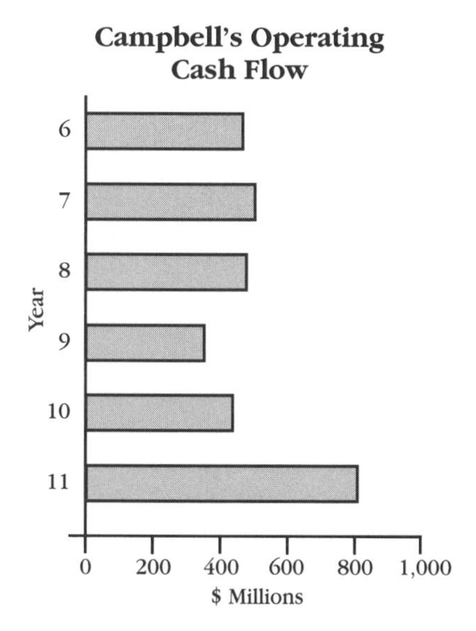

Source: Annual report.

cash, with a substantial increase in Year 11 ($805 million). The slight cash downturn in Year 9 is due primarily to an increase in inventories ($113 million) and a decrease in (negative) deferred taxes ($68 million). The increase in inventories is tied to management's desire to improve customer service, and the decrease in deferred taxes relates to restructuring and unusual charges that are not tax deductible, resulting in $78 million of credits to tax expense but higher current tax liabilities. We also note that the declines in net income for Years 9 and 10 are not reflected in operating cash flows. This is because these declines are from restructuring and divestiture charges having no immediate cash flow effects.

Our analysis of cash outflows reveals an increasing trend through Year 10. In Year 11, outflows decline mainly due to a $215 million decrease in cost of products sold. There is also evidence in Year 11 of improvements in cash flows due to a decrease of $38 million in inventory. These factors are partially offset by $91 million in higher taxes. Yet Campbell has successfully translated growing sales and increasingly larger margins into a steady growth in operating cash flows.

Campbell's common-size statements of cash flows for the six years ending with Year 11 are shown in Exhibit CC.15. This exhibit reveals several patterns in the company's cash flows over these six years. Transitory fluctuations in cash like those due to the high usage of cash for investing activities in Year 7 (62%) are put in perspective by including aggregate figures for the six years in a total column. Total operating cash flows constitute more than one-half of all cash inflows. This finding along with evidence that financing activities (using 7% of cash inflows) are mostly refinancing is indicative of Campbell's financial strength and financing practices. The total column reveals that cash used for acquiring assets and businesses consumes nearly 50 percent of cash inflows, and about 12 percent of cash inflows are used for dividends. Overall, cash

EXHIBIT CC.14

CAMPBELL SOUP COMPANY
Analysis of Cash from Operations: Direct Method
(millions)

	Year 11	*Year 10*	*Year 9*	*Year 8*	*Year 7*	*Year 6*
Inflows:						
Net sales	$6,204.1	$6,205.8	$5,672.1	$4,868.9	$4,490.4	$4,286.8
(Increase) decrease in accounts receivable	17.1	(60.4)	(46.8)	(104.3)	(36.3)	(3.6)
Cash collections on sales	$6,221.2	$6,145.4	$5,625.3	$4,764.6	$4,454.1	$4,283.2
Interest income	26.0	17.6	38.3	33.2	29.5	27.4
Total cash collections from operations	$6,247.2	$6,163.0	$5,663.6	$4,797.8	$4,483.6	$4,310.6
Outflows:						
Cost of products sold*	3,823.7	4,038.7	3,772.0	3,178.9	3,007.9	2,939.3
Marketing and sales expenses	956.2	980.5	818.8	733.3	626.2	544.4
Administrative expenses	306.7	290.7	252.1	232.6	213.9	195.9
Foreign exchange losses	0.8	3.3	19.3	16.6	4.8	0.7
Interest expense	116.2	111.6	94.1	53.9	51.7	56.0
(Increase) decrease in deferred taxes	(35.5)	(3.9)	67.8	(13.4)	(45.7)	(29.0)
Research and development expenses	56.3	53.7	47.7	46.9	44.8	42.2
Other expenses (income)	26.2	14.7	32.4	19.8	(9.5)	5.5
Increase (decrease) in inventories	(48.7)	(10.7)	113.2	(54.2)	3.9	(23.1)
Net change in other current assets and liabilities	(30.6)	68.8	0.6	(30.2)	(42.9)	(48.7)
Income tax expense	265.9	175.0	93.4	147.0	170.6	164.0
Net effect of equity in earnings of affiliates and minority interests†	4.8	(7.8)	(5.1)	0.0	(10.4)	(0.4)
Total cash outflows for operations	$5,442.0	$5,714.6	$5,306.3	$4,331.2	$4,015.3	$3,846.8
Cash from operations	$ 805.2	$ 448.4	$ 357.3	$ 466.6	$ 468.3	$ 463.8

* Adjusted by items not effecting cash. For Year 11 the computation is:

Cost of products sold as per income statement (item 14)	$4,095.5
Less: Depreciation and amortization as per statement of cash flows (item 57)	208.6
Less: Other, net as per statement of cash flows (item 60)	63.2
	$3,823.7

† This is aggregated for convenience. It is also appropriate to include dividend receipts under cash inflows.

inflows from operations (56%) are used for both financing (7%) and investing (48%) activities. Campbell's net cash position over these six years is stable, never deviating more than 7 percent from the prior year. Its growth for the entire six-year period is less than 1 percent.

It is often useful for us to construct a summary of cash inflows and outflows by major categories of activity. Using Exhibit CC.4, we prepare the following chart of cash inflows and outflows ($ millions):

	Year 11	*Year 10*	*Year 9*	*Year 8*	*Year 7*	*Year 6*	*Total*
Operating activities	$805.2	$448.4	$357.3	$466.6	$468.3	$463.8	$3,009.6
Investing activities	(478.7)	(387.5)	(473.2)	(462.2)	(401.0)	(387.6)	(2,590.2)
Financing activities	(219.6)	(101.8)	(163.1)	(52.8)	(88.3)	(54.5)	(353.9)
Increase (decrease) in cash	98.2	(40.2)	35.1	(59.2)	(28.1)	18.0	23.8

Exhibit CC.15

CAMPBELL SOUP COMPANY
Common-Size Statements of Cash Flows*
For Years 6 to 11

	Year 11	*Year 10*	*Year 9*	*Year 8*	*Year 7*	*Year 6*	*Total*
Cash flows from operating activities:							
Net earnings	26.89%	0.54%	1.15%	25.14%	38.42%	27.88%	21.54%
To reconcile net earnings to net cash provided by operating activities:							
Depreciation and amortization	13.97	24.58	16.82	15.67	22.47	15.84	19.33
Divestitures and restructuring provisions	—	41.49	30.00	1.61	—	—	12.95
Deferred taxes	2.38	0.48	(5.93)	1.23	7.10	3.62	1.11
Other, net	4.23	2.28	3.26	3.94	4.35	2.07	3.83
Cumulative effect of accounting change	—	—	—	(2.98)	—	—	(0.60)
(Increase) decrease in accounts receivable	1.15	(7.39)	(4.09)	(9.57)	(5.64)	(0.45)	(4.34)
(Increase) decrease in inventories	3.26	1.31	(9.90)	4.97	(0.61)	2.89	0.36
Net change in other current assets and liabilities	2.05	(8.42)	(0.05)	2.77	6.67	6.08	1.54
Net cash provided by operating activities	53.92%	54.86%	31.25%	42.80%	72.76%	57.94%	55.72%
Cash flows from investing activities:							
Purchase of plant assets	(24.18)%	(47.42)%	(24.85)%	(22.50)%	(47.19)%	(29.39)%	(33.64)%
Sale of plant assets	2.89	4.27	3.48	2.07	—	3.72	3.15
Businesses acquired	(12.06)	(5.09)	(11.88)	(43.28)	(1.13)	(2.50)	(15.86)
Sale of businesses	4.51	2.66	0.43	2.16	3.23	—	2.56
Increase in other assets	(3.87)	(2.28)	(9.36)	(3.70)	(7.78)	(2.25)	(5.40)
Net change in other temporary investments	0.65	0.45	0.79	22.86	(9.43)	(18.00)	1.24
Net cash used in investing activities	(32.06)%	(47.41)%	(41.39)%	(42.39)%	(62.31)%	(48.42)%	(47.95)%
Cash flows from financing activities:							
Long-term borrowings	26.97%	1.54%	11.07%	9.45%	0.75%	25.47%	15.80%
Repayments of long-term borrowings	(8.70)	(2.75)	(4.69)	(2.10)	(3.71)	(20.57)	(7.73)
Increase (decrease) in short-term borrowings	(9.23)	(0.33)	9.46	0.77	(3.22)	0.57	(0.74)
Other short-term borrowings	7.86	18.81	19.87	7.06	13.88	9.11	13.65
Repayments of other short-term borrowings	(13.82)	(10.99)	(16.82)	(8.03)	(10.30)	(11.06)	(13.53)
Dividends paid	(9.21)	(15.21)	(7.58)	(9.59)	(14.25)	(13.07)	(12.02)
Treasury stock purchases	(11.76)	(5.03)	(0.71)	(2.69)	—	—	(4.70)
Treasury stock issued	3.19	1.52	1.62	0.08	0.25	0.50	1.58
Other, net	(0.01)	(0.01)	2.06	0.21	2.89	2.24	1.15
Net cash provided (used in) financing activities	(14.71)%	(12.46)%	14.27%	(4.84)%	(13.72)%	(6.81)%	(6.55)%
Effect of exchange rate change on cash	(0.58)%	0.09%	(1.06)%	(0.99)%	(1.10)%	(0.46)%	(0.77)%
Net increase (decrease) in cash and cash equivalents	6.58	(4.92)	3.07	(5.43)	(4.37)	2.25	0.44

* Common-size percentages are based on total cash inflows = 100%. For Year 11 the 100 percent is composed of: CFO (53.92) + Sale of plant assets (2.89) + Sale of bus. (4.51) + Decrease in temp. invest. (0.65) + LT borrowings (26.97) + ST borrowings (7.86) + Treas. st. issued (3.19).

The picture emerging from this summary is that Campbell has major outlays for (1) investing—$2,590.2 million, and (2) financing (including dividends)—$353.9 million. Through this, Campbell experienced a slight cumulative increase of $23.8 million in cash. Notably, these activities are funded by Campbell's net operating cash inflows of $3,009.6 million. Notice that in Years 7, 8, and 10 the cash balances are drawn down to fund investing and financing activities. Yet operating cash flows for this six-year period are sufficient to fund *all* of Campbell's investing and financing needs and still leave excess cash of $23.8 million.

Our next stage of analysis is forecasting short-term cash flows. This forecasting analysis supplements the above static measures of short-term liquidity. A first step in forecasting operating cash flows is predicting earnings. We prepare forecasts for Campbell's statement of earnings for Year 12 (see Exhibit CC.16 and its footnotes for assumptions). We begin with a forecast of net sales—predicted to be 2.35 percent higher than the prior year. We forecast net earnings in Year 12 at $480 million, about 20 percent higher than the previous year (this reflects Campbell's five-year earnings growth of 13% plus an increment for predictably good business strategy). This earnings increase reflects more a predicted increase in operating margin than in sales. The increase in operating margin is primarily due to decreases in overall manufacturing costs. While labor costs are slightly higher, the costs of metal food containers are considerably lower due to increased competition and production in the aluminum industry. We also expect financing costs to decline from a drop in short-term interest rates. Because of their restructuring we expect Campbell to benefit from favorable operating leverage. Details behind these forecasts are reported in the notes to Exhibit CC.16.

Forecasts for the statement of cash flows for Years 12 and 13 appear in Exhibit 9.7 (pages 460–461). These forecasts use the assumptions above plus a few additional ones. The forecasted statements of cash flows expect Campbell to finance investing

EXHIBIT CC.16

CAMPBELL SOUP COMPANY
Forecasted Statement of Earnings
For Year Ended Year 12
($ millions)

	Forecast	*Percent*
Net sales*	$6,350.0	100.00%
Costs and expenses†		
Cost of products sold	4,095.8	64.50
Marketing and selling expenses	990.6	15.60
Administrative expenses	308.0	4.85
Research and development expenses	57.2	0.90
Interest expense	114.3	1.80
Interest income	(31.8)	−0.50
Other expense (income), including foreign exchange losses	88.9	1.40
Total costs and expenses	$5,623.0	88.55%
Earnings before taxes‡	$ 727.0	11.45%
Taxes on earnings§	(247.0)	−3.89
Net earnings	$ 480.0	7.56%

* Projected at 2.35 percent higher than Year 11 sales of $6,204.1 (The Value Line Investment Survey, Feb. 21, Year 12).

† Forecasts for costs and expenses are based on the following expectations:
(1)Cost of products sold is expected to be 64.5 percent of Year 12 sales. This is consistent with the Year 9 through Year 11 average and recognizes the increase in gross margin in recent years.
(2)Marketing and selling expenses are expected to approximate the Year 9 through Year 11 average with a slight increase due to an increase in advertising.
(3)Administrative expenses are expected to increase slightly from the average for Year 9 through Year 11.
(4)All other items are expected to approximate the same level as their average for Year 9 through Year 11.

‡ Effects of equity in earnings of affiliates and minority interests are considered immaterial.

§ At the expected federal statutory rate of 34 percent.

EXHIBIT CC.17

CAMPBELL SOUP COMPANY
Analysis of Cash Flow Ratios
($ millions)

(1) Cash flow adequacy ratio* $= \dfrac{\text{6-year sum of sources of cash from operations}}{\text{6-year sum of capital expenditures, inventory additions, and cash dividends}}$

$= \dfrac{3{,}009.6}{(1{,}817.1 + 856.7) + (113.2 + 3.9) + 649.4}$

$= 0.875$

(2) Cash reinvestment ratio† $= \dfrac{\text{Cash provided by operations} - \text{Dividends}}{\text{Gross PPE} + \text{Investments} + \text{Other assets} + \text{Working capital}}$

Year 6 to Year 11 average $= \dfrac{3{,}009.6 - 649.4}{15{,}183.7 + 1{,}888.3 + 2{,}929.7} = 11.8\%$

Year 11 $= \dfrac{805.2 - 137.5}{2{,}921.9 + 404.6 + 240.5} = 18.7\%$

Year 10 $= \dfrac{448.4 - 124.3}{2{,}734.9 + 349.0 + 367.4} = 9.4\%$

Year 9 $= \dfrac{357.3 - 86.7}{2{,}543.0 + 323.1 + 369.4} = 8.4\%$

Year 8 $= \dfrac{466.6 - 104.6}{2{,}539.7 + 241.2 + 499.6} = 11.0\%$

Year 7 $= \dfrac{468.3 - 91.7}{2{,}355.1 + 310.5 + 744.1} = 11.0\%$

Year 6 $= \dfrac{463.8 - 104.6}{2{,}089.1 + 259.9 + 708.7} = 11.7\%$

* All amounts are from the statement of cash flows.
† Numerator amounts are from the statement of cash flows and denominator amounts are from the balance sheet.

activities primarily from operating cash flows and redeem some of its high coupon long-term debt. If these forecasts are realized, Campbell will have enough cash for dividends and other uses.

Two additional measures of Campbell's cash flows are reported in Exhibit CC.17. The cash flow adequacy ratio provides us insight into whether Campbell generates sufficient cash from operations to cover capital expenditures, investments in inventories, and cash dividends. Campbell's cash flow adequacy ratio for the six-year period is 0.875, implying that funds generated from operations are insufficient to cover these items (see denominator) and that there is a need for external financing. We must remember this is an aggregate (six-year sum) ratio. When we look at individual years, including Year 11, the cash flow adequacy ratio suggests sufficient cash resources. The exceptions are Years 7 and 9. A second measure, the cash reinvestment ratio, provides us insight into the amount of cash retained and reinvested into the company for both asset replacement and growth. Campbell's cash reinvestment ratio is 11.8 percent for the six-year period. This reinvestment rate is satisfactory for the industry. The Year 11 reinvestment ratio is much higher (18.7%) than normal. Years 9 and 10 show a lower ratio due to decreases in operating cash flows.

Capital Structure and Solvency

We next analyze Campbell's capital structure and solvency (the analysis above related to cash forecasting is relevant to solvency). Changes in the company's capital structure are measured using various analyses and comparisons. Campbell's capital structure for the six years ending in Year 11 is depicted in Exhibit CC.18. For analytical purposes, one-half of deferred taxes is considered a long-term liability and the other half as equity. Exhibit CC.19 shows a common-size analysis of capital structure. For Year 11, liabilities constitute 53 percent and equity 47 percent of Campbell's financing.

Selected capital structure and long-term solvency ratios are reported in Exhibit CC.20. The total debt to equity ratio increases markedly in the past three years, yet remains at or below the industry norm (1.17). The source of this increase is attributed to long-term debt, see Exhibit CC.8. In particular, Exhibit CC.8 shows the trend index of long-term debt (213) exceeds that for current liabilities (204), total liabilities (192), and shareowners' equity (117). This is also evident in Campbell's long-term debt to equity ratio, where in Year 11 the ratio for Campbell (48%) exceeds the industry composite of 43 percent. We also compute the analytically adjusted long-term debt to equity ratio. For Campbell this ratio does not differ markedly from its unadjusted counterpart. These measures suggest that Campbell is moving away from its historically conservative capital structure toward a more aggressive one. This is corroborated by a lower level of fixed charge coverage ratios using both earnings and operating cash flow compared with Years 6–8. Consistent with our analysis, Campbell's long-term debt is rated AA by the major rating agencies—down from the AAA rating the company enjoyed previously, but still an excellent rating. The company's creditors enjoy sound asset protection and superior earning power.

Campbell's Financing Sources

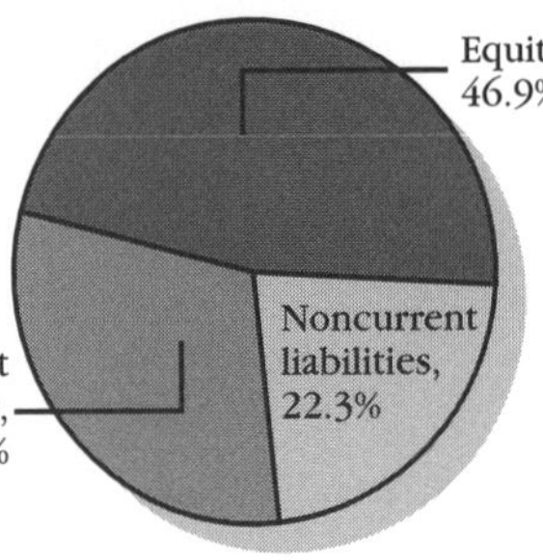

Equity, 46.9%
Noncurrent liabilities, 22.3%
Current liabilities, 30.8%

Source: Annual report.

EXHIBIT CC.18

CAMPBELL SOUP COMPANY
Analysis of Capital Structure
(millions)

	Year 11	*Year 10*	*Year 9*	*Year 8*	*Year 7*	*Year 6*
Long-term liabilities:						
Notes payable	$ 757.8	$ 792.9	$ 610.3	$ 507.1	$ 358.8	$ 346.7
Capital lease obligation	14.8	12.9	18.9	18.7	21.4	15.6
Total long-term debt	$ 772.6	$ 805.8	$ 629.2	$ 525.8	$ 380.2	$ 362.3
Deferred income taxes*	129.3	117.6	109.0	140.3	124.0	99.6
Other long-term liabilities	23.0	28.5	19.6	15.6	15.8	16.3
Total long-term liabilities	$ 924.9	$ 951.9	$ 757.8	$ 681.7	$ 520.0	$ 478.2
Current liabilities†	1,278.0	1,298.1	1,232.1	863.3	693.8	626.1
Total liabilities	$2,202.9	$2,250.0	$1,989.9	$1,545.0	$1,213.8	$1,104.3
Equity capital:						
Common shareholders' equity	$1,793.4	$1,691.8	$1,778.3	$1,895.0	$1,736.1	$1,538.9
Minority interests	23.5	56.3	54.9	29.3	23.5	20.1
Deferred income taxes*	129.2	117.5	109.0	140.3	124.0	99.5
Total equity capital	$1,946.1	$1,865.6	$1,942.2	$2,064.6	$1,883.6	$1,658.5
Total liabilities and equity	$4,149.0	$4,115.6	$3,932.1	$3,609.6	$2,097.4	$2,762.8

* For analytical purposes 50 percent of deferred income taxes are considered debt and the remainder equity.

† Including notes payable—current.

EXHIBIT CC.19

CAMPBELL SOUP COMPANY
Common-Size Analysis of Capital Structure

	Year 11	Year 10	Year 9	Year 8	Year 7	Year 6
Long-term liabilities:						
Notes payable	18.26%	19.27%	15.52%	14.05%	11.59%	12.55%
Capital lease obligation	0.36	0.31	0.48	0.52	0.69	0.56
Total long-term debt	18.62%	19.58%	16.00%	14.57%	12.28%	13.11%
Deferred income taxes*	3.12	2.86	2.77	3.88	4.00	3.61
Other long-term liabilities	0.55	0.69	0.50	0.43	0.51	0.59
Total long-term liabilities	22.29%	23.13%	19.27%	18.88%	16.79%	17.31%
Current liabilities†	30.80	31.54	31.34	23.92	22.40	22.66
Total liabilities	53.09%	54.67%	50.61%	42.80%	39.19%	39.97%
Equity capital:						
Common shareholders' equity	43.22%	41.11%	45.22%	52.50%	56.05%	55.70%
Minority interests	0.57	1.37	1.40	0.81	0.76	0.73
Deferred income taxes*	3.12	2.85	2.77	3.89	4.00	3.60
Total equity capital	46.91%	45.33%	49.39%	57.20%	60.81%	60.03%
Total liabilities and equity	100.00%	100.00%	100.00%	100.00%	100.00%	100.00%

* For analytical purposes 50 percent of deferred income taxes are considered debt and the remainder equity.
† Including notes payable—current.

Return on Invested Capital

Return on invested capital ratios for Campbell are reported in Exhibit CC.21. These ratios reveal several insights. The return on assets is stable during Years 6 through 8, declines sharply for Years 9 and 10, and then rebounds strongly to 11.75 percent in Year 11. Analysis of Years 9 and 10 shows these years' low returns are due to divestitures and restructuring charges. Yet we must keep in mind the marked increase in return for Year 11 is probably due in part to the two prior years' write-offs.

Further analysis of return on assets for Year 11 shows it is comprised of a 7.83 percent profit margin (not shown in Exhibit CC.21) and an asset turnover of 1.50. Both these components show improvement over their values from Year 8 (comparisons with Year 10 and Year 9 ratios are less relevant due to accounting charges). They also compare favorably with industry norms. Campbell's management hopes these improvements for Year 11 are reflective of their major restructuring, closings, and business reorganizations during Years 9 and 10. Because of those restructuring programs and cost-cutting efforts, profit margins are widening. Prior years' returns are depressed by several poorly performing or ill-fitting businesses. Those businesses are now divested and Campbell has streamlined and modernized its manufacturing.

Campbell's return on common equity (21.52%) exceeds both the industry norm and its most recent performance. The source of improvement is due to a solid net income margin and leverage ratio. Like the profit component in return on assets, the improved net income margin likely benefits from write-offs in Years 10 and 9. Disaggregation of Campbell's return on equity (item 6 in Exhibit CC.21) shows that changes in the net income margin are primarily responsible for fluctuations in return on equity during

EXHIBIT CC.20

CAMPBELL SOUP COMPANY
Capital Structure and Solvency Ratios

	Year 11	*Year 10*	*Year 9*	*Year 8*	*Year 7*	*Year 6*	*Year 11 Industry Composite*
1. Total debt to equity	1.13	1.21	1.02	0.75	0.64	0.67	1.17
2. Total debt ratio	0.53	0.55	0.51	0.43	0.39	0.40	0.54
3. Long-term debt to equity	0.48	0.51	0.39	0.33	0.28	0.29	0.43
4. Adjusted long-term debt to equity	0.49	0.50	0.38	0.33	0.27	0.28	—
5. Equity to total debt	0.88	0.83	0.98	1.34	1.56	1.50	0.86
6. Fixed assets to equity	0.92	0.92	0.79	0.73	0.72	0.70	0.46
7. Current liabilities to total liabilities	0.58	0.58	0.62	0.56	0.58	0.57	0.61
8. Earnings to fixed charges	5.16	2.14	1.84	6.06	6.41	6.28	—
9. Cash flow to fixed charges	7.47	5.27	5.38	8.94	8.69	9.26	—

Computations for Year 11:

(1) $$\frac{\text{Total debt}^*}{\text{Equity capital}^*} = \frac{2{,}202.9}{1{,}946.1} = 1.13$$

(2) $$\frac{\text{Total debt}^*}{\text{Total debt and equity } \boxed{55}} = \frac{2{,}202.9}{4{,}149.0} = 0.53$$

(3) $$\frac{\text{Long-term debt}^*}{\text{Equity capital}^*} = \frac{924.9}{1{,}946.1} = 0.48$$

(4) $$\frac{\text{Long-term debt}^* + \text{Estimated present value of operating lease obligations } \boxed{143}}{\text{Equity capital}^* + \text{Excess of FIFO over LIFO inventory } \boxed{153}} = \frac{924.9 + 64.1^{\ddagger}}{1{,}946.1 + 89.6} = 0.49$$

(5) $$\frac{\text{Equity capital}^*}{\text{Total debt}^*} = \frac{1{,}946.1}{2{,}202.9} = 0.88$$

(6) $$\frac{\text{Plant assets } \boxed{37}}{\text{Equity capital}^*} = \frac{1{,}790.4}{1{,}946.1} = 0.92$$

(7) $$\frac{\text{Current liabilities } \boxed{45}}{\text{Total liabilities}^*} = \frac{1{,}278.0}{2{,}202.9} = 0.58$$

(8) $$\frac{\text{Pre-tax income } \boxed{26} + \text{Interest expense } \boxed{18} + \text{Interest portion of rent expense}^{\dagger} - \text{Undistributed equity in earnings in affiliates } \boxed{24}, \boxed{169A}}{\text{Interest incurred } \boxed{98} + \text{Interest portion of rent expense}^{\dagger} \boxed{143}} = \frac{667.4 + 116.2 + 20 - (2.4 - 8.2)}{136.9 + 20} = 5.16$$

(9) $$\frac{\text{Cash flows from operations } \boxed{64} + \text{Current tax expense } \boxed{124A} + \text{Interest expense } \boxed{18} + \text{Interest portion of rent expense}^{\dagger} \boxed{143}}{\text{Interest incurred } \boxed{98} + \text{Interest portion of rent expense}^{\dagger} \boxed{143}} = \frac{805.2 + 230.4 + 116.2 + 20}{136.9 + 20} = 7.47$$

* From Exhibit CC.18.

† One-third of rent expense under operating leases. For Year 11: 1/3 of $59.7 [143].

‡ Computed as $\$71.9/1.1^{1.204}$ (see Appendix 10C for explanation).

recent years. Net income margin is as low as 0.07 percent in Year 10 from the divestitures and restructurings, and is as high as 6.47 percent in Year 11 partly due to the rebound from prior years' changes and potential cost overprovisions. The other two components are reasonably stable. Asset turnover declined slightly in Year 7 from Year 6, but remained relatively level through other years, while the leverage ratio increases gradually during the six-year period because of Campbell's increasingly leveraged capital structure.

Comparison of these disaggregated components with industry norms reveals a favorable asset turnover ratio (1.50 versus 1.38), a typical leverage ratio (2.22 versus 2.17), and a normal or slightly unfavorable net income margin (6.47 versus 6.60).

EXHIBIT CC.21

CAMPBELL SOUP COMPANY
Return on Invested Capital Ratios

	Year 11	*Year 10**	*Year 9**	*Year 8*	*Year 7*	*Year 6*	*Year 11 Industry Composite*
1. Return on assets (ROA)	11.75%	2.08%	2.13%	9.42%	9.57%	9.90%	9.20%
2. Return on common equity* (ROCE)*	21.52%	0.24%	0.67%	14.07%	14.14%	14.40%	19.80%
3. Return on long-term debt and equity	17.07%	3.04%	2.96%	12.27%	12.35%	12.90%	13.50%
4. Financial leverage index (ROCE ÷ ROA)	1.83	0.12	0.31	1.49	1.48	1.46	2.15
5. Equity growth rate	13.85%	−6.30%	−3.67%	8.59%	8.79%	8.96%	—
6. Disaggregation of return on common equity*							
Adjusted profit margin	6.47%	0.07%	0.23%	5.63%	5.51%	5.10%	6.60%
	×	×	×	×	×	×	×
Asset turnover	1.50	1.54	1.50	1.45	1.53	1.68	1.38
	×	×	×	×	×	×	×
Financial leverage ratio	2.22	2.18	1.92	1.72	1.68	1.68	2.17
	21.52%	0.24%	0.67%	14.07%	14.14%	14.40%	19.80%

Computations for Year 11:

(1) $\text{ROA} = \frac{\text{Net income + Interest expense (1 − Tax rate) + Minority interest (MI)}}{\text{Average total assets}} = \frac{401.5 + 116.2\,(1 - 0.34) + 7.2}{(4{,}149.0 + 4{,}115.6)/2} = 11.75\%$

$\text{ROA disaggregated} = \frac{\text{Net income + Interest expense (1 − Tax rate) + Minority interest}}{\text{Sales}} \times \frac{\text{Sales}}{\text{Average total assets}}$

$= \left[\frac{401.5 + 116.2\,(1 - 0.34) + 7.2}{6{,}204.1} = 7.83\%\right] \times \left[\frac{6{,}204.1}{(4{,}149.0 + 4{,}115.6)/2} = 1.5\right] = 11.75\%$

Industry ROA composite = 6.6% × 1.4 = 9.24%

(2) $\text{ROCE} = \frac{\text{Net income − Preferred dividend}}{\text{Average common equity}^{\dagger}} = \frac{401.5}{[(1{,}946.1 - 23.5) + (1{,}865.6 - 56.3)]/2} = 21.52\%$

$\text{ROCE disaggregated} = \text{Adjusted profit margin} \times \text{Asset turnover} \times \text{Financial leverage ratio} = \frac{401.5}{6{,}204.1} \times \frac{6{,}204.1}{(4{,}149.0 + 4{,}115.6)/2} \times \frac{(4{,}149.0 + 4{,}115.6)/2}{1{,}865.95^{\dagger}}$

$= 6.47\% \times 1.50 \times 2.22 = 21.52\%$

(3) $\text{Return on LTD and equity} = \frac{\text{Net income + Interest expense (1 − Tax rate) + MI}}{\text{Average long-term liabilities}^{\ddagger} + \text{Average equity}^{\ddagger}} = \frac{401.5 + 116.2\,(1 - 0.34) + 7.2}{(924.9 + 951.9)/2 + (1{,}946.1 + 1{,}865.6)/2} = 17.07\%$

(4) $\text{Financial leverage index} = \frac{\text{Return on common equity}}{\text{Return on assets}} = \frac{21.52\%}{11.75\%} = 1.83$

(5) $\text{Equity growth rate} = \frac{\text{Net income − Dividends paid}}{\text{Average common equity}^{\dagger}} = \frac{401.5 - 137.5}{(1{,}946.1 + 1{,}865.6)/2} = 13.85\%$

* Excluding the effect of divestitures, restructuring, and unusual charges, net of tax, of $301.6 million in Year 10, and $260.8 million in Year 9, drastically changes these ratios. For example, ROA, for Year 10 and Year 9 becomes 9.57 percent and 9.03 percent, respectively.

† Including 50 percent of deferred taxes assumed as equity, and excluding minority interests (MI). See Exhibit CC.18.

‡ Including 50 percent of deferred taxes. See Exhibit CC.18.

This implies Campbell's higher asset turnover (1.50) and higher leverage ratio (2.22) are primarily responsible for the favorable return on equity (21.52%) compared to the industry norm (19.8%). Recall that Campbell's increased leverage ratio yielded costs in the form of a lower credit rating.

The leverage ratio for Year 11 implies that Campbell is borrowing $1.22 on each dollar of equity. This inference is based on considering 50 percent of deferred taxes as interest-free debt. The total $2.22 in funds are then able to generate $3.33 in sales because assets are turning over at a rate of 1.50 times. This $3.33 in sales earns 6.47 percent in net income, yielding a return on equity of 21.52 percent.

Campbell's return on long-term debt and equity displays a pattern similar to return on equity over the past six years. For Year 11, return on long-term liabilities and equity is 17.07 percent. This compares favorably with the industry composite of 13.50 percent. Campbell's financial leverage index (1.83) is positive and reasonably stable, the exception being Years 9 and 10 for reasons discussed earlier. In Year 11, it rebounds strongly and improves from earlier years. This ratio confirms what we already know from our other evidence—Campbell utilizes its debt profitably.

Notice that Campbell's Year 11 equity growth rate (13.85%) markedly improved relative to prior years. Even if we exclude Years 9 and 10, this rate is nearly double the level for Years 6 through 8. The negative ratios for Years 9 and 10 are because Campbell maintained its dividend payout with its divestitures and restructuring. The strong rebound in this ratio for Year 11 bodes well for future growth in sales and earnings. A higher level of reinvestment frees Campbell from reliance on outside financing sources to fund its growth. The Year 11 net income of $401.5 million and dividends of $142.2 million leave sufficient funds for reinvestment and internally financed growth.

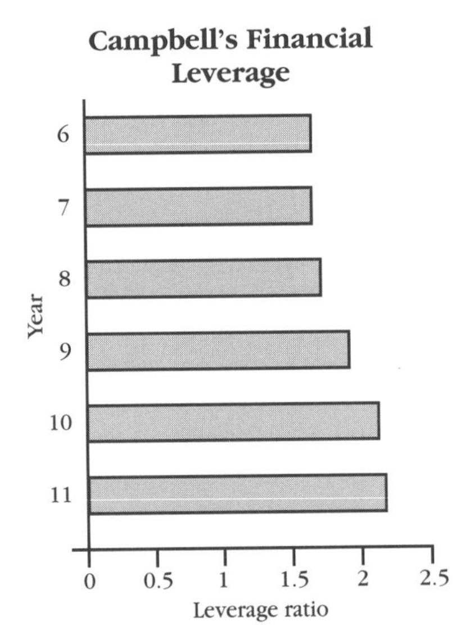

Source: Annual report.

Analysis of Asset Utilization

Campbell's asset utilization measures are reported in Exhibit CC.22. Campbell's asset turnover (1.5 for Year 11) is stable over the past six years. Yet this stability in asset turnover masks significant changes in turnover for individual asset components. Cash and cash equivalents evidence the most significant variability during this period. Variability in cash and cash equivalents is also evidenced in both the sales to working capital turnover ratio and in the common-size balance sheet in Exhibit CC.7. Exhibit CC.7 reveals a gradual disposal of temporary investments. The sizeable $98.2 million increase in Year 11 cash and cash equivalents is primarily due to improvements in operating performance (see Exhibit CC.4).

Campbell's accounts receivable turnover shows a slight improvement in Years 8 through 11 relative to earlier years. The continued improvement in Year 11 is helped by this year's decrease of $97.1 million in receivables. Regarding inventory turnover, Campbell's expressed desire to decrease inventories at every stage of its manufacturing process is revealing itself through an improved turnover ratio (8.8). It is important to

EXHIBIT CC.22

CAMPBELL SOUP COMPANY
Asset Utilization Ratios

	Year 11	*Year 10*	*Year 9*	*Year 8*	*Year 7*	*Year 6*	*Year 11 Industry Composite*
1. Sales to cash and equivalents	34.7	76.9	46.9	56.8	31.0	27.6	40.6
2. Sales to receivables	11.8	9.9	10.5	10.0	13.2	14.3	8.4
3. Sales to inventories	8.8	7.6	7.0	7.3	7.2	7.0	3.6
4. Sales to working capital	25.8	16.9	15.4	9.8	6.0	6.1	4.9
5. Sales to fixed assets	3.5	3.6	3.7	3.2	3.3	3.7	6.6
6. Sales to other assets*	7.4	8.5	7.2	6.6	14.5	16.5	7.5
7. Sales to total assets	1.5	1.5	1.4	1.4	1.5	1.6	1.4
8. Sales to short-term liabilities	4.9	4.8	4.6	5.6	6.5	6.9	4.2

* Including intangible assets.

Exhibit CC.23

CAMPBELL SOUP COMPANY
Analysis of Profit Margin Ratios

Profit margins	*Year 11*	*Year 10*	*Year 9*	*Year 8*	*Year 7*	*Year 6*	*Year 11 Industry Composite*
1. Gross profit margin	34.00%	31.38%	29.45%	30.32%	29.17%	28.09%	29.30%
2. Operating profit margin	12.63%	4.69%	3.54%	9.09%	10.46%	10.34%	—
3. Net profit margin	6.47%	0.07%	0.23%	5.63%	5.51%	5.21%	6.60%

Computations for Year 11:

(1) $\text{Gross profit margin} = \dfrac{\text{Net sales} - \text{Cost of products sold}}{\text{Net sales}} = \dfrac{6{,}204.1 - 4{,}095.5}{6{,}204.1} = 34\%$

(2) $\text{Operating profit margin} = \dfrac{\text{Income before taxes and interest expense}}{\text{Net sales}} = \dfrac{667.4 + 116.2}{6{,}204.1} = 12.63\%$

see that Campbell's asset and asset component turnover ratios often compare favorably to industry norms. In several key areas like receivables (11.8 versus 8.4), inventories (8.8 versus 3.6), and working capital (25.8 versus 4.9), its turnover ratio is better than the industry composite.

Analysis of Operating Performance and Profitability

Selected profit margin measures for Campbell are reported in Exhibit CC.23. We see that Campbell's gross profit ratio margin for Year 11 is better than the industry norm (34.0% versus 29.3%). However its net profit margin is at or slightly below the industry level (6.47% versus 6.60%). After the divestitures and restructuring of Years 9 and 10, Campbell's net profit margin is better than it was in Years 6 through 8. These moves included eliminating administrative personnel and unsuccessful divisions. Results in Year 11 already show indications of tighter control over several areas of operating expenses. Continued cost control should allow Campbell to further improve its profitability and exceed industry norms.

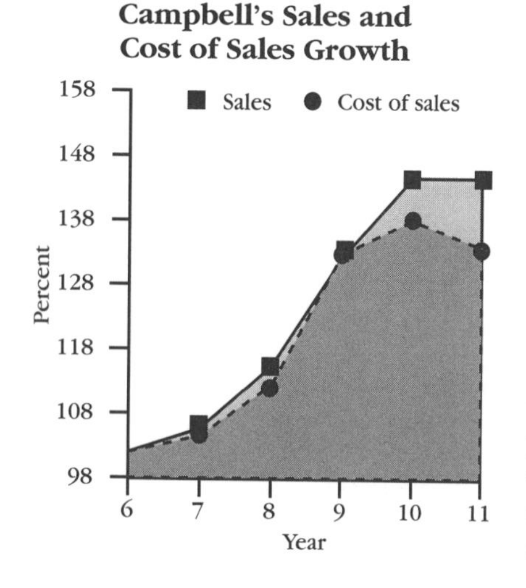

We link these profitability measures with evidence in earlier analyses. Improvement evidenced in the gross profit margin confirms earlier results in Exhibit CC.6 showing a gradual decline in cost of products sold (66.01% in Year 11 versus 71.91% in Year 6). While continued improvement in gross profit margin is possible, it will be difficult to achieve. The key for a profit ratio to benefit from improved gross profit margin is continued control over administrative and marketing expenses. This analysis is corroborated by our earlier trend index analysis. Exhibit CC.8 shows sales in Year 11 are 145 percent higher than for Year 6. Yet cost of products sold is only 133 percent greater, and the total of costs and expenses is 142 percent greater. This combination yields a net income that is 180 percent larger than the Year 6 level. The general inference from these trend indexes is that sales, gross margin, and net income are growing at a relatively faster rate than costs and expenses.

Exhibit CC.8 reveals that interest expense grew throughout the six-year period but at a relatively lower rate than did total liabilities, except for Year 11. This reflects a lower cost of borrowing resulting primarily from lower interest rates. We also note that Campbell is probably a more risky borrower compared to three to five years earlier as reflected in its increasing debt to equity ratio.

The Supplemental Schedule of Sales and Earnings in Campbell's annual report (item 1) shows the contributions of international operations to Year 11. International earnings total $92.3 million, including $35.3 million from Campbell Canada, $17.6 million from International Biscuit, and $39.4 million from Campbell International. International earnings represents about 11.6 percent of total operating earnings. In Years 10 and 9, international operations contribute negatively to total earnings. This is due to the restructuring in those years, reducing total operating earnings by $134.1 million in Year 10 and by $82.3 million in Year 9. These negative contributions are in addition to losses from foreign currency translation of $3.8 million and $20.0 million in Years 10 and 9, respectively. Foreign currency translation is not significant in Year 11. Nevertheless, international operations for the past six years comprise nearly 20 percent of total sales (see Exhibit CC.1). International operations are expected to continue to exert a significant impact on Campbell's profitability.

Campbell's effective tax rate (note 9) is 39.8 percent in Year 11, 97.5 percent in Year 10, and 87.7 percent in Year 9. The extraordinarily high rates for the latter two years are due mainly to the large amounts of nondeductible divestiture, restructuring, and unusual charges, representing 56.5 and 48.7 percent of earnings before taxes, respectively (note 9). If we exclude these divestitures, the effective tax rate declines to about 40 percent. Campbell is also taking advantage of tax loss carryforward benefits from international subsidiaries. At the end of Year 11 the company has $77.4 million remaining in unused tax loss carryforward benefits. About one-half of these expire by Year 16 and the remainder are available indefinitely. Most deferred taxes result from pensions, depreciation timing differences, divestiture, restructuring, and unusual charges. Deferred taxes due to depreciation differences are relatively large through Year 10, then decline to a low of $5.9 million in Year 11.

Analysis of depreciation data for Campbell is reported in Exhibit CC.24. This evidence shows that accumulated depreciation as a percent of gross plant assets remains stable (44.6% in Year 11). Stability in depreciation expense, as a percent of either plant assets or sales, is also evident in Exhibit CC.24. Accordingly, there is no evidence that earnings quality is affected due to changes in depreciation.

Analysis of discretionary expenditures in Exhibit CC.25 shows spending in all major categories during Year 11 declines compared to most prior years. This potentially results from more controlled spending and enhanced efficiencies. Recall our common-size analysis of factors affecting net earnings in Exhibit CC.6. This analysis is corroborative of some of the factors evidenced in Exhibit CC.25. For example, gross margin is increasing while (on a relative basis) increases in marketing, selling, interest, and "other" expenses outpace increases in sales. Administrative expenses and research and development expenses are not increasing with sales. Statutory tax rates decline over this period, thereby holding down growth in tax expenses. Profitability increases because the growth in gross margin is not offset with increases in expenses.

Recast income statements of Campbell for the most recent six years were reported in Exhibit 13.1. These recast statements support many of the observations recognized in this section. Campbell's adjusted income statements for this same period are shown in Exhibit 13.2. The adjusted statements reveal an increasing trend in net

Exhibit CC.24

CAMPBELL SOUP COMPANY
Analysis of Depreciation

	Year 11	*Year 10*	*Year 9*	*Year 8*	*Year 7*	*Year 6*
1. Accumulated depreciation as a percent of gross plant assets*	44.6%	42.3%	43.1%	43.7%	46.6%	48.6%
2. Annual depreciation expenses as a percent of gross plant	7.7%	7.7%	7.6%	6.9%	6.4%	6.4%
3. Annual depreciation expenses as a percent of sales	3.1%	3.0%	3.1%	3.3%	3.1%	2.8%

Computations for Year 11:

(1) $\frac{1{,}131.5 \ \boxed{162}}{758.7 \ \boxed{159} + 1{,}779.3 \ \boxed{160}} = 44.6\%$

(2) $\frac{194.5 \ \boxed{162A}}{758.7 \ \boxed{159} + 1{,}779.3 \ \boxed{160}} = 7.7\%$

(3) $\frac{194.5 \ \boxed{162A}}{6{,}204.1 \ \boxed{13}} = 3.1\%$

* Exclusive of land and projects in progress.

Exhibit CC.25

CAMPBELL SOUP COMPANY
Analysis of Discretionary Expenditures
($ millions)

	Year 11	*Year 10*	*Year 9*	*Year 8*	*Year 7*	*Year 6*
Net sales	$6,204.1	$6,205.8	$5,672.1	$4,868.9	$4,490.4	$4,286.8
Plant assets (net)*	1,406.5	1,386.9	1,322.6	1,329.1	1,152.0	974.1
Maintenance and repairs	173.9	180.6	173.9	155.6	148.8	144.0
Advertising	195.4	220.4	212.9	219.1	203.5	181.4
Research & development (R&D)	56.3	53.7	47.7	46.9	44.8	42.2
Maintenance and repairs ÷ sales	2.8%	2.9%	3.1%	3.2%	3.3%	3.4%
Maintenance and repairs ÷ plant	12.4	13.0	13.1	11.7	12.9	14.8
Advertising ÷ sales	3.1	3.6	3.8	4.5	4.5	4.2
R&D ÷ sales	0.9	0.9	0.8	1.0	1.0	1.0

* For analytical purposes 50 percent of deferred income taxes are considered debt and the remainder equity.
† Including notes payable—current.

income from Year 9 to Year 10—this contrasts with reported income. The average earning power calculation for the six-year period includes all charges and is $193.9 million.

Summary Evaluation and Inferences

Our comprehensive case analysis considered all facets of Campbell Soup Company's operating results and financial position. We also forecasted accrual and cash flow figures. This type of analysis, modified for our analysis perspective, is valuable for informed business decisions. While these data and information from our analysis are indispensable, they are not sufficient in arriving at a final decision. This is because other qualitative and quantitative factors should be brought to bear on our decision. For example, our earlier banker's decision on whether to extend short-term credit must take into consideration the character of management, prior loan experience, and the bank's relationship with the loan applicant. If this involved a long-term loan decision, our banker would also want to assess collateral arrangements, event risk, solvency of the applicant, and possible loan restrictions. An equity investor would be interested in earning power and other earnings-based analyses before making an investment decision. Financial analysis gives us information on what earnings are and are likely to be. It also gives us insight into price-to-book and price-to-earnings ratios. An equity investor would also want information on a company's business risk, earnings volatility, and the breadth and quality of the market for its securities. These additional factors determine whether an investment fits with one's portfolio and investment objectives.

Since our lending, investing, or other business analysis decisions require more information than provided in financial analysis, we often summarize our analysis and its inferences in a financial analysis report. This report (see the discussion earlier in this chapter) lists the most relevant and salient findings from our analysis, which depend on our analysis perspective. The remainder of this section provides a brief listing of the main findings of our analysis of Campbell Soup Company.

Short-Term Liquidity

Our assessment of Campbell's short-term liquidity is a mixed one. Both current and acid-test ratios do not compare favorably with industry norms. Yet Campbell's cash position compares favorably with its industry, and its accounts receivable and inventory turnover ratios are better than industry norms. Moreover, Campbell's conversion period is better (less) than that of the industry, and its cash position is strong, allowing for cash to be used for nonoperating activities like acquisitions and retirement of debt.

Cash Flows and Forecasts

Campbell has substantial and increasing operating cash flows, the only exception is Year 9 due to inventory increases. Its operating cash flows comprise over half of all cash inflows. Purchases and acquisitions of plant assets represent outflows totaling nearly 50 percent of the cash inflows. Another 12 percent of cash inflows are used for dividends.

Cash forecasts for Years 12 and 13, using various assumptions, suggest that Campbell will likely finance expected investments in plant assets from its growing operating cash flows. We predict little to no additions to liabilities. Campbell's cash flow adequacy ratio confirms these inferences and implies that operating cash flows are sufficient to cover most capital expenditures, investment in inventories, and cash dividends. Campbell's average cash reinvestment ratio is at a solid 16.5 percent for the past six years.

Capital Structure and Solvency

Campbell has aggressively transformed its capital structure in recent years to a less conservative one. This inference is drawn from absolute and industry comparative measures. Total liabilities comprise about 53 percent of total financing, and long-term liabilities alone equal about one-half of equity. On the positive side, both earnings to fixed charges and cash flow to fixed charges ratios are strong, the exception being earnings-coverage ratios for Years 9 and 10 (due to restructuring). These strong ratios imply solid protection for Campbell's creditors. The company also has the strength to take on additional debt, and the market continues to assign Campbell a superior credit rating (AA).

Return on Invested Capital

Campbell's return on assets varies. In Years 6 through 8 it is stable at around 9.5 percent, but in Years 9 and 10 it declines to a low of around 2 percent due primarily to divestiture, restructuring, and unusual charges. In Year 11, return on assets rebounds to a strong 11.75 percent, comprised of a 6.47 percent profit margin and an asset turnover of 1.50. Campbell's return on assets for Year 11 compares favorably to the industry average of 9.2 percent. Campbell's return on common equity is 21.52 percent for Year 11 and exceeds the industry average of 19.8 percent. This return also evidences setbacks in Years 9 and 10 for the same reasons as the return on assets. An important factor affecting return on common equity (beyond the same components comprising return on assets) is financial leverage. The leverage ratio equals 2.22 in Year 11 and is higher than in prior years mainly due to a more risky capital structure. Another favorable finding is Campbell's increased equity growth rate for Year 11, due in large part to strong earnings and a higher rate of earnings retention.

Asset Turnover (Utilization)

Campbell's asset turnover is relatively stable. While its turnover of cash and cash equivalents fluctuates from year to year, Campbell's accounts receivable and inventory turnovers are improving and exceed industry norms. These improvements are due mainly to Campbell's efforts to reduce working capital through, among other activities, less receivables and inventories. Nevertheless, asset turnover compares favorably to the industry despite the relatively low cash turnover and fixed assets turnover.

Operating Performance and Profitability

Campbell's gross profit margin is steadily improving and above the industry average. Yet its net profit margin is not as solid. This is due primarily to increased operating expenses, and the limitations with Campbell's management in controlling these expenses. Recent activities suggest that Campbell is attempting to gain greater control over these expenses.

Financial Market Measures

Selected financial market measures for Campbell are shown in Exhibit CC.26. The first four measures reflect the market's valuation of Campbell's equity securities, while the fifth (dividend payout) reflects more management discretion. Earnings per share figures for Years 9 and 10 are adjusted to exclude the effect of divestitures, restructuring, and unusual charges. Without these adjustments, the market measures are less relevant for our analysis. While earnings per share increases from $1.72 in Year 6 to $3.16 in Year 11, the earnings yield declines over the same period because of steadily increasing price-to-earnings and price-to-book ratios. This is mainly due to strong equity markets. Similarly, while dividends per share increase from $0.65 in Year 6 to $1.12 in Year 11, the dividend yield declines from 2.5 percent to 1.74 percent over the same period. Declines in earnings yield and dividend yield are attributable mainly to steady increases in price-to-earnings and price-to-book ratios. Both ratios reflect the market's appreciation and confidence in Campbell's prior and expected performance. Our analysis shows Campbell's operating performance is strong despite temporary declines in Years 9 and 10.

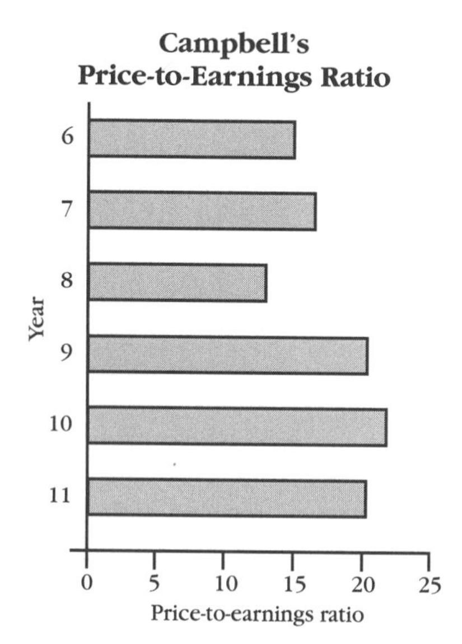

Source: Exhibit CC.26.

Higher price-to-earnings and price-to-book ratios benefit a company in several ways. These include the ability to raise a given amount

Exhibit CC.26

CAMPBELL SOUP COMPANY
Market Measures

	Year 11	*Year 10**	*Year 9**	*Year 8*	*Year 7*	*Year 6*
1. Price-to-earning (range)	27–14	26–18	29–12	16–11	19–14	20–10
2. Price-to-book (range)	6.0–3.1	4.7–3.2	4.5–1.8	2.3–1.6	2.7–2.0	2.9–1.5
3. Earnings yield	4.91%	4.53%	4.91%	7.45%	6.20%	6.61%
4. Dividend yield	1.74%	1.88%	2.08%	2.85%	2.32%	2.50%
5. Dividend payout ratio	35.44%	41.53%	42.45%	38.21%	37.37%	37.79%

Computations for Year 11:
(1) High and Low for the year: High—84.88/3.16=27; Low—43.75/3.16=14 [see item **184**].
(2) High and Low for the year: High—84.88/14.12=6.0; Low—43.75/14.12=3.1 [see item **185**].
(3) Earnings per share/Average market price = 3.16/ [(84.88 + 43.75)/2] = 4.91%.
(4) Dividend per share/Average market price = 1.12/64.32 = 1.74%.
(5) Dividend per share/Earnings per share = 1.12/3.16 = 35.44%.
* Year 10 and Year 9 results are shown for EPS *before* effects of divestitures, restructuring, and unusual charges of $2.33 and $2.02 per share, respectively.

of equity capital by issuing fewer shares and the ability to use common stock as a means of payment for acquisitions. Yet increasing stock valuations expose existing and particularly new common shareholders to increasing risks, including the risk of stagnating or reversing stock valuations. This occurs because, unlike in early stages of a bull market, prices can potentially deviate from company fundamentals in reflecting upward price momentum. When stock valuations reflect this price momentum, experience shows it is promptly erased once information on the fundamentals fails to support it. Assessing price momentum, as important and crucial as it is for equity investing, cannot be gauged by means of the analysis tools here. They involve our study of market expectations and cycles. The difference between Campbell's return on its invested capital and an equity investor's return on investment is discussed in Chapter 11.

Using Financial Statement Analysis

Our comprehensive analysis of the financial statements of Campbell Soup Company consisted of two major parts: (1) detailed analysis, and (2) summary and inferences. In our *analysis report*, the summary and inferences (executive summary) often precedes detailed analysis. The detailed analysis section is usually directed at a specific user. For example, our bank loan officer who must decide on a short-term loan application typically directs attention to short-term liquidity and cash flow analysis and forecasting. A secondary objective of the loan officer is to assess capital structure and operating performance. Regarding the investment committee of our insurance company scenario, it would take a more long-term perspective. This implies primary attention directed at capital structure and long-term solvency. Its secondary focus is on operating performance, return on invested capital, asset utilization, and short-term liquidity (in order of emphasis). Finally, the potential investor in Campbell shares has varying interest in all aspects of our analysis. The emphasis across areas is different, and the likely order of priority is operating performance, return on invested capital, capital structure, long-term solvency, and short-term liquidity. A competent financial statement analysis contains sufficient detailed evaluation along with enough information and inferences to permit its use by different users with varying perspectives.

QUESTIONS

CC–1. What type of investigation should precede analysis of financial statements?

CC–2. What are the analytical implications of recognizing that financial statements are an abstraction of a company's underlying business transactions and events?

CC–3. Identify and describe the six major building blocks of financial statement analysis. What does the building block approach involve?

CC–4. What are the attributes of a good financial analysis report? What distinct sections comprise a complete financial analysis report?

CC–5. What additional knowledge and analytical skills must our analysis bring to bear on companies operating in specialized or regulated industries?

EXERCISES

Exercise CC–1

Distinguishing Industry Classification by Company Financial Statements

Reproduced below are condensed common-size financial statements of companies operating in nine different industries. The nine industries represented are:

a. Tobacco manufacturing
b. Pharmaceuticals
c. Health care
d. Utilities
e. Investment advising
f. Breweries
g. Grocery stores
h. Computer equipment
i. Public opinion surveys

Required:

Examine the relations in the balance sheets and income statements below and match the (1) through (9) companies with the (*a*) through (*i*) industries. It might be helpful to consult published industry ratios.

Company Balance Sheets*

Account	*(1)*	*(2)*	*(3)*	*(4)*	*(5)*	*(6)*	*(7)*	*(8)*	*(9)*
Current receivables	9.77%	19.20%	3.35%	25.96%	0.55%	8.10%	26.34%	17.38%	15.33%
Inventories	6.22	14.87	5.18	0.00	7.91	20.11	31.69	0.00	0.00
Net plant and equipment	224.39	28.20	51.20	24.52	6.94	26.25	31.36	88.97	3.19
Other assets	46.56	29.15	5.48	26.65	3.71	18.50	16.91	24.35	219.59
Total assets	286.94%	91.42%	65.21%	77.13%	19.11%	72.96%	106.30%	130.70%	238.11%
Cost of P&E (gross)	279.83%	39.06%	70.33%	35.78%	9.64%	39.31%	45.91%	106.64%	6.29%
Current liabilities	18.78%	22.70%	11.19%	29.92%	7.31%	13.31%	19.30%	19.33%	76.89%
Long-term liabilities	158.69	9.22	26.65	10.19	6.06	16.40	4.11	73.32	72.18
Shareholders' equity	109.47	59.50	27.37	37.02	5.74	43.25	82.89	38.05	89.04
Total liabilities and equity	286.94%	91.42%	65.21%	77.13%	19.11%	72.96%	106.30%	130.70%	238.11%

*All numbers expressed as a percent of total revenues.

Company Income Statements

Account	*(1)*	*(2)*	*(3)*	*(4)*	*(5)*	*(6)*	*(7)*	*(8)*	*(9)*
Revenues	100.00%	100.00%	100.00%	100.00%	100.00%	100.00%	100.00%	100.00%	100.00%
Cost of sales*	49.50	31.11	67.48	63.29*	77.20	68.16	56.24	81.06*	16.55*
Depreciation expense	8.36	2.26	2.47	3.51	1.14	3.50	4.76	4.33	0.81
Interest expense	8.81	1.14	2.03	0.47	0.59	1.26	0.31	4.04	10.75
Advertising expense	0.00	2.39	4.82	0.12	3.89	6.97	3.86	0.00	6.24
R&D expense	0.76	7.95	0.24	0.00	0.00	0.00	11.06	0.00	0.00
Income taxes	11.47	8.11	2.44	6.80	0.77	4.71	2.98	4.44	33.01
All other items (net)	6.63	29.08	15.59	18.54	15.50	8.89	14.15	(0.46)	0.73
Total expenses	85.53%	82.04%	95.07%	92.73%	99.09%	93.49%	93.36%	93.41%	68.09%
Net income	14.47%	17.96%	4.93%	7.27%	0.91%	6.51%	6.64%	6.59%	31.91%

* Companies (4), (8), and (9) carry zero inventory, where cost of sales is primarily operating expenses.

Exercise CC–2

Evaluating Relative Price-to-Earnings (PE) Ratios

Discuss factors determining the relative price-to-earnings ratios assigned to each of two manufacturers of mountain bikes for which the following financial data are available:

	AXEL	*BIKE*
Capital structure:		
5% 20-year notes	$10,000,000	None
Common equity	20,000,000	$30,000,000
Number of common shares	500,000	750,000
Earnings per share:		
Year 6	$ 4.25	$ 3.00
Year 5	3.50	2.50
Year 4	2.25	1.67
Year 3	2.75	2.00
Year 2	1.70	1.95
Sales (Year 6)	30,000,000	30,000,000
Net income	2,125,000	2,250,000
Balance sheet data at end of Year 6:		
Cash and cash equivalents	3,000,000	5,850,000
Accounts receivable	5,000,000	3,750,000
Inventories	12,000,000	10,000,000
Total current assets	$20,000,000	$19,600,000
Accounts payable	4,000,000	3,500,000
Accrued expenses	2,000,000	2,000,000
Taxes payable	1,000,000	1,100,000
Total current liabilities	$ 7,000,000	$ 6,600,000
Net plant and equipment	13,000,000	15,900,000
Patents, net	4,000,000	100,000

(CFA Adapted)

PROBLEMS

Problem CC–1 Forecasting Future Profitability

Refer to the financial statement data of ABEX Chemicals, Inc., reproduced in Case 10–3.

Required:

a. Prepare a forecast of ABEX's total operating income for Year 10.

b. Identify additional information necessary to prepare a forecast of earnings per share (EPS) for Year 10, and identify five primary sources where you can obtain this information (you should identify *primary* sources and not necessarily external sources for the information needed).

c. Forecast and explain incremental changes in ABEX's earnings per share based on each of the following two independant scenarios for the petrochemical division only.
1. Price of polyethylene in Year 10 is 8 percent higher than shown in the selected key statistics.
2. Volume of production and sales of polyethylene is 8 percent higher than shown in the selected key statistics.

(CFA Adapted)

Problem CC–2 Analysis of Bond Investment

You are the portfolio manager of a high-yield bond portfolio at Solomon Group. You are concerned about the financial stability of Florida Gypsum Corporation (FGC), whose bonds represent one of the holdings in your portfolio at the *middle of Year 6.* The bonds you hold, 13.25 percent senior subordinated debentures due in Year 16, were issued at par in Year 5, and are currently priced in your portfolio at 53. Your high-yield bond sales staff is not optimistic they can even develop a bid at that level. FGC is a large producer of gypsum products, accounting for approximately one-third of total gypsum sales in the United States. The company also manufactures ceiling tile, caulks, sealants, floor and wall adhesives, and other specialty building products. In addition, FGC operates 137 distribution centers, where it markets many of its building products, particularly gypsum wallboard.

In Year 5, FGC did a leveraged recapitalization of its balance sheet. This involved paying a large dividend to common shareholders financed with several new subordinated debt financings, including the 13.25 percent debentures that you hold. The company's primary competitor, American Gypsum, is highly leveraged, following its acquisition by a large Canadian concern. Due to a downturn in residential and commercial construction activity beginning in Year 4, demand for gypsum wallboard fell off markedly through the middle of Year 6. However, capacity continues to expand at a rate of nearly 2 percent per year. As a result, capacity utilization has declined to 85 percent currently, from 87 percent in Year 4 and a peak of 95 percent in Years 1 and 2. The price of 1/2-inch wallboard, which peaked in Year 2 at about $121 per 1,000 square feet, has declined to about $83 currently.

To help you in analyzing FGC's prospects, you assemble various financial data that are reproduced below. The director of fixed income research at Solomon Group suggests that you look carefully at ratios of short-term liquidity and operating performance, specifically the quick ratio, accounts receivable turnover ratio, inventory turnover ratio, and operating profit margin. You prepare the table below and schedule a meeting with the director to discuss what the firm should do with FGC.

FLORIDA GYPSUM CORPORATION
Selected Liquidity and Operating Performance Ratios

	Year Ended		*Six Months Ended*
	Year 4	*Year 5*	*Mid-Year 6*
Quick (acid-test) ratio	0.73	0.78	0.77
Accounts receivable turnover	8.9	8.1	7.4
Inventory turnover	11.4	12.4	13.3
Operating profit margin	16.6%	13.3%	14.9%

Financial statement data for Florida Gypsum Corporation include the following:

FLORIDA GYPSUM CORPORATION
Balance Sheets
(millions)

	As of Year 4	*As of Year 5*	*As of middle of Year 6*
Assets			
Current assets:			
Cash & cash equivalents	$ 31.3	$ 250.0	$ 95.6
Accounts receivable	274.1	278.3	320.4
Inventories	144.1	124.6	128.4
Net assets of discontinued operations	415.1	20.4	—
Total current assets	$ 864.6	$ 673.3	$ 544.4
Property, plant, & equipment	909.0	906.4	878.4
Purchased goodwill	148.9	146.5	144.5
Other assets	35.0	95.0	90.0
Total assets	$1,957.5	$1,821.2	$1,657.3
Liabilities and shareholders' equity			
Current liabilities:			
Commercial paper & notes payable	$ 38.3	$ 1.3	$ 1.6
Accounts payable	141.6	125.4	125.2
Accrued expenses	188.2	256.9	244.0
Other current liabilities	14.8	38.7	13.7
Current portion of long-term debt	33.0	259.3	154.5
Total current liabilities	$ 415.9	$ 681.6	$ 539.0
Long-term debt	724.9	2,384.3	2,344.0
Deferred income tax	194.1	206.2	212.6
Minority interest	12.8	20.0	22.0
Shareholders' equity	609.8	(1,470.9)	(1,460.3)
Total liabilities and shareholders' equity	$1,957.5	$1,821.2	$1,657.3

FLORIDA GYPSUM CORPORATION
Income Statements
(millions)

	Year Ended		***Six Months Ended***
	Year 4	*Year 5*	*Mid-Year 6*
Net sales	$2,254.4	$2,248.0	$1,107.7
Cost of goods sold	(1,598.6)	(1,671.9)	(841.4)
Gross profit	$ 655.8	$ 576.1	$ 266.3
Selling and administrative expenses	(268.7)	(253.7)	(122.9)
Interest expense	(69.2)	(178.3)	(148.9)
Interest income	5.3	12.7	4.8
Recapitalization & restructuring expenses	(53.4)	(20.0)	—
Other expenses, net	34.3	(15.9)	17.0
Pre-tax earnings from continuing operations	$ 304.1	$ 120.9	$ 16.3
Income taxes	(130.9)	(48.2)	(5.9)
Earnings from continuing operations	$ 173.2	$ 72.7	$ 10.4

FLORIDA GYPSUM CORPORATION
Selected Cash Flow Data
($ millions)

	Year Ended		Six Months Ended
	Year 4	*Year 5*	*Mid-Year 6*
Cash Flow from Operations:			
Earnings from continuing operations	$173.2	$ 72.7	$ 10.4
Depreciation, depletion, & amortization	76.6	83.0	42.5
Noncash interest expense	—	19.1	22.3
Minority interest	13.2	9.1	4.0
Deferred income taxes	1.5	12.6	6.4
Other noncash items relating to operations	15.2	(6.1)	(11.7)
(Increase) decrease in working capital (excluding cash)	43.8	91.8	(84.1)
Other cash flows from operations	(24.0)	(62.0)	3.9
Total net cash flow from operations	$299.5	$220.2	$ (6.3)
Net Liquid Balance:			
Cash and cash equivalents	$ 31.3	$250.0	$ 95.6
Less notes payable	(38.3)	(1.3)	(1.6)
Less current portion of long-term debt	(33.0)	(259.3)	(154.5)
Net liquid balance	$(40.0)	$(10.6)	$(60.5)
Net liquid balance as percent of total assets	(2.0)%	(0.6)%	(3.7)%

Required:

a. The director of fixed income research argues that the four ratios you compute do not reveal changes in the financial condition of FGC. Discuss limitations of these ratios in assessing liquidity and operating performance of a company like FGC.

b. You suggest there are better measures of short-term liquidity and operating performance for FGC. Identify two such measures, calculate their values, and discuss their trend over the period Year 4 through middle of Year 6. Explain why these measures better reflect FGC's financial condition.

c. Based on the analysis performed in *(b)* and on the background information provided, recommend and justify whether you should attempt to sell the FGC bonds, retain them, or buy more FGC bonds.

(CFA Adapted)

Problem CC–3 Analysis of Credit Quality

Selected financial ratios from the (i) S&P 400, (ii) the brewing industry, and (iii) Anheuser-Busch Companies, Inc. (BUD), for Years 2 through 6 are reproduced on the next page.

Required:

a. Using these financial ratios, analyze the relative credit position of:
1. Brewing industry compared with the S&P 400.
2. Anheuser-Busch compared with the brewing industry.
3. Anheuser-Busch compared with the S&P 400.

b. Using these financial ratios and your analysis from (*a*), describe the current position of Anheuser-Busch and discuss whether you feel there has been a change in the credit quality of Anheuser-Busch during this five-year period.

	Year 2			Year 3			Year 4			Year 5			Year 6		
	S&P 400	*Brewing Industry*	*BUD*	*S&P 400*	*Brewing Industry*	*BUD*	*S&P 400*	*Brewing Industry*	*BUD*	*S&P 400*	*Brewing Industry*	*BUD*	*S&P 400*	*Brewing Industry*	*BUD*
Current ratio	1.5	1.3	1.1	1.5	1.4	1.2	1.5	1.3	1.1	1.4	1.5	1.2	1.4	1.4	1.0
Quick ratio	0.9	0.7	0.4	0.9	0.8	0.7	0.8	0.7	0.05	0.8	1.0	0.6	0.7	0.8	0.4
Long-term debt/total assets (%)	24	21	25	23	18	22	25	15	18	26	15	17	27	17	19
Total debt ratio (%)	43	37	41	42	36	39	44	31	34	48	32	33	48	34	37
Times interest earned	4.0	7.2	12.2	4.6	7.5	12.7	4.8	7.6	13.3	4.2	10.1	14.9	3.6	11.0	9.8
Cash flow/long-term debt (%)	54	52	43	61	70	55	65	84	71	57	88	79	51	80	73
Cash flow/total debt (%)	23	29	26	25	35	32	25	39	38	20	40	40	20	38	38
Total asset turnover	1.2	1.2	1.2	1.2	1.4	1.4	1.2	1.5	1.6	1.2	1.3	1.5	1.1	1.3	1.4
Net profit margin (%)	3.95	5.36	6.3	4.42	5.58	5.8	4.77	5.12	6.0	3.84	5.73	6.3	3.75	6.16	6.17
Return on assets (%)	4.64	6.46	7.4	5.10	7.98	8.0	5.80	7.47	8.7	4.41	7.66	8.7	3.97	7.90	8.89

* Total debt is defined as long-term debt plus current liabilities.

CASES

Case CC–1 Comprehensive Financial Analysis

Select a company from a nonregulated industry for which you can obtain complete financial statements for at least the most recent six years.

Required:

Based on these financial statements, the company's background, industry statistics, and other market and company information, prepare a financial statement analysis report covering the following points:

a. Executive summary of the company and its industry.

b. Detailed evaluation of:
1. Short-term liquidity (current debt-paying ability).
2. Cash forecasting and pro forma analysis.
3. Capital structure and solvency.
4. Return on invested capital.
5. Asset turnover (utilization).
6. Profitability and earnings-based analysis.
   Note: You are expected to use a variety of financial analysis tools in answering (*b*). Your analysis should yield inferences for each of these six areas.

c. Comment on the usefulness of the financial statements of this company for your analysis.

d. How did accounting principles used in the financial statements affect your analytical measures?

Case CC–2 Comprehensive Financial Analysis

Financial statements and notes of ZETA Corporation are reproduced below.

Required:

Answer the following questions and identify supporting calculations. Explain the accounts and amounts used in analyses.

a. What caused the $7,000 increase in stockholders' equity for Year 6?

b. Note 6 discloses "capitalized lease obligations" of $1,000. What journal entry is made in Year 6 to record these leases? How are these leases reflected in the statement of cash flows?

c. Use T-account analysis to determine how much long-term debt is paid in Year 6? Does your answer agree with the amount reported by ZETA?

d. Note 1 describes a change in accounting principle.
1. What effect did this change in accounting have on the Year 6 balance sheet and income statement?

ZETA CORPORATION
Consolidated Balance Sheets
As of December 31, Year 6 and Year 5
(thousands)

	Year 6	Year 5
Assets		
Current assets:		
Cash	$ 2,000	$ 2,000
Receivables	25,000	20,000
Inventories (notes 1 and 2)	56,000	38,000
Prepaid expenses	1,000	1,000
Total current assets	$ 84,000	$ 61,000
Investment in associated companies	14,000	11,000
Property, plant, and equipment	61,000	52,000
Less: accumulated depreciation	(23,000)	(19,000)
Net property, plant, and equipment	$ 38,000	$ 33,000
Goodwill	2,000	—
Total assets	$138,000	$105,000
Liabilities and Stockholders' Equity		
Current liabilities:		
Notes payable to banks	$ 16,000	$ 14,000
Accounts payable and accruals	29,000	23,000
Income taxes payable	7,000	2,000
Current portion of long-term debt (note 6)	2,000	1,000
Total current liabilities	$ 54,000	$ 40,000
Long-term debt (note 6)	25,000	15,200
Deferred income taxes (note 5)	3,600	2,000
Minority interest	1,400	800
Stockholders' equity (note 7):		
Common stock, $5 par value	5,500	5,000
Paid-in capital	24,500	15,000
Retained earnings	24,000	27,000
Total stockholders' equity	$ 54,000	$ 47,000
Total liabilities and stockholders' equity	$138,000	$105,000

2. Describe how the Year 5 balance sheet and income statement should be adjusted for our analytical comparison of Year 5 with Year 6.
3. How would the $1,000 "cumulative effect" for Year 6 be reported in a statement of cash flows (direct method). Your description must be sufficiently clear for someone else to prepare a cash statement using your description. (*Hint:* You need to discuss figures, and start by reconstructing the journal entry to record the $1,000.)

e. Note 3 describes ZETA's acquisition of TRO Company.
1. Is TRO a separate legal entity at December 31, Year 6, or is it dissolved into ZETA?
2. What effect did the acquisition of TRO Company have at December 31, Year 6 (date of acquisition), on the:
   i. ZETA balance sheet?
   ii. Consolidated balance sheet?
3. What are TRO's revenues for Year 6?

f. For the asset "investment in associated companies":
1. Explain all changes during Year 6.
2. Identify all effects in the statement of cash flows relating to this investment.

ZETA CORPORATION
Consolidated Income Statement
For Years Ended December 31, Year 6, and Year 5
(thousands)

	Year 6	*Year 5*
Net sales	$186,000	$155,000
Equity in income (loss) of associated companies	2,000	(1,000)
Expenses:		
Cost of sales	120,000	99,000
Selling and administrative expenses	37,000	33,000
Interest expense	10,000	6,000
Total costs and expenses	$167,000	$138,000
	$ 21,000	$ 16,000
Income tax expense (note 5)	10,000	7,800
	$ 11,000	$ 8,200
Minority interest	200	—
Income from continuing operations	$ 10,800	$ 8,200
Discontinued operations (note 4):		
Operations, net of tax	(1,100)	(1,200)
Loss on disposal, net of tax	(700)	—
Total gain (loss) from discontinued operations	$ (1,800)	$ (1,200)
	$ 9,000	$ 7,000
Cumulative effect of change in accounting, net of tax (note 1)	1,000	—
Net income	$ 10,000	$ 7,000
Pro forma income (assuming change in accounting is applied retroactively):		
Income from continuing operations	$ 10,800	$ 8,500
Discontinued operations	(1,800)	(1,200)
Total pro forma net income	$ 9,000	$ 7,300

g. For the minority interest reported in the balance sheet:
1. Explain all changes during Year 6.
2. Show how this account relates to the asset "investment in associated company."

h. If the FIFO method of inventory valuation is used (instead of LIFO), how much would Year 6 net income be increased or decreased?

i. Note 4 describes "discontinued operations":
1. What journal entries are made on October 31, Year 6, to record the loss on disposal?
2. What effect did the loss on disposal of $700 have on the statement of cash flows? (Identify specific items and amounts.)
3. How should the discontinued operation and $1,100 operating loss be reported in a statement of cash flows using the direct format, assuming we desire to include these operations among cash inflows and outflows?

j. How is goodwill reflected in the Year 7 (next year) statement of cash flows?

k. Explain all changes during Year 6 in the Net Property, Plant, and Equipment account.

ZETA CORPORATION
Consolidated Statement of Cash Flows
For Years Ended December 31, Year 6, and Year 5
(thousands)

		Year 6	*Year 5*
Cash provided from (used for) operations:			
Net income		$ 10,000	$ 7,000
Add (deduct) adjustments to cash basis:			
Depreciation		6,000	4,000
Deferred income taxes		1,600	1,000
Minority interest		200	—
Undistributed income of associated companies		(1,400)	1,300
Loss on discontinued operations		700	—
Increase in accounts receivable (5,000 – 2,000†)		(3,000)	(2,400)
Increase in inventories (18,000 + 100* – 2,200†)		(15,900)	(6,000)
Increase in prepaid expenses		—	(200)
Increase in accounts payable and accruals (6,000 – 300* – 3,200†)		2,500	2,000
Increase in income taxes payable (5,000 + 700)*		5,700	1,000
Net cash provided from (used for) operations		$ 6,400	$ 7,700
Cash provided from (used for) investing activities:			
Additions to property, plant, and equipment		$ (6,500)	$(5,800)
Acquisition of TRO Company (excluding cash of $4,200):			
Property, plant, and equipment	$(6,000)		
Goodwill	(2,000)		
Long-term debt	4,800		
Minority interest	400		
Current assets (receivables and inventories)	(4,200)		
Current liabilities	3,200	(3,800)	—
Investment in associated companies		(1,600)	—
Proceeds from disposal of equipment		500	—
Net cash used for investing activities		$(11,400)	$(5,800)
Cash provided from (used for) financing:			
Issuance of long-term debt		$ 7,500	$ 5,000
Reduction in long-term debt		(1,500)	(1,000)
Dividends paid		(3,000)	(2,000)
Increase (decrease) in notes payable to bank		2,000	(3,500)
Net cash provided from (used for) financing activities		$ 5,000	$(1,500)
Net increase (decrease) in cash‡		$ 0	$ 400

*Adjustments of noncash transactions arising from discontinued operations (see note 4).

†Adjustments relating to acquisition of TRO Co (note 3).

‡Supplemental disclosures of cash flow information:	Year 6	Year 5
Cash paid for interest	10,000	6,000
Cash paid for income taxes	2,600	4,800

Schedule of noncash activities:
Capital lease of $1,000 incurred on the lease of equipment

ZETA CORPORATION
Notes to Consolidated Financial Statements
For Years Ended December 31, Year 6, and Year 5
(all amounts in thousands)

Note 1: Change in accounting principle

During Year 6, the company broadened its definition of overhead costs to be included in the determination of inventories to more properly match costs with revenues. The effect of the change in Year 6 was to increase income from continuing operations by $400. The adjustment of $1,000 (after reduction for income taxes of $1,000) for the cumulative effect for prior years is shown in the net income for Year 6. The pro forma amounts show the effect of retroactive application of the revised inventory costing assuming that the new method had been in effect for all prior years.

Note 2: Inventories

Inventories are priced at cost (principally last-in, first-out [LIFO] method of determination) not in excess of replacement market. If the first-in, first-out (FIFO) method of inventory acounting had been used, inventories would have been $6,000 and 4,500 higher than reported at December 31, Year 6, and December 31, Year 5, respectively.

Note 3: Acquisition of TRO Company

Effective December 31, Year 6, the company purchased most of the outstanding common stock of TRO company for $8,000 in cash. The excess of the acquisition cost over fair value of the net assets acquired, $2,000, will be amortized on a straight-line basis over a 40-year period. The following unaudited supplemental pro forma information shows the condensed results of operations as though TRO company had been acquired as of January 1, Year 5.

	Year 6	*Year 5*
Revenues	$205,000	$172,000
Net income	10,700	7,400

Details of acquisition:

Cash	4,200	
Accounts Receivable	2,000	
Inventories	2,200	
Property, Plant, & Equipment	6,000	
Long Term Debt		4,800
Accounts payable & Accruals		3,200

Note 4: Discontinued operations

As of October 31, Year 6, the board of directors adopted a plan authorizing the disposition of the assets and business of its wholly owned subsidiary, Zachary Corporation. The "Loss on Disposal" is $700 (net of income tax credits of $700) and is based upon the estimated realizable value of the assets to be sold plus a provision for costs of $300 for operating the business until its expected disposition in early Year 7. Property, plant, and equipment has been reduced by $1,000 and inventories were reduced by $100 to net realizable value. The provision for costs of $300 was included in "Accounts payable and accruals" and has been reduced to $200 at year-end. Net sales of the operations to be discontinued were $18,000 in Year 6 and $23,000 in Year 5.

Note 5: Income taxes

The income tax expense consists of the following:

	Year 6	*Year 5*
Current	$ 8,400	$6,800
Deferred	1,600	1,000
Total	$10,000	$7,800

The effective tax rates of 47.6 percent and 48.8 percent for Year 6 and Year 5, respectively, differ from the statutory federal income tax rate of 50 percent* due to research and development tax credits of $500 in Year 6 and $200 in Year 5.

Deferred taxes result from the use of accelerated depreciation methods for income tax reporting and the straight-line method for financial reporting.

Note 6: Long-term debt

	Year 6	*Year 5*
10% promissory notes to institutional investors payable in annual installments of $900 through Year 10	$13,000	$13,900
Unsecured notes to banks—interest 1% over prime	4,000	—
Capitalized lease obligations—payable to Year 9 with an average interest rate of 8%	1,000	—
11% subordinated note payable in annual installments of $500 from Year 7 through Year 16	5,000	—
Other mortgages and notes	4,000	2,300
	$27,000	$16,200
Less current maturities	2,000	1,000
Total long-term debt	$25,000	$15,200

The various loan agreements place certain restrictions on the corporation including the payment of cash dividends on common stock and require the maintenance of working capital, as defined, of not less than $18,000. Approximately $10,000 of retained earnings was available for payment of cash dividends on common stock at December 31, Year 6. The corporation entered into several long-term noncancelable leases of equipment during Year 6 which have been capitalized for financial reporting. There are no other significant lease arrangements.

Note 7: Stockholders' equity

The corporation has 5 million shares of authorized common stock, par value $5. There were 1 million shares outstanding at December 31, Year 5, and this was increased by a 10 percent dividend payable in common stock during Year 6. The changes in retained earnings are as follows:

	Year 6	*Year 5*
Beginning balance	$27,000	$22,000
Add net income	10,000	7,000
Less cash dividends	(3,000)	(2,000)
Less 10% stock dividend	(10,000)	—
Ending balance	$24,000	$27,000

Case CC–3

Comprehensive Analysis of Equity Investments

The Policy Committee of your company decides to change investment strategies. This change entails an increase in exposure to the stocks of large companies producing consumer products dominated by leading brands. The committee decides the soft drink industry, specifically Coca-Cola Company (KO) and Coca-Cola Enterprises (CCE), qualify as potential purchases for your company's portfolio. As the company's beverage industry expert, you must prepare a financial analysis of these two soft drink producers.

KO owns the brands included in its broad product line. Its marketing efforts center on worldwide advertising promoting these soft drinks. KO manufactures primarily soft drink extract. The production process requires only low-cost raw materials and relatively limited fixed asset investment. Extract is inexpensive to ship and requires only 44 production facilities throughout the world. KO's position as a leading soft drink extract producer is protected by the technical nature of its manufacturing process, the restricted formula for its product, and strong brand names established from over a century of operations. Competition is limited essentially to one competitor, PepsiCo, Inc. KO plays almost no direct role in domestic manufacturing and distribution beyond the output of soft drink extract.

CCE's business is also dominated by soft drinks. CCE purchases extract from KO and transforms it into completed products sold in a wide variety of retail outlets throughout the United States. This costly, complex production and distribution system requires approximately 300 plants and warehouses, and approximately 18,000 vehicles. Marketing efforts emphasize local promotion. Competition consists of a large number of highly automated, similarly organized companies also manufacturing soft drinks from extract.

Selected financial statements and notes for these two companies are reproduced below:

Consolidated Balance Sheets
December 31, Year 8
($ millions)

	Coca-Cola Company (KO)	*Coca-Cola Enterprises (CCE)*
Assets		
Current assets:		
Cash & cash equivalents	$1,231	$ —
Trade accounts receivable	627	294
Inventories	779	125
Other current assets	608	69
Total current assets	$3,245	$ 488
Other investments:		
Investments in affiliates	1,912	—
Other	478	66
Total other investments	$2,390	$ 66
Fixed assets:		
Land	117	135
Plant and equipment	2,500	1,561
Other	293	42
Total fixed assets	$2,910	$1,738
Less: accumulated depreciation	(1,150)	(558)
Total net fixed assets	$1,760	$1,180
Goodwill	57	2,935
Total assets	$7,451	$4,669
Liabilities & shareholders' equity		
Current liabilities:		
Short-term debt	$1,363	$ 148
Accounts payable	1,081	402
Other	425	—
Total current liabilities	$2,869	$ 550
Long-term debt	761	2,062
Deferred income taxes	270	222
Other long-term liabilities	206	27
Shareholders' equity:		
Preferred stock	300	250
Common stock	3,045	1,558
Total shareholder's equity	$3,345	$1,808
Total liabilities & shareholders' equity	$7,451	$4,669

Year 8 Consolidated Statements of Income
(millions except per share data)

	Coca-Cola Company (KO)	*Coca-Cola Enterprises (CCE)*
Revenue	$8,338	$3,874
Cost of goods sold	(3,702)	(2,268)
Gross profit	$4,636	$1,606
Selling & administrative expenses	(3,038)	(1,225)
Provision for restructuring	—	(27)
Operating profit	$1,598	$ 354
Interest expense	(231)	(211)
Gain on sale of operations	—	104
Equity in income of affiliates	48	—
Other income	167	21
Pre-tax income	$1,582	$ 268
Income taxes	(538)	(115)
Net income	$1,044	$ 153
Preferred cash dividends	(6)	(10)
Income available for common	$1,038	$ 143
Earnings per share	$ 2.85	$ 1.03

Data Extracted from Financial Statement Footnotes

Coca-Cola Company (KO)

1. Certain soft drink and citrus inventories are valued on the last-in first-out (LIFO) method. The excess of current costs over LIFO stated values amounted to approximately $30 million at December 31, Year 8.
2. The market value of the company's investments in publicly traded equity investees exceeded the company's carrying value at December 31, Year 8, by approximately $291 million.
3. The company is contingently liable for guarantees of indebtedness owed by some of its licensees and others, totaling approximately $133 million at December 31, Year 8.
4. Pension plan assets total $496 million. The projected benefit obligation for all plans totals $413 million.

Coca-Cola Enterprises (CCE)

1. Inventory cost is computed principally on the last-in first-out (LIFO) method. At December 31, year 8, the LIFO reserve was $2,077,000.
2. In December Year 8, the company repurchased for cash various outstanding bond issues. These transactions resulted in a pre-tax gain of approximately $8.5 million.
3. The company leases office and warehouse space, and machinery and equipment under lease agreements. At December 31, Year 8, future minimum lease payments under noncancellable operating leases were as follows ($ thousand):

Year 9	$11,749
Year 10	8,436
Year 11	6,881
Year 12	4,972
Year 13	3,485
Later years	11,181
Total	$46,704

4. Pension plan assets total $197 million. Total projected benefit obligation for all plans is $151 million.

Selected Financial Ratios*
For Year 8

	Coca-Cola Company (KO)	*Coca-Cola Enterprises (CCE)*
Return on assets	0.16	0.06
Total debt ratio	0.55	0.61
Net profit margin	0.13	0.04
Receivables turnover	13.30	13.18
Property, plant, & equipment turnover	4.74	3.28
Return on common equity	0.34	0.09
Current ratio	1.13	0.89
Inventory turnover	4.75	18.14
Long-term debt to equity	0.23	1.14
Gross profit margin	0.56	0.41
Acid-test ratio	0.65	0.53
Asset turnover	1.12	0.83
Times interest earned	7.85	2.27

* For simplicity, ratios are computed on year-end data rather than on Year 8 average data.

Required:

Use *only* the financial information reproduced here in answering questions (*a*)–(*c*).

a. Your comparative analysis of these two soft drink companies requires using the ratios reported above. You identify four key areas of comparison in your analysis:
   1. Short-term liquidity.
   2. Capital structure and solvency.
   3. Asset utilization.
   4. Profitability.

   Discuss differences between KO and CCE in each of these four areas.

b. Using the financial statement information, identify *five* adjustments to the financial statements you feel enhance their comparability and usefulness for financial analysis. For each of your five adjustments, discuss the effects of these adjustments on your answer to (*a*).

(CFA Adapted)

Internet Activities

Internet CC–1

Comprehensive Financial Analysis

Access one of the financial statement databases available on the Internet (http://www.mhhe.com/business/accounting/wild). Retrieve current financial statements of a company from a nonregulated industry selected by either you or your instructor. Be certain you can obtain financial statements for at least the most recent five years

Required

Based on these financial statements, the company's background, its industry statistics, and other market and company information (e.g., analysts' forecasts and recommendations), prepare a financial statement analysis report covering the following:

a. Executive summary of the company and its industry.

b. Detailed evaluation of:
   1. Short-term liquidity (current debt-paying ability).

2. Cash forecasting and pro forma analysis.
3. Capital structure and solvency.
4. Return on invested capital and asset turnover (utilization).
5. Profitability and earnings-based analysis.

Note: You are expected to use a variety of financial analysis tools in answering part *b*. Your analysis should yield inferences for each of these five areas.

c. Comment on the usefulness of the financial statements of this company for your analysis.

d. How did the accounting principles used in the financial statements affect your measures for analysis?

Internet CC–2

Comparative Financial Analysis

Access one of the financial statement databases available on the Internet (http://www.mhhe.com/business/accounting/wild). Retrieve current financial statements of two companies in the same industry selected by either you or your instructor.

Required:

a. Conduct a comparative analysis of these two companies using the financial analysis tools discussed in this chapter and throughout the book. Your analysis should cover four key areas of comparison:

1. Short-term liquidity.
2. Capital structure and solvency.
3. Asset turnover (utilization).
4. Profitability and earnings-based analysis.

Write a comparative financial statement analysis report for these two companies covering these four areas.

b. Using these companies' financial statement, identify five adjustments that you feel enhance your comparative financial analysis.

c. For each of your five adjustments identified in *b*, discuss the effects of each for your answer in *a*.

S U P P L E M E N T

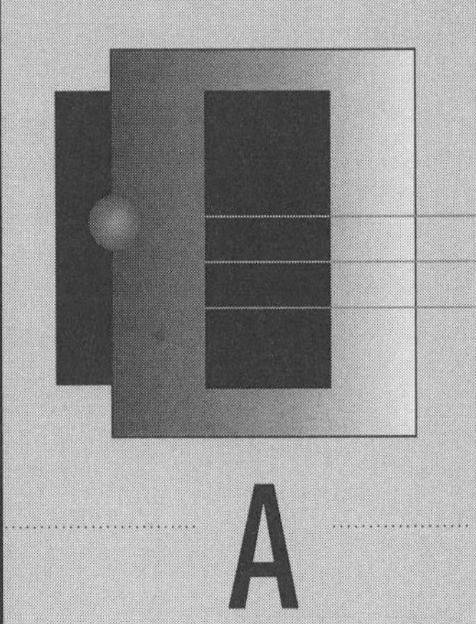

A

Financial Statements

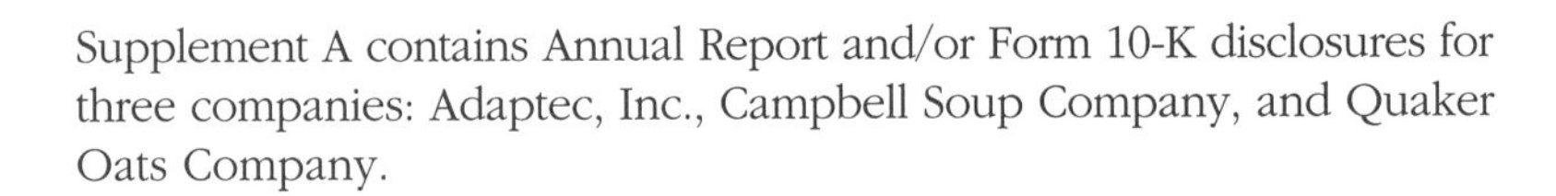

Supplement A contains Annual Report and/or Form 10-K disclosures for three companies: Adaptec, Inc., Campbell Soup Company, and Quaker Oats Company.

For ease in referencing, selected items are identified by key numbers [1]–[187].

Quaker is an international marketer of consumer food products, including cereals, mixes, grain-based snacks, syrup, corn products, rice and pasta products, chocolates, beans, edible oils, beverages, and pet foods. The company has plant facilities in 16 U.S. states and in western Europe, Canada, and LatinAmerica. Approximately 11,000 of Quaker's 21,000 employees are located in the United States. The auditor's opinion on the company's annual report is unqualified.

For ease in referencing, selected items are identified by numbers [1]–[162].

ABC & D

All About
Being Connected
to Data

ADAPTEC 1996 ANNUAL REPORT

Dear Shareholders,

Adaptec had an outstanding year in fiscal 1996. We are pleased to report that we achieved our 47th consecutive profitable quarter and again posted record revenues and profits. Our financial results reflect our strengths in providing several important market segments with the high-performance I/O, connectivity, and network products they require. The results also underscore our ability to expand opportunities and increase the number of solutions we offer. We are proud of Adaptec's leading role as a provider of foundation technology to the burgeoning global information infrastructure.

For the year, revenues were $659 million, a 41 percent increase over the prior year's $466 million. After a one-time charge for acquired in-process technology, net income was $103 million, an 11 percent increase over last year's $93 million. Earnings per share for the fiscal year were $1.89, an 8 percent increase over fiscal year 1995. Excluding this one-time charge of $0.73 per share, earnings grew 50 percent over fiscal 1995, to $2.62 per share. Adaptec's cash and investments at the end of the fiscal year were $295 million, compared to $247 million in the previous fiscal year.

Demand for our products during the fiscal year was very strong. All our major business areas grew substantially, including host adapter solutions for both high-performance desktop systems and network servers and embedded controller chips for peripherals. We also achieved our first revenues from our entry into the market for ATM network interface cards.

Our OEM customer list now includes all major PC system manufacturers such as Compaq, Dell, Digital, Gateway, Hewlett-Packard, IBM, Intel, Siemens, as well as other well-known brands. As these companies continued to supply the high-end market, we experienced growth in the number of servers and desktops using our products. PCI-based products also became dominant in the PC and server markets, and our introduction of UltraSCSI products saw immediate strong market acceptance. And, with our continued focus on high-performance solutions, we also achieved new design wins with RISC systems manufacturers.

The explosive growth of Internet and Intranet applications is driving new demands for bandwidth — demand that is being met by Adaptec's range of host adapters. The rapid acceptance of PCI-based servers and our introduction of Fast SCSI and Ultra Wide SCSI host adapters are enabling Web sites to move more data from storage to the Internet. In fact, server performance can be more restricted by the I/O bandwidth than by the CPU performance, which is why there is such a growing market for the expandability and speed offered by Adaptec's products.

Developments in our international business were also positive. Throughout the year we saw good growth in Europe. Growth in Japan was extremely strong as the entire country upgrades its computing infrastructure, including corporate networks.

Our mass storage electronics business achieved strong sales, particularly in Asia and Japan where we have achieved strategic supplier status with several important customers. Subsequent to the fiscal year end, our leadership position in this market was further underscored by the acquisition of Western Digital's Connectivity Solutions Group business unit, which has been consolidated with our business. We are particularly pleased by the growth in backlog of design wins and the penetration we are achieving in new markets. We anticipate further growth with the market acceptance of new peripherals such as recordable CD and popular removable storage devices.

Throughout the year we took advantage of healthy cash flows from operations to make strategic investments. This included acquiring complementary companies and technologies, selected for their potential to help us gain market share, expand our business reach, leverage our core competencies, and enable us to add value on a long-term basis.

In our second fiscal quarter we acquired Trillium Research, Inc., a developer and manufacturer of RAID software solutions for the Apple market. In the same quarter we acquired Future Domain Corporation, which added a complementary set of desktop I/O products to our portfolio and has added to our processor-independent solutions for the RISC-based systems market.

Also in the second quarter we acquired Incat Systems Software USA, Inc., which develops and markets application and I/O management software for recordable CD peripherals. And in the third quarter we acquired Power I/O Corporation, a developer of high-speed I/O and networking technologies that will enhance our offering in the client-server computing environment.

Assuring a high-quality, uninterrupted source of semiconductors for our products was a critical success factor for the year. We supported this goal through an agreement with Taiwan Semiconductor Manufacturing Company Ltd. to guarantee silicon supply into the next century for both current and future technologies. We also signed a significant agreement with AT&T Microelectronics, which expands our technology base as well as assures silicon supply. And, as part of our Western Digital transaction, we obtained capacity with SGS-Thomson Microelectronics, a world-class supplier of foundry services.

Looking forward, we expect the percentage of systems using SCSI to continue to grow and for SCSI to retain its position as the dominant high-functionality, high-performance I/O interface. We also continue to prepare for new market opportunities in the longer term through ongoing development of products based on serial interfaces such as 1394 and Fibre Channel.

In the last year, we achieved a significant share of the ATM market for network interface cards. As we move ahead, we anticipate bringing our proven core competencies to other high-performance networking areas with products based on technologies other than ATM.

Since our inception, Adaptec's technologies and products have grown and evolved in breadth and sophistication, until they have become a keystone to high-performance computing. Yet the shorthand term we use to refer to our business — bandwidth management — often conceals its enormous value.

The ability to achieve high-performance connectivity and to move digital data quickly and reliably is critical to a growing information infrastructure that is global in scale. Whether it takes place between the desktop PC and its high-capacity peripherals, between a mobile computer and a remote server, or between enterprise clients and servers on a network, the ability to manage and transfer data streams at ever faster speeds represents a fundamental contribution to productivity. This foundation technology is as important to computing performance as are multitasking operating systems or the latest generation of central processing unit.

With the adoption of exciting applications and tools like distributed storage, data warehousing, and RAID, the need for reliable, high-performance connectivity is expanding rapidly.

Businesses today are built around the availability of computers and data. The value of the data to the business can be incalculable, yet the cost of the devices storing and using it is really very small. This is where Adaptec's core competencies of performance, compatibility, reliability, and ease of use, add sustainable value to our customers. We enable our customers to exploit the full value of their data by reliably, easily, and speedily moving it to wherever users need it.

Despite our many products, our expertise in silicon design, and our broad software competencies, Adaptec's business is elegantly simple: we provide technology to manage the bandwidth our customers need to use information more quickly and more easily. As in past years, our annual report's thematic section is designed to communicate our business and its value in a memorable, straightforward way. Together with the information in our financial section, we hope it tells a compelling story of Adaptec's value. As always, we thank our employees, shareholders, partners, suppliers and customers for their support. We look forward to sharing our future with you.

Results of Operations

The following table sets forth the items in the consolidated statements of operations as a percentage of net revenues:

Year Ended March 31	1996	1995	1994
Net revenues	100%	100%	100%
Cost of revenues	42	44	51
Gross margin	58	56	49
Operating expenses			
Research and development	13	13	11
Sales and marketing	13	13	12
General and administrative	5	5	5
Write-off of acquired in-process technology	8	—	—
	39	31	28
Income from operations	19	25	21
Shareholder settlement	—	—	(1)
Interest income, net	2	2	1
Income before income taxes	21	27	21
Provision for income taxes	5	7	5
Net income	16%	20%	16%

Management's Discussion and Analysis

OF FINANCIAL CONDITION AND RESULTS OF OPERATIONS

Fiscal 1996 Compared to Fiscal 1995

The Company experienced growth worldwide as net revenues increased 41% to $659 million in fiscal 1996 from $466 million in fiscal 1995. The Company's continued increase in net revenues was driven by growth of client-server networking environments, complex microcomputer based applications requiring high-performance I/O, and the expanded adoption of various peripheral devices. This growth combined with the Company's market leadership in SCSI solutions resulted in increased net revenues from the Company's host adapters. During the year, the Company also began shipping products incorporating newer technologies such as RAID, ATM and CD-Recordable (CD-R) software. Fiscal 1996 net revenue from sales of mass storage integrated circuits (ICs) also increased from the prior year as the Company benefitted from next-generation design wins for higher capacity disk drives that are required for advanced applications.

Gross margin of 58% in fiscal 1996 increased from 56% in fiscal 1995. Gross margin was favorably affected by the increased revenues from the Company's higher margin products. The Company's focus on design for manufacturability allowed it to continue to experience efficiencies in the manufacturing process and accelerate time to customer volume.

Research and development expenditures in fiscal 1996 were $88 million, an increase of 44% over fiscal 1995. As a percentage of net revenues, research and development expenses were 13% for both fiscal 1996 and fiscal 1995. The Company's research and development efforts continue to be focused on solutions which enhance performance in single-user desktop, enterprise-wide computing, and networked environments. This commitment included investing in its current core SCSI business as well as several emerging technologies encompassing RAID, CD-R, ATM, and serial architectures such as 1394 and Fibre Channel. The Company believes these expenditures, consisting primarily of increased staffing levels, have allowed the Company to maintain its position in technical leadership and product innovation. The Company believes it is essential to continue this significant level of investment in research and development and anticipates actual spending in fiscal 1997 will increase.

Sales and marketing expenses increased to $82 million in fiscal 1996, an increase of 39% over fiscal 1995. As a percentage of net revenues, fiscal 1996 sales and marketing expenses were 13% in both fiscal 1996 and fiscal 1995. The increase in actual spending was a result of advertising and promotional programs aimed at generating demand in the consumer and enterprise computer markets and increased staffing levels to support the continued growth of the Company. The Company's promotional and advertising programs have allowed it to leverage its brand image around the globe. The Company believes that sales and marketing expenditures will increase in fiscal 1997 primarily to support its existing products as well as products resulting from newer technologies.

General and administrative expenses as a percentage of net revenues were consistent at

5% for both fiscal 1996 and fiscal 1995. Actual spending increased from fiscal 1995, primarily due to increased staffing to support the continued growth of the Company. The Company anticipates general and administrative expenditures will increase in fiscal 1997 to support its growth.

During the year, the Company acquired Trillium Research, Inc. (Trillium), Future Domain Corporation (Future Domain), Incat Systems Software USA, Inc. (Incat), and Power I/O, Inc. (Power I/O). These acquisitions were accounted for using the purchase method of accounting. Among the assets acquired was in-process technology, resulting in write-offs totaling $52 million. Excluding these write-offs, the Company's results of operations for fiscal 1996 were not materially affected by these acquisitions.

Interest income, net of interest expense, was $12 million in fiscal 1996, an increase of $5 million over fiscal 1995. The increase was primarily due to the increase in cash and cash equivalents and marketable securities partially offset by lower interest expense.

The Company's effective tax rate for fiscal 1996 was 25%, the same as fiscal 1995. During fiscal 1996, the Company concluded negotiations with the Singapore government extending the tax holiday for the Company's manufacturing subsidiary. The terms of the tax holiday provide that profits derived from certain products will be exempt from tax for a period of 10 years, subject to certain conditions. In addition, profits derived from the Company's remaining products will be taxed at a rate of 15%, which is lower than the statutory rate of 27%, through fiscal 1998.

While the Company has experienced significant growth in revenues and profitability, various factors could adversely affect its results of operations in the future including its reliance on the high-performance microcomputer and server markets, changes in product mix, competitive pricing pressures, fluctuations in manufacturing yields, changes in technological standards, availability of components, changes in product costs, timing of new product introductions and market demand for these products, capacity for wafer fabrication, the accounting effect of acquisitions of other companies or businesses that the Company may make from time to time, or general economic downturns.

Fiscal 1995 Compared to Fiscal 1994

Net revenues increased 25% to $466 million in fiscal 1995 from $372 million in fiscal 1994. The continued adoption of SCSI in personal computers (PCs) resulted in increased sales of the Company's SCSI host adapter products across all performance ranges. Additionally, demand for the Company's host adapters was driven by the growing use of file servers where SCSI usage approaches 100%. During fiscal 1995, the Company introduced several new IOware® solutions ranging from connectivity products for the single-user and small-office markets, to high-performance products for enterprise-wide computing and networked environments. The market acceptance of the Company's high-performance host adapters for the PCI local bus market resulted in the fastest product ramp in the Company's history. The Company's fiscal 1995 revenue from mass storage ICs was comparable to the prior year. The Company believes this was due to the timing of design win cycles at original equipment manufacturers (OEMs) coupled with significant fluctuations in demand experienced in the disk drive market. During fiscal 1995 the Company won key designs for next-generation products at major OEMs in the Pacific Rim.

Gross margin of 56% in fiscal 1995 increased from 49% in fiscal 1994. Gross margin was favorably affected by the increased revenues from the Company's higher margin SCSI host adapters. The Company also continued to experience component cost reductions and manufacturing efficiencies, including the move of the IC production test facility to Singapore where costs are lower. This also allowed the Company to shorten the manufacturing cycle time and better serve its customers.

Research and development expenditures in fiscal 1995 were $61 million, an increase of 52% over fiscal 1994. As a percentage of net revenues, research and development expenses increased to 13% in fiscal 1995 compared to 11% in fiscal 1994. This was primarily due to increased staffing levels. The Company continued to invest in its SCSI products, where it has captured a leadership position by improving system performance as the computer industry has become more I/O intensive with more powerful CPUs, multitasking operating systems, and a new generation of intelligent peripherals. While SCSI solutions remained the core of the Company's business, fiscal 1995 saw the Company broaden its portfolio of solutions to include ATM, RAID, serial I/O and infrared technology.

Sales and marketing expenses increased to $59 million in fiscal 1995, an increase of 27% over fiscal 1994. As a percentage of net revenues, fiscal 1995 sales and marketing expenses were 13% compared to 12% in fiscal 1994. The increase in actual spending was a result of increased staffing levels to support the continued growth of the Company, including expansion of the Company's international sales and marketing infrastructure. Additionally, increases in advertising and promotional expenses were aimed at strategies to further accelerate and expand SCSI acceptance in the marketplace and drive demand for the Company's products.

General and administrative expenses as a percentage of net revenues in fiscal 1995 were consistent with fiscal 1994 at 5%. Actual spending increased from fiscal 1994, primarily due to increased staffing to support the continued growth of the Company.

Interest income, net of interest expense, was $7 million in fiscal 1995, an increase of $3 million over fiscal 1994. The increase was primarily due to the increase in cash and cash equivalents and marketable securities coupled with slightly higher average yields on cash and investment balances.

The Company's effective tax rate for fiscal 1995 was 25%, the same as fiscal 1994.

Liquidity and Capital Resources

Operating Activities Net cash generated from operating activities during fiscal 1996 was $103 million compared to $118 million in fiscal 1995. This aggregate decrease was a result of the increase in the Company's current assets to support its overall growth. During fiscal 1996, the majority of funds generated from operations resulted from $103 million of net income adjusted by non-cash items including a non-recurring write-off of acquired in-process technology (net of taxes) of $40 million and depreciation and amortization of $18 million. Additionally contributing to favorable operating cash flows was an increase in accrued liabilities of $22 million reflecting the overall growth of the Company. Offsetting these were increases in current assets, excluding cash and investments, of $60 million. This increase in assets primarily resulted from the Company's continued overall growth.

During fiscal 1996, the Company signed an agreement with Taiwan Semiconductor Manufacturing Co., Ltd. (TSMC) that will ensure availability of a portion of the Company's wafer capacity for both current and future technologies. The agreement, which runs through 2001, provides the Company with a guarantee of increased capacity for wafer fabrication in return for advance payments. The Company made advance payments of $20 million during fiscal 1996 relating to this agreement. This agreement is in addition to an existing contract with TSMC for guaranteed supply and technology.

During fiscal 1995, the majority of funds generated from operations resulted from $93 million of net income adjusted by non-cash items including depreciation and amortization of $16 million. Also contributing to favorable cash flows was a decrease in net inventories of $7 million and increases in accrued liabilities and accounts payable of $7 million. During fiscal 1995, the Company paid an additional advance payment on a deposit and supply agreement to support its silicon wafer requirements.

During fiscal 1994, the Company's net cash generated from operating activities primarily resulted from $59 million of net income adjusted by non-cash items including depreciation and amortization of $11 million. An increase in accrued liabilities of $9 million also contributed to positive cash flows. These items were mainly offset by increases in accounts receivable and other assets totaling $24 million.

Investing Activities The Company made payments of $31 million in connection with the acquisitions of Trillium, Future Domain, and Power I/O during the year. Additionally, the Company acquired Incat through the issuance of 385,000 shares of common stock with a fair market value of $17 million. Also in fiscal 1996, the Company continued to invest in equipment for product development and manufacturing to support increased demand for its products and future business requirements. Additionally, to provide for future growth the Company purchased land for $12 million.

During fiscal years 1996, 1995, and 1994, the Company continued to invest significant amounts of funds in marketable securities consisting mostly of highly rated municipal instruments.

During the 1997 fiscal year, the Company anticipates it will invest approximately $75 million in equipment for future product innovation and development as well as land and facilities to support its growth. Also, during fiscal 1996, the Company signed an agreement with AT&T Corporation (AT&T), acting through its Microelectronics business division, that will ensure availability of a portion of the Company's wafer capacity for both current and future technologies. This contract, which runs through 2001, provides the Company with a guaranteed supply of wafers in return for an investment in fabrication equipment of up to $25 million for AT&T's fabrication facility located in Madrid, Spain. The sources for capital expenditures are expected to be funds generated from operations and available sources of financing as well as working capital presently on hand.

Subsequent to year end, the Company acquired certain assets and the ongoing business of Western Digital's Connectivity Solutions Group (CSG) which primarily designs, manufactures and markets controller ICs for high-capacity disk drives. In connection with the acquisition, the Company was assigned capacity for wafer fabrication. The Company paid $33 million cash for CSG and will pay future consideration based on certain performance criteria. The Company will account for this acquisition using the purchase method of accounting and will evaluate the allocation of the purchase price to assets acquired, which includes in-process technology that will be written off. The results of operations for CSG were immaterial relative to the Company's financial statements.

Financing Activities During fiscal 1996, the Company continued to receive proceeds from the issuance of common stock under its Employee Stock Option and Employee Stock Purchase Plans totaling $27 million. Also, the Company repurchased 260,000 shares of its common stock through open market transactions totaling $8 million. In fiscal 1995, two million shares totaling $37 million were repurchased. In connection with the TSMC agreement, the Company also issued a $46 million note payable due in June 1996.

Subsequent to year end, the Company acquired all of the outstanding capital stock of Cogent Data Technologies, Inc. (Cogent) in a $68 million stock transaction. Cogent provides high-performance Fast Ethernet products for the networking market. The Company will record this acquisition using the pooling method of accounting and will record acquired assets and assumed liabilities at their book values as of the acquisition date. The results of operations for Cogent for the three year period ended March 31, 1996 were immaterial relative to the Company's financial statements.

The Company has an unsecured $17 million revolving line of credit under which there were no outstanding borrowings as of March 31, 1996. The Company's liquidity is affected by various factors, some based on its continuing operations of the business and others related to the industry and global economies. Although the Company's cash situation will fluctuate based on the timing of these factors, the Company believes that existing working capital combined with expected cash generated from operations and available sources of bank and equipment financing will be sufficient to meet its cash requirements throughout fiscal 1997.

Consolidated Statements of Operations

IN THOUSANDS, EXCEPT PER SHARE AMOUNTS

Year Ended March 31	1996	1995	1994
Net revenues	$659,347	$466,194	$372,245
Cost of revenues	275,939	205,596	189,526
Gross profit	383,408	260,598	182,719
Operating expenses			
Research and development	87,628	60,848	39,993
Sales and marketing	81,548	58,737	46,192
General and administrative	35,784	23,229	19,399
Write-off of acquired in-process technology	52,313	—	—
	257,273	142,814	105,584
Income from operations	126,135	117,784	77,135
Shareholder settlement	—	—	(2,409)
Interest income	12,694	7,932	5,183
Interest expense	(840)	(1,179)	(1,306)
	11,854	6,753	1,468
Income before income taxes	137,989	124,537	78,603
Provision for income taxes	34,614	31,135	19,653
Net income	$103,375	$ 93,402	$ 58,950
Net income per share	$ 1.89	$ 1.75	$ 1.10
Weighted average number of common and common equivalent shares outstanding	54,569	53,357	53,602

See accompanying notes.

Consolidated Balance Sheets

IN THOUSANDS

As of March 31	1996	1995
Assets		
Current assets		
Cash and cash equivalents	$ 91,211	$ 66,835
Marketable securities	204,283	179,911
Accounts receivable, net of allowance for doubtful accounts of $4,220 in 1996 and $4,431 in 1995	89,487	56,495
Inventories	55,028	31,712
Prepaid expenses and other	25,271	15,519
Total current assets	465,280	350,472
Property and equipment, net	92,778	67,863
Other assets	88,428	17,373
	$646,486	$435,708
Liabilities and Shareholders' Equity		
Current liabilities		
Current portion of long-term debt	$ 3,400	$ 3,400
Note payable	46,200	—
Accounts payable	23,974	22,008
Accrued liabilities	56,717	31,006
Total current liabilities	130,291	56,414
Long-term debt, net of current portion	4,250	7,650
Commitments (Note 7)		
Shareholders' equity		
Preferred stock		
Authorized shares, 1,000		
Outstanding shares, none	—	—
Common stock		
Authorized shares, 200,000		
Outstanding shares, 53,020 in 1996 and 51,677 in 1995	182,932	140,191
Retained earnings	329,013	231,453
Total shareholders' equity	511,945	371,644
	$646,486	$435,708

See accompanying notes.

Consolidated Statements of Cash Flows

IN THOUSANDS

Year Ended March 31	1996	1995	1994
Cash Flows From Operating Activities:			
Net income	$103,375	$ 93,402	$ 58,950
Adjustments to reconcile net income to net cash provided by operating activities:			
Write-off of acquired in-process technology, net of taxes	39,686	—	—
Depreciation and amortization	17,593	15,662	11,489
Provision for doubtful accounts	250	150	2,069
Changes in assets and liabilities:			
Accounts receivable	(30,727)	(1,311)	(13,020)
Inventories	(20,516)	7,228	(5,563)
Prepaid expenses	(8,973)	460	(5,470)
Other assets	(19,111)	(4,107)	(11,478)
Accounts payable	(167)	2,354	(2,781)
Accrued liabilities	21,969	4,251	8,867
Net Cash Provided by Operating Activities	103,379	118,089	43,063
Cash Flows From Investing Activities:			
Purchase of Trillium, Future Domain and Power I/O, net of cash acquired	(31,177)	—	—
Investments in property and equipment	(39,748)	(31,576)	(17,314)
Investments in marketable securities, net	(24,372)	(32,291)	(20,250)
Net Cash Used for Investing Activities	(95,297)	(63,867)	(37,564)
Cash Flows From Financing Activities:			
Proceeds from issuance of common stock	27,459	17,174	13,511
Repurchase of common stock	(7,765)	(36,548)	—
Principal payments on debt	(3,400)	(3,400)	(2,968)
Net Cash Provided by (Used for) Financing Activities	16,294	(22,774)	10,543
Net Increase in Cash and Cash Equivalents	24,376	31,448	16,042
Cash and Cash Equivalents at Beginning of Year	66,835	35,387	19,345
Cash and Cash Equivalents at End of Year	$ 91,211	$ 66,835	$ 35,387

See accompanying notes.

Consolidated Statements of Shareholders' Equity

IN THOUSANDS

	Common Stock		Retained	
	Shares	Amount	Earnings	Total
Balance, March 31, 1993	50,714	$124,806	$100,349	$225,155
Sale of common stock under employee purchase and option plans	1,577	7,728	—	7,728
Income tax benefit of employees' stock transactions	—	5,783	—	5,783
Net income	—	—	58,950	58,950
Balance, March 31, 1994	52,291	138,317	159,299	297,616
Sale of common stock under employee purchase and option plans	1,426	11,245	—	11,245
Income tax benefit of employees' stock transactions	—	5,929	—	5,929
Repurchases of common stock	(2,040)	(15,300)	(21,248)	(36,548)
Net income	—	—	93,402	93,402
Balance, March 31, 1995	51,677	140,191	231,453	371,644
Sale of common stock under employee purchase and option plans	1,218	16,512	—	16,512
Issuance of common stock in connection with acquisition	385	17,232	—	17,232
Income tax benefit of employees' stock transactions	—	10,947	—	10,947
Repurchases of common stock	(260)	(1,950)	(5,815)	(7,765)
Net income	—	—	103,375	103,375
Balance, March 31, 1996	53,020	$182,932	$329,013	$511,945

See accompanying notes.

Notes to Consolidated Financial Statements

NOTE ONE: SUMMARY OF SIGNIFICANT ACCOUNTING POLICIES

Basis of Presentation The consolidated financial statements include the accounts of the Company and its wholly-owned subsidiaries after elimination of intercompany transactions and balances. Foreign currency transaction gains and losses are included in income as they occur. The preparation of financial statements in conformity with generally accepted accounting principles requires management to make estimates and assumptions that affect the reported amounts of assets and liabilities and disclosure of contingent assets and liabilities at the date of the financial statements and the reported amounts of revenues and expenses during the reporting period. Actual results could differ from those estimates.

Revenue Recognition The Company recognizes revenue generally at the time of shipment or upon satisfaction of contractual obligations. The Company records provisions for estimated returns at the time of sale.

Fair Value of Financial Instruments The Company measures its financial assets and liabilities in accordance with generally accepted accounting principles. For certain of the Company's financial instruments, including cash and cash equivalents, marketable securities, accounts receivable, accounts payable and accrued expenses, the carrying amounts approximate fair value due to their short maturities. The amounts shown for long-term debt also approximate fair value because current interest rates offered to the Company for debt of similar maturities are substantially the same.

Marketable Securities At March 31, 1996, the Company's marketable securities are classified as available for sale and are reported at fair market value which approximates cost. Marketable securities with maturities after one through three years totaled $153,996,000 with all remaining securities maturing less than one year. Realized gains and losses are based on the book value of the specific securities sold and were immaterial during fiscal 1996, 1995 and 1994.

Concentration of Credit Risk Financial instruments that potentially subject the Company to significant concentrations of credit risk consist principally of cash and cash equivalents, marketable securities and trade accounts receivable. The Company places its marketable securities primarily in municipal securities. The Company, by policy, limits the amount of credit exposure through diversification and investment in highly rated securities. Sales to customers are primarily denominated in U.S. dollars. As a result, the Company believes its foreign currency risk is minimal.

The Company sells its products to original equipment manufacturers and distributors throughout the world. The Company performs ongoing credit evaluations of its customers' financial condition and, generally, requires no collateral from its customers. The Company maintains an allowance for uncollectible accounts receivable based upon the expected collectibility of all accounts receivable. There were no significant amounts charged to this allowance during the current year.

Inventories Inventories are stated at the lower of cost (first-in, first-out) or market.

Property and Equipment Property and equipment are stated at cost and depreciated or amortized using the straight-line method over the estimated useful lives of the assets. During 1995, the Financial Accounting Standards Board issued Statement of Financial Accounting Standards No. 121 "Accounting for the Impairment of Long-Lived Assets and for Long-Lived Assets to be Disposed Of" (SFAS 121) which will be effective for the Company in fiscal 1997. The Company does not expect that adoption of SFAS 121 to have a material impact on its financial position or results of operations.

Income Taxes The Company accounts for income taxes under the asset and liability method. Under this method, deferred tax assets and liabilities are recognized for the future tax consequences attributable to temporary differences between the financial statement carrying amounts and the tax basis of existing assets and liabilities measured using enacted tax rates expected to apply to taxable income in the years in which the temporary differences are expected to be recovered or settled.

Net Income Per Share Net income per share is computed under the treasury stock method using the weighted average number of common and common equivalent shares from dilutive options outstanding during the respective periods.

Cash and Cash Equivalents Cash and cash equivalents consist of funds in checking accounts, money market funds and marketable securities with original maturities of three months or less.

NOTE TWO: SUPPLEMENTAL FINANCIAL INFORMATION

Marketable Securities

IN THOUSANDS	1996	1995
Municipal securities	$203,305	$169,972
U.S. Government securities and other	978	9,939
	$204,283	$179,911

Inventories

IN THOUSANDS	1996	1995
Raw materials	$23,415	$12,230
Work-in-process	12,865	5,839
Finished goods	18,748	13,643
	$55,028	$31,712

Property and Equipment

IN THOUSANDS	Life	1996	1995
Land	—	$ 25,154	$ 13,240
Buildings and improvements	5–40 years	20,328	18,088
Machinery and equipment	3–5 years	59,290	42,810
Furniture and fixtures	3–8 years	22,944	17,005
Leasehold improvements	Life of lease	5,245	3,968
		132,961	95,111
Accumulated depreciation and amortization		(40,183)	(27,248)
		$ 92,778	$ 67,863

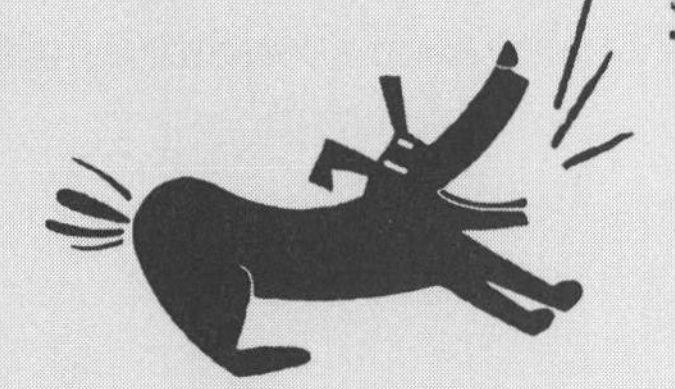

Accrued Liabilities

IN THOUSANDS	1996	1995
Accrued compensation and related taxes	$22,440	$15,740
Sales and marketing related	7,443	4,877
Tax related	16,218	5,746
Other	10,616	4,643
	$56,717	$31,006

Supplemental Disclosures of Cash Flows

IN THOUSANDS	1996	1995	1994
Interest paid	$ 764	$ 1,125	$ 1,300
Income taxes paid	$32,869	$29,411	$14,927

NOTE THREE: LINE OF CREDIT

The Company has available an unsecured $17 million revolving line of credit which expires on December 31, 1997. Of the total line of credit available, $7 million has been issued as an irrevocable standby letter of credit to guarantee component purchases from a supplier (see Note 7) at a fee of ¾% per annum. As of March 31, 1996, no borrowings were outstanding under this line of credit. The Company may select its own method of interest payment on borrowings based upon the bank's CD rate plus one percent, Eurodollar rate plus one percent or prime lending rate. A commitment fee of ¼% per annum is payable on the unused line of credit. In addition, the arrangement requires the Company to comply with certain financial covenants. The Company was in compliance with all such covenants as of March 31, 1996.

NOTE FOUR: LONG-TERM DEBT

The Company entered into a $17 million term loan agreement in June 1992 bearing interest at 7.65%, with principal and interest payable in quarterly installments of $850,000. All outstanding principal and accrued but unpaid interest is due and payable in June 1998. The arrangement requires the Company to comply with certain financial covenants. The Company was in compliance with all such covenants as of March 31, 1996.

NOTE FIVE: ACQUISITIONS

During fiscal 1996, the Company acquired all of the outstanding capital stock of Future Domain, Power I/O, Trillium, and Incat for $25 million, $7 million, $3 million, and 385,000 shares of the Company's common stock with a fair market value of $17 million, respectively. Also in connection with the Incat acquisition, the Company will pay consideration, contingent upon certain future performance criteria. These companies design and develop high-performance I/O products, networking technologies and software for recordable CD peripherals for both the consumer and enterprise computing markets.

The Company accounted for these acquisitions using the purchase method of accounting, and excluding the aggregate $52 million write-off of purchased in-process technology from these companies, the aggregate impact on the Company's results of operations from the acquisition date was not material.

The allocation of the Company's aggregate purchase price to the tangible and identifiable intangible assets acquired and liabilities assumed was based on independent appraisals and is summarized as follows:

IN THOUSANDS	
Tangible assets	$ 8,108
In-process technology	52,313
Goodwill	8,200
Assets acquired	68,621
Accounts payable and accrued liabilities	3,125
Deferred tax liability	12,627
Liabilities assumed	15,752
Net assets acquired	$52,869

Subsequent to year end, the Company acquired certain assets and the ongoing business of Western Digital's Connectivity Solutions Group (CSG), which primarily designs, manufactures and markets controller ICs for high-capacity disk drives. In connection with the acquisition, the Company was assigned capacity for wafer fabrication. The Company paid $33 million cash for CSG and will pay future consideration based on certain performance criteria. The Company will account for this acquisition using the purchase method of accounting and will evaluate the allocation of the purchase price to assets acquired, which includes in-process technology that will be written off. The results of operations for CSG were immaterial relative to the Company's financial statements.

Also subsequent to year end, the Company acquired all of the outstanding capital stock of Cogent Data Technologies, Inc. (Cogent) in a $68 million stock transaction. Cogent provides high-performance Fast Ethernet products for the networking market. The Company will record this acquisition using the pooling method of accounting and will record acquired assets and assumed liabilities at their book values as of the acquisition date. The results of operations for Cogent for the three year period ended March 31, 1996 were immaterial relative to the Company's financial statements.

NOTE SIX: STOCK PLANS

1986 Employee Stock Purchase Plan The Company has authorized 2,800,000 shares of common stock for issuance under the 1986 Employee Stock Purchase Plan (1986 Plan). Qualified employees may elect to have a certain percentage (not to exceed 10%) of their salary withheld pursuant to the 1986 Plan. The salary withheld is then used to purchase shares of the Company's common stock at a price equal to 85% of the market value of the stock at the beginning or ending of a three-month offering period, whichever is lower. Under this Plan, 139,275 shares were issued during fiscal 1996, representing approximately $4,578,000 in employee contributions.

1990 Stock Plan The Company's 1990 Stock Plan allows the Board of Directors to grant to employees, officers and consultants options to purchase common stock or other stock rights at exercise prices not less than 50% of the fair market value on the date of grant. The expiration of options or other stock rights is not to exceed ten years after the date of grant. To date, the Company has issued substantially all incentive and nonstatutory stock options under this Plan at exercise prices of 100% of fair market value on the respective dates of grant. Generally, options vest and become exercisable over a four year period.

Option activity under the 1990 Stock Plan is as follows:

	Options Available	Options Outstanding Shares	Price
Balance, March 31, 1993	2,280,412	3,751,052	$ 2.47 to $13.88
Authorized	2,000,000	—	—
Granted	(1,837,500)	1,837,500	$11.31 to $21.38
Exercised	—	(859,513)	$ 2.47 to $15.44
Terminated	330,662	(330,662)	$ 2.85 to $16.50
Balance, March 31, 1994	2,773,574	4,398,377	$ 2.47 to $21.38
Authorized	2,500,000	—	—
Granted	(1,914,500)	1,914,500	$15.63 to $35.88
Exercised	—	(930,574)	$ 2.47 to $21.38
Terminated	599,053	(599,053)	$ 2.84 to $27.63
Balance, March 31, 1995	3,958,127	4,783,250	$ 2.47 to $35.88
Authorized	2,193,900	—	—
Granted	(2,294,750)	2,294,750	$22.88 to $56.00
Exercised	—	(1,017,131)	$ 2.47 to $44.75
Terminated	241,038	(241,038)	$ 3.06 to $45.75
Balance, March 31, 1996	4,098,315	5,819,831	$ 2.47 to $56.00

At March 31, 1996, there were 1,956,767 exercisable options under this Plan at prices ranging from $2.47 to $45.88 per share.

1990 Directors' Option Plan The 1990 Directors' Option Plan provides for the automatic grant to non-employee directors of non-statutory stock options to purchase common stock at the fair market value on the date of grant, which is generally the last day of each fiscal year except for the first grant to any newly elected director. Each current director receives an option at the end of each fiscal year for 10,000 shares, which vests and becomes exercisable over a four year period. Each newly elected director receives an initial option on the date of his or her appointment or election for 40,000 shares, which also vests and becomes exercisable over a four year period. The options expire five years after the date of grant.

Option activity under the 1990 Directors' Option Plan is as follows:

	Options Available	Options Outstanding Shares	Price
Balance, March 31, 1993	40,000	157,500	$ 2.91 to $13.88
Authorized	500,000	—	—
Granted	(50,000)	50,000	$18.38
Exercised	—	(5,000)	$ 2.91
Balance, March 31, 1994	490,000	202,500	$ 2.91 to $18.38
Granted	(50,000)	50,000	$33.00
Exercised	—	(21,250)	$ 2.91 to $13.88
Balance, March 31, 1995	440,000	231,250	$ 2.91 to $33.00
Granted	(150,000)	150,000	$44.50 to $48.25
Exercised	—	(55,000)	$ 2.91 to $18.38
Balance, March 31, 1996	290,000	326,250	$ 7.69 to $48.25

At March 31, 1996 there were 93,750 exercisable options under this Plan at prices ranging from $7.69 to $33.00 per share.

Rights Plan The Company has reserved 120,000,000 shares of common stock for issuance under the Rights Plan which was amended and restated as of June 30, 1992. Under this plan, shareholders will receive one Common Share Purchase Right ("Right") for each outstanding share of the Company's common stock. Each Right will entitle shareholders to buy one share of common stock at an exercise price of $50.00 per share. The Rights will trade automatically with shares of the Company's common stock. The Rights are not exercisable until ten days after a person or group announces acquisition of 20% or more of the Company's outstanding common stock or the commencement of a tender offer which would result in ownership by a person or group of 20% or more of the then outstanding common stock.

The Company is entitled to redeem the Rights at $.005 per Right anytime on or before the tenth day following such an acquisition or tender offer. This redemption period may be extended by the Company in some cases. If, prior to such redemption, the Company is acquired in a merger or other business combination, a party acquires 20% or more of the Company's common stock, a 20% shareholder engages in certain self-dealing transactions, or the Company sells 50% or more of its assets, each right will entitle the holder to purchase from the surviving corporation, for $50.00 per share, common stock having a then current market value of $100.00 per share.

At March 31, 1996, the Company has reserved the following shares of authorized but unissued common stock:

1986 Employee Stock Purchase Plan	869,187
1990 Stock Plan	9,918,146
1990 Directors' Option Plan	616,250
Rights Plan	120,000,000
	131,403,583

NOTE SEVEN: COMMITMENTS

The Company leases certain office facilities, vehicles and certain equipment under operating lease agreements that expire at various dates through fiscal 2001. As of March 31, 1996, the minimum future payments on existing leases totaled $7,290,000. Rent expense was approximately $3,715,000, $2,377,000 and $1,640,000 during fiscal 1996, 1995 and 1994, respectively.

During fiscal 1996, the Company signed an agreement with TSMC totaling $66 million that ensures availability of a portion of the Company's wafer capacity for both current and future technologies. The agreement runs through 2001 providing the Company with a guarantee of increased capacity for wafer fabrication in return for advance payments. As of March 31, 1996, the Company made advance payments to TSMC totaling $20 million and has signed a $46 million promissory note payable which becomes due June 30, 1996. The majority of these amounts are included in other assets in the fiscal 1996 consolidated balance sheets.

In addition to this agreement, the Company has an existing deposit and supply agreement with TSMC to secure supply of silicon wafers. Under the deposit and supply agreement, the Company has made deposits aggregating $14,650,000 which are classified as other assets in the accompanying consolidated balance sheets. These advances are repayable at the expiration of the agreement in June 1997. The supplier has provided an irrevocable standby letter of credit to the Company in an equal amount to guarantee the repayment of deposits made by the Company. Under the agreement, the Company is committed to minimum purchases of $19,800,000 and $4,950,000 in fiscal 1997 and 1998, respectively.

During fiscal 1996, the Company signed an agreement with AT&T, acting through its Microelectronics business division, that will ensure availability of a portion of the Company's wafer capacity for both current and future technologies. This contract, which runs through 2001, provides the Company with a guaranteed supply of wafers at a specified level in return for an investment in fabrication equipment of up to $25 million for AT&T's fabrication facility located in Madrid, Spain. As of March 31, 1996 the Company has not made any payments in connection with this agreement.

NOTE EIGHT: INCOME TAXES

The components of income before income taxes for the years ended March 31 are as follows:

IN THOUSANDS	1996	1995	1994
Domestic	$ 57,882	$ 74,397	$54,972
Foreign	80,107	50,140	23,631
Income before income taxes	$137,989	$124,537	$78,603

The split of domestic and foreign income was impacted mainly by the acquisition related write-offs of in-process technology, which reduced domestic income by $52,313,000.

The components of the provision for income taxes for the years ended March 31 are as follows:

IN THOUSANDS	1996	1995	1994
Federal			
Current	$22,066	$26,455	$13,899
Deferred	(4,263)	(311)	2,658
	17,803	26,144	16,557
Foreign			
Current	15,074	1,106	317
Deferred	(1,491)	—	—
	13,583	1,106	317
State			
Current	3,611	3,177	3,474
Deferred	(383)	708	(695)
	3,228	3,885	2,779
Provision for income taxes	$34,614	$31,135	$19,653

Significant components of the Company's deferred tax assets, included in prepaid expenses in the accompanying consolidated balance sheets as of March 31 are as follows:

IN THOUSANDS	1996	1995
Inventory reserves	$ 3,426	$ 1,048
State taxes	1,323	990
Bad debt reserve	1,901	1,829
Compensatory accruals	5,091	4,355
Various expense accruals	5,581	3,725
Other, net	764	2
Net deferred tax assets	$18,086	$11,949

The provision for income taxes differs from the amount computed by applying the federal statutory tax rate to income before income taxes for the years ended March 31 as follows:

	1996	1995	1994
Federal statutory rate	35.0%	35.0%	35.0%
State taxes, net of federal benefit	2.7	2.2	2.9
Foreign subsidiary income at other than the U.S. tax rate	(11.8)	(9.9)	(10.5)
Tax-exempt interest income, net	(2.1)	(1.7)	(1.6)
Other	1.3	(.6)	(.8)
Effective income tax rate	25.1%	25.0%	25.0%

The Company's effective tax rate for fiscal 1996 was 25%, the same as fiscal 1995 and 1994. During fiscal 1996, the Company concluded negotiations with the Singapore government extending the tax holiday for the Company's manufacturing subsidiary. The terms of the tax holiday provide that profits derived from certain products will be exempt from tax for a period of 10 years, subject to certain conditions. In addition, profits derived from the Company's remaining products will be taxed at a rate of 15%, which is lower than the statutory rate of 27%, through fiscal 1998. As of March 31, 1996, the Company had not accrued income taxes on $186,100,000 of accumulated undistributed earnings of its Singapore subsidiary, as these earnings will be reinvested indefinitely.

NOTE NINE: SEGMENT INFORMATION

Adaptec operates in the microcomputer input/output industry and is a leading supplier of high-performance intelligent subsystems and associated software and very large-scale integrated circuits used to control the flow of data between a microcomputer's CPU and its peripherals. The Company focuses its worldwide marketing efforts on major OEM customers through its direct sales force located in the United States, Europe and Far East and also sells through distributors and sales representatives in each of these geographic areas.

Income from operations consists of net revenues less cost of revenues and operating expenses incurred in supporting the revenues of each geographic area. The Company's write-offs of acquired in-process technology are included in the corporate income from operations. All of the Company's identifiable assets are used to support the operations in each geographic area. Corporate assets include cash and cash equivalents, marketable securities, deferred tax assets and certain other assets. Intercompany sales are made at arms-length prices, and revenues for the European subsidiaries consist mainly of commissions earned in connection with obtaining foreign orders.

NOTE NINE: SEGMENT INFORMATION CONTINUED

IN THOUSANDS	United States	Singapore, Far East, Other	Europe	Corporate	Adjustments and Eliminations	Consolidated Total
Fiscal 1996						
Revenues						
Sales to customers	$609,060	$ 49,211	$1,076	$ —	$ —	$659,347
Intercompany sales between geographic areas	7,205	399,036	6,175	—	(412,416)	—
Net revenues	$616,265	$448,247	$7,251	$ —	$(412,416)	$659,347
Income from operations	100,838	76,942	668	(52,313)	—	126,135
Identifiable assets	201,128	259,179	2,644	322,910	(139,375)	646,486
Fiscal 1995						
Revenues						
Sales to customers	$464,707	$ 1,487	$ —	$ —	$ —	$466,194
Intercompany sales between geographic areas	10,401	191,360	3,905	—	(205,666)	—
Net revenues	$475,108	$192,847	$3,905	$ —	$(205,666)	$466,194
Income from operations	68,594	48,847	343	—	—	117,784
Identifiable assets	122,097	123,044	1,070	262,383	(72,886)	435,708
Fiscal 1994						
Revenues						
Sales to customers	$371,863	$ 382	$ —	$ —	$ —	$372,245
Intercompany sales between geographic areas	10,344	119,305	2,375	—	(132,024)	—
Net revenues	$382,207	$119,687	$2,375	$ —	$(132,024)	$372,245
Income from operations	53,945	23,074	116	—	—	77,135
Identifiable assets	153,340	74,512	347	207,591	(77,315)	358,475

Export Revenues The following table represents export revenues by geographic region as a percentage of total revenues:

	1996	1995	1994
Singapore, Far East, Other	32%	37%	38%
Europe	24	25	20
	56%	62%	58%

Major Customers In fiscal 1996, sales to one distributor represented 10% of net revenues. In fiscal 1995 and 1994, no customer accounted for more than 10% of net revenues.

NOTE TEN: LEGAL MATTERS

A class action lawsuit alleging federal securities law violations and negligent misrepresentation was filed against the Company, its directors, and certain of its officers on February 21, 1991. That action was settled by letter agreement on July 29, 1993. The Company has made all payments required under the terms of the letter agreement. Final settlement of the class action lawsuit was made on May 15, 1995 pursuant to the Court's final judgment and order of dismissal.

NOTE ELEVEN: COMPARATIVE QUARTERLY FINANCIAL DATA UNAUDITED

Summarized quarterly financial data is as follows:

IN THOUSANDS, EXCEPT PER SHARE AMOUNTS	Quarters				
	First	Second	Third	Fourth	Year
Fiscal 1996					
Net revenues	$138,025	$149,110	$176,187	$196,025	$659,347
Gross profit	81,359	86,451	101,986	113,612	383,408
Net income*	31,163	557	30,587	41,068	103,375
Net income per share*	$ .58	$ .01	$ .56	$ .75	$ 1.89
Weighted average shares outstanding	53,942	54,461	54,792	55,061	54,569

*The second and third quarters of fiscal 1996 include write-offs of acquired in-process technology, net of taxes, totaling $33 million and $7 million, respectively.

	First	Second	Third	Fourth	Year
Fiscal 1995					
Net revenues	$106,061	$106,574	$123,367	$130,192	$466,194
Gross profit	54,888	57,413	71,563	76,734	260,598
Net income	17,592	18,458	27,403	29,949	93,402
Net income per share	$ .33	$ .35	$ .52	$ .56	$ 1.75
Weighted average shares outstanding	53,944	53,182	52,958	53,802	53,357

Report of Management

Management is responsible for the preparation and integrity of the consolidated financial statements and other financial information presented in the annual report. The accompanying financial statements were prepared in conformity with generally accepted accounting principles and as such include some amounts based on management's best judgments and estimates. Financial information in the annual report is consistent with that in the financial statements.

Management is responsible for maintaining a system of internal business controls and procedures to provide reasonable assurance that assets are safeguarded and that transactions are authorized, recorded and reported properly. The internal control system is continuously monitored by management review, written policies and guidelines, and careful selection and training of qualified people who are provided with and expected to adhere to the Company's standards of business conduct. Management believes the Company's internal controls provide reasonable assurance that assets are safeguarded against material loss from unauthorized use or disposition and the financial records are reliable for preparing financial statements and other data and maintaining accountability for assets.

The Audit Committee of the Board of Directors meets periodically with the independent accountants and management to discuss internal business controls, auditing and financial reporting matters. The Committee also reviews with the independent accountants the scope and results of the audit effort.

The independent accountants, Price Waterhouse LLP, are engaged to examine the consolidated financial statements of the Company and conduct such tests and related procedures as they deem necessary in accordance with generally accepted auditing standards. The opinion of the independent accountants, based upon their audit of the consolidated financial statements, is contained in this annual report.

F. Grant Saviers
President and Chief Executive Officer

Paul G. Hansen
Vice President, Finance and
Chief Financial Officer

Christopher G. O'Meara
Vice President and Treasurer

Andrew J. Brown
Corporate Controller and
Principal Accounting Officer

Report of Independent Accountants

To the Board of Directors and
Shareholders of Adaptec, Inc.:

In our opinion, the accompanying consolidated balance sheets and the related consolidated statements of operations, of cash flows and of shareholders' equity present fairly, in all material respects, the financial position of Adaptec, Inc. and its subsidiaries at March 31, 1996 and 1995, and the results of their operations and their cash flows for the years then ended in conformity with generally accepted accounting principles. These financial statements are the responsibility of the Company's management; our responsibility is to express an opinion on these financial statements based on our audits. We conducted our audits of these statements in accordance with generally accepted auditing standards which require that we plan and perform the audit to obtain reasonable assurance about whether the financial statements are free of material misstatement. An audit includes examining, on a test basis, evidence supporting the amounts and disclosures in the financial statements, assessing the accounting principles used and significant estimates made by management, and evaluating the overall financial statement presentation. We believe that our audits provide a reasonable basis for the opinion expressed above. The financial statements of Adaptec, Inc. as of and for the year ended March 31, 1994 were audited by other independent accountants whose report dated April 25, 1994 expressed an unqualified opinion on those statements.

Price Waterhouse LLP

San Jose, California
April 22, 1996

Selected Financial Data

IN THOUSANDS, EXCEPT PER SHARE AMOUNTS

	1996	1995	1994	1993	1992
Statement of Operations Data					
Year Ended March 31					
Net revenues	$659,347	$466,194	$372,245	$311,339	$150,315
Cost of revenues	275,939	205,596	189,526	174,179	84,549
Gross profit	383,408	260,598	182,719	137,160	65,766
Operating expenses					
Research and development	87,628	60,848	39,993	26,324	17,514
Sales and marketing	81,548	58,737	46,192	32,525	21,338
General and administrative	35,784	23,229	19,399	15,568	10,517
Write-off of acquired in-process technology	52,313	—	—	—	—
	257,273	142,814	105,584	74,417	49,369
Net income	$103,375	$ 93,402	$ 58,950	$ 49,390	$ 14,614
Net Income Per Share					
Net income per share	$ 1.89	$ 1.75	$ 1.10	$ .96	$ .35
Weighted average shares outstanding	54,569	53,357	53,602	51,652	41,664
Balance Sheet Data as of March 31					
Working capital	$334,989	$294,058	$243,451	$191,693	$105,671
Total assets	646,486	435,708	358,475	282,896	138,615
Long-term debt, net of current portion	4,250	7,650	11,050	14,450	423
Shareholders' equity	511,945	371,644	297,616	225,155	117,742

Common Stock Prices and Dividends The Company's common stock is traded in the over-the-counter market under the NASDAQ symbol ADPT. The following table sets forth the range of the high and low prices by quarter as reported by the NASDAQ National Market System.

	1996		1995	
	High	Low	High	Low
First quarter	$39⅞	$29¼	$19½	$14
Second quarter	47¼	34½	21¼	16¼
Third quarter	48⅜	35⅝	24¾	17¼
Fourth quarter	56⅜	35⅛	37	21¾

In March 1992 and January 1994, the Company's Board of Directors approved a two-for-one-split of its common stock. The above net income per share information has been adjusted to reflect the stock splits.

At March 31, 1996, there were 724 holders of record of the Company's common stock. The Company has not paid cash dividends on its common stock and does not currently plan to pay cash dividends to its shareholders in the near future.

Adaptec in the Community

PROVIDING OPPORTUNITIES

Wally and Molly are the information users of tomorrow. But they are the children of today, and often children need our help. Adaptec believes in the importance of giving back to the communities where Wally and Molly are growing and learning. In fiscal 1996 we helped the groups and agencies below in their efforts to make our world more livable for children.

Through our commitment to children, Adaptec in fiscal 1997 is making a special $150,000 donation to support literacy and reading programs to help children get a head start on their futures.

The Children's Health Council
Make-A-Wish Foundation
United Way
The Tech Museum of Innovation
Leavey School of Business, Santa Clara University
Reading Research Center, Mission San Jose Elementary School
Junior Achievement
Second Harvest Food Bank
Ronald McDonald House
Leukemia Society of America
Adaptec Scholarship
Indian Peaks Elementary School
Milpitas High School
San Jose State University
Bellarmine College Preparatory
Girl Scouts of Santa Clara County
Los Altos Educational Foundation
Keys School

Campbell Soup Company
ANNUAL REPORT
WINNING AGAIN!
SWANSON
Salisbury Steak
Dinner
Salisbury Steak with Gravy, Mashed Potatoes, Corn in Seasoned Sauce and Cherry-Apple Crumb
Delacre
LOOK-SAFETY BUTTON
CRANBERRY HONEY
New!
PEPPERIDGE FARM
Wholesome Choice
SOFT COOKIES
Campbell's
Cream of Broccoli
NEW LABEL SAME GREAT SOUP
Garden Combinat
Prego

SUPPLEMENTAL SCHEDULE OF SALES AND EARNINGS

(million dollars)

	Year 11		Year 10		Year 9	
	Sales	***Earnings***	Sales	Earnings	Sales	Earnings
1 **CONTRIBUTIONS BY DIVISION:**						
Campbell North America						
Campbell U.S.A.	***$3,911.8***	***$632.7***	$3,932.7	$370.8	$3,666.9	$242.3
Campbell Canada	***352.0***	***35.3***	384.0	25.6	313.4	23.8
	4,263.8	***668.0***	4,316.7	396.4	3,980.3	266.1
Campbell Biscuit and Bakery						
Pepperidge Farm	***569.0***	***73.6***	582.0	57.0	548.4	53.6
International Biscuit	***219.4***	***17.6***	195.3	8.9	178.0	11.7
	788.4	***91.2***	777.3	65.9	726.4	65.3
Campbell International	***1,222.9***	***39.4***	1,189.8	(168.6)	1,030.3	(117.8)
Interdivision	***(71.0)***		(78.0)		(64.9)	
TOTAL SALES	***$6,204.1***		$6,205.8		$5,672.1	
TOTAL OPERATING EARNINGS		***798.6***		293.7		213.6
Unallocated corporate expenses		***(41.1)***		(16.5)		(31.3)
Interest, net		***(90.2)***		(94.0)		(55.8)
Foreign currency translation adjustments		***.1***		(3.8)		(20.0)
Taxes on earnings		***(265.9)***		(175.0)		(93.4)
NET EARNINGS		***$401.5***		$4.4		$13.1
NET EARNINGS PER SHARE		***$3.16***		$.03		$.10

Contributions by division in Year 10 include the effects of divestitures, restructuring and unusual charges of $339.1 million as follows: Campbell U.S.A. $121.8 million, Campbell Canada $6.6 million, Pepperidge Farm $11.0 million, International Biscuit $14.3 million, and Campbell International $185.4 million. Contributions by division in Year 9 include the effects of restructuring and unusual charges of $343.0 million as follows: Campbell U.S.A. $183.1 million, Campbell Canada $6.0 million, Pepperidge Farm $7.1 million, International Biscuit $9.5 million, and Campbell International $137.3 million.

2 RESULTS OF OPERATIONS

Overview

Campbell had record net earnings in Year 11 of $401.5 million, or $3.16 per share, compared to net earnings of $4.4 million, or 3 cents per share, in Year 10. Excluding Year 10's divestiture and restructuring charges, earnings per share increased 34% in Year 11. In Year 11, the Company sold five non-strategic businesses, sold or closed several manufacturing plants, and discontinued certain unprofitable product lines. Net sales of $6.2 billion in Year 11 were even with Year 10. Sales were up 4% excluding businesses that were divested and product lines that were discontinued in Year 11.

In Year 10 the Company incurred charges for divestitures and restructuring of $2.33 per share, reducing net earnings to 3 cents per share. In Year 9 restructuring charges of $2.02 per share reduced earnings to 10 cents per share. Excluding these charges from both years, earnings per share rose 11% in Year 10. Sales increased 9%. In Year 10 the company's domestic divisions had strong earnings performances, excluding the divestiture and restructuring charges, but the International Division's performance was disappointing principally due to the poor performance of United Kingdom frozen food and Italian biscuit operations. The Italian biscuit operations were divested in Year 11.

The divestiture and restructuring programs were designed to strengthen the Company's core businesses and improve long-term profitability. The Year 10 divestiture program involved the sale of several low-return or nonstrategic businesses. The Year 10 restructuring charges provided for the elimination of underperforming assets and unnecessary facilities and included a write-off of goodwill. The restructuring charges in Year 9 involved plant consolidations, work force reductions, and goodwill write-offs.

Year 11 Compared to Year 10

3 RESULTS BY DIVISION

CAMPBELL NORTH AMERICA—Operating earnings of Campbell North America, the Company's largest division, were $668.0 million in Year 11 compared to $396.4 million in Year 10 after restructuring charges of $128.4 million. Operating earnings increased 27% in Year 11 over Year 10, excluding the restructuring charges from Year 10. All of the division's core businesses had very strong earnings growth. Continued benefits of restructuring drove significant improvements in operating margins.

Sales were $4.26 billion in Year 11. Excluding divested businesses and discontinued product lines, sales increased 2% with overall volume down 2%. Soup volume was off 1.5% as a result of reduced year-end trade promotional activities. Significant volume increases were achieved in the cooking soup, ramen noodle and family-size soup categories and "Healthy Request" soup. Exceptionally strong volume performances were turned in by "Swanson" frozen dinners, "Franco-American" gravies and "Prego" spaghetti sauces with positive volume results for "LeMenu Healthy" entrees, Food Service frozen soups and entrees, and Casera Foods in Puerto Rico.

CAMPBELL BISCUIT AND BAKERY—Operating earnings of the Biscuit and Bakery division, which includes Pepperidge Farm in the United States, Delacre in Europe and an equity interest in Arnotts Limited in Australia, were $91.2 million in Year 11 compared with $65.9 million in Year 10 after restructuring charges of $25.3 million. Operating earnings were flat in Year 11 excluding the restructuring charges from Year 10. Sales increased 1%, however, volume declined 3%.

Pepperidge Farm operating earnings in Year 11 increased despite a drop in sales, which reflects the adverse effect of the recession on premium cookies. Several new varieties of "Hearty Slices" bread performed well. Delacre, benefiting from new management and integration into the worldwide biscuit and bakery organization, turned in significant improvement in Year 11 sales and operating earnings. Arnotts' performance in Year 11 was disappointing and included restructuring charges. Its restructuring program should have a positive impact on fiscal Year 12 results. The Year 11 comparison with Year 10 was also adversely impacted by gains of $4.0 million realized in Year 10 on the sales of businesses by Arnotts.

CAMPBELL INTERNATIONAL—Operating earnings of the International division were $39.4 million in Year 11 compared to an operating loss of $168.6 million in Year 10 after restructuring charges of $185.4 million.

In Year 11, Campbell International achieved a significant turnaround. Operating earnings for the year more than doubled above the pre-restructuring results of the prior year. There were margin improvements throughout the system. Europe led the division's positive results. A key component was the United Kingdom's move from a loss position to profitability, driven by the benefits of restructuring and product line reconfiguration.

European Food and Confectionery units turned in another year of solid earnings growth. Mexican operations, strengthened by a new management team, also turned around from a loss to a profit position. Sales were $1.22 billion in Year 11, an increase of 6%, excluding divested businesses and discontinued product lines, and the effects of foreign currency rates. Volume was approximately the same as in Year 10.

4 STATEMENTS OF EARNINGS

Sales in Year 11 were even with Year 10. Excluding divested businesses and unprofitable product lines discontinued during Year 11, sales increased 4% while volume declined approximately 2%. The decline in volume was caused by reduced year-end trade promotional activities and the adverse effect of the recession on certain premium products.

Gross margins improved 2.6 percentage points to 34.0% in Year 11 from 31.4% in Year 10. All divisions improved due to the significant benefits from restructuring and the divestitures and product-pruning activities. Productivity improvements worldwide and declining commodity prices also contributed to the higher margins.

Marketing and selling expenses, as a percentage of net sales, were 15.4% in Year 11 compared to 15.8% in Year 10. The decrease in Year 11 is due to more focused marketing efforts and controlled new product introductions. For each of the prior 10 fiscal years, these expenses had increased significantly. Advertising was down 11% in Year 11. Management expects advertising expenditures to increase in Year 12 in order to drive volume growth of core products and to support the introduction of new products.

Administrative expenses, as a percentage of net sales, were 4.9% in Year 11 compared to 4.7% in Year 10. The increase in Year 11 results principally from annual executive incentive plan accruals due to outstanding financial performance and foreign currency rates.

Interest expense increased in Year 11 due to timing of fourth quarter borrowings in order to obtain favorable long-term interest rates. Interest income was also higher in Year 11 as the proceeds from these borrowings were invested temporarily until needed. Interest expense, net of interest income, decreased from $94.0 million in Year 10 to $90.2 million in Year 11 as the increased cash flow from operations exceeded cash used for share repurchases and acquisitions.

Foreign exchange losses declined principally due to reduced effects of currency devaluations in Argentina.

Other expense was $26.2 million in Year 11 compared to $14.7 million in Year 10. The increase results principally from accruals for long-term incentive compensation plans reflecting changes in Campbell's stock price.

As discussed in the "Overview" section above, Year 10 results include divestiture, restructuring, and unusual charges of $339.1 million ($301.6 million or $2.33 per share after taxes).

Equity in earnings of affiliates declined in Year 11 principally due to the disappointing performance at Arnotts and to a $4.0 million gain on sales of businesses realized by Arnotts in Year 10.

Year 10 Compared to Year 9

5 RESULTS BY DIVISION

Campbell North America—In Year 10, Campbell North America had operating earnings of $396.4 million after restructuring charges of $128.4 million. In Year 9 the division had operating earnings of $266.1 million, after restructuring charges of $189.1 million. Excluding restructuring charges from both Year 10 and Year 9 operating earnings increased 15% in Year 10, led by strong performances by the soup, grocery, "Mrs. Paul's" frozen seafood, and Canadian sectors. The olives business performed poorly in Year 10.

Sales increased 8% in Year 10 to $4.32 billion on a 3% increase in volume. There were solid volume increases in ready-to-serve soups, "Great Starts" frozen breakfasts, and "Prego" spaghetti sauces. Overall soup volume was up 1%. "Mrs. Paul's" regained the number one share position in frozen prepared seafood.

Campbell Biscuit and Bakery—In Year 10, Campbell Biscuit and Bakery had operating earnings of $65.9 million after restructuring charges of $25.3 million. In Year 9, the division's operating earnings were $65.3 million after restructuring charges of $16.6 million. Excluding restructuring charges from both Year 10 and Year 9, operating earnings of the division increased 11% in Year 10. The increase in operating earnings was driven by Pepperidge Farm's biscuit and bakery units along with Arnott's gain on sales of businesses. Pepperidge Farm's frozen unit and Delacre performed poorly. Sales increased 7% to $777.3 million. Volume increased 1%, with Pepperidge Farm's biscuit, bakery and food service units and Delacre the main contributors to the growth.

CAMPBELL INTERNATIONAL—In Year 10, Campbell International had an operating loss of $168.6 million after restructuring charges of $185.4 million. In Year 9, the division sustained an operating loss of $117.8 million after restructuring charges of $137.3 million. Excluding restructuring charges from both Year 10 and Year 9, operating earnings declined 14% in Year 10, as strong performances in the European Food and Confectionery and Argentine operations were more than offset by poor performances in the United Kingdom frozen food and Italian biscuit operations. Sales in Year 10 were $1.19 billion, an increase of 15%. Volume was up 14% of which 11% came from acquisitions.

6 STATEMENTS OF EARNINGS

In Year 10 sales increased 9% on a 5% increase in volume, about half of which came from established businesses.

Gross margins improved by 1.9 percentage points to 31.4% in Year 10 from 29.5% in Year 9. All divisions had improved margins in Year 10, with Campbell North America operations posting substantial improvements.

Marketing and selling expenses, as a percentage of net sales, were 15.8% in Year 10 compared to 14.4% in Year 9. The Year 10 increase was due to heavy marketing expenditures by Campbell U.S.A. at both the national and regional levels.

Administrative expenses, as a percentage of net sales, were 4.7% in Year 10 compared to 4.4% in Year 9. The increase in Year 10 was driven by some unusual one-time expenditures, employee benefits, the weakening dollar and acquisitions.

Interest expense increased in Year 10 due to higher debt levels resulting from funding of acquisitions, higher inventory levels during the year, purchases of Campbell's stock for the treasury and restructuring program expenditures. Interest income declined in Year 10 because of a shift from local currency to lower-yielding dollar denominated temporary investments in Latin America to minimize foreign exchange losses.

Foreign exchange losses resulted principally from currency devaluations in Argentina. There was a large devaluation in Argentina in Year 9. Also, Year 10 losses were lower due to the shift in temporary investments described in the previous paragraph.

Other expense was $14.7 million in Year 10 compared to $32.4 million in Year 9. This decline results principally from reduced accruals for long-term incentive compensation plans reflecting changes in Campbell's stock price.

As discussed in the "Overview" section above, results include divestiture, restructuring and unusual charges of $339.1 million ($301.6 million or $2.33 per share after taxes) in Year 10 and $343.0 million ($260.8 million or $2.02 per share after taxes) in Year 9.

Equity in earnings of affiliates increased in Year 10 principally due to a $4.0 million gain on sales of businesses realized by Arnotts in Year 10.

7 Income Taxes

The effective income tax rate was 39.8% in Year 11, 97.5% in Year 10 an 87.7% in Year 9. The principal reason for the high tax rates in Year 10 and Year 9 is that certain of the divestiture, restructuring and unusual charges are not tax deductible. Excluding the effect of these charges, the rate would be 41.0% in Year 10 and 38.9% in Year 9. The variances in all years are principally due to the level of certain foreign losses for which no tax benefit is currently available.

8 Inflation

The Company attempts to mitigate the effects of inflation on sales and earnings by appropriately increasing selling prices and aggressively pursuing an ongoing cost improvement effort which includes capital investments in more efficient plants and equipment. Also, the divestiture and restructuring programs enacted in Year 9 and Year 10 have made the Company a more cost-effective producer, as previously discussed with reference to cost of products sold.

9 Recent Developments

In December Year 10, the Financial Accounting Standards Board issued Statement of Financial Accounting Standards No. 106, "Employer's Accounting for Postretirement Benefits Other Than Pensions," which requires employers to account for retiree health obligations on an accrual basis beginning with the Company's Year 14 fiscal year. For a discussion of its impact on the Company, see Note 8 to the Consolidated Financial Statements.

10 LIQUIDITY AND CAPITAL RESOURCES

The Consolidated Statements of Cash Flows and Balance Sheets demonstrate the Company's continued superior financial strength.

11 Statements of Cash Flows

Operating Activities—Cash provided by operations was $805.2 million in Year 11, an 80% increase from $448.4 million in Year 10. This increased cash flow was driven by the Company's record earnings level and reduced working capital resulting from improved asset management and the restructuring program.

Investing Activities—The majority of the Company's investing activities involve the purchase of new plant assets to maintain modern manufacturing processes and increase productivity. Capital expenditures for plant assets amounted to $371.1 million in Year 11, including $10.0 million of capital lease activity, down slightly from Year 10. The Company expects capital expenditures in Year 12 to be about $400 million.

Another key investing activity of the Company is acquisitions. The total cost of acquisitions in Year 11 was $180.1 million, most of which was spent to acquire the publicly held shares of the Company's 71% owned subsidiary, Campbell Soup Company Ltd. in Canada. This will allow Campbell North America to more efficiently integrate its U.S. and Canadian operations to provide Campbell with competitive advantage in North America.

One of the Company's strategies has been to prune low-return assets and businesses from its portfolio. In Year 11 the Company realized over $100 million in cash from these activities, with $67.4 million coming from sales of businesses and $43.2 million realized from asset sales.

Also, during Year 11 the Company made contributions to its pension plans substantially in excess of the amounts expensed. This was the principal reason for the increase in other assets.

Financing Activities—During Year 11, the Company issued debt in the public markets for a total of $400 million: $100 million of 9% Notes due Year 18. $100 million of Medium-Term Notes due Year 21 at interest rates from 8.58% to 8.75%, and $200 million of 8.875%. Debentures due Year 41. The proceeds were used to reduce short-term debt by $227 million, pay off long-term debt maturing in Year 11 of $129.9 million, and to fund the purchase of the minority interest of Campbell Canada.

During Year 11, the Company repurchased approximately 3.4 million shares of its capital stock at a cost of $175.6 million. Cash received from the issuance of approximately 1.1 million treasury shares pursuant to the stock option and long-term incentive plans amounted to $47.7 million in Year 11.

Dividends of $137.5 million represent the dividends paid in Year 11. Dividends declared in Year 11 were $142.2 million or $1.12 per share, an increase of 14% over Year 10.

12 Balance Sheets

Total borrowings at the end of fiscal Year 11 were $1.055 billion compared to $1.008 billion at the end of Year 10. Even after the effects of the borrowing and treasury stock activity previously discussed, total debt as a percentage of total capitalization was 33.7%—the same as a year ago. The Company has ample sources of funds. It has access to the commercial paper markets with the highest rating. The Company's long-term debt is rated double A by the major rating agencies. It has filed a shelf registration with the Securities and Exchange Commission for the issuance from time to time of up to $100 million of debt securities. Also, the Company has unused lines of credit of approximately $635 million.

Debt-related activity is discussed in the Statements of Cash Flows section above. In addition to that, the debt balances on the Balance Sheets were affected by current maturities of long-term debt and by the classification of commercial paper to be refinanced as long-term debt in Year 10.

Aggressive management of working capital and the effect of divested businesses are evidenced by a $235.5 million decrease in current assets exclusive of changes in cash and temporary investments. Receivables are down $97.1 million and inventories declined $113.1 million from Year 10. Accounts payable are down $42.8 million because of the reduced inventory levels and divestitures. Accrued liabilities and accrued income taxes declined $61.9 million as increases due to higher earnings levels and the timing of certain payments were offset by payments and charges resulting from the divestitures and restructuring programs.

Plant assets increased $72.7 million due to capital expenditures of $371.1 million offset by the annual provision for depreciation of $194.5 million, asset sales and divestitures. Intangible assets increased $52.1 million as the acquisitions resulted in $132.3 million of additional goodwill. Amortization and divestitures accounted for the remainder of the change. Other assets increased principally as the result of the pension contribution.

Other liabilities decreased $14.9 million as the reduction of minority interest resulting from the purchase of the publicly-held shares of Campbell Canada and changes in foreign currency rates of other liabilities offset the annual deferred tax provision.

CONSOLIDATED STATEMENTS OF EARNINGS Campbell Soup Company

(millions)

		Year 11	Year 10	Year 9
13	**NET SALES**	**$6,204.1**	$6,205.8	$5,672.1
	Costs and expenses			
14	Cost of products sold	**4,095.5**	4,258.2	4,001.6
15	Marketing and selling expenses	**956.2**	980.5	818.8
16	Administrative expenses	**306.7**	290.7	252.1
17	Research and development expenses	**56.3**	53.7	47.7
18	Interest expense (Note 3)	**116.2**	111.6	94.1
19	Interest income	**(26.0)**	(17.6)	(38.3)
20	Foreign exchange losses, net (Note 4)	**.8**	3.3	19.3
21	Other expense (Note 5)	**26.2**	14.7	32.4
22	Divestitures, restructuring and unusual charges (Note 6)	—	339.1	343.0
22A	Total costs and expenses	**5,531.9**	6,034.2	5,570.7
23	Earnings before equity in earnings of affiliates and minority interests	**672.2**	171.6	101.4
24	Equity in earnings of affiliates	**2.4**	13.5	10.4
25	Minority interests	**(7.2)**	(5.7)	(5.3)
26	Earnings before taxes	**667.4**	179.4	106.5
27	Taxes on earnings (Note 9)	**265.9**	175.0	93.4
28	**NET EARNINGS**	**$401.5**	$4.4	$13.1
29	**NET EARNINGS PER SHARE (NOTE 22)**	**$3.16**	$.03	$.10
30	Weighted average shares outstanding	**127.0**	129.6	129.3

The accompanying Summary of Significant Accounting Policies and Notes are an integral part of the financial statements.

CAMPBELL SOUP

CONSOLIDATED BALANCE SHEETS

Campbell Soup Company

(million dollars)		July 28, Year 11	July 29, Year 10
	CURRENT ASSETS		
31	Cash and cash equivalents (Note 12)	**$178.9**	$80.7
32	Other temporary investments, at cost which approximates market	**12.8**	22.5
33	Accounts receivable (Note 13)	**527.4**	624.5
34	Inventories (Note 14)	**706.7**	819.8
35	Prepaid expenses (Note 15)	**92.7**	118.0
36	Total current assets	**1,518.5**	1,665.5
37	**PLANT ASSETS, NET OF DEPRECIATION (NOTE 16)**	**1,790.4**	1,717.7
38	**INTANGIBLE ASSETS, NET OF AMORTIZATION (NOTE 17)**	**435.5**	383.4
39	**OTHER ASSETS (NOTE 18)**	**404.6**	349.0
	Total Assets	**$4,149.0**	$4,115.6
	CURRENT LIABILITIES		
40	Notes payable (Note 19)	**$282.2**	$202.3
41	Payable to suppliers and others	**482.4**	525.2
42	Accrued liabilities (Note 20)	**408.7**	491.9
43	Dividend payable	**37.0**	32.3
44	Accrued income taxes	**67.7**	46.4
45	Total current liabilities	**1,278.0**	1,298.1
46	**LONG-TERM DEBT (NOTE 19)**	**772.6**	805.8
47	**OTHER LIABILITIES, PRINCIPALLY DEFERRED INCOME TAXES (NOTE 21)**	**305.0**	319.9
	SHAREOWNERS' EQUITY (NOTE 22)		
48	Preferred stock; authorized 40,000,000 shares; none issued	—	—
49	Capital stock, $.15 par value; authorized 140,000,000 shares; issued 135,622,676 shares	**20.3**	20.3
50	Capital surplus	**107.3**	61.9
51	Earnings retained in the business	**1,912.6**	1,653.3
52	Capital stock in treasury, 8,618,911 shares in Year 11 and 6,353,697 shares in Year 10, at cost	**(270.4)**	(107.2)
53	Cumulative translation adjustments (Note 4)	**23.6**	63.5
54	Total shareowners' equity	**1,793.4**	1,691.8
55	Total liabilities and shareowners' equity	**$4,149.0**	$4,115.6

The accompanying Summary of Significant Accounting Policies and Notes are an integral part of the financial statements.

CONSOLIDATED STATEMENTS OF CASH FLOWS Campbell Soup Company

(million dollars)

		Year 11	Year 10	Year 9
	CASH FLOWS FROM OPERATING ACTIVITIES:			
56	Net earnings	***$401.5***	$4.4	$13.1
	To reconcile net earnings to net cash provided by operating activities:			
57	Depreciation and amortization	***208.6***	200.9	192.3
58	Divestitures and restructuring provisions		339.1	343.0
59	Deferred taxes	***35.5***	3.9	(67.8)
60	Other, net	***63.2***	18.6	37.3
61	(Increase) decrease in accounts receivable	***17.1***	(60.4)	(46.8)
62	(Increase) decrease in inventories	***48.7***	10.7	(113.2)
63	Net change in other current assets and liabilities	***30.6***	(68.8)	(.6)
64	Net cash provided by operating activities	***805.2***	448.4	357.3
	CASH FLOWS FROM INVESTING ACTIVITIES:			
65	Purchases of plant assets	***(361.1)***	(387.6)	(284.1)
66	Sales of plant assets	***43.2***	34.9	39.8
67	Businesses acquired	***(180.1)***	(41.6)	(135.8)
68	Sales of businesses	***67.4***	21.7	4.9
69	Increase in other assets	***(57.8)***	(18.6)	(107.0)
70	Net change in other temporary investments	***9.7***	3.7	9.0
71	Net cash used in investing activities	***(478.7)***	(387.5)	(473.2)
	CASH FLOWS FROM FINANCING ACTIVITIES:			
72	Long-term borrowings	***402.8***	12.6	126.5
73	Repayments of long-term borrowings	***(129.9)***	(22.5)	(53.6)
74	Increase (decrease) in borrowings with less than three month maturities	***(137.9)***	(2.7)	108.2
75	Other short-term borrowings	***117.3***	153.7	227.1
76	Repayments of other short-term borrowings	***(206.4)***	(89.8)	(192.3)
77	Dividends paid	***(137.5)***	(124.3)	(86.7)
78	Treasury stock purchases	***(175.6)***	(41.1)	(8.1)
79	Treasury stock issued	***47.7***	12.4	18.5
80	Other, net	***(.1)***	(.1)	23.5
81	Net cash provided by (used in) financing activities	***(219.6)***	(101.8)	163.1
82	Effect of exchange rate changes on cash	***(8.7)***	.7	(12.1)
83	**NET INCREASE (DECREASE) IN CASH AND CASH EQUIVALENTS**	***98.2***	(40.2)	35.1
84	Cash and cash equivalents at beginning of year	***80.7***	120.9	85.8
85	**CASH AND CASH EQUIVALENTS AT END OF YEAR**	***$178.9***	$80.7	$120.9

The accompanying Summary of Significant Accounting Policies and Notes are an integral part of the financial statements.
Prior years have been reclassified to conform to the Year 11 presentation.

CAMPBELL SOUP

CONSOLIDATED STATEMENTS OF SHAREOWNERS' EQUITY Campbell Soup Company

(million dollars)

		Preferred stock	Capital stock	Capital surplus	Earnings retained in the business	Capital stock in treasury	Cumulative translation adjustments	Total Shareowners' Equity
86	Balance at July 31, Year 8	—	$20.3	$42.3	$1,879.1	$(75.2)	$28.5	$1,895.0
	Net earnings				13.1			13.1
	Cash dividends ($.90 per share)				(116.4)			(116.4)
	Treasury stock purchased					(8.1)		(8.1)
	Treasury stock issued under Management incentive and Stock option plans			8.5		12.6		21.1
	Translation adjustments						(26.4)	(26.4)
87	Balance at July 30, Year 9	—	20.3	50.8	1,775.8	(70.7)	2.1	1,778.3
	Net earnings				4.4			4.4
	Cash dividends ($.98 per share)				(126.9)			(126.9)
	Treasury stock purchased					(41.1)		(41.1)
	Treasury stock issued under Management incentive and Stock option plans			11.1		4.6		15.7
	Translation adjustments						61.4	61.4
	Balance at July 29, Year 10	—	20.3	61.9	1,653.3	(107.2)	63.5	1,691.8
88	**Net earnings**				***401.5***			***401.5***
89	**Cash dividends ($1.12 per share)**				***(142.2)***			***(142.2)***
90	**Treasury stock purchased**					***(175.6)***		***(175.6)***
91	**Treasury stock issued under Management incentive and Stock option plans**			***45.4***		***12.4***		***57.8***
92	**Translation adjustments**						***(29.9)***	***(29.9)***
93	**Sale of foreign operations**						***(10.0)***	***(10.0)***
94	**Balance at July 28, Year 11**	—	***$20.3***	***$107.3***	***$1,912.6***	***$(270.4)***	***$23.6***	***$1,793.4***

95 **CHANGES IN NUMBER OF SHARES**

(thousands of shares)	Issued	Out-standing	In Treasury
Balance at July 31, Year 8	135,622.7	129,038.6	6,584.1
Treasury stock purchased		(250.6)	250.6
Treasury stock issued under Management incentive and Stock option plans		790.6	(790.6)
Balance at July 30, Year 9	135,622.7	129,578.6	6,044.1
Treasury stock purchased		(833.0)	833.0
Treasury stock issued under Management incentive and Stock option plans		523.4	(523.4)
Balance at July 29, Year 10	135,622.7	129,269.0	6,353.7
Treasury stock purchased		***(3,395.4)***	***3,395.4***
Treasury stock issued under Management incentive and Stock option plans		***1,130.2***	***(1,130.2)***
Balance at July 28, Year 11	***135,622.7***	***127,003.8***	***8,618.9***

The accompanying Summary of Significant Accounting Policies and Notes are an integral part of the financial statements.

CAMPBELL SOUP

(million dollars)

96 **1 SUMMARY OF SIGNIFICANT ACCOUNTING POLICIES**

CONSOLIDATION—The consolidated financial statements include the accounts of the Company and its majority-owned subsidiaries. Significant intercompany transactions are eliminated in consolidation. Investments in affiliated owned 20% or more are accounted for by the equity method.

INVENTORIES—Substantially all domestic inventories are priced at the lower of cost or market, with cost determined by the last-in, first-out (LIFO) method. Other inventories are priced at the lower of average cost or market.

INTANGIBLES—The excess of cost of investments over net assets of purchased companies is amortized on a straight-line basis over periods not exceeding forty years.

PLANT ASSETS—Alterations and major overhauls which substantially extend the lives of properties or materially increase their capacity are capitalized. The amounts for property disposals are removed from plant asset and accumulated depreciation accounts and any resultant gain or loss is included in earnings. Ordinary repairs and maintenance are charged to operating costs.

DEPRECIATION—Depreciation provided in costs and expenses is on the straight-line method. The United States, Canadian and certain other foreign companies use accelerated methods of depreciation for income tax purposes.

PENSION PLANS—Pension costs are accrued over employees' careers based on plan benefit formulas.

CASH AND CASH EQUIVALENTS—All highly liquid debt instruments purchased with a maturity of three months or less are classified as Cash Equivalents.

FINANCIAL INSTRUMENTS—In managing interest rate exposure, the Company at times enters into interest rate swap agreements. When interest rates change, the difference to be paid or received is accrued and recognized as interest expense over the life of the agreement. In order to hedge foreign currency exposures on firm commitments, the Company at times enters into forward foreign exchange contracts. Gains and losses resulting from these instruments are recognized in the same period as the underlying hedged transaction. The Company also at times enters into foreign currency swap agreements which are effective as hedges of net investments in foreign subsidiaries. Realized and unrealized gains and losses on these currency swaps are recognized in the Cumulative Translation Adjustments account in Shareowners' Equity.

97 **2 GEOGRAPHIC AREA INFORMATION**

The Company is predominantly engaged in the prepared convenience foods industry. The following presents information about operations in different geographic areas:

	Year 11	Year 10	Year 9
Net sales			
United States	***$4,495.6***	$4,527.2	$4,233.4
Europe	***1,149.1***	1,101.4	983.7
Other foreign countries	***656.0***	673.6	542.9
Adjustment and elimination	***(96.6)***	(96.4)	(87.9)
Consolidated	***$6,204.1***	$6,205.8	$5,672.1
Earnings (loss) before taxes			
United States	***$694.8***	$427.8	$294.5
Europe	***48.8***	(178.7)	(21.3)
Other foreign countries	***55.0***	44.6	(59.6)
	798.6	293.7	213.6
Unallocated corporate expenses	***(41.1)***	(16.5)	(31.3)
Interest, net	***(90.2)***	(94.0)	(55.8)
Foreign currency translation adjustment	***.1***	(3.8)	(20.0)
Consolidated	***$667.4***	$179.4	$106.5
Identifiable assets			
United States	***$2,693.4***	$2,535.0	$2,460.5
Europe	***711.3***	942.2	886.9
Other foreign countries	***744.3***	638.4	584.7
Consolidated	***$4,149.0***	$4,115.6	$3,932.1

Transfers between geographic areas are recorded at cost plus markup or at market. Identifiable assets are all assets identified with operations in each geographic area.

3 INTEREST EXPENSE

	Year 11	Year 10	Year 9
98 Interest expense	***$136.9***	$121.9	$97.6
99 Less interest expense capitalized	***20.7***	10.3	3.5
100	***$116.2***	$111.6	$94.1

(million dollars)

101 **4 FOREIGN CURRENCY TRANSLATION**

Fluctuations in foreign exchange rates resulted in decreases in net earnings of $.3 in Year 11, $3.2 in Year 10 and $19.1 in Year 9.

The balances in the Cumulative translation adjustments account are the following:

	Year 11	Year 10	Year 9
Europe	***$ 5.6***	$43.2	$(3.5)
Canada	***3.8***	3.6	(2.5)
Australia	***13.4***	16.1	7.3
Other	***.8***	.6	.8
	$23.6	$63.5	$ 2.1

5 OTHER EXPENSE

Included in other expense are the following:

	Year 11	Year 10	Year 9
102 Stock price related incentive programs	***$15.4***	$ (.1)	$17.4
103 Amortization of intangible and other assets	***14.1***	16.8	16.4
104 Other, net	***(3.3)***	(2.0)	(1.4)
	$26.2	$14.7	$32.4

105 **6 DIVESTITURES, RESTRUCTURING AND UNUSUAL CHARGES**

In Year 10, charges for divestiture and restructuring programs, designed to strengthen the Company's core businesses and improve long-term profitability, reduced operating earnings by $339.1; $301.6 after taxes, or $2.33 per share. The divestiture program involves the sale of several low-return or non-strategic businesses. The restructuring charges provide for the elimination of underperforming assets and unnecessary facilities and include a charge of $113 to write off goodwill in the United Kingdom.

In Year 9, charges for a worldwide restructuring program reduced operating earnings by $343.0; $260.8 after taxes, or $2.02 per share. The restructuring program involved plant consolidations, work force reductions, and goodwill write-offs.

106 **7 ACQUISITIONS**

Prior to July Year 11, the Company owned approximately 71% of the capital stock of Campbell Soup Company Ltd. ("Campbell Canada"), which processes, packages and distributes a wide range of prepared foods exclusively in Canada under many of the Company's brand names. The financial position and results of operations of Campbell Canada are consolidated with those of the Company. In July Year 11, the Company acquired the remaining shares (29%) of Campbell Canada which it did not already own at a cost of $159.7. In addition, the Company made one other acquisition at a cost of $20.4. The total cost of Year 11 acquisitions of $180.1 was allocated as follows:

107

Working capital	$ 5.1
Fixed assets	4.7
Intangibles, principally goodwill	132.3
Other assets	1.5
Elimination of minority interest	36.5
	$180.1

During Year 10 the Company made several small acquisitions at a cost of $43.1 which was allocated as follows:

108

Working capital	$ 7.8
Fixed assets	24.7
Intangibles, principally goodwill	18.5
Long-term liabilities and other	(7.9)
	$43.1

During Year 9, the Company made several acquisitions at a cost of $137.9, including a soup and pickle manufacturing business in Canada. The cost of the acquisitions was allocated as follows:

109

Working capital	$ 39.9
Fixed assets	34.6
Intangibles, principally goodwill	65.5
Long-term liabilities and other	(2.1)
	$137.9

These acquisition were accounted for as purchase transactions, and operations of the acquired companies are included in the financial statements from the dates the acquisitions were recorded. Proforma results

CAMPBELL SOUP

(million dollars)

of operations have not been presented as they would not vary materially from the reported amounts and would not be indicative of results anticipated following acquisition due to significant changes made to acquired companies' operations.

110 8 PENSION PLANS AND RETIREMENT BENEFITS

Pension Plans—Substantially all of the employees of the Company and its domestic and Canadian subsidiaries are covered by noncontributory defined benefit pension plans. Plan benefits are generally based on years of service and employees' compensation during the last years of employment. Benefits are paid from funds previously provided to trustees and insurance companies or are paid directly by the Company or its subsidiaries. Actuarial assumptions and plan provisions are reviewed regularly by the Company and its independent actuaries to ensure that plan assets will be adequate to provide pension and survivor benefits. Plan assets consist primarily of shares of or units in common stock, fixed income, real estate and money market funds.

Pension expense included the following:

	Year 11	Year 10	Year 9
For Domestic and Canadian trusteed plans:			
111 Service cost-benefits earned during the year	**$ 22.1**	$ 19.3	$ 17.2
112 Interest cost on projected benefit obligation	**69.0**	63.3	58.8
113 Actual return on plan assets	**(73.4)**	(27.1)	(113.8)
114 Net amortization and deferral	**6.3**	(38.2)	57.8
	24.0	17.3	20.0
115 Other pension expense	**7.4**	6.4	6.8
116 Consolidated pension expense	**$ 31.4**	$ 23.7	$ 26.8

Principal actuarial assumptions used in the United States were:

	Year 11	Year 10	Year 9
Measurements of projected benefit obligation—			
117 Discount rate	**8.75%**	9.00%	9.00%
118 Long-term rate of compensation increase	**5.75%**	5.50%	5.00%
119 Long-term rate of return on plan assets	**9.00%**	9.00%	9.00%

The funded status of the plans was as follows:

120	**July 28, Year 11**	July 29, Year 10
Actuarial present value of benefit obligations:		
Vested	**$(679.6)**	$(624.4)
Non-vested	**(34.8)**	(35.0)
Accumulated benefit obligation	**(714.4)**	(659.4)
Effect of projected future salary increases	**(113.3)**	(101.0)
Projected benefit obligation	**(827.7)**	(760.4)
Plan assets at market value	**857.7**	773.9
Plan assets in excess of projected benefit obligation	**30.0**	13.5
Unrecognized net loss	**122.9**	86.3
Unrecognized prior service cost	**54.9**	55.9
Unrecognized net assets at transition	**(35.3)**	(39.5)
Prepaid pension expense	**$ 172.5**	$ 116.2

Pension coverage for employees of the Company's foreign subsidiaries, other than Canada, and other supplemental pension benefits of the Company are provided to the extent determined appropriate through their respective plans. Obligations under such plans are systematically provided for by depositing funds with trusts or under insurance contracts. The assets and obligations of these plans are not material.

Savings Plans—The Company sponsors employee savings plans which cover substantially all domestic employees. After one year of continuous service the Company matches 50% of employee contributions up to five percent of compensation within certain limits. In fiscal Year 12, the Company will increase its contribution by up to 20% if certain earnings' goals are achieved. Amounts charged to costs and expenses were $10.0 in Year 11, $10.6 in Year 10, and $10.7 in Year 9.

(million dollars)

Retiree Benefits—The Company and its domestic subsidiaries provide certain health care and life insurance benefits to substantially all retired employees and their dependents. The cost of these retiree health and life insurance benefits are expensed as claims are paid and amounted to $15.3 in Year 11, $12.6 in Year 10, and $11.0 in Year 9. Substantially all retirees of foreign subsidiaries are provided health care benefits by government sponsored plans. The cost of life insurance provided to retirees of certain foreign subsidiaries is not significant.

In December Year 10, the Financial Accounting Standards Board issued Statement of Financial Accounting Standards No. 106, "Employer's Accounting for Post-retirement Benefits Other Than Pensions," which will require the Company to account for retiree health obligations on an accrual basis beginning with the Year 14 fiscal year. The Company is in the process of studying the effects of this complex new accounting standard. The standard permits an employer to recognize the effect of the initial liability either immediately or to amortize it over a period of up to 20 years. The Company has not yet decided which option to select. Management expects that the adoption of this standard will increase annual expense, but the amount has not yet been determined.

121 9 TAXES ON EARNINGS

The provision for income taxes consists of the following:

		Year 11	Year 10	Year 9
	Currently payable			
122	Federal	***$185.8***	$132.4	$118.8
123	State	***23.4***	20.8	20.9
124	Foreign	***21.2***	17.9	21.5
124A		***230.4***	171.1	161.2
	Deferred			
125	Federal	***21.9***	1.2	(49.3)
126	State	***7.5***	2.6	(8.0)
127	Foreign	***6.1***	.1	(10.5)
127B		***35.5***	3.9	(67.8)
127C		***$265.9***	$175.0	$ 93.4

The deferred income taxes result from temporary differences between financial statement earnings and taxable earnings as follows:

		Year 11	Year 10	Year 9
128	Depreciation	***$ 5.9***	$ 18.6	$ 11.9
129	Pensions	***13.6***	11.7	8.3
130	Prefunded employee benefits	***(3.3)***	(4.8)	(3.4)
131	Accruals not currently deductible for tax purposes	***(11.4)***	(5.8)	(5.3)
132	Divestitures, restructuring and unusual charges	***29.3***	(11.1)	(78.2)
133	Other	***1.4***	(4.7)	(1.1)
		$35.5	$ 3.9	$(67.8)

The following is a reconciliation of effective income tax rates with the statutory Federal income tax rate:

		Year 11	Year 10	Year 9
134	Statutory Federal income tax rate	***34.0%***	34.0%	34.0%
135	State income taxes (net of Federal tax benefit)	***3.0***	3.7	3.6
136	Nondeductible divestitures, restructuring and unusual charges		56.5	48.7
137	Nondeductible amortization of intangibles	***.6***	.9	1.1
138	Foreign earnings not taxed or taxed at other than statutory Federal rate	***(.3)***	1.2	.2
139	Other	***2.5***	1.2	.1
140	Effective income tax rate	***39.8%***	97.5%	87.7%

The provision for income taxes was reduced by $3.2 in Year 11, $5.2 in Year 10 and $3.5 in Year 9 due to the utilization of loss carryforwards by certain foreign subsidiaries.

Certain foreign subsidiaries of the Company have tax loss carryforwards of approximately $103.4 ($77.4 for financial purposes), of which $10.5 relate to periods prior to acquisition of the subsidiaries by the Company. Of these carryforwards, $54.8 expire through Year 16 and $48.6 may be carried forward indefinitely. The current statutory tax rates in these foreign countries range from 20% to 51%.

(million dollars)

Income taxes have not been accrued on undistributed earnings of foreign subsidiaries of $219.7 which are invested in operating assets and are not expected to be remitted. If remitted, tax credits are available to substantially reduce any resultant additional taxes.

The following are earnings before taxes of United States and foreign companies.

		Year 11	Year 10	Year 9
141	United States	***$570.9***	$277.0	$201.5
142	Foreign	***96.5***	(97.6)	(95.0)
		$667.4	$179.4	$106.5

143 **10 LEASES**

Rent expense was $59.7 in Year 11, $62.4 in Year 10 and $60.2 in Year 9 and generally relates to leases of machinery and equipment. Future minimum lease payments under operating leases are $71.9.

11 SUPPLEMENTARY STATEMENTS OF EARNINGS INFORMATION

		Year 11	Year 10	Year 9
144	Maintenance and repairs	***$173.9***	$180.6	$173.9
145	Advertising	***$195.4***	$220.4	$212.9

146 **12 CASH AND CASH EQUIVALENTS**

Cash and Cash Equivalents includes cash equivalents of $140.7 at July 28, Year 11, and $44.1 at July 29, Year 10.

13 ACCOUNTS RECEIVABLE

		Year 11	Year 10
147	Customers	***$478.0***	$554.0
148	Allowances for cash discounts and bad debts	***(16.3)***	(19.9)
		461.7	534.1
149	Other	***65.7***	90.4
150		***$527.4***	$624.5

14 INVENTORIES

		Year 11	Year 10
151	Raw materials, containers and supplies	***$342.3***	$384.4
152	Finished products	***454.0***	520.0
		796.3	904.4
153	Less—adjustments of inventories to LIFO basis	***89.6***	84.6
		$706.7	$819.8

Liquidation of LIFO inventory quantities had no significant effect on net earnings in Year 11, Year 10, or Year 9. Inventories for which the LIFO method of determining cost is used represented approximately 70% of consolidated inventories in Year 11 and 64% in Year 10.

15 PREPAID EXPENSES

		Year 11	Year 10
154	Pensions	***$19.8***	$ 22.3
155	Deferred taxes	***36.6***	37.7
156	Prefunded employee benefits	***1.2***	13.9
157	Other	***35.1***	44.1
		$92.7	$118.0

16 PLANT ASSETS

		Year 11	Year 10
158	Land	***$ 56.3***	$ 63.8
159	Buildings	***758.7***	746.5
160	Machinery and equipment	***1,779.3***	1,657.6
161	Projects in progress	***327.6***	267.0
161A		***2,921.9***	2,734.9
162	Accumulated depreciation	***(1,131.5)***	(1,017.2)
		$1,790.4	$1,717.7

Depreciation provided in costs and expenses was $194.5 in Year 11, $184.1 in Year 10 and $175.9 in Year 9. Approximately $158.2 of capital expenditures is required to complete projects in progress at July 28, Year 11.

(million dollars)

17 INTANGIBLE ASSETS

		Year 11	Year 10
163	Cost of investments in excess of net assets of purchased companies (goodwill)	**$347.8**	$281.1
164	Other intangibles	**129.8**	134.0
		477.6	415.1
165	Accumulated amortization	**(42.1)**	(31.7)
		$435.5	$383.4

18 OTHER ASSETS

		Year 11	Year 10
166	Investment in affiliates	**$155.8**	$169.4
167	Noncurrent prepaid pension expense	**152.7**	93.9
168	Other noncurrent investments	**44.2**	52.0
169	Other	**51.9**	33.7
169A		**$404.6**	$349.0

Investment in affiliates consists principally of the Company's ownership of 33% of the outstanding capital stock of Arnotts Limited, an Australian biscuit manufacturer. This investment is being accounted for by the equity method. Included in this investment is goodwill of $28.3 which is being amortized over 40 years. At July 28, Year 11, the market value of the investment based on quoted market prices was $213.8. The Company's equity in the earnings of Arnotts Limited was $1.5 in Year 11, $13.0 in Year 10 and $8.7 in Year 9. The Year 10 amount includes a $4.0 gain realized by Arnotts on the sales of businesses. Dividends received were $8.2 in Year 11, $7.4 in Year 10 and $6.6 in Year 9. The Company's equity in the undistributed earnings of Arnotts was $15.4 at July 28, Year 11 and $22.1 at July 29, Year 10.

170 19 NOTES PAYABLE AND LONG-TERM DEBT

Notes payable consists of the following:

	Year 11	Year 10
Commercial paper	**$ 24.7**	$191.8
8.25% Notes due Year 11		100.3
13.99% Notes due Year 12	**182.0***	
Banks	**23.6**	91.1
Other	**51.9**	69.4
Amounts reclassified to long-term debt		(250.3)
	$282.2	$202.3

**Present value of $200.0 zero coupon notes, net of unamortized discount of $18.0.*

At July 29, Year 10, $150 of outstanding commercial paper and $100.3 of currently maturing notes were reclassified to long-term debt and were refinanced in Year 11.

Information on notes payable follows:

171	Year 11	Year 10	Year 9
Maximum amount payable at end of any monthly accounting period during the year	**$603.3**	$518.7	$347.1
Approximate average amount outstanding during the year	**$332.5**	$429.7	$273.5
Weighted average interest rate at year-end	**10.1%**	10.7%	12.1%
Approximate weighted average interest rate during the year	**9.8%**	10.8%	10.6%

The amount of unused lines of credit at July 28, Year 11 approximates $635. The lines of credit are unconditional and generally cover loans for a period of a year at prime commercial interest rates.

CAMPBELL SOUP

(million dollars)

Long-term debt consists of the following:

172

Fiscal year maturities	Year 11	Year 10
13.99% Notes due Year 12	$	$159.7***
9.125% Notes due Year 14	**100.6**	100.9
10.5% Notes due Year 16*	**100.0**	100.0
7.5% Notes due Year 18*	**99.6**	99.5
9.0% Notes due Year 18	**99.8**	
8.58%–8.75% Medium-Term Notes due Year 21**	**100.0**	
8.875% Debentures due Year 41	**199.6**	
Other Notes due Year 12–24 (interest 4.7%–14.4%)	**58.2**	82.5
Notes payable, reclassified		250.3
Capital lease obligations	**14.8**	12.9
	$772.6	$805.8

*Redeemable in Year 13.
**$50 redeemable in Year 18.
***Present value of $200.0 zero coupon notes, net of unamortized discount of $40.3.

173 Future minimum lease payments under capital leases are $28.0 and the present value of such payments, after deducting implicit interest of $6.5, is $21.5 of which $6.7 is included in current liabilities.

Principle amounts of long-term debt mature as follows: Year 12-$227.7 (in current liabilities); Year 13-$118.9; Year 14-$17.8; Year 15-$15.9; Year 16-$108.3 and beyond-$511.7.

The Company has filed a shelf registration statement with the Securities and Exchange Commission for the issuance from time to time of up to $300 of debt securities, of which $100 remains unissued.

Information on financial instruments follows:

At July 28, Year 11, the Company had an interest rate swap agreement with financial institutions having a notional principal amount of $100, which is intended to reduce the impact of changes in interest rates on floating rate commercial paper. In addition, at July 28, Year 11, the Company had two swap agreements with financial institutions which covered both interest rates and foreign currencies. These agreements have a total notional principal amount of $103, and are intended to reduce exposure to higher foreign interest rates and to hedge the Company's net investments in the United Kingdom and Australia. The Company is exposed to credit loss in the event of nonperformance by the other parties to the interest rate swap agreements; however, the Company does not anticipate nonperformance by the counterparties.

At July 28, Year 11, the Company had contracts to purchase approximately $109 in foreign currency. The contracts are mostly for European currencies and have maturities through Year 12.

20 ACCRUED LIABILITIES

	Year 11	Year 10
174 Divestiture and restructuring charges	**$ 88.4**	$238.8
175 Other	**320.3**	253.1
	$408.7	$491.9

21 OTHER LIABILITIES

	Year 11	Year 10
176 Deferred income taxes	**$258.5**	$235.1
177 Other liabilities	**23.0**	28.5
178 Minority interests	**23.5**	56.3
	$305.0	$319.9

(million dollars)

179 **22 SHAREOWNERS' EQUITY**

The Company has authorized 140 million shares of Capital Stock of $.15 par value and 40 million shares of Preferred Stock issuable in one or more classes, with or without par as may be authorized by the Board of Directors. No Preferred Stock has been issued.

The following summarizes the activity in option shares under the Company's employee stock option plans:

(thousands of shares)	*Year 11*	Year 10	Year 9
Beginning of year	***4,301.1***	3,767.9	3,257.0
Granted under the Year 4 long-term incentive plan at average price of $63.64 in Year 11; $47.27 in Year 10; $30.37 in Year 9	***2,136.3***	1,196.0	1,495.5
Exercised at average price of $29.82 in Year 11; $24.78 in Year 10; $20.65 in Year 9 in form of:			
Stock appreciation rights	***(14.9)***	(110.2)	(137.3)
Shares	***(1,063.7)***	(367.2)	(615.1)
Terminated	***(216.9)***	(185.4)	(232.2)
End of year	***5,141.9***	4,301.1	3,767.9
Exercisable at end of year	***2,897.0***	2,654.4	2,104.1
Shares under option-price per share:			
Range of prices: Low	***$14.68***	$ 6.98	$ 6.98
High	***$83.31***	$57.61	$34.31
Average	***$46.73***	$33.63	$28.21

In addition to options granted under the Year 4 long-term incentive plan, 233,200 restricted shares of capital stock were granted to certain key management employees in Year 11; 168,850 in Year 10; and 162,000 in Year 9.

There are 4,229,111 shares available for grant under the long-term incentive plan.

Net earnings per share are based on the weighted average shares outstanding during the applicable periods. The potential dilution from the exercise of stock options is not material.

23 STATEMENTS OF CASH FLOWS

	Year 11	Year 10	Year 9
180 Interest paid, net of amounts capitalized	***$101.3***	$116.3	$ 88.9
181 Interest received	***$ 27.9***	$ 17.1	$ 35.5
182 Income taxes paid	***$199.3***	$152.8	$168.6
183 Capital lease obligations incurred	***$ 10.0***	$ 9.7	$ 18.0

184 **24 QUARTERLY DATA (unaudited)**

	Year 11			
	First	***Second***	***Third***	***Fourth***
Net sales	***$1,594.3***	***$1,770.9***	***$1,490.8***	***$1,348.1***
Cost of products sold	***1,082.7***	***1,152.6***	***981.6***	***878.6***
Net earnings	***105.1***	***135.3***	***76.4***	***84.7***
Per share				
Net earnings	***.82***	***1.07***	***.60***	***.67***
Dividends	***.25***	***.29***	***.29***	***.29***
Market price				
High	***54.00***	***60.38***	***87.13***	***84.88***
Low	***43.75***	***48.50***	***58.75***	***72.38***

	Year 10			
	First	***Second***	***Third***	***Fourth***
Net sales	$1,523.5	$1,722.5	$1,519.6	$1,440.2
Cost of products sold	1,057.2	1,173.0	1,049.3	978.7
Net earnings (loss)	83.0	105.2	54.6	(238.4)
Per share				
Net earnings (loss)	.64	.81	.42	(1.84)
Dividends	.23	.25	.25	.25
Market price				
High	58.50	59.63	54.13	62.00
Low	42.13	42.50	45.00	50.13

The fourth quarter of Year 10 includes divestitures, restructuring and unusual charges of $301.6 after taxes, or $2.33 per share.

ELEVEN YEAR REVIEW–CONSOLIDATED

(millions except per share amounts)

Fiscal Year	**Year 11**	Year 10	Year 9
[185] **SUMMARY OF OPERATIONS**		*(a)*	*(b)*
Net sales	***$6,204.1***	$6,205.8	$5,672.1
Earnings before taxes	***667.4***	179.4	106.5
Earnings before cumulative effect of accounting change	***401.5***	4.4	13.1
Net earnings	***401.5***	4.4	13.1
Percent of sales	***6.5%***	.1%	.2%
Return on average shareowners' equity	***23.0%***	.3%	.7%
FINANCIAL POSITION			
Working capital	***$ 240.5***	$ 367.4	$ 369.4
Plant assets–net	***1,790.4***	1,717.7	1,540.6
Total assets	***4,149.0***	4,115.6	3,932.1
Long-term debt	***772.6***	805.8	629.2
Shareowners' equity	***1,793.4***	1,691.8	1,778.3
PER SHARE DATA			
Earnings before cumulative effect of accounting change	***$ 3.16***	$ .03	$ .10
Net earnings	***3.16***	.03	.10
Dividends declared	***1.12***	.98	.90
Shareowners' equity	***14.12***	13.09	13.76
OTHER STATISTICS			
Salaries, wages, pensions, etc.	***$1,401.0***	$1,422.5	$1,333.9
Capital expenditures	***371.1***	397.3	302.0
Number of shareowners (in thousands)	***37.7***	43.0	43.7
Weighted average shares outstanding	***127.0***	129.6	129.3

(a) Year 10 includes pre-tax divestiture and restructuring charges of $339.1 million; 301.6 million or $2.33 per share after taxes.
(b) Year 9 includes pre-tax restructuring charges of $343.0 million; $260.8 million or $2.02 per share after taxes.
(c) Year 8 includes pre-tax restructuring charges of $49.3 million; $29.4 million or 23 cents per share after taxes. Year 8 also includes cumulative effect of change in accounting for income taxes of $32.5 million or 25 cents per share.
(d) Includes employees under the Employee Stock Ownership Plan terminated in Year 7.

Year 8	Year 7	Year 6	Year 5	Year 4	Year 3	Year 2	Year 1
(c)							
$4,868.9	*$4,490.4*	*$4,286.8*	*$3,916.6*	*$3,636.9*	*$3,292.4*	*$2,955.6*	*$2,797.7*
388.6	*417.9*	*387.2*	*333.7*	*332.4*	*306.0*	*276.9*	*244.4*
241.6	*247.3*	*223.2*	*197.8*	*191.2*	*165.0*	*149.6*	*129.7*
274.1	*247.3*	*223.2*	*197.8*	*191.2*	*165.0*	*149.6*	*129.7*
5.6%	*5.5%*	*5.2%*	*5.1%*	*5.3%*	*5.0%*	*5.1%*	*4.6%*
15.1%	*15.1%*	*15.3%*	*15.0%*	*15.9%*	*15.0%*	*14.6%*	*13.2%*
$ 499.6	$ 744.1	$ 708.7	$ 579.4	$ 541.5	$ 478.9	$ 434.6	$ 368.2
1,508.9	1,349.0	1,168.1	1,027.5	970.9	889.1	815.4	755.1
3,609.6	3,097.4	2,762.8	2,437.5	2,210.1	1,991.5	1,865.5	1,722.9
525.8	380.2	362.3	297.1	283.0	267.5	236.2	150.6
1,895.0	1,736.1	1,538.9	1,382.5	1,259.9	1,149.4	1,055.8	1,000.5
$ 1.87	$ 1.90	$ 1.72	$ 1.53	$ 1.48	$ 1.28	$ 1.16	$ 1.00
2.12	1.90	1.72	1.53	1.48	1.28	1.16	1.00
.81	.71	.65	.61	.57	.54	.53	.51
14.69	13.35	11.86	10.69	9.76	8.92	8.19	7.72
$1,222.9	$1,137.3	$1,061.0	$ 950.1	$ 889.5	$ 755.1	$ 700.9	$ 680.9
261.9	328.0	251.3	212.9	183.1	154.1	147.6	135.4
43.0	41.0	50.9*(d)*	49.5*(d)*	49.4*(d)*	40.1	39.7	41.6
129.4	129.9	129.5	129.1	129.0	129.0	129.0	129.6

CAMPBELL SOUP

186 Form 10-K

Schedule V
CAMPBELL SOUP COMPANY AND CONSOLIDATED SUBSIDIARIES
Property, Plant, and Equipment at Cost
(million dollars)

	Land	*Buildings*	*Machinery and equipment*	*Projects in progress*	*Total*
Balance at July 31, Year 8	$53.2	$735.5	$1,624.4	$126.6	$2,539.7
Additions	2.8	47.6	216.4	35.2	302.0
Acquired assets*	4.8	13.6	22.6	—	41.0
Retirements and sales	(4.5)	(88.4)	(238.3)	—	(331.2)
Translation adjustments	(.5)	(2.5)	(5.9)	.4	(8.5)
Balance at July 30, Year 9	55.8	705.8	1,619.2	162.2	2,543.0
Additions	3.2	69.2	219.6	105.3	397.3
Acquired assets*	3.8	14.1	6.8	—	24.7
Retirements and sales	(2.8)	(64.0)	(222.9)	(1.1)	(290.8)
Translation adjustments	3.8	21.4	34.9	.6	60.7
Balance at July 29, Year 10	63.8	746.5	1,657.6	267.0	2,734.9
Additions	1.5	70.2	239.5	59.9	371.1
Acquired assets*	.5	3.3	.9	—	4.7
Retirements and sales	(7.5)	(49.3)	(99.9)	—	(156.7)
Rate variance	(2.0)	(12.0)	(18.8)	.7	(32.1)
Balance at July 28, Year 11	$56.3	$758.7	$1,779.3	$327.6	$2,921.9

*See "Acquisitions" in Notes to Consolidated Financial Statements.

187 Form 10-K

Schedule VI
CAMPBELL SOUP COMPANY AND CONSOLIDATED SUBSIDIARIES
Accumulated Depreciation and Amortization of Property, Plant and Equipment
(million dollars)

	Buildings	*Machinery and Equipment*	*Total*
Balance at July 31, Year 8	$285.4	$745.4	$1,030.8
Additions charged to income	31.5	144.4	175.9
Retirements and sales	(57.8)	(143.5)	(201.3)
Translations adjustments	(.8)	(2.2)	(3.0)
Balance at July 30, Year 9	258.3	744.1	1,002.4
Additions charged to income	34.2	149.9	184.1
Retirements and sales	(32.5)	(154.7)	(187.2)
Translations adjustments	5.2	12.7	17.9
Balance at July 29, Year 10	265.2	752.0	1,017.2
Additions charged to income	35.3	159.2	194.5
Retirements and sales	(17.4)	(52.1)	(69.5)
Translations adjustments	(2.8)	(7.9)	(10.7)
Balance at July 28, Year 11	$280.3	$851.2	$1,131.5

Quaker

Focused on Value Creation...

QUAKER OATS

The Quaker Oats Company and Subsidiaries

Consolidated Statements of Income

Dollars in Millions (Except Per Share Data)

	Year Ended June 30	Year 11	Year 10	Year 9
1	**Net Sales**	**$5,491.2**	$5,030.6	$4,879.4
2	Cost of goods sold	**2,839.7**	2,685.9	2,655.3
3	Gross profit	**2,651.5**	2,344.7	2,224.1
4	Selling, general and administrative expenses	**2,121.2**	1,844.1	1,779.0
5	Interest expense—net of $9.0, $11.0 and $12.4 interest income	**86.2**	101.8	56.4
6	Other expense—net	**32.6**	16.4	149.6
7	**Income from Continuing Operations Before Income Taxes**	**411.5**	382.4	239.1
8	Provision for income taxes	**175.7**	153.5	90.2
9	**Income from Continuing Operations**	**235.8**	228.9	148.9
10	Income (loss) from discontinued operations—net of tax	**(30.0)**	(59.9)	54.1
11	**Net Income**	**205.8**	169.0	203.0
12	Preferred dividends—net of tax	**4.3**	4.5	—
13	**Net Income Available for Common**	**$ 201.5**	$ 164.5	$ 203.0
	Per Common Share:			
14	**Income from Continuing Operations**	**$ 3.05**	$ 2.93	$ 1.88
15	Income (loss) from discontinued operations	**(.40)**	(.78)	.68
16	**Net Income**	**$ 2.65**	$ 2.15	$ 2.56
17	Dividends declared	**$ 1.56**	$ 1.40	$ 1.20
18	**Average Number of Common Shares Outstanding** (in 000's)	**75,904**	76,537	79,307

See accompanying notes to the consolidated financial statements.

Consolidated Statements of Cash Flows

Dollars in Millions

	Year Ended June 30	Year 11	Year 10	Year 9
	Cash Flows from Operating Activities:			
19	Net income	**$ 205.8**	$ 169.0	$ 203.0
	Adjustments to reconcile net income to net cash (used in) provided by operating activities:			
20	Depreciation and amortization	**177.7**	162.5	135.5
21	Deferred income taxes and other items	**45.3**	15.2	79.9
22	Provision for restructuring charges	**10.0**	(17.5)	124.3
	Changes in operating assets and liabilities—continuing operations:			
23	Change in receivables	**(97.8)**	(55.9)	(77.1)
24	Change in inventories	**30.7**	(2.2)	(90.3)
25	Change in other current assets	**(13.7)**	(14.1)	(48.9)
26	Change in trade accounts payable	**26.1**	31.4	102.2
27	Change in other current liabilities	**43.2**	83.4	(53.1)
28	Other—net	**9.5**	0.4	(8.4)
29	Change in payable to Fisher-Price	**29.6**	—	—
30	Change in net current assets of discontinued operations	**66.0**	74.9	14.5
31	Net Cash Provided by Operating Activities	**532.4**	447.1	381.6
	Cash Flows from Investing Activities:			
32	Additions to property, plant and equipment	**(240.6)**	(275.6)	(223.2)
33	Cost of acquisitions, excluding working capital	—	—	(112.9)
34	Change in other receivables and investments	**(10.7)**	(22.6)	(5.7)
35	Disposals of property, plant and equipment	**17.9**	11.9	26.7
36	Other—discontinued operations	**(19.8)**	(58.4)	(46.7)
37	Net Cash Used in Investing Activities	**(253.2)**	(344.7)	(361.8)
	Cash Flows from Financing Activities:			
38	Cash dividends	**(123.0)**	(110.5)	(95.2)
39	Proceeds from issuance of debt for spin-off	**141.1**	—	—
40	Change in deferred compensation	**(0.2)**	3.5	(248.4)
41	Change in short-term debt	**(265.6)**	(7.2)	42.1
42	Proceeds from long-term debt	**1.8**	252.1	251.2
43	Reduction of long-term debt	**(39.7)**	(34.8)	(30.1)
44	Issuance of common treasury stock	**25.6**	12.8	10.1
45	Purchase of common stock	—	(223.2)	(68.5)
46	Issuance of preferred stock	—	—	100.0
47	Purchase of preferred stock	**(0.7)**	—	—
48	Net Cash Used in Financing Activities	**(260.7)**	(107.3)	(38.8)
49	**Effect of Exchange Rate Changes on Cash and Cash Equivalents**	**(6.0)**	1.6	(7.4)
50	**Net Increase (Decrease) in Cash and Cash Equivalents**	**$ 12.5**	$ (3.3)	$ (26.4)
51	**Cash and Cash Equivalents—Beginning of Year**	**$ 17.7**	$ 21.0	$ 47.4
52	**Cash and Cash Equivalents—End of Year**	**$ 30.2**	$ 17.7	$ 21.0

See accompanying notes to the consolidated financial statements.

The Quaker Oats Company and Subsidiaries

Consolidated Balance Sheets

	Assets			
	June 30	**Year 11**	Year 10	Year 9
	Current Assets:			
53	Cash and cash equivalents	**$ 30.2**	$ 17.7	$ 21.0
54	Short-term investments, at cost which approximates market	**—**	.6	2.7
55	Receivables—net of allowances	**691.1**	629.9	594.4
	Inventories:			
56	Finished goods	**309.1**	324.1	326.0
57	Grain and raw materials	**86.7**	110.7	114.1
58	Packaging materials and supplies	**26.5**	39.1	39.0
59	Total inventories	**422.3**	473.9	479.1
60	Other current assets	**114.5**	107.0	94.2
61	Net current assets of discontinued operations	**—**	252.2	328.5
62	Total current assets	**1,258.1**	1,481.3	1,519.9
63	**Other Receivables and Investments**	**79.1**	63.5	26.4
64	Property, plant and equipment	**1,914.6**	1,745.6	1,456.9
65	Less accumulated depreciation	**681.9**	591.5	497.3
66	**Properties—Net**	**1,232.7**	1,154.1	959.6
67	**Intangible Assets, Net of Amortization**	**446.2**	466.7	484.7
68	**Net Non-current Assets of Discontinued Operations**	**—**	160.5	135.3
69	**Total Assets**	**$3,016.1**	$3,326.1	$3,125.9

See accompanying notes to the consolidated financial statements.

Dollars in Millions

	Liabilities and Common Shareholders' Equity			
	June 30	**Year 11**	Year 10	Year 9
	Current Liabilities:			
70	Short-term debt	**$ 80.6**	$ 343.2	$ 102.2
71	Current portion of long-term debt	**32.9**	32.3	30.0
72	Trade accounts payable	**350.9**	354.0	333.8
73	Accrued payrolls, pensions and bonuses	**116.3**	106.3	118.1
74	Accrued advertising and merchandising	**105.7**	92.6	67.1
75	Income taxes payable	**45.1**	36.3	8.0
76	Payable to Fisher-Price	**29.6**	—	—
77	Other accrued liabilities	**165.8**	173.8	164.9
78	Total current liabilities	**926.9**	1,138.5	824.1
79	**Long-term Debt**	**701.2**	740.3	766.8
80	**Other Liabilities**	**115.5**	100.3	89.5
81	**Deferred Income Taxes**	**366.7**	327.7	308.4
82	**Preferred Stock,** no pay value, authorized 1,750,000 shares; issued 1,282,051 of $5.46 cumulative convertible shares in Year 9 (liquidating preference $78 per share)	**100.0**	100.0	100.0
83	**Deferred Compensation**	**(94.5)**	(98.2)	(100.0)
84	**Treasury Preferred Stock,** at cost, 10,089 shares at June 30, Year 11	**(.7)**	—	—
	Common Shareholders' Equity:			
85	Common stock, $5 par value, authorized 200,000,000 shares; issued 83,989,396 shares	**420.0**	420.0	420.0
86	Additional paid-in capital	**7.2**	12.9	18.1
87	Reinvested earnings	**1,047.5**	1,164.7	1,106.2
88	Cumulative exchange adjustment	**(52.9)**	(29.3)	(56.6)
89	Deferred compensation	**(168.0)**	(164.1)	(165.8)
90	Treasury common stock, at cost, 7,660,675 shares; 8,402,871 shares; and 5,221,981 shares, respectively	**(352.8)**	(386.7)	(184.8)
91	Total common shareholders' equity	**901.0**	1,017.5	1,137.1
92	**Total Liabilities and Common Shareholders' Equity**	**$3,016.1**	$3,326.1	$3,125.9

The Quaker Oats Company and Subsidiaries

Consolidated Statements of Common Shareholders' Equity

Dollars in Millions

		Common Stock Issued		Additional Paid-in	Reinvested	Common Stock in Treasury		Cumulative Exchange	Deferred	
		Shares	Amount	Capital	Earnings	Shares	Amount	Adjustment	Compensation	Total
93	Balance at June 30, Year 8	83,989,396	$420.0	$19.5	$ 998.4	4,593,664	$(132.9)	$(36.5)	$ (17.4)	$1,251.1
94	Net income				203.0					203.0
95	Cash dividends declared on common stock				(95.2)					(95.2)
96	Common stock issued for stock option, stock purchase and profit-sharing plans			(1.4)		(601,383)	16.7			15.3
97	Repurchases of common stock					1,229,700	(68.6)			(68.6)
98	Current year foreign currency adjustments (net of allocated income taxes of $1.2)							(20.1)		(20.1)
99	Deferred compensation								(148.4)	(148.4)
100	Balance at June 30, Year 9	83,989,396	$420.0	$18.1	$1,106.2	5,221,981	$(184.8)	$(56.6)	$(165.8)	$1,137.1
101	Net income				169.0					169.0
102	Cash dividends declared on common stock				(106.9)					(106.9)
103	Cash dividends declared on preferred stock				(3.6)					(3.6)
104	Common stock issued for stock purchase and incentive plans			(5.2)		(522,110)	21.3			16.1
105	Repurchases of common stock					3,703,000	(223.2)			(223.2)
106	Current year foreign currency adjustments (net of allocated income taxes of $6.4)							27.3		27.3
107	Deferred compensation								1.7	1.7
108	Balance at June 30, Year 10	83,989,396	$420.0	$12.9	$1,164.7	8,402,871	$(386.7)	$(29.3)	$(164.1)	$1,017.5
109	Net income				205.8					205.8
110	Cash dividends declared on common stock				(118.7)					(118.7)
111	Cash dividends declared on preferred stock				(4.3)					(4.3)
112	Distribution of equity to shareholders from spin-off of Fisher-Price				(200.0)					(200.0)
113	Common stock issued for stock purchase and incentive plans			(5.7)		(742,196)	33.9			28.2
114	Current year foreign currency adjustments (net of allocated income taxes of $3.0)							(23.6)		(23.6)
115	Deferred compensation								(3.9)	(3.9)
116	Balance at June 30, Year 11	83,989,396	$420.0	$ 7.2	$1,047.5	7,660,675	$(352.8)	$(52.9)	$(168.0)	$ 901.0

See accompanying notes to the consolidated financial statements.

QUAKER OATS

The Quaker Oats Company and Subsidiaries

Eleven-Year Selected Financial Data

Dollars in Millions (Except Per Share Data)

	Year Ended June 30	5-Year Compound Growth Rate	10-Year Compound Growth Rate	Year 11	Year 10	Year 9	Year 8	Year 7	Year 6	Year 5	Year 4	Year 3	Year 2	Year 1
118	**Operating Results** *(a)(b)(c)(d)*													
	Net sales	13.1%	10.7%	**$5,491.2**	$5,030.6	$4,879.4	$4,508.0	$3,823.9	$2,968.6	$2,925.6	$2,830.9	$2,172.4	$2,114.7	$1,989.8
	Gross profit	15.3%	14.5%	**2,651.5**	2,344.7	2,224.1	2,111.0	1,751.9	1,299.1	1,174.7	1,085.7	879.1	790.6	683.7
	Income from continuing operations before income taxes	10.0%	11.1%	**411.5**	382.4	239.1	314.6	295.9	255.8	238.8	211.3	180.1	158.9	144.1
	Provision for income taxes	9.2%	10.7%	**175.7**	153.5	90.2	118.1	141.3	113.4	110.3	99.0	81.9	68.4	63.7
	Income from continuing operations	10.6%	11.4%	**235.8**	228.9	148.9	196.5	154.6	142.4	128.5	112.3	98.2	90.5	80.4
	Income (loss) from discontinued operations—net of tax			**(30.0)**	(59.9)	54.1	59.2	33.5	37.2	28.1	26.4	14.1	26.8	24.8
	Income (loss) from the disposal of discontinued operations—net of tax			—	—	—	—	55.8	—	—	—	(55.5)	(20.4)	—
119	Net income	2.8%	6.9%	**$ 205.8**	$ 169.0	$ 203.0	$ 255.7	$ 243.9	$ 179.6	$ 156.6	$ 138.7	$ 56.8	$ 96.9	$ 105.2
	Per common share:													
	Income from continuing operations	11.5%	12.5%	**$ 3.05**	$ 2.93	$ 1.88	$ 2.46	$ 1.96	$ 1.77	$ 1.53	$ 1.35	$ 1.19	$ 1.11	$ .94
	Income (loss) from discontinued operations			**(.40)**	(.78)	.68	.74	.43	.47	.35	.32	.17	.34	.31
	Income (loss) from the disposal of discontinued operations			—	—	—	—	.71	—	—	—	(.70)	(.26)	—
120	Net income	3.4%	7.8%	**$ 2.65**	$ 2.15	$ 2.56	$ 3.20	$ 3.10	$ 2.24	$ 1.88	$ 1.67	$ .66	$ 1.19	$ 1.25
121	Dividends declared:													
	Common stock	16.5%	14.0%	**$ 118.7**	$ 106.9	$ 95.2	$ 79.9	$ 63.2	$ 55.3	$ 50.5	$ 44.4	$ 39.5	$ 35.3	$ 31.9
	Per common share	17.4%	14.6%	**$ 1.56**	$ 1.40	$ 1.20	$ 1.00	$ .80	$ .70	$ .62	$ .55	$ .50	$ .45	$ .40
	Redeemable preference and preferred stock			**$ 4.3**	$ 3.6	—	—	—	$ 2.3	$ 3.6	$ 3.9	$ 4.1	$ 4.3	$ 4.6
122	Average number of common shares outstanding (000's)			**75,904**	76,537	79,307	79,835	78,812	79,060	81,492	80,412	79,008	77,820	80,322

(a) Excludes the operating results of businesses reported as discontinued operations (see Note 2).

(b) See Management's Discussion and Analysis for discussion of fiscal Year 9 through Year 11 restructuring charges and credits.

(c) Fiscal Year 9 net income was decreased by $16 million (after tax) or $20 per share due to the adoption of the last-in, first-out ("LIFO") method of valuing inventories.

(d) Per share data reflect the November Year 6 and Year 4 two-for-one stock split-ups.

The Quaker Oats Company and Subsidiaries

Eleven-Year Selected Financial Data

Dollars in Millions (Except Per Share Data)

	Year Ended June 30	5-Year Compound Growth Rate	10-Year Compound Growth Rate	Year 11	Year 10	Year 9	Year 8	Year 7	Year 6	Year 5	Year 4	Year 3	Year 2	Year 1
	Financial Statistics *(a)(b)(c)*													
123	Current ratio			**1.4**	1.3	1.8	1.4	1.4	1.4	1.7	1.6	1.6	1.6	1.6
	Working capital	2.2%	2.8%	**$ 331.2**	$ 342.8	$ 695.8	$ 417.5	$ 507.9	$ 296.8	$ 400.7	$ 316.8	$ 261.9	$ 266.6	$ 252.4
	Working capital turnover *(d)*			**16.3**	9.7	8.8	9.7	9.5	8.5	8.2	9.8	8.2	8.1	7.7
124	Property, plant and equipment—net	12.3%	8.4%	**$1,232.7**	$1,154.1	$ 959.6	$ 922.5	$ 898.6	$ 691.0	$ 616.5	$ 650.1	$ 533.0	$ 533.8	$ 552.2
125	Depreciation expense	16.2%	14.3%	**$ 125.2**	$ 103.5	$ 94.2	$ 88.3	$ 81.6	$ 59.1	$ 56.3	$ 57.4	$ 40.1	$ 35.2	$ 32.9
126	Total assets	9.2%	8.3%	**$3,016.1**	$3,326.1	$3,125.9	$2,886.1	$3,136.5	$1,944.5	$1,760.3	$1,726.5	$1,391.9	$1,383.3	$1,360.3
127	Long-term debt			**$ 701.2**	$ 740.3	$ 766.8	$ 299.1	$ 527.7	$ 160.9	$ 168.2	$ 200.1	$ 152.8	$ 162.1	$ 164.5
128	Preferred stock net of deferred compensation, and preference stock			**$ 4.8**	$ 1.8	—	—	—	—	$ 37.9	$ 38.5	$ 41.3	$ 45.4	$ 46.7
129	Common shareholders' equity			**$ 901.0**	$1,017.5	$1,137.1	$1,251.1	$1,087.5	$ 831.7	$ 786.9	$ 720.1	$ 639.4	$ 630.5	$ 612.6
130	Book value per common share			**$ 11.80**	$ 13.46	$ 14.44	$ 15.76	$ 13.68	$ 10.64	$ 9.76	$ 8.89	$ 8.02	$ 8.04	$ 7.99
131	Return on average common shareholders' equity			**24.1%**	20.8%	12.5%	16.8%	16.1%	17.3%	16.6%	15.9%	14.8%	13.9%	12.7%
132	Gross profit as a percentage of sales			**48.3%**	46.6%	45.6%	46.8%	45.8%	43.8%	40.2%	38.4%	40.5%	37.4%	34.4%
133	Advertising and merchandising as a percentage of sales			**25.6%**	23.8%	23.4%	24.9%	22.9%	21.7%	19.4%	18.4%	18.6%	16.6%	15.3%
134	Research and development as a percentage of sales			**.8%**	.9%	.8%	.8%	.8%	.8%	.7%	.8%	.8%	1.0%	1.0%
135	Income from continuing operations as a percentage of sales			**4.3%**	4.6%	3.1%	4.4%	4.0%	4.8%	4.4%	4.0%	4.5%	4.3%	4.0%
136	Long-term debt ratio *(e)*			**43.6%**	42.1%	40.3%	19.3%	32.7%	16.2%	16.9%	20.9%	18.3%	19.4%	20.0%
	Total debt ratio *(f)*			**47.4%**	52.3%	44.2%	33.8%	50.2%	35.7%	28.9%	35.4%	32.9%	32.4%	35.2%
	Common dividends as a percentage of income available for common shares			**58.9%**	65.1%	46.9%	31.3%	25.9%	31.2%	33.0%	32.9%	75.8%	37.8%	32.0%
	Number of common shareholders			**33,603**	33,859	34,347	34,231	32,358	27,068	26,670	26,785	27,943	29,552	30,418
	Number of employees worldwide			**20,900**	28,200	31,700	31,300	30,800	29,500	28,700	28,400	25,200	26,000	30,900
137	Market price range of common stock—High			**$ 64 7/8**	$ 68 7/8	$ 66 1/4	$ 57 3/8	$ 57 5/8	$ 39 3/4	$ 26 1/8	$ 16 1/8	$ 12 7/8	$ 10 7/8	$ 9 3/8
	Low			**$ 41 3/4**	$ 45 1/8	$ 42 5/8	$ 31	$ 32 5/8	$ 23 1/2	$ 14 1/4	$ 10 5/8	$ 8 3/4	$ 7 3/4	$ 6 3/8

(a) Income-related statistics exclude the results of business which have been reported as discontinued operations. Balance sheets and related statistics have not been restated for discontinued operations other than Fisher-Price due to immateriality.

(b) Per share data reflect the November Year 6 and Year 4 two-for-one stock split-ups.

(c) During fiscal Year 11 common shareholders equity and book value per common share, as well as number of employees worldwide, were reduced by the split-off of Fisher-Price (see Note 2).

(d) Net sales divided by average working capital.

(e) Long-term debt divided by long-term debt plus total equity including preferred stock net of related deferred compensation and preference stock.

(f) Total debt divided by total debt plus total equity including preferred stock net of related deferred compensation and preference stock.

Management's Discussion and Analysis

[138] **Financial Review**

On June 28, Year 11, the Company completed the distribution of Fisher-Price to its shareholders and Fisher-Price, Inc., an independent, free-standing company, was created (see Note 2). Fisher-Price has been presented as a discontinued operation within these financial statements for all periods shown. Also in fiscal Year 11, the Company recorded a $10 million pretax restructuring charge, or 8 cents per share, to close a Golden grain pasta manufacturing plant.

In fiscal Year 10, the Company reassessed a previously announced plan to close two European pet food facilities and invest in a new pet food plant. This reassessment resulted in management's decision to upgrade existing facilities and forego building a new plant. As a result, reserves of $17.5 million, 18 cents per share, charged to fiscal Year 9 earnings were reversed in fiscal Year 10.

In fiscal Year 9, the Company recorded a variety of restructuring charges aimed at improving productivity and lowering costs. The most significant of these related to the closure of its Marion, Ohio Pet Foods Division plant, which resulted in a $70 million pretax charge to income. Also in fiscal Year 9, the Company recorded a charge of $20.7 million for the planned consolidation of European pet food facilities (referenced above). In total, these restructuring charges reduced pretax income by approximately $125 million, or $1.00 per share.

[139] **Fiscal Year 11 Compared with Fiscal Year 10**

Operations

Fiscal Year 11 consolidated sales reached a record $5.5 billion, up 9 percent over fiscal Year 10, aided by a solid unit volume increase of 5 percent. U.S. and Canadian Grocery Products sales of $3.9 billion were up 7 percent on a 5 percent volume increase. Most businesses had volume increases, led by *Gatorade* thirst quencher, up over 15 percent. International Grocery Products sales of $1.6 billion were up 15 percent on a 5 percent volume increase. The sales gain was driven by the European and Mexican businesses, due to favorable currency trends and strong volume gains in *Gatorade* and pet foods.

Gross profit margin rose to 48 percent of net sales versus 47 percent in fiscal Year 10 due largely to lower commodity and packaging costs in the domestic grocery business.

Selling, general and administrative expenses of $2.1 billion rose 15 percent over fiscal Year 10, and were also higher as a percentage of sales versus last year. The increases in both dollar and percentage terms were due to higher planned advertising and merchandising (A&M) expenditures in the domestic cereals and *Gatorade* business as well as the expansion of *Gatorade* thirst quencher in Europe.

[140] Net interest expense declined 15 percent to $86.2 million due primarily to lower financing costs in Brazil due to the hyper-inflationary environment in that country in fiscal Year 10.

Fiscal Year 11 other expense included foreign exchange gains of $5.1 million compared to losses of $25.7 million in fiscal Year 10, due largely to improvement in Brazil. Restructuring items included in other expense were a $10 million Golden Grain plant closing charge in fiscal Year 11 and a $17.5 million credit in fiscal Year 10.

Consolidated operating income was $533 million compared to $544.2 million last year. Excluding restructuring charges and credits in both years, operating income would have been $543 million in fiscal Year 11, or 3 percent higher than the $526.7 million of a year ago. Operating income for U.S. and Canadian Grocery Products for fiscal Year 11 was $429 million, up 15 percent from last year's $372.5 million. Excluding the fiscal Year 11 restructuring charge of $10 million, operating income rose 18 percent for the year. International Grocery Products operating income in fiscal Year 11 was $104 million, versus last year's $171.7 million. The year-to-year comparisons largely reflect the impact of a hyper-inflationary economic environment in Brazil in fiscal Year 10, and a downturn in the business in fiscal Year 11 because of deteriorating economic conditions in that country, as well as the fiscal Year 10 restructuring credit of $17.5 million. The operating income shortfall in Brazil was largely offset by lower financing costs in that country. In addition, significant A&M expenditures were incurred to launch *Gatorade* thirst quencher into Germany, France, Spain and Mexico. A more detailed discussion of operating performance by segment is provided in the Operations Review section of this report.

Income from continuing operations of $235.8 million increased 3 percent over fiscal Year 10. See Note 2 for a discussion of discontinued operations, which include the Company' Fisher-Price business.

In December Year 7, the Financial Accounting Standards Board (FASB) issued Statement #96, "Accounting for Income Taxes," which introduces an asset-and-liability approach to financial accounting and reporting for income taxes. This statement has not yet been adopted, although adoption is required by fiscal Year 13. Based on preliminary evaluation, Statement #96 is not expected to have a material impact on the Company's financial results.

In December Year 10, the FASB issued Statement #106, "Employers' Accounting for Postretirement Benefits Other Than Pensions." This new standard requires that the expected cost of these benefits be charged to expense during the years that the employees render service. This is a significant change from the company's current policy of recognizing these costs on the cash basis. The Company is required to adopt the new accounting and disclosure rules no later than fiscal Year 14, although earlier implementation is permitted. See Note 11 to the consolidated financial statements for a further discussion of Statement #106.

[141] **Fiscal Year 10 Compared with Fiscal Year 9**

Operations

Fiscal Year 10 sales of $5 billion rose 3 percent above fiscal Year 9, driven by solid gains in International Grocery Products. U.S. and Canadian Grocery Products sales of $3.6 billion were essentially even with the prior year, although volumes declined 6 percent.

The gross profit margin increased to 47 percent of net sales versus 46 percent in fiscal Year 9 due primarily to sharply higher margins from the Company's Brazilian business. This resulted from aggressive pricing during a period of dramatic inflation in that country and from lower commodity costs, especially oats, in the domestic grocery business. Partially offsetting the benefit of lower commodity costs were charges of approximately $15 million, recorded in fiscal Year 10 for oat bran inventory write-downs.

Selling, general and administrative expenses increased 4 percent over fiscal Year 9 to $1.8 billion but remained steady with fiscal Year 9 as a percent of net sales. The dollar increase was driven by higher advertising and merchandising spending, especially for the expansion of *Gatorade* thirst quencher in Europe.

Net interest expense increased 80 percent to $101.8 million due primarily to higher financing costs in Brazil and, to a lesser extent, domestic interest expense incurred on debt used for the repurchase of the Company's common stock.

Fiscal Year 9 other expense included approximately $125 million in restructuring charges.

Operating income increased 56 percent from fiscal Year 9. The increase is attributable to the above-mentioned restructuring charges in fiscal Year 9 and credits in fiscal Year 10 as well as significantly higher operating income from the Brazilian business. The higher Brazilian operating income was achieved in that country's hyper-inflationary environment and was largely offset by accompanying higher financing costs.

Income from continuing operations increased 54 percent over fiscal Year 9 due primarily to the restructuring charges in fiscal Year 9 and credits in Year 10.

[142] **Liquidity and Capital Resources**

The ability to generate funds internally remains one of the Company's most significant financial strengths. Net cash flow from operations of $532.4, $447.1 and $381.6 million during fiscal Year 11, Year 10 and Year 9 respectively, was well in excess of the Company's dividend and capital expenditure requirements. Capital expenditures for fiscal Year 11, Year 10, and Year 9 were $240.6, $275.6 and $223.2 million, respectively, with no material individual commitments outstanding.

Short-term and long-term debt (total debt) decreased $301.1 million from last year, due primarily to proceeds from debt spun off with the Fisher-Price business. Total debt increased $216.8 million from June 30, Year 9 to June 30, Year 10, driven primarily by the common share repurchase program (see Note 7). During fiscal Year 10, the company repurchased 3.7 million shares of outstanding common stock as part of a 7 million share repurchase program announced in May Year 9. No shares were repurchased in fiscal Year 11, because of the impending spin-off of Fisher-Price, leaving 3.3 million shares available to repurchase under this program. The Company's debt to total capitalization ratio was 47.4 percent at June 30, Year 11 compared to 52.3 percent and 44.2 percent at June 30, Year 10 and June 30, Year 9 respectively.

On January 31, Year 10, the Company filed a shelf registration with the Securities and Exchange Commission covering $600 million of debt securities. As of June 30, Year 11, no securities have been issued under this registration statement.

Commercial paper has been the Company's primary source of short-term financing. Quaker's ratings of "A1" (Standard & Poor's) and "P1" (Moody's) have been maintained throughout the year. The available levels of borrowings are adequate to meet the Company's seasonal working capital needs. The Company maintains domestic and non-U.S. bank lines of credit for future corporate general requirements. For a discussion of these lines of credit, see Note 5.

Notes to the Consolidated Financial Statements

143 **Note 1**

Summary of Significant Accounting Policies

Consolidation. The consolidated financial statements include The Quaker Oats Company and all of its subsidiaries ("the Company"). All significant intercompany transactions have been eliminated. Businesses acquired are included in the results of operations since their acquisition date. The Company's toy and juvenile products segment ("Fisher-Price") is reflected in the accompanying financial statements as a discontinued operation (see Note 2). Accordingly, unless otherwise indicated, the following notes relate to continuing operations only.

Foreign Currency Translation. Assets and liabilities of the Company's foreign affiliates, other than those located in highly inflationary countries, are translated at current exchange rates, while income and expenses are translated at average rates for the period. For entities in highly inflationary countries, a combination of current and historical rates is used to determine currency gains and losses resulting from financial statement translation and those resulting from transactions. Translation gains and losses are reported as a component of shareholders' equity, except for those associated with highly inflationary countries, which are reported directly in the Consolidated Statements of Income.

Cash and Cash Equivalents. Cash equivalents are composed of all highly liquid investments with an original maturity of three months or less. All other temporary investments are classified as short-term investments.

Inventories. Inventories are valued at the lower of cost or market, using various cost methods, and include the cost of raw materials, labor and overhead. The percentage of year-end inventories valued using each of the methods is as follows:

June 30	Year 11	Year 10	Year 9
Last-in, first-out (LIFO)	**61%**	62%	63%
Average quarterly cost	**27%**	27%	22%
First-in, first-out (FIFO)	**12%**	11%	15%

If the LIFO method of valuing certain inventories were not used, total inventories would have been $18.9 million, $27.9 million, and $31 million higher than reported at June 30, Year 11, Year 10 and Year 9, respectively.

The Company takes positions in the commodity futures and options markets as part of its overall raw materials purchasing strategy in order to reduce the risk associated with price fluctuations of commodities used in manufacturing The gains and losses on futures contracts and options are included as a part of product cost.

Properties and Depreciation. Property, plant and equipment are carried at cost and depreciated on a straight-line basis over their estimated useful lives. Useful lives range from 5 to 50 years for buildings and improvements and from 3 to 20 years for machinery and equipment.

Intangibles. Intangible assets consist principally of excess purchase price over net tangible assets of businesses acquired (goodwill).

Goodwill is amortized on a straight-line basis over periods not exceeding 40 years. Accumulated goodwill amortization as of June 30, Year 11, Year 10 and Year 9 is $86.5 million, $71.2 million and $55.6 million, respectively.

Income Taxes. Deferred income taxes are provided when tax laws and financial accounting standards differ in respect to the recording of depreciation, capitalized leases and other items. Federal income taxes have been provided on $96.1 million of the $311.5 million of unremitted earnings from foreign subsidiaries. Taxes are not provided on earnings expected to be indefinitely reinvested.

Interest Rate Futures, Currency Swaps, Options and Forward Contracts. The Company enters into a variety of interest rate futures, currency swaps, options and forward contracts in its management of interest rate and foreign currency exposures. Realized and unrealized gains and losses on interest rate futures and options are deferred and recognized as interest expense over the borrowing period. Realized and unrealized gains and losses on foreign currency options and forward contracts which hedge operating income are recognized currently in other income and expense. Realized and unrealized gains and losses on foreign currency options that hedge exchange rate exposure on future raw material purchases are deferred and recognized in cost of sales in the period in which purchases occur. Realized and unrealized gains and losses on foreign currency options, currency swaps, and forward contracts which are effective as net investment hedges are recognized in shareholders' equity.

Income Per Common Share. Income per common share is based on the weighted average number of common shares outstanding during the period.

Software Costs. As of July 1, Year 9, the Company began deferring significant software development project costs, which had previously been expensed as incurred. Software costs of $12.2 million and $6.8 million were deferred during fiscal Year 11 and Year 10, respectively, pending capitalization at the projects' completion. In fiscal Year 11, $3 million of the deferred costs were capitalized and are being amortized over a three-year period.

144 **Note 2**

Discontinued Operations

In April Year 10, the Company's Board of Directors approved in principle the distribution of Fisher-Price to the Company's shareholders. Accordingly, Fisher-Price has been reflected as a discontinued operation in the accompanying financial statements for all periods presented. The tax-free distribution was completed on June 28, Year 11 and Fisher-Price, Inc., an independent free-standing company, was created. The distribution reduced reinvested earnings by $200 million. The $29.6 million payable to Fisher-Price at June 30, Year 11 represents an estimate of the final cash settlement pursuant to the Distribution Agreement. Each holder of Quaker common stock on July 8, Year 11 received one share of Fisher-Price, Inc., common stock for every five shares of Quaker common stock held as of such date. Fisher-Price, Inc., common stock is publicly traded.

The loss from discontinued operations for fiscal Year 10 was $59.9 million, or 78 cents per share, including $25.5 million, or 33 cents per share, for the loss from the first nine months of fiscal Year 10 and an after-tax provision of $34.4 million, or 45 cents per share, recorded in the fourth quarter. The third-quarter results included charges of $10.7 million, or 8 cents per share, for the East Aurora, New York manufacturing facility closing and $17 million, or 23 cents per share, for anticipated transaction expenses of the planned spin-off and projected operating losses (including allocated interest expense) through the expected completion date of the spin-off. The fourth-quarter provision included charges of $8.6 million, or 7 cents per share, for the pending closing of Fisher-Price's Holland, New York manufacturing facility and $4.8 million, or 4 cents per share, for costs relating to staff reductions. The fourth-quarter provision also included $25.4 million, or 21 cents per share, for inventory write-downs and the cost of maintaining related trade programs and $18.1 million, or 13 cents per share, for higher projected operating losses through the spin-off date due to lower than previously anticipated sales volumes.

During fiscal Year 11, the Company recorded an additional $50 million pretax charge ($30 million after tax), or 40 cents per share to discontinued operations. The charge related primarily to receivables credit risk exposure, product recall reserves and severance costs.

The following summarizes the results of operations for discontinued operations:

Dollars in Millions	Year 11	Year 10	Year 9
Sales	**$601.0**	$702.6	$844.8
Pretax earnings (loss)	**$(50.0)**	$(96.2)	$89.6
Income taxes (benefit)	**(20.0)**	(36.3)	35.5
Income (loss) from discontinued operations	**$(30.0)**	$(59.9)	$54.1

Fisher-Price operating loss for fiscal Year 11 was approximately $35 million.

Fisher-Price operating losses for the fourth quarter of fiscal Year 10, including the Holland, New York plant closing and severance charges, were $40 million, including allocated interest expense of $1.2 million. Interest expense of $6.7 million, $7.4 million and $7.1 million was allocated to discontinued operations in fiscal Year 11, Year 10 and Year 9, respectively.

145 **Note 3**

Accounts Receivable Allowances

Dollars in Millions	Year 11	Year 10	Year 9
Balance at beginning of year	**$16.5**	$16.5	$18.1
Provision for doubtful accounts	**5.8**	3.8	2.8
Provision for discounts and allowances	**15.8**	6.7	7.2
Write-offs of doubtful accounts, net of recoveries	**(4.6)**	(2.0)	(5.3)
Discounts and allowances taken	**(14.8)**	(8.5)	(6.3)
Balance at end of year	**$18.7**	$16.5	$16.5

QUAKER OATS

146

Note 4
Property, Plant and Equipment

Dollars in Millions Year 11	Balance at Beginning of Year	Additions	Retirements and Sales	Other Changes	Balance at End of Year
Gross property:					
Land	$ 31.0	$ .8	$ (.2)	$ (.6)	$ 31.0
Buildings and improvements	395.2	41.5	(4.4)	(5.1)	427.2
Machinery and equipment	1,319.4	198.3	(38.1)	(23.2)	1,456.4
Total	$1,745.6	$240.6	$ (42.7)	$(28.9)	$1,914.6
Accumulated depreciation:					
Buildings and improvements	$ 94.1	$ 13.6	$ (1.8)	$ (1.8)	$ 104.1
Machinery and equipment	497.4	115.0	(23.0)	(11.6)	577.8
Total	$ 591.5	$128.6	$ (24.8)	$(13.4)	$ 681.9
Year 10					
Gross property:					
Land	$ 30.6	$ .5	$ (1.1)	$ 1.0	$ 31.0
Buildings and improvements	348.2	36.4	(1.5)	12.1	395.2
Machinery and equipment	1,078.1	238.7	(36.1)	38.7	1,319.4
Total	$1,456.9	$275.6	$ (38.7)	$ 51.8	$1,745.6
Accumulated depreciation:					
Buildings and improvements	$ 80.9	$ 11.3	$ (.7)	$ 2.6	$ 94.1
Machinery and equipment	416.4	95.2	(26.2)	12.0	497.4
Total	$ 497.3	$106.5	$ (26.9)	$ 14.6	$ 591.5
Year 9					
Gross property:					
Land	$ 30.1	$ 3.9	$ (3.7)	$ .3	$ 30.6
Buildings and improvements	341.7	36.4	(24.3)	(5.6)	348.2
Machinery and equipment	1,031.3	208.4	(142.5)	(19.1)	1,078.1
Total	$1,403.1	$248.7	$(170.5)	$(24.4)	$1,456.9
Accumulated depreciation:					
Buildings and improvements	$ 75.0	$ 11.1	$ (3.7)	$ (1.5)	$ 80.9
Machinery and equipment	405.6	85.9	(66.2)	(8.9)	416.4
Total	$ 480.6	$ 97.0	$ (69.9)	$(10.4)	$ 497.3

The "Additions" column for fiscal Year 9 includes acquisitions made by the Company during that year. Included in the "Other Changes" column for fiscal Year 11, Year 10 and Year 9 are net increases (decreases) of $(18.1), $22.7 and $(13.2) million, respectively, reflecting the effect of translating non-U.S. property at current exchange rates as required by SFAS #52.

147

Note 5
Short-Term Debt and Lines of Credit

Dollars in Millions	**Year 11**	Year 10	Year 9
Notes payable—			
Non-U.S. subsidiaries	**$ 67.6**	$127.1	$ 49.6
Commercial paper—U.S.			
Dealer-placed on the open market	**13.0**	216.1	302.6
Commercial paper to be refinanced	—	—	(250.0)
	$ 80.6	$343.2	$ 102.2
Weighted average interest rates on debt outstanding at end of year—			
Notes payable to banks—non U.S.	**12.1%**	17.4%	14.5%
Commercial paper—U.S.	**5.9%**	8.2%	9.4%
Weighted average interest rates on debt outstanding during the year—			
Notes payable to banks—non US (computed on month-end balances)	**50.7%**(a)	76%(a)	50.5%(a)
Commercial paper—U.S. (computed on daily balances)	**7.2%**	8.5%	8.9%
Average amount of debt outstanding during the year	**$263.5**	$264.6	$ 357.7
Maximum month-end balance during the year	**$391.4**	$355.7	$ 486.5

(a) The interest rate on debt outstanding was driven principally by periods of high real interest rates in Latin America combined with proportionately lower devaluation of local currencies resulting in high interest rates in dollar terms.

The consolidated balance sheet at June 30, Year 9 reflects the reclassification of $250 million of short-term debt, reflecting the Company's intent to refinance this debt on a long-term basis. During fiscal Year 10, the Company issued $250 million of medium term notes. (See Note 6).

The Company has a Revolving Credit Agreement with various banks, which supports its commercial paper borrowings and is also available for direct borrowings. The amount of available borrowings under the agreement was $500 million. The Agreement, which expires no sooner than June 30, Year 16, requires a commitment fee of one-eight percent per annum, payable on any available and unused portion. There were no borrowings under the Agreement during fiscal Year 11, Year 10 or Year 9. As of July 2, Year 11, the amount available borrowings under the Agreement was reduced to $300 million.

The Company's non-U.S. subsidiaries have additional unused short-term lines of credit of approximately $195 million at June 30, Year 11.

Under the most restrictive terms of the various loan agreements in effect at June 30, Year 11, minimum working capital of $250 million must be maintained.

148

Note 6
Long-Term Debt

Dollars in Millions	**Year 11**	Year 10	Year 9
Sinking Fund Debentures:			
7.7% due through Year 21	**$ 16.1**	$ 18.5	$ 21.5
8% due through Year 19	**8.4**	9.5	10.6
Industrial Revenue Bonds:			
6%-11.5% due through Year 30, tax exempt	**39.0**	46.0	46.0
4.5%-8.375% due through Year 23, taxable	**7.1**	8.2	7.4
Non-interesting bearing installment note due Year 34	**3.1**	2.7	2.4
7.83% Senior ESOP Notes due through Year 22	**94.5**	98.2	100.0
8.07% Senior ESOP Notes due through Year 22	**148.2**	150.0	150.0
8.75% ESOP installment loan due through Year 16	**12.2**	14.1	15.8
7.2%-7.9% Series A Medium-term Notes due through Year 20	**119.6**	134.6	157.1
5.415% and 6.63% deutsche mark swaps due Year 13 and Year 18	**25.6**	27.9	23.8
8.15%-9.34% Series B Medium-term Notes due Year 13 through Year 40	**250.0**	250.0	—
Commercial paper to be refinanced	—	—	250.0
Other	**10.3**	12.9	12.2
	$734.1	$772.6	$ 796.8
Less: Current portion	**32.9**	32.3	30.0
Net Long-term Debt	**$701.2**	$740.3	$ 766.8

All maturity dates presented refer to fiscal years.

Aggregate required payments of maturities on long-term debt for the next five fiscal years are as follows:

Year ended June 30	Year 12	Year 13	Year 14	Year 15	Year 16
Required Payments	$32.9	$45.3	$48.5	$46.1	$38.9

Dollars in Millions

During fiscal Year 10, the Company issued $250 million of Series B Medium-term Notes bearing interest rates ranging from 8.15 percent to 9.34 percent per annum with maturities from 3 to 30 years. The debt issuance was covered under a $250 million shelf registration filed with the Securities and Exchange Commission during March Year 7. Although none of these securities were issued as of June 30, Year 9, the consolidated balance sheet as of that date reflects a reclassification of $250 million of commercial paper to long-term debt due to the Company's intent to issue the medium-term notes in fiscal Year 10.

During January Year 10, the Company filed a shelf registration with the Securities and Exchange Commission covering $600 million worth of debt securities. No securities have been issued under the registration statement as of June 30, Year 11.

The Quaker Employee Stock Ownership Plan (ESOP) was expanded during fiscal Year 9 through two separate transactions:

—In January Year 9, the ESOP through a trust issued $150 million. Senior ESOP Notes bearing interest at a rate of 8.07 percent per annum. The proceeds from these notes were used to purchase the Company's common stock on the open market.

—In June Year 9, the ESOP incurred an additional $100 million of indebtedness through the issuance via a trust of 7.83 percent Senior ESOP Notes. The proceeds from these notes were used to acquire shares of the Company's Series B ESOP Convertible Preferred Stock.

Both issues of Senior ESOP Notes are due through fiscal Year 22 and are unconditionally guaranteed by the Company. See Note 8 for a further description of these transactions.

In July Year 7, $25 million of 8.55 and 9.2 percent medium-term notes were issued, completing the $200 million Series A Medium-term Note offering begun in January Year 7. The notes mature during fiscal years Year 13 and Year 18. This note offering was concurrently swapped into deutsche marks at interest rates of 5.415 percent and 6.63 percent. The swap is effective as a net investment hedge.

The non-interest bearing note for $55.5 million (due fiscal Year 34) has an unamortized discount of $52.4 million, $52.8 million and $53.1 million as of June 30, Year 11, Year 10 and Year 9, respectively, based on an imputed interest rate of 13 percent.

The 7.7 percent sinking fund debenture requires annual payments of $1.8 million through fiscal Year 20 and a final payment of $6.8 million due in June Year 21. The 8 percent sinking fund debenture, which is an obligation of Stokely-Van Camp, Inc., a subsidiary of the Company, requires annual payments of $1.3 million through October Year 17 with a final payment of $5.3 million due in October Year 18. Amounts held in treasury for these sinking fund requirements were as follows:

			Dollars in Millions
June 30	**Year 11**	Year 10	Year 9
7.7% Sinking Fund Debenture	**$6.9**	$6.3	$5.1
8% Sinking Fund Debenture	**$5.2**	$5.2	$5.2

149 **Note 7**
Capital Stock

In May Year 9, the Company announced its intent to repurchase, from time to time, up to seven million shares of its outstanding common stock through open market purchases and privately negotiated transactions. As of June 30, Year 11, 3,703,000 shares have been repurchased. In June Year 9, the ESOP through a trust issued $100 million of Senior ESOP Notes due through fiscal Year 22, and bearing interest at a rate of 7.83 percent per annum. Concurrently, the company sold 1,282,051 shares of the newly authorized issue of Series B ESOP Convertible Preferred Stock to the ESOP. Each share of the preferred stock, of which 1,750,000 shares are authorized, is convertible into one share of the Company's common stock and pays a dividend of $5.46. The preferred stock will be issued only for the ESOP and will not trade on the open market.

In June Year 9, the Company completed the repurchase of two million shares under a program announced in fiscal Year 8, and in January Year 8 completed a two million share repurchase program (adjusted for the November Year 6 stock split-up), announced in fiscal Year 6. Repurchased shares are used for general corporate purposes including stock option and incentive plans.

The Company is authorized to issue one million shares of redeemable preference stock and an additional ten million shares of a new class of preferred stock to be issued in series, whose term will be fixed by resolution of the Board of Directors. As of June 30, Year 11, none of the preference stock and 1,282,051 shares of the preferred stock have been issued.

The Dividend Reinvestment and Stock Purchase Plan exists for eligible employees and shareholders. The Plan allows for the use of open market, unissued or treasury shares. The shares used in fiscal Year 11, Year 10 and Year 9 were open market shares.

150 **Note 8**
Deferred Compensation

The Quaker Employee Stock Ownership Plan (ESOP) was expanded during fiscal Year 9 through two separate transactions. In January Year 9, the ESOP through a trust issued $150 million Senior ESOP Notes due through fiscal Year 22 and bearing interest at a rate of 8.07 percent per annum. The proceeds from the notes, which were received by the trust, were used to purchase 2,813,152 shares of the Company's common stock on the open market. The Senior ESOP Notes are unconditionally guaranteed by the Company.

During May Year 9, the Company announced that its Board of Directors authorized the ESOP to incur up to an additional $125 million of indebtedness, which would also be guaranteed by the Company. The Company announced that a new issue of up to $125 million of convertible preferred stock for the ESOP would be purchased with the proceeds of the ESOP debt. In June Year 9, the ESOP through a trust issued $100 million of Senior ESOP Notes due through fiscal Year 22 and bearing interest at a rate of 7.83 percent per annum. The proceeds from these notes were used to acquire 1,282,051 shares of Series B ESOP Convertible Preferred Stock.

These transactions represent an expansion of the original ESOP, which was adopted during fiscal Year 6. The loans from the original and expanded ESOP programs are included as long-term debt on the Company's consolidated balance sheets. Deferred compensation of $262.5 million represents primarily the Company's payment of future compensation expense related to the original and expanded ESOP programs.

As the Company makes annual contributions to the ESOP, these contributions, along with the dividends accumulated on the Company's common and preferred stock held by the ESOP, will be used to repay the outstanding loans. As the loans are repaid, common and preferred stock is allocated to ESOP participants, and deferred compensation is reduced by the amount of the principal payment on the loans.

The following table presents the ESOP loan repayments:

			Dollars in Millions
	Year 11	Year 10	Year 9
Principal payments	**$ 7.4**	$ 3.5	$1.6
Interest payments	**20.9**	17.4	1.5
Total ESOP payments	**$28.3**	$20.9	$3.1

As of June 30, Year 11, 883,395 shares of common stock and 166,470 shares of preferred stock have been allocated to the accounts of ESOP participants.

151 **Note 9**
Employee Stock Option and Award Plans

During fiscal Year 10, Quaker shareholders approved the adoption of The Quaker Long-Term Incentive Plan of Year 10 ("the Plan"). The purpose of the Plan is to promote the interests of the Company and its shareholders by providing the officers and other key employees with additional incentive and the opportunity through stock ownership to increase their proprietary interest in the Company and their personal interest in its continued success. The Plan provides for benefits to be awarded in the form of options, stock appreciation rights, restricted stock (with corresponding cash awards), performance shares, performance units, and other stock based awards. Six million shares of common stock have been authorized for grant under the Plan. Previously, stock options were issued under the Year 4 Long-Term Incentive Plan, which expired by its terms on December 31, Year 10. Restricted stock awards were previously issued under the Year 4 Restricted Stock Plan, which was terminated during fiscal Year 10. Officers and other managerial employees may be granted options for the purchase of common stock at a price not less than the fair market value at date of grant. Options are generally exercisable after one or more years and expire no later than ten years from date of grant. As of June 30, Year 11, 534 persons held such options. Changes in stock options outstanding are summarized as follows:

	Shares	Options Price (Per Share)
Balance at June 30, Year 8	3,226,408	$ 5.64-44.25
Granted	796,820	53.88
Exercised	(651,108)	5.64-44.25
Expired or terminated	(87,633)	10.67-53.88
Balance at June 30, Year 9	3,284,487	$ 6.74-53.88
Granted	809,300	57.00
Exercised	(535,194)	6.74-53.88
Expired or terminated	(103,356)	6.74-57.00
Balance at June 30, Year 10	3,455,237	$ 7.08-57.00
Granted	781,100	49.50
Exercised	(600,065)	7.08-57.00
Expired or terminated	(210,554)	28.69-57.00
Balance at June 30, Year 11	3,425,718	$ 8.30-57.00

During July Year 11, the number and exercise price of all options outstanding at the time of the Fisher-Price spin-off (see Note 2) were adjusted to compensate for decreases in the economic value of the options as a result of the distribution to shareholders. This adjustment increased the number of options outstanding by 293,241 and decreased the exercise price of the options outstanding by approximately 8 percent.

At June 30, Year 11, options for 2,664,490 shares were exercisable. As of June 30, Year 11, the average per share option price of unexercised options expiring during the period January 13, Year 12 to January 9, Year 21 was $43.46.

Since fiscal Year –3, the stock option plans have provided for the granting of stock appreciation rights in tandem with the granting of stock options. At June 30, Year 11, 42,156 stock appreciation rights were attached to outstanding options.

Restricted stock awards grant shares of the Company's common stock to key officers and employees. These shares are subject to a restriction period from the date of grant, during which they may not be sold, assigned, pledged or otherwise encumbered. The number of shares of the Company's common stock awarded were 172,700, 3,700 and 10,200 in fiscal years Year 11, Year 10, and Year 9, respectively. Restrictions on these awards lapse after a period of time designated by the Plan committee. In addition, participants may receive a cash award at the end of the restricted period not to exceed 200 percent of the current market value of the shares received as designated by the committee.

[152] **Note 10**
Shareholder Rights Plan

The Company's Shareholder Rights Plan, adopted July 9, Year 6, and amended July 12, Year 9, is designed to deter coercive or unfair takeover tactics and to prevent a person or group from gaining control of the Company without offering a fair price to all shareholders.

Under the terms of the plan, all common shareholders of record on July 30, Year 6 received for each share owned one "Right" entitling them to purchase from the Company one one-hundredth of a newly issued share of Series A Junior Participating Preferred stock at an exercise price of $300.

The Rights become exercisable (1) ten days after a public announcement that a person or group has acquired shares representing 20 percent or more of the voting power of the Company's capital stock, (2) ten business days following commencement of a tender offer for more than 20 percent of such voting power, or (3) ten business days after a holder of at least 15 percent of such voting power is determined to be an adverse person by the Board of Directors. The time periods can be extended by the Company. Unless the Board of Directors has made a determination that any person is an adverse person, the Company can redeem the Rights for $.05 per Right at any time prior to their becoming exercisable. The Rights will expire on July 30, Year 6 unless redeemed earlier by the Company.

If after the Rights become exercisable the Company is involved in a merger or other business combination at any time when there is a holder of 20 percent or more of Quaker's stock, the Rights will then entitle a holder, upon exercise of the Rights, to receive shares of common stock of the acquiring company with a market value equal to twice the exercise price of each Right. Alternatively, if a 20 percent holder acquires the Company by means of a reverse merger in which the Company and its stock survive, or if any person acquires 20 percent or more of the Company's voting power or acquires 15 percent of Company's voting power and is determined by the Board to be an adverse person, each Right not owned by such 20 percent shareholder or adverse person would, upon exercise of the Right, entitle the holder to common stock of the Company (or in certain circumstances other consideration) having a market value equal to twice the exercise price of the Right. The rights described in this paragraph shall not apply to an acquisition, merger or consolidation which is determined by a majority of the Company's independent directors, after consulting one or more investment banking firms, to be fair and otherwise in the best interest of the Company and its shareholders.

[153] **Note 11**
Pension Plans and Other Post-Employment Benefits

The Company has various pension plans covering substantially all of its domestic and certain foreign employees. Plan benefits are based on years of service and earnings. Company policy is to make contributions to its U.S. plans within the maximum amount deductible for federal income tax purposes. Plan assets consist primarily of equity securities as well as government, corporate and other fixed-income obligations.

The components of net pension cost for defined benefit plans are detailed below:

Dollars in Millions	**Year 11**	Year 10	Year 9
Service cost (benefits earned during the year)	**$ 28.5**	$ 26.7	$ 22.7
Interest cost on projected benefit obligation	**39.7**	36.5	34.1
Actual return on plan assets	**(70.5)**	(66.7)	(51.6)
Net amortization and deferral	**9.8**	10.6	(3.3)
U.S. and Canadian pension cost	**7.5**	7.1	1.9
Multi-employer plans	**.7**	.8	.7
Foreign plans	**3.2**	.6	3.7
Net pension cost	**$ 11.4**	$ 8.5	$ 6.3

Reconciliations of the funded status of the Company's defined benefit plans to the accrued pension asset (liability) included in the consolidated balance sheets are as follows:

	Overfunded			Underfunded		
Dollars in Millions	**Year 11**	Year 10	Year 9	**Year 11**	Year 10	Year 9
Vested benefits	**$363.6**	$336.8	$307.7	**$ 43.6**	$ 42.8	$ 37.8
Non-vested benefits	**8.1**	12.9	10.5	**.2**	.6	.3
Accumulated benefit obligation	**371.7**	349.7	318.2	**43.8**	43.4	38.1
Effect of projected future salary increases	**54.2**	61.7	56.7	**5.4**	11.8	7.1
Projected benefit obligation	**425.9**	411.4	374.9	**49.2**	55.2	45.2
Plan assets at market value	**588.2**	543.7	499.3	**28.0**	26.7	25.5
Projected benefit obligations less (greater) than plan assets	**162.3**	132.3	124.4	**(21.2)**	(28.5)	(19.7)
Unrecognized net (gain)	**(81.3)**	(39.5)	(12.4)	**(14.1)**	(5.7)	(6.3)
Unrecognized prior service cost	**10.4**	9.1	9.5	**5.6**	6.3	1.6
Unrecognized net (asset) liability at transition	**(83.8)**	(90.8)	(109.0)	**5.6**	6.3	7.1
Prepaid (accrued) pension costs (in the Balance Sheet)	**$ 7.6**	$ 11.1	$ 12.5	**$(24.1)**	$(21.6)	$(17.3)

Assumptions:
Weighted average discount rate: 9%
Rate of future compensation increases: 6%
Long-term rate of return on plan assets: 9%

Foreign pension plan assets and accumulated benefit obligations are not significant in the aggregate. Therefore, SFAS #87 disclosures have not been presented for these plans.

In addition, the Company provides certain health care and life insurance benefits to its retired employees. A substantial number of the Company's domestic employees and certain employees in foreign countries become eligible for these benefits if they meet retirement age and service requirements while still working for the Company. These costs are expensed as incurred and amounted to $7.4 million, $6.9 million and $6.4 million in fiscal Year 11, Year 10 and Year 9, respectively.

In December Year 10, the Financial Accounting Standards Board issued Statement #106, "Employer's Accounting for Postretirement Benefits Other Than Pensions." This new standard requires that the expected cost of these benefits be charged to expense during the years that the employees render service. This is a significant change from the Company's current policy of recognizing these costs on the cash basis. The Company is required to adopt the new accounting and disclosure rules no later than fiscal Year 14, although earlier implementation is permitted. The Company may adopt the new standard prospectively or via a cumulative catch-up adjustment.

The Company has not decided when it will adopt the new standard or if it will adopt the new accounting method prospectively or by recording a cumulative catch-up adjustment in the year of adoption. Because of the complexities of the new standard, management has not yet determined the effect that the change in accounting will have on the Company's reported financial position and results of operations. However, management expects that the annual postretirement benefit expense computed in accordance with the new standard will be significantly greater than the annual cash payments.

[154] **Note 12**
Leases and Other Commitments

Certain equipment and operating properties are rented under non-cancelable operating leases that expire at various dates through Year 22. Total rental expense under operating leases was $44.5 million, $44.3 million and $42.4 million in fiscal Year 11, Year 10 and Year 9, respectively. Contingent rentals and subleases are not significant. Capital leases, which are included in fixed assets, and minimum lease payments under such leases are not significant.

The following is a schedule of future minimum annual rentals on non-cancelable operating leases, primarily for sales offices, warehouses and corporate headquarters in effect at June 30 Year 11.

Dollars in Millions	*Year 12*	*Year 13*	*Year 14*	*Year 15*	*Year 16*	*Later*	*Total*
Total payments	$16.5	$16.5	$15.7	$15.2	$15.0	$66.8	$145.7

[155] **Note 13**
Supplementary Expense Data

Dollars in Millions	**Year 11**	Year 10	Year 9
Advertising, media and production	**$ 277.5**	$ 282.8	$ 256.5
Merchandising	**1,129.9**	912.5	886.2
Total advertising and merchandising	**$1,407.4**	$1,195.3	$1,142.7
Maintenance and repairs	**$ 96.1**	$ 96.6	$ 93.8
Depreciation expense	**$ 125.2**	$ 103.5	$ 94.5
Research and development	**$ 44.3**	$ 43.3	$ 39.3

[156] **Note 14**
Interest (Income) Expense

Dollars in Millions	**Year 11**	Year 10	Year 9
Interest expense on long-term debt	**$ 43.3**	$ 38.3	$ 25.7
Interest expense on short-term debt and other	**60.5**	84.7	52.4
Interest expense capitalized—net	**(1.9)**	(2.8)	(2.2)
Total interest expense	**101.9**	120.2	75.9
Interest income on securities	**(5.5)**	(7.2)	(7.3)
Interest income, other	**(3.5)**	(3.8)	(5.1)
Total interest income	**(9.0)**	(11.0)	(12.4)
Net interest allocated to discontinued operations	**(6.7)**	(7.4)	(7.1)
Total net interest expense	**$ 86.2**	$101.8	$ 56.4

157 **Note 15**
Other (Income) Expense

Dollars in Millions	**Year 11**	Year 10	Year 9
Foreign exchange (gains) losses—net	**$(5.1)**	$ 25.7	$ 14.8
Amortization of intangibles	**22.4**	22.2	18.2
Losses (gains) from plant closings and operations sold or to be sold—net	**8.8**	(23.1)	119.4
Miscellaneous—net	**6.5**	(8.4)	(2.8)
Net other expense	**$32.6**	$ 16.4	$149.6

158 **Note 16**
Provision for Income Taxes

Provisions for income taxes applicable to continuing operations were as follows:

Dollars in Millions	**Year 11**	Year 10	Year 9
Currently payable—			
Federal	**$103.0**	$ 72.7	$12.7
Non-U.S.	**36.6**	44.3	26.9
State	**21.8**	17.9	10.0
Total currently payable	**161.4**	134.9	49.6
Deferred—net			
Federal	**6.7**	13.4	30.8
Non-U.S.	**4.1**	5.4	8.2
State	**3.5**	(.2)	1.6
Total deferred—net	**14.3**	18.6	40.6
Total income tax provision	**$175.7**	$153.5	$90.2

158A
The components of the deferred income tax provision were as follows:

Dollars in Millions	**Year 11**	Year 10	Year 9
Accelerated tax depreciation	**$ 8.4**	$14.5	$15.0
Receipt of tax benefits	**(1.3)**	(2.8)	(2.1)
Long-term tax liability	—	—	18.2
Tax benefits—ANC(*a*)	—	—	(1.7)
Other—net	**7.2**	6.9	11.2
Total deferred income tax provision	**$14.3**	$18.6	$40.6

158B
The sources of pretax income from continuing operations were as follows:

Dollars in Millions	**Year 11**	Year 10	Year 9
U.S. sources	**$328.7**	$265.2	$162.2
Non-U.S. sources	**82.8**	117.2	76.9
Total income before taxes	**$411.5**	$382.4	$239.1

A reconciliation of the statutory federal income tax rate to the effective income tax rate follows:

158C	**Year 11**		Year 10		Year 9	
Dollars in Millions	**Amount**	**% of Pretax Income**	Amount	% of Pretax Income	Amount	% of Pretax Income
Tax provision based on the federal statutory rate	**$139.9**	**34.0%**	$130.0	34.0%	$81.3	34.0%
State and local income taxes, net of federal income tax benefit	**16.7**	**4.1**	11.9	3.1	7.7	3.2
ANC benefit(*a*)	—	—	—	—	(1.7)	(.7)
Repatriation of foreign earnings	**4.3**	**1.0**	4.8	1.3	(2.1)	(.9)
Non-U.S. tax rate differential	**8.2**	**2.0**	9.8	2.5	8.8	3.7
U.S. tax credits	**(.2)**	—	(.1)	—	(.7)	(.3)
Miscellaneous items—net	**6.8**	**1.6**	(2.9)	(.8)	(3.1)	(1.3)
Actual tax provision	**$175.7**	**42.7%**	$153.5	40.1%	$90.2	37.7%

(a) In fiscal Year 9, the Company recognized $1.7 million of tax benefits in its provision for income taxes related to Alaskan Native Corporation (ANC) agreements. The ANC agreements granted the Company the right to utilize net operating losses of the ANC's for tax purposes during fiscal Year 7 and Year 8. At June 30, Year 11, $67.8 million relating to these agreements are included in deferred taxes.

159 **Note 17**
Supplemental Cash Flow Information

Dollars in Millions	**Year 11**	Year 10	Year 9
Interest paid	**$101.7**	$96.8	$ 73.8
Income taxes paid	**$ 88.7**	$90.7	$140.0

Interest paid and income taxes paid include amounts related to Fisher-Price. The Company assumed liabilities in conjunction with acquisitions in fiscal Year 9 of $13.6 million.

160 **Note 18**
Financial Instruments

Foreign Currency Forward Contracts. At June 30, Year 11, the Company had forward contracts for the purchase and sale of European and Canadian currencies to hedge foreign exchange operating income and balance sheet exposure, purchases totaling $47.2 million and sales totaling $148.9 million. While the contracts generally mature in less than 12 months, the total sales include obligations to sell $8.2 million in British pounds in fiscal Year 18 and $7.6 million in Canadian dollars in fiscal Year 14.

Deutsche Mark Swap. During fiscal Year 8, the Company swapped $25 million for deutsche marks in two separate transactions. The Company is committed to re-exchange 18.5 million deutsche marks for $10 million in August Year 12, and 27.9 million deutsche marks for $15 million in August Year 17. The Company is also committed to make semi-annual interest payments of 1.4 million deutsche marks through August Year 12 and, thereafter, 0.9 million deutsche marks through August Year 17.

161 **Note 19**
Litigation

On December 18, Year 10, Judge Prentice H. Marshall of the United States District Court for the Northern District of Illinois issued a memorandum opinion stating that the Court would enter judgment against the Company in favor of Sands, Taylor & Wood Co. The Court found that the use of the words "thirst aid" in advertising *Gatorade* thirst quencher infringed the Plaintiff's rights in the trademark THIRST-AID. On July 9, Year 11, Judge Marshall entered a judgment of $42.6 million, composed of $31.4 million in principal, plus prejudgment interest of $10.6 million, and fees, expenses and costs of $0.6 million. The order enjoins use of the phrase "THIRST-AID" in connection with the advertising or sale of *Gatorade* thirst quencher in the United States. The Company and its subsidiary, Stokely-Van Camp, Inc., ceased use of the words "thirst aid" in December Year 10. The Company on the advice of inside and outside counsel, strongly believes that it will prevail in an appeal of the judgment. Therefore, no provision for loss has been made in the accompanying financial statements.

The Company is not a party to any other pending legal proceedings which it believes will have a material adverse effect on its financial position or results of operations.

162 **Note 20**
Quarterly Financial Data (Unaudited)

Year Ended June 30 — *Dollars in Million (Except Per Share Data)*

Year 11	First Quarter	Second Quarter(*a*)	Third Quarter	Fourth Quarter(*b*)
Net sales	$1,326.5	$1,293.8	$1,334.6	$1,536.3
Cost of goods sold	685.2	689.0	682.3	783.2
Gross profit	$ 641.3	$ 604.8	$ 652.3	$ 753.1
Income from continuing operations	$ 33.2	$ 33.1	$ 63.1	$ 106.4
(Loss) from discontinued operations, net of tax	—	(30.0)	—	—
Net income	$ 33.2	$ 3.1	$ 63.1	$ 106.4
Per common share:				
Income from continuing operations	$ 0.42	$ 0.43	$ 0.82	$ 1.38
(Loss) from discontinued operations	—	(0.40)	—	—
Net income	$ 0.42	$ 0.03	$ 0.82	$ 1.38
Cash dividends declared	$ 0.39	$ 0.39	$ 0.39	$ 0.39
Market price range:				
High	$ 50⅛	$ 53	$ 60¾	$ 64⅞
Low	$ 41¼	$ 42⅞	$ 47¾	$ 55⅛

(a) Includes a provision for discontinued operations of $30 million after-tax ($.40 per share) for Fisher-Price receivables credit risk exposure, product recall reserves, and severance costs.
(b) Includes a charge of $6.6 million after-tax ($.08 per share) for the closing of a Golden Grain pasta manufacturing facility. Also includes a $4.2 million after tax ($.05) per share) credits for favorable LIFO price variances that were not projected in the prior fiscal Year 11 quarters.

SUPPLEMENT

B

Auditing and Financial Analysis

Learning Objectives

- Describe the relevance of auditing for financial statements.
- Explain the importance of the audit firm for our analysis of financial statements.
- Describe the audit report (opinion) and its relevance and limitations for our analysis.
- Analyze implications of variations in the audit report for financial statement analysis.
- Interpret auditing standards specifying an auditor's responsibilities in attesting to the fair presentation of financial statements.

Preview of Supplement B

Financial statements of a company are the representations of its management. Management bears the primary responsibility for the fairness of presentation and the information disclosed in financial statements. Because of the importance of financial statements, there is demand for their independent verification. Public accounting meets this demand through attestation, or auditing, services. It is probably not coincidental that the more developed an economy and its financial markets, the more important is public accounting. In the United States, the title Certified Public Accountant is acquired by passing a series of examinations and, in many cases, obtaining sufficient experience. While no profession can ensure quality and character in its members, the successful completion of these examinations ensures a minimum level of competence in accounting and auditing practices. Since public accounting firms make up the largest segment of public accounting practice, we confine our consideration of the auditing function and opinion to that segment. There are several real and perceived limitations of auditors' work in practice. Yet the audit firm's function is of critical importance for our analysis. The audit firm's attestation to the fair presentation of financial statements greatly increases their reliability for our analysis as well as the degree and quality of disclosure. Partial or incomplete knowledge of the auditing process is more harmful than none at all. This truth applies to our understanding and knowledge of the audit firm's work and the relevance of the audit opinion. This supplement provides an overview of the relevance of auditing for our analysis. It also discusses the types of audit reports and their analysis implications. The content and organization of this supplement are as follows:

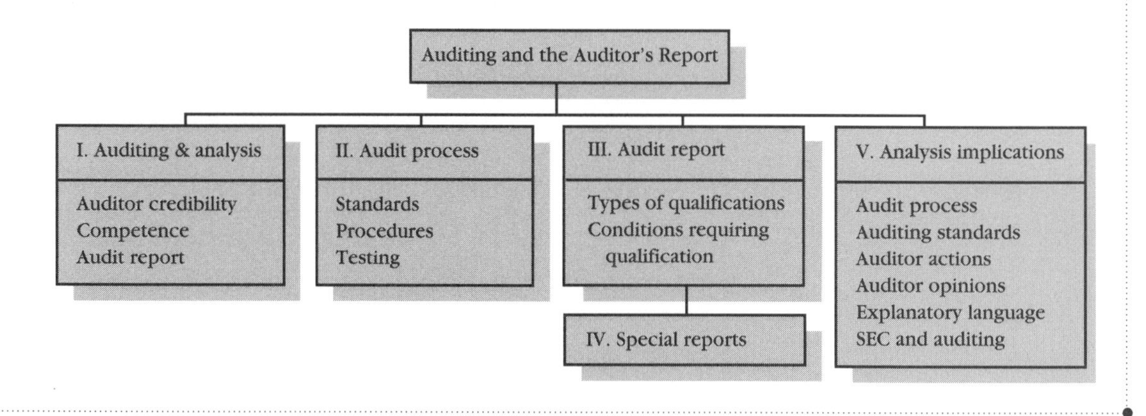

Relevance of Auditing to Analysis

The audit opinion relates to the financial statements, the accompanying notes, and certain other items. Its relevance to our analysis implies that we must both:

- Assess the credibility and competence of the audit firm.
- Know the relevance and limitations of the audit report.

This section discusses both of these tasks.

Credibility and Competence of the Audit Firm

Licensed auditors provide us a reasonable degree of confidence in the audit. However, like any profession, differences in credibility and competence are considerable. The relationship between the audit firm and users of the audit opinion differs markedly from similar relationships in other professions. While the audit firm has both an obligation and a responsibility to users, it is in most cases neither appointed nor compensated by users. An audit firm looks to management and the board of directors for both its appointment and its fee.

When management's financial reporting is in conflict with the interests of users, the audit firm's credibility, integrity, and independence are tested. One criterion of the audit firm's reliability is its reputation for integrity and independence. Whatever other attributes the audit firm possesses, without integrity and independence nothing else matters.

The competence of an audit firm is assessed in several ways. The auditor's credentials, including the length, breadth, and quality of experience, are one element. Membership and standing in state and national accounting associations are another. And participation in professional organizations are still another factor. Certainly, an audit firm's current and past performances in attesting to financial statements are of paramount importance. We are often able to form a judgment about an audit firm's reputation for quality. Since there is some latitude in adhering to auditing standards and in applying accounting principles, an audit firm's track record of actual performance provides a measure of competence. Our analysis should recognize instances where an audit firm (1) accepts less than preferable accounting principles, (2) is unnecessarily evasive in its opinion, (3) is found wanting in adherence to auditing standards, or (4) accepts clients with less than credible reputations.

Sources of information on both the credibility and competence of an audit firm include lenders, investment bankers, attorneys, directors, bond raters, and the findings and orders involving auditor performance issued by the SEC.

Relevance and Limitations of the Audit Report

The **auditor's report**, or *opinion*, is the culmination of the audit firm's attestation function. The audit report identifies the nature of the audit work and the degree of responsibility the auditor assumes. While an auditor's influence is indirectly felt in the financial statements by the presentation, description, and note disclosure, the audit opinion is its exclusive domain. The opinion and its references to the financial statements should be carefully read. To ignore the auditor's report, or to assume it means more or less than what it says, is unwarranted.

The audit firm's responsibility to users is considerable, and its exposure to liability arising therefrom is immense. The obligations that auditing standards impose on it, while extensive, are also defined and limited. Our analysis is not justified in assuming that association of the audit firm's name with the financial statements goes beyond what the auditor's opinion says. It is not a form of insurance on which we can rely to bail us out of bad decisions. The accounting profession continues to confront an "expectations gap." This gap reflects a difference in the audit firm's responsibility per professional standards and the responsibility the public thinks it assumes in attesting to statements. A classic definition of audit firm responsibility is one from Chief Justice Burger in a unanimous decision of the U.S. Supreme Court:

> By certifying the public reports that collectively depict a corporation's financial status, the independent auditor assumes a public responsibility transcending any employment relationship

> with the client. The independent public accountant performing his special function owes ultimate allegiance to the corporation's creditors and stockholders, as well as to the investing public. The "public watchdog" function demands that the accountant maintain total independence from the client at all times and requires complete fidelity to the public trust.
> It is not enough that financial statements be accurate; the public must also perceive them as being accurate. Public faith in the reliability of a corporation's financial statements depends upon the public perception of the outside auditor as an independent professional . . . if investors were to view the auditor as an advocate for the corporate client, the value of the audit function itself might well be lost.

The court's definition of the auditor's responsibility laid down expectations the public is entitled to have regarding an audit opinion. But applying this doctrine to specific cases remains difficult and controversial. For example, does the financial failure of a company soon after an unqualified opinion is rendered imply the auditors fell short in their reporting responsibility? An answer to this question and many like it is complex and depends on many factors, all weighed by a public that believes the auditor's report is like a "good housekeeping seal."

Audit Process

Our analysis must understand what the audit opinion implies for users of financial statements. Our analysis must also appreciate the limitations of the opinion and their implications for analysis of financial statements. To obtain this understanding, we must consider the standards governing auditors' behavior and the nature of audit work.

Generally Accepted Auditing Standards

Auditors typically refer to an audit made in accordance with **generally accepted auditing standards**. Audit standards are the measuring sticks assessing the quality of audit procedures. A comprehensive definition of auditing standards is included in the professional literature. These auditing standards are broad generalizations classified under three headings. *General standards* define the personal qualities required of the auditor. *Standards of fieldwork* embrace the actual execution of the audit and cover the planning of work, the evaluation of a client's system of internal control, and the quality and sufficiency of audit evidence. *Reporting standards* govern the preparation and reporting of the auditor's report. These standards are intended to ensure the auditor's responsibilities are clearly and unequivocally stated and that the degree of responsibility assumed is made clear to users.

Auditing Procedures

Auditing procedures reflect auditing theory brought to bear on a specific investigation. They also reflect the audit firm's discretion in carrying out its responsibilities. Auditing requires successful mastery of several investigative procedures. While users do not require the same knowledge of auditing procedures as the auditor, we should possess an understanding of how an audit firm obtains assurance about the fair presentation of financial statements.

The basic objective of a financial statement audit is identifying errors and irregularities, which if undetected would materially affect these statements' fairness of presentation or their conformity with generally accepted accounting principles (GAAP).

Errors are distinguished from irregularities in that errors do not result from intentional misconduct while irregularities do. To be economically feasible and justifiable, auditing aims for a reasonable level of assurance about the data under review. This means that under a testing system assurance is never absolute. Audit reports are subject to this inherent probability of error.

A key initial step in the audit process is assessing a company's system of internal control. An **internal control system** consists of all procedures and methods designed to safeguard a company's assets and ensure that all relevant economic events are accurately reflected in the financial statements. After ascertaining, by means of investigation and inquiry, management's plan and design for the system of internal control, the auditor proceeds to test the system. This is to ascertain whether it exists and is being implemented as intended. This is called *compliance testing*.

If after application of compliance testing, the control structure is shown to be well conceived and in proper operation, then the amount of detailed testing of specific account balances is reduced. The latter type of testing, called *substantive testing*, is increased if compliance testing reveals the control structure to be deficient or not operational. This method of evaluating the internal control system and performing tests based on this evaluation involves considerable professional judgment. Judgment is subject to risk of failure. However, a competent examination in accordance with generally accepted auditing standards reduces the likelihood of material misstatements in financial statements.

Audit Report

There is considerable debate among auditors, users, and other interested parties (courts, regulators) concerning the phrase ***present fairly*** in the auditor's report. Most auditors maintain that financial statements are fairly presented when they conform to accepted accounting principles and fairness is meaningful only when measured against this standard. Yet in several court cases, financial statements supposedly prepared in accordance with accounting principles were found to be misleading. This is especially apparent in the landmark Continental Vending case where the lack of disclosure of certain dubious transactions was defended as not being, at that time, required by accounting standards. In refusing to instruct the jury that conformity with accounting principles is a defense to the charge of fraud, the trial judge maintained the critical question is whether Continental's financial statements, taken as a whole, "fairly presented" its financial picture. The judge found that while conformity with accounting principles might be persuasive evidence of an auditor's good faith, it is not necessarily conclusive evidence.

The audit report's language has been revised to narrow the gap between the responsibility auditors intend to assume and the responsibility the public believes them to assume. The language is intended to be nontechnical and to more explicitly address the responsibility the audit firm assumes, the procedures it performs, and the assurance it provides. The report indicates:

- Financial statements are audited. This is intended to be descriptive of the process.
- Financial statements are the responsibility of management and the auditor's responsibility is to express an opinion on the financial statements. This gives users notice of responsibilities assumed by each party.

- The audit is conducted in accordance with generally accepted auditing standards and is designed to obtain reasonable assurance the financial statements are free of material misstatement.
- Auditors apply procedures to reasonably assure the financial statements are free of material misstatement, including: (1) examining on a test basis evidence supporting the amounts and disclosures in financial statements, (2) assessing accounting principles used and estimates made by management, and (3) evaluating overall financial statement presentation.
- Whether financial statements present fairly in all material respects the financial position, results of operations, and cash flows of the company for the period reported on.

The introductory and scope paragraphs of the auditor's report set forth the financial statements examined, the period of time they cover, and the scope of the audit to which they and the underlying records are subjected. The scope section describes auditing procedures considered necessary in the circumstances.

The opinion paragraph of an auditor's report addresses: (1) fairness of presentation for financial statements, (2) statements' conformity with accepted accounting principles, and (3) disclosure when a material change in accounting principle occurs. The standard short-form report is a "clean opinion"—this implies the auditor has no qualifications regarding any criteria. A modification of substance in the language of the auditor's opinion paragraph is considered a "qualification." Whenever an audit firm expresses a qualified opinion, it must disclose the substantive reasons for the qualification. The explanatory paragraph should disclose the principal effects of the subject matter of the qualification on financial position, results of operations, and cash flows, if reasonably determinable. All qualifications must be referred to in the opinion paragraph, and a qualification due to scope or lack of sufficient evidential matter must be also referred to in the scope paragraph.

Not all modifications are of equal significance to users. Some deviations in language are explanatory in character, reflecting matters that the auditor wishes to emphasize but which may not affect the auditor's opinion significantly. For example, references to the work of other auditors is not regarded as a qualification but rather an indication of divided responsibility for financial statements. Other explanatory comments may not carry over to affect the auditor's opinion and, at times, one may wonder why mention of them is necessary. On the other hand, certain qualifications are so significant as to cast doubt on the reliability of the financial statements or their usefulness for business decisions. We next examine the major types of audit qualifications, the occasions where they are used, and their relevance to our analysis of financial statements.

Types of Audit Qualifications

There are several major types of qualifications that an auditor can express.

"Except for" Qualification

"Except for" qualifications express an opinion on the financial statements *except for* repercussions stemming from conditions that must be disclosed. They may arise from limitations in the scope of the audit that, because of circumstances beyond the auditor's control or because of restrictions imposed by the audited company, result in a failure to obtain reasonably objective and verifiable evidence. They can also arise from a lack of conformity of the financial statements to accepted accounting principles.

When there are uncertainties about future events that cannot be resolved or the effect of which cannot be estimated or reasonably provided for at the time an opinion is rendered, a separate paragraph is added. An example is a company with operating losses or in financial distress calling into question the company's ability to continue operating as a going concern. This paragraph refers users to the note to the financial statements providing details about the uncertainty. In cases of pervasive uncertainty that cannot be adequately measured, an auditor can, but is not required to, issue a disclaimer of opinion rather than merely call the user's attention to the uncertainty.

Companies With Uncertainties in the Audit Report

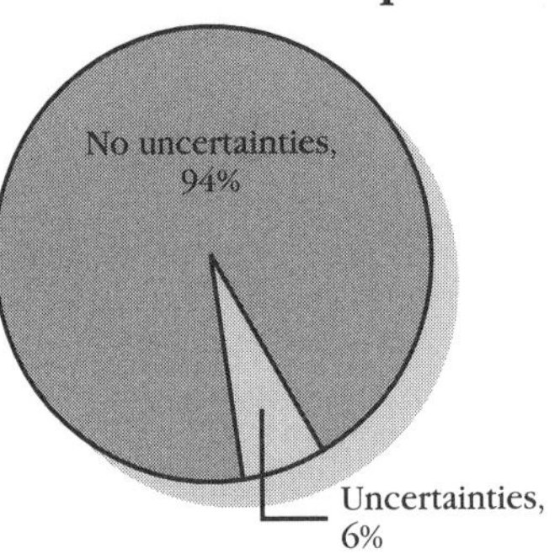

Source: *Accounting Trends & Techniques.*

Types of Uncertainties

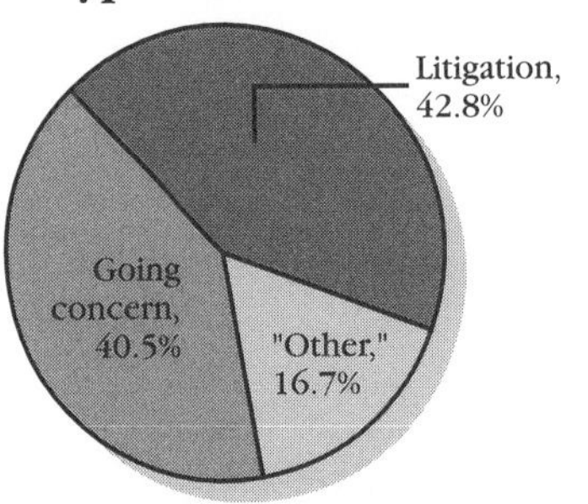

Source: *Accounting Trends & Techniques.*

Adverse Opinion

An adverse opinion is rendered in cases where financial statements are not prepared in accordance with accepted accounting principles, and this has a material effect on the fair presentation of the statements. An adverse opinion results generally from a situation where the audit firm is unable to convince its client to either amend the financial statements so that they reflect the auditor's estimate about the outcome of future events or adhere to accepted accounting principles. Issuing an adverse opinion must always be accompanied by the reasons for this opinion.

Disclaimer of Opinion

A disclaimer of opinion is a statement of inability to express an opinion. It must be rendered when, for whatever reason, insufficient competent evidential matter is available to the audit firm to enable it to form an opinion on the financial statements. It can arise from limitations in the scope of the audit as well as from the existence of uncertainties, the ultimate impact of which cannot be estimated. Material departures from accepted accounting principles do not justify a disclaimer of opinion. The difference between adverse opinions and disclaimers of opinion is best understood in terms of the difference existing between exceptions affecting the quality of financial statements on one hand, and those expressing uncertainties affecting the auditor's opinion on the other. For example, a situation calling for an "except for" opinion can in certain cases result in major disagreements with management requiring an adverse opinion.

Conditions Yielding Audit Qualifications

In this section we consider four conditions requiring audit opinion qualifications.

Limitation in Audit Scope

A material limitation in the scope of an auditor's examination results in a qualification or disclaimer of opinion. Limitation in scope implies an inability of the audit firm to perform audit procedures necessary to fulfill its responsibilities. Some limitations in scope of an auditor's examination arise from an inability to perform certain audit steps because of conditions beyond the auditor's and the client's control. An example is the inability to observe the opening inventory because the audit appointment is not made until the close of the year. Other limitations can result from a client-imposed restriction on the auditor's work. Whatever the reason for an incomplete examination, the auditor must report the inadequacy of the examination and the conclusions resulting from the inadequacy. For example, the accounting profession gives special status to procedures regarding observation of inventories and the confirmation of accounts receivable. If these procedures cannot be reasonably or practically performed, the audit firm must, to issue an unqualified opinion, satisfy itself about the inventories and accounts receivable by alternative means. For ending inventory, there are no alternative procedures to making or observing counts of inventory items.

Financial Statements Not Conforming to GAAP

The audit firm applies auditing procedures to attest to the existence, ownership, and validity of account balances, notes, and certain other information comprising financial statements. The auditor judges the fairness of presentation of financial statements and their conformity with GAAP. This conformity judgment is an important function of the auditor's opinion.

Fair presentation depends on the extent of informative disclosure. Accounting principles require adequate or full disclosure. If the auditor concurs with a company's use of an accounting principle differing from accepted practice but believes it enjoys the support of other authoritative sources, the auditor need not qualify the opinion. In this case, the auditor must disclose that the principle differs from GAAP. This puts the onus on the auditor in justifying departures from accepted principles. If, because of lack of adequate disclosure or the use of accounting principles not enjoying authoritative support, the audit firm concludes the financial statements are not fairly presented, it must qualify the opinion or render an adverse opinion. A decision of whether to make the opinion an "except for" type or to render an adverse opinion stating "financial statements do not present fairly . . . " depends on the materiality of this deficiency for the financial statements as a whole. The concept of *materiality* in accounting and auditing lacks precise definition and is unquantified. A qualification due to a lack of disclosure or a lack of adherence to GAAP implies the audit firm was unable to persuade its client to modify the financial statements. In this instance an "except for" opinion is inappropriate. Rather, an adverse opinion is called for along with full disclosure of shortcomings in the financial statements and their related impact. The following is an excerpt from an opinion *qualified* because of lack of adherence to GAAP:

> As explained in Note A, the financial statements include interest expense that has not been capitalized as required by *SFAS 34* . . . In our opinion, except that in interest expense has not been capitalized as described in the preceding paragraph, the financial statements present fairly . . .

Known Uncertainties

When known uncertainties are unresolved, or their effect cannot be estimated or reasonably measured at the time of issuing the auditor's opinion, an unqualified opinion with a required explanatory paragraph is necessary. These uncertainties can extend to lawsuits, tax matters, or other contingencies, the outcome of which depends on decisions or actions of parties other than management. Uncertainties can also extend to the recovery of the investment in certain assets through future operations or through their disposition. The explanatory paragraph discloses the uncertainty. The practical effect of this explanatory paragraph is to state the auditor's inability to assess the impact of the contingency, or the likelihood of its occurrence, and to pass the burden of evaluation to users. One cause for the explanatory paragraph is when a company is a doubtful going concern. This can arise when a company is incurring continuing operating losses, deficits in stockholders' equity, working capital insufficiencies, or defaults under loan agreements or litigation. In these cases, the auditor expresses doubt about the propriety of applying accounting principles that assume a company is a going concern (e.g., valuing plant assets at cost). Following is the pertinent portion of the auditor's report relating to a going-concern uncertainty (the explanatory paragraph follows the opinion paragraph):

> The accompanying consolidated financial statements have been prepared assuming that the Company will continue as a going concern. As discussed in note 2 to the consolidated financial statements, the Company has negative working capital . . . , negative cash flows from operations . . . , and anticipates that negative cash flows from operations will continue. These factors raise substantial doubt about the Company's ability to continue as a going concern. Management's plans in regard to these matters are also described in note 2. The consolidated financial statements do not include any adjustments, other than the current classification of long-term debt in technical default, that might result from the outcome of this uncertainty.
>
> —Gulf USA Corporation

Inconsistent Application of GAAP

When there is a material change between periods in accounting principles or in the method of their application, the auditor adds explanatory language following the opinion paragraph. An example of an accounting change where the auditor expresses an unqualified opinion but adds explanatory language follows:

> As discussed in Note 1 to the financial statements, the Company has given retroactive effect to the change in accounting for certain inventories from the last-in, first-out (LIFO) method to the first-in, first-out (FIFO) method.
>
> —United Foods, Inc.

Special Assurance Reports

The standard audit report is not appropriate in certain cases because of special circumstances or the limited scope of examination. It is particularly important our analysis properly interpret these reports so we are not misled into believing the auditor is assuming the usual measure of responsibility. Following are some types of **special reports** we can encounter:

- Reports by companies on a cash, modified cash, or tax basis of accounting.
- Reports by regulated companies using regulatory accounting practices.

- Reports prepared for specific purposes (usually limited to a certain aspect of the financial statements like compliance with provisions of bond indentures or computation of royalties, rentals, or profit-sharing agreements).

The accounting profession offers nonpublic entities **compilation** and **review** services that, while falling short of a full audit, provide users with some reduced level of assurance. *Compiled financial statements* are accompanied by a report indicating a compilation is performed and this service is limited to presenting, in financial statement format, information that is the representation of management or owners. The compilation report also states the financial statements are not audited or reviewed. Accordingly, the auditor expresses no opinion or any other form of assurance. No reference is made to any other audit procedures performed before or during the compilation.

Reviewed financial statements are accompanied by a report indicating a review is performed in accordance with accounting standards. This report describes a review, states the information in financial statements is the representation of management (or owners), and disclaims an opinion on the financial statements as a whole. The report also states: "The accountant is not aware of any material modifications that should be made to the financial statements in order for them to be in conformity with generally accepted accounting principles, other than those modifications, if any, indicated in the report." No reference is made to any other audit procedures performed before or during the review.

Analysis Implications from Auditing

The auditing process and the auditor's opinion as a means of assurance are often misunderstood. Responsibility for this misunderstanding does not solely rest with auditors because the profession earnestly endeavors to explain its role. Similarly, users of financial statements do not entirely bear the responsibility for this misunderstanding because the profession's message is often couched in technical and cautious language and requires considerable effort and background for complete understanding. Our discussion of the implications of the current state of auditing for users of audited financial statements focuses on a number of issues.

Analysis Implications of the Audit Process

Auditing is based largely on a *sampling approach* to the data and information under audit. Statistical sampling is an example of a rigorous approach to this process, lending itself to a quantification of inferences. Still, many audit tests are judgment-based and rely on samples of data selected according to an auditor's intuition or evaluation of many factors. Sample size is also limited by the costs of auditing practice. Users must recognize the audit firm does not aim at, nor can ever achieve, complete certainty. Even a review of every single transaction—a process economically unjustifiable—does not achieve complete assurance.

Auditing is a social science. Its theoretical underpinnings are complex and dynamic. It is difficult, for example, to precisely specify the relation between an auditor's evaluation of internal controls, the extent of audit testing employed, and the nature of audit procedures. If we add the variance in judgments across auditors, we must expect a past with at least some failures. Yet the percent of failure to the number of audits performed is small.

While audited financial statements provide us some assurance about the results of the audit process, we must remember there are varying risks to our relying on audit results. These risks relate to many factors, including (1) the auditor's inability and/or unwillingness to detect fraud at the highest level and to apply necessary audit tests to this end, (2) the auditor's inability to grasp the extent of a deteriorating situation, (3) the auditor's conception of the extent of responsibilities to probe and disclose, and (4) overall audit quality. We must be aware the entire audit process is a probabilistic one subject to risks. Flawless application does not yield complete assurance, and cannot ensure the auditor has elicited all the facts. This is especially the case if high-level management collusion is involved. Dependence of the auditing process on human judgment also yields varying degrees of audit quality.

Cases of Audit Failure

Our analysis often benefits from experience with prior audit failures. This section identifies and discusses three such cases.

Illustration B.1

Insight into what can be missed, and why, in the internal and external audit of a large corporation is provided by the case of Gulf Oil Corporation. Gulf's internal financial controls failed to detect or curb the expenditure of large amounts of corporate funds with "off the books" accounts for unlawful purposes. A review committee concluded that (1) internal control committees chose not to control, (2) the corporate comptroller did not exercise the control powers vested in him, (3) the internal auditing department (reporting to the comptroller rather than to an audit committee of the board) lacked independence and stature, and (4) the external auditors had some knowledge of certain unusual transactions but the extent of their knowledge could not be determined.

To provide us with further insights into auditing failures, we present the case the case of ZZZ Best Company, a carpet cleaning company organized and controlled by a 20-year-old.

Illustration B.2

ZZ Best Company received a clean audit opinion after booking fictitious receivables and revenues from nonexistent fire damage restoration contracts. This fraud included renting by ZZZ Best of a building for a weekend for the sole purpose of persuading auditors that work on a fictitious contract was actually proceeding.

Finally we describe the landmark Equity Funding case in Illustration B.3. This case includes elements of greed, fraud, deception, and audit failure. It also includes a less common occurrence of accountants being charged with knowing complicity in a fraud extending over many years.

In relying on audited financial statements, we must be aware of the risks of failure inherent in an audit. We must pay attention to the identity of the auditors and to what their prior performance suggests. Armed with knowledge of what auditors do and how they do it, our analysis must assess areas of potential vulnerability in financial statements.

Illustration B.3

The Equity Funding Corporation of America (EFCA) sold mutual fund shares and used these as security against which investors could borrow money for the payment of life insurance premiums on their behalf (the "funding" concept). From its inception as a public company, the major holders of its stock were obsessed with a desire to keep aloft the market price of its stock by fraudulently inflating reported earnings. As the fraud progressed and grew, vanity, pride, and the fear of being discovered provided added incentives to keep the fraud going. An amazing aspect of this case is the relatively crude and unsophisticated design and execution of the fraud, which relied on fictitious manual accounting entries lacking real support. In its early stages, the fraud consisted of recording nonexistent commission income with the charge (debit) going to a greatly inflated Funding Loans Receivable asset, supposedly representing borrowings by customers for life insurance premiums. Over the years, $85 million in bogus income was recorded. As is true with most frauds, the fictitious entries did not create cash. To provide cash and at the same time keep the mushrooming Funding Loans Receivable in check, the conspirators borrowed money (on the basis of glowing earning results). And instead of booking the corresponding liabilities, management credited the Funding Loans Receivable account. Other shams involved foreign subsidiaries.

As the cash-hungry fraud monster grew, the expanding circle of fraud participants, now including senior and lower management, had to invent new cash raising schemes. This led to the involvement of Equity Funding Life Insurance Company (EFLIC), a unit involved in reinsurance (i.e., the sale to others of insurance risks in force). This ultimately evolved into a practice of creating fictitious products (insurance policies) that were sold to unsuspecting reinsurers who provided significant cash inflows. This process involved the creation of all needed documentation and related fictitious records. But it also created the need for EFLIC to remit increasing amounts of cash to these reinsurers representing the premium payments that the company presumably collected from fictitious policyholders. This created monumental documentation problems and severe cash flow problems (reaching $1.7 million in cash flow deficit). These ever-growing fictions and problems created a house of cards that collapsed of its own weight even without the whistle blowing of a disgruntled dismissed employee.

The sheer size of this deception and its duration gives pause to any user. Over a nine-year period, at least $143 million in fictitious pre-tax income was reported in EFCA's financial statements. During the same period, the net income reported by the company amounted to about $76 million. This company whose reported success captured the imagination of Wall Street never earned a dollar. Subsequent bankruptcy proceedings and investigations reveal a number of startling facts. Latecomers to the fraud benefited from and were motivated by prestigious and well-paying positions. This in turn led to a climate of dishonesty including theft, expense account padding, and other manifestations of a breakdown of restraint and morality. A small audit firm performed its audit with such incompetence that it can only be inferred they knew of the fraud. A successor audit firm that purchased the practice of the smaller audit firm changed practically nothing in their careless audit process. The audit firm of EFLIC failed to review internal controls and based its audit inferences almost solely on internal records and omitted the crucial audit steps of independent outside verification. The auditors eventually settled for nearly $40 million in damages.

Rigorous financial analysis should have revealed the propensities of the defrauders if not the specific elements of the fraud. For example, a comparison of quarterly reports reveals the derived fourth-quarter earnings as inflated, with the related expenses understated in relation to revenue. The EFCA fraud provides us important lessons about the dynamics of a fraudulent process and weak points that can be revealed with a solid analysis of financial statements.

Audit Risk and Its Implications

Earlier chapters discussed accounting risk. Audit risk, while related, is of a different dimension and represents an equal danger to users of audited financial statements. While it is impossible for us to substitute our judgment for that of the auditor, we can use our understanding of the audit process and its limitations to make a better assessment of the degree of audit risk. The following are attributes pointing to potential areas of vulnerability:

- Growth industry or company with pressure to maintain a high market price or pursue acquisitions.
- Company in financial distress requiring financing.
- Company with high market visibility issuing frequent progress reports and earnings estimates.
- Management dominated by one or more strong-willed individuals.
- Signs of personal financial difficulties by members of management.
- Deterioration in operating performance or profitability.
- Management compensation or stock options dependent on reported earnings.
- Deterioration in liquidity or solvency.
- Capital structure too complex for the company's operations or size.
- Management displaying a propensity for earnings management.
- Declining industry with problems in receivables collection, inventories, cost overruns, and limited diversification.
- Insider or related party transactions or stockholder lawsuits.
- Turnover in key officers, legal counsel, or auditors.
- Company with audit firm subject to higher than normal incidence of audit failures.

While none of these situations can by itself yield higher audit risk, experience shows us they often appear in a sufficient number of problem cases to warrant our close attention.

Analysis Implications of Auditing Standards

In relying on audited financial statements, our analysis must be aware of limitations in the audit process. Moreover, we must understand what the auditor's opinion means and does not mean.

We begin by considering the unqualified, or clean, opinion. Auditors maintain that they express opinions on management's statements. This is an important point for the auditor. It implies the audit firm did not prepare the financial statements nor choose the accounting principles used in them. Instead, the audit firm asserts it reviews the financial statements presented to it by management and ascertains whether they are in agreement with the records it audits. The audit firm also determines whether accepted principles of accounting are employed in preparing the financial statements, but does not claim to represent they are the best principles. It is known that management often relies on the auditor, as an expert in accounting, to help select an accepted principle that will come nearest to meeting their reporting objectives. The auditor must be assured that minimum standards of disclosure essential to a fair presentation of the financial statements are met.

Does it make a difference whether the audit firm prepared the statements or not, so long as it expresses an unqualified opinion on them? The profession does not precisely explain what the implications of this distinction are for users of financial statements. However, a number of possible implications should be recognized in our analysis:

1. An auditor's knowledge of business activities underlying financial statements is not as strong as the preparer's. The audit firm knows only what it can discern on the basis of a sampling process and does not know all the facts.
2. Many financial statement items are incapable of exact measurement and the auditor merely reviews these measurements for reasonableness. Unless the auditor can show otherwise (e.g., estimating asset service lives), management's determination prevails.
3. While the audit firm is often consulted in selecting accounting principles, it is the preparer that selects and applies the principles. Auditors cannot insist on using the "best" principle any more than they can insist on a degree of disclosure above the minimum acceptable.
4. There exist limitations in the auditor's ability to audit certain areas. For example, is the audit firm able to audit the value of inventory work in progress? Can it competently evaluate the adequacy of insurance reserves? Can it estimate the value of problem loans? Can it second-guess the client's estimate of the percent of completion of a large contract? While these questions are rarely raised in public, they present important challenges to the profession.
5. The auditor's error tolerance is higher. The auditor looks to the concept of *materiality* implying that the audit firm need not concern itself with trivial or unimportant matters. What is important or significant is a matter of judgment, and the profession has yet to precisely define the concept nor set established criteria of materiality. This yields reporting latitude.

It is important to understand, from the point of view of accounting and audit risk, that new industries and practices (like novel financial instruments) spawn abuses not foreseen. Moreover, some auditors refuse to address emerging issues in the absence of specific professional guidance. Unfortunately, guidance often follows publicity attending an accounting transgression or audit failure. This is too late to reverse the adverse consequences our analysis confronts.

Auditors must pay attention to the economics of their profession and to limits on their responsibilities. Irrespective of whether the foregoing limitations on the auditor's function and responsibility are justified, our analysis must recognize them as standards applied by auditors and consider our reliance on audited financial statements with full understanding.

An auditor's reference to generally accepted accounting principles in its opinion should also be understood by users of financial statements. This reference means the auditor is satisfied that principles, or standards, have authoritative support and they are applied "in all material respects." Aside from understanding the concept of materiality, our analysis must understand that the definition of what constitutes *generally accepted* is often vague and subject to latitude in interpretation and application. For example, auditing standards state "when criteria for selection among alternative accounting principles have not been established to relate accounting methods to circumstances (e.g., as in case of inventory and depreciation methods) the auditor may conclude that more than one accounting principle is appropriate in the circumstances."

Similarly ambiguous are standards relating to disclosure. While minimum standards are increasingly established in professional and SEC pronouncements, accountants do not always adhere to them. The degree to which lack of disclosure impairs fair presentation of financial statements remains subject to the auditor's judgment and discretion. There are no definite standards indicating the point where lack of disclosure is material enough to impair fairness of presentation, requiring a qualified audit report.

Analysis Implications of Auditor Behavior

An auditor's misperception of the audit process presents a problem for our analysis and use of financial statements. To illustrate, take a seemingly simple question of who the client is, or who the auditor is working for. Despite court decisions, many auditors consider their relationships with companies they audit as like privileged attorney-client relationships where everything can be kept private. Moreover, some auditors believe they can determine when revelations of fraud or irregularities should be disclosed to forestall unfavorable economic or other adverse effects resulting from disclosure (see Illustration B.4).

Illustration B.4

Auditors for the Bank of Credit and Commerce International issued a clean opinion. These auditors later admitted at the time this opinion was issued they had knowledge of serious fraud or irregularities, the extent of which was not yet determined. The audit firm's senior partner defended its actions by stating: "*You simply can't go around qualifying the accounts of a bank without creating all sorts of problems, without the whole thing collapsing*." Must users of audited financial statements now consider whether other factors have priority over their right to know?

This confusion about auditor role and function manifests itself in other areas. Auditing is a major part of the profession, yet it often takes a back seat, sometimes as *loss leader*, to tangential services like headhunting, information systems, and consulting.

Auditing did not fare well in the savings and loan debacle. In the decision regarding the *Lincoln Savings and Loan v. Office of Thrift Supervision* case, the judge noted the audit partner in charge of the failed audit quit his audit firm to assume a high-paying position with Lincoln, his former client and beneficiary of favorable reports. This, in the judge's view, raises questions about the auditor's independence. In his summation of this massive audit failure the judge said: "What it is hoped the accounting profession will learn from this case is that an accountant must not blindly apply accounting conventions without . . . determining whether a transaction makes any economic sense . . . and without finding that the transaction is realistic and has economic substance."

Analysis Implications of Auditor Opinions

When an audit firm qualifies its opinion, our analysis is faced with a problem of interpretation. That is, what is the meaning and intent of the qualification? Also, what effect does qualification have for our reliance on financial statements? The usefulness of this qualification for our analysis depends on the extent supplementary information and data enable us to assess its impact. An added dimension of confusion and difficulty of interpretation arises when the audit firm includes explanatory information in its report, merely for emphasis, without a statement of conclusions or of a qualification. We are often left wondering why the matter is emphasized and whether the auditor is attempting to express an unstated qualification or reservation.

Illustration B.5

> An annual report of Manville Corporation asserted the company had substantial defenses to legal actions against asbestos-related lawsuits. However, in less than one year, it declared bankruptcy because of these suits.

Another case is that of Columbia Gas.

Illustration B.6

> Columbia Gas failed to disclose its take-or-pay contracts to buy gas at fixed prices. These contracts later proved to be far above market when gas prices declined. The subsequent sharp drop in the company's stock took many investors by surprise.

When an audit firm is *not* satisfied with the fairness in presentation of financial statements, it issues an "except for" type of qualification, and when there are *uncertainties* that cannot be resolved it adds explanatory language after the opinion paragraph. At some point, the size and importance of items under qualification are so large to result in an adverse opinion or disclaimer of opinion. Where is this point? At what point is a qualification no longer meaningful and an overall disclaimer of opinion necessary? Our analysis will not find any explicit guidelines in auditing standards. We must rely on the auditor's judgment with appropriate caveats.

Analysis Implications of Explanatory Language for Uncertainties

When an auditor is uncertain about the carrying amount of an asset or liability, or cannot assess the implications from uncertainties or contingencies on financial statements, these items are described in the audit report and users are referred to relevant notes to the statements. Our analysis of financial statements including this explanatory language is confronted with a case where the auditor has passed the uncertainty described to the user. Consequently, the task of evaluating its potential impact is similarly passed to the user. Our analysis should recognize this case for what it is and not assume we are dealing with a mere formality designed only for the auditor's self-protection. We must also remember the auditor's ability to estimate uncertainties is unlikely to exceed that of management.

When explanatory language is included because of uncertainties that cannot be resolved, we can understand why an auditor wishes to shift the burden of evaluation to the user. At the same time, we must remember the auditor (because of access to proprietary information on the company) is better equipped to evaluate the nature of uncertainties and their probabilities of occurrence. We are entitled to expect, but will not always get, a full explanation of factors surrounding uncertainties.

We must also remember the absence of explanatory language on uncertainties in the auditor's report does not imply none exist. There are many contingencies and uncertainties not requiring explanatory language that impact the company's financial condition or results of operations. Examples of these contingencies or uncertainties are:

- Obsolescence of a major product line.
- Loss of a significant customer.
- Overextension of a business beyond management's capabilities.
- Difficulties in getting production processes operating efficiently and effectively.

These matters can sometimes affect a company's ability to continue as a going concern. Activities like these should be discussed by management in its Management's Discussion and Analysis report.

Analysis Implications of the SEC

The Securities and Exchange Commission has moved more aggressively to monitor auditor performance and to strengthen the auditor's position in dealings with clients. Disciplinary proceedings against auditors were expanded with innovative remedies in consent decrees to include requirements for improvements in internal administration procedures, professional education, and reviews of a firm's procedures by outside professionals (peer review). In moving to strengthen the auditor's position, the SEC requires increased disclosure of the relationship between auditors and their clients, particularly in cases where changes in auditors take place. Disclosure must include details of past disagreements including those resolved to the satisfaction of the prior auditor, and note disclosure of the effects on financial statements of methods of accounting advocated by a former auditor but not followed by the client. The SEC has also moved to discourage "opinion shopping," a practice where companies allegedly canvass audit firms to gain acceptance of accounting alternatives they desire to use before hiring auditors.

This chapter shows our analysis must carefully consider the auditor's opinion and the supplementary information it refers to. While our analysis can place some reliance on the audit, we must maintain an independent and guarded view toward assurances conveyed in the auditor's report.

QUESTIONS

B–1. In relying on an auditor's opinion, what should our analysis consider about the audit firm and its work?

B–2. What are generally accepted auditing standards?

B–3. What are auditing procedures? What are some basic objectives of a financial statement audit?

B–4. What does the opinion section of the auditor's report usually cover?

B–5. What are the major conditions requiring that the audit report include (1) explanatory language, (2) qualification, (3) disclaimer, or (4) adverse opinion?

B–6. What is an "except for" type of audit report?

B–7. What is (*a*) a disclaimer of opinion, and (*b*) an adverse opinion? When are these rendered?

B–8. What is the practical effect of explanatory language due to an uncertainty in the audit report?

B–9. How does the auditor report on an inconsistency in the application of GAAP?

B–10. What are some implications to financial analysis stemming from the audit process?

B–11. The auditor does not prepare the financial statements but instead samples and investigates data to render a professional opinion on whether the statements are "fairly presented." List the potential implications of the auditor's responsibility to users relying on financial statements.

B–12. What does the auditor's reference to generally accepted accounting principles imply for our analysis of financial statements?

B–13. Of what significance to our analysis is explanatory language because of uncertainties?

B–14. What are some circumstances suggesting higher audit risk?

B–15. Examine Adaptec's Report of Independent Accountants; *(a)* identify the external auditor and discuss its implications for analysis, and *(b)* describe any departures from the standard short form report.

S U P P L E M E N T

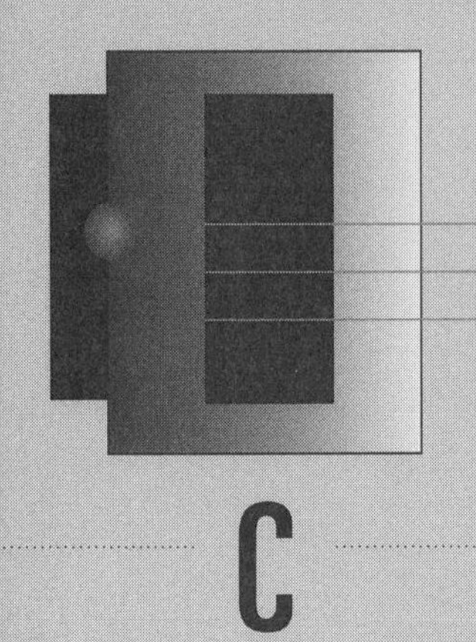

C

Changing Price Levels and Financial Analysis

Learning Objectives

- Describe the effects of changing price levels on financial statements.
- Explain capital maintenance and income determination when price levels change.
- Describe current cost and constant dollar accounting.
- Analyze financial statements restated for the effects of changing price levels.
- Interpret financial statements adjusted for changing price levels.

Preview of Supplement C

Comparability over time periods of accounting measures expressed in dollars (monetary unit) is fully valid only if the general purchasing power of the dollar remains unchanged. This is rarely the case. The value of the dollar in terms of purchasing power almost always changes over any length of time. Experience suggests these price-level changes more typically reflect inflation, or a decline in purchasing power. When inflation occurs, the monetary unit becomes increasingly distorted as a measure of actual or physical dimensions of business activities. While the distortive effect of general price-level changes on accounting measures is recognized, preparers of financial statements often prefer to rely on education and disclosure rather than on a restatement of financial statements as a means of conveying price-level effects to users. In times of severe inflation there is increased demand for more formal and systematic measures to adjust for the distortions arising from changes in price levels. The accounting regulatory agencies experimented with supplementary disclosure requirements for price-level adjustments. But these disclosures are currently voluntary. While an important source of company-generated data on the effects of price-level changes on financial statements is no longer available, our analysis needs to understand the nature of the problem and the basic approaches to a solution. Also, certain companies still provide price level–adjusted information and international financial statements often reflect adjustments made necessary by their more serious price-level changes. This supplement provides an overview of the methods available for adjusting financial statements for the effects of changing prices and how to interpret these results. The content and organization of this chapter are as follows:

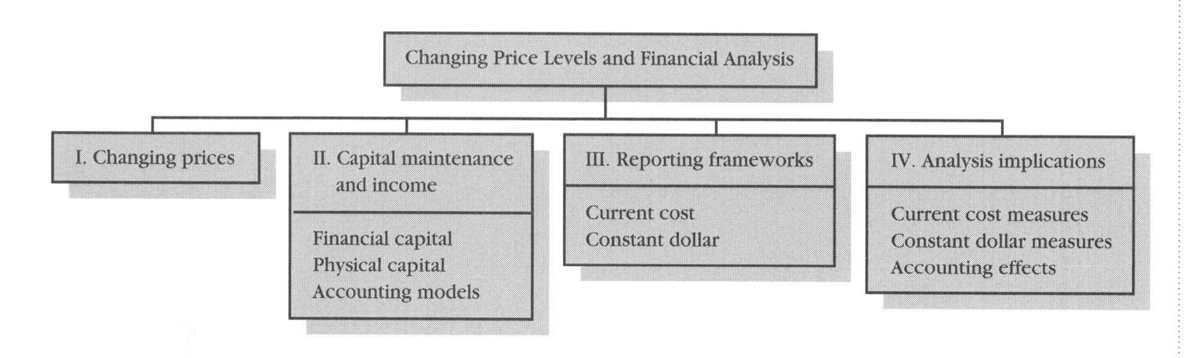

Analysis When Price Levels Change

By making the reporting of the effects of changing prices voluntary, regulators have essentially sanctioned its elimination. A review of financial statements reveals almost no companies report these data voluntarily. The decision to suspend these disclosures was by a four-to-three vote. Substantial forces were at work to bring this about. Some research indicated price level–adjusted data are not widely used. Companies did not like the work entailed nor did they like the results they had to report. For example, at one time AT&T reported accrual earnings of $7 billion and current cost earnings of only $1.4 billion. Exxon's conventional earnings of $4.2 billion became a loss when converted to the current cost basis. The double-digit inflation rate prevailing at the time the disclosure requirements were adopted eventually subsided. After several years of declining inflation, even the SEC (an earlier champion of such disclosures) withdrew its support.

All these forces are readily discerned and understood, but where does this leave us in our financial analysis? And what about our need for information in this crucial area? A few points deserve mention in this regard. Inflation is as important a political problem as a measurement problem. Politicians are against inflation but largely support policies encouraging it. If experience is a guide to the future, inflation will again be a problem sometime in the future. The cumulative effect of inflation is substantial, and so is the distortion it causes in conventional historical cost financial statements. It leads to illusory reported profits, masks the erosion of capital, and invalidates many analytical measures. For example, a plant built in 1995 with money borrowed in 1990 on land bought in 1985 and using raw materials purchased in 1997 is included in results expressed in 1997 dollars. In this case, profits tend to be overstated because depreciation and other costs are understated. Balance sheets understate the value of many assets and owners do not know whether the purchasing power of their capital is being maintained.

While there are many flaws in the methods devised to measure profits and the maintenance of physical or financial capital under price-level changes, it is better to build on and perfect our analysis tools than to abandon their "approximate" results for "precise" results using less relevant historical cost measures. Some users claim that mandatory disclosure requirements are unnecessary because they have developed their own methods of adjusting financial information for changing prices. This view is not well founded. If analytical adjustments are difficult using company-provided supplementary information, then they are even more difficult without relevant disclosures. Moreover, it is difficult to see the value in having many users approximate price-level effects when companies are in a better position to provide relevant disclosures. The elimination of supplementary disclosures about the effects of price-level changes reduces the availability of reliable information on price-level effects for financial analysis.

Capital Maintenance and Income Determination

To help us understand the analysis problems when prices change, we examine a simple but useful case example (ignoring taxes). Assume a fuel dealer needs an inventory of 100,000 gallons of oil in order to conduct business. The current inventory of fuel is purchased on January 1, Year 1, at $1 per gallon when the general price-level index (GPI) stands at 100. On March 1, Year 1, the dealer sells 10,000 gallons for $2 per gallon—at that time the fuel's replacement cost is $1.50 per gallon and the GPI is 110. The historical cost accounting model shows a profit of $10,000 (sales of $20,000 minus $10,000 cost of sales). Most users agree that this accounting does *not* fully reflect reality. But there is not complete agreement on an alternative measure.

Financial Capital Maintenance

While most users agree income is earned only after a provision is made to keep capital intact, there is disagreement on the nature of that capital. Users who are concerned with maintaining the general purchasing power of their invested capital adhere to the **financial capital** concept. Under this concept, the $10,000 cost of 10,000 gallons of oil on January 1, Year 1, is equivalent to $11,000 ($10,000 × 110/100) in *constant dollars* on March 1, Year 1. Since the general price level increased by 10 percent, it takes, on average, 10 percent more dollars or $11,000 to buy the same goods and services costing $10,000 on January 1. Because receipts for the sale of oil are in March 1 dollars, we must measure the cost in the same, or constant, dollars ($11,000). A charge of $11,000 as cost of oil sold recovers the financial capital invested in the 10,000 gallons sold and results in a profit of $9,000 (i.e., sales of $20,000 less costs of $11,000). Any distribution to owners in excess of $9,000 reduces the purchasing power of the end-of-period invested capital in relation to the beginning-of-period amount.

Physical Capital Maintenance

Users adhering to the **physical capital** maintenance concept claim a company cannot earn income unless it first provides for the maintenance of existing operating capability. In terms of our example, this means the cost of sales of the 10,000 gallons of oil is computed as $15,000 (10,000 gallons × $1.50 current cost at time of sale). Profit is then $5,000 ($20,000 – $15,000 cost). Any distribution of profit in excess of $5,000 prevents the fuel dealer from fully replenishing the 10,000 gallons of oil sold and from carrying the 100,000-gallon inventory of oil needed to conduct business.

Two Accounting Models

The two general views about the nature of capital maintenance give rise to two accounting models of price level–adjusted financial statements:

- *Current cost accounting* is advocated by users who want to focus on changes in specific prices affecting a firm's operations and who are concerned with the maintenance of the physical capital of the enterprise.
- *Constant dollar* (or *general price-level) accounting* is advocated by users who want to deal with the effects of the decline in the purchasing power of the currency and who prefer the financial concept of capital maintenance.

While current cost accounting focuses on the attribute being measured, constant dollar accounting focuses on the measuring unit. Although they are often discussed as alternative models, this is somewhat misleading. Constant dollar accounting retains the historical cost accounting model but changes the unit of measurement to a constant dollar. Current cost accounting changes the historical cost accounting model because it presumably does not deal satisfactorily with price changes. Reflecting its inability to decide which model is better in dealing with financial reporting and price changes, the FASB included both in its earlier supplementary disclosure requirements. They subsequently decided to eliminate the constant dollar accounting disclosure requirements in favor of disclosure under the current cost accounting model.

Four Reporting Frameworks

Our subsequent discussions implicitly refer to four different reporting frameworks:

1. *Historical cost/nominal dollars (HC/ND).* This is the framework under which the conventional primary financial statements are now prepared.
2. *Historical cost/constant dollars (HC/CD).* Financial statements are restated for general price-level changes and expressed in a constant dollar of a given date.
3. *Current cost/nominal dollars (CC/ND).* Financial statements are restated for specific price-level changes.
4. *Current cost/constant dollars (CC/CD).* Financial statements are restated for both specific and general price-level changes.

Current Cost Accounting

Current cost accounting uses the current cost/nominal dollar (CC/ND) framework and is advocated by users who believe the more useful way to account for price changes is to depart from historical cost. They argue historical costs, even when restated for general price-level changes, are not fully relevant to decision making. Rather, they argue, companies are directly affected by price changes of the specific goods and services they use rather than by general price-level changes. Consequently, specific price changes are more useful in preparing financial statements. There are a number of concepts of current cost, but we focus on the concept as adopted by the FASB. This focus is on the current cost of replacing the service potential of specific existing assets of the company.

Restatement Approach

Assets like cash, investment securities, accounts receivable, and current liabilities are usually stated at their cash equivalent value. The current cost of inventories and of plant and equipment can be obtained from price lists or standard manufacturing cost computations, or by use of specific price indexes. Debt often requires adjustment to reflect current market rates of interest if they differ from rates prevailing at the time the debt is issued. Revenues and most expenses (except cost of goods sold and depreciation) are likely to approximate current cost. Cost of goods sold must be restated to the current cost of goods at time of sale based on sources like price lists or invoice prices. Computing current cost depreciation is controversial. The earlier FASB requirement measured it as the current cost of the service potential used up, even when value changes in the remaining asset offset this expense. We use Illustration C.1 to explain current cost income.

Illustration C.1 raises two additional points. First, unlike constant dollar accounting, current cost accounting changes only the timing (not the amount) of the total profit recognized. For example, when the 10 CD players are finally sold, the profit under both historical and current cost bases is identical, but the timing is not. This is because under current cost accounting we recognize both current costs and holding gains.

Illustration C.1

CD World has for sale 10 CD players purchased at a cost of $20 each. This constitutes its starting capital of $200. In one week, three CD players are sold for $30 each and the inventory is replenished at a price of $25 each. Chapter 4 showed that historical cost accounting can provide at least three different profit figures for this transaction—$30 under FIFO, $26.50 under average cost, and $15 under LIFO. LIFO yields a profit figure most closely approximating current cost.

Current cost accounting departs from both historical cost and the concept of realization. Assuming units sold had a cost equal to the units replacing them, the operating profit of $15 is arrived at by deducting the current cost of sales $75 (3 × $25) from sales $90 (3 × $30). This profit is reflected with cash that can be distributed without affecting CD World's ability to carry its normal inventory of 10 CD players (that is, 10 × $25=$250). A basic principle of current cost accounting is that no profit should be reported as earned until the replacement of inventory (or of productive capacity) is provided for. The increment in the current cost of the original seven CD players still in inventory $35 (7 × $5) is recognized as an unrealized holding gain. There is also a "cost saving" or realized holding gain of $15 from having bought the three CD players that are sold at a cost of $20 each instead of the $25 current cost. Adding the $50 total holding gain to operating profit of $15, we get a net income of $65 (assuming no other expenses). This separation of operating profit and holding gain is an advantage of current cost accounting. CD World's current cost balance sheet appears as:

Cash	$ 15	Owner's equity, beginning		$200
Inventory (10 × $25)	250	Add operating profit		15
		Add holding gains (losses):		
		Realized holding gain	$15	
		Unrealized holding gain	35	50
Total assets	$265	Total liabilities and equity		$265

CD World's income statement appears as:

Sales (3 × $30)	$90.00
Cost of sales (3 × $25)	75.00
Sustainable income*	$15.00
Realized holding gains	15.00
Realized income† (equals conventional net income)	$30.00
Unrealized holding gains	35.00
Net income	$65.00

* Income that would enable CD World to sustain present level of operations were price changes to stop.

† Sustainable income plus realized holding gains (income realized in transactions with outsiders).

Second, some users believe unrealized holding gains do not belong in income. These users argue such gains should bypass the income statement and be shown directly in stockholders' equity.

Constant Dollar Accounting

One problem with HC/ND financial statements is that they include dollar amounts representing a variety of purchasing power units. Because of the decline in the purchasing power of the dollar, \$500,000 spent on a plant 15 years ago represents a far greater sacrifice in purchasing power than does \$500,000 spent on a plant today. Yet HC/ND financial statements do not recognize this difference, but rather add up the dollar costs of these two assets even though they are not expressed in a common unit of measure.

A primary purpose of financial statements restated for general price-level changes (HC/CD financial statements) is to report all elements of the financial statements in terms of units of the same general purchasing power restated by means of a general price-level index. General price-level financial statements differ from historical cost financial statements only in the unit of measure used. They do not depart from the historical cost principle. Moreover, they are subject to the same accounting standards used in preparing HC/ND financial statements with the exception that gains or losses in the purchasing power of the dollar are recognized in HC/CD statements.

The restatement of financial statements with the HC/CD basis requires a distinction between monetary and nonmonetary items. *Monetary items* represent (1) claims to fixed numbers of dollars like cash, accounts and notes receivable, and investments in bonds; and (2) obligations to pay fixed numbers of dollars like accounts and notes payable, and bonds payable. *Nonmonetary items* represent claims to other than a fixed number of dollars. Examples are inventory; property, plant, and equipment; investments in common stock; and equity accounts like capital stock and retained earnings. If an item does not qualify as monetary, it is regarded nonmonetary, as are, for example, prepaid expenses, which represent claims to future services.

We need mention that a general price-level index measures the price behavior of a group or "basket" of representative items. While there are a number of indexes measuring general purchasing power, we use a widely used index—the Consumer Price Index for All Urban Consumers (CPI-U).

Restatement Approach

Monetary items representing the general purchasing power of dollars at any given point in time require no restatement. Because monetary items represent a claim or an obligation of a fixed number of dollars rather than a given amount of purchasing power, they give rise to purchasing power gains and losses. Holding monetary assets in times of inflation results in a loss of purchasing power, while owing monetary liabilities results in a gain of purchasing power. Because nonmonetary items do not represent a fixed number of dollars, they must be restated. For example, if a piece of land is bought on January 1, Year 2, for \$100,000 when the price-level index is 100, it is converted (restated) to December 31, Year 2, dollars (when the index is 120) by multiplying the January 1 cost of \$100,000 by a conversion factor expressed as:

$$\frac{\text{Index at measurement date}}{\text{Index at acquisition date}} = \frac{120}{100} = 1.2$$

The restated cost of \$120,000 (\$100,000 × 1.2) expresses the \$100,000 January 1 acquisition in terms of December 31 dollars. Stated differently, when inflation is 20 percent, it takes 20 percent more dollars to have the same general purchasing power residing in this piece of land. A more complete illustration (Illustration C.2) follows:

Illustration C.2

On January 1, Year 3, when the price-level index is 100, FedIn's assets and equities were as reported below. No transactions occurred until December 31, Year 3, when the index is 110. The loss on monetary assets is computed by taking what these assets would have been stated at had they maintained their purchasing power ($1,000 × 110/100 = $1,100) and comparing it with their actual purchasing power on December 31, Year 3, ($1,000). Similarly, the monetary liabilities yield a gain because, had the purchasing power inherent in these obligations been maintained, it would have amounted to $2,000 × 110/100 or $2,200 on December 31, Year 3, but it is only $2,000 on this date. The net monetary gain is added to capital as part of retained earnings. The restatement of non-monetary items completes the conversion and remeasures all items in terms of December 31, Year 3, dollars.

	January 1, Year 3, Dollars	*Restatement Ratio*	*Purchasing Power Gain (loss)*	*On December 31, Year 3, C$**
Monetary assets	$1,000	None—but holding results in	($100)	$1,000
Inventories	2,000	110/110		2,200
Land	4,000	110/110		4,400
Total assets	$7,000			$7,600
Liabilities (monetary)	$2,000	None—but owing results in	200	$2,000
Capital accounts	5,000	110/110		5,500
Net general purchasing power gain	—		100	100
Liabilities & equity	$7,000			$7,600

* C$ signifies costant dollar on a particular date.

The two prior illustrations acquaint us with the general concepts underlying both current cost and constant dollar accounting for price changes. Yet, as we discussed, there are four reporting frameworks. Illustration C.3 shows all four frameworks with an example of accounting for a single transaction.

Analysis Implications of Price-Level Changes

As we know, accounting is a measurement system. If we superimpose on it the problem of an unstable measurement unit (money), its complexity increases. The larger the price-level changes, the more necessary it becomes for our analysis to adjust for price-level changes in financial statements and to understand the implications from these changes. Price changes have many causes, including changes in technology and product quality. Moreover, even without changes in the purchasing power of money, historical cost accounting is not entirely relevant. The major problem here is purchasing power changes, or specifically, inflation. Earlier in the chapter we examined two

Illustration C.3

Assume Edwards, Inc., acquires a truck on January 1, Year 1, for $4,000 when the relevant consumer price index (CPI) is 120. On June 30, Year 8, the truck is sold for $2,200 and accumulated depreciation on the truck is $3,000. On the date the truck is sold, the CPI stands at 198 and the current cost of the truck is $2,100. Computation of the gain on sale of the truck under the four reporting frameworks is reported on December 31, Year 8, when the CPI stands at 203, as follows:

	(1) HC/ND	*(2) HC/CD*	*(3) CC/ND*	*(4) CC/CD*
Selling price:				
Nominal price	$2,200		$2,200	
CD price = $\$2{,}200 \times \frac{203 \text{ (year-end)}}{198 \text{ (time of sale)}}$		$2,256		$2,256
Less adjusted cost:				
HC/ND ($4,000[a] – $3,000[b])	1,000			
HC/CD $\$1{,}000^{(d)} \times \frac{203 \text{ (year-end)}}{120 \text{ (acquisition)}}$		1,692		
CC/ND (given)			2,100	
CC/CD $\$2{,}100 \times \frac{203}{198}$				2,153
Gain on sale (before realized holding gain)	$1,200	$ 564	$ 100	$ 103
Plus realized holding gain:				
CC/ND $2,100[c] – 1,000[d]			1,100	
CC/CD $\left(\$2{,}100^{(c)} \times \frac{203}{198}\right) - \left(\$1{,}000^{(d)} \times \frac{203}{120}\right)$				461
Total gain on sale of truck	$1,200	$ 564	$1,200	$ 564

[a] Original cost.
[b] Accumulated depreciation on date of sale.
[c] CC on date of sale.
[d] Net book value on date of sale (HC/ND).

Column *1* reports the HC/ND computation of gain on sale of the truck. Column *2* measures this transaction in terms of December 31, Year 8, dollars. Column *3* accounts for the transaction on a CC/ND basis and separates the gain on sale of equipment based on current cost on date of sale from the holding gain occurring between the date of acquisition and date of sale. Column *4* expresses both the gain on sale and the holding gain in terms of dollars of December 31, Year 8, purchasing power.

major schools of thought on how accounting can deal with and reflect the effect of price changes. In this section we consider both constant dollar and current cost accounting for analysis of financial statements.

Analysis of Current Cost Measures

Current cost accounting overcomes criticism that companies experience, but it doesn't report specific price changes. Under current cost accounting, profits are reported only when the sales price exceeds the current cost of the item sold—physical capital maintenance is at the heart of this system. The excess of current cost over historical cost is considered as a holding gain. While both realized and unrealized holding gains are often considered part of net income, their exact treatment is controversial. Because profit determination under current cost accounting more closely parallels management decision processes, it provides a more consistent basis for the evaluation of management's actions and performance. As the rate of inflation increases, the separation of operating income from holding gains becomes more important in terms of capital maintenance.

A current cost accounting system is a form of *current value* accounting. Opponents of current cost accounting worry that it encourages income recognition on a prerealization basis. This is not necessarily so because while unrealized holding gains can be considered as income, they can also be considered as capital maintenance adjustments. A current cost accounting system is most effective in reflecting the effect of price changes on nonmonetary items. Yet it does not deal with erosion in the value of monetary assets or the declining economic significance of liabilities.

The strengths of constant dollar accounting are the weaknesses of current cost accounting and vice versa. Current cost accounting in nominal dollars fails to recognize that the unit of measure used in calculating current cost is not uniform. Therefore, comparability is impaired when current cost amounts of one period are compared with those of another. Current cost accounting also fails to recognize the effects of inflation on monetary items in the form of monetary gains and losses.

Analysis of Constant Dollar Measures

Two observations about the effect of price-level changes on historical cost financial statements are relevant in assessing constant dollar measures. One is that money, whether expressed in dollars or any other currency, is worth only what it can buy. If price level changes, the value of money changes with it. A dollar received or spent in one period may not be comparable with that received or spent in another period. The distortion is in proportion to the cumulative change in the general price level. It is part of the "money illusion" to consider a dollar a dollar and to forget that a 1998 dollar represents a much smaller unit of general purchasing power compared with a 1990 dollar.

We should also recognize that when prices change, the income statement is composed of at least two elements: (1) results of operating activities expressed in terms of units of equal purchasing power, and (2) changes resulting from price-level changes. Our analysis of these results requires a separation and an understanding of these two elements.

Illustration C.4

When prices are rising (inflation), a loan company with primarily monetary assets must charge a rate of interest to compensate it for *both* the use of its funds and for the loss of purchasing power of the funds lent. Our interpretation of its interest income, which by historical cost standards can seem large, must recognize the offsetting general price-level loss incurred on its monetary assets.

A major objective of financial statements expressed in constant dollars is to report them in uniform units of purchasing power rather than in terms of units of money that distort interperiod and intercompany comparisons.

General versus Specific Price Changes

A major objection to constant dollar accounting is that it focuses on general price-level changes rather than on changes in the prices of specific goods and services. For example, when prices of petroleum products skyrocket, adjustment by a general price-level index fails to reflect the price increase in these specific commodities. Conversely, prices of calculators or of semiconductors often experience price declines, and the restatement by a general price index of financial statements of companies in this field can distort performance. Opponents of constant dollar accounting object also to the abstract nature of the unit of measure. They claim that business is transacted with money, not with bundles of purchasing power. Moreover, they claim that statements expressed in constant dollars are not useful in predicting cash flows, an important function of financial analysis.

Monetary Gains and Losses

A controversial product of constant dollar accounting is monetary gains and losses. In concept, monetary losses reflect the loss of holding claims to a depreciating currency. Conversely, monetary gains reflect the gain in holding obligations in a depreciating currency. One reason these gains and losses are misunderstood is that they produce no parallel cash inflows or outflows. Moreover, there is no identifiable change in accounts as a result of changes in the purchasing power of assets and liabilities. These gains and losses are basically arrived at by means of a retrospective analysis.

Another difficulty is that the advantage of borrowing differs from company to company depending on how profitable are the assets acquired with debt. Moreover, the largest monetary gains likely occur with highly leveraged companies, including those near insolvency. This emphasizes the need for concurrent cash flow analysis. Any evaluation of purchasing power gains and losses also requires an understanding of their relation with interest expense. The interest rate charged by lenders and agreed to by borrowers reflects their expectations of future inflation. Both recognize that the higher the expected inflation, the higher the nominal interest rate must be to compensate the lender for being paid back in "depreciating" currency. Accordingly, the borrower's interest expense should be offset by purchasing power gains recorded on monetary liabilities. The following reflects McDonald's view on information reflecting price-level changes:

> The effect of inflation on property and equipment is inseparable from its effect on debt used to finance such assets. The purchasing power gain on the debt is an economic benefit to the company since, with inflation, the debt is paid back in cheaper dollars. Accordingly, we believe that this gain should be viewed as an adjustment to interest and therefore have included it in arriving at constant dollar net income.
>
> —McDonald's Corporation

Interestingly, in its comprehensively restated HC/CD financial statements, McDonald's reports interest expense of $95 million and at the same time credits income with $146 million in "purchasing power gains on net amounts owed." As a result, reported HC/CD net income is considerably higher than its HC/ND counterpart.

Accounting Effects of Inflation

Inflation acts as a "tax" on cash balances. It is a more devastating tax than anything enacted formally by legislation. It yields losses on monetary assets, gains on monetary liabilities, and changes in values (expressed in terms of money) of other assets. It effects changes in cash flows, the demand for cash, and the uncertainties and risks confronting companies. The effects of price-level changes on a company's financial statements depend not only on the rate of price-level changes but also on the composition of assets, liabilities, and equities. The following are some useful generalizations regarding these effects in times of inflation:

- The larger the proportion of depreciable assets and the greater their age, the more unadjusted income tends to be overstated. For example, the income of capital-intensive companies tends to be affected more than others from price-level restatements. Accelerated depreciation reduces this effect.
- Rate of inventory turnover is relevant to assessing price-level effects. The lower the inventory turnover, the more operating income tends to be overstated, unless LIFO costing is used.
- The mix of assets and liabilities between monetary and nonmonetary is important. A net investment in monetary assets, in times of rising price levels, leads to purchasing power losses. Conversely, purchasing power gains result from a net monetary liability position.
- Methods of financing have an important bearing on financial results. The larger the amount of debt, at fixed and favorable rates relative to the inflation rate, and the longer its maturity, the better is the protection against purchasing power losses or the better is the exposure to purchasing power gains.

While concerns about the impact of inflation on financial statements vary, the recent savings and loan crisis highlights the need for information on the current value of assets and liabilities. Accounting standards now require companies to report fair values of many financial instruments, both assets and liabilities on and off the balance sheet. This step within a broader financial instruments project represents a potential trend away from historical cost reporting.

QUESTIONS

C–1. What are the implications for our analysis of making the reporting of the effects of changing prices voluntary?

C–2. Differentiate between financial capital maintenance and physical capital maintenance. Use an example to illustrate the difference.

C–3. Differentiate among the four reporting frameworks described in the chapter.

C–4. Distinguish between monetary and nonmonetary items.

C–5. Why are monetary gains and losses sometimes misunderstood?

C–6. Identify four useful generalizations regarding the effects of price-level changes on a company and its financial statements in times of significant inflation.

EXERCISES

Exercise C–1

Accounting for the Effects of Changing Prices

Financial reporting should provide information to help investors, creditors, and other users of financial statements.

Required:

a. Describe the historical cost/constant dollar (HC/CD) method of accounting. Include in your discussion how historical cost amounts are used to make HC/CD measurements.

b. Describe the principal advantage of the HC/CD method of accounting over the historical cost method of accounting.

c. Describe the current cost method of accounting.

d. Why would depreciation expense for a given year computed using the current cost method of accounting differ from the expense computed with the historical cost method of accounting? Include in your discussion whether depreciation expense is likely to be higher or lower using the current cost method of accounting or the historical cost method of accounting in a period of rising prices, and why.

Exercise C–2

Determining Monetary Losses

Assume you deposit $20,000 in a savings account at a local bank on January 2, Year 1. The balance on December 31, Year 1, is $21,200. You make no withdrawals during the year. The general price-level index on January 1 is 110, but it increases to 121 by December 31. Inflation progresses evenly throughout the year.

Required:

a. Compute the interest rate and amount of interest earned.

b. Compute the loss due to inflation on principal, if any.

c. Compute the net increase or decrease in your wealth caused by the savings account, inclusive of interest earned.

Exercise C–3

Historical Cost versus Current Cost Earnings

Certain companies and industries show comparatively small differences between earnings as reported under historical cost and current cost accounting.

Required:

Identify and explain five financial characteristics of companies that reduce the difference between historical cost and current cost earnings.

(CFA Adapted)

Exercise C–4

Effects of Inflation on Financial Statements

Financial policies advantageous in an extended inflationary period can lead to liquidity problems for a company in a business slowdown.

Required:

a. Illustrate this point by discussing appropriate balance sheet items.

b. How can inflation result in overstating net income?

c. How can inflation result in overstating a company's return on common equity?

(CFA Adapted)

PROBLEMS

Problem C–1

Preparing a Restated Balance Sheet

On January 1, Year 2, Trek Company, a sole proprietorship, is formed. Mr. Trek contributes $200,000 cash. On the same day, land and a building are purchased for $50,000 and $200,000, respectively, paid for by $150,000 cash and $100,000 mortgage. No payments are made on the mortgage, and no other transactions occur during the year. The consumer price index is 150 on January 1 and 165 on December 31. Depreciation is computed over 25 years on a straight-line basis (no salvage value).

Required:

Prepare a balance sheet, restated for general price-level changes, at December 31, Year 2, and any necessary supporting schedules.

Problem C–2

Preparing Current Cost / Nominal Dollar Financial Statements

Historical cost financial statements of Eddy Company for Year 2 are reproduced below:

EDDY COMPANY
Comparative Balance Sheets
As of December 31 Year 2, and Year 1
(in thousands)

	Year 2	*Year 1*
Assets		
Current assets:		
Cash	$ 5,000	$ 10,000
Accounts receivable	30,000	25,000
Inventories	65,000	35,000
Total current assets	$100,000	$ 70,000
Property, plant, and equipment	270,000	270,000
Less: accumulated depreciation	(75,000)	(50,000)
Total assets	$295,000	$290,000
Liabilities and Equity		
Liabilities:		
Current liabilities	$ 47,000	$ 46,000
Long-term debt	60,000	60,000
Deferred income taxes	3,000	8,000
Total liabilities	$110,000	$114,000
Equity:		
Capital stock	$165,000	$165,000
Retained earnings	20,000	11,000
Total equity	$185,000	$176,000
Total liabilities and equity	$295,000	$290,000

EDDY COMPANY
Income Statement
For the Year Ended December 31, Year 2
(in thousands)

Sales		$400,000
Cost of goods sold:		
Beginning inventory	$ 35,000	
Purchases	135,000	
Goods available for sale	$170,000	
Less: Ending inventory	65,000	
Cost of goods sold		105,000
Gross profit		$295,000
Selling and administrative expenses	$ 50,000	
Depreciation expense	25,000	
Interest expense	25,000	100,000
Pretax income		$195,000
Income tax expense		42,000
Net income		$153,000

Additional Information:

1. Current cost estimates provided by management at December 31:

	Year 2	*Year 1*
Inventories	$ 75,000	$ 41,000
Property, plant, and equipment	300,000	290,000
Accumulated depreciation	(84,000)	(55,000)

Current cost estimates from management for year ending December 31:

Cost of goods sold at dates of sale	150,000
Depreciation expense	30,000

2. Sales, purchases, expenses (except depreciation),taxes, and dividends are assumed to occur evenly throughout the year.

Required:

Prepare current cost/nominal dollar (CC/ND) financial statements of Eddy Company for December 31, Year 2.

Interest Tables

Table 1: Future Value of 1, $f = (1 + i)^n$

Periods	*2%*	*2½%*	*3%*	*4%*	*5%*	*6%*	*7%*	*8%*	*9%*	*10%*
1	1.02000	1.02500	1.03000	1.04000	1.05000	1.06000	1.07000	1.08000	1.09000	1.10000
2	1.04040	1.05063	1.06090	1.08160	1.10250	1.12360	1.14490	1.16640	1.18810	1.21000
3	1.06121	1.07689	1.09273	1.12486	1.15763	1.19102	1.22504	1.25971	1.29503	1.33100
4	1.08243	1.10381	1.12551	1.16986	1.21551	1.26248	1.31080	1.36049	1.41158	1.46410
5	1.10408	1.13141	1.15927	1.21665	1.27628	1.33823	1.40255	1.46933	1.53862	1.61051
6	1.12616	1.15969	1.19405	1.26532	1.34010	1.41852	1.50073	1.58687	1.67710	1.77156
7	1.14869	1.18869	1.22987	1.31593	1.40710	1.50363	1.60578	1.71382	1.82804	1.94872
8	1.17166	1.21840	1.26677	1.36857	1.47746	1.59385	1.71819	1.85093	1.99256	2.14359
9	1.19509	1.24886	1.30477	1.42331	1.55133	1.68948	1.83846	1.99900	2.17189	2.35795
10	1.21899	1.28008	1.34392	1.48024	1.62889	1.79085	1.96715	2.15892	2.36736	2.59374
11	1.24337	1.31209	1.38423	1.53945	1.71034	1.89830	2.10485	2.33164	2.58043	2.85312
12	1.26824	1.34489	1.42576	1.60103	1.79586	2.01220	2.25219	2.51817	2.81266	3.13843
13	1.29361	1.37851	1.46853	1.66507	1.88565	2.13293	2.40985	2.71962	3.06580	3.45227
14	1.31948	1.41297	1.51259	1.73168	1.97993	2.26090	2.57853	2.93719	3.34173	3.79750
15	1.34587	1.44830	1.55797	1.80094	2.07893	2.39656	2.75903	3.17217	3.64248	4.17725
16	1.37279	1.48451	1.60471	1.87298	2.18287	2.54035	2.95216	3.42594	3.97031	4.59497
17	1.40024	1.52162	1.65285	1.94790	2.29202	2.69277	3.15882	3.70002	4.32763	5.05447
18	1.42825	1.55966	1.70243	2.02582	2.40662	2.85434	3.37993	3.99602	4.71712	5.55992
19	1.45681	1.59865	1.75351	2.10685	2.52695	3.02560	3.61653	4.31570	5.14166	6.11591
20	1.48595	1.63862	1.80611	2.19112	2.65330	3.20714	3.86968	4.66096	5.60441	6.72750
21	1.51567	1.67958	1.86029	2.27877	2.78596	3.39956	4.14056	5.03383	6.10881	7.40025
22	1.54598	1.72157	1.91610	2.36992	2.92526	3.60354	4.43040	5.43654	6.65860	8.14027
23	1.57690	1.76461	1.97359	2.46472	3.07152	3.81975	4.74053	5.87146	7.25787	8.95430
24	1.60844	1.80873	2.03279	2.56330	3.22510	4.04893	5.07237	6.34118	7.91108	9.84973
25	1.64061	1.85394	2.09378	2.66584	3.38635	4.29187	5.42743	6.84848	8.62308	10.83471

Periods	*11%*	*12%*	*14%*	*15%*	*16%*	*18%*	*20%*	*22%*	*24%*	*25%*
1	1.11000	1.12000	1.14000	1.15000	1.16000	1.18000	1.20000	1.22000	1.24000	1.25000
2	1.23210	1.25440	1.29960	1.32250	1.34560	1.39240	1.44000	1.48840	1.53760	1.56250
3	1.36763	1.40493	1.48154	1.52088	1.56090	1.64303	1.72800	1.81585	1.90662	1.95313
4	1.51807	1.57352	1.68896	1.74901	1.81064	1.93878	2.07360	2.21533	2.36421	2.44141
5	1.68506	1.76234	1.92541	2.01136	2.10034	2.28776	2.48832	2.70271	2.93163	3.05176
6	1.87041	1.97382	2.19497	2.31306	2.43640	2.69955	2.98598	3.29730	3.63522	3.81470
7	2.07616	2.21068	2.50227	2.66002	2.82622	3.18547	3.58318	4.02271	4.50767	4.76837
8	2.30454	2.47596	2.85259	3.05902	3.27841	3.75886	4.29982	4.90771	5.58951	5.96046
9	2.55804	2.77308	3.25195	3.51788	3.80296	4.43545	5.15978	5.98740	6.93099	7.45058
10	2.83942	3.10585	3.70722	4.04556	4.41144	5.23384	6.19174	7.30463	8.59443	9.31323
11	3.15176	3.47855	4.22623	4.65239	5.11726	6.17593	7.43008	8.91165	10.65709	11.64153
12	3.49845	3.89598	4.81790	5.35025	5.93603	7.28759	8.91610	10.87221	13.21479	14.55192
13	3.88328	4.36349	5.49241	6.15279	6.88579	8.59936	10.69932	13.26410	16.38634	18.18989
14	4.31044	4.88711	6.26135	7.07571	7.98752	10.14724	12.83918	16.18220	20.31906	22.73737
15	4.78459	5.47357	7.13794	8.13706	9.26552	11.97375	15.40702	19.74229	25.19563	28.42171
16	5.31089	6.13039	8.13725	9.35762	10.74800	14.12902	18.48843	24.08559	31.24259	35.52714
17	5.89509	6.86604	9.27646	10.76126	12.46768	16.67225	22.18611	29.38442	38.74081	44.40892
18	6.54355	7.68997	10.57517	12.37545	14.46251	19.67325	26.62333	35.84899	48.03860	55.51115
19	7.26334	8.61276	12.05569	14.23177	16.77652	23.21444	31.94800	43.73577	59.56786	69.38894
20	8.06231	9.64629	13.74349	16.36654	19.46076	27.39303	38.33760	53.35764	73.86415	86.73617
21	8.94917	10.80385	15.66758	18.82152	22.57448	32.32378	46.00512	65.09632	91.59155	108.42022
22	9.93357	12.10031	17.86104	21.64475	26.18640	38.14206	55.20614	79.41751	113.57352	135.52527
23	11.02627	13.55235	20.36158	24.89146	30.37622	45.00763	66.24737	96.88936	140.83116	169.40659
24	12.23916	15.17863	23.21221	28.62518	35.23642	53.10901	79.49685	118.20502	174.63064	211.75824
25	13.58546	17.00006	26.46192	32.91895	40.87424	62.66863	95.39622	144.21013	216.54199	264.69780

Table 2: Present Value of 1, $p = \frac{1}{(1+i)^n}$

Periods	2%	2½%	3%	4%	5%	6%	7%	8%	9%	10%
1	.98039	.97561	.97087	.96154	.95238	.94340	.93458	.92593	.91743	.90909
2	.96177	.95181	.94260	.92456	.90703	.89000	.87344	.85734	.84168	.82645
3	.94232	.92860	.91514	.88900	.86384	.83962	.81630	.79383	.77218	.75131
4	.92385	.90595	.88849	.85480	.82270	.79209	.76290	.73503	.70843	.68301
5	.90573	.88385	.86261	.82193	.78353	.74726	.71299	.68058	.64993	.62092
6	.88797	.86230	.83748	.79031	.74622	.70496	.66634	.63017	.59627	.56447
7	.87056	.84127	.81309	.75992	.71068	.66506	.62275	.58349	.54703	.51316
8	.85349	.82075	.78941	.73069	.67684	.62741	.58201	.54027	.50187	.46651
9	.83676	.80073	.76642	.70259	.64461	.59190	.54393	.50025	.46043	.42410
10	.82035	.78120	.74409	.67556	.61391	.55839	.50835	.46319	.42241	.38554
11	.80426	.76214	.72242	.64958	.58468	.52679	.47509	.42888	.38753	.35049
12	.78849	.74356	.70138	.62460	.55684	.49697	.44401	.39711	.35553	.31863
13	.77303	.72542	.68095	.60057	.53032	.46884	.41496	.36770	.32618	.28966
14	.75788	.70773	.66112	.57748	.50507	.44230	.38782	.34046	.29925	.26333
15	.74301	.69047	.64186	.55526	.48102	.41727	.36245	.31524	.27454	.23939
16	.72845	.67362	.62317	.53391	.45811	.39365	.33873	.29189	.25187	.21763
17	.71416	.65720	.60502	.51337	.43630	.37136	.31657	.27027	.23107	.19784
18	.70016	.64117	.58739	.49363	.41552	.35034	.29586	.25025	.21199	.17986
19	.68643	.62553	.57029	.47464	.39573	.33051	.27651	.23171	.19449	.16351
20	.67297	.61027	.55368	.45639	.37689	.31180	.25842	.21455	.17843	.14864
21	.65978	.59539	.53755	.43883	.35894	.29416	.24151	.19866	.16370	.13513
22	.64684	.58086	.52189	.42196	.34185	.27751	.22571	.18394	.15018	.12285
23	.63416	.56670	.50669	.40573	.32557	.26180	.21095	.17032	.13778	.11168
24	.62172	.55288	.49193	.39012	.31007	.24698	.19715	.15770	.12640	.10153
25	.60953	.53939	.47761	.37512	.29530	.23300	.18425	.14602	.11597	.09230

Periods	11%	12%	14%	15%	16%	18%	20%	22%	24%	25%
1	.90090	.89286	.87719	.86957	.86207	.84746	.83333	.81967	.80645	.80000
2	.81162	.79719	.76947	.75614	.74316	.71818	.69444	.67186	.65036	.64000
3	.73119	.71178	.67497	.65752	.64066	.60863	.57870	.55071	.52449	.51200
4	.65873	.63552	.59208	.57175	.55229	.51579	.48225	.45140	.42297	.40960
5	.59345	.56743	.51937	.49718	.47611	.43711	.40188	.37000	.34111	.32768
6	.53464	.50663	.45559	.43233	.41044	.37043	.33490	.30328	.27509	.26214
7	.48166	.45235	.39964	.37594	.35383	.31393	.27908	.24859	.22184	.20972
8	.43393	.40388	.35056	.32690	.30503	.26604	.23257	.20376	.17891	.16777
9	.39092	.36061	.30751	.28426	.26295	.22546	.19381	.16702	.14428	.13422
10	.35218	.32197	.26974	.24718	.22668	.19106	.16151	.13690	.11635	.10737
11	.31728	.28748	.23662	.21494	.19542	.16192	.13459	.11221	.09383	.08590
12	.28584	.25668	.20756	.18691	.16846	.13722	.11216	.09198	.07567	.06872
13	.25751	.22917	.18207	.16253	.14523	.11629	.09346	.07539	.06103	.05498
14	.23199	.20462	.15971	.14133	.12520	.09855	.07789	.06180	.04921	.04398
15	.20900	.18270	.14010	.12289	.10793	.08352	.06491	.05065	.03969	.03518
16	.18829	.16312	.12289	.10686	.09304	.07078	.05409	.04152	.03201	.02815
17	.16963	.14564	.10780	.09293	.08021	.05998	.04507	.03403	.02581	.02252
18	.15282	.13004	.09456	.08081	.06914	.05083	.03756	.02789	.02082	.01801
19	.13768	.11611	.08295	.07027	.05961	.04308	.03130	.02286	.01679	.01441
20	.12403	.10367	.07276	.06110	.05139	.03651	.02608	.01874	.01354	.01153
21	.11174	.09256	.06383	.05313	.04430	.03094	.02174	.01536	.01092	.00922
22	.10067	.08264	.05599	.04620	.03819	.02622	.01811	.01259	.00880	.00738
23	.09069	.07379	.04911	.04017	.03292	.02222	.01509	.01032	.00710	.00590
24	.08170	.06588	.04308	.03493	.02838	.01883	.01258	.00846	.00573	.00472
25	.07361	.05882	.03779	.03038	.02447	.01596	.01048	.00693	.00462	.00378

Table 3: Future Value of an Ordinary Annuity of n Payments of 1 Each, $F_0 = \frac{(1+i)^n - 1}{i}$

Periods (n)	*2%*	*2½%*	*3%*	*4%*	*5%*	*6%*	*7%*	*8%*	*9%*	*10%*
1	1.00000	1.00000	1.00000	1.00000	1.00000	1.00000	1.00000	1.00000	1.00000	1.00000
2	2.02000	2.02500	2.03000	2.04000	2.05000	2.06000	2.07000	2.08000	2.09000	2.10000
3	3.06040	3.07563	3.09090	3.12160	3.15250	3.18360	3.21490	3.24640	3.27810	3.31000
4	4.12161	4.15252	4.18363	4.24646	4.31013	4.37462	4.43994	4.50611	4.57313	4.64100
5	5.20404	5.25633	5.30914	5.41632	5.52563	5.63709	5.75074	5.86660	5.98471	6.10510
6	6.30812	6.38774	6.46841	6.63298	6.80191	6.97532	7.15329	7.33593	7.52333	7.71561
7	7.43428	7.54753	7.66246	7.89829	8.14201	8.39384	8.65402	8.92280	9.20043	9.48717
8	8.58297	8.73612	8.89234	9.21423	9.54911	9.89747	10.25980	10.63663	11.02847	11.43589
9	9.75463	9.95452	10.15911	10.58280	11.02656	11.49132	11.97799	12.48756	13.02104	13.57948
10	10.94972	11.20338	11.46388	12.00611	12.57789	13.18079	13.81645	14.48656	15.19293	15.93742
11	12.16872	12.48347	12.80780	13.48635	14.20679	14.97164	15.78360	16.64549	17.56029	18.53117
12	13.41209	13.79555	14.19203	15.02581	15.91713	16.86994	17.88845	18.97713	20.14072	21.38428
13	14.68033	15.14044	15.61779	16.62684	17.71298	18.88214	20.14064	21.49530	22.95338	24.52271
14	15.97394	16.51895	17.08632	18.29191	19.59863	21.01507	22.55049	24.21492	26.01919	27.97498
15	17.29342	17.93193	18.59891	20.02359	21.57856	23.27597	25.12902	27.15211	29.36092	31.77248
16	18.63929	19.38022	20.15688	21.82453	23.65749	25.67253	27.88805	30.32428	33.00340	35.94973
17	20.01207	20.86473	21.76159	23.69751	25.84037	28.21288	30.84022	33.75023	36.97370	40.54470
18	21.41231	22.38635	23.41444	25.64541	28.13238	30.90565	33.99903	37.45024	41.30134	45.59917
19	22.84056	23.94601	25.11687	27.67123	30.53900	33.75999	37.37896	41.44626	46.01846	51.15909
20	24.29737	25.54466	26.87037	29.77808	33.06595	36.78559	40.99549	45.76196	51.16012	57.27500
21	25.78332	27.18327	28.67649	31.96920	35.71925	39.99273	44.86518	50.42292	56.76453	64.00250
22	27.29898	28.86286	30.53678	34.24797	38.50521	43.39229	49.00574	55.45676	62.87334	71.40275
23	28.84496	30.58443	32.45288	36.61789	41.43048	46.99583	53.43614	60.89330	69.53194	79.54302
24	30.42186	32.34904	34.42647	39.08260	44.50200	50.81558	58.17667	66.76476	76.78981	88.49733
25	32.03030	34.15776	36.45926	41.64591	47.72710	54.86451	63.24904	73.10594	84.70090	98.34706

Periods (n)	*11%*	*12%*	*14%*	*15%*	*16%*	*18%*	*20%*	*22%*	*24%*	*25%*
1	1.00000	1.00000	1.00000	1.00000	1.00000	1.00000	1.00000	1.00000	1.00000	1.00000
2	2.11000	2.12000	2.14000	2.15000	2.16000	218000	2.20000	2.22000	2.24000	2.25000
3	3.34210	3.37440	3.43960	3.47250	3.50560	3.57240	3.64000	3.70840	3.77760	3.81250
4	4.70973	4.77933	4.92114	4.99338	5.06650	5.21543	5.36800	5.52425	5.68422	5.76563
5	6.22780	6.35285	6.61010	6.74238	6.87714	7.15421	7.44160	7.73958	8.04844	8.20703
6	7.91286	8.11519	8.53552	8.75374	8.97748	9.44197	9.92992	10.44229	10.98006	11.25879
7	9.78327	10.08901	10.73049	11.06680	11.41387	12.14152	12.91590	13.73959	14.61528	15.07349
8	11.85943	12.29969	13.23276	13.72682	14.24009	15.32700	16.49908	17.76231	19.12294	19.84186
9	14.16397	14.77566	16.08535	16.78584	17.51851	19.08585	20.79890	22.67001	24.71245	25.80232
10	16.72201	17.54874	19.33730	20.30372	21.32147	23.52131	25.95868	28.65742	31.64344	33.25290
11	19.56143	20.65458	23.04452	24.34928	25.73290	28.75514	32.15042	35.96205	40.23787	42.56613
12	22.71319	24.13313	27.27075	29.00167	30.85017	34.93107	39.58050	44.87370	50.89495	54.20766
13	26.21164	28.02911	32.08865	34.35192	36.78620	42.21866	48.49660	55.74591	64.10974	68.75958
14	30.09492	32.39260	37.58107	40.50471	43.67199	50.81802	59.19592	69.01001	80.49608	86.94947
15	34.40536	37.27971	43.84241	47.58041	51.65951	60.96527	72.03511	85.19221	100.81514	109.68684
16	39.18995	42.75328	50.98035	55.71747	60.92503	72.93901	87.44213	104.93450	126.01077	138.10855
17	44.50084	48.88367	59.11760	65.07509	71.67303	87.06804	105.93056	129.02009	157.25336	173.63568
18	50.39594	55.74971	68.39407	75.83636	84.14072	103.74028	128.11667	158.40451	195.99416	218.04460
19	56.93949	63.43968	78.96923	88.21181	98.60323	123.41353	154.74000	194.25350	244.03276	273.55576
20	64.20283	72.05244	91.02493	102.44358	115.37975	146.62797	186.68800	237.98927	303.60062	342.94470
21	72.26514	81.69874	104.76842	118.81012	134.84051	174.02100	225.02560	291.34691	377.46477	429.68087
22	81.21431	92.50258	120.43600	137.63164	157.41499	206.34479	271.03072	356.44323	469.05632	538.10109
23	91.14788	104.60289	138.29704	159.27638	183.60138	244.48685	326.23686	435.86075	582.62984	673.62636
24	102.17415	118.15524	158.65862	184.16784	213.97761	289.49448	392.48424	532.75011	723.46100	843.03295
25	114.41331	133.33387	181.87083	212.79302	249.21402	342.60349	471.98108	650.95513	898.09164	1054.79118

Table 4: Present Value of an Ordinary Annuity of n Payments of 1 Each, $P_0 = \dfrac{1 - \dfrac{1}{(1+i)^n}}{i}$

Periods (n)	2%	2½%	3%	4%	5%	6%	7%	8%	9%	10%
1	.98039	.97561	.97087	.96154	.95238	.94340	.93458	.92593	.91743	.90909
2	1.94156	1.92742	1.91347	1.88609	1.85941	1.83339	1.80802	1.78326	1.75911	1.73554
3	2.88388	2.85602	2.82861	2.77509	2.72325	2.67301	2.62432	2.57710	2.53129	2.48685
4	3.80773	3.76197	3.71710	3.62990	3.54595	3.46511	3.38721	3.31213	3.23972	3.16987
5	4.71346	4.64583	4.57971	4.45182	4.32948	4.21236	4.10020	3.99271	3.88965	3.79079
6	5.60143	5.50813	5.41719	5.24214	5.07569	4.91732	4.76654	4.62288	4.48592	4.35526
7	6.47199	6.34939	6.23028	6.00205	5.78637	5.58238	5.38929	5.20637	5.03295	4.86842
8	7.32548	7.17014	7.01969	6.73274	6.46321	6.20979	5.97130	5.74664	5.53482	5.33493
9	8.16224	7.97087	7.78611	7.43533	7.10782	6.80169	6.51523	6.24689	5.99525	5.75902
10	8.98259	8.75206	8.53020	8.11090	7.72173	7.36009	7.02358	6.71008	6.41766	6.14457
11	9.78685	9.51421	9.25262	8.76048	8.30641	7.88687	7.49867	7.13896	6.80519	6.49506
12	10.57534	10.25776	9.95400	9.38507	8.86325	8.38384	7.94269	7.53608	7.16073	6.81369
13	11.34837	10.98318	10.63496	9.98565	9.39357	8.85268	8.35765	7.90378	7.48690	7.10336
14	12.10625	11.69091	11.29607	10.56312	9.89864	9.29498	8.74547	8.24424	7.78615	7.36669
15	12.84926	12.38138	11.93794	11.11839	10.37966	9.71225	9.10791	8.55948	8.06069	7.60608
16	13.57771	13.05500	12.56110	11.65230	10.83777	10.10590	9.44665	8.85137	8.31256	7.82371
17	14.29187	13.71220	13.16612	12.16567	11.27407	10.47726	9.76322	9.12164	8.54363	8.01255
18	14.99203	14.35336	13.75351	12.65930	11.68959	10.82760	10.05909	9.37189	8.75563	8.20141
19	15.67846	14.97889	14.32380	13.13394	12.08532	11.15812	10.33560	9.60360	8.95011	8.36492
20	16.35143	15.58916	14.87747	13.59033	12.46221	11.46992	10.59401	9.81815	9.12855	8.51356
21	17.01121	16.18455	15.41502	14.02916	12.82115	11.76408	10.83553	10.01680	9.29224	8.64869
22	17.65805	16.76541	15.93692	14.45112	13.16300	12.04158	11.06124	10.20074	9.44243	8.77154
23	18.29220	17.33211	16.44361	14.85684	13.48857	12.30338	11.27219	10.37106	9.58021	8.88322
24	18.91393	17.88499	16.93554	15.24696	13.79864	12.55036	11.46933	10.52876	9.70661	8.98474
25	19.52346	18.42438	17.41315	15.62208	14.09394	12.78336	11.65358	10.67478	9.82258	9.07704

Periods (n)	11%	12%	14%	15%	16%	18%	20%	22%	24%	25%
1	.90090	.89286	.87719	.86957	.86207	.84746	.83333	.81967	.80645	.80000
2	1.71252	1.69005	1.64666	1.62571	1.60523	1.56564	1.52778	1.49153	1.45682	1.44000
3	2.44371	2.40183	2.32163	2.28323	2.24589	2.17427	2.10648	2.04224	1.98130	1.95200
4	3.10245	3.03735	2.91371	2.85498	2.79818	2.69006	2.58873	2.49364	2.40428	2.36160
5	3.69590	3.60478	3.43308	3.35216	3.27429	3.12717	2.99061	2.86364	2.74538	2.68928
6	4.23054	4.11141	3.88867	3.78448	3.68474	3.49760	3.32551	3.16692	3.02047	2.95142
7	4.71220	4.56376	4.28830	4.16042	4.03857	3.81153	3.60459	3.41551	3.24232	3.16114
8	5.14612	4.96764	4.63886	4.48732	4.34359	4.07757	3.83716	3.61927	3.42122	3.32891
9	5.53705	5.32825	4.94647	4.77158	4.60654	4.30302	4.03097	3.78628	3.56550	3.46313
10	5.88923	5.65022	5.21612	5.01877	4.83323	4.49409	4.19247	3.92318	3.68186	3.57050
11	6.20652	5.93770	5.45273	5.23371	5.02864	4.65601	4.32706	4.03540	3.77569	3.65640
12	6.49236	6.19437	5.66029	5.42062	5.19711	4.79322	4.43922	4.12737	3.85136	3.72512
13	6.74987	6.42355	5.84236	5.58315	5.34233	4.90951	4.53268	4.20277	3.91239	3.78010
14	6.98187	6.62817	6.00207	5.72448	5.46753	5.00806	4.61057	4.26456	3.96160	3.82408
15	7.19087	6.81086	6.14217	5.84737	5.57546	5.09158	4.67547	4.31522	4.00129	3.85926
16	7.37916	6.97399	6.26506	5.95423	5.66850	5.16235	4.72956	4.35673	4.03330	3.88741
17	7.54879	7.11963	6.37286	6.04716	5.74870	5.22233	4.77463	4.39077	4.05911	3.90993
18	7.70162	7.24967	6.46742	6.12797	5.81785	5.27316	4.81219	4.41866	4.07993	3.92794
19	7.83929	7.36578	6.55037	6.19823	5.87746	5.31624	4.84350	4.44152	4.09672	3.94235
20	7.96333	7.46944	6.62313	6.25933	5.92884	5.35275	4.86958	4.46027	4.11026	3.95388
21	8.07507	7.56200	6.68696	6.31246	5.97314	5.38368	4.89132	4.47563	4.12117	3.96311
22	8.17574	7.64465	6.74294	6.35866	6.01133	5.40990	4.90943	4.48822	4.12998	3.97049
23	8.26643	7.71843	6.79206	6.39884	6.04425	5.43212	4.92453	4.49854	4.13708	3.97639
24	8.34814	7.78432	6.83514	6.43377	6.07263	5.45095	4.93710	4.50700	4.14281	3.98111
25	8.42174	7.84314	6.87293	6.46415	6.09709	5.46691	4.94759	4.51393	4.14742	3.98489

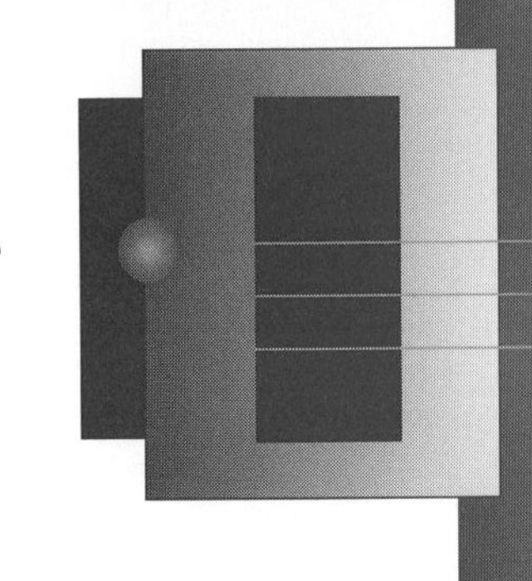

References

Chapter 1

Abarbanell, J. S. "Do Analysts' Earnings Forecasts Incorporate Information in Prior Stock Price Changes?" *Journal of Accounting and Economics,* June 1991, pp. 147–166.

Atiase, R. K. "Predisclosure Information, Firm Capitalization and Security Price Behavior Around Earnings Announcements." *Journal of Accounting Research,* Spring 1985, pp. 21–36.

Atiase, R. K.; L. S. Bamber; and R. N. Freeman. "Accounting Disclosures Based on Company Size: Regulations and Capital Markets Evidence." *Accounting Horizons* 2, no. 1 (March 1988), pp. 18–26.

Ball, R.; and P. Brown. "An Empirical Evaluation of Accounting Income Numbers." *Journal of Accounting Research,* Autumn 1968, pp. 159–78.

Collins, D. W.; S. P. Kothari; and J. Rayburn. "Firm Size and the Information Content of Prices with Respect to Earnings." *Journal of Accounting and Economics,* March 1987.

Easton, P. D.; and T. S. Harris. "Earnings as an Explanatory Variable for Returns." *Journal of Accounting Research,* Spring 1991, pp. 19–36.

Freeman, R. N. "The Association between Accounting Earnings and Security Returns for Large and Small Firms." *Journal of Accounting and Economics,* July 1987, pp. 195–228.

Hagerman, R. L.; M. E. Zmijewski; and P. Shah. "The Association Between the Magnitude of Quarterly Earnings Forecast Errors and Risk-Adjusted Stock Returns." *Journal of Accounting Research,* Autumn 1984, pp. 526–40.

Kross, W.; and D. Schroeder. "Firm Prominence and the Differential Information Content of Quarterly Earnings Announcements." *Journal of Business, Finance and Accounting,* Spring 1989, pp. 55–74.

Lev, B.; and S. Thiagarajan. "Fundamental Information Analysis." *Journal of Accounting Research,* Autumn 1993, pp. 190–215.

Ou, J. A.; and S. H. Penman. "Accounting Measurement, Price-Earnings Ratio, and the Information Content of Security Prices." *Journal of Accounting Research,* Supplement 1989, pp. 111–44.

———. "Financial Statement Analysis and the Prediction of Stock Returns." *Journal of Accounting and Economics,* November 1989, pp. 295–329.

Wild, John J.; and Sung S. Kwon. "Earnings Expectations, Firm Size, and the Informativeness of Stock Prices." *Journal of Business Finance and Accounting* 21, no. 7 (October 1994), pp. 975–96.

Chapter 2

Bauman, M. P. "A Review of Fundamental Analysis Research in Accounting." *Journal of Accounting Literature,* 1996, pp. 1–33.

Bernard, V. "The Feltham-Ohlson Framework: Implications for Empiricists." *Contemporary Accounting Research,* Spring 1995, pp. 733–47.

Dechow, P. M. "Accounting Earnings and Cash Flows as Measures of Firm Performance: The Role of Accounting Accruals." *Journal of Accounting and Economics,* July 1994, pp. 3–42.

Easton, P. D.; T. S. Harris; and J. A. Ohlson. "Accounting Earnings Can Explain Most of Security Returns: The Case of Long Event Windows." *Journal of Accounting and Economics,* June/September 1992, pp. 119–42.

Ohlson, J. A. "Earnings, Book Values, and Dividends in Equity Valuation." *Contemporary Accounting Research,* Spring 1995, pp. 661–87.

Penman, S. H. "Return to Fundamentals." *Journal of Accounting, Auditing and Finance*, Fall 1992, pp. 465–83.

Warfield, T. D. and J. J. Wild. "Accounting Recognition and the Relevance of Earnings as an Explanatory Variable for Returns." *The Accounting Review,* October 1992, pp. 821–42.

Chapter 3

Abdel-khalik, R. A. *Economic Effects on Leases of FASB Statement No. 13, Accounting for Leases*. Stamford, CT: Financial Accounting Standards Board, 1981.

"Accounting by Creditors for Impairment of a Loan." *Statement of Financial Accounting Standards No. 114*. Norwalk, CT: 1993.

"Accounting by Creditors for Impairment of a Loan—Income Recognition and Disclosures." *Statement of Financial Accounting Standards No. 118*. Norwalk, CT: Financial Accounting Standards Board, 1994.

"Accounting for Leases: A New Approach." *FASB Special Report*. Norwalk, CT: Financial Accounting Standards Board, 1996.

"Accounting for Transfers and Servicing of Financial Assets and Extinguishments of Liabilities. *Statement of Financial Accounting Standards No. 125*. Norwalk, CT: Financial Accounting Standards Board, 1996.

"Derivatives and Hedging: Questions, Answers, and Illustrative Examples." *FASB Staff Paper*. Norwalk, CT: Financial Accounting Standards Board, 1996.

"Disclosure of Accounting Policies for Derivative Financial Instruments and Derivative Commodity Instruments and Disclosure of Quantitative and Qualitative Information about Market Risk Inherent in Derivative Financial Instruments." *SEC Release 33-7386*. Washington, DC: SEC, 1997.

Disclosure of Information about Capital Structure." *Statement of Financial Accounting Standards No. 129*. Norwalk, CT: 1997.

Duke, J. C., and H. G. Hunt. "An Empirical Examination of Debt Covenant Restrictions and Accounting-Related Debt Proxies." *Journal of Accounting and Economics*, January 1990, pp. 45–63.

"Earnings per Share." *Statement of Financial Accounting Standards No. 128*. Norwalk, CT: 1997.

El-Gazzar, S. M.; S. Lilien; and V. Pastena. "Accounting for Leases by Lessees." *Journal of Accounting and Economics*, October 1986, pp. 217–237.

"Employers' Accounting for Postemployment Benefits." *Statement of Financial Accounting Standards No. 112*. Norwalk, CT: Financial Accounting Standards Board, 1992.

Fesler, R. D. "Disclosure of Litigation Contingencies." *Journal of Accountancy,* July 1990, p. 15.

"Impact of FASB Statement No. 125, 'Accounting for Transfers and Servicing of Financial Assets and Extinguishments of Liabilities,' on EITF Issues." *FASB Staff Paper*. Norwalk, CT: Financial Accounting Standards Board, 1996.

Leftwich, R. W. "Accounting Information in Private Markets: Evidence from Private Lending Agreements." *The Accounting Review*, January 1983, pp. 23–42.

"Liability Recognition for Certain Employee Termination Benefits and Other Costs to Exit an Activity (Including Certain Costs Incurred in a Restructuring)." *EITF 94-3*. Norwalk, CT: Financial Accounting Standards Board, 1994.

Mellman, M.; and L. A. Bernstein. "Lease Capitalization under APB Opinion No. 5." *The New York Certified Public Accountant*, February 1966, pp. 115–122.

Nakayama, M.; S. Lilien; and M. Benis. "Due Process and FAS No. 13." *Management Accounting*, April 1981, pp. 49–53.

Press, E. G., and J. B. Weintrop. "Accounting-Based Constraints in Public and Private Debt Agreements." *Journal of Accounting and Economics*, January 1990, pp. 65–95.

"Recognition of Liabilities in Connection with a Purchase Business Combination." *EITF 95-3*. Norwalk, CT: Financial Accounting Standards Board, 1994.

Smith, C., and J. B. Warner. "On Financial Contracting: An Analysis of Bond Covenants." *Journal of Financial Economics*, June 1979, 117–161.

Smith, C.; and L. M. Wakeman. "Determinants of Corporate Leasing Policy." *Journal of Finance*, July 1985, pp. 895–908.

Chapter 4

"Accounting for the Costs of Computer Software Developed or Obtained for Internal Use." *AICPA Proposed Statement of Position*. New York: American Institute of Certified Public Accountants, 1997.

"Accounting for the Impairment of Long-Lived Assets to Be Disposed Of." *Statement of Financial Accounting Standards No. 121*. Norwalk, CT: Financial Accounting Standards Board, 1995.

Bernard, V.; and J. Noel. "Do Inventory Disclosures Predict Sales and Earnings?" *Journal of Accounting, Auditing and Finance,* Spring 1991, pp. 145–181.

Biddle, G. C.; and W. E. Ricks. "Analyst Forecast Errors and Stock Price Behavior Near the Earnings Announcement Dates of LIFO Adopters." *Journal of Accounting Research,* Autumn 1988, pp. 169–194.

"Consolidation of Special-Purpose Entities under FAS 125." *EITF Report 96-20*. Norwalk, CT: Financial Accounting Standards Board, 1996.

Cushing, B. E.; and M. J. LeClere. "Evidence on the Determinants of Inventory Accounting Policy Choice." *The Accounting Review,* April 1992, pp. 355–366.

Dopuch, N.; and M. Pincus. "Evidence of the Choice of Inventory Accounting Methods: LIFO versus FIFO." *Journal of Accounting Research,* Spring 1988, pp. 28–59.

Elliott, J. A. "Repeated Accounting Write-Offs and the Information Content of Earnings." *Journal of Accounting Research,* Supplement 1997.

Elliott, J. A; and W. H. Shaw. "Write-Offs as Accounting Procedures to Manage Perceptions." *Journal of Accounting Research,* Supplement 1988, pp. 91–119.

Gill, S.; R. Gore; and L. Rees. "An Investigation of Asset Writedowns and Concurrent Abnormal Accruals." *Journal of Accounting Research,* Supplement 1997.

Jennings, R.; D. Mest; and R. B. Thompson. "Investor Reaction to Disclosures of 1974–75 LIFO Adoption Decisions." *The Accounting Review,* April 1992, pp. 337–354.

Lev, B.; and S. Thiagarajan. "Fundamental Information Analysis." *Journal of Accounting Research,* Autumn 1993, pp. 190–215.

Liu, C.; J. Livnat; and S. G. Ryan. "Forward-Looking Financial Information: The Order Backlog as a Predictor of Future Sales." *The Journal of Financial Statement Analysis,* Fall 1996, pp. 89–99.

Chapter 5

"Business Combinations Prior to an Initial Public Offering and Determination of the Acquiring Corporation," *SEC Staff Accounting Bulletin 97*. Washington DC: SEC, 1996.

"Consolidated Financial Statements: Policy and Procedures," *FABB Exposure Draft*. Norwalk, CT: Financial Accounting Standards Board, 1996.

Davis, M. L. "Differential Market Reaction to Pooling and Purchase Methods." *The Accounting Review,* July 1990, pp. 696–709.

Dunne, K. M. "An Empirical Analysis of Management's Choice of Accounting Treatment for Business Combinations." *Journal of Accounting and Public Policy,* July 1990, pp. 111–133.

Hong, H.; R. S. Kaplan; and G. Mandelker. "Pooling vs. Purchase: The Effects of Accounting for Mergers on Stock Prices." *The Accounting Review,* January 1978, pp. 31–47.

Morck, R.; A. Shleifer; and R. W. Vishny. "Do Managerial Objectives Drive Bad Acquisitions?" *Journal of Finance,* March 1990, pp. 31–48.

Robinson, J.R., and P.B. Shane. "Acquisition Accounting Method and Bid Premia for Target Firms." *The Accounting Review,* January 1990, pp. 25–48.

"Streamlining Disclosure Requirements Relating to Significant Business Acquisitions," *SEC Release 33-7355.* Washington, DC: SEC, 1996.

Chapter 6

Bublitz, B.; and M. Ettredge. "The Information in Discretionary Outlays: Advertising, Research and Development." *The Accounting Review*, January 1989, pp. 108–124.

Dukes, R. E. "An Investigation of the Effects of Expensing Research and Development Costs on Security Prices." In *Proceedings of the Conference on Topical Research in Accounting,* ed. M. Schiff and G. Sorter. New York: Ross Institute of Accounting Research, New York University, 1976.

Shevlin, T. J. "Taxes and Off-Balance-Sheet Financing: Research and Development Limited Partnerships." *The Accounting Review*, July 1987, pp. 480–509.

"The Valuation of R&D Firms with R&D Limited Partnerships." *The Accounting Review*, January 1991, pp. 1–22.

Chapter 7

Backer, M.; and M. L. Gosman. Financial Reporting and Business Liquidity. New York: National Association of Accountants, 1978.

Bernard, V. L.; and T. Stober. "The Nature and Amount of Information in Cash Flows and Accruals." *The Accounting Review*, October 1989, pp. 624–652.

Bowen, R. M.; D. Burgstahler; and L. A. Daley. "The Incremental Information Content of Accrual Versus Cash Flows." *The Accounting Review,* October 1987, pp. 723–747.

Hawkins, D. F.; and W. J. Campbell. *Equity Valuation: Models, Analysis and Implications*. New York: Financial Executives Research Foundation, 1978.

Klammer, T. P.; and S. A. Reed. "Operating Cash Flow Formats: Does Format Influence Decisions?" *Journal of Accounting and Public Policy,* 1990, pp. 217–235.

Livnat, J.; and P. Zarowin. "The Incremental Informational Content of Cash-Flow Components." *Journal of Accounting and Economics,* May 1990, pp. 25–46.

Rayburn, J. "The Association of Operating Cash Flow and Accruals with Security Returns." *Journal of Accounting Research,* Supplement 1986, pp. 112–133.

Wilson, P. G. "The Relative Information Content of Accruals and Cash Flows: Combined Evidence at the Earnings Announcement and Annual Report Release Date." *Journal of Accounting Research,* Supplement 1986, pp. 165–200.

Chapter 10

Guenther, D. A.; and M. A. Trombley. "The 'LIFO Reserve' and the Value of the Firm: Theory and Empirical Evidence." *Contemporary Accounting Research,* Spring 1994, pp. 433–452.

Hand, J. "Resolving LIFO Uncertainty—A Theoretical and Empirical Reexamination of 1974–1975 LIFO Adoptions and Non-adoptions." *Journal of Accounting Research,* Spring 1993, pp. 21–49.

Kang, S. "A Conceptual Framework for the Stock Price Effect of LIFO Tax Benefits." *Journal of Accounting Research,* Spring 1993, pp. 50–61.

Sougiannis, T. "The Accounting Based Valuation of Corporate R&D." *The Accounting Review* (January 1994): pp. 44–68.

Trombley, M. A.; and D. A. Guenther. "Should Earnings and Book Values Be Adjusted for LIFO?" *The Journal of Financial Statement Analysis,* Fall 1995, pp. 26–32.

Chapter 11

Ball, B. "The Mysterious Disappearance of Retained Earnings." *Harvard Business Review,* July–August 1987.

Bernard, V. L. "Accounting-Based Valuation Methods, Determinants of Market-to-Book Ratios and Implications for Financial Statements Analysis." University of Michigan (December 1994).

Fairfield, P. M.; R. J. Sweeney; and T. L. Yohn. "Accounting Classification and the Predictive Content of Earnings." *The Accounting Review*, July 1996, pp. 337–356.

Hickman, W. B. *Corporate Bond Quality and Investor Experience*. Princeton, NJ: Princeton University Press, 1958.

Penman, S. H. "An Evaluation of Accounting Rate-of-Return." *Journal of Accounting, Auditing and Finance*, Spring 1991, pp. 233–255.

Selling, T. I.; and C. P. Stickney. "Disaggregating the Rate of Return on Common Shareholders' Equity: A New Approach." *Accounting Horizons*, December 1990, pp. 9–17.

Chapter 12

Baldwin, B. A. "Segment Earnings Disclosure and the Ability of Security Analysts to Forecast Earnings per Share." *The Accounting Review,* July 1984, pp. 376–389.

Bowman, R. G. "The Theoretical Relationship between Systematic Risk and Financial Variables." *Journal of Finance,* June 1979, pp. 617–630.

Collins, D. W. "Predicting Earnings with Subentity Data: Some Further Evidence." *Journal of Accounting Research,* Spring 1976, pp. 163–177.

Hopwood, W.; P. Newbold; and P. A. Silhan. "The Potential for Gains in Predictive Ability Through Disaggregation: Segmented Annual Earnings." *Journal of Accounting Research,* Autumn 1982, pp. 724–732.

Lev, B. "On the Association between Operating Leverage and Risk." *Journal of Financial and Quantitative Analysis,* September 1974, pp. 627–640.

Mandelker, G. M.; and S. G. Rhee. "The Impact of the Degrees of Operating and Financial Leverage on Systematic Risk of Common Stock." *Journal of Financial and Quantitative Analysis,* March 1984, pp. 45–57.

Swaminathan, S. "The Impact of SEC Mandated Segment Data on Price Variability and Divergence of Beliefs." *The Accounting Review,* January 1991, pp. 23–41.

Chapter 13

Bauman, M. P. "A Summary of Fundamental Analysis Research in Accounting." *Journal of Accounting Literature,* 1996.

Fairfield, P. M.; R. J. Sweeney; and T. L. Yohn. "Non-Recurring Items and Earnings Predictions." *The Journal of Financial Statement Analysis,* Summer 1996, pp. 30–40.

Givoly, D; and C. Hayn. "Transitory Accounting Items: Information Content and Earnings Management." Tel Aviv University and Northwestern University, 1993.

Kormendi, R; and R. Lipe. "Earnings Innovation, Earnings Persistence, and Stock Returns." *Journal of Business*, July 1987, pp. 323–345.

Penman, S. H. "The Articulation of Price-Earnings Ratios and Market-to-Book Ratios and the Evaluation of Growth." *Journal of Accounting Research,* Autumn 1996.

Subramanyam, K. R.; and J. J. Wild. "Going Concern Status, Earnings Persistence, and Informativeness of Earnings." *Contemporary Accounting Research* 13, no. 1 (Spring 1996), pp. 251–273.

Index

World's Major St

Buenos Aires S.E.
Yerevan S.E.
Australian S.E.
Vienna S.E.
Dhaka S.E.
Bahrain S.E.
S.E. of Barbados
Brussels S.E.
Bolivian S.E.
Santa Cruz S.E.
Stockbrokers Botswana
Sao Paulo S.E.
Rio de Janeiro S.E.
Bulgarian S.E.
Toronto S.E.
Montreal S.E.
Vancouver S.E.
Santiago S.E.
S.E. of Hong Kong
Shanghai S.E.
Shenzhen S.E.
Bogota S.E.
Medellin S.E.
Cali (Occidente) S.E.
Natl. S.E. of Costa Rica
Abidjan S.E.
Zagreb S.E.
Cyprus S.E.
Prague S.E.
Copenhagen S.E.
Santo Domingo S.E.
Guayaquil S.E.
S.E. of Quito
Cairo S.E.
El Salvador S.E.
Helsinki S.E.
Paris Bourse S.E.
German S.E.
Ghana S.E.
Athens S.E.
S.E. of Honduras
Budapest S.E.
Iceland S.E.
Bangalore S.E.
Bombay S.E.

OTC Exch. of India
Natl. S.E. of India
Calcutta S.E.
Madras S.E.
Delhi S.E.
Jakarta S.E.
Surabaya S.E.
Tehran S.E.
Irish S.E.
Tel-Aviv S.E.
Italian S.E.
Jamaica S.E.

Fukuoka S.E.
Hiroshima S.E.
Kyoto S.E.
Nagoya S.E.
Niigata S.E.
Osaka S.E.
Tokyo S.E.
Sapporo S.E.
Amman Fin. Mkt.
Nairobi S.E.
Korea S.E.
Kuwait S.E.
Riga S.E.